SOUTHERN BRITAIN

The starting points of the 250 tours are indicated on this map and on the map of Northern Britain on the end-papers at the back of the book. The tours are grouped into eight regions, as shown at the foot of ... on how to reach the ... on the larger-scale ... indicated.

D0712867

... r of tour and ... point
... oundary of region
Motorway
Main road

WHERE TO FIND THE TOURS

WEST COUNTRY	EASTERN ENGLAND
Tours 1–32	Tours 136–151
Map on pages 8–9	Map on pages 222–223

THE SOUTH-EAST	NORTH COUNTRY
Tours 33–72	Tours 152–197
Map on pages 62–63	Map on pages 248–249

WALES	SCOTTISH LOWLANDS
Tours 73–102	Tours 198–224
Map on pages 124–125	Map on pages 326–327

CENTRAL SHIRES	SCOTTISH HIGHLANDS
Tours 103–135	Tours 225–250
Map on pages 170–171	Map on pages 368–369

MILES   20   40   60
KM   20   40   60   80

250 TOURS OF BRITAIN

250 TOURS OF BRITAIN
was edited and designed by
The Reader's Digest Association Limited
for Drive Publications Limited
Berkeley Square House, London W1X 5PD

First Edition Copyright © 1986
Drive Publications Limited

Printed in Great Britain
The typeface used for text in this book is
7½ pt Palatino

Page 1: Tal-y-llyn, Gwynedd (Tour 88).
This page: Lacock Abbey, Wiltshire (Tour 25).
Pages 4-5: Berwyn mountains near Llangynog, Powys (Tour 91).
Pages 6-7: Moors, near Lealholm, North Yorkshire (Tour 163).

250 TOURS OF BRITAIN

MAPS AND EASY-TO-FOLLOW ROUTE INSTRUCTIONS FOR
DAY AND WEEKEND DRIVES THROUGH ENGLAND, WALES AND SCOTLAND,
WITH DESCRIPTIONS OF THE NATURAL WONDERS
AND MAN-MADE ATTRACTIONS TO BE SEEN ON THE WAY

Published by Drive Publications Limited
for the Automobile Association
Fanum House, Basingstoke, Hampshire RG21 2EA

The publishers would like to thank the
following people for major contributions to this book:

WRITERS

John Burke   Martyn F. Chillmaid
Neil Coates   Ross Finlay   Ted Forrest   Ron Freethy
John M. Gittens   Ned Halley
Marjorie Caton Jones   Andrew Lawson
Philip Llewellin   Charles MacLean   John Man
Richenda Miers   Chris Mole
David Moore   Julian Plowright   Robert Sackville-West
Donald Seaman   Anna Selby
Colin Speakman   Keith Spence   Roger Thomas
K.J. Williams

PHOTOGRAPHERS

Nigel Cassidy   Martyn F. Chillmaid
Richard Dudley-Smith   David Gallant   Neil Holmes
Andrew Lawson   Susan Lund
Colin Molyneux   Jason Shenai   John Sims
Tim Woodcock   Jon Wyand

CONTENTS

ENGLAND, WALES AND SCOTLAND, ARRANGED IN EIGHT REGIONS

BYWAYS THROUGH BRITAIN

From John o'Groats to Land's End, from Pembrokeshire's wild shore to the fenlands of East Anglia, the 250 tours in this book weave a web of discovery through the length and breadth of Britain. Each itinerary includes a selection of the natural and man-made attractions that blend to make Britain such splendid touring country. Steep climbs zigzag over spectacular mountain passes and flat roads meander across green river valleys. From market towns steeped in centuries of history, lanes reach outwards across countryside with few marks of human habitation. Ancient castles look down upon new nature reserves, and stately homes sit comfortably beside humble cottages.

The tours are designed to allow maximum flexibility in planning a drive according to the time available. Most are circular, varying in length from a dramatic 130 mile safari through the north-west Highlands of Scotland to a 25 mile afternoon's drive among the Sussex downs. Many of the longer tours can be shortened at will. Guided by the map, the motorist can take a short cut back to the starting point, or make an overnight stop at a town on the way. There are also 19 cross-country tours which show the motorist how to escape the motorways and travel by attractive byways instead.

Each map shows a tested and recommended route which uses largely minor roads to link a choice of stopping places of special interest. Other interesting sites reached by easy detours just off the route are also marked. Route instructions on the map make it clear which way to turn at awkward junctions. The eight regional maps show how to reach the starting point of each tour, and also indicate how two or more tours can be combined to make a week's holiday motoring.

nly half an hour's drive across Cornwall's narrow instep connects two contrasted coastlines. To the north, the Atlantic waves snarl against high granite cliffs, topped by the relics of tin mines and punctuated by bays where surfboarders ride the rollers. To the south lies the softer Channel coast, scalloped by estuaries which force traffic inland along flower-banked lanes.

Across the broad Tamar rise the flanks of Dartmoor, one of Britain's last true wildernesses, splendid in the sunshine but menacing in the mist. From tors as old as the Earth itself, roads drop north and south to ports that reared yesterday's sea dogs and resorts that lure today's holidaymakers. Beside the Bristol Channel, Exmoor's heathery combes give way to the airy ridge of the Quantocks, and beyond the Somerset Levels rise the limestone Mendips, honeycombed by gorges and caves.

Through the red farmlands of South Devon, sunken lanes link villages of cob and thatch. Dorset's green crescent of hills has a magic blended from the brooding presence of ancient hill-forts and the undying spirit of Thomas Hardy's Wessex. Green lanes descend to a coast of horseshoe-shaped coves, backed by the Purbeck Hills that have given their stone to buildings all over Britain. Among these is Salisbury Cathedral, whose tall spire is the focus of rivers tumbling from Salisbury Plain.

Through Cornwall's far west to Land's End

Around England's westernmost tip, granite cliffs are broken by rocky coves and stretches of yellow sand. Across the moors lies Mount's Bay, dominated by its island monastery and fortress.

PENZANCE

The main thoroughfare of this former fishing village, the oddly named Market Jew Street, curves grandly up from the Quay to the domed, granite Market House, now a bank. Immediately below its imposing Ionic colonnade stands a statue of Sir Humphry Davy, inventor of the miner's safety lamp, who was born in the town two centuries ago. The name Market Jew Street is a corruption of the Cornish *Marghas Yow*, 'Thursday Market', thought to have been transferred long ago to Penzance from the older market town of Marazion.

Elegant Georgian and Regency buildings line the scored granite pavements of Chapel Street; unusually for West Cornwall, with its abundance of stone, they include a number of brick-built houses faced with granite. The Egyptian House was built in 1835 to house a geological museum; today it is a National Trust shop. Farther down is the Union Hotel, where the first news in Britain of Nelson's death at Trafalgar was announced from the minstrel gallery in the dining room. The Nautical Museum is laid out like a wooden-hulled four-decker man-of-war, and exhibits pieces of eight and other artefacts recovered from wrecks off the Isles of Scilly; it is open daily except Sundays in summer.

NEWLYN

Terraced cottages of local stone lead through the narrow streets of this tourist fishing port to the quays and fish-cellars of the market. Every morning sees the harbour busy with boats unloading their catches, ice spilled on the cobbles, and gulls screaming raucously from every wharf.

The smell of the sea, and of fish, is all around. Old men sit and smoke their pipes outside the Ship Institute as they watch the traditional scene of a Cornwall living by and from the sea.

MOUSEHOLE

The little harbour, with its curved stone quays and narrow entrance, was once the busiest in Mount's Bay, with nearly 1000 people engaged in the fishing industry; today there are only a few working boats, but outwardly little has changed. Sturdy, stone-built cottages, their diminutive gardens bright red in summer with fuchsias, line the narrow, twisting streets. Three inns take their names from the sea: The Ship, The Lobster

ISLAND OF LEGEND *Miracle cures and the story of Jack the Giant-killer are associated with St Michael's Mount.*

FISHING FLEET *Trawlers crowd the quays at Newlyn, one of Cornwall's busiest ports and the home of thriving communities of fishermen and artists.*

MINING RELIC *Derelict mines such as Botallack dot the Cornish cliff tops.*

PAINTERS' PARADISE *Below a green headland, white sands and stone houses face the sheltered harbour at St Ives.*

Pot, and The Old Coastguard. Nearby, the old hilltop village of Paul has two Celtic crosses, believed to be more than 1000 years old, in its churchyard. In the north aisle of the church, a granite boulder brought from Lamorna Cove bears an inscription commemorating the eight Mousehole men aboard the Penlee lifeboat *Solomon Brown* who were drowned on December 19, 1981, off Lamorna as they attempted to rescue the crew of the coaster *Union Star*.

ST BURYAN

The tower of the village church has for centuries been a landmark for ships rounding Land's End. Inside the 15th-century church is a superb wooden screen. Its upper part is carved to depict a rare hunting scene: a stag, dragon, bear, dogs, birds, fish and a donkey all take part in the chase through foliage scrolls, said to portray the eternal struggle between good and evil.

The screen is thought to have been carved in the 15th century. Incredibly it was pulled down during 'restoration' in 1814 and much of it was thrown into the tower where it remained for 100 years.

LAND'S END

Like survivors from an ancient shipwreck, jagged rocks battle their way through waves and surf from the Longships Lighthouse, a mile offshore, to reach the westernmost tip of mainland England. The first impression is of the awesome bareness of the place. There is no village, no church, no tree, no natural shelter from the wind, save the great granite boulders scattered along the cliff tops.

The view from the cliffs, rising 200 to 250ft above the Atlantic Ocean, is majestic. The Longships, built on a reef to raise its light more than 100ft above sea level, looks almost toy-like;

the Wolf Rock Lighthouse, 8 miles south, is a needle in the haystack of the ocean. On a clear day the Isles of Scilly, 30 miles off, can also be seen.

There is a maritime exhibition, and a crafts centre with workshops engaged in spinning, knitwear, pottery, leatherwork, jewellery-making and glass-blowing.

SENNEN

King Arthur is said to have defeated the Danes at Sennen in the great battle of Vellan-Drucher. Table Maen, the great granite block on which he is traditionally supposed to have feasted with seven Cornish kings to celebrate victory, lies in the garden of a cottage behind the village shop.

A mile past Churchtown, a side road drops to Sennen Cove, where green cliffs hug the sandy curve of Whitesands Bay.

ST JUST

From medieval times, and especially during the Industrial Revolution, the little town of St Just was a prosperous mining centre. Its big 15th-century church, two-storey Methodist chapel and Market House are all built of local stone, as are the old terraced cottages with their pale-grey slate roofs. An ancient 'Playing Place' – where plays were once performed by the Cornish clergy – stands in the town square.

A left turning by the clock tower winds to the sombre but beautiful headland of Cape Cornwall. A single chimney marks the derelict Cape Cornwall mine, perched on the tip of the cape high above the sea.

PENDEEN

The Geevor Mine at the western entrance to Pendeen is one of a handful still producing tin in Corn-

wall. Its maze of underground workings includes the Levant Mine which runs out under the ocean. Half of Geevor's 370 workforce today mines underground, at depths of up to 2000ft. The mine is open to the public on normal working days for guided tours of the surface plant, and there is a museum.

Pendeen's modern Church of St John the Baptist, built of local stone entirely by local labour, is a replica of the cathedral on the Isle of Iona, off the coast of Mull.

A minor road opposite the museum leads to Pendeen Watch, the headland site of the Pendeen Lighthouse. It is open on weekday afternoons in summer. The views are superb.

ZENNOR

Almost everything in this ancient village is built of stone, from its 12th-century church, slate-roofed cottages and farm buildings, to the mysterious, 5000-year-old Zennor Quoit, crouching on the windswept moorland above. The author and miner's son D.H. Lawrence came here in 1916 with his German-born wife Frieda to try to escape from the hatreds aroused by the First World War. They failed, and the police ordered them to leave on suspicion of being spies.

The 'Mermaid's Chair' in the church, carved from old bench ends, is thought to be 600 years old. According to legend the Zennor Mermaid entered the church and lured the squire's son to a nearby cove where he vanished, never to be seen again. The chair shows her, mirror in one hand, comb in the other. The Wayside Museum in the old mill

house has old mining tools, fishing nets, oil lamps, chairs and utensils from the cottage kitchens of an earlier Zennor.

Follow the main road for 1 mile towards St Ives. Opposite the first large house on the left, a path leads across moorland to the ruin of an old mine building; some 300yds to the right is the Stone Age tomb of Zennor Quoit. The huge capstone, 18ft long and estimated to weigh 25 tons, has slipped from its supporting stones and it now leans against the tomb like a weary giant.

ST IVES

As pilchard fishing and tin exports began to decline, the arrival of the railway in 1877 brought with it a new future for St Ives. Holidaymakers, as well as artists following in the footsteps of Turner, Whistler and Sickert, came in ever-increasing numbers.

The old fishing quarter is built round The Island, where St Ia, the Irish saint, is said to have landed in a coracle in the 5th century. Behind The Island, now silted into a headland, lies a maze of narrow, cobbled alleyways and slate-hung cottages with names such as Rope Walk, Wheal Dream, Fish Street, Salubrious Place and Teetotal Street.

The September arts festival reflects the continuing influence of the art colony. There are galleries in the harbour area, and a Barbara Hepworth Museum in the house off Fore Street where the sculptress lived for 25 years.

A glimpse of the St Ives that has gone for ever can be found in the tiny fishermen's chapel of St Leonard, between the piers below The Island. It measures about 18ft by 12ft and dates back to medieval times, when the fishermen paid a friar to bless their boats before they sailed.

ST MICHAEL'S MOUNT

This great rockpile with a castle on top has played many parts in its day, from busy tin port before the time of Christ to church, priory, place of pilgrimage, fortress and stately home.

The Mount is dedicated to the Archangel St Michael, who according to legend appeared to fishermen there in AD 495. The Benedictine priory was built in the 12th century by the Norman abbot of Mont St Michel in Normandy for a prior and 12 monks. At low tide the mount can be reached on foot, across the same cobbled causeway used in medieval times. The island rises 230ft to the tower, chapel and battlements of the castle-cum-mansion house which has been the home of the St Aubyn family since 1659; it was presented to the National Trust in 1954, but the family still lives there.

Among the rooms open to the public is the Chevy Chase Room, named after its superb plaster frieze.

St Michael's Mount is open to the public in summer at varying times (not at weekends) and in winter for guided tours only (Penzance 710507).

Tourist information: Penzance 62207/62341; St Ives 797600.

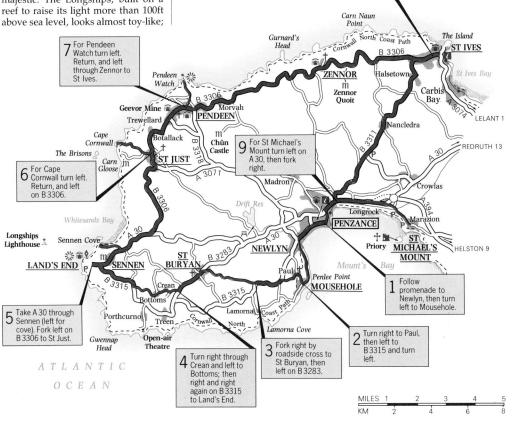

7 For Pendeen Watch turn left. Return, and left through Zennor to St Ives.

8 Return on B 3306, then left on B 3311.

6 For Cape Cornwall turn left. Return, and left on B 3306.

9 For St Michael's Mount turn left on A 30, then fork right.

5 Take A 30 through Sennen (left for cove). Fork left on B 3306 to St Just.

4 Turn right through Crean and left to Bottoms; then right and right again on B 3315 to Land's End.

3 Fork right by roadside cross to St Buryan, then left on B 3283.

2 Turn right to Paul, then left to B 3315 and turn left.

1 Follow promenade to Newlyn, then turn left to Mousehole.

From rolling surf to Roseland's gardens

TOUR

2

---

40 MILES

On Cornwall's Atlantic coast, pounded by great rollers, sand dunes serve as windbreak and sea wall. Over the centuries the sands buried the oldest known church in south-west England.

NEWQUAY

A legacy of sandy beaches and the arrival of the railway transformed an ancient fishing village into one of Cornwall's biggest holiday resorts. Its name stems from the stone quay built in the 15th century to shelter its little pilchard boats from Atlantic gales.

Reminders of Newquay's past are all around. Iron Age chieftains lie buried in the barrows that dot the coast, from Whipsiderry to Kelsey Head and beyond. The old huer's hut – a 'huer' was lookout for the pilchard fleet – stands near the Atlantic Hotel.

CRANTOCK

Some fine old thatched cottages stand in the village square, and the stocks last used in 1817 to punish a robber named William Tinney now imprison his effigy in the churchyard. The 16th-century Old Albion Inn has a smuggler's hole in the bar, leading to the church. Church and village take their name from the Celtic saint Carantacus, who is said to have established his oratory here in the 5th century.

HOLYWELL

The sand dunes at Holywell form the outer defences against wind and sea; the village itself shelters below the slopes of Penhale Point, a little way inland. The two 'holy wells' from which it takes its name lie a mile apart. The first, a roofed shrine with clear running water, is generally regarded as the authentic holy well of St Cubert. It stands by the stream north of Trevornick Farm, an easy walk from the east of the village.

The second well is 20ft up in a cave below the south-west corner of Kelsey Head, where fresh water seeps into rock pools. It is accessible only at low tide by steps cut into the rock and slippery with seaweed. Visitors should consult tide tables or local knowledge before setting out across the beach.

ST PIRAN'S ROUND

Most famous of all Cornwall's 'playing places', where Mystery Plays were enacted by the clergy in the Middle Ages, this earthwork amphitheatre can seat an audience of hundreds. Its age is uncertain. The 'rounds' were built originally as fortified farmsteads, long before the Romans invaded Britain. St Piran's Round measures about 130ft in diameter, with grassed seats sloping down from an 8ft high embankment.

ST PIRAN'S ORATORY

Half a mile above Rose, from the road bordering Penhale Sands, a line of white stones picks out the route to the site of a tiny oratory, or chapel, built by an Irish saint, Piran, in the 6th or 7th century. A second chapel built on the site some 300 years later was engulfed by sand around AD 1000, only to be partly uncovered by movement of the sand 800 years later and found to be well preserved. An attempt was made to protect it with a concrete shell, but after further encroachment the ancient oratory was reburied. Today a 12ft high cross points the way; the exact location of the lost chapel, some 150yds away, is marked by a simple granite stone.

A further Church of St Piran was built among the same dunes during the 12th century, and enlarged in the 15th century. But when this Norman church, in its turn, became buried in sand a new church was built at Lambourne in 1804. The site of the original Norman church is marked by an old Celtic cross pierced with three holes.

PERRANPORTH

The white sands of Perran Beach have brought new prosperity to the ancient mining village of Perranporth. It takes its name from St Piran, the patron saint of tin miners; in the middle of the last century Cornish mines supplied nearly half the world's tin. Today the old engine houses and dressing floors have been replaced by hotels.

The coastal path runs south from Droskyn Point past Cligga Head to St Agnes. Much of it was once the way to work for Perranporth's miners, and disused shafts and ventilation bores can still be seen through the cliff face. The views are magnificent; even the abandoned mines have a sad, haunting beauty.

ST AGNES

Another ancient tin-mining village which has become a thriving holiday centre, St Agnes has fine stone-built shops and cottages, some dating back to the early 18th century. At the top of Town Hill, a row of old slate-roofed cottages glorying in the name of 'Stippy Stappy' points the way down a steep incline to Trevaunance Cove, good for swimming and surfing.

A second beach, at Chapel Porth below St Agnes Beacon, has fine sands as well as a nature trail. The third beach, little more than a rocky cove but peaceful beneath its guardian cliffs, is at Trevellas Porth. A footpath winds through the steep-sided valley of Trevellas Coombe.

A road running west from St Agnes Hotel leads to St Agnes Beacon, rising more than 600ft above the Atlantic. An unmade road on the lower slopes leads to Wheal Coates Mine, with its engine house and chimney clinging spectacularly to the cliff's edge, 300ft above the sea.

ST NEWLYN EAST

An ancient village which looks as if it has slumbered through the centuries, St Newlyn East was in 1846 the scene of Cornwall's worst mining disaster. A cloudburst flooded the East Wheal Rose lead mine, leaving 39 men and boys drowned underground.

The part Norman Church of St Newlina, restored in the late 19th century, has a fig tree growing from its south wall said to carry a curse that anyone who plucks a leaf will die within 12 months.

A mile to the north-east is Benny Halt, terminus of the Lappa Valley Railway. Built originally as a branch

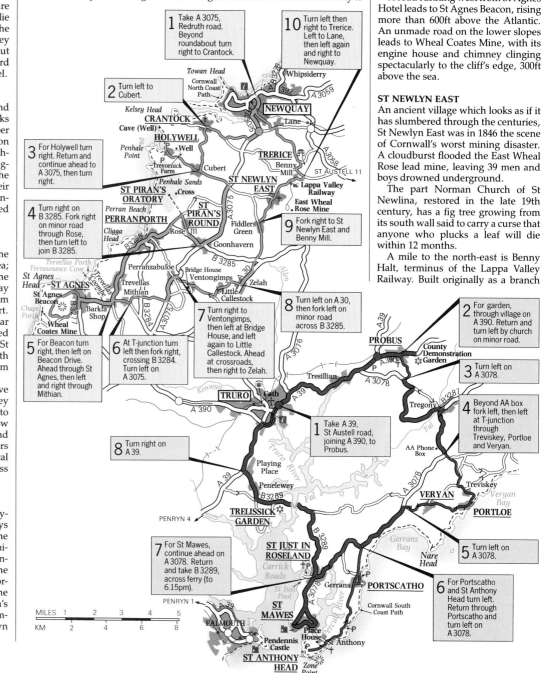

ST MAWES CASTLE *Stones from a monastery were used in the castle walls.*

TRERICE *Stone mullioned windows adorn the Elizabethan house.*

EVERYMAN'S CORNWALL *Portloe is typical of the Cornish fishing villages beloved by holidaymakers. White-painted houses cling to the sides of a narrow break in the cliffs leading down to a rocky harbour, still used by a few crab boats.*

line to the doomed East Wheal Rose, it was taken over by the old Great Western Railway but later axed in the Beeching cuts of the 1960s. An enthusiast, Eric Booth, restored it in 1968 and transformed it into today's narrow-gauge steam railway running through 1 mile of green countryside. It visits the East Wheal Rose mine, where there is a modern maze.

The railway is open daily from Easter to September, and on Sundays and school holidays in October.

TRERICE

The superb Elizabethan manor house of Trerice is one of the treasures of Cornwall. The original structure, dating back to the 14th century, was rebuilt in 1571 under the direction of Sir John Arundell, later Sheriff of Cornwall.

The broad front of the house, with its two-storey porch and splendid gables, is imposing enough; but the crowning glory of Trerice is its great mullioned window, containing 576 panes to brighten the Great Hall. The hall is two storeys high with an elaborate plaster ceiling and a minstrel gallery. The house and its grounds are owned by the National Trust and open daily from April to October.

Tourist information: Newquay 71345/6.

TOUR 3

—— 47 MILES ——

Palm trees flourish in the Roseland peninsula's sheltered climate. Winding lanes lead to a castle built by Henry VIII, an ancient church, and a headland with fine coastal views.

TRURO

Cornwall's only city, Truro stands amidst a bowl of green hills, where the diminutive Allen and Kenwyn rivers join to become the Truro river. Georgian and Regency streets are dominated by the towers and spires of Truro's cathedral, completed after 30 years in 1910 to become the first built in England since St Paul's.

High metal prices made Truro prosperous in the 18th and 19th centuries. Lemon Street, the centre of 19th-century fashion, is lined by splendid Georgian houses. It sweeps grandly up from the river to the fluted granite memorial to the Truro-born West African explorer Richard Lander.

PROBUS

The 16th-century church at Probus boasts the tallest (123ft 6in) and the most richly ornamented tower in Cornwall. Gargoyles lurk beneath the pinnacles; the pierced stone screens of the exterior belfry windows have a lace-like quality; and a hound hunts the fox across the tower's granite north face.

Just outside the village, on the St Austell road, is the County Demonstration Garden – a permanent demonstration of all the things the amateur gardener needs to know. Displays show how to build a patio garden, how to raise trees and shrubs, how to care for a suburban lawn. The garden is run by the County Council Education Committee, and is open Monday to Friday all year and Sunday afternoons from May to September.

PORTLOE

At the foot of a valley leading into Veryan Bay, tiny Portloe looks every inch the traditional Cornish fishing village. Boats lie hauled up on a pebble beach by the harbour mouth, lobster pots crowd the quay behind, men in blue jerseys paint their boats and mend their nets.

In the village above, a single winding street climbs past stone-built cottages to the inn. The post office by the harbour has a small front garden filled with flowers in summer. The Methodist chapel stands across the street, and the tiny All Saints' Church occupies the site of a former lifeboat house.

VERYAN

Protected from sea winds by the great mass of Nare Head, subtropical shrubs and flowers grow in Veryan's well-tended gardens, and many of its old, whitewashed stone cottages are roofed with thatch.

Five tiny, whitewashed, circular cottages, topped by a cross, date back to the early 19th century. They were believed to be 'Devil-proof' – for in a house without corners, Satan has no place to hide.

PORTSCATHO

Seen from across Gerrans Bay, Portscatho gleams white and clean against a background of low green hills. A fine seafront promenade called 'The Lugger' is backed by late Georgian, stone-built houses. The car park above lies within easy walk of the village square, with whitewashed cottages grouped round the inn.

ST ANTHONY HEAD

A lighthouse points to the shelter of the Carrick Roads, busy with ocean-going ships and sailing craft and guarded by the Tudor castles of Pendennis and St Mawes. Across Falmouth Bay to the west, the wild Lizard coastline runs down past Rosemullion Head.

Follow the minor road down from the point left to Place House, above a wooded inlet off the Percuil river.

13

Originally a monastery, then a manor house, Place House is no longer open to the public; yet it is still worth viewing from the riverside, for the sheer beauty of its setting. Green lawns sweep down from the stucco neo-Gothic building to the water's edge, and yachts bob at anchor.

The coastal path winds through Place churchyard to the tiny medieval Church of St Anthony which, like Place House, is privately owned.

ST MAWES

The road following the sea wall through St Mawes leads past stone-built cottages, some thatched, to St Mawes Castle, built in the shape of a clover leaf by Henry VIII in the days when Britain feared an invasion from Europe. Together with Pendennis Castle, below Falmouth a mile to the west, it was designed to command the entrance to the Carrick Roads.

In the Civil War it was surrendered to Cromwell's Roundheads without a shot being fired. It is open daily. Its sheltered position and gentle climate make St Mawes a popular yachting centre. A coast path leads to St Just in Roseland.

ST JUST IN ROSELAND

The ancient church stands above St Just Pool, a wooded inlet leading off the Carrick Roads. The church is surrounded by a churchyard land-scaped out of the hillside and ablaze with Chilean fire bushes, rhodo-dendrons and camellias.

The church is dedicated to St Just the Martyr. The present structure dates from 1261, and its tower and pillars are 15th century. A Roman coin of the Constantine era, AD 274-388, thought to have been worn in a necklace, was discovered under the floorboards when repairs were carried out this century.

TRELISSICK GARDEN

The gatehouse leading to Trelissick mansion and its garden, set in 376 acres of woodland splendour, lies immediately above the King Harry ferry exit. The house was rebuilt in the early 19th century in neo-Greek style, with Ionic portico and tall fluted columns, for Thomas Daniell – the son of a Cornish tin magnate. Today it is owned by the National Trust, but not open to the public.

Lawns slope down to the banks of the River Fal, mossy paths lead through the woodland, and slate steps zigzag up to an ancient granite cross. A footbridge leads back over the ferry road to more gardens, loud with birdsong. Trelissick Garden is open to the public from March to the end of October.

Tourist information: Truro 74555.

IN THE WAKE OF NELSON *Only small boats tie up in St Just Pool today, but once Britain's great wooden warships anchored there. Men-of-war of Nelson's fleet were held in quarantine there after returning from the Battle of Trafalgar.*

Round the Lizard to Frenchman's Creek

TOUR
4

————— 56 MILES —————

Winding roads follow the coast of the Lizard peninsula, dropping down into fishing villages between high cliffs. Beyond the windswept Goonhilly Downs lies the calm Helford River.

HELSTON

Two open channels of water, fed by moorland streams, babble noisily through Coinagehall Street as it curves grandly down towards the Cober river. The street's name recalls Helston's former status as a stannary town, established by King John for the assaying of tin, when a *coin*, or corner, of each ingot of tin was cut off for testing.

At the top of Coinagehall Street stands the Guildhall, built of local granite in the early 19th century; at its foot is a Gothic gateway honouring a former mayor. Halfway down the street is the Angel Hotel, 500 years old and formerly the town house of the Godolphins, one of Cornwall's leading families; the original Tudor minstrels' gallery still overlooks the restaurant. A web of lanes and narrow medieval streets leads off Coinagehall Street.

The folk museum behind the Guildhall contains mementos of two famous Helston men – Henry Trengrouse (1772-1854), inventor of the life-saving maritime rocket apparatus, and Bob Fitzsimmons (1863-1917), Britain's only triple world boxing champion.

The one major event in Helston's past that cannot be dated is the origin of the Furry Dance. All that is known is that it was danced in pre-Christian times, so long ago that even the derivation of the name is obscure. On the day of the dance, various processions of dancers weave on a 3 mile route through the streets, in and out of the old town houses and elegant gardens and through shops and offices. The dance is held on May 8, except when that date is a Sunday or Monday, when the dance is held on the preceding Saturday.

CORNWALL AERO PARK

Visitors to this family leisure centre can see a tableau which spans the history of aviation from the daredevil days of the Cody Kite to Concorde. Outside, fixed-wing aircraft stand side by side with helicopters and hovercraft, while helicopters from neighbouring Culdrose Royal Naval Air Station often chatter overhead.

In 1979 the Aero Park displayed two replica aircraft which had been built for the TV serial *Flambards*, the story of a family who became involved in the pioneer days of flying. Now Flambards Village has been faithfully re-created to show the everyday life of the period – including a horse-drawn cab and grocer's and apothecary's shops. There is also a re-creation of a street at the time of the Blitz.

The park is open daily from Easter to October.

POLDHU COVE

History was made here in 1901, when the world's first radio transmission – the letter 'S', three dots in Morse code – was sent from Poldhu and received 3000 miles away in Newfoundland by the Italian inventor Guglielmo Marconi. This demonstration that radio waves would follow the curve of the Earth revolutionised communications.

Poldhu became the site of the first experimental wireless station, but this was demolished in 1933, and little trace of it remains. Only a footpath leads over the cliffs to Poldhu Point, where a simple stone monument – standing in 50 acres of headland, donated by the Marconi Company to the National Trust – records the triumph of the Italian genius and his British colleagues.

Half a mile below, Poldhu Cove slumbers quietly on, a beautiful sandy bay ringed by low green hills and scoured clean each day by the wind and rolling Atlantic combers.

MULLION

Bronze and Iron Age burial mounds ring the approaches to this peaceful village, where centuries-old cottages and little shops, built of stone and painted cream and white and yellow, front onto the narrow streets.

The exact age of Mullion's lovely old church is uncertain. Its chancel and font are 13th century, while its black-and-white tower, built of serpentine and granite, was erected around AD 1500. Fine 16th-century carved bench ends show the symbols of the Passion and the Crucifixion.

Beyond the village the road winds south-west through a green valley to the jagged rocks, dark islets and stone jetties of Mullion Cove, owned by the National Trust. Lobster pots are piled on the walls and boats drawn up.

KYNANCE COVE

From the car park at the end of a privately owned toll road a flight of 109 stone steps leads down to the pale sands and coloured pebbles of Kynance Cove. Rocks pierced by blowholes form teeth in the mouth of the cove. The changing light at early morning and sunset picks out the

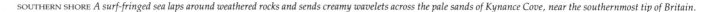

SOUTHERN SHORE *A surf-fringed sea laps around weathered rocks and sends creamy wavelets across the pale sands of Kynance Cove, near the southernmost tip of Britain.*

natural colours of the serpentine rock – olive-green, black, red and cream. The sands are accessible only in the 2½ hours before and after low tide; and the rocks can be slippery.

LIZARD

Until comparatively recent times, farming was the only industry in the Lizard. With the advent of tourism in the 19th century, a brisk trade arose in souvenirs made from serpentine, which cuts and polishes beautifully and was much admired by Queen Victoria.

A minor road leads south to Lizard Point and the twin towers of its lighthouse, completed in 1751; today its beam is 4 million candlepower, and can be seen 35 miles away. The view from the top is awe-inspiring.

On the road to nearby Church Cove, the ancient Church of St Wynwallow has snowdrops and daffodils growing from its graves each spring and roses in summer: the Celtic cross surmounts many of its headstones.

CADGWITH

Handsome old cottages built of serpentine, many roofed with thatch, adorn the slopes of Cadgwith Cove on either side of a tumbling brook. Boats hauled up on the pebbles fill the entrance to the harbour; lobster pots overflow from the walls into every available space around The Todden, the central point of Cadgwith's steep, winding street.

Fishermen mend their nets in the big loft nearby, where tallies of the once-prodigious catches of pilchard – and the prices they fetched – survive on the beams overhead. Another reminder of those golden days is the lone huer's hut on the cliff top. The huer, or lookout, kept watch for shoals of pilchards so big that they gave a blood-red tint to the sea, then signalled to the seine boat crews with 'flags' of gorse.

The route across Goonhilly Downs, the high moorland plateau that forms the backbone of the Lizard peninsula, winds past ancient bowl barrows – burial mounds of Celtic chieftains who died some 2500 years ago. By supreme irony the downs today are dominated by the latest in space-age technology, the giant 'tracking saucers' of the Satellite Earth Station, which is open in summer.

ST KEVERNE

The church, shops, terraced cottages and two inns which make up the heart of this old village form a hollow square, like a company of soldiers on parade. The square is dominated by the church, a place of worship for more than 1300 years. Its medieval spire was destroyed by lightning in 1770 but was quickly replaced, to fulfil its ancient role as a warning to ships that they were nearing The Manacles reef; the name stems from the Cornish words *Maen eglos*, 'Church rocks'.

The route continues to Porthallow, a secluded fishing village whose few cottages shelter alongside the Five Pilchards inn. Above the cove, clifftop walks lead north to Nare Head and east to Porthkerris Point, with fine views across Gerran Bay.

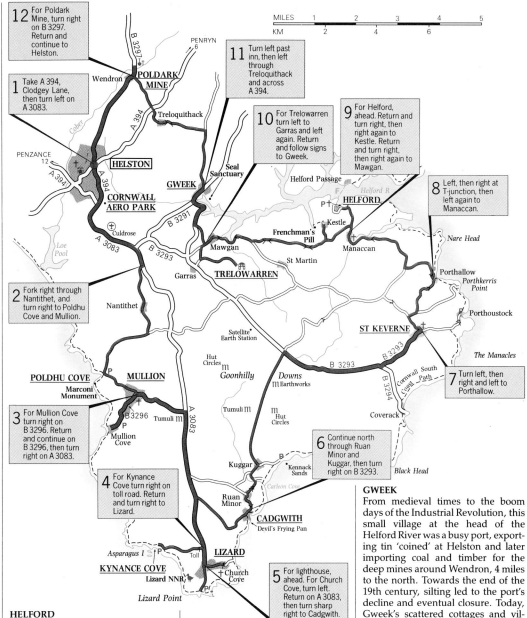

HELFORD

Narrow lanes lead like the threads of a spider's web through green countryside from the hilltop village of Manaccan to the lower reaches of the beautiful Helford River, with its oyster beds, sailing boats and thickly wooded banks. On an inlet leading off the river stands the tiny village of Helford, considered by many to be the loveliest in the Lizard peninsula.

Cottages built of stone, many of them thatched, have gardens ablaze in summer with fuchsias, hydrangeas, roses and honeysuckle. Ducks waddle along the single street, which winds round the wooded inlet, crossed at its head by a wooden footbridge.

A passenger ferry which dates back to the 16th century still plies between The Ferry Boat Inn, on the north bank at Helford Passage, to the quay near the Shipwright's Arms in Helford village.

Parking in Helford is banned from June to September, and visitors must use the car park by the small church above the inlet. From Kestle a footpath leads through the woods to Frenchman's Pill, the setting for Daphne du Maurier's novel *Frenchman's Creek*, the Cornish *pill* meaning 'creek'. Frenchman's Pill, which belongs to the National Trust, is a silent, haunting place even on the brightest summer's day.

TRELOWARREN

The drive leads through an avenue of dark ilex trees to an imposing two-storey, grey-stone house, home of the Vyvyan family for more than 500 years. The first lord of the manor was Earl Harold, killed at the Battle of Hastings and succeeded at Trelowarren by William the Conqueror's half-brother, Robert Mortain.

The Vyvyans, who acquired the estate in the 15th century, supported the royalists in the Civil War. Charles II, then Prince Charles, is believed to have stayed at Trelowarren during his escape to the Isles of Scilly.

The Vyvyans still live at Trelowarren, but the house is open for conducted tours on certain afternoons in summer.

GWEEK

From medieval times to the boom days of the Industrial Revolution, this small village at the head of the Helford River was a busy port, exporting tin 'coined' at Helston and later importing coal and timber for the deep mines around Wendron, 4 miles to the north. Towards the end of the 19th century, silting led to the port's decline and eventual closure. Today, Gweek's scattered cottages and village inn doze peacefully near the stone-built bridge.

A signpost points the way to Britain's only seal sanctuary, where injured grey Atlantic seals washed up on the beaches of Cornwall and the Isles of Scilly are brought for treatment before being returned to the sea. The sanctuary is open daily.

POLDARK MINE

Visitors to Poldark don safety helmets before going underground to see the old workings where tin miners stood on shelves to hack out the ore. The main lode they worked, its vein of tin, and the timbered galleries are all on view. Mining relics including tin samples and ingots, old lamps and assaying tools are also on display.

Above ground are a beam engine, corn mills and other exhibits. There are also craft shops, picnic gardens and a children's playground. The mine is open from the week before Easter until October.

Tourist information: Camborne 712941.

Map labels:

12 For Poldark Mine, turn right on B 3297. Return and continue to Helston.

1 Take A 394, Clodgey Lane, then turn left on A 3083.

11 Turn left past inn, then left through Treloquithack and across A 394.

10 For Trelowarren turn left to Garras and left again. Return and follow signs to Gweek.

9 For Helford, ahead. Return and turn right, then right again to Kestle. Return and turn right, then right again to Mawgan.

8 Left, then right at T-junction, then left again to Manaccan.

2 Fork right through Nantithet, and turn right to Poldhu Cove and Mullion.

3 For Mullion Cove turn right on B 3296. Return and continue on B 3296, then turn right on A 3083.

4 For Kynance Cove turn right on toll road. Return and turn right to Lizard.

7 Turn left, then right and left to Porthallow.

6 Continue north through Ruan Minor and Kuggar, then turn right on B 3293.

5 For lighthouse, ahead. For Church Cove, turn left. Return on A 3083, then turn sharp right to Cadgwith.

MILES 1 2 3 4 5
KM 2 4 6

PENRYN
B 3297
Wendron POLDARK MINE
A 394 Treloquithack
Cober
PENZANCE 12
A 394 HELSTON
CORNWALL AERO PARK
Culdrose
A 3083 B 3291 GWEEK
Seal Sanctuary
Helford Passage
HELFORD
Kestle
Frenchman's Pill
Manaccan
Mawgan St Martin
Garras TRELOWARREN
Nantithet
Nare Head
Porthallow
Porthkerris Point
Porthoustock
ST KEVERNE B 3293
The Manacles
Satellite Earth Station
Hut Circles Goonhilly
Downs Earthworks
Cornwall South Coast Path
Coverack
B 3294
Tumuli Hut Circles
POLDHU COVE MULLION
Marconi Monument
B 3296 Tumuli
Mullion Cove
Black Head
Kuggar
Kennack Sands
Carleon Cove
Ruan Minor
CADGWITH
Devil's Frying Pan
Asparagus I Toll
LIZARD
KYNANCE COVE Church Cove
Lizard NNR
Lizard Point
Loe Pool
A 3083

Through the 'Cornish Alps' to the sea

TOUR 5

61 MILES

The moonscapes of Cornwall's china clay country give way to some of its finest coastal scenery. Narrow roads wind between 'hedges' of stone built on banks aglow with wild flowers.

ST AUSTELL
For centuries tin was king in Cornwall, now it is china clay. The prosperity both brought has transformed St Austell from a small medieval village into a thriving market town. Links with the past remain in its narrow streets and fine stone buildings. All is dominated by Holy Trinity Church, chiming the hour from the hill above Fore Street from a tower of ivory-yellow Pentewan stone.

The countryside north of St Austell has changed in shape and colour since the discovery of china clay more than 200 years ago by William Cookworthy, a Plymouth chemist. Giant tips of waste soil turned once-green valleys into a range of towering white hills, known as the 'Cornish Alps'; these in turn are gradually being restored to grass.

CARTHEW
Signs in this tiny village point the way to the Wheal Martyn Museum – wheal means 'mine' in Cornish – where visitors can learn something of the china-clay industry which contributes to products as various as teacups and talcum powder, wellington boots and fireworks. The museum has a picnic area, and a three quarters of a mile nature trail to show how wildlife has adapted to the changed environment. The museum is open daily from April to October.

LUXULYAN
The wooded beauty of the mile-long Luxulyan valley, with its riot of bluebells and its pale, tumbling river, makes it a good spot for picnics. But the main attraction is man-made – the Treffry Viaduct, a stone colossus of ten arches, 216yds long and 93ft high. In building it to link Cornwall's north and south coasts, by a railway line above and an aqueduct below, the engineer Joseph Treffry in 1839 became the first man to transport ore by taking a 'canal' to the mine.

Luxulyan was once a centre of England's stone-quarrying industry. Silent monuments to those days are the enormous boulders, some weighing hundreds of tons, lying in the fields like great stone mushrooms. A museum in an old Methodist chapel records Luxulyan's past. Part of it is devoted to stone quarrying, showing old photographs and rock-splitting tools; among these are 'jumper rods', made to pierce holes in granite. Staffed by volunteers, the museum is open on Tuesday and Thursday afternoons during school holidays at Easter and in summer.

ROCHE ROCK
An outlying spur of the 1024ft high Hensbarrow Beacon rises 100ft above the windswept moorland near Roche village. Perched on top is the hermit's

cell and ruined Chapel of St Michael, built in 1409. Iron ladders clamped to the rock lead to a bird's eye view of the moorland heights and white clay tips all around.

CASTLE-AN-DINAS
It stands 702ft above sea level – yet the motorist may drive past without recognising this Iron Age earthwork fortress, consisting of four great circular ramparts. It provides views from Bodmin Moor to the 'Cornish Alps', and west and north to the Atlantic Ocean. To reach this ancient green 'castle', park carefully at the roadside then follow the sign to 'The Rings' for about half a mile.

ST MAWGAN
Church and village inn stand cheek by jowl above the green, with a trout stream flowing by. The village was once the home of the Arundells, Cornwall's richest and most powerful family before the Reformation. Their Elizabethan mansion above the church has been a Carmelite convent since 1794, when it was established by nuns fleeing the French Revolution; the chapel is open to the public.

The well by the church lich gate is believed to mark the site of the Welsh St Mawgan's 6th-century cell. The largely 13th-century church named after him has some of the finest brasses in Cornwall, the earliest dated 1374.

The Falcon Inn opposite dates from the 16th century. Across the road a path lined by yew and holly leads to a Carmelite chapel above.

TREWITHEN GARDENS
An early Georgian country house built of fine Pentewan stone, Trewithen stands in open parkland, with 28 acres of gardens renowned for their flowering trees and shrubs.

The elegant two-storey house has nine bays of windows centred on an arched doorway, and faces north onto parkland and meadows, with a lake and circular lawn set within a forecourt close by. The gardens blend with natural woodland to form a rich blaze of colour from scarlet tree rhododendrons, Japanese azaleas, maples and magnolias, as well as the deep green of native trees. There are also a walled garden, with an ornamental pond, and a water garden.

Trewithen House is open every afternoon from April to July. The gardens are open every afternoon except Sundays from March to September.

PORTHLUNEY COVE
The towers and turrets of Caerhays Castle are set against a backcloth of beech, pine and giant Asiatic flowering trees, with meadows running down to the white sands of Porthluney Cove. The castle, converted from a Tudor manor house in the early 19th century, appeared as 'Manderley' in the TV production of Daphne du Maurier's novel *Rebecca*. It was built by John Nash, architect of London's Marble Arch and the Royal Pavilion at Brighton.

The Williams family, owners of Caerhays Castle since the mid-19th century, have created magnificent

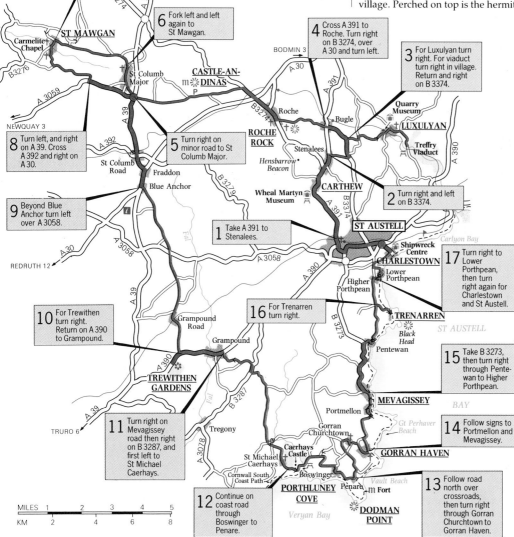

gardens of natural woodland intermingled with tall flowering trees and shrubs grown from seed brought back from Burma, China, India and Taiwan. The gardens are open to the public on Easter Sunday and either the first or second Sunday in May.

A car park adjoins the beach, making it an ideal place to picnic, while coastal paths round the cliffs on each side offer views past Nare Head to the Lizard, or from Dodman Point beyond Gribbin Head.

DODMAN POINT
A footpath leads in less than a mile from the tiny hamlet of Penare, past the mound of an Iron Age fort to a great granite cross on Dodman Point, nearly 400ft above the sea.

The 20ft cross represents a burning declaration of Christian faith: its inscription reads: 'In the firm hope of the second coming of our Lord Jesus Christ and for the encouragement of those who strive to serve Him this cross is erected AD 1896.'

A small stone-built hut roofed with slate standing among the gorse 50yds back was formerly used by excise men patrolling this remote stretch of coast. The headland and the hamlet below it are owned by the National Trust. Seabirds abound, and there are sweeping views across Veryan Bay to the Lizard, and north-east towards Plymouth.

GORRAN HAVEN
Once a thriving fishing village with its own boat-building yards, Gorran Haven is now a holiday resort of quiet beauty. Its three sandy beaches – Great Perhaver to the north, the harbour enclave itself, and Vault (or Bow) beach to the south – are sheltered by green cliffs. Most of its houses are modern, but some old, stone-built cottages with traditional slate roofs lie huddled by the harbour below the medieval Chapel of St Just. And some of the street names (such as 'Rattle Street', from the sound of iron-rimmed wheels of fishermen's barrows on former cobblestones) tell their own story of the haven's past.

Smuggling, as well as fishing and farming, was once an industry here; in 1825, even the local coastguards were accused of 'a total want of order and discipline' after broaching casks of contraband spirits and helping themselves.

The quay was built in 1888 by the Williams family of Caerhays. Records of that period show that 30 boats worked out of Gorran Haven. The handful left – crabbers mostly – are today heavily outnumbered by visitors and their pleasure boats.

MEVAGISSEY
Though its fleet of little boats was reduced by the disappearance of the pilchard, Mevagissey remains a busy fishing village. Old slate-roofed cottages, with walls of stone and cob 2ft thick, line the streets around the harbour. More houses, some decorated in bright colour-wash, cling to the slopes above.

Noisy hordes of gulls escort each working boat back into port with its catches of many kinds of fish,

MEVAGISSEY 'DUCK' *Pleasure craft throng the harbour whose fishermen once supplied 'duck' – pilchards – to feed the Royal Navy.*

CALM HAVEN *Secluded St Mawgan lies only 2 miles from the wild Atlantic.*

TREWITHEN GARDENS *The Cornish name Trewithen means 'the house in the spinney'. Over 200 years, imaginative gardening and nature have combined to produce a delight of parkland and gardens, noted for their trees and shrubs, especially rhododendrons.*

including mackerel, pollack and whiting. Other boats take anglers out to sea, and turn the double harbour with its inner and outer quays into a scene of colourful, non-stop bustle.

The ancient, narrow streets of Mevagissey, with their one-way routing, present traffic problems in summer, but there is ample parking space within easy walking distance of the harbour.

TRENARREN
A sign by the manor house at the top of the hill warns that the way down to Trenarren is 'Impracticable to motorists'; but the quarter-mile walk to the secluded hamlet in a wooded valley below Black Head is well worth while.

It passes detached stone-built houses and cottages, all with pleasant gardens, and a stone stile at the far end leads to a rocky, sheltered cove.

CHARLESTOWN
The road sweeps down through an avenue of fine beech trees before turning into this tiny port and former pilchard-fishing village, named after a land owner, Charles Rashleigh. Charlestown owes much of its prosperity to the harbour he built here – one of the smallest in Britain – towards the end of the 18th century.

Today, small freighters ply from Bremen, Hamburg and other European and British ports, carrying fertiliser and clay in and out of Charlestown's Tom Thumb harbour.

Sheltering cliffs enclose a small pebble beach. A line of handsome stone-built cottages, most of them terraced and all with bright, colour-washed walls and neat flower gardens, gaze down on the quay. Behind the cobbled car park of The Rashleigh inn a Shipwreck Centre is open daily from Easter to September. The coastal path above Charlestown leads north towards the sands of Carlyon Bay, and south towards Lower Porthpean and Black Head.

Tourist information: Truro 74555; (Lostwithiel) Bodmin 872207; Newquay 71345/6; (Summercourt) St Austell 860747 (summer).

From a cliff-top castle to the Cornish Riviera

TOUR
6
── 63 MILES ──

Northwards from Bodmin Moor lies a land steeped in legends of King Arthur. Headlands give dramatic views along a wild, rocky coast punctuated by coves and tiny fishing harbours.

BODMIN
Streets of brownstone and granite buildings cluster together on the south-west edge of Bodmin Moor. Bodmin is the only Cornish town recorded in Domesday Book which, together with the Crown Jewels, was placed for safe keeping in Bodmin Gaol during the First World War.

The Regimental Museum of the Duke of Cornwall's Light Infantry in Lostwithiel Road is open daily, and the Old Colours carried by the regiment can be seen in St Petroc's Church.

BLISLAND
A cluster of Georgian houses and cottages grouped around a village green makes an unexpected sight in Cornwall. The village church is dedicated to St Protus and St Hyacinth – two brothers who were martyred in Italy in the 4th century – and has a dazzling interior. Richly carved wagon roofs, granite columns, slate floors and old benches contrast with a highly coloured medieval-style rood screen and Renaissance-style high altar.

The screen and altar were designed by Frederick Charles Eden, who in 1894 restored the church in a way that successfully blends old with new.

CAMELFORD
A reconstruction of a moorland cottage at the turn of the century is a centrepiece of the North Cornwall Museum and Gallery in Camelford. Its fascinating display of aspects of Cornish life over the past century includes a wide variety of tools of various trades, as well as domestic items ranging from lace bonnets to early vacuum cleaners. The museum is open daily, except Sundays, from April to September.

A short detour off the main road leads to the start of a path to the top of Rough Tor, at 1311ft the second highest hill in Cornwall. The effort is rewarded by spectacular views, including Brown Willy (1377ft), the highest point in the county.

King Arthur's last battle, according to local legend, was fought at Slaughterbridge, 1 mile north of Camelford.

BOSCASTLE
The harbour entrance looks impossibly narrow – but fishing boats tied up alongside the quay prove the passage can be made. Local craft shops include the Camelot Pottery, where

ON THE WATERFRONT *Across the estuary from Polruan, the buildings of Fowey jostle for space below green slopes.*

ANCIENT WAY *A medieval clapper bridge, built of stone slabs, spans the De Lank river at Bradford, on the road to Blisland.*

STATELY PORTAL *With lordly dignity the 17th-century gatehouse commands the entrance to Lanhydrock House.*

visitors can watch a family of potters producing Mochaware, decorated with ferns, trees and bushes in Chinese-style patterns.

Round the corner, another family craft enterprise produces handmade perfumed candles, and next door there are paintings on stone for sale. A Museum of Witchcraft on the quay is open in summer.

ST NECTAN'S GLEN
One of North Cornwall's least publicised and most magical spots is reached from a car park just off the road from Boscastle to Tintagel. A well-defined path leads through St Nectan's Glen, a peaceful, wooded valley filled with bird song. At its top a waterfall plunges 40ft, thundering through a hole in a stone basin.

The waterfall may be approached in summer through the Hermitage Tea Garden. A path leads down to duckboards at the foot of the waterfall, and to an upper platform which is a fine viewpoint.

ROCKY VALLEY
A continuation of St Nectan's Glen towards the sea, Rocky Valley can be reached only by a footpath starting farther down the road, near a layby. The footpath leads through a trout farm and down a wooded valley. It passes the ruins of an old mill, behind which is a rock with small maze-like carvings said to date from 1600 BC.

The river flows through a miniature gorge, with several small waterfalls, and the half-hour walk ends on rocks above the sea.

TINTAGEL
Tradition says Tintagel was the seat of King Arthur and his knights, and the nearby village makes the main part of its living from Arthurian lore. But the existing castle ruins, reached by footpath from the village, have nothing to do with Arthur and date from no earlier than the 12th century. There are, however, the remains of a much older Celtic monastery on The Island, at the end of a climb of 300 steps.

In the village, the Old Post Office is a small 14th-century manor house, used as a post office in Victorian times and now owned by the National Trust and open daily from April to October. King Arthur's Hall, a three-storey building of 1933, has 73 stained-glass windows illustrating the legends associating King Arthur with Tintagel which Tennyson popularised in *The Idylls of the King.*

DELABOLE SLATE QUARRY
From the visitors' viewing platform, workers at the bottom of this enormous hole in the ground – more than 500ft deep and 1 mile in circumference – look like ants with toy trucks rather than quarrymen with mechanical diggers. Quarrying for the distinctive blue-grey slate has been carried on here for more than 400 years.

PORT ISAAC
The only way to see Port Isaac is on foot. There are no parking spaces, and reversing in the narrow, steep streets

is a nightmare. Entering the village from Portgaverne there is a large car park at the top of the hill. From there an attractive walk leads round the cliffs to the harbour and back up through the village. Fresh lobsters and crabs can often be bought at the slipway.

PENTIRE POINT
From Pentire Farm, where cars may be parked, there are easy walks to the Rumps, to the right, or Pentire Point to the left. The Cornwall North Coast Path joins the two headlands to complete a circular route, with marvellous views up the Camel Estuary, taking about an hour to cover.

PENCARROW
A tour of this beautiful Georgian house is a journey through the history of the Molesworth St Aubyn family, its owners since the reign of Elizabeth I. The family's portraits have been painted by most of the famous painters of their day; the dining room alone is hung with 11 portraits by Sir Joshua Reynolds.

The house also contains other fine paintings, furniture, fabrics and china. It stands in gardens bright in spring and summer with rhododendrons, camellias and hydrangeas. Pencarrow is open every afternoon except Fridays and Saturdays from Easter to September; the gardens are open daily in summer.

Tourist information: Bodmin 4159; Camelford 212954 (summer).

Riverside villages offer unusual extra attractions in the form of displays of music, art and the American railroad. On the coast, cliffs shelter holiday resorts which are still busy fishing villages.

LOOE
The Looe river divides the seaside resort and fishing port into two towns, West Looe and East Looe. Summer holidaymakers throng the quays to watch the departure and return of the brightly coloured fishing boats, or set off themselves on fishing trips for shark and mackerel. Cars are barred from the old part of East Looe, so that visitors can wander unhindered around its narrow streets.

There are good beaches – East Looe's is the sandier – and during the holiday season there are trips to Looe Island, about a quarter of a mile offshore. After leaving Looe, the route turns north through Kiln Wood, named after the old limekilns which stand beside the road.

ST KEYNE
The road northwards from Sandplace to St Keyne runs alongside the single-track Liskeard to Looe railway line, perhaps the prettiest branch line in the West Country. Near St Keyne

station is housed the Paul Corin Musical Collection, one of Europe's finest collections of automatic musical instruments.

The exhibits include fairground organs, continental café organs and orchestrions. Player-pianos, which are worked by perforated paper rolls, reproduce performances of famous pianists, such as Rachmaninov, while a relic from a later age is the mighty Wurlitzer organ from the Regent Cinema, Brighton.

Many of the mechanical marvels in the Musical Collection may be heard playing daily from Easter to the end of September.

RAILROAD PARK
Miniature replicas of American locomotives draw passengers on two railroad networks through extensive parkland. One ride simulates a trip through the Colorado forests, the other the Wyoming plains. There are also locomotive sheds, an American Railroad Exhibition, picnic areas, a lake for radio-controlled boats, a trading post and a display explaining the history of the enterprise.

The park was started by John Southern and his family as a hobby. Another of Southern's enthusiasms is reflected in the adjoining Archibald Thorburn's Edwardian Countryside exhibition. Southern has been collecting the paintings of the British bird artist Archibald Thorburn (1860-1935) since he was 11 years old. They are displayed in a vivid reconstruction of the countryside in which Thorburn painted, complete with authentic sights, sounds and smells.

The Railroad Park is open daily from Easter to the end of October. Thorburn's Edwardian Countryside is open daily.

GOLITHA FALLS
A signposted footpath to Golitha Falls starting opposite the car park runs through beech woods alongside the Fowey river – here only a stream. The setting is as attractive in winter, with frost crackling underfoot, as it is in high summer. The walk to the falls and back takes about half an hour.

ST NEOT
This large and attractive village is best known for the stained glass in its 15th-century church. Much of it was restored in the last century, but a dozen windows retain the original 16th-century glass. The Creation window, at the east end of the south aisle, is the earliest and least restored. Among the subjects depicted are the creation of fish and birds and the stories of Adam and Eve and Cain and Abel. The upright of the granite cross outside the church door is thought to date from the 10th century.

In a meadow some 300yds away stands a Holy Well; it is reached by a riverside track starting beside the Carlyon Garage.

SLATE CAVERNS
Apart from slender pillars of slate left by old-time quarrymen, the majestic domed roofs rising to 50ft high are without support, an enduring testimony to the skill of the men who fashioned them and to the strength and stability of the slate.

The most spectacular sight is an underground lake, the stillness of its turquoise-coloured water disturbed only by an occasional drip of water from the roof. There are guided tours daily in the summer.

LANHYDROCK HOUSE
Only the gatehouse of 1651 and the north wing, with its 116ft long gallery, survive of the original 17th-century building, which was largely destroyed by fire in 1881. The gallery has

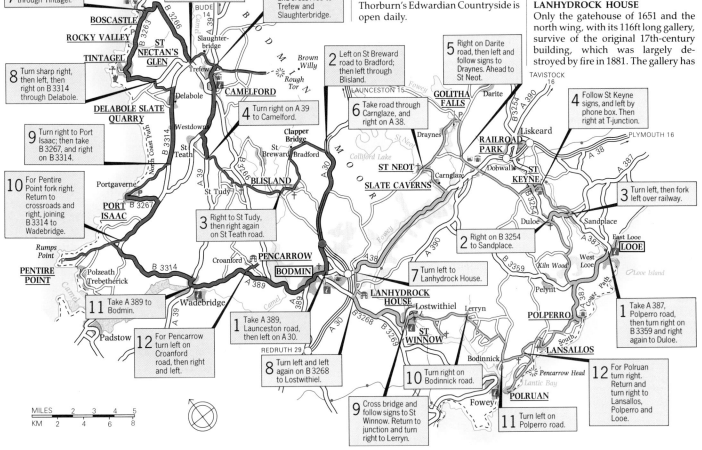

21

a magnificent plaster ceiling decorated with scenes from the Old Testament. For the rest, Lanhydrock gives a very 'lived-in' feeling of life in late Victorian times. The servants' quarters still have their brass beds and washstands, and the kitchen quarters their coal ranges and cooking utensils.

The house and its grounds, owned by the National Trust, are open daily from April to October.

ST WINNOW

The Church of St Winnow is romantically sited in a tiny peaceful village on the banks of the River Fowey. Despite much restoration last century, the old carved wagon roofs and several 16th-century bench ends remain. There is a 15th-century font, and the east window of the south side contains exquisite late-15th-century glass depicting kneeling figures, standing saints and coats of arms.

POLRUAN

This unspoilt village has a ruined blockhouse, a handful of shops, a flourishing boatyard, two pubs and a waterfront bistro and bar open in summer. There is a regular passenger ferry service to Fowey on the other side of the river. Visitors must park at the top of the village, from where there are superb views across the harbour.

The 14th-century parish church of Lanteglos-by-Fowey stands alone in farmland. Pencarrow Head, a magnificent headland overlooking Lantic Bay, is a favourite picnic spot.

LANSALLOS

One of the most attractive and accessible small beaches on this stretch of coast is reached by a 15 minute walk starting by the gate of Lansallos church.

Nearly all the beams and bosses in the 15th-century Church of St Ildierna are original, and on the south wall is a slate coffin slab featuring an Elizabethan lady. Some of the early 16th-century carved pews are decorated with animal heads and bodies.

POLPERRO

Strung along a narrow combe, Polperro's streets lead down to a tiny harbour where the water laps against the walls of colour-washed cottages. There is a car park at the top of the village from which visitors can walk down or take a bus.

The Land of Legend and Model Village at the Old Forge, open from mid-March to October, includes a photographic exhibition showing the history of Polperro up to the floods of 1976 and tableaux portraying Cornish life and history. A museum illustrates the history of smuggling.

Tourist information:
Looe 2072 (summer).

LANTIC BAY *The Cornish Coast Path dips and climbs along the rugged cliffs, and a pathway starting opposite a National Trust car park zigzags down to the secluded beach in its tiny cove.*

Tors, tin mines and towers beside the River Tamar

Between Bodmin Moor and Dartmoor lies some of the most bleakly beautiful upland scenery in the West Country. Roads climb to windy viewpoints and explore a spectacular gorge.

LAUNCESTON

The streets of Cornwall's ancient capital are lined with eye-catching features, large and small. There are grand rows of Georgian houses, the epitome of red-brick harmony, and a wealth of individual details such as the gilded phoenix, traditional sign of the chemist, in the High Street.

The castle, its grey keep astride the summit of a steep, grass-covered mound, has seen service as a Civil War stronghold, assize court and prison. Views from the lofty keep, which leans 3ft out of the vertical, together with an aerial photograph of the town in the small castle exhibition, put everything into perspective. Below winds the River Kelsey, with the town a maze of narrow streets to the south and east.

Medieval Launceston was the only walled town in Cornwall. Isolated fragments of these fortifications still remain, particularly in the green parklands beneath the castle and at the South Gate, one of the three original entrances. The 16th-century St Mary Magdalene's Church is startling in appearance, almost every available surface on its Cornish granite exterior being decorated with carvings of legendary figures, animals, plants and fruit. Below the east window is a carved figure of St Mary Magdalene.

From a terminus below the castle, Launceston Steam Railway's veteran locomotive runs westwards for 1¼ miles along the Kensey valley. Services operate daily from the end of May to mid-October, at Easter and Christmas, and on Sunday afternoons from Christmas to May.

LYDFORD GORGE

The romantic notions of landscape expressed by the poets and artists of the 19th century are evoked in this sombre defile, cutting through high moorlands. From the first of two car parks two footpaths lead to the White Lady waterfall, which slides 100ft down a rocky chute to join the River Lyd in the wooded valley below.

A footpath from the second car park, 1 mile north-east, zigzags through woods into the depths of a sheer-sided valley. From the bridge across the river, turn right along a narrow path cut into the cliff for the Devil's Cauldron, where the Lyd crashes through a narrow cleft in the rocks, their vertical black walls covered in dripping moss.

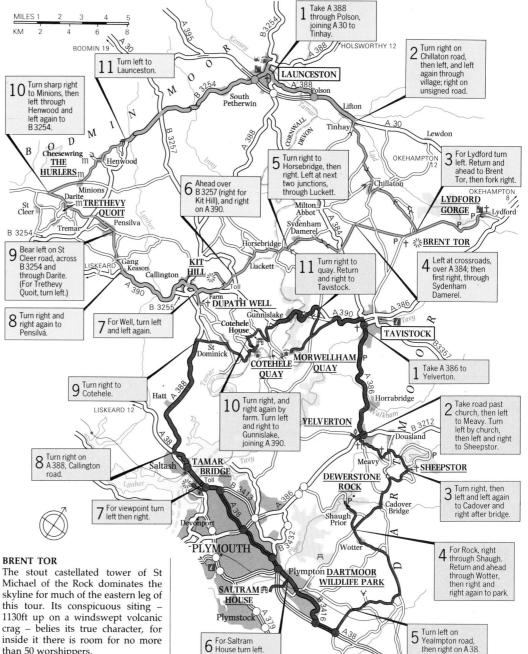

BRENT TOR

The stout castellated tower of St Michael of the Rock dominates the skyline for much of the eastern leg of this tour. Its conspicuous siting – 1130ft up on a windswept volcanic crag – belies its true character, for inside it there is room for no more than 50 worshippers.

The stiff walk to the summit is rewarded by one of the broadest views in the West Country. It takes in the mass of the Dartmoor National Park, the sea beyond Plymouth, Bodmin Moor and distant Exmoor.

KIT HILL

A towering chimney tops the conical granite outcrop of Kit Hill. The stack is a memorial to the once-booming Kit Hill Mine, closed early this century. For hundreds of years, rich deposits of tin, copper, zinc and arsenic attracted feverish mining activity. Huge cubes of granite scattered about the hillside are relics of quarrying.

DUPATH WELL

Hidden in a small, grassy enclosure off a muddy track through Dupath Farm is a well covered by a small 16th-century granite chapel, roofed with hefty slabs of moorstone and crowned by a crooked pinnacle. The well is, in fact, a spring which rises a few feet away and flows through the chapel into a shallow trough.

According to legend, the well originates from Saxon times when a remorseful victor of a duel put it up as an act of repentance for his sins.

TRETHEVY QUOIT

Among the most spectacular of Cornwall's prehistoric monuments is Trethevy Quoit, on the south-eastern edge of Bodmin Moor. Huge upright slabs nearly 15ft high support a slanting capstone more than 11ft long – the bare bones of a burial chamber, once covered by an earthen mound and probably used as a collective tomb between 1800 and 1200 BC.

THE HURLERS

Mysterious man-made and strange natural rock formations are scattered about Bodmin Moor just west of Minions. Three stone circles known as The Hurlers may have been placed by Bronze Age people to mark the sunset in early spring and late autumn; local legend, however, says they were men turned to stone for the sin of hurling a ball on the Sabbath.

A ragged mound of strangely shaped rocks fills the horizon 1 mile to the north and includes the Cheesewring, a precariously balanced stack of slabs which narrows towards its base.

Tourist information: Launceston 2321.

The open flanks of Dartmoor National Park give way to wooded river valleys. The River Tamar separates Devon from Cornwall and flows through a countryside rich in industrial relics.

TAVISTOCK

One man's fortune was largely responsible for Tavistock's spacious and gracious town centre. Francis, Duke of Bedford, a copper-mining magnate of the mid-19th century, ploughed part of his wealth into remodelling Tavistock. His statue, standing near the square named after him, surveys his neo-Gothic buildings of sea-green volcanic stone.

In 1281 Tavistock became a stannary town – a centre for the weighing and stamping of tin from the mines of western Dartmoor. Wool also played a part in the town's prosperity.

YELVERTON

A kaleidoscopic array of more than 800 glass paperweights of all shapes, sizes, colours and designs from all over the world can be seen at the Yelverton Paperweight Centre. Some are antique, some are modern. Many seem to contain their own miniature, multicoloured worlds filled with countless flowers and intricate patterns.

SHEEPSTOR

The typical Dartmoor church in this isolated hamlet, which lies beneath the treeless heights of Sheeps Tor, has most untypical associations. A stone-flagged pathway leads into a churchyard containing the Rajah's Tomb, resting place of the Rajah of Sarawak.

James Brooke, an officer in the East India Company, was granted the title of Rajah in 1841, by the Rajah of Borneo. Brooke later returned to England and lived at nearby Burrator House, where he died in 1868. The colourful and adventurous story of the Brookes of Sarawak is recounted in full on a commemorative plaque in the church.

DEWERSTONE ROCK

A craggy rib of granite stands above the confluence of the Plym and Meavy, rivers which rise on Dartmoor and rush down to meet in a boulder-strewn, wooded gorge. From the car park a number of paths lead up to the Dewerstone's irregularly shaped trio of peaks, the Devil's Rock, Needle Buttress and Raven Buttress.

DARTMOOR WILDLIFE PARK

A 30 acre hillside site is the home of a veritable Noah's Ark of reptiles, birds and beasts; inhabitants include the rare Siberian tiger, which has been successfully bred here. Every afternoon from Easter to September the park stages an event called 'Close encounters of the animal kind': this takes the form of an informal lecture followed by a session in which the

GOOD AS NEW *Cotehele House, built in the late 15th century, is one of the least-altered examples of a medieval squire's house.*

SAINTS AND SINNERS *Lydford Castle was built in 1195 as a prison for offenders against local laws. Its 13th-century neighbour is dedicated to St Petrock.*

ROCK PILE *The Cheesewring crowns Stowe's Hill, on Bodmin Moor.*

public can stroke and handle many of the animals, including racoons, birds of prey, iguanas and snakes.

SALTRAM HOUSE

Despite the suburbia that lays siege to its grounds, Saltram manages to preserve an historic calm. The house, owned by the National Trust, incorporates substantial Tudor and Stuart remains, though it is essentially a remarkable survival of a mid-18th-century mansion.

The Parker family were Saltram's most influential owners. Much of the lavish interior reflects their tastes and the skills of such artists as the designer Robert Adam and the painter Sir Joshua Reynolds. The saloon is an opulent, mirrored room in which two magnificent chandeliers hang from a pale blue and fawn ceiling, its design complemented by the carpet pattern.

TAMAR BRIDGE

The clean, modern lines of the suspension bridge, opened in 1961 to carry road traffic, contrast with the complex web of grey-painted tubular arches and girders of the railway bridge of 1859. The railway bridge was designed by the Victorian engineer Isambard Kingdom Brunel, whose name and profession are proudly emblazoned on its framework.

COTEHELE QUAY

The Tamar's past role as a thriving commercial waterway is remembered at this beautiful quayside where the river loops through a steep-sided wooded valley. In the last century the slopes of the Tamar valley were alive with the activity of miners and quarrymen, and the river below was a major trading highway.

The once-derelict quayside and wharf buildings have been restored and brought to life again by the National Trust. A museum in the main wharf building recalls the time when Cotehele's waterfront was all bustle as lime and coal were unloaded and tin, lead, copper and barrels of arsenic filled the quayside. On a hillside stands Cotehele House, surrounded by beautiful grounds.

MORWELLHAM QUAY

Visitors to Morwellham step back into the 19th century, when Morwellham was the greatest copper exporting port in Britain. They can meet and talk to blacksmiths, quay workers, assayers and the like – all dressed in period costume – and learn something of life and work in the Victorian boom years.

This period dress is just one aspect of Morwellham's living past. There are workshops, a 19th-century farm and cottage, working water wheels, a port museum, tramway and canal, and riverside and woodland trails. Horse-drawn carriages follow the Duke's Drive, named after Morwellham's 19th-century landowner, the Duke of Bedford.

Below ground, electric-powered trams take passengers deep into the George and Charlotte copper mine for a fascinating look at 18th and 19th-century mining conditions.

Tourist information: Tavistock 2938 (summer); Plymouth 23806 (summer), 264849.

Ports and resorts between high cliffs

Long lanes, banked high with wild flowers and ferns in summer, link a glorious surfing beach, a wave-torn headland and villages that descend steep slopes down to the sea.

BUDE
Ocean rollers pile in with 3000 miles of muscle behind them to collapse on the shore in slow-motion majesty. Experts say there is no better surfing anywhere between Bude and Bondi. At low tide, the sea can be very dangerous, but the beaches are superb: Crooklets is best for surfing, while Summerleaze has a massive breakwater and a river and canal that flow side by side to the sea.

Bude grew up on the canal, built in the 1820s to take barges as far as Launceston, but only a mile or so is navigable now. Beside it survive some fine Georgian buildings – a folk exhibition and a few stone cottages.

Stratton, to the north-east, is older than Bude and looks it. There are some Georgian and older buildings in the town centre, from which narrow streets of thatched, deep-windowed cottages swing steeply uphill to the church.

Near the top is one of the West Country's most characterful inns, The Tree, dating from the 13th century. The beams are timbers from wrecked ships, and long ago it was a manor house of the Grenvilles. In 1643 the inn was the headquarters of the Royalist commander, Sir Bevil Grenville, during the Battle of Stamford Hill fought nearby.

COOMBE VALLEY
A high green ridge is crowned by a tracking station and surrealistic trees, bent over and shaven by the wind off the sea. Below, remote from all this, is the Coombe Valley, a quiet place of oak woods and a stream that may be explored along nature trails.

A scattering of cottages once housed workers in a now disused water mill, and Stowe Barton, a solid 17th-century farm, was built by the Grenvilles, perhaps to replace a long-vanished manor house that belonged to Sir Richard Grenville of *Revenge* fame. His epic fight with the Spanish fleet off the Azores in 1591 was celebrated in a poem by Tennyson.

The stream comes to the sea at Duckpool, a popular surfing beach in good weather and pure Wagner in bad, when the waves snarl in like raging furies.

MORWENSTOW
The hamlet is entirely pervaded by the spirit of Robert Stephen Hawker, its vicar from 1834 to 1875. An eccentric poet, he wrote the *Song of the Western Men*, with the line 'And shall Trelawney die?' Beneath and around the ship's figurehead in the churchyard lie more than 40 mostly unnamed seamen whose corpses Hawker brought from the shore.

HARTLAND
The village is a pretty place of stone and slate cottages, narrow alleys, shops and craft displays. At Hartland Quay there is a white stone hotel among the dark cliffs and fearsome fangs of rock. A museum, open in summer, tells of shipwrecks down the centuries, the coastal trade and the wildlife of the cliffs.

Stoke is a hamlet as Devonian as the cream teas sold in a low, black-and-white painted stone house. Intriguing Church House was probably an outbuilding of the vanished Hartland Abbey. Beside it is the 14th-century Church of St Nectan, a tremendous building with a barrel-roofed ceiling decorated with huge, multicoloured stars, and a 128ft tower that can be seen for miles out to sea.

At Hartland Point a tough, white lighthouse stands at the foot of the cliff. Above it, a radar scanner reels like a drunken robot. The lighthouse can be reached by driving to Blagdon Farm, paying a toll and walking down the cliff path. The Somerset and North Devon Coast Path can be joined by parking at Titchberry Farm.

CLOVELLY
Nature and circumstances combine to create the perfect Devon village – with a steep High Street, also known as 'Up-a-long' and 'Down-a-long', falling in steps made up of beach pebbles down to a 14th-century quay; whitewashed cottages, no two alike and almost drowned in fuchsias, geraniums and hydrangeas; and a view all round Bideford Bay.

This unspoilt vista survives partly because there is no more building space, and even more because it has been in the hands of single owners – the Careys, the Hamlyns and now a trust. Christine Hamlyn, who died in 1936, devoted her life to preserving Clovelly's charm, and many of the cottages bear her initials. The Hamlyns provided Mount Pleasant Park and the lovely 3 mile Hobby Drive, an alternative approach to the village from the main road near Buck's Cross. The trust maintains the picture by banishing cars to the car park at the top of the village.

Clovelly was built for the herring fisheries, which declined in the 1900s, but about the quay and the Red Lion there are still reminders of the sturdier days before cream teas were thought of.

CLOVELLY CASCADE *A delightful medley of houses tumbles 400ft down to Clovelly's harbour and its 18th-century quay.*

VALLEY OF PEACE *The tiny hamlet of Coombe shelters amid the tranquil woodlands of the beautiful Coombe Valley.*

TAPELEY PARK *The mansion looks out to the sea over terraced Italian gardens noted for their rare plants.*

26

BUCK'S MILLS

A steep, secret road leads to a mini-Clovelly, a village in which stone and slate cottages drop at an ever-increasing angle to the sea. The cottages are tiny against the great masses of creeper-hung masonry beside them. This is all that remains of a 19th-century limekiln that turned limestone imported from Wales into lime for fertiliser.

TAMAR LAKES

In a county where largish bodies of fresh water – even those created by man – are rare, Tamar Lakes are a pleasant surprise. Upper Lake, a reservoir, was created only in 1975, but already with its surrounding meadows and woods seems perfectly natural. Lower Lake is reed-wrapped and wilder; it was made in 1820 to feed the Bude Canal, and is now a wildfowl reserve.

MARHAMCHURCH

The village, mostly of whitewashed stone, thatched or slated, is piled about its church.

Dating mainly from the 14th century, the church has slight remains of an anchoress's cell – that of Cecilia Moys, who had herself bricked into a tiny room whose only outlet was a small window into the church.

The building is glorious; look especially at the chequerboard floor, cleverly constructed of slates set on end, the Jacobean pulpit, and the huge cast of Charles II's Royal Arms.

Tourist information: Bude 4240 (summer); (Stamford Hill) Bude 3781 (summer).

TOUR 11

——— 33 MILES ———

Two ancient ports beside the Torridge recall Elizabethan sea dogs, and a nearby resort has associations with two Victorian writers. An inland town is noted for its glass.

BIDEFORD

Saxon *Bieda's Ford* (on the Torridge) is a market town nowadays, though for many years it was one of the busiest seaports in England. Until the War of Independence put a stop to the trade, Bideford waxed rich on tobacco from the American colonies.

Not many deep-sea vessels dock there now, but plenty of coasters still tie up at the long, tree-shaded quay. Nevertheless, memories of the old westward urge still linger. Sir Richard Grenville's *Revenge* was crewed entirely by Bideford men when she challenged the Spanish fleet off the Azores in 1591.

The focal point of the town is the many-arched bridge composed of a stone cladding over medieval oak. The site of the ford that preceded the bridge is marked by Old Ford House, now a museum.

Streets of fine houses climb as steep as ski-runs from the quay. At the top

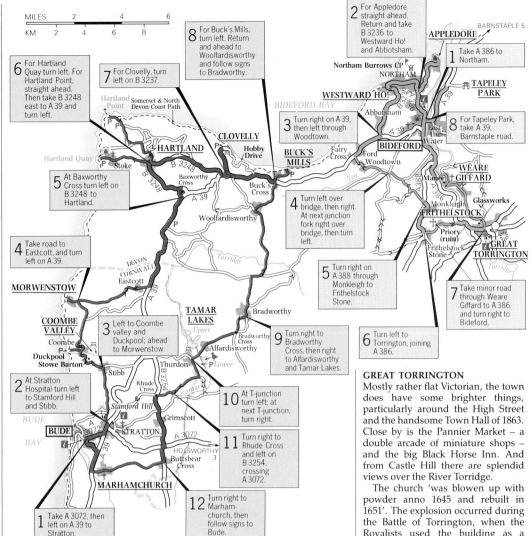

is the Market Plaza in which pannier markets (when stallholders sit beside panniers or baskets of produce) are held on Tuesdays and Saturdays.

APPLEDORE

High tide brings the married estuaries of the Taw and Torridge brimming to the edge of the quay that runs the whole length of the village, while at low tide yachts, cabin cruisers and fishing boats lie canted over on the sands. Boats and cars are parked side by side along the quay, where many of the shops and houses have been converted from chandlers' stores. Some of these flourished when the port was a power in the Newfoundland cod and Virginia tobacco trades. The story of these, and local smuggling and privateering, is told in the North Devon Maritime Museum in Odun Road.

Shipbuilding survives, producing trawlers, naval vessels, and full-size replicas of historic ships, among them the Hudson Bay Company's 17th-century *Nonsuch* and Sir Francis Drake's *Golden Hinde*.

WESTWARD HO!

The town was founded in the 1860s to rival Torquay, but it never began to compete. Some of the original features remain, notably the Royal North

Devon Golf Club, the oldest links club in England. There are lofty Victorian terraces, some of which in 1874 were converted into the United Services College, a public school for the sons of officers. Thirty years later it was amalgamated with Haileybury and would have been forgotten, had not one of its former pupils, Rudyard Kipling, based *Stalky and Co* upon it. The resort was named after the novel by Charles Kingsley.

A 1½ mile natural barrier of wave-rounded rocks protects Appledore, Westward Ho! and Northam Burrows from the sea.

FRITHELSTOCK

The essentials of a Devon village stand here – half a dozen 18th-century houses, a good-looking pub, a war memorial, a village green and a lovely church with an elegant tower. The interior of the church is touchingly simple, apart from an ornate Royal Arms of Charles II. The pews and their carving are medieval; look out for the two prelates sticking their tongues out at one another, said to be a Bishop of Exeter and the Prior of Frithelstock.

Adjoining the church is North Devon's only monastic ruin – the remains of an Augustinian priory founded in about 1220.

GREAT TORRINGTON

Mostly rather flat Victorian, the town does have some brighter things, particularly around the High Street and the handsome Town Hall of 1863. Close by is the Pannier Market – a double arcade of miniature shops – and the big Black Horse Inn. And from Castle Hill there are splendid views over the River Torridge.

The church 'was blowen up with powder anno 1645 and rebuilt in 1651'. The explosion occurred during the Battle of Torrington, when the Royalists used the building as a magazine.

WEARE GIFFARD

The nucleus of the village is delightful – a pairing of a 15th-century manor house like a miniature castle, and a church at least 100 years older. The house is not open to the public, but the church has some fascinating monuments.

Effigies of a 14th-century knight and his lady which once lay together are now separated, and it is said that the couple will haunt the building until they are reunited. There is a 15th-century wall painting thought to be of St Edmund transfixed by arrows.

TAPELEY PARK

A lovely William and Mary house overlooks the Taw and Torridge estuaries. Its 18th-century ceilings are remarkable, and there are fine collections of furniture and porcelain.

The house belonged to John Christie, founder of the Glyndebourne Opera, and it was his mother who laid out the glorious gardens, including woodland walks and a walled kitchen garden. The gardens are open daily, and tours of the house can be made between Easter and October.

Tourist information: Bideford 77676 (summer).

A rugged coastal fringe to Exmoor

——— 59 MILES ———

High cliffs broken by rocky bays face the Bristol Channel, and long sands fringe Bideford Bay. Inland a great house immortalises the gracious lady who lived there for 84 years.

ILFRACOMBE

North Devon's response to the Victorian yearning for sea bathing was to thrust a resort upon a fishing village hardly changed since the Middle Ages. Then, there was a single curved street with a church at one end and a harbour at the other, and this pattern can still be seen.

The Tunnel Baths in Bath Place and the terraces that began to climb the hill were the overture of change. The curtain rose with the coming of the railways in 1874, leading to an explosion of hotels, public gardens and yellow-brick boarding houses.

A couple of echoes of vanished days remain: the part-Norman Holy Trinity Church, with its beautifully carved roof figures, and the Chapel of St Nicholas high on its rock above the harbour. For nearly 700 years a light has burned there to guide mariners through some of Britain's most hazardous rocks and tides.

LEE

A lovely wooded combe, hemmed in by stone walls turned into hedgerows by tumbling creepers and rock plants, leads down to cottages and houses tucked anyhow into tiny creeper-hung canyons, or perched on crags.

Beyond Lee, Morte Point, a grass-covered fang of rock, gives splendid views of the coast and Lundy.

WOOLACOMBE

Until the mid-19th century, Woolacombe hardly existed at all, but it now has 1890s brick and bargeboarding, 1930s Tudor and 1960s concrete. And in what a setting – 2 miles of hard, clean sand on which line after line of marbled green and white waves roll in slow motion, while behind are Woolacombe Downs with wonderful walks.

Farther south, at Croyde, stand tiny cottages, with shapely chimneys and switchback roofs of slate or thatch. A swift stream demands a miniature bridge to each garden gate, and the village has a craft shop and a shell and gem museum.

BRAUNTON

It is claimed to be Britain's largest village, with a nucleus of church and ancient, heavy-walled cottages, and outer layers of haphazard later development. Do not miss the church. It is dedicated to St Brannock, a 6th-century Welsh missionary who voyaged to Braunton, so it is said, in a stone coffin. The present 13th-century church stands on the site of a church founded by the saint, and beneath it he lies to this day. Something of his story is told in the stained-glass windows, on one of the roof bosses and on one of the remarkable carved pew ends.

Braunton Burrows is a wild area of dune and marsh, part of which has been designated a national nature reserve. Other parts are used as a training area by the army, so if the red flags are flying, keep away.

MARWOOD HILL GARDENS

A garden as rich as only Devon gardens can be, Marwood Hill was created in the 1960s by damming a stream to form a small string of lakes. Irises and arum lilies grow among the willows and dogwoods, and the rugged slope that was once a quarry glows with seasonal plants from spring to autumn. There are also formal rose beds and dense plantations of rare or unusual trees in happy juxtaposition, and greenhouses of magnificent camellias and Australasian plants. The gardens are open to the public daily.

ARLINGTON COURT

The Chichesters lived at Arlington for 600 years, though the present house dates only from 1822. There in 1865 Miss Rosalie Chichester was born. She inherited at the age of 15 from her attractive but wildly extravagant father, and spent much of her life paying off his debts. She died, the last of her line, in 1949 and left the house to the National Trust.

Miss Chichester's personality pervades all. She is in every room, in her watercolours, her collections of ship models, trinkets, enamels, snuffboxes, fans, pewter and Victorian dresses. She is in her bedroom where her night things are still laid out, and in the park that she maintained as a wildlife reserve.

The house is open from April to October, except on Saturdays; the grounds are open daily all the year.

PARRACOMBE

The world rushes past Parracombe along the main road, so seek out the narrow road into its steep little valley. All at once the village appears below like a model, and once the houses are reached it can be appreciated just how steep and twisting the streets are.

There is a remarkable church, not the one seen from above, but the hidden-away St Petrock's. Though redundant, it is maintained with love: a village church with 18th-century box pews, stalls for clerk and musicians, a minister's reading desk, and scripture texts on the walls above the screen.

HUNTER'S INN

The road is lovely, but narrow, with the wild River Heddon on one side and a high bank on the other. It runs through Mill Wood, tier upon tier of beeches on either hand. In their midst is the big stone mill, cream plastered and converted into a private house. Beyond lies Hunter's Inn, timbered, with mullioned windows.

The frequent appearance of a Coastguard Rescue Land Rover strikes an odd note in this sylvan scene, but the sea is surprisingly close and reached by a mile-long path beside the river to Heddon's Mouth.

COMBE MARTIN

A long street is given some variety by serpentine wriggles and colour washes on the cottages and houses. The lovely 13th-century Church of St Peter ad Vincula has rare carvings and rarer paintings on the rood screen. The castle-like Pack of Cards Inn was built in 1626 by George Ley of Marwood to celebrate a phenomenal win at cards. Hence, it had 52 windows, one for each card, and four floors with 13 doors on each for the four suits of 13 cards each.

At about the point where it seems that the street will never come to an end, it does, at a cove or cutting into the cliff that was a harbour where coasters used to be beached. The skippers must have been skilful men, for the rock fangs are ominously close together and the tide can come in like an express train.

CHAMBERCOMBE MANOR

So old that it seems to have grown with the landscape, Chambercombe was a manor house of the Champernownes in Henry II's reign, and though it has shrunk since their day, it is still impressive.

In 1865, the owner discovered that the number of windows seen from the outside exceeded by one those seen from inside. He investigated, broke down a wall, and found a chamber containing a skeleton. The room is on view and, not surprisingly, the house is said to be haunted. It is open most days in summer.

At Hele, a 16th-century water mill has been restored and sells stone-ground flour to visitors.

Tourist information:
Ilfracombe 63001;
Woolacombe 870553 (summer);
Braunton 816400 (summer);
Combe Martin 3319 (summer).

——— 52 MILES ———

Steep roads plunge and climb along the coast, then pass by Dunkery Beacon, Exmoor's highest point. Villages of stone and thatch shelter in deep green combes below the moor.

LYNTON AND LYNMOUTH

An unwitting alliance between Napoleon and the Romantic poets brought fame to the two villages. In the early 19th century, Lynton was a huddle of cliff-top cottages and Lynmouth a tiny harbour below. Cut off from the Grand Tour by the French Wars, young men of taste and means looked instead to their own country. One of the first venturers westward was the poet Shelley who, with his runaway schoolgirl bride, stayed in Lynmouth for nine weeks in 1812. They were soon followed by Wordsworth and Coleridge.

Lynton nowadays is mostly staid Victorian and Edwardian. It is approached by a 1-in-4 road, or by a near-vertical cliff railway, ingeniously powered by water. There are fine

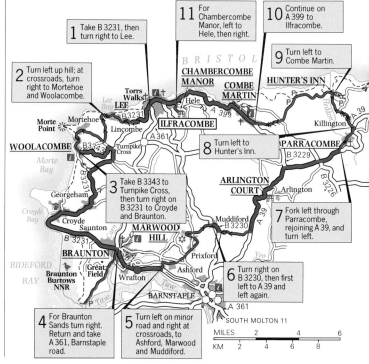

1 Take B 3231, then turn right to Lee.

2 Turn left up hill; at crossroads, turn right to Mortehoe and Woolacombe.

3 Take B 3343 to Turnpike Cross, then turn right on B 3231 to Croyde and Braunton.

4 For Braunton Sands turn right. Return and take A 361, Barnstaple road.

5 Turn left on minor road and right at crossroads, to Ashford, Marwood and Muddiford.

6 Turn right on B 3230, then first left to A 39 and left again.

7 Fork left through Parracombe, rejoining A 39, and turn left.

8 Turn left to Hunter's Inn.

9 Turn left to Combe Martin.

10 Continue on A 399 to Ilfracombe.

11 For Chambercombe Manor, left to Hele, then right.

views from everywhere, a wonderful walk west through the Valley of the Rocks to Castle Rock, and also the Lyn and Exmoor Museum. Lynmouth is still scarred by the flood of 1952, when the East and West Lyn Rivers burst their banks and tumbled hundreds of tons of rock upon the village, killing 34 people and causing great damage. But the 18th-century quay survived, as did the pretty cottages, houses and inns behind it.

COUNTISBURY COMMON
Go on a day of rain and sun and watch the clouds drop gauzy curtains of moisture and light upon the pale pewter sea, 1000ft below – a mingling of light and air and water best captured in some of Turner's paintings. The best route is the 1½ mile path over springy heather to Foreland Point and its lighthouse.

County Gate, 3 miles east, is the border between Devon and Somerset. Among all the shires, few can have such definite frontiers. The jigsaw pattern of luminous green pastures typical of North Devon changes abruptly to the copper and bronze distances of Somerset's Exmoor. The national park information centre offers magnificent views all round, to Exmoor and across the Bristol Channel. From County Gate a nature trail runs to Glenthorne Beach.

OARE
A hamlet of grey stone lies snug in the ravine of the Oare Water. The 15th-century church standing above is famous for an incident that never took place. The interior is like a small, whitewashed cave, and a notice by one of the deep-set windows says that it was through this – in R.D. Blackmore's novel *Lorna Doone* – that Carver Doone shot Lorna as she was being married to John Ridd. The plain interior of the church can have changed little since the 17th century in which the novel is set. There is a

monument to Blackmore. Oare Manor was the home of the Snow family, who also appear in *Lorna Doone*, and nearby Robber's Bridge is associated with the Doones.

PORLOCK
A throng of white cottages, their gardens crammed with fuchsias, welcome motorists who have just negotiated the 1-in-4 plunge down Porlock Hill. The small port of Porlock Weir usurped Porlock's role when the sea deserted it in the Middle Ages. Pleasure craft fill the harbour, and the remains of a submerged forest can be seen at very low water.

There are spectacular views from the wooded cliffs, and a woodland walk leads to Culbone and what is said to be England's smallest parish church. It is only 35ft long and seats just 38 people.

SELWORTHY
The village's 1010ft beacon protects it from the worst of the sea gales. It is a crowd of deep-thatched, dormer-windowed estate cottages gathered about an enclosed green, with a National Trust information centre and a walnut tree for a centrepiece.

Most of the village is focused upon a wooded knoll with the Church of All Saints, pale and pristine. Its pulpit, still with an hour glass, is early 16th century, and the carved barrel roofs are among England's finest.

WINSFORD
Bridges are the theme – there are eight of them, including a packhorse bridge – and spectacular buildings too, including Karstal House, a 15th-century maltings converted into a hotel, and the Royal Oak inn.

A mile or so down the road at Spire Cross there is a curiosity known as the Caractacus Stone from a fading inscription that might read *Caracti Nepus*, 'a relative of Caractacus'. Whether this refers to the 5th-century

St Carantacus or Caractacus, the British king who defied the Romans in AD 50, no one knows.

Another moor mystery is Tarr Steps, a 180ft long clapper bridge across the River Barle. It is widely held to be prehistoric, though it may be no earlier than 13th century. Its huge stone slabs, about 3ft above the river, are supported on massive piers.

SIMONSBATH
Standing at 1100ft, Simonsbath is the highest village on the moor. There is not much of it – some low, white-stone cottages with slate roofs, the Exmoor Forest Hotel and the Simonsbath Pottery and Gallery.

WATERSMEET
To come to Watersmeet in autumn is unalloyed, selfish delight. Then, far below, the Hoaroak Water and the East Lyn River are in grey-green and white spate, crashing down to their meeting place, and the trees clothing the sides of the ravine are a vibrant combination of colours.

Tourist information: Lynton 52225.

HIDDEN COVE *Splashes of flowers relieve the stark cliffs overlooking Lee Bay.*

ARLINGTON COURT *A pretty nature walk passes the lake, a wildfowl refuge.*

ROYAL OAK *A straw peacock perches on the thatch of the old inn at Winsford.*

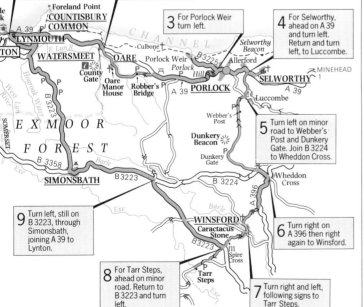

1 Take A 39 to Countisbury Common and County Gate.

2 Turn right to Oare, then left to rejoin A 39, and turn right.

3 For Porlock Weir turn left.

4 For Selworthy, ahead on A 39 and turn left. Return and turn left, to Luccombe.

5 Turn left on minor road to Webber's Post and Dunkery Gate. Join B 3224 to Wheddon Cross.

6 Turn right on A 396 then right again to Winsford.

7 Turn right and left, following signs to Tarr Steps.

8 For Tarr Steps, ahead on minor road. Return to B 3223 and turn left.

9 Turn left, still on B 3223, through Simonsbath, joining A 39 to Lynton.

Gardens by the estuary of the Dart

TOUR
14

68 MILES

Steep and narrow lanes wind through the red-earth farmlands of South Devon. The sea swirls around a rocky headland, and thrusts fingers of water far inland along sheltered estuaries.

DARTMOUTH

To most people, Dartmouth means the Naval College, nursery of princes and admirals for a century and more. Indeed, the great pinkish, towered building on the crest of the ridge does to some extent dominate the town; but Dartmouth was naval before colleges were dreamt of.

To the Angevin and Plantagenet kings, it was a place from which they could keep an eye on their French possessions and assemble fleets for the Crusades. Edward III sent 31 Dartmouth ships to the siege of Calais, and the town contributed nine vessels to the squadrons that chased the Armada up the Channel. On June 4, 1944, part of one of the greatest fleets the world has ever seen moved ponderously down the dark wooded estuary bound for the beaches of Normandy.

Not that Dartmouth had things entirely its own way over the centuries. It was attacked by raiders from Brittany and even from North Africa – hence its harbour defences, the castles of Dartmouth, Kingswear, Bearscove and Gallants Bower that were armed and manned again during the Second World War.

Between these alarms, the town grew rich on the wine trade and the Newfoundland cod fisheries, and sent its sons out to explore the New World or as merchants who did a little privateering on the side. Typical of these was Sir John Hawley, an old villain who was 14 times mayor of Dartmouth in the 14th century. His likeness in brass can be seen set between those of his two wives in St Saviour's Church.

The highlights of Dartmouth can be seen quite quickly – though days could be spent wandering its steep, haphazard alleys. The houses pile up and up the alp-like hills in ramparts of ochre, primrose, green and blue. A good deal of solid, colourful carving might have been inspired by the figurehead and ornamentation of a three-decker vessel; it includes the pillars and crowns on the Country House Inn, the cherub on the 14th-century house in Higher Street, the lovely, pillared Butterwalk, the coloured stone pulpit in St Saviour's, and griffins everywhere.

STOKE FLEMING

The road twists and turns between high stone walls into a delightfully casual village, with houses dressed in the blue, pink or green liveries much favoured in this part of the world. There are fine views down the coast to the Dancing Beggars, the gently named rocky terrors that guard Dartmouth's approaches. In the church there is a splendid monument to John Corp, who died in 1361, and to his granddaughter, Elynore; she stands on a pedestal, like a chess queen, with her headdress blowing skittishly in the breeze.

BLACKPOOL SANDS

A long succession of coves with dark gold sand and gravel are interspersed with green headlands like sphinx's paws running into the sea. Blackpool Sands is the most formal of the coves, with a paved car park and a pink brick lavatory with a belfry and a seagull weather vane. Pine-clad cliffs sweep down to a crescent of fine shingle, and rhododendrons bloom near the beach in early summer.

SLAPTON SANDS

The curious double shore of Slapton Sands has the sea on one side and the reedy, freshwater Slapton Ley on the other. The Ley is a bird sanctuary, for marsh birds in particular, and attracts many rare visitors.

Seen from above, Slapton Sands is a golden half-moon curve fringed with white breakers. Early in 1944 it was used by the American forces to practise the skills they would require on the beaches of Normandy on D-Day. One such rehearsal, Operation Tiger on April 28, became horribly authentic when two flotillas of German E-boats got inside the protective naval screen and attacked the troop transports. Some 700 US soldiers were killed, and three tank landing craft sunk just off the beach are still there.

TORCROSS

The introduction to Torcross, at the end of Slapton Sands, is a Sherman tank by the side of the road. It was one of those sunk during the E-boat attack in April 1944; recovered 40 years later by a local hotelier, it was placed at the entrance to the village as a monument to members of the US forces who lost their lives in the rehearsals held locally before the D-Day landings.

Torcross is a straggling collection of stone cottages between Slapton Sands and Slapton Ley. It was a fishing village once. The fishermen, who launched their boats straight off the beaches, kept Newfoundland dogs trained to swim ashore with the mooring ropes.

Beyond Torcross the route breaks inland to Stokenham, a village of ironstone cottages, with thatched roofs and thatched hats like tea cosies over the front doors – a feature as South Devonian as the red soil that splashes up the walls after rain and mingles with the gravel on the roads.

START POINT

The savage prow is one of the classic landfalls for mariners homeward bound from the Western Ocean. There is a car park near the point with wonderful views up the coast. Close by is the lighthouse, watching over rocks where five ships were wrecked in one night in 1891, and the spot where a pirate was hanged in chains in 1581, as a hint that like-minded sailormen should shun temptation.

KINGSBRIDGE

There is no river and therefore no bridge – and the identity of the king is anybody's guess. One of the deep inlets that make road navigation in South Devon so interesting comes to an end in a limpid stretch of water where swans, yachts and cruisers admire themselves in still reflections framed by trees and high meadows.

Steep Fore Street makes up most of the old town, with Georgian houses and shops whose upper storeys are stylishly hung with patterned slate or tiles in dark and pale grey, red, white and violet. The Shambles is an Elizabethan arcade whose overhanging

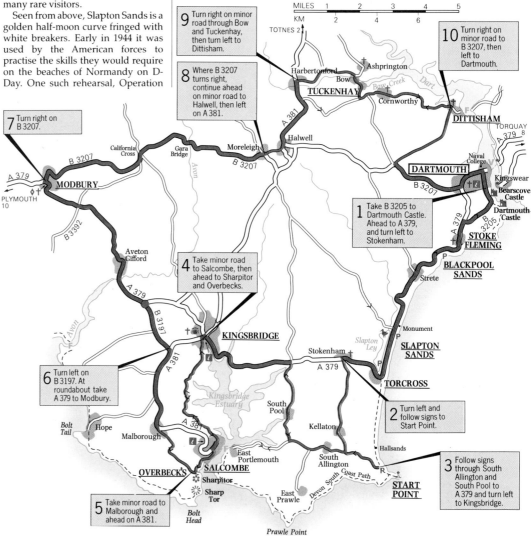

upper storey is supported on granite pillars. The Victorian building next door, with a delightful onion-shaped clock tower, combines Town Hall, theatre, cinema and market.

The interior of St Edmund's Church is big, grand, polished and parqueted. There are some medieval carvings and extravagant monuments, but most people's favourite is the one outside the door to Peter ('Comonly called Bone') Philip, who died in 1793. It reads:
Here I lie at the churchyard door
Here I lie because I'm poor
The forther in the more you'll pay
Here I lie as warm as they.

SALCOMBE

The southernmost of Devon resorts is often compared with those of the Mediterranean. This seems a little unfair, since the hills about Salcombe are much greener, its waters cleaner, and its coves and beaches filled with real sand. But the air is remarkably balmy, the approach is Corniche-like as it soars above the town, and the estuary is filled with yachts and fishing boats. There is a touch of the Mediterranean, too, in the houses painted in the colours of Neapolitan ice cream – bright pink, lime green and pistachio.

More English, though, is the notice above the Victorian drinking fountain in Fore Street; it promises fearful punishments to 'whoever is found cleaning fish or committing any other nuisance at this watering place'.

Opposite, Normandy Way leads to the quays; the name commemorates the 66 ships and hundreds of auxiliary craft of the US Navy that sailed from there on June 4, 1944, carrying the invading American armies to the French beaches code-named Utah and Omaha.

The quays are peaceful enough now, with a pink Customs House and fishermen's cottages. Among these, and often adapted from them, are bistros, boutiques and chandlers whose sailing clothes are just as chic as the garments sold in the boutiques.

High above the town are large and exuberant villas, some Victorian or Edwardian, some newly built, and all set in steep and immaculate gardens.

OVERBECK'S

This airy paradise of a garden looks down miles of estuary creeks and beaches to Salcombe, diminished to a toytown by distance. Though some of the planting was done before the First World War, most of Overbeck's steep 6 acres of exotic trees, shrubs and herbaceous borders were the work of Otto Overbeck who, when he died in 1937, left his house and garden to the National Trust. Part of the house is now a youth hostel, and the remainder is a museum containing shipbuilding tools, model boats, shells and other exhibits.

The mild South Devon air cossets palm trees among the pines and beeches, and many tender plants

such as agapanthuses, prostrate rosemary, libertias and crinums. A brick pergola supports climbing roses and wisterias, but the real showpiece of the place is the magnolia that puts out scores of large, flamingo-pink flowers in early spring.

Overbeck's is open daily all the year, and the museum is open daily from April to October.

MODBURY

Seen from even a moderate distance, St George's Church is as a great and solitary galleon parting green billows; some trick of the land conceals the town itself. Close to, the church is just as impressive; big, rough-hewn and airy within, and most of it dating from the 13th and 14th centuries.

Modbury mostly consists of three steep streets that meet close by the handsome old Exeter Inn. There are art galleries, antiques shops and teashops galore, and a goodly number of 18th-century houses; some of these are of considerable elegance, with carved and pillared porticoes. An old livery stable has been converted into a woodturners' craft centre. There is an exhibition of other local crafts – pottery, basketry, weaving – but the principal features are woodcarving and furniture making.

TUCKENHAY

The village on Bow Creek is the creation of a Mr Tucker who, at the beginning of the 19th century, built a paper mill and wharves for exporting

road stone. He put up cottages for his workers and a gasworks to give them light, at a time when gaslight was a novelty in London. Most of his buildings still stand, a monument to the theory that it was impossible to design badly during the Regency. They are being converted into holiday homes, flats, boathouses and a winery. The Maltsters' Arms and the Waterman's Arms have gardens running down to the creek.

DITTISHAM

Nothing could be nicer than to be famed for plums or cider, and Dittisham is celebrated for both. The plums are called Ploughmen, seemingly because the trees originally came from Germany, where they are called *pflaumen*. At any rate, in season, the petals lie along the ploughed furrows of neighbouring red fields like drifted snow.

Stone and thatch cottages ascend steeply from the Dart estuary at its widest point, where there is a passenger ferry across the river to the quay below Greenway House, causing some parking problems.

The church is a joy, with a Norman font, a 15th-century screen and a fantastically carved pulpit, on which figures sunk in deep niches are twined about by vines, leaves and bunches of grapes.

Tourist information: Dartmouth 4224 (summer); Salcombe 2736 (summer); Kingsbridge 3195 (summer).

SHELTERED WATERS *Pleasure craft of all kinds crowd the estuary at Salcombe, gateway to almost 2000 acres of tidal creeks stretching some 5 miles inland to Kingsbridge.*

From Dartmoor's tors to seaside sand

TOUR
15
67 MILES

Only a few miles inland from South Devon's resorts, Dartmoor looms above the Teign and Dart valleys. Mists can quickly shroud the moor and turn it into a menacing wilderness.

BOVEY TRACEY

An excellent centre for exploring southern Dartmoor, Bovey Tracey is a friendly little town, which has expanded with the growth of the tourist trade. Its main landmark is a restored water wheel over the River Bovey in the town centre.

The church, dedicated to St Thomas Becket, is said to have been built by Sir William de Tracey, after whom the town is named, to expiate his part in the saint's murder in 1170.

The information centre at Parke, on the western outskirts of Bovey Tracey, provides a useful introduction to a tour of the Dartmoor National Park. This fine classical mansion, owned by the National Trust, is the National Park headquarters. It stands in 240 acres of superb parkland, planted with oaks, Wellingtonias, sweet chestnuts and other fine trees.

Just behind the house is the Rare Breeds Farm, where traditional breeds of cattle, sheep, pigs and poultry are housed in farm buildings and paddocks. The parkland is open daily and the Rare Breeds Farm daily from April to October.

YARNER WOOD

More than 370 acres of oak and birch woodland, with patches of conifers and moorland, form a National Nature Reserve, with a waymarked nature trail of 1½ miles and a woodland walk of 3 miles.

The reserve contains traces of Dartmoor's industrial past in a stretch of the Hay Tor Granite Railway, a horse-drawn tramway built in 1820 and used for carrying stone down from the high moorland, and the ruined engine house and shaft of an old copper mine from which 2300 tons of copper were extracted between 1858 and 1867.

BECKY FALLS

The beautiful cascade, surrounded by trees, stands in a privately owned 45 acre estate. The water crisscrosses down for 70ft over a jumble of boulders, falling into pools which are ideal for paddling and splashing about on a hot summer's afternoon. The stream of which they form part is called the Becka Brook though local usage and signposts have now changed it to Becky. There is a large car park about 100yds from the entrance, on the opposite side of the road.

MANATON

The straggling village with its whitewashed thatched cottages and neat little tree-lined green is overlooked by one of Dartmoor's most impressive churches.

Dedicated to St Winifred, the granite-built church has a 15th-century tower more than 100ft high, and a fine rood screen of about 1490. Its panels, painted with saints, were mutilated at the Reformation.

WIDECOMBE IN THE MOOR

As summer approaches, the car parks at Widecombe fill up with visitors in search of Tom Pearse, his grey mare, Uncle Tom Cobleigh and all the other characters of the famous song. Though Widecombe is one of Dartmoor's main tourist magnets, full of curio shops and tearooms, it still remains basically a pretty little village of thatched cottages, nestling in the valley at the foot of Widecombe Hill.

The Church of St Pancras, the 'Cathedral of the Moor', dates mainly from the late 14th century. The tower, 135ft high, is thought to be early 16th century, built by tin-miners who had made their fortunes on Dartmoor.

Widecombe Fair is still held on the second Tuesday in September. The original Uncle Tom Cobleigh died in the 1790s, and the song was written about 1880.

ASHBURTON

Strung out along the main street of this attractive small town are many 17th and 18th-century houses, some of them hung with slates or tiles. The most striking is in North Street; now a shop, it is known as the 'House of Cards' from the spades, hearts, diamonds and clubs picked into the tiles hung on its façade.

Ashburton's small museum is open on Tuesday, Thursday, Friday and Saturday afternoons from mid-May to September.

RIVER DART COUNTRY PARK

The Dart runs swift and sparkling across this delightful park just west of Ashburton. The house is used for management courses, while the grounds have been laid out with picnic sites, nature trails, woodland adventure playgrounds and a bathing lake. A 'tree trail' identifies such magnificent trees as coast redwoods, western red cedars, and a Bhutan pine from Afghanistan. The park is open daily from April to September.

New Bridge, 2 miles farther along the road towards Two Bridges, makes a good stopping-point on the southern fringes of the moor. An information centre is open during the summer.

DARTMEET

Bubbling down from the high moors, the East and West Dart join to form the River Dart, which flows south past Dartington and Totnes to reach the sea at Dartmouth.

Just above the modern bridge are the remains of a medieval clapper bridge – horizontal stone slabs laid on uprights across the river, forming a crossing place wide enough for the packhorses that once formed Dartmoor's main means of transport.

POSTBRIDGE

Unlike the clapper bridge at Dartmeet, the bridge at Postbridge is complete, and gives a good idea of the

MOSAIC FIELDS *Red and green ribbons pattern the slopes near Compton, where every inch of the land has been exploited.*

RIVER LINE *Steam trains of the Dart Valley Railway run daily excursions from Buckfastleigh to Totnes in summer.*

BERRY POMEROY *The tall-towered St Mary's Church in the village was built by the Pomeroy family 500 years ago.*

hazards of travel across Dartmoor in former times. Probably built in the 13th century, it has recently been strengthened by modern technology, using epoxy resin to bond the stones together. The word 'clapper' is said to come from the Saxon word *cleaca*, 'a large stone'.

CHAGFORD
The pretty little stone-built town in the heart of Dartmoor was once a tin-mining centre with the status of 'Stannary' town. St Michael's Church is a sturdy granite building dating mainly from the 15th century.

CASTLE DROGO
Standing on a magnificent south-facing site high above the Teign valley, Castle Drogo looks from a distance like some baronial fortress. In fact it was built between 1910 and 1930 by Julius Drewe, who made a fortune as one of the partners in the Home and Colonial Stores grocery chain.

He chose Sir Edwin Lutyens as his architect, and together they built Drogo Castle, regardless of expense, from granite quarried on the estate. The house is owned by the National Trust, and a good deal of it, including the towering Great Hall and the chapel, can be visited daily from April to October.

MORETONHAMPSTEAD
The most distinguished buildings in this small crossroads town are a group of old almshouses outside the church-yard. Owned by the National Trust but not open to the public, they were built in 1639 and have a sturdy granite colonnade along the front.

Tourist information: Bovey Tracey 832047 (summer).

TOUR
16

— 54 MILES —

Two neighbouring resorts differ totally in character. Inland, ancient Totnes guards the lower Dart valley, and narrow, sunken lanes link villages remote from the coastal bustle.

TORQUAY
Torbay styles itself the 'English Riviera', and Torquay is certainly the queen of this particular riviera coast. It has several good beaches, elegant 19th-century terraces, a busy yachting harbour, an aquarium, and fine public gardens where palm trees grow.

The main beach is backed not by houses, shops or amusement arcades but by a broad stretch of meadow that has survived since the Middle Ages. This was once the farmland of Torre Abbey, founded in 1196 and dissolved by Henry VIII in 1539. The medieval gatehouse still survives, as does the magnificent tithe barn, known as the Spanish Barn from the Spanish sailors held prisoner there after the defeat of the Armada in 1588. A museum and art gallery is open daily in summer.

PAIGNTON
With its beaches of reddish sand, its small pier, and its streets of hotels and boarding houses, Paignton is very much the family seaside town. Its old centre, clustered round the red-sand-stone medieval Church of St John the Baptist, has been submerged by the tide of later building, but still has a distinct sense of identity.

Kirkham House is a magnificent 15th-century house, full of furniture by modern craftsmen inspired by medieval originals. It is open daily from April to September.

TORBAY AIRCRAFT MUSEUM
Tucked away in the hills 3 miles inland from Paignton is a journey into the past for those who recall dogfights between Spitfires and Messerschmitts above the fields of southern England.

As well as 20 or so complete aircraft, the museum has fragments of aircraft trawled up from the seabed, displays of flags and medals, and relics of First World War air aces. It also has a model railway, and a garden dedicated to the memory of the actor Kenneth More, who played the fighter ace Douglas Bader in the film *Reach for the Sky*. The museum is open daily from April to October.

BERRY POMEROY CASTLE
A romantic ruin, set high above a wooded ravine, Berry Pomeroy is unusual in being a double ruin, with an Elizabethan mansion inside the medieval walls. 'Beri', as the castle was called in the Middle Ages, was built about 1300 by the Pomeroy family, who came over with William the Conqueror. The south curtain wall survives, along with one of the corner towers and the main entrance.

The castle is open daily in summer, and on weekdays from late September to early March.

TOTNES
This beautiful and historic town carries its sense of the past into real life every Tuesday during summer when many of the local residents go about their business in Elizabethan costume. The old part of the town lies in and around Fore Street and High Street, which rises steeply from the River Dart to the remains of the Norman castle on its grassy mound.

The local museum, open Monday to Friday from April to October and on Saturday mornings during school holidays, is in a fine Elizabethan merchant's house. On the other side of the Dart is the Totnes Motor Museum, with a collection of sports and racing cars; it is open daily from Easter to September.

DARTINGTON
Built as an unfortified mansion in the late 14th century, Dartington Hall is the largest medieval house in the West of England; it is now the headquarters of the Dartington Hall Trust. The 2500 acre Dartington estate was bought in the 1920s by Leonard and Dorothy Elmhirst, who restored the derelict mansion, founded a co-educational boarding school and established Dartington as a centre for music and the visual arts. Visitors can walk round the courtyard and gardens and enter the Great Hall when it is not in use.

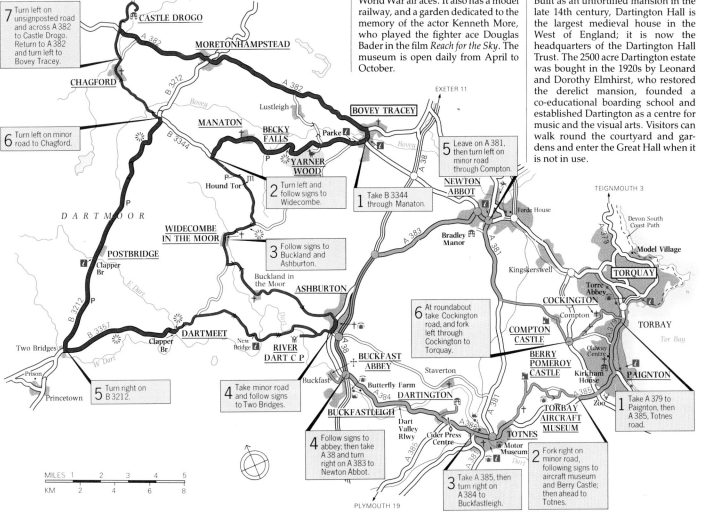

BUCKFASTLEIGH

The small country town is the head-quarters and terminus of the Dart Valley Railway, which follows the course of the Dart to Totnes. Re-opened by enthusiasts in 1969, it operates three trains in each direction daily from mid-June to early September, and occasionally in April, May and late September. A Steam Museum is open when trains are running.

At Buckfast Butterfly Farm, visitors in summer can see exotic butterflies in near-natural surroundings.

BUCKFAST ABBEY

Founded by King Canute in 1018, Buckfast was dissolved by Henry VIII in 1539 and re-established in 1882 by Benedictine monks from France. The present buildings, including the huge church with its lofty tower, were built by the monks and completed in 1938. An exhibition in the crypt describes the history of the monastery since Saxon times.

NEWTON ABBOT

The busy market town, rapidly expanding, is almost linked to Torquay by continuous housing. Its chief landmark is the 14th-century St Leonard's Tower, which had a chapel attached to it until 1836, when the chapel was pulled down and a new church built nearby.

On the town's southern outskirts the medieval Bradley Manor stands in sweeping parkland with open country beyond. It belongs to the National Trust and is open every Wednesday afternoon from April to September.

COMPTON CASTLE

A neat little stone castle is hidden away in a valley just outside the fringes of Torbay. Yet for all its small size, it was quite capable of defending itself, as it has slots for portcullises, arrow-slits, holes through which boiling oil could be poured, and a high wall round three of its sides.

Compton was begun in the 14th century by the Gilbert family. It is now owned by the National Trust and is open on Monday, Wednesday and Thursday from April to October.

COCKINGTON

Apart from modern housing along the skyline, the village of thatched cottages has been lovingly preserved. The cottages today are mainly curio shops and tearooms. The forge has been there since the 14th century.

The parish church of St George and St Mary is now isolated, since much of the village was pulled down in the 18th century to open up the view from Cockington Court.

Tourist information: Torquay 27428; Paignton 558383; Totnes 863168 (summer); Newton Abbot 67494.

DEVIL'S DOMAIN *The granite stack of Hound Tor was once believed to be the Devil's home on Dartmoor, and horses were said to shy away from it. Sir Arthur Conan Doyle used its grim surroundings for his 'Hound of the Baskervilles'.*

Farmlands below the Devon moors

TOUR
17
69 MILES

Between the Exmoor and Dartmoor National Parks lie the rich red farmlands of mid-Devon. There are churches grand and small and country mansions both opulent and modest.

TIVERTON

Wool brought wealth to this busy market town as early as the 1200s, and despite fire after fire in the centuries that followed, evidence of its early prosperity still survives. The Great House in St Peter Street, used today as council offices, preserves its original dignity as an impressive Jacobean mansion, built about 1613 for a wool merchant, George Slee. The humbler dwelling adjoining, also built by Slee, is one of a number of almshouses scattered around the town.

The wealth of the wool trade is reflected even more emphatically in St Peter's Church, part sandstone and part white stone from Beer. Slee's table-top tomb of grey stone lies within a church which benefited greatly from the patronage of 15th and 16th-century merchants.

The church was founded in 1073. Tiverton Castle, which stands close by on the same wooded rise above the River Exe, came a little later, in 1106. Visitors enter through the medieval main gate, once protected by a moat, drawbridge and portcullis, into a peaceful little courtyard and garden. Romantic ruins lead off from a wing of restored rooms which contain various collections, including a clock collection and a gallery devoted to Joan of Arc. A relative of the Campbell family who lived at Tiverton Castle was Joan's chief military adviser.

Tiverton's superb museum provides a concentrated look at the town's past, well-stocked as it is with penny-farthing bicycles, horse-drawn carts and wagons, a 17th-century cider press – and even an immaculately polished full-size tank engine in the green livery of the Great Western Railway.

The town's evolution as a textile centre is highlighted in the Heathcoat Lace Machine Gallery, named after John Heathcoat who established his lace factory here in 1816. One of his machines, 23ft long, is part of a display which also features the use of Tiverton lace in the wedding veils of royal brides, including that of the Princess of Wales.

Tiverton's canal basin, which stretches east from the town, commands wide views of this rambling town. The Grand Western Canal, built between 1810 and 1814, was to have been part of a waterway link connecting the Bristol and English Channels. This plan came to nothing, and the canal was abandoned in the 1920s. It is now restored along its entire 11 mile length between Tiverton and Loudwalls, and forms a country park. Horse-drawn narrow boats carry passengers along part of the tranquil waterway.

KNIGHTSHAYES COURT

The spirit of Victorian success and self-confidence is perfectly captured in this opulent house. Its grand design came from the eccentric, idiosyncratic mind of the architect William Burges, though the house, started in 1869, was finished only after Burges's replacement by the artist-designer J.D. Crace.

Whimsical figures make an appearance on the corbelling in the hall beneath a fabulously painted bookcase. The drawing room is particularly lavish, culminating in a huge white marble chimneypiece which is, in fact, a later Burges import given by Worcester College, Oxford, in 1981.

The exterior is no less arresting. A profusion of projecting gargoyles and gables gives the mansion a brooding Gothic countenance rather at odds with the beautiful gardens, in which specimen trees, alpine plants, formal terraces, scented woodland groves, azaleas and rhododendrons spread along a gently sloping hillside overlooking Tiverton. The 40 acre garden is also noted for its topiary, the most amazing example of which is a hunting scene cut into the hedgerows.

Knightshayes Court is owned by the National Trust and open daily from April to October; the house is closed on Fridays.

DULVERTON

Steep hillsides cloaked in a thick tangle of woodlands separate this small, cosy town from the open moorlands to the north. Dulverton, on the fringes of the Exmoor National Park, is a compact, pretty settlement of narrow medieval streets and passageways which has grown up around a five-arched stone bridge – one of the oldest on Exmoor – across the River Barle.

Antiques shops, craftshops, bookshops, little groceries, traditionally fronted inns and a sturdy, stone-built town hall line the triangle of main streets below the ornate Church of All Saints. The church, restored in Victorian times though retaining its 13th-

BY THE RIVERSIDE *The River Exe makes its unhurried way past Bickleigh, where thatched cottages and a riverside inn cluster beneath a ridge of low hills.*

century tower, contains fine stained glass given by Sir George Williams, founder of the YMCA, who lived locally. The red-bricked studio building directly below the church is the home of Dulverton Weavers, where visitors can watch wool and silk being woven and made into garments.

Dulverton is the headquarters of the Exmoor National Park, whose riverside building, Exmoor House, was once a workhouse. A visitor centre, open daily, provides information on the park and on local riverside and woodland walks. A plaque high on the wall near The Bridge Inn indicates the level to which the Barle rose at the time of the disastrous Lynmouth floods in August 1952.

EGGESFORD FOREST
On the roadside in what is now a conifer forest the Forestry Commission, on December 8, 1919, planted its first trees. A large stone unveiled by the Queen on May 8, 1956, commemorates the planting by the commission of 1 million acres in Britain.

The stone stands in a shady spot close to a forest car park and picnic site. Two waymarked walks lead through the woodlands; the Hilltown Trail heads for the higher ground, while the Home Valley Walk follows a stream as it flows through the forest on its way to join the River Taw.

LAPFORD
A pretty village of buff-washed dwellings, cream-painted terraces and farm buildings spreads itself out on a steep, south-facing hillside. Opposite the Old Malt Scoop, an arched inn dating from the 16th century, stands the Church of St Thomas of Canterbury.

The interior of the church is a tribute to the art of the Tudor woodcarver. It contains superb pew bench ends, each one individually decorated with deeply incised carvings depicting complex patterns and designs. The 16th-century rood screen, running the entire width of the church, has fluted columns of wood opening into an upper section laden with intricate detail.

CREDITON
The rosy red-sandstone Church of the Holy Cross at the eastern end of the town's long main street appears almost too grand and stately for its present-day surroundings. But in Saxon times Crediton was the cathedral city for Devon. The town is also celebrated as the reputed birthplace in AD 680 of St Boniface, the missionary who helped spread the Christian faith throughout Europe.

St Boniface's monastery probably stood on or near the site of the original Saxon cathedral which was, in turn, replaced by a Norman collegiate church and the present building, Perpendicular in style, which dates largely from the 15th century. A statue of St Boniface, 'Bishop and Martyr', carved in light-toned wood, stands near the entrance. Scenes from the saint's life, culminating in his martyrdom in Germany in 755, are depicted in stained glass on the great east window.

Crediton's church is one of a handful of 'Royal Peculiar' churches, so called because it operates by Royal Charter granted by Edward VI in 1547 and has its own board of governors. They still meet in the Governors' Room within the Chapter House which, together with the Lady Chapel, is 13th century. The room has an uneven 13th-century wooden floor cut from a single elm tree, while its rough roof beams are ships' timbers brought from Exeter. Cromwellian mementos are kept here, including armour, a buckskin coat and a pair of boots which look almost new.

FURSDON
The appeal of the house lies not in its size, for it is not huge, but in the tale it tells of the one family who lived here

for over 700 years. The family tree on display in the entrance hall begins with Walter de Fursdon, who founded the estate in the 13th century. On certain days in summer visitors can tour the main hall, dining room and library – all still in use by the Fursdon family – and a small museum and costume gallery.

BICKLEIGH CASTLE
This historic site tucked away down a leafy lane beside the River Exe spans many centuries. All that remains of the original Norman castle is a little chapel, authentically austere from the cold stones of its flagged floor to the thatch of its roof.

The castle's evolution from stronghold to comfortable manor house begins at the 14th-century gatehouse, built on the ruins of the Norman fortification. An armoury, its walls stripped of the original rugged stonework, contains Cromwellian armour, pistols, swords and cannon. Opposite is the old guard room which, in complete contrast, is decorated in domestic style with Tudor furniture and portraits.

Visitors step into yet another era of Bickleigh's history in the farmhouse wing. This pink-washed, thatched extension, dating from the Stuart period, houses an old farm kitchen with a cavernous fireplace and bread ovens, and an elegantly furnished

room overlooking beautifully tended gardens.

Bickleigh's most recent claim to fame comes from its connections with the Tudor warship Mary Rose. Vice-Admiral Sir George Carew, one of the family that lived at Bickleigh from the Middle Ages until 1922, perished when the Mary Rose, which he commanded, sank in 1545. Items found in the wreck are on display, together with an exhibition illustrating the salvage operation in 1982. There is also a display of ingenious secret gadgets invented by Charles Fraser-Smith – the 'Q' of the James Bond novels – to help undercover agents and prisoners of war to escape during the Second World War. The castle is open most afternoons in summer.

BICKLEIGH MILL
Huge wooden cogs, powered by a water wheel, mesh silently in this old mill building, renovated to house a place for craftsmen to make and sell their wares. There are large craft shops and small 'workshop cabins' specialising in everything from pottery to corn-dolly making.

Farming is the other main attraction here. Shire horses are still used on a farm which re-creates Devon country life at the turn of the century.

Tourist information: Tiverton 255827 (summer); Dulverton 23665.

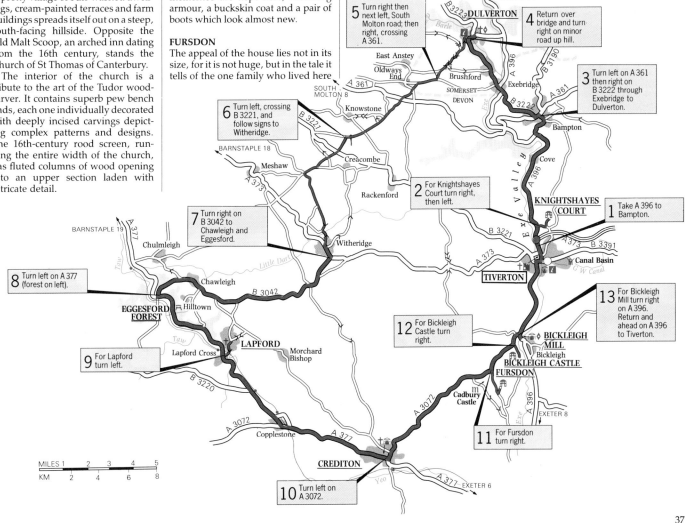

Along the red lanes of South Devon

TOUR

18

—— 40 MILES ——

Between the Exe and the Teign lanes wander over hills slashed by curves of red ploughland. There are forest walks, secluded villages and a long coast with room for holidaymakers and sea birds.

DUNCHIDEOCK

Around Dunchideock even the gravel on the roads glows red, as does the tower of Dunchideock's Church of St Michael, off the main road to the right. A monument in the church commemorates Major-General Sir Stringer Lawrence who died in 1775 'For ... French and Indian Armies Defeated and Peace concluded in the Carnatic'. Next to him lies Sir Robert Palk, Governor of Madras.

Sir Stringer bequeathed his entire fortune to Sir Robert, part of which was spent on building Lawrence Castle – actually a Gothic tower or folly – on the nearby hilltop in Sir Stringer's memory. It is open daily from May to September and otherwise at weekends, to give splendid views over the quilted countryside. Close by, Great Haldon offers a car park, picnic sites and forest walks among tall pines.

THE ASHTONS

Higher Ashton by the church and Lower Ashton by the Teign river are both tucked away among tall trees in a green-gold valley. The houses are mostly of whitewashed stone and smooth dark thatch, with the 15th-century church rising above them on an embankment.

The church's carved bench ends are exquisite, and the screens are bright with late medieval colour. One of them depicts saints and their attributes – St George's dragon, St Lawrence's gridiron, and so on – while another depicts the Annunciation of the Virgin. Latin inscriptions float about the heads of the people rather in the manner of modern strip cartoons, and the portraits are remarkably vivid – perhaps the artist used local people as models. There are some fine monuments to the Chudleigh family.

CHUDLEIGH

This small market town has some colourful small shops and houses, and one or two grander Georgian ones, but the principal attraction is the Wheel Community Craft Centre in Old Town Mills. The huge water wheel that powered the mill still develops a steady 30 horsepower, and around it have gathered a blacksmith's shop, potters, leatherworkers, textile workers, toymakers and other craftsfolk. Their wares are sold from a crafts shop.

To the south-west of the town is Chudleigh Rocks, a fantastical limestone outcrop that incorporates Pixies' Hole. This has a rock called the Pope's Head, which is supposed to grant a wish if a pin stuck onto it does not fall out.

UGBROOKE HOUSE

Despite its unmusical name, Ugbrooke is one of the loveliest of south-western houses. It was built towards the end of the 18th century for the 4th Lord Clifford of Chudleigh – whose family still own it – by Robert Adam, who gave it the castle-like appearance popular in that romantic age – his first in that style.

Ugbrooke is open to the public every afternoon from Spring Bank Holiday until September, when it presents a magnificent collection of embroidery, portraits, silverware, uniforms and furniture.

LITTLE HALDON

On a 780ft common of heath and pines are plenty of good, easy walks and picnic sites. Car parks and viewpoints survey serene, patchwork fields, the lowering bleakness of Dartmoor, the Teign estuary and, as evening falls, the twinkling galaxies of Exeter and Newton Abbot.

BISHOPSTEIGNTON

From the top of the village there is a wonderful view over the Teign estuary to hills softly patterned in reds and greens. The village itself has white houses of all shapes and sizes and a red-stone church, St John's, behind which are the remains of a 13th-century Sanctuary Chapel. A carving on the wall of the church dates from the same century.

SHALDON

Jammed between steep wooded hills and the red sands of the Teign estuary, Shaldon has had little choice than to miniaturise. A web of narrow streets, no more than alleys, widen briefly into tiny squares like Crown Square and The Green, where exquisite little Georgian houses sit about flowerbeds and a bowling green.

The walls of Shaldon's cottages are primrose, green and pink, and their gardens are crammed with flowers. The resort comes to an abrupt end at The Ness, a great red headland, pierced by Smugglers' Tunnel. Alas, investigation proves the smugglers insubstantial; the tunnel was actually constructed about 150 years ago by Lord Clifford as a more convenient route to his bathing beach.

TEIGNMOUTH

A few pretty Regency streets, some big Edwardian houses, amusement arcades and gift shops form the heart of Teignmouth. But there is evidence still of the port and fishing town that existed before the watering place.

From prehistoric times to the late Middle Ages, Teignmouth panned and exported salt. By the time this trade faded, the town had a fleet of fishing boats working the Newfoundland Grand Banks, and as this became less profitable, it began to export

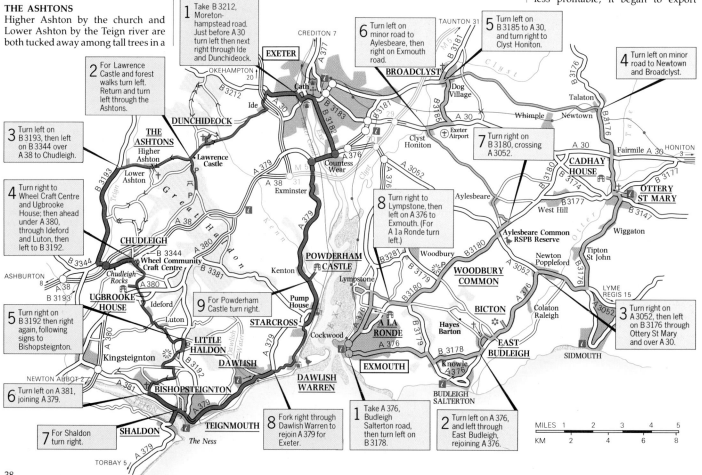

38

potter's clay and granite. The port is still active, exporting clay and importing wood, cattle meal and grain.

DAWLISH
Among Regency, Victorian and Edwardian houses runs the Dawlish Water, edged by lawns and palms, on its way in little cascades to the sea. Ducks jump to the top of the cascades and slide down, and black swans paddle along the edges. The railway line pops in and out of tunnels through the red cliffs.

DAWLISH WARREN
Rabbits surrendered Dawlish Warren long ago when their place of sandy burrows became a place of chalets, caravans, railway holiday homes, go-kart tracks and ice-cream parlours. The beach stretching out from a rocky sea wall is pleasant, and at the seaward end of the Warren a Nature Reserve occupies 505 acres of sandspit.

STARCROSS
The railway that hugs the South Devon coast was the work of Isambard Kingdom Brunel, giant of the Industrial Revolution and innovator of several of its most spectacular might-have-beens. One of these is commemorated in the rough, red-stone building at Starcross, the last surviving pumping station of Brunel's Atmospheric Railway, ancestor of the coastal line.

Brunel's railway was built in the 1840s, its trains being powered by atmospheric pressure and a vacuum created in a cast-iron pipe between the rails. The pipe contained a piston, connected through a leather seal to the front of the train. The pump houses sucked the air out of the pipe and pulled the piston along like fluff in a vacuum cleaner tube. The idea was not a success and, within a few years, locomotives replaced the pipe. Eventually Brunel's 7ft gauge was narrowed to the standard 4ft 8½in.

The pump house at Starcross is the Atmospheric Railway's sole monument, apart from one at Totnes which is now part of a factory. It contains many railway relics, and presents an audio-visual display and a working model of the railway – powered, appropriately, by vacuum cleaners – on which visitors may ride. The building is open daily in summer.

POWDERHAM CASTLE
Most of the present building – a fortified manor house rather than a castle – dates from the 1390s, when the Courtenays arrived from France in the train of Eleanor of Aquitaine, Henry II's queen. They were given the manor of Powderham and have lived there ever since.

The interiors are largely 18th century, incorporating splendid plasterwork ceilings and early Georgian and Regency furniture; there is a fine collection of family portraits. Powderham is open to the public in the afternoons from the end of May to mid-September, except on Fridays and Saturdays.

Tourist information: Exeter 72434; Teignmouth 6271; Dawlish 863589.

RIVERMOUTH RESORT *Shaldon climbs the wooded hills above the Teign estuary.*

HAYES BARTON *Sir Walter Raleigh was born in the thatched manor house in 1552.*

TOUR
19
38 MILES
Villages of simple cob and thatch cottages lie close to the grand manors of Tudor times. High commons clad with pine and furze give long views over miles of Devon to the sea.

EXMOUTH
The place is rather more given to year-round liveliness than the resorts on the other side of the Exe. On the Esplanade, tall cream and white houses and hotels look out over a vista of sand flats, luscious Devon countryside, headlands and open sea. The Beacon is a terrace of elegant Georgian houses.

Behind the Esplanade is a many-pinnacled church tower and behind that again, a different kind of Exmouth of crammed, small red houses and shops dating from the town's Victorian and Edwardian heyday.

EAST BUDLEIGH
The village of cream walls and thatch has a handsome square-towered church perched high over all. A clue to the carefully maintained prettiness is provided in the name of the pub, the Sir Walter Raleigh. The hero was born in the big thatched manor house of Hayes Barton, which is still a working farm and shows its age only in the clipped yews about its door and by its mullioned and leaded win-

dows. It lies in a cup of rounded, cattle-dotted pasture about a mile west of the village along Hayes Lane.

Hayes Barton is not open to the public, but the Church of All Saints still has the Raleigh family pew and some remarkable carved bench ends portraying local people in Tudor times, ships, animals and what might be the first likeness of a Red Indian chief made in this country.

BICTON
Trees do well in Bicton's 50 acres, as is apparent from the lofty conifers in the Pinetum and the huge cedar on the upper terrace.

Among five separate gardens at Bicton is the Italian Garden, with its formal pool, fountain and statuary. There is a round Victorian summerhouse, an 18in gauge railway for train rides and the James Countryside Museum whose theme is the farming year, illustrated by implements and machinery of the past.

OTTERY ST MARY
What is most worth stopping in for in the village is the Church of St Mary, rebuilt in the 14th century by John de Grandisson, Bishop of Exeter. His work is noble in the extreme, and later additions do nothing but enhance it. There is superb 16th-century fan tracery in the vaulted Dorset Aisle, for example, and the roof bosses are little jewels.

The monuments, too, are fascinating. There is a red-breeched, booted and spurred cavalier of the 17th century and an effigy of Sir Otto de Grandisson, the Bishop's brother who

died in 1358; he wears full armour and sports a droopy moustache. A humbler stone commemorates the Reverend John Coleridge, Vicar of Ottery St Mary in the late 18th century. He was a studious man who read Hebrew to his farming congregation each week because it was 'the language of the Holy Ghost'. He also sired 13 children, the youngest of whom was the poet Samuel Taylor Coleridge.

CADHAY HOUSE
In the 1540s, John Haydon, a lawyer of Lincoln's Inn, did well out of negotiating deals in West Country Church lands that had been confiscated during the Dissolution of the Monasteries. He celebrated by building a house at Cadhay.

The result was perhaps the finest Tudor house in Devon. Parts of a medieval building were retained, and there were alterations in the 18th and 19th centuries, but basically the house is as the Haydons left it. There are some fine interiors, but the most striking feature is the chequerboard stone Court of Sovereigns with niches holding statues of four Tudor monarchs. Cadhay is very much lived in, but is open to the public on certain afternoons in summer.

BROADCLYST
Tall trees gather about the green, Church Lane has a row of rough red-stone almshouses, and there are thatched cottages in front of the Close and behind the big, tile-hung Red Lion pub. Prior's Court looks Georgian, but is much older and was once a monastic cell; Broadclyst House really is Georgian, pink, white and splendidly opulent. The church has a pinnacled tower with gargoyles.

WOODBURY COMMON
A huge car park gives all-round views to vast and purple distances. In the middle background are pastures surrounded by neat little woods of deciduous trees, but the immediate surroundings are tall stands of pine, acres of gorse and patches of heath. Clumps of ancient beeches have bony-fingered branches reaching far out, and writhing roots gripping the ground like dragons' claws.

A LA RONDE
A charming curiosity built in 1798, A la Ronde is the work of two maiden ladies, the Misses Parminter, who apparently drew their inspiration from things seen on a ten-year grand tour of the Continent. The building is not truly round but 16 sided, and incorporates 20 rooms. Most radiate from an octagonal hall and from an upper gallery.

The Misses Parminter undertook the decoration themselves. The walls of the gallery are covered with shells, there are seaweed pictures and a room decorated in feathers. Some of the ladies' dresses and nightgowns have survived, and are shown to visitors daily in summer by members of the family who still live there.

Tourist information: Exmouth 263744 (summer); Ottery St Mary 3964 (summer); Exeter 72434.

Villages behind the Lyme Bay cliffs

TOUR
20

──── 70 MILES ────

Between woods covering the scars of a historic landslide and golden cliffs facing Lyme Bay, Devon shades into Dorset. Inland, high-banked lanes lead to villages of faded sandstone.

HONITON
A disastrous fire in 1765 left Honiton in ruins in the midst of one of the best decades in history for rebuilding an English town. The result is a fine, nearly all-of-a-piece Georgian town with roof lines as delicate and precise as the crafts for which Honiton is famous. The present age has added colour to the walls – apple blossom, daffodil and bluebell.

Most of Honiton is the long High Street stoppered by tremendous cedars at one end. Here are bookshops, print shops, health foods and antiques galore, and teashops with bow windows. In their midst is the Honiton Lace Shop, full of froths and foamings of lace, and bobbins and cushions for lacemaking. The delicate craft has been practised in Honiton since the 16th century, when it was introduced by Protestant refugees from the Low Countries. Its story is told in the Honiton and Allhallows Museum of Lace and Natural History. Next to the lace shop is the workshop of a glass engraver, and at the head of the town another of Honiton's traditional crafts is carried on at the Honiton Pottery. Its patterns are strong on flower motifs as in Honiton lace, and the works are open to visitors on weekdays.

St Paul's Church, built in 1837, is lofty and airy, the nicest of early Victorian, with a beautifully carved reredos, a splendidly detailed east window, and a vast royal coat of arms above the chancel arch.

BLACKBURY CASTLE
An Iron Age hill-fort occupied by cattle farmers from 200 BC to AD 100 is today an impressive amphitheatre filled with tall, slim beeches and carpeted with bluebells in the spring. It also possesses that odd silence that sometimes clings to sites of great antiquity. Bird calls, a woodpecker drumming, a man whistling to his dog – the sounds float through the trees as through the aisles of a ruined abbey. It is a marvellous place, if eerie, for a picnic.

BRANSCOMBE
The road twists and dives down steep, sharp bends to a village scattered haphazardly on the rising slopes of a steep, green bowl. There is white stucco and slate, and long, low, stone and thatched houses reminiscent of Ireland or the Western Isles. Smoke stands above the chimneys in unwavering blue lines against the dark woods.

Where the centre of the village might be is anyone's guess. There is a wondrous pub, the Mason's Arms, with thatched hats over the doors and thatched gnomes' caps for table umbrellas; there is a forge, run by a lady who is a registered farrier and blacksmith; and Branoc's Well, named after a Celtic saint, invites contributions with the inscription:
'With each groat thee heft in thicke well,
May thee one wish to Branoc tell.'

St Winifred's Church is a worn, stony happy building with deep windows, a three-decker pulpit and monuments among the pews as though the people remembered were parishioners still.

BEER
Down the main street a stream hurries along a stone channel beneath slab bridges to a pebbly, cliff-backed cove where fishing boats are drawn up beside piles of lobster pots. Beside it is a Memorial Garden containing a fishermen's capstan, and a memorial to Hamilton Macallum, a local painter who died in 1896.

There are some attractive buildings in the village, almost all of stone, since Beer stone has been quarried from Roman times and was used in cathedrals and abbeys throughout the country. The quarries are still there, some bright, white and working, others disused, with creepers and rock plants pouring down their sides; there are guided tours through the ancient quarry caves.

Beer also offers a Modelrama and Pleasure Garden, mostly devoted to model railways of various gauges, one of which is large enough to carry passengers.

COLYTON
In the 16th century, Colyton was a prosperous wool town owned mostly by Henry Courtenay, Marquis of Exeter, who fell out with Henry VIII and lost his head and lands. Twenty Colyton merchants and yeomen farmers clubbed together £1000 and purchased the manor from the Crown by a Deed of Feoffment; 16 feoffees, elected from among the townspeople, direct Colyton's affairs to this day.

There are a number of fine buildings: Old Church House; the chequerboard-fronted Great House and the Vicarage, both Tudor; and the Old Court House, where Judge Jeffreys tried local participants in the Monmouth Rebellion. St Andrew's Church, with its octagonal tower and exuberant weathercock, has 16th-century effigies of Sir John and Lady Elizabeth Pole, and the grave of 'Little Chokebone', granddaughter of Edward IV, who choked to death on a fishbone in 1512.

An open-topped tram runs between Colyton, Colyford and Seaton.

LYME REGIS
Dorset's frontier town begins at The Cobb, the massive breakwater that figures in John Fowles's novel and

SMUGGLER'S BEACH *Contraband was landed at Beer until well into the 19th century. One of Devon's best-known smugglers, Jack Rattenbury, was a native of the village.*

film *The French Lieutenant's Woman*. An earlier literary association is with Jane Austen's *Persuasion*, in which Louisa Musgrove falls from The Cobb's rough steps.

The Aquarium is nearby, and beside it an 1872 list of harbour dues: a mule or ass cost 2d, a trawler with 20 tons of fish was charged a shilling. The harbour area is overlooked by tiers of coloured cottages that climb up the hill behind. Lyme Regis is a pretty town of hotels and inns and browsable shops, and great sea walls on which the waves smack sullenly below Gun Cliff.

Fossils occur in the Blue Lias deposits of shale and limestone laid down by tropical seas 150 million years ago. Visitors can seek the fossils themselves; or they can buy them in the shops or see them in the excellent Philpot Museum. There are tiny fish, and ammonites up to 3ft across etched into stone, and huge prehistoric marine reptiles.

West of Lyme Regis, and reached along a footpath starting at Underhill Farm, stretch 4 miles of wooded slopes cut off from the mainland cliff in 1839 by a huge landslide. The area is now the Axmouth to Lyme Regis Undercliffs National Nature Reserve. A path, slippery in places, runs the length of the reserve.

WHITCHURCH CANONICORUM
The 'capital' of Marshwood Vale has an ecclesiastical title because its tithes were once split between the chapters of Wells and Salisbury. The church dates mostly from the 13th century, but there is even some Roman tile in its construction.

The church has the rare distinction of harbouring what are thought to be the bones of its patron saint, St Wite, also called Candida, a Saxon woman who, according to tradition, was slain by Danish raiders. She lies in a tomb pierced by three oval holes through which medieval pilgrims thrust their crippled limbs in hope of a cure.

BRIDPORT
In an area of helter-skelter towns, Bridport, by comparison, does little more than undulate. Its streets are immensely wide – the reason is said to be that new-spun strands of hemp were hung along them to dry – and end in green views of far-off hills. The town is therefore uncrammed and gracious, an air enhanced by the Georgian red-brick Town Hall, topped by the gold and green cupola of its clock tower. The building is supported on either side by Georgian shops and inns.

At the bottom of West Street is the rope and net factory, reflecting Bridport's principal industry for more than 700 years. The town made ropes for anchors and for gallows; Thomas Hardy wrote of the rope-makers 'walking backwards, overhung by appletrees and bushes'. A museum in South Street illustrates the history of the industry.

BEAMINSTER
The old nutmeg-coloured stone town has the good sense to keep its modern development well tucked away. Much of the town was rebuilt in the late 18th century after one of those disastrous fires that smote so many West Country towns about that period. It has a goodly collection of pubs; the enormous White Hart Inn and the tiny Pickwick's Inn are two of many. The 15th-century St Mary's Church is a mini-cathedral. It is supported by cathedral-like columns and has cathedral-like monuments, mostly elaborate portraits of the Strodes of Parnham, and a lovely angel roof. The 16th-century tower has pinnacled buttresses. It is said that after Judge Jeffreys' Bloody Assizes at Dorchester in 1685 the remains of the judge's victims – probably local men – were suspended from the tower.

The Strodes' old abode, Parnham House, just outside the town, is approached by neat beech and yew hedges flanking a railed drive; it is built of stone the warm side of grey, and has pretty mullioned windows. Built in the 1550s, it was given a facelift by John Nash in the early 19th century, and now houses the John Makepeace Furniture Workshops and The School for Craftsmen in Wood. House, gardens, workshops and picnic areas are open to the public on certain days from April to October.

LAMBERT'S CASTLE HILL
This is one of the Iron Age hill-forts that guard Marshwood Vale. Covered with gorse and bracken and patches of old woods, it reaches nearly 900ft and offers distant but tremendous views eastward to Chesil Bank and deep into Dartmoor to the west. Its 167 acres belong to the National Trust.

AXMINSTER
Long before it wove its first carpet in 1755 Axminster was a renowned market centre, its prosperity assured by its position in the Axe valley at the junction of two ancient roads, the Icknield and the Foss Ways. Markets are still its chief concern, as can be seen on Thursdays when all three, including one for cattle, are open, and so are the pubs, all day.

The principal streets, governed by the course of the main road, form slow curves of mainly Georgian and early Victorian houses. Among them is The George Hotel with its Adam Assembly Room and musicians' gallery, and Oak House, once an Academy for Young Gentlemen and now converted to flats. Chard Street has Regency shop fronts and an 18th-century United Reformed Church in whose cemetery lies Thomas Whitty, the founder of the local carpet industry in 1755.

Whitty was a local cloth weaver who saw a Turkey carpet in London and copied the design. His first carpets were hand-knotted, a task best performed by 'the pliant fingers of little children'. He employed the pliant fingers of his own five daughters first, and soon became famous and rich.

The heart of Axminster is Trinity Square. There stands the Church of St Mary, whose 13th-century tower was badly damaged during the Civil War when the Royalists turned it into a strong point. The pews are pushed far back so that the altar is seen down a long length of choir and chancel. Before the pews lies a great red-patterned sea of Axminster carpet. When Thomas Whitty was making his carpets the church bells were rung each time a carpet was finished.

SHUTE
One of the most important non-castellated houses of the Middle Ages, Shute Barton was begun in 1380 and later became the property of the Grey family, Dukes of Suffolk. They lost it, and their heads, in 1554 when the family made their bid to put Lady Jane Grey on the throne; it then passed to the de la Poles.

The interior is fascinating, with a huge, original fireplace in the kitchen and trussed roofs. On the exterior, the stone heads of witches, strange birds, griffins and demons jut from the top of the tower and from the battlements of the gatehouse which fronts upon the green. The gatehouse forms the entrance to Shute Park in which stands the privately owned Shute House, built in the 18th century.

The church contains the Pole chapel with splendid monuments, of which the finest is to Sir William Pole, Master of the Household to Queen Anne. He wears a beautifully embroidered coat, and holds his wand of office.

Shute Barton is owned by the National Trust and is open on Monday, Wednesday, Friday and Sunday afternoons from April to October.

Tourist information: Honiton 3716 (summer); Seaton 21660 (summer); Lyme Regis 2138; Bridport 24901 (summer); Axminster 34386 (summer).

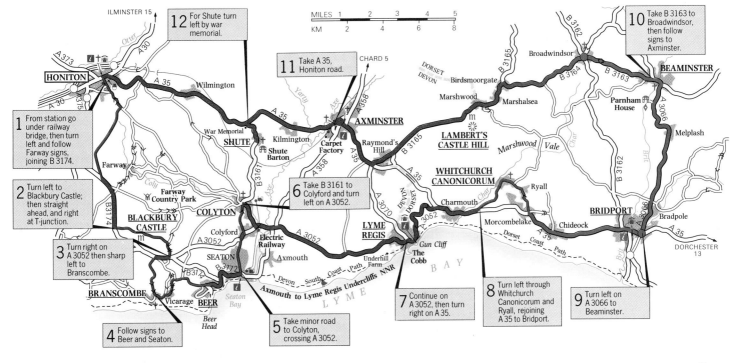

A fenland battlefield below the breezy Quantocks

Memories of a rebellion are recalled on the battlefield of Sedgemoor, amid the Somerset Levels. Lanes lead west through wooded combes to a largely unspoilt coastline.

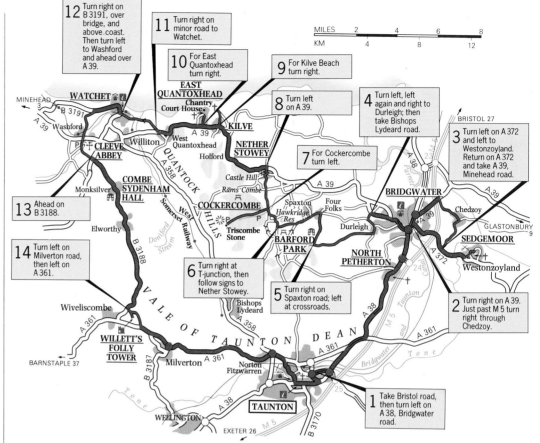

TAUNTON

The skyline of Taunton is dominated by the towers of the Churches of St Mary Magdalene and St James. The taller of the two, St Mary's, 163ft high, is visible from miles away across the fens to the east.

From the windows overlooking Taunton's spacious streets the townsfolk 300 years ago hung bunting to welcome the troops of the Duke of Monmouth, the illegitimate son of Charles II, who had come to rally Protestants and seize the throne from the Roman Catholic James II. The scenes of joy in Fore Street, East Reach and Corporation Street were followed a few weeks later by defeat – and the terror of the Bloody Assize.

Taunton's streets are still pleasant places to wander in, for the town has escaped the worst ravages of modern redevelopment. On an island in the centre of the town is the Market House, and facing this across the road is the Tudor House, where Judge Jeffreys is thought to have dined before the assize. The house is now a restaurant, so visitors can follow the notorious judge's precedent.

The Somerset County Museum is housed in Taunton Castle, behind Corporation Street. The building dates from the 13th century and contains the Great Hall where the assize was held. The museum contains a geological and natural history of Somerset, as well as the Somerset Light Infantry Museum; one of the most extensive military exhibitions in the country. It is open from Monday to Friday throughout the year, and also on Saturdays from June to September.

NORTH PETHERTON

The handsome 14th-century church, with its impressive 15th-century tower, faces the main road across a spacious green. There is parking space just south of the church. North Petherton is the scene of an annual winter carnival in November, when hundreds of decorated floats parade through the town.

BRIDGWATER

A walk along West Quay from Blake Gardens leads to the wharves where there is a new marina. Castle Street, running down to West Quay, is a perfect Georgian street, and contains the first arts centre in England, opened in 1946. In the centre of the town is the Church of St Mary, with a tower topped by a 14th-century spire. It was from this tower that the Duke of Monmouth surveyed King James's troops drawn up against him at Westonzoyland.

A museum is housed in the birthplace of Robert Blake, who defended Taunton for Parliament during the Civil War and later, as Admiral Blake, won renown under Cromwell. The museum is open daily, and includes a room devoted to exhibits connected with the Battle of Sedgemoor.

The library has an unusual freestanding bookcase in the shape of a donkey made from the materials of an old printing frame, with type blocks for teeth. Known as 'Caxton', it is the work of Hans Schwarz, a sculptor who had his studio in Stogursey.

St Matthew's Fair, lasting four days from the last Wednesday in September each year, includes a sheep fair and stalls of all kinds, and a large firework carnival is held in November. There are two town trails.

SEDGEMOOR

The tower of Westonzoyland's St Mary's Church rises high above the fens of the Somerset Levels, and can be seen stark against the skyline shortly after leaving Bridgwater. From a sharp bend in the road north of the village a track leads to the site of the last pitched battle to take place on English soil.

On the evening of July 5, 1685, the Duke of Monmouth climbed the tower of St Mary's, Bridgwater, and could see the king's cavalry ranging the moor just west of the village. Judging that he could surprise them under cover of darkness, he set out with a local guide and about 3000 followers, armed only with three guns, a few muskets and great numbers of pitchforks. Skirting the village of Chedzoy, the rebels were held up by Bussex Rhine, an artificial waterway dug to drain the fields. A nervous rebel accidentally fired a pistol, and the king's troops were alerted. Surprise was lost, and facing disciplined troops the rebels stood no chance.

About 700 rebels were killed, and some 500 prisoners were herded into the church at Westonzoyland to await trial. Monmouth himself fled towards the New Forest, where he was captured a few days later, conveyed to London and beheaded on Tower Hill. Such was the vengeance taken by King James and Judge Jeffreys at the Bloody Assize that two generations later Jeffreys' granddaughter was hounded out of the area.

The Sedgemoor Memorial Stone stands near the Bussex Rhine, where some of the heaviest fighting took place.

BARFORD PARK

A mellow red-brick Queen Anne house is surrounded by extensive parkland with fine trees. There is a walled flower garden, a water garden and a woodland garden. The house is in daily family use, but can be visited on Wednesdays and Thursday afternoons from May to September, and at Bank Holiday weekends.

COCKERCOMBE

A road leads up the combe through woods owned by the Forestry Commission, with a purling brook on the right; the hills on either side are so steep that even at midday the combe is in shadow. Nearing the ridge of the Quantocks the trees thin out until at the top, from the car park, there are magnificent views in all directions.

To the left is the Triscombe Stone with a vista over the Vale of Taunton Deane. A little way to the right is open heathland, with breathtaking views over the sea to Wales 20 miles away.

About four-fifths of the way up the combe a footpath turns off to the right. This leads north to a picnic site in Rams Combe.

NETHER STOWEY

The front door of the cottage in which the poet Samuel Taylor Coleridge lived for three years opens directly onto the pavement. In this modest little house was written most of his best verse, including *The Rime of the Ancient Mariner*, and here the poet entertained William and Dorothy Wordsworth who were frequent visitors.

The cottage now belongs to the National Trust, and the parlour, with the desk and other furniture that Coleridge used, can be visited on most afternoons in summer. The village is overlooked by the grassy mound of Castle Hill. On its summit the layout of the Norman keep can still be traced, and there are magnificent views across the Bristol Channel.

KILVE
A turning off the main road leads to a car park by Kilve church. Nearby stand the ivy-clad ruins of an old chantry that was burnt down by a 19th-century blaze – fuelled, it is said, by smuggled liquor concealed within. A path leads to the beach about 100yds away. In the low crumbling cliffs may be found fossils of ammonites and other creatures.

EAST QUANTOXHEAD
A peaceful village pond, where white ducks dabble, is set against the backdrop of the church and partly Jacobean Court House which has remained unaltered since the east front was added in 1610. A path leads to the beach, with views across to South Wales.

WATCHET
The tiny harbour dries out at low tide, and the cargo ships that trade mainly with Spain and Portugal lie upright on the mud. It is said that it was here that Samuel Taylor Coleridge met his 'ancient mariner' – an old sailor whose seafaring tales inspired Coleridge's famous poem.

A museum in the old Market House facing the harbour has a display of local history from prehistoric times to the present day; exhibits include Roman remains, the products of a Saxon mint and items from the iron mines of the Brendon Hills. The museum is open daily in summer.

Britain's longest, privately owned passenger railway, the West Somerset Railway, has a station at Watchet, with services throughout the summer and occasionally in winter. The trains use 20 miles of the 23 mile line which runs along the coast from Minehead to Watchet, then up the valley between the Brendon and Quantock Hills to Bishops Lydeard.

A minor joy of Somerset lies in the picturesque names of villages – Stogursey, Stogumber, Bicknoller, Monksilver and many others. It is said that Philip Gosse, the son of the writer Sir Edmund Gosse, when a doctor during the First World War, recited the names of the stations on the West Somerset line to a severely wounded soldier who came from these parts. Accidentally he included Stogursey instead of Stogumber. 'There bain't no station at Stogursey', whispered the soldier – and Dr Gosse claimed that the man's recovery dated from that moment.

CLEEVE ABBEY
This small religious house, founded for Cistercian monks in 1198, is sufficiently well preserved to convey a vivid feeling of late medieval monastic life. The refectory, the dormitories and many of the cells, on two floors, can be visited daily. The refectory, rebuilt in the late 15th century, has a superb timber roof. Through the slit windows of the convent buildings there are long views over the fields and hills.

MAN-MADE LAKE *The route runs beside Hawkridge Reservoir, whose waters add a splash of blue to the wooded Quantock foothills.*

TALL TREES *Walkers in Great Wood, in the Quantocks, may spot red deer.*

BLOSSOM TIME *From the churchyard in the pretty little village of East Quantoxhead there are views southwards up to the Quantock Hills.*

BATTLE SCENE *The Battle of Sedgemoor raged near Westonzoyland church.*

LATE REPAIRS *The gatehouse at Cleeve Abbey was rebuilt just before the Dissolution, when there were 17 'priests of honest life who keep great hospitality'.*

COMBE SYDENHAM HALL
Handsome Elizabethan walled gardens, ornamental tree nurseries and a deer park surround the home of Elizabeth Sydenham, Sir Francis Drake's wife, on the edge of the Exmoor National Park. Tall hedges of clipped yew surround a series of gardens, including a rose garden and herb garden, and there, hidden from view, it is easy to imagine Drake's contemporaries indulging in the courtly intrigues that characterised the age. There are woodland walks in the grounds, now a country park. One of them goes south-westwards, up past valley ponds made for Sir Francis, and now used as a trout farm.

Also in the park is the British Bird of Prey Care Centre, where injured hawks and owls are cared for and then returned to their natural habitat. The house, still a family home, and its grounds are open to the public on Monday to Friday from Easter to the end of October.

WILLETT'S FOLLY TOWER
This curious edifice, reached by a footpath off the Milverton road, just after turning off the B3188, was built in the early 19th century, from the materials of a ruined church. The climb is rewarded by splendid views of the Quantock Hills.

Tourist information: Taunton 74785/ 70479; Bridgwater 427652/424391 ext 419 (summer); Watchet 31824 (summer).

Gorges and green lanes among the Mendip Hills

TOUR

22

———— 56 MILES ————

A long headland once occupied by prehistoric man guards the sands of Weston Bay. Inland one of England's scenic wonders, Cheddar Gorge, cuts a canyon into the limestone Mendip Hills.

WESTON-SUPER-MARE

Once a fishing village, Weston was put firmly on the tourist map by the arrival of the Great Western Railway in 1841, and by the steamers which brought trippers across the Bristol Channel from Cardiff and Newport. Today it has two piers, the Winter Gardens and a bracing 2 mile promenade.

A reminder of Weston's ancient past is the local history trail to Weston Woods and Worlebury Camp, the hilltop site of an Iron Age settlement begun 2500 years ago. The trail begins at Prince Consort Gardens, opposite Birnbeck Pier, and follows a 3 mile route through the hill-fort, past the Worle Windmill, built around 1760.

BREAN DOWN

The peninsula guarding the southern approach to Weston Bay affords commanding views from its 320ft summit. Iron Age settlers fortified the landward end of what was then an island, before the draining of the Bleadon Level. Centuries later, around AD 350, the Romans built a temple on the down, close to a massive mound that is probably a Bronze Age barrow.

An energetic walk up the military road – so called because it leads to a fort built in 1867 to repel possible invasion by the French – passes the down's historic sites.

BRENT KNOLL

Legend has it that on this curious 450ft hill, rising in solitary splendour from the Somerset Levels, King Arthur came upon one of his knights, Ider, killed in battle after dispatching three giants. Blaming himself for the hero's fate, the king gave land and property to Glastonbury's monastery in penance. The legend enhances the knoll's atmosphere of ancient mystery. The best approach to the hill is by a half-mile walk starting from the leafy churchyard of East Brent.

WEDMORE

Among this ancient village's many fine buildings are some sublime Victorian private houses, two hotels and the ancient Church of St Mary, which in part dates back to the late 12th century. A modern stained-glass window in the church commemorates King Alfred, who came to Wedmore to sign the treaty of 879 that concluded his defeat of the Danes in Wessex. The impeccably restored Ashton Windmill, which overlooks

CHEDDAR GORGE *Cascading drapes of greenery cloak the sheer cliff faces of the gorge, cut by a river that now runs underground.*

Allerton Moor, is open on Sunday and Bank Holiday Monday afternoons from Easter to October.

BLACK ROCK NATURE RESERVE

Entered by a gate and stile to the right of the road at the head of the Cheddar Gorge, the reserve offers an introduction to the wildlife of the Mendips. Its 183 acres are home to more than 200 species of wild flowers and trees, and two trails wind through ash woodland, pine forest and open grassland.

At the Black Rock Reserve's northern end begins the Long Wood Nature Reserve, where a mile-long trail passes through ash, maple and oak.

CHEDDAR GORGE

The approach to one of Britain's most spectacular sights is made all the more dramatic by the gradual deepening of the road along the gorge's floor. At first, it leads through gentle, boulder-strewn slopes, passing on to craggy, steeper rises; then, quite suddenly, the road plunges into a breathtaking

canyon, its sheer limestone sides towering up a dizzying 400ft.

Gough's Cave, open daily, has spectacular stalagmites and stalactites. The Cheddar Museum shows the lifestyle of the Stone Age cave-dwellers and their successors.

The little town of Cheddar retains few signs of its medieval origins, other than the 14th to 15th-century church and a fine market cross.

AXBRIDGE

Beyond the sprawl of new housing, the road emerges into a town square that delights the eye. The beautifully maintained buildings, cheerfully painted in green, brown, yellow and blue, crowd round their brick-paved precinct.

The oldest building in the square is the so-called King John's Hunting Lodge, in fact constructed around 1500, more than 200 years after the king's death; its name is a reminder that John used the Mendips as a royal hunting ground. The three-storey

house is now a museum of local history, open every afternoon from April to September.

WINSCOMBE

Strung out along lovely wooded slopes at the heart of the Mendips, Winscombe has a fine old church, St James's. It is noted for its 15th-century stained glass, in particular two windows in the Lady Chapel. The churchyard is dominated by a magnificent 500-year-old yew.

BANWELL

The road up the hill into the village passes what appears to be a pristine medieval castle. It is in fact a piece of Victorian whimsy, a rather grand private house. The village has more ancient origins, having been built round a natural spring after King Alfred founded a minster here in 885.

Tourist information: Weston-super-Mare 26838; Brent Knoll 466 (summer); Cheddar 742769.

Inland from the Bristol Channel, hedged lanes link stone-built villages on the slopes of Avon's hills. A hymn, an epic poem and a historical novel were inspired by the area and its inhabitants.

CLEVEDON

Modest villas, with the occasional restaurant or antiques shop, look across the similarly modest promenade to Clevedon Bay and the breezy Bristol Channel beyond. A once-fashionable Victorian watering place, this quiet resort is understated and elegant – and free of the neon-signed attractions of many seaside towns.

Clevedon's very earliest days are recalled by the Norman Church of St Andrew, which stands on Wain's Hill, the town's southerly headland. Buried here is Arthur Hallam, in whose memory his close friend Alfred Tennyson wrote *In Memoriam*.

YATTON

St Mary's Church, like other village churches along this part of the tour, illustrates the eager rivalry that existed between even the tiniest communities of 500 years ago to build bigger and better places of worship.

The church at Yatton, with its curious part-spire emerging from the Perpendicular tower, probably lacked the foundations to support the ambitiously tall steeple originally built in the 1450s, but the present arrangement has maintained its high profile since 1595.

CONGRESBURY

From the churchyard of St Andrew's there is a good view of Yatton church across the mere mile of Congresbury (pronounced 'Coomsbury') Moor that separates the two parishes. Equally grand, St Andrew's is reached from the main road by a gate to the left, immediately after the Old School Rooms.

The church itself dates from the 13th century and has good medieval stonework including the corbels supporting the roof vaulting. These are decorated with the painted figures of headache and toothache sufferers – in commemoration of the famed healing powers of William Button, Bishop of Bath and Wells from 1248 to 1264.

WRINGTON

Another small village with a large church, Wrington lies idyllically along the Mendip foothills. John Locke, the philosopher, was born here in 1632, and Hannah More, the writer and philanthropist, lived here from 1785 until her death in 1833. During her lifetime Hannah More wrote many religious tracts and set up Sunday schools in Somerset.

BURRINGTON COMBE

The car park at the north end of this miniature gorge is a good point from which to investigate Burrington's caves and towering cliffs. Opposite is the cleft in which the curate of nearby Blagdon, Augustus Toplady, sheltered from a thunderstorm, and was thus inspired to write the hymn *Rock of Ages* in 1775.

About 150yds down the road to the left is Aveline's Hole, one of many caves in the gorge that were once the homes of Stone Age families.

HINTON BLEWETT

Facing the green, the Ring O' Bells pub all but conceals the enchanting little Church of St Margaret, which basks in its secluded, sunlit churchyard behind the inn and the delightful old cottages that flank it. Originally built by the Bluet family, manorial lords here during the 14th and 15th centuries, the church has a chancel arch made to a 13th-century design.

CHEW VALLEY LAKE

This scenic stretch of water is, in fact, a modern reservoir, popular among trout fishermen and birdwatchers; as many as 240 different species of bird have been spotted here. Off the lakeside road are two picnic areas.

CHEW MAGNA

Crossing the 15th-century bridge over the Chew river, the road leads onto the picturesque main street of the village. The Old School Room at the church gate was built around 1500, and has served as a shelter for the poor and as an alehouse as well as a school. Today, with its beautiful original timber roof still intact, it is the village hall.

STANTON DREW

This brief diversion offers a lingering glance over the fine old farm buildings and cottages that cluster round the river to the east of Chew Magna. Beside the turning to Stanton Drew is a tiny six-sided house with a thatched conical roof. A double-arched bridge leads into the village, which is dominated by large Georgian houses. Beyond it are stone circles dating from the Bronze Age.

CLEVEDON COURT

Built in 1320, Clevedon's manor house has miraculously survived in its entirety, and even incorporates a tower and hall from the preceding century. The manor's south front has a two-storey porch with a mock-medieval portcullis.

The house was bought by Abraham Elton, a Bristol merchant, in 1709 and remained in the hands of his family until it passed to the National Trust in the 1950s. In the 19th century Clevedon Court was visited by many of the Eltons' literary friends. Thackeray wrote part of his novel *Henry Esmond* while staying here.

The house and its terraced gardens are open on Wednesday, Thursday, Sunday and Bank Holiday Monday afternoons between April and September.

Tourist information:
Weston-super-Mare 26838.

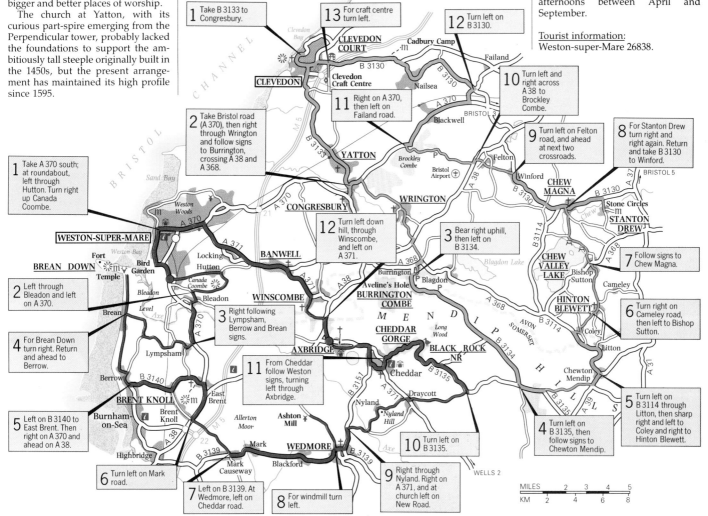

1 Take B 3133 to Congresbury.

13 For craft centre turn left.

12 Turn left on B 3130.

2 Take Bristol road (A 370), then right through Wrington and follow signs to Burrington, crossing A 38 and A 368.

11 Right on A 370, then left on Failand road.

10 Turn left and right across A 38 to Brockley Combe.

9 Turn left on Felton road, and ahead at next two crossroads.

8 For Stanton Drew turn right and right again. Return and take B 3130 to Winford.

1 Take A 370 south; at roundabout, left through Hutton. Turn right up Canada Coombe.

12 Turn left down hill, through Winscombe, and left on A 371.

3 Bear right uphill, then left on B 3134.

7 Follow signs to Chew Magna.

2 Left through Bleadon and left on A 370.

6 Turn right on Cameley road, then left to Bishop Sutton.

3 Right following Lympsham, Berrow and Brean signs.

4 For Brean Down turn right. Return and ahead to Berrow.

11 From Cheddar follow Weston signs, turning left through Axbridge.

5 Turn left on B 3114 through Litton, then sharp right and left to Coley and right to Hinton Blewett.

5 Left on B 3140 to East Brent. Then right on A 370 and ahead on A 38.

4 Turn left on B 3135, then follow signs to Chewton Mendip.

6 Turn left on Mark road.

7 Left on B 3139. At Wedmore, left on Cheddar road.

8 For windmill turn left.

10 Turn left on B 3135.

9 Right through Nyland. Right on A 371, and at church left on New Road.

MILES
KM

45

Manors of the Wiltshire downlands

TOUR
24
—— 50 MILES ——

Just off the busy motorway, leafy lanes wind through Wiltshire. Beyond two lovely old market towns lie one of the finest arboretums in Europe and a village with a maypole.

SWINDON

Until 1841 Swindon was a quiet market town set on a hilltop. In that year, however, the final link of Isambard Kingdom Brunel's Great Western Railway was made a few miles west of Swindon, and a few years later the town was chosen as the site for the railway company's locomotive works. Those works employed some 12,000 workers who were housed in a specially designed 'village' of terraced cottages on the north side of Faringdon Road. The cottages have been restored and one, furnished as a typical foreman's home of the late 1800s, is open daily.

The Great Western Railway Museum, also in Faringdon Road, displays many railway relics, including the old locomotives *North Star* and *Lode Star*. One room in the museum is devoted to Isambard Kingdom Brunel.

LYDIARD TREGOZE

An unsignposted drive, through a gateway bearing the nameplate Lydiard Park Management Committee, leads to Lydiard Mansion and the Church of St Mary. There was a village here once called simply Lydiard in the Domesday Book of 1086; the Tregoze was added in the 12th century, when the manor passed to the family of that name. All that remains now is the house, the church and a modern office block housing the estate offices, isolated among trees at the end of the drive which is punctuated by ramps.

The house looks out over some 140 acres of parkland and was remodelled in 1743 by John Viscount St John from an older building. It was built of Bath stone and in the classical style of that period. Open daily, Lydiard Mansion contains furniture, china and paintings in rooms with richly decorated ceilings.

The church is much older, dating from the 13th century, and contains splendid memorials to the St Johns, especially that of Edward St John who died in 1645 fighting for Charles I at the second battle of Newbury. His gilded effigy, standing beneath a purple, white and gold canopy, has been called the 'golden cavalier'.

MALMESBURY

The rivers Avon and Ingleburn flow on either side of Malmesbury and meet just east of the town, which is served by six bridges. Approached from the east the town is reached by St John's Bridge, beside which stands the first clue to Malmesbury's past identity. Like most Wiltshire towns, Malmesbury once prospered as a weaving centre, and the massive, five-storey mill by the bridge is one of several mills that thrived until the 19th century. Built in 1798, the building was first a woollen mill and later a silk mill, and is now a block of private apartments.

After crossing the bridge the road winds up to the High Street, and there stands a second monument to Malmesbury's past, the 15th-century market cross sitting like an enormous stone crown in the centre of the road. Octagonal in form, it stands 41ft high and has a vaulted roof with battlements, pinnacles and flying buttresses. From it radiate streets full of character, and behind rise the honey-coloured walls and pinnacled buttresses of Malmesbury Abbey.

The abbey was founded in Saxon times by St Aldhelm, who is buried there in an unidentified site, but most of the present structure dates from the 12th century. The soaring arches and pillars in the nave are superb examples of Norman architecture, and the south porch is carved with figures representing Biblical stories. Also in the abbey is the tomb of King Athelstan, grandson of King Alfred who in 880 made Malmesbury a borough.

A pleasant riverside walk starts at The Flying Monk pub, named after a monk called Elmer who in 1010 became the first British 'aeronaut'. He made wings and jumped from the tower of the abbey, and actually 'flew' for about 200yds before falling to earth and breaking both legs.

TETBURY

The charm of Tetbury begins with its Town Hall, which for 300 years has been the hub of the town, serving both as a meeting place and market. It stands on sturdy stone pillars four-square in the centre of the town, defying the rumble of traffic and dominating its neighbours with a regal 'I was here first' air. It is certainly an architectural gem, one of the finest of its kind in England, with mullioned windows and a stone roof topped by a cupola with a bell and a weather vane flying a pair of dolphins.

The Town Hall looks down Long Street, which seems to consist almost entirely of antiques shops. The mixture of stone and stuccoed buildings is brightened by the eye-catching ochre and black façade of the Gentle Gardener Hotel.

The original market was in The Chipping – meaning 'market' – at the end of Chipping Street. The square is now a car park overlooked on one side by fine Georgian houses. Steps lead down beside medieval cottages and houses with low stone walls enclosing pretty little front gardens.

WESTONBIRT ARBORETUM

In 1829 Robert Stayner Holford of Westonbirt House began planting trees in downland to the west of the house. He did so for his own interest, but as a result the public can today enjoy one of the finest collections of trees and shrubs in Europe.

The arboretum covers about 600 acres, and a visitor centre explains some of the features to be seen and identifies which trees and shrubs are currently in flower. The building itself is constructed of several different timbers, including Douglas fir, Baltic pine and red cedar. There is a series of walks through the arboretum, among giant cedars, alder, oaks, whitebeam and maple towering to almost 100ft. Flowering shrubs and trees include rhododendron, camellia, magnolia, azalea, syringa and cherry, while in autumn the Acer Glade is afire with the scarlet foliage of Japanese maple. The arboretum is open daily.

HORTON COURT

A winding lane leads up to Horton Court from the village of Horton, and the first glimpse of the house at the

BIRTHPLACE OF PHOTOGRAPHY *William Fox Talbot's first recognisable photograph was of a window in Lacock Abbey.*

end of a drive lined with trees and flowering shrubs is quite charming. The house, built in the 12th century, was heavily restored in the 19th century, though the original hall remains. Only the hall is open to the public, together with a fine covered walk in the gardens modelled on the Italian loggia, even down to four stucco medallions of emperors' heads. It was built in the 16th century by William Knight who served Henry VIII as an intermediary with the Holy See on several foreign missions.

Horton Court is in the care of the National Trust, and open on Wednesday and Saturday afternoons in summer.

IRON ACTON

There is more to this rambling village than first meets the eye. The main street winds past the parish church of St James the Less, which dates from the late 14th century. A carved stone figure of the saint stands in a niche on a buttress of the tower. Inside the church a richly carved, canopied pulpit bears the date 1624, and in the aisle there is a candelabra of 1725.

Beyond the church a pleasant mixture of Georgian cottages and houses ends at the White Hart, which boasts a wood-burning clay oven. It also sports, on its front wall, one of those old yellow and black AA plaques which not only proclaims the name of the village but also gives its distance from London as being 112¾ miles. To the right of the inn is a wide green with a striped maypole.

Tourist information: Swindon 30328/26161; Malmesbury 2143/3748; Tetbury 53552 (summer).

TOUR
25
61 MILES

A scenic route through the Wiltshire downlands seems a world away from the motorway it accompanies. Villages of beauty and historic houses are strung along the route.

BRISTOL

The heart of Bristol, torn out during the bombing raids of the Second World War, is now a complex of shops and offices, but fragments of the old city are tucked away in odd corners. In cobbled King Street is the Theatre Royal, opened in 1766 and Britain's oldest working theatre; farther along the street is the Llandoger Trow, the 17th-century inn said to be the 'Spyglass Inn' of Robert Louis Stevenson's *Treasure Island*.

Bristol Cathedral, which stands on College Green, was founded in the 1140s and became a cathedral in 1542. Its Norman chapter house is said to be the finest in England.

Several old houses are open to the public. They include the 16th-century Red Lodge in Park Row; Chatterton House, birthplace of the poet Thomas Chatterton in 1752; and the Georgian House, with period furniture, in Great George Street.

In Gasferry Road Isambard Brunel's steamship *Great Britain* stands in the dock in which she was built, a reminder that Bristol was once the gateway to the New World. Soaring above the awesome Avon Gorge, Brunel's Clifton Suspension Bridge, completed after his death in 1859, serves both as a memorial to the Victorian engineer and as an enduring symbol of this gracious and vibrant city.

DYRHAM PARK

Pretty though it is, Dyrham's street climbing between green verges and stone-built cottages gives no hint of the architectural treasure that lies beyond. At the top of the hill a road leads up to St Peter's Church, and at the end of a footpath the church and the upper storeys of Dyrham Park come into view. The two buildings stand so close together that they appear to be one.

The church dates from the 13th century and stands on the side of a wooded hill, its churchyard sloping steeply among the trees. Behind an immaculately trimmed box hedge, the west front of the house rises from a wide terrace where peacocks strut among flowerbeds and close-shaven lawns.

Dyrham Park is reached through imposing gates on the Bath to Stroud road. A driveway winds down into a deep wooded hollow, at the foot of which Dyrham Park looks almost like a very splendid doll's house in its superb panoramic setting.

The house was built late in the 17th century by William Blathwayt, a Secretary of State to William III. The bold east front is surmounted by a balustrade, with stone urns and a spread eagle which is part of the Blathwayt crest.

The rooms contain period furniture, Delftware china and paintings mainly by Dutch artists. The house is in the care of the National Trust and is open daily in the afternoon, except Fridays in summer, and Thursdays and Fridays in spring and autumn.

CASTLE COMBE

In 1962 Castle Combe was chosen as England's prettiest village, and from any point in the village the eye is caught by some delightful feature – the honey-coloured cottages of Cotswold stone, the steep, stone-tiled roof on the market cross, or the gentle hump of the pack bridge spanning the sparkling little Bybrook.

Perhaps the best view is from the bridge, looking up the main street curving up to the market cross and the Castle Hotel. On the right, the lattice-windowed bays of the post office peep out from under a stone-tiled canopy and flower baskets hang below mullioned windows. Farther along is the Old Rectory, facing an antiques shop that was once the village chapel, and at the top of the street rises the gleaming white façade of the White Hart.

The village church, St Andrew's, is tucked away behind the houses facing the market cross, and has a tower built in 1434.

Castle Combe was once a centre for cloth weaving, and by the bridge are weavers' cottages and Weavers House, which was the home of the master weaver. Here, it is said, lived the Blanket brothers who gave a new word to the English language when they devised a warm covering for their bed.

BIDDESTONE

A spacious green crisscrossed by roads forms the heart of Biddestone, with a duck pond in one corner and stone-built cottages and houses facing each other across buttercup-speckled verges. The White Horse inn dominates the green, its whitewashed walls bedecked with old wagon wheels and hanging flower baskets.

About a mile east of the village, a lane beside Biddestone Manor leads

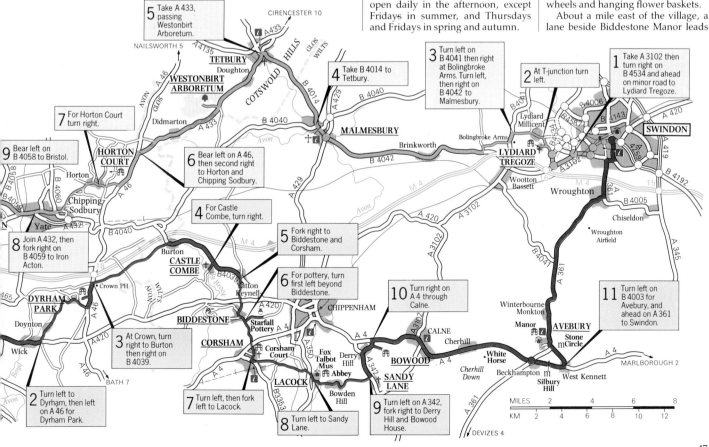

MELLOW STONE *Time-worn cottages stand in Lacock's Church Street.*

LYDIARD MILLICENT *All Saints' Church dates mostly from the 14th century.*

DYRHAM PARK *A herd of fallow deer roams the spacious parkland.*

COTTAGE INDUSTRY *Weavers' cottages stand near the bridge in Castle Combe.*

MYSTIC STONES *Grey boulders form a 4000-year-old ring round Avebury.*

IRON ACTON *A 15th-century preaching cross stands in the churchyard.*

to Starfall Pottery. Two potters have set up their wheel in a tumbledown stone barn, part of Starveall Farm, and make a range of stoneware and commemorative pottery.

CORSHAM

Like so many Cotswold towns Corsham thrived on the cloth-weaving trade in the 17th century, and most of its oldest buildings date from that time. There are Flemish-gabled houses in High Street, and more gabled cottages in Church Street, where there is also a stately Georgian house. At the top of Church Street the arched gateway to Corsham Court stands close to St Bartholomew's Church.

Corsham Court dates from 1582 and has been the home of the Methuen family since 1745. It is a mixture of neatly blended styles, the original Elizabethan front leading onto 18th-century additions built to house the priceless Methuen collection of paintings by British, Flemish, Spanish and Italian Old Masters. The grounds were laid out by Capability Brown and Humphry Repton. The house is open to the public every afternoon except on Mondays and Fridays.

LACOCK

If Castle Combe is England's prettiest village, then Lacock must run a close second. Its wide High Street is lined on one side with timber-framed cottages and houses, including the imposing Porch House with a two-storey timber-framed porch that gives it its name; on the other side is a pleasing array of stone-built cottages.

High Street forms one side of a square of streets, each with its own charm. Every corner turned brings some fresh delight, such as the pretty Sign of the Angel in Church Street with its overhanging upper storey, and the 14th-century tithe barn next to the domed lockup in East Street.

To the east of the village is Lacock Abbey, founded in the 13th century as a nunnery and converted to a house in 1540 by Sir William Sharington when it was one of the last religious orders dissolved by Henry VIII. Sir William retained many of the abbey's features, such as the cloisters and sacristy, which can still be seen. The house later passed into the ownership of the Talbot family, and in the 19th century William Fox Talbot made some of the earliest experiments with photography at the abbey. Examples of his work, including his first recognisable photograph taken in 1835, and some of his equipment are displayed in the Fox Talbot Museum, open daily in summer, housed in a 16th-century building near the abbey entrance.

Lacock Abbey, like most of the village, is owned by the National Trust and is open daily in summer in the afternoon, except on Tuesdays when only the grounds are open.

SANDY LANE

This pretty little village strung out along the Devizes to Chippenham road is a masterpiece in thatch. The smart-as-paint cottages stand behind trim hedges and colourful gardens,

and in a minor road forking off at the southern end of the village there is a thatched church. Dedicated to St Nicholas, it was built in 1892 and is tiny, its timber walls enclosing a simply furnished interior just about large enough for a couple of dozen worshippers who sing their hymns to the accompaniment of a hand-pumped organ.

BOWOOD

Early summer visitors to Bowood can enjoy the magnificent rhododendron gardens set out in a woodland south of Bowood House and reached by an entrance on the Devizes to Chippenham road. Walks in the woodland, carpeted with bluebells in early

summer, provide vistas of breath-taking beauty with every step.

Bowood House dates from the 18th century and is the home of the Lansdowne family, Earls of Shelburne. The architecture is superb, as well it might be since such famous names as Robert Adam, George Dance, Robert Smirke and Charles Barry all had a hand in its construction. Adam's south front is particularly elegant and looks out onto wide terraces, trim lawns and rose beds and soldierly conical yew trees.

Behind Adam's façade is his orangery, cool and serene and now displaying paintings and classical marble sculptures where orange and lemon

trees once grew. At the end of the orangery is a room called the Laboratory; it was used by Dr Joseph Priestley when he was tutor to the first Lord Lansdowne's sons, and it was here that he discovered oxygen in 1774.

In contrast to the formal terraces the grounds of Bowood are a superb example of landscaping by the master of the art, Capability Brown. The lake, made by damming a stream, looks completely natural in its setting in a shallow valley, and on a small promontory stands a Doric temple.

Bowood House is open daily from April to September. The rhododendron walks are open from mid-May until mid-June, daily.

AVEBURY

The road to Avebury passes Silbury Hill, a man-made mound standing 130ft high and dating from at least 2500 BC. Excavations have failed to reveal its purpose, and it makes a fitting prologue to Avebury, which itself has an air of mystery, a mystery locked in the ancient grey stones standing like misshapen aliens encircling the village. And alien to Avebury they are, for they were hauled from the Marlborough Downs in the late Stone Age and set up at least 200 years before Stonehenge. That much is known, but the purpose of the stones has eluded archaeologists down the centuries: a site for pagan rituals perhaps, or a temple to the sun? The heaviest of the stones, in the outer ring, weighs about 40 tons. Inside the outer ring are two incomplete circles, their gaps marked by concrete posts. It has been suggested that some of the stones may represent human figures.

Whatever their purpose, there is nothing sinister about the stones on a warm summer's day when sheep graze in their shadows and schoolboys scramble, notebooks in hand, on the grassy banks. Nor is there much mystery about Avebury itself, sitting snugly within the ring of stones and secure in its own history, from its Norman church to its 16th-century manor house and 17th-century thatched barn.

HIGH HORSE *The white horse on Cherhill Down, carved in 1780, marks the highest point on the Downs between London and Bath. Its creator, a Dr Alsop from Calne, directed his workmen from a mile away, using a megaphone.*

Avebury Manor, which has fine plasterwork, panelling and furniture, is open to the public daily in summer. Finds from local excavations are displayed in the Alexander Keiller Museum, and there is a museum of rural life in the thatched barn.

Tourist information: Bristol 293891; Corsham 714867; Avebury 425/555 (summer).

Green lanes around Arthur's Camelot

Narrow lanes wind among Dorset's green hills to a chalk-cut giant. Somerset presents a broad man-made lake, villages of golden stone, and a hilltop where King Arthur may have held court.

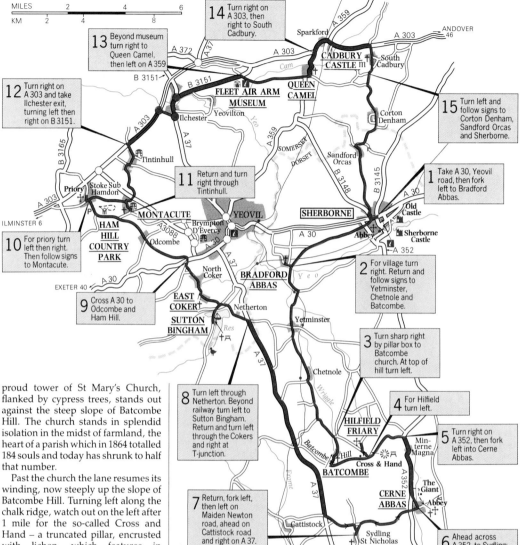

13 Beyond museum turn right to Queen Camel, then left on A 359

14 Turn right on A 303, then right to South Cadbury.

12 Turn right on A 303 and take Ilchester exit, turning left then right on B 3151.

15 Turn left and follow signs to Corton Denham, Sandford Orcas and Sherborne.

11 Return and turn right through Tintinhull.

1 Take A 30, Yeovil road, then fork left to Bradford Abbas.

10 For priory turn left then right. Then follow signs to Montacute.

2 For village turn right. Return and follow signs to Yetminster, Chetnole and Batcombe.

9 Cross A 30 to Odcombe and Ham Hill.

3 Turn sharp right by pillar box to Batcombe church. At top of hill turn left.

8 Turn left through Netherton. Beyond railway turn left to Sutton Bingham. Return and turn left through the Cokers and right at T-junction.

4 For Hilfield turn left.

5 Turn right on A 352, then fork left into Cerne Abbas.

7 Return, fork left, then left on Maiden Newton road, ahead on Cattistock road and right on A 37.

6 Ahead across A 352, to Sydling; keep left at ford.

SHERBORNE

Sir Walter Raleigh, so they say, fell off his horse in amazement at his first sight of Sherborne from the rocky knoll on which the 12th-century Old Castle stands. From the ruins that remain after Civil War bombardment, Raleigh's view is today enhanced by the new Sherborne Castle that Raleigh built just below it, seen across the lake which his successors, the Digbys, added in the 18th century.

As if two castles were not enough, this gem of a town has also Bishop Aldhelm's abbey, with its breathtaking 15th-century fan-vaulting; a pinnacled Gothic memorial to the Digbys who restored the abbey; 15th-century almshouses, still in use, set round a tiny cloistered courtyard; and a roofed conduit house where monks washed and shaved their heads. All this within 50yds of Half Moon Street at the heart of Sherborne, where a map on the stone wall of another of the town's ancient buildings gives a potted history of all its showpieces.

As a grace note, townsfolk earlier this century staged a pageant to commemorate the first 1200 years of their abbey. To mark the occasion, the Digbys presented a plot of land beside the River Yeo and the town carpeted it with an attractive sweep of gardens. The Old Castle is open on Thursday, Saturday, Sunday and Bank Holiday afternoons from April to September.

BRADFORD ABBAS

With its pinnacles, turrets and battlemented parapet, the tower of St Mary's Church wears the aspect of a medieval castle keep, standing guard over the pub and cottages at its foot in a perfect Dorset village grouping. Inside the church, the beautiful carved desk and pew ends, worn shiny with age, show vine and ivy foliage, ogres, a griffin, a monkey and an owl. The heavy grey pointing, which in Victorian times replaced the plaster covering of the walls, gives an unusual homely impression, suggesting the external walls of a newly restored country cottage.

Beyond Bradford Abbas the road crosses the River Yeo by a humpbacked bridge, then heads south along narrow lanes between highhedged banks.

BATCOMBE

A last bend in the narrow lane which has followed the aptly named Wriggle river from Yetminster – and ahead the proud tower of St Mary's Church, flanked by cypress trees, stands out against the steep slope of Batcombe Hill. The church stands in splendid isolation in the midst of farmland, the heart of a parish which in 1864 totalled 184 souls and today has shrunk to half that number.

Past the church the lane resumes its winding, now steeply up the slope of Batcombe Hill. Turning left along the chalk ridge, watch out on the left after 1 mile for the so-called Cross and Hand – a truncated pillar, encrusted with lichen, which features in Thomas Hardy's *Tess of the D'Urbervilles*.

Near the breezy 870ft summit of the ridge is the well-laid out Batcombe picnic area, with broad panoramas over the Blackmoor Vale and a view indicator that picks out the distant contours of Exmoor and the Quantocks. A 1½ mile hill walk winds through the firs, beeches and red cedars that clothe the slopes.

HILFIELD FRIARY

The plainchant of friars at their Mass issues from the open door of a converted cattle shed at the head of a green valley. Joining with the brown-cassocked brothers in prayer are ordinary tourists in holiday attire. The Anglican Society of Saint Francis has converted the buildings of an old farm to house a lively and friendly community where brothers test their vocation and wayfarers are cared for.

Visitors have the run of the friary, and there is a trail leaflet to guide them through chapel, refectory and library and out into the gardens, where the brothers grow their own food in the lee of wooded Batcombe

Hill. A modern statue of St Francis stands in the colonnaded courtyard, and a shop sells honey, bird boxes and pottery.

CERNE ABBAS

If the chalk-carved giant on the hill above the village is Cerne Abbas's main claim to fame, the flint that often goes with chalk comes into its own in the village streets. Time and again it appears, set in parallel bands between the stones of the church walls, or partner to brick as the infilling of half-timbered buildings in the main street.

A walk along Abbey Street, beside the broad, brightly lit St Mary's Church, spans the centuries. Half-timbered houses rub shoulders with Georgian porticoes, pillared and pastel-painted; there are medieval stocks outside the church . . . and a Falklands War victim of 1982 is commemorated on the village war memorial. A rivulet runs along one side of the street, with bridges across it to the houses. At the top of the street ducks

swim on a pond in front of the slight remains of Cerne Abbas's 10th-century abbey.

A path through the abbey burial ground leads onto the slopes of Giant Hill. But to see the famous chalk figure in perspective, go down Mill Lane, opposite the burial ground, and follow the river bank for a quarter of a mile to a bridge. From a stile on the right a path leads back across the lower slopes of the hill.

SUTTON BINGHAM

In sharp contrast to the narrow, high-banked lanes on the Dorset side of the border, Somerset at once asserts its individuality with a gleaming expanse of water set in a broad valley. Sutton Bingham Reservoir, owned by the Wessex Water Authority, is roughly T-shaped. A causeway carries the road across the crosspiece of the T, with model boats to the right and full-sized dinghies to the left, to a wide viewing area, open in summer, with picnic benches set high above the water. On the long leg of the T, devotees with binoculars gather to watch water birds.

Half hidden in woods beside the viewing area is a lovely little Norman church, roofed with stone slabs that increase in size from the ridge down to the eaves. Inside, a huge triple arch, with wavy motifs, forms a massive division between a nave with seats for some 40 worshippers and a chancel with ancient wall paintings.

EAST COKER
From a main street of thatched stone cottages, reached by little bridges over a rushing stream, a hill leads to the left past a row of tall, gabled and green-doored almshouses to St Michael's Church and the neighbouring Coker Court.

Two famous sons of East Coker are remembered in the church. One is the poet T.S. Eliot, whose ancestors emigrated from East Coker to America; he is commemorated by a simple tablet quoting from his poem *East Coker – 1940* the lines 'In my beginning is my end . . . in my end is my beginning'. The other local hero, commemorated by a brass memorial, is William Dampier, the navigator who explored the west coast of Australia, and also rescued Alexander Selkirk, the real-life Robinson Crusoe.

HAM HILL COUNTRY PARK
High-banked sandstone lanes with overarching trees tunnel upwards to the country park at the crest of the hill. There are car parks on both sides of the road, but the best views are obtained from the lay-by near the entrance to the Prince of Wales pub.

Here the land drops away to the Somerset Levels, a counterpane of green and brown hedged fields broken only by the spires of village churches.

Behind, by contrast, are the bumps and hillocks created by settlers who fortified the hilltop in prehistoric times and by later centuries of quarrying for building stone. Sandy paths provide opportunities for strolls or scrambles, and an information caravan is open in summer.

At the foot of the hill, golden-stone houses in the village of Stoke Sub Hamdon show the use to which the stone from the nearby quarries was put. The priory at the west end of the village is a complex of medieval buildings, preserved by the National Trust; it includes two thatched barns with nesting holes for doves, and an early 14th-century great hall which is open to the public.

MONTACUTE
Just as the main road seems about to sweep straight up to the front door of Montacute House it swings sharply right then left, along a narrow street lined with buildings of Ham stone, into the village's spacious central square, The Borough. Golden stone gleams in the sun on buildings old and not-so-old, from the immense Elizabethan mansion of Montacute House itself to the tiny drinking fountain in The Borough, completed only in 1983.

At the opposite end of Middle Street is St Catherine's Church, which contains the ornate tombs of the Phelips, owners of Montacute House for 300 years; outside in the church-

yard are the simple, lichened graves of ordinary parishioners dating back as many centuries.

Over the churchyard wall can be seen the battlemented gatehouse of a former 12th-century Cluniac priory, standing at the foot of St Michael's Hill – the 'pointed hill', *mons acutus*, that gave the village its name. The pepper-pot tower on top of the hill is a folly built by the Phelips in 1760.

Montacute House, which has a 189ft gallery running the whole length of the second floor, is owned by the National Trust and open every afternoon except Tuesdays in summer; the grounds are open daily.

FLEET AIR ARM MUSEUM
The Falklands War makes its second appearance on the tour in a display of captured Argentine aircraft and equipment in the grounds of the Royal Naval Air Station at Yeovilton. But the planes by the roadside proclaim the main business of the museum, which is a display of some 50 aircraft tracing the history of naval flying since 1903.

Cut off from their natural element by the roof of a huge hangar, the planes take on the aspect of elaborate sculptures, in a variety of shapes and colours ranging from the fragile elegance of First World War biplanes to the pencil-thin profile of Concorde. The museum is open daily.

QUEEN CAMEL
A quiet pathway called Grace Martin's Lane leads between cottages at the north end of the village towards the tall square Norman tower of St Barnabas's Church. A niche over the west

door holds a modern glass-fibre figure of St Barnabas, his face averted from the flying stones of his martyrdom, his hand clasping a hayrake, symbol of his feast day of June 11. The church's finest treasure is a remarkable rood screen, its fan-vaulted canopy carved with interlaced foliage and richly coloured.

It does no harm to imagine this village's unusual name as being linked with King Arthur's Camelot – even if etymologists more prosaically explain that the Old English *cant mael* meant a 'bare ridge', and that Edward I gave the manor to his wife Eleanor in the 13th century.

CADBURY CASTLE
Just beyond the attractive Church of St Thomas Becket in South Cadbury, a path called Castle Lane leads steeply up through beech woods onto the huge grassy plateau of an ancient hill-fort. The ramparts, thrown up by successive defenders from Iron Age to Saxon times, still form a green wall completely encircling the 18 acre fort except for gateways at the east and west ends. It must have been a well-nigh unassailable position, for on all sides the land drops some 300ft onto a patchwork of hedged fields.

Was this King Arthur's Camelot? Nobody knows. Certainly, standing on the ramparts today and looking north as the setting sun casts a last ray towards Glastonbury Tor, islanded on its hilltop, there is a strong sense of England's history.

Tourist information: Sherborne 815341 (summer); (Yeovilton) Ilchester 841083 (summer).

FROM A DORSET HILLTOP *A lane winds uphill from the lonely tower of Batcombe church, and Blackmoor Vale unrolls its green patchwork to the horizon.*

From Hardy's Wessex to Studland Bay

TOUR
29
—— 40 MILES ——

Memories of Thomas Hardy are strong in his native Wessex. Towns and villages depicted in his novels are passed on a tour which crosses the meandering Frome to woods and heathland.

DORCHESTER

Thomas Hardy reigns supreme in this splendid market town, the 'Casterbridge' of his novel *The Mayor of Casterbridge* and one of the most delightful centres in the West Country. The novelist's statue stands at the top of High West Street, while another Dorset writer, the dialect poet William Barnes, has his monument beside the medieval St Peter's Church.

However, Dorchester is a much older town than Hardy's Casterbridge. The Romans founded a town here in about AD 70, calling it Durnovaria. The grassy horseshoe amphitheatre where their gladiators fought, known as Maumbury Rings, is a prominent landmark almost in the centre of the town, and a large Roman town house has been excavated in Colliton Park, behind the county council offices.

In later centuries, Judge Jeffreys held his Bloody Assizes in Dorchester after the Monmouth Rebellion of 1685, and in 1834 the Tolpuddle Martyrs were tried in the Old Crown Court, virtually unchanged since their day and open to the public from Monday to Friday.

The history and prehistory of Dorset can be traced in the County Museum, which has an outstanding archaeological gallery centred on the discoveries at Maiden Castle, the huge Iron Age earthwork just outside the town; the museum is open daily except Sundays. Dorset's military history is displayed in the Military Museum, open daily except Sundays, while the Dinosaur Museum, open daily in summer, illustrates the prehistoric reptiles that once roamed the Dorset swamplands.

There is a Wednesday market.

WHITCOMBE CHURCH

A pretty little church with no known dedication stands next to a farm beside the main road. A simple building in grey-white stone, the church is mainly 12th century, with a 16th-century west tower. Inside there are considerable remains of medieval wall painting, including St Christopher, painted about 1400. The church is now maintained by the Redundant Churches Fund. The poet William Barnes was curate of Whitcombe in 1847. He is buried under a tall Celtic cross outside the south-west corner of the church at nearby Winterborne Came, where he was rector from 1862 until his death in 1886.

MORETON

A compact village beside the Frome, Moreton has a curious Gothic Revival church, rebuilt in the 1770s, and perched up on a mound. Unusually wide for its length, it has a rounded apse at the eastern end. In 1940 the church was shattered by a bomb, and the windows were blown out. They have been replaced with a complete set of clear glass windows engraved by Laurence Whistler.

In 1935, T.E. Lawrence, 'Lawrence of Arabia', was killed near Moreton on his motorcycle. His funeral service was held in Moreton church, and he is buried in the cemetery just along the main road.

CLOUDS HILL

In the cream-painted cottage beside the road, T.E. Lawrence lived from 1925 until his death in 1933. Owned by the National Trust, it contains Lawrence's furniture and some literary relics. The cottage is open most afternoons in summer and on Sundays in winter.

BOVINGTON TANK MUSEUM

The museum, at the southern end of Bovington Camp, contains the largest collection of armoured fighting vehicles in the world – more than 150 examples, from the lumbering tanks of the First World War to the latest products of arms technology. It includes famous tanks like the German Tiger of the Second World War, and curiosities such as a 1933 flamethrower. Visitors can test their skills on the 'Drive-a-tank Simulator', a tank-recognition slot machine, and tank video games. The museum is open daily.

BERE REGIS

It was the Turberville family tombs in the church at Bere Regis, Hardy's 'Kingsbere', that set in motion the tragic events of *Tess of the D'Urbervilles*. The village clusters round St John's, one of the finest parish churches of the region. The remarkable nave ceiling is decorated with painted wooden figures that look as though they are flying across the church; the ceiling is said to have been given by Cardinal Morton at the end of the 15th century.

The church retains traces of Saxon stonework, and there is Norman stone-carving on the nave arcades.

TOLPUDDLE

In the early 1830s six agricultural labourers met under a sycamore tree, known as the 'Martyrs' Tree', on Tolpuddle's small village green to establish a workers' union. This so alarmed the local landowners that they had the six arrested, tried and condemned to seven years' transportation. Pardoned before their sentences were completed, most of them emigrated subsequently to Canada.

CORFE CASTLE *Majestic even in their ruin, the shattered towers of Corfe loom above the grey-roofed village below the castle mound.*

LORD MAYOR'S SHOW *The lovely Athelhampton Hall was built about 1485 by Sir William Martyn, a Lord Mayor of London.*

GREENWOOD HOME *In his birthplace at Higher Bockhampton Thomas Hardy wrote 'Under the Greenwood Tree'.*

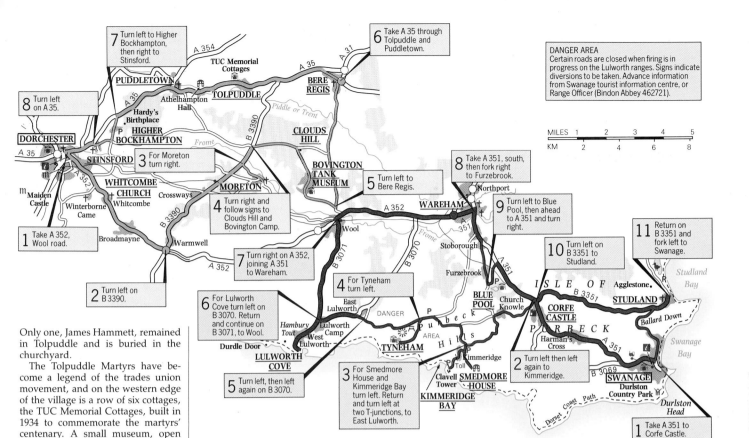

Map labels:

7 Turn left to Higher Bockhampton, then right to Stinsford.

6 Take A 35 through Tolpuddle and Puddletown.

8 Turn left on A 35.

3 For Moreton turn right.

1 Take A 352, Wool road.

4 Turn right and follow signs to Clouds Hill and Bovington Camp.

7 Turn right on A 352, joining A 351 to Wareham.

2 Turn left on B 3390.

5 Turn left to Bere Regis.

8 Take A 351, south, then fork right to Furzebrook.

9 Turn left to Blue Pool, then ahead to A 351 and turn right.

10 Turn left on B 3351 to Studland.

11 Return on B 3351 and fork left to Swanage.

6 For Lulworth Cove turn left on B 3070. Return and continue on B 3071, to Wool.

4 For Tyneham turn left.

5 Turn left, then left again on B 3070.

3 For Smedmore House and Kimmeridge Bay turn left. Return and turn left at two T-junctions, to East Lulworth.

2 Turn left then left again to Kimmeridge.

1 Take A 351 to Corfe Castle.

Only one, James Hammett, remained in Tolpuddle and is buried in the churchyard.

The Tolpuddle Martyrs have become a legend of the trades union movement, and on the western edge of the village is a row of six cottages, the TUC Memorial Cottages, built in 1934 to commemorate the martyrs' centenary. A small museum, open daily, is devoted to their lives and to the history of the TUC.

Tolpuddle itself is a pretty village beside the River Piddle or Trent. The name Piddle comes from an Old German word *pedel*, meaning 'lowland' or 'marsh'.

Athelhampton, 1½ miles west, is a Tudor manor house with a 15th-century great hall, surrounded by walled and terraced gardens. The house is open most afternoons in summer.

PUDDLETOWN

Unlike most of the villages on the Dorchester to Bere Regis road, which are constantly shaken by heavy traffic, the attractive centre of Puddletown, Hardy's 'Weatherbury', is off the road, on the north side. The imposing Church of St Mary still has its west gallery, supported on bulbous pillars, where church bands like those in Hardy's *Under the Greenwood Tree* accompanied the Sunday services. There are several fine effigy tombs and memorial brasses, and a superb oak nave roof, constructed in the 15th century.

HIGHER BOCKHAMPTON

The thatched cottage where Thomas Hardy was born in 1840 is tucked away below soaring beech woods in this little hamlet.

It is reached by a ten-minute walk through woods from the car park. Built by the novelist's great-grandfather in 1800, the cottage is now owned by the National Trust, and contains a small collection of Hardy relics. The outside of the house can be viewed daily in summer except on Tuesday morning. The interior can be viewed by arrangement with the tenant (Dorchester 62366).

STINSFORD

A cul-de-sac hamlet above the Frome, Stinsford was Hardy's 'Mellstock', where the old church band was ousted by the young lady organist in *Under the Greenwood Tree*. In tiny St Michael's Church, reached down a little lane, is a plan drawn up by Hardy showing the position in 1835 of the members of the band, three of them from the Hardy family. The musicians' gallery was removed early this century.

Hardy's heart is buried in the churchyard; his ashes are in Westminster Abbey. Another grave in the churchyard is that of Cecil Day Lewis, poet laureate from 1968 until his death in 1972.

Tourist information: Dorchester 67992.

TOUR
30
64 MILES

The limestone uplands of Purbeck contrast with the lush farmland of the rest of Dorset. Along the coast, crumbling cliffs alternate with horseshoe-shaped coves scooped out by the sea.

SWANAGE

Once the centre of the Purbeck stone trade, which dealt in the Purbeck marble used as decoration in many great cathedrals, Swanage is now a popular seaside resort. Traces of old Swanage survive around the Mill Pond, surrounded by sturdy stone houses, just off the High Street.

Swanage has two architectural curiosities. One is the Wellington clock tower, which once stood at the southern end of London Bridge and was moved to Swanage in 1867. The other is the façade of the Victorian town hall, which was designed by a pupil of Sir Christopher Wren and once adorned the front of the Mercers' Hall in London's Cheapside.

The Tithe Barn Museum contains a collection of fossils and displays of local history; it is open every morning except Sunday from Easter to early September, and in the evenings in midsummer. Steam-rail enthusiasts have recently reopened 1 mile of the line which once ran from Swanage to Corfe Castle, and there are regular excursions from Swanage station throughout the summer.

South of Swanage a superb stretch of countryside and cliff round Durlston Head forms the Durlston Country Park. Its main man-made feature is a massive stone globe, 10ft in diameter and weighing 40 tons, carved with the countries of the world. Known as the Great Globe, it was placed there in 1887 by John Mowlem, founder of the firm of building contractors.

The information centre makes a good starting point for exploring the park; it offers guides to local topics from bird life to stone-quarrying.

CORFE CASTLE

First fortified by the Saxons, Corfe Castle guards a strategic gap in the Purbeck range. In 978 it was the scene of a notorious murder, when the young Saxon King Edward was stabbed to death there at the instigation of his stepmother, Queen Elfrida. He was later canonised as St Edward the Martyr. The mighty keep was built about 1105, and the outer walls and towers date mainly from about 1270. During the Civil War the castle was defended against the Cromwellians, but it was finally captured and blown up – hence the lopsided angles of the remaining walls and turrets.

Corfe Castle is owned by the National Trust and open daily from March to October, and at weekend afternoons in winter.

SMEDMORE HOUSE

A remote country mansion of grey Purbeck stone, Smedmore is a mixture of architectural styles, its dignified Georgian front concealing a largely Jacobean house behind. It was built about 1620 by Sir William Clavell, who ruined himself by various industrial projects – extracting alum from the cliffs at Kimmeridge Bay, producing salt by boiling seawater, and making glass using the local bituminous shale as a fuel.

The house contains some fine furniture and paintings, and the old kitchen has been turned into a museum. The house and garden are open on Wednesday afternoons from June to mid-September, and on the late summer Bank Holiday Sunday.

KIMMERIDGE BAY

The low, shaly cliffs at Kimmeridge, reached by a toll road from the village of Kimmeridge, have eroded into ledges and are rich in fossils. Owing to their crumbly nature, they are extremely dangerous. The varied marine life includes many types of seaweed, which shelter crabs, anemones and other animals.

The eastern side of the bay is dominated by the Clavell Tower, a folly or summerhouse built in 1831 by the Reverend John Clavell, owner of Smedmore House. On the low cliffs to the right is a 'nodding donkey' oil-well pump.

TYNEHAM

A deserted village, in the middle of the Royal Armoured Corps Lulworth Range, Tyneham is open most week-ends and for longer periods in sum-mer. There was a village here from Saxon times, and it survived until 1943, when the army range was extended and the villagers had to move out. The village church, surviv-ing amid the eerie ruins of the remainder of the village, contains a small exhibition on the history of the valley.

LULWORTH COVE

The road ends beside a beautiful little horseshoe-shaped inlet, which can be a brilliant blue on a summer after-noon, or lashed by waves when a gale blows in from the south. The cliffs rise sharply on either side, reaching their highest point, more than 400ft, at Hambury Tout.

WAREHAM

The Saxons would not feel out of place today in Wareham, since it has hardly outgrown the huge earth bank that they built round it, and which still survives in large sections, now over-grown with gorse and scrub. Ware-ham has a simple layout, divided into quarters by North, South, East and West Streets, which intersect at its centre. It was built as a *burh* or 'fort' to guard Wessex against Viking raiders.

The principal church, of Lady St Mary, is at the southern end of the town, above the River Frome. Orig-inally a Saxon church, it was largely rebuilt in Victorian times and given an unusually high nave. The north-west

section of the surrounding earth bank is known as 'Bloody Bank', from the executions carried out there after the Monmouth Rebellion of 1685.

BLUE POOL
The water in this extraordinary man-made pool varies in colour from deepest blue to shades of green, depending on the variations in sun or cloud cover. It was originally a clay pit, dug in the 19th century to provide clay for famous potteries such as Wedgwood, Royal Worcester, Spode and Minton. The colour is due to the reflective properties of the clay particles held in suspension in the water.

A museum illustrates the history of clay-mining on the estate. It is open daily from April to October.

STUDLAND
Separated from Swanage by the high ridge of Ballard Down, Studland has kept its identity as a small Purbeck village, built around the Norman Church of St Nicholas. From the car park just north of the village, a nature trail winds through scrubland behind the sand dunes, while the Dorset Coast Path runs above the high-tide level of Studland Bay.

A mile walk from the village leads to the Agglestone, a 17ft high boulder of ironstone. According to legend it was dropped by the Devil who had carried it from the Isle of Wight with the intention of dropping it on Salisbury Cathedral.

Tourist information: Swanage 422885.

WISE FOLLY *The sweeping view of Kimmeridge Bay no doubt inspired local landowner John Clavell to build his tower on a lofty headland where the green Purbeck Hills drop to the sea.*

Ancient forests of Cranborne Chase

TOUR
31
—— 66 MILES ——

Roads follow the edges of the centuries-old royal hunting forest of Cranborne Chase. Northwards lie villages of pale-beige stone cut from the local Chilmark quarries.

SHAFTESBURY

The site of Shaftesbury, 700ft up, was a naked spur until AD 888, when Alfred the Great founded an abbey upon it. The foundation thrived, especially after 979 when it gained the battered corpse of the boy King Edward; he was reputedly murdered by his stepmother at Corfe Castle, and was afterwards canonised. Miraculous cures were reported at his tomb, and pilgrims came in droves, so that by the Middle Ages there were 12 churches and a market town to serve them.

Of the religious buildings, only the parish church of St Peter remains; the others vanished at the Reformation. Thomas Hardy considered living in Shaftesbury, but these vanished churches induced a mood of 'pensive melancholy'. However, he liked the town well enough to make it the 'Shaston' of his Wessex.

Shaftesbury is not really melancholy. From Park Walk, which follows the line of the old abbey, there are the happiest views over Blackmoor Vale. At the end of Park Walk is Gold Hill, a giddy downward steep of cobbles, with the abbey on one side and tiled and thatched cottages on the other.

High Street, too, has some attractive buildings, including the bow-fronted tearoom called King Alfred's Kitchen, and the stone-built Mitre Inn. Tiny Pump Court is just as picturesque as Gold Hill, and the grand Grosvenor Hotel has a carved oak sideboard depicting a theme fairly remote from Dorset – the Battle of Chevy Chase fought between the Scots and English in 1388.

IWERNE MINSTER

The enormous Claysmore School was the house built by Lord Wolverton, the banker and politician, in 1878. He also built much of the 'model' village, in red brick and black-and-white Tudor style. Each pretty shop has its descriptive sign, and little streams run before the houses. St Mary's Church predates everything else by about seven centuries.

Iwerne Courtenay, more often called Shroton, is less formal than its sister village. Sheep graze almost to the doors of the older stone and strawberry brick houses, and to those of Shroton's own St Mary's Church.

Two vast Iron Age hill-forts lean over the villages, and both provide magnificent viewpoints. Hambledon

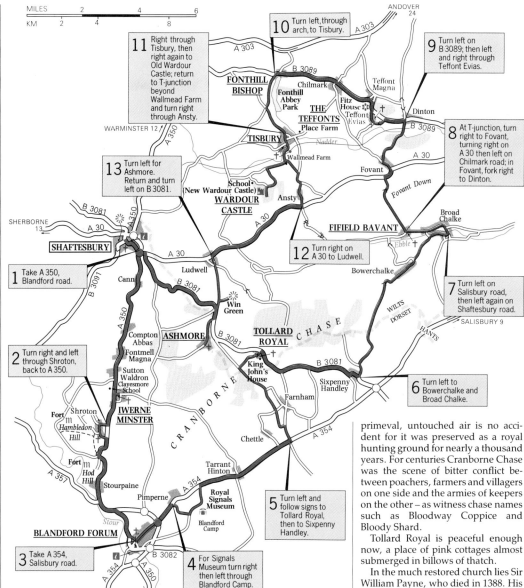

Hill's defences were sufficiently strong during the Civil War for 4000 local men, sick of both sides, to make a protest for peace. Cromwell routed them with 50 Ironsides.

Hod Hill was one of the Celtic strongholds taken by the future Emperor Vespasian and his fearsome 2nd Legion Augusta in their sweep across southern Britain in AD 43.

BLANDFORD FORUM

The name is probably a piece of medieval snobbery. Instead of being called 'Market' or 'Chipping' – its equivalent in Middle English – some monk chose to Latinise it and write the name as Blandford Forum. It bears the dignity well, being another handsome Georgian town of the West Country that was reborn after a fire. After a blaze on June 4, 1731, reduced the town to ashes, the work of rebuilding was entrusted to two talented local builders, John and William

Bastard. They gave the town its shops and houses of chequered brick, its handsome Market Place and gracious Corn Exchange. Their greatest achievement was the Church of St Peter and St Paul. Built of greenish stone, it shows the influence of Sir Christopher Wren, and has one of the finest 18th-century organs in England.

Also in the church is the laid-up standard of the Royal Naval Division, which trained at Blandford Camp in 1914. One of its young officers was Sublieutenant Rupert Brooke, the poet. The military presence is still strong in Blandford, though nowadays it belongs mostly to the Royal Corps of Signals, whose depot is at Blandford Camp. The corps museum is open to the public.

TOLLARD ROYAL

The old capital of Cranborne Chase is tucked into a wooded hollow. All about is the lonely and aloof chase. Its

primeval, untouched air is no accident for it was preserved as a royal hunting ground for nearly a thousand years. For centuries Cranborne Chase was the scene of bitter conflict between poachers, farmers and villagers on one side and the armies of keepers on the other – as witness chase names such as Bloodway Coppice and Bloody Shard.

Tollard Royal is peaceful enough now, a place of pink cottages almost submerged in billows of thatch.

In the much restored church lies Sir William Payne, who died in 1388. His effigy's sword is about to be drawn and its crossed feet, chain-mailed and spurred, rest upon a heraldic lion. Whoever carved it was a master.

Next to him is buried General Augustus Pitt-Rivers (1827-1900). From an interest in ballistics, he progressed to weapons in general, then to tools, and later to the new science of archaeology. His methods of meticulous excavation and recording gave rise to those employed now, and his monument shows the tools of his last craft.

FIFIELD BAVANT

A row of cottages and a couple of farms flank the serpentine River Ebble. St Martin's, 35ft long, is one of the contenders for the title of smallest church in England; it stands on a knoll approachable only through a farmyard. It is a hospitable place with chequered flint and stone walls about the same age as the 13th-century font.

The road to Fovant crosses another wide, sunlit valley filled with the

KING'S CHOICE *The 700ft spur of the Dorset hills chosen by King Alfred as the site of his abbey at Shaftesbury looks out across Blackmoor Vale, over the parish of St James.*

COUNTRY IDYLL *The 13th-century King John's House at Tollard Royal now provides a theatre and picnic arbours.*

DOWNS VILLAGE *Village and church at Shroton make an attractive grouping below a shoulder of the downs.*

NOBLE RUIN *Old Wardour Castle rises to four storeys, looking blitzed rather than crumbled.*

voices of sheep. It was filled with voices more stentorian once. In the First World War it was a training ground for Kitchener's New Armies, and they cut the badges of their volunteer units into the chalk of the hillside; still visible, they include Post Office Rifles, Devonshires, Wiltshires, Anzacs, London Rifle Brigade, Signals and others.

THE TEFFONTS
The name of Teffont Evias is derived from Ewas in Herefordshire, whose manorial lords also held lands in this village. There are some good stone houses, for the Chilmark quarries are practically next door. They are closed now, but were reopened recently to supply the stone for the restoration of Salisbury Cathedral.

The village also possesses a charming manor house and church, united within the same sweep of lawn. The church, with its tall, slim steeple, was almost entirely rebuilt in the 1820s, but retains some of its ancient features, including Elizabethan tombs. The Manor House, now flats, is mostly 17th century.

The Church of St Edward, almost entirely 13th century, has a bell of the same age on the windowsill, and the shaft of an Anglo-Saxon cross, at least 400 years older. Fitz House is mostly early 17th century, and its gardens are

open at Easter, then on Wednesday, Sunday and Bank Holiday afternoons from May to October.

FONTHILL BISHOP
The great surprise of the place is the monumental gatehouse through which passes the road to Tisbury, while at the same time it forms the entrance to Fonthill Abbey Park. Gatehouse and park are nearly all that remain of several ambitious abbeys, including that begun by William Beckford in 1796.

He inherited a vast fortune at the age of ten, and conceived a passion for building. He set out to create the greatest Gothic palace in England. With the aid of 500 men working round the clock – except for a three-day break in 1800 to give a party for Lord Nelson – he achieved his dream. Its tower was 275ft high.

Sadly, Beckford's patience would not await secure foundations for his buildings, which began to crumble. After the tower collapsed, he retired to Bath where he died – and there is nothing left of his dream house.

TISBURY
The most immediately impressive building in Tisbury is the Church of St John the Baptist, mostly 12th century. It contains some notable monuments to the Arundells of Wardour Castle,

and Rudyard Kipling's mother and father are buried in the churchyard. There are some partly 17th-century almshouses near the church, and several pleasant old houses scattered through the village.

The real treasure, though, is Place Farm, built in the 14th century as a grange farm for Shaftesbury Abbey. Its gatehouse is like that of a fort, and the tithe barn, 200ft long, is one of the largest in England.

WARDOUR CASTLE
The route runs through steep and stately pine plantations to a placid lake beside which is the ruin of Old Wardour Castle. In 1643, Lady Blanche, widow of the Royalist Lord Arundell who had died of wounds at Oxford, held the castle for several days against 1300 Parliamentarian troops, with a garrison of a few servants and estate workers. No sooner had she surrendered than her son, the 3rd Lord Arundell, set about recapturing it. He did so at last by exploding gunpowder in the passage leading to the castle cellars, thus rendering the building forever uninhabitable. It is open daily.

New Wardour Castle, across the park, is the grandest Georgian building in Wiltshire. It was built in the 1770s by James Paine for the 8th Lord Arundell, and is one of the great

triumphs of the 18th century. The central block has a staircase 60ft high and 47ft in diameter.

The castle is now Cranborne Chase School, but is open on Monday, Wednesday, Friday and Saturday afternoons from mid-July to early September.

ASHMORE
All roads in Cranborne Chase seem to lead towards the tree-crowned summit of Win Green Hill, which at 910ft is one of the highest vantage points in southern England. Steep roads they are too. In Hardy's *Tess of the d'Urbervilles*, Alec d'Urberville takes the heroine for a wild ride over them, to frighten her.

Ashmore, a couple of hundred feet lower, is the highest village in Dorset, easily cut off in bad winters. In fine weather it has views to the Isle of Wight, 40 miles off.

Thatched cottages and houses of grey-green stone, the 18th-century Old Rectory and the part medieval St Nicholas Church are grouped around a large duck pond. On the Friday evening closest to Midsummer Eve a morris dancing celebration called Filly Loo is held by the pond.

Tourist information:
Shaftesbury 2256;
Blandford Forum 51989 (summer).

Valleys and streams that edge Salisbury Plain

TOUR

32

──── 63 MILES ────

River valleys wind through chalk downlands to meet close to Salisbury Cathedral. The open grasslands of Salisbury Plain are dotted with the evidence of its importance to early man.

OLD SARUM

This turfed moonscape of craters, bumps and deep ditches would, if sliced through, summarise much of the early story of southern Britain. The defensive advantages of the site towering 240ft above the Avon were improved upon by Iron Age farmers, who added a bank and ditch. The Romans made the hill a junction on their network of roads to the south and west, and established a settlement close by called Sorviodunum.

After the legions left, the Romano-British held the old fort for a while, but were driven out by the Saxons who turned it into a fortified town. The Normans built a royal castle upon the hill, and next to it a cathedral. The town that grew up about them became known as Salisburia, 'the town of salt'; Sarum seems simply to have been a clerical abbreviation.

In time the clerics complained of the lack of water, the bitterness and loudness of the wind and the blinding white of the chalk, and looked with longing at the lush lands by the Avon. At the beginning of the 13th century they walked down the hill, followed by most of the townsfolk, and began to build the new cathedral, and beside it the town of New Sarum.

Old Sarum is a wonderful place to explore, with its moats and ramparts and its ruins, military and ecclesiastical, mixed up together. But New Sarum, or Salisbury, is the rightful capital of Salisbury Plain. The great cathedral, a joyous hymn in stone, gathers to it all the rivers of the chalk, the Avon, the Wylye, the Nadder and the Bourne, and lies in its downland cup like a jewel.

WOODHENGE

A group of concrete stumps within a circular ditch and bank marks the positions of the massive timber posts that once supported a Stone Age temple. What rites or ceremonies were carried out in the temple can never be known, but during excavation the skeleton of a three-year-old child was discovered; the skull had been split, suggesting at least one human sacrifice.

Just to the north is Durrington Walls, another and much larger monument. It is much eroded by ploughing, but the ditch was originally 60ft across and 20ft deep. This circle, too, once contained at least two wooden buildings thought to have been some 100ft across.

BISHOP'S MOVE *Bishop Richard Poore moved Old Sarum's cathedral in the 13th century, leaving only the foundations.*

GREAT WISHFORD *The Victorians gave St Giles's Church a Gothic tower.*

PALLADIAN BRIDGE *In 1736 the 9th Earl of Pembroke and his architect Roger Morris built this elegant structure across the River Nadder in the grounds of Wilton House.*

STONEHENGE

Lonely in time and alien to its present surroundings of chain-link fencing and guard dogs, Stonehenge yet retains much of its majesty and all of its mystery and aloofness.

Stonehenge was built in several stages. The first was a circular ditch and bank erected in about 3100 BC; stone posts at the circumference may have marked the position of sun and moon at the summer and winter solstices. In the second stage, begun 1000 years later, a 2 mile avenue to the Avon was built, more clearly marking the line of sunrise on Midsummer's Day. In addition, some 80 bluestones were imported from the Preseli Mountains in South Wales; their 240 mile journey by sea, river and overland must have been epic in itself. The third stage, between 2000 and 1500 BC, included the familiar trilithons, the heart of the tremendous temple whose worn remains are with us still.

Stonehenge was old when Helen of Troy was young, its meaning forgotten by the time Julius Caesar landed his legions at Deal. But see it stark on an autumn afternoon when clouds like galleys row across the Plain on oars of light, and explanations are not really necessary.

TILSHEAD

There are probably more soldiers hereabouts than ever were present at the field of Waterloo – which the Plain quite closely resembles. For Tilshead is a kind of frontier post between the Plain that is partly army and the one that is almost entirely so.

The village is a brief and brave straggle of cottages and houses against the wide prairie. The walls of the church and of many of the cottages are decorated in a chequerboard pattern, picked out in stone and split flint. The church is Norman, and massively built.

EDINGTON

Good building materials and medieval wool ensured that there is no shortage of handsome churches about Salisbury, but the fortress-like Church of St Mary, St Katherine and All Saints at Edington just off the main road is remarkable, even for this region.

For once, wool had little to do with it. The church was built in 1352 at the request of the Black Prince by William of Edington, Bishop of Winchester, as a priory for a minor order of Augustinians. It might also have been a rehearsal for the rebuilding of

Winchester Cathedral. St Mary's is certainly on the grand scale, with its battlemented tower and parapets. Even the yew in the churchyard is reputedly the largest and oldest in the county, while the interior of the church has floors of patterned marble and ceilings of sumptuous browns, creams and pink. A medieval, faceless clock tells the hour by chime only.

The village is tiny for so large a church, and stands against a background of hills eroded into huge green and olive furrows, as though they had been ploughed and left fallow by giants of long ago.

WESTBURY HILL
White horses have long been a popular subject with Wessex hill-doodlers. The one on Westbury Hill was carved into the hillside in 1778, allegedly obliterating another that commemorated King Alfred's victory over the Danes at the Battle of Ethandun (Edington) in AD 878.

Just above the creature's head is Bratton Castle, a massive Iron Age fort whose double walls enclose 25 acres and a large mound that is probably a long barrow. There are wonderful views from the airy ramparts, and splendid strolls among the wild flowers of spring and summer.

WESTBURY
Within the satellite rings of Victorian and Edwardian building, the area about the Market Place and the church is Georgian, or mostly so. There is a pale gold, classical Town Hall of 1815, while three inns, including the Lopes Arms, are said to date from the 14th century. The unusual name is repeated in a frieze on the Town Hall – Sir Massey Lopes, Bart, Recorder of the Borough, who paid for the building. Up a lane towards the church, with its central tower, a

little gathering of brick and painted stone houses makes an oasis of unfussedness. Among Georgian survivors in the town are the former Laverton's Cloth Mills, stark but well proportioned. They made the woollens and worsteds for which Westbury was famed.

WARMINSTER
The high, broad gateways and old stableyards of the Anchor, the Bath Arms and the Old Bell tell of the days when Warminster was a famous stopping place for coaches on the Bath Road. The traffic now rushes through in a bellowing spate, but a good deal remains of the market town that was renowned through England for its wool and corn sales.

The wide main streets still suggest market days, but look their best from the first floors upwards, where the good stonework begins. Many of the shop fronts clash with the 17th and 18th-century buildings they occupy; a charming exception is the old-fashioned grocers' next to the Old Bell. Church Street is probably the most graceful, with its strawberry-coloured, 18th-century buildings. The Minster Church of St Denys is grand 15th century, with a Victorian polish and interesting monuments.

The Downs crowd about the town, whose favourite hill – mascot, almost – is Cop Heap. There are walks to the summit and the beech-tree aisles that surround a great long-barrow burial ground of the Bronze Age.

HEYTESBURY
The road skirts the bases of one hillfort after another. Enormous buttresses of sheep-nibbled turf lead the eye up to the deep-cut ramparts.

Their palisades have gone long ago and their edges are blurred by 2000 and more winters, yet still they advertise the enormous labour that went into their building, the great number of people involved, and the sheer urgency of the tasks. What were the builders so anxious about? Each other? Or the way the Romans were behaving as they moved across Europe, ever closer to the Channel?

The Hospital of St John and St Katharine in Heytesbury comprises 17th-century almshouses, repaired after a fire 100 years later. There is an impressive church that dates partly from Norman times, an agreeable Jacobean parsonage and Georgian maltings. Heytesbury House looks Georgian, but the façade conceals much older beginnings, perhaps of the early Middle Ages.

WYLYE
This is a pretty, all-of-a-piece village of thatched or mossy-tiled chequerboard cottages. The Bell Inn, so it says, dates from the 14th century, and by the bridge a red-brick water mill swallows the Wylye river in great swirls of green water.

The tower of St Mary's Church is 15th century, but the remainder was rebuilt in the 1840s. The ornately carved Jacobean pulpit is incongruous, but a remarkably fine piece of craftsmanship.

GREAT WISHFORD
The village consists of stone cottages and small Georgian houses, suavely and lovingly maintained. Among them are stone almshouses of 1628, and a chequered brick village school of 1722. The church, restored in 1863, is crammed with treasures.

A sign on the Royal Oak pub commemorates the village's Grovely ceremony, held annually before daybreak on Oak Apple Day – May 29. The young people of Great Wishford march up the hill to Grovely Wood, returning with the dawn to

deck houses and church with branches of oak. This they do by 'auntient custome and tyme out of mynde' to affirm the village's right to gather firewood in Grovely Wood. Later, the villagers take their branches to Salisbury, where four of the women dance on the cathedral green and the rector declaims the village charter within the cathedral.

WILTON
A crowded little town, Wilton has played many roles through its long history – Saxon capital, medieval monastic centre, haven for the Elizabethan intelligentsia, one of the first manufacturing centres in England, and market centre for the surrounding countryside.

In the Market Place is the early 18th-century Market Hall with its lofty clock tower, and nearby the market cross that seems to be made up of any bits and pieces of monumental sculpture that happened to be around at the time.

The town's biggest surprise is the Church of St Mary and St Nicholas. It was built in 1842 by T.H. Wyatt who, gripped by a dream of Tuscany, built a complete Italian church, separate bell tower, mosaics, coloured marbles, medieval stained glass and all.

Wilton House has been the home of the Herbert family, Earls of Pembroke, since 1544. They have always been a lively and distinguished family, and their house reflects it. All the bright stars of the Elizabethan Age visited it – the queen herself, Spenser, Ben Jonson, Sir Philip Sidney, and perhaps Shakespeare, with the first performance of *Twelfth Night*.

Wilton Carpets, born in the 17th century, are still going strong. A Royal Weavers' Shop has working looms and carpets for sale.

Tourist information: Salisbury 334956; Amesbury 22833; Warminster 216047.

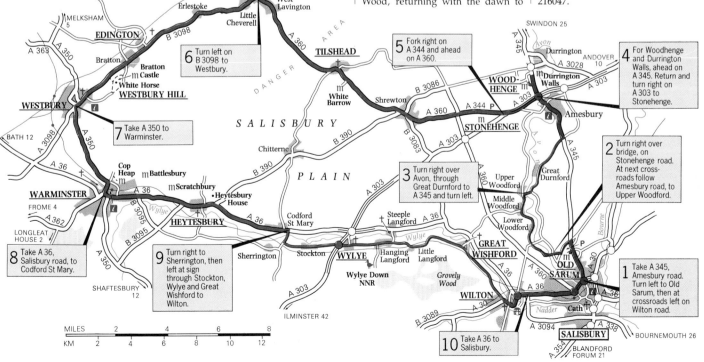

The South-East

*C*halk downs straddle south-east England, and though nowhere reaching 1000ft high their commanding summits have been prized by man since prehistoric times. Here Stone Age men built their hill-forts, Elizabethan defenders lit their warning beacons when Spanish invasion threatened, and in modern times intrepid aeronauts launch themselves into space on silent wings.

On the coast, the New Forest spreads its leafy 90,000 acres from the Hampshire Avon to the Beaulieu River, and offshore lies the green diamond of the Isle of Wight. East of the broad Test valley the North Downs begin their curving sweep across to Kent's eastern shore, embracing the orchards and hop fields of the Weald, the white cliffs of the South Downs and the misty Romney Marsh. To the north, the River Thames cuts a gap between the Berkshire Downs and the Chilterns, whose beech-clad heights roll northwards to the Bedfordshire plain. A gentle counterpane of farmland and leafy lanes spreads eastward to the rivers and creeks of the Essex coast, and westward to the edge of the Cotswolds.

South-east England is the foundation stone of modern Britain. On its southern shore William the Conqueror poured his powerful armies into a land ruled by an uneasy throne – and established his own. At Berkhamsted he accepted the crown from the defeated nobles, from Winchester he ruled his new realm, and at Windsor he built the world's most famous castle.

Ipswich

MALDON
Southend-
on-Sea

BRIDGE
S

ASTINGS

61
58
59
CANTERBURY
60
ASHFORD
56
HYTHE
55

A 45
A 12
A 12
A 131
Stour
Colne
Medway
Rother
A 28
A 2
M 2
A 20
M 20
A 28
A 21
A 259

STRAIT OF DOVER

45 ● EPSOM
Number of tour
and starting point
Route of tour

Through the New Forest to Beaulieu

TOUR

33

——— 77 MILES ———

Descendants of the deer hunted by William the Conqueror roam the New Forest, mingling with forest ponies among the gorse and bracken. To the south, deep inlets cut a shingle coast.

LYMINGTON

Rising on the high ground of the New Forest plateau, the Lymington River flows into The Solent past the pretty little estuary town of Lymington. Though in former centuries its harbour rivalled Portsmouth and Southampton in importance, Lymington is now a yachting centre, full of the noise of rigging slapping in the wind, and ferry terminal for the Isle of Wight.

From the quayside, where ships' chandlers and yacht brokers jostle with restaurants, boutiques and antiques shops, the cobbled Quay Street leads up to the Georgian town centre. Close by, in Bath Road, is the 19th-century Harbour Master's Office and Pressgang Cottage, once the headquarters of an 18th-century pressgang.

HURST CASTLE

One of several stone fortresses built by Henry VIII to guard The Solent from French invasion, Hurst Castle stands at the end of a shingle causeway, which is like a small relation of

Dorset's Chesil Beach. Henry's castle was strengthened in the 17th and 19th centuries and today incorporates a lighthouse. Charles I was held there briefly in 1648, after being taken from the Isle of Wight to face trial and execution in London.

The castle can be reached either on foot along the causeway, or by ferry from the inlet at Keyhaven. Keyhaven Marshes are preserved in part as a bird sanctuary. The long-distance Solent Way footpath, which runs along the shore above the salt marshes, affords splendid views to sea.

BURLEY

This scattered village near the western edge of the New Forest has attractive cottages and antiques shops and a red-brick village pub, the Queen's Head. A saddlery workshop also makes carts and carriages for competition driving.

Castle Hill, 1 mile north-west, was once an Iron Age fortress whose ditches and earthworks can still be traced among the gnarled trees on its summit.

RINGWOOD

A breezy, open market town, just outside the western boundary of the New Forest, Ringwood's oldest part lies down by the Hampshire Avon, which flows through peaceful gardens and is noted for the quality of its trout.

At Monmouth House in West Street the Duke of Monmouth was held briefly after his capture at the Battle of Sedgemoor in 1685; the building now

houses a dental surgery. Next to it is Old Cottage, a long, timber-framed and thatched building that is now a restaurant. The High Street has a number of dignified Georgian buildings.

DEER MEADOW

Visitors who want to observe the New Forest's most typical inhabitants and find out more about them should stop at the large Bolderwood car park. Just a few minutes' walk away, former farm fields are now used as a deer meadow; it is closed to the public but there is a viewing platform, accessible by wheelchair, from which the shy creatures can be studied.

In 1079 William the Conqueror enclosed some 150 square miles of Hampshire as his favourite hunting preserve, calling it his Nova Foresta, or 'New Forest'. The Norman kings loved hunting and enacted savage laws to deter poachers from killing the deer. Death was the usual penalty, and even merely disturbing the deer carried a penalty of blinding. A later Act of Parliament passed in 1851 provided for the 'removal' of the deer because of the damage they were causing to the trees. Fortunately it proved impossible to exterminate them all, and the present healthily large fallow deer population is mainly descended from the few that escaped the guns of the Victorians.

There are now about 1500 deer in the New Forest. Most are red, roe, sika and fallow, but there are also a few muntjac, hardly larger than a spaniel, which came originally from

Asia. Display boards on the viewing platform show graphically the antler growth rate according to the age of the fallow deer. Other displays show what visitors may expect to see at different seasons of the year: for example, in the summer the bucks shed their old antlers and grow new ones, and the fawns are born.

BOLDERWOOD

From the Bolderwood car park, three waymarked walks of different lengths lead through some of the New Forest's most beautiful scenery.

The Radnor Walk is named after the 7th Earl of Radnor who was a Forestry Commissioner from 1942 to 1963. It leads through Douglas firs dating from 1860, their slender, pencil-straight trunks rising to almost 100ft. In a green glade is a memorial to the Earl of Radnor, carved from Westmorland slate.

Another short walk takes in about 40 different species of trees, which are labelled for identification. Californian redwoods, Japanese cedar, Italian poplar, Norway spruce, Chinese fir and Corsican pine make up this forestry 'United Nations', and presiding over all is a 140ft tall Noble fir from Washington State, USA. A 3 mile walk through North Oakley Inclosure plunges deep into the forest, where some trees are so close to each other that their branches have become joined.

ORNAMENTAL DRIVE

In 1964 a 3 mile forest track was turned into a public highway, giving access to magnificent trees that formerly were seen only by foresters. The road leads between giant conifers before dropping down to mixed woodland, where beech trees rise

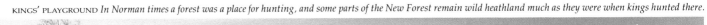

KINGS' PLAYGROUND *In Norman times a forest was a place for hunting, and some parts of the New Forest remain wild heathland much as they were when kings hunted there.*

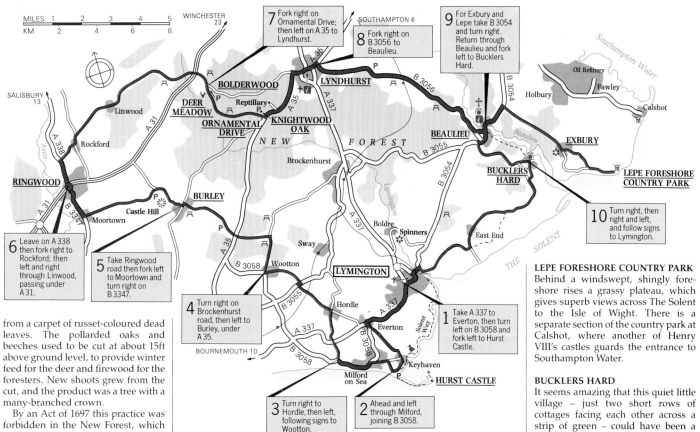

from a carpet of russet-coloured dead leaves. The pollarded oaks and beeches used to be cut at about 15ft above ground level, to provide winter feed for the deer and firewood for the foresters. New shoots grew from the cut, and the product was a tree with a many-branched crown.

By an Act of 1697 this practice was forbidden in the New Forest, which means that any ancient pollarded oak or beech must date from the mid-17th century or earlier.

KNIGHTWOOD OAK

Inside a small fenced enclosure 200yds from the car park stands a venerable pollarded oak, with five lesser trunks shooting upwards from the giant main trunk which has a girth of 21ft. Ring counts put the tree's age at about 375 years, though tradition makes it far older.

Nearby is the solitary Queen's Oak, planted when the Queen visited the New Forest in 1979 to commemorate its 900th anniversary. Also in the enclosure is an unusual example of 'inosculation' – tree branches that have joined together. This is common among trees of the same species, but here an oak and a beech are joined.

LYNDHURST

The administrative centre of the New Forest, Lyndhurst has a history going back to Saxon times, though most of today's village is Victorian or later. Its most prominent building is the large, multicoloured parish church of St Michael and All Angels, built in the 1860s in red, yellow and white brick; it has a fresco behind the altar painted by Lord Leighton, and stained-glass windows by Sir Edward Burne-Jones and William Morris. In the churchyard is the grave of Alice Liddell (Mrs Hargreaves), who was the original of Lewis Carroll's Alice.

Next to the church is the Queen's House, the old royal manor house of Lyndhurst. It is largely 17th century but with traces of much earlier building. It is used as offices by the Forestry Commission and also by the Ancient Court of Swainmote, or Verderers' Court, which sits every two months to administer forest matters and settle disputes.

Several fine houses in Lyndhurst include Foxlease House, built in 1700 and now headquarters of the county Girl Guides Association, and Northerwood House, now flats, where George III often stayed.

About half a mile west of Lyndhurst is Swan Green, a charming hamlet of thatched Tudor cottages set around a green.

BEAULIEU

Standing at the head of the gently winding Beaulieu River, Beaulieu lives up to its medieval name of *Bellus Locus* or *Beau Lieu*, the 'beautiful place' chosen by the Cistercian monks who founded an abbey there in 1204. Their gatehouse, now incorporated into Palace House, the family home of Lord Montagu of Beaulieu, still looks out across a tranquil mere fringed with reeds; but their great church was torn down by Henry VIII at the Dissolution of the Monasteries in 1538. Of the monastic buildings only the cloister survives, now partly a museum of Cistercian monastic life.

The outlines of the buttressed gatehouse stand out against the rest of Palace House, added by the 1st Lord Montagu in 1870. The style is 'Scottish Baronial', with round, conical-roofed turrets and a square battlemented tower. Several of the rooms have wax figures in period dressing, adding realism to the scene.

At the National Motor Museum more than 200 historic vehicles, from vintage limousines to historic racing cars, are displayed in a futuristic hall. The museum includes a sound-and-vision show on the world of transportation, and visitors can travel around the grounds by a monorail which passes through the roof of the museum. The museum, Palace House and ruins are open daily.

Beaulieu village is a quietly attractive little place, full of red-brick Georgian cottages, now largely tea-rooms and curio shops.

EXBURY

The view between Beaulieu and Exbury is dominated by the serried chimneys of the Fawley oil refinery a couple of miles across the fields, with its flare towers shooting jets of flame high into the air. The impact of such technology is soon forgotten, however, among the rhododendrons and azaleas of Exbury's superb gardens, which extend over more than 200 acres beside the Beaulieu River.

The gardens were created by Lionel de Rothschild soon after the First World War. For a decade an army of 150 gardeners and workmen created shrubberies, water gardens, display beds and a rockery covering about an acre and said to be the largest in Europe. Rothschild financed plant-hunting expeditions to the Himalayas to bring back seed, and himself bred more than 1200 varieties of rhododendrons and azaleas. Many of these, together with other ornamental trees and shrubs, can be bought at Exbury's plant centre. A number of walks lead through Home Wood, Yardwood, Witcher's Wood and Bog Garden – each with different characteristics. The gardens are open daily from March to mid-July.

LEPE FORESHORE COUNTRY PARK

Behind a windswept, shingly foreshore rises a grassy plateau, which gives superb views across The Solent to the Isle of Wight. There is a separate section of the country park at Calshot, where another of Henry VIII's castles guards the entrance to Southampton Water.

BUCKLERS HARD

It seems amazing that this quiet little village – just two short rows of cottages facing each other across a strip of green – could have been a bustling shipbuilding centre where men-of-war were built for Nelson's navy. They included his favourite ship, *Agamemnon*. What Bucklers Hard actually looked like is shown by a model of the village in the excellent Maritime Museum; in the model, two hulls are under construction on the slipways above the Beaulieu River, and tree-trunks and sawn planks are piled between the cottages.

The museum includes a reconstruction of the New Inn, in the actual rooms that the inn occupied in the 18th century. Lifelike models sit at rough wooden tables, and a tape recording of the general hubbub of conversation adds startling realism.

Several of the cottages in the village have been restored so perfectly that their original occupants would recognise them immediately. Among them are the shipwright's cottage, with its four-poster bed upstairs and its spit above the open range, and the rougher and simpler labourer's cottage.

Behind a window of the Master-Builder's House Hotel, a lifelike model of the master-builder Henry Adams pores over a ship's blueprint, while below him the Beaulieu River dances with the small craft of today's sailors. The village, cottages and museum are open daily.

Boats are still built at Bucklers Hard, in the Agamemnon Boatyard from where a riverside footpath leads through water meadows to Beaulieu, 2 miles upstream. At the start of the walk stands a Scots pine known to be at least 200 years old.

Tourist information: Lyndhurst 2269 (summer), 3121 (winter); Beaulieu 612345.

Chalk streams round Alfred's capital

TOUR
34
———— 44 MILES ————

On the downlands near England's ancient capital stand an Iron Age hill-fort and a modern country park and arboretum. Abbeys stand beside the rivers that flow down from the chalk hills.

WINCHESTER

The ancient capital of Wessex, and of England, stands on the River Itchen, sheltered by the surrounding chalk downs. Every street and old building in the city centre carries some tale of historic fact or legend. No one really knows where or when King Alfred burnt the cakes, but his statue at the bottom of the Broadway is magnificent: the black figure, twice life size, holds a sword upraised before him and directs an authoritative yet benevolent gaze up towards the High Street.

At the top of the High Street is one of Winchester's two remaining gateways, Westgate, which is in excellent condition although traffic no longer passes through the main arch. The ground rises towards the Great Hall, all that remains of a former Norman castle. Dating from 1222, it is deemed to be the finest aisled medieval hall in Britain. Inside hangs what is said to be the top of The Round Table of King

Arthur and his 24 knights; but its origin is unknown.

From the castle return eastwards down St Clement Street and through little alleys to The Square, which provides the best view of Winchester Cathedral. Work started on the cathedral in 1079 and it underwent many alterations over the centuries; its size and grandeur are awe-inspiring.

FARLEY MOUNT

Superb views over downland and woods are obtained from a 280 acre country park on the old Roman Road from Winchester to Salisbury. The views over the woodland to the north are at their most spectacular in the autumn when birch, beech, hazel, oak and pine combine to produce a kaleidoscope of colours. Part of the area is a nature reserve, and trail leaflets are available.

A side turning on the way to Stockbridge leads to Crawley, a pleasant little hamlet with a half-timbered pub, thatched cottages and all the old-world charm of a 'film set' village.

STOCKBRIDGE

Stockbridge Down, just outside the town, is the site of an ancient earthwork, and being devoid of tall trees offers far-reaching views over the surrounding countryside. Now in the care of the National Trust, it is a nature reserve with many wild flowers and rare chalk-loving butterflies.

With faster motor routes opened to the West Country, tranquillity has

returned to Stockbridge, but the broad main street recalls busier times, when travellers halted at the huge pillared porch of the Grosvenor Hotel. Most of the buildings are on the main street, with fields behind.

DANEBURY RING

Enclosed by three ramparts, which are still intact, this Iron Age hill-fort gives views to the north-west and to the south, where the ruins of the old Stockbridge racecourse grandstand can just be seen. Peaceful in summer, Danebury Ring is an exhilarating place for a walk in the winter winds.

MOTTISFONT ABBEY

A large and comfortable Tudor and Georgian house converted from an Augustinian priory stands amid lawns sweeping down to the River Test. Cedar trees shade the lawns, and a London plane rises 100ft above the river. A spring rising to the west of the house feeds a stream.

A walled rose garden contains almost every species of old European rose still in cultivation, and towards the end of a summer's day their scent fills the air. The house, owned by the National Trust, is open on Wednesday and Sunday afternoons from April to September: the grounds are open on most days in summer.

ROMSEY

At first sight it seems incongruous that such a small market town should have such a large abbey. It began as

the church for a community of nuns established in 907, but was greatly enlarged in the 12th century and survived the Dissolution to be recognised today as one of Europe's finest Norman buildings.

The abbey is built to the traditional plan of a cross, and three storeys of lofty arches soar roofwards on either side of the nave. Romsey's treasures span some ten centuries. On one wall hangs an Anglo-Saxon sculpture depicting the Crucifixion, while the richly coloured east windows, through which the early morning sun gleams, were added in Edwardian times.

A marble slab in the south transept marks the simple grave of Earl Mountbatten of Burma, murdered in 1979. The earl's superb Georgian home at Broadlands, 1 mile south of Romsey, is open to the public while preserving the homely touches of a house that is still very much lived in by Lord Mountbatten's heirs Lord and Lady Romsey.

The Mountbatten Exhibition, in the converted stables, contains a wide-ranging display of the earl's life and public service. Mementos range from his christening robes to his diaries, inventions, medals and uniforms. A corridor has been turned into a replica of part of a warship. Broadlands is open daily except Monday from April to July, and daily in August and September.

HILLIER ARBORETUM

In case a visit to what is probably the world's largest collection of ornamental trees and shrubs, spread over 160 acres, should sound a daunting experience, its custodians have devised

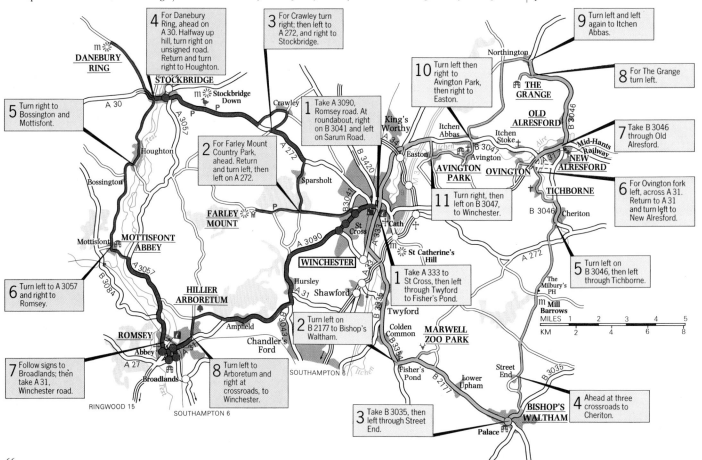

an ingenious series of colour-coded trails, each taking about an hour to walk. They make an easy introduction to such highlights of the arboretum as the huge collection of pines, the midsummer pond-side plants, the woodlands ablaze with colour in autumn, the heather garden and the Centenary Border, 200yds long, containing a variety of dwarf shrubs. Guided tours are also available.

The arboretum was founded by Sir Harold Hillier in 1953 and given to Hampshire County Council in 1977. It is open daily from Monday to Friday, and on Saturday and Sunday afternoons from March to mid-November.

TOUR
35
——— 39 MILES ———

A bishop's palace and an unusual zoo lie amid countryside dotted with picturesque villages beside the River Itchen. The Tichborne family still live in the village named after their ancestor.

MARWELL ZOO PARK
In the wooded country park of Marwell Hall a latter day 'Noah's Ark' houses some of the world's rarest and near-extinct animals. The enclosures are skilfully designed to blend naturally with the landscape and its native oak trees. Some of the animals are now believed to be extinct in the wild; these include Przewalski's horse, named after a Russian Count and the only true wild horse still alive, the Indian or Asiatic lion and the snow leopard.

The large Gothic mansion is now the zoo's headquarters, and its gardens are used to house some of the smaller animals, such as monkeys and red pandas. Deer and zebra graze the outer fields of the park.

BISHOP'S WALTHAM
Grey ruined walls towering high above the grass give some indication of the huge area once covered by the palace of the Bishops of Winchester. It was built by Henry of Blois, King Stephen's brother, in 1135, greatly extended in the 15th century, and then largely destroyed in the Civil War. The Great Hall still has its tall traceried windows, and the carved corbels which once supported the timber roof. A display in the Dower House illustrates the palace's long history.

From the palace a short walk across the main road leads to St George's Square, where a curious Victorian lamp standard, probably sited on the base of the town cross, is topped by a bishop's mitre. The High Street is lined by little shops occupying 18th and 19th-century buildings; on the left the Oddfellows Hall, now a shop, has ornate brick walls.

TICHBORNE
Overlooking the village on the side of the hill the small Church of St Andrew is unusual in containing a chapel dedicated to the Roman Catholic

AVINGTON PARK *At the rear of the house, two orangeries linked by a colonnade were added in the 19th century.*

REBORN HAMLET *Crawley was an untidy farming settlement until the early 1900s, when an industrialist, Ernest Philippi, transformed it to its present beauty.*

KING'S ABBEY *Edward, son of Alfred the Great, founded Romsey Abbey.*

faith. Set behind an ornate iron railing, the chapel contains lifelike effigies of Sir Benjamin Tichborne and his wife, dating from 1621. It was Sir Benjamin's loyalty to James I that allowed him to have a 'mixed' church.

The Tichborne family is believed to have lived in the village from 1135 or even earlier and their home, Tichborne House, is still owned by the family. Every year villagers observe the ceremony of Tichborne Dole, when flour is distributed to all parishioners. It is said to date from the 13th century when Sir Roger Tichborne's dying wife asked that he should make this bequest for the poor; he agreed to grant for the purpose all the corn from the land she could walk round while a brand was burning. Too weak to walk, she crawled round 23 acres; the field is still known as 'The Crawls'.

OVINGTON
Beside the ancient Pilgrims' Way from Winchester to Canterbury lies the Bush Inn on the River Itchen. From the inn, with its low ceilings and open fires, a footpath leads north across the river, wide and fast at this point, then turns to run between the main stream and a mill stream. After a quarter of a

mile the path turns to Itchen Stoke village, where a little green is overlooked by half-timbered cottages. Here the Victorian Church of St Mary has an unusual round chancel, its altar being set in the middle below a colourful east window, also circular.

THE ALRESFORDS
New Alresford and Old Alresford are separated by a causeway which acts as a dam for the large pond built in the late 12th century by the Bishop of Winchester. The 'New' half centres on a well preserved main street, Broad Street, lined by 17th and 18th-century houses and leading to Mill Hill. A footpath leads past the old mill and watercress beds. South lies the western terminus of the Mid-Hants Railway, the 'Watercress Line', a steam railway running to Alton.

THE GRANGE
A long driveway and an avenue of lime trees lead to the shell of a house whose exterior has been restored to its former glory. The building was designed by William Wilkins in 1804 for a banker, Henry Drummond. He gave it a temple-like portico supported on six Doric columns. Below the columns steep steps lead down to lawns, once

the site of formal gardens. There are waterfowl on a lake; the former parkland is now farmland.

AVINGTON PARK
From the wrought-iron gates of Avington Park a long drive sweeps up to the classical portico of a red-brick mansion dating from the 16th century and re-modelled in the late 17th century in the style of Inigo Jones.

The ballroom has a magnificent painted ceiling in gold plasterwork, with wall paintings depicting the four seasons. The adjoining red drawing room also has exquisitely painted walls and ceiling, with the homely atmosphere of a room that is still in regular use by the owner. The house is open on Saturday, Sunday and Bank Holiday afternoons from May to September.

Set between house and village is a perfect Georgian church built in 1770 by Margaret, Marchioness of Caernarvon. Her memorial to the left of the altar praises her beauty and fine character, and asks the reader to spare a thought for the bereaved husband.

Tourist information: Winchester 68166; Romsey 512987 (summer).

Cliffs and green downland on the Isle of Wight

An ancient forest survives close to the island's capital. Three Victorian forts look out across The Solent, and the jagged Needles rise beyond the tip of a chalky headland.

WHITE CLIFFS OF WIGHT *On the island's southern coast, rolling downs end abruptly in rugged chalk cliffs facing Freshwater Bay.*

NEWPORT
In the busy High Street stands the Guildhall with its clock tower commemorating Queen Victoria's Golden Jubilee. Built in 1816, the Guildhall stands on the site of a much earlier building where in 1648 Charles I met the Parliamentary Commissioners in an effort to keep his throne.

The River Medina runs through the town, and the old docks were once busy with commercial shipping. Today only pleasure craft berth there, but many old warehouses remain. A restored quayside building houses the Quay Arts Centre, which is open daily except Mondays.

The Roman villa in Cypress Road contains a bathhouse of which enough survives to show how the water was heated by a furnace. The villa is open daily, except Saturdays, from May to September.

PARKHURST FOREST
More than 1000 acres, mainly of conifers and oak trees, survive of the ancient wood which existed before the Domesday survey. Today Parkhurst is managed by the Forestry Commission.

From the car park and picnic area a 2½ mile waymarked walk leads through oaks planted in the early 19th century for building wooden warships. Beyond is a larger area of conifers planted this century. Native red squirrels can be seen in one of the few remaining forests in Britain where they are unmolested by the grey squirrel.

NEWTOWN
Beyond the stone bridge across the Newtown river stands the Old Town Hall, dating from 1699. The simple brick building is the only surviving relic of the days when Newtown was the leading town on the island.

The town hall was virtually a ruin in 1933 when an anonymous group of benefactors handed it over to the National Trust. The building has been restored and is open on certain days from April to September.

From the village, a footpath leads to the Newtown estuary, a National Trust nature reserve covering more than 800 acres of mud flats and salt marsh. It is an important wintering area for wildfowl. Oysters have been harvested in the estuary since Roman times, and the industry has been revived since the end of the Second World War.

YARMOUTH
The road reaches the coast at the outskirts of Yarmouth, where there are views across The Solent to the Hampshire coast. Beside the harbour stands Yarmouth Castle, a small, square fortress built by Henry VIII as part of his coastal defence system. It is open daily from April to September. A car park near the Lymington ferry terminal is the start of a 4½ mile nature trail beside the River Yar.

FORT VICTORIA
The remains of a long, low brick fort stand on a grassy point looking across the narrowest stretch of The Solent. Fort Victoria was built by Lord Palmerston in 1852-3 at a time when fear of a French invasion led to the construction of several fortresses along England's south coast. The defences were never tested, and they have been dubbed 'Palmerston's Follies'.

The main body of the fort was dismantled in the 1960s, but the remainder is being restored and houses an exhibition of the island's military heritage and a marine aquarium which are open daily from the end of March to the end of October. Beside the fort is a picnic and barbecue site with magnificent views across The Solent to Hurst Castle.

From the picnic site a 1½ mile nature trail leads through the Fort Victoria Country Park – 50 acres of woodland sloping up from the seashore.

GOLDEN HILL FORT
The white walls of the fort crown a hilltop just beyond the village of Norton. The hexagonally shaped fort was built in 1869 with its walls hidden behind mounds of earth. The earth has now been removed and the brick walls whitewashed.

Part of the restored fort is now a museum which includes a restored barracks room and the powder room. Other rooms have been converted into craft workshops. The fort is open daily in summer.

Golden Hill Fort is another of 'Palmerston's Follies' built to defend the south coast. No shot was ever fired from it in anger; the guns were once tested to see whether they would reach the sea but the shot fell short, breaking the window of a shop in Freshwater, 1 mile away. The fort is open daily in summer.

ALUM BAY
The cliffs behind the pebbly bay are striped with yellow, brown, red, green, grey, white and many other shades. The unusual colours have been created by the action of the weather on the quartz, iron oxide and other minerals in the rock.

The beach is reached down a steep path, which includes 231 wooden steps; a chair lift operates in summer. In the car park stands a monument to the radio pioneer, Guglielmo Marconi, who transmitted messages from here to a tug in Alum Bay in 1897, and set up the world's first wireless station at the site in the same year.

THE NEEDLES
White chalk cliffs curve round from Alum Bay then dive down steeply to the sea. Beyond this point rise three jagged pinnacles called The Needles. A fourth rock, 120ft high and known as Lot's Wife, collapsed into the sea in

1764: its stump can still be seen at low tide. A striped red and white lighthouse clings to the westernmost rock. There are boat trips to The Needles from Alum Bay in summer.

Reached by a walk of about a mile along the cliff top from Alum Bay is The Needles Old Battery, the remains of an old fort built on the headland in 1863. It has been restored by the National Trust and contains a museum of old guns, magazines and searchlight positions.

The fort and museum are open most days in summer. A 200ft long tunnel leads to a lookout point with magnificent views of The Needles.

TENNYSON DOWN
A steep, half-hour climb from the car park at Alum Bay leads to the summit of the down where the poet Alfred Lord Tennyson used to make a daily pilgrimage from his home at nearby Farringford House. He would sit for hours gazing out to sea across the cliffs to the south.

The view in other directions is equally magnificent, extending from Cowes to St Catherine's Point and the Dorset coast. A stone cross in memory of Tennyson stands on the summit of the down.

CALBOURNE
Tucked away off the main road is a row of delightful, 18th-century stone cottages with flowerbeds along their front walls. This is Calbourne's Winkle Street, reached across an old stone bridge over the Caul Bourne from which the village takes its name. Beside the sloping green is a 13th-century church with views over the village to the downs.

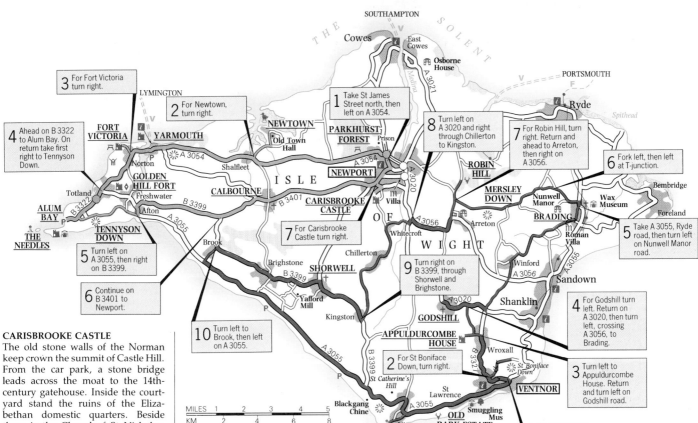

Map labels and route directions:

SOUTHAMPTON

THE SOLENT

Cowes — East Cowes — Osborne House — A 3021 — PORTSMOUTH

Ryde — Spithead

1 Take St James Street north, then left on A 3054.

8 Turn left on A 3020 and right through Chillerton to Kingston.

7 For Robin Hill, turn right. Return and ahead to Arreton, then right on A 3056.

6 Fork left, then left at T-junction.

3 For Fort Victoria turn right.

LYMINGTON

2 For Newtown, turn right.

NEWTOWN — Old Town Hall

PARKHURST FOREST — Prison

ROBIN HILL

Wax Museum — Bembridge

4 Ahead on B 3322 to Alum Bay. On return take first right to Tennyson Down.

FORT VICTORIA — YARMOUTH — Norton — A 3054 — Shalfleet

ISLE — NEWPORT — A 3054

MERSLEY DOWN — Nunwell Manor — BRADING — Foreland

GOLDEN HILL FORT — Freshwater — CALBOURNE

Totland — B 3399 — B 3401 — CARISBROOKE CASTLE — Villa — A 3020 — A 3056 — Arreton — Roman Villa

ALUM BAY — Afton — A 3055 — OF — WIGHT — Whitecroft

5 Take A 3055, Ryde road, then turn left on Nunwell Manor road.

THE NEEDLES — TENNYSON DOWN — Brook — Chillerton — Winford — A 3056 — Sandown

7 For Carisbrooke Castle turn right.

5 Turn left on A 3055, then right on B 3399.

6 Continue on B 3401 to Newport.

Brighstone — B 3399 — SHORWELL — Yafford Mill — Kingston

9 Turn right on B 3399, through Shorwell and Brighstone.

GODSHILL — A 3020 — Shanklin

4 For Godshill turn left. Return on A 3020, then turn left, crossing A 3056, to Brading.

APPULDURCOMBE HOUSE

2 For St Boniface Down, turn right.

St Boniface Down — Wroxall — A 3327

3 Turn left to Appuldurcombe House. Return and turn left on Godshill road.

10 Turn left to Brook, then left on A 3055.

A 3055 — B 3399 — St Catherine's Hill — St Lawrence — VENTNOR

MILES 1 2 3 4 5
KM   2   4   6   8

Blackgang Chine — Niton — A 3055 — Smuggling Mus — OLD PARK ESTATE

1 Take B 3327 to Wroxall.

CARISBROOKE CASTLE

The old stone walls of the Norman keep crown the summit of Castle Hill. From the car park, a stone bridge leads across the moat to the 14th-century gatehouse. Inside the courtyard stand the ruins of the Elizabethan domestic quarters. Beside them is the Chapel of St Nicholas, built as a memorial to Charles I who was imprisoned at Carisbrooke in 1647 and 1648.

The Great Chamber is now part of a museum which contains some of Charles's possessions and many other relics of the castle's history.

At the far end of the courtyard is the castle well, housed in a 16th-century building. The well is worked by donkeys working in shifts of an hour each. The castle is open daily.

Tourist information: Newport 524343; Yarmouth 760015 (summer).

TOUR
37

49 MILES

Steep chalk cliffs fringe the Isle of Wight's south coast. Inland, rolling farmland rises to grassy downland summits, from which there are superb views across the island and The Solent.

VENTNOR

Behind a curving sandy beach, Ventnor climbs a steep, wooded hillside in a series of terraces. The town faces due south, and most of its houses are built with balconies and wide windows to catch the sun. The mild winter climate attracted the Victorians, and Ventnor grew from a fishing hamlet to a resort between 1830 and 1900.

One mile west of the town, on a hill overlooking the sea, are the Ventnor Botanic Gardens where many subtropical plants grow, including camellias, jasmine, Mexican orange blossom and palm trees. A Smuggling Museum depicts every known method of smuggling on the island for more than 700 years; it is open daily from April to September.

From Ventnor the route climbs steeply to St Boniface Down, at 787ft the highest point on the island.

APPULDURCOMBE HOUSE

A short, steep climb from the car park leads to the gaunt shell of a baroque mansion standing in parkland. Appuldurcombe House was built in 1701 by Sir Robert Worsley, the wealthiest man on the island at the time. The grounds were landscaped by Capability Brown.

The east façade of the house is supported by giant pilasters, and on either side are magnificent pavilions. The four chimneys are built in the form of triumphal arches. A museum in the grounds tells the history of the house, which is open daily.

GODSHILL

Approaching this pretty village of thatched cottages, the eye is drawn to the square tower of the church standing high on a hill. A short walk between the cottages leads up to the 14th-century Godshill church, known as 'The Church of the Lily Cross', because of the mural on its east wall showing Christ crucified on a triple-branched lily. The painting, dating from about 1450, is the only one of its kind in Britain. It was whitewashed over at the time of the Reformation and only rediscovered in the middle of the last century.

BRADING

The High Street, lined with attractive colour-washed buildings, straggles up a hill to the Church of St Mary the Virgin. Standing on the spot where, it is claimed, St Wilfrid preached to the heathens in the 680s, the church has a 12th-century nave and 13th-century tower and spire.

Next to the church a timbered Tudor house of 1499 houses the Osborn-Smith Wax Museum and Animal World. The museum contains lifelike wax models depicting the history of the island, while Animal World displays stuffed animals, birds, reptiles and butterflies from all over the world; both are open daily.

On the other side of the High Street the Lilliput Museum of Dolls and Toys houses more than 1000 items, some dating from 2000 BC.

Brading Roman villa, reached by a signposted turning off the Sandown road just south of the town, contains some well-preserved mosaic flooring. There is a museum with Roman pottery, coins, tools and fragments of wall paintings. The site is open daily from April to September.

MERSLEY DOWN

The route climbs steeply to Ashey Down, then follows a ridge to the 420ft summit of Mersley Down. From the car park there are magnificent views across The Solent. On a clear day it is possible to see along the coast eastwards as far as Sussex.

ROBIN HILL

From the car park of the Robin Hill Zoological and Adventure Park a nature trail leads through 10 acres of woodland where squirrels, foxes and badgers roam and hawks, pheasants and magpies can be seen. Snakes and lizards sun themselves in an old clay pit and brightly coloured butterflies flit among the flowers. The park is open daily from the end of March to the end of October.

SHORWELL

One of a cluster of attractive villages in this part of the island, Shorwell has several pretty, thatched stone cottages grouped near the inn which is beside the stream.

Down a minor road about a mile beyond the village is Yafford Mill, a restored 18th-century water mill. It is open daily from Easter to October.

ST CATHERINE'S POINT

The route runs along the edge of the downs above the coast. Just beyond Blackgang Chine is a car park from which there are magnificent views.

From this car park a steep, 1½ mile path leads up across fields to the 781ft summit of St Catherine's Hill. On the hilltop stands a curious obelisk, 35ft high. This is the remains of St Catherine's Tower, known locally as the 'Pepperpot', which was built as a lighthouse in 1323. In 1785, work started on a second lighthouse nearby, but it was never finished. All that remains is a circle of bricks about 6ft high known as the 'Salt Cellar'.

The route continues through the village of Niton. Park in the village and walk down a road to the right signposted to St Catherine's Lighthouse. The lighthouse is open to the public in summer at the discretion of the keeper.

OLD PARK ESTATE

The road between Niton and St Lawrence is overhung with trees, with occasional glimpses of the sea below. On the hillside below St Lawrence, a tropical bird park surrounds a large pond in the Old Park Estate. Visitors can walk through aviaries which house more than 300 exotic birds. The park is open daily.

Tourist information: Ventnor 853625 (summer); Shanklin 862942.

Waterside ways in north Hampshire

TOUR
38

——— 36 MILES ———

Leafy lanes climb to the breezy Hampshire Downs, then wind through the remnants of ancient forests where King John hunted. High walls mark the site of a large Roman town.

BASINGSTOKE

Commercial development has given Basingstoke some spectacular modern architecture. The best new buildings are off Churchill Way East: one award-winning office block climbs like a Babylonian ziggurat in terraces of dark brown brick and dark glass, its successive roof levels planted with trees and hanging gardens.

An older Basingstoke survives, however, behind the new shopping area. Here stands the parish church of St Michael, dating mostly from the 16th century, whose south wall bears the marks of Civil War musket fire. The adjacent half-timbered Tudor Church Cottage has been used as vicarage and tithe barn and now houses the parish offices and church hall.

Walk up Church Street to Market Place, where a classical-style Old Town Hall accommodates the Willis Museum. This contains an excellent collection of clocks and watches from the 16th century to the present day, together with exhibits depicting the history of Basingstoke.

HANNINGTON

From the Beach Arms Hotel the road winds up through farmland and woods to Hannington, a hamlet set high on the downs. On its little green is the village sign and a wellhead with a wooden tiled canopy, erected to celebrate Queen Victoria's Diamond Jubilee in 1897.

The small flint-built Church of All Saints beside the green has an airy, white-painted interior, with roof timbers more like those of a farm building than a church. One window was engraved by Laurence Whistler in memory of William Whistler, a distant relative; it depicts a sheaf of corn and a scythe, against chalk downland.

WHITE HILL

The car park at the summit provides breathtaking views, on a clear day, over Kingsclere and the Kennet valley towards the Berkshire Downs.

The long-distance Wayfarer's Walk ascends from the south onto White Hill and continues westwards along the ridge to Inkpen Beacon. After 1½ miles the path reaches the top of Watership Down, the inspiration for Richard Adams' novel about a community of rabbits. The patient observer may see the real-life models for Hazel, Fiver and the rest of the warren, but more in evidence are the racehorses which are trained regularly on the gallops.

KINGSCLERE

One of Hampshire's most attractive villages lies on the banks of a small stream. Its pleasing medley of building styles is seen at its best in Swan Street, where Queen Anne, Georgian and Victorian dwellings blend beautifully.

The focal point of the village is its Norman Church of St Mary, which has a curious weather vane in the shape of a bug. This is said to have been given by King John after he was bitten by bedbugs while staying at a local monastery. John was a frequent visitor to the area for hunting in the nearby forests; the name Kingsclere means 'king's hunting ground'.

WOLVERTON

One of Britain's finest Georgian churches is set in open countryside on the edge of Wolverton Park. The exquisite red-brick Church of St Catherine was built in 1717, and its original interior is little altered.

From the north-east corner of the churchyard a footpath leads through the park to a lake, from which there is a view of Wolverton House. The house is not open to the public.

PAMBER PRIORY

A tree-lined avenue leads to a farm and the remains of a large Norman priory. The surviving chancel and tower now serves as the church, and though it is only a small part of the original building it retains much of the atmosphere of a Benedictine priory. In the south wall lies a 14th-century wooden effigy of a knight in chain mail, his feet resting on a lion.

SILCHESTER

Near Silchester Common a tiny museum in a wooden hut contains photographs and plans and a reconstruction of a 4th-century Christian church in the Roman town of Calleva Atrebatum, which once stood nearby. The site was excavated to reveal the site of the market place and town hall, baths, an inn, temples and the church. The soil has now been replaced, restoring the site to open farmland; but the town walls, in places up to 15ft high, still survive.

For the best views of the walls, drive a mile farther on to St Mary's Church and follow the footpath through the churchyard to the centre of the site. From here it is easy to visualise the extent of the town, which once covered 100 acres and was the capital of the Atrebates tribe before the Romans came to Britain.

Just outside the walls, by Manor Farm, an open banked hollow ringed by trees was once an amphitheatre which in Roman times accommodated several thousand people watching wrestling and beast-baiting.

THE VYNE

This warm red-brick house, in an idyllic sheltered park and garden, was built in 1510 by Lord Sandys, who became Lord Chamberlain to Henry VIII in 1526. Its interior combines a homely atmosphere with some spectacular decorative effects.

The grand Palladian staircase, designed by John Chute in 1770, is an intricate combination of painted ceilings, mouldings and columns. The first floor oak gallery is panelled; each of the 798 panels bears a different coat of arms or other motif.

Outside the house, lawns sweep down to the lakeside and there is a choice between a gentle stroll around the grounds or a longer signposted walk through tranquil woodlands. The house and grounds are open most afternoons in summer.

HOME AND BEAUTY *Wolverton House and park and the red-brick tower of St Catherine's Church combine in a stately English scene.*

ARTISTRY IN BRICK *Purple bricks set in a crisscross pattern, called diapering, ornament the exterior walls of The Vyne.*

HEARTBREAK HOUSE *Plague victims of the 17th century were isolated in the Pest House at Odiham, and few ever left.*

Large farmhouses in the wooded Hampshire countryside reflect years of agricultural prosperity. There are memories of a novelist, and a country park surrounds the home of a great military hero.

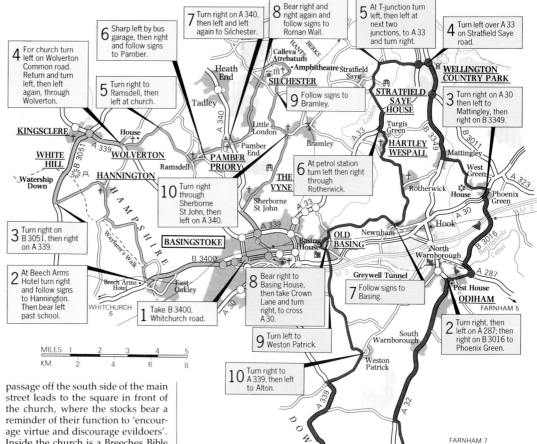

ALTON

Set at the source of the River Wey, Alton has a bustling High Street where majestic Georgian buildings survive amongst modern structures. Side streets running north off the High Street towards Market Square contain charming little shops, unchanged for centuries, with half-timbered walls and red-tiled roofs.

The fortunes of Alton were founded on various industries from brewing to papermaking; the tools of these crafts are exhibited in the Curtis Museum, at the northern end of the High Street, which also contains displays of 19th-century botany and dolls and dolls' houses. Near the museum the 17th and 18th-century Allen Gallery contains a large display of English ceramics and pottery from 1550 to the present; behind the gallery is a tranquil garden. The museum is open daily except Sunday, and the gallery daily except Sunday and Monday.

Set on a knoll is St Lawrence's Church, largely 15th century but with a Norman tower of 1070. The church was the scene of a dramatic siege in 1643, when Colonel Boles and his detachment of Royalists took refuge in the church from a Roundhead attack. The colonel is said to have made his 'last stand' from his pulpit command post; the church door bears bullet scars from the battle, and some lead shot can still be seen embedded in one of the columns.

Alton station, to the east of the town, is the terminus of the steam railway known as the Watercress Line after the beds of watercress visible from the train. The 1½ hour return trip to Alresford behind a gleaming locomotive passes through delightful woodland and meadow scenery.

The village of Chawton, signposted off the main road 1 mile south-west of Alton, was the home of the novelist Jane Austen. The red-brick farmhouse in which she lived from 1809 to 1817, and which, she said in a poem, 'will all other houses beat', is still very much as it was in the novelist's time, and full of mementos of Jane's life and work. Here she wrote *Mansfield Park*, *Emma* and *Persuasion*, before moving to Winchester. The house is open daily except on Monday and Tuesday in winter.

ODIHAM

The Georgian façades – some painted, some red brick – of the buildings flanking Odiham's wide High Street testify to the village's 18th-century prosperity. They were grafted onto earlier timber-framed houses, as a glance down the side alleys reveals. A

passage off the south side of the main street leads to the square in front of the church, where the stocks bear a reminder of their function to 'encourage virtue and discourage evildoers'. Inside the church is a Breeches Bible of 1578; unlike the Authorised Version it recounts that Adam and Eve wore breeches not aprons. South of the church are 17th-century almshouses set around a courtyard.

A signposted road from the east end of the High Street leads to the Basingstoke Canal, which has been restored for recreational use. The towpath makes a pleasant 2 mile walk westwards to Greywell Tunnel past the ruins of King John's castle at North Warnborough. By the Water Witch inn boats can be hired for a cruise on the canal, passing between thick woods.

Beyond Phoenix Green, the gardens of West Green House have a wealth of flowering shrubs. Owned by the National Trust, they are open on Wednesday, Thursday and Sunday afternoons in summer.

WELLINGTON COUNTRY PARK

Woods cover large tracts of the Wellington Country Park, and five nature trails of varying lengths wind beside the shore of a large lake and through plantations of beech, oak, fir and Scots pine. There is a deer enclosure, a children's farm with many breeds of domestic animals, an adventure playground and a miniature steam railway. Boats can be hired on the lake, but the island in the middle is a bird sanctuary with geese, mallards, coots and moorhens. Patient watchers may also see dabchicks, kingfishers and woodpeckers.

The 400 acre park is part of the Duke of Wellington's Stratfield Saye Estate. The National Dairy Museum, near the entrance, chronicles the history of milk production and distribution

since the time of Waterloo. It includes a reconstruction of a Victorian farmhouse dairy and the window of a Victorian dairy shop. The park is open daily in summer and at weekends in winter.

STRATFIELD SAYE HOUSE

Rolling parkland surrounds the mansion given by the nation to the first Duke of Wellington after his victory at the Battle of Waterloo. The house, built in 1635, is the home of the present duke and contains art treasures and personal possessions of his ancestor, including even his underwear and false teeth. Also on display are the Iron Duke's Coronation carriage and massive funeral carriage. In the gardens there are walks through an arboretum, rose garden and wildfowl sanctuary.

The house is open daily except Friday from May to September and on Saturday and Sunday in April.

HARTLEY WESPALL

This little hamlet amid farmland is notable for its tiny Church of St Mary. Victorian restoration by George Gilbert Scott included the re-siting of the tower and spire at the side of the church, revealing huge 14th-century timbers in the west wall. The neat flintwork of the other walls is made up of stones removed from the Roman remains at nearby Silchester.

Farther on, the compact village of Rotherwick has an unusually wide main street, flanked with some pretty half-timbered cottages. Over the nave of the church is a splendid oak roof dating from the 15th century, while one of its six bells is believed to date from the 14th century.

OLD BASING

From a car park outside the village a path goes along the bank of the River Loddon and past a superb tithe barn to the ruins of Basing House. Originally the house was a motte-and-bailey castle, but it was later converted into a fortified house.

The Marquis of Winchester defended the house for two years against Cromwell's army between 1643 and 1645, but he was defeated when the heavy artillery arrived. Today the walls and extensive foundations survive, together with cellars revealed by recent excavations and a dovecote which has survived the ravages of time intact.

Tourist information: Basingstoke 56222.

71

Backwaters below the Berkshire Downs

TOUR
40
—— 58 MILES ——

Dramatic chalk downs extend from Berkshire into rural Wiltshire. In their shelter lie handsome towns and villages at ease with their long, eventful histories.

HUNGERFORD
In the 18th and 19th centuries as many as 200 coaches a week passed through Hungerford, situated midway along the old London to Bath road on the Kennet valley's southern slopes. They were served by a dozen inns along Bridge Street and Charnham Street. One inn that remains is The Bear, where in 1688 historic negotiations were held between envoys of the fleeing James II and his son-in-law the Prince of Orange, later William III.

Bridge Street spans the Kennet and Avon Canal, which brought the town further prosperity after its completion in 1810, and leads into the wide and gracious High Street. Dominated by the Victorian brick and terracotta town hall and clock in Byzantine style, the gently rising street has many fine old buildings, a number of which now house antiques shops. An antiquity displayed in the town hall is the brass horn said to have been given to Hungerford by its one-time manorial lord, John of Gaunt.

About half a mile east of Hungerford is Denford Mill House, an attractive converted mill on the Kennet.

INKPEN HILL
The drive south from the village of Inkpen leads to England's highest chalk downs. Along the way, a replica of the 17th-century Combe Gibbet is grimly visible on the site of a Stone Age burial mound on top of Inkpen Hill's stark ridge. At the summit crossroads there is car parking and a short walk west to the Gibbet, with an awe-inspiring view across the great sweep of the downs.

Combe Gibbet is today a popular launching spot for hang-gliding enthusiasts. East of the crossroads, a prehistoric track leads to the 974ft summit of Walbury Hill, the site of an ancient fortification.

GREAT BEDWYN
Approached across twin humpbacked bridges over the canal and railway, the village high street and Brown's Lane are lined with beautiful old houses. Although small today, Great Bedwyn was classed as a city in Saxon times, and through its borough status returned two members to Parliament from around 1300 to the last century.

In Church Street, the stonemasonry incorporates a fascinating museum of busts and statues, tombstones and plaques. The flint-built Church of St Mary the Virgin dates from the 11th century and contains the Tudor tomb of Sir John Seymour. Sir John's ten children included Jane, third wife of Henry VIII, who died shortly after giving birth to his heir Edward VI.

CROFTON PUMPING STATION
Two restored beam engines dating from 1812 and 1845 remain in steam to raise tons of water from the foot of the hill to the Kennet and Avon Canal's high point a mile to the west. The working engines are open to the public on Sundays from April to October and at various times in summer (Goring 874072). The site with its massive chimney and pumphouse is open daily.

SAVERNAKE FOREST
Magnificently lined by towering beeches, the straight road known as Grand Avenue gives a fine introduction to the 4500 acres of woodland, formerly a royal hunting forest, given to the Seymour family by Edward VI. The forest is open to the public and its roads are quite motorable. The signposted picnic area at Postern Hill has tables and even barbecue hearths set in green glades among the tall beeches, chestnuts and oaks. Trails lead off into the forest in all directions.

MARLBOROUGH
At Marlborough's western end, in the grounds of the town's famous public school, is Castle Mound, the prehistoric earthwork that is the traditional burial place of Merlin, the wizard of Arthurian legend. Known locally as Maerl's Barrow, the mound thus gives the town its name. From the 11th century, a royal castle stood at the ancient site; the town grew with it, receiving its charter in 1204 from King John, who had been married in the castle chapel 15 years earlier.

Today the market town has a wide High Street of Jacobean and Georgian buildings, with projecting upper floors over colonnaded walkways. Most of the buildings date from 1653, when a fire destroyed much of the High Street. At the west end, however, the lovely 15th-century Perpendicular Church of St Peter and St Paul escaped damage. It probably looks much today as it did in 1498 when Cardinal Wolsey was ordained there. Sadly, the church is now redundant; but it is preserved by a local trust and houses a tourist information centre, open during the summer.

MILDENHALL
Invisible from the main road at the foot of the gentle slope down to the Kennet river, St John's Church is a blissfully secluded backwater among ancient thatched farm buildings, lush pasture and majestic trees in which ring doves coo. The serene little church is mainly Norman, but retains part of an Anglo-Saxon tower. Inside, the superb oak box pews and panelling are 19th century – and yet look very much at home.

ALDBOURNE
From the wind-blown heights of Aldbourne Chase, more than 800ft up on the ancient Ridgeway, the road

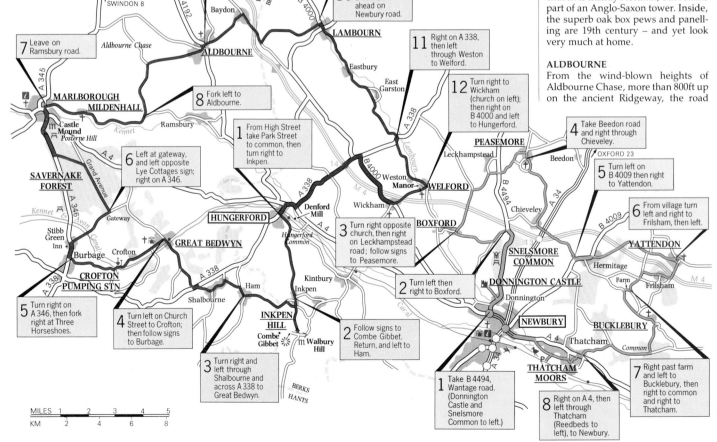

9 Right at square and left to Baydon; then right and follow signs to Lambourn.

10 Right on B4000, then ahead on Newbury road.

11 Right on A338, then left through Weston to Welford.

12 Turn right to Wickham (church on left); then right on B4000 and left to Hungerford.

7 Leave on Ramsbury road.

8 Fork left to Aldbourne.

6 Left at gateway, and left opposite Lye Cottages sign; right on A346.

1 From High Street take Park Street to common, then turn right to Inkpen.

4 Take Beedon road and right through Chieveley.

5 Turn left on B4009 then right to Yattendon.

6 From village turn left and right to Frilsham, then left.

3 Turn right opposite church, then right on Leckhampstead road; follow signs to Peasemore.

2 Turn left then right to Boxford.

5 Turn right on A346, then fork right at Three Horseshoes.

4 Turn left on Church Street to Crofton; then follow signs to Burbage.

3 Turn right and left through Shalbourne and across A338 to Great Bedwyn.

2 Follow signs to Combe Gibbet. Return, and left to Ham.

1 Take B4494, Wantage road. (Donnington Castle and Snelsmore Common to left.)

7 Right past farm and left to Bucklebury, then right to common and right to Thatcham.

8 Right on A4, then left through Thatcham (Reedbeds to left), to Newbury.

MILES 1 2 3 4 5
KM 2 4 6 8

descends steeply into an enchanting village in a valley hollow. At the centre of its sprawl of old houses, with their beautiful red-tiled roofs, is a rectangular green enclosed by terraced cottages on three sides and overlooked by St Michael's Church.

The largely 13th and 15th-century church has some fine brasses and monuments and, curiously, two fire engines. These were given to the village in 1778 following a disastrous fire in the previous year.

LAMBOURN
At the head of the narrow valley of the Lambourn river, a Kennet tributary noted for its trout-fishing, this market town is a racehorse-training centre. Thoroughbred horses are exercised on the surrounding downs, and Lambourn's streets teem with riders in jodhpurs and flat caps. In Newbury Street, the saddlers E.J. Wicks welcome visitors to their workshop.

WELFORD
A delightful little village on the Lambourn, Welford has a massive, but privately owned manor house with a deer park, hidden behind high walls and hedges but partly visible from the grounds of St Gregory's Church. The church, half hidden from the road by old yews and a vast cedar, has ancient origins: when it was rebuilt in 1852 a pre-Conquest coin was found in its stonework.

Tourist information:
Marlborough 52989 (summer).

TOUR
41
— 34 MILES —
From a town where cloth was king, roads wind across countryside where the Civil War has left its marks. There are breezy commons on the downs and secluded villages in their lee.

NEWBURY
The wide thoroughfare of Northbrook Street, with its handsome three-storey red-brick houses, leads southward to Newbury Bridge, built in 1769. From this, the latest in a succession of bridges built over the Kennet here since before the Conquest, can be seen the fine 17th and 18th-century buildings that still line the canalside.

Beyond the bridge, in Bartholomew Street, is St Nicolas Church, elaborately constructed in buttressed, pinnacled Perpendicular style. The church's rather grand interior is at its best on sunny mornings when light filtering through the fine stained glass floods the great vaulted space with a mysterious, rose-pink glow.

Opposite the town hall is Wharf Street and the magnificent Cloth Hall, built in 1626, which now houses the town's museum and tourist information centre. The museum, open daily except on Wednesdays and winter Sundays, traces Newbury's

DONNINGTON CASTLE *Thomas Chaucer, son of the poet, once owned the fortress which Cromwell's cannons battered.*

PEACEFUL CORNER *A sprinkling of daffodils between weatherworn headstones brings a splash of colour to the quiet country churchyard in Bucklebury.*

DENFORD MILL *The Kennet drove the 18th-century mill, now a private house.*

history from earliest days. The Granary, adjoining the Cloth Hall, was built in the early 18th century when Newbury became a grain-trading centre; it is remarkable for its timber frame and external all-wood gallery.

DONNINGTON CASTLE
Approached up a grand avenue of beeches, the six-storey gatehouse on top of a steep mound is all that remains of a 14th-century fortress that withstood a 20-month siege by Cromwell's troops from 1644 to 1646. The castle surrendered only on the orders of the defeated king.

SNELSMORE COMMON
Ample parking space and secluded picnic spots are close to the entrance of this attractive country park. A 2 mile nature trail winds through birch woodland and through areas of open heath where green woodpeckers and jays can be seen.

BOXFORD
Though only a mile from the uproar of the motorway, this quaint village in a woody dell has the air of a community little touched by the outside world. Exquisite timbered and thatched cot-

tages of the 17th century cluster along the Lambourn river, with their green gardens running right to the water's edge. The rambling Old Mill, with its higgledy-piggledy and ancient red-tiled roofs, is said to have been built round a tree.

PEASEMORE
Up on the edge of the downs, this spread-out village has a number of very large houses, the grandest of them carefully concealed behind high red-brick walls. At the centre is St Barnabas, a large, spired church rebuilt around 1840. In the churchyard, sheep sometimes graze and the heights of a tall cedar are home to a raucous colony of rooks.

YATTENDON
From the car park at the entrance to the village it is only a few steps round the corner to the Square, surrounded by marvellous 17th and 18th-century brick houses, among them the attractive Royal Oak Hotel. Beyond to the left is Yattendon Manor, built around 1780 and the former home of Alfred Waterhouse, an eminent local architect who designed several houses in the village. The neighbouring St

Peter's and St Paul's Church is largely Victorian but retains part of its original nave roof of 1450 and a splendid Jacobean pulpit.

BUCKLEBURY
The drive up the gentle, wooded slope from Bucklebury village leads to the common where in October 1644 the Earl of Manchester's 20,000-strong Parliamentary army encamped before the second Battle of Newbury. The common's Avenue is flanked by monumental oak trees, said to have been planted in the reign of Elizabeth I, with later additions to celebrate the victories of the Duke of Marlborough and Nelson.

THATCHAM MOORS
Just on the other side of the Kennet and Avon Canal from Newbury racecourse, 32 acres of wetland have been set aside as a nature reserve. In the small parking area a board gives guidance on visiting the reserve.

Birds breeding here include snipe, reed warbler and sedge warbler, and the reedbeds provide a valuable refuge for many migrant species.

Tourist information: Newbury 30267.

Pages of history beside the noble Thames

TOUR
42

───── 57 MILES ─────

English history revolves around Windsor, from the castle built by William the Conqueror to the Thameside spot where democracy was born. Along the leafy ways are gardens and a Tudor mansion.

WINDSOR

The towers and walls of Windsor Castle soar above the town in splendid majesty, as befits the world's most famous royal residence and largest inhabited castle. Its lofty site was chosen by William the Conqueror, who built the mound and crowned it with a wooden fort to command the River Thames and the approaches to London. Edward III made it into a comfortable residence, and many of his successors lived there. George IV made additions, including the distinctive crown to Henry II's Round Tower.

Within the castle precincts is St George's Chapel, started in 1475 by Edward IV and completed in the reign of Henry VIII. Many kings and queens are buried there, including Edward VII and Queen Alexandra, George V and Queen Mary, and George VI. The castle is open daily.

The town at the castle's feet has a long history of service to monarchs and their staff. Like the castle its buildings date from many periods; some of the oldest, huddled beneath the massive walls between Castle Hill and Church Street, date from Tudor and early Stuart times. In St Alban's Street is the 17th-century Burford House, built for Nell Gwyn by Charles II, and in Market Street the Three Tuns Hotel dates from 1518. Nearby is the superb classical style Guildhall, designed by Sir Thomas Fitch but completed by Sir Christopher Wren after Fitch's death in 1689.

One mile west of the castle is Windsor's oldest building, Clewer Parish Church. It was largely completed before the end of the 11th century and parts of it are 150 years older than the castle. It has a Norman font and a tomb with Saxon lettering, suggesting that an even earlier building once stood on the site.

Not surprisingly, pageantry plays a part in this royal town. Every morning at 11am the castle guard is changed. The new guard marches from The Royal Mews to the castle, and after the ceremony of the changing of the guard the old guard marches back to the mews.

The panoplies of both pageantry and war are well displayed in the Household Cavalry Museum, in Combermere Barracks. This museum, one of the largest of its kind in Britain, contains weapons, uniforms, equipment and pictures of the Life Guards, Royal Horse Guards and 1st Royal Dragoons. The museum is by the

ROYAL WINDSOR *The Long Walk leads to the King George IV Gateway into Windsor Castle's State and Private Apartments.*

EARLY POST *Beside Eton timber-framing stands a Victorian pillar box.*

FAR FROM HOME *The columns of a Roman temple, brought from Libya and now standing beside Virginia Water, were intended for the portico of the British Museum.*

main entrance to Combermere Barracks in St Leonards Road and is open Mondays to Fridays and also on Sundays from May to September.

WINDSOR GREAT PARK

South of Windsor some 5000 acres of parkland, with drives and walks leading through dells, glades and avenues, make up the Great Park. On its south and west edges are remnants of the original royal chase, the Windsor Forest which in Norman times extended as far as Guildford to the south and Reading to the west. In the forest and park many ancient oaks still survive, alongside beeches, cedars and pines. Notable specimens are the King's Oak, the largest tree in the park, and the Four Queens, three oaks and a beech.

Running north to south from the castle is the Long Walk, a 3 mile avenue that crosses the Home Park and rises to Snow Hill and the Copper Horse, a statue of George III on horseback. The Long Walk was planted with an avenue of elm trees in 1685 by Charles II, but in 1945 the trees became diseased and were replaced by London planes and chestnuts. The statue, erected by George IV, was the work of Sir Richard Westmacott. Nearby is the Royal Lodge, the private home of the Queen Mother.

RUNNYMEDE

On the slopes of Cooper's Hill above the Thames stand three memorials – each in its way dedicated to liberty and democracy and the defence of those ideals. The classical temple close to the river is the Magna Carta Memorial, built by the American Bar Association in 1957. It stands near the spot – the exact location is not known – where in 1215 King John was forced by his barons to fix his seal to Magna Carta, a document that paved the way for constitutional democratic government.

Close by is the Kennedy Memorial, a Portland stone block in memory of President John F. Kennedy, assassinated in 1963. The memorial stands on an acre of ground given to the people of the USA by the people of Britain.

The third memorial, standing on the brow of Cooper's Hill, is a shrine to 20,456 airmen of the Allied Forces who died during the Second World War and have no known grave. Their names are recorded in the cloister which forms part of the memorial complex.

The Magna Carta and Kennedy memorials are reached by footpath from the car park beside the river. The Air Forces Memorial is in Cooper's Hill Lane, a turning off the road to Englefield Green.

SAVILL AND VALLEY GARDENS
These two gardens, both reached from the Savill Garden car park, are in a corner of Windsor Great Park. In their splendour and variety of plants they rival London's Kew Gardens, and cover some 435 acres.

Savill Garden is named after Sir Eric Savill, Deputy Ranger of Windsor Great Park when the garden was first laid out in 1932. Its pathways lead through banks of rhododendrons, by ponds and streams and across immaculate lawns bordered by flowerbeds set with azaleas, primulas, hydrangeas and roses.

Valley Garden, the larger of the two, borders Virginia Water and has a heather garden and a rhododendron species collection. The heather garden was developed in 1954 on the site of a disused gravel pit. The area has been landscaped informally to include some 200 species of heather, and it is claimed that there is a heather in flower on every day of the year. The rhododendrons cover some 50 acres and include species introduced into Britain during the last century. Both gardens are open daily.

VIRGINIA WATER
A glistening sheen of water stretches for more than 2 miles in the south-east corner of Windsor Great Park. It was created in the 18th century by the 1st Duke of Cumberland and is one of the largest ornamental lakes in England. So vast is it that it was drained during the Second World War so that it would not provide a landmark for enemy aircraft seeking to bomb Windsor Castle.

On the south bank of the lake stand columns from the Roman city of Leptis Magna, in Libya, brought to England in 1816 and presented to the Prince Regent. Nearby is a waterfall made in the 18th century with boulders from Farnham. On the opposite bank, a 100ft high totem pole towers above the trees. It was erected in 1958 to commemorate the centenary of British Columbia, Canada, and was carved from a 600-year-old Western red cedar. Its carved figures represent mythical ancestors of tribes in the province. A key to the figures can be found at the base.

Woods of beech, sweet chestnut, oak and pine border the lake, which is a haven for wildfowl. Some of the trees were planted almost 200 years ago, and plaques show their ages.

CHOBHAM
The approach to Chobham is across Chobham Common, largely used as a military vehicle testing station but including a Surrey County Council nature reserve. The common comprises wet and dry heathland and is noted for its rare insect life.

On the northern outskirts of Chobham a large green, complete with village pump, is faced on three sides by attractive old cottages. In one corner of the green is The Forge, where a farrier and blacksmith carries

on his trade. Horses are shod here, though the forge furnace is gas-fired. A showroom has brass, copper and wrought-iron work for sale.

LIGHTWATER COUNTRY PARK
The park is part of Bagshot Heath, said to be one of the haunts of the highwayman Dick Turpin. Some 143 acres of heathland, with birch and pine woods and three lakes, make up the park, which has two waymarked paths and a nature trail. One path leads to High Curley, a viewpoint with views across the heath.

WINDSOR SAFARI PARK
In 150 acres near Windsor Great Park, a small part of Africa has been set down in the heart of Berkshire. Here visitors can drive through game reserves where lions, giraffes and elephants roam. There is also a herd of rare White rhinos. Dolphins display their extraordinary talents in the dolphinarium, and there is a killer whale. The safari park, which also includes a pets' corner and children's farm, is open daily.

BRAY
Black-and-white cottages and houses line every street in this delightful Thameside village, from the quaint village hall crowned with a tiny bell cote to the Hind's Head Hotel facing down the main street. Down by the river is the elite Waterside Hotel, with its own landing stage, and a small beach from which there are fine views across the river.

Above the village towers the massive St Michael's Church, standing in a churchyard entered by a 15th-century gatehouse, timber-framed with an overhanging gable and red-brick infilling. Bray's 16th-century vicar, Simon Aleyn, became famous in song as the turncoat who lived through four reigns and adjusted his religious and political views to suit those of each monarch.

MAIDENHEAD
A railway bridge built by Isambard Brunel in 1838 spans the Thames at Maidenhead. Across this bridge in the 1920s and 1930s steamed the 'Greasepaint Special', the train that brought actors and other stage personalities from London to their homes by the river. Maidenhead between the wars was the favourite place of residence not only for theatre folk but also for the fun-loving high society, and its champagne parties, hotels and drinking clubs became notorious.

All that is in the past now, but some of the atmosphere survives down by the river where river steamers ply from the western bank and rowing boats can still be hired. Each August Maidenhead holds its regatta, when the splash of oars and the cheers of straw-boatered supporters once again echo across the water.

Boulter's Lock, a mile upriver, has been a favourite Thames beauty spot since Edwardian times, when young men in punts crowded the river. Today gleaming motorboats queue to pass through the 200ft long lock.

DORNEY COURT
Pass through the gateway in the red-brick wall and enter the 16th century, for Dorney Court stands as it has done for some 500 years – a many-gabled pink-brick and timbered manor house steeped in the atmosphere of Tudor times. The house has been the home of the Palmer family for almost 400 years, and here Charles II came to seek the charms of Barbara Palmer, Countess of Castlemaine.

The rooms are furnished with furniture of several periods, including 17th-century lacquer furniture and 18th and 19th-century tables, and the walls are hung with family portraits. The spacious gardens are noted for their immaculately clipped yew hedges. The house is open on certain days in summer.

Adjoining Dorney Court is St James's Church, also built of brick with white-stone corner facings and a turreted tower. House and church are a perfect blend set in this quiet corner of Buckinghamshire.

ETON
England's famous public school holds sway in this Thameside town across the river from Windsor. The college was founded in 1440 by Henry VI, and its buildings, some dating from that time, occupy one end of the High Street. Eton College Chapel, the School Yard, the Museum of Eton Life in the Cloisters and the Natural History Society Museum can be visited.

Eton's narrow High Street is a picturesque jumble of 18th-century shop fronts and timber-framed buildings where restaurants, antiques shops and book shops can be found. The High Street is linked to Windsor by an 18th-century bridge which is closed to traffic but open to pedestrians.

Tourist information: Windsor 851046; Maidenhead 781110.

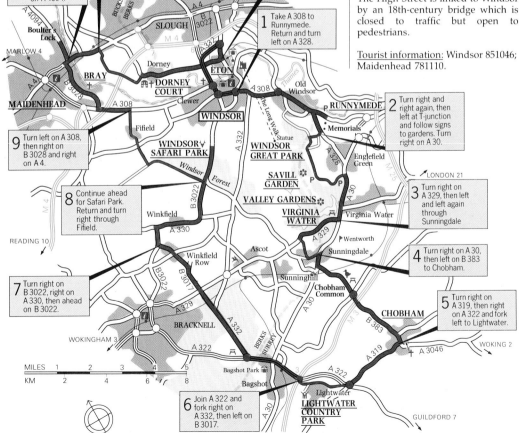

Heathland panoramas towards the North Downs

<table>
<tr><td>

TOUR
43
— 58 MILES —

</td></tr>
</table>

A ruined abbey on the River Wey gives its name to Surrey's District of Waverley. Historic towns are surrounded by heathlands, and a scenic drive runs along the ridge of the North Downs.

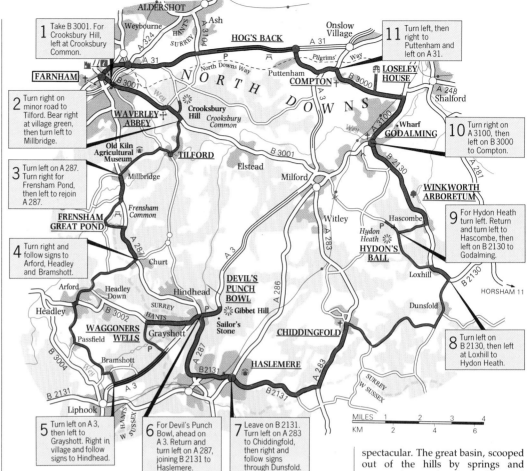

1 Take B 3001. For Crooksbury Hill, left at Crooksbury Common.

2 Turn right on minor road to Tilford. Bear right at village green, then turn left to Millbridge.

3 Turn left on A 287. Turn right for Frensham Pond, then left to rejoin A 287.

4 Turn right and follow signs to Arford, Headley and Bramshott.

5 Turn left on A 3, then left to Grayshott. Right in village and follow signs to Hindhead.

6 For Devil's Punch Bowl, ahead on A 3. Return and turn left on A 287, joining B 2131 to Haslemere.

7 Leave on B 2131. Turn left on A 283 to Chiddingfold, then right and follow signs through Dunsfold.

8 Turn left on B 2130, then left at Loxhill to Hydon Heath.

9 For Hydon Heath turn left. Return and turn left to Hascombe, then left on B 2130 to Godalming.

10 Turn right on A 3100, then left on B 3000 to Compton.

11 Turn left, then right to Puttenham and left on A 31.

FARNHAM

Though its history can be traced back to prehistoric times, Farnham grew around its 12th-century castle, whose substantial remains stand on Castle Hill north of the town. The castle was built as a residence for the Bishops of Winchester, and Bishop Wayneflete's tower, built 1470-5, is said to be the earliest and best example of patterned brickwork in England. The keep, now only a shell, is open daily, and the Great Hall, kitchens and late 17th-century chapel are open on Wednesday afternoons.

Farnham prospered as a centre of the wool trade in medieval times, and in the late 17th and early 18th centuries it was one of the major corn markets in southern England; hop-growing was also a thriving industry. That period of prosperity is reflected in the many Georgian façades built onto medieval buildings in the town. On the north side of West Street, Farnham's main thoroughfare, is Timber Close where, it is believed, the hammerbeam roof of London's Westminster Hall was carved. Close by is Factory Yard, with workers' cottages and workshops where hop sacks were made.

The radical politician and author of *Rural Rides*, William Cobbett, was born in Farnham in 1763. His birthplace, The Jolly Farmer in Bridge Square, is still an inn, now called The William Cobbett. He is buried in the graveyard of St Andrew's Church, near the porch.

WAVERLEY ABBEY

In a meadow by the River Wey stand the grey, crumbling ruins of the first Cistercian abbey in England, founded in 1128. Hospitality was the special vocation of the monks, and several kings stayed at the abbey, including King John, Henry III and Edward I. The abbey prospered for 400 years, until the Dissolution of the Monasteries. It is open daily from March 15 to October 15.

At this point the road takes a sharp turn to the left and crosses the River Wey, an idyllic spot where willows line the river bank. The water tumbles over a small weir and seethes in foam as it cascades beneath the low arches of the medieval bridge.

TILFORD

A long, six-arched medieval bridge crosses the River Wey at Tilford, leading to a large triangular green faced by houses, cottages and an inn which dates from 1700. At each corner of the sloping green there is an oak tree, two with seats around; the one at the bottom corner, called The British Oak, was planted in 1897 in honour of Queen Victoria's Diamond Jubilee. The Tilford Institute by the green dates from 1893 and is an early work by Sir Edwin Lutyens, better known as the designer of the Cenotaph in Whitehall, London. The Church of All Saints was built in 1867.

The road leaves the village by another medieval bridge, with four arches, that crosses a branch of the Wey. On Reeds Road, about a mile from the village, is the Old Kiln Agricultural Museum, set in 10 acres of garden, arboretum and woodland. Restored agricultural implements are on display, and among the buildings are a smithy, a wheelwright's shop and a farmhouse kitchen. The smithy's and wheelwright's crafts are boldly represented at the museum entrance – a fine pair of gates comprising four iron wheels in wrought-iron frames. The museum is open on Wednesday to Sunday and on Bank Holidays.

FRENSHAM GREAT POND

Despite its name the Great Pond is one of the largest lakes in southern England, about half a mile square. It was excavated in the 13th century to supply fish to the Bishops of Winchester when they visited Farnham Castle. The pond is set in 958 acres of heathland that make up Frensham Common, which straddles the Farnham to Hindhead road. The common is owned by the National Trust.

WAGGONERS WELLS

A lane from the village of Grayshott leads down to a wooded valley in which lie three lakes, the Waggoners Wells, once known as Wakeners Wells. The origin of two of the lakes possibly dates back to medieval times when streams were dammed to form fish ponds. The third lake dates from the 18th century. At the head of the lakes a small bridge and a ford cross the stream which rises a few hundred yards upstream. Marsh marigolds bloom here in spring, and kingfishers nest in the banks.

Beech trees and silver birch clothe the valley sides down to the water's edge. There are paths through the woods and alongside the lakes, with seats conveniently placed for admiring the view at leisure or simply for basking in the sun.

DEVIL'S PUNCH BOWL

Among the many beauty spots throughout England attributed to the work of the Devil, the vast hollow just north of Hindhead is one of the most spectacular. The great basin, scooped out of the hills by springs and streams, is more than 2 miles long and half a mile wide, its slopes plunging 350ft to a stream that flows into the River Wey. At the north-west corner of the hollow are three humps known as the Devil's Jumps, were the Devil was said to exercise himself daily by hopping from one to another.

The best view of the valley is from the National Trust car park on the Hindhead to Guildford road, and there are footpaths along both sides of the hollow. On the north side of the Devil's Punch Bowl is Gibbet Hill, its 895ft summit bearing a granite cross erected in 1851 to mark the spot where a gibbet once stood. Here, until the late 18th century, criminals were hanged in chains and their bodies left for months as a warning to travellers that local justice was swift and terrible.

A footpath from the road leads to the top of the hill, passing the Sailor's Stone, which stands on the spot where a sailor was murdered by thugs in 1786. An inscription records that a curse is laid on anyone who moves the stone. The three murderers ended up on the gibbet on April 7, 1787.

HASLEMERE

A long High Street is lined with modern and Victorian shop fronts and a few half-timbered houses. The road climbs gently to the Town Hall of 1814, which stands behind a triangular green, facing north along the High Street. Near the town hall are the

18th-century White Horse Hotel and the Georgian Hotel. Close by is the Town House of 1725 which has a carved oak panelled staircase said to be the work of Inigo Jones. To the right of the town hall, Shepherds Hill and Lower Street both have 17th and 18th-century houses, some with tile-hung upper storeys – typical of this part of Surrey.

At the northern end of the High Street is the Haslemere Educational Museum, devoted to geology, botany, zoology, archaeology and local history.

Haslemere's motto is 'Life is more satisfying through the muses or arts', a fitting motto for a town where the Dolmetsch family have been making harpsichords, lutes, recorders and other early musical instruments since 1917. Dr Carl Dolmetsch and other members of the family direct recitals of early music at the Haslemere Festival, which is held each year in the second fortnight of July. Begun in 1925, it is the longest running music festival held in the same place in England.

CHIDDINGFOLD
A village pond where goldfish dart among the water plants lies in the heart of a village which in the 13th century was the centre of a glass-making industry. Charcoal from nearby woods fired the furnaces, but in 1615 the use of charcoal was banned because of the danger of deforestation and the industry moved to coal-producing centres. The glass-makers have gone, but some of their names are recorded on brass plates in the Church of St Mary, and the glass they made was used in many notable buildings including Westminster Abbey and St George's Chapel, Windsor.

Around the green are buildings of several periods, including the fine old half-timbered Crown Inn, which has a crown for its inn sign. It is believed to date from 1285 and claims to be the oldest licensed house in Surrey.

Other buildings, such as Chantry House at the top of the green, are brick-faced and tile-clad. The elegant Manor House and Glebe House have 18th-century façades. The Church of St Mary is built of local stone and has a fine lich gate with the timber slab, where the coffin was rested, still in place.

HYDON'S BALL
A conical wooded hill 586ft high stands on Hydon Heath, whose sandy soil was used for Chiddingfold's glass industry. The hill belongs to the National Trust, along with 125 acres of the heath, and on the summit is a memorial to Octavia Hill, a social reformer and one of the founders of the National Trust formed in 1894. On clear days the view from Hydon's Ball stretches across the Weald to the South Downs.

WINKWORTH ARBORETUM
Rare trees including species from the Himalayas, Japan and North America grow alongside the more common British trees on this 96 acre hillside owned by the National Trust. The first 60 acres were given in 1952 by Dr Wilfrid Fox who had devoted himself to the care of neglected woodlands. At the bottom of the hill two lakes reflect the glorious hues of the seasons – the reds, oranges and golds of autumn, the rich greens of summer, and the softer greens of spring which are complemented by blue and yellow carpets of bluebells and daffodils. The arboretum is open daily throughout the year.

GODALMING
A Town Hall of 1814, octagonal and standing on arches, stands in Godalming's High Street: it houses the local museum, and is known affectionately as 'the pepperpot'. An old coaching inn, the King's Arms Royal Hotel, is a reminder of the days when Godalming was a staging point. It bears the date 1753 but is older – Peter the Great of Russia dined there in 1689. Two other inns, the Great George and the Angel, are now shops. They stand in the High Street where many buildings have Georgian façades on much earlier premises.

The River Wey flows through the town, and there is a pleasant walk along the towpath to Catteshall Wharf, nearly a mile to the east.

Just outside the town is Charterhouse School, founded in London in 1611 and moved to Godalming in 1872. The 150ft Founder's Tower dominates the buildings.

LOSELEY HOUSE
Stone from Waverley Abbey was used in the building of this house, built in 1562 by an ancestor of the present owner and set in glorious parkland. Elizabeth I slept there three times, and James I stayed there twice. A feature of the house is a carved chalk chimneypiece. It also contains panelling bought from Henry VIII's now-vanished Nonsuch Palace, fine ceilings, furniture and tapestries. The house is open most afternoons in summer.

COMPTON
The Pilgrims' Way runs just to the north of this village, and its Church of St Nicholas has memories of the days when pilgrims passed that way to Canterbury after the murder of Thomas Becket in 1170. Inside are Norman columns carved from the hard chalk of the Hog's Back.

The church has a double chancel, unique in England, and the lower chancel has a small east window, the focus of the pilgrim's devotions, with Norman stained glass depicting the Virgin and Child. A wooden balustrade in the upper sanctuary is also Norman and is one of the oldest surviving examples of church timberwork. A large gallery is devoted to the Victorian artist G.F. Watts, who lived in the village.

HOG'S BACK
The road into Farnham from the east runs along this chalk ridge on the northern edge of the North Downs. There are wayside car parks along the road, with fine views across the Weald. Along the southern edge of the ridge parts of the Pilgrims' Way from Winchester to Canterbury can be traced.

Tourist information: (Farnham) Godalming 4104; Guildford 575857.

DOWNLAND AND WEALD *Wooded valleys and sandy heathland sprawl below Hydon's Ball, with views stretching northwards across the Weald to the distant North Downs.*

Villages sheltered by the North Downs

TOUR 44

——— 75 MILES ———

Looping lanes follow river valleys and climb the North Downs, passing tile-hung and timbered villages. Often these routes meet the ancient Pilgrims' Way from Winchester to Canterbury.

GUILDFORD

In the middle of a busy shopping area, the High Street, still cobbled, draws the eye down its long slope between tall Tudor, baroque and Georgian buildings. Abbot's Hospital, with its turreted gateway in glowing brick and its enclosed courtyard, was originally planned for housing 12 old men and eight widows or spinsters. The 17th-century Guildhall adds a delightful break in the façade of the street, with its hexagonal bell turret and a 17th-century clock projecting far out over the pavement.

The castle is an early 12th-century keep within gardens set into the old defensive ditch. The grounds are open daily, the keep from April to September; and a museum of local history and needlework in a cottage built into the castle outworks is open on weekdays.

There are riverside walks past the site where a pilgrims' ferry once crossed the River Wey, and in summer pleasure boats ply between the landing stage and Godalming.

CLANDON PARK

The road runs beside an alluring expanse of parkland laid out by Capability Brown, from a massive pair of ornate gates to the turn-off through West Clandon to the main entrance. Set in this rolling landscape was a large Jacobean house, which was entirely rebuilt for the Onslow family in the early 18th century by the Venetian architect Giacomo Leoni.

Beyond his impressive Palladian marble entrance hall are collections of pictures, furniture, Oriental porcelain birds, and the Museum of the Queen's Royal Surrey Regiment.

In the gardens near the house a flint and brick grotto shelters a cuddlesome trio of the Three Graces. Incongruous in this setting is a Maori house brought from New Zealand.

The park is not open to the public, but house and gardens are owned by the National Trust and are open in the afternoons from April to mid-October, except on Mondays and Fridays. A Garden Centre is open daily.

NEWLANDS CORNER

One of the loftiest viewpoints on the North Downs looks out over wooded slopes and the grounds of Albury Park towards the South Downs, with the Pilgrims' Way climbing up from the sheltered valley below. A short distance along the road is parking space for the Silent Pool. In reality there are two secluded pools, one of them especially dark and still even on the brightest day: legend has it that a peasant girl was frightened here by King John and drowned.

GREAT BOOKHAM

Although the original village has expanded into a sprawling offshoot of Leatherhead, its heart is still unspoilt and friendly, around a church with a pretty weatherboarded tower and shingled spire. Most of St Nicholas's dates from Norman times, with brasses from the 15th, 16th and 17th centuries, and a medieval rood screen which, once cut up to make pews, was later painstakingly reconstructed. The east window was blown out during the Second World War, but restored with stained glass made in the Rhineland in the 16th century.

South of the village is the Regency house of Polesden Lacey, refitted for an Edwardian hostess in 1906 on the site of the former home of the 18th-century playwright Richard Brinsley Sheridan. The terrace which, from some yards back from its edge, seems as if it must lead to a sheer drop onto the richly wooded landscape below, was planned by Sheridan himself. Statues lurk like eavesdroppers within clipped hedges, and there is an agreeably intimate, secretive atmosphere within the walled rose garden.

The house's exhibits include furniture, silver and porcelain, and photographs from Mrs Ronald Greville's Edwardian albums. King George VI and Queen Elizabeth spent part of their honeymoon here.

Polesden Lacey is owned by the National Trust. The gardens are open daily; the house is open in the afternoons from April to October, except on Mondays and Fridays; and on Saturday and Sunday afternoons in March and November.

BOX HILL

Seen from the road descending past Westhumble station, the soaring escarpment of Box Hill is an imposing canvas of light and shade, sometimes dusted by cloud shadows, darkened by clumps of the trees which give it its name. Just below its summit stands a 'pulpit' in stone, commemorating Leopold Salomons of Norbury Park who gave the property to the nation in 1914. Carved in the parapet are markers identifying distant landmarks: on a clear day there are views right across the Weald to the South Downs and Chanctonbury Ring.

CHALDON

The flinty little Church of St Peter and St Paul on its steep knoll dates mainly from the 12th and early 13th centuries, with an odd-looking tower and spire which seem to have been tacked onto the end of the south aisle as if by an afterthought. Nothing prepares one for the horrific wall painting within. Covering the west wall is a white and yellow Doom painting on a rust-coloured background. A ladder climbs to heaven, but most of the characters portrayed seem to be more interested in indulging themselves in the seven deadly sins, to the great delight of the Devil and his henchmen.

The picture was lost for centuries beneath layers of whitewash, but researchers have established that it must have been painted around the year 1200.

GODSTONE

Brick and tiled frontages, which disguise far older buildings, stand discreetly back from a wide green and village pond sheltered by lime and chestnut. Godstone was once a centre of the medieval iron industry and then of the Elizabethan leather trade, with later prosperity from some sturdy coaching inns. Bay Path leads to Bay Pond Nature Reserve around what was once an ironfounder's hammer pond, and the church set well outside the village.

LIMPSFIELD

Near the bottom of the sloping village street of timbered houses with trim little porches is St Peter's Church, which has a Norman tower and restored 14th-century lich gate. Among the gravestones are those of the composer Frederick Delius who, after many years abroad, asked that he should lie in 'a quiet country churchyard in a south of England village'.

Detillens, a hall house containing collections of orders and decorations from all over the world, is open on Saturday afternoons from May to June and also on Wednesdays from July to September and on August Bank Holiday.

WESTERHAM

One end of the triangular village green is dominated by a statue of General Wolfe, the market town's most famous son, brandishing a sword. Farther down the tapering slope sprawls a representation of Winston Churchill, whose Chartwell home lies 2 miles south. In the churchyard is buried Colonel Peter Nissen, who designed the Nissen hut, used as temporary accommodation for the armed services during the Second World War.

Squerryes Court, a late 17th-century manor house owned by the Warde family for over 250 years, has displays of Dutch paintings, china, glass, tapestries, furniture, and relics of General Wolfe. In the grounds a cenotaph marks the spot where Wolfe, a friend of the family, received his officer's commission at the age of 14. The court is open on Wednesday, Saturday and Sunday afternoons from April to September, and also on Sundays in March.

Wolfe's own home, originally Spiers but later renamed Quebec House in honour of his great victory, is open every afternoon except Thursday and Saturday from April to the end of October, and on Sunday afternoons in March.

EYNSFORD

Three historic buildings of widely separated centuries stand in the delectable valley of the shallow, winding, sparkling River Darent. A Romano-British villa is set on a terrace above what were once gardens sloping gently down to the water's edge; ruins of a Norman castle can be found just north of Eynsford Bridge; and the Tudor brickwork of Lullingstone Castle gatehouse gleams in a shaded hollow above which are the walks, bridlepaths and golf course of Lullingstone Park.

The castle and its grounds, featuring an apple orchard, are open on Saturday, Sunday and Bank Holiday afternoons from April to October. Eynsford Castle and the Roman villa are open daily.

Mosaic flooring in Lullingstone Villa was rediscovered in the 18th century, but the site was not thoroughly excavated until after the Second World War. The excavations revealed a sumptuous dwelling which, starting life as a simple wooden farmhouse, was developed

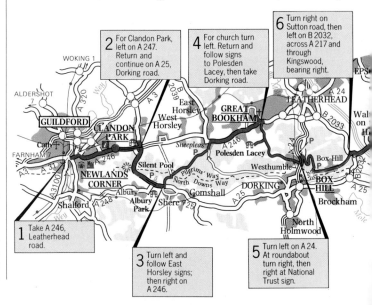

in stone and included a bath suite, a deep room with richly coloured frescoes, and a fascinating juxtaposition of pagan motifs and evidence of early Christian worship.

TROSLEY COUNTRY PARK
Of all the nature reserves and woodland spaces open to the public in this region, such as Andrews Wood, Holly Hill Wood and the Sheepleas, the most extensive and varied is Trosley Country Park. The Pilgrims' Way and North Downs Way march hand in hand across it; woods and scarps of the Downs can be explored; and along the 3½ mile Trosley Ramble are the Coldrum Stones, remains of a Neolithic burial chamber more than 4000 years old.

A visitor centre is open on Saturday, Sunday and Bank Holiday afternoons. When it is shut, there is a dispenser of waymarked walk leaflets adjacent.

AYLESFORD
The medieval bridge leading into the centre of this large village marks an important river crossing since prehistoric times. Beyond it are waterside terraces of tall houses, with gables, timber-framing and watchful windows. Stone, Bronze and Iron Age remains have been found in the neighbourhood, and on the slopes above are Kit's Coty House long barrow and the 'Countless Stones' of a tomb renamed in later years as Little Kit's Coty House. Aylesford is believed to have been the scene of the Jute invaders' first major battle, when Horsa himself was killed.

To the west is the priory of The Friars, a monastic retreat and conference centre built around a 13th-century Carmelite foundation dissolved by Henry VIII but reborn in 1949. A shrine is open daily to the weather and to visitors. The 16th-century courtyard and surrounding ranges have been preserved.

The eastward road passes Cobtree Manor Country Park and then the Museum of Kent Rural Life, open from April to mid-October.

Tourist information: Guildford 575857; Maidstone 671361.

SURREY SUMMIT *A zigzag road climbs like an Alpine pass to the 563ft summit of Box Hill, one of the best viewpoints in Surrey.*

VENERABLE TIMBERS *The Old Bell at Oxted dates from about 1500.*

HOUSE OF DISTINCTION *Squerryes Court, built in 1681, stands in a woodland setting that beautifully sets off this elegant William and Mary period manor house.*

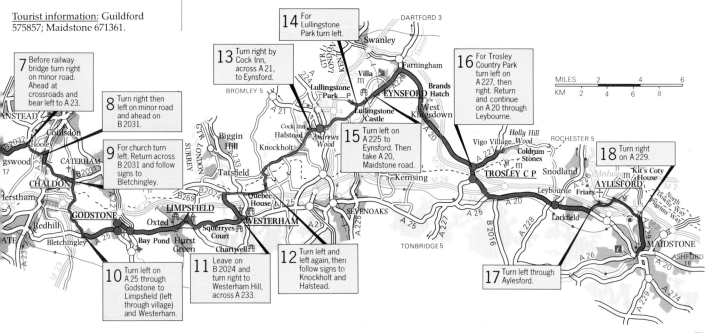

7 Before railway bridge turn right on minor road. Ahead at crossroads and bear left to A 23.

8 Turn right then left on minor road and ahead on B 2031.

9 For church turn left. Return across B 2031 and follow signs to Bletchingley.

10 Turn left on A 25 through Godstone to Limpsfield (left through village) and Westerham.

11 Leave on B 2024 and turn right to Westerham Hill, across A 233.

12 Turn left and left again, then follow signs to Knockholt and Halstead.

13 Turn right by Cock Inn, across A 21, to Eynsford.

14 For Lullingstone Park turn left.

15 Turn left on A 225 to Eynsford. Then take A 20, Maidstone road.

16 For Trosley Country Park turn left on A 227, then right. Return and continue on A 20 through Leybourne.

17 Turn left through Aylesford.

18 Turn right on A 229.

Woods and waters in the Surrey Hills

TOUR
45
59 MILES

Open downs where racehorses gallop give way to wooded hills where lanes run deep between sandstone banks. At the foot of the North Downs the Tilling Bourne links a string of villages.

EPSOM

From the end of Epsom's busy High Street there is an easy escape down West Street and West Hill to the calm oasis of Stamford Green, where a clapboarded pub beside a duck pond faces a wide village green. Beyond the green lies Epsom Common, a wide expanse of gorse, birch and hawthorn surprisingly close to the town centre, with the flint-walled Christ Church half hidden in trees at its edge.

Paths wind across Epsom Common to The Wells, a housing estate arranged in concentric rings around the railed-off enclosure that protects Epsom's original well. A plaque identifies the source of 'the medicinal waters that in the 17th century made Epsom a place of great resort and its name known throughout Europe'.

There are a few traces of Epsom's heyday as a spa town in the handsome brick upper storeys of some buildings in the High Street, where visitors as celebrated as Samuel Pepys, Charles II and Nell Gwyn once stayed. Alleys between the buildings lead to Epsom's roofed-over modern shopping centre, all dark red brick outside and marble, glass and rubber plants within.

The popularity of Epsom's wells declined after 1727 as the bitter waters began to run dry. But by then the town's visitors had discovered the more enduring delights of horseracing, and so the focus of Epsom life moved to the Downs. As the route heads south from Epsom, the huge Grandstand overlooking the Derby course gleams on the horizon like a pink-iced wedding cake.

HEADLEY

Drivers stopping at the Cock Inn share the car park with horses at their lunch-time nosebags. If Epsom Downs have been left behind this is still prime riding country, where four wheels should give way to four legs on the narrow roads.

St Mary's Church dates only from the 1850s, but its walls of knapped flint and its shingled spire give it a sturdy and well-established appearance. The Faithfull family vault, in the churchyard near the porch, was built from the rubble of an older church.

Headley Heath, just to the south, is a wide expanse of National Trust land on the gentle northern slope of the North Downs. There are footpaths and riding tracks across the heathland and up and down the chalk hillsides among birches, oaks and rowans; and there are picnic areas beside the information caravan and by the ancient Brimmer Pond, near the car park half a mile farther south.

BROCKHAM

Hiding its treasures until the last moment, the sloping village suddenly reveals itself as the road sweeps over a narrow bridge and round a bend. Park near the church at the top of the wide triangular green for the best view of the village, spread out like a stage set against the backdrop of the wooded North Downs.

Comfortably disposed around the green are two pubs and a wealth of attractive houses – several with tile-hung upper storeys beneath half-timbered gables, others black and white or colour-washed. Beside the village pump an ornamental sign commemorates an obviously well-merited 'best-kept village' award.

The church, in white stone, is Victorian, with a striking wood carving of the Last Supper behind the altar. Beyond it, on the road south, is a pond.

At Highridge Wood, 2 miles south on the Holmwood road, walks radiate from a car park along avenues of fir trees crisscrossed by grassy rides. Holmwood Common, a little farther on, offers the bonus of a large pond by the roadside, from which riders set off in single file along a network of bridleways.

OCKLEY

The huge village green sloping away from the main road is large enough to swallow up, almost unnoticed, a duck pond and a soccer pitch. On the green in AD 851 two armies found room to fight a pitched battle, in which a force of marauding Danes took a mauling from King Ethelwulf's West Saxons.

A well is covered by a roof on pillars and surrounded by seats, and along the lower end of the green are some attractive cottages with steep half-timbered gables projecting at all angles. Ockley's Church of St Margaret, beside a rambling farm, is passed on the way to the village.

LEITH HILL

A turret on the skyline, visible from Ockley, leads the eye towards the summit of Leith Hill. The road snakes up the wooded slopes to a large car park near the crest of the hill, from which an easy half-mile walk up a sandy track leads to the 64ft high Leith Hill Tower in its grassy summit clearing.

The tower is a folly, built in 1766 by a local landowner, Richard Hull of Leith Hill Place, to increase the hill's natural height of 965ft – the highest point in south-east England – to just over the more satisfying 1000ft. From the top of the tower avid observers armed with a map can, on a clear day, play the game of counting the counties visible: 13 are claimed.

WHERE FURNACES ROARED *Friday Street's hammer pond powered bellows and forge hammers during the 17th century, when the Surrey Weald was a centre of the iron industry.*

FRIDAY STREET

A dark lake at the foot of a pine-clad hillside ... a cluster of old cottages beside the bridge ... a single pub beyond which footpaths lead off into the surrounding woodlands. Friday Street is today a place of great stillness, where visitors instinctively find themselves talking more quietly. It helps that cars are banished to a car park outside the hamlet, from which a railed path, starting high above the road, drops 170yds down to the lake.

The hamlet's unusual name is derived from the Scandinavian goddess Frig, perhaps once honoured by a shrine beside the stream which flows down through a green valley to join the Tilling Bourne. The spot has not always been so peaceful: in the late 17th century the descending stream powered the tilt-hammer of a forge, when the surrounding woodlands echoed to the clangour of iron foundries. A forge at Abinger Hammer was in operation until the late 18th century.

ABINGER COMMON

Malefactors in 18th-century Abinger Common must have been numerous, for the stocks on the village green have holes for no fewer than three pairs of legs. The small green is overlooked on one side by an inn dating from the 17th century and on the other by the parish church.

As befits a church standing near the old Pilgrims' Way from Winchester to Canterbury, this one is dedicated to St James, patron saint of pilgrims. It dates back to the 12th century but was severely damaged by a flying bomb in 1944. Modern restoration has created a spacious interior, chancel and north chapel being joined in a single stone-flagged space and lit by an east window of richly coloured modern stained glass.

Beside the church a path leads down past the grounds of Abinger Manor; the huge mound on the left of the path is a motte built around 1100 as a lookout tower to help defend the manor. After about 50yds the path emerges from the trees beside a field gate, from which there is a glorious view across the broad Tilling Bourne valley towards the North Downs.

Over the slight rise in the field to the left, a corrugated iron hut covers a remarkable prehistoric find – the remains of a pit-dwelling occupied in about 4000 BC and believed by Dr Louis Leakey, who excavated it in 1950, to be the oldest man-made dwelling found in Britain.

The key to the hut can be obtained from the manor, but a large window gives an ample view of the pit dug by Stone Age man into the sandy clay soil, now chemically hardened to preserve it just as Dr Leakey found it. Around the pit are the holes for posts which once supported some sort of roof of skins or bracken, and cabinets displaying the flint axes, scrapers and arrowheads found on the site.

SHERE

The main road which runs through Tilling Bourne villages such as Abinger Hammer and Gomshall happily bypasses Shere and leaves its

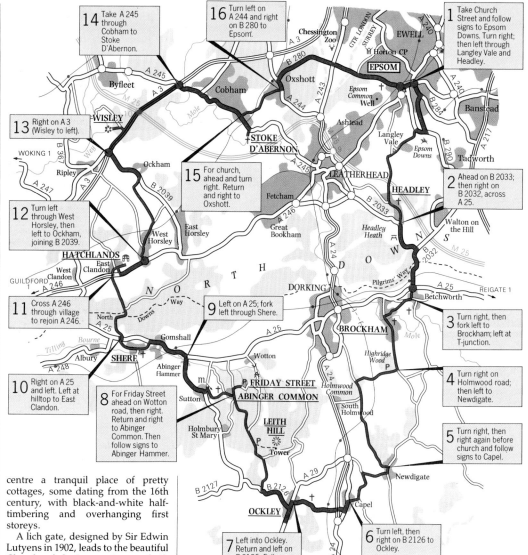

centre a tranquil place of pretty cottages, some dating from the 16th century, with black-and-white half-timbering and overhanging first storeys.

A lich gate, designed by Sir Edwin Lutyens in 1902, leads to the beautiful Church of St James. It was built mainly around 1190 and has the characteristic pointed arches of the Early English style; its Norman tower is topped by a broach spire of cedar-wood shingles. Apart from its fine structure, the church has another claim to fame in the curious tale of the anchoress Christine Carpenter, who in 1329 had herself walled up in a cell built onto the north wall of the chancel. Still visible inside the church are the squint window through which she could see the altar and the quatrefoil through which she received the bread and wine of communion.

HATCHLANDS

The mellow red-brick façade of Hatchlands glows warmly among the trees as the approach drive sweeps past a lake and across the parkland towards it. The house was built in the 1750s by Admiral Edward Boscawen, from the prize money he gained by naval actions against the French in the Seven Years' War, as recounted in one room of the house.

The Scottish architect Robert Adam designed much of the interior, including some fine ceilings and chimneypieces, but redecoration and furnishing by a later owner, Lord Rendel, today gives the house an Edwardian feeling. A monument to

Lord Rendel stands in the flint-walled St Thomas's Church, in the village of East Clandon outside the gates.

Hatchlands is owned by the National Trust and open on Wednesday, Thursday and Sunday afternoons in summer.

WISLEY

One spot the amateur gardener would not select to create his ideal garden is on thin, sandy soil where the climate is generally dry and what rain does fall drains swiftly away. Yet it is on just such a site that the Royal Horticultural Society has created one of England's best known gardens.

For the gardening enthusiast Wisley offers the fruits of decades of experimental horticulture in demonstrating what plants grow best in particular situations – shady corner, rocky bank or town-house plot – and how to provide colour at all seasons. Non-gardeners can simply let themselves be dazzled by the sheer prodigality of the display, which ranges from low banks of heather to lofty oaks and dawn redwoods, and from the luxuriance of massed banks of

rhododendrons and azaleas to the simple pleasures of a wild alpine garden where daffodils, wood anemones and spotted orchids blow. The gardens are open daily; members only are admitted on Sunday mornings.

STOKE D'ABERNON

In its brass of Sir John D'Abernon, dating from 1277, St Mary's Church possesses the oldest monumental brass in England. The life-size effigy of the knight, clad in chain mail, with a 6ft lance at his side and blue enamel still clinging to his shield, lies on the floor of the chancel; his son, the second Sir John, lies close by.

The flint-walled church is reached by a signposted drive through the grounds of Parkside School. Its south wall dates from the 7th century, and incorporates bricks from a Roman villa which once stood on the site of the adjoining manor house. The fireplace in the chantry may date from the chapel's use in Tudor times as the village schoolroom.

Tourist information: Guildford 575857.

Villages of the South Downs and Weald

TOUR

48

—— 75 MILES ——

Lanes wind inland to villages half hidden in the folds of the South Downs and the Weald. Legends hang about their settlement, and ruined castles testify to their place in history.

WORTHING

A 5 mile seafront draws the summer visitors, but Worthing has out-of-season attractions as well. A geological display in the town's museum lays bare the underlying structure of a gigantic slice through Sussex, from its golden beaches through the Downs to the Weald. The museum also identifies the area's animals and plants, while paintings and old postcards show the development of Worthing as a resort over the centuries.

Another of Worthing's surprises is its 'village within a town' of Tarring. Although surrounded by the houses of Worthing itself and Goring, Tarring retains the air of a country village, with a pub, a village store and a little church. Two 15th-century timber-framed buildings known as Parson's Row stand in Tarring High Street.

HIGHDOWN TOWER

Cut into a bluff of the South Downs, the terraced chalk garden at Highdown Tower gives broad views along the coast from the Isle of Wight, 30 miles west, to beyond Brighton in the east. The gardens, the property of Worthing, also include a rose garden and a tree and shrub garden.

A footpath from the car park leads over the open Downs to the hill-fort on Highdown Hill, affording fine views over Worthing and the sea.

POLING

At the end of a mile-long cul-de-sac lies one of the most isolated of all Sussex villages. The road stops at St Nicholas's Church and beyond there are only footpaths that lead across the fields to Preston and Lyminster.

Stone from Caen in France and the Isle of Wight, Purbeck marble and local Sussex chalk have all gone into the present church, which dates from the 12th century. In the north wall is a window from the original Saxon building.

ARUNDEL

Stark against the skyline, the battlements and towers of the medieval castle and the soaring nave roof of the modern Roman Catholic cathedral dominate the little town of Arundel. The castle, seat of the Dukes of Norfolk, was founded in Norman times to guard a strategic gap through the Downs. It was held for the king in the Civil War, but surrendered to besiegers in 1644 when the water supply became tainted. After this it

was almost completely destroyed, and not rebuilt until the 19th century. A reconstruction of the siege is on show in the Museum and Heritage Centre in the High Street.

Also in the High Street is Potter's Museum of Curiosities, which has a collection of Victorian tableaux of small stuffed animals at work and play. Guinea pigs play cricket, squirrels duel, and mice and rabbits learn their lessons in school. In the Toy and Military Museum nearby are displayed toys, medals and military relics ranging over the centuries, right up to the Falklands War.

A mile north of Arundel Castle is the Arundel Wildfowl Reserve. More than 80 species of birds have been recorded here, and a network of walkways and hides provide opportunities for the birdwatcher and photographer. Across the road lies Swanbourne Lake, around which runs a 2 mile footpath; another footpath leads from the northern tip of the lake to Houghton and Amberley. The narrow road beyond the wildfowl reserve ends at the quiet villages of Offham and South Stoke, by the River Arun.

AMBERLEY

The past of the Sussex countryside comes alive in the open-air Amberley Chalk Pits Museum, approached through the forecourt of Amberley station. Here are a blacksmith's forge, a pottery, a woodturner's shop, a boat-builder, early traction engines

and narrow-gauge railway locomotives. A nature walk leads through woods which are a haunt of the chalkhill blue and other butterflies.

In Amberley, 1 mile north, is a craft centre where visitors can watch potters and weavers at work, and corn dollies being made.

PARHAM

A winding drive through a deer park leads to a stately Elizabethan house of grey stone, which combines historical magnificence with a feeling of homely domesticity. The beautifully proportioned rooms contain a collection of portraits from the 16th century onwards, including works by Romney and Lely, many fine pieces of Jacobean furniture and much lovely embroidery.

The grounds include a walled garden of about 4 acres set in a deer park, from which there are fine views to the Downs a mile to the south and across the Arun valley to the west. The house and gardens are open on

Sunday, Bank Holiday, Wednesday and Thursday afternoons from Easter to early October.

Just south of the house, and within its park, is the little Church of St Peter, all that remains of the village of Parham. In the late 18th century the village was regarded as a possible source of infection – as well as spoiling the view for the squire – so it was pulled down and its people were rehoused in the village of Rackham, a mile to the west.

The church has high box pews, and the squire's pew occupying the whole north transept has its own open fireplace. It is said that if the squire took exception to the length of the sermon, he would signify his displeasure by noisily shovelling coal on the fire.

SHIPLEY

For more than 40 years this tiny, isolated village was the home of Hilaire Belloc, the poet, essayist and historian. In the grounds of King's Land, Belloc's home, is King's Mill, the only working smock mill in West Sussex; it can be visited on the first weekend of each month from May to October, and on Bank Holidays. The

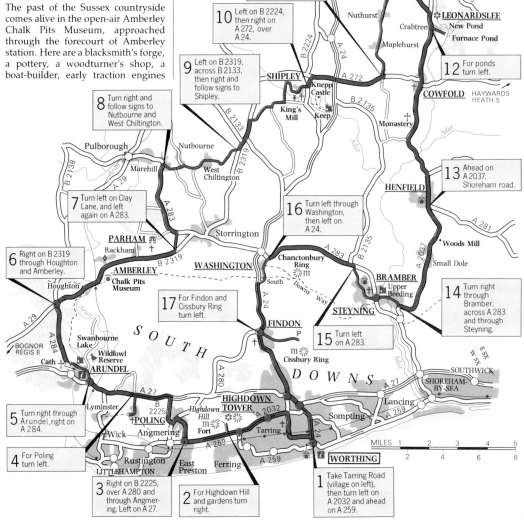

mill contains an exhibition of the life and work of Hilaire Belloc, who loved Sussex. It is said that Belloc bribed porters at Horsham station to call out 'Horse-ham, Horse-ham' to retain the old Sussex pronunciation, which puts equal stress on each syllable of a name.

North of the Church of St Mary the Virgin, a footpath leads eastwards through the woods and the grounds of Knepp Castle. The path leads past Kneppmill Pond – whose waters once drove iron-smelting hammers – to the forlorn remains of an old Norman keep alongside the Worthing road. Another footpath leads from the southern end of the pond through Pound Farm back to the village.

LEONARDSLEE
The landscaped gardens beside a chain of stream-fed hammer-ponds are noted for their early summer blaze of rhododendrons, azaleas, magnolias and camellias. Lilies of the valley grow wild in woods of oak, birch and beech, and there is a second blaze of colour in autumn from the leaves of Japanese maples, liquidambars and a 112ft high tulip tree. The gardens are open daily from mid-April to mid-June, and at weekends from late June to the end of October.

At Crabtree, half a mile beyond Leonardslee, is a turning to the left called Mill Lane. Where this road bends right, by an isolated cottage on the left, a bridleway through the woods leads to Furnace Pond and New Pond, two more typical Sussex hammer-ponds.

COWFOLD
A crossroads divides this compact village. The Church of St Peter, tucked away in the south-western quarter, dates from the 13th century, and has some fine stained glass and one of the largest brasses in the country, a 10ft 1in figure of Prior Thomas Nelond, who died in 1429.

In the uprights of the churchyard fence are carved the names of free-holders of the village who in the 17th century set up boundary markers to indicate the extent of their individual holdings; under the lich gate is a plan of these boundary marks. The 13th-century St Peter's Cottage, outside the churchyard, is now a restaurant.

Just over 1 mile south of Cowfold, the 200ft spire of the Carthusian Monastery of St Hugh soars above the trees that conceal the building from the road. One of the first monasteries to be founded in Britain after their dissolution in the 16th century, it was begun in 1876 and consecrated seven years later. It is the only Carthusian monastery in Britain.

HENFIELD
This large, rambling village has one of the most varied museums in the county. Housed in the village hall, it has been stocked entirely by local residents, and boasts amongst other oddities an 'ambulance' – more like a stretcher on wheels – which was last used in 1932, relics of the Beeching-axed railway, and natural history exhibits such as a woodpecker's nest and a wasps' nest. There are bright

BELOW THE RAMPARTS *Undulating fields and the village of Findon lie in a gentle valley to the west of the Cissbury Ring hill-fort.*

PROUD PARHAM *Tall mullioned windows grace the house built in 1577 by Sir Thomas Palmer, a Freeman of the Mercers' Company.*

military uniforms made by a local tailor, and a comprehensive collection of farm implements. Roland Emett, creator of the eccentric Emett trains, lived in the village and was inspired by the local line.

Woods Mill, 1 mile south of Henfield, is a restored 18th-century water mill with a nature trail where many local varieties of plants are labelled for the visitor.

BRAMBER
The village huddles beneath the 76ft high ruined wall of its Norman castle. At the time of the Norman Conquest, both Bramber and Steyning belonged to the Abbey of Fecamp in France. To break the monks' monopoly, William granted Bramber to William de Braose, who built the castle and a Benedictine college. It was de Braose also who built Knepp Castle near Shipley.

The House of Pipes displays pipes of all kinds, samples of tobaccos, old cigarette machines, and cigarette cards from the 1920s and 1930s. There are also 40,000 other items covering many fields of bygones.

STEYNING
A late-19th-century traveller recorded that when passing through Steyning (pronounced 'Stenning') he saw a

signwriter working on the first letter of his sign. When the traveller passed again, five weeks later, the same signwriter was working on the second letter. The tale is belied by present-day Steyning, which is a lively, go-ahead community.

The story goes that the earliest church in Steyning was founded by St Cuthman in the 8th century. When his father died, Cuthman fashioned a wheelbarrow in which he conveyed his aged mother to find a new home near the village. Some haymakers laughed at this rude conveyance, but Cuthman brought upon them the wrath of God by calling up a violent storm of rain, which ruined their hay. While he was building his first church, a traveller gave him help with the roof, and when Cuthman asked the stranger's name, he replied 'I am He in whose name you are building this church', and vanished from sight.

The history of the village can be traced in a series of coloured maps, drawings and old photographs in the museum in the High Street.

WASHINGTON
The village is most famous for the natural landmark that towers above it. Opposite the Frankland Arms, to the north of Washington, a footpath leads by a stiff 1½ mile climb up to

Chanctonbury Ring. This circular stand of beech trees on top of the Downs, planted in 1760 in an oval prehistoric earthwork, is visible from Crowborough Beacon, 25 miles away to the east, and from Box Hill, as far to the north.

To the east of the village is Wiston Park and its mansion, once the home of Sir Charles Goring who planted the trees on Chanctonbury when he was a boy. The house is now a conference centre.

FINDON
A 17th-century inn and 18th-century houses form the heart of Findon, clustering round a square just east of the main Worthing road. The church, separated from the rest of the village by the main road, is of Saxon foundation, but has traces of all styles from Norman times onwards. It is built of flint and contains a rare 13th-century oak screen.

From the square, Nepcote Lane runs eastwards to the Iron Age hill-fort of Cissbury Ring; one of the best preserved of the South Downs hill-forts. There are fine views over Worthing to the sea, and northwards to Chanctonbury Ring.

Tourist information: Worthing 210022; Arundel 882268.

Green ways through the forest of iron

The boundaries between West and East Sussex, Kent and Surrey snake invisibly along leafy lanes and across quiet pasture and wooded parkland. Each village has its individual charm.

EAST GRINSTEAD

The name of the town comes from the Saxon Greenstede, a green clearing in what was once the great Wealden forest. The most inviting feature of today's wide High Street is a stepped terrace on the south side, graced by lime trees and pleasant modern shops with upper storeys of weatherboarding, half-timbering and an appealing unevenness of gables and rooftops. Parts of Sackville College, a superb group of almshouses, are open on summer afternoons, except Saturdays.

STANDEN

This country house, built in 1891-4 around a medieval house, was designed by Philip Webb as a weekend home for a wealthy London solicitor. Webb's friend, William Morris, designed the textiles and wallpapers, many of which survive, while others have been lovingly restored from the original patterns. The terraced garden and lawns offer a fine panorama of the Weald and glimpses of shimmering Weir Wood Reservoir. The house, owned by the National Trust, is open most afternoons in summer.

BURSTOW

In this sprawling parish the secluded Church of St Bartholomew is a marvel – lonely and embowered by trees. The unusual, three-stage tower is all of timber, with a broad base of rough elm planking, a shingled square tower and, to top it all, a cedarwood shingled spire. The massive supporting posts and beams are more than 500 years old.

The east window, depicting the Magi and the star in the east, is a memorial to John Flamsteed, rector from 1684 until his death in 1719, but better known as the first Astronomer Royal.

OUTWOOD

The great black-and-white post mill at Outwood, built in 1665, is now the oldest working windmill in England.

The mighty body and sails are reproduced in miniature in the village sign on the green.

There is ample parking and picnic space by stretches of Outwood Common, cared for by the National Trust.

HAXTED MILL MUSEUM

The western section of the double-fronted water mill was built around 1580 and added to in 1794. It ground corn for flour until the end of the First World War, and continued grinding meal for local farmers until 1945. Now it is kept as a museum with working models of mill machinery.

The museum is open on Saturdays, Sundays and Bank Holidays from Easter to September, and on Monday to Thursday afternoons from July to September.

EDENBRIDGE

Since Roman times there has been a bridge at this point over the River Eden, a tributary of the Medway, and quantities of Romano-British pottery were unearthed about a mile west of the town in 1912.

The 14th-century Crown Inn, with its 'gallows' sign spanning the main street, brought the town into ill repute in the 17th century when it became a haunt of the ruthless Romney gang of smugglers.

HAMMERWOOD PARK

Benjamin Latrobe, architect of the Capitol in Washington, designed this house before he emigrated to America in 1796. In summer, it is the palatial setting for concerts and cavalcades.

The collection of costumes and displays of musical instruments and domestic items can be seen by visitors on Wednesdays, Saturdays, Sundays and Bank Holidays, from Easter to September, and also on Thursdays in August.

Ashdown Forest offers expanses of heath with gaunt sentinels of Scots pine. Names like Forge Lane and Hammerwood recall the clangour of the thriving iron industry of the 17th century.

UCKFIELD

Once an iron-working centre, Uckfield lives on as a market town and shopping centre. Its steep main street has some dignified timber-framed buildings and the fine bow-windowed frontage of a Georgian hotel, the Maiden's Head.

Four miles north, beyond Fairwarp, is the vineyard of Barnsgate Manor, one of the largest in England. For conducted tours of the vineyard and wine-tasting, an appointment is essential (Nutley 2854).

KING'S STANDING

A dark clump of trees crowns King's Standing, one of the finest vantage points in Ashdown Forest. It is supposedly named after Edward II,

BRIGHTON LINE *Near Balcombe, the 37 elegant arches of a viaduct carry the London to Brighton line across the Ouse valley.*

VETERAN WORKER *Outwood's mill is more than 300 years old.*

SACKVILLE COLLEGE *The almshouses at East Grinstead were founded in 1609 by Robert Sackville, Earl of Dorset, for his retired servants: 21 men and ten women.*

who stood here to shoot deer driven towards him from the surrounding woodlands. Grassy slopes offer ideal picnic places, and in every direction there are vistas over moorland and coppice. Ten ancient packhorse tracks have been identified as converging at this spot.

HARTFIELD
On the approach to Hartfield the tour enters Winnie the Pooh country. The writer A.A. Milne created the famous bear and his friends when he was living south of the village at Catchford Farm. A footpath through Posingford Wood crosses the bridge which was the setting for the game of 'Poohsticks'.

The name Hartfield recalls the days of deer-hunting in the forest. On a sunny day, the local white weatherboarding can be dazzling; it is offset, from spring to autumn, by the multi-coloured glow of tiny gardens, public flowerbeds and hanging baskets.

FOREST ROW
From the car park beside the Foresters' Arms Hotel, a short walk across the green leads to the Forest Way Country Park, a 9½ mile stretch of disused railway line linking East Grinstead and Groombridge. It is now a sheltered path and cycle track where wild flowers flourish.

SPRING HILL WILDFOWL PARK
This wildfowl collection was begun in the early 1970s beside the 15th-century Spring Hill Farmhouse. Springs or brooks provided the present lakes for cranes, flamingos, geese, swans and ducks – in all, nearly 1000 birds from about 100 species.

BLUEBELL RAILWAY
The smell of smoke and steam and the whistle of an engine often issue from the dense woodlands between the village of Horsted Keynes and the great acres of Sheffield Park. The Bluebell Railway, running limited services off-season, does a brisk daily trade in summer along the 5 mile line, which was saved from extinction in 1960. At Horsted Keynes station there is a large picnic site; at Sheffield Park a station is maintained in the original style of the London to Brighton and South Coast Railway, and is home to a collection of veteran locomotives and rolling stock equalled only by the National Railway Museum in York.

WEST HOATHLY
This drowsy little village hides its charms down secretive lanes which converge on the central group of inn, tile-hung houses, timber and plaster and rust-tinted stone cottages, dominated by the tall shingled spire of the buttressed church tower.

The Priest House, a 15th-century estate office, administered the local property of the Priory of St Pancras in Lewes. It is a sturdily timbered house roofed with heavy Horsham stone slabs, and is now a museum of local life with displays of embroidery, tapestries, costume dolls, old craftsmen's tools and clothing, and many domestic items. It is open daily from April to October.

WAKEHURST PLACE GARDENS
Lakes originating from the hammerponds of the old ironworkers reflect the varied shades of bluebells, trees and shrubs in the gardens of this spacious estate. There are numerous walks – one of them running through impressive rock formations and outcrops of grossly misshapen tree roots. Another leads through a valley where a stream runs through a ravine.

The gardens, which were laid out early this century, are owned by the National Trust and administered by the Royal Botanic Gardens as a country annexe to Kew. They are open daily all the year.

BORDE HILL GARDEN
The garden and woodland walks around the graceful manor house display magnolias, azaleas and a selection of rare trees and shrubs. The scene is most colourful in late spring and early summer. The garden, which has a picnic site, is open most days in summer, and at weekends in March and October.

DITCHLING
Away from the centre of the village, narrow back lanes reveal many fine old buildings. They include the demure, red-brick, little Old Meeting House of 17th-century dissenters, the weatherboarded Candles, which was once a candlemaker's workshop, and in High Street the red-brick house where the sculptor and typographer Eric Gill worked for several years.

Below the church stands an exuberant tangle of brick, timber and plaster. This is Wings Place – better known as Anne of Cleves' House because its site was given by Henry VIII to his fourth wife in her divorce settlement.

SHEFFIELD PARK GARDEN
In spring, bright rhododendrons and azaleas fringe lakes laid out by Capability Brown in the late 18th century and altered and enlarged this century. Autumn brings a vivid display of golden foliage.

Now the garden belongs to the National Trust, while the house remains privately owned. The garden is open on weekdays – except Mondays – from April to mid-November, and on Sunday and Bank Holiday afternoons.

FLETCHING
One of the most appealing villages in East Sussex is graced by one of its loveliest churches. Here in May 1264 Simon de Montfort and his troops kept vigil the night before they defeated Henry III at the Battle of Lewes, and some knights killed in combat are said to lie buried in full armour below the nave.

Tourist information: Tunbridge Wells 40766/26121.

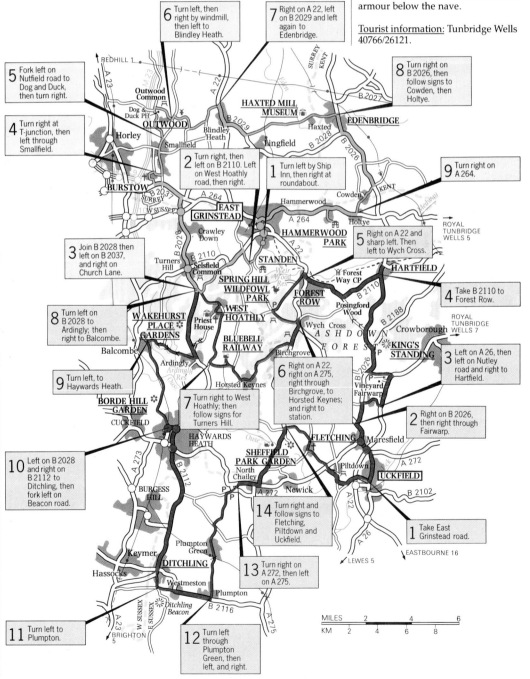

87

Cliff colossus of the downland trail

TOUR
51
—— 65 MILES ——

The beaches of a busy seaside resort shelter behind a broad sweep of the South Downs. Inland, old towns and a moated castle guard the strategic routes through the hills.

EASTBOURNE
The centrepiece of Eastbourne's fine seafront is the cheerful blue-and-white pier, backed to landward by brilliantly planted flowerbeds. Nearby is the Wish Tower, a Martello tower now housing a museum devoted to Napoleon's invasion threats.

The development of Eastbourne as a resort began in about 1850. The original East Bourne, a mile or so inland, consists of a few streets of old houses around the medieval parish church. The Towner Art Gallery was once the manor house.

PEVENSEY
In 1066 William the Conqueror came ashore with his Norman army somewhere near Pevensey – then on the coast but now a mile inland. The village is dominated by the mighty walls of Pevensey Castle, one of the Roman 'forts of the Saxon Shore'. It was built towards the end of the 4th century to guard against Saxon raiders, and the original walls still stand.

Near the castle are the magnificent half-timbered Mint House, built in the 14th century and now an antiques shop; St Nicolas's Church used in the 17th century for storing smuggled brandy; and the white-painted court house and jail, now a small museum.

The Roman fort is always open. The Norman castle and the court house are open daily in summer.

HERSTMONCEUX CASTLE
On the journey north across the pastureland of Pevensey Levels, a silver dome appears glinting in the distance. This signals the approach to the Royal Greenwich Observatory, which in 1957 moved from London to the less-polluted atmosphere of Sussex. The observatory is run from Herstmonceux Castle, a palatial, moated building of brick, which was built in the 1440s by Sir Roger de Fiennes, a veteran of Agincourt.

Two exhibition rooms display the current state of astronomy, and an astronomer is usually present on weekday afternoons to answer visitors' questions. Also on view is the observatory's 26in telescope, housed in one of the smaller green domes.

ABBOT'S WOOD
The wood is part of Wilmington Forest, itself a fragment of the vast Saxon Andredeswald (shortened to Weald), which once covered much of south-eastern England. It is now owned by the Forestry Commission, who have laid out forest walks.

MICHELHAM PRIORY
Above Michelham's 14th-century stone gatehouse flutters a brilliant banner displaying a red eagle on a gold ground – the arms of Gilbert de Aquila, Lord of Pevensey, who founded the priory in 1229. The monks made a moat from the River Cuckmere, and the tranquil scene of water, grass and ancient stones is a favourite with artists. Though the church and cloister have vanished, parts of the buildings survive.

Near the entrance, the monks' water mill has been restored and grinds flour, which is on sale. The mill also contains displays of milling and millwrights' implements. Michelham Priory is open daily in summer.

BENTLEY
A myna bird says 'Hello!' to greet visitors to Bentley, where a wildfowl reserve has more than 1300 birds, of 114 species, in pens around a chain of pools. There are three walks taking about 30, 60 and 90 minutes.

The motor museum has a constantly changing loan collection, with vehicles of all ages and types, from Rolls-Royces to tricycles, nearly all in perfect working order. Bentley House, surrounded by superb formal gardens, is an old farmhouse with modern 'pavilions' added at either end in the 1960s. One of the pavilions is a gallery devoted to bird paintings by Philip Rickman.

The wildfowl reserve and motor museum are open daily in summer, and at weekends in winter, except December. The house is open only in the afternoons.

GLYNDE PLACE
The pretty brick-and-flint village of Glynde straggles down the steep hill below Glynde Place and the odd little 18th-century classical church beside it. Built in the 16th century on the site of a medieval house, Glynde Place is a magnificent country mansion, with flint walls and stone-mullioned windows. Though Elizabethan on the outside, it has a largely Georgian interior, with some fine 18th-century portraits. Glynde Place is open on Wednesday and Thursday afternoons from June to September, and on Bank Holidays.

FIRLE PLACE
This imposing mansion seems to crouch below the escarpment of the South Downs. From the outside it looks an 18th-century building, but it is in fact an Elizabethan courtyard house, built in the 16th century by a member of the Gage family, who still own it. The house is open on Sunday, Wednesday and Thursday afternoons from June to September, on Thursday afternoons in August, and on Bank Holidays.

Overlooking Firle Place is Firle Beacon, at 713ft the highest point of this stretch of the Downs. On fine days it gives breathtaking views

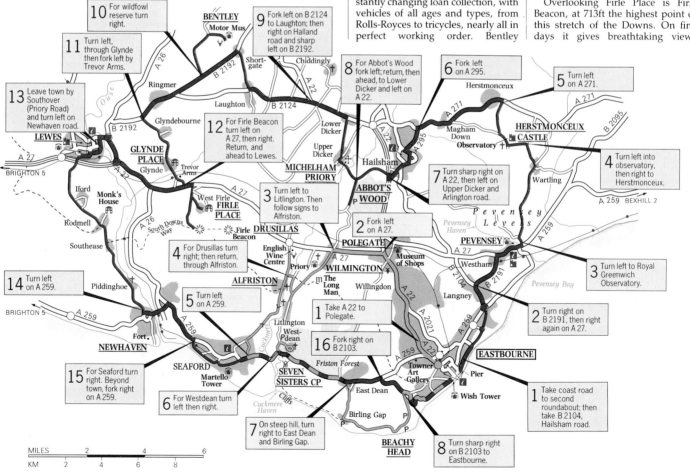

WINDING WATERS *Below Exceat the Cuckmere meanders towards Cuckmere Haven, where wildfowl seek winter refuge, migrating birds rest and flowers bloom in summer.*

southwards across Newhaven to the sea, and northwards over the rich farmland of the Weald.

LEWES
The county town of East Sussex has been an important place since Saxon times, commanding the gap where the Ouse meanders through the Downs. The Normans built a mighty castle here. Part of it still stands and is reached through an imposing barbican.

Lewes is crammed with fine buildings of all periods. The High Street has some of the best of them, and it is well worth exploring steep little streets, such as Church Twitten, which run down to Southover.

The castle is open on weekdays all the year and on Sundays in summer. Lewes also has the Military Heritage Museum, open from Monday to Friday; the Barbican House Museum, open the same times as the castle, and Anne of Cleves's House and Museum in Southover, open on weekdays from February to November, and on Sunday afternoons from April to October.

Farther down the Ouse valley is the village of Rodmell, where the novelist Virginia Woolf lived at Monk's House, now a National Trust property open on Wednesday and Saturday afternoons in summer.

NEWHAVEN
In this small cross-Channel port is the recently restored Fort Newhaven, on the heights overlooking the harbour. The fort was one of a chain built during the French war scare in the 1860s. It is now a leisure centre, with an underground museum, craft shops and picnic areas.

TOUR
52
—— 25 MILES ——
A tall windmill and downland giant point the way to a vineyard, a cool forest and a cliff-top country park. Beyond, the high bastion of Beachy Head towers above the English Channel.

POLEGATE
Though linked to Eastbourne, Polegate still has a separate character. Its restored smock windmill is open on Sunday afternoons in summer, on Wednesdays in August, and on Bank Holidays. The Museum of Shops is a delightful shopping display in the High Street, open daily in summer.

WILMINGTON
On the green slopes of the Downs above this pretty Sussex village, the giant outline of a man cut in the chalk stands out in brilliant white. The Long Man, as he is known, grasps a staff 226ft long in either hand. Of all the chalk-hill figures in England, he is perhaps the most enigmatic. Theories abound as to his age, purpose and creators. He may represent a pagan god, a saxon cult figure or even a medieval pilgrim. Roman coins found nearby and bearing a similar figure suggest a possible Roman origin.

At the southern edge of the village are the remains of a priory founded soon after the Conquest. It has a small museum of farming implements from old-time Sussex, open from mid-March to mid-October on weekdays,

except Tuesdays. The church used by the Benedictine monks is now the parish church.

DRUSILLAS
A small zoo, butterfly house, miniature railway, and playground are among the attractions on this converted farm near Alfriston. The zoo includes a nocturnal area with animals such as bush babies that only move at night in the wild.

Adjoining Drusillas is the English Wine Centre, with its own vineyard, where many English wines can be sampled. An English wine festival is held there every September.

ALFRISTON
The busy main street is crammed with tearooms and antiques shops. The large church with a massive central tower, stands by a broad green and beside it is the half-timbered Old Clergy House – the first building to belong to the National Trust, which bought it in 1896 for £10. It is open daily in summer.

St Andrew's Church dates from the 14th century and is known as the 'Cathedral of the Downs'. Its stonework of small flints is unusual in Sussex.

Beyond Alfriston lies Friston Forest covering almost 2000 acres of chalk downland, a wonderful oasis of shade on a hot day. There is a waymarked walk of 2¾ miles, and other paths crisscross the forest. At its heart is the tiny hamlet of Westdean, with a fine old church, and a pond complete with geese. At the northern edge of the forest is Charleston Manor, whose beautiful gardens are open daily from April to October.

SEVEN SISTERS COUNTRY PARK
The Seven Sisters cliffs form a superb chalk rampart that runs from the mouth of the Cuckmere to Birling Gap. A path leads from the Exceat car park along the meandering river to its mouth and the beach below the Sisters. There are two marked trails, 3 and 1½ miles long, through the park.

On the north side of the road a cluster of fine 18th-century barns has been turned into a visitor centre, with a 'Living World' exhibition of natural history, open daily.

BEACHY HEAD
From Birling Gap, once used by smugglers landing their contraband, the road sweeps up through downland to the mighty chalk bastion of Beachy Head, more than 500ft high. The Normans called it *Beau Chef*, 'beautiful headland', and it still deserves the name. The views on a clear day extend to the Isle of Wight in the west and to Dungeness in the east. Below the sheer cliff pounding waves send up fountains of wind-driven spume, and the red-banded lighthouse off the shore looks like a toy, though its powerful beam penetrates 16 miles out to sea.

Between the road and the cliff edge there are enough acres of grassland and hidden dells to absorb the largest summer crowds. Sea birds wheel in dizzying circles above the stony foreshore far below. A small natural history centre is open in the afternoons on summer weekends.

Tourist information: Eastbourne 27474/21333; Lewes 471600; Hailsham 840604.

Manors in the Garden of England

TOUR
53
——— 54 MILES ———

The upper Medway and its tributary the Eden flow through green and fertile valleys. Along them, and on the wooded ridge above, stands a dazzling array of great houses.

TONBRIDGE

Overlooking the River Medway at Tonbridge are the remains of a medieval castle, whose massive 13th-century gatehouse stands three storeys high. The 'motte' or castle mound was originally fortified by the Normans, to guard the important Medway crossing-point.

Though Tonbridge now sprawls north and south of the river, the old centre around the castle and church can be explored in half an hour or so. The High Street has a fine group of gabled, half-timbered buildings.

PENSHURST

From Bidborough ridge, the road plunges sharply down to a narrow bridge across the Medway, beyond which Penshurst village clusters around its high-pinnacled church, with the palatial mansion of Penshurst Place just visible behind. The mansion's centrepiece is its magnificent medieval hall, built by Sir John de Pulteney, four times Lord Mayor of London, in the 1340s. In 1552 Penshurst was given to the Sidney family by Edward VI and it was enlarged and remodelled in Elizabethan times by Sir William Sidney and his descendants – whose formal portraits line the walls. As well as the paintings, there are magnificent tapestries and furniture and a children's toy museum. The house is open daily except Mondays from April to early October, and on Bank Holidays.

CHIDDINGSTONE

Tucked away in a maze of byroads, the short village street of Chiddingstone looks like a relic from the Tudor world. The single row of half-timbered houses, with projecting upper storeys carried on massive beams, some of them elaborately carved, belongs to the National Trust.

The 14th-century parish church of St Mary the Virgin has numerous memorials to the Streatfeild family of ironmasters, who lived at Chiddingstone Castle, west of the village. The building's mock-medieval façade, turreted and battlemented, dates from the early 19th century and conceals a 17th-century interior. The castle is open most days from late March to the end of October and also Sundays and on Bank Holidays.

Opposite the church, a pathway leads to the 'Chiding Stone', where village scolds were brought to be 'chided' for their behaviour.

FAIR DEAL *Henry VIII gave Hever Castle to Anne of Cleves as a sop for a divorce.*

SCOTNEY CASTLE *A round 14th-century tower adjoins a Tudor manor.*

IGHTHAM MOTE *The house has been continuously occupied since 1340.*

HEVER

If the ghost of Anne Boleyn still lingers anywhere, it will probably be at the exquisite little castle at Hever, where she was born and spent her early years – before being wooed, married and executed by Henry VIII. After Anne's execution in 1536, and the death soon afterwards of her father, Henry took over the moated castle and gave it to his fourth wife, Anne of Cleves.

In 1903 Hever was bought by an American millionaire, William Waldorf Astor, who transformed the interior, added a house in the form of a 'village' of cottages in mock-Tudor style, and created the magnificent Italian garden and large ornamental lake. Though Hever is no longer owned by the Astor family, many of the art treasures they collected are still on display. The castle and grounds are open daily except Thursdays from early April to early October, and daily in mid-summer.

CHARTWELL

Hidden from the road behind a high brick wall, Chartwell was the country home of Sir Winston Churchill, who bought the house in 1922. In the 1920s and 1930s he spent much of his 'years in the wilderness' at Chartwell. The house stands high on the slope, with wide views across the Weald. The interior is much as it was in Churchill's day and displays the gifts and honours he accumulated, the books he read and wrote and the pictures he painted.

Round the kitchen garden runs the vast brick wall which Churchill built as a kind of occupational therapy during his 'wilderness' years. Chartwell is open daily except Mondays and Fridays from April to October, and on weekends and Wednesday in March and November.

KNOLE

Set in rolling parkland, where deer graze among gnarled and ancient trees, Knole's fascinating jumble of stone walls, turrets and courtyards make it more of a miniature village than a country house. Now owned by the National Trust, it is said to have 365 rooms for the days of the year, 52 staircases for the weeks, and seven courtyards for the days of the week.

The building was begun by Thomas Bourchier, a 15th-century Archbishop of Canterbury. It was taken over by a later archbishop, Thomas Cranmer, who dutifully handed it to Henry VIII

on royal 'request'. In 1566 Queen Elizabeth gave Knole to her cousin, Thomas Sackville, who greatly extended it. Members of the Sackville family have lived there ever since.

Inside it is a treasure-house of paintings and furniture, including the original drop-end sofa or 'Knole settee', dating from the time of James I, which has given its name to innumerable copies.

Knole Park, stretching over 1000 acres, is a magnificent open space for walking and picnicking. The park is open daily and the house is open daily except Mondays and Tuesdays from April to October.

SEVENOAKS

Sevenoaks grew up as a village at the gates of Knole, but its origins are far older. Its name probably derives from a clump of seven oak trees which stood on the site in Saxon times. Now a popular commuting town, it stands high on a greensand ridge, looking north towards the Downs. At the southern end of the town, near the entrance to Knole, are the Church of St Nicholas, with its tall Perpendicular tower, the 18th-century classical buildings of Sevenoaks School, and a number of superb red-brick Georgian houses.

IGHTHAM MOTE

This beautiful little moated manor house, which was acquired in 1985 by the National Trust, is tucked away in a hollow on a hillside. The house's name is said to derive from *moot* – a Saxon assembly place. Externally, it looks much as it did in the 14th century – but, in fact, it consists of several building styles, with a medieval Great Hall, a Tudor chapel and an 18th-century Palladian window. It is open from Easter to October, on Monday, Wednesday, Friday and Sunday.

Tourist information: Sevenoaks 450305.

TOUR
54
——— 67 MILES ———

Hop gardens, with handsome oast-houses, alternate with vineyards, orchards and woods. Spick and span towns and villages lead to one of England's most beautiful formal gardens.

ROYAL TUNBRIDGE WELLS

It is easy to conjure up a picture of bewigged beaux and their belles strolling and chatting across the piazza of The Pantiles, with its arcaded row of shops, restaurants and inns graced by a line of lime trees and a sprightly little bandstand. The town acquired a fashionable reputation as a spa after the discovery of a chalybeate spring in 1606. A cold bath was installed in 1701 at the end of The Pantiles, and the surviving bathhouse (no longer in use) was built above it in 1804. However, the iron-laden water can still be tasted on occasions at the nearby 'Dippers' Well'. Fine Georgian terraces flank steep hills and gardens. A green oasis is the Common, with the twisted shapes of the Wellington Rocks at its northern end, and some 250 acres of grass, fern, bracken and birch trees reaching almost to the edge of The Pantiles.

BAYHAM ABBEY
The monks who built their tall and beautiful abbey in the vale of the River Teise in the early 13th century chose a tranquil setting for their devotions. The lofty remains of the abbey are in a meadow in Sussex, and across the stream in Kent is Bayham mansion. When Humphry Repton landscaped the mansion's gardens in 1800, he did so with an eye for picturesque angles on the abbey ruins. And the prospect still includes impressive sections of the gatehouse, chapter house, nave and church. The abbey is open daily from April to September.

LAMBERHURST
One of the finest stretches of Lamberhurst, complete with colourful old inns, hugs the busy northbound road. A turning off this, at the northern end of the village, leads to the Owl House Gardens, spread around a 16th-century cottage named after the 'owlers' – wool smugglers who used an owl hoot as their signal. The gardens are open daily (with occasional Tuesday and Thursday closing).

Beside the broad village green are the Lamberhurst Vineyards, where visitors can explore a vineyard trail.

SCOTNEY CASTLE
Romantically landscaped gardens provide a perfect setting for a fairytale 14th-century tower and crumbling walls, reflected in a moat which seems designed more for sheer beauty than defence. It is owned by the National Trust and is open from April to mid-November from Wednesday to Friday (and afternoons only on Saturday, Sunday and Bank Holiday Monday). The castle itself is open from May to August.

BEWL BRIDGE RESERVOIR
The reservoir, built in the 1970s to supply water to parts of north and west Kent, is also a popular leisure area for the family. A visitor centre offers technical and recreational information, with craft exhibitions and activities at summer weekends. Beside it is an adventure playground for children; and there are footpaths and picnic sites all along the shores.

FINCHCOCKS
An early Georgian baroque mansion in rolling parkland now houses a collection of early keyboard instruments: harpsichords, chamber organs and early pianos are played during opening hours, and concerts are held on weekends in September. The house and gardens are open on Sundays and Bank Holiday Mondays from Easter until September, and every afternoon in August except Mondays and Tuesdays.

GOUDHURST
Soaring red-roofed and red-tiled on a crest above white-cowled oasthouses, the village coaxes the traveller up a steep hill and then, after a brief respite beside its rippling pond, up a further climb between elegant houses and shops, no two the same, elbowing each other at steep angles. Most of these have brief flights of steps and protective railings or low walls. High up the curve of the street is a gazebo once used as a lookout for stagecoaches toiling up the slope.

Finally, at the very top, stands the golden, stony grandeur of St Mary's Church, with the timbered, galleried Star and Eagle Hotel nearby. Inside the church are brasses and monuments of the local Culpeper family, including two painted wooden effigies.

SISSINGHURST CASTLE GARDEN
This lightly fortified, moated Tudor manor house was largely built in the mid-16th century by Sir Richard Baker. In the 18th century it was used to house French prisoners of war who called it *le château*, 'the castle', and so gave it the name of Sissinghurst Castle. Its few remains – overshadowed by a tall, Elizabethan tower – are a wonderful visual foil for the garden laid out in the early 1930s by the diplomat Sir Harold Nicolson and his novelist wife, Vita Sackville-West. The garden is open daily except Monday from April to mid-October.

BEDGEBURY NATIONAL PINETUM
In 1924 the administrators of Kew Gardens established this coniferous plantation for scientific study far from the sooty climate of London. Together with the Forestry Commission, who own the property, they designed Bedgebury as a large estate with walks, streams, a small lake, ferns and rhododendron bushes. The estate is open daily.

WADHURST
The village sign symbolically combines three vigorous local occupations in its grouping of oak tree, anvil and oast-houses. Proudly the tree recalls that all the timber used in the hammerbeam roof of London's Westminster Hall came from an estate just outside Wadhurst. The anvil represents one of the busiest phases in the region's history, of which there is weighty evidence in the Church of St Peter and St Paul. The floor is inlaid with more than 30 huge, black memorial slabs of Wealden iron dating between 1617 and 1799; there is another slab in the porch, and one in the churchyard.

The oast-houses in the sign relate to the hops grown in the district.

HIGH ROCKS
The sandstone formations from which Tunbridge Wells's iron-rich spring emerged have produced a number of freakishly eroded outcrops in the neighbourhood. The highest fault scarp is that of High Rocks, which provides a challenge for experienced climbers. Within the entrance gate, open daily, are a scenic walk, hanging rocks, bridges and a rhododendron maze.

Tourist information: Tunbridge Wells 26121.

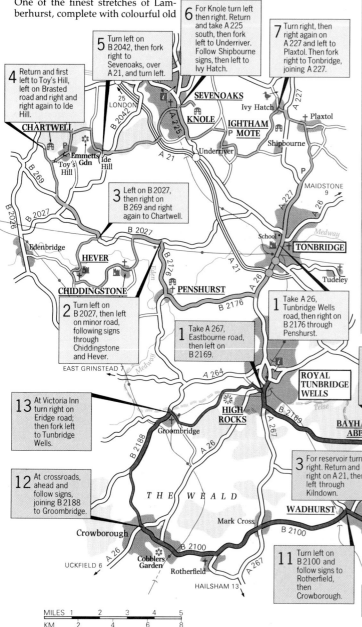

6 For Knole turn left then right. Return and take A225 south, then fork left to Underriver. Follow Shipbourne signs, then left to Ivy Hatch.

7 Turn right, then right again on A227 and left to Plaxtol. Then fork right to Tonbridge, joining A227.

5 Turn left on B2042, then fork right to Sevenoaks, over A21, and turn left.

4 Return and first left to Toy's Hill, left on Brasted road and right and right again to Ide Hill.

3 Left on B2027, then right on B269 and right again to Chartwell.

2 Turn left on B2027, then left on minor road, following signs through Chiddingstone and Hever.

1 Take A267, Eastbourne road, then left on B2169.

1 Take A26, Tunbridge Wells road, then right on B2176 through Penshurst.

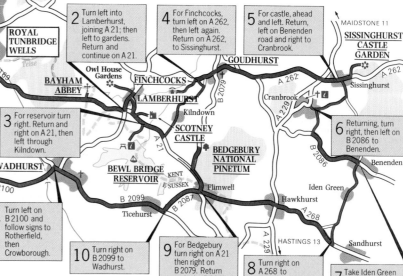

2 Turn left into Lamberhurst, joining A21; then left to gardens. Return and continue on A21.

4 For Finchcocks, turn left on A262, then left again. Return on A262, to Sissinghurst.

5 For castle, ahead and left. Return, left on Benenden road and right to Cranbrook.

13 At Victoria Inn turn right on Eridge road; then fork left to Tunbridge Wells.

12 At crossroads, ahead and follow signs, joining B2188 to Groombridge.

3 For reservoir turn right. Return and right on A21, then left through Kilndown.

6 Returning, turn right, then left on B2086 to Benenden.

11 Turn left on B2100 and follow signs to Rotherfield, then Crowborough.

10 Turn right on B2099 to Wadhurst.

9 For Bedgebury turn right on A21 then right on B2079. Return and take B2087 to Ticehurst.

8 Turn right on A268 to Hawkhurst and Flimwell.

7 Take Iden Green road, then Sandhurst road.

From Romney Marsh to the Weald

From the Cinque Port of Hastings the coast road leads to two former ports now stranded well back from the sea. Inland lie the woods, farmlands and villages of the East Sussex Weald.

HASTINGS
The first of many castles that William of Normandy built throughout the land was a wooden fort above Hastings. This was later expanded into a stone stronghold whose skeletal ruins and dungeons are open to visitors. There are also smugglers' caves under West Hill.

In the Town Hall, Queen's Road, are displayed a 243ft long embroidery of British historical events, commissioned in 1966 to mark the 900th anniversary of the Battle of Hastings, and a scale model of the battle.

Footpaths from East Hill, or a minor road towards Fairlight, off the main road climbing out of the town, lead to the Hastings Country Park. The visitor centre is the starting point of several nature trails, leading to beauty spots such as Ecclesbourne Glen and Fairlight Glen, and along the Fire Hills – so called because of their blaze of gorse along the cliff top 500ft above the sea.

WINCHELSEA
The town, on its commanding hilltop, was laid out by Edward I on a gridiron system of streets after the old town below the hill had been destroyed by the sea.

Some of the old town gates still stand; remains of the New Gate are to be found on the lane to Pett; the Pipewell Gate guards the road to the railway station; and, most impressive of all, the Strand Gate dominates the precipitous hill down to the Rother Levels and the Royal Military Road to Rye.

The Methodist chapel was opened by John Wesley, who preached his last outdoor sermon under a tree near the New Inn.

RYE HARBOUR
Just by the turn-off over the river there begins a footpath to Camber Castle, built by Henry VIII in the shape of a Tudor rose. Restoration work has been in hand for some years, and entry is restricted.

In November 1928 the Rye lifeboat with its crew of 17 put out in a gale to answer a distress call, but the boat capsized with the loss of all hands. The bodies of the crew now lie in the churchyard, which is almost swamped by gravel diggings. Inside the tiny church the crew are commemorated by a tablet of Manx stone presented by the Isle of Man, birthplace of the Royal National Lifeboat Institution.

RYE
Defiant on its church-crowned hill, Rye glows with red roofs set at bewildering angles. The heart of the once walled town is reached through the 14th-century Landgate, with its massive drum towers. Cobbled streets enclose the churchyard; the name of one of them, Watchbell Street, recalls the many alarms which for centuries had to be sounded against French raiders.

On the south-eastern tip is the Ypres Tower, a small Norman keep which in time of municipal penury in the 15th century was sold off to John de Ipres. The tower later served as a prison and mortuary. Today it is an excellent museum of local history.

NORTHIAM
On the left of the road into the village is the dazzling black-and-white, half-timbered Brickwall House, built in the 16th century by a Rye shipbuilding family, and now a school. Parts of the house and gardens are open on Wednesday and Saturday afternoons from late April to early July.

The village street, embowered, like the side lanes, by trees which almost obscure the church, presents beautiful examples of tile-hanging and timbering, and especially white weatherboarding. Most impressive of all is the three-storeyed frontage of Oak Side. A footpath to pretty little Ewhurst across the valley starts opposite the car park.

From the northern end of Northiam a lane leads to Great Dixter, a 15th-century, half-timbered manor house restored by Sir Edwin Lutyens, who also designed most of the extensive gardens. House and gardens are open in the afternoons, except Monday, from April to October. The nurseries are open every weekday.

BODIAM
A shallow cleft of the Rother valley shelters a fairy-tale moated castle, surrounded by a spacious park. In spite of its apparently vulnerable

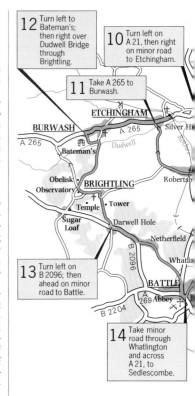

position, it was designed in 1386 as a strong defence against the French.

The village was once the centre of a prosperous hop-growing region, served by 'The Hoppers' Line' of the Kent and East Sussex Railway. Many hop gardens have now been stripped out, because of falling demand.

ETCHINGHAM
The Church of the Assumption of Blessed Mary and St Nicholas was built in the 14th century by Sir William de Echyngham, who gave his name to the village. He is commemorated by an imposing brass, unfortunately headless, in the floor before the high altar. Other fine memorials include a well-preserved triple brass of Sir William, his wife and son, and a modern brass tablet of 1962. The choir has some imaginatively carved, 14th-century misericords, one of them showing a fox in priest's clothing preaching to six geese.

BURWASH
A gracious, tree-lined village, Burwash has not a dull note nor eyesore anywhere. Halfway along the southern pavement, a map on a plinth identifies outstanding buildings, including Rampyndene near the church, with its beautifully moulded shell-like porch and wrought-iron gates. The village sign of hammer and anvil recalls the once booming iron industry of the Weald.

St Bartholomew's Church has what is thought to be the earliest Sussex iron grave slab dating from the 14th century. Just below the ridge is Bateman's, a 17th-century ironmaster's house which was the home of Rudyard Kipling from 1902 to 1936. Kipling's initials are woven into the wrought-iron gate. Bateman's is open daily except Thursday and Friday from April to October.

ROMNEY MARSH *Dykes pattern the landscape and sheep graze in broad pastures reclaimed from the sea in the 17th century.*

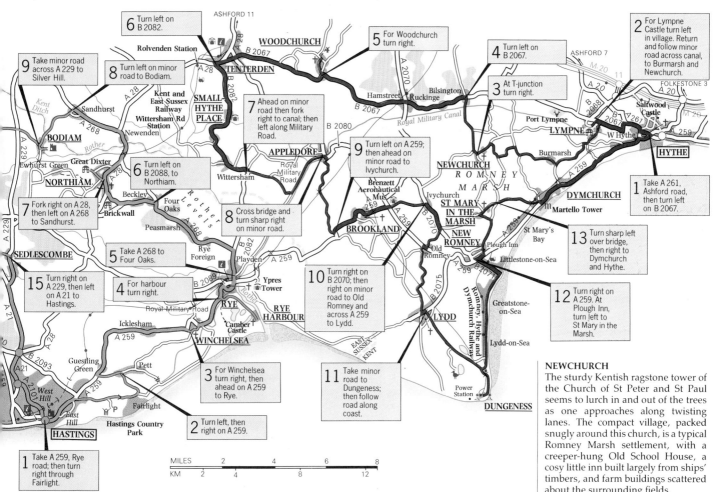

6 Turn left on B 2082.

ASHFORD 11

WOODCHURCH

5 For Woodchurch turn right.

4 Turn left on B 2067.

ASHFORD 7

2 For Lympne Castle turn left in village. Return and follow minor road across canal, to Burmarsh and Newchurch.

9 Take minor road across A 229 to Silver Hill.

8 Turn left on minor road to Bodiam.

Rolvenden Station

TENTERDEN

Hamstreet Ruckinge

Bilsington

3 At T-junction turn right.

M 20

FOLKESTONE 3

Saltwood Castle

Kent Ditch

Sandhurst

Kent and East Sussex Railway Wittersham Rd Station

SMALL-HYTHE PLACE

7 Ahead on minor road then fork right to canal; then left along Military Road.

Port Lympne

LYMPNE

W Hythe

HYTHE

BODIAM

Great Dixter

Newenden

APPLEDORE

Royal Military Canal

Burmarsh

9 Turn left on A 259; then ahead on minor road to Ivychurch.

NEWCHURCH

ROMNEY MARSH

1 Take A 261, Ashford road, then turn left on B 2067.

NORTHIAM

6 Turn left on B 2088, to Northiam.

Wittersham

Brenzett Aeronautical Mus

Ivychurch

DYMCHURCH

Martello Tower

7 Fork right on A 28, then left on A 268 to Sandhurst.

Beckley

Brickwall

8 Cross bridge and turn sharp right on minor road.

ST MARY IN THE MARSH

Four Oaks

Peasmarsh

BROOKLAND

NEW ROMNEY

Plough Inn

St Mary's Bay

13 Turn sharp left over bridge, then right to Dymchurch and Hythe.

SEDLESCOMBE

5 Take A 268 to Four Oaks.

Rye Foreign

Playden

10 Turn right on B 2070; then right on minor road to Old Romney and across A 259 to Lydd.

Old Romney

Littlestone-on-Sea

15 Turn right on A 229, then left on A 21 to Hastings.

4 For harbour turn right.

Ypres Tower

Royal Military Road

RYE

Camber Castle

RYE HARBOUR

Greatstone-on-Sea

12 Turn right on A 259. At Plough Inn, turn left to St Mary in the Marsh.

Icklesham

WINCHELSEA

3 For Winchelsea turn right, then ahead on A 259 to Rye.

LYDD

Lydd-on-Sea

Guestling Green

Pett

EAST SUSSEX KENT

11 Take minor road to Dungeness; then follow road along coast.

Fairlight

West Hill

East Hill

Hastings Country Park

2 Turn left, then right on A 259.

Power Station

DUNGENESS

HASTINGS

1 Take A 259, Rye road; then turn right through Fairlight.

MILES   2   4   6   8
KM   2   4   8   12

BRIGHTLING

The rolling countryside around Brightling affords tantalising glimpses of a number of architectural fantasies, all of them the 'follies' of Squire John Fuller, a local Member of Parliament, often known as Mad Jack. Inheriting a family fortune made from the iron industry, he gave employment in the early 19th century at a time of serious depression by setting local men to build the long wall which to this day surrounds Brightling Park.

A keen amateur scientist, Fuller built a working observatory. More eccentrically he built a tower beside the Brightling to Darwell Hole road, an obelisk high on the hill, a rotunda temple, a cone called the Sugar Loaf at Woods Corner (supposedly to win a bet that he could see the similarly shaped Dallington church spire from his house), and a pyramidal mausoleum in Brightling churchyard.

BATTLE

The Battle of Hastings took place on the slopes below this town, not in Hastings itself. Down one section of hillside above the road to Catsfield the National Trust cares for an area which includes a clayey stream often running dark red – with blood, according to legend, since this is thought to be the stream into which slaughtered Saxons were flung. In fact, the red colouring is caused by iron in the soil.

William the Conqueror founded an abbey on the site of his victory, placing the high altar on the spot

where Harold was killed. Additions were made later. A school now occupies most of the surviving premises, but a large part of the grounds and impressive monastic buildings is open to the public.

SEDLESCOMBE

The village street descends gently past an idyllic green with, on its far side, a narrower road lined by trim, appealing houses. Perkily set on the green is a pump which, until well into this century, was the community's only water supply. Today it is still a focus for locals to gather and chat.

Tourist information: Hastings 424242; Rye 222293; Battle 3721.

TOUR

56

— 78 MILES —

Between the Royal Military Canal and the English Channel, lanes meander through a secretive world. There are whispers of wind, reed and water, silver mists and summer hazes.

HYTHE

The coats of arms on the town signs of Hythe, Hastings, Dover, Romney and Sandwich proudly proclaim membership of the Cinque Ports, the medieval confederacy of south-east coast towns

which supplied ships and crews for the defence of the realm in return for many special charters and privileges. On one of the hillside terraces which make up the town stands St Leonard's Church on the site of an early Norman building. In its crypt is a gruesome collection of thigh bones and skulls dating back many centuries, probably put there when the churchyard became overfull.

On the northern outskirts stands Saltwood Castle, where Thomas Becket's four murderers sheltered on the night before their crime. It is privately owned, but opened at times by prior arrangement.

LYMPNE

In Roman times the Saxon Shore fort of Portus Lemanis, the village now sits tranquilly above the great chunks of Roman masonry tumbling down the hillside. Lympne Castle, open occasionally in summer, was begun in 1360 around earlier fortifications, but by the 17th century had become just a manor house, centre of a large farm. The great hall, with its Tudor fireplace, and other parts of the building were restored to their original form this century. On top of the east tower, a Second World War concrete observation post provides a marvellous vista of Romney Marsh.

Another fine vantage point is the stone staircase of 125 steps at Port Lympne, an extensive zoo park and gardens west of the village, which is open daily.

NEWCHURCH

The sturdy Kentish ragstone tower of the Church of St Peter and St Paul seems to lurch in and out of the trees as one approaches along twisting lanes. The compact village, packed snugly around this church, is a typical Romney Marsh settlement, with a creeper-hung Old School House, a cosy little inn built largely from ships' timbers, and farm buildings scattered about the surrounding fields.

WOODCHURCH

Turning off the Hamstreet to Tenterden road, the village street climbs a gentle slope past a huge triangular green flanked by tile-hung houses and weatherboarded and rose-hung cottages, until it reaches the tall shingled spire of the Church of All Saints on the crown of the hill.

Across the road from the church, a shaded public footpath leads between two spacious inns to a restored smock mill, open on Sundays from April to September.

TENTERDEN

The wide main street of this distinguished market town is lined with timbered houses, glowing tiled frontages, old inns and tempting shops.

In Station Road a museum displays mementos of the weaving trade, and hop-picking days. At the foot of the road is the terminus of the Kent and East Sussex Railway, a preserved stretch of line along which steam trains run 50 minute trips to and from Rolvenden and Wittersham Road.

SMALLHYTHE PLACE

The actress Ellen Terry lived in this 16th-century, half-timbered manor house from 1900 until her death in 1928. It is now a theatrical museum, with a collection of the actress's personal mementos, open to the public every afternoon except Tuesday and Friday from April to the end of October. Smallhythe – 'hythe' is an

93

MEDIEVAL DETERRENT *Bodiam Castle was built to deter raiders from France, and served its purpose well. But it fell easily to Cromwell's forces during the Civil War when it was threatened by bombardment by modern cannon.*

old word for harbour – was a port before the channel from the Rother estuary silted up in the 17th century, and in the museum grounds remains of an old ship repair dock can still be traced.

APPLEDORE
From Rye to Appledore, a finely preserved stretch of the Royal Military Road runs parallel with the Royal Military Canal. During the threat of invasion by Napoleon, squat Martello towers were built along the coast, and between 1804 and 1809 a canal was dug farther inland to seal off the marsh. Sluices could be used to flood the levels if necessary.

BROOKLAND
There are many local legends to explain why the shingled octagonal bell tower, with its iron dragon weather vane, is set apart from its church. The probable truth is that the marshy ground would not support a tower on the main building, which itself has an alarming tilt to the aisle arcades.

Just over a mile along the road to Ivychurch is the Brenzett Aeronautical Museum, featuring fragments of British and German aircraft excavated from Romney Marsh after the Second World War. The museum is open on Sundays and Bank Holidays from Easter to September, and also on Tuesday, Wednesday and Thursday afternoons in July and August.

LYDD
In spite of the nearby army ranges, where the explosive known as lyddite was developed, the little town itself has an attractive, welcoming heart.

Beside the square is a beautifully proportioned half-timbered house, a scheduled Kent Historic Building. The Church of All Saints, twice bombed during the Second World War, once had Thomas (later Cardinal) Wolsey as rector.

DUNGENESS
The great hulks of the nuclear power station buildings loom ahead on the road from Lydd. In spite of this space-age intrusion, Dungeness remains the most important bird site in south-east England. On the wind-lashed shingle spit stand two lighthouses and the base of an earlier one built in 1792 and now converted into accommodation for the keeper.

Construction of the power station partially obscured the sightline of the 1901 High Light, which had to be replaced by a new tower in 1961; the original lighthouse has been retained for the benefit of visitors, and is open daily throughout spring and summer.

NEW ROMNEY
The 14 mile track of the world's smallest public railway, the Romney, Hythe and Dymchurch Railway, crossed several times on this tour, is visible up a number of side lanes along the coastal road and over Romney Marsh towards Hythe. Its headquarters at New Romney, opposite an inn named after Captain Howey, who founded the line and opened it in 1927, incorporates a lavish model railway layout. Outside the holiday season, trains carry children to and from school.

ST MARY IN THE MARSH
Church, old vicarage, village inn, post box and telephone box make up the perfect hamlet, lulled by background music of sheep, birds and the sighing of wind in the grass. Edith Nesbit, the author of stories such as *Railway Children*, lived in two converted army huts near the railway. She is buried in St Mary's churchyard below a barge-

POET'S CORNER *Rudyard Kipling lived at Bateman's, and based 'Puck of Pook's Hill' on the surrounding countryside.*

RYE COBBLES *Weatherboarded houses line the medieval Mermaid Street.*

SMALLHYTHE PLACE *The actress Ellen Terry lived here for almost 30 years.*

ANCIENT ENTRY *Winchelsea's Strand Gate was built in the 13th century.*

EAST MEETS WEST *A Moorish patio is a feature of the mansion built by Sir Herbert Baker at Port Lympne.*

GREAT DIXTER *The gardens were laid out by Sir Edwin Lutyens in 1911.*

board carved by her husband, a sea captain. There is a tablet to her memory inside the homely little church.

DYMCHURCH
One of the steam engines on the light railway is named *Dr Syn*, after Russell Thorndike's fictional Dymchurch parson-cum-smuggler who embodies so much of Romney Marsh legend. Dymchurch's holiday camps and amusement arcades do not make a picturesque background, but a walk along the sea wall evokes many centuries of history.

A Martello tower has been restored as a museum, and between Dymchurch and Hythe are substantial relics of defences against both Napoleon Bonaparte and Adolf Hitler. The massive sea wall may date from Roman times.

Tourist information: Tenterden 3572 (summer); New Romney 64044.

SACRED STONES *Northiam's Church of St Mary is Norman and has a stone spire.*

COASTAL DEFENDERS *Martello towers at Hythe were part of a chain built to guard against the threat of invasion by Napoleon.*

Ways where Chaucer's pilgrims rode

TOUR
57
— 79 MILES —

Centuries ago, pilgrims bound for Canterbury passed this way. Historic towns and villages set among Kent's orchards and hopfields still evoke the atmosphere of Chaucer's tales.

DARTFORD

Although factories and modern housing crowd in on it, the centre of Dartford still has a hospitable air and a lingering sense of its own historic importance. It was a major Roman station by a crossing of the Darent – little more than a stream now, but once a wider river. Near its railway station are the gateway and other remnants of a priory founded by Edward III which, after the Dissolution, became a royal palace.

The parish church has fine brasses and contains memorials to Sir John Spielman and Richard Trevithick. Spielman was given a licence by Elizabeth I to 'gather all manner of rags, scrolls, scraps of parchment, clippings of cards' as raw material for paper mills which he founded at Dartford. His name is of German origin and means 'jester'; his watermark of a jester probably gave rise to the word 'foolscap'. The area still abounds in paper mills.

Richard Trevithick, the railway pioneer, died in poverty at the Bull Hotel in 1833. This brilliant but improvident man had been working locally on some of his inventions, and mechanics who knew him clubbed together to give him a decent funeral.

The Bull, like its namesake in Rochester, was renamed the Royal Victoria and Bull after the young Princess Victoria visited it. Built in 1703, it is one of the few surviving galleried inns in the county – tastefully incorporated in the corner of a modern pedestrian precinct, with a brightly painted and polished old stagecoach in its now enclosed courtyard.

On East Hill there is a memorial to three martyred Protestants who were burnt at the stake on July 17, 1555.

SUTTON AT HONE

Cloaked by trees, St John's Jerusalem Garden stands on the banks of the Darent, which supplies its moat. This property, given to the National Trust by Sir Stephen Tallents, was once a headquarters of the Knights Hospitallers, and the 13th-century chapel was extended in the 16th and 18th centuries to form a private house. The eastern end was retained for private worship, but later became a billiard room; now it is the only part of the building open to visitors, along with the beautifully laid-out gardens, on Wednesday afternoons from April to October.

MEOPHAM GREEN

The first recorded cricket match played on the wide, gently sloping green was between Meopham and Chatham in 1778. The green is surrounded by houses and cottages worthy of the setting. At one corner stands a handsome converted oasthouse; diagonally across the green is an inn predictably called The Cricketers.

Towering above the inn is an 1801 smock mill which continued to work by wind power until 1927. It was restored in 1962, though its 27ft long sails no longer turn, and is open on Sunday and Bank Holiday afternoons in July and August.

North-east of the village is Camer Country Park – 46 acres of landscaped parkland open daily.

LUDDESDOWN

Lonely on its secluded slope, above sunken lanes and overshadowing beech trees, the Church of St Peter and St Paul has a solid, square tower with some Roman tiles mixed into its flint and rubble, and a squat spire roofed with shingle.

Close to it – and with so much flint in its own walls as almost to seem part of the church – is Luddesdown Court, one of the oldest continuously inhabited houses in England. Thought to date from about 1100, its additions cover almost every style up to Tudor times, and there are a few more recent renovations and adaptations. It is privately owned and can be visited by appointment only.

COBHAM

A right turn into Cobham reveals the warm, red-brick façade of Owletts, a modest, ingratiating house from the time of Charles II. This National Trust property has a notable staircase and fine plasterwork ceilings; outside are a kitchen garden and pleasure area. It is open on Wednesday and Thursday afternoons from April to the end of September.

Cobham was a favourite haunt of Charles Dickens, and part of *The Pickwick Papers* was written in the luxuriantly timbered and gabled Old Leather Bottle inn. On the other side of the road, the church has probably the finest collection of monumental brasses in the country. Behind it is a long, low range of medieval almshouses on the foundations of a monastic college endowed in the 14th century by Sir John de Cobham. The buildings are open to the public daily, except Thursday, from April to September, and on most days from October to March. Neighbouring Stone House was once a hostel for visitors to the college.

Other buildings of note are the Ship Inn, thought to have been built from the timbers of a ship which foundered off Sheerness, and The Darnley Arms, which possibly dates from the 12th century.

Cobham Hall, for many generations the home of the Earls of Darnley, was often visited by the cricketer W.G. Grace. It was in the park that Dickens took his last walk. Today the hall is a girls' school, but it can be viewed at Easter and in August.

ROCHESTER

Drivers racing above the River Medway on the bypass are likely to regard Rochester as an ungainly industrial sprawl. But the compact centre of the old city within its medieval walls is a colourful medley of richly gabled houses and inns, with little paved and cobbled lanes offering inviting glimpses of the cathedral and the castle.

The castle keep is surrounded by generous expanses of grass. A twisting road and flights of steps lead down to the long esplanade where seats and picnic places offer ever-changing views of the river traffic. On the far side of the water is Temple Manor, a 13th-century store hall of the Knights Templars with 17th-century extensions. It is open to the public at certain times during the summer.

The Roman settlement of Durobrivae guarded this important river crossing. The Normans erected a great rectangular keep which in 1215, during the barons' rebellion against King John, defied all the king's attempts to storm it until sappers undermined the south-east corner.

Work on the cathedral began in 1080, and the see of Rochester is second only to that of Canterbury in age. The cathedral library is outstanding and contains valuable old Bibles.

Charles Dickens spent much of his childhood in Rochester and later lived in the area at Gad's Hill Place. A Charles Dickens Centre is established in the 16th-century brick mansion of Eastgate House. In the garden stand the Swiss-style chalet from Dickens' Gad's Hill home, in which his last words were written, and the machinery of a horse-driven water pump from the well at the house. The centre is open daily.

QUEEN DOWN WARREN

Stiles give access to paths across a reserve administered by the Kent Trust for Nature Conservation. Its records stretch back to the 15th century when it was a commercially run rabbit warren producing meat and fur. And today, despite myxomatosis, rabbits are plentiful.

Queen Down Warren has fine chalk grassland, scrub and woodland, and is noted for its orchids. Butterflies abound, and there are breeding colonies of both common and chalk-hill blue species. Woodpeckers and warblers are among the birds that can be seen.

SITTINGBOURNE

This old market town and small port is on Milton Creek, off the River Swale. In medieval times it was a stopping place on the Canterbury Pilgrims' Way, and in later centuries an important coaching station. Henry V rested here on his way home from the victory at Agincourt, and Henry VIII stayed here in 1532.

The great Thames and Medway sailing barges trade no more, but at Dolphin Yard off Crown Quay Lane there is a museum where some survivors have been restored and are exhibited. The museum is open on Sundays and Bank Holidays from Easter to mid-October.

From a station off Milton Road a narrow-gauge steam railway carries passengers 2 miles to and from Kemsley along a track once used for hauling the produce of the local paper mills. It operates on Sunday afternoons from Easter to October; on Wednesday, Thursday and Saturday afternoons in August; and on Bank Holidays.

TONGE

Restored in the 1970s, Tonge's weatherboarded water mill stands on a site recorded in Domesday Book. Its stables, in gardens beside the millstream, are now open as a craft centre on weekday afternoons and all day on Saturdays. Visits to the mill house are by appointment only.

St Giles's Church is mainly 12th to 14th century and has 15th-century carved stalls. Near the church is Tonge Castle, a grass-covered mound with a dry moat. A few miles farther on is Teynham, the birthplace of Kent's luscious orchards. It was developed by Henry VIII's fruiterer Richard Harris, from cherries and apples brought from the Continent.

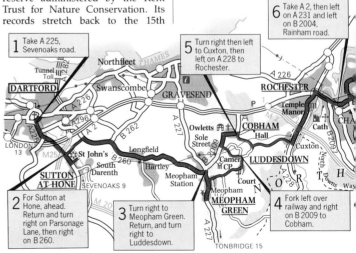

CHILHAM CASTLE *The lovely Jacobean house overlooking the Stour valley stands in 25 acres of gardens, originally laid out by the botanist John Tradescant.*

FAVERSHAM

Ospringe, once a settlement in its own right, is now part of the borough of Faversham. The dust of the main road adds a grey film to the stones of its special treasure, the Maison Dieu. Since the 13th century, pilgrims have lodged here on their way to Canterbury, and royalty too, when heading for the Channel ports. Displays from different centuries show Roman finds, the story of the Maison Dieu itself, and exhibits organised by the Faversham Society. The creek which contributed so much to Faversham's trading prosperity runs from The Swale through marshes rich in wildlife, past Oare's old wharves and the landmark of a windmill converted into a private dwelling.

In Faversham itself the beautifully proportioned Market Place, with its timber-pillared Guildhall, built as a Market Hall in 1574, and graceful houses – mostly of 17th and 18th-century origin – is the heart of a conservation area containing no fewer than 400 listed buildings.

The Fleur de Lis Heritage Centre and Museum was once the inn where in 1550 the plot to murder Arden of Faversham was concocted, at the instigation of his wife. The killing is the subject of a play once attributed to Shakespeare. The centre has displays of local brewing, brickmaking and hop-picking, an Edwardian barber's shop, and records of the explosives industry, which is linked locally to Chart Mills.

It is claimed that Chart Mills, near Stonebridge Pond, is the oldest gunpowder factory of its kind in the world. It dates from 1561, flourished in the Napoleonic and Crimean wars, and was operating until the 1930s. Visits can be made on Sunday and Bank Holiday afternoons from Easter until October.

PERRY WOOD

Down a lane from Selling lie 150 acres of unspoilt woodland, with picnic areas and forest walks, opened to the public in 1980 by the local council after being owned for centuries by Corpus Christi College, Oxford. There was once a semaphore telegraph station on a raised structure at the highest point of the wood, 504ft above sea level; it is now a vantage point known as The Pulpit.

CHILHAM

Approached along a rich trail of hop gardens and orchards, Chilham is reached by a narrow uphill road which opens out breathtakingly onto the village square – with the turreted St Mary's Church, the 15th-century White Horse inn and the gate of Chilham Castle.

The Normans built a keep and bailey here; some remnants survive beside the red-brick Jacobean mansion built in 1616 and attributed to Inigo Jones. England's first mulberry trees and wisteria were introduced into its gardens. Medieval jousting and displays of falconry are staged on occasional Sundays and Bank Holidays.

Tourist information: (Rochester) Medway 43666; Faversham 534542, Canterbury 66567.

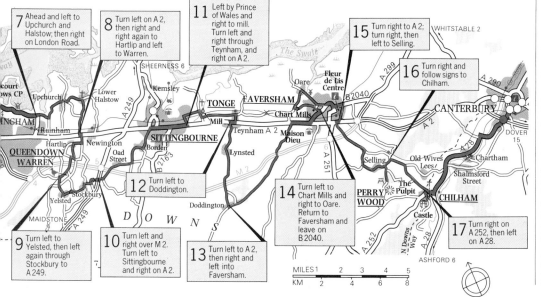

7 Ahead and left to Upchurch and Halstow; then right on London Road.

8 Turn left on A 2, then right and right again to Hartlip and left to Warren.

11 Left by Prince of Wales and right to mill. Turn left and right through Teynham, and right on A 2.

15 Turn right to A 2; turn right, then left to Selling.

16 Turn right and follow signs to Chilham.

12 Turn left to Doddington.

14 Turn left to Chart Mills and right to Oare. Return to Faversham and leave on B 2040.

9 Turn left to Yelsted, then left again through Stockbury to A 249.

10 Turn left and right over M 2. Turn left to Sittingbourne and right on A 2.

13 Turn left to A 2, then right and left into Faversham.

17 Turn right on A 252, then left on A 28.

White cliffs of an invaders' coast

TOUR
58
——— 48 MILES ———

To a coastline of shallow shores and gentle cliffs, Roman and Saxon invaders were followed by Flemish weavers and brickmakers. Inland lie mellow towns and villages.

CANTERBURY
Despite Civil War demolition, and a German air raid in 1942 which destroyed a large part of the city within its medieval walls, half of those walls and most of Canterbury's historic buildings survive. Modern shopping precincts and pedestrian ways have been skilfully integrated with dignified old stone halls and soaring timbered gables. Leisurely river trips start near the overhanging Old Weavers' House.

Dominating all this is the superb Gothic 'Bell Harry' tower of Christ Church Cathedral, mother church of the Anglican communion. Thomas Becket was murdered in the cathedral in 1170, and his tomb became a shrine, the focus of pilgrimages from all over Europe.

WEALDEN FOREST PARK
More than 20 acres of forest provide the visitor with a chance to see owls, foxes, deer and, in a covered garden, English and tropical butterflies flying free. The park is open daily from Easter to October.

HERNE
Under the shadow of housing estates spilling over the coastal ridge, Herne retains all the weatherboarded, brick and tile-hung charm of a self-sufficient Kentish village clinging to its tight twist of road. The picture is completed by an 18th-century smock mill on the slope above.

HERNE BAY
A breezy, unpretentious holiday resort since Victorian times, Herne Bay has 7 miles of seafront and shingle beach, with shelving stretches of sand at low tide. Until the late 1970s Herne Bay had a pier nearly three-quarters of a mile long, but gales tore it apart, leaving only a pavilion beside the promenade and a forlorn white superstructure on stilts out in the water.

RECULVER
On the outskirts of Herne Bay, Bishopstone Lane, off the road to Reculver, leads to car-parking spaces on the cliff tops at the start of exhilarating walks high above the sea.

From the land, the two Norman towers of St Mary's Church can be seen from miles away. From the sea they look even more dramatic – which is why they were taken over by Trinity House as navigational aids when the rest of the church was demolished in

1809. Below the site are a few stony fragments of Regulbium, one of the string of Romano-British forts which defended the Saxon Shore.

ST NICHOLAS AT WADE
A flawless little village overawed by its long, wide church, this was a busy trading centre with its own ferry to Thanet before the Wantsum channel silted up. The lofty church tower is still a landmark for shipping. Two old brick cottages face the church porch, one with Dutch gables – recalling the days when Flemish weavers brought their techniques to Kent.

QUEX PARK
Big game specimens are mounted in African and Asian settings in the Powell-Cotton Museum in Quex Park. There are collections of tribal arts and

crafts, and antique cannon and other weapons in galleries attached to a Regency and Victorian mansion.

PEGWELL BAY
In AD 449 the Jutish warriors Hengist and Horsa landed on the bleak saltings of the bay, and after a series of battles in which they defeated the Britons they set up the powerful kingdom of Kent. In 1949, on the 1500th anniversary of their landing, a Danish crew rowed a replica longship from Jutland to the bay. Their craft, the *Hugin*, now lies with its dragonhead prow and brightly painted shields above the modern Hoverport.

RICHBOROUGH
On what was in Roman times a broad river, the fortified harbour of Rutupiae was the bridgehead for the

invasion of AD 43 ordered by the Emperor Claudius. Three sturdy stone walls are still in place. Within the stone ramparts of Richborough Castle can be seen the base of a triumphal arch, built to proclaim that Rome had effectively subjugated Britain, and a site museum which contains thousands of excavated relics. Half a mile south is a typical Roman amphitheatre. The museum and amphitheatre are open daily.

FORDWICH
Tucked away above the Stour, the village, with its secretive lanes and ancient buildings, seems almost like an artificially preserved showpiece of timber and plaster, with pretty displays of brick nogging here and there. In medieval times Fordwich was Canterbury's main river supply port, and it was at the town quays that imported Caen stone was unloaded to build Christ Church Cathedral. The brick and timber-framed town hall was rebuilt in 1555.

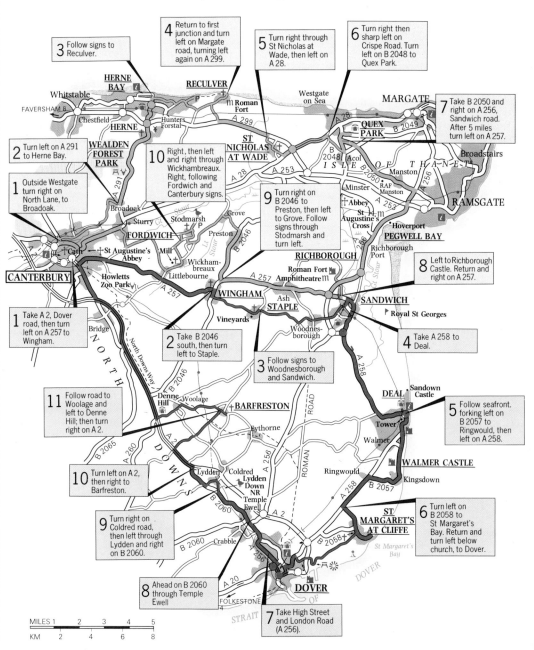

BAY OF AMBITION *From St Margaret's Bay many a hopeful swimmer has set out in the quest for a new cross-Channel record.*

SCRIPTURES IN STONE *Barfreston's Church of St Nicholas is noted for its Norman carvings, depicting Biblical scenes, the lives of the saints and mythical beasts.*

WICKHAMBREAUX MILL *The weather-boarded mill stands by the Little Stour.*

TOUR 59

—— 51 MILES ——

Old castles still watch over the English Channel, across which so many invasions have threatened. From Dover there are fine views over the water – and inland to fruit and hop-farming land.

WINGHAM

The slim copper-clad spire on the sturdy church tower, with its spiky corner turret, stands sentinel on the edge of the village. Along the tree-lined main street are houses of plaster and timber and of Georgian brick. Wingham's two inns date from the 13th century, and both in their time have housed magistrates' courts.

STAPLE

A village scattered over several fields and lanes, Staple takes its name from the 'staple' or market place for wool, an industry once important in the region. Its Church of St James the Great has a venerable 17th-century lich gate and a single-handed clock which has to be wound daily from inside the tower. Opposite the church are Staple vineyards. Conducted tours can be arranged, but from June to September visitors can make their own way round the vineyard.

SANDWICH

Winding narrow streets of high gabled, timbered houses, some tilting and bulging at alarming angles, testify to the wealth and good taste of the merchants who flourished when Sandwich was one of the busiest of the Cinque Ports. By the middle of the 15th century it was the most important naval base in England, but over the next hundred years the harbour silted up. The arrival of Flemish weavers kept the town prosperous, and mementos of their craft can be seen in the Guildhall Museum.

DEAL

The seafront is invigorating, not just because of the sea breezes rustling over the shingle, but also on account of the lively contrasts visible on the other side of the road, where gleaming white and colour-washed houses and inns of the old fishing community stare out to sea over boats drawn directly up onto the beach. There are substantial Georgian and Edwardian hotels and boarding houses, and also two relics of older times: the Time Ball Tower, which until 1927 relayed Greenwich time signals to shipping in The Downs, and Deal Castle, one of Henry VIII's chain of coastal fortresses, laid out in the shape of a vast Tudor rose.

A museum of maritime and local history in St George's Road is open every afternoon from May to the end of September.

WALMER CASTLE

Julius Caesar is thought to have made his landing in 55 BC between Deal and Walmer. Much later, Henry VIII built Walmer Castle to guard the coast from any future invaders. From 1708 onwards the castle has been the official residence of the Lord Warden of the Cinque Ports. Its little arc of cannon facing out to sea is now decorative rather than defiant. The Wellington Museum in the fortress has many souvenirs of the Iron Duke, who served as Lord Warden from 1829 until his death there in 1852.

The castle and gardens are open daily, except for Mondays (other than Bank Holidays) and Sunday mornings when the Warden is in residence.

ST MARGARET'S AT CLIFFE

Set at the top of a steep slope down to the water's edge, the Church of St Margaret of Antioch has some of the richest late-Norman decorated stone-work in the country. Light floods in through continuous clerestory arcading along the entire length of the nave.

Across from the church is the Cliffe Tavern, an 18th-century schoolhouse with a typical Kent-style weather-boarded exterior.

A narrow, tortuous road leads down between trees – through which there are glimpses of the sea – and comes out at St Margaret's Bay, where a short stretch of promenade fronts a beach between two mighty out-thrusts of white cliff.

DOVER

South-east of the road leaving St Margaret's at Cliffe is the South Foreland Lighthouse. On the other side of the road, undulating fields roll away over gentle slopes. Then, all at once, Dover Castle floats up ahead, rising higher to reveal its keep and walls, the Saxon Church of St Mary-in-Castro and the Roman *pharos* – one of a pair of lighthouses which guided galleys into the harbour.

There was once an Iron Age fort where the castle now stands. Then came the Romans, one of whose town houses just outside the naval base of Dubris was discovered in 1970. Known as 'The Painted House', it still has 400sq ft of painted wall plaster, fragments of painted floors, and a hypocaust for underfloor heating. The house is open daily, except Mondays, from April to October.

The tantalising 21 miles of water between England and France has challenged intrepid pioneers for many years. On the promenade are statues of Captain Matthew Webb, who in 1875 was the first man to swim the Channel, and of Charles Rolls who flew the Channel both ways in a single flight in 1910.

BARFRESTON

The tiny village is set on the North Downs Way, a footpath following much of the Pilgrims' Way from Winchester to Canterbury.

The small Church of St Nicholas, without porch or tower – the church bell hangs from a yew tree in the churchyard – might be regarded as stark were it not for the elaboration of its carvings. Corbels of half-eroded faces grimace down from the eaves; round the eastern wheel window is a frieze of angels and beasts; and there are carvings of lions and a crocodile on the exterior.

Tourist information: Deal 361161; Dover 205108; Canterbury 66567; Herne Bay 66031.

Ancient walls of the Kentish Weald

TOUR
60

--- 63 MILES ---

Two rivers, the Beult and the Great Stour, meander through water meadows, orchards and hop gardens. Protected to the north by the rampart of the Downs lies a string of Wealden villages.

ASHFORD
In recent years Ashford has restored its old buildings and barred several streets to traffic, which makes it an unworrying town to wander about in.

In the heyday of the railways, Ashford manufactured rolling stock for all parts of the world and was a major depot for locomotives. It is still an important junction, with railways entering it from five directions, but the rail workshops have now given way to light industries of all sorts.

Round St Mary's Church, which dates from the 13th and 15th centuries, is a warren of ancient streets and alleyways, with plenty of overhanging half-timbered houses. The broad High Street, traffic-free at its upper end, has some fine Georgian buildings – reminders of the days before the coming of the railways, when Ashford was already a prosperous market town.

A market is held on Saturdays, and a street market on Fridays. One of Kent's major cattle markets is held early on Tuesday and Wednesday mornings.

Ashford's military links are recalled by the Intelligence Corps Museum in the Templer Barracks, off the main road just north of the town. It contains documents, maps, photographs and other items relating to British military intelligence in both world wars. Open Monday to Friday.

BETHERSDEN
The suffix 'den', found in dozens of village names in the area, shows that in Saxon times this compact Wealden village was a *denn* or clearing in the thick Wealden Forest where pigs were pastured. St Margaret's Church has a big battlemented west tower, built in the 15th century and used as recently as the Second World War as an observation post for warning of approaching enemy aircraft.

The so-called 'Bethersden marble', used in Canterbury and Rochester cathedrals and many smaller churches, is a greyish stone which was quarried nearby. It can take a high polish, and so was known as 'marble'.

SMARDEN
One of the gems of the Weald, Smarden has won the title of Kent's best-kept village on several occasions. More than 100 of the parish's superb, half-timbered, weatherboarded and brick-built houses are listed buildings. Standing beside the River Beult, Smarden was a noted cloth-working centre in the Middle Ages and Tudor times, and many of its finest houses were built by wealthy cloth merchants.

St Michael's Church, reached under the first floor of the overhanging Penthouse, is mainly 14th century, with a large tower added about 1475. Because of its vast size, unencumbered by supporting pillars, it has been nicknamed the 'Barn of Kent'. The magnificent roof is 36ft wide, and is of a type known as scissors-beam, because the timbers intersect. The fine cloth hall beside the churchyard has a hoist used for lifting bales of cloth still projecting from its gable.

BIDDENDEN
The village sign portrays Biddenden's unusual pair of heroines – the Siamese twins Eliza and Mary Chulkhurst, who were born about 1100, joined at hip and shoulder, and founded a local charity which exists to this day. Biddenden was a cloth-weaving village, and the most imposing of its many half-timbered buildings is the gabled Old Cloth Hall, a little way north of the green, which contained workshops for the weavers and was the headquarters of the local cloth trade.

All Saints' Church, at the end of the short main street, has a noble 15th-century tower, and contains some fine Tudor brasses, protected by carpeting, in front of the altar.

Two miles south of the village, down a small side road, the fruit trees give way to rows of neatly trimmed vines, looking more like the South of France than the Weald. These belong to the Biddenden Vineyards, where visitors can sample and buy home-grown wines and go on a tour of the 18 acre vineyard. The vineyards are open daily, except Sundays in winter.

HEADCORN
The straight village street is lined with fine old houses, some of them, like the tall-gabled, half-timbered Shakespeare House, of superb quality. Like Smarden and Biddenden, Headcorn was a cloth-weaving centre, and the Old Cloth Hall, now offices, stands at the corner of the churchyard.

The Church of St Peter and St Paul is set well back from the High Street. Built in the 1400s, it has magnificent roof timbering. On the south side is a vast hollow oak tree, almost 50ft in circumference and said to be a survivor of the ancient Wealden Forest which once covered most of Kent. There is a tradition that King John, in about 1200, held a bull-baiting beneath its spreading branches.

SUTTON VALENCE
The main road north from Headcorn shoots steeply up past the side road on which the village stands, making it easy to drive right past it. Seen from the valley, the bulky buildings of Sutton Valence boys' public school lie along the ridge, dominating the view. Once the village is reached, they are less obtrusive, though they are still its main feature. The school was founded in 1578 by William Lambe, a wealthy cloth-maker. In London, he is commemorated by Lamb's Conduit Street, named after the conduit he built to bring fresh water to the people of Holborn.

The village has plenty of old houses, built on different levels round an elliptical green. On its eastern outskirts, high on a grassy knoll, are the remains of a small Norman castle.

LEEDS CASTLE
No castle in England enjoys a more romantic setting than Leeds, rising as it does from a tranquil lake where

CASTLE OF QUEENS *Leeds Castle was bought by Queen Eleanor in 1278, and for 300 years it was a favourite retreat for eight of England's medieval queens.*

black swans glide over the reflections of its turrets and battlements. Built on two small islands, Leeds is a marvellous blend of fortification and domesticity. Dating from 857, the stone castle was rebuilt from 1119 by a Norman knight, Robert de Crevecoeur. In the late 13th century it became the favourite country retreat of Edward I and Eleanor of Castile, and it was greatly improved in the early 16th century by Henry VIII. The Heraldry Room, once the castle's great hall, encapsulates the whole history of Leeds, with coats of arms, portraits and memorabilia of many of the families associated with Leeds from the 16th to 19th centuries. The Henry VIII Banqueting Hall has a carved oak ceiling and ebony wood floor; the massive stone fireplace is 16th century and the walls are hung with tapestries including one portraying the Adoration of the Magi and dating from the late 15th century.

The castle gatehouse contains a unique museum – a collection of antique dog collars. The collection ranges over 400 years and includes collars in leather, bronze, brass and silver. The magnificent parkland, laid out by Capability Brown, includes a woodland garden, a golf course, a vineyard and the Culpeper Flower Garden. The castle, now used as a conference centre, and grounds are open daily from April to October and on Saturdays and Sundays from noon in winter.

Leeds village, just south of the castle entrance, has a striking medieval church with a massive and fortress-like wooden rood screen right across the church.

HOLLINGBOURNE
Heavy lorries thunder through Hollingbourne's single narrow street, distracting the attention from some fine old houses in the lower part of the village, known as Eyhorne Street. Godfrey House is half-timbered and dates from 1587. Eyhorne Manor is a yeoman's house dating from about 1410 and has a good collection of furniture and old laundry equipment; it is open on Saturday, Sunday and Bank Holiday afternoons from May to August, and also on Tuesdays, Wednesdays and Thursdays in August.

HARRIETSHAM
The main road splits Harrietsham into two. The northern half, known as West Street, has some good Tudor and Georgian houses. A little to the north, below the steep escarpment of the Downs, is the medieval Church of St John the Baptist, which has an unusual tower with upper room and pitched roof, tucked away behind it in the north side.

The southern half of the village has a delightful row of a dozen 18th-century almshouses, originally built by Mark Quested of the Fishmongers' Company in 1642, and rebuilt by the company in 1770.

LENHAM
A bypass leaves Lenham's superb little central square virtually traffic-free. The old houses are of every style

from medieval to Georgian, and make a leading landmark, leading back to St Mary's Church. This was largely rebuilt in the 14th century after a fire. Inside it has some superb woodwork, and on the south wall is a faded medieval mural painting showing St Michael weighing the souls of the dead.

CHARING
Approaching Charing, the main road falls headlong down Charing Hill, giving a magnificent view across the Weald – though it only lasts a minute or so, as there are no lay-bys where one can stop and enjoy it.

Charing itself is on a gentler hill, fairly free from traffic. Its single main street is lined with good Georgian and Tudor houses, and down a lane beside the churchyard are the remains of one of the great medieval palaces of the Archbishops of Canterbury. The gatehouse survives, as do the lower walls of the rest of the palace, which incorporates a Tudor farmhouse.

The Church of St Peter and St Paul has a magnificent 15th-century tower, and a roof of elaborately painted beams. It was built in 1592 to replace the original roof which was burnt out when a careless sportsman shot at a bird on the tinder-dry shingles and set them on fire.

PLUCKLEY
A pretty little hillside village above the valley of the Beult, Pluckley owes its reputation to the number of its ghosts. These include a highwayman pinned to a tree by the sword of a victim who fought back; a lady of the Dering family of local squires searching for her unbaptised child in the churchyard; a Cavalier caught and killed by the Roundheads; a 'screaming man' who worked at the local brickworks in Victorian times and fell into a mixing-trough filled with knives; a 'smiling monk' executed at Tyburn in the time of Henry VIII; and a gypsy watercress woman, who fell asleep smoking her pipe and burnt to death when her gin-soaked shawl caught alight.

HOTHFIELD COMMON
This ancient stretch of peaty land just north of Hothfield village has never been cultivated, though it was used in former centuries for grazing stock and as a source of firewood and peat. When the country was wilder than it is today, highwaymen used to lurk here to rob travellers on the road to Dover.

The common, now a nature reserve, is rich in plant life, including several varieties of heather, bog asphodel and sundew. More than 60 species of bird have been recorded,

among them green woodpeckers, nuthatches and yellowhammers, while adders and grass snakes have been seen.

The 140 acre common is owned by Ashford Borough Council and run by the Kent Trust for Nature Conservation. There is a picnic site, and a waymarked nature trail across heathland and through woods.

GODINTON PARK
Only 2 miles from the centre of Ashford, this red-brick Jacobean mansion, set in wide parkland, still seems remote from any contact with urban life. Its great hall dates from the 15th century, but its present appearance is due to Captain Nicholas Toke, who lived at Godinton for most of the 17th century, and died there in 1680 at the age of 93.

The main rooms are decorated with carved woodwork, illustrating the captain's sporting interest in pig-sticking and bear-baiting. There are also carvings of soldiers carrying out the movements of drill with pikes and muskets.

Among the ancient trees in the park are the remains of a vast oak, known as the Domesday Oak, so called from the date it was supposed to have been planted. On September 3, 1939, it split and collapsed at the moment that Neville Chamberlain was broadcasting Britain's declaration of war on Germany.

Godinton Park is open to the public at Easter, then on Sundays and Bank Holiday afternoons from June to September.

Tourist information: Ashford 37311.

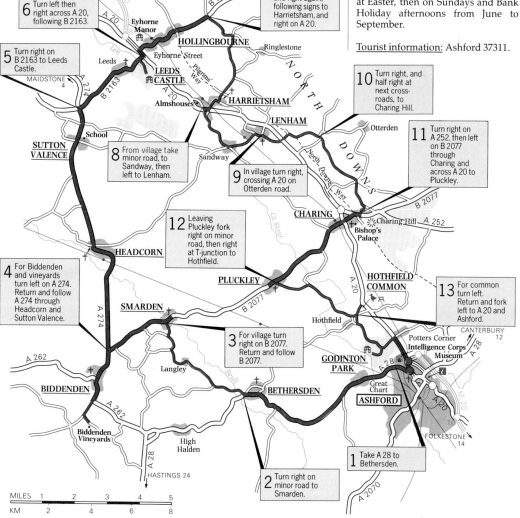

Across the gentle uplands of Essex

TOUR

61

——— 83 MILES ———

Beyond an ancient harbour where sail is still king stands the tower of a palace that was never built. A hilltop bears the marks of an army that waited for an enemy who never came.

MALDON

From the landward side the ancient hilltop town of Maldon offers no clue to its long association with the sea. This is only revealed at the Hythe, Maldon's harbour on the Blackwater estuary – an important port in the days of sail, and still important to those who sail for fun. Among the modern pleasure craft which crowd the haven are some splendid old sailing barges, which once carried a large trade out of Maldon to London and other east coast ports; their story is told in the Maldon Maritime Centre on the Quay.

The Hythe has had its own church since Saxon times, though the present building behind the Quay is Norman; its white shingled spire has been a beacon to sailors since 1740. From the Hythe, High Street curves gently uphill to the town centre past buildings of all ages from medieval to modern. Not that street-level appearance is any clue to age; many 15th and 16th-century timber-framed buildings are hidden behind later frontages. Maldon Museum, open on Saturdays, is housed in a 16th-century house which looks the part. But the Rose and Crown Hotel, despite its 19th-century cast-iron balcony on pillars, is a masterpiece of medieval brickwork.

The 'church' on the corner above the museum is in fact the library, bequeathed to the town in 1704 and one of the oldest public lending libraries in Britain. The benefactor's original collection of 6000 books is housed on the upper floor.

At the top of the High Street is Maldon's parish church of All Saints. Its 13th-century triangular tower, topped by a hexagonal spire, is unique in England, and its memorials include a stained-glass window in memory of Lawrence Washington, the great-great-grandfather of the first US president, who is buried there.

TOLLESHUNT D'ARCY

The D'Arcys are long gone, but they are not forgotten in the village to which they gave such a splendid name. Their moated manor house of about 1500 is on the right, just before the church. How the D'Arcys reached the house in its early years is not recorded; but the only way over the moat today is a four-arched bridge, not built until 1585.

The 14th-century Church of St Nicholas is noted for its brasses, four

LADIES IN RETIREMENT *Thames sailing barges lie at rest at Maldon's Hythe Quay.*

TOP TOWER *The Layer Marney Tower is the tallest Tudor gateway in England.*

CROWNING GLORY *Cottages at Pleshey show the thatcher's art at its best.*

of which commemorate D'Arcys. The last of the D'Arcys of Tolleshunt, Thomas D'Arcy III, died in 1593. His memorial, in marble, shows him kneeling at a prayer desk facing his wife.

The Georgian D'Arcy house, with evergreen oaks in its walled garden, was the home of Margery Allingham, the writer of detective novels. At the village centre, where the road forks, stands a maypole, protected by a wicket fence and topped by a weather vane. It is faced by the Queen's Head public house, a pottery and a rambling old cottage with a clock in a dormer window, where the glass would normally be.

ABBERTON RESERVOIR

Drive carefully into the car park beside the reservoir, because numbers of wildfowl seem to prefer it to the reserve established there to protect them. The entire 1300 acre reservoir and its surrounding land is a bird sanctuary, visited every year by thousands of migrating ducks, geese, swans and other birds.

A fenced refuge beside the car park encloses a large pond where visitors can see many of the migrants. For serious birdwatchers, a 100ft long hide overlooks the reservoir. There are fine views over the water from the churchyard at Layer de la Haye.

LAYER MARNEY TOWER

The massive red-brick tower which rises 80ft above green lawns is the gatehouse to a mansion that was never built. Only the tower and its wings were complete when its owner, Henry, Lord Marney, died in 1523, and work stopped. The square core of the tower is flanked by four turrets, ringed at the top with figures of dolphins and pineapples instead of battlements. Visitors can climb to the top of the tower, from which there are extensive views.

Lord Marney did finish the church next door, where he is buried. He lies in effigy, surrounded by ancestors whom he had transferred from an earlier church on the site. The tower and gardens are open on Sunday and Thursday afternoons and on Bank Holidays from April to September, and also on Tuesday afternoons in July and August.

COGGESHALL

Paycocke's, one of the finest timber-framed houses in England, sits among a supporting cast of contemporaries. All are a legacy from the Middle Ages when the town grew wealthy, first on wool, then on cloth. Sheep were brought onto the rich meadows of the River Blackwater by Cistercian monks, the ruins of whose abbey stand a short distance up a bridleway on the southern approach to the town. Laymen prospered along with the monks, among them John Paycocke who built the house in West Street around 1505; the rich carving of its timbers makes it outstanding among houses of its period. It belongs to the National Trust and is open on Wednesday, Thursday, Sunday and Bank Holiday Monday afternoons from April to mid-October. More

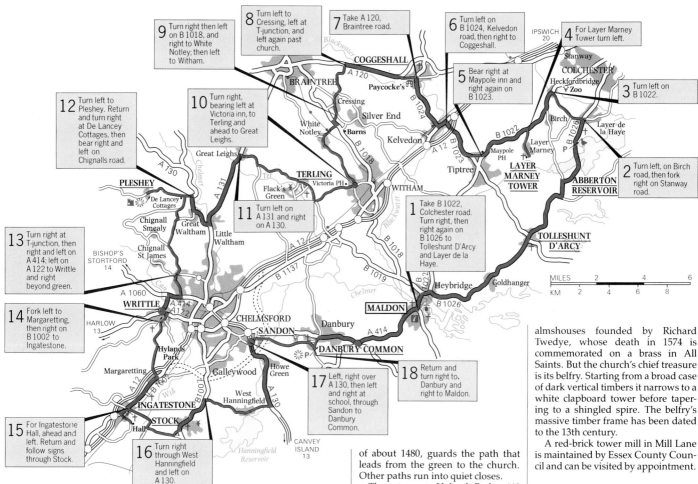

9 Turn right then left on B 1018, and right to White Notley; then left to Witham.

8 Turn left to Cressing, left at T-junction, and left again past church.

7 Take A 120, Braintree road.

6 Turn left on B 1024, Kelvedon road, then right to Coggeshall.

4 For Layer Marney Tower turn left.

5 Bear right at Maypole inn and right again on B 1023.

3 Turn left on B 1022.

12 Turn left to Pleshey. Return and turn right at De Lancey Cottages, then bear right and left on Chignalls road.

10 Turn right, bearing left at Victoria inn, to Terling and ahead to Great Leighs.

2 Turn left, on Birch road, then fork right on Stanway road.

13 Turn right at T-junction, then right and left on A 414; left on A 122 to Writtle and right beyond green.

11 Turn left on A 131 and right on A 130.

1 Take B 1022, Colchester road. Turn right, then right again on B 1026 to Tolleshunt D'Arcy and Layer de la Haye.

14 Fork left to Margaretting, then right on B 1002 to Ingatestone.

15 For Ingatestone Hall, ahead and left. Return and follow signs through Stock.

16 Turn right through West Hanningfield and left on A 130.

17 Left, right over A 130, then left and right at school, through Sandon to Danbury Common.

18 Return and turn right to Danbury and right to Maldon.

MILES 2 4 6
KM 2 4 6 8

COGGESHALL · BRAINTREE · Cressing · Silver End · Paycocke's · White Notley · Barns · Kelvedon · Great Leighs · TERLING · Victoria PH · Flack's Green · WITHAM · PLESHEY · De Lancey Cottages · Chignall Smealy · Great Waltham · Little Waltham · Chignall St James · BISHOP'S STORTFORD 14 · WRITTLE · A 414 · A 122 · HARLOW 13 · Hylands Park · Margaretting · Galleywood · Howe Green · West Hanningfield · INGATESTONE · STOCK · Hall · Hanningfield Reservoir · CANVEY ISLAND 13 · CHELMSFORD · SANDON · Danbury · DANBURY COMMON · MALDON · Heybridge · Goldhanger · TOLLESHUNT D'ARCY · LAYER MARNEY TOWER · Tiptree · Maypole PH · Layer Marney · ABBERTON RESERVOIR · Birch · Layer de la Haye · COLCHESTER · Heckfordbridge Zoo · Stanway · IPSWICH 20

16th-century houses, spaced by later intruders, lead up Church Street to the Woolpack Inn, whose timbers rival Paycocke's in all but carving.

Opposite the Woolpack Inn stands the Church of St Peter-ad-Vincula, evidence that if the woolmen of Coggeshall built richly for themselves, they also built richly for God. Completed in 1426, St Peter's is 125ft long and 63ft wide, its lofty roof creating a vast airy interior. There are a number of brasses, some of which commemorate members of the Paycocke family.

A few miles beyond Coggeshall, just beyond Cressing, two huge buildings loom across the fields to the left. They are the barns of Cressing Temple and were used in the Middle Ages by the Knights Templar. The Barley Barn dates from between 1000 and 1060; the Wheat Barn is probably late 13th century. They are still in use, and with a third barn of the 17th century they form the courtyard of a working farm.

TERLING
At the ancient heart of Terling the 13th-century Church of All Saints stands beside an immaculate village green. Opposite is a beautifully preserved old manor house of about 1480. It is complemented by colour-washed cottages which follow a bend in the road past the iron gates of Terling Place, which is not open to the public.

Flacks Green, a sort of suburb of Terling, is pinpointed by a windmill on the other side of the River Ter. It is approached either by road, past church and green, or over a footbridge beside a ford. The detour leads to another broad green surrounded by attractive old cottages. The old smock mill, now a private house, is tucked away up a side lane.

PLESHEY
A mile-long earthen rampart encircles the village of Pleshey, and from the castle mound its line is easy to follow. The ramparts protected the village when it huddled around the great castle built by the de Mandeville Earls of Sussex in the 12th century. By the 14th century it had passed to Thomas of Woodstock, Duke of Gloucester and uncle of Richard II.

It was probably from Gloucester's ownership that the only above-ground part of the castle survives. This is a red-brick bridge that spans the moat – the only bridge of its type and age in England. The top of the 60ft high mound is one of the highest points in Essex and offers fine views.

WRITTLE
The urban sprawl of Chelmsford has surrounded but not swallowed the old village of Writtle. Its broad triangular green, with the Rose and Crown at one end and the pond at the other, is still overlooked by houses that have stood there from the 15th century onwards. The finest of them, a timber-framed double-gabled house

of about 1480, guards the path that leads from the green to the church. Other paths run into quiet closes.

The entrance to Hylands Park, a 440 acre estate surrounding an 18th-century mansion, is at the end of Paradise Road. The unspoilt parkland, open daily, contains fine woods, lakes and ponds.

INGATESTONE
A bypass allows the timber-framed and Georgian houses of the main street to look forward to a few more centuries of useful life. The Church of St Edmund and St Mary lies back from the main road, sheltering behind its colossal red-brick tower. Among its many fine monuments are a series devoted to the Petre family.

Sir William Petre, who died in 1572, was Secretary of State to Henry VIII and served all three of his successors as Privy Councillor. He built the magnificent rose-brick Ingatestone Hall, where his descendants still live, half a mile south of the church across the fields. The present Lord Petre has leased the north wing to Essex County Council as a centre for historical exhibitions. The Long Gallery is lined with portraits of generations of Petres, while the Garden Chamber contains Tudor and Stuart furniture.

STOCK
There are two Stocks – the old village strung out along the through road, and newer development along Mill Road and Mill Lane. Both are equally well cared for. The old is the traditional Essex mix of soft red brick, clapboarding and colour-washed plaster. Four tiny single-storey cottages behind a neat thorn hedge were

almshouses founded by Richard Twedye, whose death in 1574 is commemorated on a brass in All Saints. But the church's chief treasure is its belfry. Starting from a broad case of dark vertical timbers it narrows to a white clapboard tower before tapering to a shingled spire. The belfry's massive timber frame has been dated to the 13th century.

A red-brick tower mill in Mill Lane is maintained by Essex County Council and can be visited by appointment.

SANDON
The small village green at Sandon must be unique in England. The houses that surround it are a mixture of cottages and larger properties of several periods, all beautifully maintained and embowered in colourful gardens. The Crown Public House, tucked away in one corner, is all that a village pub should be. But what catches the eye and dominates the whole scene is a single tree that stands at the centre of the green. Its branches writhe out to seemingly impossible lengths to cover virtually the whole green. The tree is a Spanish oak, rare in Britain – which is perhaps just as well. For charming though Sandon's unusual green is, there is something to be said for the traditional type with room for a pond and a cow or two.

DANBURY COMMON
An open area of heather, gorse and bracken, dotted with strands of silver birch and oak, the common belongs to the National Trust and offers a maze of paths and bridleways. The Danbury Ridge commands views over the Blackwater estuary, a possible route inland for any invader, so it has long had great appeal to the military mind. Just beyond Danbury Country Park can be seen the Napoleonic redoubt – an earthwork dug by an army which camped on the common throughout the Napoleonic Wars to guard against a French landing on the coast below. Soldiers were based there again in the Second World War.

Tourist information: Maldon 56503.

Winding ways to Cambridge through the Rodings

TOUR
62

——— 83 MILES ———

Of all the exits from London, the way out through Epping Forest is arguably the finest. Another forest, a quiet river valley and a chain of ruined castles mark the route to Cambridge.

EPPING FOREST

Just 9 miles from the City the sprawl of London comes to an abrupt end by the Warren Wood public house. From there, Epping Forest stretches unbroken for 6 miles. At more than 6000 acres, the forest is one of the largest stretches of native woodland in southern England – and all of it is open to the public.

In low-lying areas the dominant trees are oaks – many of great age and size. On higher ground beeches take over, rivalling the oaks in size and grandeur. But the trees for which the forest is famous are its hornbeams; smaller than oaks and beeches, their gnarled branches make them look ancient beyond their years.

There is one small community in the forest, at High Beach. Its church, known as the church in the woods, stands embowered by trees at a meeting point of several forest lanes. Lord Tennyson lived at High Beach for several years.

The name High Beach refers to a great outcrop of gravel on a scarp where no trees grow. From the car park there are views down into the valley of the Lea, where the stumpy tower of Waltham Abbey, the reputed burial place of King Harold, can be seen. Beyond the car park is the Epping Forest Conservation Centre, where information on the forest's wildlife and history is available.

GREENSTED CHURCH

The little wooden Church of St Andrew at Greensted is a lone survivor from an age when most English buildings were built of wood. Modern scientific techniques date its timbers back to about 850, making it the oldest wooden church in the world.

From the outside the nave has the look of a log cabin, consisting as it does of timbers standing side by side to support the roof. The timbers – black with age, but sturdy as ever – are trunks of oak, split vertically with the smooth side facing inwards. There is also a wooden tower, weatherboarded and topped by a jaunty little spire, possibly dating from Tudor times.

THE RODINGS

The River Roding cuts a modest valley through West Essex from its source near Great Dunmow to the Thames, linking, in its upper reaches, eight villages and hamlets with Roding in their names. They are not named after

PALACE AND PLAYERS *With Audley End as a noble spectator, a game of cricket completes the wholly English scene.*

AYTHORPE RODING *The weatherboarded post mill is a prominent landmark.*

BEAUTY TREATMENT *The 15th-century Sun Inn at Saffron Walden has some of the finest decorative plasterwork, called pargeting, in East Anglia.*

the river – the river is named after the settlements, founded by a Saxon tribe called the Hrothingas.

Beauchamp Roding's church, in the fields to the right about 2 miles north of Fyfield, is reached by a quarter-mile footpath from the road. Beauchamp Roding itself is another quarter of a mile away across the fields on the other side of the church.

Abbess Roding, where church and hall sit cheek by jowl, owes its name to the Abbey of Barking which owned the manor until the Dissolution. Next comes White Roding, typical of Essex villages in its timber houses and stone-built church.

The River Roding itself appears just before Leaden Roding – so named, it is said, because it was the first of the

Rodings to have its church roofed with lead. At Aythorpe Roding the sails of a white-painted post mill soar above a group of old thatched houses. The mill is open on the last Sunday of each month.

The last, and biggest, of the Rodings, is High Roding, an example of medieval ribbon development along a length of Roman road. Among the old colour-washed houses sits the comparatively young Old School of 1861, forlornly bereft of children, and a couple of comfortable pubs which are still attended.

STANSTED MOUNTFITCHET

The Norman family who gave this small town its full name died out in the 13th century, but not before

building the castle whose mound rises above the railway station. A few ruins of the foundations and ramparts are all that remain among the earthworks. Below the mound, in Lower Street, is a row of 16th-century houses, some with their timbers exposed, others clad in decorative plasterwork.

Monuments in St Mary's Church, half a mile away, include the simple 13th-century figure of a crosslegged knight in armour, whose turnout contrasts with that of Hester Salusbury's effigy. Her smart hat, elaborately coifed hair, lace collar and cuffs and well-cut gown seem more suited to presentation at court than an appointment with her maker.

Up Chapel Hill, to the left, is a well-restored tower windmill of 1787. Its machinery is maintained in working order, and it can be visited on the first Sunday afternoon in the month from April to October, every Sunday in August, and on Bank Holidays.

CLAVERING
One of the few castles existing in England before the Norman Conquest was built at Clavering in 1052 by a Breton, Robert Fitzwimarc, a sheriff of Essex. All that remains of his castle – in a meadow beside the church – is the moat, fed by ditches linked to the River Stort.

The Church of St Mary and St Clement almost makes up for the missing castle with a riot of battlements. It dates from the 14th century.

WENDENS AMBO
Colour-washed cottages, some roofed in thatch and some tiled, perch on a grassy bank above the short lane which leads to the Church of St Mary. Facing the cottages is the gable end of an enormous timber-framed barn, also with a thatched roof.

The sturdy squat tower of St Mary's is topped by a short slender spire of the type known as a Hertfordshire spike. The village name dates from 1662 when the parishes of Little Wenden and Great Wenden were combined: *ambo* is Latin for 'both'.

SAFFRON WALDEN
The tangle of 15th and 16th-century timber-framed buildings at the town centre is a delight to the eye – but even they are modern when compared with the streets in which they stand. For the layout of the town centre is the same today as it was in 1141 when Geoffrey de Mandeville established a market below his castle walls. What is left of his castle – a decayed stump or two – stands on a grassy knoll at the highest point of the town.

The church's soaring 193ft spire dominates castle and town. Though the spire was a 19th-century afterthought, it sits beautifully on the tower of the largest church in Essex – 184ft long by 80ft wide. The church was rebuilt in the 15th century, and its grandeur reflects Walden's prosperity at that time.

Walden's original wealth came from wool and cloth, then in the 14th century it was discovered that the saffron crocus grew well in the local soil. This produced a new source of wealth, and Chipping ('Market') Walden became Saffron Walden. The trade in saffron – used in dyeing, medicine and cooking – continued until the end of the 18th century.

AUDLEY END
Large as it is, the handsome Jacobean mansion which presides over a park landscaped by Capability Brown is only one wing of the original house. It was built for Thomas Howard, 1st Earl of Suffolk and Lord High Treasurer to James I. Work started in 1603 and continued until 1616, by which time it was the biggest house in England, bigger even than the king's own palace of Hampton Court.

Suffolk's successors found the upkeep of the place too expensive and it

was eventually sold by the 3rd Earl to Charles II. The king never finished paying for it, and William II returned the house to the Suffolks. In 1721 the 7th Earl called in the architect Sir John Vanbrugh, who had more than half the building demolished.

The present interior owes much to Robert Adam, who also designed the bridge over the River Cam and several elegant garden 'ornaments', including temples, lodges and a hilltop column. The house and gardens are open every afternoon except Mondays from April to September, and on Bank Holidays.

DUXFORD AIRFIELD
More than 90 historic aircraft are on permanent display at Duxford Airfield. These range from tiny, fragile-looking veterans of the First World War to Concorde 01. This, the British pre-production model, has flown faster than any other Concorde, attaining 1450mph over Tangier in 1974.

In the Second World War Duxford was first a fighter base – Group Captain Douglas Bader flew Spitfires there – and later a station of the US Air Force, which flew Thunderbolt and Mustang fighters.

WANDLEBURY
In the flat Cambridgeshire landscape the Gog Magog Hills loom like the Himalayas, although they rise to only 300ft. The top is crowned by an Iron Age fort whose ramparts enclose 15 acres.

The nearby building is the stable block of a now demolished mansion. Beneath its central arch is buried the Godolphin Arabian, one of the four arab stallions from which all modern racehorses are descended. He died in 1753 aged 29. The block belongs to the Cambridge Preservation Society, who have laid out a nature trail in the grounds.

GRANTCHESTER
If there is such a thing as a literary village, then Grantchester is it. And it is pretty, too. The village stands beside the River Cam, known there by its older name of Granta, and it is the river which has attracted writers down the ages. The spot they sought, now called Byron's Pool, is reached by a footpath signposted off the Trumpington Road just before the village.

Chaucer, Spencer, Milton and Dryden all knew the spot long before Byron, and in more recent years Rupert Brooke immortalised the village in his poem *The Old Vicarage, Grantchester*, which ends with the lines: 'Stands the church clock at ten to three? And is there honey still for tea?' Brooke lived in the village for several years, first at a cottage, called the Orchard – now a tearoom – and later at the Old Vicarage.

For the rest, Grantchester is a colourful jumble of substantial villas and ancient cottages of plaster and thatch, tucked in well-kept gardens behind hedges and walls of flint and brick. And the clock? It still stands at ten to three.

Tourist information: Saffron Walden 24282; Cambridge 322640.

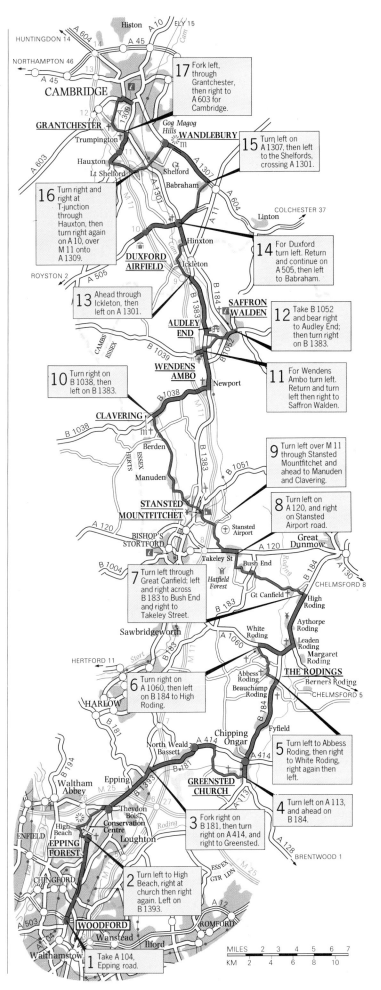

17 Fork left, through Grantchester, then right to A 603 for Cambridge.

15 Turn left on A 1307, then left to the Shelfords, crossing A 1301.

16 Turn right and right at T-junction through Hauxton, then turn right again on A 10, over M 11 onto A 1309.

14 For Duxford turn left. Return and continue on A 505, then left to Babraham.

13 Ahead through Ickleton, then left on A 1301.

12 Take B 1052 and bear right to Audley End; then turn right on B 1383.

11 For Wendens Ambo turn left. Return and turn left then right to Saffron Walden.

10 Turn right on B 1038, then left on B 1383.

9 Turn left over M 11 through Stansted Mountfitchet and ahead to Manuden and Clavering.

8 Turn left on A 120, and right on Stansted Airport road.

7 Turn left through Great Canfield; left and right across B 183 to Bush End and right to Takeley Street.

6 Turn right on A 1060, then left on B 184 to High Roding.

5 Turn left to Abbess Roding, then right to White Roding, right again then left.

4 Turn left on A 113, and ahead on B 184.

3 Fork right on B 181, then turn right on A 414, and right to Greensted.

2 Turn left to High Beach, right at church then right again. Left on B 1393.

1 Take A 104, Epping road.

MILES 1 2 3 4 5 6 7
KM 2 4 6 8 10

105

Progress through Bunyan's country

Villages in the peaceful valley of the Great Ouse have an abundance of thatched cottages, giving them an old-world charm. Lanes wind through green pastures and broad fields of wheat.

BIDDENHAM

Although very close to Bedford, this attractive village retains its rural atmosphere. Its main street with wide grass verges is lined with large houses dating mostly from the 19th century, and colour-washed cottages. Many of the buildings are magnificently thatched; they include the large Three Tuns pub. Across the road, on the corner of Nodder's Way, a long, low barn has been converted into the village hall.

At the end of the village stands the 12th-century Church of St James. It has a Jacobean screen. A blue-gold cloth behind the altar was used in Westminster Abbey during the Coronation of Elizabeth II.

STAGSDEN

In Turvey Road, leading from the parish church of Stagsden, are the Stagsden Bird Gardens, a bird-breeding and conservation centre specialising in pheasants, waterfowl and poultry.

The gardens contain more than 150 species of birds, many of them rare breeds such as guans and gallinules, black-necked swans, the sacred ibis and Siberian red-breasted geese. Open daily, the gardens also contain a display of shrub roses, and there are picnic areas.

TURVEY

On a warm summer's day the tree-shaded banks of the Great Ouse provide a cool resting place by Turvey's 13th-century bridge, and the air is clean and fresh when a light breeze ripples the waters streaming beneath the low arches. Beside the bridge is the 17th-century Ye Three Fyshes Inn, and a little farther along the road are imposing houses of the mid-19th century.

The houses were built by Charles Longuet-Higgins, lord of the manor at that time, who also spared no expense in restoring the parish church. During the restoration a 14th-century wall painting was uncovered; it can be seen on the south wall of the chapel.

FELMERSHAM

Buildings of cream-coloured stone and neatly trimmed thatch are attractively grouped in this village on a hill rising from the banks of the Great Ouse. A five-arched stone bridge spans the river.

The Church of St Mary the Virgin is 13th century, with an impressive arcaded west front and lofty, abbey-like interior. Next to the church stands a medieval tithe barn, its long, low roof tiled and the walls buttressed.

ST NEOTS

In a broad swath of steely-grey water the Great Ouse sweeps to the west of the town close to the market square; it is joined by its tributary the Hen Brook just beyond the concrete bridge which carries the main road into the town. At the junction of these waters a monastery was founded in the 10th century by Earl Leofric and dedicated to St Neot, the saint most venerated by Alfred the Great.

Nothing remains of the monastery, but the town that grew around it prospered and took its name from the patron saint. By the 15th century local merchants were trading with the cities of both north and south Europe. Their prosperity is reflected in the church they built, the magnificent St Mary's which dominates the town.

Georgian buildings with façades in shades of yellow and ochre face the market square, and by the bridge the 17th-century Bridge Hotel has waterside terraces and a small quay. To the

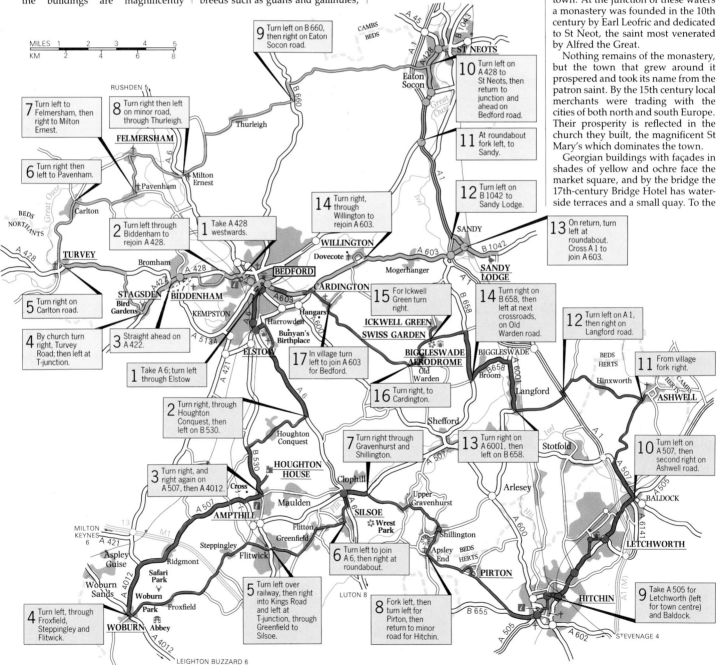

MILES 1 2 3 4 5
KM 2 4 6 8

RUSHDEN 5

9 Turn left on B 660, then right on Eaton Socon road.

CAMBS
BEDS

7 Turn left to Felmersham, then right to Milton Ernest.

8 Turn right then left on minor road, through Thurleigh.

Thurleigh

ST NEOTS

10 Turn left on A 428 to St Neots, then return to junction and ahead on Bedford road.

Eaton Socon

FELMERSHAM

Milton Ernest

6 Turn right then left to Pavenham.

Pavenham

11 At roundabout fork left, to Sandy.

Carlton

BEDS
NORTHANTS

2 Turn left through Biddenham to rejoin A 428.

1 Take A 428 westwards.

14 Turn right, through Willington to rejoin A 603.

12 Turn left on B 1042 to Sandy Lodge.

SANDY

13 On return, turn left at roundabout. Cross A 1 to join A 603.

TURVEY

Bromham

WILLINGTON
Dovecote

A 603

B 1042

SANDY LODGE

5 Turn right on Carlton road.

STAGSDEN
Bird Gardens

BIDDENHAM

BEDFORD

Mogerhanger

4 By church turn right, Turvey Road; then left at T-junction.

3 Straight ahead on A 422.

KEMPSTON

Harrowden

CARDINGTON

Hangars

15 For Ickwell Green turn right.

14 Turn right on B 658, then left at next crossroads, on Old Warden road.

12 Turn left on A 1, then right on Langford road.

BEDS
HERTS

1 Take A 6; turn left through Elstow

ELSTOW

Bunyan's Birthplace

ICKWELL GREEN
SWISS GARDEN

BIGGLESWADE AERODROME
Old Warden

BIGGLESWADE

Broom

Langford

Hinxworth

11 From village fork right.

ASHWELL

17 In village turn left to join A 603 for Bedford.

16 Turn right, to Cardington.

2 Turn right, through Houghton Conquest, then left on B 530.

Houghton Conquest

Shefford

7 Turn right through Gravenhurst and Shillington.

13 Turn right on A 6001, then left on B 658.

Stotfold

10 Turn left on A 507, then second right on Ashwell road.

BALDOCK

3 Turn right, and right again on A 507, then A 4012.

Cross

HOUGHTON HOUSE

Clophill

Maulden

Upper Gravenhurst

Arlesey

MILTON KEYNES 6

AMPTHILL

Flitton
Greenfield

SILSOE
Wrest Park

Shillington

Apsley End

LETCHWORTH

Steppingley

Flitwick

6 Turn left to join A 6, then right at roundabout.

BEDS
HERTS

Aspley Guise

Safari Park

Ridgmont

5 Turn left over railway, then right into Kings Road and left at T-junction, through Greenfield to Silsoe.

PIRTON

Woburn Sands

Woburn Park

Froxfield

LUTON 8

8 Fork left, then turn left for Pirton, then return to minor road for Hitchin.

9 Take A 505 for Letchworth (left for town centre) and Baldock.

HITCHIN

4 Turn left, through Froxfield, Steppingley and Flitwick.

WOBURN Abbey

LEIGHTON BUZZARD 6

STEVENAGE 4

OLD WARDEN *Green parkland and brown stubble share the fertile sandstone countryside round Old Warden Park, built in 1872 and now an agricultural college.*

south of the bridge the river winds between tree-lined banks where pleasure craft moor, and on the western side a footpath crosses grassy open spaces running to the water's edge.

SANDY LODGE
This 19th-century house on the outskirts of Sandy has been the headquarters of the Royal Society for the Protection of Birds since 1961. It stands in 104 acres of heath and woodland where a nature trail has been laid out. More than 100 different species of birds have been recorded at Sandy Lodge, and 50 or more have been known to breed there.

Though principally a bird reserve, other wildlife can be seen along the nature trail. Grey squirrels are common in the woodland and there are muntjac deer in the areas of bracken. Common lizards live on the heath, and wolf spiders like to sun themselves on the warm, sandy soil.

Sandy Lodge is open to the public daily except Sundays in summer, and on weekdays only in winter.

WILLINGTON
This village is notable for its fine church, dedicated to St Lawrence and dating mostly from the 16th century. It is a bluff, square-looking building with a stocky tower and battlemented parapet. The church was built in the time of Sir John Gostwick, a member of the court of Henry VIII.

Sir John's manor house has not survived, but its huge dovecote has. It has two roofs set one above the other and separated by louvres through which the birds could pass in and out.

The dovecote is owned by the National Trust but is open only by appointment. It can be seen quite clearly, however, from the road leading from the church.

TOUR
64

——— 75 MILES ———

Across the fertile Bedfordshire Plain, strode Christian in Bunyan's *Pilgrim's Progress*; from these fields, too, in October 1930, the airship R101 began its ill-fated maiden voyage.

BEDFORD
The Great Ouse river flows through the centre of the town, passing within a few yards of the busy market square. The five-arched Town Bridge, dating from 1813, gracefully spans the river and there are riverside walks, open spaces and gardens beside the water.

Most of Bedford's architecture dates from the 18th century and later, including the Meeting House of 1849 which stands on the site of the barn where John Bunyan once preached. It has bronze doors which are divided into five panels depicting scenes from *Pilgrim's Progress*.

Adjoining the Meeting House is the Bunyan Museum which displays relics of the author's life. His statue stands on St Peter's Green, in front of St Peter's Church.

ELSTOW
Here, in 1628, John Bunyan was born; his cottage birthplace has long since vanished, but the site is marked by a stone in a field near the hamlet of Harrowden. The late 15th-century Moot Hall is now a museum illustrating 17th-century life and traditions associated with John Bunyan.

Elstow's Abbey Church of St Helena and St Mary contains the font

at which Bunyan was christened, and two stained-glass windows installed in 1880 depict scenes from *Pilgrim's Progress* and *The Holy War*. Bunyan's mother, father and sister are buried in the graveyard.

HOUGHTON HOUSE
Before he became a nonconformist preacher, John Bunyan was a tinker, and as such he visited Houghton House to mend kitchen utensils. Even today, though the house is a gaunt ruin, it is possible to imagine the impact it must have made on the young man as he climbed the hill on which it stands, probably the 'Hill Difficulty' that Christian had to climb.

From the top of the hill it is possible to see, on a clear day, the Chiltern Hills in the far distance – the 'Delectable Mountains' which Christian saw when he left 'House Beautiful'.

AMPTHILL
Georgian houses and bow-windowed shop fronts line the streets converging on Ampthill's town centre, overlooked by a splendid Dutch-gabled building surmounted by a small clock tower with a cupola.

In 1533 Henry VIII sent his first wife Catherine of Aragon to Ampthill Castle while arranging the divorce that led to the break with Rome. The castle fell into ruin in the 17th century, and only an 18th-century cross now marks the spot; but the 300 acre parkland in which it stands is open to the public.

WOBURN
The route into the village runs alongside the high brick walls of Woburn Park, the 3000 acre estate of the Duke of Bedford. His house, Woburn Abbey, was built in the 18th century by Henry Flitcroft and Inigo Jones, and

later additions were made by Henry Holland. The State Apartments contain paintings by Canaletto, Van Dyck, Rembrandt, Gainsborough and Reynolds. There are also collections of French and English 18th-century furniture, silver and porcelain.

The park contains herds of several species of deer, including the rare Père David's deer. There is also the Wild Animal Kingdom, a safari park where visitors can drive through pastures in which lions, giraffes and elephants roam free. It is open daily in summer.

SILSOE
A bypass has brought peace to this attractive village on the London to Bedford road. Its colour-washed cottages with their brightly painted front doors and tread-worn stone steps stand quietly along narrow pavements. Behind the main street stand houses of thatch and timber.

To the east of the village is Wrest Park, with a house built in the French Renaissance style in 1834. Some rooms and the landscaped gardens are open on summer weekends.

PIRTON
On the corner of Pirton's High Street stands a row of cottages which are a sheer delight. A steep thatched roof, with windows peeping out from under the eaves, sweeps down to timber-framed walls, and roses climb to upper-floor level. A white picket fence encloses front gardens tall with hollyhocks.

HITCHIN
This Hertfordshire market town centres upon its original market place, from whose corners lead four streets. For the most part they are streets full of charm, especially Churchyard

PIGEONS' FANCY *Sir John Gostwick, a courtier of Henry VIII, built this dovecote with 1500 nesting boxes in Willington.*

CARDINGTON CHURCH *St Mary's has Norman origins but was largely restored this century by the Whitbread family.*

CALM WATERS *At St Neots today only pleasure craft ruffle the Great Ouse, which was once busy with barges.*

VILLAGE VIEWPOINT *At 568ft one of Bedfordshire's highest villages, Shillington looks over country that Bunyan knew.*

STAR ROLE *A star-shaped pavilion with a central room is the focal point of Wrest Park's formal 18th-century gardens.*

TURVEY TOMB *A lavish mausoleum in Turvey churchyard honours the 19th-century Higgins family.*

WREST PARK *A 19th-century French Renaissance-style mansion stands in landscaped gardens near Silsoe.*

which has a Georgian terrace and almshouses dated from the 17th century. The 15th-century Church of St Mary stands in beautiful grounds, with lawns leading down to the tiny River Hiz which runs through the town. The Baptist Church of 1844 stands on the site of an earlier chapel where John Bunyan preached. Its pulpit chair was a gift from Bunyan.

Among the timber-framed houses in Bridge Street stands The Priory, built of stone in 1771, with Venetian windows and a semicircular pillared porch. It is now business premises.

LETCHWORTH
Only a few miles east of medieval Hitchin lies a town that is pure 20th century – the dream come true of Ebenezer Howard who, in the early 1900s, built this garden city. It clings like a flowering bud to the stem of the ancient Icknield Way, lined for a mile of its length with almond trees.

In the town centre are spacious gardens with tall poplars soaring high above neat flowerbeds and dwarfing the red-brick Georgian-style buildings around. Spreading out from the centre are roads, avenues, squares and gardens planted with 7000 trees of some 50 different varieties.

Letchworth was Britain's first garden city, and a museum in the town contains items relating to the garden city movement.

ASHWELL
At the eastern end of Ashwell a spring bubbles up in a dell surrounded by ash trees. Thus Ashwell got its name, and grew up around the spring which is the source of the River Cam. During the 19th century plaiting straw for the Luton hat industry was a major village craft.

The tower of the 14th-century St Mary's Church is the highest of any parish in Hertfordshire, and can be seen for miles around. In 1896 it was fitted with a clock, which has only three faces because a farmer whose lands lay to the north complained that if his workers in the fields could see the clock they would waste time watching it.

Many of Ashwell's buildings date from medieval times; they include Bear House, on the corner of Bear Lane, the Chantry House and the Rose and Crown pub.

BIGGLESWADE AERODROME
In the late 1920s a young man named Richard Shuttleworth began collecting veteran cars and aeroplanes. This was the start of the Shuttleworth Collection now housed at Biggleswade Aerodrome. Shuttleworth joined the Royal Air Force at the outbreak of the Second World War and was killed in 1940, but his mother endowed a trust to maintain the collection as a memorial to him and it now contains some 40 old aeroplanes, cars, carriages and bicycles.

By far the most exciting of the exhibits are the aircraft, ranging from a 1909 Blériot to a 1941 Spitfire, many of which take to the air for public flying displays on the last Sunday of every month in summer. The museum is open daily in summer.

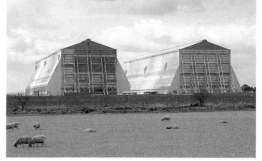

SWISS GARDEN

This garden, part of the Old Warden Park estate, was laid out in the early 19th century and is presumably so named because of the pretty little Swiss cottage that stands on a knoll in the centre of lawns, ponds and flowerbeds. The garden was conceived by the Ongley family, owners of Old Warden Park at that time.

In a mere 8 acres the design captures a romantic mood with its rock gardens, the cottage, ornamental ponds and a stone grotto to which is attached a fern house in a glass and cast-iron structure. Waymarked paths wind through the garden, which is open most days in summer.

ICKWELL GREEN

A short detour leads to a pretty village built around a vast green where, on May Day, revellers dance around the permanent maypole. Cottages are scattered around the green, their faces cheerfully made up in shades of primrose, ochre and brick red; and here and there thatched roofs rise steeply from low eaves, including the yellow-washed cricket pavilion.

On one side of the green is the old forge, no longer in use as such, with a doorway in the shape of a horseshoe. In the 17th century it was the workshop of Thomas Tompion, the father of English clock-making. His nearby cottage is marked by a plaque given by the Clockmakers' Company.

CARDINGTON

Looming over the flat countryside surrounding Cardington the giant airship hangars, built in the days when airships seemed to be the aerial transport of the future, are landmarks for miles around. For more than 50 years the village has lived in their shadow, and has shared the triumphs and the grief of the airship building programme that was abandoned after the tragic loss of the R101. In Cardington's church the airship's tattered ensign is a sad reminder of the October day in 1930 when she crashed in France on her maiden voyage with the loss of 48 lives.

The houses of Cardington, and the Kings Arms pub, are set around a wide green. Most were built by the Whitbread family whose fortunes were made in the brewing firm founded by Samuel Whitbread in the 18th century. He was born in Cardington in 1720. The Whitbread family continued to take an interest in the village, and a later Samuel Whitbread restored the church. It contains a font which is a rare example of Josiah Wedgwood's work in black basalt – a gift from Harriet Whitbread in 1783.

The airship hangars served as workshops for the barrage balloons built to defend London during the Second World War. No one expected them ever to fulfil their original purpose again, yet today the silver cigar-shaped aircraft are once more a familiar sight in Bedfordshire's skies, carrying the hopes of a new breed of airship designers who still believe that these graceful craft have a future.

Tourist information: Bedford 215226; Ampthill 402051; Hitchin 34738.

OLD ELSTOW *Cottages in Elstow's main street have been restored to look much as they did in Bunyan's day.*

HIGH HANGARS *The ill-fated R101 was among the airships built in these giant hangars near Cardington.*

BUNYAN MUSEUM *The late 15th-century Moot Hall in Elstow is now a museum of the life and times of Bunyan.*

SPACIOUS CHURCH *St Mary's in Hitchin, with its fine two-storey porch, is the largest parish church in Hertfordshire.*

BEAUTIFUL RUIN *Houghton was probably the 'House Beautiful' visited by Christian in 'Pilgrim's Progress'.*

STAGSDEN SWANS *Many rare waterfowl are among more than 1500 birds in Stagsden Bird Gardens.*

PEACEFUL REFLECTIONS *The placid waters of the Great Ouse mirror the trees that line its banks near Felmersham.*

A martyr's shrine and a writer's corner

TOUR
65
—— 70 MILES ——

Leafy lanes climb to the northernmost ridges of the Chilterns. On the way are one of England's finest Jacobean houses, and the home of the playwright George Bernard Shaw.

ST ALBANS

The cathedral city surrounds an abbey church built in 1077 on the site of the shrine of St Alban, Britain's first Christian martyr. Alban, a Roman soldier based at Verulamium, was put to death in 303 for sheltering a Christian priest. The Roman town occupied a site by the River Ver; it was sacked by Boudicca in AD 60, but soon rebuilt. Parts of its massive walls can still be seen, as well as its theatre – the only known example which has a stage instead of an amphitheatre.

The town of St Albans – it became a city in 1877 – grew up around the abbey, and there are many fine buildings dating from medieval and later periods. There are timber-framed shops in French Row, with overhanging upper storeys, and close by is the clock tower dating from the early 15th century. It was built as a curfew tower and is one of only two in England – the other is at Morpeth in Northumberland. Fishpool Street has Georgian frontages covering older structures, and Holywell Hill has attractive Georgian houses and the 15th-century White Hart Hotel.

The cathedral is 550ft long, one of the longest in Britain, and its square Norman tower was built with Roman bricks from Verulamium. Nearby is the abbey gateway, once the main entrance to the monastery that was destroyed at the Dissolution of the Monasteries in 1539. A road from the gateway leads to the medieval Ye Old Fighting Cocks inn, originally a fishing lodge for the monks and once a venue for cock-fighting. It claims to be the oldest inhabited licensed house in England.

To the west of the city is Gorham-bury House, home of the Earl of Verulam. It dates from 1784 and stands near the ruins of a Tudor house that was built by Sir Nicholas Bacon, Lord Keeper to Elizabeth I, and inherited by his son Sir Francis Bacon. Gorhambury House is open on Thursday afternoons in summer.

SALISBURY HALL

During the Second World War this Jacobean house became the secret workshop for one of the most successful aircraft of the war – the de Havilland Mosquito. Built mostly of wood, the component parts of the prototype aircraft were made at Salisbury Hall and then transported to the de Havilland factory at Hatfield, where various versions of

the Mosquito went into full-scale production.

The grounds now contain the Mosquito Aircraft Museum, which includes the original prototype along with many other de Havilland aircraft. The museum is open on Sundays in summer, and also Thursdays from July to September.

HATFIELD HOUSE

For more than 350 years Hatfield House has been the home of the Cecil family, marquises for 200 years and now Earls of Salisbury. It was Robert Cecil, favourite of Elizabeth I and her successor James I, who conceived the magnificent building, which is a superb example of Jacobean architecture, with just a touch of Tudor styling linking it with a departing age. Previously a royal palace had stood here, and in its grounds Elizabeth heard of her accession to the throne.

One wing of the palace, containing the banqueting hall, still stands 100yds away from Robert Cecil's house. He acquired Hatfield when James I offered it in exchange for Cecil's house at Theobalds, near Enfield. Between 1607 and 1611 Cecil

employed the finest craftsmen available in Europe to build Hatfield House. Its south front, perfect in its symmetry and noble in its majestic elegance, has altered little in 350 years, its red-brick projecting wings thrusting out from the white stone facing of the long gallery with its clock tower and Dutch gables.

The Great Hall stands two storeys high with a carved wooden screen at one end, and at the other a door leading to the Grand Staircase carved with lions and cherubs. The Marble Hall, named for its chequered marble floor, has a minstrels' gallery, reflecting Cecil's nostalgia for the Tudor age.

There are relics of both Elizabeth I and Mary, Queen of Scots in the house – Elizabeth's stockings, gloves and straw hat, and a draft of Mary's execution warrant. These, and the paintings, furniture, tapestries and armour set out in the rooms, can be seen daily except Mondays in summer.

HATFIELD

In 1948 Hatfield became one of the first post-war 'new towns', but in Old Hatfield the character of the old

coaching town survives. There are a number of half-timbered and red-brick Georgian buildings, and the Eight Bells Inn, which dates from the 17th century. The oldest building is the 13th-century St Ethelreda's Church which has a chapel·for the Cecil family.

AYOT ST LAWRENCE

In 1906 the playwright George Bernard Shaw was seeking a country home, and while visiting Ayot St Lawrence he saw a gravestone in the churchyard inscribed with the epitaph 'Her time was short'. The lady buried there had lived to the age of 70 and Shaw, then 50, decided that a place where 70 years was considered a short life span was the place for him.

It was a prophetic decision, for Shaw lived at Ayot St Lawrence for the next 44 years, at the house he renamed Shaw's Corner. In 1944 he gave the house to the National Trust, though he continued to live there, and after his death in 1950 Shaw's Corner became a place of pilgrimage for his many admirers.

Four of the downstairs rooms are unchanged since Shaw's death; his typewriter, pens, notebooks and dictionaries are set out on the desk in the study, and his hats still hang in the hall. At the bottom of the large garden is the revolving summerhouse where

MARTYR'S SHRINE *Abbot Paul de Caen built St Albans Abbey on the site of a Saxon shrine to Britain's first Christian martyr.*

SHAW'S CORNER *George Bernard Shaw's house was originally the New Rectory.*

ROOFTOP ODDITY *The Crooked Chimney pub at Lemsford needs no inn sign.*

OLD HATFIELD *Half-timbered cottages survive from the days of the stagecoach.*

the playwright sometimes worked. Shaw loved Ayot St Lawrence, and his last published work was a book of verse about the village. Certainly it has a charm that would inspire all but the soulless, with its ruined 14th-century church and 18th-century Grecian-style successor, rows of timber-framed cottages, the 400-year-old Brocket Arms and the 17th-century Old Rectory, all tucked away in leafy country lanes.

LILLEY

The road leading north-west from Whitwell runs through the shallow valley of Lilley Bottom, hops over the Luton to Hitchin road and then winds into this attractive village where Georgian cottages, the gleaming white Lilley Arms and a group of Tudor-style houses face a small triangular green.

The parish church of St Peter is 'new' as parish churches go – less than 150 years old. It is faced with undressed flint, and has a chequer-work parapet to its tower. A lich gate leads to a path lined with rosebushes. The oak pulpit was made from timbers from the Chapel of St John's College, Cambridge, which was pulled down and rebuilt in 1871.

HEXTON

Laburnum trees line Hexton's main street and the approach to it, and in spring when the flowers hang like golden pendants it lives up to its local name, the 'golden mile'. To the south of the village rise the wooded Barton Hills and on one of them is Ravensburgh Castle, an Iron Age hill-fort surrounded by a deep ditch.

SHARPENHOE

A crooked finger of low hills straggles across south Bedfordshire, and at Sharpenhoe the knuckle-like ridge rises to 525ft and is crowned by a leafy crest of beech trees called Clappers Wood. This, on the northernmost tip of the Chilterns, is a remnant of the great beech woods farther south, and stands like a cockscomb above the flat plains to the north.

A road leads up from the village to a small National Trust car park, and from there footpaths lead across the ridge and into the woods.

DUNSTABLE

Two mini-roundabouts mark the crossing of two ancient roads in the centre of Dunstable – the Roman Watling Street, now the A5, and the B489 which follows the line of the

prehistoric Icknield Way. The Romans established a posting station at the crossing and called it Durocobrivae, but when they left, their settlement decayed and it was not until the 12th century that Dunstable began to emerge as a market town. It grew around the Augustinian priory founded by Henry I, but all that remains of the priory now is the parish church of St Peter built in 1150. It is in this church that Archbishop Cranmer pronounced the divorce of Catherine of Aragon from Henry VIII in 1533.

There is little else of great age in Dunstable, and most of its heart is taken up by a shopping precinct and car parks. But Saturday markets are still held in front of the modern, oval-shaped Queensway Hall.

DUNSTABLE DOWNS

Only a few miles from the urban sprawl of Luton and Dunstable the grassy humps of Dunstable Downs rise dramatically above the Vale of Aylesbury, with views stretching for miles into a distant haze across fields to the dark outlines of Aylesbury on the horizon. On clear summer days gliders circle above like predatory birds and hang-gliders dart into space, their colourful wings speckling the green patchwork fields as they swoop down from the heights.

A few miles south-east of the downs is Whipsnade, famous for its zoo which covers 200 acres where animals roam in large enclosures. On Whipsnade Heath a path leads to the

Tree Cathedral. Here a local land-owner, Edmund Kell Blyth, planted trees in the 1930s in the form of a nave, transepts, chapels, cloisters and a dew pond in the position of the altar. Fifty years later the trees have matured to make a unique glade, as tranquil and peaceful as any of its stone-built counterparts.

STUDHAM

Away from the windswept heights of Dunstable Downs, Studham is sheltered in a shallow bowl of common land first settled in Saxon times. Narrow alleys and footpaths wander between groups of cottages and houses huddled together in one corner of the common, a broad expanse of coarse grass, with the tall tower of St Mary's Church rising behind the lattice-windowed and whitewashed Red Lion pub.

Most of the church is 13th century, but it has 15th-century additions by Sir Reginald Bray who built St George's Chapel at Windsor and Henry VII's Chapel in Westminster Abbey. The font is Norman, surrounded by medieval tiles, and there is a handsome Victorian pulpit of red and grey marble.

REDBOURN

The village's long High Street stretches along part of the Roman Watling Street, and Roman bricks were re-used in the Norman tower of St Mary's Church. The nave and aisle are also Norman, the rest is 14th and 15th century. Traditionally St Amphibalus, who converted Alban to Christianity, was martyred at Redbourn. To the west of the High Street, Redbourn Common is a broad greensward edged with timber-framed, thatched and Georgian houses and criss-crossed by roads.

Tourist information: St Albans 64511; Bedford 215226.

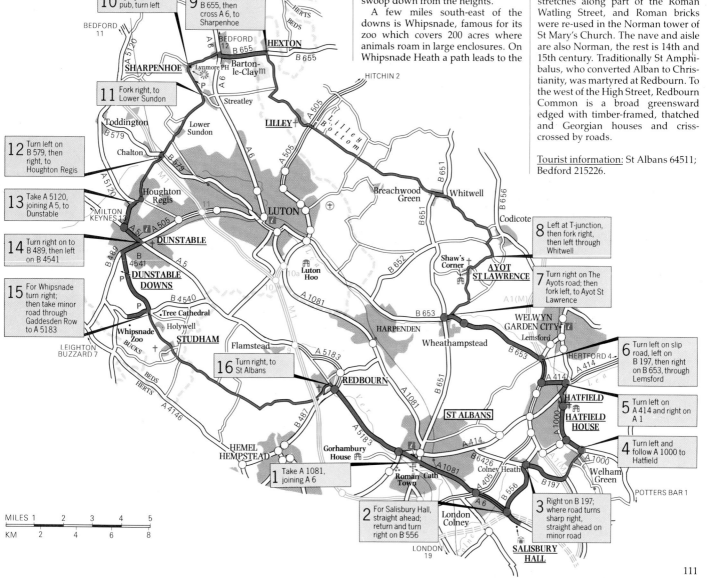

Old-time tracks through the Chilterns

TOUR
66
— 75 MILES —

From the town where Norman rule in Britain began, the way lies along ancient routes in the Chilterns. It continues into the Vale of Aylesbury and visits two stately homes.

BERKHAMSTED
Only weeks after landing near Hastings in September 1066, William the Conqueror arrived in Berkhamsted, and there he accepted the English throne from the defeated Saxon leaders. His half-brother, Robert Mortain, built a castle there in the late 11th century. It became the favourite home of many kings, queens and princes, and was the prison of King John of France after his capture at the Battle of Poitiers in 1356.

The castle is little more than a grassy mound now, but much of the town that grew around it remains. The High Street is broad and straight, following the line of the Roman road known as Akeman Street, which cut through a gap in the Chilterns. Centuries later Victorian canal-builders used the same route to take the Grand Union Canal on its way from London to Birmingham. There are several walks beside the canal,

where narrow boats and pleasure craft moor.

In Castle Street stands the 13th-century Church of St Peter, with a window dedicated to the poet and hymn-writer William Cowper, born at Berkhamsted Rectory in 1731.

TRING
This small market town seems an unlikely place in which to find a department of the British Museum. It is even more surprising to find that the huge, red-brick building tucked away in Akeman Street is devoted entirely to animals from all parts of the world. The Zoological Museum owes its existence to Lionel Walter, 2nd Baron Rothschild who, in 1892, opened his collection of mounted specimens to the public. On his death in 1937 he bequeathed the collection to the British Museum.

There are six galleries, each crammed with hundreds of species. On the ground floor lions, tigers and polar bears gaze sightlessly from huge glass cases, and apes hang immobile from branches. On the second floor are creatures of the deep. Side rooms contain reptiles, birds and insects.

CHILTERN HILLS
The road between Tring and Princes Risborough follows the Upper Icknield Way, a track which, in prehistoric times, was part of a route from East Anglia to Avebury and Stonehenge. Along the way the rolling green hills

and woodlands of the Chilterns are constant companions – with viewpoints, picnic places and forest walks a short way off the route.

Two miles beyond Tring, a road leads left up Aston Hill to Wendover Woods, at 876ft the highest point of the Chilterns. From the small car park on Aston Hill there are waymarked walks through the woods, and for the less energetic the views from the hill are rewarding enough, taking in the Vale of Aylesbury with the Tring reservoirs glittering in the distance like fragments of broken glass.

A little more than a mile south-west of Wendover is Coombe Hill, 852ft high, with a tall granite monument commemorating Buckinghamshire men killed in the Boer War.

At Princes Risborough, Whiteleaf Hill has a huge white cross cut in the chalk. The origin of the cross is not known: it may have been cut as a Christian symbol or, in pagan times, as a signpost at the crossing of ancient trackways.

THAME
The wide, mile-long main street of this market town in the Vale of Aylesbury retains an old-world charm, with its cheerful jumble of styles covering several centuries. There are medieval, timber-framed houses, their black-and-white frontages standing out against the red brick of their Georgian neighbours, and everywhere there are elegant

porches, fanlight windows and bay windows. The gabled, timber-framed, 15th-century Birdcage Inn, in Cornmarket, is believed to have once been the local lock-up.

St Mary's Church has a 13th-century chancel containing the magnificent 16th-century tomb of Lord Williams of Thame and his wife.

HADDENHAM
This sprawling village is best explored on foot, for many of its streets and alleyways are narrow and, in some cases, lead nowhere.

Haddenham is large enough to boast both a square and a village green. The square is dominated by the splendid Crown inn, a large cream-washed building with pretty bay windows and gabled porches. Across the way are brick-and-timber houses and a road leading down to Church End and the green. Here there are more old inns, the Rose and Thistle, and Red Lion facing St Mary's Church, whose great bell tower rears above the thatch of the 15th-century Church Farm House.

Many of Haddenham's boundary walls are made of wichert, a local material consisting of chalk mixed with straw, and the walls are topped with red pantiles. The style of the old walls has been matched in new buildings, using modern materials.

WADDESDON MANOR
The long drive up from the village passes through beautiful woods and parkland, and ends at a superb fountain set at the end of a broad avenue leading to the manor. Here, rural England is suddenly transformed into aristocratic France, for Waddesdon Manor is in the style of a French chateau – a riot of turrets, towers, domes and pinnacles.

The house was built by Baron Ferdinand de Rothschild between

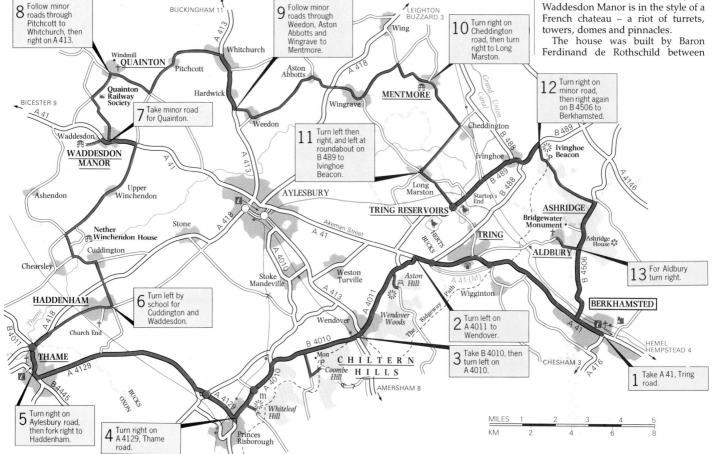

1874 and 1889, and was designed by the French architect Gabriel-Hippolyte Destailleur. The gardens at the rear of the house are also in the formal French style, with lawns and flowerbeds geometrically laid out, close-clipped yews, statues and another great fountain pool.

Inside the manor are rooms furnished in French style, with 18th-century furniture, porcelain and carpets. On the walls hang Dutch, Flemish and Italian paintings and portraits by Gainsborough, Reynolds and Romney. There is an exhibition of ladies' dresses of the 1860s.

Waddesdon Manor was bequeathed to the National Trust by James A. de Rothschild in 1957. It is open every afternoon in summer; except Mondays and Tuesdays.

QUAINTON

When a Victorian railway station is needed for a TV play or a film, the location for shooting is quite often Quainton. On the outskirts of the village are the track, station and rolling stock of the Quainton Railway Society where on summer Sundays and Bank Holidays steam locomotives draw carriages from the station along the track which is nearly a mile long.

The village stands at the top of a hill, and its landmark is the tower of a brick-built windmill dating from the 1830s. Cottages line two sides of the triangular green, on which stands the broken shaft of a 15th-century cross. Close by the Church of St Mary and Holy Cross, dating from the 14th century, is a group of 17th-century red-brick almshouses where pensioners still live.

MENTMORE

Cottages line the large village green, and in one corner stand the magnificent gates to Mentmore Towers, approached along an avenue of trees – chestnuts and giant Wellingtonia. The house is a superb piece of Victoriana, the finest surviving work of Sir Joseph Paxton – better known for the Crystal Palace, which he built for the Great Exhibition in 1851. Mentmore is built of solid Ancaster stone, though Paxton did give the Grand Hall a glass roof. Great pinnacled towers rear up from their hillside setting.

The house was built for Baron Meyer de Rothschild in 1852 and was later the home of the Earls of Rosebery. It is now the headquarters of Maharishi University of Natural Law, and is open to visitors on Sundays and Bank Holidays.

TRING RESERVOIRS

At Startop's End, 1 mile north of Tring, the Grand Union Canal goes into a series of bends as it descends 400ft from the Chilterns and passes through six locks in about half a mile. The lock gates date from 1865 and are used now only by pleasure craft, but in their heyday the constant traffic of narrow boats required the canal water to be constantly replenished from the nearby reservoir – replacing the 50,000 gallons lost downhill each time a boat passes through.

The reservoir and three others close by form the Tring Reservoirs National

INTER-CITY LINK *The Grand Union Canal between London and Birmingham passes under the road near Marsworth.*

STRIPLING RIVER *Between Lower Winchendon and Cuddington the River Thame moves slowly between reed-fringed banks amid parkland scenery.*

ASHRIDGE PILLAR *The Bridgewater Monument recalls a canal pioneer.*

OLD HADDENHAM *Ivy-clad cottages stand in a quiet corner of Church End.*

Nature Reserve, the home of many water birds including great crested grebe, mallard, heron, pochard, coot and moorhen. In winter there are also teal, wigeon and goldeneye.

ASHRIDGE

Tall beeches, oaks, birches and sycamores cloak the heights of Ashridge, forming a forest of some 2 square miles that cascades down the steep hillside to Aldbury Common in tumbling shades of green. Along the ridge a road runs through the woods, and from it a broad avenue leads to a wide clearing and the Bridgewater Monument.

The 108ft tall column was erected in 1832 in memory of the 3rd Duke of Bridgewater, the canal builder, who once lived at Ashridge House – now a college – on the eastern side of the woods. The top of the column, peeping above the trees, can be reached by climbing 172 steps.

From the Bridgewater Monument there are walks in the woods, 4000 acres of which are owned by the National Trust – with the chance of seeing fallow or muntjac deer at dusk or dawn.

The present house at Ashridge, a magnificent building in Gothic revival style, was begun in 1808 by James Wyatt for the 7th Duke of Bridgewater. It is set in fine gardens landscaped by Humphry Repton which are open at weekends in summer.

ALDBURY

This charming, unspoilt village in a lovely setting high in the Chilterns is the ideal place to end a tour. Near the small car park by the green and duck pond are the creeper-clad Greyhound pub and a pretty little teashop serving cream teas.

Around the green stand cottages of brick and tile, and nearby a row of sparkling white cottages with trim thatch and colourful front gardens catches the eye. Behind the village the great beech woods of Ashridge Park climb the hillside in billowing clouds of green.

Tourist information: Berkhamsted 4545; Aylesbury 5000; Thame 2834.

Beechwood beauty by the Thames

TOUR
67

——— 70 MILES ———

South of the Chilterns, the Thames loops its way between the beech-clad fringes of the hills. In the villages some surprises lurk – for example, a whiff of 18th-century devilry.

HENLEY-ON-THAMES

The Thames at Henley becomes crowded in summer with gleaming white cabin cruisers and noisy little motorboats. But in June and July the aristocrats are the oarsmen. The streets of the little town are thronged with blazered and white-flannelled figures. Henley Regatta, dating from 1839, is now a major international event offering the most coveted prizes in the rowing world. The regatta course, from Temple Island to Henley Bridge, is the longest straight stretch on the river.

The five-arched bridge spanning the river was built in 1786 and has keystones carved with figures representing Father Thames and the goddess Isis. The wide main street has Georgian houses and inns. Three houses in Bell Street – Elm House, Rupert's Elm and Rupert's Guard – were once the grammar school. Before that the site was the Bell Inn where, during the Civil War, Prince Rupert stayed while a Roundhead spy was hanged from an elm tree outside.

The Church of St Mary, with a striking 16th-century tower of flint and stone, stands by the bridge, and its spacious interior contains several fine monuments. A porch connects it with the Chantry House, a timbered building erected about 1400.

FAWLEY COURT

The work of two 17th-century and one 18th-century master craftsmen is embodied in Fawley Court. It was built by Sir Christopher Wren in 1684, was decorated by the great woodcarver Grinling Gibbons, and stands in grounds designed by Lancelot 'Capability' Brown.

Wren built it as a family residence for Colonel William Freeman, but it is now the Divine Mercy College of the Marian Fathers, who open it to the public on Wednesdays, Thursdays and Sundays in July and August, and on certain days in winter. The house contains a Polish museum, displaying relics of Poland's kings and its army.

MEDMENHAM

At the crossroads in Medmenham stands the Dog and Badger Inn. A sign on the wall bears the date 1390. Across the road, Ferry Lane leads down past lovely houses and gardens to a small jetty by the river, a starting point for riverside walks. In the 13th century, Medmenham had a Cistercian abbey, which five centuries later became a meeting place for the daredevil rakes of the Hell Fire Club, whose motto was 'Do what you will'. The ruins of the abbey are now part of a private house.

MARLOW

Wooded hills rise steeply above the Thames at Marlow. On a sunny summer day the green of the woodlands, the blue-grey sheen of the river, the shimmering white roadway and the towers of the suspension bridge combine in a picture of unrivalled beauty.

Downstream from the bridge the river rushes over a weir, and the lawns of the Compleat Angler Hotel stretch down to the water's edge. The narrow bridge, opened in 1836 and one of the most graceful on the Thames, is complemented by the soaring spire of All Saints' Church on the north bank.

On the other side of the river a road climbs steeply, through sharp hairpin bends among the trees of Quarry Wood, to Winter Hill, where a small roadside car park gives superb views of Marlow and Marlow Reach. Below the wooded slopes the river is a silver thread; beyond are the broad reservoirs where speedboats and water-skiers plough creamy furrows.

COOKHAM

Approached across Cookham Moor, this lovely riverside village appears as a pleasant mixture of brick cottages and timber-framed houses huddled together along a narrow main street. Here afternoon teas are served behind bow windows, and stronger refreshment is offered in the flower-decked Kings Arms.

At the far end of the main street is King's Hall, which houses the Spencer Art Gallery. Sir Stanley Spencer lived in Cookham for most of his life and painted many river scenes, some of which are displayed in the gallery.

BEACONSFIELD

The elegance of the Georgian age is everywhere apparent in Beaconsfield – particularly in the main street where the Royal White Hart and the Royal Saracen's Head survive from the days when the town was a staging post on the London to Oxford road. The town has grown considerably since those days, sprawling northwards to the beechwood hills of the Chilterns. Its growth was encouraged by the arrival

REGATTA RIVER *Rowing boats await amateur oarsmen eager to try their skills on one of the best known stretches of the Thames.*

GREYS COURT *The Great Tower is part of the mansion built by the first Lord de Grey who fought at Crecy and became one of the first Knights of the Garter.*

WEST WYCOMBE *A Tuscan portico ends one wing of the Dashwood home.*

STOKE ROW *Below the oriental dome plunges a well 368ft deep.*

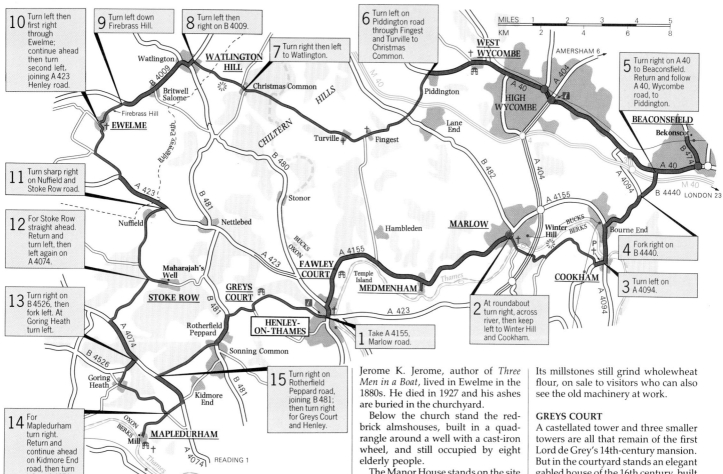

10 Turn left then first right through Ewelme; continue ahead then turn second left, joining A 423 Henley road.

9 Turn left down Firebrass Hill.

8 Turn left then right on B 4009.

7 Turn right then left to Watlington.

6 Turn left on Piddington road through Fingest and Turville to Christmas Common.

5 Turn right on A 40 to Beaconsfield. Return and follow A 40, Wycombe road, to Piddington.

11 Turn sharp right on Nuffield and Stoke Row road.

12 For Stoke Row straight ahead. Return and turn left, then left again on A 4074.

13 Turn right on B 4526, then fork left. At Goring Heath turn left.

14 For Mapledurham turn right. Return and continue ahead on Kidmore End road, then turn left on A 4074.

15 Turn right on Rotherfield Peppard road, joining B 481; then turn right for Greys Court and Henley.

4 Fork right on B 4440.

3 Turn left on A 4094.

2 At roundabout turn right, across river, then keep left to Winter Hill and Cookham.

1 Take A 4155, Marlow road.

of the railway in 1862, and many fine Victorian and Edwardian houses stand in tree-lined streets and roads between the main street and the railway line.

Near the station, in Warwick Road, is the Bekonscot Model Village, which has been delighting children since 1929. It is claimed to be the oldest model village in the world, and is open daily from April to October.

WEST WYCOMBE
Some time before reaching this National Trust village, surviving precariously on a busy main road, the eye is caught by a tower surmounted by a golden ball peeping above the trees. The tower is part of the Georgian Church of St Lawrence, and the hollow ball could hold eight men, members of the notorious Hell Fire Club.

The club was founded in the 18th century by Sir Francis Dashwood of West Wycombe Park, which has its entrance on the western edge of the village. The superb Palladian-style house has fine collections of paintings and furniture. It stands in landscaped grounds complete with lakes and classical temples, and is open to the public most afternoons in summer.

Sir Francis also built a road between the village and High Wycombe, and the material was quarried from the chalk hills nearby. In the caves left by the quarrying the Hell Fire Club are said to have held wild parties. Now, as a reminder of those times, there are

wax effigies in the caves, which are entered by a mock Gothic ruin.

The Church of St Lawrence, rebuilt by Dashwood in the 1760s, stands on top of a hill across the valley from the park, and close by is Dashwood's mausoleum. It is hexagonal in shape, with three sides built as triumphal arches and three containing niches for funeral urns.

WATLINGTON HILL
There are fine views from these 108 acres of chalk down, given to the National Trust in 1941 by the 3rd Viscount and Viscountess Esher. Carved into the hill's lower slopes is the shape of a church steeple. This is said to have been the idea of an 18th-century eccentric, who wanted to give the illusion of a steeple on Watlington Church.

EWELME
At the foot of the splendid-sounding Firebrass Hill the Chilterns level out in a series of three terraces, on which stand a church, a school and almshouses. With several pretty cottages and a Georgian manor house, they form a secluded village which has some surprising historical and literary associations.

The Church of St Mary, high on the upper terrace, contains the tomb of Alice, Duchess of Suffolk, who died in 1475. She was the granddaughter of the poet Geoffrey Chaucer, and with her husband, the Earl of Suffolk, built the church, almshouses and school.

Jerome K. Jerome, author of *Three Men in a Boat*, lived in Ewelme in the 1880s. He died in 1927 and his ashes are buried in the churchyard.

Below the church stand the red-brick almshouses, built in a quadrangle around a well with a cast-iron wheel, and still occupied by eight elderly people.

The Manor House stands on the site of an earlier residence much used by Henry VIII and Elizabeth I. In 1540 Henry spent part of one of his six honeymoons there – with Catherine Howard who, two years later, was beheaded, like Anne Boleyn.

STOKE ROW
A slight diversion into the centre of Stoke Row leads to a unique roadside feature, known simply as the Maharajah's Well. The well, complete with an iron windlass for raising the water, is set under an ornate domed canopy which bears the inscription: 'His Highness the Maharajah of Benares gave this well in 1864.'

This unusual gift, looking rather like a cross between a seaside bandstand and a piece of the Taj Mahal, stemmed from the maharajah's gratitude to Edward Reade – a local resident and brother of the author Charles Reade – for his work in supplying a water system in the Indian state.

MAPLEDURHAM
The quiet little village of Mapledurham lies on the Oxfordshire bank of the Thames, between Pangbourne and Reading, and is dominated by the lovely Elizabethan Mapledurham House. It stands in parklands running down to the river and was often visited by the poet Alexander Pope. The house is the home of the Eyston family, and is open to the public on Saturdays, Sundays and Bank Holiday afternoons during summer.

Nearby is a 15th-century water mill.

Its millstones still grind wholewheat flour, on sale to visitors who can also see the old machinery at work.

GREYS COURT
A castellated tower and three smaller towers are all that remain of the first Lord de Grey's 14th-century mansion. But in the courtyard stands an elegant gabled house of the 16th century, built of brick and stone and facing spacious lawns. Until 1969, when the house was given to the National Trust by Sir Felix Brunner, it was continuously occupied, and the rooms show the styles of several centuries. The drawing room is particularly impressive, with its ornate ceiling and marble fireplace dating from the mid-18th century.

Close to the mansion is a well which was donkey-powered and used until 1914. The well house dates from Tudor times, but the well itself, a terrifying 200ft deep, is probably as old as the medieval towers of Greys Court. Here is the largest surviving example of a donkey wheel, and also in the grounds is a horse wheel of 1870 which came from a 488ft deep well at Shabden Park, near Epsom, in 1975. Two horses turned the wheel, walking in a circle, thus operating pumps to draw water.

Also at Greys Court is the Archbishop's Maze, designed in 1981 to represent Christian symbolisms. The design of the paved pathway winding among lawns stemmed from the address given by Dr Robert Runcie on his enthronement as Archbishop of Canterbury in 1980. He urged that people should help each other to solve the secret of the maze of life.

Greys Court is open from April to September, the house on some afternoons, and the garden each afternoon except Sunday.

Tourist information:
Henley-on-Thames 578034;
High Wycombe 26100.

A green vale below a White Horse on the hilltop

—— 66 MILES ——

Beyond the Vale of White Horse, an age-old chalk figure gallops across the slope of the downs. To the north, winding lanes link villages of Cotswold stone beside the Thames and its tributaries.

FARINGDON

The gently sloping Market Place lies at the crossing of a medieval wool pack route from the Cotswolds to the south coast ports and the old main road from Oxford to Bristol. Below the 18th and 19th-century façades on the east side – many of which conceal more ancient stones within – stall-holders on Tuesdays display their wares, as they have on market days since 1218.

The 16th-century Portwell Monument in the centre marks the source of the town's first water supply. The 17th-century Town Hall, supported on stone pillars, is now the public library. Inside All Saints' Church lie and kneel finely sculpted figures of 16th and 17th-century members of the Unton family, who knew the church before its spire was toppled by Civil War cannonades. Outside, pause to admire the handsome pattern of 13th-century ironwork on the south door, and the Norman stone carving above.

From the Market Place a walk up past the cottages of London Street and into Stanford Road leads to a path, steep but short, to the top of Folly Hill. Beyond the tower erected in 1935 and claimed to be the last folly built in England there are views across the Vale of White Horse.

BADBURY HILL

A clump of trees marks the site of an Iron Age camp, and the girdle of ancient earthworks is visible east of the car park. The clump, which is owned by the National Trust, is carpeted with bluebells in spring. There are footpaths and picnic spots.

Some historians believe Badbury Hill was the site of one of King Arthur's battles.

GREAT COXWELL

After a short drive down a narrow high-banked lane, the Great Barn bursts into view on the right. This is possibly the finest surviving medieval barn in Britain, and on entering it the visitor experiences something of the awe felt in the great Gothic churches.

The barn, 152ft long and 48ft high, with walls and roof tiles of Cotswold stone, has changed little since it was built by Cistercian monks more than 700 years ago to house farm produce. The graceful oak pillars and vaulting timber bear lightly the weight of the enormous roof. Now owned by the National Trust, the barn is open daily. Farther along the road is the old Court

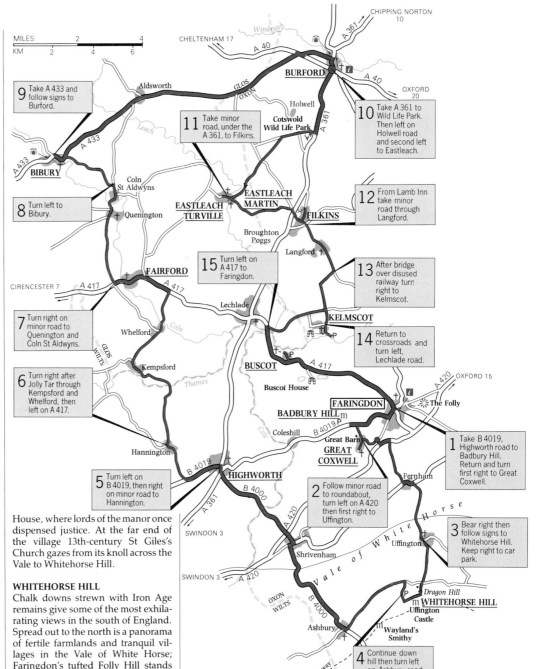

House, where lords of the manor once dispensed justice. At the far end of the village 13th-century St Giles's Church gazes from its knoll across the Vale to Whitehorse Hill.

WHITEHORSE HILL

Chalk downs strewn with Iron Age remains give some of the most exhilarating views in the south of England. Spread out to the north is a panorama of fertile farmlands and tranquil villages in the Vale of White Horse; Faringdon's tufted Folly Hill stands out clearly, and beyond is the undulating line of the Cotswolds. Gates beside the car park lead onto open downland, owned by the National Trust and surmounted by Uffington Castle, an Iron Age camp some 2500 years old, with oval earth ramparts enclosing an area 250yds long and nearly 200yds wide.

Cut into the hillside below the castle is the mysterious White Horse, perhaps as old as the fort and possibly connected with Celtic religious rites for which the tribes may have gathered in the gully beneath.

Behind Uffington Castle a stile leads onto the Ridgeway Path, a long-distance path following an ancient track along the top of the downs. A mile along it to the west is Wayland's Smithy, a long barrow perhaps 3000 years old.

HIGHWORTH

The town has exchanged the bustling activity of its former stagecoach days for a share in the commercial life of nearby Swindon. But hotels clustering around the Market Place still recall those earlier times; and around the graceful spire and weatherbeaten parapets of the Church of St Mary and All Angels rise the tall chimneys of old stone houses set back from the road amid leafy gardens.

FAIRFORD

Around the peaceful Market Place stand the calm and dignified fronts of old stone buildings, including the Bull Hotel, in stagecoach days one of the most famous posting houses in the country. Along the High Street on the left is the old Farmor's School founded in 1738 as a free school; though the school has now moved to other premises, the stately old house survives as Fairford's cultural centre.

It was a rich wool merchant, John Tame, who at the end of the 15th century built the elegant Church of St Mary that soars above the lower High Street. Wealth from wool also provided the superb set of 28 glowing stained-glass windows. Grotesque stone figures guard each corner of the clock tower, and high on the east wall the figure of a bear with a ragged staff recalls the town's association with the Earls of Warwick, whose arms incorporate such a bear. Cross to the other side of the High Street and look across at the east end of the church; it seems to be sweeping forward like a triumphant galleon.

Mill Lane leads to an old water mill by the swiftly flowing River Coln, with a view across the meadows back towards the town. The Croft, a backwater of peaceful stone houses and decorated walls, is entered through an arch across the road from Farmor's School.

BIBURY
Ducks dabble and plump trout draw dark shadows in the clear waters of the River Coln. For a closer look at the line of ancient cottages beyond, known as Arlington Row, cross the small bridge nearby. Originally a 14th-century wool store, the row was converted into weavers' cottages in the 17th century and now belongs to the National Trust.

At the other end of the village, over the bridge by the Swan Hotel, are the tanks of a trout fishery. Beside it is Arlington Mill, now the Cotswold Country Life Museum, with exhibitions of rural life and crafts. Both are open daily from March to October.

BURFORD
The view from the top of the steep High Street takes in a line of stone and slate roofs tumbling down towards the meadows beyond the River Windrush. For centuries Burford thrived on the wool trade, and much of its wealth was lavished on the building of houses and mansions from the local stone in a diversity of styles. In the 16th-century Tolsey, halfway down the High Street, market and fair dues were paid to the local guild of merchants; it is now the Tolsey Museum of Burford History, open every afternoon from Easter to October.

When legs tire of the steepness of the High Street, there are level side lanes in which to saunter and gaze. In Sheep Street, by the Tolsey, stands the 15th-century Lamb Inn, the oldest of many hostelries in the town. Lawrence Lane, at the bottom of the hill, leads to the 16th-century buildings of Burford School and to a line of 15th-century almshouses flanking the magnificent Norman and Gothic Church of St John the Baptist, a treasure-house of glass and sculpture.

In the Cotswold Wild Life Park, 2 miles south, a variety of wild animals can be seen living in the open.

THE EASTLEACHES
The twin hamlets of Eastleach Martin and Eastleach Turville, set in a Cotswold hollow, are best explored on foot. The slope beside the war memorial provides a broad view of both hamlets, framed by their two churches sitting one on each side of the River Leach.

On the east bank Eastleach Martin's church, now redundant, has the remains of a sanctus bellcote on its roof. A group of fine old farm buildings flank the churchyard, and the stone-mullioned windows of Eastleach House look down from the hill. Leave the churchyard by its north gate and cross the stream by the clapper footbridge, known as Keble's Bridge after the local lords of the manor; John Keble, initiator of the Anglo-Catholic Oxford Movement, was once curate of both the Eastleach churches. To the right stands Eastleach Turville's Church of St Andrew, with its fine Norman south doorway.

FILKINS
A few yards along the village street from the Lamb Inn, chinks in the door of an old lock-up give a glimpse of rusting instruments that lie inside. The lock-up is roofed with large stone 'slats' quarried locally; a walk down the quiet lane opposite the Post Office shows how the slats have also been used for fencing.

Farther along the road, at Cotswold Woollen Weavers, a working mill has been set up in a splendidly restored 18th-century barn. Visitors can watch the looms turning Cotswold wool into cloth, and there is a skilfully arranged small exhibition of the history of wool and weaving in the Cotswolds. The mill's products, and the work of other traditional craftsmen, are on sale. The mill is open daily.

KELMSCOT
The Elizabethan Kelmscot Manor was from 1871 to 1896 the home of William Morris, artist, designer and writer. It is privately owned, but open on certain days in summer or by arrangement with the occupier. Morris is buried in the churchyard of St George's Church, and nearby is a group of cottages built in 1902 by his widow, Jane. An unsurfaced lane leads down to a small parking area by the Thames. This quiet stretch of the river, with its *Wind in the Willows* air, is popular with anglers, and day permits may be obtained from the nearby Plough inn.

BUSCOT
The sound of rushing water accompanies the short walk from the car park to Buscot weir, and from the weir a footpath leads across a field to the peaceful old Church of St Mary. Norman in origin, the church has a pulpit with panels by the 15th-century Flemish artist Mabuse, and an east window by the 19th-century artist Sir Edward Burne-Jones. Nearby stands the early 18th-century Old Parsonage, open on Wednesday afternoons by appointment.

Half a mile along the main road to Faringdon, tall pillars flank the entrance to Buscot House, a mansion built in Adam style in 1780 and carefully restored to its original form by Lord Faringdon in the 1930s. Now owned, like the village of Buscot, by the National Trust, Buscot House contains fine art-nouveau paintings by Burne-Jones depicting the story of *Sleeping Beauty*. Buscot is open on Wednesday, Thursday and Friday afternoons, and on the second and fourth weekends in the months in summer.

Tourist information: Faringdon 22191 (summer); Burford 3590.

HILL OF LEGEND *Dragon Hill, below the White Horse, is said to be the spot where St George killed the dragon, and grass never grows where the dragon's blood was spilt.*

Winding waterways around Oxford's dreaming spires

TOUR
69
— 52 MILES —

Beyond the Victorian villas of north Oxford lies a palace built for one national hero which became the birthplace of another. Market towns and ancient villages line tributaries of the Thames.

WOODSTOCK

The high wall of the park surrounding Blenheim Palace forms the western boundary of Woodstock; but the town itself is far older than the palace. During the 18th century many of Woodstock's older houses acquired more elegant façades to keep up with their new neighbour, John Churchill, 1st Duke of Marlborough.

One such house is Fletcher's House, now containing the Oxfordshire County Museum which explains local history from Stone Age times; it is open daily, except Mondays in winter. Woodstock has long been noted for glove-making, and in Harrison's Lane the Leather Glove Workshops welcome visitors. The 17th-century wisteria-clad Chaucer's House, the successor of a much older building on the site, is named after the poet's son.

The tower of the Church of St Mary Magdalene carillons 18th-century tunes every four hours from 9am. The Bear Hotel was founded in the 13th century, and its garages were stables for 66 horses in the heyday of the stagecoach.

A Triumphal Arch at the end of Park Street leads into Blenheim Palace, built as a grateful nation's gift to the Duke of Marlborough after his victory over the French and Bavarians at the Battle of Blenheim in 1704. It was designed by Sir John Vanbrugh, and stands in a great park landscaped by Capability Brown.

Sir Winston Churchill was born at Blenheim on November 30, 1874, and the room in which he was born is on show, together with numerous Churchill relics. Blenheim Palace is open daily from mid-March to October; the park is open daily all year.

At nearby Bladon, the simple graves of Sir Winston Churchill and his wife lie by the north wall of the tower of the little Church of St Martin.

CHURCH HANBOROUGH

The slender 15th-century spire of the little Church of St Peter and St Paul is visible far across the surrounding countryside. Parts of the church date from the 12th century. These include a sculpture over the north doorway which incorporates a pun in stone. St Peter, holding the keys of Heaven and Hell, is shown sitting between a lion and a lamb. The lion, controlled by a celestial hand, offers him a stone – in Latin *petra*, the origin of the name of Peter – with a look on its face of

enjoyment at the joke. Inside is a rare 15th-century wooden rood screen with much of its painted decoration still visible, the remains of a medieval wall painting and the old 17th-century church clock mechanism. The upper level of the high north transept was probably the priest's living quarters in medieval times.

NORTH LEIGH ROMAN VILLA

As the lane descends towards the villa it becomes obvious why some unknown Roman or Romanised Briton chose to site his dwelling here. Set in a fertile fold of the Evenlode valley and circled by gentle wooded hills, the inhabitants would be assured of ample food from local farming and fishing, while Akeman Street, the Roman road between Cirencester and Alchester, ran only a mile or so north.

Little more than foundations and some mosaic floor remain, but these fragments are sufficient to give an idea of the size of the villa and its comforts, including central heating and hot baths. The villa is open daily except Thursday from April to September.

COGGES FARM MUSEUM

A working museum, Cogges recreates farming life and activity as it was round the turn of the century. Agricultural tools, carts, farmyard and outbuildings are maintained as they were at that time. Cattle, sheep, pigs and chicken typical of the period are kept, and there are demonstrations of activities such as threshing.

Parts of the farmhouse date from the 13th century, and the living rooms, kitchens and dairy are furnished in Edwardian style. Cogges is open daily from April to October.

New housing estates against the farm boundary spill out from the growing town of Witney, long known for the manufacture of woollen blankets. But Witney still retains the air of a market town. Halfway down its High Street is an unusual 17th-century Butter Cross with a clock-turret and sundial. Lime trees and handsome stone houses flank the Church of St Mary the Virgin.

MINSTER LOVELL

Glimpses of the ruins of Minster Lovell Hall are seen across the meadow on the left as the road drops towards the village. The hall, together with the adjoining church, farmhouse and dovecote, was constructed in the mid-15th century by Lord William Lovell, descendant of a long line of noblemen in royal service. Enough remains to give an impression of the size and splendour of the Gothic mansion.

The lofty hall, carved doorways and windows hint at the richness of design of ecclesiastical buildings of the period. The interior of the dovecote, adjoining the nearby farm, is domed like a basilica. A footpath runs from the hall along the River Windrush. The hall is open daily. The

RUNNING WATER *Castle Hill looks down on Day's Lock and weir across the Thames.*

RISING WATER *The Glyme has partly submerged Vanbrugh's bridge at Blenheim.*

alabaster effigy of Lord Lovell, dressed in plate armour, lies on his tomb in the Church of St Kenelm.

BABLOCK HYTHE

From this quiet leafy spot beside the River Thames there are towpath walks in both directions. A passenger ferry crosses from the Ferry Inn to the opposite bank, from which a footpath leads up to Cumnor.

In the nearby village of Stanton Harcourt, parts of the ruined Stanton Harcourt Manor date back to the 12th century. It has an old kitchen, a Tudor gatehouse and a tower in which Alexander Pope in 1718 wrote part of his translation of the *Iliad*. The manor is open on Bank Holiday Mondays and certain other days in summer.

The Church of St Michael contains numerous mementos of the service of the Harcourt family to church, army and state; they include the remains of the standard borne by Sir Robert Harcourt for Henry Tudor at the Battle of Bosworth in 1485.

CUMNOR

Still recognisable as a village, despite the encroachments of suburban Oxford, Cumnor is best known for its association with Amy Robsart, wife of the Earl of Leicester, who fell down a staircase to her death in 1650 at Cumnor Manor. Wagging tongues maintained that her death had been contrived by Leicester to free his path for a hoped-for marriage to Elizabeth I. Walter Scott used the tale in his novel *Kenilworth*.

There is today no trace of the manor, which stood at the western end of St Michael's churchyard. In the church are facsimiles of letters written by and to Amy Robsart shortly before her death, and a statue of the Queen. A wooden stairway of 1685 coils round a great central post up to the tower. The Leicester arms are commemorated in the name of the 14th-century Bear and Ragged Staff inn.

Tourist information: Woodstock 811038.

TOUR
70

50 MILES

The Cherwell, which is crossed at Magdalen Bridge, merges to the south with the Isis to form the River Thames. Hilly vantage points give views of its course through the green countryside.

IFFLEY
Though close to the heart of Oxford there are still quiet corners in Iffley, which also contains one of England's finest 12th-century Norman Romanesque churches. St Mary's was built about 1160 in a style which adds eastern decoration to the plain Norman construction. Some of the windows were later converted to the Perpendicular style, but the resplendent Romanesque west window was restored to its original Eye of God form in 1858.

The black stone font is large enough for an infant's total immersion. The groove in the wall by the north door housed a wooden bar which secured the door against attackers. The stone carvings round the original Norman south door are particularly well preserved; one portrays Henry II, who caused the death of Archbishop Thomas Becket, as a monster.

ABINGDON
One of Christopher Wren's masons built the magnificently glassed and pillared County Hall in his master's style in 1682, and this now houses the Abingdon Museum illustrating domestic life and crafts in the town over the centuries; it is open daily. Behind the late 15th-century Abbey Gate-

house across the Market Square once stood a great Benedictine abbey, from which survive the 12th-century Abbey Bakehouse, the 13th-century Checker Hall and 15th-century Long Gallery, all open every afternoon except Mondays in winter.

Abingdon's early importance was as a river port and crossing of the River Thames, which forms its southern boundary. From the 16th-century bridge steps lead down to waterside gardens and the towpath.

Overshadowing the northern end of the bridge is the early 19th-century Old Gaol, now an arts and crafts centre. East St Helen Street, with its timber-framed houses, leads down to St Helen's Church, one of only four in the country having five aisles. The churchyard is enclosed on two sides by rows of 15th and 18th-century almshouses, and at St Helen's Wharf behind it the little River Ock flows into the Thames.

CLIFTON HAMPDEN
Half-timbered cottages snuggle beneath thatch as ample as tea cosies, and little gardens bloom as they do in the pictures in children's story books. The six russet-coloured arches of G.G. Scott's 1864 bridge over the Thames are the summer haunt of house martins. From the bridge there is a delightful view of the miniature cliffs on the north side of the river, crowned by the little Church of St Michael and All Angels. From the churchyard there is a broader view of the river and water meadows.

THE WITTENHAMS
The Thames runs on the right of the road leading to Long Wittenham, a village almost totally destroyed by fire

in 1868. St Mary's Church was founded in Norman times and fragments of Bronze Age funerary urns have been found in the churchyard. Inside is a medieval decorated lead font, said to have been encased in wood during the Civil War to save it from being melted down for bullets. There is also one of the smallest sculptured monuments in England: an effigy of a crosslegged knight only 2ft long. The Pendon Museum portrays English rural life in the age of steam; it is open on Saturday, Sunday and Bank Holiday afternoons.

From the hamlet of Little Wittenham a footpath from St Peter's Church leads up to the Wittenham Clumps, from which there are extensive views across the Thames and surrounding countryside. Another path winds down past willows and over footbridges to Day's Lock.

DORCHESTER
The glory of Dorchester is its abbey, but there are many quaint corners and byways to explore. Bridge End is a village on its own, with a green from which a path leads across fields to Dyke Hills, a line of Saxon fortifications. Malthouse Lane is quiet, with timbered cottages, while old coaching inns recall the days when Dorchester lay on a main road from London to Oxford.

Dorchester was a Bronze Age and Roman settlement, but it was here that Christianity was first introduced into southern England by St Birinus in 635. The present abbey dates from the 12th century, but part of the wall of the nave survives from an earlier Saxon cathedral. First impressions on entering the abbey are of space and simplicity, and an awesome sense of

height and length. The little 12th-century windows of the sedilia contain the earliest coloured glass known in England, and the 14th-century Jesse window is one of the finest in the country. The effigy of a 12th-century Crusader Knight lying on his back and endeavouring to draw his sword, his face contorted by effort, is a very rare 'action' statue.

Outside, the Guest House is the only monastic building surviving from the Dissolution in 1537. A grammar school in the 17th century, it is now a museum, open daily in summer.

GARSINGTON
The road climbs between the stone and thatched cottages of this hillside village. On the left near the top is the 17th-century Garsington Manor with its Jacobean façade, tall chimneys and plain formal garden framed by thick high yew hedges. Between the World Wars it was the home of Lady Otteline Morrel, who kept a salon frequented by literary and political figures.

The Church of St Mary, at the summit of the hill, contains an unusual 13th-century tombstone inscribed in Norman French and a pre-Reformation stone altar dug up in the churchyard.

SHOTOVER COUNTRY PARK
The park was once part of a royal hunting ground, and across it runs the line of the old stagecoach road into Oxford from the east. Often the ascent proved too difficult for the horses, and passengers had to get out and walk. Now this stretch of unspoilt countryside offers nature trails and views over the surrounding area.

Tourist information: Abingdon 22711.

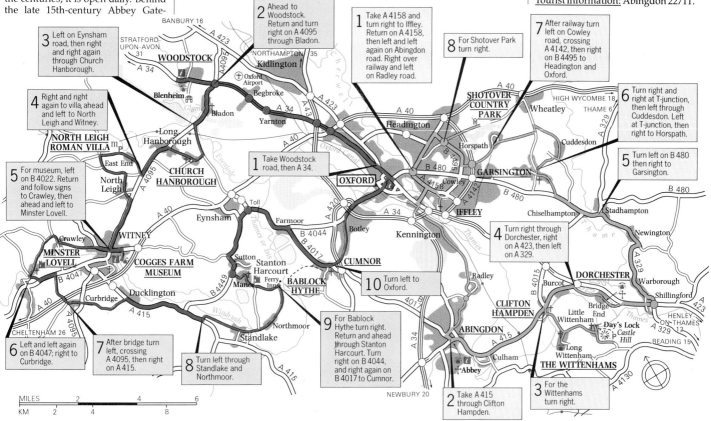

119

Ridges above the green Midland plain

TOUR
71

———— 73 MILES ————

The spires of three churches renowned in local rhyme lead like marker posts across the flat farmlands of north Oxfordshire. The waters of three rivers accompany the journey.

CHIPPING NORTON

The town clings to the northern slopes of the Cotswolds, and a tour of the Wednesday morning market stalls is like a walk across the slanting deck of a ship. Chipping Norton has survived for 1000 years, and since the decline of its early woollen trade it has found a new role as a tourist centre.

The Town Hall whose classical profile dominates the town centre is Victorian, but there are dignified houses of a century earlier around it, and the windows of the nearby Guildhall show its Tudor origins. Set endways into the slope beside hilly Church Street is a row of almshouses in Cotswold stone, built in 1640. So steep is the slope that the almshouses are almost level with the tower of St Mary's Church, framed between firs lower down the hill. Tall clerestory windows along the top of the nave admit light into a spacious interior, whose pillars look surprisingly slender to support a structure of such cathedral-like dimensions. Brasses commemorate the wealthy woolmen who rebuilt the church around 1500.

A path beside the church leads downhill past the mounds of a Norman castle to Pool Meadow. On the western outskirts of the town, reached down New Street, a tall chimney rises from the ornate Gothic façade of the Bliss Tweed Mill, which closed in 1980 after a century of production.

LITTLE ROLLRIGHT

An avenue of trees leads to a cluster of farmhouses, through which the narrow road twists uphill to a simple, 13th-century church. In its tiny interior – a congregation of 40 would fill it – the two life-size monuments which flank one side of the chancel seem oddly out of scale. A good view of the church can be seen from the road rising to the next crossroads.

ROLLRIGHT STONES

Stand at the centre of this mysterious ring of limestone boulders and look around at their pitted and lichened forms. They may well have been a matching set when they were erected 3500 years or more ago, but time has dealt unevenly with them and now no two are alike in size or shape.

On three sides the ring, known as the King's Men, is screened by hedges and trees, but to the south there is a broad view across rolling cornfields to a distant tree-topped ridge. The King Stone stands apart from the 'men' and is reached over a stile on the other side of the road.

GREAT TEW

Golden roofs of new thatch and rebuilt walls of mellow Cotswold stone testify to several years of painstaking restoration after decades of decay. Hollyhocks and sunflowers reach upwards to meet the thatch drooping low over the eaves. The village where Viscount Falkland, Secretary of State to Charles I, played host to scholars such as Ben Jonson, Edmund Waller and Abraham Cowley has now been saved by grants awarded to a conservation area 'of outstanding interest'.

At the top of the village, an ornate arch frames a broad, grassy path to the 14th-century Church of St Michael, which has a battlemented tower and a cool, spacious interior of soaring arches.

BLOXHAM

The 200ft spire of St Mary's Church dominates the countryside for miles around; and the church's spacious interior, with an east window by William Morris and Edward Burne-Jones, and ancient churchyard are good places in which to wander. Next to the church a tiny bowfronted stone museum casts a light on aspects of the large village's history. The best of Bloxham, however, lies in the maze of little streets just off the main road.

A flagstoned lane leads past the Hawk and Partridge onto Little Green, where the cottages of ironstone, many of them thatched, have gardens that spill out over the pavements. A footpath, known as The Gogs, leads steeply downhill to a little brook. Cross the bridge and turn right to Little Bridge Road, where another right turn leads back to the main road beside the war memorial and the 16th-century Joiner's Arms.

The public school of All Saints rises high beside the road at the north end of the village.

ADDERBURY

Twin streams, the Mill Stream and Sor Brook, divide Adderbury into two. A path down through the long sloping churchyard leads to a shady walk between the streams where trees arch overhead and crab apples plop into the water. On the far side the wooded banks open out to West Adderbury's broad green.

St Mary's Church stands on a knoll, and the little paths and roads round it all look up to its impressive four-square tower and sturdy spire. High up on the outside walls of the nave run two Early English carved friezes, depicting animal figures with human heads and a line of musicians holding a motley array of ancient instruments, including timbrel, bagpipes, hurdy-gurdy and kettledrum.

Opposite the lich gate, Church Lane leads up towards East Adderbury's High Street. On the way, notice the timber cruck frame, in the shape of a giant letter 'A', exposed on the south gable of a cottage on the left. There is a tree-edged green at the top of the High Street; just off the green is a mounting block beside a house in Croft Road.

KINGS SUTTON

The village is dominated by a church with a spire renowned for its 'beauty', in the words of a local rhyme which

BATTLE LONG AGO *Westward from Edge Hill and beyond the village of Radway stretches the plain where the first major battle of the Civil War was fought.*

also commends Bloxham's spire for 'length' and Adderbury's for 'strength'. Inside the church is a macabre memorial of about 1820 representing the resurrected Lord stepping forth from a grimly realistic decomposing corpse. Beside the church a footpath leads down past thatched cottages to the post office and a street called simply 'Paradise'. Around the long green in front of the church are two pubs and some thatched and half-timbered houses.

Newbottle Woods, half a mile off the main road east of the village, offers shady picnic spots.

AYNHO

The road that drops down into Aynho is flanked on one side by a dry-stone wall beyond which lies a glorious vista of farmlands – green, brown or golden, with puffs of darker green from surviving clumps of woodland. On the left, thatched houses have tiny front gardens whose petunias overflow onto the pavements.

In Aynho there are apricot trees on the walls of the houses in the main street, and a network of narrow lanes behind the Cartwright Arms. The 14th-century tower of St Michael's Church contrasts oddly with the body of the church which was rebuilt in 1725 in classical style. Inside there are 18th-century box pews and a gallery on Tuscan columns; the general austerity of the interior is relieved by some shining stained glass, and organ pipes decorated in Georgian floral motifs.

The neighbouring Aynhoe Park, in matching classical style, is divided into private apartments. Parts of the building are open on Wednesday and Thursday afternoons in summer.

THE ASTONS

The road through the Astons follows a slope above the Cherwell's broad valley, and there are fine views all the way, across the valley to the equally gentle slopes on the opposite bank. North Aston has cottages set around a green with a church and manor on the lower slopes. Middle Aston presents more the appearance of a working village, as the road descends through a farmyard with stables and silos on either side.

Steeple Aston has a 13th-century church with battlemented walls; inside is a massive Baroque tomb to an 18th-century judge, whose life-size marble effigy, in wig and robes, reclines beside that of his wife.

ROUSHAM PARK

Classical temples and statues are almost as plentiful as trees in the gardens designed by William Kent at Rousham Park. Pan and a faun peep out from box hedges over a well-stocked goldfish pond; a portico with classical columns looks across a bend in the Cherwell to sheep grazing beyond; figures of Apollo, a dying gladiator, Venus and cupids catch the eye at the end of long grassy paths under the overarching trees.

There is an attractive air of wildness about the landscaped garden that makes it a more relaxing place to wander in than anywhere too neatly ordered and clipped. In the formal gardens there is a remarkable medieval pigeon house, with 19 rows of nest holes running right round its interior and reached by a ladder which revolves on a central pivot.

The gardens at Rousham are open daily; the house is open on Wednesday, Sunday and Bank Holiday afternoons in summer.

CHARLBURY

Cross the bridge and pause near the railway station to look back and see how Charlbury lies so snugly along its tree-clad ridge on the east bank of the River Evenlode. The square tower of St Mary's Church, just visible above the trees, presides over a satisfying pattern of houses in mellow stone, with slate roofs. Near the top of Church Street is a small museum which displays local bygones such as a spinning wheel, a penny-farthing bicycle, agricultural implements and wartime mementos.

For a stroll beside the Evenlode, walk down Dyers Hill towards the bridge, then turn right just beyond the high wall on the right onto a footpath between houses; this leads over a bridge beside a tiny sluice gate onto quiet water meadows.

<u>Tourist information:</u> Chipping Norton 41320.

Villages of warm limestone set around neatly mown greens line this tour through the borderlands of three counties. Four historic houses stand amid their own broad parklands.

BANBURY

A cake and a nursery rhyme helped to make Banbury's name, so it is a pity that citizens destroyed the original Banbury Cross, around 1600, and the original Cake Shop, as recently as 1967. A Norman castle and a massive

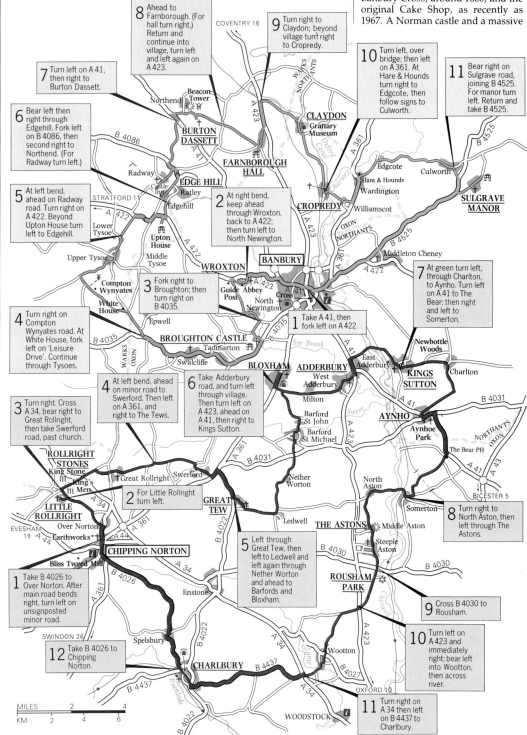

8 Ahead to Farnborough. (For hall turn right.) Return and continue into village, turn left and left again on A 423.

9 Turn right to Claydon; beyond village turn right to Cropredy.

10 Turn left, over bridge; then left on A 361. At Hare & Hounds turn right to Edgcote, then follow signs to Culworth.

11 Bear right on Sulgrave road, joining B 4525. For manor turn left. Return and take B 4525.

7 Turn left on A 41, then right to Burton Dassett.

6 Bear left then right through Edgehill. Fork left on B 4086, then second right to Northend. (For Radway turn left.)

5 At left bend, ahead on Radway road. Turn right on A 422. Beyond Upton House turn left to Edgehill.

2 At right bend, keep ahead through Wroxton, back to A 422; then turn left to North Newington.

7 At green turn left, through Charlton, to Aynho. Turn left on A 41 to The Bear; then right and left to Somerton.

3 Fork right to Broughton; then turn right on B 4035.

1 Take A 41, then fork left on A 422.

4 Turn right on Compton Wynyates road. At White House, fork left on 'Leisure Drive'. Continue through Tysoes.

4 At left bend, ahead on minor road to Swerford. Then left on A 361, and right to The Tews.

6 Take Adderbury road, and turn left through village. Then turn left on A 423, ahead on A 41, then right to Kings Sutton.

3 Turn right. Cross A 34, bear right to Great Rollright, then take Swerford road, past church.

2 For Little Rollright turn left.

5 Left through Great Tew, then left to Ledwell and left again through Nether Worton and ahead to Barfords and Bloxham.

8 Turn right to North Aston, then left through The Astons.

9 Cross B 4030 to Rousham.

10 Turn left on A 423 and immediately right; bear left into Wootton, then across river.

1 Take B 4026 to Over Norton. After main road bends right, turn left on unsignposted minor road.

12 Take B 4026 to Chipping Norton.

11 Turn right on A 34 then left on B 4437 to Charlbury.

MILES

KM

COVENTRY 16
WARKS / NORTHANTS
Northend
Beacon Tower
BURTON DASSETT
B 4086
A 41
A 423
Radway
CLAYDON
Granary Museum
Oxford Canal
EDGE HILL
Castle Inn
Ratley
Edgehill
FARNBOROUGH HALL
Edgcote
Hare & Hounds
Wardington
Culworth
STRATFORD 11
A 422
Lower Tysoe
Upton House
Middle Tysoe
Upper Tysoe
WROXTON
A 422
CROPREDY
A 423
Williamscot
SULGRAVE MANOR
B 4525
Compton Wynyates
White House
Epwell
Guide Post
Abbey
North Newington
BANBURY
Cross
Middleton Cheney
A 422
OXON / NORTHANTS
A 361
BROUGHTON CASTLE
Tadmarton
Swalcliffe
BLOXHAM
ADDERBURY
West Adderbury
East Adderbury
Newbottle Woods
KINGS SUTTON
Charlton
B 4031
WARKS / OXON
B 4035
Milton
Barford St John
Barford St Michael
Swere
A 41
AYNHO
Aynhoe Park
NORTHANTS / OXON
A 43
A 41
ROLLRIGHT STONES
King Stone
King's Men
Great Rollright
Swerford
Nether Worton
North Aston
The Bear PH
BICESTER 5
LITTLE ROLLRIGHT
EVESHAM 19
A 44
Over Norton
Earthworks
A 34
A 361
GREAT TEW
Ledwell
Somerton
Middle Aston
THE ASTONS
Steeple Aston
B 4030
CHIPPING NORTON
Bliss Tweed Mill
B 4026
Enstone
B 4022
ROUSHAM PARK
Cherwell
SWINDON 26
Spelsbury
B 4022
B 4437
CHARLBURY
Evenlode
B 4437
A 34
Wootton
A 423
B 4027
OXFORD 10
WOODSTOCK

GREAT TEW *The pub is named after the 17th-century lord of the manor.*

EDGE HILL *A battlemented tower today marks Charles I's rallying point.*

HILLSIDE CHURCH *Burton Dassett's church of dark ironstone is built into a hillside, and its floor slopes 15ft upwards from the door to the chancel.*

medieval church have, over the centuries, gone the same way.

Yet good things remain; and a glimpse of the best of old and new Banbury can be obtained by a brief walk from the town's 'new' church. This is an unusual square building of 1793, built in classical style with Corinthian columns supporting a domed roof, a pillared and domed porch, and a tall, green-domed bell tower which rises beside Horse Fair like an Italian campanile. Notice the fossil shells tightly packed into the brown Hornton stone of the church walls.

A pathway from the churchyard leads through traffic-free shopping lanes to a network of narrow streets. Here old coaching inns survive among modern shops, the beautifully lettered façade of a Victorian coal merchant dignifies a building society office, and the classical entrance of the Victorian Corn Exchange now leads into a covered modern shopping centre. Just inside the centre is a mural depicting Banbury's history, which once decorated the original Banbury Cake Shop.

Another link with the Cake Shop is the original shop front which now hangs in the museum near the 'new' Banbury Cross. This is one of those engrossing local museums whose exhibits, carefully selected and clearly labelled, give a clear insight into a town's roots to a visitor with only half an hour to spare.

WROXTON

A narrow lane of thatched red-brown cottages leads down to a quiet hamlet just off the main road. There are grassy banks in front of the cottages, and tall hollyhocks in the gardens. The squat Norman church has a huge canopied tomb of 1631 to Sir William Pope and his wife, their marble effigies still showing red paint on headdress and robe.

The road through the village follows a high wall to the gates of Wroxton Abbey, once the home of Lord North, Prime Minister at the time of the American War of Independence, and now, by one of time's ironies, an American college. The building is closed to the public, but a footpath through the ground, open on weekdays, gives a good view of the front of the 17th-century building,

and leads past a large dovecote round the far side of the abbey grounds.

Even the pub at the abbey gates – inevitably the North Arms – is thatched. A large duck pond and a post office with a sundial of 1752 complete the picture.

An even older and more unusual sundial, the vanes on its four separate faces each set at a precisely calculated angle, tops the brown-stone Guide Post beside the turn-off to North Newington. Erected in 1686, it also bears realistically carved hands pointing the way to London, Stratford, Banbury and 'Chiping' Norton.

BROUGHTON CASTLE

Beyond the broad moat and battlemented gatehouse, the likeness to a 'real' castle ends. A modest porch leads into an elegant country mansion, enlarged in the late 16th century from a manor house dating back to 1300. For five centuries Broughton Castle has been the family home of the Lords Saye and Sele, and the magnificence of its main rooms does not eclipse the house's welcoming homeliness.

The light that pours through the tall broad windows – added by ancestor Richard Fiennes in the 16th century – makes the Great Hall a light and airy place, its walls of undressed stone set off by red plush sofas and carpet. Stalactites of ornamented plaster hang from the ceiling. In the oak-panelled dining room, look out for the tiny woodcarving of the manor as it appeared before the additions of the 1550s.

Broughton was a Puritan stronghold in the 17th century, and a small room at the top of the house was the secret meeting place of Hampden, Pym, Lord Saye and other opponents of Charles I. During the Civil War Parliamentarian troops often lodged in the castle, which Charles's army captured after the battle at nearby Edge Hill.

From the secret 'council chamber' a door leads out onto a parapet walk, with fine views over the castle gardens and across the moat to the surrounding parkland. The castle is open on Wednesday and Sunday from mid-May to mid-September, also on Thursday in July and August, and at Bank Holidays. Also outside the moat is the 14th-century Church of

St Mary, its clear-glass windows making the interior as light and airy as the castle itself. The life-size effigy of Sir John de Broughton, builder of the original manor house, lies within a resplendent tomb of red, blue and gold – though, curiously, it is partly obscured by a later tomb.

The route from Broughton passes through a string of villages, including Swalcliffe with a tiny triangular green dropping steeply down to a thatched pub. In the church across the road stands a 6ft long iron hook, once used to pull burning thatch off the roofs of houses.

From the hilltop road beyond Epwell White House the pink brick walls and tall twisted chimneys of the Tudor Compton Wynyates can be glimpsed through the trees down in the valley; it is not open to the public.

EDGE HILL

Where Charles I raised his standard on the lip of the Cotswolds on October 23, 1642, an octagonal battlemented tower was built a century later. Designed by Sanderson Miller, who lived at nearby Radway Grange, the tower is today part of the Castle Inn, its ground floor forming an unusual octagonal bar.

Paths crisscross the beech-clad slopes nearby, and descend to the village of Radway, which has thatched cottages round a pond, and a church built of stone from the nearby Hornton quarries. Inside the church is an effigy of Henry Kingsmill, a knight who fell in the indecisive Edge Hill conflict.

Upton House, 1 mile south of Edge Hill, is a late 17th-century mansion, owned by the National Trust, which is approached down a broad tree-lined drive. Artists from El Greco to George Stubbs are represented on its walls, while miniature paintings, amazing in their rich detail and lustrous colour, decorate a collection of Sèvres and English porcelain.

BURTON DASSETT

Suddenly the road climbs from the flat Warwickshire Plain up onto a bumpy, breezy moorland where sheep nibble the thin turf, knapweed and stunted bushes dot the slopes, and the wide views which open up in all directions make the visitor feel magically airborne. Old iron-ore quarries, now

grassed over, pit the hills and provide sheltered picnic spots. A beacon tower crowns one hill, and on the facing Magpie Hill, 630ft up, a view indicator identifies landmarks as distant as the Malverns (40 miles away) and the Clee Hills (52 miles).

The tower of All Saints' Church peeps from the trees to the south-east, and its interior offers a further surprise. Light floods in through clear-glass windows onto a cool, white-painted interior which looks more like that of a basilica in some Mediterranean land than that of an English parish church. The absence of pews increases the sense of space. Round the tops of the columns of the north arcade runs a remarkable series of 14th-century carvings of animals and foliage.

FARNBOROUGH HALL

This charming Palladian villa has been the home of the Holbech family for three centuries, and members of the family often stand welcoming today's visitors. In the light and airy book-lined study, household belongings such as phone books, spectacle cases and walking sticks lie among the family souvenirs scattered on every available table top – press cuttings of events in Farnborough's history, war medals, a document of 1810 calling up local men to the militia. There is a pleasing continuity from the family portraits on the wall to the framed photographs of their descendants on graduation day and on the ski slopes.

In the dining room, superb plaster work by William Perritt decorates the ceiling and frames the pictures on the walls. The original Canalettos for which the room was designed were sold in 1929, but they were replaced by copies; a bill for £330 for the copying lies on a side table.

Outside, a Terrace Walk yields fine views over the surrounding parkland, which descends to a slow-moving stream, and across the Warwickshire Plain beyond to the Malvern Hills. An Ionic Temple and Oval Pavilion provide viewpoints along the terrace, and an obelisk at the far end bears the names of Italian prisoners cut into it when Farnborough was used as a hospital during the Second World War. The Terrace Walk is open on most days in summer, but the house only on Wednesdays and Sundays.

UPTON HOUSE *The mansion, dating from 1695, was remodelled this century.*

GREEN TERRACE *The lawn sweeps upwards from the south front of Farnborough Hall to a broad grassy terrace, edged by laurels, which curves south-east for nearly a mile.*

KING'S MEN *In a hilltop clearing, 70 stones have stood for 3500 years.*

CLAYDON

Farming bygones are displayed in a long low barn, but the real charm of Claydon's Granary Museum is the Aladdin's Cave of memorabilia stored in a loft room just beside the entrance gate. Here is one man's personal collection, formed over 30 years: bagatelle boards and beer-pump handles jostle for space with typewriters, gramophones and gasmasks. An 1897 Diamond Jubilee brick props the door open. It is an intriguing collection, open daily.

CROPREDY

Thatched and colour-washed stone cottages line the narrow lanes of this canal-side village. The nearby bridge over the River Cherwell was the scene of a skirmish in the Civil War, and suits of armour, helmets, bayonets and cannonballs from the 1644 engagement are displayed in the sandstone St Mary's Church.

Red Lion Street, behind the church, leads down past a pub to a humpbacked bridge which looks down onto the tiny Cropredy Lock, just wide enough for a single narrow boat, with a towpath walk along the Oxford Canal in both directions.

SULGRAVE MANOR

The home of George Washington's ancestors surprises by its modest proportions. It is a small manor house, built of local limestone in about 1560 by Lawrence Washington, a wool merchant and Mayor of Northampton. It was a century later when Lawrence's great-great-grandson John left England and settled in Virginia, where in 1732 his own great-grandson and president-to-be, George Washington, was born.

Joint British and American efforts have re-created the gentle domestic interior which Lawrence Washington, living at the time of Shakespeare, must have known. There is a stone-flagged Great Hall, a cosy kitchen with a fireplace running the length of one wall, and upstairs an oak-floored main bedroom whose ceiling slopes with the pitch of the roof.

Lawrence Washington lies buried in the 14th-century St James's Church, at the opposite end of a quiet village of thatched and stone-roofed houses.

Tourist information: Banbury 59855.

ROUSHAM PARK *The battlements were added by William Kent in the 1730s to an H-plan house built a century earlier.*

KINGS SUTTON *Gothic windows illuminate a church which dates back to 1220.*

CALM WATERS *A humpback bridge at Cropredy looks down on the Oxford Canal, where painted narrow boats lie beside a towpath walk.*

123

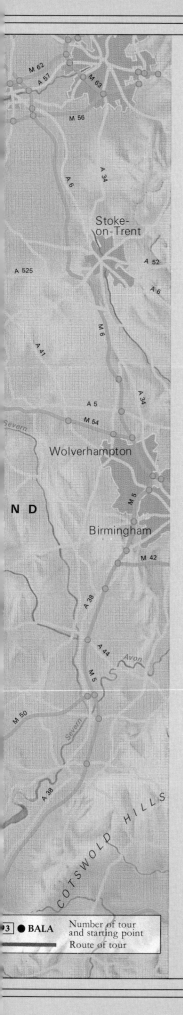

03 ● **BALA** Number of tour
and starting point
Route of tour

Wales

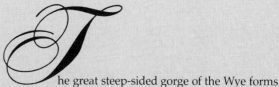

The great steep-sided gorge of the Wye forms an appropriate south-eastern border to a principality whose heart is formed of high peaks and plateaux, with the sound of rushing water never far away. Below the wave-like crests of the Brecon Beacons a green corridor beside the Bristol Channel leads past stately Caerphilly Castle into the rolling farmlands of the Vale of Glamorgan and onwards to the breezy cliffs and sandy beaches of Gower. Farther west lie the 'little England beyond Wales' of former Pembrokeshire, where quiet bays shelter between wave-lashed headlands, and the cathedral of Wales's patron saint.

Into the great sweep of Cardigan Bay to the north pour the estuaries of tumbling rivers such as the Teifi, the Ystwyth and the Dyfi. Their sources are high in the Cambrian Mountains, where lonely Plynlimon guards a chain of man-made lakes, and craggy Cadair Idris clasps its clouds and its legends. Inland, southern Britain's highest waterfall of Pistyll Rhaeadr cascades nearly 300ft down, and there are memories of the heroic Owain Glyndwr, leader in 1400 of the last bid for Welsh independence. To the north, mighty Snowdon and its attendant peaks brood over lonely lakes and dramatic mountain passes. Narrow-gauge railways that once took slate to the ports now puff up and down the fellsides carrying tourists through scenery as spectacular as any in Britain.

The roller-coaster skyline of the Snowdonia National Park provides a striking backcloth to the lower, green lands of Anglesey and the Lleyn Peninsula, where quiet lanes wriggle down to sandy beaches. Beyond Edward I's great castles at Caernarfon and Conwy, wearing their seven centuries lightly, stretch the lively modern resorts of the northern holiday coast. Between them, valleys wind inland to the hills. The River Dee contributes another section of the border with England, where more ruined castles recall the struggles of Welsh warrior-heroes against the English invaders.

From the River Wye to the Vale of Usk

TOUR

73

—— 75 MILES ——

The rural landscape of northern Gwent is dotted with castles belonging to the stormy history of the Welsh Marches. Deep in its gorge, the Wye winds round a dramatic viewpoint.

MONMOUTH

The focal point of the town, Agincourt Square, is virtually enclosed by imposing buildings of many eras. They include the Beaufort Arms Hotel and the King's Head Hotel – the former connected with Lord Nelson, the latter with Charles I – and the impressive early Georgian Shire Hall, built when this was the administrative county town of Monmouthshire.

The highest point in the town is crowned by the remains of Monmouth Castle, birthplace of Henry V. The adjoining Great Castle House, dating from 1673, is the headquarters of what is claimed to be the oldest militia in the British Army, the Royal Monmouthshire Royal Engineers (the repeated 'Royal' is unique in British regimental titles).

Two ancient ecclesiastical buildings remain. St Peter's Church at Dixton, a short walk along the banks of the Wye, and St Thomas's Church at Over

Monnow are both little altered since Norman times; the latter has a superb Norman doorway. Next to St Thomas's is the fortified Monnow Bridge, dating from the 13th century and unique in Britain in having its fortified gateway intact.

East of the town, the Kymin hill is capped by a round house and Naval Temple, dedicated to the admirals of Nelson's fleets and their victories. Views from here stretch to the Brecon Beacons far into South Wales. Some 3 miles farther into the Forest of Dean is the Suck Stone, reputed to be the largest single slab of stone in Britain. It is reached by a 2½ mile waymarked path leading deep into the forest.

SYMONDS YAT

Two settlements, Symonds Yat East and West, are separated by the Wye, here lined by huge cliffs and winding through a tortuous gorge.

Above Symonds Yat East a renowned viewpoint, Yat Rock, overlooks the river, which here curves in a massive horseshoe. Views from the rock extend north-east to the Malvern Hills and west to the Black Mountains. Several waymarked paths lead from the car park through the forest, in which the ramparts of an old British camp can be seen.

Symonds Yat West contrasts sharply with the scenic grandeur of Yat Rock. This straggling settlement on the riverside is a holiday centre with a maze and a Museum of Mazes,

open from Easter to October. It also offers fairground rides and a boat trip to the rapids at the entrance to the Wye gorge. A passenger ferry crosses the river to the east bank, where quiet riverside walks can be taken.

Two miles away the Seven Sisters rocks offer a dramatic view over the heavily wooded Wye gorge. Giant monoliths and projections of rock stand out from the side of the gorge, towering above the water. These lofty perches afford views over an unspoilt section of this noted salmon-fishing river, and the scene is uncluttered by people, cars or roads.

The Seven Sisters are reached along waymarked paths – follow the arrows – from the forest road leading to The Biblins, an adventure centre for local schools. Away from the gorge edge is King Arthur's Cave, once the home of hunters and their prey in Neolithic times.

GROSMONT

The spire of the 13th-century Church of St Nicholas can be seen from miles away; it draws the eye up to the hilltop where Grosmont nestles. The village – consisting of a main street of solid, ancient houses and a few back lanes – lies huddled between the church and the skeletal remains of Grosmont Castle, standing aloof on its dry-moated motte. The castle was built to protect this part of the southern Marcher Lordship – a Norman local government system – from

the ravages of the Welsh. In 1405 a major battle here saw Prince Henry, later Henry V, defeat Owain Glyndwr and turn the tide of that particular struggle for Welsh independence.

The River Monnow, here forming the Wales-England border, snakes through meadowland and oak woodland at the foot of the bluff beneath the castle, disguising evidence – traces of streets and buildings – of the once much larger borough of Grosmont. The size of the church is further evidence of the past: part of the nave is now used to store old agricultural implements. The Monnow is one of the few rivers in Britain still a home to wild otters. The medieval Angel Inn fronts the tiny market place, on which the 1832 market hall replaced a much earlier one.

TRE-WYN

About 2 miles north of Llanvihangel Crucorney stands the majestic mansion of Tre-wyn, built mainly in the William and Mary style. It is noted for its fine oak panelling, staircases and minstrels' gallery.

The house stands on a hillside and affords magnificent views of Ysgyryd Fawr (Skirrid Mountain). Its grounds, covering 6 acres, include terraced gardens, an arboretum and walled and rose gardens. Offa's Dyke can be seen nearby. The house and gardens are open on most days in summer.

LLANVIHANGEL CRUCORNEY

The Honddu river breaches the immense sandstone wall of the Black Mountains at Llanvihangel, flowing from the Vale of Ewyas into the lower-lying area of Gwent. The village lies

RAINBOW'S END *There may be no pot of gold buried at Lower Dyffryn, but the tiny settlement south-east of Grosmont is a gem set in green velvet.*

just above the river in an area with a long settlement history. There are Norman castle mottes (mounds) at Blaengavenny, south of the village, and Treveddw, to the north. The Skirrid Mountain Inn claims to be the oldest pub in Wales, dating from about 1110; it has been used as a courthouse and a garrison for Cromwellian troops, and is said to be haunted. The single main street is lined with several substantial, stone-built medieval buildings. St Michael's Church, though half ruined, is still in regular use.

The most impressive building in the village is Llanvihangel Court, across the new bypass from the village centre. This 15th-century building – restored in the 17th century when a splendid yew staircase was added – is noted for the fine trees in its grounds. It is open at Easter and on Sundays in July and August.

ABERGAVENNY

A labyrinth of narrow streets and alleyways at the foot of the castle hill recalls Abergavenny's long history. Elsewhere 20th-century developments reflect the town's industrial and agricultural importance.

Only a few bare walls of the Norman castle remain, for in 1645 Charles I ordered it to be destroyed so that it would not become a Parliamentarian stronghold. However, the keep was rebuilt in the early 19th century and now houses a museum.

The parish church of St Mary was originally part of a Benedictine priory founded in the 11th century. Its immense tithe barn, part of the priory buildings, is used as an auction house. In the church are several effigy tombs of the 13th and 15th centuries, and intricately carved 15th-century choir stalls. The neo-Gothic market hall, in the centre of the old town, is a dominating building.

Down a narrow side street opposite is the former Church of St John which was used as the King Henry VIII Grammar School from 1542 to 1898. Tourist and National Park information centres are in Monk Street.

At Llanfoist, 1 mile south, the Monmouthshire and Brecon Canal clings to the hillside above the River Usk. Llanfoist Wharf, on a wooded site at the foot of Blorenge, has remains of an old tramway – one of many along this section of canal – leading to Blaenavon.

East of Abergavenny, a small roadside car park gives access to a short, steep walk up Ysgyryd Fawr (1595ft), a dramatic outcrop of the Black Mountains. Views from the summit are superb. Near the summit are traces of St Michael's Chapel, a place of pilgrimage until the 18th century.

WHITE CASTLE

This is one of three castles built by the Normans to control an unstable border area; the others are Grosmont and Skenfrith. Moated White Castle is the most impressive of the three. It dates from the 12th century, and was strengthened by Edward I a century later. At one time the castle's walls were plastered white. The last of countless prisoners to walk its court-

yards was Rudolf Hess, held in the area after his landing in Scotland during the Second World War.

RAGLAN

The village lies isolated between two dual-carriageway trunk roads linking South Wales with the Midlands. Though largely a 20th-century 'dormitory', it retains a core of pleasant old buildings adjoining the late 15th-century Church of St Cadoc.

Standing aloof from the village are the spectacular remains of Raglan Castle, greatest of the Marcher fortresses. Built mostly in the 15th century on the site of an earlier motte and bailey, Raglan was one of the last major castles to be constructed. It comprises two courts linked by the hall, each served by its own gatehouse.

The massive hexagonal keep, the Great Tower, known also as the Yellow Tower of Gwent, is the oldest part. It stands apart, protected by a moat, but is linked to the rest of the building by a bridge. The castle is open daily throughout the year.

Tourist information: Monmouth 3899; Abergavenny 3254 (summer).

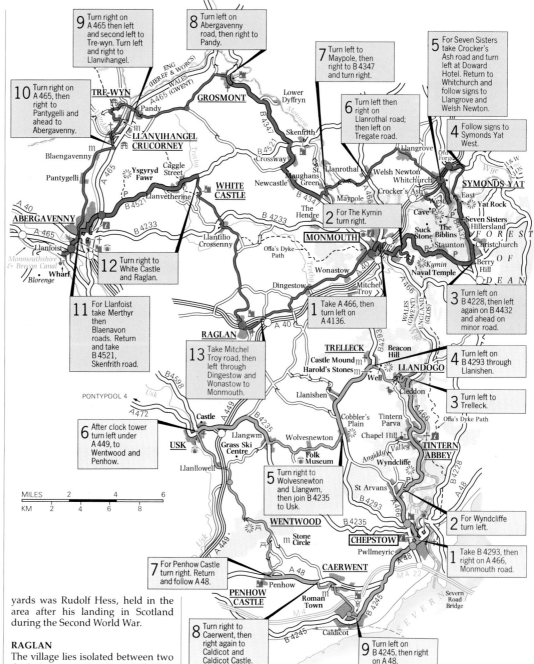

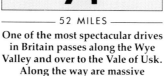

TOUR
74

52 MILES

One of the most spectacular drives in Britain passes along the Wye Valley and over to the Vale of Usk. Along the way are massive Norman castles and modern engineering wonders.

CHEPSTOW

The Wye gorge ends at Chepstow, just upstream from the point where the Wye joins the mighty Severn beyond the Severn Road Bridge. Two equally magnificent bridges span the Wye, which forms the Wales-England border at this point. One is Rennie's cast-iron road bridge of 1816. The other is Brunel's immense bridge built in 1852 to carry the former South

Wales Railway across the gorge; its centre span was replaced in 1962. Between these bridges are the remains of the port of Chepstow: old warehouses are a reminder of the days when the town was a thriving centre for trade with Europe.

The streets of the town climb steeply up the cliffside. Hocker Hill Street is the sole reminder of the port's narrow, winding, cobbled ways. Bridge Street, a terrace of bowfronted town houses, is an example of the successors to the medieval lanes.

At the lower end of Bridge Street is Chepstow Museum, and the old school, which now houses the Stuart Crystal Centre, where glass engraving may be seen. The upper end of the street leads to High Street and the remaining gate in the 13th-century Portwall, enclosing the old town.

Chepstow Castle surveys the town to the north. A steep river cliff acts as a natural moat on one side, and the other sides are defended by massive limestone walls. The castle, open daily, belonged to William FitzOsbern, Earl of Hereford and the most powerful of the Marcher Lords under William the Conqueror. Before his death in 1071, FitzOsbern endowed the Priory Church of St Mary, which retains a superb Norman doorway. In the church are fine tombs of the 2nd Earl of Worcester who died in 1559, and of Henry Marten, one of the judges at Charles I's trial.

North of the town, at Wyndcliffe, a waymarked trail leads to the edge of the Wye gorge at Eagle's Nest – with views to the Cotswolds and Somerset – and the 365 steps, a spectacular descent of the cliff face.

TINTERN ABBEY
Massive vaulted and arched remains command the floor of the Wye Valley, standing serenely at the river's edge and hemmed in by steep, thickly wooded slopes. Like all the major monasteries this Cistercian house – founded in the 12th century and rebuilt in the 13th – was an important economic centre as well as a religious settlement. Its economy was based on agriculture, which was the responsibility of the lay brothers who lived in their own quarters and attended their own services in the church. The abbey is open daily, and an exhibition near the entrance explains the abbey and its history.

The wireworks founded in the Angiddy valley were the first in Britain. These and related small industries were the lifeblood of the village of Tintern Parva right up until the early 1900s; their excavated remains stand on waymarked forest paths beside the road to Llanishen.

The village is no more than a strand of houses between the river and the steep wooded hillside, but it has been a tourist centre since William Wordsworth praised it in the 18th century. The railway stole much of the river trade in the 1870s, but this has been closed since 1964. The old bridge over the river offers access to pleasant riverside and woodland walks; one waymarked path includes a section of Offa's Dyke. The old station houses a railway exhibition and adjoins a picnic area.

LLANDOGO
The village was once a busy river port for the export of – among other things – millstones which were quarried and honed on the plateau above the steep river cliffs. Houses and cottages cling precariously to the steep, wooded embankment long ago cut into the cliffs by the Wye. Deep sunken pathways lead from the plateau to the river, offering fine walks and views.

A steep, narrow road leads from the village to the lip of the gorge at Cleddon. Here a stream plunges into the gorge in a spectacular series of waterfalls and shoots. A streamside path follows the watercourse through the Cleddon Shoots Nature Reserve, where ferns and mosses grow in the dense shade of wild cherry, oak, beech, holly and yew. Beacon Hill is the highest point on the plateau, and views extend far into South Wales.

TRELLECK
This very old settlement, in rolling country beside the Wye, has a marvellously preserved castle mound at Court Farm, beside a footpath leading to St Nicholas Church. The church dates from around 1225, when it replaced Christian buildings dating back to the 7th century.

On the road from Cleddon is St Anne's Virtuous Well, a place of pilgrimage until the 17th century and reputed to have healing properties. Three standing stones, Harold's Stones, stand in a field just south-

OPEN TO THE SKY *The roofless remains of Tintern Abbey lie among wooded hills.*

CASTLE IN THE TREES *Caldicot Castle stands at the centre of a small country park.*

west of the village. They are at least 2000 years old though at one time they were thought to be a monument to Harold, the last king of Saxon England who came nearer to conquering South Wales than any predecessor.

Views westwards from Cobbler's Plain, 4 miles south-west, stretch to the Brecon Beacons – at up to 2906ft the highest mountains in South Wales. The steep road down into the Vale of Usk passes a folk museum near Wolvesnewton, based around a model farm built in the 1790s for the Duke of Beaufort. It is open at weekends from Easter to November, and daily from June to September.

USK
The privately owned ruined castle, dating from the 12th century, overshadows the small, compact Twyn Square, lined with inns and solid old houses. Much of interest in this small market town lies to the east of its main thoroughfare, Bridge Street. New Market Street, wide and tree-lined, contains the Gwent Rural Life Museum in the old Malt Barn; it is open daily in summer. In Old Market Street is the Great House, an immense medieval building now split into several houses.

The river from which the town takes its name flows briskly beneath a five-arched bridge, where a pleasant riverside walk begins. The castle is the town's oldest building. It became a royal castle in 1424 when it was inherited by Richard Plantagenet, Duke of York. Henry VIII gave the castle to his sixth wife, Catherine Parr, as part of her dowry.

To the north of the castle is the site of the Battle of Pwll Melyn in 1405, a fierce skirmish during the rebellion of Owain Glyndwr. It ended in defeat for the Welsh hero, whose brother was among those killed while his son was captured and sent to the Tower of London.

From AD 55 until 66 Usk was a fortress and base camp for the Roman Twentieth Legion, whose task it was to subjugate South Wales. The garrison of 10,000 men occupied a 48 acre site called Burrium, one of the largest fortresses in the entire Roman Empire. It now lies beneath the town, which was originally laid out by Richard Strongbow de Clare about 1170.

In the 19th century Usk was the site of the county gaol which still stands in Maryport Street, a massive, castle-like building built by Thomas Henry Wyatt in 1841 and modelled on Pentonville Prison, London. It is now a youth custody centre. Magistrates still sit in the adjoining Court House, also by Wyatt.

The Church of St Mary's, associated once with a Benedictine priory, has some fine medieval woodwork and a Tudor rood screen. The 16th-century gatehouse was once the entrance to Priory House, rebuilt in Victorian times.

Two miles south of Usk, at Llanllowell, a grass ski centre is open at weekends.

WENTWOOD
Shady glades and forest rides in Wentwood Forest provide ample opportunities for viewing its varied habitats and wildlife. Fallow deer roam freely and badgers and foxes are also there. Magnificent banks of wild daffodils may be seen in spring.

Several picnic sites and car parks are provided by the Forestry Commission. Foresters' Oaks picnic area on the far side of the forest overlooks Wentwood Reservoir. This is the start of the Gray Hill Countryside Trail of just over 3 miles. It takes in a Neolithic stone circle and the hill's summit, with good views southwards over the Severn estuary.

PENHOW CASTLE
This Norman castle stands on a craggy hill overlooking the marshlands of the Severn estuary. It is still a family home and is the oldest inhabited castle in Wales. It is also the only intact survivor of a host of castles in this part of Gwent. It has a 15th-century great hall with a minstrels' gallery, a 12th-century bedchamber and a Victorian housekeeper's room. The castle is open from Wednesdays to Sundays in the summer.

CAERWENT
Many remains of Venta Silurum – named after the local Silures tribe – enclose the existing small village of Caerwent, the regional capital of the Romans in South Wales. Well-preserved sections of wall, with the outline of temples and other administrative buildings, make this one of Britain's leading Roman sites.

Caldicot Castle, 2 miles south-east, was partially restored in Victorian times to its original Norman design. It lies at the centre of a small country park – a green island in a sprawling new town area – and has a museum, open daily from March to October.

Tourist information: Chepstow 3772 (summer); Tintern 431 (summer).

GLORIOUS GATEWAY *Rising 400ft above the Wye, Symonds Yat Rock has glorious views of the outlying countryside. 'Yat' means 'gate' in Old English, and Symonds was a 17th-century High Sheriff of Herefordshire.*

A castle beyond the Garden of Wales

Hilly coal-bearing country is the backdrop for one of the finest castles in Britain. Southward is the fertile Vale of Glamorgan, its rolling green farmlands forming the Garden of Wales.

CAERPHILLY

The grey-green walls, squat purposeful towers and massive water defences of Caerphilly Castle occupy a 30 acre site in the middle of the town. Perhaps because of its unpretentious surroundings, the castle's rightful stature as one of Europe's greatest surviving medieval fortresses has only recently been generally recognised.

It dates from 1268, but it was three years later that the Norman lord, Gilbert de Clare – fearful of the native Welsh – began serious work on the site. His 'water-and-stone' system for the defence of Caerphilly survives largely intact. The castle is of concentric design, with a seemingly impregnable series of moats and battlements which radiate, in a succession of larger and larger circles, from its inner ward. There is a ruined tower that manages to out-lean even Pisa's.

The castle was rescued from dereliction in the 19th century by the wealthy Bute family. Restoration, rather than wholesale reconstruction, was their guiding principle. As a result, this is one of those rare sites which still convincingly evoke the spirit of medieval times. It is open daily.

CAERAU HILL-FORT

A path to the hill-fort starts from the narrow lane leading straight ahead from the road junction in Rhiwsaeson. The path itself is somewhat indeterminate, but its goal is un-mistakable. Caerau fort is a conspicuous stump on top of a 548ft hill. This undisturbed – and largely unvisited – site, clothed with groves of oak and clumps of fern and gorse, was an Iron Age fortification.

LLANTRISANT

The steep hillside site appealed to the castle-building Normans, and thanks to them Llantrisant has the tall ruined 'Tower of the Raven', its stonework completely obscured by a thick coat of ivy.

The parish church has been a place of Christian worship since the 6th century, and it contains a 7th-century decorated 'Resurrection stone'. Narrow streets lined with old buildings spread from the hilltop.

Llantrisant is now the home of the Royal Mint. Guided tours, from April to the end of August, can be arranged (Llantrisant 222111).

BEAUPRE CASTLE

Beaupre (pronounced 'Bewper'), stands south of St Hilary, a pretty village of immaculate stone dwellings with the occasional thatched roof. The castle is splendidly isolated in rolling farmland, a quarter of a mile walk from the road.

More a manor house than a military fortress, Beaupre Castle dates largely from Elizabethan times, when creature comforts had priority. The rooms are ranged round a central courtyard reached through two Italianate porches. The castle is open daily.

COWBRIDGE

This handsome, prosperous old town, known as the capital of the Vale of Glamorgan, consists basically of one long main street. Cowbridge was a market centre in Norman times, and it is still a place of bustling trade. Remnants of the medieval walled town remain. South of the main street, a narrow gateway and part of the walls can be seen.

NASH POINT

The two lighthouses that share the headland with remnants of an Iron Age fort testify to the treacherous nature of the coastline. The cliffs are striking: layers of limestone rock, looking like building blocks, have been exposed in a regular series of steps. The shoreline is an expanse of boulders and rocks washed by the grey waters of the Bristol Channel. The effect is strange, almost lunar. From the cliff-top car park there are views across to Exmoor.

ST DONATS

The earliest part of St Donats Castle dates from around 1300, though the building as it now stands, with not a stone out of place, looks as if it could have been built yesterday. In fact there was considerable restoration early in this century. Then, in 1925, the American newspaper magnate William Randolph Hearst bought the castle and incorporated into it a miscellany of buildings. In the shadow of the walls is St Donats Church.

Now the castle is the home of The United World College of the Atlantic, the world's first international sixth-form school with 360 students from more than 60 countries. There is a guided afternoon tour in June and July (Llantwit Major 2271).

LLANTWIT MAJOR

This little town has grown up haphazardly over the years. With its narrow streets meeting at acute junctions, it was not built for the motor age, and its

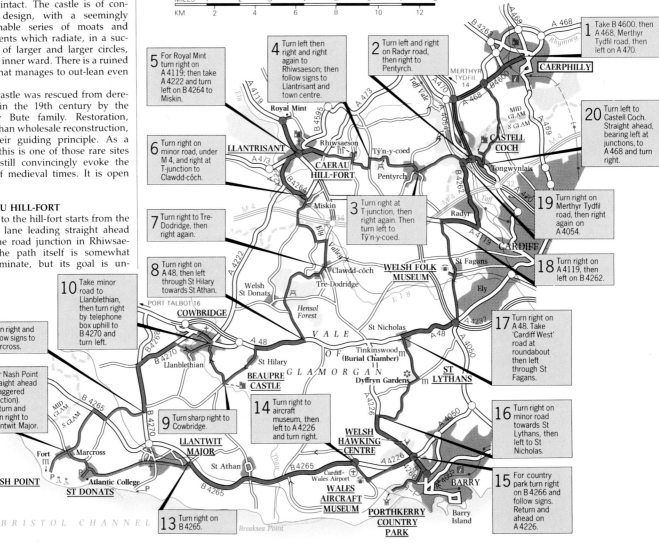

MILES 1 2 3 4 5 6 7 8
KM 2 4 6 8 10 12

5 For Royal Mint turn right on A 4119; then take A 4222 and turn left on B 4264 to Miskin.

4 Turn left then right and right again to Rhiwsaeson; then follow signs to Llantrisant and town centre.

2 Turn left and right on Radyr road, then right to Pentyrch.

1 Take B 4600, then A 468, Merthyr Tydfil road, then left on A 470.

20 Turn left to Castell Coch. Straight ahead, bearing left at junctions, to A 468 and turn right.

6 Turn right on minor road, under M 4, and right at T-junction to Clawdd-côch.

3 Turn right at T-junction, then right again. Then turn left to Tŷn-y-coed.

19 Turn right on Merthyr Tydfil road, then right again on A 4054.

7 Turn right to Tre-Dodridge, then right again.

18 Turn right on A 4119, then left on B 4262.

8 Turn right on A 48, then left through St Hilary towards St Athan.

10 Take minor road to Llanblethian, then turn right by telephone box uphill to B 4270 and turn left.

17 Turn right on A 48. Take 'Cardiff West' road at roundabout then left through St Fagans.

11 Turn right and follow signs to Marcross.

12 For Nash Point straight ahead (staggered junction). Return and turn right to Llantwit Major.

9 Turn sharp right to Cowbridge.

14 Turn right to aircraft museum, then left to A 4226 and turn right.

16 Turn right on minor road towards St Lythans, then left to St Nicholas.

15 For country park turn right on B 4266 and follow signs. Return and ahead on A 4226.

13 Turn right on B 4265.

The rugged beauty of the Pembrokeshire coast is preserved in a National Park. The Normans built a mighty castle at Pembroke, and created their 'Little England beyond Wales'.

PEMBROKE

Pembroke's main street displays Georgian ancestry with its pleasant, pastel-coloured buildings. It follows the crest of a long, narrow ridge, culminating in a castle-crowned outcrop above the river. Beyond the Great Gatehouse a grass-covered outer ward is ringed by walls and stout towers, one of which – the Henry VII Tower – was the reputed birthplace in 1457 of Harri Tudur, the Welshman who became Henry VII of England and initiator of the mighty Tudor dynasty. The Great Keep is the castle's most outstanding feature. A circular staircase cut into its wall leads to a spectacular viewpoint high above the rooftops and river. The castle is open daily.

Pembroke's early 14th-century wall runs beside the river, from the castle to the end of the town.

HOBBS POINT

The quay stands on the dividing line between the sheltered deep-water harbour of Milford Haven, with its dockyards and oil installations, and the peaceful Daugleddau, a backwater of wooded creeks. Cruises around Milford Haven run from Hobbs Point in summer.

MULLOCK BRIDGE

The stone bridge over Mullock Brook reputedly stood here when Harri Tudur, who became Henry VII by his victory over Richard III at Bosworth, passed this way with his invading army in 1485. Sir Rhys ap Thomas, a wily Welsh nobleman, kept his allegiances open by lying under the bridge as Harri's forces passed over it, thus honouring his oath to King Richard that 'only over his body would such an invasion take place'.

DALE PENINSULA

This isolated peninsula has a coastline of rugged grandeur, spectacular cliff walks and a teeming bird life. The razorbill, official symbol of the Pembrokeshire Coast National Park, is one of the many species of sea bird that colonise Dale's rock crevices and ledges. At the tip of the peninsula is St Ann's Head, where a lighthouse stands on the site of a chapel dedicated to St Ann and said to have been built by Henry VII. The village of Dale is a collection of prettily painted cottages at the end of a long beach. Its sheltered anchorage within Milford Haven is popular with yachtsmen.

MARLOES

Marloes Sands is one of the most beautiful beaches in Pembrokeshire. The half-mile walk from the car park opens out onto a huge stretch of firm sands, backed by a gently curving line of red cliffs. At the far end is Gateholm Island, which is accessible at low tide.

LITTLE HAVEN

Huddled around a cliff-backed beach, this attractive little village grew up in the 1850s as a port for shipping coal to other parts of Britain. Today it is a popular resort for swimming and boating.

Half a mile up the coast is Broad Haven, a more spacious village spread out behind long, gently shelving sands. There is good bathing, and boats can be launched from the foreshore.

HAVERFORDWEST

As with many old settlements, Haverfordwest is initially a confusing jumble of steep streets, side lanes and narrow passageways. Go first to the viewpoint on top of the hill, where the shell of a Norman castle shares the summit with the Castle Museum and Art Gallery accommodated in an old jail. The hilltop looks out across a busy town which was once a thriving port at the highest navigable point on the Western Cleddau river. Echoes of Haverfordwest's nautical days are strongest along Quay Street. This leads to the historic Bristol Trader Inn, standing among multi-storeyed wharfside warehouses.

SUTHERLAND ART GALLERY

The artist Graham Sutherland had a special affection for Pembrokeshire, an area which inspired much of his work. The largest permanent collection of his works on public display is housed in a gallery adjacent to Picton Castle. The gallery is open daily except Mondays from April to September. The gardens of the castle, which has a Norman exterior, are open most days in summer.

LLAWHADEN

The substantial ruin of the Bishop of St David's Castle at Llawhaden occupies a grassy bluff overlooking rolling countryside. Built as a castle, it evolved over the centuries into a great fortified palace. Decorated archways, the shells of private apartments, remains of vaulted storage rooms, kitchens and great hall survive.

CAREW

When the tide is high, the old arched stone bridge which still carries traffic over the Carew river is almost submerged.

Downstream from the bridge, a dam across the river traps the waters at high tide in a mill pond, used for many centuries to drive the water wheels of Carew Tidal Mill, the only one of its kind remaining in Wales. The three-storey, early 19th-century building, on the site of an earlier mill, has been restored and is open most days from Easter to October.

Nothing remains of the original early medieval stronghold built by Sir Nicholas Carew in the late 13th century. Carew, as it now stands, is a castle of great style. Military influences of the 13th century remain, but they are largely overlaid with Tudor and Elizabethan additions; the stone-mullioned windows are particularly striking. The castle is open from Easter to October.

Tourist information: Pembroke 682148 (summer); Haverfordwest 66141/3110 (summer); Broad Haven 412 (summer).

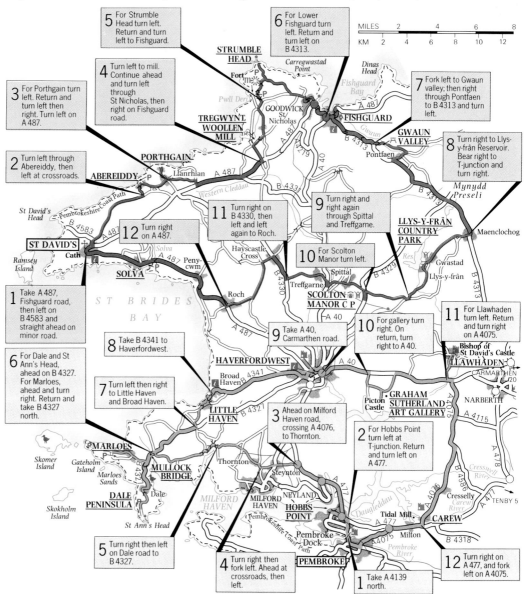

135

Sea, sands and rivers by Cardigan Bay

Narrow lanes lead to tiny coves and old fishing villages on Cardigan Bay. Inland, green farmlands follow the Teifi as it flows by market towns, wool mills and castles.

CARDIGAN

Multistoreyed quayside warehouses, some converted into holiday apartments, are reminders of the times when this handsome old town near the mouth of the Teifi flourished as a trading port. The silting up of the river and the arrival of the railways took away its trade, and now it turns inland, serving as a market town for the rich farmlands to the south.

Cardigan's historical pedigree is an ancient one: Wales's first eisteddfod is said to have been held there in 1176. Two small round towers and a stretch of outer wall are all that remain of the town's medieval castle, which is not open to the public. It looks out onto Cardigan's finest architectural feature, a five-arched stone bridge built in the 12th century.

MWNT

The beach of Mwnt lies, totally protected, beneath a towering headland, the whole scene enhanced by a small solitary building, its dazzling whitewashed walls conspicuous amongst the headland grass. This is Eglwys y Graig (Holy Cross Church), which has stood here since the 13th or 14th century.

ABERPORTH

A pretty seaside village, Aberporth spreads up a steep hillside from its twin beaches, separated by a small rocky headland. It is one of the few places on this rugged, remote coastline where the road runs right down to the sea.

Walkers can follow a coastal footpath leading east for little more than a mile, to Tresaith. Those travelling by car are advised to park on the hilltop above the beach and walk the short distance to the sea. Just to the east, a waterfall plunges from the cliffs onto the seashore rocks.

At Traeth-Penbryn (Penbryn Beach), 1 mile farther east, motorists must use the car park and walk about one-third of a mile to this delightful stretch of sands set in a break in the headlands.

LLANGRANOG

Colourfully painted cottages cling to the steep sides of a narrow, wooded vale running down to the sea. There it opens out onto a sandy beach sheltered by cliffs.

From the beach, a wild and windy walk – one of the most spectacular along the coast – leads across the cliffs, below an Iron Age hilltop fort, to the promontory of Ynys-Lochtyn, owned by the National Trust.

NEW QUAY

Activity in New Quay's harbour centres around a small fleet of trawlers which bring in fish, crabs and lobsters. The great seafaring days of Cardigan Bay, when everything was shipped in and out by ketch, may have long gone, but the list of harbour 'tolls and dues' is still on the wall. Soap, onions, limestone and coconuts were unloaded here, their prices clearly displayed in elegant writing. It cost sixpence (2½p) to take a small musical instrument off a ship, a shilling for a Bath chair, and a pound for an organ.

The poet Dylan Thomas lived in New Quay in the 1940s, and the life of the resort is believed to have provided much of his inspiration for *Under Milk Wood*.

The stone quayside and beach face east, and are completely sheltered from the westerly winds by a steep hillside. On a clear day, the views from above the harbour and sands extend across the bay and well past Aberystwyth to the purple mountains of mid and North Wales.

MAESLLYN MILL AND MUSEUM

Teifiside was once a thriving wool-producing area. The banks of the Teifi and its tributaries were lined with mills which made Welsh weaves and distinctively patterned tapestry cloths. In the area around Llandysul, quite a few are still working including Maesllyn Mill, which was reopened in 1976.

The renovated stone building stands in a peaceful valley at the end of a short, rough track. Dating from 1881, the mill contains machinery from that period, together with an earlier hand-operated loom and a range of exhibits explaining the production process from raw fleece to finished cloth. The mill shop sells a number of craft products including cloth and woollen garments.

Visitors can also wander around the 20 acres of wooded grounds on a 1½ mile waymarked nature trail. The mill and museum are open daily, except on Sunday in winter.

LLANDYSUL

Although it is one of the largest towns on the Teifi, Llandysul remains largely undiscovered by visitors. Fishermen and canoeists are the exceptions, however. The anglers pit their skills against salmon and sea trout; and the canoeists brave the tricky 'white-water' slalom course formed by the Teifi as it rushes through a rocky chasm near the road bridge.

Farther upstream, the river is more placid and flows quietly past St Tysul's Church. This 13th-century building with its substantial, square, Norman tower is somewhat dwarfed by the hills and rooftops of the town rising above it.

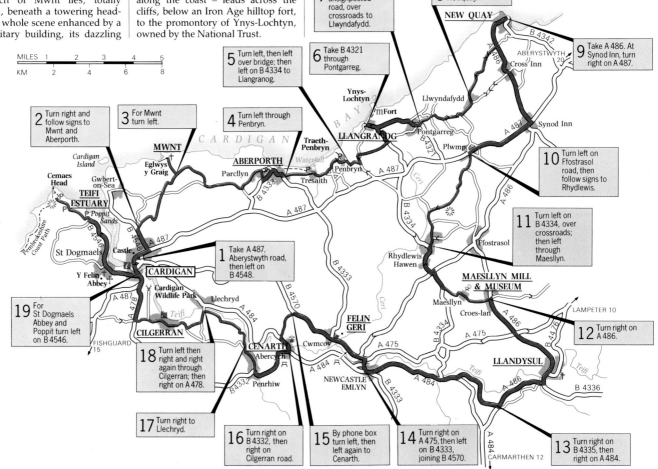

SEA, SAND AND SOLITUDE *In the tiny bay below Mwnt a steep path with steps zigzags down to a west-facing beach where a creamy surf caresses the shore.*

CHURCH IN TRUST *Mwnt's ancient Holy Cross Church is in the care of the National Trust.*

MAESLLYN MILL MUSEUM *Weaving machinery from the 19th century is on display in the museum.*

CONQUEROR'S CASTLE *The impressive twin-towered fortress at Cilgerran dates from Norman times.*

FELIN GERI

The Ceri, a little tributary of the Teifi, provides the power which drives one of Wales's few surviving water mills. Stone-ground wholemeal flour is produced by traditional means on a commercial basis, reviving a practice that dates from the 16th century. The derelict mill was renovated in the early 1970s. When the water wheel is in action, the old building creaks and groans as the stone grinder turns grain into flour.

A second water wheel drives another rarity: a water-powered sawmill. The site also has its own bakery, where cookery demonstrations are given, and a small farming museum. The mill is open daily from Easter to September.

CENARTH

The Teifi tumbles over rocks, pounding against the salmon as they leap and struggle to reach their spawning grounds upstream. Fishermen congregate on the banks as the river funnels into a narrow course before rushing beneath the old stone road bridge. Stone-built houses stand close to the river and a restored smithy stands, appropriately, opposite the Three Horseshoes Inn.

At one time coracle fishermen were also a familiar part of the scene at Cenarth. The tiny coracle, a precarious looking, wooden-framed craft, has been used in Wales for at least 2000 years. But coracle fishing is now a rarity, though races are held here every August.

Nearby is Cenarth Fishing Museum. It has a huge array of rods and reels, many of them antique, and a display explaining how coracles are made. Upstairs, the Salmon Leap Art Gallery runs a film show about the river and fishing in general. The museum is open from Easter to early October.

CILGERRAN

The stronghold at Cilgerran stands just off the main street, on a lofty crag above the Teifi. The wooded bluff on which it is perched commands spectacular views of farmlands and the snaking Teifi as it flows through a narrow, inaccessible gorge. These waters, like those at Cenarth, have long been associated with the coracle; a coracle regatta is held each August.

The entrance to Cardigan Wildlife Park is on the western edge of the village. The park is a cross between a formal zoo and a free-ranging safari area. Waymarked trails lead across fields and through woodland, past enclosures containing many types of animal, including deer, zebus and goats. Open daily, the park has picnic areas, an adventure playground, and occasional falconry displays.

TEIFI ESTUARY

St Dogmaels, over the river from Cardigan, is noteworthy mainly for its abbey, founded in 1115 by monks from the Benedictine Order of Tiron, France. The sparse remains, in pleasant green fields behind the main street, lie beside the parish church of St David. Y Felin, a water mill, also stands nearby. Built in the 1640s and recently restored to full working order, the mill's three sets of water-driven stones are once again grinding wheat, barley and oatmeal.

Poppit Sands, farther north, is an extensive stretch of beach and duneland filling the mouth of the estuary, beyond which lies open sea and rocky headlands. From Poppit, the road climbs away from the coast, narrowing into a high-sided country lane with passing places. Its end is marked, within a mile or so, by two rough-and-ready car parks. The farthest one, in the fields of Allt-y-goed Farm, is the most convenient for the footpath to Cemaes Head.

The walk, part of the long-distance Pembrokeshire Coast Path, is no more than half a mile and well waymarked. Along the way there are fine views across the estuary to Gwbert-on-Sea's white-painted houses and the grassy hump of Cardigan Island.

Tourist information: Cardigan 613230 (summer); Aberaeron 570602 (summer).

Mountains above the Teifi and Tywi valleys

TOUR

81

——— 87 MILES ———

From the farmlands of the Teifi valley, an old drovers' road crosses the lonely Abergwesyn Pass to a group of lowland market towns. The route heads back into the hills to a spectacular reservoir.

LAMPETER

The Afon Teifi meanders lazily through green pastureland on the southern fringes of this pleasant country town. Lampeter has long served as a market town for the surrounding farmlands, and its main streets are lined by coaching inns and Georgian and Victorian buildings.

Lampeter is also an historic seat of learning. St David's University College was founded in 1822 and opened five years later. A quadrangle, with corner towers, clock tower and fountain, forms the centrepiece of a neat, grassy campus.

LLANDDEWI BREFI

Llanddewi means St David, and Wales's patron saint held a meeting here in AD 519 to denounce heresy. During this Synod of Brefi, the ground is said to have risen beneath his feet so that he could be seen and heard by the crowds. The meeting was held on the site now occupied by the parish church, which stands on a slight rise above the rooftops.

The church is ancient, built around a late 12th-century tower. A statue of St David, staff in hand and dove on shoulder, looks towards the altar from a corner near the main door.

TREGARON

This small, strongly Welsh town straddles the border between settled farmlands and the high, wild country often referred to as 'the great Welsh desert'. Tregaron was an important staging post where drovers would congregate before setting off across the inhospitable Abergwesyn Pass. Today it is still a meeting place, for farmers who buy and sell sheep.

TREGARON BOG

Already the largest raised peat bog in Wales, Tregaron Bog is still growing. This bleak, 6 mile expanse of undrained moss and grass-covered wetlands is noted for its plants and birds: the red kite can sometimes be seen.

Tregaron Bog is now the Cors Caron National Nature Reserve and entry is by special permit only. However, the public can follow a nature trail leading to an observation point, on the disused railway line along the bog's north-east rim.

ABERGWESYN PASS

A thin grey line of tarmac tenuously connects Tregaron and Abergwesyn, climbing and plunging across an

CASTLE ON A ROCK *Carreg-Cennen Castle stands on a rocky height of almost 900ft, making it impregnable from the south.*

PRINCE'S ABBEY *Talley Abbey was founded in the late 12th century by the Welsh prince Rhys ap Gruffydd.*

FULL TO THE BRIM *When the level of Llyn Brianne is high, water cascades down a spillway in ever-changing patterns.*

exposed, uninhabited upland region where the views seem to go on forever. Rough pasture and barren moorland roll in waves to distant horizons; farms are few and far between; and the hairpin-bend called Devil's Staircase is aptly named.

From the start of the pass, two walks through forest lead to Llyn Berwyn, a little mountain lake hidden away in a conifer plantation.

LLANWRTYD-WELLS

The Victorian and Edwardian houses are reminders of Llanwrtyd-Wells's heyday as a spa resort, when visitors arrived in their thousands to take the waters. In recent years the late 19th-century pump room and adjoining building in the wooded parklands behind the Dol-y-Coed Hotel have been renovated. Visitors can once more sip the blue-tinged sulphur waters of *Y Ffynon Ddrewllyd*, 'The

Stinking Well', or preferably partake of an innocuous cup of tea in Victorian surroundings.

LLANDOVERY

George Borrow, the 19th-century author of *Wild Wales*, thought Llandovery 'the pleasantest little town in which I have halted'. The cobbled old market square, fine Georgian façade and verandah-fronted inns make his commendation easy to understand.

Traditional weekly livestock markets still take place. The animal pens near the town centre lie beneath a ruined medieval castle, its gnarled, shattered keep perched on top of a steep earthen mound.

CILYCWM

During the restoration of St Michael's Church in 1906, in this typical one-street Welsh hill village, remarkable mural paintings came to light. The

most memorable is *The Devil in the West Wall*, a ghoulish representation of death in the form of a skeleton brandishing a spear.

The church itself, medieval in origin, has 15th-century roof timbers over the south aisle.

RHANDIRMWYN

A village of scattered farms and cottages spreads across a steep hillside overlooking the Tywi valley.

The wilderness areas beyond Rhandirmwyn kept the Welsh Robin Hood, Twm Shon Catti, out of the clutches of the Sheriff of Carmarthen. Twm, an enigmatic 16th-century character, has been variously described as a guerrilla fighter, bandit, rogue and practical joker. He chose as his hiding place a cave high in the boulder-strewn upper reaches of Dinas Hill. The densely wooded conical hill, now a bird reserve, stands above the waters of the Tywi as they tumble over rocks in a narrow gorge. A footpath leads right around the hill – with a detour to Twm's cave – from an RSPB information centre near Ystradffin.

LLYN BRIANNE
From the car park and viewpoint above the rock-filled dam head, the waters of Llyn Brianne reach like the fingers of an outstretched hand into the folds of desolately beautiful upland country.

DOLAUCOTHI
One of the main reasons for the Romans' interest in Wales lies near the rural backwater of Pumsaint. The village's Dolaucothi Arms stands roughly on the site of a large Roman camp, built to protect the only place in Britain where it has been established that the Romans mined for gold.

The mines themselves, in the hills just east of the village, are hidden amongst thickly wooded cliffs. Dolaucothi was actively mined for over 100 years from around AD 75, and again attracted prospectors from the 1870s to 1938, when it finally closed.

CAIO
Snug and self-contained, tiny Caio has its post office, pub, chapel and rows of terraced cottages. The Church of St Cynwl overshadows everything. Medieval in origin, this large place of worship stands on raised ground, its tall, castellated west tower looking out across to grazing land and forested mountainside.

Tourist information: Llandovery 20693 (summer).

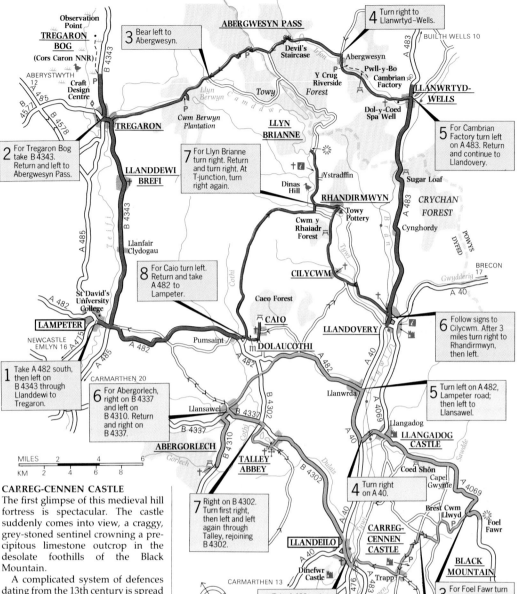

Map labels:
- Observation Point
- TREGARON BOG (Cors Caron NNR)
- ABERYSTWYTH 12
- Craft Design Centre
- TREGARON
- LLANDDEWI BREFI
- Llanfair Clydogau
- St David's University College
- LAMPETER
- NEWCASTLE EMLYN 16
- CARMARTHEN 20
- ABERGORLECH
- Llansawel
- TALLEY ABBEY
- Pumsaint
- CAIO
- DOLAUCOTHI
- LLANDEILO
- Dinefwr Castle
- CARMARTHEN 13
- CARREG-CENNEN CASTLE
- Trapp
- BLACK MOUNTAIN
- Brest Cwm Llwyd
- Foel Fawr
- Coed Shôn
- Capel Gwynfe
- LLANGADOG CASTLE
- Llangadog
- Llanwrda
- LLANDOVERY
- CILYCWM
- Caeo Forest
- RHANDIRMWYN
- Towy Pottery
- Cwm y Rhaiadr Forest
- Ystradffin
- Dinas Hill
- LLYN BRIANNE
- Cwm Berwyn Plantation
- Llyn Berwyn
- Towy
- Cambrian Factory
- Dol-y-Coed Spa Well
- Y Crug Riverside Forest
- Pwll-y-Bo
- LLANWRTYD-WELLS
- Abergwesyn
- Devil's Staircase
- ABERGWESYN PASS
- BUILTH WELLS 10
- Sugar Loaf
- CRYCHAN FOREST
- Cynghordy
- POWYS DYFED
- BRECON 17
- Gwydderig

Map instruction boxes:
- 3 Bear left to Abergwesyn.
- 4 Turn right to Llanwrtyd–Wells.
- 2 For Tregaron Bog take B4343. Return and left to Abergwesyn Pass.
- 7 For Llyn Brianne turn right. Return and turn right. At T-junction, turn right again.
- 5 For Cambrian Factory turn left on A483. Return and continue to Llandovery.
- 8 For Caio turn left. Return and take A482 to Lampeter.
- 6 Follow signs to Cilycwm. After 3 miles turn right to Rhandirmwyn, then left.
- 1 Take A482 south, then left on B4343 through Llanddewi to Tregaron.
- 6 For Abergorlech, right on B4337 and left on B4310. Return and right on B4337.
- 5 Turn left on A482, Lampeter road; then left to Llansawel.
- 7 Right on B4302. Turn first right, then left and left again through Talley, rejoining B4302.
- 4 Turn right on A40.
- 3 For Foel Fawr turn right on A4069. Return and continue through Llangadog.
- 1 Take A483 and turn left to Carreg-Cennen, then ahead on minor road.
- 2 Turn right then left following Gwynfe then Brynamman signs.

MILES 2 4 6
KM 2 4 6 8

TOUR
82
49 MILES
A 13th-century fortress at Carreg-Cennen is a dramatic introduction to the Black Mountain. Lofty viewpoints look down on winding, wooded riversides and beautifully situated villages.

LLANDEILO
A single-span stone bridge crosses the waters of the Tywi which loop and swirl around Llandeilo's foot. From this handsome bridge, put up in 1848, ranks of houses and cottages appear as steps in the hillside, leading from the valley up to a town of substantial houses, narrow passageways and steep terraces.

West of the bridge, well camouflaged by thick woods on a riverside bluff, stand the remains of Dinefwr Castle. This romantic ruin was a seat of the Lords Rhys who ruled this part of south-west Wales. It can be seen from a path which starts from Llandeilo Bridge and passes the old Llandyfeisant Church, now an interpretive centre.

The ivy-clad ruin has a massive circular keep, dating from the 13th century. Perched on top of the keep is a small tower, added as a summerhouse in the 18th century.

CARREG-CENNEN CASTLE
The first glimpse of this medieval hill fortress is spectacular. The castle suddenly comes into view, a craggy, grey-stoned sentinel crowning a precipitous limestone outcrop in the desolate foothills of the Black Mountain.

A complicated system of defences dating from the 13th century is spread across a grassy summit, accessible from the north along a steepish footpath. The south-facing battlements tiptoe on the edge of a vertical cliff face.

Views from the windswept towers and curtain walls seem to take in most of South and Mid Wales.

Another memorable sight lies below ground. An inconspicuous doorway in the south wall leads down steep steps to a narrow, walled passageway cut into the cliff face. This drops down into a cave occupied by man in prehistoric times.

THE BLACK MOUNTAIN
Beyond Carreg-Cennen, the road climbs from high-banked country lanes onto the wide, open and treeless shoulder of the Black Mountain, where nothing impedes the view. The car park 1141ft up at Brest Cwm Llwyd looks northwards across huge panoramas. Better still are the magnificent views from the north-facing car park on the main road a mile or so farther east.

From here the road continues climbing to 1618ft, while on either side moorlands rise steadily for a further 1000ft into the barren upper reaches of the Black Mountain. This is an inhospitable area of exposed, boggy, plateau lands with few landmarks.

LLANGADOG CASTLE
On the eastern side of the common on the approach to Llangadog stand the remains of a very early Norman motte-and-bailey castle. Although on private farmland, the tree-covered castle mound and the earthen bank which encloses the 2 acre bailey can be seen from the road. The Tywi river once swept around the foot of the castle.

ABERGORLECH
Pretty, peaceful Abergorlech is a hamlet of bridges and well-kept riverside gardens. A fine old three-arched stone bridge spans the Cothi, a noted salmon and trout river. The Gorlech, a fast-flowing mountain stream which here merges with the Cothi, is crossed by a simple, single-arched structure. A scenic car park, picnic site and children's play area have been laid out on the banks of the Gorlech.

St David's Church, behind the Black Lion inn, has ornate brass lamps hanging above the aisle and altar.

TALLEY ABBEY
A long avenue of oaks lines the narrow road, which then slices its way into a steep hillside overlooking Talley's twin lakes. On the shore of the southern lake, two religious sites stand side by side.

A surviving tall archway points skywards amongst the evocative ruins of Talley Abbey, founded in the late 12th century. Nearby, St Michael's Church was built in 1773 to an unorthodox plan: with no central aisle and its interior filled with box pews.

Tourist information: Cardiff 499909.

139

Valleys below the Brecon Beacons

Lakes, rivers and a canal thread a silvery necklace around the summits of the Brecon Beacons National Park. Pen y Fan, often in view, dominates a wild upland of moor and forest.

BRECON

Brecon stands at the confluence of the Honddu and Usk rivers, in a pastoral vale presided over by the peaks of the Brecon Beacons.

The Guildhall, pretty and cream-washed in its upper storeys, stands opposite the inn named after the actress Sarah Siddons, born there in 1755. Narrow streets and alleyways lead in all directions from a central square overlooked by a statue of Wellington and the tall, 16th-century sandstone tower of St Mary's Church.

Remnants of the castle still survive, incorporated today into the fabric of the Castle of Brecon Hotel.

The Cathedral Church of St John, nearby, fully deserves its grander title of Brecon Cathedral. This vast medieval church is much restored, but with many a gem, in particular the beautiful lancet windows of the chancel. Originally a priory church, it became a cathedral in 1923, serving the diocese of Swansea and Brecon.

The Brecknock Museum is housed in the old Shire Hall, and exhibits include a collection of Welsh love-spoons, intricately carved from a single piece of wood by young men as gifts for girls they were courting.

The South Wales Borderers' and Monmouthshire Regiment Museum housed in the barracks, in the Watton, includes a Zulu War Room. This recalls the defence of Rorke's Drift in 1879 by 141 men from the regiment against attack from 4000 Zulus; nine VCs were won in a single day.

MOUNTAIN CENTRE

Some of the best views of the Brecon Beacons can be enjoyed from the comfortable lounge and terraces of this superbly sited centre. Located at 1100ft, it looks out across the Tarell valley to the distinctive, table-top summits of Pen y Fan, at 2907ft the highest point in South Wales, and its neighbouring peak, Corn Du, 2863ft.

Displays, maps and films at the Mountain Centre introduce the main features of the park and its many outdoor activities. There are easy walks from the centre along Mynydd Illtud, an open common dotted with historic sites.

GARWNANT FOREST

Garwnant lies hidden amongst cool conifers above a reservoir created to supply water to Cardiff. Picnickers catch a glimpse of the Llwyn-on Reservoir through the trees, while walkers can follow a series of marked paths through the forest. The visitor centre, open from Easter to September, is housed in a converted farm building, where displays and audio-visuals introduce the work of the forest.

MORLAIS CASTLE

Grass-covered mounds, rock-cut ditches and fragments of stonework are all that remain above ground of the 13th-century Morlais Castle on an exposed lofty rise. Morlais's most unexpected feature is below ground – a basement with a central pillar and spectacular vaulted arches that have miraculously survived intact.

The quarries gouged into the mountainside below Morlais Castle were the source of the limestone which, together with local iron ore, made Merthyr Tydfil a major iron and steel centre.

BRECON MOUNTAIN RAILWAY

This pretty little line, its locomotives painted in a deep red livery, is the newest of the narrow-gauge 'Great Little Trains of Wales' – and the only one operating in the south.

From its terminus at Pant the railway runs for 2 miles into the foothills of the Beacons. The line clings to a steep-sided ledge in the valley before descending to its lakeside halt at Pontsticill, where there are walks, picnic areas and lovely views across to Pen y Fan.

From Pontsticill the route strikes north, through forests and past a string of man-made lakes. There are shady walks and picnic sites in Taf Fechan Forest, at the foot of The Glyn, a 1433ft mountain pass.

LLANFEUGAN CHURCH

The isolated Church of St Meugan in the hills above the Vale of Usk, signposted 'Llanfeugan', is older than the ancient yews that surround it. The building dates from the 14th century, and its font is even older.

An 8ft tall stone shaft near the gate is part of an old preaching cross, while inside there are the remains of a 15th-century wooden rood screen adorned with the white rose of York. The castle-like tower also dates from the 15th century.

MONMOUTHSHIRE CANAL

The road north-west of Talybont runs beside the Monmouthshire and Brecon Canal, built between 1792 and

FOAMING TORRENT *Blaen-y-glyn waterfall surges over rocks among forest and heathland, 5 miles north of Pontsticill.*

CRICKHOWELL BRIDGE *Built in the 17th century for packhorses, the bridge was widened as traffic increased. Its 13 stone arches span the Usk river below the town.*

PRIORY VIEW *Llanthony's arches frame a prospect of the Black Mountains.*

1812 to connect Brecon with Newport. Holiday craft now use the 32 mile navigable stretch from Brecon to Pontymoile, near Pontypool.

The canal follows a picturesque course cut into the side of the green Vale of Usk, running parallel to the river for most of the way. Its progress is charted from the road by the occasional wooden lift bridge and stone-arched crossing point.

There are only six locks on the entire canal. One of them, at Brynich near Brecon, is right beside the road. A short walk along the towpath leads to a fine old stone aqueduct which carried the canal's still and muddy waters across those of the swifter flowing Usk.

TOUR
84
68 MILES

The graceful Wye and Usk rivers frame the remote Black Mountains. A dramatic pass cuts across formidable heights, then drops to the Vale of Ewyas, dotted with religious sites.

BRONLLYS
Both church and castle in this scattered village share a certain air of oddness. St Mary's Church, restored in 1887, is ordinary enough in itself, but its bell tower is unusual in being completely detached from the main building.

Bronllys Castle also stands alone, a single round stone tower perched like a massive stone chimney on top of the steep conical hill. A series of near-vertical steps makes reasonably light work of reaching the tower, which was built by the Marcher Lord Walter de Clifford in the mid-13th century to control the troubled borderlands. It commands a valley looking towards Talgarth. Original stone steps survive within the narrow wall passageways.

TALGARTH
But for one or two modern shop fronts, Talgarth remains the perfect 19th-century small town. Its busy centre – a spider's web of narrow roads – is presided over by the old Town Hall, with its memorial clock tower for Queen Victoria's Golden Jubilee of 1887.

The oldest building of all stands above the river just opposite. This is an unusual medieval tower with a stone-tiled roof shaped like a pyramid.

MAESYRONNEN CHAPEL
The tiny chapel is delightful. The key, available nearby, unlocks one of the earliest chapels in Wales. Maesyronnen's discreet, out-of-the-way location is no accident: religious dissenters would meet there secretly under cover of darkness.

The present building, a rough stone long house, was converted around 1696 from a 16th-century barn. Still in use, it preserves a remarkable atmosphere of times gone by, thanks to its location and its box pews, benches, tables and pulpit of the 18th and 19th centuries.

CLYRO
This sleepy settlement beside the lazy River Wye is a magnet to those who have read and loved *Kilvert's Diaries*. The diaries begin with the record kept by Francis Kilvert of the last two years he spent in Clyro as curate, from 1870 to 1872 and vividly portray life in the area. Here, in the heart of 'Kilvert Country', visitors can track down the places the country curate wrote about, many of which have changed little, if at all, since his time.

The rather grand house where Kilvert lodged from 1865 to 1872 now bears a prominent plaque in memory of the 'priest and diarist'.

The old-established Wye Pottery, which welcomes visitors, specialises in decorative plaques, earthenware and porcelain.

HAY-ON-WYE
This borderland town is full of books, books and more books. At the last count there were 13 bookshops stocking, between them, well over a million titles, mostly second hand. Serious bibliophiles and enthusiastic browsers come to Hay-on-Wye from all over the world.

Hay preserves an older face too. There are steep streets, a covered market place, an elegant Town Hall, a ruined castle and gabled cottages.

GOSPEL PASS
South of Hay, the route ventures into deserted high country, climbing steadily to 1778ft at the summit of the Gospel Pass. This is one of the few roads that enter the remote, sparsely inhabited Black Mountains. It is narrow in parts, and congested at summer weekends.

Before reaching the summit, the road skirts Hay Bluff, a bare saddle of land 2220ft high. Views extend from the Cambrian Mountains to the Malvern Hills, the mighty Wye looking a tiny stream flowing through a patchwork of fields.

LLANTHONY PRIORY
Mountain-locked Llanthony, a red-stoned ruin set among silent hills, perfectly embodies the solitude sought by monastic communities. Augustinian canons founded a monastery there in the early 12th century, though the existing priory dates from 1175.

Even in ruin, Llanthony is still magnificent. The craftsmanship that went into its construction is evident everywhere. Its walls and towers stand tall and solid. Decorative stonework survives intact, as does the priory's greatest glory – an elegant row of pointed Early English archways, gazing out onto unchanging mountainsides.

TRETOWER
This fascinating two-in-one historic site reflects the differences between early and late medieval life in Wales. Tretower Castle came first, built strictly for military reasons. Its tall, round, stone tower was put up in the mid-13th century inside a keep buried more than a century earlier.

Those who built Tretower Court, on the other hand, were more concerned with comfort and gracious living. It was constructed in the 14th and 15th centuries, by which time such indulgences were becoming possible.

Tourist information: Brecon 3366; Hay-on-Wye 820144 (summer)/ 820847.

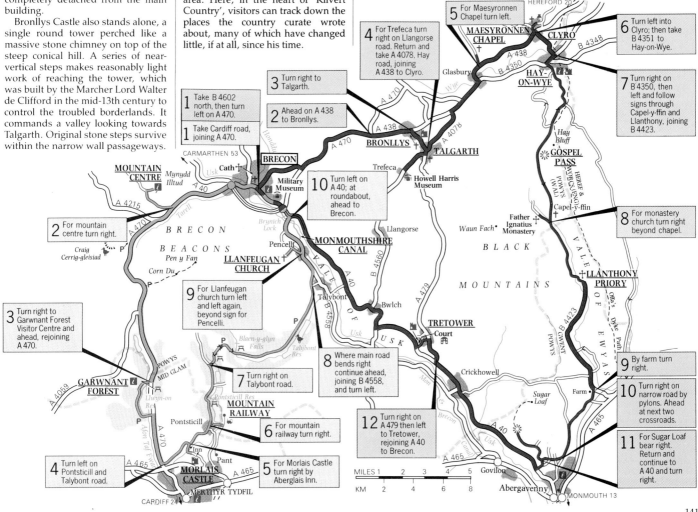

Waterfalls along the Rheidol valley

TOUR
85

— 82 MILES —

Inland from the rugged coast of Cardigan Bay lies a sparsely populated countryside of hilly sheep farms and forests. Beyond the Rheidol valley rise the heights of Plynlimon.

ABERYSTWYTH

A long, rather formal promenade lined with pastel-shaded Victorian buildings preserves the dignity of a bygone era. Nothing too brash disturbs the seafront's aura of turn-of-the-century gentility. In contrast, the town itself is a lively, rather cosmopolitan place – in term time, anyway, when the resort of Aberystwyth reflects the influence of its university college. Part of this is housed in a Victorian Gothic building by the pier. Not far away, on a headland beside the Rheidol estuary, are the ruins of Aberystwyth Castle; begun in 1277 by Edward I, it was captured by Owain Glyndwr and later destroyed in the Civil War, after which its stones were removed to build houses. A stone pier protects the estuary, which provides a haven for sailing craft and fishing boats.

The main college campus, a largely modern development, occupies the hillside above the town. Town and gown are well integrated, though. The exhibition gallery, theatre and film facilities at the superb Arts Centre on the campus are open to everyone, and the centre commands fine views of the resort and bay.

The august National Library of Wales, open most days, stands a little farther down the hill. The library contains more than 2 million books, including the 12th-century Black Book of Carmarthen, one of the oldest existing manuscripts in Welsh. In the town centre the Ceredigion Museum exhibits everything from farm and household implements to seafaring relics. These share the limelight with the building itself, for the museum is housed in the ornate Coliseum, a carefully preserved Edwardian music hall.

The Cliff Railway, at the northern end of the town, made its first journey in 1896. This near-vertical railway climbs to the 430ft summit of Constitution Hill, which is crowned with a camera obscura, claimed to be the largest in the world, giving views of 100 miles of coast and no fewer than 26 peaks.

VALE OF RHEIDOL RAILWAY

Although Wales has many narrow-gauge 'Great Little Trains', the Rheidol line is British Rail's last remaining operational link with the 'Age of Steam'. A trip on this delightful old railway gives passengers a leisurely perspective of the thickly wooded and steep-sided Vale of Rheidol, completely different from that experienced from the road. The railway travels some 12 miles from Aberystwyth Station, climbing laboriously along a narrow ledge cut into the side of the valley to its mountain terminus at Devil's Bridge.

NANTEOS

Although advertised as a stately home, Nanteos is not the usual immaculately restored mansion complete with opulent interiors – and therein lies its unorthodox appeal. This Georgian house, dating from 1739, has been more accurately described as representing 'the crumbling face of elegance'.

In its time, Nanteos has accommodated such notable people as the composer Richard Wagner. Until the 1950s, a mysterious relic thought to have been part of the Holy Grail – the cup used by Christ at the Last Supper – was kept at Nanteos. Its present whereabouts is unknown. The house is open daily.

RHEIDOL POWER STATION

The drive along the secluded floor of the upper Rheidol valley is a beautiful one. Wooded hillsides rise abruptly from the meadows beside the winding waters of the Rheidol. This setting seems the last place on earth in which to expect to find any form of industry or technology, and when the Rheidol power station does present itself it is easily missed.

The attractive, stone-fronted building looks anything but a power station. This is the nerve centre for an ambitious hydroelectric scheme which harnesses the waters of the Nant-y-Moch and Dinas Reservoirs. Guided tours are available daily from Easter to October.

Just beyond the power station are the tumbling Rheidol Falls, which can be viewed from a footbridge beside the road. An information centre 1 mile west of the power station is the starting point for a nature trail around the banks of the Rheidol Reservoir. The weir is floodlit from Easter to September.

DEVIL'S BRIDGE

Through a narrow ravine clothed in thick woodlands, the Mynach river plunges 300ft in a series of torrents to join the Rheidol river in the valley below. The falls are hidden from the road, but can be viewed by following a steep footpath from the village of Devil's Bridge down into the gloomy ravine, which was christened the 'dread chasm' by William Wordsworth in 1824. The path includes an unbroken flight of 100 steps, called Jacob's Ladder.

As its name implies, the village is also remarkable for its bridge – or bridges, to be correct, for there are three, piled one on top of another, across the Mynach gorge. The earliest bridge, a simple stone affair known as Pont-y-gwr-drwg, 'the Bridge of the Evil One', is medieval in origin. A second, wider bridge was built in 1753 to take horse-drawn traffic. On top is the newest road bridge, built in 1901 and modernised in 1983.

Devil's Bridge lies in a sheltered position on the lower slope of high mountains. The wild surrounding

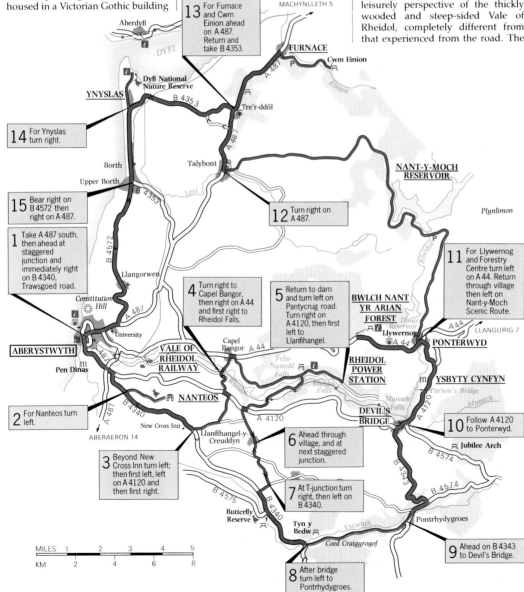

13 For Furnace and Cwm Einion ahead on A 487. Return and take B 4353.

14 For Ynyslas turn right.

15 Bear right on B 4572 then right on A 487.

1 Take A 487 south, then ahead at staggered junction and immediately right on B 4340, Trawsgoed road.

12 Turn right on A 487.

11 For Llywernog and Forestry Centre turn left on A 44. Return through village then left on Nant-y-Moch Scenic Route.

4 Turn right to Capel Bangor, then right on A 44 and first right to Rheidol Falls.

5 Return to dam and turn left on Pantycrug road. Turn right on A 4120, then first left to Llanfihangel.

10 Follow A 4120 to Ponterwyd.

2 For Nanteos turn left.

3 Beyond New Cross Inn turn left; then first left, left on A 4120 and then first right.

6 Ahead through village, and at next staggered junction.

7 At T-junction turn right, then left on B 4340.

9 Ahead on B 4343 to Devil's Bridge.

8 After bridge turn left to Pontrhydygroes.

MILES 1 2 3 4 5
KM 2 4 6 8

DYNAMIC RIVER *The Rheidol thunders over the Cwm Rheidol Dam and Felin Nywedd Falls, down river from the hydroelectric power station that exploits its pent-up energy.*

GEORGIAN GEM *The 18th-century Nanteos is as pretty as its name, which means 'valley of the nightingale'.*

GREAT LITTLE TRAIN *The Vale of Rheidol Railway, begun as a freight line in 1902, runs daily in summer.*

STEEP CLIMB *Aberystwyth's cliff railway climbs a 2-in-1 gradient to the top of Constitution Hill.*

---

countryside is seen from the mountain road which climbs from the village to a 1223ft summit, 2 miles to the east. The summit is marked by a rough stone arch erected in 1810 to mark the jubilee of George III.

YSBYTY CYNFYN
The massive stones embedded in the walls of this lonely churchyard are the remains of an ancient circle of stones, the largest of which still stands 11ft tall.

Ten minutes' walk from the church is Parson's Bridge, a little-known companion to its more familiar neighbour, Devil's Bridge. Few visitors reach this isolated spot, where a mountain stream tumbles over a precipice into a rocky gorge.

PONTERWYD
Relics of the silver and lead-mining past of mid-Wales are provided in the Llywernog Silver Lead Mine Museum, just west of Ponterwyd, which is open daily in summer.

This open-air site was a silver and lead mine from the mid-18th century until the 1880s. Its complex of water wheels and old buildings, although

carefully restored, has an authentic ramshackle look. The site also contains a waymarked miners' trail, a 'California in Wales' exhibition, and an underground prospector's tunnel, all open to the public.

BWLCH NANT YR ARIAN FOREST
A forest visitor centre is set dramatically at the crest of a lovely valley. A magnificent view extends down the valley as far as Aberystwyth and the blue horizon of Cardigan Bay. Inside the centre imaginative displays give a fascinating introduction to the Rheidol Forest, the surrounding landscape and local history. The centre is open daily from Easter to October.

The site includes waymarked walks, picnic areas – even a 10ft high piece of modern art constructed of laminated Douglas fir.

NANT-Y-MOCH RESERVOIR
The mountain road which strikes due north from Ponterwyd is one of Britain's most memorable motoring experiences. For mile after mile, a thin, grey ribbon of tarmac winds its way across lonely plateaux possessed by a forbidding, primeval beauty.

The road winds down to Nant-y-Moch, a man-made lake whose inky-black waters are held back by the buttresses of a 172ft high stone dam.

Nant-y-Moch's huge reservoir – and the smaller Dinas reservoir downstream – are 20th-century creations, part of the Rheidol hydroelectric power scheme.

From the dam, the road follows the western shores of the lake, with a view of the brooding Plynlimon which rises to 2469ft behind it.

FURNACE
The hamlet owes its existence to a sizeable old stone building and water wheel on a bend in the road. A squat, stone chimney on the slate roof indicates that this is no ordinary water mill. The wheel once powered the bellows of an early charcoal-fired metal smelting plant.

Silver was refined here in the 17th century, though the present building was an ironmaking furnace dating from the mid-18th century. The entire site is being restored. Motive power for the wheel came from the Einion river, which plunges into a waterfall behind the furnace site. A narrow

road climbs steeply from the village, following the course of the river up into Cwm Einion.

This hidden, profusely wooded valley, also known appropriately as Artists' Valley, is a sheer delight: its only concessions to the visitor are occasional riverside picnic areas and a few waymarked forest walks.

YNYSLAS
A straight road leading across the flatlands which border the southern shores of the Dyfi estuary terminates at a huge, empty beach. Close by is an information centre, open in summer, which serves as an introduction to the Dyfi National Nature Reserve.

The dunes, salt marshes and sands support a wide variety of wildlife. Butterflies are common in summer, and the estuary is a winter refuge for wildfowl and waders. The views are magnificent, especially across the mouth of the estuary to the village of Aberdyfi, whose pretty waterfront houses line up neatly beneath a steep green hillside.

Tourist information: Aberystwyth 612125/617911.

Spas and reservoirs in central Wales

TOUR
86

75 MILES

The cool interiors of calm churches contrast with the open space of a nature reserve above the Wye river. Beyond lie two former spa towns and the remains of a Roman fort.

RHAYADER
At the crossroads of this attractive market town is a 1924 war memorial and clock tower, decorated with an angel, a soldier, a dragon which has just slain an eagle, and a woman with a child. There are some substantial 18th and 19th-century houses in South Street, and Bridge Street has several inns and an Edwardian police station. The square-towered parish church of St Clement peers down from the top of a high bluff, which overlooks picnic tables and leafy footpaths along the rock-strewn Wye.

LLANFIHANGEL HELYGEN
Encircled by tall oaks, this simple little wayside church has a fragile slate roof supporting a small, pyramid-capped turret. Inside, oak box pews rest on stone flags, and there is a fine wooden roof and three-decker pulpit which half blocks the window behind it. The vestry is floored with stone blocks.

LLANBADARNFAWR CHURCH
The porch of this plain, late-Victorian church conceals a Norman doorway with a boldly carved arch; two lions eye each other from opposite sides of a plant sprouting from another beast's head. The pillar on the right shows a mythical creature and the pillar on the left shows two human figures, possibly Adam and Eve.

Easily missed is a little stone plaque in the left wall of the porch. Enscribed *Valflavini*, it is Roman and possibly from the fort at Castellcollen. The Victorian interior has three lancet windows at the east end set in deep recesses. The chancel arch and the roof are well-proportioned, and there is some finely carved woodwork.

THE PALES
A narrow, winding road leads about a mile to The Pales, an early 18th-century thatched Quaker Meeting House perched on a hillside looking southwards over unspoilt country-side. In the thatched porch are a number of clothespegs, some broken. Two doors lead from the porch: one opens into the bright, tastefully modernised meeting room with its simple benches; the other leads to the old school room, set up in 1867.

NEW RADNOR
A mixture of the old and the new, the town is dominated by a vast, tree-flanked castle hill. The vestiges of medieval, grid-planned streets can be seen, and to the west are the knobbly earth banks of the former town walls. There are some attractive farm buildings and houses including, just west of the war memorial, a trim, white Victorian house which contrasts with its ramshackle stone and half-timbered neighbour.

The Victorian church is perched on a hillside, and not far away is a memorial to the mid-Victorian Chancellor of the Exchequer, Sir George Cornwall Lewis. It has some savage-looking winged-dog gargoyles.

ALONG THE WYE *At Llandeilo Graban the Wye flows through a broad, shallow valley, patchworked with fields and more English than Welsh in character.*

WATER FOR A CITY *A green-domed, Baroque-style building marks the point where water is extracted from the Garreg Ddu Reservoir to supply the needs of Birmingham.*

NEW IDENTITY *The ornate market hall in Builth Wells is now an arts centre.*

WAYSIDE CHAPEL *Rhosgoch's chapel is functional rather than decorative.*

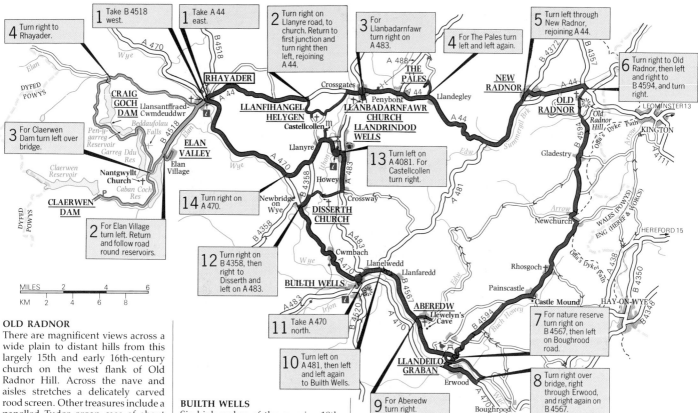

4 Turn right to Rhayader.

1 Take B 4518 west.

1 Take A 44 east.

2 Turn right on Llanyre road, to church. Return to first junction and turn right then left, rejoining A 44.

3 For Llanbadarnfawr turn right on A 483.

4 For The Pales turn left and left again.

5 Turn left through New Radnor, rejoining A 44.

6 Turn right to Old Radnor, then left and right to B 4594, and turn right.

3 For Claerwen Dam turn left over bridge.

2 For Elan Village turn left. Return and follow road round reservoirs.

13 Turn left on A 4081. For Castellcollen turn right.

14 Turn right on A 470.

12 Turn right on B 4358, then right to Disserth and left on A 483.

11 Take A 470 north.

10 Turn left on A 481, then left and left again to Builth Wells.

9 For Aberedw turn right.

7 For nature reserve turn right on B 4567, then left on Boughrood road.

8 Turn right over bridge, right through Erwood, and right again on B 4567.

DYFED POWYS · CRAIG GOCH DAM · Llansantffraed Cwmdeuddwr · Beddaufolau Falls · Pen-y-garreg Reservoir · Garreg Ddu Res · ELAN VALLEY · Elan Village · Claerwen Reservoir · Nantgwyllt Church · Caban Coch Res · CLAERWEN DAM · DYFED POWYS · RHAYADER · LLANFIHANGEL HELYGEN · Castellcollen · Llanyre · Howey · Newbridge on Wye · DISSERTH CHURCH · Crossgates · Penybont · LLANBADARNFAWR CHURCH · LLANDRINDOD WELLS · THE PALES · Llandegley · NEW RADNOR · OLD RADNOR · Old Radnor Hill · Offa's Dyke Path · KINGTON · LEOMINSTER 13 · Gladestry · Crossway · Cwmbach · Llanelwedd · Llanfaredd · BUILTH WELLS · ABEREDW · Llewelyn's Cave · Newchurch · Rhosgoch · Painscastle · Castle Mound · HAY-ON-WYE · WALES (POWYS) · ENG (HEREF & WORCS) · HEREFORD 15 · LLANDEILO GRABAN · Erwood · Boughrood

MILES 2 4 6
KM 2 4 6 8

OLD RADNOR

There are magnificent views across a wide plain to distant hills from this largely 15th and early 16th-century church on the west flank of Old Radnor Hill. Across the nave and aisles stretches a delicately carved rood screen. Other treasures include a panelled Tudor organ case of about 1500 and a massive, tub-like font probably fashioned by Celtic priests in the 6th or 7th centuries and one of the oldest in Britain.

LLANDEILO GRABAN

From Old Radnor the road meanders steeply down to a spot where the river flows between overhanging trees and gentle, grassy banks. For a circuit of the valley, take the Aberedw road and turn first left to Boughrood. This tree-lined road, overlooking the Wye, is now a wayside nature reserve. It follows the old railway line south-eastwards just above the north bank of the Wye.

ABEREDW

High limestone crags peep through trees along the magnificent approach to Aberedw. The sleepy-looking church has some remarkable wood-work: a huge porch with gaping, cloverleaf mouths over the arch and, inside, a fine roof and 15th-century rood screen. The key to the church can be obtained from the nearby Seven Stars Inn.

A lonely, man-made cave where the Welsh leader Llywelyn the Last is thought to have sheltered before his death near Builth in 1282 may be reached on foot – but the route is not signposted.

To get there, take the road east-wards out of the village, forking right and crossing a little bridge. Walk up the steep track next to a small hut. Go through the first gate on the right and follow the public footpath up the steep track, bearing left and onto another gate. Go through this and also through the first gate on the right. Follow the cliff base up to a small wooden gate. The cave lies among trees just above this.

BUILTH WELLS

Six high arches of the massive 18th-century bridge over the Wye carry roads from the north into the heart of this former spa town. On the left stands the old, high-roofed Market House, now converted into the Wye-side Arts Centre. Just to the right of the handsome, early 19th-century Lion Hotel a well-signposted path leads to some huge grassy mounds – all that is left of the castle built by Edward I between 1277 and 1283. It has excellent views across the Wye to the Royal Welsh Showground and the surrounding town. In Broad Street there are some fine houses and inns built in the 18th and 19th centuries. St Mary's Church is largely Victorian, but its tower dates from about 1300.

DISSERTH CHURCH

Beautifully situated beside the Ithon river, the Church of St Cewydd in Disserth seems to be frozen in the early 18th century. There have been no 'improvements' or restoration work, and the outside walls gleam with whitewash. Inside, numerous box pews extending on both sides of the altar date from 1666 to 1722 and bear the names of their owners. There is an impressive, three-decker pulpit of 1687, and the lime-washed walls have been left in places to show the original surface paintings of text, foliage and the Royal Arms.

LLANDRINDOD WELLS

Tall, yellow and red-brick Victorian and Edwardian hotels and terraces of shops with iron verandahs characterise this once flourishing spa town – now enjoying a new lease of life as a conference centre. Near Temple Gardens stand the town's two largest hotels: the rambling Metropole and the Glen Usk with a wrought-iron verandah. To the left of the Metropole

is a small local history museum. Temple Street leads to the Automobile Palace, a white-glazed brick garage topped by rows of white lions which houses a fascinating collection of old bicycles.

Just over a mile to the north – and reached down a farm track – are the remains of Castellcollen Roman Fort. Visitors can wander over the earth banks and stone walls.

TOUR
87

— 27 MILES —

From an old market town, the route circles a dramatic series of man-made lakes behind high dams in the remote Elan and Claerwen valleys. Above them are open moors and a waterfall.

ELAN VALLEY

A side road to the left off the route leads across a dainty little suspension bridge to Elan Village, a 'model' settlement built in 1906-9 to house waterworks maintenance staff in the Elan valley.

Beautifully designed grey-stone houses and a school have been thoughtfully arranged – partly around greens – beside the wooded river bank. Back on the main road, the way runs up to the top of the first of four dams, this one holding back Caban Coch Reservoir, the surface of which slips gently over the rim and is ruffled into a foaming white sheet by the rough concave surface.

A mile farther on, what appears to be a low, many-arched stone bridge

across the water is actually the top part of the sunken Garreg Ddu Dam, built in 1904 to hold water fed through a 73 mile aqueduct to Birmingham at a rate of 25 million gallons daily.

CLAERWEN DAM

By crossing the 'bridge' at Garreg Ddu and following the road for 5 miles – past the foundations of an unfinished dam and some rapids – the motorist reaches the impressive Claerwen Dam.

Completed in 1952 and rising 184ft, the dam is a colossal structure: its 1186ft arms outstretched to the banks; its back against a vast, bleak lake of more than 19,000 million gallons where desolate moorland ends; feet firmly anchored in the ground; mouth disgorging water. A roadway is carried on 13 arches across its span.

The traveller should then return to Nantgwyllt church, cross the 'bridge' and drive northwards along the wooded east bank of Garreg Ddu Reservoir. On the right is the sylvan cut of Beddaufolau Falls and a hairpin bend leads to Pen-y-garreg Reservoir.

CRAIG GOCH DAM

The last and most impressive of the dams, Craig Goch carries a sweeping curved road across on 13 elegant arches past the crown tower. The dam is 120ft high and holds back 2028 million gallons of water. Behind is a landscape of treeless moorland through which the route winds, eventually dropping into a gorge where water slips over large rock slabs into frothy pools.

Tourist information: Builth Wells 553307; Llandrindod Wells 2600; Rhayader 810591/810898 (summer).

From Cadair Idris down to the sea

The vast bulk of Cadair Idris looms over wooded valleys and windy mountain passes. The cliff-lined coast road leads to the Mawddach estuary, where the mountains meet the sea.

MACHYNLLETH

Looming above the tallest buildings in the centre of this handsome old market town is a flamboyant clock tower. Rising 78ft to a weather vane, it has an ornate base, and tapers to a narrow, sharp spire surrounded by four lesser pinnacles, like a Gothic church steeple. It looks down on Maengwyn Street, a wide and airy thoroughfare harmoniously lined with well-proportioned houses, shops and inns.

The clock tower was given to the town in 1873 to commemorate the coming of age of the Marquis of Londonderry's son and heir. The Marquis lived at Plas Machynlleth, a fine house dating from the 17th century and restored in the 19th century and set in spacious park-lands. The house is now used as council offices, but the park is open to the public.

Owain Glyndwr, the last native Welsh leader, held his historic parliament at Machynlleth in 1404. The stone building on the site of the supposed meeting place in Maengwyn Street houses an exhibition devoted to Owain's life and times, and is open in summer. It also contains the Dyfi Centre, open all year for displays and tourist information.

CENTRE FOR ALTERNATIVE TECHNOLOGY

About 3 miles north of Machynlleth, the road enters the 845 square mile Snowdonia National Park. As the road snakes through conifer-clad hillsides, on the horizon a strange, three-bladed aerogenerator – or windmill – comes into view.

The aerogenerator stands on a hilltop above an old slate quarry, which since the early 1970s has been the home of the Centre for Alternative Technology. Known also as 'The Village of the Future', the centre is a living experiment in self-sufficiency, producing as much of its own energy and food as possible. At the same time, it has become an unusual tourist attraction. Visitors are welcome daily and can see a wide range of devices which produce alternative sources of heat and light – including aerogenerators, solar panels, water turbines and a woodgas system.

CORRIS

This cluster of slate cottages just off the main road was once a thriving slate-mining village. Steep-sided slopes filled with deep green fir trees and screes of slate rise above the narrow streets and jet-black slate roofs, creating a picture of strange and striking beauty. A little museum in the village, open in summer, recalls the times of the former Corris narrow-gauge railway.

CADAIR IDRIS

The massive, misty bulk of the mountain comes into view on the rise above Corris. From this vantage point it is easy to see why Cadair Idris was once thought to be the highest mountain in Wales. In fact, it is 2927ft – 600ft less than that of Snowdon. Yet Cadair Idris ranks amongst the most powerful and challenging mountains in Britain. No one should venture lightly into its boulder-strewn upper reaches, where conditions can be extremely hazardous.

The dramatic, brooding presence of Cadair Idris has given rise to a variety of legends. The mountain was named 'the chair of Idris', possibly after a mythical giant or warrior. It is said that anyone who spends a night on Idris's rocky peak will awake either a poet or a madman – or become blind.

CASTELL Y BERE

Wales's reputation as a land of castles rests on the mighty medieval fortresses erected by the English king, Edward I. But Castell y Bere is quite different, having been built in the 1220s by the Welsh leader Llywelyn the Great. Today, Llywelyn's mountain stronghold is an evocative ruin, cloaked from the road by trees.

A short walk from the car park reveals the ruins on a rocky outcrop, commanding magnificent views of Cadair Idris and the green bowl of the Dysynni valley. In its prime, the castle guarded a strategic route through the mountains. The modern route takes an easier course to the south, leaving Castell y Bere in an undisturbed cul-de-sac, alone and forgotten.

A mile beyond Castell y Bere, the Mary Jones Monument stands amid the ruins of a cottage at Tyn-y-ddôl. The monument marks the starting point of a heroic walk by Mary Jones from her home to Bala, some 25 miles away. In 1800 she journeyed across the mountains to collect a Welsh Bible from the Reverend Thomas Charles.

TYWYN

A long, thin finger of stone, 7ft high, stands within St Cadfan's Church near the town centre. It bears what is

TRANQUIL TAL-Y-LLYN *Beside the road to Tywyn the lake shimmers in its valley, with reeded flats at its northern end and softly contoured mountains to the south.*

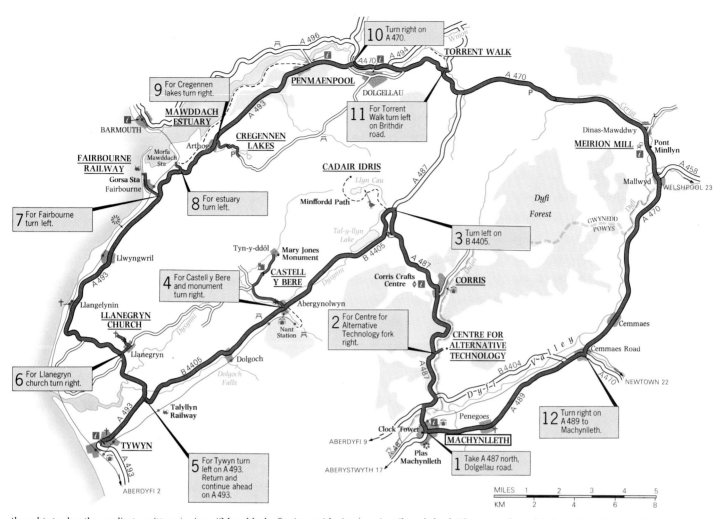

10 Turn right on A 470.

TORRENT WALK

A 496

A 470

A 494

PENMAENPOOL

DOLGELLAU

9 For Cregennen lakes turn right.

MAWDDACH ESTUARY

BARMOUTH

A 493

CREGENNEN LAKES

Arthog

Morfa Mawddach Sta

11 For Torrent Walk turn left on Brithdir road.

A 470

Dinas-Mawddwy

Pont Minllyn

MEIRION MILL

A 458

Mallwyd

WELSHPOOL 23

A 470

CADAIR IDRIS

Llyn Cau

Minffordd Path

A 487

Dyfi Forest

GWYNEDD
POWYS

FAIRBOURNE RAILWAY

Gorsa Sta
Fairbourne

8 For estuary turn left.

7 For Fairbourne turn left.

Tal-y-llyn Lake

B 4405

3 Turn left on B 4405.

Llwyngwril

A 493

Tyn-y-ddôl

Mary Jones Monument

CASTELL Y BERE

Dysynni

Corris Crafts Centre

CORRIS

Cemmaes

Llangelynin

4 For Castell y Bere and monument turn right.

Abergynolwyn

Dysynni

Nant Station

2 For Centre for Alternative Technology fork right.

A 487

CENTRE FOR ALTERNATIVE TECHNOLOGY

Cemmaes Road

LLANEGRYN CHURCH

Llanegryn

B 4405

Dolgoch

Dolgoch Falls

B 4404

D-y-f-i Valley

A 489

A 470

NEWTOWN 22

6 For Llanegryn church turn right.

A 493

Talyllyn Railway

Penegoes

A 487

12 Turn right on A 489 to Machynlleth.

Clock Tower

ABERDYFI 9

MACHYNLLETH

TYWYN

5 For Tywyn turn left on A 493. Return and continue ahead on A 493.

Plas Machynlleth

1 Take A 487 north, Dolgellau road.

ABERYSTWYTH 17

ABERDYFI 2

MILES 1 2 3 4 5
KM 2 4 6 8

---

thought to be the earliest written Welsh, possibly dating from the 7th century.

Tywyn is visited mainly for its large beach and little railway. For this quiet seaside resort is the terminus for the narrow-gauge Talyllyn Railway, a colourful line which runs for just over 7 miles to a remote halt near Abergynolwyn. Tywyn's terminus houses a Narrow Gauge Railway Museum, which, like the railway itself, is open in the summer.

LLANEGRYN CHURCH
The craft of the medieval wood carver reaches its peak in Llanegryn Church. This small, ordinary looking building contains a magnificent, intricately carved rood screen, dividing the nave from the chancel. The screen is a work of great complexity, filled with delicately carved detail. Diamonds, flowers, leaves, berries, vines and abstract forms are picked out on the panels and the loft above.

The screen's date and origin are uncertain, but one account states that it was saved from Cymer Abbey, near Dolgellau, during the Dissolution of the Monasteries in 1536.

FAIRBOURNE RAILWAY
Britain's longest place-name – all 66 letters of it – is found on the refurbished and publicity conscious Fairbourne Railway. The new name of Gorsafawddach'idraigddanheddog-leddollonpenrhynareurdraethceredi-gion ('Mawddach Station with its dragon's teeth on North Penrhyn Drive by the golden sands of Cardigan Bay') has been given to its mid-distance halt. This beats by eight letters the previous record holder – the village railway station in Anglesey, Gwynedd, usually referred to as Llanfair PG. The 'dragon's teeth' refer to concrete tank traps on Fairbourne beach, bizarre relics of the Second World War.

Fairbourne Railway has a gauge of 15in, originally a horse-drawn tramway, and its steam engines are half-size replicas of world-famous, narrow-gauge engines. Trains run from Easter to mid-September for 2 miles along an attractive, dune-backed beach from Fairbourne village to the mouth of the Mawddach estuary.

MAWDDACH ESTUARY
The Mawddach river rises near Bala, flows through gorges and picks up a few companions on the way, including the Wnion which joins it downstream from Dolgellau. Finally it broadens out into one of the loveliest estuaries in Britain.

This is William Wordsworth's 'sublime estuary' which, he said, could 'compare with the finest in Scotland'. Its swirling waters, sandbanks and wooded shoreline, protected by the smooth flanks of open mountains, form a harmonious blend of coastline and countryside, which is best seen on foot.

A rail and footbridge runs from Morfa Mawddach Station over to the holiday resort of Barmouth, providing a memorable walk across the waters. The station is also the western end of a walk following the shore of the estuary to Penmaenpool.

CREGENNEN LAKES
A steep and narrow road off the main route leads from the outskirts of Arthog up into the mountains. Looking down from the top of the 1½ mile long road, the waters of the twin Cregennen lakes stretch across a remote and open shelf of land beneath the north-facing slopes of Cadair Idris. Nothing has been allowed to spoil the scene, the entire area is cared for by the National Trust to whom the property was given by the Wynne-Jones family in memory of their two sons killed in the Second World War.

On the descent back to Arthog, there are more memorable views – particularly of the mountain-backed resort of Barmouth, at the mouth of the Mawddach estuary.

PENMAENPOOL
A 5¼ mile footpath, the Penmaenpool – Morfa Mawddach Walk, runs along the southern shore of the Mawddach estuary, following an abandoned railway line. Old railway signals still stand in front of Penmaenpool's George III Hotel, and a signal box nearby has been turned into a Wildlife Information Centre. The estuary's variety of bird life – including cormorants, oystercatchers and herons – can be observed along the walk.

TORRENT WALK
One of the most spectacular riverside walks in Britain – the Torrent Walk – lies 2 miles east of Dolgellau. It leads along the steep and thickly wooded banks of the Clywedog, passing a series of rushing falls which eventually join the Wnion river in the valley below. The tree-shaded walk, only a mile long, is well marked from beginning to end.

MEIRION MILL
The entrance gates to the wool mill stand opposite the Buckley Arms Hotel in the peaceful, single-street village of Dinas-Mawddwy. Built in the 19th century as a salt storehouse, the building has been in regular use as a mill since 1966.

In the working area the various weaving processes are demonstrated and explained, and the shop sells traditional Welsh weaves and modern patterns, made up into garments, bedcovers, rugs and so on. There is also a well-stocked mill shop. The mill is open on weekdays, and the shop daily, from April to October.

Tourist information: Machynlleth 2401; Corris 343; Tywyn 710070 (summer); Barmouth 280787 (summer).

Rolling hills in the Welsh Marches

TOUR
89

——— 73 MILES ———

On a clear day, nearly all the route can be seen from the top of Llanymynech Hill. There, one of the finest views on the border embraces Welsh mountains and the English plain.

WELSHPOOL

At the spot where hills tumble down to the River Severn as it approaches the English border lies a lively little town whose weekly market, held every Monday for more than 700 years, attracts more livestock than any other in Wales. Tucked away behind Broad Street, where the 19th-century Town Hall's clock tower contrasts with several black-and-white buildings, is the only cockpit in Wales still standing on its original site. On the other side of the street, Britannia Passage, Daxe's Row and Bear Passage are squeezed between old buildings, and recall the grid-pattern layout adopted for many 'new towns' in the Middle Ages.

The old Montgomery Canal wharf, a two-minute walk from the town centre, has an exhibition about the waterway whose completion at the end of the 18th century brought a new lease of life to Welshpool. Swans glide sedately under the warehouse's canopy, sharing the water with a narrowboat which takes passengers along a short, restored length of the canal, whose commercial life ended in 1936. Another boat is specially equipped to cater for handicapped children.

The town is the eastern terminus of the narrow-gauge Welshpool and Llanfair Light Railway. The railway has its western terminus at Llanfair Caereinion.

LONG MOUNTAIN

Rising steeply to 1338ft above the meandering Severn, the wooded Long Mountain is where Henry Tudor camped for two nights in the summer of 1485. Greatly encouraged when his army was joined by troops recruited in central Wales, Henry crossed the border and became Henry VII after defeating Richard III at the Battle of Bosworth Field.

The tour follows a Roman road with good eastward views before turning left down one of the Long Mountain's many narrow, tree-lined lanes. A few hundred yards beyond the junction stands what used to be the Welsh Harp Inn, where illegal cockfights were staged after the 'sport' was banned in 1849. It is now a farm.

BREIDDEN HILL

From the summit of The Breidden, as it is known locally, there are wide-ranging views of the Welsh hills and of the Shropshire plain sprawling

eastwards towards the Pennines. The summit, reached by a footpath from Criggion, bears a monument to Admiral Lord Rodney, who savaged a Spanish fleet off Cape St Vincent in 1780 and routed the French off Dominica two years later. He had no connections with the area, but Rodney's Pillar was erected as a tribute by the people of Montgomeryshire and Shropshire.

On the western side of the hill, extensive quarry workings face the tall masts of a British Telecom station that handles top-secret ship-to-shore communications.

After skirting The Breidden, the tour reaches England, when it crosses the River Severn on a narrow bridge originally built to carry a single-line railway.

MELVERLEY

This remote and scattered hamlet has one of Britain's most enchanting little churches. Perched above the Vyrnwy and surrounded by ancient yews, it has timber-framed walls of wattle and daub. The oak beams are joined with wooden pegs, and the 'magpie' building, with its tiny tower, shelters beneath tiles green with lichen. The

GREEN PASTURES *Trees seam a counterpane of fields near Llanfair Caereinion.*

MAGPIE CHURCH *Melverley's endearing timber-framed church was built in 1406.*

marriage register for 1776 records:
'This morning I have put a tie,
 No man could put it faster,
 Twixt Matthew Dodd, the man of
  God,
 And modest Nellie Foster.'

NESSCLIFFE

Nesscliffe Hill, where rhododendrons ramble amid the trees, is said to have been the hideout of 'Wild Humphrey' Kynaston, a 16th-century outlaw remembered as the Robin Hood of Shropshire. The cave named after him is reached by a flight of narrow steps, hollowed by countless feet and carved into a sheer cliff of red sandstone. From the top of the hill, where the remains of an Iron Age fort can be discovered amid the undergrowth, there are fine views over the Shropshire plain to Oswestry and the Berwyn mountains.

Narrow lanes take the tour from Nesscliffe to a small village with a strange name, Ruyton-XI-Towns. It was coined in 1301, when eleven local 'townships' – really rural areas – were merged to form a single local government unit.

The mile-long main street climbs a sandstone hill above the River Perry

and passes the Norman Church of St John the Baptist. In the church grounds stand the scanty remains of a small castle built by Edmund, Earl of Arundel, who created the borough. At the foot of the hill is a sandstone cross – built on the site of Ruyton's lock-up – with a plaque recording the names of the old townships.

KNOCKIN

Brick, sandstone and timber-framed 'magpie' buildings line Knockin's single street, making this one of the area's most attractive little villages. The road from Ruyton-XI-Towns runs through an avenue of trees before crossing two small bridges, each with an old sheep dip on its downstream side. Another link with the rural past is the old pound, opposite the handsome black-and-white façade of Top Farm.

LLANYMYNECH

Towering above a tangle of trees and bushes, the man-made limestone cliffs of Llanymynech Hill rise to 500ft above this 'frontier' village. Defined in 1535, the border zigzags up the main street to such an extent that several buildings can claim 'international' status. They include the Lion Hotel, where, until Montgomeryshire licensing laws were changed in 1960, Sunday drinking was legal in one bar and banned in another.

St Agatha's Church was built in 1845 and is a cheerfully eccentric little example of mock-Norman architecture. Its clock has faces big enough to be seen from Llanymynech Hill's quarry, where its designer, Richard Roberts, worked as a boy.

A footpath running south curves and climbs Llanymynech Hill on the eastern flank of the old limestone quarry. Crossed by the Offa's Dyke long-distance footpath, the hill is a magnificent vantage point with views embracing the mountains of Wales and the Shropshire plain, from which isolated sandstone hills rise like islands in a green ocean. In the middle of the golf course is the Ogof, a cave where Romans delved for lead, copper and silver.

The workings, where 60,000 tons of limestone were quarried each year in the middle of the 19th century, were abandoned before the First World War. Their cliffs now form part of the Llanymynech Rocks Nature Reserve, noted for carline thistle, clematis, wild thyme and other plants typical of limestone areas.

LLANYBLODWEL

The sparkling Afon Tanat sweeps under a handsome old bridge, only just wide enough for a car, and passes the 16th-century, black-and-white Horseshoe Inn. The timber-framed buildings of this small, scattered village contrast with the whimsical works of John Parker, Llanyblodwel's vicar from 1845 until 1860.

Parker built the former village school, now a private house, and turned the medieval Church of St Michael into a minor masterpiece of Gothic eccentricity.

The tower suggests an enormous rocket and is linked to the church by an arch bearing a carved plea for Llanyblodwel to be delivered from tempests, earthquakes and other disasters.

LLANSILIN
Flanked by steep, wooded hills where fists of naked rock break through the greenery, the Afon Cynllaith's peaceful valley makes a beautiful setting for the village. The writer and traveller George Borrow walked to Llansilin while gathering material for *Wild Wales* in the mid-19th century. He came to visit the grave of Huw Morris, the Welsh poet who died in 1709 at the age of 87. A stone still marks the poet's burial place by the south wall of the 15th-century church, whose chancel has a fine barrel-vaulted ceiling of carved oak.

TOUR
90
— 42 MILES —
Wooded hills rise steeply above valleys dotted with timber buildings in the border country. Two high points are commanded by castles – one a ruin, the other a family home and treasure-house.

MEIFOD
Llyn Du, a lovely little lake clasped in a fold of Broniarth Hill, is typical of the beautiful scenery surrounding this quiet village in the Afon Vyrnwy's broad, green valley. Georgian buildings, some clad with ivy, follow the long gentle curve of an exceptionally spacious churchyard with delightful views of meadows and steep, rounded hills thick with trees. The medieval church of higgledy-piggledy stones has a pre-Norman burial slab carved with elaborate Celtic patterns.

Princes of Powys ruled from Meifod until Wales lost its independence after Llywelyn the Last was killed in 1282. Their stronghold at Mathrafal – now just a grassy, tree-clad mound near the Afon Banwy's confluence with the Vyrnwy – stands by the road 2 miles south of Meifod.

LLANFAIR CAEREINION
Small coaches hauled by steam engines with gleaming brasswork and clanking pistons bring a delightful dash of colourful nostalgia to the outskirts of Llanfair Caereinion. Set on a steep slope above the fast-flowing Afon Banwy, the village is at the western end of the narrow-gauge Welshpool and Llanfair Light Railway, which runs through 8 miles of rolling country, patchworked with woods and fields – scenery 'soft' by Welsh standards but typical of eastern Powys.

The railway was opened in 1903 after a debate lasting 43 years. It closed in 1956 but was soon revived by enthusiasts. Now there is a regular service every weekend from Easter to early October, plus Bank Holidays, and from mid-June to August trains run virtually every day. The atmosphere of much of Llanfair Caereinion

is early 19th century, but parts of its church are medieval and it contains the effigy of a 14th-century knight. From the top of Gibbet Hill, between the village and New Mills, there are pleasant views up the valley of the Rhiw and southwards towards Newtown.

BERRIEW
A discreet sign by the gate of St Beuno's Church marks the fact that Berriew won ten Best Kept Village Awards between 1960 and 1973 – three for the whole of Wales and seven for the old county of Montgomeryshire.

Black-and-white buildings, their gardens bright with flowers, cluster round the church, while the Rhiw hurries down its wooded valley and passes a picturesque terrace of timber-framed cottages before meeting the Severn.

Although it dates from the 1870s, the church has fine marble effigies of Arthur Price, Sheriff of Montgomeryshire in 1578, and his wives, Bridget and Jane.

The effigies spent many years exposed to the elements after Berriew's

old church was demolished – 'so greatly decayed in every part that the inhabitants cannot report there to hear divine service without endangering their lives'.

Before reaching the Welshpool to Newtown road, the tour passes under a four-arched brick aqueduct built to carry the Montgomery Canal over the Rhiw. The waterway was completed in 1821, but the original stone aqueduct had to be replaced in 1889.

MONTGOMERY
The castle, set on a crag shared by trees and greenish rock tangled with ivy, is now a ruin. But it has dominated Montgomery since Henry III established the 'new town' in 1223.

The old Town Hall in Broad Street is one of many Georgian buildings. Its timber-framed neighbours in Arthur Street include the 16th-century Old Bell, a former pub now used as an exhibition centre by the Civic Society.

The 13th-century church has a wonderfully ornate canopied tomb with effigies of Richard Herbert, who died in 1596, his wife Magdalen and their eight children. Near the churchyard's north gate is the Robber's

Grave, where John Davies was buried in 1821 after being executed for theft. He proclaimed his innocence on the scaffold, saying God would prove it by not letting grass grow on his grave. Today the grave is still a barren strip.

POWIS CASTLE
Built of rich sandstone – its Welsh name means 'Red Castle' – Powis Castle stands on high ground in a park grazed by deer. Its battlemented walls and towers rise majestically above four splendid terraces which are shared by 18th-century statues, shrubs, flowers and immaculately trimmed yew hedges which extend for nearly 200 yds.

Unlike its counterpart at Montgomery, Powis Castle gradually changed from a fortress to a palatial home whose treasures include portraits by Gainsborough, Reynolds, Romney, French and English furniture and a magnificent 16th-century Italian table inlaid with marble. The castle is open most afternoons in summer.

Tourist information: Welshpool 2043; Shrewsbury 50761.

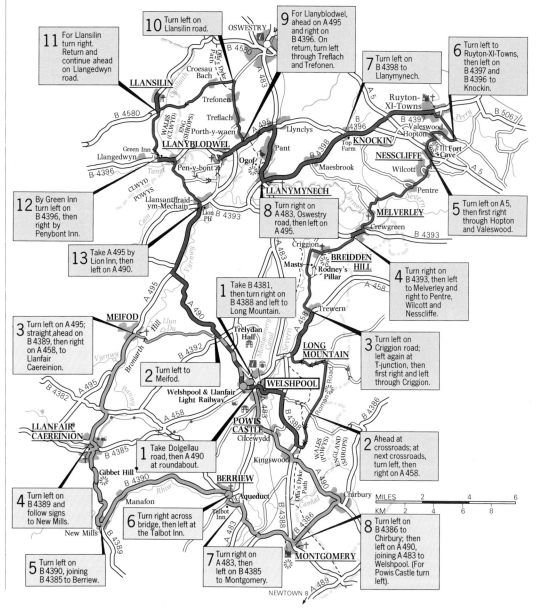

11 For Llansilin turn right. Return and continue ahead on Llangedwyn road.

10 Turn left on Llansilin road.

9 For Llanyblodwel, ahead on A 495 and right on B 4396. On return, turn left through Treflach and Trefonen.

7 Turn left on B 4398 to Llanymynech.

6 Turn left to Ruyton-XI-Towns, then left on B 4397 and B 4396 to Knockin.

12 By Green Inn turn left on B 4396, then right by Penybont Inn.

8 Turn right on A 483, Oswestry road, then left on A 495.

5 Turn left on A 5, then first right through Hopton and Valeswood.

13 Take A 495 by Lion Inn, then left on A 490.

4 Turn right on B 4393, then left to Melverley and right to Pentre, Wilcott and Nesscliffe.

1 Take B 4381, then turn right on B 4388 and left to Long Mountain.

3 Turn left on A 495; straight ahead on B 4389, then right on A 458, to Llanfair Caereinion.

3 Turn left on Criggion road; left again at T-junction, then first right and left through Criggion.

2 Turn left to Meifod.

1 Take Dolgellau road, then A 490 at roundabout.

2 Ahead at crossroads; at next crossroads, turn left, then right on A 458.

4 Turn left on B 4389 and follow signs to New Mills.

6 Turn right across bridge, then left at the Talbot Inn.

5 Turn left on B 4390, joining B 4385 to Berriew.

7 Turn right on A 483, then left on B 4385 to Montgomery.

8 Turn left on B 4386 to Chirbury; then left on A 490, joining A 483 to Welshpool. (For Powis Castle turn left).

MILES 2 4 6
KM 2 4 6 8

NEWTOWN 8

Green lanes through the Dee valley

The highest waterfall in Wales pours down its peat-stained torrents. And in the lovely valley of the Dee there are reminders of the Welsh soldier-statesman Owain Glyndwr.

LLANFYLLIN

Steep hills patchworked with woodlands and criss-crossed by a web of narrow lanes rise on every side of this quiet little town, where the Cain river is joined by the Abel river. The main street is lined with a pleasant mixture of brick, stone and timber-framed buildings, including two pubs.

The route between Llanfyllin and Llanrhaeadr-ym-Mochnant climbs to nearly 900ft and has splendid views northwards across the Tanat valley to the Berwyn mountains. Their highest point, Moel Sych, stands 2713ft above sea level and is just 1ft higher than its neighbour, Cadair Berwyn. The cairn on Cadair Bronwen is one of many sites in Wales where King Arthur is said to be buried.

LLANRHAEADR-YM-MOCHNANT

Tweed-capped farmers and their trained collies travel to Llanrhaeadr for the sheep sales that make this one of the Berwyn region's most important villages. Near the market stands a tall, slender stone whose carved Roman numerals give the distances to London and Shrewsbury.

Llanrhaeadr is also a popular base for pony-trekkers and walkers, because the surrounding mountains and valleys are laced with lanes, bridleways and footpaths. Many more pass through the village on their way to Pistyll Rhaeadr.

Solid stone buildings roofed with slate curl round the riverside church whose 16th-century vicars included William Morgan, a future Bishop of St Asaph. At Llanrhaeadr, Morgan completed the first Welsh translation of the Bible in 1588. Permission to undertake the work had been granted by Elizabeth I after her father, Henry VIII, banned any official use of Welsh. The translation did much to keep the language alive.

PISTYLL RHAEADR

A deep and peaceful valley carved by Ice Age glaciers leads to Pistyll Rhaeadr, the highest waterfall in Wales or England. Stained with peat, the Disgynfa's brown waters cascade 240ft down a glistening, mossy cliff flanked by pines, then thunder down another 50ft into a deep pool. A footbridge provides memorable views of the falls, which can also be seen by following a steep path through the trees to the cliff top.

Pistyll Rhaeadr is the most convenient starting point for a walk to Moel

Sych, the highest point in the Berwyn massif. Topped with an ancient cairn, it forms part of the rocky ridge that towers above a small lake. On a clear day the view extends from Snowdonia to the Shropshire plain, where the power station chimney at Iron-Bridge is a landmark.

Serious walkers can make for either Llandrillo or Llanarmon Dyffryn Ceiriog. But care is essential, because weather conditions change very quickly – and the 'hounds of hell' are said to prowl the Berwyns in search of lost souls.

LLANARMON DYFFRYN CEIRIOG

Memories of his beautiful birthplace inspired John Ceiriog Hughes, Llanarmon's most celebrated son, to write lyrical poems ranked with the finest in the Welsh language. The house where he was born in 1832 stands on a hillside high above the pebbled Ceiriog river as it hurries down through the Berwyns.

The village's full name, generally abbreviated to Llanarmon or Llanarmon DC, is one of the longest in Wales and means 'Garmon's

Church in the Valley of the Ceiriog'. St Garmon is said to be buried beneath the grassy mound by the entrance to the yew-shaded churchyard; but the distinction of being the Saint's last resting place is also claimed by Llanarmon-yn-Ial.

Set in a bowl of high hills stippled with the white blobs of grazing sheep, Llanarmon is a popular retreat for walkers, anglers, shooting parties and those who simply like fresh air and mountain scenery. The West Arms dates from the 16th century.

GLYN CEIRIOG

Nature has healed the scars left by the slate industry that flourished in and around Glyn Ceiriog for more than 300 years. The village's last workings were abandoned in 1946, but the Chwarel Wynne – Welsh for Wynne Quarry – vividly recalls the period when slate was the 'grey gold' of North Wales.

Chwarel Wynne was an open-cast operation from 1750 until the workings went underground in the late

1860s. When the quarry closed in 1928 there were three levels linked by more than 3 miles of passages. At its peak just before the First World War the quarry employed 77 men and produced 2000 tons of slate a year, plus 60,000 tons of waste.

Guided tours lasting 30-45 minutes explore several of the subterranean quarry's 49 immense chambers where men toiled by the flickering light of candles bought with their own money.

The museum – where visitors can try their hand at splitting and dressing slates – once housed steam-powered machinery that hauled loaded trucks from the mine. The lowest workings were 300ft below the surface.

The mine and museum are open daily from Easter to October. There are nature trails, attractive gardens, a picnic place and a craft shop on the site.

John Ceiriog Hughes, Huw Morus and other local celebrities are commemorated by stained-glass windows in the Ceiriog Memorial Institute. Its furniture includes pieces presented by Welsh families who emigrated to Patagonia in the 19th century. The 'colonists' in this Argentinian

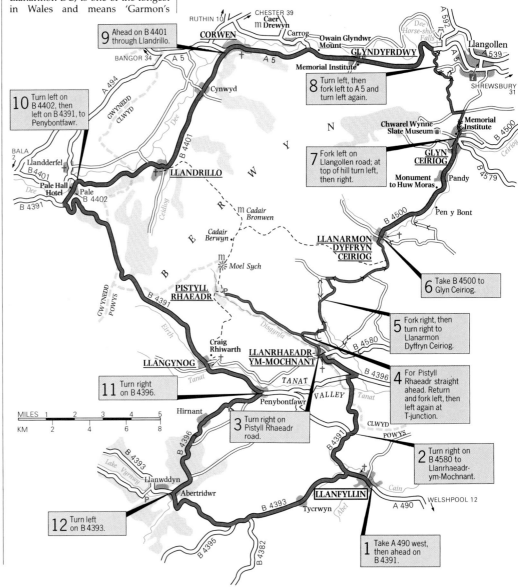

province now speak Welsh and Spanish, but not English.

Church Hill climbs a 1-in-4 gradient and has good views across the valley. The route then crosses high ground and overlooks the dramatic limestone crags behind Llangollen before twisting towards the Dee.

GLYNDYFRDWY

This little village above the Dee is believed to have been the birthplace of Owain Glyndwr, the greatest of all Welsh heroes. The exact date of his birth is not known. It was probably 1359, but 1362 is a strong contender if William Shakespeare is to be believed, because it was the year when a great comet blazed across the sky. Glyndwr (Glendower) tells Hotspur in *Henry IV, Part I*: 'At my nativity the front of heaven was full of fiery shapes, of burning cressets . . .'

A wealthy landowner, Glyndwr studied at the Inns of Court in London and served Richard II in the Scottish Wars before launching the last bid for Welsh independence in 1400. He captured Harlech Castle and was proclaimed the rightful Prince of Wales before the revolt fizzled out towards the end of the decade. It is not known where or when Glyndwr died, but there are no references to his life after 1412.

The village's Owain Glyndwr Memorial Institute has a photograph of the document that ratified the treaty signed by the Welsh leader and Charles VI of France in 1404. On the right of the road, 2 miles beyond Glyndyfrdwy, a tree-clad mound is said to be the site of Glyndwr's birthplace.

CORWEN

The Berwyns, green with conifers, tower above the rooftops of a little town whose Iron Age predecessor, the Caer Drewyn hill-fort, stands high above the Dee's opposite bank. Corwen has a very Welsh character, and the modern national eisteddfod's foundations were laid here in 1789 when a local man, Thomas Jones, staged a bardic festival at the Owain Glyndwr Hotel.

A cross-shaped incision above the parish church's south porch is said to have been made when Glyndwr hurled his dagger from a crag overlooking the town. In the grounds of the medieval church stand ivy-clad almshouses built in 1750. At the western end of the graveyard, a whimsical piece of doggerel says of Owen Owen, an engine driver who died in 1872:

When death sounds its whistle the
   steam of life falls
And his mortal clay shunteth till
   the last trumpet calls.

LLANDRILLO

A steepled church watches over the Ceidiog river as it hurries through tranquil Llandrillo to meet the meandering Dee. The village's whitewashed cottages contrast with the green-flanked Berwyns, whose highest points are only 3 miles away.

Before reaching the Bala to Llangynog road, the route skirts the grounds of the Pale Hall Hotel. Pale –

AUTUMN MORNING *The textured-glass waters of the Afon Ceiriog ripple between frost-dusted fields and hedgerows at Pen y Bont.*

pronounced 'pallay' – was built in 1875 for Henry Robertson, one of the great Victorian civil engineers. He built the majestic viaduct – 1508ft long and 147ft high – which carries the Shrewsbury to Chester railway line across the Vale of Dee.

LLANGYNOG

The road to Llangynog snakes across windswept moorland with views of the Snowdonia National Park. It climbs to 1595ft, then clings to the side of a dramatic valley where cliffs stand nearly 1000ft above the Eirth river. The mountain thwarted an optimistic 19th-century railway scheme that would have made Llangynog a station on the line to Porthmadog. The village clusters around the Eirth where it joins the River Tanat.

Slate and lead were quarried and mined on Craig Rhiwarth for nearly 300 years, but hardy plants are slowly covering the old workings. A footpath climbs the crag's eastern slope and eventually reaches Pistyll Rhaeadr.

There is a direct route back to Llanfyllin from Llangynog, but the tour turns right in Penybontfawr to explore the deep valleys and high, rolling hills east of Lake Vyrnwy.

Tourist information: Bala 520367 (summer); Llangollen 860828 (summer).

Over mountain passes to Bala Lake

TOUR

92

— 74 MILES —

The historic market town of Dolgellau sits in the shadow of the massive 2927ft Cadair Idris. It is close to cool, green forests, mirror-like lakes, high waterfalls and wild moors.

DOLGELLAU

Black is the predominant colour in Dolgellau – a wet, jet black when rain douses the slate roofs and stone houses. And the mood is unquestionably a traditional one. Welsh is spoken as a first language in the streets, and farmers come to town to sell their livestock and buy their groceries.

Dolgellau's attractive main square, with its fringe of shops and inns, sets an architectural style which the rest of the town follows faithfully. Huge blocks of dark stone are used in the buildings. The occasional archway and gabled roofline enliven the scene, but the overall impression is of robustness and uniformity.

From the road over the bridge, there is a fine view of the town spreading itself out across green river banks and wooded hillsides in the Wnion valley. Behind Dolgellau the hills rise sharply towards the open, upper reaches of Cadair Idris, its towering bulk looming menacingly over the rooftops.

LLANELLTYD

The wizened old yew trees in the graveyard of the Church of St Illtyd may be more ancient than the church itself. This immaculately kept place of worship occupies a rounded hillock, and possibly because of this is one of the few churches in Britain with a circular churchyard.

The church, restored in 1636, has ancient walls and 15th-century roof beams. Its principal relic is a stone in the shape of a coffin lid. A clearly carved footprint on it is followed by lettering of the 9th or 10th century which has been translated as: 'The footprint of Kenyric – a pilgrim – is imprinted at the head of this stone before he himself set out for foreign parts.'

RHAIADR DU

Park the car at Ganllwyd and walk the quarter mile or so to foaming Rhaiadr Du, 'The Black Waterfall'. Though the route is surfaced for most of the way, there is no parking at the waterfall. The path climbs steeply up a boulder-strewn valley, clothed in tall oak woodlands, to the dramatic falls. There are many black rocks scattered about, and the waters of the Gamlan are deep black.

Rhaiadr Du is within the National Trust's 1249 acre Dolmelynllyn Estate. The estate hall – a substantial Victorian house – is now a hotel.

COED-Y-BRENIN

Of all the Forestry Commission's plantations in Wales, Coed-y-Brenin, 'the King's Forest', is the most beautiful and accessible. Its beauty comes from a constantly changing landscape, and a variety of foliage rarely seen in commercial forests. There are waterfalls, shady valleys, conifer and broad-leaved trees, high viewpoints, craggy outcrops and a network of forest trails.

Call first at Maesgwm Visitor Centre, open from Easter to the end of September. Imaginatively presented displays and exhibitions tell the story of the forest and those who work and live there. One display deals with Dolgellau's 19th-century 'gold rush'; and today mining still takes place deep in the forest.

The centre also supplies information and maps for walks. More than 50 miles of waymarked trails take walkers on short strolls or deep into the heart of this forest of 34 square miles, named to commemorate the Silver Jubilee of King George V in 1935. Several trails run from the Ty'n-y-groes car park and there are more from Pont Dôl-gefeiliau, including two to remote waterfalls, Pistyll Cain and Rhaeadr Mawddach.

At Pont Dôl-gefeiliau drovers used to gather to shoe their cattle in preparation for the long march to London.

TRAWSFYNYDD

From a distance, Trawsfynydd Nuclear Power Station bears an uncanny resemblance to a medieval castle, the protrusions on its roofline suggesting battlements. At close quarters, illusions are put firmly in their place. This massive complex is unmistakably 20th century. Trawsfynydd, opened in 1965, was the first nuclear power station in Britain to be built inland, using Llyn Trawsfynydd – a man-made reservoir created in the 1920s – for cooling purposes. Groups may visit the station by prior arrangement.

MIGNEINT

A vast upland plateau more than 1000ft high spreads itself from Ffestiniog across to Llyn Celyn. On the approach road, just beyond the car park, is a viewpoint for Rhaeadr y Cwm. This waterfall tumbles down from Migneint's saturated, boggy moorlands, cutting a deep black scar in the precipitous green hills.

Even the hardy Welsh hill sheep are few and far between on Migneint's moors. Apart from occasional patches of conifer, this is a treeless, windy and desolately wild corner of Wales.

LLYN CELYN

Although no more than 20 years old, the man-made reservoir of Llyn Celyn has blended well with its mountain setting, thanks to sympathetic and imaginative landscaping, especially along the grass-covered dam which drivers can cross to a car park.

On the northern shore of the lake stands a poignant memorial to a chapel now submerged beneath the waters. Some of the stones from the lost chapel went to build the modern Capel Celyn Memorial, and headstones from the original chapel stand nearby in a small garden of remembrance.

A flagstone terrace at the entrance to the chapel looks out across the lake, which holds 16,280 million gallons and supplies north-east Wales and Cheshire. Just below the dam is the Tryweryn canoe slalom course.

CYFFDY FARM PARK

This traditional hill farm, on the lower slopes of the Arenig mountains, is open to the public from Easter to October.

Visitors are free to wander around the old farm buildings and paddocks stocked with sheep, cattle, pigs, horses, goats, rabbits, poultry and waterfowl, including some rare breeds. There are occasional displays of sheepshearing, sheepdog handling and hand milking.

The farmhouse, a large, three-storey stone building dating from 1600, is surrounded by historic farm machinery. Other features include craft exhibitions, a farm trail, pony trekking, fishing, picnic sites and an adventure playground.

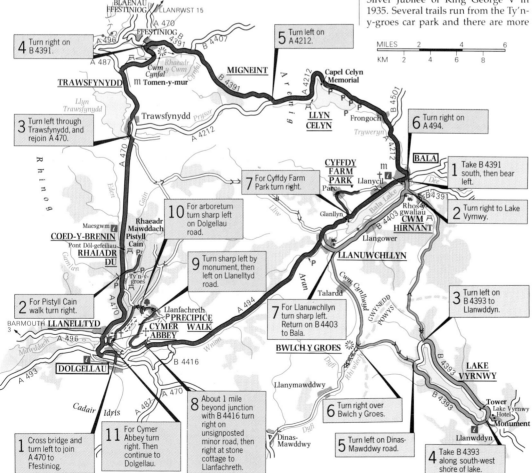

THE VALLEY BELOW *To the north-east of Precipice Walk the village of Llanfachreth sits like a tiny jewel on a green velvet gown below the slopes of Snowdonia.*

LAKE OF LEGEND *A legendary prince and his palace are said to lie beneath the waters of Bala Lake.*

GLISTENING CONTRASTS *The white water of Afon Gamlan cascades over Rhaiadr Du's black rocks.*

TEUTONIC TOWER *A 75 mile pipeline starts from the tower that flanks Lake Vyrnwy like a Rhineland castle.*

PRECIPICE WALK

Dolgellau's lovely setting can be appreciated in all its glory from the Precipice Walk. The 3 mile path runs along a high steep ridge, with views of the Mawddach estuary and the Cadair Idris, Rhinog, Aran and Arenig mountains, before returning beside the pretty Llyn Cynwch.

About 1½ miles farther on, at the edge of Coed-y-Brenin Forest, is a riverside arboretum, a plantation with a waymarked trail.

CYMER ABBEY

The abbey stands amongst farm buildings on a peaceful riverbank near the meeting place of the Mawddach and Wnion. Founded in 1198 by Cistercian monks, its most outstanding features are the three arched windows in the east wall, and fine craftsmanship on the columns.

Tourist information: Dolgellau 422888 (summer).

TOUR

93

—— 37 MILES ——

In the wild, mountainous country around Bala the roads are often steep and narrow, climbing over the highest, most spectacular pass in Wales and penetrating to remote lakes.

BALA

This is a Welsh country town through and through. Welsh is the language of its inhabitants, young and old; and many of the shops state the nature of their business in the traditional tongue. Bala has long been a stronghold of Welsh culture. The Reverend Thomas Charles (1755-1814), a leading figure of Welsh Nonconformism, preached there to packed congregations; a white statue of him,

holding his Bible, stands outside Capel Tegid, a Presbyterian chapel.

Bala's most theatrical statue is that of Thomas Edward Ellis (1859-99), the Liberal MP who advocated Welsh home rule. He stands in flamboyant pose above the wide, tree-lined main thoroughfare. A wooded mound, rising above the rooftops near the statue, is Tomen y Bala, the remains of a Norman earthwork.

The town stands at the foot of Llyn Tegid (Bala Lake), at 4 miles long and 150ft deep the largest natural lake in Wales. In its waters lurks the gwyniad, a deep-water white trout found only in this lake. According to legend the waters also cover a prince, his palace and his people, drowned for their wickedness.

CWM HIRNANT

The drive south from Bala through the Hirnant valley is a journey across the contrasting faces of upland Wales. The first part of the route runs

alongside dark, deep green forests. Views are dominated by the tall conifers that march unswervingly up the hillsides.

Farther south, the forest loosens its grip. Untamed, open countryside and treeless moorland come into view. The narrow road begins its ascent of a lonely, empty valley. Beyond the summit, it plunges back into shady forest before reaching the shores of the most beautiful man-made lake in Wales.

LAKE VYRNWY

On a calm day, the still, inky waters of Lake Vyrnwy reflect the tall pines and peaks that completely encircle it, effectively locking it away from any through traffic. The road follows the shore, passing a fairy-tale Gothic tower, with tall twin spires, jutting out of the water. Lake and tower were built by Liverpool Corporation in the 1880s, in an age when architectural eccentricity was fashionable. At the same time, the corporation constructed the Lake Vyrnwy Hotel which stands on a lush, rhododendron-covered hillside above the lake.

The hotel's wood-panelled interior is reminiscent of a Scottish shooting lodge. Old photographs in the hotel show the original village of Llanwddyn with its 37 houses, all now drowned beneath 13,100 million gallons of water.

The 'new' village, a scattering of buildings, stands south of the dam. On the hill above, a church has been built to replace the old Church of St Wddyn. On higher ground still, on a site offering panoramic views of the lake, stands an obelisk made from solid blocks of grey stone, tapering to a point. This is a monument to the 44 men who died either from natural causes or accidents during the construction of the reservoir.

The road across the giant dam leads to a chapel, now converted into the Vyrnwy Visitor Centre, open on summer afternoons. Exhibits interpret the story of the lake and the rich wildlife in the surrounding woods.

BWLCH Y GROES

Those who believe that Britain's landscape has been well and truly tamed by the motor car should drive over the high and mighty Bwlch y Groes – the 'Pass of the Cross'. Here, the motorist is the timid interloper, meekly following a tight tarmac road that climbs from the shores of Lake Vyrnwy to a 1790ft summit and viewpoint.

On a clear day, the view extends beyond the summit of the Arenigs to the peaks of North Wales. Walk a little way south along the road for a glimpse of the pass as it drops away steeply into the folds of the Dyfi valley and Llanymawddwy.

LLANUWCHLLYN

This small village, strung out to the south-west of Bala Lake, is another bastion of Welsh tradition. It has statues of two eminent Welshmen, Sir Owen Morgan Edwards (1858-1920) and his son Sir Ifan ab Owen Edwards (1895-1970), both concerned with the survival of the Welsh language and culture. The latter founded Urdd Gobaith Cymru – the Welsh League of Youth – which holds lakeside summer camps at nearby Glanllyn.

The Bala Lake Railway – one of the narrow-gauge 'Great Little Trains of Wales' – follows a lakeside route for 4½ miles from the terminus at Llanuwchllyn to the outskirts of Bala. Services operate from Easter to mid-October.

Tourist information: Bala 520367 (summer).

ROOF OF WALES *Bwlch y Groes, the highest mountain road in Wales, clings to a ledge cut into the hillside as it sweeps down from desolate moors to the valley of the Rhiwlech.*

Strongholds along the Anglesey coast

TOUR
94
——— 87 MILES ———

Low hills give broad views across Môn, Mam Cymru – 'Anglesey, Mother of Wales'. There are forts of the Romans and Normans, the remains of a Celtic village and reserves thronged with sea birds.

BEAUMARIS

A rich variety of well-preserved buildings, the oldest dating from the late 13th century, make Beaumaris one of the most enchanting small towns in Wales. It is now a fashionable holiday resort and sailing centre, with an atmosphere of the Regency and Victorian periods that belies a longer history.

Derived from Norman-French, the town's name means 'beautiful marsh', and refers to the site chosen by James of St George for the last of the eight castles built by Edward I in North Wales. Work started in 1295, shortly after Madog ap Gruffydd's brief but bloody revolt had underlined the need for a fortress on Anglesey.

The Master of the King's Works in Wales created a stronghold whose elaborate system of concentric defences set a new style. Its strength was never put to the test, but attackers would have had to cross the moat, then breach or scale the outer walls before assaulting the heart of the defences. The castle is open to the public daily.

Within a two-minute walk of the castle are the quaint little Court House, built in 1614, and the former Free Grammar School of 1603. Victoria Terrace's limestone façade looks out across The Green to the Menai Strait and Snowdonia. One of the town's architects was Joseph Hansom (1803-82), the English designer of the hansom cab. He worked on the Bulkeley Arms Hotel which shares Castle Street with the Tudor Rose, the George and Dragon and other timber-framed buildings.

The 14th-century Church of St Mary and St Nicholas, built to serve the 'new town' which grew up around the castle, contains 15th-century alabaster effigies of William Bulkeley and his wife. In the porch is the stone coffin of Princess Joan, wife of Llywelyn the Great and daughter of King John of England, who died in 1237. For many years the coffin was used as a drinking trough for horses.

In Steeple Lane, in the town centre, rise the tall, grim walls of Beaumaris Gaol, where prisoners were held from 1829 until 1878. Restored, it is a place of stone floors, shackles, studded doors secured by huge bolts, and many stern reminders of the Victorian penal system. Prisoners doing hard labour spent their days either breaking stones or toiling at the tread-wheel, the only one of its type in Britain to have survived in its original position. Beaumaris Gaol and Court House are open daily in summer.

RAF VALLEY

Jet-powered Hawk trainers, visiting Phantom fighters, and helicopters used for air, sea and mountain rescue work make Valley the liveliest RAF base in Wales. The aircraft can be watched from a car park near the main gate. RAF Valley was established in 1941, and became a 'reception centre' for United States Army Air Force bombers which flew the Atlantic to take part in the bombardment of Germany. The 'valley' from which the base takes its name was a cutting made through a small hill during the construction of Thomas Telford's London to Holyhead road in 1822.

A roadside stone near the base recalls one of Europe's most important Iron Age discoveries. War chariots, swords, shields, trumpets and other artefacts were found when a peat bog, the site of a small lake in the Iron Age, was drained in 1943. The relics are now in the National Museum of Wales at Cardiff.

SOUTH STACK

Sandy coves flank the lane from Trearddur Bay to South Stack, where visitors share spectacular cliff scenery with puffins, fulmars, razorbills, guillemots and herring gulls. The birds and their nesting ledges are seen at relatively close quarters by taking the long, steep flight of steps down through the South Stack Cliffs Reserve to the lighthouse. Built in 1809

and reached by a tiny suspension bridge, the lighthouse was manned until automatic equipment was installed in 1984.

The car park near Ellin's Tower, a Victorian summerhouse, is the starting point for walks along the cliffs from Gogarth Bay to North Stack, where grey seals may be seen basking on rocks far below the path. Holyhead Mountain's rocky summit, 720ft above the sea, is the highest point on Anglesey. On a clear day the climber is rewarded with spell-binding views right across the island to Snowdonia, the Lleyn Peninsula and the Great Orme, which shelters Llandudno.

A ruined 'village' of circular huts, inhabited between 1600 and 1800 years ago, is a short stroll from the car park. Stone slabs used as seats and beds lie among the heather and springy turf.

HOLYHEAD

Caer Gybi, a Roman fort just off the main street – Stanley Street – is one of the treasures of this old-established ferry port. The fort's high, well-preserved walls enclose the grounds of the medieval Church of St Cybi, whose late-Victorian chapel has stained-glass by Sir Edward Burne-Jones and William Morris.

Ferries gliding in and out of the harbour maintain links with Ireland that were forged in Tudor times, but Holyhead was a modest fishing village until the 19th century. This changed after the 1801 Act of Union abolished Dublin's parliament, centralised the United Kingdom's government in London, and underlined the need for greatly improved communications between the two cities. Thomas Telford's London to Holyhead road, completed in 1826, helped to provide the link. The harbour's 1¾ mile North Breakwater,

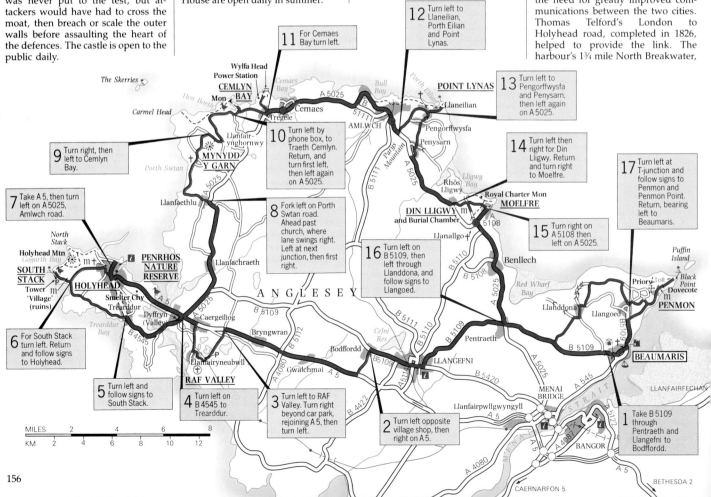

11 For Cemaes Bay turn left.

12 Turn left to Llaneilian, Porth Eilian and Point Lynas.

13 Turn left to Pengorffwysfa and Penysarn, then left again on A 5025.

14 Turn left then right for Din Lligwy. Return and turn right to Moelfre.

17 Turn left at T-junction and follow signs to Penmon and Penmon Point. Return, bearing left to Beaumaris.

9 Turn right, then left to Cemlyn Bay.

10 Turn left by phone box, to Traeth Cemlyn. Return, and turn first left, then left again on A 5025.

7 Take A 5, then turn left on A 5025, Amlwch road.

8 Fork left on Porth Swtan road. Ahead past church, where lane swings right. Left at next junction, then first right.

16 Turn left on B 5109, then left through Llanddona, and follow signs to Llangoed.

15 Turn right on A 5108 then left on A 5025.

6 For South Stack turn left. Return and follow signs to Holyhead.

5 Turn left and follow signs to South Stack.

4 Turn left on B 4545 to Trearddur.

3 Turn left to RAF Valley. Turn right beyond car park, rejoining A 5, then turn left.

2 Turn left opposite village shop, then right on A 5.

1 Take B 5109 through Pentraeth and Llangefni to Bodffordd.

MILES 2 4 6 8
KM 2 4 6 8 10 12

CAERNARFON 5   BETHESDA 2

the longest in Britain, took 28 years to build and was finished in 1873. It shelters an anchorage where yachts mingle with fishing boats, ferries and ships laden with ore for the nearby aluminium smelter – whose 420ft chimney is one of Anglesey's outstanding man-made landmarks.

PENRHOS NATURE RESERVE
Founded in 1972 by a local policeman and conservationist, the Penrhos Nature Reserve is an ideal place to stop, stroll and admire views of Anglesey's rugged north-west coast. The reserve's attractions range from a ruined gun battery – built to defend Holyhead during the Napoleonic Wars – to the animal hospital whose patients have included badgers and two young ravens which were later presented to the Tower of London. In 1966 an Arctic tern ringed on the reserve set a record when it was found in New South Wales, Australia, after a journey of 14,000 miles.

Rare bird visitors have included a sacred ibis – a bird venerated by the ancient Egyptians – but the public are more likely to see Canada geese, cormorants, and herons patrolling the 'inland sea' between the reserve and Anglesey's mainland.

Penrhos is where the tour crosses the huge Stanley Embankment. Built by Thomas Telford as part of the London to Holyhead road, it is 1300ft long and is shared by Robert Stephenson's Chester to Holyhead railway.

MYNYDD Y GARN
Reached by footpaths from the surrounding lanes, this 558ft high hill is topped with a small obelisk and has magnificent views in all directions. The obelisk was put up by the villagers of Llanrhyddlad to commemorate William Thomas, who was born there in 1837 and became a prosperous Liverpool shipmaster.

Away to the north-west, beyond Carmel Head, are the wave-swept Skerries whose light has guided seafarers since 1716. It was the last private lighthouse in Britain until control passed to Trinity House in 1841. The owners had been given the right to levy tolls on passing ships and, after a lengthy legal wrangle, received a payment of nearly £500,000 in compensation.

CEMLYN BAY
Waves rolling into this peaceful little bay break on the long arm of smooth shingle which protects a brackish lagoon whose level is maintained by a weir.

A pleasant walk along the bay's western shore passes a monument built in 1978 to commemorate the 150th anniversary of the launching of Anglesey's first lifeboat. The slipway remains, but the lifeboat station was closed in 1919. Other paths lead to Hen Borth, a lonely cove with a shingle shore, and to Carmel Head with its views of The Skerries.

The massive buildings of Wylfa nuclear power station dominate the coast between Cemlyn Bay and Cemaes Bay. The 1000 megawatt power station's nuclear reactor is cooled by pumping 55 million gallons of water from the sea every hour. Guided tours are available during the summer. At Wylfa Head there is a grassy picnic area and an eight-stage nature trail.

POINT LYNAS
The bracing walk from Porth Eilian to Point Lynas ends at what appears to be a small, whitewashed Victorian fort or folly. It is actually a lighthouse and the base for pilots who guide ships to Liverpool. The headland had a semaphore signalling system before electricity revolutionised communications in the second half of the 19th century. Given good visibility, the old system could relay shipping information from Holyhead to Liverpool in less than a minute.

DIN LLIGWY
A field crossed by a footpath lies between the lane and trees which shelter the bulky remains of Din Lligwy. Inhabited during the 4th century AD, it is believed to have been the stronghold of a Celtic chief in the years before the Romans withdrew from Britain. Ruined limestone walls 5ft thick surround half an acre of land where the substantial traces of nine buildings rise from the grass.

Nearby, the 3000-year-old Lligwy burial chamber stands in a field looking like a gigantic tortoise. The huge capstone alone is estimated to weigh 25 tons. The bones of 30 people were found when the grave was excavated in 1908. Remains of an early Celtic chapel were also found.

MOELFRE
Cottages cluster round a shingle beach at Moelfre. From low cliffs east and north of the village there are excellent views of the Great Orme, Puffin Island and Snowdonia. The walk passes the lifeboat station whose most famous coxswain, Richard Evans, was awarded his second Royal National Lifeboat Institution's gold medal in 1959. Braving 100mph winds, Evans and his colleagues rescued the eight-man crew of the *Hindlea*, a coaster whose barnacle-encrusted remains, draped with seaweed, can be seen on the rocks below the Coastguard's lookout station.

But in 1859, for all their bravery, the men of Moelfre could do little to help the steam-clipper *Royal Charter* when she was wrecked near the village. A small memorial on the cliff-top path to Lligwy Bay commemorates the 452 passengers and crew who perished when the vessel was driven ashore by a hurricane. She was on the last stage of a voyage from Australia to Liverpool. A slightly larger memorial stands in Llanallgo churchyard, where 140 victims of the disaster are buried.

Many of the passengers were gold miners and their families, and the cliff-top memorial stands near the spot where a breeches buoy was set up in a desperate attempt to save them. Many of the victims died trying to swim ashore with pockets full of gold. Most of the ship's cargo was salvaged, but the strongroom is thought still to contain gold and silverware valued at £4 million.

BLACK POINT *An automatic lighthouse signals the hazards near Puffin Island.*

TABLE FARE *Penmon's dovecote bred birds for a local landowner's table.*

VILLAGE STONES *Din Lligwy was a Celtic settlement in Roman times.*

BUILT TO LAST *Beaumaris Castle took 35 years to build, and much of it remains intact.*

PENMON
This small, scattered community on Anglesey's eastern tip is a wonderful area for walkers, anglers and those who simply enjoy unspoilt coastal scenery. In the 'Age of Saints' it was associated with St Seiriol, a Celtic monk who lived on Puffin Island, off the coast, in the 6th century AD.

Trees surround the holy well where St Seiriol is said to have baptised converts, and nearby are the ruins of a 13th-century Augustinian priory. The building succeeded an earlier settlement founded by relatives of St Seiriol. Among the ruins is a three-storey section of the south range, comprising cellar, refectory and dormitory.

The adjoining Church of St Seiriol was rebuilt in the 12th century, and has a Celtic cross in the south transept. Slate headstones in the churchyard mark the graves of seafarers whose ships went down in the Menai Strait. A stone dovecote near the church, built about 400 years ago, has nesting places to accommodate 1000 birds.

Another ancient cross, representing the Temptation of St Anthony, stands in the hillside Deer Park.

A toll road, free to walkers, runs from Penmon to Black Point and the fast-flowing channel between Anglesey and Puffin Island. Seafarers are warned of its perils by a jaunty little black-and-white lighthouse, complete with battlements. Low rocks make this a favourite spot for fishermen when mackerel shoals come close to the shore.

Tourist information: Llangefni 724666; Holyhead 2622 (summer); Menai Bridge 712626 (summer).

157

Castles and bridges of the Menai Strait

TOUR
95

———— 90 MILES ————

On one side of the Menai Strait lie the soft green landscapes of Anglesey. On the other the heights of Snowdonia look down upon the mighty walls of Caernarfon Castle.

CAERNARFON

The battlemented walls and tall, angular towers of Caernarfon Castle have watched over this busy little town on the Menai Strait for 700 years. Built by Edward I after Llywelyn the Last's death in 1282, the castle is seen at its best from the far bank of the Seiont, where ships laden with Snowdonia's slate have given way to yachts and small, sturdy fishing boats. The castle is open to the public daily.

At Caernarfon, Edward I proclaimed his baby son Prince of Wales in 1301. Subsequent ceremonies were held elsewhere until 1911, when the future Edward VIII received the title. Thanks to television, Prince Charles's investiture as Prince of Wales in 1969 was watched by 500 million people throughout the world.

Walls dating from the same period as the castle surround the compact gridiron of narrow streets established when the 'new town' of Caernarfon became the seat of English government in North Wales. A short walk from the castle is the Victoria Dock, where a dredger launched in 1937 is the focal point of a small museum devoted to the area's seafaring history.

Caernarfon's earliest days are recalled at Segontium, a Roman fort on the road to Beddgelert. It has fine views of Snowdonia and a museum telling how a Celtic community of dwellings, shops and taverns gradually developed at the fort's main entrance. Segontium's first garrison of about 1000 men is believed to have come from a regiment raised by the Romans in northern Spain.

The road to Anglesey is carried high above the Menai Strait by the Pont Britannia. The original bridge, designed by Robert Stephenson, was opened in 1850 to carry the London to Holyhead railway. Its track ran through square-section tubes of cast iron, but these collapsed during a fire in 1970. Ten years later the bridge was reopened as a 'double decker', with the railway running below a new road.

LLANFAIR PG

Rising 112ft from its wooded hillock, a fluted column commemorating the 1st Marquis of Anglesey dominates the village which has Britain's second longest (and unofficial) place name. Llanfairpwllgwyngyllgogerych-wyrndrobwllllantysiliogogogoch was almost certainly strung together in the 19th century to attract, amuse and baffle English visitors. Its 58 letters mean 'St Mary's church in a hollow by the white hazel close to the rapid whirlpool by the red cave of St Tysilio'. However, it was recently exceeded by eight letters by a made-up name for a stop on the Fairbourne Railway beside Cardigan Bay.

The village also has an immaculate, whitewashed tollhouse designed by Thomas Telford when he engineered the London to Holyhead road in the 1820s. The green building next to it has an inscription recalling how Britain's first Women's Institute was founded at Llanfair PG in 1915.

PLAS NEWYDD

From this mansion hung with Virginia creeper there are beautiful views across the Menai Strait to Snowdonia. Inside there are fine paintings, furniture and mementos of links with the Napoleonic Wars. Plas Newydd was the home of William Henry Paget, the 1st Marquis of Anglesey. Born in 1768, he became an MP at the age of 22, raised a regiment three years later and became one of the Duke of Wellington's most able and trusted commanders.

The column at Llanfair PG was erected after the hero died in 1854,

having fathered 18 children who produced 73 grandchildren.

Although dating from the 16th century, Plas Newydd has been altered several times and reveals no traces of its Tudor origins. The dining room's main wall consists of a 58ft long painting by Rex Whistler. Full of whimsical jokes and references to the Paget family, it depicts a romantic seaport viewed from the terrace of a great house.

A short detour from the road between Plas Newydd and Brynsiencyn leads to Bryncelli Ddu, a 'passage grave' dating from about 2000 BC. The name means 'Mound in the Dark Grove', but the burial chamber now stands in an open field and is reached after a five-minute walk.

A lane from Brynsiencyn wriggles down to the Mermaid Inn on the Menai Strait, where views of Caernarfon are framed by Snowdonia's peaks. Shark, ray, skate, lobster and many other denizens of Welsh coastal waters live in tanks at nearby Anglesey Sea Zoo.

NEWBOROUGH

Despite its name, Newborough was founded at the end of the 13th century by people whose homes on the Menai Strait had been cleared to make way for Beaumaris Castle. The village stands on the edge of a huge tract of land, crossed by many footpaths, where neat regiments of Forestry Commission conifers contrast with Newborough Warren's wilderness of sand dunes.

The drive through Newborough Forest, a Site of Special Scientific

SPANNING THE CENTURIES *Beyond the 14th-century Church of St Tysilio, islanded at high tide, Telford's suspension bridge of 1826 strides 1000ft across the Menai Strait.*

Interest, ends on Llanddwyn Bay, where Llanddwyn Island – joined to the shore by a natural causeway – is reached after a 1 mile walk. Superb views, a ruined 16th-century church and several sheltered coves make the island a delightful place to stroll, picnic and relax while watching cormorants and shags diving for fish.

Newborough Warren National Nature Reserve extends from Abermenai Point to Llanddwyn Island, then onto the Afon Cefni's broad estuary, where shelduck, lapwing, curlew, several species of swan and many other birds feed and breed. Walkers on the Warren, one of Britain's biggest expanses of sand dunes, make their way across what used to be fertile fields. These were buried, together with the village of Rhosyr, when a series of great storms displaced offshore sandbanks in the 14th century. Visitors wishing to leave the marked paths must obtain a permit.

The route from Newborough runs along a low ridge above the Cefni valley. The river formed a navigable link between the sea and Llangefni until the end of the 18th century, when it was turned into a canal to drain the valley, turning marsh into farmland.

MENAI BRIDGE

From the Belgian Promenade – a footpath built by refugees who settled here during the First World War – there are memorable views of the bridge from which this little Victorian town on the fast-flowing Menai Strait takes its name. Designed by Thomas Telford, the bridge cost £120,000 and was the most important feature of his great highway which cut the travelling time between London and Holyhead from several hazardous days to little more than 24 hours.

Sheltered by trees, the footpath goes across a causeway to the 'island' where St Tysilio built a church in the 7th century. Its medieval replacement stands amid slate headstones. From the nearby hillock's Celtic cross war memorial there are views of the Pont Britannia, which forged Anglesey's second link with the mainland in 1850.

BRYN BRAS CASTLE

Towers, turrets and battlements ideal for archers belie the fact that Bryn Bras Castle dates from the early 19th century, not the Middle Ages when Wales was at war with England. It was built in the 1830s by Thomas Williams, a wealthy solicitor, and has been lived in ever since. Williams almost certainly entrusted the romantic project to Thomas Hopper, the architect whose most famous work, Penrhyn Castle, was built near Bangor during the same period.

Sheltered by Snowdonia's northern slopes, Bryn Bras stands in 32 acres of well-kept gardens and woodland – where lawns, pools, shrubs and flowering trees bring softer colours and contours to the grandeur of North Wales.

The castle's interior is notable for stained glass, elaborately carved furniture, an elegant drawing room, galleried stairs and a huge slate fireplace whose mantelpiece alone weighs half a ton. Bryn Bras is open to the public daily in summer except on Saturdays.

BETWS GARMON

Spectacular mountains flank the route into Snowdonia National Park. On the far side of the village, the Gwyrfai cascades over rocks and under a picturesque old bridge before passing Hafodty garden, where hydrangeas and azaleas bloom.

Llyn Cwellyn, a beautiful lake beneath the steep slopes of Mynydd Mawr, is overlooked by the Snowdon Ranger path to Snowdon's summit, 3560ft above sea level. The walk there and back takes about five hours and must not be attempted without appropriate footwear, clothing and equipment. Another path starts from Rhyd-Ddu.

The route of the tour turns west and crosses a pass through the craggy mountains before reaching Nantlle, where mounds of slate loom above the terraced cottages. The village's Dorothea quarry, worked from 1829 until 1970, can be seen from a track which starts opposite the post office.

FELIN FAESOG

An 18th-century 'man plough' used by farmers unable to afford a horse or donkey is one of many evocative exhibits in this delightful little Museum of Old Welsh Country Life, housed in a former water mill reached by crossing a shallow ford. It was known to be operating in the 1680s, but appears to be much older. Felin Faesog also has an enchanting Victorian bedroom and a country kitchen where brass and copper utensils gleam by the fireplace. The museum is open daily in summer.

Narrow lanes lead from the mill to Clynnog-fawr, the village where St Beuno founded a monastery and died in about AD 630. According to legend, he brought his niece, St Winefride, back to life after she was decapitated by a frustrated suitor. Clynnog-fawr's fine 16th-century church, one of the noblest in North Wales, is linked by a passageway to the chapel where the saint's tomb survived until the end of the 18th century. Sick pilgrims were said to have been cured of all ills after sleeping on the grave's stone slab.

LLANDWROG

The slender spire of St Twrog's Church rises 110ft above this attractive, peaceful village built to serve the Newborough estate in the 1830s. The family home, Glynllifon Park, is now a college, but the church of 1864 has memorials to the 1st Lord Newborough, his father and other members of the family.

Dinas Dinlle, a mile north-west of Llandwrog, is an Iron Age hill-fort battered by waves. It commands memorable views of Anglesey and the Lleyn Peninsula's highest peaks.

Tourist information: Caernarfon 2232 (summer); Llangefni 724666.

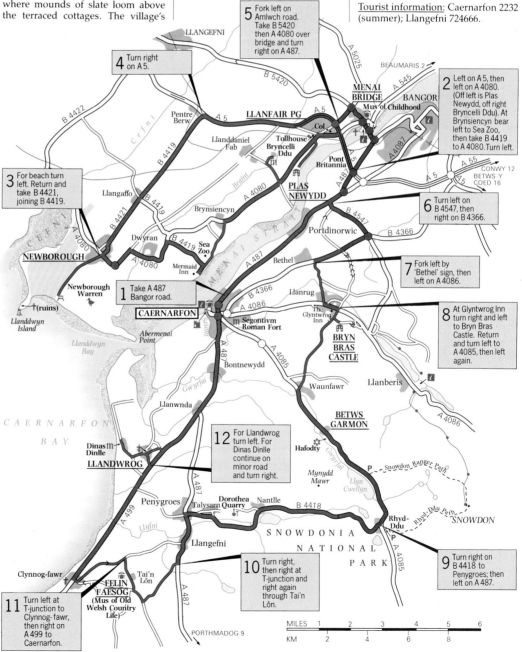

Bays and hills on the Lleyn Peninsula

On a crooked finger of land rich in Welsh tradition, Welsh is overwhelmingly the language of the people. It is an area of wild, dramatic scenery and also quiet, sandy beaches.

PWLLHELI

Lleyn's main market and shopping centre is at the end of British Rail's scenic Cambrian Coast line, which hugs the shore all the way from Aberystwyth. The railway station is on the divide between the old town and the new.

Pwllheli had its first charter in the 14th century – at the time of the Black Prince. The traditional part is to the north, where tall buildings line the narrow High Street. Above and beyond the modern shop façades are architectural delights from the past. An alley leads to a little Georgian arcade fronted by substantial grey-stone arches, and rows of canopied shopfronts survive from Victorian and Edwardian days.

South of the station, the seaside takes over. Pwllheli's large, almost land-locked harbour sits behind a long stretch of sandy beach. A wide road runs beside the beach into the districts of South Beach and West End, where well-designed, modern houses share the seafront with more traditional buildings.

TREFOR

The silent quarries cut into the mountain above Trefor tell the story of the village. Now it looks too large for its out-of-the-way location, but it was once a busy place where people living in its granite-built cottages walked to work each morning up the steep slope to the quarries. There is a striking view of a 1700ft mountain rising almost vertically above the sea.

NANT GWRTHEYRN

A walk down a steep forest path leads to the hidden valley of Nant Gwrtheyrn, the 'valley of Vortigern' – a place of mystery, shadowy and isolated. It has been described as 'the gloomy hollow'. When the sun is low and the shadows are long it is easy to associate it with the legend of Vortigern, the 5th-century king who is said to have died a fugitive here after inviting the Saxons to Britain to help fight the Picts.

Adding to the other-worldly atmosphere of Nant Gwrtheyrn is the ghost village of Porth-y-nant. This is no more than L-shaped rows of cottages and two other buildings overlooking the sea. Porth-y-nant, a village built in the 19th century to house the quarry workers, slowly died when the granite quarries in the hillside above were abandoned in 1959. But now it is coming alive again: a number of cottages have been renovated and are used as a centre for Welsh language studies.

Towering above the village is Yr Eifl, 'the Fork', the Lleyn's most prominent mountain with its three-pronged peaks thrusting to 1850ft.

PORTH NEFYN

One of several lovely bays scooped out by the sea along Lleyn's coastline, Porth Nefyn is on the doorstep of Nefyn, one of the peninsula's most popular little holiday towns. Cliff walks and a beautiful, gently shelving beach of firm sand are the main attractions for summer visitors.

The town is an ancient one – it was made a borough in medieval times – and has strong links with the sea. These would have been even stronger had a 19th-century plan been realised. This was to turn nearby Porth Dinllaen – the only good anchorage for miles – into an alternative to Holyhead for serving the Irish ferries.

The plan came to nothing, and Porth Dinllaen has changed little. A neat cluster of houses, self-contained in their sandy cove, shelters in the lee of a protective headland at the end of the long, crescent-shaped bay.

PORTH OER

A short walk from the car park leads down a grassy valley opening into the isolated cove of Porth Oer. The sandy beach, backed by low cliffs, is known as Whistling Sands because its sand granules whistle or squeak underfoot at certain stages of the tide. The sound is said to be due to the compression of the uniform-size quartz grains.

MYNYDD MAWR

Lleyn is at its glorious best on the National Trust's Mynydd Mawr headland in the far south-west. From the upper car park at this Land's End of North Wales some of Britain's finest coastal views can be seen.

The promontory takes a shuddering nose-dive into the sea at the Braich y Pwll cliffs. Bardsey Island thrusts itself out of the water 2 miles offshore, across a strait that looks deceptively innocent on a calm day. Bardsey's Welsh name of Ynys Enlli ('the Isle of the Eddies') conveys the dangers of this stretch of water. Pilgrims crossed it at their peril when Bardsey was also known throughout early Christian Britain as the Isle of 20,000 Saints. The island is now owned by a trust.

PLAS-YN-RHIW

A small manor house of medieval origin, with Tudor and Georgian additions, stands almost hidden amid vegetation of near-Amazonian profusion on a hillside which offers views, through the trees, of Porth Neigwl. The house and grounds of Plas-yn-Rhiw are open most summer afternoons. They have been restored by the National Trust, but the gardens – a tangle of shrubs, flowers, trees and subtropical plants – have an appealingly undisciplined look.

PORTH NEIGWL

A magnificent, 4 mile long bay, framed by low cliffs and two rugged headlands, takes up a large part of Lleyn's south-western tip. Through the centuries the peninsula's treacherous, rockbound coast has been a mariners' graveyard, and the bay's alternative name of Hell's Mouth is more forceful than Porth Neigwl, which means the 'gateway, harbour or landing place of Neigwl'.

Today's surfers and walkers are mostly unaware that Hell's Mouth once had a reputation among sailors for a siren-like invitation to doom. Any ship blown inshore by south-west gales risked being trapped within the bay and eventually driven onto the rocks.

ABERSOCH

The harbour and adjoining yards are packed with all kinds of craft – mostly holiday boats, for this thriving resort is popular among weekend sailors. There are two beaches.

Tiny Llangian, about a mile inland, provides a complete contrast. Not a blade of grass looks out of place in this immaculate village of stone houses and beautifully tended gardens.

Tourist information: Pwllheli 613000 (summer).

Lloyd George's boyhood home and a fantasy Italianate village face the arc of Tremadoc Bay. Between are superb coastal views, and the chance of an exciting railway trip into the mountains.

CRICCIETH

This little seaside town has a castle – small by North Wales standards perhaps, but conspicuously sited. Its round towers and ruined walls crown a grassy, rock-bound headland which separates Criccieth's two beaches. Built around 1230, the castle has an unorthodox history, having served as a Welsh native stronghold and, later, a fortress of the English invaders after Edward I captured it in 1282. The castle is open daily all the year, except Sunday mornings in winter.

The great twin-towered gatehouse, its most outstanding feature, appears high above Criccieth's rooftops. The town spreads itself out in a sheltered, south-facing position, and shows its development as a Victorian resort.

LLANYSTUMDWY

This peaceful little village was the boyhood home of the political firebrand David Lloyd George, Prime Minister from 1916 to 1922. Born in Manchester in 1863, he lived here

DISTANT HILLS *From Penygarn, a hill behind Pwllheli, there are views over Lleyn.*

PORTH DINLLAEN *Cottages and a water-front inn face a sheltered sandy cove.*

PORTMEIRION *Bell towers and piazzas create an Italianate fantasy.*

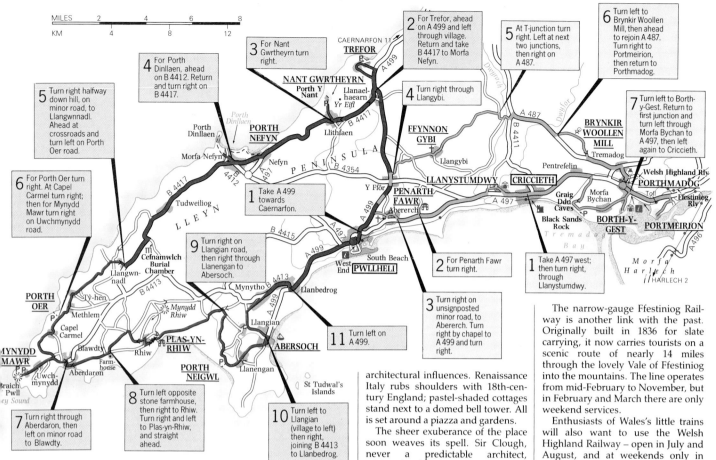

Take A 499 towards Caernarfon.

1 Take A 499 towards Caernarfon.
2 For Trefor, ahead on A 499 and left through village. Return and take B 4417 to Morfa Nefyn.
3 For Nant Gwrtheyrn turn right.
4 For Porth Dinllaen, ahead on B 4412. Return and turn right on B 4417.
4 Turn right through Llangybi.
5 Turn right halfway down hill, on minor road, to Llangwnnadl. Ahead at crossroads and turn left on Porth Oer road.
5 At T-junction turn right. Left at next two junctions, then right on A 487.
6 For Porth Oer turn right. At Capel Carmel turn right; then for Mynydd Mawr turn right on Uwchmynydd road.
6 Turn left to Brynkir Woollen Mill, then ahead to rejoin A 487. Turn right to Portmeirion, then return to Porthmadog.
7 Turn right through Aberdaron, then left on minor road to Blawdty.
7 Turn left to Borth-y-Gest. Return to first junction and turn left through Morfa Bychan to A 497, then left again to Criccieth.
8 Turn left opposite stone farmhouse, then right to Rhiw. Turn right and left to Plas-yn-Rhiw, and straight ahead.
9 Turn right on Llangian road, then right through Llanengan to Abersoch.
10 Turn left to Llangian (village to left) then right, joining B 4413 to Llanbedrog.
11 Turn left on A 499.
1 Take A 497 west; then turn right, through Llanystumdwy.
2 For Penarth Fawr turn right.
3 Turn right on unsignposted minor road, to Abererch. Turn right by chapel to A 499 and turn right.

from 1864 to 1880 in a humble cottage now identified by a slate plaque.

A bust of the statesman stands a few yards away in front of a small museum dedicated to him – open on weekdays in summer and also weekends in July and August. Lloyd George was buried on the banks of the Dwyfor river, a short walk from the museum, and his grave is marked by a great boulder inscribed 'DLG 1863-1945'. It was designed by Sir Clough Williams-Ellis, architect of Portmeirion. Shortly before his death Lloyd George took the title of Earl Lloyd George of Dwyfor.

PENARTH FAWR

Farmlands and woodlands surround one of the few surviving stone hallhouses in Wales, the view from which can have changed little since it was built in the 15th century.

Plain on the outside, Penarth Fawr has a simple interior, too: essentially one large room where the entire household, including servants, would live and sleep. The hall contains a well-preserved timber-framed roof, wooden columns and a grand 17th-century fireplace. Penarth Fawr is open daily.

FFYNNON GYBI

The ancient belief in the restorative, healing power of water is almost palpable at Ffynnon Gybi, 'St Cybi's Well'.

The fields behind Llangybi's village church drop into an enchanting valley where a moss-covered stone path leads to a ruined cottage. At one end, its rough stone walls enclose a well chamber of clear, icy water. Traditionally associated with St Cybi, a 6th-century saint who travelled widely in Wales, its water once had a reputation as a cure for warts.

BRYNKIR WOOLLEN MILL

Visitors can see traditional Welsh cloths decorated with striking patterns made at Brynkir. This is a working mill, open on weekdays throughout the year, where the entire manufacturing process, from raw wool to finished cloth, takes place.

The mill has been in continuous production since 1830; it was originally water-powered and the old wheel still turns. Fluffy bundles of wool are fed into machines on the ground floor. More clanking, noisy machines are at work elsewhere in the three-storey mill, winding the wool from colourful rows of bobbins before building up the complicated patterns on the weaving frames.

PORTMEIRION

This is the most un-Welsh village in Wales. Sir Clough Williams-Ellis's fantasy creation, standing on its own peninsula, has been variously described as Italianate, bizarre ... or a sheer folly. The visitor's initial impression is one of disorientation – perfectly in accord with the theme of the television series The Prisoner, which was filmed at Portmeirion.

Sir Clough began work on his dream in 1925. The village, built into a steep rocky slope leading to the water's edge, is a riot of different architectural influences. Renaissance Italy rubs shoulders with 18th-century England; pastel-shaded cottages stand next to a domed bell tower. All is set around a piazza and gardens.

The sheer exuberance of the place soon weaves its spell. Sir Clough, never a predictable architect, achieved what he called his 'gay, light-opera sort of approach' with a wealth of improbable, humorous touches. Huge butterflies are stuck on the entrance arch; painted-in fake windows are momentarily convincing; a Buddha figure sits in his roadside shrine; and on the seafront, a life-size concrete ship lies permanently moored to the harbour wall.

There are beautiful walks in the grounds, the paths leading through thick shrubs and woodland to a sparkling white-sand beach.

Sir Clough died in 1978, aged 94. During his lifetime the future of his creation was assured: the buildings were officially designated as being of historical and architectural interest. The village is open daily in summer.

PORTHMADOG

Porthmadog's life still revolves around its harbour. More than 100 years ago, the wharfsides would have been full of tall-masted sailing ships taking on their cargoes of slate from the mines in Blaenau Ffestiniog for destinations all over the world.

Today, modern marina-style housing mixes with traditional stone-and-slate buildings. Colourful, sleek holiday craft bob about in the harbour, though there is an echo from bygone times in the SS Garlandstone, a black-painted old sailing ketch moored to the harbour wall. Like exhibits in an adjacent wharfside building, the Garlandstone is now part of the Gwynedd Maritime Museum, which illustrates harbour life in the heyday of slate, and it is open daily in summer.

The narrow-gauge Ffestiniog Railway is another link with the past. Originally built in 1836 for slate carrying, it now carries tourists on a scenic route of nearly 14 miles through the lovely Vale of Ffestiniog into the mountains. The line operates from mid-February to November, but in February and March there are only weekend services.

Enthusiasts of Wales's little trains will also want to use the Welsh Highland Railway – open in July and August, and at weekends only in spring and early autumn. This line runs from near Porthmadog's British Rail station – initially only for a short distance, but eventually it is hoped to extend it to the Aberglaslyn Pass.

Among the craft shops in this friendly, busy town is the Porthmadog Pottery, instantly recognisable from its wall mural of heroic proportions. It is housed in a mill that used to grind corn for ships' biscuits in the days of sail. Guided tours of the workshops are available, and visitors can try to throw their own pot.

One of the many figures on the mural, William Maddocks (1774-1828), was a tireless local entrepreneur who gave Porthmadog its outstanding physical landmark, the Cob. This is a mighty, mile-long embankment which carries road traffic and the Ffestiniog Railway across the mouth of the estuary. When it was built early in the 19th century it reclaimed 7000 acres of land from the river's mud flats.

BORTH-Y-GEST

Borth-y-Gest's miniature bay, fringed with waterside houses, protects a tiny beach. A few miles farther west, Black Rock Sands stretch as far as the eye can see.

A drive through dunelands leads to an exposed, open stretch of sands which looks out across Tremadog Bay to the mountains above Harlech. The beach ends abruptly to the north-west at the rocky headland and sea caves of Graig Ddu.

Tourist information: Porthmadog 2981 (summer).

Peaks and lakes in wild Snowdonia

TOUR
98
—— 85 MILES ——

The summits of Snowdon, the Glyders and Tryfan, all rising above 3000ft, form the heart of the Snowdonia National Park. Medieval castles of Welsh princes guard the valleys.

BETWS-Y-COED

The village is beautifully set among conifer-clad crags rising steeply above the Llugwy's confluence with the Conwy. It has been a gateway to Snowdonia ever since Thomas Telford's Shrewsbury to Holyhead road was driven through North Wales early in the 19th century. Memories of the days when trail-blazing tourists relied on horse-powered transport are evoked by the National Park's visitor centre in what used to be the Royal Oak Hotel's stables.

Nearby, the Llugwy, flanked by mossy oaks, foams between glistening boulders and races beneath Pont y Pair bridge. Pont y Pair's stonework contrasts with the cast iron of Telford's graceful but untypically ornate bridge over the Conwy. Embellished with the national emblems of Wales, England, Scotland and Ireland, it was completed in 1815. The words 'This arch was constructed in the same year the Battle of Waterloo was fought' span the river as it emerges from a deep, wooded gorge. There are well marked walks in the surrounding Gwydir Forest.

Following the main road out of Betws-y-Coed, the tour passes the dramatic Swallow Falls, where the Llugwy cascades through a wooded ravine. There is a lay-by for parking and the falls are reached through a turnstile.

The 15th-century Ugly House (Ty Hyll), built of rough boulders, is a notable landmark halfway between Betws-y-Coed and Capel Curig, and is open daily in summer. One of the Gwydir Forest walks starts from a car park on the steep, narrow lane above the house.

LLYN OGWEN

The rocky flanks of Tryfan, one of Snowdonia's most impressive mountains, rise majestically above this shallow lake whose waters overflow over a small waterfall down into Nant Ffrancon.

The mountains surrounding Llyn Ogwen, itself nearly 1000ft above sea level, have attracted climbers since the 19th century, but no special equipment is needed to explore the 2 mile nature trail in Cwm Idwal National Nature Reserve. It circles Llyn Idwal, a lake visited by herons and cormorants, passes the Idwal Slabs where climbers may often be seen, and has splendid views down Nant Ffrancon to Bethesda.

Visitors with less time can take a two-minute walk from the Ogwen Cottage car park to the waterfall at the head of the valley. The vantage point also reveals the remains of an ancient bridge huddled beneath the one built by Thomas Telford.

PENRHYN CASTLE

Unlike most castles in North Wales, Penrhyn is not a ruined relic of the 13th century's Anglo-Welsh Wars. Its mighty towers and battlemented walls look strong enough to defy a medieval army, but actually date from 1820. They are the work of Thomas Hopper, a pioneer of the Norman revival style of architecture, who built Penrhyn for George Hay Dawkins Pennant. The Pennants' wealth originally came from sugar plantations in Jamaica, and was later supplemented by immense profits from the slate quarries of Bethesda.

The 5 acre castle's interior is equally elaborate and astonishing. Hopper's masterpiece, the finest building of its style and period in Britain, is notable for carved oak doors and panelling, richly decorated plasterwork and sculpted stone.

Now owned by the National Trust, the castle and its grounds are open daily from Easter to October, except on Tuesday. The castle also houses a doll museum and a railway museum. It commands fine views across the Menai Strait to Anglesey.

LLANBERIS

Snowdon's northern slopes sweep down to this small, lakeside town whose Dinorwic Quarry was one of the world's greatest sources of slate in the 19th century. The quarry closed in 1969, but terraces rising nearly 2000ft above the dark waters of Llyn Peris are reminders of the years when the 'grey gold' was shipped as far afield as South America and Japan.

Despite their size, the workings did not extend far enough to destroy Coed Dinorwig, a beautiful oak wood which climbs the steep hillside above Llyn Padarn and is part of the 350 acre Padarn Country Park. Footpaths look down on the park's Welsh Slate Museum, where machinery powered by the British mainland's biggest water wheel recalls the period when the quarry employed 3000 men.

The quarry hospital, built in 1876, is now a visitor centre. Sheltered by Coed Dinorwig's lichen-covered oaks, it overlooks the narrow-gauge Llanberis Lake Railway. Trains run along 2 miles of the track that once took slate to Port Dinorwig on the Menai Strait. Llanberis is also the starting point of the narrow-gauge Snowdon Mountain Railway, opened in 1896, whose steam-powered locomotives climb to within yards of the 3560ft summit. The track runs roughly parallel to one of Snowdon's most popular footpaths.

Oriel Eryri, a gallery of the National Museum of Wales, open daily in summer, houses tourist information centres and exhibitions concerning the Welsh environment.

As it leaves Llanberis, the tour passes ruined Dolbadarn Castle. Perched on a rocky outcrop surrounded by trees, the fortress dates from the early 13th century, and was probably built by Llywelyn the Great.

PASS OF LLANBERIS

The road up the pass climbs to nearly 1200ft, and is one of the most spectacular in Britain. Squeezed between the flanks of Snowdon, Glyder Fawr

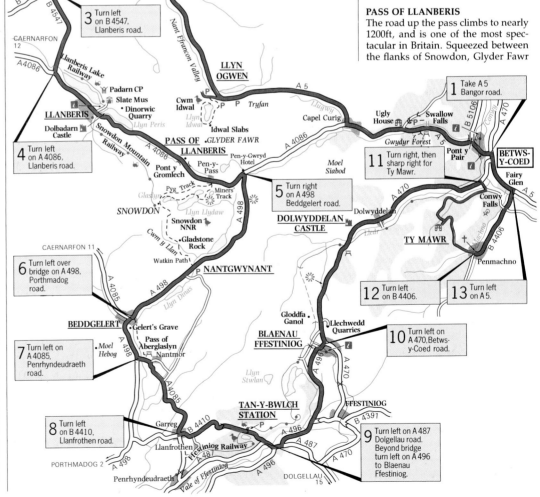

MOUNTAIN LAKE *At the north-western end of Llanberis Pass the towering peaks of Snowdonia hem in Llyn Peris, and cast dark shadows over its calm waters.*

and Y Garn, it snakes below vertical cliffs which tower above scree punctuated by boulders as big as houses. The small parking area at Pont y Gromlech, where the road crosses a turbulent stream, is an excellent vantage point from which to watch climbers tackling some of Snowdonia's classic ascents.

Many walkers follow the Pyg Track from the head of the pass to Snowdon's summit. A shorter and easier walk follows the Miners' Track nature trail in the Snowdon (Y Wyddfa) National Nature Reserve to Llyn Llydaw, a lake overlooked by buildings where copper ore was crushed until the workings were abandoned in 1916. Higher up the track, on the way to the summit, is Glaslyn, a lonely lake below the crags where King Arthur is said to have died in battle.

The road sweeps down from Pen-y-Pass to the Pen-y-Gwryd Hotel, where the future Lord Hunt and his team met to plan the first successful assault on Mount Everest in 1953. There are breathtaking views of Snowdon's jagged peaks and ridges before the route plunges into Nantgwynant.

NANTGWYNANT

In this lovely wooded valley the Watkin Path starts its 3300ft climb to Snowdon's summit. The last part of the path involves a scramble up steep slopes of treacherous scree, but the first section is a pleasant exploration of Cwm y Llan, a valley in the Snowdon National Nature Reserve. Welsh Mountain sheep and wild

goats share the valley with ravens, ring ouzels, choughs and pied flycatchers.

The path was established by Sir Edward Watkin, a wealthy Victorian businessman. It was officially opened by William Gladstone in 1892, when the statesman was 83. He walked up to Gladstone Rock, where a plaque commemorates the ceremony.

BEDDGELERT

The dramatic beauty of Beddgelert's setting is equalled by few British villages. It stands where three valleys meet, and looks southwards towards the gorge-like Pass of Aberglaslyn. Snowdon rises to the north, while 2566ft Moel Hebog dominates the west and is seen at its best from the riverside path to Gelert's Grave.

According to legend, Gelert was a dog owned by Llywelyn the Great, who united most of Wales during the 13th century. He left Gelert to guard his son, but returned to find the dog covered in blood and the child missing. Gelert was killed before Llywelyn realised that his heir was alive. The faithful hound had saved the baby from a wolf whose body was discovered nearby. The old story was embroidered by an 18th-century innkeeper anxious to foster Beddgelert's tourist trade. He and his friends were responsible for the 'grave'.

TAN-Y-BWLCH STATION

This picturesque little station and vantage point on the narrow-gauge Ffestiniog Railway has views across the Vale of Ffestiniog and is the

highest point of the short but fascinating Coed Llyn Mair nature trail in Coedydd Maentwrog National Nature Reserve. Oaks more than 200 years old shelter the walk down to the lakeside.

BLAENAU FFESTINIOG

Vast accumulations of slate, climbed by zigzag paths and near-vertical tramways, dwarf this small town. Slate is still quarried and mined, though on a much smaller scale than in the past, and two old-established sites are open to visitors.

At Llechwedd, Welsh slate's story is told on film by the actor and author Emlyn Williams, and special trains tour caverns where tableaux depict working conditions around the end of the last century. Gloddfa Ganol, once the world's most extensive slate mine, has walks through some of its 42 miles of tunnels. Both give visitors an opportunity to watch the ancient craft of splitting slate, and are open daily from Easter to October.

Slate was the reason why the narrow-gauge Ffestiniog Railway was built between Blaenau Ffestiniog and Porthmadog in 1836, when power was provided by a combination of horses and gravity. The line switched to steam in the 1860s, closed in 1946, and was acquired by enthusiasts eight years later.

Huffing and puffing up the wooded Vale of Ffestiniog, the colourful little trains blend industrial history with superb scenery. They run from mid-February to November, but only at weekends in February and March.

DOLWYDDELAN CASTLE

North of Blaenau Ffestiniog, the road reaches 1263ft at the Crimea Pass, named after a pub built in the 1870s when Britain's seventh-longest railway tunnel was built. The navvies were too rowdy for the locals, so their tavern was closed and demolished. Its site is now a car park with splendid views over a wild landscape overlooked by Moel Siabod.

Lower down the valley, the Lledr flows close to the crag from which ruined Dolwyddelan Castle's square keep still dominates its beautiful surroundings. Like the majority of native Welsh castles, Dolwyddelan was intended to command a strategic route through the mountains. It was almost certainly the birthplace of Llywelyn the Great in 1173.

TY MAWR

A narrow, gated lane climbs from the Lledr's wooded valley to Ty Mawr, the sturdy little stone house where William Morgan was born in 1545. He completed the first Welsh translation of the Bible in 1588 and later became Bishop of St Asaph. Sheltered by high hills, Ty Mawr is one of the few buildings on the road to Penmachno, where Bishop Morgan is commemorated by a window in the church. Ty Mawr, owned by the National Trust, is open daily, except on Mondays and Saturdays, from Easter to October.

Tourist information: Betws-y-Coed 426/665 (summer); Llanberis 870765 (summer); Blaenau Ffestiniog 830360 (summer).

163

Castles guarding Clwyd's green hills

Soft green hills rise between the fertile Vale of Clwyd and the Dee's broad, sandy estuary. Ruined castles recall border wars, and a mountain top gives magnificent views.

DENBIGH

This ancient market town is clustered on a steep hillside overlooking the fertile Vale of Clwyd, with views beyond to the smooth Clwydian hills. Above the town stands the ruined castle, a limestone fortress that became a major border stronghold after Edward I defeated Llywelyn the Last in 1282. The castle has a magnificent gatehouse with three towers.

Near the castle stands the shell of Leicester's church, begun by the Earl of Leicester in 1579 and intended as a replacement for St Asaph Cathedral. However, the project ran short of money and was abandoned after Leicester's death in 1588.

Castle Hill slopes down from the 13th-century Burgess Gate to the town centre whose layout has changed little since the Middle Ages. High Street, enlivened by a market

every Wednesday, is overlooked by the 16th-century County Hall. In the neighbouring Bull Hotel, a staircase, decorated with carved hands recalls the time when Denbigh was noted for glove-making.

Denbigh was the birthplace in 1841 of the explorer Henry Morton Stanley. He was born out of wedlock, as John Rowlands, and changed his name before being sent to Africa by the *New York Herald* on a long, hazardous quest which ended with the famous greeting: 'Doctor Livingstone, I presume.' Stanley was later knighted by Queen Victoria, and died in 1904.

On the outskirts of Denbigh stands the ruined church of a 13th-century Carmelite friary.

ST ASAPH

Though little more than a village, St Asaph is technically a city containing Britain's smallest cathedral – founded in AD 560 by St Kentigern. The cathedral is dignified and impressive despite being smaller than many a parish church. The present building was begun at the end of the 13th century, after two predecessors had been reduced to ruins during the Anglo-Welsh Wars.

Inside the cathedral is a copy of the first Welsh Bible, published in 1588. The translation was made by William Morgan, Bishop of St Asaph from 1601 until his death in 1604. Statues of

Bishop Morgan and other translators stand in the niches of an elaborate Victorian monument in the grounds of the cathedral.

BODELWYDDAN CHURCH

Rich in tracery, ornate pinnacles and delicate flying buttresses, the exquisite Victorian Church of St Margaret has a slender limestone spire that spears 202ft above the Vale of Clwyd. Completed in 1860, it is known as the 'Marble Church' because it contains 14 different varieties of marble from Anglesey, Ireland, France, Sicily and elsewhere.

A font of white Italian marble, given by Sir Hugh Williams, depicts his elder daughter kneeling with a shell while the younger stands beside her. The oak lectern, representing an eagle perched on a crag, is a superb example of the 19th-century woodcarver's art.

In the churchyard among the war graves are those of five Canadian soldiers who died in a riot in 1919. It flared up because the troops, anxious to get home, were frustrated by a series of postponed sailings.

RHUDDLAN

The pancake-flat road from Bodelwyddan to Rhuddlan crosses a tract of what was once desolate fenland. It became suitable for farming after Edward I's engineers spent about three years diverting and canalising the Clwyd between Rhuddlan and Rhyl. The king's motives were in fact military, because he wanted to make

a navigable link between the sea and his new castle at Rhuddlan which was the hub of England's power in North Wales. The castle is now a ruin. Its walls and drum towers stand on a grassy plateau above the river and make a fine sight from Rhuddlan's 16th-century bridge.

A five-minute walk upstream leads to Twthill, a steep-sided mound where William the Conqueror built the present castle's predecessor.

In High Street stands the old Parliament Building, now a private house. Here, Edward I is believed to have held the parliament which passed the Statute of Rhuddlan in 1284. It gave Wales an English-style system of local government and created shires which retained their identities for nearly 700 years.

BODRHYDDAN HALL

In this handsome mansion of mellow red brick is preserved the charter by which Edward I granted borough status to Rhuddlan in 1284. The charter is one of a rich variety of treasures collected by the Rowley-Conwy family whose links with Bodrhyddan go back at least 700 years.

Suits of armour dating from the 15th century share the Front Hall with swords, muskets, crossbows and a Civil War helmet dented by a shot. The Egyptian Room contains the mummified body of a priest who died more than 3000 years ago.

Other highlights include a pair of gloves given to the family by Charles I, carved panels from a galleon of the Spanish Armada wrecked off Anglesey, Hepplewhite chairs and the dress sword presented to Conwy Shipley by the Patriotic Fund for capturing a French warship in 1804. One of the many family portraits was painted by Sir Joshua Reynolds.

The gardens contain a small pavilion built by Inigo Jones in 1612.

DYSERTH

This little village at the foot of the Clwydian hills is notable for what Dr Samuel Johnson described as 'a very striking cataract' when he visited Dyserth in 1774. The waterfall tumbles 60ft down a wooded, limestone cliff opposite the Red Lion Hotel.

A short detour north of Dyserth leads to Graig Fawr, a craggy limestone peak 500ft high. A footpath leads to the summit, from where there are magnificent views along the coast to the Great Orme whose cliffs tower above Llandudno. Blackthorn, sycamore and wild cherry grow on the north-eastern slopes.

The tour continues through Prestatyn, a popular seaside resort, before meeting the Dee's broad estuary where glistening low-tide sandbanks sprawl towards the Wirral peninsula.

GREENFIELD

From this little hamlet, a footpath leads from a car park up a lovely wooded valley to Holywell, 1 mile away. The valley is full of relics from the heyday of the Industrial Revolution, when it echoed to the clang of water-powered factories producing copper, brass, cotton goods, paper

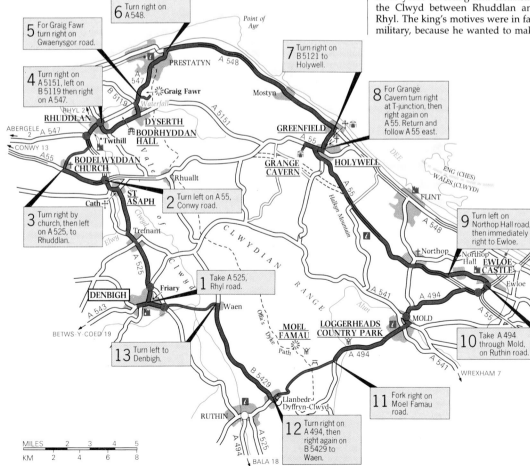

SEAT OF POWER *Edward I built Rhuddlan Castle in 1277-82 as part of his chain of castles designed to suppress the Welsh, and held court beside the Clwyd for three years.*

BODRHYDDAN HALL *A house has stood on the site of the hall for some 700 years, but the present building with its ornamented garden dates from the 1700s.*

WHITE WATER *A stream foams and cascades over a cliff at Dyserth.*

SHINING SPIRE *Magnesium limestone makes Bodelwyddan church gleam.*

and flannel. Its decline began in the 1830s, when silt started choking the Dee estuary. The walk from Greenfield follows the track of an abandoned railway past ponds, weirs, millraces and old buildings.

The Abbey Farm Museum contains agricultural implements and working machinery. An audio-visual presentation tells the story of the valley since the 7th century. Nearby stand the ruins of Basingwerk Abbey, a Cistercian house founded in 1131 for pilgrims visiting St Winefride's Well in Holywell.

The woodlands around the valley attract many butterflies in summer, and mute swans and moorhens share their year-round homes with tufted ducks and other winter migrants.

HOLYWELL
This workaday town is an unlikely setting for one of the most romantic of all Welsh legends and a holy well to which pilgrims have travelled for more than 1300 years. The legend tells how Caradoc, a local chieftain, decapitated Winefride, the daughter of a prince, after she firmly resisted his advances. A spring appeared where her head fell to the ground. Winefride's head was replaced by her uncle, St Beuno, whose prayers brought the maiden back to life. St Winefride's Well became known as the 'Lourdes of Wales', and has been credited with many cures.

The spring flows into a stone-lined pool, sheltered by the crypt of a chapel built by Lady Margaret Beaufort. Her son became Henry VII in 1485. The crypt's Victorian statue of St Winefride has a thin line round the neck to show where her head was severed by Caradoc's sword.

GRANGE CAVERN
The cavern, 2½ acres in area and some 100ft below the surface, was quarried for its limestone in the 19th century. During the Second World War it was used to store 11,000 tons of bombs. Today it houses a military museum, with more than 70 military vehicles and displays of mortars, shells, mines, badges, buttons and medals.

The museum is open daily from Easter to the end of October, and at weekends in February and March.

EWLOE CASTLE
The deep, secluded valley of the Wepre Brook, thick with noble oaks, makes a magical if puzzling site for a castle. Most medieval strongholds were built to dominate their surroundings. Ewloe hides in its valley and is not visible until the end of the five-minute walk from the road.

The castle was almost certainly begun by Llywelyn the Great at the start of the 13th century, and its D-shaped tower is typical of the period. Ewloe ceased to be important after Edward I gained control of north-east Wales in 1277 and built the first of his many coastal castles at Flint.

LOGGERHEADS COUNTRY PARK
This 67 acre country park borders the Afon Alun, beneath the conifer-clad slopes of Moel Famau. Its most dramatic feature is a lofty limestone cliff which forms part of a 1½ mile nature trail and has fine views of the Clwydian hills. In summer the cliff top is speckled with common rockrose, wild thyme, blood-red cranesbill and other lime-loving plants. Jaunty

little dippers search for food in the river whose energies were diverted in the 1820s to pump water from lead mines lower down the valley. The 'leat', or channel, has not been used since 1845, but traces survive near the information centre. Today, a corn mill in working order is driven by the river.

MOEL FAMAU COUNTRY PARK
This 2000 acre country park takes its name from the 1817ft Moel Famau whose summit is reached by a footpath through woodland where skylarks and ring ouzels abound. Views from the summit range from Snowdonia to the Isle of Man, the Lake District and the Pennines.

Moel Famau is capped with the base of the Jubilee Tower planned to mark the 50th anniversary of George III's reign. The foundation stone was laid in 1810, but the tower never reached its intended 150ft and collapsed in a storm in 1862.

Tourist information: Holywell 780144 (summer); Mold 59331 (summer); Colwyn Bay 31731.

169

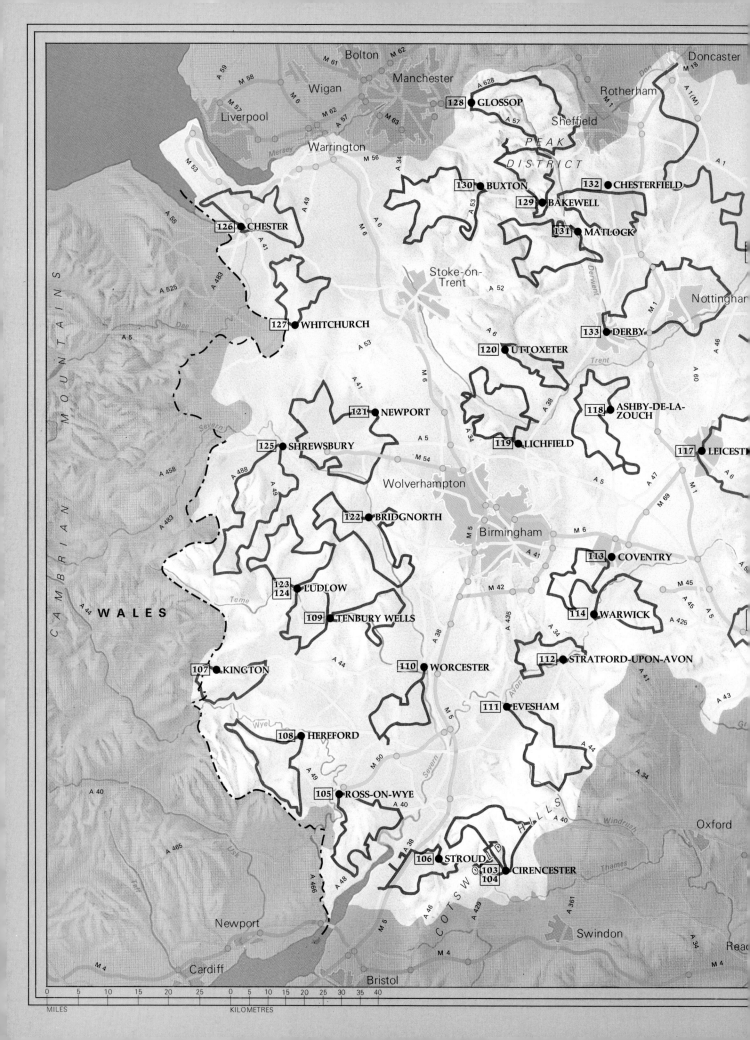

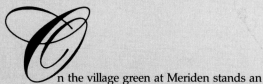

On the village green at Meriden stands an ancient cross which, it is claimed, marks the centre of England. The countryside surrounding it justly claims to be the heart of England – a heart whose arteries are two of England's loveliest rivers, the Avon and the Severn, pulsing through fertile valleys. On the south-western and eastern fringes their valleys are sheltered by gentle hills: the Malverns, rising like a miniature mountain range from a flat landscape, and the rugged limestone uplands of the Cotswolds. They embrace historic country towns such as Cirencester, Worcester and Evesham, and a host of villages brimming with old-world charm.

The Avon, the river that Shakespeare knew, laps the mighty walls of Warwick Castle, then flows through quiet meadows to join the Severn at Tewkesbury. The Severn loops around Shrewsbury and cuts through the Shropshire Hills before heading south through the Ironbridge Gorge, where an open-air museum re-creates the days when the Industrial Revolution was forged there. Farmlands and forest roll towards the Welsh border, with valley orchards that form a sea of colour in blossom time. The Cheshire Plain, dotted with black-and-white houses, descends to the estuary of the Dee, and eastwards are the Derbyshire dales and the crags of the Peak District, whose bubbling springs brought fame and prosperity to towns such as Buxton and Matlock.

To the east, the rolling cornfields of Leicestershire surround a hilltop where, in 1485, Henry Tudor vanquished Richard III and changed the course of English history. Country lanes weave a tranquil circle round busy cities such as Leicester and Derby. The M1 carves a straight line across countryside which can be enjoyed more fully by the motorist with time to spare; cross-country tours starting from Northampton and Newark-on-Trent offer alternatives to the bustle of the motorway, taking to quiet byways that link peaceful villages, great country houses, tree-studded deer parks and romantic castles.

6 ● STROUD Number of tour and starting point
Route of tour

A Roman trail through the Cotswolds

TOUR
103

— 60 MILES —

From a Roman regional capital to the edge of the Cotswold Hills this tour follows the line of a Roman road. Around stretch fields farmed by the Romans from estates such as Chedworth.

CIRENCESTER

The mellow old market town has some houses dating from the 17th century and many elegant Georgian buildings. But they all overlie the much older Roman town of Corinium, which was second only to London in size. Major roads radiated from the town; Ermin Way and Foss Way form the basis for modern roads followed on this tour.

The remains of an amphitheatre are seen in a grassy hollow mound called the Bullring to the south-west of the town, and the Corinium Museum in Park Street contains a wealth of Roman material. Several outstanding mosaic floors have been excavated at Cirencester and re-laid in the museum; the Four Seasons mosaic provides the floor for a reconstructed Roman dining room.

Dominating the Market Place is the Church of St John the Baptist, the largest parish church in Gloucestershire. The three-storey porch was the town hall until the 18th

century, and it has a dole table where bread was distributed to the poor.

The poet Alexander Pope helped the 1st Earl Bathurst in the early 18th century to lay out the huge park of Cirencester House. The house is not open to the public, but walkers can roam the park.

PAINSWICK

One of the Cotswolds' loveliest small towns, Painswick grew up in the 17th and 18th centuries as an almost self-sufficient community. The pale cream stone of its handsome merchants' houses was quarried on Painswick Hill, while the stream at the foot of the town powered cloth mills that brought the town its prosperity. A local family of outstanding stonemasons created the ornately carved table-tombs in the churchyard, which are framed by a regiment of immaculately clipped yew trees.

PRINKNASH ABBEY

On opposite sides of a bowl-shaped park on the edge of the Cotswold escarpment, a venerable old manor house faces a starkly modern building in radiantly golden stone. These are the old and new monasteries of Prinknash.

Visitors are welcome at the new monastery, where Benedictine monks manage the estate. Clay dug from the foundations of the new building was used to start a pottery. This became so successful that assistants from outside the community are now employed; visitors can watch the potters

at work from a public viewing gallery. There is a 9 acre bird park, with peacocks, golden pheasants and Australian black swans. The wooded park has views to Gloucester and the Severn Vale. The old mansion house, which is not open, dates mainly from about 1514.

COOPER'S HILL

Half a mile north of Prinknash a lay-by gives access to Cooper's Hill, near the scar of a quarry on the wooded slopes. A nature trail leads through the woods, and an observation point gives magnificent views through the beech trees down to the Severn Vale.

A maypole marks the summit of Cooper's Hill. From there on Spring Bank Holiday Monday a large cheese is rolled down the precipitous slopes with local youths in pursuit.

CRICKLEY HILL

Three trails lead through the public park of Crickley Hill. A geology trail follows the edge of the escarpment, where quarrying has exposed the formations of limestone rock; an archaeology trail explores the Iron Age promontory fort; and an ecology trail leads through scrub woodland.

For many, however, it will be enough just to sit and absorb the stunning views and enjoy the air filled with the sound of skylarks.

WITHINGTON

The main street leads down through high banks, and tall trees cast dappled shade on old stone houses. Yew trees

encircle the graveyard of St Michael's Church, which has a fine Norman doorway with zigzag mouldings decorated with flower motifs.

Below the church a footpath runs between stone walls below a pleasant garden and into the meadows through which the Coln runs; they are ablaze with buttercups in summer.

CHEDWORTH ROMAN VILLA

It is not difficult to imagine why the Romans chose to build a country villa in this delightful spot, on the gentle slopes above the little Coln. A spring still trickles into a basin which the Romans lined with cement.

Excavations beginning in 1865 revealed three wings of the villa, which was first occupied around AD 120 as the centre of an agricultural estate owned probably by a Romanised Briton. Its rooms included two elaborate bathhouses with mosaic floors and hollow channels beneath them, forming the hypocaust through which hot air circulated from furnaces.

A museum displays finds from the site, including stone carvings, coins and a pair of iron shears similar to the hand shears still used today for sheepshearing. The Roman villa is open daily except Monday from March to October, and at certain times in winter.

NORTHLEACH

The long High Street threads between rows of ancient stone cottages, some dating from the 17th century and having half-timbered first storeys overhanging the pavement. Several coaching inns survive from the days when Northleach was on the main coach road between London and Gloucester. Above the small market

WEALTH FROM WOOL *Bow-windowed shops in Cirencester's Dollar Street – once the site of a Dole Hall – date back to the 17th century, when the town was a wool centre.*

CIRENCESTER PARK *The view from the tower of St John's Church peers over the yew hedge surrounding Lord Bathurst's home.*

ON THE TILES *Spring is depicted in mosaic as a girl with a bird and a basket of flowers, at Chedworth Roman Villa.*

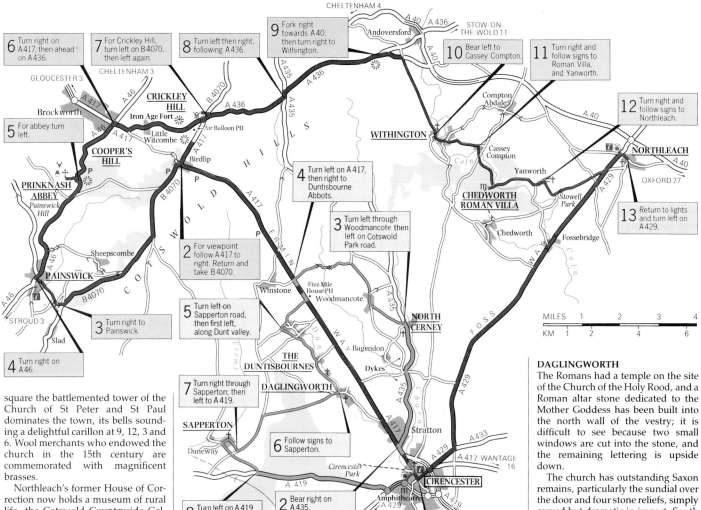

6 Turn right on A417, then ahead on A436.

7 For Crickley Hill, turn left on B4070, then left again.

8 Turn left then right, following A436.

9 Fork right towards A40; then turn right to Withington.

10 Bear left to Cassey Compton.

11 Turn right and follow signs to Roman Villa, and Yanworth.

12 Turn right and follow signs to Northleach.

5 For abbey turn left.

13 Return to lights and turn left on A429.

4 Turn left on A417, then right to Duntisbourne Abbots.

3 Turn left through Woodmancote then left on Cotswold Park road.

2 For viewpoint follow A417 to right. Return and take B4070.

5 Turn left on Sapperton road, then first left, along Dunt valley.

3 Turn right to Painswick.

4 Turn right on A46.

7 Turn right through Sapperton; then left to A419.

6 Follow signs to Sapperton.

8 Turn left on A419 to Cirencester.

2 Bear right on A435.

1 Take Gloucester road A417.

GLOUCESTER 3 · CHELTENHAM 3 · CHELTENHAM 4 · STOW-ON-THE-WOLD 11 · OXFORD 27 · STROUD 3

CRICKLEY HILL · Iron Age Fort · Brockworth · Little Witcombe · Air Balloon PH · Birdlip · COOPER'S HILL · PRINKNASH ABBEY · Painswick Hill · Sheepscombe · PAINSWICK · Slad · Andoversford · WITHINGTON · Compton Abdale · Cassey Compton · Yanworth · CHEDWORTH ROMAN VILLA · Chedworth · Stowell Park · Fossebridge · NORTHLEACH · Winstone · Five Mile House PH · Woodmancote · THE DUNTISBOURNES · DAGLINGWORTH · SAPPERTON · Daneway · Bagendon · Dykes · NORTH CERNEY · Stratton · Cirencester Park · CIRENCESTER · Amphitheatre · A417 WANTAGE 16 · CHIPPENHAM 20 · SWINDON 13 · COTSWOLD HILLS · ERMIN WAY · FOSS WAY

MILES 1 2 3 4
KM 1 2 4 6

---

square the battlemented tower of the Church of St Peter and St Paul dominates the town, its bells sounding a delightful carillon at 9, 12, 3 and 6. Wool merchants who endowed the church in the 15th century are commemorated with magnificent brasses.

Northleach's former House of Correction now holds a museum of rural life, the Cotswold Countryside Collection. There are displays of farm implements and country crafts.

Tourist information: Cirencester 4180; Painswick 812569; Northleach 715 (summer).

TOUR 104

─── 20 MILES ───

Villages slumber in the valleys of the Churn, the Dunt and the Frome. Above them stretch the wolds, where sheep graze between dry-stone walls and beech thickets crown the slopes.

NORTH CERNEY

An inn and a millhouse border the Churn, and behind them the village climbs the hillside, with pretty cottages bordering a tiny green. The Church of All Saints has an unusual saddleback tower, gabled like a house, and inside there are exquisite details from many periods. These include a Norman doorway, medieval glass and a pulpit carved around 1480 from a single piece of stone.

At Bagendon Dykes, 1 mile south, are the remains of the Iron Age settlement which was the capital of the Dobunni tribe at the time of the Roman invasion.

THE DUNTISBOURNES

Two villages and four hamlets, which look as old as time, are strung along the valley of a bubbling stream called the Dunt, after a Saxon chief who

lived in the area. There are several fords across the stream where ducks dabble in the shelter of ancient farm buildings, with stone walls, stone steps, stone troughs and mushroom-shaped staddle stones that were used for raising hayricks to keep them dry.

At Duntisbourne Abbots the Norman Church of St Peter looks downhill past old cottages towards a tiny lane where drivers splash along the bed of the Dunt for 50yds. Carters used to clean the wheels of their wagons here; walkers today have the option of a raised path at the side.

The lane, and the drier road along the valley side, lead to Duntisbourne Leer, a tiny cluster of stone houses and farm barns, with pigeon nesting holes in their gables, round a ford. The hamlet is named after its one-time owners, the abbey of Lire in Normandy.

From the next tiny hamlet of Middle Duntisbourne, which has its own ford, a path leads through woods parallel with the road to the little Church of St Michael at Duntisbourne Rouse, which was standing before the Normans came. The herringbone stonework on the outside of the north wall and the simple doorway are Saxon. There are tiny stained-glass windows, and an organ given in memory of the author Katherine Mansfield by her three sisters, one of whom lived nearby.

DAGLINGWORTH

The Romans had a temple on the site of the Church of the Holy Rood, and a Roman altar stone dedicated to the Mother Goddess has been built into the north wall of the vestry; it is difficult to see because two small windows are cut into the stone, and the remaining lettering is upside down.

The church has outstanding Saxon remains, particularly the sundial over the door and four stone reliefs, simply carved but dramatic in impact. South of the church a path leads to the lower end of the village where the old manor house has a round dovecote in the garden.

SAPPERTON

Perched on the steep side of a ridge facing the River Frome's 'Golden Valley' – so called because of the colour of its beech woods in autumn – Sapperton is attractive for walkers, but is also a place of pilgrimage for canal and crafts enthusiasts. The 2¼ mile Sapperton tunnel – now abandoned – was cut through the hill in 1789 to convey the canal that linked the Thames with the Severn. The classical eastern entrance to the canal, at Coates, has been restored.

At the turn of the century the village was the home of Ernest Gimson and the brothers Ernest and Sidney Barnsley, who were architects, furniture makers and leaders of the Arts and Crafts Movement inspired by William Morris. Gimson had his workshops in Daneway House, a 14th-century manor across the valley. The group designed several houses in the village, following the style of its earlier 17th-century cottages, and are buried in St Kenelm's churchyard.

The church is decorated with powerful Elizabethan and Jacobean carved oak panelling and other woodwork brought from a manor house, now demolished, which stood to the north of the church.

Tourist information: Cirencester 4180.

Forest and vale beside the Severn

TOUR
105
— 67 MILES —

The Forest of Dean forms a great triangle bordered by the Wye and Severn. Through the woods rumble the trains of a restored steam railway, while a castle stands on a green hill.

ROSS-ON-WYE
Perched on sandstone cliffs above the placid Wye, Ross is a town of narrow, winding streets. At every turn, tall black-and-white buildings come into view. The impressive sandstone Market House stands above an arcaded market place, and there is a pleasing jumble of shop-front styles ranging from Georgian to modern. The alms-houses in Church Street date from 1575.

Wye Street curves down steeply to the river bank where there is an inn, the Hope and Anchor; wide stretches of grass line the water's edge. This spot affords a charming view of the town, with its church spire soaring above the trees, red-sandstone cliffs, and shimmering river.

MAY HILL
Crowning this 971ft high hilltop are tall pines planted in 1887 to commemorate Queen Victoria's Golden Jubilee. More were planted in 1977 and in 1980 to honour the Queen's Silver Jubilee and the Queen Mother's 80th birthday. A footpath leads to the top, with superb views over the Forest of Dean and, on a clear day, as far as the mountains of Wales.

WESTBURY COURT GARDEN
This water garden laid out in the late 17th century is in the Dutch style, with two canals set among formal flowerbeds, trim lawns and precision-cut box hedges. It is the earliest of its kind remaining in England.

At the head of the Long Canal is the Tall Pavilion, consisting of an upper storey with high windows above a colonnaded porch. A cupola on the roof was intended to give visitors a bird's-eye view of the gardens and panoramic views across the River Severn. The gardens are open most days in summer.

NEWNHAM
A car park at the northern end of the town extends to the water's edge of the Severn, where it loops in a dramatic U-bend. This is an excellent point for seeing the sometimes spectacular Severn bore, a tidal wave which rushes up the river's estuary several times a year.

LITTLEDEAN HALL
Excavations in the grounds of this lovely house have shown that this was the site of a Roman temple built over a spring. The house itself has Roman stonework in its foundations. It is not known whether it was put there by the Romans or taken later from the temple site, but the house dates back at least to Saxon times and developed from Norman times to the early 14th century. Littledean Hall is open daily in summer.

SUTTON BOTTOM
In this part of the Forest of Dean the road goes through a deep, pine-clad valley belonging to the Forestry Commission. There is a car park and picnic place, and a forest drive leads up to Blaize Bailey, with fine views across the River Severn.

DEAN HERITAGE MUSEUM
The 19th-century Camp Mill, standing by the millpond in Soudley, houses a museum devoted to the life and history of the Forest of Dean. Before its acquisition by the Dean Heritage Museum Trust, the building served in turn as an iron foundry, sawmill, brush factory, corn mill, leather-board mill and car dump.

Now the restored mill looks much as it did 100 years ago, and includes workshops where woodturning, pottery and other crafts may be seen. It is open daily all the year.

DEAN FOREST RAILWAY
A 1½ mile railway line between Lydney and Norchard Steam Centre once again carries the trains of the Dean Forest Railway. The Steam Centre has a fascinating collection of locomotives, rolling stock and railway buildings, including a complete station from the old Severn and Wye Railway and a ticket office from the Bristol to Weston-super-Mare line.

The centre is open daily, and trains run on Sundays in summer.

CLEARWELL CAVES
Deep in the limestone beneath the Forest of Dean lies a world of caverns and passages hacked out over thousands of years in man's quest for metal. Long before the Romans came, ancient Britons worked the iron mines in the forest, and at Clearwell a honeycomb of passages and vast chambers can be explored.

One cavern, called Barbecue Churn, is sometimes used for social functions and will comfortably hold 500 people. In Old Churn the pick marks of old-time miners can be seen, and one of the men, dressed in 14th-century mining clothes, is said to haunt the cavern. The caves are open to the public in summer every day except Mondays.

GOODRICH CASTLE
High on a green hill above the Wye stand crumbling towers and walls that, from afar, look like a child's sandcastle partly washed away by an incoming tide. The red-sandstone fortress was built to guard a river crossing made by the old Roman road from Gloucester to Caerleon, and no doubt in Norman times it did so very well. But the guns of Cromwell's army breached its walls, and even the deep moat cut into solid rock could not stop the castle surrendering in 1646.

Tourist information: Ross-on-Wye 62768; (Cinderford) Dean 22581.

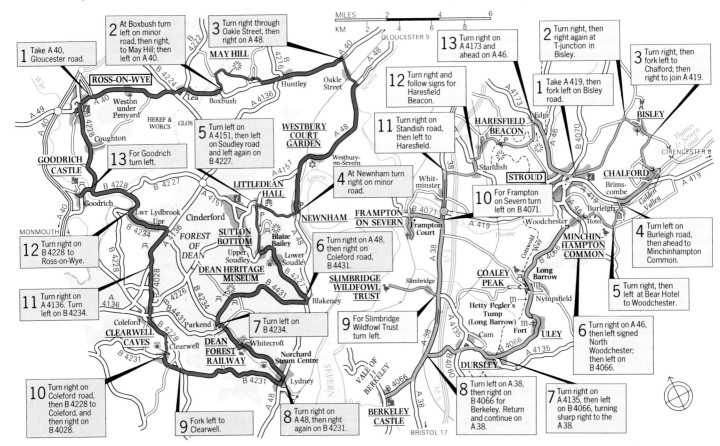

BORDER RIVER *At Lower Lydbrook the gentle Wye flows through a misty valley, forming the boundary between Gloucestershire and Hereford and Worcester.*

TOUR 106

55 MILES

At the heart of the southern Cotswolds the glorious pale gold limestone is everywhere, in humble cottages and in the graceful Georgian houses of the old wool towns.

STROUD
Where five deep valleys meet, Stroud, on the banks of the Frome, prospered from the wool trade, with its mills and dyeworks stretching for miles beside the river. Once there were 150 of them, and though today only a handful remain, Stroud is the only place in the Cotswolds where textiles are made on any scale.

The centre of the town is modern, with a large shopping area, but the Old Town Hall in The Shambles is late 16th century, and another civic building, the Subscription Rooms, dates from 1833.

BISLEY
Set high on a windswept hill, Bisley was once a market town and textile centre, but its remoteness led to its decline at the time of the Industrial Revolution. Its narrow streets are lined with grey-stone, gabled houses, and at the top of George Street stands the 17th-century Bear Inn.

CHALFORD
Houses clinging to the hillside in steep terraces give the village an alpine appearance. The disused Thames-Severn Canal runs through the valley, and alongside it is the River Frome, lined with old mill buildings – some now part of an industrial estate. A stone-built 'roundhouse' was once a canal-worker's house.

MINCHINHAMPTON COMMON
The road to the common climbs and twists steeply, with houses perched precariously on the sides of the valley below. The common stands high on a ridge, with superb views over the Frome valley. The land, now National Trust property, was given to Minchinhampton by Henry VIII. Some of it is still used for cattle grazing. Grass-covered ridges, early earthworks known as The Bulwarks, extend down to Dane Bottom, where Saxons defeated the Danes.

COALEY PEAK
A large car park and picnic area afford splendid views from this windy peak. Below lies the Vale of Berkeley, with the golden strand of the Severn.

The peak is part of the limestone escarpment known as Frocester Hill, mostly owned by the National Trust and preserved as a nature reserve. The Cotswold Way runs along the top of the ridge and nearby is the Nympsfield long barrow, a Neolithic burial mound.

ULEY
A village of Cotswold stone, set on the side of a hill, is built around a small, triangular green overlooked by the Crown Inn. The main street winds down into the Ewelme valley, and on either side are cottages and houses where little front gardens are bright with flowers in spring and summer.

A footpath leads along the side of St Giles's churchyard and then climbs the steep, wooded hill to Uley Bury Fort, an Iron Age hill-fort.

DURSLEY
French and Flemish weavers once lived in this pleasant town beneath the Cam valley's wooded hills. The prosperity of the weaving days has left its mark in many fine Georgian buildings.

The Market House dates from 1738 and has an upper floor above a stone-columned arcade decked with hanging flower baskets. The Old Bell Hotel in Long Street and two banks are also early 18th century.

BERKELEY CASTLE
Few people can have enjoyed a more stately, majestic and romantic home than the succession of Berkeleys who have lived in Berkeley Castle for more than 800 years. Its walls, turrets and towers of rough-hewn sandstone and pale grey puffstone are at the same time both grim and hauntingly beautiful, especially when the late afternoon sun casts purple shadows and picks out the delicate hues of the stones.

These are walls that shelter a long, colourful and sometimes gruesome history. Here, in 1327, Edward II was imprisoned in a cell close to the castle dungeon, a hideous device consisting of a deep pit into which rotting carcasses and half-alive prisoners were thrown. It was thought that the stench would overpower the prisoner in the adjoining cell, but Edward survived for five months before being tortured to death by his jailers.

The castle has its more pleasant sides, particularly the magnificent Long Drawing Room with its gilded furniture, the Picture Gallery with seascapes by Van de Velde, and the magnificent oak-beamed Great Hall, 62ft long and 32ft wide.

Berkeley Castle is open to the public most days in summer.

SLIMBRIDGE WILDFOWL TRUST
Here, it is claimed, can be seen the world's finest collection of wildfowl in their natural surroundings, the wetlands. In the pens set among shrubbery walks are waterfowl from many parts of the world. The most spectacular are the flamingos, with rich pink plumage seen against a background of pampas grass in the South American pen. There are rare Hawaiian geese, Bewick's swans and white-fronted geese.

In one corner of the grounds is a picnic area, and nearby is the 51ft Acrow Tower with superb views across the Severn.

FRAMPTON ON SEVERN
This charming riverside village is set around a vast village green – large enough for three ponds and a cricket ground, and with room enough to spare for walking. The ducks on the ponds are sometimes joined by peacocks drinking at the water's edge – they come from the grounds of Frampton Court, which stands behind trees on the eastern side of the green. The building dates from 1731.

Most of the local cottages and houses, as well as the Bell Inn, are Georgian. At one end of the green are some pretty timber-framed cottages leaning at odd angles, like playing-card houses on the point of collapse.

HARESFIELD BEACON
From the 713ft summit of this National Trust property there are views extending across the Severn valley to the Brecon Beacons in Wales, and as far south as Exmoor in Devon. A footpath from the car park by the road leads to the summit.

Tourist information: Stroud 4252.

Down the Wye to a Golden Valley

TOUR
107
——— 40 MILES ———

Rolling wooded ridges separate the tributaries of the River Wye into valleys of orchards and meadows. Medieval villages are built in the black-and-white style typical of the Welsh Marches.

KINGTON

High Street and Bridge Street thread their way between the close-packed buildings of this small market town, and narrow courtyards and alleyways are vestiges of the town's medieval gridiron street pattern. In the courtyard beside the Burton Hotel, the Old Gospel House has close associations with John Wesley, who is said to have written many of his sermons there. From the same courtyard a path winds to the River Arrow, emerging beside a fine Georgian mill-owner's house; the mill is still in partial use.

A lane opposite the church leads to Hergest Croft gardens, noted for azaleas and rhododendrons. Beyond the bypass a narrow road leads up to a fine viewpoint on Bradnor Hill.

PEMBRIDGE

Few modern buildings intrude into the lanes of this tiny medieval village. Eight immense ancient timbers support the roof of the 16th-century market hall. The nearby New Inn, itself over 600 years old, is a black-and-white timber-framed building.

On a slight hill above the market place, the sparse remains of a motte-and-bailey castle adjoin the churchyard of the 14th-century St Mary's Church. The separate bell tower was used as a place of refuge during the Welsh border wars.

Along the one short main street, worn flagstone steps lead steeply from street level to the front doors of tiny gabled cottages. The eastern end of the village is marked by the neat Trafford Hospital, dating from 1686, while at the west end one of the oldest and most striking buildings in the village is now an antiques saleroom. On all sides meadows and orchards hem the village in like a green sea around a black-and-white island.

EARDISLAND

The River Arrow meanders through this sleepy village, along whose back lanes and footpaths the main road traffic is soon forgotten. The moated motte of an old castle adjoins the medieval St Mary's Church, which has an Early English chancel roof and 15th-century carvings.

Beside the solid two-arch bridge stands Staick House, an example of the small black-and-white manor at its best, with gables, lattice windows, crucks and massive timber frames. From the narrow road alongside Staick House can be seen Monks Court mound, its origin a mystery, while standing sentry on the river bank opposite Staick House is a tall brick dovecote.

The Georgian façade of Burton Court, half a mile south, conceals a medieval old hall. It houses a varied collection of costumes; open in summer on Wednesdays and Thursdays and at weekends.

WEOBLEY

The graceful spire of the Church of St Peter and St Paul dominates the gentle valley in which this ancient village lies. The village itself is best viewed from the remains of a massive motte and bailey on the south side, from which an avenue of oaks leads to the grassed-over site of several old houses burnt down in the 1960s.

The fire spared most of the buildings in the village, leaving a collection of black-and-white buildings unsurpassed anywhere – with seemingly impossible overhangs, huge timber frames at drunken angles, gabled rooflines and moss-covered tiles.

ALMELEY

This tiny village, hidden down quiet twisting back roads, once boasted two castles and a railway station. None survive intact, although the solid conical earth mound of one of the castles still stands next to the mainly 14th-century Church of St Mary.

Completing the traditional medieval threesome of castle, church and manor is the seat of the local landowner, the timber-framed Almeley House, opposite the churchyard. A small area of commonland still survives behind the main street.

EARDISLEY

Breaking up a patchwork quilt of orchard and pastureland, the straggling village of Eardisley closely hugs its one main street, its buildings spanning 1000 years of history. The medieval character of the timeless village is established by the large number of small black-and-white cottages, many of them dwarfed by enormous chimney breasts.

The Church of St Mary Magdalene, adjoining two substantial rows of well maintained black-and-white houses, has one of the finest Norman fonts in Britain, intricately carved 800 years ago. It also has one of the earliest known tombs – that of Edward Fitz-John Fiest, dating from the late 11th century – and fine wall monuments.

GLADESTRY

Set in a gap in one of Radnor Forest's sandstone ridges, this hamlet is typical of many in mid-Wales. Church, chapel, inn, court house and cottages huddle together beside Gladestry Brook, overshadowed by heather and bilberry-clad sheepwalks. This is where lowland arable and livestock farming gives way to upland sheep-farming territory; the nearby hills reach more than 1600ft high. Tiny St Mary's Church, dating from 1060, is unusual in having memorials mounted on its outside walls.

Tourist information: Kington 230202.

ABBEY DORE COURT *The 4 acre garden of this Dore valley farmhouse accommodates rare plants and shrubs.*

WINSOME WATERWAY *At Eardisland the River Arrow winds past cottages whose gardens embroider the water's edge.*

SAFE AND SOUND *Skenfrith's massive and solid church tower was probably a refuge for villagers during border wars.*

176

—— 61 MILES ——

The majestic buzzard soars over a landscape dotted with ancient churches, tiny villages and country estates. Castles and castle mounds stand amid rolling farmlands and cider orchards.

HEREFORD

The city skyline is dominated by ecclesiastical buildings, notably All Saints with its crooked spire, and the Cathedral Church of St Mary the Virgin and St Ethelbert. This immense sandstone building has a notable array of effigy tombs, some dating back to the founding of the church in the 11th century, and an inspiring nave ceiling. It also counts amongst its treasures a chained library of some 1500 books, including an 8th-century Gospel, and the Mappa Mundi, a map of the world drawn in about 1290.

Hereford's major product, cider, is celebrated by a Museum of Cider in Grimmer Road. Other museums include a Waterworks Museum at Broomy Hill, the St John Coningsby Museum in Widemarsh Street, and Bulmers Steam Centre in Whitecross Road, home to famous steam locomotives including the *King George V*.

High Town, the traffic-free city centre, has for its centrepiece The Old House, built in 1621 and moved to its present site this century. South and south-east of High Town a number of narrow streets and alleyways retain something of the character of bygone Hereford.

KILPECK

In this tiny hamlet is one of Britain's architectural masterpieces, the early Norman Church of St Mary and St David. Unchanged since the 1100s, its walls incorporate some Saxon remains, and the bold yet intricate carvings, especially on the south door, are world-famous. They show a tree of life, birds, dragons and angels. A frieze running around the outside of the church has some 70 carvings of human and animal heads. The simple interior includes a fine chancel arch and a wooden gallery.

ST WEONARDS

The church tower is a landmark from many miles around, and around it church farm, village mound and mellow sandstone houses cluster tightly together. Largely of 14th-century origin, the church has fragments of 15th-century Flemish glass, possibly made by Flemish glassmakers who settled near the village at that time.

The village mound, or rump, is the reputed burial place – in a golden coffin – of St Weonard. It is in fact a prehistoric structure, emphasising the long history of settlement in the area.

SKENFRITH

The distinctive sight and sound of a large water wheel emphasises the timelessness of this compact border village, just in Wales. The mill stream is fed from a weir on the River Monnow, and the mill still grinds corn in the time-honoured way. The Monnow also forms part of the moat of Skenfrith Castle, whose remains, owned by the National Trust, lie at the heart of the village; the filled-in, grassed-over moat facing Skenfrith's single row of houses is now the village green.

St Bridget's Church was built in the early 13th century. The dark, cool interior is a jumble of old graveslabs, medieval pews, a minstrels' box and the Morgan tomb, carved with effigies in Tudor costume. The Monnow washes the edge of the churchyard, entering and leaving the village in a steep-sided and wooded valley.

ABBEY DORE

A forest of gravestones witnesses the past importance of Dore Abbey, founded on a terrace on the west bank of the River Dore in 1147. Virtually derelict after its suppression in the 1530s, the truncated remains of the abbey church were restored in the 1630s. The lavishly vaulted super-structure shelters 17th-century wall paintings, a minstrels' gallery, richly carved side aisles, monumental tombs and well preserved 13th-century tiles.

The wide, flat Dore valley provided excellent agricultural land around the abbey. One of the valley farms, Abbey Dore Court, has a walled garden which is open daily from March to October.

VOWCHURCH

Known as the Golden Valley, the broad gentle valley of the River Dore (a corruption of the French *d'or* – 'of gold') is a deeply rural area. Vowchurch has an ancient church, a few houses, and several solid, brick-built farms. The tiny Norman church has an unusual wooden bell turret built in the 1520s.

DORSTONE

Old stone cottages line narrow lanes radiating from a small green. The Pandy Inn, more than 500 years old, gives evidence of past industrial activity in the village – Pandy is Welsh for mill. A wooded castle mound rises west of the village, while St Faith's Church is an 1890s reconstruction on a site dating back to the time of Thomas Becket, one of whose murderers founded the original church.

The Golden Valley comes to an abrupt end north-west of Dorstone, where high hills sweep in from three sides. Near the crest of one hill stands Arthur's Stone, a chambered tomb from which there are commanding views down the Golden Valley and across to Waun Fach, at 2660ft the highest of the Black Mountains.

BREDWARDINE

A wide meander of the River Wye skirts the foot of steep Bredwardine Hill, where the village's few houses cluster around the imposing 17th-century Red Lion Hotel. A former patron of the hotel was the Reverend Francis Kilvert, diarist of daily events in a rural parish a century ago. The church of which he was curate stands apart from the village on a cliff above the river. Its largely Norman architecture has long outlasted the old Norman castle, whose mound, bailey, fishponds and ivy-covered walls survive just south of the churchyard.

MADLEY

Ancient and modern meet in Madley, a straggling village set amidst orchards in the flat plains above the River Wye. The cold, white, functional dishes of a satellite-tracking station – floodlit at night – contrast starkly with the grandiose medieval architecture of the Church of the Nativity of the Blessed Virgin Mary.

Wormhill Farm Museum, just outside the village, has a display of bygone farming paraphernalia. It is open on Thursday and Saturday afternoons from June to August.

Tourist information: Hereford 268430.

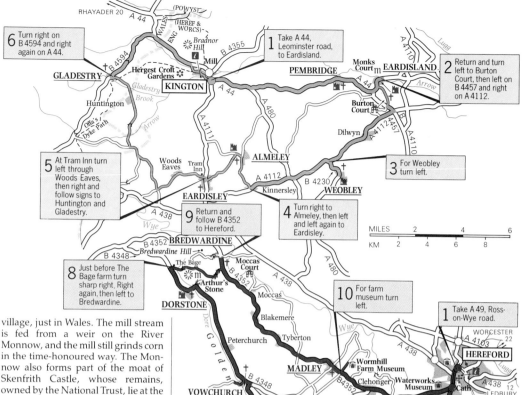

Orchards and meadows beside the Teme

TOUR
109

—— 43 MILES ——

Between the sparkling Teme at Tenbury and the limpid Severn at Bewdley lies a land of red soil and half-timbered farmhouses. From the hills there are views south to the Malvern Hills.

TENBURY WELLS

'The town in the orchard', announces a sign welcoming visitors to Tenbury Wells – an appropriate title, as the approach roads are lined with fruit farms, hop and nursery gardens. Henry III granted Tenbury a charter for a weekly market in 1249, and growers still flock in from outlying farms to sell their produce every Tuesday.

Some farmers arrive early to secure a good pitch at the market house in the centre of the town. This curious, oval-shaped brick building, with arched windows and an overhanging roof, was built in 1811 as a corn and butter market.

Several ancient inns testify to Tenbury's importance as a coaching town on the road between London and Wales before the railway. The Royal Oak, which probably dates from the 16th century, is a magnificent black-and-white building, its timbers forming an intricate web of squares, circles and diamond shapes. The Pembroke Inn is another timber-framed house with its first floor overhanging the pavement; its walls have settled over the centuries into delightfully crooked angles.

Oddest of all Tenbury's buildings – and the one that gave the town its title of 'Wells' – is the Spa building, a dilapidated folly at the rear of the

Crow Hotel. Mineral waters were discovered there in 1839, and Tenbury enjoyed a short-lived boom as a health resort.

The baths were housed in a curiously decorated conservatory, with a metal-clad tower that looks like a space rocket with four nose cones, one above the other. Relics of the spa and other curiosities are housed in Tenbury Museum in Cross Street, which is open at weekends.

St Mary's Church has monuments to the Cornewall family, including a unique painted memorial in the form of a triptych. Its doors open to reveal three life-size Elizabethan portraits. They are of Richard Cornewall, 9th Baron of Burford, his wife and eldest son, Edmund, who succeeded him.

The River Teme skirts the north of the town and marks the Shropshire border. Across the medieval bridge and 1 mile west of the town is the hamlet of Burford, flanked by the fast-flowing Teme. The gardens of Burford House are immaculately laid out, and roses galore grow up the mellow red-brick walls of the Georgian mansion built in 1728. Each plant is labelled, tempting visitors to the nursery next door where most species on display can be bought. The gardens are open daily in summer.

LOWER ROCHFORD

Behind a screen of trees the Teme winds through a valley where apple orchards are ablaze with blossom in spring. Fields neatly strung with hops

are interspersed among the orchards, and several of the farms have oast houses with rows of wooden air vents like small ships under sail. The warm red brick of the farm buildings matches the glowing red soil through which the Teme cuts its swathe.

Set back from the road, between a farm and the river, St Michael's is an unspoilt little Norman church. An outstanding 12th-century doorway, with a Tree of Life carved within its arch, is set into the north wall, blocked up now but visible from outside.

The fine stained glass in the east window is an early work by William Morris.

CLIFTON UPON TEME

Despite its name, Clifton is in fact perched high on a hill several hundred feet above the Teme – and over a mile away as the crow flies.

A seat girdles the trunk of a huge horse-chestnut tree beside a little green at the heart of the village. Generations of villagers have lingered in its shade for a gossip beside the village pump which stands there. Black-and-white cottages of a venerable age cluster around the green.

St Kenelm's Church has a handsome octagonal spire, clad with cedarwood shingles. In the south aisle is a

14th-century effigy of a knight, Sir Ralf Wysham, who lies with his legs crossed and his feet resting on a lion.

Among the memorials to the Jeffreyes family on the nave wall, look out for the mis-carved stone that alleges that William died some nine months before he was born. The tablet is the work of Thomas White, who designed Worcester Guildhall. The adjacent memorial was carved by Grinling Gibbons, the 18th-century sculptor also famous for his wood carvings, and is of Italian marble.

From the main street of the village a footpath cuts between hedges beside Chapel House, and leads past the village football pitch into open fields from which there are magnificent views east to the Teme valley and south to the Malvern Hills.

SHELSLEY WALSH

A jewel of a little church, plain on the outside but with a fine interior, snuggles at the foot of a steep wooded hill. Only a farm and handsome, 16th-century manor house keep it company.

The splendour of the Church of St Andrew's breathtaking interior lies in its woodwork. The 15th-century oak screen, intricately carved with vine motifs and fruit, doubles back into the nave of the church to form a little private chapel. Above the screen a huge beam spans the nave; this, too, is carved with vine leaves, and surmounted by a bold wooden cross. A century older than the screen are the

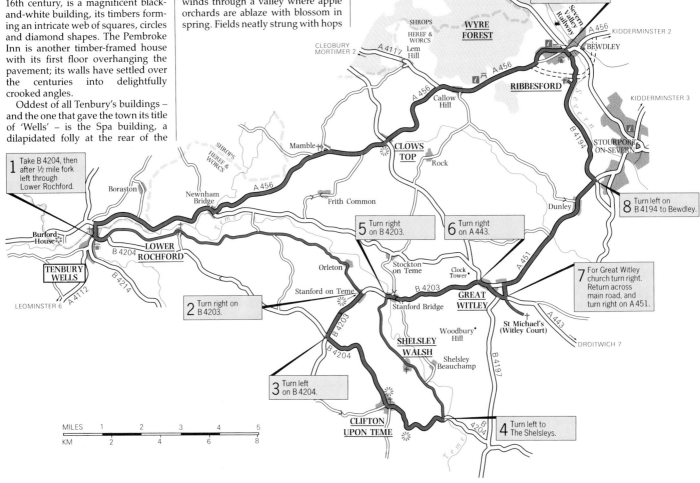

timbers of the roof, with sturdy rough-hewn beams and planks simply painted with stars.

The private road behind the church climbs so steeply that it is used as a motorsport hill-climbing venue; spectators enjoy a magnificent view through the trees to the Teme valley below.

GREAT WITLEY

Where peacocks once strutted, jackdaws now swoop from the ruined shell of one of England's most sumptuous houses. Edward VII, when Prince of Wales, often used to stroll in the gardens of Witley Court; today only bumps in the grass reveal where the terraces stood, while a few bedraggled yews mark the lines of the formal walks.

Two magnificent fountains stand relatively unscathed by the fire, demolition and vandalism that have left the house a roofless and unstable ruin. One fountain has an immense statue of Perseus on a horse prancing 26ft above the ground. It used to throw a jet of water 90ft into the air, but has been dry since 1937, the year of the fire, when the long decline began.

In contrast, St Michael's Church, attached to the ruined house, is immaculately restored, with a baroque interior of unbridled opulence that would seem more at home in Italy than in the heart of the English countryside. Built by Lord Foley and consecrated in 1735, it was lavishly embellished 20 years later by the 2nd Lord Foley. Every available surface was decorated by the finest craftsmen of the time and in the best materials – though surprisingly the ceiling mouldings are of papier-mâché, which had just been invented when the church was built.

The glorious paintings on the ceiling, by the Italian artist Antonio Bellucci, once graced the Duke of Chandos's mansion at Canons near Edgware, Middlesex. When that house was broken up in 1747 the paintings were brought to Great Witley together with the painted glass windows and the ornate case of the organ which Handel used to play at Canons.

This beautiful church is now the parish church of the village, and some of the atmosphere of its past grandeur is re-created at concerts of baroque music which are held there occasionally.

RIBBESFORD

Beside the road the Severn runs broad, deep and slow compared with its boisterous tributary the Teme. An avenue of horse chestnuts leads to the hamlet of Ribbesford, which consists of no more than a farm, a cluster of dwellings, a big house aloof across the fields, and St Leonard's Church.

The church dates from about 1100, and over its Norman doorway is a carving of a hunter shooting with a bow and arrow at a strange creature – perhaps a duck-billed platypus or a seal.

Inside, the church is sombre from Victorian refurbishment. However, there is a fine stained-glass west

VALLEY OF FARMS *Wooded undulating slopes overlook the fertile meadows of the Teme valley east of Shelsley Walsh.*

VILLAGE ON A HILL *Clifton upon Teme's Church of St Kenelm rises beyond the cottages grouped around a village green 650ft above the Teme valley.*

SENTIMENTAL JOURNEY *The Severn Valley Railway makes a call at Bewdley.*

window in delicate colours designed by Edward Burne-Jones, and medieval painted glass showing St George and the dragon survives in another window.

An ancient barn opposite the church has unusual oval windows beside the doors, which look like the eyes of two faces peering from the mellow pink stone.

WYRE FOREST

Fallow deer roam the 6000 acres of Wyre Forest, which is the remaining part of a vast Royal hunting forest mentioned in the Domesday Book. Walkers can wander for miles along three main tracks through the forest.

Large tracts of Wyre are natural oak woodlands, with plantations of larch and Douglas fir among them. Above

the wild flowers that dot the forest floor in summer, silver-washed fritillary butterflies glide in and out of the trees' shade. Meadows among the woodlands are bright with flowers and scented by wild thyme.

Photographs in the Forestry Commission's information centre evoke forest life in the past, when oak bark used to be collected for tanning leather, and when basket-makers and charcoal-burners earned a living working right in the heart of the forest.

CLOWS TOP

A hamlet at the peak of the long climb out of the Severn valley, Clows Top offers magnificent views in all directions. To the south-east, the Victorian clock tower of Abberley Hall school

looks like Big Ben miraculously transported into the woody countryside . It is a landmark too from many other points along the tour. Eastwards lie the Clent Hills near Birmingham, and to the west are the hills of the Welsh Border. Southwards the Malverns may be seen in the distance.

At Mamble, 2 miles farther on, St John the Baptist's Church has a tall doorway, built to enable knights to ride into the church on horseback to be blessed at the altar before departing to fight in the Crusades. One such knight is commemorated with a cross-legged effigy. In the east window is a small but exquisite panel of early 14th-century stained glass, with a powerful image of the Crucifixion.

<u>Tourist information</u>: Bewdley 403303.

Down the Severn to the Malvern Hills

TOUR
110

—— 45 MILES ——

The Severn valley broadens south of Worcester, and to the west the lofty Malvern Hills rise abruptly from an elegant Victorian spa. Beyond lie broad hop fields and cider-apple orchards.

WORCESTER

Though Worcester's broad High Street is now a pedestrianised walkway, the past is never very far away in this ancient city. Many of its streets are lined with medieval houses whose upper storeys jut boldly above narrow pavements, and on the banks of the Severn the cathedral's great tower soars above the rooftops.

Built between the 11th and 14th centuries, Worcester Cathedral was once part of a monastery. It is the burial place of King John, who died in 1216, and his tomb stands in the centre of the magnificent nave. The marble lid of the original coffin forms the top of the tomb and dates from between 1230 and 1240. The effigy of the king is said to be the earliest royal effigy in England. Near the cathedral is the 14th-century Edgar Tower, once the gateway to the monastery.

Worcester's other famous connection with royalty stands in New Street and has the inscription 'Love God, honour ye King' above the doorway. Called King Charles' House, the 16th-century, half-timbered building is where Charles II took refuge after his defeat at the Battle of Worcester in 1651. His stay was short and he is said

to have left hurriedly by the back door as his Parliamentary pursuers entered by the front.

Worcester's unswerving loyalty to the Stuarts is depicted on the façade of the magnificent Guildhall, which has statues of Charles I and II and an effigy of Cromwell's head nailed by the ears above a doorway. The building dates from 1721 and was designed by Thomas White, a pupil of Sir Christopher Wren.

Royalty is also associated with the name of Worcester's world-famous porcelain, manufactured by the Worcester Royal Porcelain Company. The original company was founded in 1751 by Dr John Wall and a group of local businessmen, but the present name was first used in 1862. The Dyson Perrins Museum, next door to the factory in Severn Street, has the world's finest collection of Worcester porcelain and is open on weekdays all the year, and also on Saturdays in summer.

UPTON UPON SEVERN

A modern bridge arches gracefully across the Severn at Upton, but the town's chief landmark is the massive Bell Tower which stands close by. The tower dates from the 14th century and is Upton's oldest building, yet bridge and tower harmonise perfectly.

The tower was once part of the Church of St Peter and St Paul, which was badly damaged when it was held by Parliamentarian troops during the Battle of Upton Bridge in 1651. It was rebuilt in 1754, and in 1770 the church spire was replaced by the lantern and

cupola which is a distinctive feature of the tower and has given it the local nickname The Pepperpot. The nave of the church was dismantled in 1937 and the churchyard was laid out as a public garden, leaving the tower to stand alone. It now houses the Pepperpot Heritage Centre which has displays showing the development of the town and the Battle of Upton Bridge. The centre is open daily in summer.

A walk around Upton's streets is a pleasant excursion among buildings of several periods, from the black and white of Tudor timber-framed cottages to the handsome façades and bow windows of Georgian houses. A footpath along the river bank leads past several riverside inns, notably the 19th-century Plough Inn and the King's Head; and some 18th-century warehouses are reminders that Upton was once a small port handling wine, wool and silk brought up the river from Bristol and Gloucester.

HEREFORDSHIRE BEACON

With breathtaking views at every turn, the road up from the Severn vale winds across the broad back of the 1114ft Herefordshire Beacon. From the large car park, steps and a footpath lead to the summit. In the valley below a glint of water between

the trees is the British Camp Reservoir, which supplies water to Great Malvern. It was opened in 1895 by Princess Mary, later Queen Mary, wife of George V.

To the south the summit is covered by the earthworks of British Camp, one of the most impressive Iron Age hill-forts in Britain. Its lower rampart is more than a mile long and the entire fort covers 32 acres. Tradition says that here the British chief Caratacus made his last stand against the Romans.

A footpath through the camp leads to Clutter's Cave, hacked from an outcrop of volcanic rock. It is 6ft high and 10ft deep, and may have been a hermit's cell or a shepherd's shelter.

EASTNOR

Many villages in England have a castle, but Eastnor has two. Or rather it has a great house built like a castle in 1812, when the fashion for fortresses stemmed more from romanticism than the need for protection against unfriendly neighbours, and the remains of a 15th-century castle which failed to survive the Civil War.

Bronsil Castle, the older of the two, was built by Richard Beauchamp, son of John Beauchamp who was Lord Treasurer to Henry VI, and all that remains is the moat and part of the gatehouse. Eastnor Castle, however, still stands as boldly as it did when it was built to the design of Sir Robert Smirke, designer of the British Museum. It looks every inch a Norman castle, with tall, turreted towers at each corner and a central keep. It contains collections of armour, tapestries and paintings. In the days of steam locomotives one of the Great Western Railway's Castle Class locomotives bore the name *Eastnor Castle*, and its nameplates are displayed in the entrance hall. The castle is open to the public on certain days in summer.

Opposite Eastnor Castle's gatehouse stands a pretty thatched cottage, which is also the post office; close by is a small village green with a roofed drinking well.

LEDBURY

'A little town of ancient grace', was how the poet John Masefield described his birthplace, and no one today would argue with the sentiments of the man who was poet laureate from 1930 until 1967. Ledbury's ancient grace begins in its main street, where the splendid timber-framed, 17th-century Market Hall stands on wooden pillars in the centre of the road. Beyond the Market Hall, in The Homend, are steps and houses many of which are timber-framed with brick or stucco frontages added in the 18th century. At the end of the road is The Knapp, birthplace of John Masefield in 1878.

Just behind the Market Hall is Church Lane, a narrow cobbled street where the overhanging upper storeys of the black-and-white houses almost meet. Farther along the High Street the 16th-century Feathers Hotel is a dazzling example of the period when timber-framed construction was at its peak. It stands three storeys high. Ledbury may also have been the

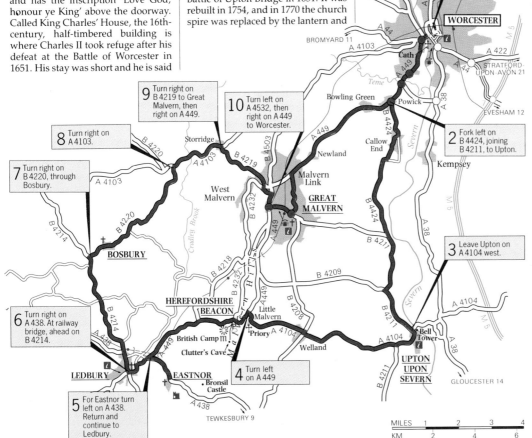

ON A CLEAR DAY *From Herefordshire Beacon the switchback hills of the Malverns roll northwards like miniature mountains, and the air is as heady as the local cider.*

LEDBURY *Church House, in Church Lane, is a fine example of 17th-century timber-frame building.*

TEMPLE OF STEAM *Great Malvern's Victorian railway station has cathedral-like adornments.*

SMALL ORDER *Little Malvern Priory is well named, as its Benedictine monks never numbered more than 12.*

birthplace of the 14th-century poet William Langland – the other claimant is Cleobury Mortimer in Shropshire. He is best known for his poem *The Vision of William Concerning Piers Plowman*, which is thought to have been inspired by the Malverns.

BOSBURY
Hopfields surround Bosbury, and for many years the hop-pickers from South Wales and the Midlands moved in by the hundred each September, until mechanisation put an end to this old tradition. As for the village itself, its houses and cottages are a pleasing mixture of timber frame, stone and brick, but it is the church, and particularly its tower, which immediately catches the eye. The Church of the Holy Trinity dates from the 12th

century and the tower dates from the mid-13th century. It stands apart from the church and is a massive fortress-like building with battlements and narrow windows. It was built as a refuge against marauding Welsh raiders who pillaged the borderlands until the 15th century. It is now a bell tower, with six bells installed in the 16th century.

Near the church porch is a 14th-century preaching cross, a rare survivor from the days when the Puritans destroyed such crosses as symbols of popery.

GREAT MALVERN
The pure spring water produced by the hard rocks of the Malvern Hills has been bottled and sold since the 18th century, when Malvern became a

fashionable spa rivalling Bath and Cheltenham. More than 1 million bottles are sold throughout the world each year. In 1842 it became the home of England's first hydrotherapy establishment, and continued to be a popular place for 'taking the waters' throughout the Victorian and Edwardian periods.

Traces of those days can still be seen, in the Georgian Mount Pleasant Hotel, the Regency ironwork of the Foley Arms, and the Victorian buildings lining the steep hillsides and tree-lined avenues leading to Great Malvern Station.

Great Malvern's greatest treasure, however, is its priory church, founded in 1085 but dating mainly from the 15th century. Its collection of 15th and early 16th-century stained-

glass windows are second in England only to those of York Minster.

The north transept window, a gift from Henry VII, is particularly beautiful in glorious yellows. It contains portraits of the king and his elder son, Arthur, Prince of Wales.

Opposite the priory, in Grange Road, is Priory Park which has a lake that was once the monks' fishpond. There is also an elegant Victorian bandstand where bands play on summer Sunday afternoons. Malvern Museum, housed in the Abbey Gateway, shows Malvern through the ages and is open daily in summer.

Tourist information: Worcester 23471; (Upton upon Severn) Malvern 4200 (summer); Ledbury 2461; Malvern 4700.

Beside the Windrush and the Avon

Above the flat orchard country of the Vale of Evesham rise the limestone uplands of the north Cotswolds. Stone buildings, ancient and weathered, create showpiece towns and villages.

EVESHAM

If the Vale of Evesham is one of England's gardens, Evesham itself is its market. It is an airy town with wide tree-lined streets and grassy walks alongside the River Avon, which loops sedately through the town. An open park at the heart of the town is the site of the Benedictine Abbey of Evesham, founded in 714 and demolished after the Dissolution of the Monasteries in 1539.

The great constitutional reformer Simon de Montfort was buried under the high altar of the abbey church after he had been slain at the Battle of Evesham in 1265. All traces of the church have now vanished, but a memorial to de Montfort stands in the open on the wide lawns. Some of the abbey buildings survive, including the bell tower, a masterpiece of Perpendicular architecture.

BROADWAY

The long broad High Street is lined with houses ranging in period from Tudor to the 20th century but uniform in their use of golden stone. With stone tiles on the roofs, stone-mullioned windows, stone chimneys and stone garden walls, the village looks as though it has grown spontaneously from its own quarry.

The main street forks at the west end of the village to form the Green, framed by old inns and shops. The street is bright in early summer with the flowers of horse chestnut trees. Several of Broadway's finest houses are now hotels.

Broadway Beacon, second highest point in the Cotswolds, rises to 1024ft east of the village. At the summit, visible for miles around, is Broadway Tower, built as a folly by the Earl of Coventry in 1800. It is now the centre of a country park, reached on foot from Broadway, or by road from a turning beside the Fish Inn.

SNOWSHILL

Crouching in a dip on the side of a steep hill, Snowshill presents itself first as a roofscape of steeply pitched stone tiles with views north-west through the trees onto the Vale of Evesham. The manor house is a treasure house of objects collected by an eccentric 'magpie', Charles Wade, who died in 1956. Wade scoured the country for clocks, oriental oddities, dolls and toys, early prams and bicycles and bric-a-brac of every description.

COTSWOLD FARM PARK

Some 50 acres of small fields on a high plateau among the Cotswold hills comprise a living museum of English agriculture, where rare breeds of farm animals are bred and saved from possible extinction. Fenced walkways give close access to such unusual varieties as Longhorn cattle, Cotswold sheep, Shetland geese and Gloucester Old Spot pigs. The farm park is open daily in summer.

TEMPLE GUITING

The narrow Windrush has carved a gently sloping valley and kept it green with waterside alders and oaks. At Temple Guiting an ancient Tudor farmhouse seems suspended among the trees above a widening of the river. At Kineton, 1 mile farther on, two stone slab footbridges cross the stream, and at Guiting Power the houses are arranged round a sloping green in little squares and terraces, the walls hung with roses, honeysuckle and clematis.

Naunton squats in a hollow alongside the stream; one of its oldest buildings is a square dovecote of 1600.

BOURTON-ON-THE-WATER

The Windrush cuts the village in two, and is crossed by five stone bridges. Wide grassy banks border the stream and trees overhang the water. At Birdland penguins can be watched from an underwater viewing chamber.

The model railway in High Street is laid out on 400sq ft of miniature countryside. Behind the unusually named Old New Inn is one of Britain's finest model villages – an exact replica of Bourton itself, built in natural stone and complete with a mini Windrush, a water mill, strains of choral music from the model church – and even a model of the model village itself.

STOW-ON-THE-WOLD

At 750ft the highest Cotswold town, Stow-on-the-Wold, 'where the wind blows cold' according to an old rhyme, is a meeting point of eight roads. The broad market square, with its restored stone market cross, is flanked by fine stone houses, with St Edward's Church standing back a little to the west.

ADLESTROP

Noted for its former railway station where a train carrying the poet Edward Thomas stopped and inspired a poem, Adlestrop still displays the station sign and bench – housed now in a bus shelter. In Thomas's poem no one left the train and no one came, and Adlestrop still has the air of a forgotten little place, reposing in its comfortable little stone cottages, with roses and clematis around their doors.

HARMONY IN STONE *Dry-stone walls across the flanks of the Windrush valley blend with the stone church and homes of Naunton.*

CHARLECOTE PARK *The house stands in parkland where, legend says, William Shakespeare was caught poaching deer in 1583.*

SNOWSHILL STONE *The handsome Tudor manor house once belonged to Catherine Parr, the sixth wife of Henry VIII.*

CHASTLETON

Built by a successful wool merchant in 1603-9, Chastleton has an imposing façade of golden stone, topped by five gables and two short towers.

The original furniture is still in place, and there are fine carved panelling, screens and plasterwork as well as a secret room, the hiding place of a Royalist, Arthur Jones, after the Battle of Worcester. Even the 17th-century garden survives, with box hedges trimmed to curious shapes and enclosed within a wall of yew.

Chastleton is open in summer on Friday afternoons and at weekends and Bank Holidays.

MORETON-IN-MARSH

There is no marsh at Moreton: the name is a corruption of March, meaning boundary, and the town used to mark the meeting point of the Roman Foss Way with Icknield Street. Among the houses of golden stone that line this street are several venerable old coaching inns.

On the corner of the Oxford road stands a little stone tower in which the old curfew bell still hangs. The clock on the tower is 17th century, and the windowless room on the ground floor used to be the town lockup.

BATSFORD

Two great estates face each other from opposite sides of a broad ridge. At Batsford Park, 50 acres of gardens around the Victorian house have been replanted to create an aboretum, vivid with colour in spring and autumn.

At Sezincote, opposite, the gardens are more formal, designed by Humphry Repton and Thomas Daniell around a stream which drops to a large lake. An oriental flavour is created by statues of Indian deities and cast-iron Brahmin bulls.

Batsford Arboretum is open daily from April to October. At Sezincote the gardens are open on Thursday, Friday and Bank Holiday afternoons, and the house on Thursday and Friday from May to July and in September.

CHIPPING CAMPDEN

The wealth of Chipping Campden's wool merchants in the Middle Ages has left its mark on the town, as many of the buildings put up at that time have survived. The finest is St James's Church, originally a Norman building but transformed in 1450-1500.

The handsome stone gateway beside the church survives from the old Manor House, built in 1613 by the 1st Viscount Campden but burnt down by Royalists in the Civil War. Lord Campden was also responsible for the Market Hall, built of stone in 1627 with a rough cobbled floor and a roof of magnificent oak timbers. Its central position in the High Street gives fine views of the gently curving street, with its delightful variety of dark, golden-stone houses.

Tourist information: Evesham 6944 (summer); Broadway 852937 (summer); Stow-on-the-Wold 30352 (summer); Moreton-in-Marsh 50881; (Chipping Campden) Evesham 840289 (summer).

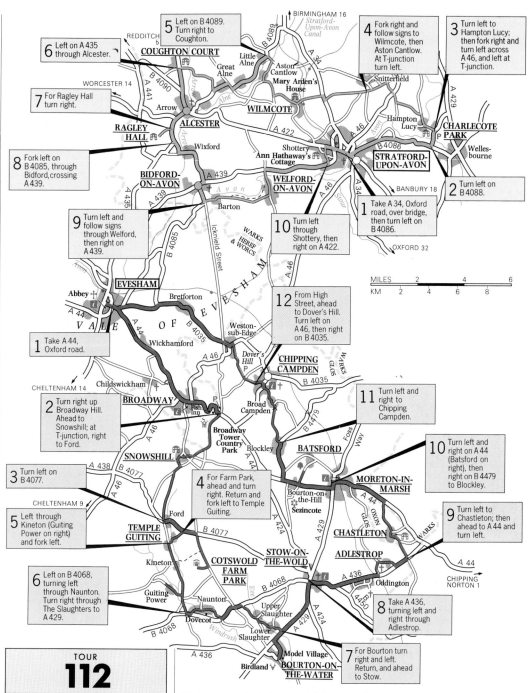

TOUR
112
— 48 MILES —

Stratford and the surrounding countryside nurtured the genius of Shakespeare. Little changed since his day are the churches and timber-framed homes of villages beside the placid River Avon.

STRATFORD-UPON-AVON

Authenticated details of William Shakespeare's life are sketchy but his spirit seems to walk the streets of Stratford, so intense is the association of the town with his name. Pilgrims from all over the world converge on the poet's birthplace in Henley Street. The beamed upstairs room where he was born is austerely furnished, and the windows are engraved with the signatures of earlier visitors, including Sir Walter Scott and Ellen Terry.

The site of New Place, where Shakespeare died, is occupied by a beautiful old English knott garden – with 4 'knotts' or beds of herbs interlaced with flowers.

At Shottery, 1 mile west of the town, is the cottage of Anne Hathaway, the poet's wife. Dozing under an eiderdown of thatch, the half-timbered house is surrounded by a cottage garden ablaze with blossom in the spring.

CHARLECOTE PARK

The red-brick house, begun by Sir Thomas Lucy in 1551, stands on a terrace above the slow-flowing River Avon, overlooking the flat meadows where Charles I camped with his army in 1642 on the night before the Battle of Edgehill. Although some of Sir Thomas Lucy's Great Hall survives, the house was largely remodelled in the 19th century, with heavy carved fireplaces, elaborate

plasterwork and sombre decorations. Outside, though, the beautiful pink-bricked Elizabethan gatehouse escaped 'improvement', and now houses a small museum of sporting life. Charlecote Park is open on most days in summer.

WILMCOTE

Shakespeare's mother, Mary Arden, was brought up on a farm in the little village of Wilmcote. The farmhouse is there still, its venerable timber-framed walls bent with age and seeming to follow the rolling contours of the ground on which they stand. Inside, the stone and polished oak floors undulate too, and there is a delightful irregularity in the beams and rafters overhead. The house is furnished in 17th-century style, with polished oak furniture, including a linen cupboard, a dough chest and even a wooden rat trap. The farm buildings contain a fine collection of country bygones, among them a huge cider press and a painted gypsy wagon.

COUGHTON COURT

The impressive honey-coloured stone tower which is the gatehouse to Coughton Court was the refuge in 1605 of the wives of the Gunpowder Plotters as they awaited the results of their husbands' trial. Later, in the Civil War, the great gatehouse withstood Royalist bombardment.

Today the house enjoys a peaceful retirement from its violent history. It contains fine furniture and family portraits, and there is a small museum of wartime aircraft relics.

ALCESTER

A market grew up in Roman times at the meeting point of two Roman roads and two rivers, the Arrow and the Alne, from which Alcester derived its name. No longer a market town, Alcester has a quiet elegance, its 16th-century black-and-white houses mingling with Georgian red-brick façades. The Town Hall, half timbered on the first floor, was built in 1618.

RAGLEY HALL

From its stately perch on a hill of rolling parkland, Ragley Hall surveys the Arrow Valley and the Cotswold hills beyond. The grey-stone house, with sweeping stone stairs leading up to the grand classical columns of the entrance, was designed in the Palladian style by Robert Hooke in 1680 for the Seymour family, who have lived there ever since.

One of the largest murals in the country, the *Temptation* by Graham Rust, was completed in 1983 and covers 5000sq ft in the south hall.

BIDFORD-ON-AVON

A Roman road forded the Avon near where Bidford's Church of St Laurence now stands, and the village remained an important crossing point when the fine eight-arched stone bridge was built in the 15th century. Shakespeare knew the village as 'drunken Bidford' on the strength of his experiences at the Falcon Inn. Although it is no longer an inn, the building still stands, with thick stone walls and stone-mullioned windows.

WELFORD-ON-AVON

A wealth of half-timbered thatched cottages grace the broadly spaced village of Welford. The idyllic Englishness of the place is underlined by the attractive cottage gardens. A footpath follows the Avon through the willow hung water meadows south-west of the village.

<u>Tourist information:</u> Stratford-upon-Avon 293127.

HAMLET OF YESTERYEAR *Tucked away in a wooded vale, Upper Slaughter's grey-roofed houses and cottages date mostly from the 16th, 17th and 18th centuries; no house has been built there since 1904.*

Canals and castles at England's centre

A short drive from the cathedral city of Coventry leads to a village at the centre of England. A Norman castle and a great Tudor house survive in an area that was once part of the Forest of Arden.

MERIDEN

A 15th-century wayside cross on Meriden's village green marks, it is claimed, the geographical centre of England. At the other end of the green a monument honours cyclists who died in two World Wars. On a Sunday in May cyclists from all over England gather by the memorial for a service of remembrance, for Meriden's claim has made the village a cyclists' rallying point.

West of the village is the 18th-century Forest Hall, home of England's oldest archery society, the Woodmen of Arden. Archery contests are held on the lawns of the hall, near the spot where, it is said, Robin Hood once competed.

BERKSWELL

Red-brick almshouses, the village school and a bowfronted post office and shop face Berkswell's triangular green, where stocks stand beneath the trees. Behind the almshouses is a well which once belonged to a lord of the manor named Bercul, and thus Bercul's well gave the village its name.

Also behind the almshouses is the Berkswell Museum, a collection of farm implements, Victorian domestic items and church and parish documents housed in a timber-framed cottage built about 1500. The museum is open on Sundays and Bank Holidays from April to September, and on Saturdays from May to August. Nearby is the Church of St John the Baptist, a red-sandstone Norman building with a two-storey timber-framed porch.

BERKSWELL MILL

The mill stands in Windmill Lane at Balsall Common, some 1½ miles south of the village from which it takes its name. The four-storey tower mill was built in 1826 and the sails, 60ft in diameter, drove two pairs of millstones. Most of the mill's machinery is intact and was driven by a diesel engine from 1933, when the sails were destroyed in a gale, to 1948 when it was last used for grinding corn. The mill has been fully restored and can be visited on Sundays in summer.

KNOWLE

The village has the distinction of having a church with three dedications – St John the Baptist, St Lawrence and St Anne. A chapel was founded here in 1396, the church was consecrated in 1402 and a college was founded in the church in 1416. Its west tower, buttressed and battlemented, soars above the 15th-century Guildhouse, a timber-framed building with close-set timbers and stone mullioned windows.

Chester House in the High Street also dates from the 15th century, and has an overhanging upper storey and two large gables. It contains the village library.

PACKWOOD HOUSE

The house is a fine example of Tudor building, dating from between 1556 and 1560, with 17th-century additions. Its 50 acres of gardens include the Carolean Garden, which has a gazebo at each corner. One of these, dating from the reign of Charles II, has a furnace and flue used to heat an adjacent wall against which peach trees were grown.

The most remarkable feature, however, is the yew garden where clipped yew trees are said to be set out to represent the Sermon on the Mount. One large tree is known as 'The Master', and on each side are the Evangelists and Apostles. Rows of smaller trees stand for the listening Multitude. The garden was laid out by John Fetherston, owner of Packwood in the mid-17th century. The rooms of the house contain fine tapestries and English furniture.

HATTON LOCKS

From the bridge crossing the Grand Union Canal, lock gates stretch away in the distance – 17 to the east, and 4 to the west. Beside the bridge stands the British Waterway Board's maintenance depot, a Victorian building of red and plum-coloured brick with a three-legged crane at the dockside. There is a car park on the north side of the canal.

KENILWORTH CASTLE

There are better preserved castles in England than Kenilworth, but few can match it for grandeur and nobility. The red-sandstone keep dates from Norman times, and additions were made in every century up to the 16th, including an outer court and towers built by King John, the banqueting hall of John of Gaunt and the gatehouse added by Robert Dudley, Earl of Leicester. Dudley was Elizabeth I's favourite, and she often visited him at Kenilworth.

The best preserved building is the stables, built for the Earl of Leicester. The lower walls are of dressed stone and support the upper brick and timber-framed walls. Nearby is the Tiltyard, and it is probably here that the Great Tourney of Kenilworth took place in 1279, with more than 100 knights taking part.

In its long and chequered history Kenilworth's most famous event was the siege of 1266 when the followers of the rebellious Simon de Montfort were encircled for eight months by the forces of Henry III. The king offered terms of surrender to the garrison, who cut off the hand of the royal envoy before sending him back. The Archbishop of Canterbury then excommunicated the garrison, whereupon the garrison's surgeon dressed in ecclesiastical clothes and excommunicated the archbishop, the king and all his followers. The defenders were brought low by disease.

The keep was partially destroyed after the Civil War and was never occupied after the Restoration. The castle is open daily.

Tourist information: Kenilworth 52595.

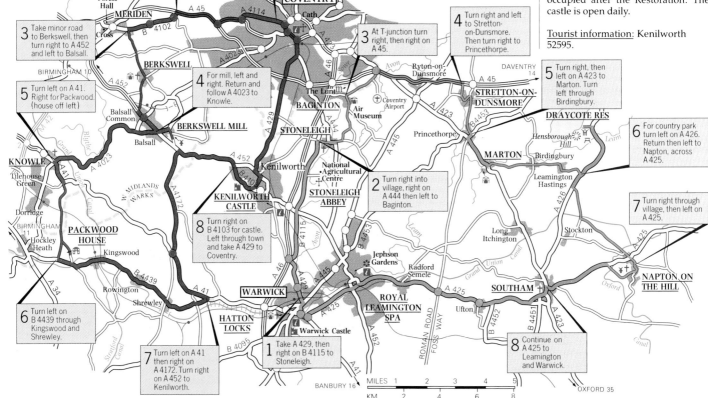

In England's heartland a great castle stands above the River Avon, Regency terraces grace a royal spa and farming research is conducted in the grounds of a Georgian mansion.

WARWICK

The majestic walls and towers of Warwick Castle rear above the town, where Georgian houses built after a fire in 1694 blend happily with buildings which survived the blaze.

The castle dates mainly from the 14th century, and in 1978 was sold by the Earl of Warwick to the waxworks company of Madame Tussaud's. Until then it had been one of the oldest inhabited castles in England; now its inhabitants are waxwork figures depicting a 'Royal Weekend Party of 1898'. The figures stand or sit in lifelike poses in several rooms, and in the Kenilworth Bedroom the Prince of Wales, the future Edward VII, is seen talking to his staff.

Reminders of the castle's less pleasant past can be seen in the dungeon, torture chamber and armoury. The castle is open daily.

In the town two of the most interesting buildings to escape the fire are the Lord Leycester Hospital and the Market Hall. The hospital, or almshouses, was founded in 1571 by Robert Dudley, Earl of Leicester, for disabled soldiers and is occupied by 12 ex-servicemen today. The Market Hall of 1670 now houses the Warwickshire County Museum and the tourist information centre. The museum, which displays the geology, history and natural history of the county, is open on weekdays and also on Sundays in summer.

On the south side of the town the 18th-century Castle Bridge spanning the Avon provides one of the best viewpoints of the castle. Here the massive walls, towers and turrets come into perspective, towering above the river and casting their reflections on the placid waters.

STONELEIGH ABBEY

The original abbey was founded about 1154 by Cistercian monks. The present building dates from the 13th century but was substantially enlarged in Georgian times. In the abbey grounds is the National Agriculture Centre, where research is carried out into farming techniques, and these techniques are demonstrated to the public on certain open days during the year. The abbey and grounds are open on Sundays, Mondays and Thursdays. Stoneleigh Abbey is also the venue for the Royal Show, held in the grounds every July in summer.

STONELEIGH

Timber-framed houses and cottages with brick infilling stand on high grassy banks in Stoneleigh's main street, which runs down to a 19th-

LEISURELY WATERWAY *A quiet stretch of the Oxford Canal winds below Napton Hill.*

HOME IMPROVEMENT *Packwood's red-brick addition was built in the 17th century.*

century bridge crossing the River Sowe. The red-sandstone Church of St Mary is Norman, and contains monuments to the Leigh family of Stoneleigh Abbey. Alice Leigh married Sir Robert Dudley in 1596, and in 1645 was made Duchess Dudley by Charles I.

BAGINTON

The runways and buildings of Coventry airport lie close to the village, and the tower blocks and church spires of the city itself punctuate the horizon to the north. Inside the airfield grounds is the Midland Air Museum, with exhibits of jet fighters and rare historic aircraft. There is an exhibition dedicated to Sir Frank Whittle, pioneer of the jet engine, who was born in Coventry.

Near the airport is 'The Lunt', a reconstruction of a Roman fort. The fort was built after Boudicca's uprising in AD 60 and includes a stockade thought to have been a training ground for military horses.

STRETTON-ON-DUNSMORE

A tiny triangular green and a stream spanned by low brick bridges form the heart of the village. Around the green stand timber-framed houses and red-brick farm buildings.

Each year on St Martin's Day, November 11, the people of Stretton join with villagers from 24 other parishes at sunrise to observe a Saxon custom – the payment of Wroth Silver. They gather together in a field near the village and the agent for the lord of the manor, the Duke of Buccleuch, collects the Wroth Silver, which preserves the villagers' rights to drive cattle across the duke's lands.

MARTON

The village stands on the Oxford to Coventry road. The River Leam skirts the village to the north, and the road bridge that crosses it still has masonry from the 15th century.

In Louise Close, off the High Street, is the Museum of Country Bygones. The museum began from the private

collection of Mr George Tims, now the museum's curator. Everything in the museum comes from local farms and villages, and includes craftsmen's tools, dairying implements and agricultural machinery. The museum is open daily in summer.

DRAYCOTE RESERVOIR

A country park surrounds the reservoir, 2 miles long and ¾ mile wide, at the foot of Hensborough Hill. From the hilltop there are fine views across the reservoir and the surrounding countryside. Beside the water there are picnic places and a children's adventure playground.

NAPTON ON THE HILL

Napton Hill stands 500ft high above the Oxford Canal, and the village clings precariously to its southern and eastern slopes in terraces of houses and cottages. On the hilltop stands the Church of St Lawrence, of Norman origin but mostly 13th century, and a restored windmill of the early 19th century, converted to a private house.

SOUTHAM

Red-brick, bowfronted shops and the whitewashed Black Dog inn face Southam's Market Hill. The town grew up on the old cattle droving road from Wales to London; less peaceful visitors were the Royalist and Parliamentarian troops during the Civil War, and Charles I stayed there overnight on his way to the first major battle of the war at Edgehill in 1642.

The parish church of St James has a handsome, 16th-century timber roof, a 14th-century tower and a 15th-century octagonal spire.

ROYAL LEAMINGTON SPA

Leamington became 'Royal' in 1838 when Queen Victoria visited the spa, and during the 19th century the town reached the peak of its fame as invalids flocked to take advantage of the town's mineral springs. Many stayed at the Regent Hotel, the largest hotel in England when it was opened in 1819; its guests included the Prince Regent, who allowed the hotel to take his name.

A local doctor, Dr Jephson, did much to publicise the waters, and he is remembered by the Jephson Gardens on the banks of the Leam which runs through the town. In the gardens stands a marble statue of Dr Jephson, erected in 1849.

The gardens and river are overlooked by elegant Regency and Victorian terraces. Newbold Terrace has houses probably built by John Nash, who designed London's Regent Park terraces. The Royal Pump Rooms, opposite the entrance to Jephson Gardens, were built in 1814 over one of Leamington's seven springs. South of the river is All Saints' Church, built in the Gothic style in the mid-19th century. It is one of the largest parish churches in England.

Leamington remains a popular spa town, and more than 50,000 invalids are treated there each year.

Tourist information: Warwick 492212; Leamington Spa 311470.

Farms and forests by the River Nene

TOUR
115

——— 48 MILES ———

South and west of Northampton lie broad farmlands, royal forests and two rivers, the Nene and Great Ouse. The tour visits a village which a poet loved and an Elizabethan house.

NORTHAMPTON
Most of Northampton's medieval buildings were destroyed by fire in 1675. The rebuilt town was neatly laid out around one of the largest market squares in England, where markets are still held on Wednesdays, Fridays and Saturdays.

Northampton's boot and shoemaking industry is highlighted in the Central Museum and Art Gallery, whose exhibits include Queen Victoria's wedding slippers and Margot Fonteyn's ballet shoes. Another link with the town's medieval past stands on the southern outskirts; this is an Eleanor Cross erected in 1291 in memory of Edward I's wife, whose body rested there while being taken from Nottinghamshire to London for burial. The cross is one of only three that have survived from the original 12 on the route.

SALCEY FOREST
The road south from Quinton plunges suddenly into unfenced woodlands, with parking areas and a picnic place at the roadside. There are walks into the forest which, in medieval times, was part of the royal hunting grounds that once covered a large part of south Northamptonshire.

Five nature trails starting from the picnic place lead through oaks, horse chestnuts, hawthorns, beeches and conifers.

GAYHURST
About a quarter of a mile south of Gayhurst village stands Gayhurst House, the earliest parts of which date from 1520. In 1581 the manor was conferred on Sir Francis Drake by Elizabeth I, and he is remembered by the Sir Francis Drake pub which occupies part of a building that was once a bathhouse erected over a chalybeate spring.

From the pub a drive leads up to the house, which is privately owned and cannot be visited. Close by, however, is St Peter's Church, built in the early 18th century and one of the best examples of Georgian church architecture in England. The architect is not known; for many years the design was attributed to Sir Christopher Wren, its style so closely resembling Wren's with its elegant tower topped by a cupola, arched windows and tall columns flanking the south entrance.

Inside the church all is whiteness and light, there being no stained glass to filter the daylight that streams across the nave and spotlights the superb monument to Sir Nathan Wrighte, Keeper of the Great Seal of England to Queen Anne, and his son George. The Wrightes owned Gayhurst, and father and son are represented by standing effigies, be-wigged and wearing frock coats, knee breeches and stockings.

OLNEY
Olney's Market Place forms the hub of this small town, with a small triangular green, war memorial and bench seats beneath shady trees. Facing Market Place is a large Georgian house which is now a museum devoted to the works of the poet and hymn-writer William Cowper. There, between 1768 and 1786, he wrote some of his best-known works, including *The Task*, *John Gilpin* and the *Olney Hymns*.

Cowper wrote his hymns in collaboration with his friend John Newton, who was the curate of Olney's 14th-century Church of St Peter and St Paul. Inside the church is Newton's pulpit, and a stained-glass window depicting Cowper and three pet hares that shared his home.

GRENDON
Stone-built cottages and houses hug the twisting road through this quiet village in the Nene valley, and the 12th-century Church of St Mary, with its distinctive brown-and-grey tower, is a landmark for miles around. Grendon Hall, on the northern edge of the village, dates from the early 18th century and was once the home of the Compton family, earls and marquises of Northamptonshire. It is now owned by the Northamptonshire County Council and is used as a youth centre. Its fine frontage with mullioned windows can be seen from the entrance gate at the roadside.

CASTLE ASHBY
Like so many Englishmen's homes this 'castle' is in fact a house, though it does have pretty octagonal turrets rising from a roof with a parapet. It was begun around 1574 and was added to in the 17th century by William Compton, 1st Earl of Northampton. The front of the house is said to be by Inigo Jones, and there is more of his work inside, including some fine ceilings, staircases and panelling.

The gardens were laid out in the 1860s by Matthew Digby Wyatt, in grounds that had already been landscaped 100 years before by Capability Brown. Those grounds, with walks through woodlands and by a lake, can be explored by a nature trail that starts from the churchyard.

The Church of St Mary Magdalene dates partly from the 14th century and stands in a tree-shaded corner of the grounds. Inside there are monuments to the Compton family and a pulpit said to be by Inigo Jones. Outside are a gnarled mulberry on props and an Italian-style orangery. Castle Ashby is open to the public occasionally in summer; the grounds are open daily.

BILLING AQUADROME
Northampton's playground is set among lakes, lawns, woods and parkland. There is boating and fishing on the lakes and along half a mile of the River Nene that runs through the park. Parking space and picnic places are provided round the lakes. In one corner of the aquadrome a water mill stands astride the Nene, its giant wheel gently turning to operate a mill wheel. The building also contains a mill museum with exhibits of old-time milling and domestic life of the Nene valley. The museum is open daily in mid-summer.

TOUR
116

——— 67 MILES ———

Away from the ever-busy M1 are old coaching towns and villages, locks and canalside communities along the Grand Union Canal, and at each end of the route a fine 18th-century house.

ALTHORP
Approaching the family home of the Princess of Wales from the tree-shaded car park, the first building the visitor sees is the stable block – and surely no horse ever had a grander home. The block was built in the 18th century, using the local beige iron-stone, in the style of Inigo Jones, with a square tower at each corner and a tall-columned portico at the entrance to the courtyard.

In contrast the house is faced with light grey brick, the work of the architect Henry Holland who carried out extensive alterations to the Elizabethan dwelling in the late 18th century for the 2nd Earl Spencer. Set in formal gardens the house has a quiet dignified air set off by acres of greensward and broad gravel paths.

In superbly furnished rooms, corridors and galleries are paintings by Rubens, Van Dyck and Reynolds, and rare porcelain from leading factories. Althorp is open every afternoon, and from 11am in July, August and September and on Bank Holidays.

PASTORAL LANDSCAPE *Flore's 13th-century All Saints' Church sits amid green pastures on the edge of the village.*

GREAT BRINGTON

The reddish-yellow ironstone church of St Mary the Virgin stands at the northern end of the village, close to Althorp. It was Sir John Spencer who in 1514 added the Spencer Chapel to the church, and he is buried there along with some of his descendants and their wives.

The chapel is guarded by tall, spiked railings, but through the bars can be glimpsed the black marble columns of William, the 2nd Baron Spencer's tomb, the long, decorated pendants and fluted columns of the tomb of Robert, 1st Baron Spencer, and the colourful tomb of the 2nd Sir John Spencer, grandson of the chapel's founder.

FLORE

Narrow streets and alleyways with thatched cottages and houses built of brown ironstone and cream limestone give Flore a special charm. South of the village a brick-built bridge crosses the River Nene, and by it stands Mill Farm. Though the mill is no longer there, it is a pretty spot, with the river running placidly among reeds beneath overhanging trees.

BLISWORTH

Canal enthusiasts know Blisworth for its tunnel, which starts just south of the village and ends at Stoke Bruerne. Its most attractive features for the casual visitor, however, are the stone-built houses and cottages that line the streets. They are built of brown ironstone and cream-coloured limestone, some using the two colours to give an attractive mottled effect and others with alternate courses looking like chocolate layer cakes.

TOWCESTER

This town straddling the old Watling Street claims to be one of the oldest in England, for the Romans established a settlement called Lactodorum there soon after the road was built 2000 years ago. But it was as a coaching town in the 18th and 19th centuries that Towcester prospered, and its narrow main street, still looking a little weary from the days when it carried the bulk of northbound traffic, has changed little since.

Towcester's several coaching inns include the Saracen's Head, where Mr Pickwick stayed after a wet ride from Birmingham, as told by Charles Dickens in *Pickwick Papers*.

The Talbot, once called the Tabard, was bought by Archdeacon Sponne in 1440 to found a charity. It is no longer a hotel but still stands, as does the Archdeacon's Chantry House in the small market square.

STOKE BRUERNE

Narrow boats lying nose to tail at their moorings, a white-painted bridge, lock gates and a canalside inn recall the days when Stoke Bruerne was a hive of industry. Northbound boatmen on the Grand Union Canal stopped for a glass of ale in the Boat Inn before tackling the 3074yd Blisworth tunnel, or had their horses freshly shod at the smithy and bought new rope from the ropeworks. Boats coming down from the Midlands

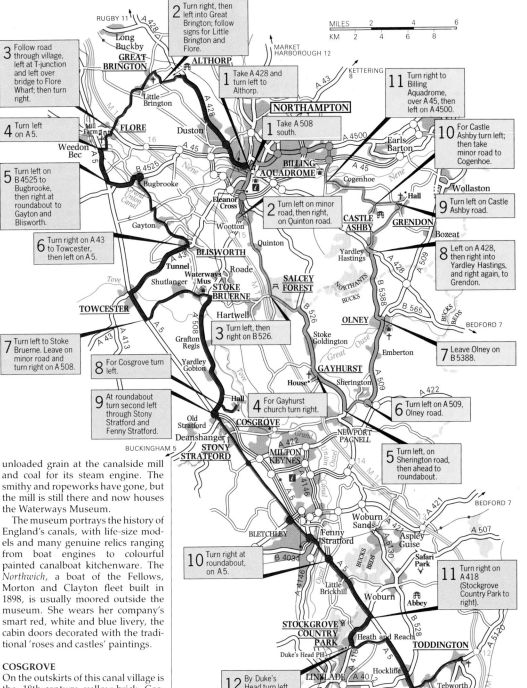

unloaded grain at the canalside mill and coal for its steam engine. The smithy and ropeworks have gone, but the mill is still there and now houses the Waterways Museum.

The museum portrays the history of England's canals, with life-size models and many genuine relics ranging from boat engines to colourful painted canalboat kitchenware. The *Northwich*, a boat of the Fellows, Morton and Clayton fleet built in 1898, is usually moored outside the museum. She wears her company's smart red, white and blue livery, the cabin doors decorated with the traditional 'roses and castles' paintings.

COSGROVE

On the outskirts of this canal village is the 18th-century yellow-brick Cosgrove Hall, not open to the public but clearly visible from the road. Also visible, and immediately catching the eye, is the pretty lodge house, a white, L-shaped cottage with a deep thatch and arched windows beneath the eaves. The cottage stands close to the roadside, and behind its low chain fence grow masses of flowers.

STONY STRATFORD

In coaching days Stony Stratford was an important stop on the London to Holyhead road, and competition for the trade must have been fierce, for several old coaching inns line the road. Both the Bull and the Cock hotels have large signs projecting above the pavement. Behind the main street is the market place, overlooked by the black-and-white Crown inn and stone-built houses. The house on

the corner of Church Street has a large sundial above the door.

STOCKGROVE COUNTRY PARK

Part heath and part woodland, this lovely park on the Bedfordshire-Buckinghamshire border lies in a shallow valley, with a lake where mallard and coot paddle among the tall reeds. There are picnic tables on the ridges where a lakeside walk starts.

South of the park lies the charming little village of Heath and Reach, its tiny green taken up almost entirely by the village pump housed in a brick-built shelter with a clock tower. The

thatched Duke's Head inn faces the green, from which a narrow lane leads past thatched cottages.

TODDINGTON

A large village green is divided into four by crisscrossing roads and bordered by Georgian cottages and a church proudly dedicated to 'St George of England'. On the green stands a village pump, and nearby is the old forge where petrol pumps have replaced anvil and hammer.

Tourist information: Northampton 22677, 34881; Milton Keynes 678361; Dunstable 608441.

Villages of stone in a hunting shire

Cottages of honey-coloured stone lend an unaffectedly pretty appearance to a cluster of villages east of Leicester. The rolling farmland between them is noted hunting country.

BARKBY

Oak trees shade the cricket pitch amid the parkland of Barkby Hall, and it would be hard to imagine a more rural English scene.

In St Mary's Church the 13th-century masons used several designs for the decorated tracery of the nave windows – of the 12 windows, only one pair share the same pattern. A glass case in the south aisle reveals the mechanism of the old clock that was originally installed in the tower in 1773, when it cost £25. The present clock was installed in 1887.

QUENIBOROUGH

The village's wide main street has often echoed with the clatter of horses' hoofs. The horses are hunters these days, but warhorses were stabled here in the Civil War when Prince

Rupert set up his headquarters in the village. The charm of the street lies in the variety of its houses – some thatched, some tiled, some brick, some half-timbered.

GADDESBY

An incongruous monument adorns the chancel of one of Leicestershire's finest medieval churches, St Luke's at Gaddesby. It is a Victorian carving in marble of a local squire, Colonel Edward Hawkins Cheney of the Royal Scots Greys, shown almost life-size astride a horse which is dying in agony. The colonel was a hero of Waterloo in 1815. Four horses were killed under him in the battle, but he lived to tell the tale until 1848.

From the church gate a footpath passes alongside the privet hedge that borders the gardens of Gaddesby Hall. The path leads to Park Hill, the village's main street with its houses of mellow brick and stone.

LITTLE DALBY

Herds of Friesian cows pattern the rolling green hills between Great and Little Dalby. This has been prime dairy country at least since the 18th century, when Little Dalby's herds were the tiny village's main claim to fame. Mrs Orton, housekeeper at Little Dalby Hall, is given credit for having made, in 1720, the first Stilton

cheese. The rich, blue-veined cheese was originally sent to London by coach from Stilton, Cambridgeshire, hence its name.

BURROUGH HILL

The earth banks of an Iron Age hill-fort enclose a large area of the plateau at the hill's summit, some 690ft above sea level. From the grassy ramparts there are panoramic views across a patchwork of fields in this pleasant corner of Leicestershire.

BRAUNSTON

Houses in the little upland villages of Burrough, Somerby, Knossington and Braunston are built of a honey-coloured ironstone that glows in the evening sun. Roses and clematis trained against these golden walls provide a striking contrast of colour.

At Braunston a huge lime tree – planted in 1897 for Queen Victoria's Diamond Jubilee – stands on the green, with a seat below it.

BROOKE

A few scattered houses in the hamlet of Brooke are all that remain of a once quite large village. The Church of St Peter looks equally modest from outside. But beyond the dog-toothed Norman doorway lies an exquisite interior, with light flooding through plain glass windows onto white-

washed walls. This is a rare example of an Elizabethan church superimposed on a Norman framework. The 16th-century woodwork in the church – pulpit, pews and screens – is fashioned in dark polished oak.

Beside the Braunston road the large brick-built farmhouse called Brooke Priory was built in the 17th century near the site of a 12th-century Augustinian priory. Later a grand country house stood here, but all that remains of this is a lodge, converted to a dovecote, that stands in the corner of the farmhouse garden.

PRESTON

An attractive little village, all of a piece in mellow gold ironstone, Preston has a thatched pub, the Fox and Hounds, and a five-gabled Manor House that dates from the 17th century. Proud of their Rutland origins, many villagers hereabouts are loath to acknowledge that their county has been absorbed into Leicestershire.

UPPINGHAM

A small market town and home of a famous public school, Uppingham stands on a plateau surrounded by farmland. At the heart of the town is a small market place, fringed by delightful old-fashioned shops. The Victorian Falcon Hotel faces the Church of St Peter and Paul across the square and between them stands the drinking fountain, built to commemorate Queen Victoria's Golden Jubilee in 1887.

The church was largely rebuilt in 1861, but on the wall just inside the door there are two lively Norman carvings – one of Christ and one of an unnamed saint.

For nearly 270 years from its foundation in 1584, Uppingham School was housed in a single building that still stands south-east of the church. But in 1853 the school's best-known

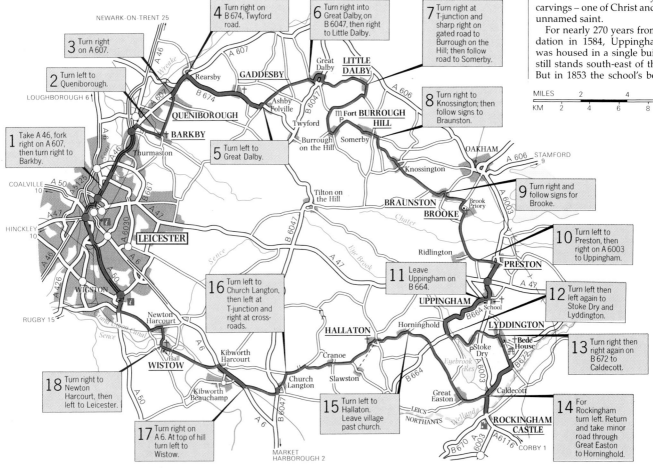

headmaster, Edward Thring, was appointed, and under him, Uppingham expanded from 23 boarders to more than 300. The handsome stone buildings of the school back onto the western end of the High Street, and there are glimpses through the gates to the courtyards within.

LYDDINGTON
The hamlet of Stoke Dry, perched high above the Eyebrook Reservoir, gives fine views to the west. On the other side of the hill – as the slope turns eastwards – there are fine views down to the enchanting village of Lyddington. The village is ranged along one main street, a double row of ancient stone houses roofed with local stone slates.

At its centre stands the Church of St Andrew, noted for its fine wall paintings and brasses. Beside it stands a remarkable medieval building called the Bede House. This was built in the 15th century as a residence for Bishops of Lincoln, who had had a house there since before the reign of King John. In 1602 it became an almshouse, but now it is empty and open to the public daily in summer. (It is closed on Sunday mornings.)

The finest room in the Bede House is the spacious hall on the first floor where the bishops used to hold audience. This has stone-mullioned windows and a magnificent oak ceiling with an intricately carved cornice.

In fields to the east of the village, depressions in the ground are the remains of a network of ponds where fish were bred in the Middle Ages. On islands between the ponds, birds were fattened for the table.

ROCKINGHAM CASTLE
Ancient Britons built a fort on the hill that overlooks the Welland valley, and William the Conqueror ordered that a castle should be raised on the same site. For more than 400 years Rockingham Castle was a royal residence much frequented by the English kings who came to hunt in Rockingham Forest, which covered most of what is now Northamptonshire.

The twin round towers of the entrance gate, with slit windows for defending archers, are very much as they were in Edward I's time. The Walton family bought the castle from Henry VIII, and it has been the family's home ever since.

Inside the gate the castle is largely Tudor, and there is a fine collection of English paintings from the 18th century to the present day. The castle is open on two or three afternoons each week in summer.

Climbing the steep hill at the foot of the castle is the little village of Rockingham, built of the local ironstone. One or two cottages are thatched, but most have stone slates from the nearby quarries of Collyweston.

HALLATON
The nucleus of the village is a square in which there are two stone crosses – one the war memorial, the other an unusual conical market cross, sur-

RAMPARTS VIEW *From the hill-fort on Burrough Hill there are views northward over chequered wheatfields and pastureland.*

WISTOW HALL *The home of the Cottesloe family is Jacobean, but its stuccoed façade was added in 1810. It was used as a hospital in the First World War.*

BALL AND CONE *An ancient market cross stands in Hallaton's square.*

SEAT OF LEARNING *Uppingham's school badge can be seen on the library building.*

mounted by a stone ball. This cross is the focal point of an ancient Easter Monday game called bottle-kicking, in which a Hallaton team battles with neighbouring Medbourne. Each team tries to carry off the bottle – a small iron-bound barrel. The game is very rough and can last up to five hours. The custom may survive from rites connected with the Germanic goddess Eostre, from whose name Easter is said to derive.

St Michael's Church is on a grand scale, with a fine Early English tower and an octagonal spire. A footpath leaves the main street through an arch near the Bewicke Arms, crosses a stream and continues over the fields to Slawston.

WISTOW
The name of this village is derived from Wistanstowe, 'Holy place of Wistan'. For it was here in 847 that Wistan, a Christian prince of the Saxon kingdom of Mercia, was murdered by his uncle, Brifardus, who wanted his throne.

The present Church of St Wistan began as a Norman building – and a blocked-up Norman arch can be seen beside the south door. It has a perfect 18th-century interior, with box pews and pulpit in oak. The Halford family memorials dominate the north transept. They include a reclining effigy of Sir Richard Halford, who sheltered Charles I at Wistow Hall on the night before his defeat at the Battle of Naseby in 1645.

If the church is locked the key may be obtained from Wistow Hall, the handsome house with a Regency façade which stands across the road.

Tourist information: Leicester 556699; Oakham 2918; (Wigston) Leicester 887381.

Hilltop where a king lost his crown

TOUR

118

———— 84 MILES ————

Stones carved in England's early history are found in churches among rolling cornfields. A banner on a hilltop marks the battlefield of Bosworth, where Richard III lost his crown.

ASHBY-DE-LA-ZOUCH

The houses and shops that line broad Market Street span a period from the 14th century, when the Bull's Head inn was erected, to the present day. The half-timbered Queen's Head bears a huge Elizabethan-style window above the courtyard gateway.

Ashby's ruined castle was besieged for more than a year by Parliamentarian forces in the Civil War of the 1640s, and a model depicting the siege can be seen in the little town museum, a short walk away. The museum is open daily in summer.

Before the days of careful preservation, cattle grazed in the castle grounds and the ruin was capped with stunted trees. This landscape inspired the painter J.M.W. Turner, and was the location of several scenes in Sir Walter Scott's novel *Ivanhoe*. The huge keep, Hastings Tower, was built by the 1st Lord Hastings in the 15th century. Only half of its massive walls still stand. The castle is open daily except Thursdays.

STAUNTON HAROLD

A church stands in the grounds of Staunton Harold Hall, a Georgian house. The church was one of the few built during Cromwell's Commonwealth, when the Anglican faith was under siege. Its painted ceiling, dark with storm clouds, seems to depict not only the Creation but also the tumult of the 1650s, and an inscription tells how 'Sir Robert Shirley, Baronet, Founded this church, whose singular praise it is To have done the best things in ye worst times, and hoped them in the most calamitous'.

The church belongs to the National Trust and is open most days in summer.

BREEDON ON THE HILL

A short detour leads to the church on the summit of Breedon Hill, close to a quarry precipice. It was built on the site of an Iron Age hill-fort, whose earthworks still form the cemetery boundary.

Set into the interior walls of the church are about 30 major fragments of Anglo-Saxon stone carving, in which beasts, birds and symbols of a pagan age contrast with Biblical figures and an angel.

Down in the village, near the quarry entrance, is a 17th-century lock-up, a tiny cylindrical cell surmounted by a huge conical roof of mossy stone.

MELBOURNE

On Melbourne Pool, a short walk from the village centre, terns dive after minnows and gliding swans lead their young in search of food. Melbourne Hall, once the home of Queen Victoria's first prime minister, Lord Melbourne, peers out over the pool. This mansion, built in the 17th century and incorporating a medieval house, was greatly enlarged in the 18th century.

Formal gardens descend in steps to a pond, beside which stands a wrought-iron pergola adorned with golden suns and moons, flowers and leaves. It was made by Robert Bakewell, the 18th-century ironsmith, and is known as 'the birdcage'. Statues and cherubs hide at the corners of shrub-lined walks, and at

UNTROUBLED HEART *Looking east from Breedon on the Hill the peaceful fields of emerald and gold justify Leicestershire's claim to be 'the heart of the Shires'.*

HASTINGS TOWER *Ashby Castle's 80ft keep was built in 1474 as a self-contained dwelling.*

BIRDS OF A FEATHER *Caribbean flamingos are among the exotic species that have bred at Twycross Zoo.*

BACK AT WORK *A 1940s loco now runs on the Market Bosworth Light Railway at Shackerstone.*

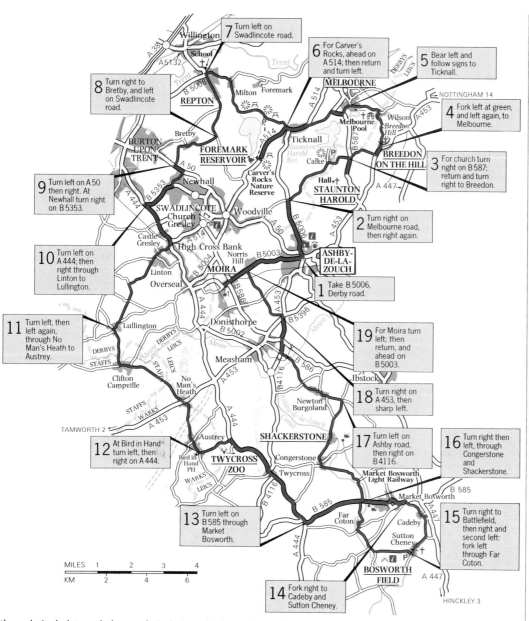

7 Turn left on Swadlincote road.

8 Turn right to Bretby, and left on Swadlincote road.

6 For Carver's Rocks, ahead on A 514; then return and turn left.

5 Bear left and follow signs to Ticknall.

4 Fork left at green, and left again, to Melbourne.

3 For church turn right on B 587; return and turn right to Breedon.

9 Turn left on A 50 then right. At Newhall turn right on B 5353.

2 Turn right on Melbourne road, then right again.

10 Turn left on A 444; then right through Linton to Lullington.

1 Take B 5006, Derby road.

11 Turn left, then left again, through No Man's Heath to Austrey.

19 For Moira turn left; then return, and ahead on B 5003.

18 Turn right on A 453, then sharp left.

12 At Bird in Hand turn left, then right on A 444.

17 Turn left on Ashby road, then right on B 4116.

16 Turn right then left, through Congerstone and Shackerstone.

13 Turn left on B 585 through Market Bosworth.

15 Turn right to Battlefield, then right and second left; fork left through Far Coton.

14 Fork right to Cadeby and Sutton Cheney.

MILES 1 2 3 4
KM 2 4 6

---

the end of a dark tunnel of yews, their branches clasping overhead, water sparkles in a fountain jet. The gardens are open daily; the hall is open on Sunday afternoons in summer.

The nave of Melbourne church displays the full robust splendour of Norman church architecture. Massive columns support clean curved arches, adorned only by a chevron pattern. In contrast, carvings on the capitals of the pillars under the tower show men and beasts writhing in combat.

In Potter Street are thatched and whitewashed cottages, dazzling in sunlight, while in the High Street is the Cruck House, which gets its name from the A-shaped timber-frame which has supported its ancient roof and walls for centuries.

FOREMARK RESERVOIR
On the southern shores of Foremark Reservoir are the birch woods and steep cliff faces of Carver's Rocks Nature Reserve, through which runs a short nature trail. The woods enclose a sheltered finger of the reservoir where great crested grebe shepherd their young, which some-

times hitch a ride on their mother's back. Between the silvery trunks there are glimpses of the main body of water, where bright sailing boats manoeuvre around orange buoys.

On the northern shore there are two more car parks, from which a 3 mile walk leads to Carver's Rocks and back. Picnic benches dot the grassy slopes leading down to the water's edge.

REPTON
In the north aisle of Repton's part Saxon Church of St Wystan lies an alabaster knight covered in the graffiti of centuries. At his feet a short, narrow tunnel descends to the crypt, whose vaulted ceiling is supported by solid stone pillars. The air is damp and smells of age; the floor is of broken and uneven stones. Look closely at the barley-sugar design that spirals down the pillars carved by masons in the 9th century.

Through a graceful archway at the side of the church lies Repton School, which was founded in 1557 on the site of an ancient priory. From the court-yard a cobbled causeway leads to the

Prior's Hall, and to its right is a flight of steps to Pear's School – a 19th-century part of Repton School named after a headmaster. Permission can be obtained at the gatehouse to walk around the schoolyard.

The Repton Trail, a leaflet for which is obtainable at the church, leads from the church and school, past the column of the old market cross and down the High Street. Here the architecture spans four centuries, and some houses incorporate masonry from the priory that was destroyed after the Dissolution of the Monasteries by Henry VIII.

TWYCROSS ZOO
At the entrance to Twycross Zoo a black-and-white Malayan tapir may often be seen lurking in the undergrowth, its trunk-like nose testing the breeze. Flamingos in pink plumage squabble over nest mounds in their pond, while the ring-tailed lemur and his mate use their tiny hands to search each blade of grass for insects.

Primates form a substantial part of the collection, but there are also lions, tigers, camels, elephants, snakes and

penguins, all in clean and modern enclosures. The zoo is in park-like grounds, with sheltered picnic spots and a play area for children, and is open daily.

BOSWORTH FIELD
The land at Bosworth Field sweeps down on all sides in fields of gold and green, bordered with wild flowers. At its breezy summit flies a huge standard bearing a white boar – the emblem of Richard III. Visitors can follow a trail across the battlefield from the site where, on August 22, 1485, King Richard's forces stood looking down to Henry Tudor's little army. Within hours Richard was dead, Henry VII was king, and a new royal lineage, the Tudors, had begun to rule.

In the Battlefield Centre the drama of the clash that ended the Wars of the Roses is re-created with hundreds of model knights, archers and foot soldiers clashing in conflict and an audio-visual display. The centre is open in the afternoons in summer. By the shady picnic ground at the centre is King Dick's Well. Admirers have set up a simple cairn guarding the spring, which is set about by white roses representing the House of York.

King Richard's Field lies in the shadow of a canal embankment, and a rough boulder marks the place where the last Plantagenet king fell. Canal trips by traditional horse-drawn or diesel narrow boats start at the canal side above King Richard's memorial.

Sutton Cheney church, close by, is said to have been the scene of Richard's last mass, and the hassocks are emblazoned with the designs of his standards.

SHACKERSTONE
On weekends at Shackerstone Station the smells of hot steam and oiled metal emanating from the Market Bosworth Light Railway conjure up memories of an earlier railway era. On a summer Sunday or Bank Holiday afternoon, visitors can take a leisurely journey in a Pullman coach through countryside bright with ripening grain and wild flowers. In the stationmaster's office are lamps, levers, clocks, dials and posters – and railway enthusiasts eager to chat about their use and history.

The railway is run and preserved by volunteers, and the station and museum are open at weekends throughout the year. Trains run only on Sunday and Bank Holiday afternoons from Easter to September.

MOIRA
The night sky over Moira, a 19th-century mining village, once glowed from streams of liquid iron disgorged from a roaring blast furnace. For more than a century the furnace has been cold, but a trail starting from its gaping maw leads to other relics of this area's industrial past. A guide to the 1¼ mile trail can be obtained from the Ashby-de-la-Zouch or Coalville tourist information centres.

Tourist information: Coalville 35951; Ashby-de-la-Zouch 415603 (summer).

From Cannock Chase to the Dove

TOUR 119
— 51 MILES —

Between the heaths and woodland of Cannock Chase and ancient Needwood Forest stand a mansion rich in tradition, a romantic castle and a village that stages an ancient hunting dance.

LICHFIELD

Lichfield Cathedral's three great spires pierce the sky above the city, forming a distinctive skyline that is recognisable from several points on this tour. A fourth spire, nearby, belongs to the Church of St Mary in the market square, which now houses the Lichfield Heritage and Treasury Exhibition, open daily. A model of a Roundhead soldier guards the stairway to the exhibition's gallery.

The cathedral dates from the 13th century and its magnificent west front contains more than 100 statues. The 17th-century Bishop's Palace stands in the quiet cathedral close.

In the market place the statue of Samuel Johnson, lexicographer and literary giant, broods on the world passing below. The front door of his father's house is opposite. Johnson was born here and it remained his home until he was 27. The house contains books, manuscripts and Johnson relics. It is open on weekdays throughout the year, and also on summer Sunday afternoons.

There is a marked town trail through the gridiron of streets around the house. It leads to fine old timber buildings in Bore Street and Quonians Lane, and in Vicars Close a secluded grassed courtyard shaded by a tree is lined by 16th-century cottages.

CANNOCK CHASE

From the Marquis Drive Information Centre two trails lead over Brindley Heath through marsh, birch groves, pine woods and heather. Here at twilight, fallow deer may emerge from thickets that ring with the nightjar's note.

The history and life of Cannock Chase and its inhabitants are the theme of a permanent exhibition at the information centre. During the First World War the Chase was used for military training and there was a camp for prisoners of war. The remains of the encampments can be followed by a car trail, with marked walks from six car parks.

The road zigzags through pine plantations and emerges at the country park, part of which is set aside for recreation and picnics.

At the north-west end of the park, a small nature reserve has been created around a flooded quarry.

Guides to the walking trails on the Chase can be obtained from the information centres at Marquis Drive and Milford Common. Guides to the walks through Forestry Commission plantations are available from the Forest Centre at Ladyhill.

SHUGBOROUGH

An imposing Ionic portico dominates the east front of this mainly 18th-century mansion. The west front of the house is almost as impressive, with a three-storey bay window set between two cast-iron verandahs.

The interior of the mansion reflects the scholarly tastes of the Anson family, Earls of Lichfield, who have

been at Shugborough since 1624. The Red Drawing Room, designed by Samuel Wyatt in 1794, has a coved ceiling decorated with magnificent plasterwork. Owned by the National Trust, Shugborough is open daily except Monday from mid-March to mid-October.

The park surrounding the house is open all year and contains an unusual collection of monuments. Some, like the Tower of Winds, are copies of Classical Greek buildings. Two marked tours of the monuments start from the car park. Picnicking is allowed in the grounds, and there are several easy walks.

The Staffordshire County Museum is housed in the domestic buildings of the house, and includes the restored brewhouse, coach-house and laundry, and a reconstructed tailor's shop and village general store. It is open from Tuesday to Sunday, but closes on Saturdays in winter.

Adjoining the estate is the Shugborough Park Farm, open at the same times as the museum. Its livestock are mainly Staffordshire breeds of cattle, sheep and pigs, and a small museum displays farm equipment.

CHARTLEY CASTLE

From the road, a short uphill walk leads to the ruin of Chartley Castle. In contrast to castles that are fenced off

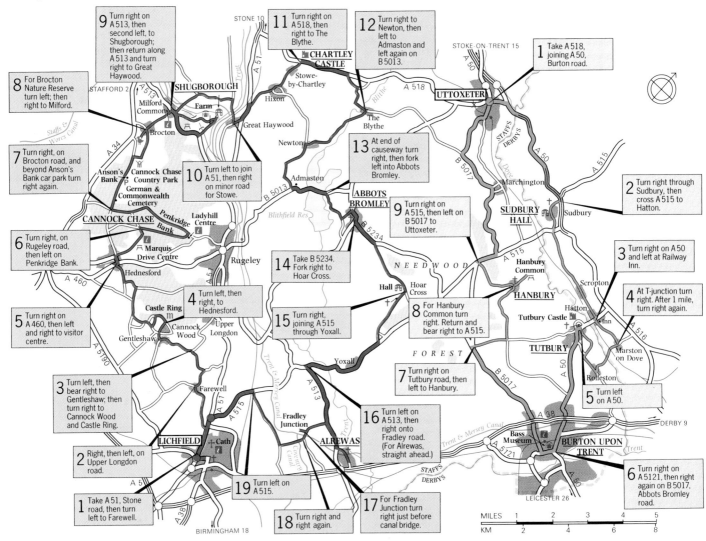

194

and carefully tended, Chartley still wears an air of romantic neglect, with scrubby trees growing from its crumbling stonework.

ABBOTS BROMLEY
The road through the village squeezes between Georgian brick and Elizabethan timber buildings that suddenly give way to an open square. Massive timbers support the roof of the butter cross, beside a green.

Inside the Church of St Nicholas hang reindeer horns set in dummy heads. Reputed to date from Saxon times, they are carried every September by performers in the Abbots Bromley Horn Dance, a hunting rite that may be pre-Christian.

ALREWAS
Pretty gardens surround many of the half-timbered, thatched cottages that line the main street of Alrewas and the narrow lanes that adjoin it.

A rough road starting beside the canal bridge at Fradley leads to Fradley Junction, where the Coventry Canal joins the Trent and Mersey Canal. Locks and bridges evoke the atmosphere of the canal's heydays.

Tourist information: Lichfield 252109.

TOUR
120
—— 36 MILES ——

Green hills line the valley of the lower River Dove, where villages are dotted among meadows grazed by cattle. In Burton upon Trent, the history of brewing is captured in a museum.

UTTOXETER
The handsome half-timbered buildings that overlook Uttoxeter market belong to the 19th century. But in one corner of the market place is a genuine Elizabethan house and shop, carefully restored by a local butcher. Bright awnings of stalls that crowd the narrow streets still enliven the town centre on Wednesdays and Saturdays.

A regular stallholder in Uttoxeter market 250 years ago was a Lichfield bookseller named Michael Johnson. When Johnson lay on his deathbed his son, Samuel, refused to go to the market in his father's place. The memory of this ignoble act so haunted Dr Samuel Johnson that as an elderly man he stood bareheaded in the rain in the market place for a day. A plaque commemorating this act of penitence is set in the wall of a stone kiosk.

SUDBURY HALL
This solid 17th-century brick mansion is a marriage of Jacobean and Elizabethan styles. It is the creation of one man, George Vernon, who built it on or near the site of an old manor house of his ancestors. The plasterwork of the Great Staircase is almost overpowering in its complexity. The Long Gallery, a wide corridor running the length of the house, has oil paintings, mainly of the Vernon family.

CANNOCK CHASE *Bracken carpets part of the former hunting ground of kings stretching north from Brocton Coppice.*

FRADLEY JUNCTION *Some of the magic of the old waterways is recaptured where two canals – the Coventry and the Trent and Mersey – join near Alrewas.*

SUDBURY HALL *This 17th-century mansion is a showcase of the period's arts.*

ONE FOR THE ROAD *A converted 1924 Daimler stands in the Bass Museum.*

The hall and museum are open from April to the end of October in the afternoons, from Wednesday to Sunday, and also Bank Holidays.

TUTBURY
The shattered towers and breached walls of Tutbury Castle crown a wooded hill that can be seen for much of the tour. The castle dates from the 12th century, but most of what remains is 15th century. Mary, Queen of Scots had two spells of imprisonment here, between 1569 and 1587, after she fled from Scotland.

The ruin overlooks the meandering River Dove, flanked on the south by the remnants of Needwood Forest.

There is a car park near the 14th-century John of Gaunt's Gateway. Below it, a steep wooded slope can be explored by nature trails leading down to the river.

The castle is open from April to October, and the well-kept grounds make a good spot for a picnic.

The village of Tutbury has a long history of glass-making, and near the village centre glassblowers may be seen in action in their workshops.

BURTON UPON TRENT
The aroma of hops and malt is everywhere in a town where beer has been brewed since the Middle Ages. It became the centre of Britain's brewing industry in the 18th century when the coming of the Trent and Mersey Canal made the transport of beer easier.

The town's Victorian Gothic town hall is among several fine 19th-century buildings given by Michael Bass, who became Lord Burton. The Bass Museum, which is open daily, illustrates 200 years of brewing history. Displays explain the alchemy by which hops, grain and water are transmuted into beer.

HANBURY
At the edge of this little village, the Church of St Werburgh stands on a hill. Light from a window falls on the figure of a peacefully resting knight, probably John de Hanbury who died in 1303. If so, it is probably the oldest alabaster tomb in England; it is known that masons specialising in alabaster were operating locally as early as the 16th century.

Tourist information:
Burton upon Trent 45454.

195

A river gorge where history was made

TOUR

121

─── 80 MILES ───

The steep-sided Severn valley, spanned by the world's first iron bridge, is rich in relics of the Industrial Revolution. To the north, the great bulk of The Wrekin guards a green plain.

NEWPORT

The Normans built Newport as a 'new town', designed around a winding main street with the Church of St Nicholas on an island at the centre. The red-sandstone church still stands at the town's northern end, and though massively restored in the 19th century retains its medieval character. Along the main street pleasant timber-framed shops and houses contrast with rows of Georgian and Victorian red brick.

Newport's most eye-catching building is the Town Hall, now used as business premises. Built in 1860, it is in Italian style with tall arched windows, stone facings and an ornate clock. The windows and stone facings are painted a dazzling white, while the rest of the brickwork is pale blue, giving the building a distinctly 'Wedgwood' look.

LILLESHALL

On a rocky knoll above the village stands a 70ft high monument to the 1st Duke of Sutherland, a local landowner who died in 1833. According to the lengthy inscription on its base, he was 'the most just and generous of landlords' who 'went down to his grave with the blessings of his tenants on his head'. The monument was erected in 1833, and from its plinth there are superb views across the flat plains stretching westwards to The Wrekin.

South-east of the village is Lilleshall Abbey, founded in 1148 for Arroasian canons. Though now a ruin, the sandstone building is still impressive, particularly the arched doorway to the roofless nave and the tall Gothic window arch at the eastern end.

WESTON PARK

The industrious Capability Brown laid out the gardens and parkland surrounding this 17th-century mansion built by Lady Wilbraham and the home of the Earls of Bradford for almost 300 years. The house is one of the best examples of Restoration period architecture and contains a collection of pictures by English, Flemish and Italian painters.

In the spacious grounds are three lakes, and there are walks through woodland. There is also a butterfly farm, a miniature railway, an aquarium and a museum of country bygones. The house and park are open most days in summer, and at weekends in spring and autumn.

COALPORT

Beside the still, weed-covered waters of a disused canal stand the abandoned buildings and kilns of a china works which was one of the foremost names in fine porcelain for 200 years. The Coalport Company occupied this site from the mid-18th century until 1926, when it moved to Staffordshire; the buildings now form a museum showing the history of the porcelain china industry, and of Coalport in particular. The old kilns and workshops can be visited, and one kiln now houses a dazzling display of Coalport china.

Though now part of the Wedgwood Company, Coalport still retains its name, and in the entrance hall of the museum are displays of present-day products ranging from elegant tableware to the delicate flower-design ornaments for which Coalport is noted. The museum is open daily.

BLISTS HILL

Blists Hill Open Air Museum brings history to the present day. A hundred years ago Blists Hill must have resembled an inferno, with flames belching from three blast furnaces, smoke pouring from the kilns of a brick and tile works, and steam winding-engines hauling coal, clay and iron ore from mines 600ft down.

Today the furnaces and kilns are cold, the engines silent, but around them has been built a small community showing what life was like in a typical East Shropshire industrial community of the 1890s. In gas-lit streets are shops, a pub, a candle factory, blacksmith's and plasterer's premises, a sawmill and a printer's workshop – all staffed by people in period dress and operating exactly as they did at the turn of the century.

In a valley below the little township stand a reconstructed ironworks and a pair of steam engines, called *David* and *Sampson*, which once pumped air into a nearby blast furnace. At the far end of the valley is the remarkable Hay Inclined Plane, which carried boats up and down between the Shropshire Canal and the wharfs at Coalport, a drop of 207ft.

SWEET SEVERN *Britain's longest river flows gently through the Ironbridge Gorge, where the brown trout rises in limpid waters that once glowed red in the glare of furnace fires.*

OLD TIMER *The iron clock tower at Coalbrookdale dates from 1843.*

STAUNCH SUPPORTERS *The ribs of the iron bridge weigh 5 tons each.*

IRON-BRIDGE

This small town rising in terraces above the River Severn takes its name from the world's first bridge of iron. The bridge was cast in the nearby works of Abraham Darby and assembled using carpentry joints, since bolts and rivets were still inventions of the future. Its graceful 100ft arch has spanned the gorge since 1779, and only in the 1930s was it closed to traffic; it is still open to pedestrians.

A footpath on the river bank below the bridge affords a good view of the bridge's unique construction, particularly the five ribs which are secured to the uprights by wedges, and the base-plates held together by dovetail joints.

The new technology caused the builders to err on the side of caution, preferring strength rather than economy of material. Consequently the weight of iron in the bridge is just over 378 tons – considerably more than later bridges of similar size.

The buildings close to the bridge date from the late 18th century and seem to have been influenced by that soaring arch; or perhaps the arched windows and arcaded shop fronts are no more than reflections of the Georgian style. The rest of the town clings to the side of the gorge, connected by terrifyingly steep hills and vicious hairpin bends.

COALBROOKDALE

In 1709 Abraham Darby, the ironmaster at the Coalbrookdale ironworks, began to smelt iron ore using coke rather than charcoal as his fuel. This change was forced upon him because in the early 18th century charcoal was becoming scarce. It took 100 tons of timber to produce 25 tons of charcoal – and timber was needed for many other uses. Darby's innovation revolutionised ironmaking, making it cheaper and quicker to produce, and paved the way for the manufacture of iron wheels, rails, bridges, ships and high-pressure steam engines.

By 1838 Coalbrookdale was one of the largest foundries in the world, and the Great Warehouse built in that year now houses a Museum of Iron which illustrates the history of ironmaking and the story of the Coalbrookdale Company. Prominent among the exhibits are examples of ornamental cast-iron work, including the 'Cupid and Swan' fountain made for the Great Exhibition of 1851. Of a more practical nature are a locomotive, a haystack boiler and iron chimney pots and cauldrons.

In the grounds of the museum stands a tent-like canopy of glass and steel which protects Coalbrookdale's holy of holies – the Old Blast Furnace in which Abraham Darby first produced his coke-smelted iron. In this brick-built structure, only rediscovered in 1959, a revolution was revolutionised.

BUILDWAS ABBEY

Only the main body of this once lovely abbey still stands, though roofless and without its aisle walls. It dates from the 12th century and has a serene simplicity, particularly in the seven arched bays of each side of the

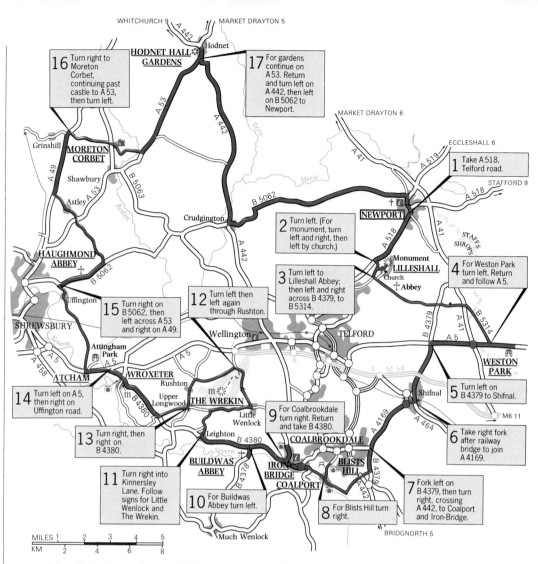

nave and the tall, slender windows at the eastern end.

Buildwas Abbey, never a powerful house, had a fairly uneventful history until its last abbot, Stephen Greene, surrendered it to Henry VIII in 1536.

THE WREKIN

The brooding, whale-back hump of The Wrekin is something of a geological oddity, for it rises abruptly from the flat Severn Plain, remote from the nearest range of hills, as if dumped there by some strange force. Not surprisingly there are legends to account for its presence, mostly involving giants, but in fact The Wrekin was formed from lava, ash and debris disgorged from a volcano some 900 million years ago.

Its 1334ft summit is crowned by earthworks that were the ramparts of the tribal capital of the Cornovii, one of the last tribes to resist the Roman invasion. A footpath to the top of the hill leads through the fort's inner and outer entrances, known as Hell Gate and Heaven Gate.

WROXETER

The Romans established a fort at Wroxeter during the 1st century, and when the legions left it became the fourth largest town in Roman Britain – Viroconium. The town covered some 200 acres and excavations have exposed a market hall and a swimming pool. The most impressive relic at

Wroxeter is one wall of the exercise hall adjacent to the baths. This 20ft high wall contains a square entrance which had double doors leading to the frigidarium, or 'cooling off' room. A museum displays coins, pottery and painted plaster from the site.

ATCHAM

Two bridges span the Severn at Atcham, one dating from 1769 and the other, which carries today's traffic, built in 1929. On one side of the main road close to the modern bridge is the elegant gateway to Attingham Park, an 18th-century house built for the 1st Lord Berwick and now owned by the National Trust.

In 1805 the architect John Nash added a picture gallery and circular staircase, using cast iron from Coalbrookdale. The grounds were laid out by Humphry Repton.

Attingham Park is open to the public on certain days in summer.

HAUGHMOND ABBEY

This 12th-century Augustinian foundation was the victim of two major events in English history. First, in common with most abbeys, it was partly demolished in 1539 at the Dissolution of the Monasteries. What remained was converted into a private house, which was burnt down during the Civil War.

The ruins are still impressive, however, especially as they contain

features from the abbey's two roles – as a church and as a private house. The entrance is through a 17th-century garden gate, and attached to what was the abbot's lodgings there is a 16th-century bay window.

MORETON CORBET

A Norman castle stood at Moreton Corbet until Cromwell dismantled it; what stands there now and bears the name Moreton Corbet Castle is the stark ruin of a once-magnificent house built in 1579 by Sir Andrew Corbet. The flat surrounding countryside accentuates the bold outlines of the house, its tall gables reaching to the sky where rooks take flight from empty windows.

HODNET HALL GARDENS

In a valley below the Victorian Hodnet Hall are 60 acres of lakes and pools set among trees, flowers and shrubs. Primulas and irises grow beside the water, and in spring the banks are ablaze with daffodils and early flowering shrubs.

Hodnet Hall is the home of the Heber-Percy family, and it was Brigadier Heber-Percy who created the water garden in 1921. The gardens are open to the public daily from April to September.

Tourist information: Newport 814109; Iron-Bridge (Telford) 882753 (summer).

197

Wooded ridges and dales of Shropshire

TOUR
122
— 83 MILES —

In the peaceful Severn valley are the shady glades of the Wyre Forest. The heights of Kinver Edge and Wenlock Edge frame this delightful western part of the English Midlands.

BRIDGNORTH
There are two towns at Bridgnorth – Low Town, which sits on the banks of the Severn, and High Town, perched on a sandstone cliff rising sheer from the opposite river bank. The two towns are connected by a six-arched road bridge, a winding road and a cliff railway.

The 17th-century Town Hall stands solidly in the middle of High Town's High Street, and traffic passes through the arches on which it is built. Close to the cliff edge are the remains of a castle whose ruined Norman keep leans at an angle of 17 degrees, the result of undermining by Parliamentarians after the Civil War. Nearby is the 'top' station of the cliff railway, said to be the steepest in Britain with a 1 in 1½ gradient. A walk along the cliff edge gives views across the Severn, with Low Town and the bridge looking like a miniature town far below.

Cartway leads down to the river from the High Street, and was once the only link between the two levels. In this road is Bridgnorth's oldest house, the timber-framed Bishop Percy's House built in 1580 and the birthplace in 1729 of Thomas Percy

who became Bishop of Dromore. Also in Cartway are caves cut into the sandstone cliff and used as dwellings well into Victorian times.

Low Town also has its share of old buildings. They include Diamond Hall and a post office, both dating from 1700.

Looking up to High Town from the far bank of the river, the outstanding feature is the Church of St Mary Magdalene, a dignified classical building built in 1792 by Thomas Telford, better known for his roads, bridges and canals.

Bridgnorth is the northern terminus of the Severn Valley Railway, which runs steam trains to Kidderminster, 16 miles away, during the summer. The line runs through the lovely countryside, following the course of the river for most of the way. At times it clings to the valley side, with the river a silvery ribbon below, then descends to pass through riverside stations still looking as they did when the Severn valley line was part of Britain's railway network.

CLAVERLEY
This delightful village set on a wooded slope is a study in black and white. The main street curves gently as it climbs to the top of the hill, from where the view is a charming perspective of timber-framed houses and cottages, and the handsome Crown Inn. In summer, window boxes and hanging baskets glow with the vibrant red of geraniums, and even the stone trough beneath the village pump overflows with aubrietia. There

are one or two sandstone buildings in the village, including the imposing All Saints' Church, whose lofty tower soars above the rooftops.

On the north wall of the nave is a painting, believed to date from 1200, of a battle between armed knights on horseback, illustrating the Battle of the Virtues and the Vices. Near the church is the rectory, a timber-framed building with timbers arranged in a herringbone design.

MIDLAND MOTOR MUSEUM
The setting for this impressive museum, containing more than 90 historic cars and motorcycles, is Stanmore Hall, which stands in 24 acres of beautiful parkland. The museum specialises in sports and racing cars, and among the models on display are Jaguars, Ferraris, Bugattis and Porsches. The majority of the cars on display have been completely restored, and it is claimed that each is capable of the performance for which it was designed.

Also in the museum is the 1933, 24 litre Napier-Railton driven by John Cobb at Brooklands, where it made the fastest-ever lap of 143.44mph.

While motoring enthusiasts browse among the machinery of yesteryear, the less mechanically minded can explore the impressive grounds. The museum and grounds are open daily.

DUDMASTON HALL
This impressive 18th-century house contains a fine collection of furniture, 17th-century flower paintings and modern painting and sculpture,

including works by Matisse, Barbara Hepworth and Henry Moore. The house is surrounded by an attractive shrub garden.

The house and garden are open on Wednesdays and Sundays from April to September.

UPPER ARLEY
The steep little main street, clinging to the east bank of the Severn, dips down to the water's edge, climbs up to the church and goes no farther. A slipway leads down to a shingly little beach, giving Upper Arley the appearance of a seaside fishing village, were it not for the grassy bank across the water where patient anglers sit, and the line of the Severn Valley Railway.

A ferry once operated here – its steel cable still spans the river – but now a footbridge leads across to the Old Harbour Inn and the smart little railway station.

As the road climbs away from the river it passes the Valentia Arms inn and restaurant, which takes its name from Viscount Valentia who is buried in the 14th-century St Peter's Church at the top of the rise. Next to the restaurant stands Arley House, a mock-Gothic private residence with battlements and a turreted tower.

KINVER
Some fine old houses survive in Kinver's main street, mostly dating from the Georgian period when the village's main industry was the manufacture of iron screws and nails. There are also humbler dwellings from the same period, the red-brick cottages built to house the nail workers, and a coaching inn, the White Harte.

High above the village, on a 298ft sandstone spur, stands St Peter's

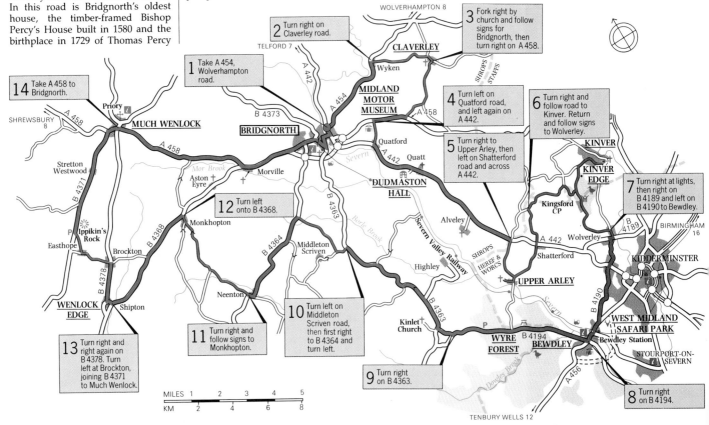

Church, mostly 14th century but with traces of a Norman church. Among its many monuments is one dating from the early 16th century and commemorating Sir Edward Grey of nearby Enville and his two wives, three sons and ten daughters.

KINVER EDGE
This sandstone bluff towering some 300ft above the village of Kinver has a formation of rocks with cave dwellings carved into the soft, pink stone. Some probably date back to the Iron Age, but others were occupied during this century. One cave, Holy Austin Rock, was a hermitage and another, in the bottom of Nanny's Rock, has windows and a chimney flue.

Kinver Edge is owned by the National Trust, and the rest of it is a nature reserve covered by heath and woodland. Views from the summit extend as far as the Malvern Hills, the Cotswolds and Wenlock Edge.

To the south is the Kingsford Country Park, with woodland walks and picnic places in shady glades.

WEST MIDLAND SAFARI PARK
Lions, tigers, giraffes, elephants, rhinos, zebras, camels and monkeys are among more than 50 species of wild animals that roam through 200 acres of grass and woodland at the West Midland Safari and Leisure Park. From the car park, a road winds through an African reserve, a Eurasian reserve including deer, an American reserve containing wolves and bison, and a monkey jungle. Near the animal reserves is an amusement park and lakes with boats. There is a pool with sea lions and a pets' corner where visitors can feed the animals. The safari park is open daily from mid-March to October.

BEWDLEY
Its name a corruption of the French *beau lieu*, Bewdley is still a 'beautiful place' situated on the edge of the Wyre Forest and on the banks of the Severn, though some of its ancient black-and-white buildings and red-brick Georgian terraces have seen better days. In its heyday Bewdley was a prosperous inland port, handling goods sent up river from Bristol; today the traffic on the river are skiffs from the local rowing club and pleasure boats.

But Bewdley enjoys two time capsules that whirl the visitor back into the past. The Bewdley Museum is housed in a cobbled alleyway of small shops, called the Shambles, where butchers used to kill their own beef. A ropewalk, brass foundry and cooper's shop are so realistically set up that it looks as though the craftsmen have just gone off for a tea break – an illusion that is made even more real by the presence of modern craftsmen at work, among them a blacksmith and a glass-blower.

Across Thomas Telford's handsome stone bridge over the river is Bewdley Station, on the Severn Valley Railway. As well as the gleaming locomotives and the immaculate cream and brown coaches, the fittings of the station evoke nostalgia in any visitor who can recall the golden age of steam. Enamel signs advertise long-forgotten merchandise. Stacks of trunks and leather suitcases might be the luggage of a colonel or a tea planter on his way out to the colonies. There are daily excursions in the summer to Bridgnorth or Kidderminster.

WYRE FOREST
From Bewdley the road runs northwest for about 2 miles through an avenue of trees. All along the way are parking places and picnic sites on both sides.

Footpaths lead down to the swift-flowing Dowles Brook, a tributary of the Severn, at the heart of a nature reserve, noted for its wide variety of forest types. A permit is needed to leave the footpaths.

WENLOCK EDGE
The great tree-clad escarpment of Wenlock Edge runs for 16 miles across Shropshire, a massive limestone ridge shelving steeply on its western face to the patchwork fields of Ape Dale, and on its eastern side sloping gently into the lovely Corve Dale.

Disused quarries pepper the northern section, and near Lilleshall Quarry is Ippikin's Rock, a projecting crag which gives good views towards the Stretton Hills. According to legend, Ippikin was a notorious robber who lived in a cave in the cliff. A landslide buried the cave and its hoard of stolen goods, and the ghost of Ippikin still stands guard ready to push over the cliff anyone who approaches his treasure.

Near Stretton Westwood the sheer face of the edge is called Major's Leap, after Major Thomas Smallman, a Civil War Royalist officer who rode his horse over the cliff to avoid capture by pursuing Parliamentarians. His horse was killed, but the major's fall was broken by a tree and he escaped to Shrewsbury.

MUCH WENLOCK
The streets of this old market town are narrow and lined with black-and-white buildings; even the 16th-century old Gaol House is half-timbered, and the Guildhall of the same period stands on sturdy oak pillars. It is open daily in summer.

The town grew around St Milburga's Priory, established in 680, pillaged by the Danes and rebuilt by Leofric, husband of Lady Godiva. The ruins of this once lovely building rise from well-kept lawns dotted with flowerbeds and clipped box hedges.

Much Wenlock was the birthplace of Dr Penny Brookes, a pioneer of physical education in schools. The people of Much Wenlock, however, claim that he was also the true founder of the modern Olympic Games. Dr Brookes held Olympic Games in Much Wenlock in 1850, though they were not international and it was ten years before they were opened to all England. The first modern International Olympiad was held in Athens in 1896, one year after Dr Brookes' death.

Tourist information: Bridgnorth 3358; Bewdley 403303; Much Wenlock 727679 (summer).

CHURCH IN A PARK *Kinlet's part-Norman parish church stands in Kinlet Park and was built to serve a village which has now vanished, leaving only a small hamlet.*

From Wenlock Edge to the Clee Hills

TOUR
123

— 63 MILES —

The wooded escarpment of Wenlock Edge runs north-east from Craven Arms. Behind and below it a network of narrow lanes zigzags across a landscape of streams and small valleys.

LUDLOW

There is no finer townscape in England than the view of Ludlow from the Wigmore road, just south of the River Teme. From this point the whole town lies spread out. Below are the massive walls and square towers of the castle; a little to the right, the

pinnacles of the magnificent church tower soar 135ft above the clustered streets of Tudor and Georgian houses; and farther right again the distant slopes of Titterstone Clee Hill stand like a bastion on the horizon.

Ludlow was built as a 'new town' by the Normans, soon after the Conquest. The castle was begun about 1090, and reached the height of its glory under the Mortimer family in the late Middle Ages. Under the Tudors and Stuarts it became the headquarters of the Council of the Marches set up to administer the wild Welsh border region.

Built of greenish and pinkish limestone and sandstone, Ludlow Castle is still magnificent in decay, with notable features such as the round Chapel of St Mary Magdalene, built around 1100. The castle is open daily

except Sundays in winter. The nearby St Laurence's Church is as splendid as the castle. Built mainly in 15th-century Perpendicular style, it is entered through an unusual hexagonal south porch. Inside, its vast size gives it an almost cathedral-like impact. The oak misericords under the choir stalls are carved with mermaids, musicians and everyday scenes from medieval life, and the choir ceiling is decorated with gilded angels and heraldic roof bosses.

Finest of Ludlow's many half-timbered buildings is the ornate Feathers Hotel, in the Bull Ring. The three-storey hotel is a profusion of carved timberwork dating from 1619, from its elegant first-floor balcony to its three-gabled roof.

Ludlow's town museum, in an elegant 18th-century stone building

known as the Butter Cross, is open daily from April to September. Dinham House, a graceful 18th-century town house next door to the castle, is now a centre for craftsmen from all over Shropshire, and open daily.

BROMFIELD

Among the water meadows where the River Onny joins the Teme stands the ruin of what was once an important Benedictine priory. All that survives is the gateway, half-timbered above and stone-built below.

Next to it stands St Mary's Church, much reduced in size by Henry VIII at the Dissolution of the Monasteries but still impressive, with its strong 13th-century tower and magnificent timber roof. The barrel-vaulted ceiling of the chancel is painted with Biblical texts in scrolls, cherubs' heads and other decoration.

STOKESAY CASTLE

Crab-apple trees grow in the moat of this attractive little castle, giving a rustic touch. Built mainly in the late 13th century by Laurence de Ludlow, a wealthy wool merchant, Stokesay is a fortified manor house, rather than a castle built purely for defence.

The two lower storeys of the north tower were built by the Say family – the name Stokesay means 'dairy farm of the Says'. De Ludlow built nearly all the rest, which consists of a great hall with an attached solar and a battlemented south tower.

The solar appeared in many 13th-century houses, and was the place where the family withdrew after meals. Stokesay's solar measures 29ft by 19ft, and its fittings date from the 17th century. Presumably because the sun could not always be relied upon to provide warmth, the room has a stone medieval fireplace with an elaborately carved Flemish overmantel. The timber-framed Elizabethan gatehouse, still inhabited, has fine carving on the external timbers.

The castle is open daily except for Mondays and Tuesdays in November.

ASTON ON CLUN

In the centre of the village stands an ancient black poplar, known as the Arbor Tree, which is ceremonially decorated with flags and bunting each May 29 – Royal Oak Day. The custom celebrates the marriage of a local landowner on May 29, 1786. Many of the decorations remain throughout the year, and the tree is a popular centrepiece for weddings.

At Hopesay, 1 mile north, a footpath leads to the top of Hopesay Hill. From the summit, which is National Trust land, there are fine views of The Long Mynd to the north and the Welsh hills to the west.

ACTON SCOTT FARM MUSEUM

The farming clock has been turned back a century at Acton Scott, where superbly groomed Shire horses plough the upland soil, russet-coloured Tamworth piglets squeak among their straw, and Norfolk black turkeys strut round the farmyard. Far from being just a showplace, it is a working mixed farm of 22 acres, within sight of Wenlock Edge, using

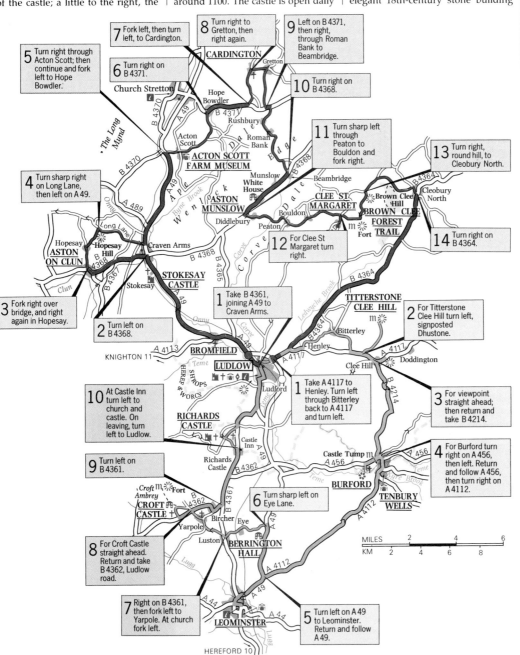

PEACEFUL HILLS *A patchwork counterpane climbs the broad back of Hopesay Hill, in a landscape that the poet A.E. Housman called 'the quietest under the sun'.*

19th-century techniques which can still teach the modern farmer valuable lessons. Displays of traditional crafts include regular demonstrations of butter-making in a churn.

Apart from the barns and other farm buildings, Acton Scott has a fishpool, paddocks and meadows, a waymarked nature trail, café and picnic tables. Warm clothing and strong shoes or gumboots are recommended, as this is an outdoor site and conditions are often wet and muddy. The farm is open daily from April to October, and near the entrance there is a large picnic site.

CARDINGTON
This remote village of stone-built houses lies just north of a bleak stretch of hilly moorland. Its medieval Church of St James, standing in an unusually large and irregular churchyard, has a massive tower that looks strong enough to be defended. The church has superb timbers in its roof, and an ancient door that has survived since the Middle Ages.

ASTON MUNSLOW
Overlooking the village, medieval, Elizabethan and Georgian building styles amalgamate in a fascinating architectural jumble known as the White House. In Saxon times there was a manor here known as Estune, held by Lord Elmund in 1042, but the earliest part of the present house dates from the 14th century. The vast beams of the original medieval hall are still visible in places.

In the 16th century a gabled cross wing was added; in the 18th century this was partly destroyed by fire and replaced by a Georgian addition. Near the house are the ruins of a 13th-century dovecote, a 17th-century cider house complete with cider press, a 17th-century coach house and a large 16th-century stable block. These outbuildings now form part of a Museum of Buildings and Country Life.

The White House is open on Wednesdays and Saturdays from Easter to October, and also on Thursdays during July and August.

CLEE ST MARGARET
At the bottom of a leafy lane below Brown Clee Hill, this village of pretty cottages and magnificent stone barns crowds down the hill to a watersplash. Just above the village, on the eastern side, is the bracken-covered mound of the Nordybank hill-fort. From its summit, best reached from the lane north-east of the village, there are fine views over the surrounding countryside.

BROWN CLEE FOREST TRAIL
Unlike the grassy slopes on the western side of Brown Clee Hill, its eastern flanks are largely covered in trees, most of them close-packed conifers, with forest rides between. The Brown Clee Forest Trail, which takes about 45 minutes to walk, is an easy waymarked ramble among pine and spruce along which there may be glimpses of foxes, badgers, grey

squirrels and hares, while many different birds may be seen including woodpeckers, buzzards and jays. The walk starts from a stile opposite a row of oak trees, where there is room to park, and covers a loop of about 1¼ miles rising from 1000ft to 1250ft above sea level.

About halfway along the trail, a path leads up to the top of Brown Clee Hill, at 1772ft the highest point in Shropshire. From here there are views across rolling farmlands to Wenlock Edge in the west and The Wrekin to the north.

TOUR
124

—— 59 MILES ——

East of Ludlow, which has no rivals among the gems of the Welsh Marches, rises the dramatic silhouette of Titterstone Clee Hill. Beyond lie water meadows beside the Lugg and the Teme.

TITTERSTONE CLEE HILL
This solitary escarpment dominates the landscape east of Ludlow. From its windswept, desolate upper slopes there are vast panoramas westwards towards the Welsh hills, and southwards across the rich farmlands of Herefordshire.

Titterstone Clee Hill was mined for coal during the Middle Ages, and the black basalt – 'dhustone', or black

stone – which forms its upper part, is still quarried today for road-building. On either side of the road to the summit is a moon landscape of worked-out pits and quarry workings, contrasting with the modern radomes and aerials on the hill's eastern edge.

Beyond Clee Hill village a short detour down the Doddington road leads to a public viewpoint. Cars can be parked on the south of the road, from where there are wide-ranging views south towards the Malvern Hills.

BURFORD
A pretty cul-de-sac hamlet consisting of a fine, red-brick Georgian house, a fascinating church and a few cottages, stands beside the gently flowing waters of the River Teme.

Burford House is a graceful, early 18th-century country mansion, built for a wealthy glass manufacturer. It stands in gardens which are a plantsman's delight, full of shrubs and flowers collected over the years by John Treasure, a leading clematis specialist, who has his own clematis nursery at Burford. The handsome stable block contains a small museum on the history and development of the clematis, from Elizabethan times. The gardens are open from April to October.

Across the lane is the little Church of St Mary, which has a 13th-century priest's doorway on the south side of its Norman chancel. The church contains memorials to the Cornewall

WOOD AND STONE *The timber-framed gatehouse was added to Stokesay Castle in about 1600.*

OLD AND NEW *Richards Castle's All Saints' Church, though Victorian, is 14th century in style.*

GABLED GATE *The gateway of timber and stone is all that survives of 12th-century Bromfield Priory.*

family who lived at Burford Castle, on the site of the present house. Edmund Cornewall, who died in 1585, was 7ft 3in tall and known as the 'Burford Giant'; there is a life-size painting of him on the triptych on the north wall of the sanctuary.

The main doors of the triptych open to reveal a triple portrait of members of the Cornewall family, including Edmund, painted in 1588. The heart of an earlier Edmund who died in 1436 is buried in the rare 'heart shrine', on the south side of the chancel.

TENBURY WELLS

The River Teme and its tributary Kyre Brook flow through this pleasant market town. An elegant, six-arched bridge spans the fast-flowing Teme, while the Kyre Brook, though bridged at several places, has steppingstones linking Godson's Walk and Cross Street. In a recess off Cross Street stands Tenbury Museum, which includes a village cobbler's shop and a display of items connected with local hop-picking in the days when this was done by hand. In Church Street is the so-called Round Market – in fact oval in shape – of 1811.

Close to Teme Bridge is Castle Tump, a tumulus that is the remains of a fortified castle, probably Saxon, built to guard the river approaches. Local legend gives it a more romantic history, for here, it is said, was buried the English warrior king Caratacus when he died after his return from captivity in Rome.

LEOMINSTER

An important crossroads town for centuries, Leominster (pronounced 'Lemster') is less glamorous than Ludlow, but nevertheless an attractive market town with some interesting old buildings unmarred by modern additions.

The magnificent Church of St Peter and St Paul stands on the site of a nunnery founded before the 9th century. The present church, with its huge west window, 45ft high, and mighty buttresses, was built by the Benedictines from the 12th century, and is only part of the cathedral-like building that once stood there. In 1699 a disastrous fire all but destroyed the church and it was not fully restored until the late 19th century, when the architect was Sir Gilbert Scott. In the north aisle there is a ducking stool, last used in 1809.

Leominster's old Town Hall, the intricately half-timbered Grange Court, no longer stands at the town centre where it was built; it was shifted in the 19th century to its present site, on an expanse of lawn known as The Grange. It was originally built in 1663 by John Abel, the king's carpenter, who is also thought to have been responsible for several houses in the town. The town's history can be followed in the Folk Museum in Etnam Street, mainly devoted to the farm life of the region; it is open daily from April to October, and at weekends for the remainder of the year.

SIDE BY SIDE *The detached belfry at Yarpole is 13th century, and older than the church.*

CROFT CASTLE *The ancient pink-stone home of the Croft family is now in the care of the National Trust.*

DALE FARMS *East of Munslow, wide farmlands spread across the gentle slopes of Corve Dale.*

BERRINGTON HALL

Surrounded by superb parkland, Berrington Hall is a dignified classical building, imposing and austere outside but cheerfully elegant within. It was built in 1778 by Henry Holland, architect to the future George IV.

Early in the 19th century the hall passed to the eldest son of Lord Rodney, the 18th-century admiral, whose victories are commemorated by paintings hung in the dining room. Among its outstanding features are the grand central staircase, and the delicate plasterwork and ceiling decoration.

The 455 acre park was laid out by Capability Brown, around a 14 acre lake at the foot of lawns sloping down from the house. From the steps in front of the house there are tremendous views, taking in Brecon Beacons, the Black Mountains, Radnor Forest and the Iron Age hill-fort of Croft Ambrey. The hall and gardens are open from Wednesday to Sunday, April to September.

CROFT CASTLE

Like Berrington Hall, Croft Castle offers a striking contrast between exterior and interior. In this case, medieval walls and turrets enclose a fanciful Georgian 'Gothick' interior.

The castle has been the home of the Croft family since soon after the Norman Conquest, apart from a gap of 170 years from 1746. The interior dates from the 1760s, when Croft was owned by the Knight family of iron-masters, from Coalbrookdale in Shropshire. Croft Castle is open from Wednesday to Sunday, April to September.

The little Church of St Michael beside the castle contains a fine portrait monument to Sir Richard Croft – who died in 1509 – and his wife Eleanor.

The park surrounding the castle is planted with magnificent trees, among them avenues of oaks, limes and Spanish chestnuts said to be 350 years old. From the car park, a track about a mile long leads up to the summit of Croft Ambrey, an Iron Age fort with a triple row of earthworks. From this vantage point 14 counties in England and Wales can be seen on a clear day.

RICHARDS CASTLE

This romantic ruin, with an overgrown moat, and fragments of stone jutting among the trees and brambles, stands high on a hill. It is reached through the churchyard of the beautiful medieval Church of St Bartholomew. Inside, the church still has its 18th-century box pews.

Tourist information: Ludlow 3857 (summer); Leominster 2291.

FAIR PROSPECT *Mellow castle, red rooftops, soaring parish church and the backcloth of the gentle Clee Hills combine to make the view of Ludlow from Whitcliffe one of the most spectacular of English townscapes.*

Magpie cottages in rural Cheshire

The marshes of the Dee estuary are an eerie fringe between land and sea. Inland the pastures of the Cheshire Plain, dotted with woods and villages, are crossed by steep sandstone slopes.

CHESTER

The city was already ancient when William the Conqueror, in the 1070s, made it the seat of an earldom. Impressive medieval walls, with Roman and Saxon fragments, enclose Chester, and a walk around them is a fine introduction to the city. The walls command memorable views of the city, the cathedral, the river and the Welsh hills; the prospect from the Eastgate arch is outstanding.

Steps down from the walls lead to the maze of narrow streets that characterise Chester. From the Eastgate there is a descent to the Rows, two-tier shopping arcades dating from medieval and Victorian times, which spread out from the old cross at the city centre.

Off Northgate Street is the cathedral, approached through the massive 14th-century Abbey Gateway. Built as St Werburgh's Abbey in 1092, the cathedral was consecrated in 1541 after Henry VIII's dissolution of the Benedictine abbey.

In St John Street, the 12th-century Church of St John the Baptist has impressive Norman architecture. Streets nearby reflect the city's prosperity in Georgian times.

Chester Zoo, 2 miles north, has few cages, as moats are used to confine the animals. The zoo is noted particularly for its polar bears, elephants and giraffes and the gardens are magnificent.

BURTON

Buildings of varied ages and styles, from medieval times onward, can be seen in the winding village street. Half-timbered and thatched cottages on the sandstone bedrock mix in with Georgian brick houses and the stone church. At the lower end is the Edwardian Burton Manor, formerly a home of the Gladstones.

A footpath climbs gently to a hill, clothed with oak and beech, which is owned by the National Trust and provides wide views across the Dee estuary.

A turn down Station Road leads to the edge of some of the most extensive marshlands in England. Across the creeks, alive with wildfowl, the horizon is dominated by the Clwydian mountains of North Wales. Near Burton are the Liverpool University Botanical Gardens at Ness, where the grounds of an Edwardian mansion have been turned into 'theme' sections including a water garden and a rhododendron plantation.

ELLESMERE PORT

The Shropshire Union Canal meets the Manchester Ship Canal amid a remarkable group of buildings alongside the canal dating from the height of the inland waterway era. A series of locks drops the canal between old offices and warehouses, while a growing collection of narrow boats floats in the canal basins. All form part of Ellesmere Port's Boat Museum, one of the foremost of its kind in Britain.

FRODSHAM

The 20th century seems an interloper in Frodsham's wide, tree-lined Main Street. The Bear's Paw Inn, dating from 1632, is a fine relic from before coaching days. Thatched and black-and-white cottages, such as the Old Cottage of 1580, join with spacious Georgian and Victorian town houses.

St Laurence's Church, of 12th-century origin, stands above the town beneath the steep north face of Overton Hill – the end of the Sandstone Ridge, Cheshire's 'backbone'. From the war memorial near Mersey View Club there are extensive views.

DELAMERE FOREST

The name is taken from a great Norman hunting forest which once covered much of Cheshire. The present forest consists largely of conifer plantations, but oaks and beeches lining the roads still give the impression of a native woodland. Details of the many marked paths, taking from 15 minutes to a whole day, are in a leaflet available from the Forestry and Information Centre at Linmere Moss.

LITTLE BUDWORTH

Mill Lane cuts between an old water mill and its power source, Budworth Pool, before reaching the centre of this village. The parish church of St Peter is a squat sandstone building on a small mound in the village centre. Other old buildings, including the almshouses, line the village street.

A mile to the west, Little Budworth Common Country Park offers walks – the peace occasionally disturbed by the roar of engines from Oulton Park racing circuit.

TARPORLEY

Tarporley is virtually a one-street village. The imposing buildings lining the High Street back almost directly onto lush pastureland. A system of courtyards, alleyways and back lanes links those buildings not actually in the High Street. The Old Manor House (1585) is dwarfed by the fine Georgian and Victorian buildings which make up the bulk of the village. The Swan Hotel, a splendid coaching inn, has a cobbled courtyard now enclosed by modern mews cottages instead of stables.

Tourist information: Chester 313126.

BORDER VIEW *Looking west from Maiden Castle hill-fort, countryside like a vast park rolls away to the distant hills of Wales.*

MAGPIE HOUSE *Churche's Mansion, in Nantwich, dates from 1577.*

WALL WALK *Chester's North Wall leads towards the Bridge of Sighs, which crosses the canal between the Chapel of Little St John and former dungeons below Northgate.*

—— 53 MILES ——

Hedged lanes join a cluster of tiny villages with black-and-white 'magpie' cottages. Settlement in the area since medieval times has left a legacy of fine old houses and country estates.

WHITCHURCH
This town is just inside Shropshire's border with Wales, and its Highgate pub claims to be the last in England.

St Alkmund's Church, with its distinctive, airy Queen Anne style of architecture, dominates the town. The original church collapsed one night in 1711, and the new one was paid for partly from taxes levied on visitors to the town's inns.

Downhill from the church, the High Street is lined with a remarkable variety of buildings. They include an unusual structure clad in cast iron – once the Alexandra Temperance Hotel and later the works of J.B. Joyce, makers of clocks. The courtyard off the Bullring, which fronts the White Bear Inn, is the sole survivor of many such courtyards to be seen in the town until the 1950s.

MARBURY
Until 20,000 years ago, what is now Cheshire was, like most of northern England, covered by an enormous ice sheet. On melting, the sheet in this part of Cheshire left many deep hollows which soon filled with water to form the Cheshire meres. Marbury lies at the end of Big Mere, which is overlooked from the opposite end by a palatial Georgian hall. An old village farm, pub and cottages cluster around the natural mound where the solid 13th-century St Michael's Church stands.

WRENBURY
The immense village green is bordered by a number of thatched cottages and the substantial St Margaret's Church. Rebuilt in the 16th century, this church has an impressive array of alabaster memorials to the Cotton family, who lived at Combermere Abbey. Half a mile north-west, the Llangollen branch of the Shropshire Union Canal is crossed by a lift bridge of a type more commonly found in Holland. An old mill beside the canal is now a boat hire centre.

NANTWICH
Welsh Row, by which the route enters Nantwich, is a delight. One of the oldest local buildings is here – the Cheshire Cat Inn, dating from around 1500. Additions to the street over the centuries have created a mixture of styles hard to match anywhere.

Across the River Weaver in the town centre, half-timbered buildings outnumber Georgian and Victorian houses. Rooflines pitch and tumble like boats in a rough sea, yet none reach the modest height of the octagonal tower of St Mary's Church. The magnificent interior of the church

reflects the wealth that came from salt. Nantwich was the centre of England's salt industry from Roman times until 150 years ago.

A mile to the west of Nantwich is Dorfold Hall, a magnificent Jacobean house which is open on Tuesday and Bank Holiday afternoons in summer.

BUNBURY
The hamlets of Bunbury Heath, Lower Bunbury and Bunbury are linked to make a straggling settlement with a mixture of modern housing and ancient dwellings. Medieval St Boniface's Church contains a fine collection of delicately carved alabaster and stone effigies, including those of the founder, Sir Hugh Calveley, and Sir George Beeston who, at the age of 88, commanded a ship against the Spanish Armada.

Not far past the church, an unsurfaced lane leads down to Bunbury Mill, a restored water mill open at weekends and Bank Holidays from Easter to September.

BEESTON
Houses and timber-framed cottages which make up this hamlet are dwarfed by Beeston Hill, an isolated hump of Cheshire's Sandstone Edge, crowned by the ruins of a substantial castle. The outer walls enclose a vast area, riddled with caves, which rises steeply to the inner bailey and keep, separated from the surrounding hillside by a massive dry moat.

BROWN KNOWL
The village is a straggling settlement consisting largely of former farmworkers' cottages. To the south of the

village rises Bickerton Hill, crowned by the earth ramparts of Maiden Castle, an Iron Age hill-fort. This, with Beeston Castle, is evidence of the strategic importance of the Sandstone Edge. The walk to the fort from the village or from the signposted Sandstone Trail car park is rewarded with views across Wales and Shropshire.

MALPAS
Built on the course of an old Roman road from Whitchurch to Chester, the township spreads down the hillside from the medieval St Oswald's Church. In the churchyard is a grassy mound, the motte of an old castle built nearly 1000 years ago.

Much of Malpas dates from the 16th and 18th centuries. Its old buildings include a pillar-fronted market hall.

Tourist information: Whitchurch 4577; Nantwich 623914.

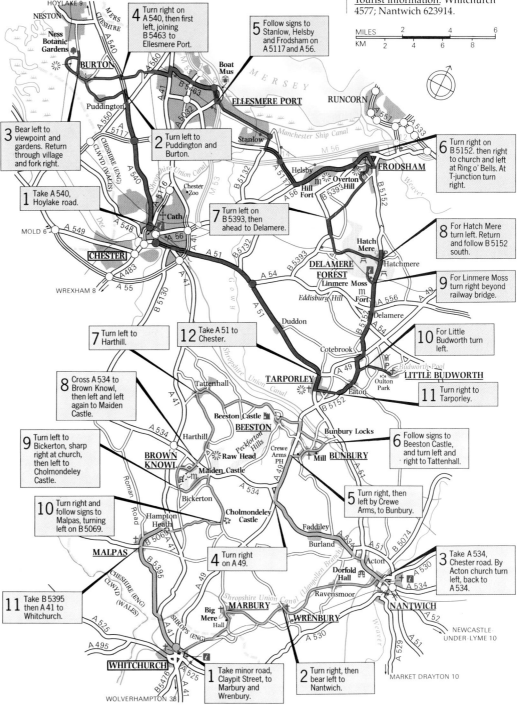

Moors and vales of the Peak District

TOUR
128

——— 68 MILES ———

There is an air of magnificent desolation about the high peat moors of Derbyshire's Dark Peak. Dry-stone walls line the route beside broad reservoirs and along river valleys.

GLOSSOP

The story of Glossop is a tale of two towns – the industrial 19th-century town with huge Victorian cotton mills and dark terraces clinging to steep hills, and the unspoilt 17th-century village of Old Glossop with its cobbled streets and fine buildings.

At the heart of Old Glossop is an irregularly shaped 'square' with a market cross, behind which rises the impressive parish church.

There was a still earlier Glossop, a Roman fort known locally as Melandra, though properly called Ardotalia. The scant remains of fort, walls, the headquarters and part of a bathhouse can still be seen on high ground above the junction of the River Etherow and Glossop Brook.

Dinting Railway Centre has a display of locomotives, a miniature railway and steam train rides on Sundays in summer. The centre is open daily.

LANGSETT

Approaching the tiny hamlet of Langsett, the bleak openness of the Derbyshire Dark Peak gives way to rolling daleland around Langsett Reservoir. The gentle hills continue to Ewden Beck and the Bradfields – with wide views over tiny green meadowlands divided by dry-stone walls, dense copses and steep river valleys.

RIVELIN NATURE TRAIL

A car park on the right of the crossroads, 1½ miles beyond Stannington, is the start of the Rivelin Nature Trail. It runs through a pleasant river valley to the Rivelin Dams, which are surrounded by woodland.

More paths lead beyond to Redmires Reservoirs and eventually along a Roman road to Stanage Edge, the longest gritstone edge in the Peak District, 100ft high and popular with rock-climbers.

HATHERSAGE

A century ago, Hathersage had four needle factories, but today there is little sign of its industrial past and the gritstone village wears an altogether rural face. The 14th-century St Michael's Church has a collection of brasses to the Eyre family who gave their name to Charlotte Brontë's Jane. The writer made a long visit here with her school friend Ellen Nussey, sister of the vicar of Hathersage.

In the churchyard is a grave said to be that of Little John, Robin Hood's best-loved 'Merry Man'. When his grave was opened in the last century, a thigh bone was discovered, measuring 30in, suggesting it belonged to a man more than 7ft tall.

LADYBOWER RESERVOIR

The thickly wooded shores of Ladybower Reservoir are a perfect spot for walking, picnicking or simply relaxing. Picnic areas and car parks are dotted along the shores up to the dam which divides Ladybower and Derwent Reservoirs, and many footpaths are signposted along the way.

The drive beyond the dam along the shores of Derwent Reservoir goes through some lovely open moorland, but this stretch is closed to cars on Sundays and Bank Holidays from Easter to the end of October. The road continues as a footpath along the shore of Howden Reservoir to Slippery Stones and a 17th-century packhorse bridge spanning the Derwent.

The bridge originally stood in the village of Derwent Woodlands; it was moved when the Ladybower Reservoir was built and the village disappeared beneath its waters.

SNAKE PASS

A long, sinuous climb up from the Derwent valley leads through the Snake Pass to skirt Kinder Scout, at 2088ft the highest point in the whole Peak District. As the road winds through thick plantations of conifers and high, barren moorland, it is easy to assume that Snake Pass was named after its twistings and turnings; in fact, it was named after the Snake Inn, which is on the right of the road in Hope Forest. The inn bears the coat of arms of the Cavendish family which features a snake. The Cavendishes, Dukes of Devonshire, have their main seat at Chatsworth, near Bakewell.

For much of its way, Snake Pass follows the course of the Roman road to Glossop from the fort of Navio at Brough. The Pennine Way crosses the road on its way from Kinder Scout to Bleaklow Moor.

Kinder Scout and Bleaklow Moor are the very essence of the Dark Peak country. On this bleak plateau, outcrops of bare, dark rock are often sculpted and broken into extraordinary shapes, set among black peat moorland with only the barest scrub, bracken and heather for vegetation. The few habitations are huddled against the hills, their backs to the wind.

Tourist information: Glossop 5920.

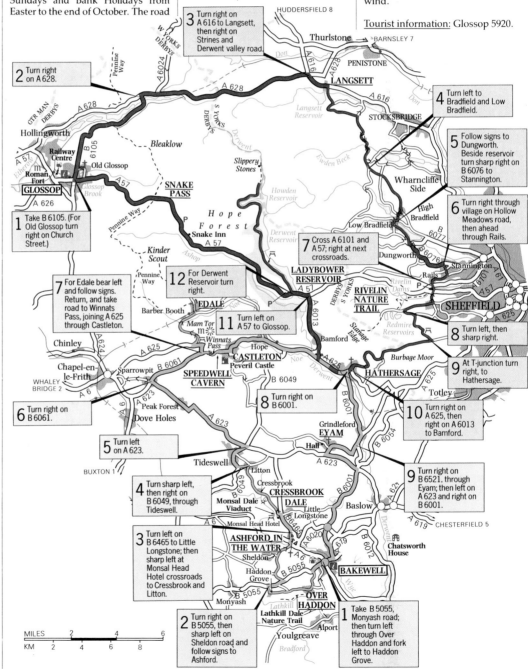

208

TOUR
129

55 MILES

The brooding gritstone landscape of the Dark Peak contrasts with the pretty valleys and bright villages of the White Peak, an area of pale limestone which lies to the south.

BAKEWELL

Set among hills at the heart of the Peak District, this small, handsome market town built of local yellow-grey stone is dotted with well-kept public gardens and laced with higgledy-piggledy narrow alleys. The broad River Wye flows through the town; a pleasant walk along its banks starts from Bakewell Bridge, carried on five pointed arches, which was built about 1300.

Bakewell's fine buildings include the 16th-century Old House Museum, in Cunningham Place behind the church, which still has its original wattle-and-daub walls. The museum includes collections of craftsmen's tools and farm implements. It is open in the afternoons in summer.

The traditional Bakewell Pudding – it is *not* called a tart here – is still sold in the town's two pudding shops. It is made according to the original 19th-century recipe which arose, it is said, from a cook's mistake. The cook at the Rutland Arms Hotel in the square intended to make a strawberry tart but absent-mindedly poured egg mixture over strawberry jam instead of mixing it into the pastry. The result proved an enduring success.

OVER HADDON

A path from the car park in the village leads down to lovely Lathkill Dale. A walk upstream follows the River Lathkill through ash woods and past abandoned lead mines. A path downstream passes beside the river as it tumbles spectacularly over 11 weirs in quick succession. It continues for about 2 miles to the tiny hamlet of Alport, where the Lathkill joins the River Bradford.

ASHFORD IN THE WATER

Bypassed by the main road, this quiet village grew up around a busy ford over the River Wye. Three old bridges still arch gracefully over the river. The narrow Sheepwash bridge recalls the days when trains of packhorses passed through Ashford.

CRESSBROOK DALE

Turning left from the Monsal Head Hotel, there are panoramic views of the dale and of the huge Monsal Dale Viaduct, now disused, which was flung across the valley in the 1860s. The narrow road drops steeply down to lovely Cressbrook Dale and breathtaking views continue all the way through this deep river valley.

The imposing Cressbrook Mill, a textile mill built in 1815, and the 18th-century hostel for its apprentices stand near a millpond by a valley known as Water-cum-Jolly-Dale. The

RUGGED EDGE *A winding, dry-stone-walled road climbs from Burbage Moor – only a few miles from the heart of Sheffield.*

WINNATS PASS *Weatherworn rocks, like crudely sculpted faces, tower above the steep-sided gorge west of Castleton.*

WATERY GRAVE *Two villages were submerged under the Ladybower Reservoir, which was completed in 1943.*

road, overhung with trees, twists and turns through the valley to the grey-stone village of Cressbrook, clinging to the hillside.

EDALE

As the road climbs from Sparrowpit up to Edale, the gentle White Peak countryside gives way to the open, often bleak aspect of the Dark Peak. After the sharp right turn to Barber Booth, the huge, rounded hills have ever-stranger formations in this striking wilderness. There are several stopping places with views down to tiny fields below.

To the right of the road is Mam Tor, with the remains of a late Bronze and Iron Age fort at its summit and magnificent views to Kinder Scout.

SPEEDWELL CAVERN

From an opening in the hillside at the foot of beautiful Winnats Pass, steps lead down to a boat which takes visitors through this illuminated, flooded, 18th-century lead mine.

The tour takes 45 minutes and at its farthest point reaches the so-called Bottomless Pit. This is a natural cavern, where a platform hangs over a natural underground lake some 70ft below.

The Blue John and Treak Cliff Caverns are the only places where the famous Blue John stone is still mined. This beautiful, purple-blue stone has been made into vases, clocks and furniture, and other Blue John artefacts can be seen in craft shops in nearby Castleton, including the Ollerenshaw Collection at the Blue John Craft Shop.

The entrance to Blue John Cavern is at the foot of Mam Tor's footpath; Treak Cliff Cavern is signposted from Castleton village. All the caverns are open daily.

CASTLETON

At the top of a sheer rock face stands the impregnable castle which gave Castleton its name. Peveril Castle was built in the 11th century by William Peveril, the illegitimate son of William the Conqueror, the keep was added in 1176 by Henry II. The castle, which is open daily, can be reached only on foot by a steep climb, and has magnificent views over Castleton and the surrounding countryside.

The village is a tightly knit jumble of steep narrow streets and pretty cottages, split by a tumbling millstream. It is a perfect centre from which to explore the nearby caves.

EYAM

The handsome Jacobean hall, set in a fine walled garden, is not open to the public, but can be seen through tall gates. It stands next to Plague Cottages, named after the tragic events of the most terrible year in the village's long history.

In 1665, a tailor living in Eyam was sent some clothes from London, which brought with them the plague. The infection spread rapidly through the village, and the terrified villagers prepared to flee.

However, Eyam's rector, William Mompesson, persuaded 350 of the inhabitants to stay and so prevent the contamination of nearby villages. There followed 13 months of isolation, when supplies were left by neighbouring villagers at Mompesson's Well north of the village. Only 83 of the original 350 survived, and the rector's wife, one of the victims, lies buried in the churchyard.

The village's original stocks stand opposite Eyam Hall, and the carved stone cross in the churchyard is a remarkable 9th-century survivor.

Tourist information: Bakewell 3227; (Edale) Hope Valley 70207; (Castleton) Hope Valley 20679 (summer).

209

From high peaks to wooded waterside

Rugged moors rise above a beautiful valley, and to the west lie pasture and woodland on the Cheshire Plain. Man-made marvels range from a medieval hall to a radio telescope.

BUXTON

A gracious town, with a predominant shade of soft yellow, Buxton stands on the River Wye, 1000ft up in the Peak District. Around are even higher hills. The old name of 'Bucks' Town' is a reminder that it was part of the Royal Peak Forest where the king's deer roamed.

Its magnificent position and its warm-water springs have made Buxton a delightful spa town and one of Britain's leading inland resorts. The first baths were built by the Romans, who took advantage of the clear blue water that bubbles up at a constant 28°C (82°F). In medieval times the springs were dedicated to St Ann, mother of the Virgin Mary, and people hoping for a divine cure left gifts at the shrine-like well.

It was in Georgian times that Buxton truly developed. In 1780 William Cavendish, the 5th Duke of Devonshire, who owned much of the town and lived at nearby Chatsworth, commissioned the Yorkshire architect John Carr to design accommodation which would attract elegant and wealthy visitors. In four years, using stone quarried in the area, Carr had completed The Crescent – a superb three-storeyed terrace with Doric pilasters and a paved, pillared arcade.

Today, part of The Crescent is still a hotel, and it also houses a tourist information centre and a library. The library's Adam-style ceilings date from its time as Buxton's assembly rooms. To the left of The Crescent is a colonnaded square which was completed in 1811.

Opposite is the elegant Victorian Pump Room, built in 1894 by the 7th Duke of Devonshire. This now houses a Micrarium – a museum displaying wonders of the natural world invisible to the naked eye. At the touch of a button, some 50 powerful microscopes project images magnified 1500 times onto television-sized screens. The pictures take viewers inside a living ants' nest, and show such miracles in miniature as crystals changing shape, snails' hearts beating and crickets scraping their legs together.

Next to the Pump Room is St Ann's Well, where the waters can be sampled; bottled water can be bought from the information centre. In the spa's heyday the treatment offered in Buxton for gout, rheumatism and heart disease included massage and baths as well as drinking the water.

The old thermal and natural baths adjoining The Crescent are now a shopping arcade, but the water is pumped from the natural baths into a modern swimming pool in Pavilion Gardens. Originally the Devonshire Royal Hospital, behind The Crescent, was built in 1790 as stables for the hotels. Its huge dome, 156ft in diameter, was added in 1881 following its conversion to a hospital in 1859 and was at the time the largest in Europe.

The nearby Opera House, built in 1903-5, is a delightful confection mixing classical style and Edwardian opulence. Since 1979 it has staged the Buxton International Festival of Music and the Arts. Behind the Opera House is the Conservatory which overlooks Pavilion Gardens – 23 acres of landscaped walks through which the Wye meanders.

Other fine local buildings are the Church of St John the Baptist, tiny St Anne's Church off the High Street, and the Old Hall Hotel.

POOLE'S CAVERN

Poached Egg Chamber and Flitch of Bacon are among the names given to some of the extraordinary limestone formations seen on a 40 minute tour of Poole's Cavern. The Flitch of Bacon is a huge stalactite almost 5ft long; the Poached Egg Chamber gets its name from its stalagmites stained orange by iron oxide. The name Mary, Queen of Scots Pillar which is given to one great stalactite commemorates Mary's visit to the cavern while she was in Buxton taking the waters as a cure for rheumatism. The temperature of the cavern remains a constant 9°C (48°F) in summer and winter.

The cavern is named after a medieval outlaw who is said to have used it as his lair. It would certainly make a perfect hide-out, but Poole was not the first man to live there. Stone Age man had lived in its entrance, and it is thought that the Romans used it as a place of worship. A visitor centre has an exhibition on the story of limestone, and there are relics from the Iron Age and Roman Britain on display, including jewellery, coins and pottery. The cavern is open daily in summer, and by its entrance is a picnic area.

Above Poole's Cavern is Grin Low now part of Buxton Country Park, planted on the site of a former wasteland of quarries and limekilns. A delightful walk passes through woods and glades to Solomon's Temple, a folly built at the end of the last century by public subscription, to give work to the unemployed. There are superb views from the temple's top to Buxton, Mam Tor, Axe Edge and Kinder Scout, at 2088ft the highest point in Derbyshire.

AXE EDGE

Leaving Buxton, the road hugs Axe Edge, a long exposed ridge, with Axe Edge Moor behind it. There are exceptional views from the road looking north-east to Buxton, and eastwards towards the Dove valley. On this bleak moor rise five rivers – Dove, Wye, Manifold, Goyt and Dane.

DROWNED VALLEY *The silvery surface of Fernilee Reservoir, completed in 1938 to supply water for Stockport, mirrors the wooded slopes of the Goyt Valley.*

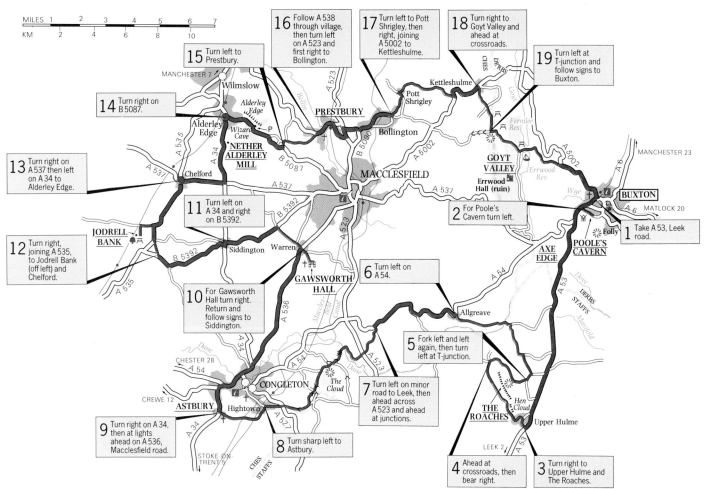

MILES 1 2 3 4 5 6 7
KM 2 4 6 8 10

15 Turn left to Prestbury.

16 Follow A538 through village, then turn left on A523 and first right to Bollington.

17 Turn left to Pott Shrigley, then right, joining A5002 to Kettleshulme.

18 Turn right to Goyt Valley and ahead at crossroads.

19 Turn left at T-junction and follow signs to Buxton.

MANCHESTER 7

Wilmslow

Alderley Edge

Kettleshulme

Pott Shrigley

PRESTBURY

Bollington

CHES
DERBS

Fernilee Res.

MANCHESTER 23

14 Turn right on B5087.

Alderley Edge

Wizard Cave P

NETHER ALDERLEY MILL

A535

A34

B5087

B5090

A5002

GOYT VALLEY

Errwood Hall (ruin)

Errwood Res.

BUXTON

13 Turn right on A537 then left on A34 to Alderley Edge.

Chelford

A537

MACCLESFIELD

A537

Wye

A6

MATLOCK 20

11 Turn left on A34 and right on B5392.

2 For Poole's Cavern turn left.

Folly

1 Take A53, Leek road.

12 Turn right, joining A535, to Jodrell Bank (off left) and Chelford.

JODRELL BANK

B5392

Siddington

Warren

A523

B5392

GAWSWORTH HALL

6 Turn left on A54.

AXE EDGE

POOLE'S CAVERN

A535

A54

A53

Dove

DERBS
STAFFS

10 For Gawsworth Hall turn right. Return and follow signs to Siddington.

A34

A536

Macclesfield Canal

Allgreave

A54

Manifold

5 Fork left and left again, then turn left at T-junction.

CHESTER 28
A54

Dane

A523

The Cloud

Hen Cloud

CREWE 12

CONGLETON

Hightown

A527

7 Turn left on minor road to Leek, then ahead across A523 and ahead at junctions.

THE ROACHES

Upper Hulme

ASTBURY

A34

9 Turn right on A34, then at lights ahead on A536, Macclesfield road.

8 Turn sharp left to Astbury.

STOKE-ON-TRENT 5

CHES
STAFFS

LEEK 2

A53

4 Ahead at crossroads, then bear right.

3 Turn right to Upper Hulme and The Roaches.

THE ROACHES

The weirdly shaped Roaches and their splintered sister, Hen Cloud, are formed by a mile-long outcrop of dark Millstone Grit. The tall rocks rise majestically out of the wild moorland, and footpaths lead up to them from the road. From their summit, and from the road that skirts them, there are fine views into Cheshire and Staffordshire.

The road from the Roaches to Allgreave offers views of an ever-changing countryside – bare moorland, undulating meadows with dry-stone walls, and wooded hillsides.

ASTBURY

The village clusters around a triangular green, and the magnificent Church of St Mary. The church has a beautiful carved and painted ceiling, panelled oak pews and a 1000-year-old yew tree in the churchyard. With the exception of the stone church and its gateway, Astbury makes a striking contrast to the gritstone villages of the Peak District National Park. It is a happy mixture of pretty red-brick cottages and the black-and-white Tudor houses that abound in Cheshire.

GAWSWORTH HALL

Standing well back from the road, the half-timbered Gawsworth Hall and Gawsworth parish church are reflected in a long lake. The hall has a handsome library and a chapel dating from 1365 which leads to a cloister with stained-glass windows by William Morris (1834-96). A gallery reveals a wonderfully complicated timber construction of massive oak trusses. The rest of the house dates mainly from the 15th century.

One tiny room is known as Mary Fitton's Bedroom. Mary, the second daughter of Gawsworth's owner, Sir Edward Fitton, became maid of honour to Elizabeth I. She was noted for her beauty, and some claim she is the 'dark lady' of Shakespeare's sonnets. Her days at court came to an abrupt end when, in 1602, she was found to be pregnant. Her lover, the Earl of Pembroke, was sent to prison, and she gave birth to a son who died shortly after.

In the summer, picnickers can watch opera and Shakespeare productions in the gardens. The hall and park are open each afternoon from the end of March to the end of October – and for a week at Christmas.

JODRELL BANK

The 250ft dish of Jodrell Bank's radio telescope towers over the Cheshire Plain – a saucer the size of a cathedral. It is one of the largest, fully steerable instruments in the world.

The telescope, designed by Sir Bernard Lovell, was built in 1957 for Manchester University. It picks up radio waves from stars and planets, enabling it to 'see' much farther into space than conventional telescopes. In the Concourse Building there is a permanent exhibition showing how the telescope works and telling the history of radio astronomy.

The Planetarium gives a 30 minute presentation on the sky at night. The gardens include a picnic area, and a 40 acre arboretum contains heather and rose gardens as well as an outstanding collection of shrubs and trees.

In summer, Jodrell Bank is open daily; in winter at weekends only.

NETHER ALDERLEY MILL

The red-sandstone walls of Nether Alderley Mill are almost hidden under a huge sweep of its stone-tiled roof. Inside, the original Elizabethan woodwork and Victorian machinery survive in full working order. Two wheels are driven by water flowing from two 16th-century reservoirs. From July to September the mill is open every afternoon except Monday. In April, May, June and October it is open on Wednesday, Sunday and Bank Holiday Monday afternoons.

About a mile north of the mill is Alderley Edge, a pink-sandstone escarpment with vast beech woods and views north to Lancashire. A car park lies to the left of the road. Nearby is the cave of the Wizard of Edge where, according to legend, an army of knights waits to ride out on white horses if called upon to save their country. Also close are some Bronze Age lead and copper mines.

PRESTBURY

At the centre of the village stands its fine sandstone church, thought to have been started about 1220. Many later additions include a fine 18th-century screen of carved oak. A stone coffin dating back to 1250 and a restored Saxon cross stand in the churchyard. There are also the remains of a small Norman chapel with a beautifully carved doorway, built on the site of a Saxon one.

Along the main street are substantial half-timbered houses, including the former priest's house, tiny cottages, and old inns and shops.

GOYT VALLEY

Hills surround the Cheshire hamlet of Pott Shrigley, which has a 14th-century church of millstone grit, a handsome hall and a handful of smaller buildings round the church.

From Pott Shrigley the road passes through distinctive Peak countryside, providing magnificent views over undulating pastureland, river valleys, woods and chequered fields. This is the way into the wild and beautiful Goyt Valley. Its steep slopes sweep down to the tranquil waters of Fernilee Reservoir, and to Errwood Reservoir, which is dotted with sailing boats in the summer months.

There are pleasant walks to the romantic ruins of Errwood Hall, surrounded by its banks of rhododendrons. The hall was allowed to fall into majestic ruin when the valley was flooded to create reservoirs. Now it is the last sign of human habitation in what was once a busy community with farms, school, mill, railway – and a gunpowder factory.

Tourist information: Buxton 5106; Congleton 271095.

Proud homes by the Dove and Derwent

TOUR
131
—— 80 MILES ——

Between the Derwent gorge at Matlock and the lovely dales to the west, glorious scenery unfolds. The spirit of ancient times broods on among burial mounds and giant stones.

MATLOCK
Two towns of very different character roll into one along the banks of the River Derwent. Matlock is a bustling commercial centre which grew up around an ancient stone bridge across the river. Matlock Bath is a tourist resort which developed around the warm springs that made it a popular spa in Victorian times.

The greatest attraction of the Matlocks is the natural beauty of the Derwent gorge. The river cuts through high limestone hills, whose steep, tree-clad slopes are studded with impressive crags.

The hills are pocked with caves – some natural formations, some the result of lead-mining which was the local industry from Roman times into the present century. The Peak District Mining Museum at Matlock Bath is open daily.

STANTON MOOR
The high heather-clad plateau of Stanton Moor was sacred to Bronze Age settlers, who buried no fewer than 70 of their chieftains or elders in mounds there between 2000 and 1000 BC. Some of these barrows are hidden now beneath the heather, bracken and scrub that cloak the moor. The most prominent Bronze Age remains are the Nine Ladies, a circle of upright stones around a small cairn, with the larger King's Stone nearby.

HADDON HALL
One of Britain's most perfectly preserved medieval stately homes, Haddon Hall has passed down through only two families, the Vernons and the Manners, since 1170.

Backed by gently sloping wooded hills, and bordered by the fast clear waters of the Wye, Haddon is a tight-knit complex of weathered grey-stone towers and turrets, intimate court-yards and gardens laid out along walled terraces that step down to the river. There are traces of the 11th-century house begun by William Peverel, illegitimate son of William the Conqueror, but much of the building dates from the 14th to 16th centuries. It is open to the public on most days in summer.

ARBOR LOW
Like great white bones projecting above the turf, the mystic stones of Arbor Low, reached by turning left up a farm track, have lain in a circle among the bare windswept fields of the White Peak since they were first put there by Stone Age people almost 4000 years ago.

Some powerful religious motivation drove men to arrange more than 40 stones, weighing 8 tons apiece, into the 'Stonehenge of the North', and the site retained its mystic significance for up to 1000 years, judging by the number of Bronze Age burial mounds nearby.

HARTINGTON
The youthful River Dove is a sparkling ribbon that snakes through Beresford Dale – now shaded by trees, now flashing through rich green fields bordered by walls of pale stone. Hartington shelters under the hills on the eastern side of the dale. A quiet, pretty little village of stone, it was an important centre of lead-mining from medieval times to the 19th century, and was the market town for the area.

DOVE DALE
For 2 miles or more the River Dove tumbles down over the natural stone steps of its rocky bed, through a dramatic limestone gorge.

Along the river bank, erosion has shaped the limestone into weird formations – pillars and crags and caverns – from which the gorge has earned the name Little Switzerland.

At Milldale, a hamlet at the head of Dove Dale, a stone packhorse bridge arches over the river. Izaak Walton gave it the name of Viator Bridge in *The Compleat Angler*.

Ilam Hall's lovely parkland, with several walks, is owned by the National Trust and open all year.

ASHBOURNE
One of Derbyshire's most handsome market towns, Ashbourne has terraces of red-brick houses with several stone buildings among them – a reminder that the town is a gateway to the limestone belt of the Peak District.

Leading from the triangular cobbled market place, St John Street has fine Georgian and half-timbered

HARDWICK HALL *The impressive mansion set in parkland stands as a monument to the woman for whom it was built – the redoubtable Elizabethan, Bess of Hardwick.*

TISSINGTON HALL *The FitzHerberts, owners of this Jacobean house, have held the manor for 500 years.*

EDENSOR *The village was transplanted in the last century because it spoilt a duke's view.*

ILAM HALL *This mansion set in a country park in beautiful Dove Dale is now a youth hostel.*

212

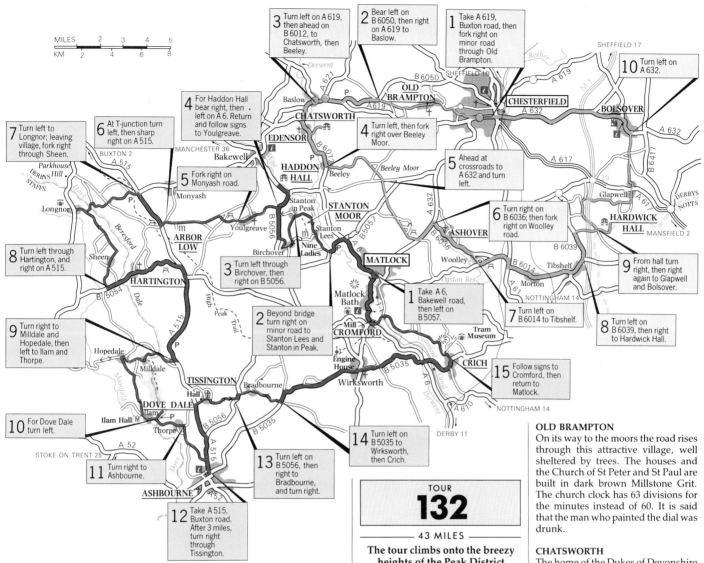

TOUR
132

— 43 MILES —

The tour climbs onto the breezy heights of the Peak District National Park. Chatsworth and the mansion of the formidable Bess of Hardwick are two of England's stateliest homes.

houses. The Green Man and Black's Head Hotel combines two earlier inns, and its sign spans the street.

St Oswald's Church has a 212ft spire and fine monuments.

TISSINGTON

An idyllic village of mellow stone houses in open formation around a spacious green, Tissington is approached through a stone gateway and avenue of lime trees that give the impression of a driveway to a private house. In fact, most of the village is still part of the private estate of the FitzHerbert family, who built Tissington Hall. It is an impressive house, long and low in proportion, with fine wrought-iron gates.

There are memorials to the FitzHerberts in St Mary's Church, including one of the 17th century showing two tiers of kneeling figures and so bulky that it almost blocks the chancel arch.

CRICH

An eccentric site for a museum of that most urban means of transport, the tram, is a disused limestone quarry above the rural village of Crich. The museum has some 40 trams built between 1873 and 1953, and visitors can ride in them along a mile-long track, with spectacular views.

CROMFORD

A cradle of the industrial revolution, Cromford was the site where Sir Richard Arkwright built Britain's first water-powered cotton mills. His original mill of 1771 still stands, though disused, while the red-brick Masson Mill of 1783 is still a factory. Arkwright built the stone village of Cromford to house his workers.

Arkwright was also the pioneer of the Cromford Canal, built to link the Erewash Canal and to transport the products of his factories to the industrial cities. A stretch of the canal has been restored for leisure use, and a horse-drawn passenger boat operates at weekends in summer.

The Cromford and High Peak Railway was a magnificent feat of engineering, opened in 1830 and involving steep inclines up which the trains were hauled on chains drawn by stationary steam engines.

The Middleton incline, near Cromford, is 708yds long with a gradient of 1 in 8¾. The engine house at the top of the incline has been restored and is open to the public at weekends. The disused track is now the High Peak Trail, 17½ miles long.

<u>Tourist information:</u> Matlock Bath 55082; Ashbourne 43666.

CHESTERFIELD

Rising out of a huddle of grey slate roofs and red-brick terraces, one of England's architectural oddities proclaims the town's identity. The twisted and seemingly precarious spire of the parish church of St Mary and All Saints is more than 9ft off the vertical. But it has been like that for 200 years, and engineers check its safety every year. The spire is 228ft and made of lead-covered wood which has warped.

Set in the Derbyshire hills, Chesterfield is an ancient market town. Its centre was redeveloped in the 1970s, when the large market place and Victorian Market Hall, which bustle with trade every Monday, Friday and Saturday, were refurbished. Nearby, a restored 16th-century timbered building houses the Peacock Heritage Centre and information centre. George Stephenson (1781-1848), the railway pioneer, spent his last years in the town and is commemorated in the Stephenson Memorial Hall, which houses the Pomegranate Theatre.

OLD BRAMPTON

On its way to the moors the road rises through this attractive village, well sheltered by trees. The houses and the Church of St Peter and St Paul are built in dark brown Millstone Grit. The church clock has 63 divisions for the minutes instead of 60. It is said that the man who painted the dial was drunk.

CHATSWORTH

The home of the Dukes of Devonshire is on a grand scale. The approach from the west through parkland yields a breathtaking view of the house's classical stone façade, which can glow like gold when the sun gleams on it. Woods clothe the hills above the house, and in the foreground the River Derwent flows gracefully below an elegant three-arched stone bridge.

The present house was started by the 1st Duke of Devonshire in 1686. Later dukes collected the priceless treasures that seem almost to overflow the house's 175 rooms.

Chatsworth's superb gardens are largely the result of the 6th Duke's long association with the great Victorian engineer Joseph Paxton, later to become architect of the Crystal Palace. As a young man, Paxton was employed at Chatsworth as head gardener. He designed the great Emperor Fountain that is capable of gushing to a height of 260ft by the natural pressure of water draining from a large pond on a hilltop.

The house and gardens are open daily from late March to October.

EDENSOR

Not least among the 6th Duke of Devonshire's landscaping projects was the shifting of an entire village because it spoilt the view. Under Joseph Paxton's direction the estate village of Edensor was entirely rebuilt to the west of Chatsworth.

The village is a unity by virtue of its mellow golden stone; its separate houses, however, are a splendid jumble of styles, some with ornate overhanging gables, some with Tudor or Georgian features.

ASHOVER

The village's name means 'ash tree slope', and there are ash trees in abundance, as well as pines, birches and oaks, on the slopes up to the moors. The village of warm, dark brown Millstone Grit huddles in the hills which once yielded lead, the former source of Ashover's prosperity.

A rarity in All Saints' Church is the Norman lead font, dating from about 1200 and decorated with figures of the Apostles. Many such fonts were melted down for ammunition by the Parliamentarians in the Civil War, but the rector saved this one by burying it in his kitchen garden.

HARDWICK HALL

The spirit of one of Elizabethan England's most formidable characters stalks the great rooms of Hardwick Hall. Bess of Hardwick, the Dowager Countess of Shrewsbury, stamped her personality on the great mansion she built beside her old ancestral home in 1590 – on a ridge above the valley where the M1 now runs. Such was her pride that she had her initials carved in letters 6ft high around the balustrades of Hardwick's six towers, and such was her wealth that she decked out the rooms with priceless tapestries and textiles.

Neatly trimmed yew hedges line the formal gardens to the south of the house, and the large park rolls down towards the motorway to the west. Hardwick Hall is owned by the National Trust and open to the public on Wednesday, Thursday, Saturday, Sunday and Bank Holiday Monday afternoons in summer. The gardens are open daily in summer.

BOLSOVER

Aloof from the industrial clutter of its surroundings, Bolsover Castle perches on a wooded bluff like a romantic castle from a fairy tale. From the valley below, the buildings make an impressive group, with the stone towers and turrets of the 'Little Castle' to the north, and a long ruined terrace beside it.

The castle dates from the 17th century and was built by Sir Charles Cavendish on the site of a medieval castle. It was severely damaged during the Civil War.

Tourist information: Chesterfield 207777/8; (Bolsover) Chesterfield 823179.

IN THE DARK PEAK *Dry-stone walls flank the lane leading from the upper Dove valley, just south-east of Longnor. The gritstone ridge on which the village stands looks across the valley to the limestone moorlands of Parkhouse Hill.*

Through Sherwood Forest to the Trent

TOUR
133

85 MILES

A rural circuit around Derby and Nottingham embraces lovely villages and the homes of two writers. Country parks are restoring landscapes scarred by the Industrial Revolution.

BREADSALL
Despite its closeness to Derby, the village of Breadsall is comfortingly peaceful. The Church of All Saints contains a medieval alabaster carving of a Pieta – buried under the floor of the nave at the time of the Reformation to save it from destruction, and discovered in 1877. Opposite the church is a half-timbered Tudor house, the Old Hall.

SHIPLEY PARK
A country park has been created in the grounds of what was once a great mansion. Shipley Hall was demolished in the 1940s and only the foundations remain; signs indicate where the various rooms stood.

From the car park a network of footpaths and bridleways radiates through woodland and pasture. Anglers and naturalists can enjoy the peaceful Mapperley Reservoir which is set in a nature reserve.

EASTWOOD
Mining is no longer the heart of Eastwood's life as it was when the author D.H. Lawrence was born there. His father was a miner, and several of Lawrence's novels, such as *Sons and Lovers*, conjure up vividly the tight-knit mining community set against a background of idyllic rural life. Today in Eastwood the contrast still exists. Across the roofs and

chimneys of the well-restored red-brick terraces of miners' cottages can be seen the green fields and woods beyond.

The spirit of Lawrence lingers throughout Eastwood, but nowhere more evocatively than in the little house, two rooms up and two down, at 8a Victoria Street where he was born. Period furnishings capture the atmosphere of the tough but cosy life of a miner's family; the house is open to the public daily.

In Scargill Walk, next to the museum, are craft workshops also open to visitors.

PAPPLEWICK
With cottages of pink stone and red tiles, Papplewick is a pretty village with few reminders of its hard, industrial past. In the 18th century there were cotton mills here and in neighbouring Linby, where children laboured in appalling conditions. No fewer than 42 child apprentices are buried in Linby churchyard.

Papplewick's Church of St James is set apart from the village among the fields. It is reached by a narrow lane that skirts the grounds of Papplewick Hall, which is not open to the public. The 18th-century squire of Papple-wick, Frederick Montagu, built the church in Gothic style and furnished the interior with a gallery down one side, complete with a fireplace to warm his own pew. Emblems of their trades decorate memorials to former estate workers.

NEWSTEAD ABBEY
It would be difficult to imagine a greater contrast between D.H. Lawrence's humble birthplace and Newstead Abbey, the grandiose home of the poet Lord Byron. Yet Newstead was almost a ruin when Byron went to live there in 1808, having inherited it from his great-uncle, who had been known as the 'wicked lord'.

Byron relics at the house include the memorial on the lawn to his pet dog, Boatswain. The glorious grounds, which are open daily, have a large lake where the 'wicked lord' staged mock naval battles, a Japanese garden, and extensive woods and rhododendron plantations.

PAPPLEWICK PUMPING STATION
This water-pumping station, 2½ miles east of Papplewick village, once pumped drinking water for Nottingham from an underground source. The interior of the red-brick

building is like a temple of Victorian engineering, with classical wrought-iron columns and stained-glass windows. The station is open on Sunday afternoons, and the steam-powered pumping engines, built by James Watt's Company in 1884, are in operation two or three times a month.

The station is on the edge of an area of woodland, plantations and heath – one of several fragments of Sherwood Forest. At Burntstump Country Park there are well-marked forest trails.

OXTON
Cornfields brush the edge of the red-brick village, and there is a shallow ford across the stream. The Church of St Peter and St Paul has a Jacobean screen with carved figures of children, one blowing pan pipes, the other bagpipes. The woodwork of the choir stalls has a carved inscription dated 1617. Two white ensigns in the church commemorate members of the Sherbrooke family who commanded ships in both World Wars.

EPPERSTONE
Strung out along a wide and leafy main street, Epperstone's attractive red-brick houses have spacious gardens, and there are footpaths leading to open fields. A high stone wall holds back the mound on which the Church of the Holy Cross stands. Near the pub is a dovecote in mellow red brick.

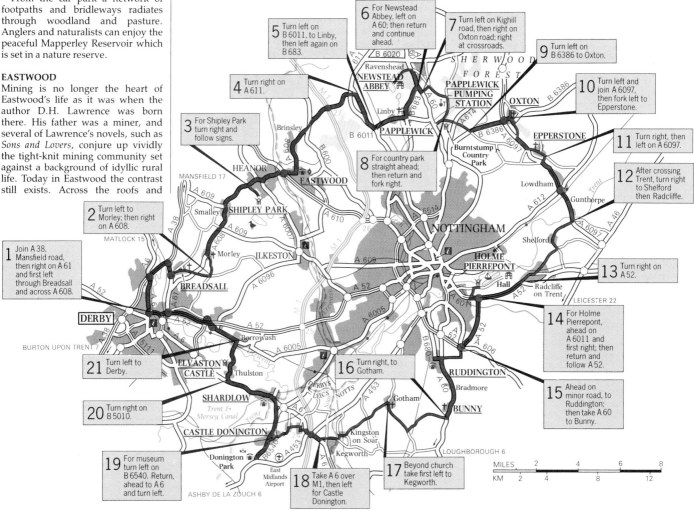

5 Turn left on B 6011, to Linby, then left again on B 683.

6 For Newstead Abbey, left on A 60; then return and continue ahead.

7 Turn left on Kighill road, then right on Oxton road; right at crossroads.

9 Turn left on B 6386 to Oxton.

4 Turn right on A 611.

10 Turn left and join A 6097, then fork left to Epperstone.

3 For Shipley Park turn right and follow signs.

8 For country park straight ahead; then return and fork right.

11 Turn right, then left on A 6097.

12 After crossing Trent, turn right to Shelford then Radcliffe.

2 Turn left to Morley; then right on A 608.

1 Join A 38, Mansfield road, then right on A 61 and first left through Breadsall and across A 608.

13 Turn right on A 52.

14 For Holme Pierrepont, ahead on A 6011 and first right; then return and follow A 52.

16 Turn right, to Gotham.

15 Ahead on minor road, to Ruddington; then take A 60 to Bunny.

21 Turn left to Derby.

20 Turn right on B 5010.

19 For museum turn left on B 6540. Return, ahead to A 6 and turn left.

18 Take A 6 over M1, then left for Castle Donington.

17 Beyond church take first left to Kegworth.

MILES 2 4 6 8
KM 2 4 8 12

HOLME PIERREPONT

In an imaginative leisure development, disused gravel pits beside the Trent have been transformed into the National Water Sports Centre. The main lake is an Olympic-standard rowing and canoeing course. It is also used for sailing, windsurfing, fishing and water-skiing.

From the world of 20th-century water sports it is only a short step to the splendid environment of Tudor nobility, as represented by Holme Pierrepont Hall. The hall faces open meadows, with only St Edmund's Church for company. Built by the Pierreponts in the early 16th century, it has a handsome façade of brick, surmounted by battlements added about 1800. The hall and its courtyard garden are open on summer afternoons except Mondays.

RUDDINGTON

In Chapel Street, the Framework-knitters' Museum carefully re-creates the living and working conditions of 19th-century stocking-makers. The stocking-knitting frame, invented by the Reverend William Lee of Woodborough, Nottinghamshire, in 1589, was used by cottage craftsmen in Ruddington for more than 200 years.

In 1829 a factory and cottages were built around a courtyard in Chapel Street, and the complex has been preserved in the museum as an example of the transition from cottage to factory methods. The museum is open on Wednesday evenings, or by appointment.

BUNNY

An eccentric 18th-century squire of Bunny, Sir Thomas Parkyns, has left his very personal mark on the village. A sporting fanatic, Sir Thomas employed two professional wrestlers at Bunny Hall to be his opponents. He designed his own memorial in St Mary's Church; this shows him poised for a wrestling bout, with a diminutive wrestler sprawled at his feet, and Father Time as the referee taking the count.

Sir Thomas fancied himself as an architect, too. He designed his own house, Bunny Hall, whose curious brick tower, with family hatchments and openings like blocked fireplaces, is visible from the road, but is not open to the public.

CASTLE DONINGTON

An attractive small town on a steep hill, Castle Donington is best known for the motor-racing circuit at Donington Park, 1½ miles south-west. Race meetings take place most weekends. An avenue of antique petrol pumps leads to a museum with more than 120 historic Grand Prix racing cars, the earliest dating from 1911, and the Mike Halewood and Barry Sheene collection of racing motorcycles.

SHARDLOW

The Trent and Mersey Canal runs through the middle of Shardlow which, two centuries ago, was a bustling inland port, a key staging post on the canal which had been completed in 1777. At Shardlow,

INLAND PORT *Boats passed under the arch of the Clock Warehouse beside Shardlow canal port's western and earliest basin.*

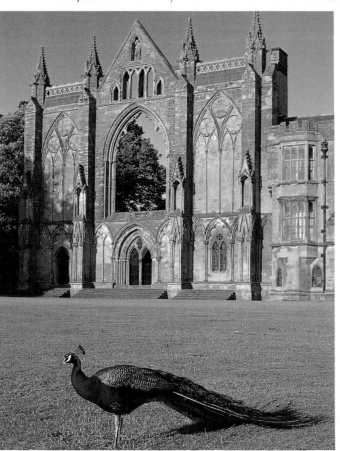

POET'S HOME *Lord Byron lived at Newstead Abbey, a priory that had been converted to a house in the 1540s. Byron sold the house in 1818 to pay off his debts.*

UPSTAIRS, DOWNSTAIRS *In this small house at Eastwood the writer D.H. Lawrence was born in 1885.*

RURAL RELIC *An old wagon is part of the Elvaston Castle Museum.*

cargoes were unloaded from broad seagoing Trent barges into canal narrow boats for the journey westwards.

An industrial village sprang up, with mills, warehouses, craftsmen's shops, and cottages and taverns for the canal people. Much of the canal village has survived. The main warehouse, which dates from 1780, now houses a museum of canal life, open daily. There are models of the original canal port, and displays and photographs of the vanished commercial life of the canals.

ELVASTON CASTLE

Visitors are free to roam the 200 acres of woodland, parks and gardens that surround Elvaston Castle, formerly the seat of the Stanhope family, among them the Earls of Harrington. The gardens, noted in the 19th century for their arrangements of conifer hedges and topiary, have been restored with clipped hedges of box and yew. There are large plantations of rhododendrons, and the kitchen garden has been replanted as an Old English garden of herbaceous plants.

The castle itself, a gaunt stone pile that dates from the Gothic Revival of the early 19th century, is not open; but the Working Estate Museum set up in the stables and workshops is a hive of activity. In its heyday, Elvaston was almost self-sufficient, with its own blacksmiths, carpenters and carriage makers. Now the craftsmen's workshops are restored and are open on summer afternoons.

<u>Tourist information:</u> Derby 31111; Nottingham 470661/823823.

Through the Vale of Belvoir to an inland 'sea'

The flat Trent valley soon gives way to the gently undulating Vale of Belvoir. Between Oakham and Stamford lie a man-made lake and a ribbon of villages built in the warm local stone.

BOTTESFORD

The diminutive River Devon winds through the village, and a notice warns visitors to watch out for ducks crossing the road. The river almost encircles St Mary's Church, as if to provide a moat to guard the tombs of the Lords of Belvoir buried there. There are monuments to eight Earls of Rutland, and the chancel is practically blocked by rows of magnificent life-size effigies.

Most curious of the effigies is the tomb of Francis, the 6th Earl of Rutland, who died in 1632. The earl's effigy reclines beside those of his two wives, and above them towers a canopy of marble with a family crest so massive that a roof rafter had to be cut away to accommodate it.

The monument to the 6th Earl is known as the Witchcraft Tomb from the inscription which records that two of Francis's sons '. . . died in their infancy by wicked practice and sor-cerye'. Between the lines of this chilling statement lies the tale of the witches of Belvoir. After a woman had been dismissed from service at Belvoir Castle she and two other Bottesford women were alleged to have sought revenge by inflicting sickness and convulsions upon the Rutland family. At their trial for witchcraft in 1618, one of the accused called for bread and butter to prove her innocence, claiming that it would 'never go through her if she were guilty'. No sooner had she taken it into her mouth than she died.

St Mary's needle-like spire is the highest in Leicestershire, soaring to 207ft. A stone cross in the centre of the village is a relic of Bottesford's medieval market, and beside it stands the village stocks and whipping post.

BELVOIR CASTLE

Visible for miles around, the romantic, golden, stone battlements and turrets of Belvoir (pronounced 'beever') Castle peer over their fringe of trees high up on an escarpment above the cornfields of the Vale of Belvoir. William the Conqueror's standard-bearer, Robert de Todeni, built the first castle on this commanding site. The present building, despite its medieval-looking fortifications, dates mainly from the early 19th century.

The home of the Duke of Rutland, the castle is a treasure house of furniture and fine oil paintings, among them a portrait of Henry VIII by Holbein and three of Poussin's

paintings from the series of the 'Seven Sacraments'. The ornate stone hall is hung with military banners and decorated with displays of swords, muskets and hunting trophies.

The castle also houses the museum of the 17th/21st Lancers. The regiment is the successor of the 21st Light Dragoons which were first raised in 1760 by John Manners, Marquis of Granby, eldest son of the 3rd Duke of Rutland.

Belvoir means beautiful view, and from the castle terraces there are spectacular views down into the vale. The fields bordered by oak and ash trees are punctuated by the spires and towers of village churches nestling in the shelter of the gentle hills.

THE JUBILEE WAY

One of the best ways to enjoy the delights of the countryside of the Vale of Belvoir is to stroll a few miles along the Jubilee Way. This waymarked footpath crosses the Belvoir estate on its way from the nearby village of Woolsthorpe to Melton Mowbray, 15 miles south.

The section of the Jubilee Way west of Belvoir Castle runs to Stathern through attractive woodlands of mature oak, beech and sweet chestnut, where birds abound. At Woolsthorpe the Jubilee Way joins another long-distance path, the Viking Way, linking Oakham and the Humber Bridge.

COLSTON BASSETT

As the road from Belvoir rises and dips, there are frequent glimpses between hawthorn hedges of fields of reddish earth rolling away into the distance. The narrow thread of the disused Grantham Canal still weaves a wandering line across the patchwork countryside, and the River Smite runs through the village.

At the heart of Colston Bassett, red-brick cottages with roses round their doors are shaded by high trees. Little more than a hamlet now, the village was once important enough to have a weekly market, and the market cross still stands between the Martin's Arms and the post office. The base of the cross is medieval, but the classical column above it was added in 1831 to mark the coronation of William IV the year before.

St John's Church, whose tall spire rises above the trees, was built in Gothic Revival style in 1892.

WALTHAM ON THE WOLDS

Enjoying an airy position some 560ft above sea level, Waltham is an attractive, tight-knit village of creamy local limestone. Most of the houses have roofs of blue-black tiles, but there are also several thatched buildings, including the Royal Horseshoes Inn. On a prominent position south of the church the stump of a windmill has been incorporated into a private house.

The spire of St Mary Magdalene's Church provides a landmark for miles

around. The oldest fitment in the church is the Norman stone font, decorated with fine carvings of an arcade and leaf patterns. Wood carvings of monastic figures carrying scrolls, books and shields adorn the ancient roof.

EXTON

This enchanting little village of creamy stone and thatched cottages has two greens. The little triangular green has a small domed and pillared building known as the town pump. It covers a sealed-off well which was

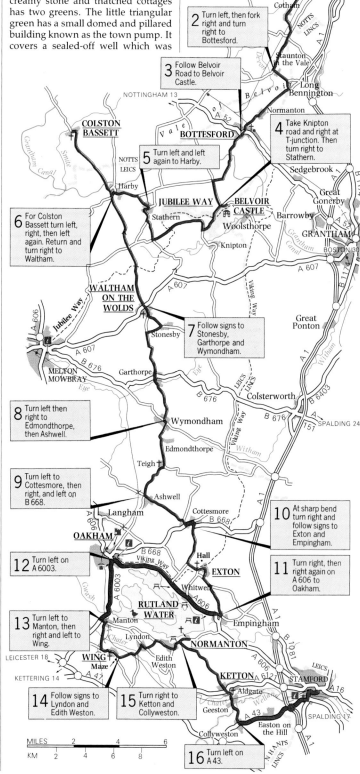

1 Take minor road to Staunton.

2 Turn left, then fork right and turn right to Bottesford.

3 Follow Belvoir Road to Belvoir Castle.

4 Take Knipton road and right at T-junction. Then turn right to Stathern.

5 Turn left and left again to Harby.

6 For Colston Bassett turn left, right, then left again. Return and turn right to Waltham.

7 Follow signs to Stonesby, Garthorpe and Wymondham.

8 Turn left then right to Edmondthorpe, then Ashwell.

9 Turn left to Cottesmore, then right, and left on B 668.

10 At sharp bend turn right and follow signs to Exton and Empingham.

11 Turn right, then right again on A 606 to Oakham.

12 Turn left on A 6003.

13 Turn left to Manton, then right and left to Wing.

14 Follow signs to Lyndon and Edith Weston.

15 Turn right to Ketton and Collyweston.

16 Turn left on A 43.

once the village's water supply. On the larger green, facing the Fox and Hounds Hotel, grow 12 magnificent sycamore trees.

A high dry-stone wall skirts Exton Park, and a gap in the wall gives access to the track which leads to the Church of St Peter and St Paul. The limestone gravestones in the churchyard are beautifully engraved and carved with decorative swags and cherubs, but it is for the monuments inside the church that Exton is justly famous.

These memorials provide magnificent examples of English sculpture spanning the centuries, from the simple effigy of a 14th-century knight to the swaggering sophistication of the 18th-century marble carvings. Probably the finest monument is by the sculptor Grinling Gibbons (1648-1721); it shows the 3rd Viscount Campden with his four wives and their children.

In the park just north of the church stand the ruins of the old Hall which was burnt down in 1810, although the chimneys and ragged walls remain. Behind the ruins, among the stately beech trees of the park, stands the imposing, gabled stone Victorian building of the new Hall.

RUTLAND WATER
In the 1970s the tranquil valley of the River Gwash east of Oakham was transformed by a dam at Empingham into one of Europe's largest man-made lakes, Rutland Water. Comparable in size to Windermere, the reservoir covers 3100 acres and has a shoreline of 24 miles. Far from destroying the natural beauty of the valley, a new beauty was created as this vast sheet of water slowly grew, edging its way into the folds of the landscape. Coot, wildfowl and waders have adopted the reservoir, and more than 215 species of birds have been recorded here.

Rutland Water has superb leisure facilities. Anglers fish for the large brown and rainbow trout, yachtsmen skim the waters and nature trails explore the banks.

At the western end of the lake is a 350 acre nature reserve, with a 1 mile nature trail which starts and finishes at picnic sites. There are hides overlooking the water.

OAKHAM
Until it was absorbed by Leicestershire in 1974, Rutland was England's smallest county and Oakham its county town. A compact little town of stone and red-brick houses, Oakham has an ancient market place dominated by a buttercross with an eight-sided roof of stone tiles supported by massive oak pillars.

A step away, on the grassy plateau, stands Oakham Castle, modest-looking on the outside because only the hall survives. But the interior of the hall is remarkable. Dating from 1180-90, this stone building is one of the finest examples of domestic Norman architecture in Britain. Like a church, the hall is divided into a nave and aisles by two arcades of columns. The stone capitals above the columns are decorated with carvings so similar to

those at Canterbury Cathedral that they were probably the work of the same sculptors. The carvings include six figures of musicians, four human and two animal, though all are headless.

Used as a courtroom in the early 19th century, the hall is still furnished with court benches. But its most unusual feature is the display of more than 200 gigantic horseshoes that line the walls from floor to ceiling. By tradition, any peer of the realm passing through Oakham presents an inscribed horseshoe to the Lord of the Manor. In recent years several members of the Royal Family have added horseshoes to the collection.

Rutland County Museum, housed in a converted 18th-century riding school in Catmose Street, contains a wealth of domestic and agricultural relics and an exhibition of local history from prehistoric times.

WING
There are attractive stone houses around the Church of St Peter and St Paul, but Wing's chief curiosity is the turf maze beside the playing fields to the east of the village. The maze consists of patterns in gravel separated by 9in turf walls. Some 40ft in diameter, the maze has an identical pattern to mazes on floors in French Gothic cathedrals such as Chartres.

NORMANTON
Seven farmhouses and 16 cottages were submerged for ever when Rutland Water was created. One building that escaped a similar fate was the Church of St Matthew, Normanton, which stands in isolation on the south side of the lake. To save the church the floor level was raised inside almost up to the arches, and a bank of stone built up against the outside walls. The church was deconsecrated in 1970 and

now houses a Water Museum, open daily from April to October.

Even when it was first built, the church looked like an urban intruder, as its tower and portico were based on the baroque designs of St John's, in Smith Square, Westminster.

KETTON
There is an abundance of pretty stone villages east of Rutland Water, and Ketton is among the prettiest. At the centre of the village the houses are all of a piece, built of local stone with slates from nearby Collyweston.

Ketton's main street curves past St Mary's Church, with its magnificent spire that dates from around 1300 and reaches a height of about 150ft, down to the stone bridge over the River Chater, overhung with trees.

Tourist information: Newark-on-Trent 78962; Oakham 2918.

RURAL RUTLAND *The route winds unobtrusively through a patchwork of green and brown fields near the village of Wing.*

EARL'S CHURCH *The battlemented Holy Trinity Church at Teigh dates from 1782 and is one of several built in Leicestershire by the 4th Earl of Harborough.*

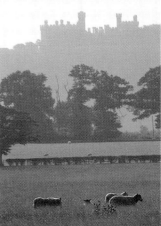

CASTLE IN THE AIR *A gentle mist softens the stark outlines of Belvoir Castle.*

Parklands and caves of the Dukeries

TOUR

135

——— 79 MILES ———

When parts of Sherwood Forest were incorporated into ducal estates they became known as the Dukeries. Some areas look much as they did at the time of the legendary Robin Hood.

NEWARK-ON-TRENT

The ragged walls of Newark Castle rear up above the Trent like a cliff face, with gaping caverns where the windows used to be. Below the walls fishermen crouch beside the sluggish river under umbrellas that look like rows of green mushrooms.

Newark Castle has been a ruin since the Civil War when, as a Royalist stronghold, it was besieged three times. During the sieges of Newark the governor of the town used to live in the fine half-timbered house with overhanging upper floors that still stands in Stodman Street, just off the great market place.

A diagonal line of stones across the cobbles of the square marks the line of the path that the governor used to take to the Church of St Mary Magdalene. The church is built on the

scale of a cathedral, with a peal of ten bells and a spire that soars to 252ft. Dating mainly from the 15th century, the church has magnificent carvings on the screen and choir stalls, and one of the largest brasses in the country, a memorial to Alan Fleming, a Newark merchant who died in 1363.

At the south-east corner of the market place stands the immaculately restored White Hart Hotel, a 14th-century, timber-framed building decorated with rows of sculptured figures. Delightful arcades and alleys of 17th- and 18th-century brick and half-timbered houses lead off from the square. In Appletongate a 16th-century stone building, formerly the old Magnus Grammar School, now houses the Newark Museum which has a collection that ranges from Roman pottery found on sites along the Foss Way to a hoard of 465 silver coins buried during the Civil War.

At Winthorpe, 2 miles east, Newark Air Museum has more than 30 historic aircraft on display, including one of the last Lancaster bombers.

WELLOW

A huge maypole painted red, white and blue and topped by a weather vane stands permanently on the green at Wellow. On Spring Bank Holidays stalls are set up on the green and children dance with ribbons

around the pole. Beside the green there are brick cottages with roofs of red tiles. The little Church of St Swithin, built of pinkish stone, stands back behind the Olde Red Lion Inn.

Wellow stands on the site of an early settlement, as revealed by the earthwork called Gorge Dyke that almost surrounds the village. Villagers enjoy an ancient privilege of grazing their animals on land in the area enclosed by the earthworks.

LAXTON

Laxton is unique. It is the last village in England where medieval agricultural methods survive. By some freak of history the ancient system of strip farming in open fields survived here long after it was swept away elsewhere when farms were enclosed in the 18th and 19th centuries.

At first sight it is not obvious that Laxton is such a special place. Its red-brick houses are strung out on a long main street, with the stone-built St Michael's Church on a slight rise at the centre. Many of the buildings in the main street are farmhouses, and this is the first clue to the curiosity of Laxton.

In the Middle Ages farmhouses were clustered in village communities; in later centuries they were set on the edges of villages, or among the fields the farmer works. The fields of

Laxton are different too. Some 483 acres are arranged in three open fields, and each farmer cultivates broad strips within each field. A committee, called the 'Court Leet', allocates the strips to the farmers each year. The court acts on behalf of the Lord of the Manor, at present the Crown.

At Egmanton, 1 mile farther north, the Church of Our Lady has been a shrine and a place of pilgrimage since the Middle Ages, when a woman of the parish had a vision of the Virgin Mary. The church was magnificently restored in 1897-8 by Sir Ninian Comper who painted the rood screen in bright reds, greens and golds, much as it would have appeared originally.

THORESBY HALL

One of a string of great estates in The Dukeries, Thoresby Hall is a vast Victorian mansion surrounded by 12,000 acres of parkland, lakes and farms. Built for the Pierrepont family by Anthony Salvin, architect of the restoration of Windsor Castle, the house was begun in 1864 and took 11 years to complete.

Inspired by Elizabethan palaces, Thoresby is like a great wedding cake in stone, with little towers and gables and cupolas creating a riot of decoration along the rooftops. The hall is open occasionally in summer, and its rooms are as richly decorated as their wrappings suggest. The Great Hall is 64ft long with two storeys of galleries rising to a great hammerbeam roof.

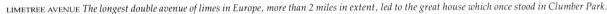

LIMETREE AVENUE *The longest double avenue of limes in Europe, more than 2 miles in extent, led to the great house which once stood in Clumber Park.*

Ornate wall hangings, gilded plaster-work and opulent furnishings are a monument to Victorian taste.

From the hall a Grand Staircase rises towards a statue of Charles I on horseback. In the Library, statues of Robin Hood and Little John flanking the fireplace support a carving of the Major Oak at Edwinstowe.

CLUMBER PARK
A magnificent avenue of lime trees threads through the 4000 acres of Clumber Park. Now a country park owned by the National Trust and open all year, Clumber is like a crown without a jewel, for the mansion, Clumber House, was demolished in 1938 after a series of fires. The foundations of the great house, home of the Dukes of Newcastle, are clearly visible beside the 85 acre lake.

The original grandeur of the estate can be imagined from the scale of the stable complex that houses the visitor centre. A handsome stone bridge spans the River Poulter as it widens into the lake. Clumber church, a monumental Victorian creation in pink and grey stone, stands in splendid isolation beside the lake.

The houses in the little estate village of Hardwick have the same generous scale – with high-pitched gables and tall brick chimneys. Great open spaces of parkland surround the village, with miles of tracks among the birch and conifer scrubland and through woods of oak and beech. Bicycles can be hired, and there is excellent coarse fishing on the lake.

CRESWELL CRAGS
Wild bears, hyenas, reindeer and even mammoths used to roam the limestone hills of Derbyshire, according to the bones found in the caves of Creswell Crags. As the glaciers of the last Ice Age retreated, ancestors of modern men occasionally took shelter in the caves, leaving behind tools and arrowheads made from stone and from the bones of the reindeer and wild horses that they hunted. One fragment of bone on display at the visitor centre is a replica of a bone engraved with the head of a horse some 13,000 years ago. The original bone is in the British Museum, and others discovered in the caves are in the Manchester University museum.

A footpath extends along the length of the gorge, following the narrow lake. Gaunt cliffs of limestone, swathed in trees, overhang the caves. The largest cave, Church Hole Cave, penetrates some 170ft into the rock, and evidence that it was occupied by prehistoric men has been found in the form of hand axes and other stone tools. Most of the caves however, are small, like Mother Grundy's Parlour, named after a witch who was said to have lived there in the 19th century. Iron grilles guard the caves' entrances, but they are opened to parties by making an appointment.

WORKSOP
A town on the River Ryton, Worksop has a fine priory church, dedicated to Our Lady and St Cuthbert. The opposite ends of the church represent two extremes of architecture. The

venerable stonework of the round arches in the nave are Norman work, dating from about 1170 when the church served the community of Augustine monks. The east end of the church has been restored in an uncompromisingly modern style, with crisp new stonework supporting a short needle-sharp spire.

Most of the monastic buildings have long vanished. The gatehouse, however, still stands, a stone building with a large mullioned window above the gateway, and with niches for carvings along its façade; it is used now as a community centre.

BLYTH
Among Blyth's red-brick Georgian houses are several coaching inns that testify to the village's earlier role as a staging post on the Great North Road. There was already an Angel Inn in Blyth in 1274, though the present building of whitewashed brick dates from the 18th century.

Bypassed now by the A1, Blyth dozes beside its green, shaded by lime trees. An avenue of acacias leads up the hill to the Church of St Mary and St Martin, surmounted by a magnificent 14th-century tower with pinnacles as decorative as lacework.

In about 1420, monks of the priory that was attached to Blyth church quarrelled with the villagers and erected a wall to separate the choir of the church, which they used, from the nave, used by the villagers.

After the priory was dissolved in the 1530s its buildings were demolished up to the wall that had cut the church in half. This explains why the church comes to such an abrupt and surprising end.

ROCHE ABBEY
Pheasants croak in the covers of scrub that cloak the craggy valley sheltering the ruins of Roche Abbey. Cliffs of white limestone create their own Gothic architecture beside the vaults and arches of the ruin, which was founded for the Cistercians in 1147.

The gentle, soothing sound of a stream tumbling over a small weir enhances the stillness of the site. The stream ran through the middle of the abbey buildings, and the refectory and monks' dormitory were built over it.

CONISBROUGH CASTLE
Although it is 800 years old, the cream, dressed stonework of the keep at Conisbrough Castle looks immaculate, as if it were built yesterday. The shape looks modern too, being cylindrical with six bold supporting buttresses and giving the impression of a rocket in its launching gantry aimed at the sky.

The surrounding walls and buildings are of a rougher stone, their crumbling outlines more in keeping with their age. This great Norman castle, high on its grassy mound above the town of Conisbrough, features in Sir Walter Scott's novel *Ivanhoe*.

Tourist information: Newark-on-Trent 78962; Worksop 475531; Doncaster 734309.

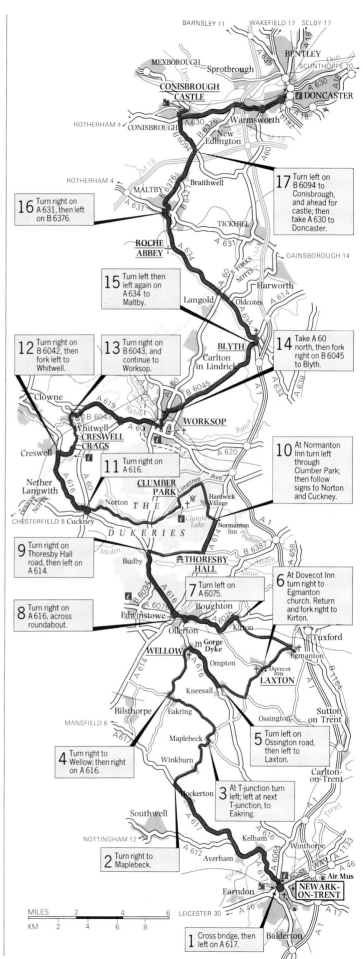

NORTH

Doncaster

Grimsby

M 62

Nottingham

Leicester

Northampton

Bedford

149 ● LOUTH

151 ● LINCOLN

150 ● BOSTON

THE WASH

144 ● SHERINGF

148 ● SPALDING

145 ● KING'S LYNN

146 ● STAMFORD

147 ● PETERBOROUGH

THE

FENS

136 ● HUNTINGDON

138 ● BURY ST EDMUNDS

137 ● CAMBRIDGE

139 ● SUDBURY

140 ● HADLEIGH

Ip

150 ● BOSTON Number of tour and starting point

──── Route of tour

MILES

KILOMETRES

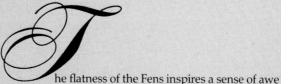

The flatness of the Fens inspires a sense of awe and wonder. The horizons seem to stretch to infinity, and the sky takes on an importance of its own. Its changing moods are like transformation scenes on a giant stage; there are no skies bluer, no cloud formations so impressive and no sunsets more glorious than those seen over the shimmering Fens. A fringe of handsome cities and towns, each with its own long and individual history, looks out across the flat lands, where high embankments carry roads above the rivers and drainage channels threading their way to The Wash, and tall church towers stand sentinel over compact villages.

Farther east are gentle hills, forests, heathland and the lovely Stour valley that inspired the painter John Constable. Along the coast, low cliffs and long beaches stretch almost continuously from Southwold to Sheringham. In Suffolk whole villages have disappeared beneath the waves; in Norfolk, man has succeeded where Canute failed, and acres of marshland have been reclaimed from the sea. Inland, East Anglia's capital and ancient cathedral city of Norwich is surrounded by fertile farmlands. To its north-east are the reed-fringed Broads, teeming with wildlife and speckled with brightly coloured sails that flit across the waters like darting butterflies.

Tulips bring spring colour to the aptly named South Holland district of Lincolnshire, centre of Britain's bulb-growing industry, and Boston's tall church tower is visible for miles across the Fens. North of The Wash lie the chalk uplands of the Lincolnshire Wolds, praised by the poet Lord Tennyson who was born among them, and the limestone ridge of Lincoln Edge. The rich fenland soil between them supports acres of wheat and vast crops of peas, barley, sugarbeet and potatoes. On Lincoln Edge, at a gap through the limestone ridge made by the River Witham, stands the city of Lincoln, the three slender towers of its cathedral presiding majestically over the patchwork landscape spread out below.

Cromwell and the cloud-kingdom of the Fens

Huntingdon was the birthplace of Oliver Cromwell, and the area has many reminders of the Lord Protector. A string of attractive villages lines the banks of the Great Ouse.

HUNTINGDON

A handsome old town survives behind the shopping precincts of Huntingdon. The High Street consists of Georgian houses with shops of earlier and later times.

In 1599, Oliver Cromwell was born in a building on a site now occupied by a small office building of classical aspect. He attended the Grammar School – as did Samuel Pepys some 20 years later – in what had been part of the 12th-century Hospital of St John; it is now the Cromwell Museum, open daily except Monday.

Echoes of the Lord Protector linger everywhere. His great-grandfather owned Hinchingbrooke House on the way to Brampton, and his grandfather had what is now the George Hotel. Cromwell's father is buried in All Saints' Church.

During the Second World War, bomber airfields surrounded Huntingdon, and the Pathfinder squadrons set up their headquarters here in huts. Pathfinder House, now council offices, stands on the site.

A bridge over the Great Ouse, dated 1332, joins Huntingdon to Godmanchester, a smaller town of separate character. It has a generous share of 17th and 18th-century houses and a vast, partly 13th-century church.

Near the junction of Cambridge Street, Post Street and The Causeway, the Chinese Bridge leads over to a recreation ground, which affords the best view of Godmanchester.

HOUGHTON

A massive brick-and-timber water mill on a backwater of the Great Ouse ground the local corn until 1930. The building, which belongs to the National Trust, dates mostly from the 17th century and is now a youth hostel.

Other local attractions include the brick-and-thatch Water Close Cottages by the church and the black-and-white houses in St Ives and Thicket Roads. These lead charmingly to the centre of Houghton with its bowfronted shops and thatched clock tower.

ST IVES

A Persian bishop named St Ivo inexplicably lived and died on the banks of the Ouse, at a place called Slepe, in about AD 600. Some four centuries later his grave was found and a priory was built on the spot. A market grew

up about the priory and, as the place grew in importance, the old name of Slepe gave way to St Ives.

The river is crossed by a wonderful 15th-century bridge with pointed arches. In the middle is a rare two-decker bridge chapel jutting out over the water. The riverside street called The Quay has pretty houses and, with the spire of the 15th-century church soaring above, an air reminiscent of Bruges or Amsterdam. Market Hill has a statue of Oliver Cromwell, who may have lived in the town for a while.

HEMINGFORD GREY

By the banks of the Great Ouse stands one of the loveliest riverside groupings in England. The keynote is the Church of St James with its oddly truncated spire – the top, removed by a gale in the 18th century, lies on the riverbed. There is a girdle of deep-thatched white and ochre cottages. In their midst are two notable houses – the 12th-century Manor House, said to be the longest-inhabited home in the country, and the red-brick, 300-year-old Hemingford Grey House.

FENSTANTON

Some colour-washed cottages, a few Georgian houses, a 1650 lock-up and a largely 14th-century church by a triangular green – these are all that remain of old Fenstanton.

But no true gardener could ever pass it by, for buried in the church is Lancelot 'Capability' Brown (1715-83), the greatest of landscape designers. His epitaph commands: 'Ye Sons of Elegance . . .Come from the sylvan Scenes his Genius grac'd, and offer here your tributary sighs.'

BOURN

A charming High Street with cottages of varying age snakes up to a triangular green. The Church of St Helen and St Mary is topped by a lead-sheathed spike set jauntily askew. The choir stalls and benches are medieval. Behind the church, on the site of a Norman castle, is the restored Jacobean Bourn Hall, now a clinic. By the Caxton road the black and somewhat sinister-looking Bourn Mill waves white skeletal arms. It dates from at least 1636 and is said to be the oldest post mill in England.

BUCKDEN

On the approach to Buckden from Offord Cluny is a vast marina filled with cabin cruisers. Buckden's wide High Street was once part of the Great North Road; the Lion and the George are coaching inns that recall the busy past.

The remaining fragments of Buckden Palace – a gatehouse and a massive, rose-red tower of the 15th century – loom over the wall like a miniature Hampton Court. The palace was a residence of the Bishops of Lincoln until 1838, when it was abandoned. It was rescued in the 1950s by the Claretian Missionaries, a religious order who roofed the tower and built a chapel nearby.

KIMBOLTON

Once an important market town, Kimbolton is now much smaller, but the streets of old pantiled houses still have rather an urban air. The Church of St Andrew has fine sculptures – monuments to earls, countesses and duchesses of Manchester. The chief

treasure is a painted medieval screen showing various saints and the Virgin Mary as a child.

The tough old Norman castle has long vanished. It was replaced by a Tudor manor house where Catherine of Aragon spent the last two unhappy years of her life after her marriage to Henry VIII was annulled. This building was impressively remodelled in 1707 by Vanbrugh for the 4th Earl of Manchester. Robert Adam added the gatehouse in 1764. The building is now a school, but it is open at spring and late summer Bank Holiday weekends, and on Sundays in school summer holidays.

BRAMPTON

Samuel Pepys, the diarist, was born at Brampton in 1633, at the farm named after him. He returned to the village frequently and made a lengthy stay in 1665 when the Great Plague was raging in London. It is said that he buried his money there when a Dutch invasion threatened.

Brampton's lovely 13th-century church has carved misericords depicting life in the Middle Ages. One represents a knight and his lady and the others show a clerk, a haymaking scene, sheepshearing and harvesting.

On the Huntingdon road is the Tudor Hinchingbrooke House, built by Richard Cromwell, Oliver Cromwell's great-grandfather. After the restoration of Charles II the house passed to the 1st Earl of Sandwich who added to the house. It was damaged by fire in 1830, but was restored and is now a school. It is open on spring and summer Sunday afternoons and on Bank Holidays.

KINDLY LIGHT *Ely Cathedral's octagonal lantern guided travellers across the treacherous fens in the Middle Ages.*

The Fenland drainage begun by the Romans reached its peak in the 17th century. North of Cambridge, the region's beauty unfolds, with cloud formations rolling above flat fields.

STRETHAM

A tall-chimneyed building stands beside the wind-ruffled Great Ouse. Inside are a grandly ponderous beam engine of 1831 and a row of massive boilers. The engine was used in a fen drainage scheme, driving a scoop-wheel 37ft across which lifted 30 tons of water at each revolution and dumped it into a dyke. Steam power was replaced by diesel in 1925, and the engine operated until 1941.

In St James's Church, a plough stands at the edge of the chancel, and there is a fine 15th-century brass of a lady with a gentle, expressive face.

ELY

The cathedral tower beckons for more than 20 miles across the flat landscape. In the enormous fields the soil is black, showing its marshy origins. The marshland was partly drained by the Romans but later reverted to a reedy wilderness with the Isle of Ely – 'island of the eels' – in its midst.

Here, in AD 673, the Anglian queen St Etheldreda founded an abbey. It was destroyed by the Danes nearly 200 years later, but rose again to survive further raids and Hereward the Wake's long, unavailing struggle against the Norman invaders.

The cathedral, originally the abbey church, was begun in the 11th century. Its central tower collapsed in 1322 and was replaced by a magnificent octagon with a 400 ton, timber-framed lantern at the top. Over a town where many buildings proclaim their great age, the walls of the cathedral tower like cliffs, and its windows glow magically as dusk falls.

SOHAM

As with several other Fenland settlements, Soham hides from the world behind a garland of post-war brick. But persevere, for the centre is old and attractive, governed by the cruciform, 12th-century St Andrew's Church, a building so enormous that it appears to be emulating Ely Cathedral.

WICKEN

Henry Cromwell, fourth son of Oliver, is buried in the small grey church at the entrance to the village. He was a distinguished Parliamentarian soldier and a shrewd administrator who became Lord Lieutenant of Ireland, but at the Restoration he was stripped of his offices.

At nearby Wicken Fen the National Trust has pumped water back into the land, re-creating a piece of Fenland as near its former state as possible. This is a fine nature reserve, with wildfowl, butterflies and moths, and some rare plants. Only part of the fen is open to the public.

NEWMARKET

This could be called the capital of the horse world. Its countryside is all racecourses, training areas and paddocks. In the wide, gracious High Street is the Rutland Arms, full of small trilby hats, riding macs and spidery legs in jodhpurs. Here, too, is the Jockey Club, the august arbiter of racing destinies, and next door the National Horse Racing Museum.

Other attractions are the National Stud, the autumn and winter bloodstock sales at Tattersalls, and the occasional antiques fairs in winter.

DEVIL'S DITCH

This is the most impressive of the great Cambridgeshire earthworks built to defend the Icknield Way, the prehistoric trackway running from The Wash to Salisbury Plain which served East Anglia for more than 2000 years. The earthworks were probably built in the period after the Roman legions had left Britain.

The Romano-British may have put up the defences against Danish invaders. However, the defences generally face south-west, and it is now more widely believed that the Danes built the ditch to defend themselves against the natives. It runs for more than 7 miles across country and still measures 15ft from the ditch bottom to the top of the bank.

THE SWAFFHAMS

Swaffham Bulbeck was once an inland port trading in cereals with the Continent. The 18th-century wharves remain; so do the Dutch-style Merchant's House, the warehouse and the maltings of the same period. St Mary's Church, probably dating from the 13th century, has a lovely portable altar of the Italian Renaissance.

Swaffham Prior has two churches, St Mary's and St Cyriac's, within the same churchyard.

ANGLESEY ABBEY

From 1135 until the Dissolution of the Monasteries, Anglesey was a small priory housing 11 Augustinian canons. Then it crumbled into a ruin which in about 1600 was incorporated into a house by Thomas Hobson, a livery stable owner. He would never let a customer choose a horse, but would part with the animals in strict rotation; hence the saying 'Hobson's choice'.

Anglesey's present glory dates from 1926, when it was bought by Huttleston Broughton, 1st Lord Fairhaven, who created one of England's finest gardens out of the fenland landscape. The principal feature is the wonderful collection of trees, but there are formal and waterside gardens too.

The house and garden now belong to the National Trust. The house is open in the afternoons in summer, from Wednesday to Sunday; the gardens are open each afternoon in summer.

FULBOURN

The centre of Fulbourn village is a triangular green. Around it are flint or pink-washed buildings, a post office, stores and a pub. The flint-and-pantiled church is dedicated to St Vigor, a 6th-century Bishop of Bayeux whose name was brought to England by the Normans. Big, handsome Fulbourn Manor has a statue of William III as a Roman general.

Tourist information: Cambridge 322640; Ely 2062.

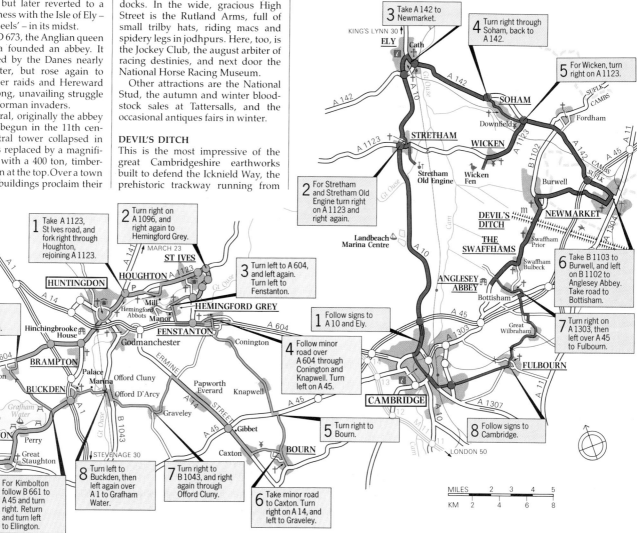

Forests and ancient mines of Breckland

TOUR
138

——— 75 MILES ———

Farmlands around a king's burial place give way to 'brecks', or tracts of heath, and forests. Sparsely populated today, the landscape bears the marks of greater use by early man.

BURY ST EDMUNDS

Four tall sentinels rise out of the Breckland plain to greet the traveller from Cambridge. These are the silos of a beet sugar refinery which, though prominent, are a far cry from the towers that beckoned to the medieval wayfarer when St Edmundsbury was one of the great centres of European pilgrimage.

The story began in AD 870, when King Edmund of the East Angles was murdered by marauding Danes. He was transfixed by arrows and then beheaded; according to legend his body was soon recovered by his soldiers, but the head could not be found until searchers were guided to it by the howls of a she-wolf that stood guard over it.

Edmund was later buried on the site of the town now named after him, and was quickly canonised. Long before the Norman Conquest St Edmund was a major cult figure, and he continued to be so throughout the Middle Ages.

About his tomb a great abbey grew, whose size can be guessed at by that of the enormous gatehouse on Angel Hill. In fact, it occupied the 6 acres of gardens behind the gatehouse, out of which fragments of the ruined abbey rise like reefs. Among them is the Appleby Rose Garden, a monument to the USAAF 94th Bombardment Group which operated from airfields in the vicinity during the Second World War.

Two of the old monastic churches remain – St James's, now the cathedral, and St Mary's. The cathedral was restored by the Victorians, whose bright carvings look down upon the 1000 colourful hassocks in the pews, each one representing a Suffolk parish. In St Mary's Church is the grave of Mary Tudor, Queen of France and sister of Henry VIII, and monuments to the Suffolk Regiment.

WOOLPIT

The houses of Woolpit are Georgian brick or timber-framed and plastered in pink, soft yellow and green; their chimneys are twisted like barley sugar, or lean at rakish angles. In the square, pretty and highly useful shops – Post Office, Old Bakery and General Store – look over a covered pump commemorating the Diamond Jubilee of Queen Victoria to the handsome Swan pub.

St Mary's Church is spectacular, with a flying buttressed Victorian spire and a 15th-century porch that may have been built by the architect of King's College Chapel, Cambridge. The building has a glorious hammerbeam ceiling with spread-winged angels decorating the beam ends.

PAKENHAM

This village is unique, for it has two working mills. One is a restored 18th-century water mill which replaced an earlier one recorded in the Domesday survey. In it there are regular milling demonstrations between Easter and September. The other is a five-floor, 19th-century tower mill.

The fine Jacobean Newe House was the home of 'American' Reeve, a 19th-century local lad who ran away to the USA, where he became a buffalo hunter and made a fortune which he spent on buying the big house in his native village.

IXWORTH

The grandest building in Ixworth is the abbey, reached down Conister Lane opposite the Pickeral Inn. It is a 16th, 17th and 18th-century building incorporating the 13th, 14th and 15th-century remains of an Augustinian priory. The 1st lord temporal of the manor was Richard Codington, who lies with his wife in the chequered flint church almost next door.

The abbey is open to the public on Tuesdays, Sundays and Bank Holiday afternoons from May to August. In the nearby Waterfowl Farm, dozens of species are bred in paddocks beside The Black Bourn.

EUSTON

A solidity of wall, a neatness and uniformity of dormer window and thatch and grandeur of cedars suggest an estate village and the proximity of a great house. In this case it is Euston Hall, a vast and lovely red-brick building dating from the 17th and 18th centuries. It is the seat of the Dukes of Grafton, the first of whom was the son of Charles II and his aristocratic mistress, Barbara Villiers. The nearby Church of St Genevieve dates from the 17th century and is in the style of Sir Christopher Wren.

Euston has one of the finest collections of family portraits in the country, many of them royal, and by such painters as Reynolds, Lely and Van Dyck. The hall and church are open to the public on Thursday afternoons from June to September.

THETFORD

Older buildings of finely dressed flint, emphasised by door and window frames of white-painted brick or stone, shine through the modern architecture of Thetford.

It is a town of sites. There is the site of the castle, thought to have been built by William de Warenne shortly after the Norman Conquest and marked by an 80ft mound. Then there are the sites of the great Cathedral of St Mary, the Cluniac priory, the Benedictine Nunnery of St George – the 12th-century Augustinian Priory of St Sepulchre and several other ecclesiastical foundations.

Near the meeting of the Little Ouse and Thet rivers there is a water mill – as well as the attractive Nuns' Bridges and the 18th-century Spring House that was the pump room of the short-lived Thetford Spa. The Bell Hotel is Tudor, and the King's House, now the council offices, is 18th century. Outside is a statue of the philosopher Tom Paine, who was born in the town. His writings, including *The Rights of Man* and *Age of Reason*, inspired the American and French Revolutions.

SANTON DOWNHAM

A modern forestry village of timber and brick houses is almost overwhelmed by the dark and solemn pines of Thetford's forests. Probably the most profitable of Breckland's crops, the trees, planted by the Forestry Commission, cover some 70 square miles and are harvested for construction and saw-milling materials, pit props, fencing, paper and

---

MILES / KM scale

9 Turn left on A 134. Turn left and left again on A 1065 through Brandon.

8 Fork right to Santon Downham, then turn right.

7 Take A 11, Newmarket road, then turn right on B 1107, Brandon road.

6 Turn left on A 1088 to Thetford.

5 Follow signs to mill and ahead to A 143, then turn right to Ixworth.

4 Turn left to Pakenham.

10 Turn left on B 1112, across A 11, then left on A 1101 through Icklingham.

11 Turn left to West Stow. (For Anglo-Saxon village, left again.)

12 Turn right and right again to Flempton. Cross A 1101 and then over A 45 to Little Saxham.

13 Turn left to crossroads then right to Horringer.

14 Follow A 143 to Bury St Edmunds.

1 Take A 45, Stowmarket road.

2 Turn off on minor road to Beyton and Hessett, then turn left to Woolpit.

3 Take Thetford road over A 45, then turn left on A 1088.

SWAFFHAM, GRIME'S GRAVES, Breckland, Weeting, Hall, BRANDON, Brandon Country Park, Thetford Forest, SANTON DOWNHAM, Lakenheath Airfield, (Rems of), Nuns' Bridges, THETFORD, EUSTON, Little Fakenham, Honington, Ixworth Thorpe, The King's Forest, Anglo-Saxon Village, Icklingham, WEST STOW, Flempton, Risby, CAMBRIDGE, Little Saxham, ICKWORTH, Cath Horringer, Abbey, IXWORTH, Waterfowl Farm, Water Mill, Newe House, PAKENHAM, BURY ST EDMUNDS, Norton, Beyton, Hessett, Drinkstone, WOOLPIT, STOWMARKET

chipboard. The Commission's district office is in Santon, and a forest trail 3 miles long begins at the car park.

A little forlorn among all the modern bustle is the Norman church which is all that remains of the old Santon Downham village that was smothered in sand in the 1660s.

GRIME'S GRAVES

The craters and scattered debris are quite obviously the works of man – as obvious as the Second World War runways of the area that are slowly disappearing under crops. But at Grime's Graves the flint chippings that crunch underfoot were whittled some 2000 years before the birth of Christ, and the visitor is looking at the substantial remains of one of the oldest mines in the world.

In the 34 acres occupied by Grime's Graves there are some 360 craters, each one of which is a filled-in shaft. One of them, the first of several, was reopened in 1869 and found to connect with a system of galleries at about 30ft, where there is a strata of large flint nodules. These were dug out with antler picks and brought to the surface where they were split and chipped into axe blades, arrowheads and scrapers.

One of the mines is generally open to the public. The smoke stains of the miners' animal fat lanterns can still be seen on the walls, and the workers' fingerprints on the antler picks.

BRANDON

A long, strung-out town that is much admired for the flint work in its buildings. Though somewhat masked now by overspill estates and concrete lampposts like Martian invaders, a good deal remains, especially in the older streets where the dark flint is generally cut into small squares and set in brick frames into the walls. The material is used too with good effect in some of the grander houses such as the 18th-century Brandon Hall, where it is attractively alternated with strawberry bricks.

Flint knapping or splitting was the older of Brandon's two crafts. The raw material was obtained from little bell-shaped mines, just as it was in the Stone Age, and used as building material – or was ground down for mixing with potter's clay, or, most importantly, was knapped into gunflints. The Brown Bess muskets and rifles that stopped the Old Guard at Waterloo were sparked by Brandon flints. Brandon's other industry was fur, obtained from rabbits living on the sandy heaths round about.

WEST STOW

An Anglo-Saxon community was established at West Stow on a hillock beside the River Lark, and when the site was excavated a few years ago, enough evidence was discovered to give a fairly clear idea of what life was like in the Suffolk of about AD 450-650. So much so in fact, that the county archaeologists' department has been able to rebuild a number of the houses. They are remarkably solid with their walls of timber, wattle and daub, their thatched roofs and clay fireplaces. A number of outhouses –

THETFORD CHASE *The forest has grown since 1922, when the Forestry Commission first planted conifers on the sandy heathland.*

IXWORTH THORPE *The church has a thatched roof and wooden belfry.*

THETFORD PRIORY *A Cluniac house stood here in the 12th century.*

SPRING AT ICKWORTH *Trees in bud arch over a carpet of snowdrops and aconites in the grounds of Ickworth, which were planned by Capability Brown. The rotunda, with its fine carved frieze, is partly modelled on the Pantheon in Rome.*

storage rooms and weaving sheds – have also been rebuilt.

The village lies within the West Stow Country Park, which also has a nature reserve.

ICKWORTH

From its outer pavilions and across its linking corridors and central rotunda, Ickworth is 700ft wide while the top of the dome stands 100ft high. The house was begun towards the end of the 18th century by the 4th Earl of Bristol, who was also the Bishop of Derry. He intended the pavilions as galleries for his collection of antiquities and the rotunda as living quarters. But Napoleon's invading armies confiscated the collection before it left Italy, and the earl-bishop was dead long before the house was completed in the 1830s.

Now the original plan has been reversed; the pavilions are living quarters, and the huge oval rotunda is a gallery that beautifully sets off the gatherings of family portraits, the furniture, silver and antique toys. The house and grounds, owned by the National Trust, are open to the public on Bank Holidays and on most afternoons in summer.

Tourist information:
Bury St Edmunds 64667 (summer); Thetford 2599.

A valley home of weavers and artists

TOUR
139

—— 49 MILES ——

Clothiers prospered in East Anglia before the Industrial Revolution. Their legacy lives on today in great churches, noble merchants' houses, and sturdy stone-built cottages.

SUDBURY

Jibed at by Charles Dickens as corrupt, greedy 'Eatanswill' in *Pickwick Papers*, Sudbury is in fact an engaging, hospitable market town. Its long tradition of weaving is remembered in the ample first-floor windows behind which the looms once stood. The silk used in the Princess of Wales's wedding dress was woven in the town.

Thomas Gainsborough was born in a house in what is now Gainsborough Street. Open daily except on Mondays, it displays many of his works.

The railway station now houses the town museum, open on Thursday, Saturday and Sunday afternoons. A nearby car park leads to Friars Meadow and the Valley Walk along the old Stour Valley Railway to a picnic site near Rodbridge Corner. A restored Stour barge floats near the Quay Theatre, which has been imaginatively constructed from an 18th-century granary.

LAVENHAM

The stone and flint tower of the Church of St Peter and St Paul looms over the horizon, to be finally revealed in unobscured splendour on the crown of its hill. A curving street of weavers' cottages falls gently away to the timbered richness of the finest of all medieval wool towns.

The half-timbered Guildhall, owned by the National Trust, contains exhibitions telling the story of the wool trade and Lavenham's speciality, blue broadcloth. A splendid Wool Hall was added to one corner of the Swan Hotel.

The church was endowed by John de Vere, 13th Earl of Oxford, and Thomas Spring, 'the Rich Clothier'. Its 141ft tower has the de Vere star emblem set in the flintwork, and the Spring coat of arms repeated around the top.

Little Hall, a 15th-century hall house beside the market place, is open on Saturday, Sunday and Bank Holiday afternoons in summer. The restored priory in Water Street, another medieval house, with some fine Elizabethan frescoes, is open every afternoon in summer.

LONG MELFORD

Arriving in the village beside the old timber-framed Bull Inn, a right turn leads towards the warm Tudor brickwork and pepperpot towers of Melford Hall, with a row of Tudor almshouses and the church at the summit of a sloping green. Holy Trinity Church has some of England's finest patterns of trimmed flint and freestone 'flushwork'. For 200 years its Lady Chapel was used as a school, and it still has multiplication tables painted on one wall.

Melford Hall contains naval pictures, Chinese porcelain, fine furniture, and some mementos of Beatrix Potter who frequently stayed there. It is owned by the National Trust and is open on Wednesday, Thursday, Sunday and Bank Holiday afternoons in summer.

Kentwell Hall, a Tudor mansion behind the church, reached by a mile-long avenue of lime trees, offers concerts, an open-air theatre season and displays of Tudor domestic life.

On the Essex side of the Stour the meadows are overlooked by the 14th-century round tower of Pentlow's church. It is Saxon in origin but largely Norman in character, with a lavishly carved Norman font.

CAVENDISH

The wide, slanting village green is backed by the church above a little group of beautifully restored almshouses. Three stags' heads on the village sign come from the coat of arms of the Cavendish family, one of whom, Sir John Cavendish, hid his valuables in St Mary's belfry during the Peasants' Revolt but was pursued to Bury St Edmunds and beheaded.

Nether Hall, a sumptuous Tudor house close to the church, is open to visitors daily, together with the vineyard trail and crafts museum of Cavendish Manor Vineyards. Another museum, near the duck pond, is housed in the Old Rectory and shows the work done throughout the world by the Sue Ryder Foundation for the Sick and Disabled. It is open daily.

CLARE

'Go about your business' enjoins the 18th-century sundial over the south porch of the Church of St Peter and St Paul, and the inhabitants of this tiny yet always busy town have been doing so to good effect since the height of the place's prosperity in the 13th century. At that time the Clare family established a friary here, and after the male line was wiped out at the Battle of Bannockburn a surviving sister, Elizabeth de Burgh, founded Clare College at Cambridge.

Beside the church, the 15th-century Ancient House is covered with decorative plasterwork as deep and convoluted as the icing on a florid wedding cake. It now serves as a local museum, open every afternoon in summer except on Mondays.

A toothy fragment of the Norman castle keep rises jaggedly from its tree-choked motte, with footpaths ascending the mound. Other paths lead to a nature trail through Clare Castle Country Park, based on the abandoned railway station.

CASTLE HEDINGHAM

The two grey towers of the Norman castle keep glower possessively over lands which once belonged to the de Vere family, who lived here for some 500 years.

Four floors of the keep survive, containing a banqueting hall with a minstrels' gallery, all reached by a Tudor brick bridge across a dry moat. Visitors can picnic in the grounds when the keep is open, at Easter and daily from May to October.

In the village, brick shines warmly also in the conflicting styles of the church, which has Norman walls crowned by Tudor battlements, and a 17th-century tower whose stair turret sprouts an 18th-century cupola and weather vane. The gloriously coloured glass of the east window is framed within the spokes of one of the few surviving Norman wheel windows in the country.

A stretch of track from the old Colne Valley Railway has been reopened for steam train and railcar trips between April and December. The station has been reconstructed in the style of a typical Victorian branch line, open daily for viewing even when trains are not running.

LITTLE MAPLESTEAD

Between a thin veil of trees on the exposed Essex farmlands appears a strange, squat round tower topped with a six-sided wooden belfry. At close range it is revealed as the round church of Little Maplestead, based, like other places of worship of the Knights Hospitallers, on the Church of the Holy Sepulchre at Jerusalem.

The hospitallers established a Hospital and Church of St John here in the 11th century, and rebuilt their church around 1335. It has been left looking starkly white and bare inside since ruthless 'restoration' in the 1850s.

HALSTEAD

The bright and breezy town derives its name from Saxon words meaning 'place of health'. Its broad main street runs steeply down between shops old and new to a bridge across the River Colne, which offers a splendid view of a historic water mill. Built in 1788 as a corn mill, it was bought in·1825 by Samuel Courtauld, who converted it for the weaving of silk fabrics. A terrace of workers' houses along The Causeway ends near a jolly little clocking-on office, rather like a miniature glassed-in bandstand.

St Andrew's Church has imposing monuments and tombs of the Bourchier family, one of whom fought beside the Black Prince at the Battle of Crécy in 1346.

Tourist information: Sudbury 72092.

CHURCH AND CHARITY *A 14th-century church stands by almshouses at Cavendish.*

HALL OF PROSPERITY *Lavenham's merchant clothiers met in the Guildhall of 1529.*

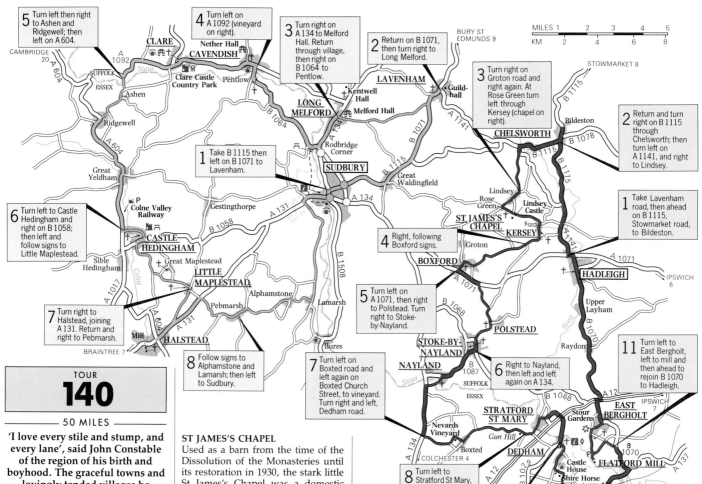

5 Turn left then right to Ashen and Ridgewell; then left on A 604.

4 Turn left on A 1092 (vineyard on right).

3 Turn right on A 134 to Melford Hall. Return through village, then right on B 1064 to Pentlow.

2 Return on B 1071, then turn right to Long Melford.

3 Turn right on Groton road and right again. At Rose Green turn left through Kersey (chapel on right).

2 Return and turn right on B 1115 through Chelsworth; then turn left on A 1141, and right to Lindsey.

1 Take B 1115 then left on B 1071 to Lavenham.

1 Take Lavenham road, then ahead on B 1115, Stowmarket road, to Bildeston.

6 Turn left to Castle Hedingham and right on B 1058; then left and follow signs to Little Maplestead.

4 Right, following Boxford signs.

7 Turn right to Halstead, joining A 131. Return and right to Pebmarsh.

5 Turn left on A 1071, then right to Polstead. Turn right to Stoke-by-Nayland.

11 Turn left to East Bergholt, left to mill and then ahead to rejoin B 1070 to Hadleigh.

8 Follow signs to Alphamstone and Lamarsh; then left to Sudbury.

7 Turn left on Boxted road and left again on Boxted Church Street, to vineyard. Turn right and left, Dedham road.

6 Right to Nayland, then left and left again on A 134.

8 Turn left to Stratford St Mary, then right to Dedham.

9 Turn left on Manningtree road, then left by Castle House and ahead at crossroads.

10 Turn left on A 137, then left on B 1070.

TOUR 140

— 50 MILES —

'I love every stile and stump, and every lane', said John Constable of the region of his birth and boyhood. The graceful towns and lovingly tended villages he painted have changed little.

HADLEIGH

The long main street offers a lively display of colour washes in green, ochre, pink and yellow, with richly pargeted frontages. The eye is tempted by a score of different façades; the feet are tempted into side streets graced by oversailing upper storeys and the sudden surprise of elegant Georgian town houses, a Victorian neoclassical corn exchange, and a lovely churchyard.

The church's slim leaden spire carries a projecting bell. In the south aisle a tomb canopy known as Guthrum's Tomb commemorates the fact that the Christianised Danish king to whom King Alfred conceded the monarchy of East Anglia was buried somewhere beneath the present building.

CHELSWORTH

With its double-humped, 18th-century bridge crossing the little River Brett, this is a village for connoisseurs of all that is gentlest yet sturdiest in England. Its scattered, uneven houses are neighbourly; its gardens compete in beauty, but always in good fellowship; and it inspired an affectionate literary tribute in *Suffolk Scene* by the poet Julian Tennyson, killed in the Second World War. To the west of the village is Cobbold's Mill, once the home of Sir Francis Meynell, founder of the Nonesuch Press, and now a picture gallery.

ST JAMES'S CHAPEL

Used as a barn from the time of the Dissolution of the Monasteries until its restoration in 1930, the stark little St James's Chapel was a domestic 'free' chapel of the 13th century probably attached to Lindsey Castle, of which a few lumpy earthworks remain some 250yds south-east.

KERSEY

Lindsey gave its name to linsey-woolsey, a light material for women's clothing, while the cottages of Kersey produced the tougher kerseymere for men's trousers and other garments. One of the most beautiful villages in England, Kersey ravishes the eye with its steep slope descending to a ford where ducks take priority over motorists, and rising again to the majestic church tower.

Houses cling to the sides of the two hills, many with twisting flights of steep steps serving high-set front doors. In the lanes off the main street, timbered and plastered buildings are set at conflicting angles. Nothing is straight, nothing ordinary. The bar of the Bell Inn has beams exposed to the roof ridge, interlocking in geometric patterns, a lesson in timber-framing.

BOXFORD

The compact village centre is fed by lanes bedecked with timbered medieval houses. One of the finest ranges is in Butcher's Lane, part of which combines oversailing upper timbered storeys with pargeted ground-floor panels, and some eccentric examples of patched-up repairs. Opposite the church is a characteristic weavers' hall house with a high latticed window.

The 15th-century Church of St Mary has a wooden north porch of the 14th century. Within, the font has an unusual Jacobean octagonal painted cover with hinged doors. A tablet commemorates Elizabeth Hyam who in 1748 was 'at last hastened to her end . . . in her 113th year'. The east window, showing the Transfiguration, is a beautiful example of modern stained glass, completed in 1972.

POLSTEAD

Little groups of cottages with diminutive but smart gardens cluster above a veritable lagoon of a duckpond. Among the buildings is the home of Maria Marten, murdered in 1827 in the Red Barn which burnt down long ago. Her gravestone in the churchyard was so badly chipped away by souvenir hunters that now only a noticeboard names her, without identifying the exact spot. Nave arcades and windows contain brickwork from Norman times, when there was little brickmaking in England.

STOKE-BY-NAYLAND

A succession of lofty gables and the timbers of the Guildhall and old maltings look down on an almost complete square of streets. These form a multi-hued palisade around the soaring pinnacled tower of the Church of St Mary the Virgin, which in one of Constable's paintings rides like a mighty galleon beneath the shining arc of a rainbow.

NAYLAND

The little spire jutting above the compact, drowsy little village is a 1963 replacement of the original, which was removed in 1834 because it was unsafe. Above the altar is a painting by John Constable showing Christ blessing the bread and wine.

On the outskirts of Boxted, the tiny Nevards Vineyard welcomes visitors. An appointment is recommended (Nayland 36325).

STRATFORD ST MARY

From the summit of Dedham Gun Hill the view over Dedham Vale appears, apart from the gash of the main road, much as in Constable's paintings. It was by the Swan, an inn dating from Tudor times, that the 18-year-old John waited for the coach to London on his first vain attempt to interest the art world in his early work.

The first stretch of street runs beside the Stour, then swings right on the corner graced by the 16th-century

229

timbered house called Gooseacres, to reveal more sturdy timber and some plastered frontages.

DEDHAM

St Mary's great tower dominates Dedham Vale and many of Constable's paintings. Within the church, the ceiling is enriched by a great display of heraldic bosses. British and US airmen who flew from nearby airfields in the Second World War are commemorated in modern pews.

In the centre of the village, a small Countryside Information Centre has displays mounted by the National Trust and local conservation groups, open daily in summer except on Sundays. An old church has been transformed into Dedham Centre of Arts and Crafts, open daily, where embroiderers, potters, glass workers and other designers can be seen at work; and there is a toy museum.

A painter of our own century, Sir Alfred Munnings, lived at Castle House, which has a display of his paintings. Munnings was noted as a portrayer of horses, and it is appropriate that nearby is the 50 acre Shire Horse and Farm Centre. It has show horses, rare breeds of cattle, exhibitions of vintage horse vehicles and demonstrations of grooming and driving. The centre is open at Easter, every Sunday from April to September, Wednesdays from mid-April to mid-September, and daily in July and August.

FLATFORD MILL

Close to a wooden bridge over the placid Stour are the water mill and Willy Lott's cottage, owned by the National Trust, and the lock, some of Constable's favourite subjects. The mill, seen at its most radiant from the Essex towpath, is now a Field Studies Council centre, open only to students on residential courses.

EAST BERGHOLT

The lane from Flatford emerges opposite the strange bulk of East Bergholt church. Its tower was begun by Cardinal Wolsey but never finished, so the bells hang in a wooden cage in the churchyard. Constable's birthplace, a short stroll along the street, has been demolished, but its site is marked by a plaque. In the churchyard of St Mary the Virgin are buried his parents and his old friend Willy Lott.

The gardens of the late Randolph Churchill's home, Stour, offer an uninterrupted panorama of the vale. They are open daily, with a craft centre and shop next door.

Tourist information: (Hadleigh) Ipswich 822922; (Dedham) Colchester 323447 (summer).

RIVER OF TRANQUILLITY *Bridge Cottage stands beside the peaceful Stour just upstream from Flatford Mill. The timber-framed and thatched 16th-century building is owned by the National Trust, and provides information about the area whose scenes, said Constable, 'made me a painter'.*

Inland from Suffolk's threatened coast

TOUR

141

—— 77 MILES ——

Small ports shelter behind rugged breakwaters and unstable dunes, and footpaths crisscross heath and marsh. Farmhouses inland are covered with decorative plaster, and often moated.

SOUTHWOLD

Three fingers thrust skywards from the elegant little town – the steeple of St Edmund's Church, the white column of the lighthouse, and the slender metal chimney of one of the country's most renowned real ale breweries. Set well back from the edge of the low cliff and surrounded by houses, the lighthouse looks down on one of the nine greens laid out as firebreaks after a devastating blaze in 1659. Today the most attractive is South Green, shelving away between Georgian houses and fishermen's cottages converted into modern homes, with a view across the Town Marshes.

Gun Hill Green sports six ancient cannons, and a coastguard lookout in what used to be a camera obscura. Long Victorian terraces stand back above a shallow promenade where a line of beach huts adds a turn-of-the-century air to this amiable resort in which nothing noisy or garish could ever hope to flourish.

Inland along the banks of the River Blyth straggle the happily untidy sheds and tackle of a fishing and sailing harbour. The bridge, which once carried a narrow-gauge railway across the river, is part of a footpath to Walberswick and Blythburgh along old railway tracks and over a bridge. Walberswick was once a fishing and trading port of some consequence, but is now a residential backwater for retired folk and a number of artists and craftsmen.

BLYTHBURGH

In any weather Holy Trinity Church is a ravishing sight, riding like a great ship above the reflections of the tidal water or glistening mud flats, sometimes hazy, sometimes stark against the sky. Floodlit at night, it seems to float above the heath and marsh.

Inside, it has a 'Jack-o'-the-Clock' – a painted wooden figure which strikes a bell to signal the beginning of a service. Traces of tethering rings in the nave pillars recall the days when Cromwell's cavalry used the vast, bright interior as a stable, and the fanatical William Dowsing smashed religious emblems and fired bullets into the angels in the roof. This superb building deserves its reputation as the 'Cathedral of the Marshes'.

DUNWICH

Most eerie and echoing of all east-coast communities, Dunwich is now a small hamlet and only a remnant of its former self. In the time of Henry II it was recorded as having 15 religious establishments, and was a major shipbuilding centre and supplier of royal galleys. But storms struck again and again, the sandy cliffs on which the town stood crumbled, and building after building was clawed into the sea; in our own century the last surviving church of the old town went bit by bit over the edge. A well-kept museum tells the dramatic story, while the walls of a former monastery now shelter farm implements.

DUNWICH HEATH

The National Trust car park at the end of Dunwich Heath commands a spreading prospect of Minsmere Nature Reserve with its rushes, ponds and creeks abounding in wildlife, backed by Sizewell Nuclear Power Station. Admittance to the reserve is controlled by the Royal Society for the Protection of Birds, whose information centre can be reached from the road to Westleton, but below the heath a footpath passes a public hide for viewing birds.

Back on the main route, Westleton Heath National Nature Reserve is one of the last surviving expanses of the once extensive East Suffolk heathland. Footpaths as rough and natural as those trodden since Neolithic times lead across tracts of sandy, acid soil on which flourish heather, bracken and birch, whispering with the secretive, strange melodies which inspired Benjamin Britten to compose so much of his music.

THEBERTON

The round tower of St Peter's Church, rising from a Norman base and topped by an octagonal belfry added in the 14th century, stands on a steep knoll at the entrance to the village. The tower is guarded by ferocious gargoyles which seem poised to spit venom upon the churchyard.

Within, the vestry has a perfect Norman arch with two orders of zigzag moulding, rediscovered earlier this century. In a glass case near the font is a grim memento of war – a fragment of Zeppelin L48, shot down in flames near the village in June 1917.

Behind the flamboyantly painted south aisle arcade is the Doughty Chapel, which was renovated in 1846 by the Doughty family of Theberton Hall whose most famous son was C.M. Doughty, author of *Travels in Arabia Deserta*.

LEISTON ABBEY

A skeleton of eroded stone plays tricks on the eyes of the passer-by: between the stumps of the old fabric are glimpses of an incongruous Georgian house quite at odds with the original grey walls. Closer examination reveals substantial remains of a 14th-century Premonstratensian foundation, with a Tudor brick gatehouse with turrets. Originally built in

CHANGING COASTLINE *Year by year the low, sandy cliffs at Minsmere are changing shape, sculpted by the remorseless sea.*

CASTLE OF FEAR *At Framlingham in 1553, Mary Tudor began the reign that earned her the nickname of 'Bloody Mary'.*

POST MILL *The 18th-century mill at Saxtead Green, turning on a central post, stands on a brick roundhouse.*

the 12th century on a dank site in Minsmere Marshes, the abbey was rebuilt at Leiston in 1363.

The Lady Chapel and the house now house a music school, but the ruins are open to the public daily.

SIZEWELL
Access to the Sizewell Nuclear Power Station is by a road opposite the Vulcan Arms public house, so named long before the power station was ever dreamt of. The road is a private CEGB one, but visitors to the information centre may use it.

The centre and neighbouring exhibition rooms display models and diagrams explaining the production of electricity from nuclear energy. There is a cinema, a recreational area for children and space for picnics. The centre is open from Monday to Friday and on Saturday afternoons in July and August.

ALDEBURGH
The approach through Thorpeness puzzles many a visitor, with its pseudo 'olde-worlde' townscape adorned by a 'House in the Clouds' (actually a water tower with living accommodation), a windmill, mock Tudor dwellings, and a man-made lake with islands known as The Pirate's Lair, Treasure Island, and so on. All this was the brainchild of Glencairn Stuart Ogilvie, an enthusiast earlier this century who wanted to create 'a corner of Merrie England'.

Aldeburgh itself is bleaker and tougher. The Regency poet George Crabbe painted dour poetic pictures of surly inhabitants in their storm-ridden setting, and the composer Benjamin Britten immortalised one of those characters in his 1945 opera *Peter Grimes*. Certainly the sea is forever threatening, and the lifeboat is forever alert, poised on its cradle ready to plough spectacularly through the shingle into the waves.

The brick and timber Moot Hall once stood in the centre of the town, but erosion has taken its toll, and now it serves as a little museum close to the water's edge.

SNAPE MALTINGS
Benjamin Britten and Peter Pears founded the annual Aldeburgh Festival in Aldeburgh's cramped Jubilee Hall, but later moved to the superb complex of buildings by Snape Bridge and created a concert hall within a former malt house. In summer there are trips on the River Alde; and a riverside walk is rich in birdlife, reeds, grasses, and views over the marshes.

GLEMHAM HALL
The red-brick, largely Elizabethan house stands in spacious parkland with a picnic site and, behind it, a fine avenue of yews, a walled rose garden, and a lily pond. Indoors, family mementos and personal possessions lying around show that the house is still lived in. There are fine pieces of furniture, four-poster beds, some notable panelling, and paintings by Gainsborough and Constable. The hall is open on Wednesday, Sunday and Bank Holiday afternoons from Easter Monday to September.

EASTON
Easton Hall no longer exists, but its grounds are still surrounded by the longest serpentine or ribbon wall – 'crinkle-crankle' in Suffolk idiom – in the world, and neighboured by a whole colony of *cottages ornées*, many of them circular with a central chimney and a stumpy little wing behind.

Easton Farm Park, open daily from Good Friday until late September, operates as a working farm in which many old crafts are still practised; there is a blacksmith's shop and demonstrations of threshing are given. Vintage farm machinery is on display and there is a nature trail.

A few minutes down a minor road is Letheringham Watermill, with gardens and water meadows populated by peafowl and ornamental birds. The mill is open on Sunday and Bank Holiday afternoons from mid-April until the end of September, and also on Wednesday afternoons from June until September.

FRAMLINGHAM
Framlingham Castle's high walls and spindly chimneys rise high above a jumble of pantiled roofs twisting uphill, downhill, and around the wayward streets of the brisk little market town.

The narrow parapet high up behind the castle walls offers dizzying views down on the sloping market place, the 16th-century Crown Hotel, and St Michael's Church. Among the

church's treasures are a characteristic East Anglian font and the 'Flodden Helmet' worn by Thomas Howard in the English vanguard at the Battle of Flodden Field in 1513. There are monuments to other Howards including the 4th Duke of Norfolk, beheaded for collaborating with Mary, Queen of Scots.

SAXTEAD GREEN
The sails of the village's 18th-century post mill, on a site where a mill has stood since the 14th century, can often be seen in action across the fields or across Saxtead's broad green. In full working order, the mill is open daily except Sundays from April to September.

DENNINGTON
Now little more than a cluster of pleasant little houses by a village green so denuded by horses' hoofs and modern parking that it has become known simply as 'The Square', Dennington was once the centre of a very large parish and the scene of huge horse and cattle fairs. Until the beginning of this century the inn served as a charitable institution for the distribution of food and fuel to the needy.

LAXFIELD
The long, wide village street swings abruptly at its eastern end between a nicely balanced assembly of church, inn, and half-timbered, brick-nogged Guildhall. The Guildhall houses a

small museum run by local volunteers. Laxfield was the birthplace of the infamous William Dowsing, Oliver Cromwell's destroyer of statues, 'superstitious pictures', glass and crucifixes. He seems, however, to have been lenient on his own parish: the church still has its fine seven-sacrament font, as well as a muddled mixture of old carved benches and box pews.

BRAMFIELD
St Andrew's round tower stands well away from the thatched, colour-washed body of the church. With its 5ft thick foundation walls, the tower looks toughly defensive rather than religious, and it was almost certainly used for sheltering villagers during 13th-century baronial squabbles.

Inside the church, the eye is delighted by an exquisite, lacy rood screen, and a touching marble monument to the Coke family who lived nearby.

Across the road, a rosy 'crinkle-crankle' wall twists round the grounds of Bramfield Hall.

The church in neighbouring Wenhaston has a large 'Doom' painting, painted on boards in about 1480. It shows the righteous being welcomed into Heaven and naked sinners being plunged into the torments of Hell.

Tourist information: Southwold 722366 (summer); Aldeburgh 3637 (summer).

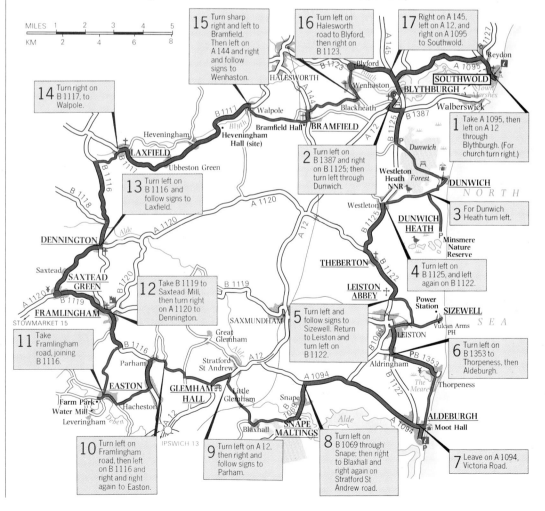

Meadows and marshes around Norwich

TOUR
142
54 MILES

Flinty church towers and pantiled farmhouses punctuate the flat farmlands south-west of Norwich. A majestic abbey church at Wymondham rivals Norwich's own cathedral in splendour.

KETTERINGHAM

St Peter's Church, flint-walled and sturdy, and an immaculate white-walled thatched cottage hide among trees in the grounds of the privately owned Ketteringham Hall. Inside the church, a gallery looks down into a nave spanned by scrubbed wooden pews. The chancel is a fine clutter of marble memorials, many of them commemorating members of the Boileau family who restored the church in the 19th century.

Other treasures of the church include a font of 1494 and a neoclassical white marble memorial tablet designed by John Flaxman, creator of the classical figures on Wedgwood pottery. The church key, appropriately massive, is kept at the tiled cottage opposite the lich gate.

WYMONDHAM

Held aloft for three centuries on its wobbly looking wooden stilts, Wymondham's market cross is a little octagonal half-timbered room with mullioned windows, once used for meetings of the town's market court and as a library.

From the cross, narrow streets drop away in all directions, and nearly every one of the buildings lining them deserves a second look. Most date from after 1615 when much of Wymondham (pronounced 'Windham') was burnt to the ground: scorch marks are still visible on the timbers of the 15th-century Green Dragon pub, one of the few buildings to survive the fire.

Timber-framed houses, their first storeys jutting out over the pavements, alternate with handsome Georgian façades in grey, pink, cream and white, and pantiled roofs drop in higgledy-piggledy lines towards the twin towers of the abbey.

The majestic 60ft high arch framed between Scots pines that first confronts the visitor to Wymondham's abbey church gives some idea of the scale of the enormous abbey which stood here before the Dissolution. What remains, though half the size of the original, is massive enough. The nave soars high upon sturdy Norman columns to a hammerbeam roof with carved angels flying out over the congregation; and the high altar is backed by a screen glittering with golden high-relief figures of Christ and the saints, surmounted by a huge golden canopy.

The fire of 1615 left the abbey church unharmed. The more modest Guild Chapel of St Thomas also escaped, and is now a dignified, high-ceilinged public library.

WICKLEWOOD MILL

Grinding corn in 1942 . . . derelict in 1975 . . . restored by 1985 to working order. The story of Wickle-wood Mill is an outstanding example of what painstaking work by a devoted team – in this case the Norfolk Windmills Trust – can achieve. The mill stands five storeys high, with a black-painted brick tower and a gleaming white cap to turn the sails into the wind. Visitors can explore the mill on certain Sundays in summer, and at other times by arrangement with the keyholder at Mill House (Wymondham 606161 or 604815).

HINGHAM

Eye-catching Georgian houses face a spacious triangular village green. The sign on the green shows the Pilgrim Fathers sailing for the New World, and in the huge St Andrew's Church there is a memorial to Abraham Lincoln. Among many Hingham folk who emigrated to America in the 17th century was an apprentice weaver named Samuel Lincoln, ancestor of the American president.

ATTLEBOROUGH

Rescued by a new bypass, Attleborough looks inwards again onto its small, railed-in village green. Elegant pink-washed and red-brick façades stand out among the medley of surrounding buildings. But Attleborough's glory stands within the flint-walled Norman Church of St Mary. The oak rood screen, 52ft across and spanning the nave and both side aisles, is a masterpiece of the medieval woodcarver's art. Beneath the delicate filigree vaulting are painted panels showing the saints, while above the screen are fragments of wall paintings dating from 1500.

THE BUCKENHAMS

The 'village green' of Old Buckenham is a broad field with attractive houses, some thatched and half-timbered, around its edges. Flint-walled church, duck pond and pub form a quiet group at one corner. The village sign shows a spectrum of local interests – miller, blacksmith, cricketer and monk – set within the embrasures of a castle.

New Buckenham is more compact: a couple of streets of attractive houses, mainly Georgian, around a 17th-century market house. Chapel Street leads past the village pump along a terrace of colour-washed cottages. Nearby, the ramparts of a Norman stronghold enclose the remains of one of England's earliest round keeps. The ruins are not open to the public. But a good view of them is obtained from a field path that starts

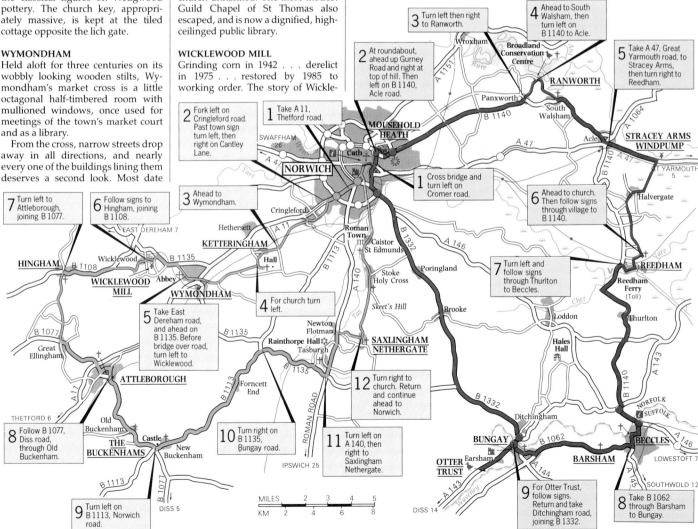

from the footpath sign just beyond St Martin's Gardens, past the church. The path circles the castle mound to the road at the entrance to the village.

SAXLINGHAM NETHERGATE
An Old Hall dating from 1290, with cream gables and mullioned windows, an Old Rectory built by Sir John Soane in 1784, and the square-towered Norman Church of St Mary gather round a small sloping green.

The undulating minor road back to Norwich offers hilltop views rare in Norfolk. At the brow of one hill rises the Church of Stoke Holy Cross. On the next is Caistor St Edmund; here the path to the church crosses the deep ditch which once surrounded the ramparts of the Roman town of Venta Icenorum, built as the capital of the Iceni to pacify the tribe after the quelling of Boudicca's rebellion.

TOUR
143

—— 62 MILES ——

Boats cruise reed-fringed Broads, and windpumps rear their sails above wide marshes. A long, straight road leads towards a toll ferry across the River Yare on the way to a Georgian town.

MOUSEHOLD HEATH
From the breezy hill just across the River Wensum, Norwich's claim to have a church for every week of the year is credible. Some 20 visible towers and spires are identified on the view indicator at the crest of the grassy ridge. In the foreground the lofty spire of the cathedral rises just beyond the winding river, with plenty of green space to insulate it from the remainder of the city. On the slope behind, landmarks such as the cathedral-like Roman Catholic Church of St John, the flat-topped castle and the tall-towered City Hall rise above the cluster of narrow streets and alleyways at the heart of the city. At night the scene is a fairyland of floodlit stonework.

Beside the car park on the heath are the Britannia Barracks of the Royal Norfolk Regiment, housing a museum of the regiment's history; it is open from Monday to Friday.

RANWORTH
The clamber to the top of the tower of St Helen's Church at Ranworth involves 89 steep stone stairs and two ladders, but for those with a head for heights the view is ample reward. To the north, Ranworth Dike stretches away into the distance, pleasure craft looking like toy boats on its still waters. Beyond, the River Bure meanders in wide loops through the marshes whose reeds are in nationwide demand for quality thatching. Closer at hand are the display area and floating gallery for birdwatching of the imaginative Broadland Conservation Centre, open daily in summer except Mondays.

Inside Ranworth Church, clear glass windows illuminate the superb 15th-century screen, one of Britain's finest. Spanning the broad nave, it is covered with paintings of saints, apostles and martyrs, recently restored to their original glowing colours after being painted over in the 16th century.

STRACEY ARMS WINDPUMP
Leaving Acle, a tall four-sailed tower soon comes into sight on the left-hand side of the road. This is an excellently restored specimen of the wind-powered pumps built to drain the marshes, whose keepers' lonely vigil in earlier times is part of East Anglian lore. In the summer visitors can climb into the cap of the brick-built tower.

REEDHAM
A sharp turn at the foot of Mill Road and suddenly the quay comes into view beside a wide stretch of the River Yare. The Ship Inn at one end and the Nelson at the other emphasise the nautical flavour of a village where most visitors are messing about in boats – or even behaving quite seriously in them.

Reedham's flint-walled church, with its battlemented tower, stays aloof from all this, high on the ridge behind the village. Near it is Feather-craft – an aviary where peacocks and other exotic birds strut about, oblivious of the workshop where their moulted feathers are turned into ornaments.

Reedham Ferry is the only crossing point of the Yare for 26 miles between Norwich and Great Yarmouth, so the little chain ferry, operating from 8am to 10pm, is well used in summer. But the wait and the toll are seldom costlier than the long detour downriver, and the crossing between the reed-fringed banks is an unusual experience.

BECCLES
Every doorway at the heart of Beccles seems to be flanked by clean, white-painted classical columns and surmounted by a triangular pediment. The town has preserved its Georgian heritage with exceptional care. The two showpiece streets, Ballygate and Northgate, extend in opposite directions from St Michael's Church along a ridge beside the River Waveney. Their frontages present an appealing medley of colours – plain brick, patterned brick, stucco in pink, grey, green, brown and beige. Rooftops are a roller-coaster of elegantly curved pantiles, many in the black glaze typical of the area. Between the houses, lanes drop down towards the river and its bobbing cabin cruisers.

The church, built in 1350, has a detached four-storey bell tower 97ft high, added in 1500. It was handed over to Beccles Town Council in 1977 for the token sum of one penny, which is today embedded in a plaque at its base.

BARSHAM
Across a field to the right of the Bungay road, just outside Beccles, stands Barsham's Church of the Holy Trinity, its round flint tower and thatched nave nicely framed among the trees. Inside is an impressive early

FERTILE FIELDS *At Skeet's Hill, the open countryside comes close to busy Norwich.*

MARKET HOUSE *Nine wooden pillars support New Buckenham's centrepiece.*

TALL TOWERS *Two great towers frame Wymondham's abbey church.*

RANWORTH DIKE *A floating observation platform looks out onto birds and boats.*

Jacobean screen, above which figures of the Virgin Mary and St John reach up to a painted wooden arch. The chancel has decorated plasterwork.

BUNGAY
Two semicircular stone towers, on a mound just behind the buildings of Bungay's main street, once flanked the gatehouse of a castle built by Robert Bigod in about 1294. It is reached through an alleyway opposite the Butter Cross.

The streets radiating from the Butter Cross are lined with elegant buildings, most of them dating from after 1689 when a fire devastated the town. The tall pinnacled tower whose gilded pennants catch the sun belongs to St Mary's Church, once the nave of a Benedictine nunnery church whose ruined walls poke up among the surrounding gravestones. Inside, St Mary's has the unhappy air of disuse, for it is classed as redundant and the nearby Trinity Church, with its Saxon round tower of herringbone masonry, serves the parish.

OTTER TRUST
Beside the River Waveney at Earsham are the headquarters of the Otter Trust, open from April to October. The display of otters in near-natural surroundings is allied to the practical purpose of breeding them for release into the wild, to save the species from extinction. There are lakes, woods, riverside walks and a picnic area.

Tourist information: Norwich 666071/2; Beccles 713196 (summer); (Ranworth) South Walsham 453 (summer).

Stern sea and waterway wonderland

TOUR
144

—— 101 MILES ——

North-east Norfolk is dominated by water – by the sea, sometimes threatening, and by the Broads and their linking rivers. On the skyline are great churches founded on wealth from wool.

SHERINGHAM

The sturdy buttresses of the sea wall, supporting separate stretches of promenade, look almost too massive for the small town – like military fortifications rather than a coastal defence. Below are inviting sweeps of shingle and sand which in the 19th-century railway boom attracted holidaymakers. Brick houses and hotels were built around the original flint fishing village – still noted for its crabs and whelks.

A reminder of old times is a lifeboat built with oars and sail. This is on show at the town's west end, with its present-day successor close by. Steam trains still travel along the North Norfolk Railway's Poppy Line – so named because of the poppies growing in the fields along its route – to Weybourne in spring and summer. Diesels extend the service to Kelling.

On the wooded ridge 1 mile south of the town is Pretty Corner, a beauty spot with parking and picnic sites from which long or short walks can be taken over heathland and through mixed woodlands.

CROMER

Like Sheringham, Cromer is a fishing port turned holiday centre, but it is rather brasher and busier than its neighbour. The Cromer lifeboat service has a distinguished history, and the present boat is always at the ready to race down the dizzying ramp from the pier – often to rescue seamen in trouble in the shoals which give this stretch of coastline the nickname of the Devil's Throat.

At the foot of The Gangway – from which a second boat operated until 1966 – is a lifeboat museum. This is open from May to September, as is the local history museum in Tucker Street. The town's most famous son was the heroic lifeboat coxswain Henry Blogg, who was three times awarded the Gold Medal of the RNLI – 'the lifeboatman's VC'. After his death in 1954 a memorial bust of him was put up beside the cliff path east of the town.

FELBRIGG HALL

The drive through parkland landscaped by Humphry Repton gives a faraway glimpse of a wing of the Jacobean house – a National Trust property. But its full glory is not revealed until it stretches its full length before the beholder, resplendent with tall windows, graceful

bays, a clock tower and a parapet above the south front lettered GLORIA DEO IN EXCELSIS.

Inside, the original furniture still graces the rooms. There are fine pictures and a magnificent library. Outside are a walled garden, an orangery, and lakeside and woodland walks. The estate is open every afternoon except Tuesday and Friday from mid-April to October.

NORTH WALSHAM

An unusual three-tiered market cross has stood at the foot of the sloping market place since the middle of the 16th century, and was renovated after a great fire which swept through the town in 1602. It has eight timber pillars supporting a roof with dome and lantern, on top of which the

design is repeated – rather like a giant wedding cake.

St Nicholas's Church is one of the largest in East Anglia. In the chancel a large monument to Sir William Paston recalls the celebrated family who lived 4 miles from North Walsham and whose collected letters give a matchless picture of life in the 14th and early 15th centuries.

WORSTEAD

The village was once a busy town which gave its name to a cloth made from closely twisted yarn of fine, long-staple wool. The manufacture of worsted was introduced in medieval times by Flemish immigrants, and continued as a cottage industry until the Industrial Revolution took trade to the northern mills.

Clothiers' riches contributed to the great 14th-century Church of St Mary, with its 109ft high tower, box pews and fine hammerbeam roof. Below it

is the square of Georgian and Queen Anne houses known as Church Plain. In and around the village are weavers' houses, in which 12ft high looms were used, with wide windows in the rooms where the weavers worked.

BEESTON HALL

An 18th-century mansion in Gothic style, the hall has an unusual facing of knapped flint, giving it a dark silvery dazzle in its setting of luxuriant gardens. In piquant contrast are the classical Georgian interiors and furniture, together with some Russian souvenirs brought back by one of the Preston family who built the hall.

House, orangery and gardens are open Friday, Sunday and Bank Holiday afternoons in summer.

HORNING

Disciplined little watery inlets serve as parking slots for dinghies and cabin cruisers moored close to bright bungalows, boathouses and more splendid dwellings with lawns sloping down to the River Bure. Thatch adds a picturesque touch to the smart modern village street.

Horning has an ancient history. There was probably once a Roman

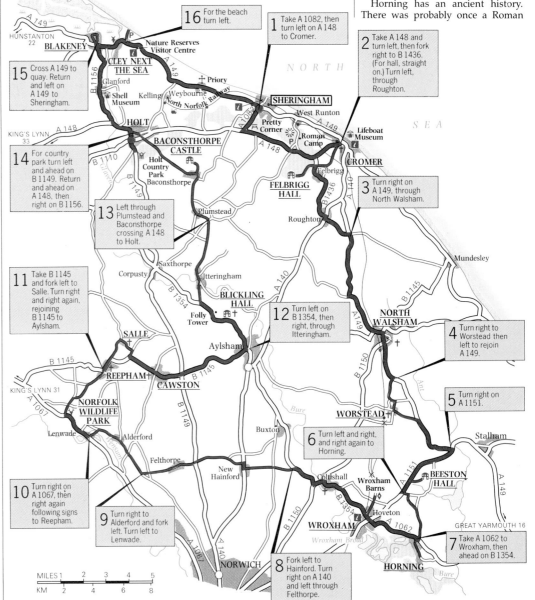

236

staging post, and a ferry is said to have operated for 1000 years near the present Horning Ferry Inn. A colourful Mississippi-style paddle-boat churns up and down the river on most days in summer.

WROXHAM

Near the bridge at Wroxham, under which the Bure flows before widening out into Wroxham Broad, are bustling boatyards and departure points for day cruises and hired craft which make this 'the capital of the Broads'. Shops catering for the needs of boating enthusiasts include one which claims to be the 'largest village store in the world'.

A mile and a half north along a signposted minor road are Wroxham Barns, a complex of large and small farm buildings imaginatively converted into workshops where lace-makers, glass engravers, wood turners, boatbuilders and other craftsmen can be seen at work.

NORFOLK WILDLIFE PARK

In 40 acres of parkland the naturalist Philip Wayre began in 1961 to build up what is now thought to be the largest collection of European mammals and birds in the world. Badgers, otters, wolves and waterfowl live in spacious semi-natural enclosures, and many endangered species have been successfully bred and reintroduced to the wild. The park is open daily.

REEPHAM

Sumptuous Georgian houses and half-timbered and plaster dwellings cling tightly together along the road which twists through the heart of the village, broadening into a square dominated by the red-brick Old Brewery House.

SALLE

The 111ft high tower of Salle church dominates an expanse of otherwise featureless fields. There is no real village; just a few scattered houses and the soaring church, in size and atmosphere more like a cathedral. Wealthy 15th-century wool merchants contributed to its cost among them the family of Anne Boleyn.

CAWSTON

In the north aisle of the Church of St Agnes stands a plough – souvenir of a ritual which used to be observed on the first Monday after Epiphany, when a plough was dragged through the parish begging for 'plough money' to spend in the local inn. The guildhall at Sygate in Cawston became in due course the Plough Inn; when this closed in 1950 its sign was presented by the brewers to the church and hangs on the north wall.

BLICKLING HALL

The slope of the road is shielded by trees and the church until the great sweeping façade of the Jacobean hall glows into view with its pinnacles, gables, chimneys and clock tower – set back behind smooth lawns and immaculately trimmed yew hedges.

Once the home of the Boleyn family, the property passed into the hands of the 11th Marquis of Lothian, who left it to the National Trust. As well as caring for the lovely gardens and the rooms furnished with period furniture and tapestries, the Trust have their main textile conservation workshop on the premises.

The hall is open every afternoon except Monday, Thursday and Good Friday from March to November; also mornings from May to September.

BACONSTHORPE CASTLE

A medieval fortified manor with its moat shimmering around the curtain walls, Baconsthorpe was the home of the Heydon family, noted for their rapacity during the Wars of the Roses. The most substantial remains are two huge gatehouses: one commanding the bridge across the moat, the other set farther out and used as a dwelling long after the rest had crumbled. One of the second gatehouse's two pepperpot towers is still virtually intact. The castle is open daily.

HOLT

The streets and lanes of the little market town weave in and out of islets of houses and shops like rivulets rather than roadways. Behind the smart colour-washed shops are flint and pebble cottages.

A country park 1 mile to the south has woodland walks, an observation tower and a picnic site beside a sheltered lake.

Beside the route to Blakeney is the Glandford museum of seashells from all over the world, together with jewellery and pottery from Pompeii. It is open daily from Monday to Thursday except for the last two weeks in October – and on Friday and Saturday afternoons.

BLAKENEY

From the main road the High Street has some of the stony, whitewashed charm of a Cornish fishing village. It is narrow until it reaches broad Blakeney Quay, where fishing boats and pleasure craft bob on a tide or sit drowsily on the mud of the channel which winds out to sea through marshes noisy with birds.

CLEY NEXT THE SEA

One of Norfolk's many deserted ports, Cley (pronounced 'Cly') silted up largely due to land reclamation by an entrepreneur in the time of Charles I. Still the sea breezes add their tang to the narrow lanes; the 18th-century Custom House still stands beside the River Glaven; and a drive to the beach reveals a windswept lookout post.

The return drive offers a splendid view of Cley's fine windmill, more than 160 years old, which has a splendid outlook from its upper floors. The mill is open on summer afternoons from Wednesday to Sunday, and on Bank Holiday afternoons.

Tourist information: Sheringham 824329 (summer); Cromer 512497/ 513811 (summer); Hoveton 2281 (summer).

HIGH AND DRY *Cley next the Sea's 19th-century windmill stands on land reclaimed from the sea a century earlier.*

GARDEN GEOMETRY *Blickling Hall's formal garden, with its precision-clipped yews, ruler-straight paths and close-shaven lawns, was laid out in 1729.*

TWO IN ONE *A 13th-century priory is part of All Saints' Church, Weybourne.*

Royal acres beside the Norfolk coast

Towns and villages built of pebbles and flint are scattered amid wide farmlands near The Wash. The royal estate of Sandringham is here, and the area has reminders of Nelson.

KING'S LYNN

Modern shopping precincts have changed the character of much of the town, but around St Margaret's Church colourful lanes of tall warehouses and the sumptuous homes of bygone merchants remain to recall Lynn's most prosperous days as a port. The most distinguished of these buildings is Hampton Court, which probably gets its name from a 17th-century owner, John Hampton, who was a master baker.

Behind the house's half-timbered frontage on Nelson Street, a cobbled courtyard is enclosed by lovingly restored wings dating from as early as the 14th century.

On Saturday Market Place stands Holy Trinity Guildhall faced with elaborate chequered flushwork, an ornamental combination of knapped flint and freestone. Behind Tuesday Market Place – a huge square with imposing offices, houses and old inns – is the medieval Guildhall of St George, which in its time has been a theatre, a corn store and a wool store. Now it is again a theatre, combined with an arts centre.

CASTLE RISING

A short diversion out of the cosy centre of this unpretentious village leads to the huge, solid keep of a moated Norman castle. Here in the 14th century Edward III incarcerated his mother, Queen Isabella, after her implication in the murder of his father, Edward II.

In the early 17th century a block of rosy red-brick almshouses, rebuilt in 1807, was built near the church around a grassy quadrangle, entered through a turreted miniature gatehouse. All the roofs sport variegated tiles, and the whole complex is in perfect harmony with the brick and carstone – a velvety, chocolate-coloured local stone – of the village cottages. The hall and chapel are open to the public on Tuesday, Thursday, Saturday and Sunday throughout the year.

SANDRINGHAM ESTATE

Once the royal train would arrive at Wolferton to deliver or collect Edward VII and Queen Alexandra and their guests visiting Sandringham House. No railway line runs through it now, but the station, complete with its little clock tower and signal box, houses a nostalgic museum of railway travel in the ornate royal waiting rooms. This

ROYAL RETREAT *Springs rising in the grounds feed the lakes at Sandringham, which has been a royal residence since 1862.*

is open daily except Saturdays from April to September.

Sandringham Country Park – open between April and September except on Fridays and Saturdays – is flanked by woodland walks available to the public even outside those times. Sandringham House and its gardens, holiday home of the Queen, are open over the same period as the park unless the royal family are in residence. The attractions include a nature trail, a car museum and a collection of dolls.

PEDDARS WAY

The road running over the sandy heaths and scatterings of stone and flint between Sandringham and the parkland of Houghton crosses a much older route – the prehistoric Peddars Way. Taken over by the Romans as a supply route to and from The Wash, it drives straight down into Breckland, sometimes almost obscured but frequently an easily distinguishable 'green road'. Long sections can still be walked through the Norfolk farmlands, dipping now and then into the

shade of trees and hedges, including a stretch north of the Anmer to Houghton road towards Fring.

HOUGHTON HALL

In the 18th century Sir Robert Walpole, the first politician to be called Prime Minister, had a Palladian-style mansion built for himself which involved the removal of the original village of Houghton. Today all that remains of the village is a double row of squared-up whitewashed houses like a military guard of honour at the

238

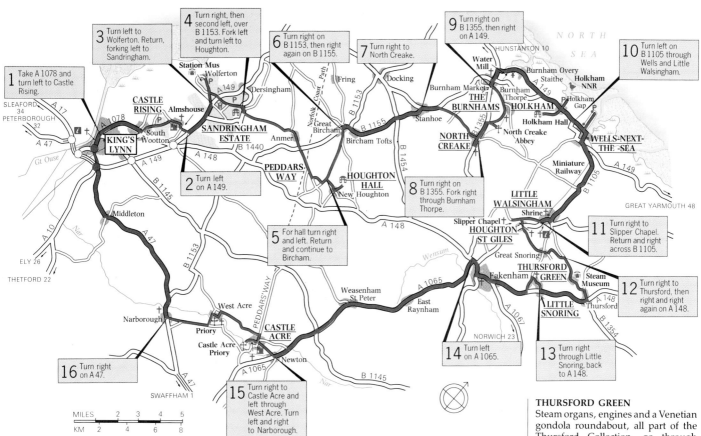

1 Take A 1078 and turn left to Castle Rising.

2 Turn left on A 149.

3 Turn left to Wolferton. Return, forking left to Sandringham.

4 Turn right, then second left, over B 1153. Fork left and turn left to Houghton.

5 For hall turn right and left. Return and continue to Bircham.

6 Turn right on B 1153, then right again on B 1155.

7 Turn right to North Creake.

8 Turn right on B 1355. Fork right through Burnham Thorpe.

9 Turn right on B 1355, then right on A 149.

10 Turn left on B 1105 through Wells and Little Walsingham.

11 Turn right to Slipper Chapel. Return and right across B 1105.

12 Turn right to Thursford, then right and right again on A 148.

13 Turn right through Little Snoring, back to A 148.

14 Turn left on A 1065.

15 Turn right to Castle Acre and left through West Acre. Turn left and right to Narborough.

16 Turn right on A 47.

MILES 2 3 4 5
KM 2 4 6 8

approach to the white gates of the hall.

In the house – topped by four corner cupolas adding a touch of frivolity to the Norfolk landscape – is a collection of thousands of model soldiers and other militaria, and there are lavish furnishings in the state rooms. The house is open on Thursday, Sunday and Bank Holiday afternoons from Easter to September.

NORTH CREAKE
As well as its fine wall paintings and brasses, the Church of St Mary the Virgin has a tasteful modern chapel commemorating a young parishioner who died in 1978. Above an altar incorporating a stone from Creake Abbey, close to where he lived, are four worthily mounted medieval painted panels.

Creake Abbey was a foundation untouched by the greed of Henry VIII: it fell empty before his day, when all the resident canons died of the plague one week in 1504. Fragments of the transept and choir survive.

THE BURNHAMS
On a wall by the road entering the straggling hamlet of Burnham Thorpe, beside the little Burn river, is a plaque marking the birthplace of Horatio, Admiral Lord Nelson. This was his father's rectory, which was demolished two years before the Battle of Trafalgar. All Saints' Church has been heavily restored in Nelson's honour, with a lectern made from timbers of the *Victory*, flags flown at the Battle of Jutland, and the ship's crest of HMS *Nelson* from the Second World War. The village hall is the

Nelson Memorial Hall; the post office is the Trafalgar Stores; and the pub, in Horatio's time called the Ship, is now the *Lord Nelson*.

In neighbouring Burnham Market the narrow road opens out dazzlingly upon a fine grassy boulevard lined with dignified Georgian houses and neat little shops.

Burnham Overy Staithe, closer to the sea, is reached past a round-towered church, a water mill beside a pond, and an abandoned but impressive windmill.

HOLKHAM
Set in the heart of 2987 acres of landscaped parkland, Holkham Hall, built in 1734-62, has a severe Palladian façade in yellow brick, giving no hint of its flamboyant entrance hall of pink marble and soaring columns. Up the great staircase are a green state bedroom, a statue gallery, and displays of tapestries and 18th-century furniture.

In summer the house and grounds are open on Sunday, Monday and Thursday afternoons and on Bank Holidays – also on Wednesday afternoons in July and August. There are Victorian and Edwardian collections; a garden centre; and a pottery where afternoon demonstrations are given.

At Holkham Gap there is a car park for the beach, with trails through a National Nature Reserve.

WELLS-NEXT-THE-SEA
An agreeable mixture of the genteel and the garish, Wells has not been 'next the sea' for some centuries, but the winding creek still brings coastal traffic to the waterfront with its cafés,

bingo and amusement arcades; and fishing boats still go out for sprats and whelks. A few paces up Staithe Street lead into a different world: the shops are mainly little family concerns, amiable and welcoming, while side lanes and fishermen's yards are lined with rough pebbled cottages.

LITTLE WALSINGHAM
The small village square and its 16th-century octagonal pump house are almost eclipsed by tall timbered houses with overhanging upper storeys. These buildings have brick, pebble and flint forming patterns between the timbers.

A shrine of the Virgin Mary, founded in the 11th century, soon became a place of pilgrimage and was later supplemented by an Augustinian friary and a Franciscan priory. The priory ruins, including the fine east window of its church, are open to the public on certain summer afternoons and are approached by a 15th-century gateway in High Street.

The parish church of St Mary was burnt out in 1961, but rebuilt in 1964. Its interior is suffused with light from generously large, clear windows, with one radiant stained-glass window over the altar.

HOUGHTON ST GILES
Pilgrims on their way to Little Walsingham used to walk the last mile barefoot, leaving their shoes here in a little 14th-century, grey-stone Slipper Chapel. In sharp contrast is the large modern chapel of red brick and tile with stone panels – dedicated as the Roman Catholic Shrine of Our Lady and Chapel of Reconciliation.

THURSFORD GREEN
Steam organs, engines and a Venetian gondola roundabout, all part of the Thursford Collection, go through their paces every afternoon from Easter until the end of October, and on Sundays during March and April before Easter and during November. There are also rides on a miniature steam train.

Among the gleaming, painted and polished splendours are a showman's engine weighing 17 tons, a 98-key Parisian organ from the turn of the century, a Wurlitzer theatre organ whose pipes occupy two separate chambers, and a wealth of colourful fairground models including charioteers, dancers, dragons and flying horses.

LITTLE SNORING
Flinty and isolated on its little knoll above the village, the pre-Norman detached round tower of St Andrew's Church looks like the watchtower of some central European fortress. In fact, it was a lookout and place of refuge from marauding Danes.

CASTLE ACRE
A haunted and haunting village of flint and cobbles, softened by warm red-tiled roofs, Castle Acre stands guard on a hill beside a huge Norman castle mound, with the prehistoric and Roman track of Peddars Way running through it. The enclosed village green is one of the most inward-looking yet delightful in East Anglia, with its stockade of houses and little shops. The green was once part of the castle bailey, which is dramatically entered through a 13th-century stone bailey gate.

Tourist information: King's Lynn 763044; Little Walsingham 510 (summer).

Splendid skies over Hereward's Fenland

TOUR
146
—— 45 MILES ——

To the east of Stamford lie the drained fenlands of Lincolnshire and Cambridgeshire. Here, in what was once desolate swamp, Hereward the Wake harried the Norman invaders.

STAMFORD

Mellow local stone enhances Stamford's air of antiquity, as can be seen in the fine Georgian houses, the six churches and the public buildings which tell of a great social life brought to the town by the Great North Road. The River Welland, spanned by a 19th-century bridge, flows through the town.

Stamford prospered first in Norman times, when the religious orders built houses and schools, then from the wool trade in the 12th century, and later from the stagecoaches. Travellers were well catered for at several coaching inns, and The George Hotel still has a room marked 'London' where southbound passengers rested.

MARKET DEEPING

Travellers in bygone stagecoach days were catered for by several coaching inns in this small town on the River Welland. One is called the Deeping Stage – which stands alongside other Georgian buildings of pale grey stone facing the Market Place, which is now a car park.

NORTHBOROUGH

The large, vaulted gatehouse of Northborough Manor dominates a bend in the road running through this village. The building dates from the 14th century and at one time was the home of John Claypole, Oliver Cromwell's son-in-law. The manor is not open to the public. On the opposite corner to the manor is the delightful Packhorse inn, an 18th-century hostelry of dressed stone.

A road running eastward from inn and manor leads to St Andrew's, a church of Norman origin without a tower or visible roof. In the churchyard are buried the wife and four of the seven children of the 'peasant poet' John Clare, born in 1793 in nearby Helpston, who lived in Northborough for ten years. His thatched stone cottage stands opposite Pingle Lane and is a private dwelling.

CROWLAND

The squat tower and ruined Norman arch of Croyland Abbey tower above Georgian and timber-framed cottages. Crowland or Croyland – the name means soft and muddy land – was built on an island in the fens, and the abbey was founded in AD 716 by King Ethelbald of Mercia to the memory of St Guthlac. The beautiful Norman nave of the abbey church stands open to the sky – a peaceful retreat with wooden bench seats among lawns and rose bushes. The 15th-century north aisle is now used as the parish church.

In the centre of the village is the 14th-century triangular (or trinity) bridge. Its three arches, joined at the centre, once spanned waterways that flowed through Crowland's streets. A mutilated stone figure on one of the parapets is thought to represent either Christ or King Ethelbald.

THORNEY

On this island in the fens, Hereward the Wake, the Saxon rebel, made one of his last stands against the Normans before disappearing into the mists of swampland and legend. The Saxon abbey, built on the 'isle of thorns' by Benedictine monks, was Hereward's refuge when the Normans besieged him there, and suffered some damage. In 1085 it was rebuilt and parts of it remain in the present Church of St Mary and St Botolph.

In the main street, only yards away from the twin towers and turrets of the abbey's Norman front, are rows of gabled, terraced houses built in the 1850s by the Duke of Bedford to provide better living conditions for his workers. The pale yellow bricks came from the duke's brickyard at Toneham.

PEAKIRK

Since 1956 an old gravel working just north of the village has been the site of a nature reserve of the Wildfowl Trust. Here many birds have taken refuge from the surrounding cultivated farmlands that were once fens. They share the pens and ponds of the 14 acre grounds with birds from all over the world, including black swans, Hawaiian geese, flamingos and a pair of rare trumpeter swans, a species once threatened with extinction.

BARNACK

Stone-built cottages and houses, some with thatch and some with stone roofs, line Barnack's shady, curving main street. In medieval times the name Barnack became synonymous with the tough local limestone used in the construction of many great buildings. Peterborough and Ely cathedrals and the abbeys of Ramsey (Cambridgeshire), Bury St Edmunds and Crowland were built of Barnack Rag.

The quarries south of the village were worked from Roman times until the end of the 16th century, when the area was exhausted. Part of the old quarries is now known as the Hills and Holes, a hummocky grassland which is a National Nature Reserve.

BURGHLEY HOUSE

At the end of a long drive, flanked by parkland where deer browse, stands the great house built by William Cecil, Lord Burghley, who was Elizabeth I's Lord High Treasurer. It stands on a slight rise, with its magnificent façade, domed towers and tall, slender chimneys etched boldly against the sky. The tall mullioned windows glint when caught by the evening sun. The house is a superb example of Elizabethan architecture and a tribute to the quality of the Barnack stone which appears as sound as on the day it was quarried.

Inside the house a guided tour starts in the kitchen, which gleams with some 260 copper utensils, and continues through richly furnished rooms hung with Old Masters. Also on display are the trophies of the 6th Marquis of Exeter who, as Lord Burghley, won the gold medal for the 400 metres hurdles at the 1928 Olympic Games in Amsterdam. Burghley House is open to the public daily in summer.

Tourist information: Stamford 64444.

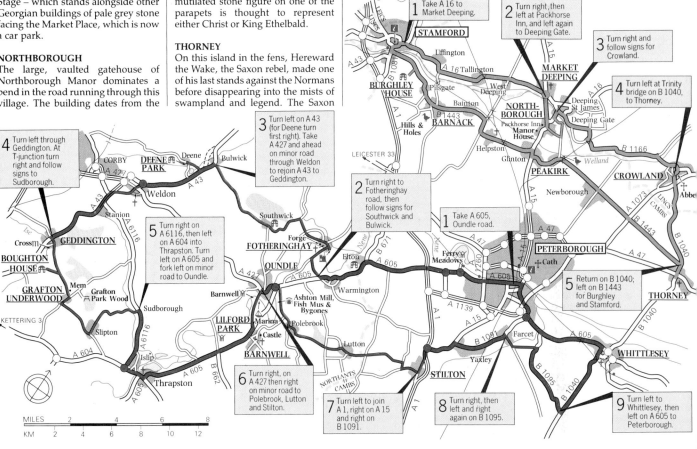

Leafy byways lead through historic villages to the fenlands, with skies of azure blue one day, great banks of clouds the next, and sunsets that paint the landscape with a red-gold hue.

PETERBOROUGH

In modern Peterborough, spacious pedestrianised streets are pleasantly laid out among large department stores, shops, banks and public buildings. The older buildings blend happily with the new. The 17th-century Guildhall and the 15th-century Church of St John the Baptist seem not at all out of place in a wide paved square at the heart of the shopping centre; and the colonnaded Town Hall, though dating only from the 1930s, lends an air of quiet dignity.

But the glory of Peterborough is its cathedral which, unlike many others, does not dominate the city. It stands quietly in its precincts, only a few yards away from the shopping centre. It is one of the finest Norman buildings in England, begun in 1118, with a magnificent west front of three soaring Gothic arches flanked by pinnacled towers.

Across Cathedral Square is the Great Gate, also of Norman origin – perfect for stepping into the old world from the new.

FOTHERINGHAY

In this peaceful village one of the grim events of English history was enacted. At Fotheringhay Castle, Mary, Queen of Scots, was executed on February 8, 1587. After the execution the castle crumbled into decay and all that remains is a grassy mound where sheep graze among elderberry and hawthorn trees. There is little to evoke the memory of the unhappy queen, but Scottish thistles grow on the mound in summer, and according to legend Mary planted thistles a short time before she was beheaded. A footpath leads to the castle, running alongside Castle Farm.

From Castle Farm the village street is lined with stone-built thatched cottages. Just off the street is Fotheringhay Forge where visitors can watch wrought ironwork being made. The forge is open on weekdays throughout the year and most Saturday afternoons.

DEENE PARK

James Thomas Brudenell, 7th Earl of Cardigan, who led the heroic but disastrous charge of the Light Brigade at Balaclava in 1854, once lived at Deene Park, home of the Brudenell family since 1514. Originally Deene Park was a medieval manor house, but it was transformed in the 16th, 17th and 19th centuries to the present elegant house, standing in superb grounds with a large lake and gardens containing old-fashioned roses, rare trees and shrubs.

The house, still occupied by the

GREEN AND PLEASANT LAND *Fotheringhay's Church of St Mary and All Saints stands amid meadows on the banks of the Nene.*

Brudenell family, and grounds are open to the public on Sundays in summer. Military uniforms and mementos are on show in the house.

GEDDINGTON

In the tiny village square stands a slender monument, one of 12 that marked the resting places of the coffin of Queen Eleanor, wife of Edward I, during its journey from Harby in Nottinghamshire to London in 1290. Only three Eleanor Crosses remain – the other two are at Waltham Cross, Hertfordshire, and Hardingstone on the outskirts of Northampton.

Geddington's is the best preserved cross, and the most striking in its simplicity. The tall, triangular column stands on a stepped plinth and contains carved stone figures in three arched niches below the tapering pinnacled top.

Sturdy stone-built houses stand around the square, and close by a medieval packhorse bridge spans the River Ise.

BOUGHTON HOUSE

Built some 500 years ago as a monastery, Boughton House has been enlarged over the centuries around seven courtyards. In 1695 it was given a French-style façade, based on Versailles, and achieved a pleasing symmetry with its rows of lattice windows, arched arcade and an absence of ornamentation.

The rooms contain 17th and 18th-century French and English furniture, tapestries, painted ceilings and works of art.

Boughton House is a home of the Duke of Buccleuch and Queensberry, and is open to the public daily, except on Fridays, in summer and on certain days in autumn.

GRAFTON UNDERWOOD

In the Second World War Grafton Underwood heard the thunder of American Flying Fortress bombers, based at an airfield west of the village.

The runways have long since gone under the plough, but at the roadside is a simple block of polished granite, a memorial to the men who flew out never to return.

Great chestnut trees line one side of the village street, and alongside flows a stream which passes under small stone bridges which lead to thatched, grey-stone cottages. To the north there is a pleasant picnic spot in Grafton Park Wood.

LILFORD PARK

Roadways through acres of parkland provide a drive-around route among paddocks containing farm animals, aviaries, rock gardens and picnic meadows. There are also good views of the impressive house in the centre of the park; this dates from the 17th century and has an imposing façade with three large gables, tall bow windows and balconied porch.

The house stands empty except when used for events such as antique and craft fairs. The park is also the venue for the Lilford May Fayre. It is open daily in summer.

BARNWELL

A tiny stone bridge crosses a stream at one end of the village, and from it extends a delightful view. The stream divides the village from end to end, and trickles quietly between green verges bordered by willows and linked here and there by more bridges – some stone, some wooden and white-painted – which give access to pretty stone and thatch cottages.

The Montagu Arms is a friendly little inn whose name gives a clue to the village's history, for it grew around the medieval castle and manor house once owned by the Montagu family and now belonging to the Duke of Gloucester.

From the bridge the street climbs to St Andrew's Church, a 13th-century building restored in 1851 by Sir Giles Gilbert Scott. There are few relics of the Montagus there; these are to be

found in the partly demolished Church of All Saints which stands at one end of the village.

OUNDLE

The River Nene loops around Oundle like a moat. The town has narrow streets lined with stone-built houses, mostly Georgian, and there are two fine 17th-century inns, the White Lion and the Talbot. The front of the Talbot was built from materials taken from the ruins of Fotheringhay Castle.

There is a marina on the Nene south of Oundle, and along the Ashton road are an old mill and a fish museum, both open at weekends in summer.

STILTON

The 17th-century Bell Inn at Stilton was a staging post where farmers from Leicestershire took their produce for delivery to London. The produce included a fine cheese which became known as Stilton although it was not made in the village.

WHITTLESEY

The compact little town breaks up the geometrical pattern of the surrounding fens, where ruler-straight roads crisscross the landscape like lines on an engineer's blueprint. No doubt the people of Whittlesey are accustomed to the vastness that surrounds them, but to the visitor this quilted land of distant horizons can be both awesome and impressive, especially when billowing clouds build up in the sky, or the sun and a sudden summer shower produce a perfect rainbow arc.

Those rich fenlands that man has wrested from wild swamps made Whittlesey what it is: a market town with a small square and a 17th-century butter cross, some fine houses of the Georgian period and a church, St Mary's, with a splendid 15th-century spire supported by flying buttresses on a pinnacled tower.

Tourist information: Peterborough 63141.

Changing landscapes in tulipland

TOUR
148

76 MILES

In spring the fields around Spalding are awash with colour as the tulip-growing season reaches its height. There are windmills, ruined castles and an abbey in which King John stayed.

SPALDING

The capital of 'Tulipland', Spalding has something in common with a typical Dutch town, especially where the River Welland runs close to the market place. The river divides the town in two and is crossed by three bridges. Along its banks are three-storey Georgian houses, and on its tree-lined eastern side stands the 15th-century Ayscoughfee Hall, now a natural history museum and tourist information centre. The hall was the home of Maurice Johnson, founder of the Spalding Gentlemen's Society in 1710. The society, which still exists, numbered the scientist Sir Isaac Newton and the poet Alexander Pope among its members.

Close to High Bridge, which leads to the market place, is the thatched White Horse Inn. Another old inn,

the 18th-century White Hart, stands in the market place, where markets are held twice weekly.

On the north-eastern outskirts of the town is Springfields Gardens, 25 acres of lawns, flowerbeds and woodlands which are ablaze with colour from spring until autumn. Tulips, naturally, are the main feature of the gardens in April and May.

Spalding celebrates its importance as Britain's major bulb-growing centre each May with a flower parade, when floats decorated with millions of flower heads parade through the streets, led by a float carrying Miss Tulipland. This colourful display also has a serious purpose: tulip growers remove the heads of the flowers in spring to promote the sturdy growth of bulbs for sale in autumn, and it is these flower heads that are used to decorate the floats.

BOURNE

The earthworks of an 11th-century castle stand in a park to the south of Bourne's town centre, and here, it is said, the Fenland hero Hereward the Wake was born. The park is beautifully set out and, close to where Bourne Eau flows through the town, attractive rose gardens surround the war memorial.

The town centre is typical of most Fenland towns, with buildings in a

mixture of styles jostling each other along the main street. A number of old inns include the Burghley Arms Hotel, which incorporates a house that was the birthplace of William Cecil who later became the 1st Baron Burghley and was Secretary of State to Elizabeth I.

EDENHAM

Solid-looking stone houses and cottages make up most of Edenham, overshadowed by the tall, pinnacled tower of the church, just as the whole village has been overshadowed by the Willoughby de Eresby family whose monuments fill the church and churchyard. Their statues and busts, almost all dressed in Roman togas and breastplates, seem to fill every corner of the chancel.

Among them is the Restoration-period tomb of the 1st Earl of Lindsey, Robert Bertie Willoughby de Eresby, who was killed at the Battle of Edgehill in 1642. He shares the tomb with his son, Montague, who was one of the four peers who attended Charles I's funeral.

GRIMSTHORPE CASTLE

The stateliest of Lincolnshire's stately homes, Grimsthorpe Castle has been the home of the Willoughby de Eresby family since 1516. Most of the building is Tudor, but in 1722-4 the house

was remodelled by Sir John Vanbrugh, whose last commission this was. Vanbrugh was responsible for the magnificent hall, 110ft long and arcaded in two tiers. Busts fill the open upper arcades at one end of the hall, and portraits of kings fill the arcades above the carved stone fireplace.

The 200 acres of parkland in which the house stands were landscaped by Capability Brown. The house, gardens and grounds are open to the public during afternoons in August and the first week in September.

IRNHAM

West of Spalding the countryside is a broad, flat landscape, where even the smallest tree on the horizon is a dominant feature and the roads run as straight as airfield runways. But at Bourne the scenery changes dramatically. The byways become more leafy and the roads rise and fall – and in a dip in one of them lies a sequestered paradise, called Irnham.

At the bottom of the dip, tall, ivy-clad trees shade the still waters of a large pond, and geese cluster together on the grassy banks. Close by, a rustic bridge spans a tiny waterfall cascading into a trickling stream, and through a veil of beeches, oaks and willows can be seen Irnham Hall, a long, low grey-stone house lording it over wide green lawns. The house is not open to the public.

By the gateway of Irnham Hall the road rises again and passes through a village of stone-built cottages. Then Irnham is left behind, a dreamlike memory that seems a million miles away from the patchwork fields and wide horizons of the fens.

FOLKINGHAM

The pale orange, brick-built Greyhound inn looks out across Folkingham's market square, at the top of a steep, wide road lined with brick and stone houses standing well back. This spacious and elegant village was once Kesteven's seat of Quarter Session Court, and to the east of the village stood the 'House of Correction'. Its forbidding, 19th-century gateway is still there.

From the square a row of white-painted houses and the pretty blue-and-white post office line the lane to St Andrew's Church, its lofty tower commanding the low Kesteven hills that slope down to the fens. Inside the church are the village stocks and whipping post.

SLEAFORD

A few grassy hummocks by the railway are all that remain of Sleaford's castle – famous in history as the place where King John was treated for fever from which he died five days later at Newark. The castle was demolished in Elizabethan times, and the building that dominates Sleaford now is St Denys's Church, which has one of the oldest stone spires in England. Built of Ancaster stone, it dates from the early 13th century and is 144ft high.

Sleaford's main street is lined with shops, but side roads, lanes and passageways lead to quiet corners,

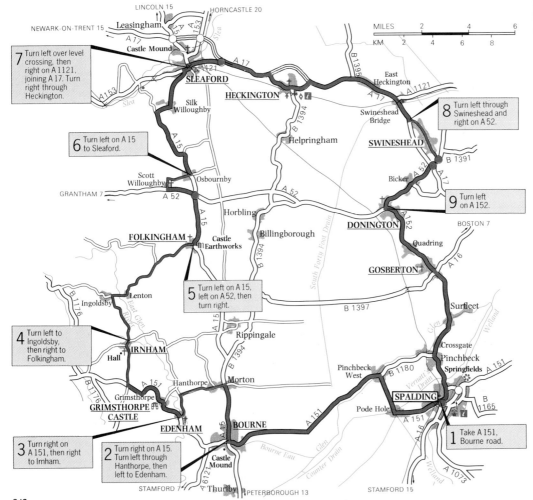

7 Turn left over level crossing, then right on A1121, joining A17. Turn right through Heckington.

6 Turn left on A15 to Sleaford.

8 Turn left through Swineshead and right on A52.

9 Turn left on A152.

5 Turn left on A15, left on A52, then turn right.

4 Turn left to Ingoldsby, then right to Folkingham.

3 Turn right on A151, then right to Irnham.

2 Turn right on A15. Turn left through Hanthorpe, then left to Edenham.

1 Take A151, Bourne road.

SERENE OASIS *Only a few miles from the open fields of fenland, Irnham Hall and village lie in a rustic dell where willows trail their tresses in a crystal pond.*

STAGING POST *Folkingham's Greyhound inn was a stop for stagecoaches between Lincoln and Peterborough.*

FLOWER POWER *Spalding's sign symbolises the town's thriving industry.*

FENLAND CHURCH *Poplars dwarf Scott Willoughby's church, built in 1826, one of the smallest in Lincolnshire.*

such as Westgate where houses and gardens are approached by bridges over the River Slea, and Langfords Passage with a row of attractive brick-built cottages only yards away from the bustling town centre. Just south of the church are almshouses of 1830, though originally founded by the Carre family in the 17th century.

HECKINGTON
In Heckington stands what must surely be the last word in windmills, with no fewer than eight sails 70ft in diameter projecting from a 60ft high tower. The mill was built in 1830 and the eight sails were fitted in 1891, their massive sail area being capable of working in the slightest winds.

This fine tower mill stopped grinding corn commercially in 1942, but is open to the public daily. The five pairs of grindstones and original machinery can be seen.

Opposite the mill is the Pearoom Craft and Heritage Centre which has souvenirs on sale.

SWINESHEAD
Little remains of the abbey at Swineshead where, it is said, King John stayed a few nights after losing his baggage in The Wash in 1216. The king died of a fever several days later; according to a local legend, however, a monk poisoned his ale and drank first from the cup to make the king believe it was safe.

DONINGTON
Most of the village lies to the west of the main road, but its heart is a small market place where a few 18th-century houses have survived. One of the oldest buildings is the former Grammar School, now a secondary school, founded by Thomas Cowley in 1719. The school was rebuilt in 1812 but still has its original windows, rooftop bell turret and large porch, which incorporates a sundial.

In 1774 Donington was the birthplace of Captain Matthew Flinders, the explorer who mapped much of Australia's coastline in the early 1800s. He named many features there after towns and villages in Lincolnshire. There are memorials to him in the church, including a fine stained-glass window.

The church has a massive tower and a spire dating from the 14th century. Inside is an unusual box-like shelter, called a hude, which protected the parson when conducting funerals in wet weather.

GOSBERTON
The 160ft spire of St Peter and St Paul heralds the approach to Gosberton from the north. The slender, octagonal spire is supported by pinnacled flying buttresses and is decorated with foliage designs, called crocketing, along each angle. Gargoyles, including the head of an elephant on the east wall, project from under the battlements of the tower.

The village is mentioned in Domesday Book and the church dates from Norman times, with 14th and 15th-century additions. Inside, the church is spacious and has a 14th-century effigy of a crosslegged knight who may have been one of the church's benefactors.

Tourist information: Spalding 5468; (Heckington) Sleaford 60765.

243

Breezy wolds and fens by The Wash

TOUR 149

─ 79 MILES ─

The Lincolnshire Wolds were much loved by Alfred, Lord Tennyson, born in 1809 in the hamlet of Somersby. In his *In Memoriam* he recalled the 'Calm and deep peace of this high wold'.

LOUTH
Approached from any direction, Louth's Church of St James is a soaring landmark for this pleasant market town. Its slim, hexagonal spire, rising to nearly 300ft, is one of the loveliest in England.

The church dates mostly from the 15th and 16th centuries, and is built of Ancaster stone. The remainder of Louth, however, grew during the Georgian, Regency and Victorian periods and is a blend of styles.

ALVINGHAM
The only church in Britain dedicated to the Saxon St Adelwold stands in a remote corner of Alvingham, and it shares its churchyard with another church, St Mary's. Once the chapel of a 12th-century priory, St Mary's is the parish church of neighbouring North Cockerington, and is equally remote from the village it serves.

The churches, with their low, squat towers lie beyond a farmyard and are partly obscured by farm buildings, but there is no difficulty in spotting Alvingham's water mill, which stands close by. The red-brick, three-storey building straddles the millstream, and massive millstones leaning against the walls are the symbols of its trade. The mill is still working and is open to visitors on certain days in spring and summer.

THEDDLETHORPE DUNES
On warm evenings in spring and early summer the grassy dunes often echo to the churring song of natterjack toads which breed in the marshy slacks among the dunes. These rare toads – recognised by the yellow line down their back and their running gait – are just one of the many forms of wildlife that live in the Saltfleetby-Theddlethorpe Dunes National Nature Reserve. The reserve comprises some 5 miles of windswept sandy banks bordering a wide, sandy foreshore where dunlins and redshanks feed, and the rare little tern nests.

ALFORD
The windmill at Alford, built in 1813, has five sails standing gaunt against the skyline atop a 95ft high tower which has a domed, white-painted cap. The mill is open to visitors on certain days in summer, when it can be seen working.

HARRINGTON HALL
This lovely manor house of mellow red brick was the home of Tennyson's *Maud*, and its terrace was the 'high Hall garden' of his poem. It dates from 1678, but stands on a medieval base and still has an Elizabethan porch. Inside, richly panelled rooms contain furniture, pictures and china of the 17th and 18th centuries.

The hall is open on Thursdays and some Sundays in summer; its gardens are open on Wednesdays and Thursdays in summer.

LANGTON
The Church of St Peter and St Paul has high walls, a steep roof with overhanging eaves and a stubby octagonal tower. It dates from the early 18th century and the interior is splendidly Georgian, with tiers of inward-facing box pews, a three-decker pulpit and a reredos and gallery in panelled oak.

Near the church stands a pretty 'roundhouse' cottage, with a conical thatched roof.

SNIPE DALES NATURE RESERVE
This 120 acre valley in the sandstone of the southern wolds is a haven for the long-billed snipe, which may be seen in its darting, zigzag flight when disturbed. In the damp valley bottom, washed by chattering streams, marsh marigolds grow, and on the slopes bluebells and primroses flower in spring. The reserve is reached by a footpath from the hamlet of Winceby.

HORNCASTLE
Most of Horncastle was rebuilt in the 19th century, and its market square is lined with red-brick shops and houses. The square stands in the centre of what was once a Roman fort, Banovallum, and parts of the Roman wall survive in St Mary's Square.

DONINGTON ON BAIN
For about 5 miles the Viking Way runs north from Donington following the eastern bank of the River Bain, here at its most attractive as it flows between high banks and tall trees. The Viking Way, its route marked by horned-helmet signs, is a long-distance footpath running through the wolds. A stretch of it can be sampled at Donington by joining the path by the mill, a picturesque, white-painted building close to the weir.

BLUESTONE HEATH ROAD
For almost all the way along the 14 miles of the Bluestone Heath Road nothing obstructs the views eastward across rolling fields of crops and westward over soft, undulating hills and valleys, dotted here and there by farms and ribboned with dark green hedgerows. The road follows the course of an ancient trackway. Beside it at Belchford is a viewpoint with an information board.

Tourist information: Louth 602391; Spilsby 52301.

TOUR 150

─ 73 MILES ─

Windmills dot the rich farmlands of the Lincolnshire Fens. There are memories of the Pilgrim Fathers and visits to a king's birthplace, a great castle and a church with an unusual clock.

BOSTON
In the 14th century, Fenland travellers and sailors on The Wash took their bearings by the 272ft tower of Boston's St Botolph's Church, affectionately known as The Stump. The tower more than dominates Boston, it commands it. Look up from almost any street and The Stump is there. Perhaps the best view is from Haven

FAR HORIZONS *Big skies and big fields merge beneath gathering clouds west of Flint Hill on the edge of the wolds.*

DAILY GRIND *Alvingham's water mill has been partly restored and is used to grind barley for animal food.*

HIGH-RISE CASTLE *Tattershall Castle's four storeys consist of four great rooms stacked one above the other.*

Bank, on the western side of the River Witham which flows through the town.

Boston has been a port since the 13th century, and it was from there that a band of Puritans set sail for America in 1630 to found the town of Boston in Massachusetts. Fydell House, built in 1726, has an American Room set aside for the use of any American visitors.

The 15th-century Guildhall now houses Boston Museum and is open on weekdays in summer.

FISHTOFT
At the end of a road leading east from the village stands a granite obelisk erected in 1957 as a memorial to the first Pilgrim Fathers. It was from near this spot, overlooking Scotia Creek near the mouth of the Witham, that 13 Puritans tried to set sail for America in 1607. They were betrayed by their ship's captain and were imprisoned in Boston Guildhall before trial at which they were found guilty of trying to emigrate illegally. In 1620 they tried again, making their epic voyage from Plymouth in the *Mayflower* to found the New World.

There is a picnic site close to the memorial, with good views across the river to The Wash.

BURGH LE MARSH
Dobson's Mill stands beside the Lincoln to Skegness road at Burgh le Marsh. The sails, shuttered and self-regulating, were added in 1870 and revolve in a clockwise direction, unlike most other mills.

The mill is open daily. Four of its floors can be inspected, and on the last Sunday of each month it can be seen in operation.

GUNBY HALL
The beautifully symmetrical house of plum-coloured brick, with white stone facings and windows, is reputedly Tennyson's 'haunt of ancient peace'. It was built in 1700 by Sir William Massingberd and was added to in 1873 by the inclusion of a large, oak-panelled drawing room in which hang portraits by Reynolds.

The house, standing in gardens ablaze with roses in summer, is owned by the National Trust and is open to the public on Thursday afternoons in summer.

OLD BOLINGBROKE
Leafy lanes on the edge of the wolds lead to this demure village – a peaceful haven with a fine church, a few houses, and an inn. Beside the inn stands a bed of red Lancastrian roses and the coat of arms of Henry IV, for only a few yards away stand the ruins of the king's birthplace in 1367, Bolingbroke Castle.

The castle dates from the 11th century, and in the 14th century it was occupied by the powerful John of Gaunt, Duke of Lancaster and father of Henry IV. It fell into decay after being captured by Cromwell following a Civil War battle at nearby Winceby in 1643, and all that remain are grassy mounds and fragments of

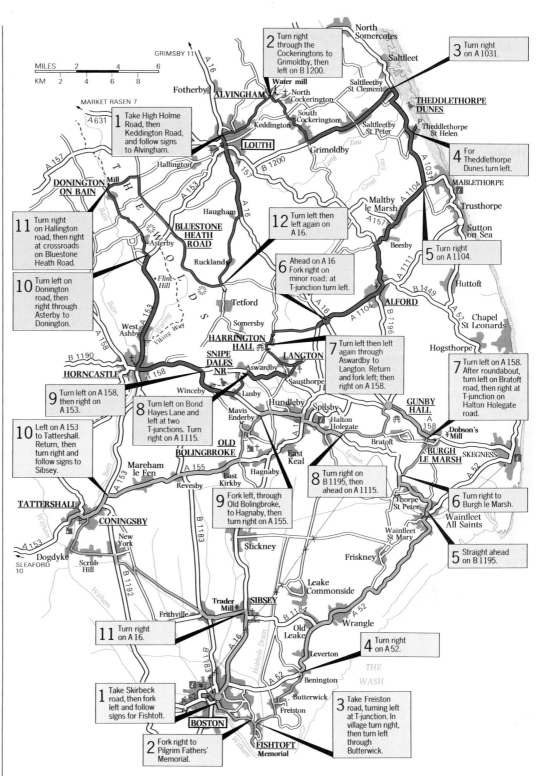

the walls. The Church of St Peter and St Paul, north of the village, is said to have been commissioned by John of Gaunt.

CONINGSBY
A clock face 16½ft in diameter is painted in white on the tower of Coningsby's Church of St Michael and All Angels. It has only one hand, indicating the hours with divisions for minutes, and is said to be the largest single-handed clock in the world.

The village lies on the southern tip of the Lincolnshire Wolds, and the church clock can be seen for miles across the flat fenlands.

TATTERSHALL
Peacocks strut on trim lawns and a rustic wooden bridge crosses the moat surrounding Tattershall's mighty keep, looming above the flat countryside like a giant's castle. Four storeys high and 110ft from its 20ft thick base walls to the top of its castellated turrets, the red-brick tower was built by Ralph, Lord Cromwell, Treasurer of England from 1433 to 1443, on the site of an earlier castle.

The tower is rectangular, with an octagonal turret at each corner and one large room on each floor. Each room has a massive fireplace, and the

chimneypiece on the ground floor has a shield bearing Cromwell's arms. The keep, owned by the National Trust, is open daily.

SIBSEY
The Trader Mill, 1 mile west of Sibsey, is England's only remaining six-sailed windmill. It is six storeys high and dates from 1877. It was one of the last windmills built in Lincolnshire, and was in operation until 1958. It has been restored and is open to the public daily in summer.

Tourist information: Boston 64601 (summer); Spilsby 52301.

Lincoln Edge and the villages of Witham Vale

TOUR

151

─── 77 MILES ───

One of England's loveliest
cathedrals stands on a hill
overlooking flat farmland watered
by the Witham and Brant rivers.
A Roman road leads to the
RAF College at Cranwell.

LINCOLN

England's first Norman bishop, Remigius, built Lincoln Cathedral, and if
it was his wish that the great church
should be near to Heaven he could
not have chosen a better site. Standing on a hill 200ft above the city, the
three towers have a celestial quality;
their pinnacled crowns point to the
sky and the golden-hued stonework
changes shade with every subtle
change of light, from pale gold in the
rays of the sun to deep bronze against
dark and brooding clouds.

It is said that the cathedral's western façade may have been built to
symbolise Heaven's Gate; certainly it
frames a glorious threshold to the
marble-pillared nave and the magnificent Angel Choir with the largest
eight-light window in England.

Men of less peaceful intentions
preceded Remigius; his king, William
the Conqueror, built a castle on the
hill in 1068 and its walls and keep,
known as Lucy's Tower, still stand in
Castle Square. In its day the castle
dominated the surrounding countryside, just as a Roman fortress had
done 1000 years earlier. To the north
of the castle stands the Newport
Arch, the only Roman gateway in
Britain still used by traffic.

Below the cathedral, medieval
buildings cling precariously to the
steep hillside. They are interwoven
with cobbled streets descending to
the modern city centre through which
flows the River Witham, bordered by
attractive riverside walks from the
Norman High Bridge. West of the
city, the river is linked to the River
Trent by the 11 mile long Fossdyke
Navigation, dug by the Romans
nearly 2000 years ago.

DODDINGTON

Rows of red-brick cottages, mostly
19th century, line Doddington's single
street, and at its head stands one of
the most beautiful Elizabethan mansions in Lincolnshire. Doddington
Hall stands close to the road behind a
Tudor-style gatehouse, and high brick
walls sheltering a garden bathed in
the scent of roses – a perfect setting for
the red-brick house with its three
projecting bays each topped by a
domed cupola.

It is believed that the house was
designed by Robert Smythson in the
1590s for Thomas Tailor, Recorder to
the Bishop of Lincoln. Today it is the
home of the Jarvis family, and is open
to the public on Wednesday and

BELTON HOUSE *Cupolas top the fine
mansion built at the Restoration.*

ELIZABETHAN ELEGANCE *The exterior of Doddington Hall has survived exactly as it
was built in 1600. The house has been continuously occupied since that time.*

STILL WATERS *Near Bassingham the Witham is a sluggish, weed-dappled river twisting and turning between grassy banks.*

Sunday afternoons in summer. Its
rooms contain 18th-century furnishings, tapestries and collections of
china. A nature trail leads through
nearby estate woods and meadows.

Close to Doddington Hall stands
the Church of St Peter, rebuilt in 1770
by Sir John Deleval, then owner of the
hall, as a burial place for his daughter.
The white stone church with its red-
tiled roof sits serenely in a leafy
churchyard, but a close inspection of
the stonework reveals legacies of a
sad occasion. Not long after the death
of his daughter, Sir John Deleval's
only son died and the grief-stricken
father had the church coated in black
paint, traces of which can still be seen.

BRANT BROUGHTON

The road runs ruler-straight through
Brant Broughton. On one side, behind trees and a grass verge, stands a

row of Georgian houses and cottages,
a study in mellow brick, red pantiles
and spotless white doorways and
windows. In the middle of this
elegant parade stands a small stone
building with a roof sweeping down
to almost head height. Through its
half-door can be seen the glow of a
forge where for centuries the Coldron
family have worked wrought iron into
fine and intricate patterns. Their work
can be seen outside and inside the
church, in the shape of the gates at the
north entrance and the attractive
chandeliers in the nave. The Church
of St Helen stands a little to the west of
the main street; but finding it is no
problem, for its lovely spire soars to
198ft above the village.

The church dates from the 13th
century, but most of what can be seen
today is the result of a 19th-century
restoration which was inspired by

Canon Frederick Heathcote Sutton,
rector from 1873 until 1888. Sutton
designed the chandeliers and also
designed and made much of the
stained glass, in a kiln at the former
rectory, the building south of the
church.

About 2 miles south of Brant
Broughton stands Stragglethorpe
Hall. It is not open to the public, but
its superb timbered porch and upper
floor can be seen from the road at the
end of a tree-lined drive. The nearby
St Michael's Church has a Saxon west
doorway and a fine late-17th-century
monument to Sir Richard Earle.

BARKSTON

The River Witham meanders through
meadowlands behind the village, and
it is crossed by a small road bridge
where there is a shady patch of grass
at the water's edge, ideal for a picnic

or a moment or two's relaxation away from the busy main road. The tiny village green stands by the roadside. Opposite is Barkston House, a fine 18th-century building with a wrought-iron porch, standing at the end of a cedar-lined drive. It was once a farmhouse but has been converted to a small country hotel; the restaurant, once the farmhouse kitchen, has the original servants' bells and bacon hooks.

BELTON

The first sight of Belton House is unforgettable. It stands in broad parklands across which there is an uninterrupted view of this neat, honey-coloured stone mansion.

For many years its building was attributed to Sir Christopher Wren; the true architect is not known, but the building is a supreme example of the domestic architecture of the late 17th century, those heady years when England followed the energetic pleasure-seeking pursuits of its new king, Charles II.

Begun in 1685, the last year of the 'merry monarch's' reign, Belton House was built for Sir John Brownlow. It remained in the Brownlow family until 1984, when it was given to the National Trust. The grey limestone, now mellowed to pale gold, was quarried at nearby Ancaster; the finest craftsmen were employed for the interior, including Edward Goudge whose superb plasterwork ceilings are impressive features of many rooms.

Fine furniture, including a bed used by Edward VIII who was a frequent visitor, and another made for Queen Adelaide, can be seen together with rich tapestries, oriental porcelain and portrait paintings. At the rear of the house are formal gardens, laid out in the late 19th century, and an orangery standing by a sunken garden and a fountain pool.

Belton House is open every afternoon in summer except Mondays and Tuesdays.

GRANTHAM

Any visitor to this old coaching town who is not aware of Grantham's associations with Sir Isaac Newton is soon reminded of them. A huge bronze statue of the scientist stands in front of the Guildhall, and the modern shopping centre bears his name. It was in the classrooms of the 15th-century grammar school, now King's School, that Newton was educated, and he left his name carved on a windowsill.

Coaching inns played a vital part in the town's history, in the days when Grantham was a stopping place for travellers on the Great North Road. The Angel and Royal in the High Street is one of the oldest inns in Britain. Here, it is said, King John held court in 1213, and in an upper room Richard III signed the Duke of Buckingham's death warrant in 1483.

The George Hotel dates from the 18th century, and was described by Charles Dickens in *Nicholas Nickleby* as 'one of the best inns in England'. Another inn, the Beehive in Castlegate, has an unusual sign – an

inhabited beehive set in a tree. Below the sign hangs the legend:
'Stop traveller, this wondrous sign explore,
And say when thou has viewed it o'er and o'er,
Grantham now two rarities are thine A lofty steeple and a living sign.'

The lofty steeple is that of St Wulfram's Church, whose 14th-century spire soars to 272ft and was described by the 19th-century architect George Gilbert Scott as 'next to that of Salisbury Cathedral, the finest in the kingdom'. The church contains a chained library established in 1598, possibly the first public library in England. Most of the books are in Latin, and the oldest, called *Lanfranc*, dates from 1472.

Also in Castlegate is Grantham House, which dates from the 14th century but was altered and enlarged in the 16th and 18th centuries. Princess Margaret, daughter of Henry VII, stayed here in 1503 on her way to marry James IV of Scotland. The house is owned by the National Trust and is open on Wednesday and Thursday afternoons in summer.

WOOLSTHORPE MANOR

In this stone-built farmhouse, small as manors go, the great scientist and mathematician Isaac Newton was born in 1642. The house stands in a quiet lane near Woolsthorpe village, and it is easy to imagine Newton sitting in the garden, as he often did when visiting his mother while at Cambridge University. It is said that it was here that an apple falling from a tree led Newton to his discovery of the law of gravitation, and an apple tree still standing is thought to be a grafting from the original.

The four rooms open to the public include the room in which Newton was born, though the massive bed is from a later date. It is believed that the bookshelves in the upstairs study were built by Newton. The study contains a bust of Newton, and a cast of his death mask hangs above the fireplace. Also in the study, in a corner darkened by partitions, it is probable that he carried out experiments with prisms, proving that white light is made up of a spectrum of colours.

Woolsthorpe Manor is owned by the National Trust and is open every afternoon except Fridays and Saturdays in the summer.

CRANWELL

Along the arrow-straight Ermine Street, which the Romans built to link London with York, the air is constantly filled with the roar and whine of jet aircraft operating out of several RAF airfields between Grantham and Lincoln. At Cranwell is the place where the men piloting those machines acquired their skills, the Royal Air Force College.

A road runs through the establishment, lined with grass verges, low hedges and flowerbeds all as smart and neat as an airman's kit laid out for inspection. Young men in air force blue go briskly about their business, small, single, jet trainers circle the airfield, and in the centre of it all

stands the splendid brick and stone college building, Georgian in style though built in 1933. It is fronted by lawns as closely trimmed as a warrant-officer's moustache.

At the roadside entrance, two lantern-topped brick pillars support massive wrought-iron gates bearing the spread eagle and crown of the RAF insignia, with its proud motto – *Per Ardua ad Astra*. Farther along the road are the married quarters, in streets with names like Airman's Square and Baghdad Road. Then Cranwell becomes the rural village from which it takes its name, and the towers of Lincoln Cathedral come into view.

Tourist information: Lincoln 29828/32151; Grantham 66444 (summer).

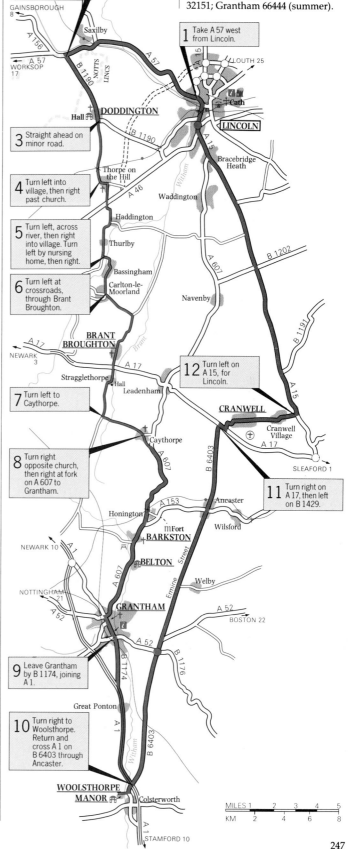

North Country

The broad Humber cleaves a way between the smooth rounded uplands of the Lincolnshire Wolds and the Yorkshire Wolds, where rich farmland rises above sheltered valley villages. The ancient city of York stands at the gateway to two great National Parks, the North York Moors and the Yorkshire Dales; their rolling heights are separated by the Vale of York where, over the centuries, travellers between England and Scotland have left a rich heritage of towns, abbeys and castles. Spectacular cliffs guard the coast, between holiday resorts on wide sandy bays.

Across the Pennines lie the Lancashire Plain and its holiday coast on the Irish Sea. Inland are secluded green oases such as the Forest of Pendle and the Forest of Bowland. To the north roads sweep past Morecambe Bay to the Lake District, where mountain passes cut between the high peaks, and long lakes give rise to rivers which run down to a coastline of sand dunes and old ports. The Eden Valley drops from the high Pennines towards the coast near Carlisle, where Hadrian's Wall begins its long stride eastwards to the North Sea.

At Newcastle, the Tyne divides the moors and valleys of Teesdale and Weardale in Durham from Northumberland's coastline of proud castles, long white sands, and islands which were once cradles of Christianity and are now the haunt of sea birds. Green dales thread their way inland towards the huge Border Forest, surrounding Northern Europe's largest man-made lake.

Farmlands south of the Humber

Inland from the River Humber, farmlands stretch to the Lincolnshire Wolds. Quiet roads lead to an abbey gatehouse and a medieval maze, and follow part of Ermine Street.

CLEETHORPES

Though Cleethorpes is now linked to Grimsby by continuous housing, it is a resort in its own right, with its own character. Its promenade gardens look out at low tide onto vast stretches of sand.

Good bathing beaches extend for more than 3 miles. The seafront is a good spot from which to observe shipping moving up and down the Humber. The few remaining old houses in the High Street recall the days when Cleethorpes was a small fishing village, famous for its oysters. Narrow Sea View Street, which rises up behind the promenade, is lined with interesting old shops, which continue round the corner into Cambridge Street. In Alexandra Road, the modern public library has a framework of massive timbers, in the style of a medieval barn.

GRIMSBY

The best way to get acquainted with Grimsby's fishy sights, sounds and smells is to turn down Fish Dock Road towards the port. There, cars have to pick their way between giant container lorries, and fish porters in long white coats and waders. The warehouses, many of them Victorian but still serviceable, are now used for refrigerated storage.

Near the harbour entrance, the Dock Tower, more than 300ft high, looks like a gigantic minaret, though it was in fact modelled on the tower of Siena's Palazzo Publico.

The old town of Grimsby lies half a mile inland. At its farther end stands Grimsby's finest building, the medieval Church of St James, mainly 13th century, with a noble tower rebuilt in 1365. Beside it is an attractive pedestrian square, where the people of Grimsby sun themselves on benches away from the traffic. Farther south, in Welholme Road, the Welholme Galleries have extensive collections of historic photographs, model ships and marine pictures. They are open from Tuesday to Saturday.

Grimsby's name ends with the *-by* suffix, which denotes a Viking settlement. Nearly every village round about has the same suffix – meaning 'farm' or 'village'; the road to Thornton Abbey passes Laceby, Keelby, Brocklesby and Ulceby.

THORNTON ABBEY

The pride and pomp of abbots in the heyday of the monasteries is nowhere better shown than at Thornton, open daily in summer. Here the abbot lived not in the abbey among his monks, but in a sumptuous gatehouse, 68ft high, and the largest ever built in England. Its upper rooms are fit for a palace.

The gatehouse is one of the earliest brick buildings of any size in Britain, having been built in 1382 as a fortress as well as a residence. It has been extensively restored. On its west front are carvings which depict the great size of the abbey, whose ruins are 200yds away across a field. Only the foundations survive of the 13th-century church and cloister, but part of the magnificent octagonal chapter house survives to about 30ft high.

Across the fields the gas flares of oil refineries stand in contrast with the ancient ruins.

BARTON-UPON-HUMBER

In the shadow of the giant Humber Bridge, Barton is an attractive riverside town, with some fine streets of Georgian houses, and two ancient churches within a stone's throw of each other. The spacious 13th-century parish church of St Mary has a large eight-pinnacled tower; St Peter's nearby is several centuries older, dating back to Saxon times, when Barton was already an important harbour town.

St Peter's tower, with its tall, narrow windows, is typical Saxon stonework. Parts of the church, thought to date back to the 10th century, have been restored.

A turning beside a windmill tower leads to Baysgarth House, a Georgian mansion now a museum of local history and wildlife. It is open from Thursday to Sunday.

RIVERSIDE GRANARY *Below the wolds near Alkborough, the fertile 'carrs' – low-lying farmland – beside the River Trent have been reclaimed from what was once a bog.*

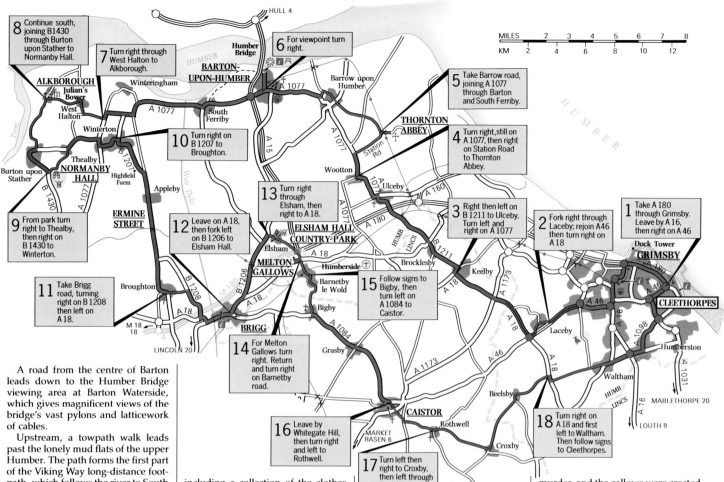

8 Continue south, joining B1430 through Burton upon Stather to Normanby Hall.

7 Turn right through West Halton to Alkborough.

6 For viewpoint turn right.

5 Take Barrow road, joining A1077 through Barton and South Ferriby.

4 Turn right, still on A1077, then right on Station Road to Thornton Abbey.

10 Turn right on B1207 to Broughton.

3 Right then left on B1211 to Ulceby. Turn left and right on A1077.

2 Fork right through Laceby; rejoin A46 then turn right on A18.

1 Take A180 through Grimsby. Leave by A16, then right on A46.

13 Turn right through Elsham, then right to A18.

9 From park turn right to Thealby, then right on B1430 to Winterton.

12 Leave on A18, then fork left on B1206 to Elsham Hall.

15 Follow signs to Bigby, then turn left on A1084 to Caistor.

11 Take Brigg road, turning right on B1208 then left on A18.

14 For Melton Gallows turn right. Return and turn right on Barnetby road.

16 Leave by Whitegate Hill, then turn right and left to Rothwell.

18 Turn right on A18 and first left to Waltham. Then follow signs to Cleethorpes.

17 Turn left then right to Croxby, then left through Beelsby.

Map labels: HULL 4, Humber Bridge, BARTON-UPON-HUMBER, Barrow upon Humber, Winteringham, A1077, THORNTON ABBEY, HUMBER, Station Rd, ALKBOROUGH, Julian's Bower, West Halton, South Ferriby, Wootton, Ulceby, A160, GRIMSBY, Dock Tower, Winterton, A15, A1077, A180, CLEETHORPES, Thealby, NORMANBY HALL, Highfield Farm, Appleby, Weir Dyke, Elsham, HUMB LINCS, Brocklesby, Keelby, A1173, A46, Burton upon Stather, ERMINE STREET, B1430, A1077, B1207, ELSHAM HALL COUNTRY PARK, Humberside, Barnetby le Wold, Bigby, Laceby, Humberston, Broughton, MELTON GALLOWS, B1208, B1206, A18, Grasby, A1084, A1173, Beelsby, A18, A46, Waltham, A1098, LINCOLN 20, BRIGG, M18, A18, HUMB LINCS, A16, MABLETHORPE 20, CAISTOR, Rothwell, Croxby, LOUTH 9, MARKET RASEN 6

MILES 2 3 4 5 6 7 8
KM 2 4 6 8 10 12

A road from the centre of Barton leads down to the Humber Bridge viewing area at Barton Waterside, which gives magnificent views of the bridge's vast pylons and latticework of cables.

Upstream, a towpath walk leads past the lonely mud flats of the upper Humber. The path forms the first part of the Viking Way long-distance footpath, which follows the river to South Ferriby, before striking south across the Lincolnshire Wolds.

ALKBOROUGH

On an escarpment high above the Trent at Alkborough, a maze known as Julian's Bower is cut in the turf. About 40ft in diameter, its date is unknown, but it may have been cut by monks during the Middle Ages. The pattern of the maze has also been set in black-and-white stone in the porch floor of the village's 11th-century parish church.

Such mazes were often called 'Julian's Bower' or 'Troy Town', both names recalling the legend that Julius, son of the Trojan hero Aeneas, brought maze games from Troy to Italy, from where they spread all over Europe. Maze patterns were adopted by the early Church as symbols of the Christian path to salvation.

Beyond Alkborough, the route runs above cliffs beside the Trent, and there are excellent views over the Trent valley, and the Yorkshire Wolds to the north.

NORMANBY HALL

A stone mansion set in 350 acres of parkland, Normanby Hall was built in the 1820s for the Sheffield family, formerly Dukes of Buckingham and owners of Buckingham Palace. Designed by Sir Robert Smirke, architect of the British Museum, it is furnished and decorated in Regency style and has fine collections of textiles and silver.

The Costume Rooms contain displays of 18th and 19th-century dress, including a collection of the clothes worn by one of Scunthorpe's leading 18th-century landowners, John Parkinson. There are also examples of 19th-century military uniform.

The hall is open daily except on Tuesdays in summer, and Saturdays in winter.

The grounds of the hall have been developed into a country park where red and fallow deer wander among magnificent old trees. There is an information centre and a picnic area. The park is open daily.

ERMINE STREET

Just beyond Highfield Farm, the route joins a long, straight stretch of Roman road, and continues along it for more than 6 miles. Built along a ridge to avoid marshy ground, Ermine Street runs between Lincoln and the River Humber. It is part of the Roman road from London to York, where it becomes Dere Street and runs north beyond Hadrian's Wall.

Ermine Street was part of the line of advance of the Roman Ninth Legion, providing a link between the governor in London and his legions in Scotland.

BRIGG

The slumbering atmosphere conjured up by Delius's tone poem *Brigg Fair* has given way to the noise of heavy traffic in this ancient market town; but there are still peaceful spots along the River Ancholme.

Built at an ancient crossing of the river, the town's name means simply 'bridge' in Old English. It was known as Glanford Brigg when a charter of 1235 granted it a weekly market and an annual fair. The name 'Glanford' is now applied to the surrounding district.

ELSHAM HALL COUNTRY PARK

At the foot of the wolds, a country park has been created in the lakeside gardens of Elsham Hall. A nature trail has been laid out round the three lakes, one of which is full of giant carp which can be hand fed. There is trout fishing in season, and organised pony trekking through the 400 acres of woods. There is a bird garden whose wardens take a special interest in the care of injured birds, and an arboretum planted with more than 80 varieties of tree.

The hall itself is not open to the public, but the outbuildings are now a crafts centre with a working forge, and exhibits by resident sculptors and other artists. The park is open daily in summer and on Sundays and Bank Holidays in winter.

MELTON GALLOWS

Beside a lay-by off the main road, opposite Gallows Wood, two upright posts with a horizontal laid across them are gallows originally set up by a king to discourage two local families from feuding.

James I built the gallows after a quarrel broke out between the Ross and Tyrwhitt families during a hunting expedition, and several members of both were killed. James decreed that if any further deaths occurred, the killer would be hanged for murder, and the gallows were erected to put his decree into effect. From then on the feuding ceased.

CAISTOR

The tower of Caistor church dominates the lowlands from a spur on the western edge of the wolds – a commanding position appreciated by the Romans, who built a stronghold there around AD 300. The town's name comes from the Latin *castra*, meaning a 'fortified camp'.

It is likely that the first English kings made use of the Roman walls and towers to build a stronghold of their own; but all that remains of the fortress today are a few fragments of wall.

The chief impression of Caistor today is of a quiet Georgian market town, with up-and-down alleys leading into unexpected little squares and open spaces.

When Christianity came to Caistor some time after 600, the first church was built inside the Roman fortifications; a fragment of the church can be seen below a wooden palisade on the south side of the churchyard. The present church, built of golden stone and dedicated to St Peter and St Paul, has a massive tower with a late Saxon or early Norman base, while the main building is 13th century.

On a clear day it is possible to see Lincoln, some 20 miles south-west, from the slopes of Caistor.

Tourist information: Cleethorpes 697472; Grimsby 53123; (Barton-Upon-Humber) Brigg 52441 (summer); Brigg 57637.

251

Fields and sands to the tip of Holderness

KINGSTON UPON HULL

The tang of the sea reaches into the heart of Kingston upon Hull, which grew up along the banks of the winding River Hull and is now one of Britain's major seaports. Its dockland stretches for miles along the River Humber. Two docks have been converted into a marina, so that once again the skyline is etched with sails and masts as it was some 170 years ago when the docks first opened.

The port was originally laid out in the late 13th century by Edward I, and the remains of the medieval old town lie near the west bank of the River Hull. The ancient High Street – somewhat down-at-heel, but gradually being restored and refurbished under a council plan – runs parallel to the river and is linked to the waterfront by narrow lanes and staithes.

At the top of the High Street is the magnificent Jacobean merchant's house in which the social reformer William Wilberforce was born in 1759. As a Member of Parliament for Yorkshire, he campaigned vigorously for the abolition of slavery in the British Empire. Success came in July 1833, when – three days before he died – Parliament passed the Abolition of Slavery Bill. His birthplace is now a museum devoted to his life and work and has pictures, models and audio-visual reconstructions of slave auctions and voyages. Wilberforce House is open daily.

Farther along the High Street is the Transport and Archaeology Museum, open daily, whose exhibits range from tramcars to flint arrowheads. The port's heyday as a deep-sea fishing centre is recalled in the Town Docks Museum in Queen Victoria Square, open daily. This building, with its three distinctive domes, has displays on whaling and trawling. Almost facing it, by the old Prince's Dock, is the Ferens Art Gallery, which has a permanent gallery of local maritime paintings, as well as works by Frans Hals and Canaletto. It is open daily.

A statue of Hull's most renowned daughter, the aviation pioneer Amy Johnson (1903-41), stands a short distance away in Prospect Street. In 1930 she was the first woman to fly solo from England to Australia. She was killed during the Second World War when a plane she was ferrying for the Royal Air Force plunged into the River Thames.

SKIDBY MILL

This lofty landmark on the road from Hull to Beverley has a black tower with a revolving white cap and four sails, each weighing 1¼ tons. Inside there is an impressive display of cogwheels, shafts and other spare parts for sale.

Skidby Mill was built in 1821. After the use of wind power was discontinued in 1954, big changes were made and it stayed in working order until 1966. It was restored in the 1970s and is once again used to grind wholemeal flour. It is open daily except Mondays from May to September, and flour is ground on every other Sunday.

BEVERLEY

Approaching Beverley from the south, the skyline is dominated by the outline of medieval Beverley Minster, whose delicate twin towers look from a distance like a single, stout block. Inside, the richly decorated Percy tomb is a monument to the powerful Percy family who owned much of the local land.

A curiosity is the 'fridstol', or sanctuary chair, beside the altar. This small stone seat dates from Saxon times. It is thought to have been occupied by an officer hearing pleas for sanctuary from fugitives – a practice which continued until sanctuaries were abolished in 1540. The minster also contains fine stone and wood carvings, and an organ dating from 1767.

The main road leading northwards out of Beverley is guarded by a gate called North Bar – the sole survivor of four 15th-century gateways. Nearby is the second of the town's two mighty churches, the parish church of St Mary. It was started in 1120 as a chapel to the minster, but by the time of its completion in 1530 it had become a masterpiece in its own right. Among its many treasures is a painting on the chancel ceiling of English kings.

Between the two churches lie a wealth of Georgian buildings, wide handsome streets and two attractive markets: Saturday Market to the north and Wednesday Market to the south. In 1984 the Museum of Army Transport opened in Flemingate, just to the east of the minster. The museum is crammed with Jeeps, tanks, general service wagons, recovery tractors and armoured cars, including the Rolls Royce used by Field-Marshal Montgomery in the Second World War. It is open daily.

HORNSEA

There are two distinct and appealing sides to Hornsea: the modern seaside resort, with its long promenade and wide sandy beach; and old Hornsea, an 'inland' village of pretty cottages with pantiled roofs, clustered around the medieval parish church of St Nicholas.

Just behind the village is Hornsea Mere, which is particularly enchanting in the evening, when the sun goes down behind the trees and birds splash in the shallows. The mere is the largest freshwater lake in Yorkshire, 2 miles long and 1 mile wide, and covering about 324 acres. A public footpath skirts the lake, giving fine views across the water. There is an information centre from which escorted afternoon birdwatching walks set out each Saturday and Monday, and on Sunday in summer.

At the south of the town, just off Rolston Road, Hornsea Pottery has a 28 acre leisure park, whose attractions include a lake with water birds, a model village, a children's playground, a small zoo and a picnic area. The park is open daily.

WITHERNSEA

Withernsea's tall, white-painted lighthouse, built in 1894, stands in the centre of the village, well away from the coast and the dangers of erosion.

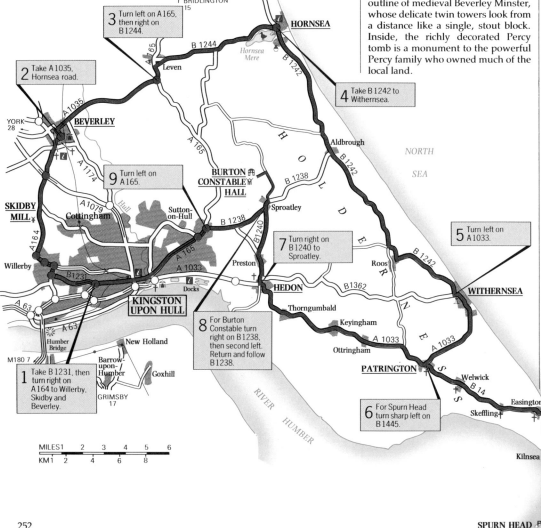

It is now disused and normally closed.

During the mid-19th century there were hopes of turning Withernsea into a major resort, but they never materialised. The seafront is small and unpretentious. The mock fortress at its southern end was once the entrance to a pier, which was destroyed in 1880 when a steamer ran into it during a storm.

PATRINGTON
Although the lofty spire of St Patrick's is visible for miles around, the church mysteriously 'disappears' as soon as the visitor enters the village. This is because the church is set back from the main street and is not seen until almost the last moment. Its perfect proportions, both inside and out, have won it the title of the 'Queen of Holderness' – and a notice in the porch proudly proclaims: 'This is England's finest village church.'

The spire rises from a delicate stone 'crown' on top of the tower, and huge windows flood the inside with light. Built mainly in the mid-14th century, the church has features which are usually found only in cathedrals – including the magnificent transepts, each with a pair of aisles. It is also noted for its superb timbered roof and 15th-century wooden screen across the chancel.

SPURN HEAD
At the southern tip of Holderness a narrow spit of sand and shingle guards the north side of the Humber Estuary. The name 'Spurn' means spur or peninsula, and the existing spur is the most recent of many, as the sea washes away the spit about every 250 years. Each time this happens, a new peninsula is formed slightly to the west of the old one.

Spurn Head has wide acres of mud flats, uncovered at low tide, where fishermen rake for lugworms and birdwatchers sit on the foreshore armed with telescopes and powerful cameras. The Head itself is a nature reserve run by the Yorkshire Wildlife Trust, who charge a toll to drive the 3 miles from the entrance to the car park at the end of the spit. It is open daily.

The drive along the Head is a dramatic one. On one side is the Humber, with the Lincolnshire shore in the distance; and on the other is the North Sea, where cargo ships and tankers queue to enter the estuary. Beyond the lighthouse, built in the late 19th century, and the car park, the tip of the Head is closed to the public; but it is possible to walk round the end at low water.

Spurn Head is one of the major sites in Europe for observing migrating birds. Wildfowl shelter here in winter, and wading birds such as dunlins, curlews and oystercatchers may be seen. Seals sometimes haul themselves onto the Spurn sandbanks and bask in the sun, and porpoises are occasionally seen offshore.

HEDON
Once a prosperous port on the banks of the Humber, Hedon was deposed by Hull in the Middle Ages, when the estuary gradually silted up, leaving Hedon stranded 2 miles inland. Its main street has a number of fine Georgian houses, and the nearby parish church of St Augustine, known as the 'King of Holderness', is one of the largest and most impressive churches in Humberside. It is 165ft long, and its tower soars 128ft above the medieval grid pattern of streets. In Souttergate are Painter's Cottages, Hedon's oldest houses dating from the mid-16th century. They were left in the will of George Painter, a chantry priest of Holy Trinity in Hull, to provide homes for three poor people.

Hedon was notorious as a 'rotten borough'. Until it was disenfranchised by the Reform Act of 1832 it returned two members to Parliament. Bribery and corruption were rife. In 1826 the two MPs were elected by only 331 freemen, most of them from outside Hedon.

BURTON CONSTABLE HALL
This imposing Elizabethan mansion was built in 1570 for the local Constable family, who still live there. The present owner, John Chichester-Constable, has the ringing title of 'Lord Paramount of the Seigniory of Holderness', which was first bestowed on a Norman ancestor who came over with William the Conqueror.

The interior of the elegant, redbrick house was lavishly remodelled and decorated in the 18th century by no fewer than four imaginative architects – Robert Adam, James Wyatt, John Carr and Thomas Lightoler. Its vast, banner-hung Great Hall was given some intricately patterned plasterwork – and other rooms were made more decorative and ornate. The Long Gallery has a library of 5000 books.

The house contains some splendid examples of the work of Robert Adam and of the furniture maker Thomas Chippendale, while Lancelot 'Capability' Brown created the beautiful parkland and lakes. The grounds contain museums of agricultural machinery and vintage motorcycles, and a collection of 18th-century scientific equipment.

In the summer such events as traction-engine rallies and light aircraft displays are held in the grounds. There are camping and caravan sites, and a large picnic area. Beside the children's playground is a model railway.

The hall is open on weekend afternoons in summer, and the grounds are open each afternoon in summer.

Tourist information: Hull 223344; Beverley 867430; Hornsea 2919 (summer).

SPLENDOUR IN STONE *Beverley's great minster, dating from 1220, is one of the finest Gothic buildings in Europe.*

HORNSEA MERE *Humberside's largest freshwater lake is a sanctuary for geese, ducks and wildfowl, and is popular for boating, yachting and fishing.*

HIGH LIGHT *Withernsea's lighthouse rises above the flat fields of Holderness.*

Broad acres of the Yorkshire Wolds

TOUR
154

— 79 MILES —

Rich farmland, crisscrossed by rivers and dotted with villages, lies between the Ouse and the Yorkshire Wolds. The market towns include the birthplace of England's tallest man.

SELBY

Driving into this lively market town from the north-east, the motorist crosses a tollbridge over the River Ouse which recalls earlier days of road travel. The bridge, built in 1969-70, replaced an old wooden bridge that had spanned the river since 1791 but which eventually proved too frail for modern traffic.

Just across the bridge loom the three pinnacled towers of Selby Abbey, founded in 1069 by Benedict, a monk from the Norman monastery of Auxerre. He absconded from France with the dried finger of St Germain, sailed up the Ouse and settled in Selby, where there was fertile land and a plentiful supply of fresh fish.

Benedict was said to have chosen the marshy site after seeing three swans alighting on the water – which he interpreted as a sign of the Holy Trinity. According to tradition, St Germain's finger became the principal relic of the abbey, which was begun by the second abbot, Hugh de Lacy, in about 1100 and completed in 1230.

Designed in the round-arched Norman style, the abbey has splendid incised carving on the outer doorways, and on the arches and columns of the nave. The arches nearest the crossing have a curious, squashed-up appearance, due to subsidence of the marshy soil. The choir and east end were added about 1300 in the Gothic Decorated style. The east window, which still has some of its original 14th-century glass, is a 'Jesse window', showing Christ's family tree, from Jesse, father of David, at the bottom, to Jesus and Mary at the top. The window includes 68 small figures.

The church brought prosperity to Selby, which, however, declined after Henry VIII dissolved the monasteries in the late 1530s. But the abbey itself has survived as the parish church, and still fills this role today. Visitors to the abbey – especially Americans – should look out for the Stars and Stripes flag below one of the south windows of the choir clerestory. The stained glass in the window above includes the coat of arms of the Washington family – which accounts for the inclusion of Selby on the 'American Heritage Trail'.

Since the Middle Ages the church has been considerably altered, first in 1690, when the central tower collapsed and damaged much of the building, and again in 1906, when fire destroyed the roof. The two west towers were built to their present height as recently as 1935. Before that, they were only as high as the nave roof.

In the 17th century two weekly markets were set up near the abbey – a general market on Mondays and a cattle market on Fridays – the Monday market is still held. By the beginning of the 19th century Selby was an important port handling some 400,000 tons of shipping a year – and today it is still a port. It is also a busy industrial centre, its giant flour mills, cattle-food factory and large sugar-making plant reflecting its role as the centre of a fertile area.

Selby's old town runs westwards from the abbey. There are some handsome Georgian houses in The Crescent and the Market Place; and the town's most elaborate and finest house, the early 18th-century Corunna House, takes pride of place in Ousegate, overlooking the river. The house was famed for the cockfights which were held there, and there is still a cockpit in the roof.

During the past few years Selby has

VALLEY VILLAGE *The slender steeple of St Edith's Church rises above Bishop Wilton, sheltered in a hollow where the Wolds sweep down towards the Derwent.*

FLOATING FLOWERS *Water lilies decorate a lake at Burnby Hall, Pocklington.*

VILLAGE PRIDE *Neatly thatched and clad with ivy, these trim cottages stand back from a quiet street in the village of Warter – 4 miles east of Pocklington.*

RUINED SPLENDOUR *The east end of Howden Minster is preserved as a ruin.*

come to prominence as the chief town of the Selby Coalfield. Its 10ft thick seams, estimated to contain enough coal to keep mining going there for the next century, spread for more than 100 square miles below the fertile Ouse valley, in the direction of York.

ALLERTHORPE COMMON
The demands of farming have left few stretches of woodland around Selby, but Allerthorpe Common is one of the survivors. Part of the once-mighty York Forest, it is owned by the Forestry Commission, which has laid out a picnic site from which paths radiate through the woods.

BISHOP WILTON
Tucked away in a narrow valley on the western edge of the wolds, Bishop Wilton is a beautiful village of red-brick houses with pantiled roofs. Their twin rows face each other across a wide swathe of grass, which slopes down to the beck flowing through the centre of the village.

The little church, St Edith's, has a Norman chancel arch and an unusual black-and-white mosaic floor, showing ducks, lapwings, magpies and other birds common in the area. At the top of the village a grassy rectangle in a meadow marks the site of a long-vanished bishop's palace, said to have been built by Archbishop Neville during the reign of Edward IV (1461-83).

POCKLINGTON
The centre of this market town at the foot of the wolds is full of twisting little alleys, which give constantly changing vistas of its old buildings. The parish church of All Saints, built mainly between 1200 and 1450, has a magnificent 15th-century tower, which in 1733 was the scene of an early unsuccessful attempt at man-powered flight. A local man named Thomas Pelling jumped off the top of the tower, attached to a rope and flapping batlike wings; but his attempt to fly ended in tragedy when he collided with the choir battlements and was killed. Inside All Saints is its most treasured possession – a churchyard cross carved in the late 14th century in memory of one John Sotheby, or Soteby. The cross was discovered in 1835, buried in the churchyard – where it was thought to have been hidden from Cromwell's troops during the Civil War.

The former Ritz Cinema in the Market Place now houses an exhibition of mechanical entertainment. It is called the 'Penny Arcadia' – a collection of amusement machines including 'Test-Your-Strength' machines, 'What-the-Butler-Saw' peepshows, fortune tellers and automatic musical machines. The arcade is open daily in summer.

At the southern edge of the town, Burnby Hall, now local council offices, stands in gardens containing one of the finest collections of water lilies in Europe. It was created in the mid-1930s by Major Percy Stewart, a local botanist and sportsman, on completing his hunting expeditions around the world. The water lilies, nurtured in two lakes, flower by the

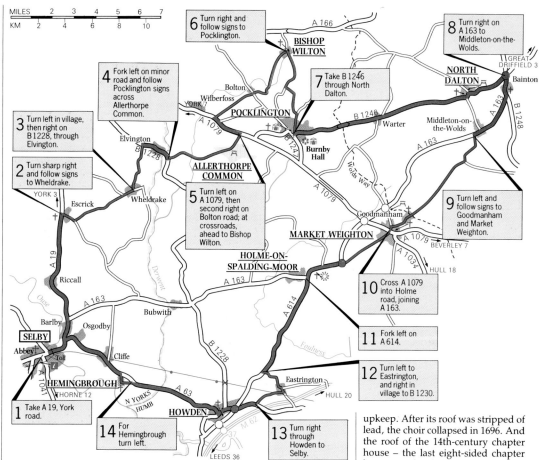

thousand from late May to October – the main display being from mid-June to early September. The Stewart Collection – made up of souvenirs of the major's travels – is housed in a small museum. The trophies include Burmese religious items and African musical instruments. The museum is open daily from May to September.

The town's traditional open-air market is still held each Tuesday.

NORTH DALTON
The road from Pocklington to North Dalton is an exhilarating 9 mile drive over rolling wolds countryside, first through parkland planted with trees, and then across an open landscape of well-tended fields. North Dalton is a village where the visitor half expects to see smock-clad countrymen driving their cattle down to the big village pond.

The road makes a dogleg through the village; at its apex is All Saints' Church, largely Norman, perched on a mound across the road from the pond. About half a mile to the north is a small field, complete with seats, which makes a delightful picnic place.

MARKET WEIGHTON
Although the centre of this pleasant market town is often congested with traffic, away from the High Street there are several peaceful backwaters with some fine 18th-century buildings. The parish church of All Saints, behind the Market Place, is mainly 13th century, with the remains of Saxon herringbone stonework in its square tower.

The town was the birthplace of William Bradley, known as the 'Market Weighton Giant', at 7ft 9in the tallest Englishman ever recorded. He died in 1820 at the age of 33 and is buried in the church, where there is a plaque to his memory. Bradley's huge chair is kept in a former coaching inn, the Londesborough Arms Hotel in the High Street, and a plaque with his enormous footprint drawn on it marks his former home – Bradley House, now a bicycle shop – on the corner of York Road. The doorways of the house had to be enlarged to accommodate Bradley, who weighed 27 stones.

HOLME-ON-SPALDING-MOOR
Aloof on a steep hill to the north-east of the village is the medieval Church of All Saints, a commanding building with an impressive tower. The views from the ground extend for miles over the surrounding moors and commons. The church is reached by a track starting from a cattle grid, a few hundred yards beyond a garage on the south side of the road from Holme to Market Weighton. There is plenty of room to park at the top of the hill, and a good stretch of grass for a picnic.

HOWDEN
From a distance the soaring tower of Howden Minster – dedicated to St Peter and St Paul – forms a graceful landmark across the level countryside. The choir fell into disrepair in the 17th century when the local gentry refused to give money for its

upkeep. After its roof was stripped of lead, the choir collapsed in 1696. And the roof of the 14th-century chapter house – the last eight-sided chapter house to be built in England – collapsed in 1750. The west end of the minster, 225ft long, is intact and still in use as a parish church, one of the largest in Humberside. The chapter house is being restored, but the east end will be preserved as the picturesque ruin it is.

The minster was established in 1267 for a college of canons, and the elegant columns of its nave date from that time. Offerings made at the shrine of St John of Howden in the Middle Ages contributed to the splendour of the building.

Since most heavy traffic now avoids Howden, it is a pleasure to wander through the streets seeking out the remaining medieval and Georgian houses in this small and attractive market town.

HEMINGBROUGH
To the west of Howden, the countryside is flat and heavily cultivated, with rich, dark, fen-like earth. Away to the south, the vast cooling towers of Drax Power Station rise dramatically above the flat landscape.

A much older and more revered landmark is the magnificent stone spire of the Church of St Mary the Virgin in the pretty village of Hemingbrough. The spire soars to 189ft, and was added in the 15th century to the 13th-century tower. Inside the church is a misericord thought to be the oldest in Britain; it has been in use since 1200.

Tourist information: Selby 703263; Beverley 867430; Goole 2187/8; York 21756/7; (Humber Bridge) Hull 640852.

Moors and valleys north of York

TOUR
155
— 90 MILES —

Tucked away in the North York Moors are lonely villages and busy market towns, while in the vale flamingos cluster on a zoo lake and a white horse strides across a hillside.

YORK

Romans, Saxons, Vikings and Normans have all left their marks in York, from the remnants of the wall that enclosed the Roman town of Eboracum to the great minster that dominates the city. Side by side with lovely old buildings from Georgian and Victorian times, they make York a city of living history.

That history is effectively displayed in the Heritage Centre in Castlegate, using models, paintings and audio-visual displays.

The centre is close to some of the city's oldest streets; narrow thorough-fares where fine old shop fronts display fine old antiques, silver and jewellery, and fine old inns sell fine old Yorkshire beers.

Some streets, such as Stonegate, follow the lines of the Roman streets, and in Coppergate there are houses of Viking days – not lining the street but below it. Discovered in the 1970s, the lower walls of the 10th-century buildings of the Viking town of Jorvik have been re-erected where they were found, and reconstructions of a market and a wharf bring to life the days of the Viking settlement.

Towering above the narrow streets is York Minster, the largest Gothic church in England. It was begun in the 13th century and is noted for its stained-glass windows, especially those in the nave which date from the 14th century. The Minster is dedicated to St Peter, whose figure stands between the west doors.

York is also a city of museums, where history lives on in realistic displays. The Castle Museum, in the 18th-century debtors' and women's prisons, reflects Victorian Yorkshire life in town and country, with its spectacular reconstruction of a cobbled street – Kirkgate – and period rooms.

In the National Railway Museum, York moves into the 20th century on the massive wheels of the great locomotives that once thundered across the English countryside.

MALTON

The York to Scarborough road curves to the west of Malton, léaving this historic market town and its neighbour, Norton, to enjoy a peaceful but still busy life beside the River Derwent. The Romans were here about AD 70 and built a fort, Derventio, relics from which can be seen in the Roman Museum in the Market Place. Malton prospered after the Derwent was made navigable during the 18th century, and many stone-built houses and shops of the period line the long, gently curving main street.

KIRBY MISPERTON

Though called 'Flamingoland', the zoo at Kirby Misperton has much more to offer than just these lovely birds which inhabit the large lake. There are lions, tigers, elephants, polar bears and many other animals in the 250 acre gardens that surround Kirby Misperton Hall, a Georgian mansion. The zoo is open daily in summer.

LASTINGHAM

The road into Lastingham dips down among tall trees and then winds into the main street where ancient stone houses cluster around a stream, the white-fenced village green and the 11th-century Church of St Mary.

In this hollow below the moors a priory was founded in the 7th century by St Cedd. The church is all that remains of the priory today; it has a Norman crypt and a 15th-century tower. A fountain honouring St Cedd, dating from the 9th century, stands in the main street.

HUTTON-LE-HOLE

High moors ring this charming village in a valley carved by the rushing waters of the Hutton Beck. The stream cascades over waterfalls and ripples between grassy banks spanned by little stone bridges, while on either side stand rows of neat, stone-built cottages.

Next door to the Crown Inn is the Ryedale Folk Museum and park. The museum has a large collection of farm implements, and in the park are reconstructions of early dwellings. A right turn beyond Lowna leads to Low Mill, in Farndale, where a walk by the River Dove is bordered by thousands of wild daffodils in spring.

KIRKBYMOORSIDE

The market place forms a thriving centre to this moorland town, especially on Wednesdays when stalls line the street as they have done every Wednesday for 600 years. The Toll Booth or Market Hall, still used on market days, dates from about 1700, and there are a number of coaching inns dating from the days when Kirkbymoorside was on the main road from Thirst to Scarborough.

The Black Swan, a well-preserved, half-timbered building dated 1634, looks across to its opposite number, the White Swan, and up the hill is the King's Head and its neighbour, Buckingham House.

KIRK DALE

Pleasant walks through the dale start from St Gregory's Minster, a tiny church with a Saxon sundial over the south porch. An inscription in Northumbrian English tells that the church was rebuilt by Orm, son of Gamal in the days of Edward the Confessor.

Kirk Dale's principal historical feature, however, is a cave in which the bones of prehistoric animals were discovered in 1821. The bones, now in the Yorkshire Museum in York, are

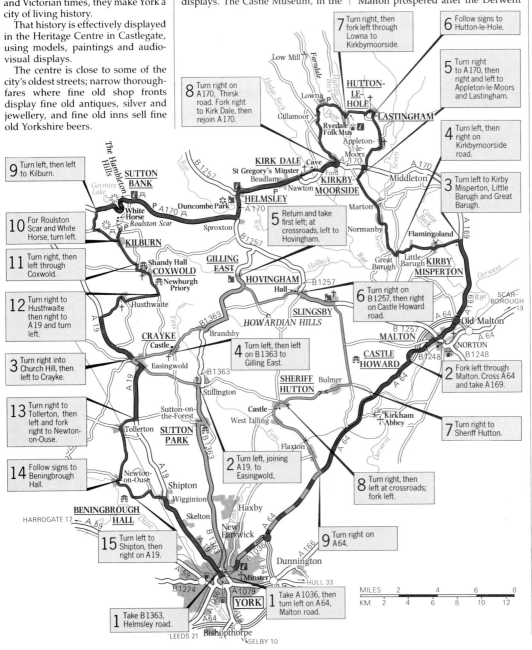

Map directions:

1. Take B1363, Helmsley road.
2. Turn left, joining A19, to Easingwold.
3. Turn right into Church Hill, then left to Crayke.
4. Turn left, then left on B1363 to Gilling East.
5. Return and take first left; at crossroads, left to Hovingham.
6. Turn right on B1257, then right on Castle Howard road.
7. Turn right to Sheriff Hutton.
8. Turn right, then left at crossroads; fork left.
9. Turn right on A64.
1. Take A1036, then turn left on A64, Malton road.
2. Fork left through Malton. Cross A64 and take A169.
3. Turn left to Kirby Misperton, Little Barugh and Great Barugh.
4. Turn left, then right on Kirkbymoorside road.
5. Turn right to A170, then right and left to Appleton-le-Moors and Lastingham.
6. Follow signs to Hutton-le-Hole.
7. Turn right, then fork left through Lowna to Kirkbymoorside.
8. Turn right on A170, Thirsk road. Fork right to Kirk Dale, then rejoin A170.
9. Turn left, then left to Kilburn.
10. For Roulston Scar and White Horse, turn left.
11. Turn right, then left through Coxwold.
12. Turn right to Husthwaite then right to A19 and turn left.
13. Turn right to Tollerton, then left and fork right to Newton-on-Ouse.
14. Follow signs to Beningbrough Hall.
15. Turn left to Shipton, then right on A19.

those of mammoths, cave lions, oxen, tigers and hippopotamuses, suggesting that the cave was a hyenas' den. The entrance is reached by a path leading from the ford at the lower end of the dale.

HELMSLEY

The wide market square in Helmsley is gay with the striped awnings of stalls and roundabouts when a travelling fair comes to town. The scene makes a vivid contrast to the Gothic pinnacles of the square's centrepiece, a memorial to the 2nd Baron Feversham whose home was at nearby Duncombe Park. Visitors from London will note the memorial's resemblance to the Albert Memorial, both having been designed by Sir Gilbert Scott.

The Town Hall on the western side of the square was built by the 1st Earl of Feversham in 1901. There are older buildings on the north side, where a half-timbered Elizabethan cottage is now part of the Black Swan hotel.

SUTTON BANK

Road signs warn motorists to engage low gear as they approach a 1 in 4 gradient that descends from Sutton Bank into the Vale of York. Before the winding descent there is a viewpoint, car park and picnic spot from where views stretch across to Swaledale, Wensleydale and the Pennines.

In between are such landmarks as Fountains Abbey and Knaresborough Castle, while below Sutton Bank lies the glistening Gormire Lake. When conditions are right, gliders from the nearby airfield soar aloft on the air currents forced up by the 700ft escarpment.

KILBURN

A white horse and a mouse have made Kilburn famous far beyond the hills and valleys of this corner of the Vale of York. The Kilburn White Horse appeared on the limestone face of the Hambleton Hills in 1857 when a local schoolmaster, John Hodgson, carved the figure, 314ft long and 228ft high, with the help of his pupils and 30 local men. Six tons of lime were used to whiten the figure, which gets a 'facelift' every few years, and it can be seen from as far away as Leeds, some 30 miles south-west.

A road up from the village leads to the base of the horse, and from there a path runs along the edge of the cliff to Roulston Scar, a 200ft limestone crag.

The mouse was the trademark of Robert Thompson, a local woodcarver whose work can be seen in churches all over Britain, including Westminster Abbey and York Minster. Thompson died in 1955, but the business is still carried on by his grandsons, and the little mouse still appears in the carvings. The workshops stand behind a pretty half-timbered house used as a showroom; both can be visited.

COXWOLD

The author Laurence Sterne lived and worked in Coxwold from 1760 until 1768. He was known locally as the eccentric vicar of St Michael's Church, and known the world over as the author of *Tristram Shandy*, or more

PASTORAL DALE *Patchwork fields, lonely farms and the gentle River Dove lie cupped in the palm of Farndale, below Spaunton Moor.*

MOORLAND SAINT *St Mary's Church at Lastingham stands on the burial place of St Cedd, who founded an abbey there.*

SMART SET *Neat and orderly Stillington is typical of many villages in North Yorkshire.*

correctly *The Life and Opinions of Tristram Shandy, Gentleman.*

The church makes a spectacular approach to the village, its 15th-century octagonal tower standing proudly above the street of limestone houses that face across grassy banks on the side of a steep hill. Sterne's home, Shandy Hall, was built about 1450, with 17th and 18th-century additions. It is open to the public on Wednesday afternoons in summer.

BENINGBROUGH HALL

A major restoration in 1979 has given new life to this 18th-century house standing in a wooded park. Built of red brick, with white stone facings, the building has few external decorative features, but inside there are carved cornices and overmantels and a staircase with treads 7ft wide and a carved balustrade.

In the principal rooms are portraits on loan from the National Gallery. There is also a Victorian laundry, and exhibitions showing domestic and public life in the 17th and 18th centuries.

The house, owned by the National Trust, is open to the public most days in summer.

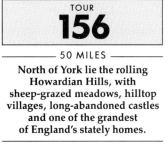

TOUR

156

—— 50 MILES ——

North of York lie the rolling Howardian Hills, with sheep-grazed meadows, hilltop villages, long-abandoned castles and one of the grandest of England's stately homes.

SUTTON PARK

This Georgian house of 1730 stands in parkland designed by Capability Brown, which offers woodland walks and a nature trail. There is also a terraced garden with roses, shrubs, herbaceous borders and a lily canal. The house has some fine plasterwork and the rooms are furnished with Chippendale, Sheraton and French furniture. The house is open twice weekly in spring and summer.

CRAYKE

Red-brick houses on wide grassy banks stand back from the road leading up from the white-painted Durham Ox inn in this hilltop village,

and at the top of the hill stand a church and a castle. Both date from the 15th century, the castle standing behind ivy-clad stone walls, on the site of a Norman fortress. It is not open to the public, but can be seen clearly from the road.

GILLING EAST

Stone lodge gates opposite the church herald the approach to Gilling Castle, which stands high on a hill above the village. A long drive winds up the hill through an avenue of trees, opening out to grass parkland and the buff-coloured stone façade of the castle.

Most of the castle dates from the 18th century, but parts are much older. The main block consists of the lower floor of a 14th-century tower house with Elizabethan additions.

The castle's entrance hall and great chamber are open to the public daily.

HOVINGHAM

Sheep-speckled meadows and a trickling stream spanned by a little stone bridge give the approach to Hovingham a delightful pastoral air. Beyond a pair of stone pillars the road leads into a spick and span village of golden stone cottages and trim greens fenced by white rails, and it is immediately apparent that such orderliness did not occur by accident. Hovingham is an estate village, laid out by Sir Thomas Worsley, George III's surveyor-general, and his successors.

Hovingham Hall, a lovely Palladian house with a gateway that houses a riding school stables, is still the home of the Worsleys, the family of the Duchess of Kent. The Worsley Arms Hotel, an attractive Georgian building with a delicate iron canopy at the doorway, faces the green.

SLINGSBY

Like the jagged pinnacles of a weatherworn rock formation, the corners of Slingsby Castle rear up from a tangled undergrowth. That is all that remains of the 17th-century house built for Sir Charles Cavendish, who fought with Charles I at the Battle of Edgehill. He is said to have fled from the house before it could be completed. The remainder of the village is built of cream-coloured stone, on a rectangular plan.

CASTLE HOWARD

Long before Castle Howard is reached, its domed cupola appears above the trees beyond the shimmering waters of a vast lake. The road runs arrow straight but not level, switchbacking through parkland and then rising to a 100ft high obelisk that marks the turn off for the castle.

Castle Howard is in fact a palace, built for the 3rd Earl of Carlisle in 1700 by Sir John Vanbrugh, aided by Nicholas Hawksmoor. The great hall is 70ft high and has a painted domed ceiling. The rooms are hung with paintings by Rubens, Gainsborough, Reynolds and Holbein, and there are statues from ancient Greece and Rome.

Castle Howard and its grounds and gardens are open daily throughout spring and summer.

SHERIFF HUTTON

Cattle graze among the neglected ruins of Sheriff Hutton Castle, and only portions of the walls and towers stand as bleak monuments to one of the most turbulent times in English history. The castle was built in the 14th century by Ralph Neville, 1st Earl of Westmorland. It was at Sheriff Hutton that Richard III imprisoned Princess Elizabeth of York and the young Earl of Warwick, who were both contenders for his throne. Elizabeth was released by Henry VII after Richard's death at Bosworth, and became his wife and the mother of Henry VIII.

Tourist information: York 21756/7; (Hutton-le-Hole) Lastingham 367 (summer); Helmsley 70401; (Sutton Bank) Thirsk 597426 (summer).

RUGGED EDGE *At Sutton Bank the high plateau of the North York Moors ends abruptly in limestone cliffs and wooded slopes plunging down to the flat plain of the Vale of York.*

A valley route through West Yorkshire

TOUR
157
— 60 MILES —

The peaceful beauty of old England flourishes in the shadow of industrial towns. Villages have kept their charm, and gracious houses stand amid rolling farmland and woods.

BOSTON SPA

There is a feeling of 18th-century elegance and spaciousness about Boston Spa, an echo of Harrogate or Bath. Its mineral springs, discovered in 1744, attracted the attention of the rich and ailing occupants of carriages and stagecoaches that passed on the newly built Tadcaster to Otley turnpike road.

Many stayed to taste and bathe in the waters; others set up home in gracious, Georgian houses that still survive. The Spa bathhouse also survives as the headquarters of an angling club down by the River Wharfe.

There are pleasant riverside and woodland walks, and a fine old bridge links the village with the much older Thorp Arch, north of the river.

CLIFFORD

Rows of cottages built of rich, honey-coloured stone give Clifford an almost Cotswold-like appearance. The magnesian limestone is the same stone that was used to build York Minster. It was quarried near Clifford and taken down the River Wharfe and up the Ouse to York.

Clifford's magnificent Roman Catholic Church, dedicated to St Edward the Confessor, was built in 1845-8 in Romanesque style. Its fine tower, modelled after Angoulême Cathedral in France by George Goldie, was added in 1859-66. The interior of St Edward's contains some fine carvings, and stained glass by Pugin.

BRAMHAM

The route passes through gently undulating countryside before dipping down into this delightful village of mellow, stone cottages and fine 18th-century houses.

Beyond Bramham at Terry Lug on the Thorner road, there is a signpost to Bramham Park, a superb Queen Anne mansion and gardens. The house was built between 1698 and 1710 for Robert Benson, 1st Lord Bingley; it is still occupied by his direct descendants, the Lane Fox family. The gardens of Bramham Park rank with Hampton Court as an outstanding example in England of French-style formal layout. Avenues lined with clipped beech hedges, a canal, cascades, ponds, groves, statues and temples have created a kind of miniature Versailles. Waymarked walks lead through extensive woodland.

The house and gardens are open most days from mid-June to the end of August.

THORNER

A pleasant drive through farms and woodland leads to the village of Thorner, clustered around St Peter's Church with its battlemented tower. Though it is a popular commuter area for Leeds, Thorner has kept much of its rural character with an attractive main street and an old ford crossed by a bridleway into the village.

BARWICK IN ELMET

An enormous maypole close to the old parish church in Barwick brings rural England close to the industrial city of Leeds. Ancient festivities continue each spring with elaborate maypole dances.

The name 'Elmet' is a survivor of an ancient independent kingdom of the same name which flourished into Anglo-Saxon times. Extensive earthworks around the village suggest there may once have been important defensive fortifications here, presumably to defend the little kingdom against successive waves of invaders.

ABERFORD

Fine old coaching inns survive as reminders that Aberford was once an important coaching town on the Great North Road. The White Swan Inn has a great arch, high enough to permit a stagecoach to enter the stable yard.

The Gascoigne Almshouses are in an astonishing neo-Gothic building in the style of a university college. It was built in 1844 by George Fowler Jones for the Gascoignes of nearby Parlington Park, to house the local aged poor, and now houses the conservation workshops of the City of Leeds Art Gallery.

LOTHERTON HALL

Set in Japanese and Italian gardens, this elegant Edwardian house was the home of Sir Alvary Gascoigne, a former British Ambassador to Russia and Japan, who gave the house, together with numerous art treasures, to the City of Leeds. It now forms one of the city's major art galleries and houses fine collections of furniture, paintings, silver and ceramics. A costume and fashion gallery displays clothes from the 18th century to the present day.

The gardens are particularly lovely in spring when semi-wild daffodils turn the lawns into a sea of colour, and the alpine rockery plants bloom.

WATERY AVENUE *Overhung by trees, this calm stretch of the River Wharfe lies some 2 miles south-east of Wetherby – between the twin villages of Thorp Arch and Boston Spa.*

Adjoining the gardens is one of the largest and most fascinating bird gardens in England, with a collection that includes giant condors, flamingos, emus and owls. There is also a deer park in the grounds.

The hall and its bird gardens are open daily except Mondays, and the grounds are open daily.

SHERBURN IN ELMET
The first glimpse of Sherburn is of its Church of All Saints, set on a hill at the edge of the village. The church dates from the late 12th century, and much of the original building survives.

Undoubtedly there was an earlier Saxon church on the site, as records note that in the 9th century King Athelstan gave the church to the people and city of York, in gratitude for their victory over the Danes.

LEDSHAM
In this tiny village at a crossroads of narrow lanes, the superb Anglo-Saxon Church of All Saints is miraculously preserved within the fabric of a later medieval building. Saxon windows, an archway, a doorway and walls give a vivid insight into what this little church must have been like in the 8th century, when it was built. At that time Christianity was still struggling against paganism, and the church was probably the only stone building in the village.

In the newer part of the church stands a statue of the 18th-century beauty and philanthropist Lady Elizabeth Hastings, who died at Ledsham in 1739.

FAIRBURN INGS
A remarkable nature reserve and bird sanctuary has been created in the Lower Aire valley around flooded mine workings which have produced great man-made lakes and marshland. The reserve, managed by the Royal Society for the Protection of Birds, attracts a variety of birdlife, both native and migrant. In the car park there is a bird identification board to help visitors recognise many of the species to be seen.

PONTEFRACT
Look carefully at Pontefract's old street names – Micklegate, Beast Fair, Shoe Market, Salter Row, Ropergate – and an impression of the old medieval town begins to emerge, a bustling crowded huddle of narrow streets, shops and inns. Some fine Georgian houses and shops have survived modern redevelopment, as has the Butter Cross, the focal point of a lively outdoor market on Wednesdays and Saturdays.

Pontefract Castle, dating from Norman times, was where Richard II ended his days in 1400, shortly after being deposed. It is thought that he either starved to death or was murdered by Henry IV's knights. During the Civil War, the castle resisted sieges by Cromwell's men; even after the execution of Charles I in 1649, local defenders refused to surrender the castle, declaring they were holding it for the king's son. Two months after Charles I's death Cromwell

demolished the castle at the request of the townsfolk, leaving the present gaunt ruins, which are open daily.

Evocative, too, are the great ruins of the medieval Church of All Saints, below the castle walls. The church was destroyed in the Civil War but has been partially restored.

Pontefract is inseparably associated with liquorice, which used to be widely grown in the area for the confectionery industry. The famous black 'Pontefract Cakes' are still made locally, though the liquorice is now imported.

TOP FARM MUSEUM
In the village of West Hardwick, there is a remarkable collection of tractors, farm implements, and various breeds of farm animals. The Top Farm Museum is the creation of a local farmer and his wife, concerned to see local farming traditions survive.

As well as the farm displays there are fairground organs and vintage cars, and a barn has been converted into a restaurant. The museum is open daily, except Mondays, from April to October.

NOSTELL PRIORY
This magnificent Palladian house designed by James Paine in 1733 and standing on the site of a vanished 12th-century priory, is one of the architectural showpieces of West Yorkshire. It is the ancestral home of Lord St Oswald, and its treasures include decoration by Robert Adam, Chippendale furniture, tapestries and paintings and a fine 18th-century doll's house.

The extensive grounds include lakeside walks and rose gardens, and a children's adventure playground. Wragby church, in the grounds, dates from the 16th century; it contains Flemish altar carvings and Italian and German carved pulpit panels. Nostell Priory belongs to the National Trust and is open at weekends from April to October, and daily, except Fridays, in July and August.

Two miles beyond Nostell Priory, the route begins to wind around the edge of Wintersett Reservoir. There is a car park and picnic spot beside the water, with views across the reservoir to rolling farmland and woodland.

WENTWORTH PARK
With almost breathtaking suddenness the elegant parkland of Wentworth appears from the pit-scarred landscape around it. Standing in the park is the house with a 600ft long façade, one of the longest in Britain – Wentworth Woodhouse, built in the 18th century for the Marquis of Rockingham. It has some 240 rooms and covers more than 1½ acres.

In the estate grounds are several elaborate 'follies', including a three-storey mausoleum which contains a statue of the 2nd Marquis of Rockingham. The extensive grounds contain several lakes and footpaths.

Wentworth House is privately owned, but a footpath through the grounds is open to the public.

Tourist information: Wetherby 62706/7; Leeds 462453/4.

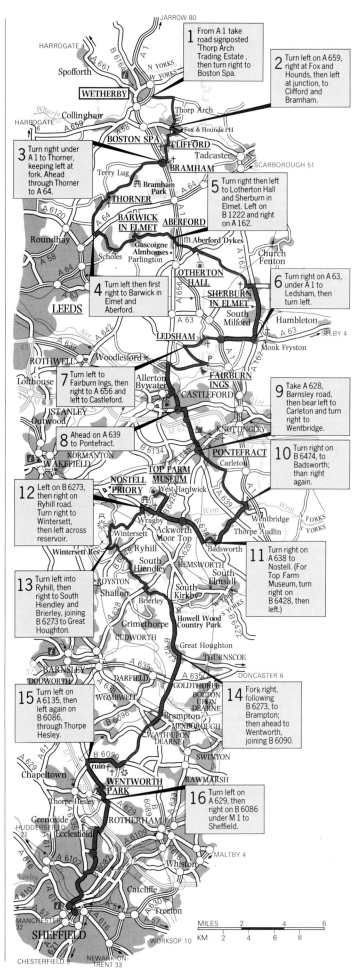

261

Ancient towns at Yorkshire's heart

Rolling countryside in the heart of Yorkshire contains many reminders of the past. There are Roman mosaics, Ripon's fine medieval cathedral and one of England's finest Norman castles.

WETHERBY
The agreeable old-fashioned feeling of this busy market town is due partly to the warm, cream-coloured stone used to build the houses and shops around the market square. A fine bridge spans the River Wharfe in the town centre, and water rushing over the old weir makes a delightful picture.

SPOFFORTH CASTLE
At the back of Spofforth village is the ruined castle which once belonged to the Percy family of Northumbria. Little remains of the early 14th-century building – a fortified manor house – apart from a tower, sections of a hall and the ground-floor walls, one of which is formed from the natural rock against which the house was built. The castle was wrecked by the enemies of Sir Henry Percy after his death in 1461. Almost two centuries later there was further dismantling. It is open daily.

PLOMPTON ROCKS
Massive gritstone rocks stand worn by thousands of years of erosion by wind and rain into fantastic and beautiful shapes. Their curious outlines are reflected in a lake, and there is a stretch of woodland nearby. The rocks are on a private estate, but the public are admitted at weekends from March to October.

KNARESBOROUGH
Terraces line the steep gorge of the River Nidd, overlooked by a medieval castle and the arches of a Victorian railway viaduct, a combination which gives the ancient town an impressive setting. The 14th-century castle is open daily in the summer and exploration in Knaresborough is rewarding, with a number of zigzagging lanes and cobbled alleys running down to the riverside.

A footpath leads to the remarkable Dropping Well, open on Sundays from mid-February and daily from April to November. The well is actually a spring in which the high mineral content 'petrifies' objects left in its waters – shoes, hats, gloves, even teddy bears. The prophetess Mother Shipton (1488-1561) is said to have been born near the Dropping Well. It has been claimed that she forecast the English Civil War of the 1640s, the Great Fire of London (1666), the coming of aircraft and the end of the world – in 1881.

Farther down the river is a medieval chapel carved out of rock, and steps lead to an 18th-century house cut out of the rock by a local weaver, Thomas Hill. This is occasionally open to visitors on special request. In the market square is another curiosity – a chemist's shop said to be the oldest in England.

ALDBOROUGH
On the site of this village once stood the capital of the Roman-British colony of Brigantia. Originally it was a camp of the Ninth Legion, but after the British tribe of Brigantes had been conquered in AD 71 it developed into an administrative centre, Isurium Brigantium.

Clues to Aldborough's importance in Roman times are extensive earthworks and fragments of wall, and two superb mosaic pavements. The pavements, dating from the 4th century, are preserved in pavilions. There is a small museum containing Roman remains, open to the public daily in the summer. Nearby, a maypole stands on the village green.

BOROUGHBRIDGE
The trunk route now bypasses the village, leaving it at peace – with massive, early 19th-century coaching inns as reminders of the days when horse-drawn traffic clattered between London and Scotland.

Boroughbridge's most remarkable feature lies immediately west of the town. The Devil's Arrows – three gigantic, fluted megaliths, each about 20ft high – stand roughly in a north to south line. The southernmost is hidden among trees on the left of the road to Roecliffe; the other two stand in the field opposite, eerie sentinels from a mysterious past.

Dating from the mid-Bronze Age, about 3000 years ago, they were massive symbols, supposedly endowed with power to increase fertility. They were hewn from millstone grit, quarried and hauled from Abbey Plain, near Knaresborough, 7 miles away. Their transport and erection on this site are extraordinary evidence of early engineering skills.

SKELTON
In 1870 a young Englishman, Frederick Vyner of Newby Hall, was captured and murdered in Greece by brigands while making a Grand Tour of Europe. His mother, Lady Mary Vyner, used the money collected for his ransom to build a magnificent church to his memory in Newby Park – dedicated to Christ the Consoler. The church, completed in 1872, is richly decorated in High Victorian style. The superb altar cloth was designed by William Burges and embroidered by Lady Mary. The church is reached from the village along a footpath through an archway of yews.

Newby Hall and gardens, open every afternoon except Monday in the summer, date from the late 17th century, but the dominant style is of the 18th century with extensive alterations and interiors by Robert Adam making this one of the most elegant houses in the north of England. A miniature steam railway carries visitors through the gardens.

RIPON
Long before the remainder of Ripon comes into view, its cathedral is a landmark across the plain. The west front gives little clue to the splendour of the interior – the soaring arches of the 16th-century nave, the fine, early 14th-century east window, and the

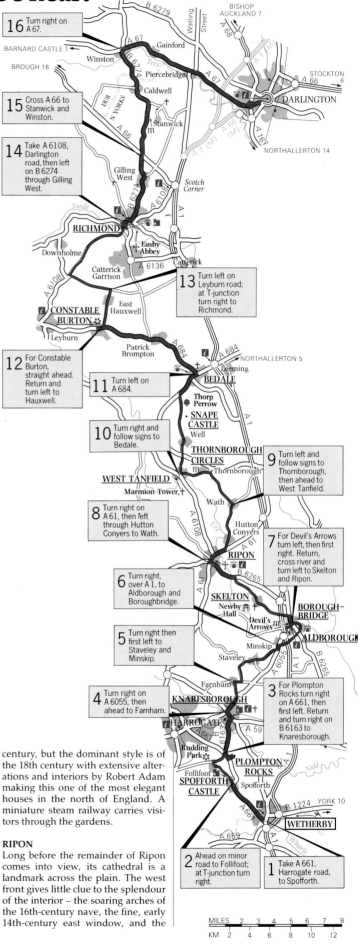

elaborately carved choir, where many of the misericords – hinged shelves on the undersides of the choir seats – date from the 15th century. Most impressive of all, perhaps, is the 7th-century Anglo-Saxon crypt – now the cathedral's treasure house – dating from 672, when St Wilfrid built the first stone church by the River Ure.

The market square has a huge 90ft obelisk that supports a gilded horn as a weather vane – a symbol of the wakeman's horn. In medieval times the wakeman, who kept order in the town with his aldermen, would sound the horn each night to impose the town watch – an early form of police patrol. A wakeman still blows a horn at 9 o'clock each evening, the original horn is kept in the Town Hall. A timber-framed, 14th-century house in the corner of the square which was once the wakeman's home now also houses the tourist information office. It is open daily in the summer. The frieze carved on the Town Hall – built in 1801 to the design of James Wyatt – carries the motto: 'Except ye Lord keep ye cittie, ye Wakeman waketh in vain.'

The obelisk itself, built in 1781, is a memorial to William Aislabie, who was Ripon's MP for 60 years in the 18th century.

A short walk from the cathedral, in St Marygate, is the former town prison – now a police museum, displaying relics of early police work in Yorkshire. It is open every afternoon in the summer except Monday.

THORNBOROUGH CIRCLES
Three Bronze Age circles, each between 550 and 780ft across, lie just to the west of this village. The easiest one to see is just to the right of the Thornborough to West Tanfield road, but it could be mistaken for a railway or a reservoir with its 6ft high embankments. These banks form a huge natural amphitheatre of earth and stones, and were almost certainly used for ceremonial or religious purposes in early Bronze Age times, some 4000 years ago.

WEST TANFIELD
The great arch and medieval oriel window of Marmion Tower make this 15th-century gatehouse to a now-vanished fortified house look almost theatrical. A staircase can be followed up to the second storey, which gives a splendid outlook over the wooded riverside. The tower is close to the medieval parish church, and open daily.

SNAPE CASTLE
Turrets and mullioned windows give an almost fairy-tale appearance to this little medieval and Tudor castle seen on the approach to the village from the main road. It was for many years the home of Catherine Parr, who was to become the sixth and surviving wife of Henry VIII. Now it is a private house.

A small car park to the right of the road half a mile from Snape lies at the entrance to Thorp Perrow Arboretum, open to the public from March to November. Grassy paths lead through avenues of trees.

BEDALE
Bedale is a typical North Yorkshire market town. Its wide main street has cobbled verges for market-day stalls, and there are fine old houses and shops. At the top of the town is the imposing parish church, dating from Saxon times with architecture of almost every period since. Local people say it was built large enough to hold the entire population of the town when marauding Scots invaded.

Bedale Hall, a classically proportioned country house dating mostly from the mid-18th century, has a great ballroom with a beautifully decorated plaster ceiling. The ballroom and a small local museum are open on Tuesday afternoons in summer.

CONSTABLE BURTON
The gardens of Constable Burton Hall are noted for their alpines, borders and mature trees, and are open daily from spring until autumn. The house, dating from 1768 and designed by John Carr of York – who also designed Harewood House, near Leeds – has some opening days during the summer.

The drive beyond Constable Burton offers glorious views along Wensleydale and into Swaledale.

RICHMOND
The magnificent Norman castle of Richmond, with its mighty keep, suddenly and dramatically comes into view on the approach to the town. The castle was founded by Alan the Red in 1071, and is superbly situated on a crag above the River Swale. It is open daily.

Quiet cobbled ways or wynds lead around the castle into elegant squares or narrow courts. Houses crowd into narrow streets behind the castle, and architectural splendours are to be seen around every corner. There is a local museum in Ryder's Wynd near the castle, open in the afternoons in the summer. And the regimental museum of the Green Howards is in the square in the former crypt of Holy Trinity Church. It is open daily except during December and January. Richmond's Georgian Theatre is the finest example in the United Kingdom of a surviving 18th-century theatre. There are tours of the theatre every afternoon from Monday to Friday, and also on Saturday afternoons in the summer.

Superb riverside and woodland walks lead from Richmond Bridge – upstream through National Trust woodland, and downstream below the castle walls along the riverside to the ruins of the 12th-century Easby Abbey.

Tourist information:
(Knaresborough) Harrogate 866886 (summer); Ripon 4625 (summer); Richmond 3525 (summer).

HIGH CHURCH *The Church of St John overlooks the viaduct over the River Nidd at Knaresborough.*

Green lanes and grey stone in the Dales

TOUR
159

76 MILES

Dramatic waterfalls, caves and cliffs are among the spectacles of the limestone scenery in the Yorkshire Dales National Park. The climax comes in the awesome Malham Cove.

SKIPTON

Two massive round towers, surmounted by the Clifford family motto *Desormais* – 'Henceforth' – guard the entrance to Skipton's castle. The moated fortress, partially destroyed by Cromwell but rebuilt by Lady Anne Clifford in the 1650s, is open daily. It has a 50ft long banqueting hall and a huge kitchen with roasting and baking hearths. A colourful market fills the High Street leading to the castle every day except Tuesday and Thursday. The nearby Craven Museum, open most days, has displays of local history.

KILNSEY

The hamlet grew around a grange of Fountains Abbey on Mastiles Lane – an ancient green road which crosses the fells from the Lake District and Malhamdale, where the abbey had

extensive estates. Mastiles Lane can be followed on foot from Kilnsey, and a fragment of the 13th-century gatehouse belonging to the original grange can still be seen.

At the Trout Farm and Visitor Centre, open daily, fresh trout can be purchased and there are displays of local wildlife.

ARNCLIFFE

The large green around which Arncliffe is built was turned into a defensive stockade against Scottish marauders in the Middle Ages. On a more peaceful note the village provided one of the settings for Charles Kingsley's novel *The Water Babies*, published in 1863. Kingsley sometimes had tea at a friend's house in the village, and he put the river which flowed by the house, the Skirfare, into his book. Nearby the river is joined by the Cowside Beck.

STAINFORTH

This orderly village huddles under the tall grey limestone face of Langcliffe Scar. Nearby is Stainforth Force, a lovely waterfall in a wooded ravine below Stainforth's 17th-century packhorse bridge over the River Ribble. It is reached by a narrow lane off the Horton road.

The stepping stones in the village centre are the start of a longer walk to Catrigg Foss waterfall.

RIBBLEHEAD

A great 24-arch railway viaduct, 1328ft long and 105ft high, towers over Ribblehead, carrying the Settle to Carlisle railway line through a bleak but breathtaking landscape. Directly ahead is Whernside, 2414ft above sea level and the highest of Yorkshire's Three Peaks; to the left is the great ridge of Ingleborough, 2373ft, and along the way is the sphinx-like profile of Pen-y-Ghent, 2277ft.

WHITE SCAR CAVES

The Yorkshire Dales are honeycombed with potholes, caverns and passages. At White Scar Show Cave, open daily, dry walkways lead into floodlit underground passages where dramatic hanging stalactites, rising stalagmites and waterfalls can be seen.

INGLETON

The spectacular waterfalls that cascade near Ingleton can be viewed from carefully constructed walkways. From the village centre a series of signs on the Thornton road lead to the falls, at the entrance to which there is a car park. The walk around the falls takes about 2½ hours.

CLAPHAM

Twin main streets run along each side of a sparkling mountain stream, crossed by stone bridges. At the top of the village is the early 19th-century church with its 15th-century tower.

Reginald Farrer (1880-1920), the explorer, botanist and plant collector, was born in Clapham, and at the National Park Information Centre in the Old Manor House by the village car park leaflets are available describing the Reginald Farrer Trail. This is a 2 mile return walk through Ingleborough Hall grounds.

SETTLE

Pale grey limestone cliffs overlook the stone roofs of this bustling market town. Settle has a handsome square, and a multitude of small courts and alleyways, some of them leading past fine merchants' houses of the 18th and early 19th centuries. The Museum of North Craven life is in Chapel Street.

Settle is an excellent centre for walks. Among the best is the two-hour walk to Victoria Cave, discovered on June 20, 1837 – the day Queen Victoria came to the throne.

SCALEBAR FORCE

At Scalebar, Stockdale Beck cascades down a steep little wooded ravine to form a foaming white torrent of water. Park on the wide verge on the road about 1½ miles from Settle, near Scalebar Bridge, and cross the stile on the right onto the path to the waterfall, about 50yds away.

MALHAM COVE

A vast curving wall of pale limestone, 240ft high, forms the backdrop of Malham Cove. This awe-inspiring

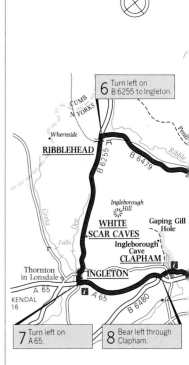

cliff was the result of ancient earth movements along the Craven Fault, when rocks to the north were pushed upwards relative to those to the south. Water once flowed in the valley above the cliff, but now emerges from its foot on its way to the River Aire.

Not far away is Gordale Scar, a dramatic gorge more than 250ft deep, where waterfalls cascade over boulders. Nearby Janet's Foss, another waterfall, rushes over a thick apron of limestone deposit down to a pool.

Walks starting at the National Park Centre in Malham village take about 30 minutes to Malham Cove, 45 minutes to Janet's Foss, and about an hour to Gordale. A walk from Watergate leads to Malham Tarn, now part of a nature reserve. Across the lake is the Malham Tarn Field Centre, where natural history is researched and taught.

TOUR
160

62 MILES

The green splendour of Wharfedale gives way to the bleak beauty of Brontë country. One of England's prettiest roads leads to Bolton Abbey and on to Yorkshire's 'lake district'.

OTLEY

Medieval courts and alleyways lie only yards away from the busy main street and Market Square of this old town. Its history is reflected in the fine part-Norman parish church. In the churchyard is a scale model of Bramhope Tunnel on the nearby Leeds to Harrogate railway line, built as a monument to the 30 men killed in

LITTONDALE SLOPES *A beck tumbles beneath a narrow bridge towards the River Skirfare, and sheep graze the steep sides of Littondale, 4 miles north of Arncliffe.*

BARDEN BRIDGE *High stone arches span the River Wharfe near Barden Tower.*

STEAM DAYS *Vintage engines operate the Keighley and Worth Valley Railway.*

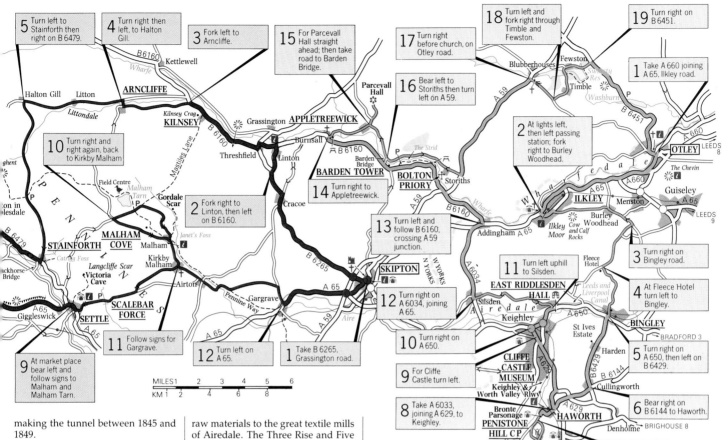

making the tunnel between 1845 and 1849.

Behind the town rises the steep wooded hillside of The Chevin, a forest park with miles of pathways and woodland rides. The walk to the cross on Surprise View takes about 40 minutes, but is rewarded by extensive views across the valley. A visitor centre at the White House has displays on local countryside features.

ILKLEY
An elegant late-Victorian shopping parade leads to tree-lined avenues of grand houses. These recall Ilkley's heyday in the 19th century, when its health-giving springs and fine moorland walks established it as a spa.

The coming of the railways in the 19th century turned Ilkley into a 'retreat' for wealthy Bradford wool merchants and manufacturers. The Elizabethan Manor House Museum – open daily except Mondays – gives a fascinating account of the town's growth since its earliest beginnings as a Roman fort and river crossing.

There is a steep but attractive walk up from the main shopping street, Brook Street, to Ilkley Moor. It is about 30 minutes' walk to White Wells, an 18th-century bathhouse, now restored and open to visitors at weekends and on Bank Holidays.

The song On Ilkla Moor baht 'at tells of the fate of any young man who goes courting on Ilkley Moor 'without a hat' – he will catch a fatal cold. The words, written at the beginning of this century, were set to a well-known hymn tune, Cranbrook.

BINGLEY
Running through this old wool town is the Leeds and Liverpool Canal, which once brought cheap coal and raw materials to the great textile mills of Airedale. The Three Rise and Five Rise 'staircase' locks are a magnificent example of late 18th-century canal engineering. Follow the towpath to the locks from the main car park by the station.

HAWORTH
Outwardly this bleak but dignified moorland village has changed little since the day in 1820 when the Reverend Patrick Brontë brought his wife and six children to live in the Georgian parsonage – now the Brontë Parsonage Museum. Here, three of the Brontë girls, inspired by the austerely beautiful countryside, wrote some of the best-loved English novels: Jane Eyre by Charlotte, Wuthering Heights by Emily, and The Tenant of Wildfell Hall by Anne.

The parsonage, at the top of Haworth's steep and cobbled Main Street, is furnished much as it was in the Brontës' time and contains many family relics. It is open daily except for three weeks in February.

PENISTONE HILL COUNTRY PARK
A stretch of heather moorland is dotted with informal picnic places and marked paths. There are fine views in all directions, and Penistone Hill is a starting point for walks into Brontë country – to the Brontë Waterfalls (about 45 minutes), for instance.

KEIGHLEY AND WORTH VALLEY RAILWAY
The 5 mile single-track railway which runs from Keighley to Oxenhope was closed in 1959 but carefully restored and reopened in 1968.

Vintage steam engines and stations were repainted and its 1950s appearance re-created with contemporary posters and advertisements. With appropriate changes, the railway is often used as a film setting, and among the films made there have been The Railway Children and Yanks.

CLIFFE CASTLE MUSEUM
Originally a Victorian mill-owner's mansion, the museum is set in extensive gardens, with a small aviary. There are displays of local natural history and geology, as well as art treasures and period furniture. It is open daily except Mondays.

EAST RIDDLESDEN HALL
The ornate, Jacobean merchant's manor house, rebuilt in 1628 by James Murgatroyd, a Halifax clothier, has some superb decorations. They include magnificent plaster ceilings and much of the original panelling. There is, reputedly, a ghost. Recently restored by the National Trust, the hall is open on most days in summer.

BOLTON PRIORY
Approaching the village of Bolton Abbey the visitor is aware of coming to a place of great charm. Leave the car in the car park and go through a small gateway in a nearby wall into parkland containing the remains of 12th-century Bolton Priory.

The beautiful location of the priory on a tree-lined bend of the River Wharfe has long attracted artists. Its best-known representation is Bolton Abbey in Olden Times, painted by Sir Edwin Landseer in 1834. The nave and west tower now serve as the parish church, and the gatehouse is a private residence – Bolton Hall.

Close by are the Strid Woods Nature Trails – six clearly marked paths through deciduous woods. Heading north towards Barden Tower, the paths go past a gorge called the Strid, where the Wharfe narrows to become 'stridable', bursting spectacularly through a crevice.

BARDEN TOWER
The ruined, 15th-century tower was once a hunting lodge of the Clifford family, Lords of Skipton. The nearby Priest's House is now a restaurant and artist's studio. A leaflet gives the history of the tower, including its restoration in the 17th century.

APPLETREEWICK
This neatly designed village was once owned by Bolton Priory, and was noted for its onion fair. There are several old merchants' and yeoman farmers' houses and cottages, and two old inns. Just beyond the village is Parcevall Hall, a restored 17th-century house, now an Anglican diocesan house. Its terraced hillside gardens are open to the public in spring and summer.

Tourist information: Skipton 2809 (summer); Horton-in-Ribblesdale 333; Otley 465151; Ilkley 602319; Haworth 42329.

Ridgeways and ruins on the moors

TOUR
161
—— 60 MILES ——

The Hambleton and Cleveland Hills rise at the edge of the North York Moors National Park. Forest hides the ruins of two abbeys, and ancient ridgeways cross the heather-clad summits.

THIRSK

The electrifying atmosphere of a test match at Lord's Cricket Ground in London seems a world apart from this tranquil little North Yorkshire town; but it was in Thirsk in 1755 that Thomas Lord was born, the son of a local labourer. A keen cricketer, Lord leased some ground in Marylebone for the White Conduit Cricket Club, forerunner of the Marylebone Cricket Club; he moved the ground to Regent's Park, and then to its present site in 1814.

Part of the cottage in Kirkgate where Thomas Lord was born is today a museum and tourist information centre.

The old market town with its huge cobbled Market Square and Victorian clock has many fine old coaching inns, recalling the days when Thirsk was a port of call for dozens of stagecoaches on the busy turnpike roads between Scotland and northern England. The imposing, early 15th-century church has among its eight bells a tenor bell dated 1410, older than the church itself, and reputed to have come from Fountains Abbey.

BORROWBY

A long street of red-pantiled cottages, verged by a steep green, climbs a low ridge to the top of the village. Above the village and along the road to Leake there are splendid views across the Vale of Mowbray to the Pennines in the west, and the Hambleton Hills directly ahead.

NETHER AND OVER SILTON

Under the great bulk of Black Hambleton – at more than 1300ft the highest of the Hambleton Hills – are the twin villages of Nether Silton and Over Silton. Between the villages the tiny Norman Church of St Mary, Over Silton, with its low bellcote and curious stepped roof, can be seen across the fields.

A narrow lane off to the right leads to a car park and picnic site hidden in the deep woodland of Cleveland Forest. Paths radiating from the car park offer short, gentle strolls among conifers, oaks and sycamores, while the rambler can enjoy a 4 mile return walk to the summit of Black Hambleton.

MOUNT GRACE PRIORY

One of the finest surviving Carthusian monastic ruins in Britain lies in a beautiful, woodland setting below the escarpment of the Cleveland Hills. Founded in 1398, the priory was the home of Carthusian monks who swore strict vows of silence and seclusion.

The tiny, two-storey cells where the monks lived can still be seen – one of them partially restored – with their own secluded gardens. Each has its own water supply and ingeniously designed serving hatches allowing food to be placed there by lay brothers without even a hand being seen. Between the cells and cloisters are the remains of a small church.

Mount Grace Priory is open daily.

OSMOTHERLEY

This old village on the edge of the Cleveland Hills was once an important market centre, close to the main roads and trackways. The old market cross still survives in the centre of the village, together with a remarkable five-legged stone table, presumably a market stall, from which John Wesley is reputed to have preached. One of the country's first Methodist chapels, dating from 1754, was built in Osmotherley, while the parish church of St Peter has Anglo-Saxon fragments and a great deal of medieval work.

SCARTH GAP

A natural gap or 'nick' through the hills, originally caused by glacial meltwater, carries the Hambleton Drove Road and other ancient roads and trackways across the edge of the Cleveland escarpment. The views from the summit of the pass are superb, across the Vale of Mowbray to Teesside.

On the open moorland of Scarth Wood Moor are a number of Bronze Age burial mounds and some ancient stone walls. The moor, which is owned by the National Trust, is also the starting point of the 39 mile Lyke Wake Walk across the North York Moors to the coast at Ravenscar.

WHORLTON

A magnificent castle gateway, the ruins of a church and a couple of farms are all that remain of one of Yorkshire's forgotten villages. Whorlton, once an important community, vanished long ago, its inhabitants perhaps victims of a medieval plague.

The castle was built by a Norman lord, Robert de Meynell. The gatehouse which survives dates from around 1400 and has over its gateway

GLORY IN STONE *The lovely vale of Rye Dale is a perfect setting for the mellowed walls of Rievaulx Abbey.*

GATEWAY TO NOWHERE *On the edge of moorland at Whorlton an imposing gatehouse is all that remains of a Norman castle that once covered 2½ acres.*

MOUNT GRACE *A church tower dominates the ruined priory.*

the carved shields of the Meynell, Darcy and Grey families. The church is an eerie part-ruin, reached along an avenue of yew trees through a graveyard which has remained in use over the centuries. Only the chancel and bell tower remain, separated by the arches of a ruined nave.

CARLTON IN CLEVELAND
The twin summits of Carlton Bank and Cringle Moor form a spectacular backcloth to a village whose fine cottages and houses include a Palladian style manor house dating from the mid-18th century. The Church of St Botolph was designed by the Victorian architect Temple Moore, in 14th-century Gothic style. It has an imposing lich gate.

The drive over Carlton Bank to Chop Gate affords glorious views across to the pointed summit of Roseberry Topping. The hillsides are pitted with the remains of alum mines. Alum was extensively used in the dyeing industry, and the stream which runs through Carlton village is still called Alum Beck. Farther east, the road offers panoramic views into Bilsdale.

From the car park below Chop Gate village there are attractive walks onto nearby moorland ridges or 'riggs'. Many of these are dotted with Bronze Age 'howes' or cairns, being burial mounds or ritual sites often set at the highest point of a moorland ridge.

NEWGATE BANK
From this Forestry Commission picnic site overlooking the top end of Rye Dale there are spectacular views across to the village of Hawnby. Pleasant walks through the Hambleton Forest from the car park and picnic site include a level track along the edge of Rievaulx Moor.

RIEVAULX TERRACE
A level lawn about half a mile long occupies the summit of the hilltop above Rievaulx Abbey and offers dramatic views over the abbey ruins. The terrace was laid out in 1758 by Thomas Duncombe, who may have intended to link it by carriageway to the grounds of his home at Duncombe Park, 3 miles away.

At each end of the terrace are temples in the classical style. The elegant Ionic temple, nearer the car park, has a superb painted ceiling depicting scenes from Greek mythology by the Italian artist Giuseppe Borgnis. At the other end the beautiful round Tuscan temple has a painted ceiling attributed to Andrea Casali, surrounded by magnificent plasterwork, and a medieval mosaic floor. The temples, which may have been built to designs by Sir John Vanbrugh, are connected by a winding footpath.

Rievaulx Terrace is owned by the National Trust and open daily from April to October.

RIEVAULX ABBEY
The road through the village of Rievaulx to Rievaulx Abbey is like a descent into an enchanted garden. The magnificent ruins of the abbey stand in a steep, richly wooded valley close to a serpentine river, and the

soaring beauty of the abbey's 13th-century Gothic arches is awe-inspiring. Little wonder the poet William Cowper said he wished he could live in the shadow of Rievaulx for ever.

The imposing arches contrast with the simple and austere late-Norman columns which date back to the founding of the abbey in 1131 by Walter l'Espec, a Helmsley noble. The abbey grew rapidly in wealth and influence to become one of the most important Cistercian houses in the north of England.

In its heyday in the late 12th century, under the rule of Abbot Ailred, it had a complement of 140 monks and 500 lay brothers, many of whom would have been involved in completing this architectural masterpiece. After the Dissolution, when many monasteries were plundered for building stone, Rievaulx Abbey survived remarkably intact.

There is evidence that the monks were also ironmasters, and developed small furnaces to work local ironstone. An early watercourse for a water wheel survives. Rievaulx Abbey is open daily.

Rievaulx Bridge, crossed on the route soon after leaving the abbey, is a fine 18th-century structure.

OLD BYLAND
There are impressive views across Rye Dale from the road between Rievaulx and Old Byland. The name recalls the fact that the monks from Furness who founded Byland Abbey, 4 miles away, came here before moving to the site where they chose to

build. The village has a broad, quiet green and a church containing some fascinating Norman winged dragons around the porch entrance.

In the eastern wall of the church tower is a carved sundial dating back to the Anglo-Danish period, which has been inserted in the wall upside down. It is inscribed in a curious and barely decipherable mixture of Anglo-Saxon and Latin – *Sumorlidan Huscarl me fecit*, which probably means 'Sumorlida the Huscarl made me'. A huscarl was a servant or bodyguard to Anglo-Saxon kings or nobles.

Old Byland is situated on a low ridge between two steep, wooded valleys, Caydale and Nettle Dale, both offering opportunities for pleasant circular walks.

HAMBLETON DROVE ROAD
Two miles beyond Old Byland the route joins one of the most remarkable prehistoric ridgeways in the north of England. The Hambleton Drove Road runs in a fairly straight line along the summits of the Hambleton Hills; men and their beasts were constantly passing along it at a time when the Great North Road was a mere track. Even into the 19th century drovers continued to use the ridgeway with their herds of sheep and cattle to avoid paying tolls on the busy turnpike roads in the

valley. Drovers from as far away as Scotland used it to bring their cattle to the markets of York and Malton, and to Hull where the cattle were sold for ships' provisions.

For much of its length the drove road remains as a rough track or green way across the hills, but short sections are followed by modern roads such as the one used on this route.

BOLTBY
Stone-built houses with pantiled roofs blend into the green hillside, and villagers have added to the effect of harmony with the landscape with strands of rambling roses that wind up every wallside. The church looks medieval, but is a skilful Victorian imitation.

FELIXKIRK
Another attractive winding lane leads to Felixkirk, passing the imposing entrance to Mount St John, a fine 18th-century house set in parkland sheltered by the hills behind. The village church, one of the very few in England dedicated to St Felix, dates from Norman times. Though largely rebuilt more than a century ago, some Norman carving and medieval effigies survive.

Tourist information: Thirsk 22755 (summer).

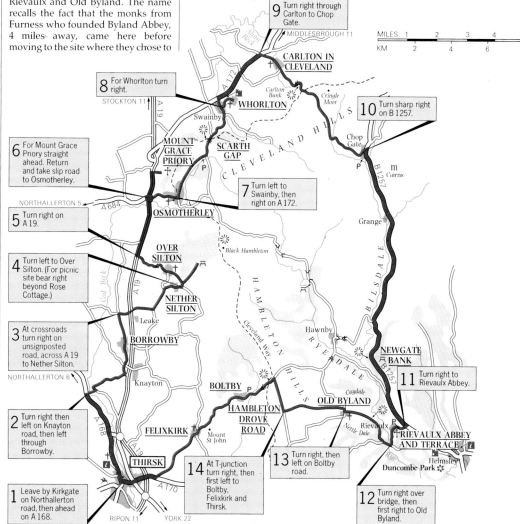

Chalk cliffs edging the Yorkshire Wolds

The North Sea pounds the cliffs between Filey and Bridlington, where Vikings invaded in the 9th century. Behind lies the farmland of the wolds, where a 'lost' medieval village hides.

FILEY

The stony finger of Filey Brigg forms a natural breakwater sheltering Filey Bay from the full fury of the North Sea and protecting the fishing cobles drawn up on Coble Landing, at the north end of the bay. Filey is a cosily genteel, largely Victorian resort. Below its handsome seaside terraces, attractive gardens lead down to a wide beach, framed by red-clay cliffs. There is easy walking at low tide round to the Brigg.

In Queen Street is the Folk Museum, in a house with the date 1696 above the door. The ground floor has a show of lifeboat equipment, while upstairs are displays depicting Filey's past.

Apart from Coble Landing, the chief survivor of bygone Filey is the partly Norman St Oswald's Church, on the northern edge of the town. Nearby, a wide sweep of grassland on top of the Brigg has been turned into a country park, with a mile-long nature trail and the site of a Roman signal station. A guide to the trail is available at the Tourist Information Centre in John Street.

BEMPTON CLIFFS

Viewing platforms take birdwatchers to the edge of sheer 400ft high cliffs. Here, thousands of sea birds squabble by their nests on the narrow ledges, or hurtle into the sea for fish.

Bempton is especially noted for its gannetry. Gannets first colonised the cliffs in the late 1920s, and more than 500 pairs now breed there.

For those who want a gentle walk with splendid sea views – as well as the chance to get close to the sea birds – there are footpaths along the cliffs westwards to Speeton and south-east to Flamborough Head.

FLAMBOROUGH HEAD

At Flamborough the chalk wolds fall into the sea in a series of dramatic cliffs. Above them is a broad expanse of turf which is ideal for picnicking.

In Flamborough village the tower of the partly medieval St Oswald's Church has a fine carving of St Oswald, the patron saint of fishermen. The tiny natural harbour at North Landing, with its crystal-clear water, shelters a small fleet of cobles which are hauled up the steep shore by a winch. From the grassland above North Landing there is a pretty cliff-top walk to the lighthouse at the end of the Head.

DANES DYKE

This deep, tree-covered ravine stretches for 2½ miles across Flamborough Head, for which it once served as a defence. It runs across farmland near Bempton, on the road from Filey to Flamborough; but the best place to see it is between Flam-borough and Sewerby. There it can be explored along a well-marked nature trail, 1¼ miles long, reached by a made-up road on the left.

The dyke's name is misleading, as it was already long in existence when the Danes landed in the 9th century. It probably dates from the Bronze Age or even late Stone Age times.

SEWERBY HALL

Standing in some 50 acres of wooded parkland, this handsome mansion has an unbroken view across the blue waters of Bridlington Bay. Apart from its beautiful setting, Sewerby has a zoo, and a museum and art gallery. Wide lawns on the seaward side look down the coast to Bridlington sands.

The house is a classical Georgian building, enlarged in Regency and Victorian times. As well as its collection of local paintings and its historical displays, it has a room of photographs, trophies and mementos of Amy Johnson, the Yorkshire aviation pioneer.

In 1930 she became the first woman to fly solo from England to Australia, for which she was made a CBE, and followed this with several epic flights to Japan, South Africa, India and the USA. She formally opened the hall and park to the public in June 1936.

The park is open daily, and the hall is open daily in summer.

BRIDLINGTON

The cheerful seafront centres on a busy harbour, where cobles and slightly larger keelboats unload their catches alongside trawlers. On either side are the Victorian terraces and more recent seafront houses of this lively resort.

Old Bridlington lies a mile or so inland, built at a safe distance from the sea in the days when pirate raids were common. At its heart is the Augustinian Priory Church of St Mary, with its twin towers, one tall and gracefully pinnacled, the other shorter and flat-topped. The towers and the magnificent nave and aisles are all that are left of the original building, destroyed in the late 1530s, after Henry VIII dissolved the monasteries.

Outside the church the medieval gatehouse, known as 'The Bayle', is now a local history museum, open in summer on Tuesday, Wednesday and Thursday afternoons.

BOYNTON

In this pretty little wolds village, a street of white-painted cottages leads down to the splendid parkland of Boynton Hall. The house, which dates mostly from about 1730, is not open to the public but can be seen from a footpath.

At the gates of the hall stands the Church of St Andrew, rebuilt in the late 1760s. Its somewhat plain outside belies an ornate interior, the highlight of which is the elaborate chancel arch. The chancel itself is full of monuments, large stone coffins and pillars. The lectern carries a wood-carved turkey, commemorating the introduction of the turkey to England by the Stricklands of Boynton Hall.

RUDSTON

Christian and pagan monuments exist only a few yards apart in the churchyard of All Saints' Church. There, looming over the gravestones, is one of Britain's largest standing stones which was set up and worshipped by prehistoric man. The stone is more than 25ft tall, almost 6ft wide and weighs about 46 tons. It probably came from the gritstone rocks at Cayton Bay, 10 miles away, and was hauled across the countryside to its site. The village's name comes from 'rood-stone', which suggests that the standing stone may have had a rood or cross fixed to it when Christianity first came to Yorkshire.

The village stream, called Gypsey Race, is also known as 'Woe Waters': it is said to reach full spate before a national disaster.

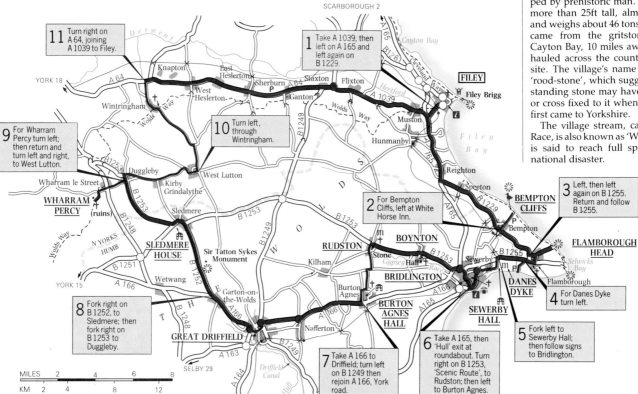

SELWICKS BAY *Chalk cliffs 150ft high have been fretted and eroded by wind and waves into fantastically shaped caves along the coast north-west from Flamborough Head*

BOYNTON CHURCH *The lectern commemorates England's first turkey.*

BURTON AGNES HALL *This beautiful red-brick mansion basks in a tranquil setting of lawns, clipped yews, statues and an ornamental pool. According to tradition, James I stayed in the King's Bedroom (left) on the way to his coronation.*

BURTON AGNES HALL

This gem of an Elizabethan country house is ornate on the outside and lavishly furnished within. It basks in a tranquil setting of lawns, clipped yews and statues.

It was built by Robert Smithson, Elizabeth I's master mason, who also designed Longleat House in Wiltshire and Hardwick Hall in Derbyshire. The house has an imposing turreted gatehouse and entrance front, with four projecting window bays.

Inside there is a wealth of elaborate Elizabethan carving, in wood and stone, and a wide and lavishly carved staircase links the floors through a tall narrow well. There is also an outstanding collection of French Impressionist and modern paintings – including works by Renoir, Pissarro, Utrillo, Gauguin and Augustus John. The hall is open daily from April to October.

GREAT DRIFFIELD

A lively jumble of a market town, Driffield calls itself the 'Capital of the Wolds'. Its long main street, Middle Street, has an extensive cattle market every Thursday.

The parish church of All Saints has a magnificent 15th-century tower, 110ft high and visible for miles around. Its stonework has twice started to crumble and it has twice been restored – in the late 19th century and in the 1960s.

SLEDMERE HOUSE

This grey stone classical mansion, set above terraces of lawn with rolling parkland beyond, was designed and built by Sir Christopher Sykes in the late 18th century. He employed Capability Brown to lay out 2000 acres of parkland and gardens.

The house has a magnificent library-cum-gallery 100ft long, while the Turkish Room, its walls covered in blue and red decorated tiles, is a copy of one of the sultan's apartments in the Valideh Mosque, Istanbul.

WHARRAM PERCY

In a hidden valley of the wolds lies one of the most haunting of England's lost villages. The road to it ends at the foot of a wooded hill, and after a 15 minute walk uphill the land opens out to reveal the sole remaining building – a ruined church, with a shattered tower.

Wharram Percy was the victim of wolds landlords who, at the end of the 15th century, turned from arable to sheep farming – which needed a much smaller work force. As a result, whole villages became deserted. Excavations are being carried out on 15th-century cottages and other buildings, and the various sites are clearly marked.

Tourist information: Filey 512204 (summer); Bridlington 673474/679626; Driffield 47644.

Valleys below the North York Moors

TOUR
163

—— 49 MILES ——

Below the windswept high moors, villages in the Esk valley are linked by steep, narrow roads. In the 1830s George Stephenson built a railway across the moors, and much of it has been restored.

WHITBY
Split into two halves by the River Esk, old Whitby has hardly changed since Captain Cook learnt seamanship in the town, or since the imagination of the author Bram Stoker let Dracula loose in its streets.

The first thing any visitor should do is to climb the 199 steps to St Mary's churchyard, from which the whole of Whitby can be surveyed. Inland, the Esk winds away to the south; across the harbour are the elegant terraces of West Cliff, with the statue of Captain Cook near an archway formed of a whale's jawbone; and down below are the tiled houses and jumble of narrow streets that make Whitby a delightful place to wander about in.

Over the churchyard wall are the ancient ruins of Whitby Abbey, which date mainly from the 13th century. The abbey's battered walls and lofty window arches form the principal landmark in the town.

GOATHLAND
Black-faced Swaledale sheep crop the wide grass verges of this moorland village to the texture of a lawn. Though dating from the 12th century, its name may have been of Norse origin, few of its buildings date from earlier than the 19th century. The stone-flagged causeway beside the road, however, is thought to be 17th century.

Goathland is the centre for walks through an entrancing countryside of sheep-cropped turf, wooded valleys and open moorland. About a mile north-west of the village the pretty hamlet of Beck Hole is tucked away in a hollow.

MALLYAN SPOUT
At Mallyan a tributary of the Esk cascades over a lip of rock to form a waterfall 70ft high, reached after a 20 minute walk down a steep, rough track that starts beside the wall of the Mallyan Hotel. The waterfall is spectacular after a downpour.

Half a mile farther on, a turning marked 'Roman Road' leads to a small car park from which a 30 minute walk across moorland leads to a well-preserved stretch of Roman road.

ESKDALE
Grassy banks slope gently down to the River Esk as it ripples along its stony bed. Past the village of Egton Bridge, the road keeps close to the river; at Glaisdale a superb packhorse bridge, still with its cobbles, crosses the Esk just by the railway bridge; and at Lealholm there are stepping stones across the river.

DANBY
South of the village the 14th-century Danby Castle has been converted into a private farmhouse, which can be viewed on application to the owner. Danby Castle is said to have been the home of Catherine Parr, and according to tradition Henry VIII courted her there before she became his sixth and last wife.

From the castle the road climbs to Danby Rigg, a magnificent expanse of heather-covered moorland, dotted with small prehistoric standing stones, and giving wide views of the Esk and its tributary valleys.

The Danby Lodge Moors Centre, just east of the village, offers a wealth of information about the North York Moors National Park. The centre is housed in a fine old stone-built shooting lodge beside the Esk and has an exhibition of the National Park's geology, archaeology, history, land use and natural history.

GROSMONT
This hillside village is the northern terminus of the 18 miles long North Yorkshire Moors Railway. One of the world's earliest lines, it was built by George Stephenson in the 1830s as a link between the port of Whitby and the farmland of the Vale of Pickering. Closed by British Rail in 1965, it was reopened in 1973 as a private railway.

From the Grosmont railway station car park an easy walk leads to the locomotive sheds, which are full of steam engines and carriages dating back to the 1890s. A 3 mile Historical Railway Trail between Grosmont and Goathland follows the track bed of the original line, which included the steep Beck Hole incline. It is walked in one direction, taking a train back.

<u>Tourist information:</u> Whitby 602674; (Danby) Castleton 60654 (summer).

TOUR
164

—— 75 MILES ——

More than 500 square miles of moors, purple with heather in the late summer, are bounded by the Vale of Pickering to the south and the Hambleton and Cleveland Hills to the west.

SCARBOROUGH
Still Yorkshire's favourite seaside 'lung', Scarborough developed as a resort in the 17th century – well before Brighton began to lure wealthy visitors with promises of cures from seawater. Behind the seafront, the narrow streets of old Scarborough rise to the walls of the castle, whose massive keep dominates the sandy bays to north and south.

The churchyard of St Mary's Church looks over a harbour crowded with fishing cobles and yachts.

HOLE OF HORCUM *A legend tells how the Devil gouged out this huge natural amphitheatre, 1 mile wide, beside the high moorland road from Pickering to Whitby.*

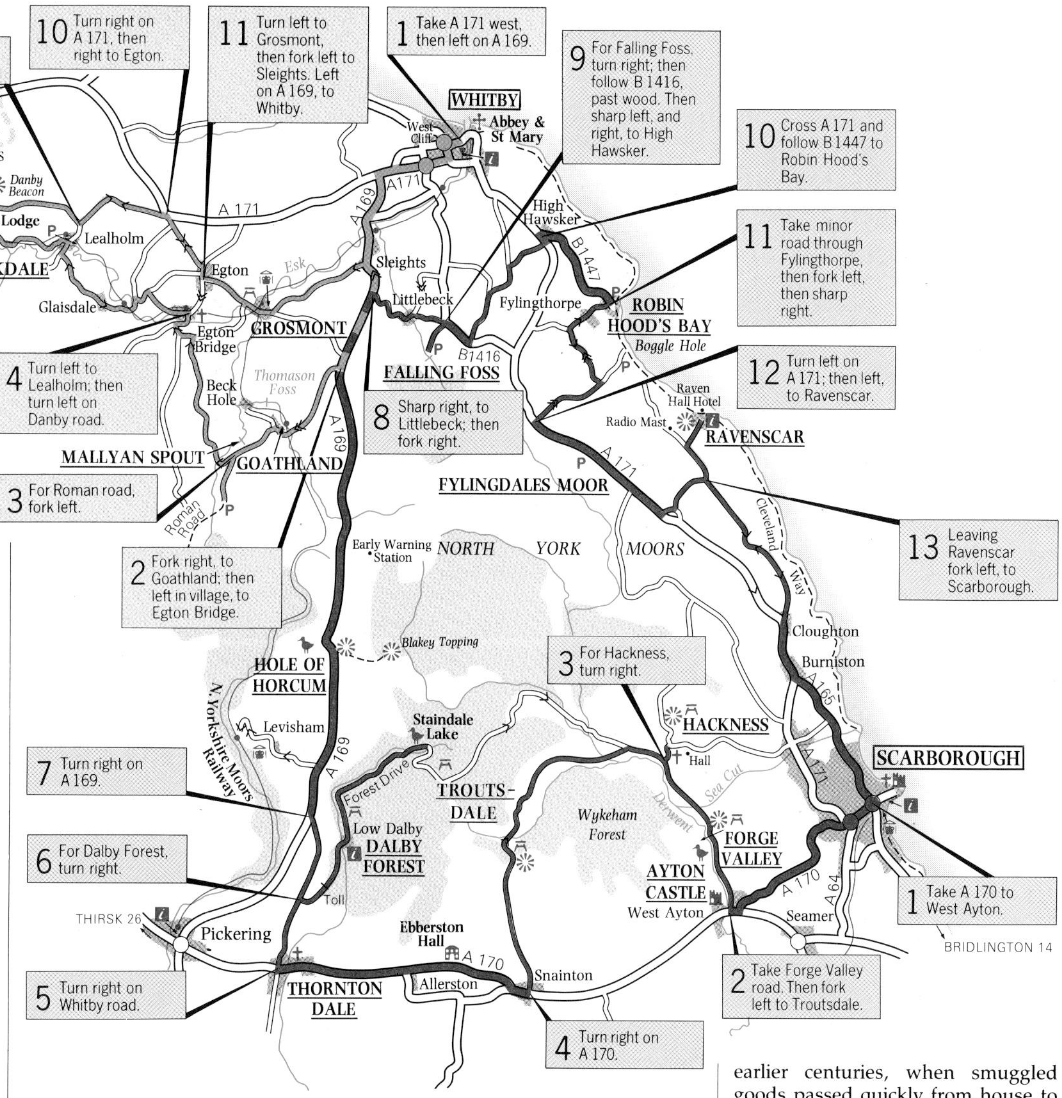

1 Take A 171 west, then left on A 169.
2 Fork right, to Goathland; then left in village, to Egton Bridge.
3 For Roman road, fork left.
4 Turn left to Lealholm; then turn left on Danby road.
5 Fork left before railway bridge, then left up lane, to Danby.
6 For Danby Rigg, turn left.
7 Turn right to Moors Centre.
8 For Danby Beacon, turn left.
9 Turn left on Whitby road.
10 Turn right on A 171, then right to Egton.
11 Turn left to Grosmont, then fork left to Sleights. Left on A 169, to Whitby.
1 Take A 170 to West Ayton.
2 Take Forge Valley road. Then fork left to Troutsdale.
3 For Hackness, turn right.
4 Turn right on A 170.
5 Turn right on Whitby road.
6 For Dalby Forest, turn right.
7 Turn right on A 169.
8 Sharp right, to Littlebeck; then fork right.
9 For Falling Foss, turn right; then follow B 1416, past wood. Then sharp left, and right, to High Hawsker.
10 Cross A 171 and follow B 1447 to Robin Hood's Bay.
11 Take minor road through Fylingthorpe, then fork left, then sharp right.
12 Turn left on A 171; then left, to Ravenscar.
13 Leaving Ravenscar fork left, to Scarborough.
MIDDLESBROUGH 15
WHITBY
Abbey & St Mary
West Cliff
DANBY
Danby Lodge
Danby Beacon
Lealholm
ESKDALE
Glaisdale
Danby Rigg
Egton
Egton Bridge
GROSMONT
Sleights
Littlebeck
Fylingthorpe
High Hawsker
ROBIN HOOD'S BAY
Boggle Hole
FALLING FOSS
Raven Hall Hotel
Radio Mast
RAVENSCAR
Thomason Foss
Beck Hole
MALLYAN SPOUT
GOATHLAND
FYLINGDALES MOOR
Roman Road
Early Warning Station
NORTH YORK MOORS
Cleveland Way
Cloughton
Burniston
Blakey Topping
HOLE OF HORCUM
N. Yorkshire Moors Railway
Levisham
Staindale Lake
Forest Drive
TROUTSDALE
HACKNESS
Hall
Sea Cut
SCARBOROUGH
Low Dalby
DALBY FOREST
Wykeham Forest
Derwent
FORGE VALLEY
AYTON CASTLE
West Ayton
Toll
THIRSK 26
Pickering
Ebberston Hall
Seamer
BRIDLINGTON 14
THORNTON DALE
Allerston
Snainton
MILES 1 2 3 4 5 6
KM 1 2 4 6 8

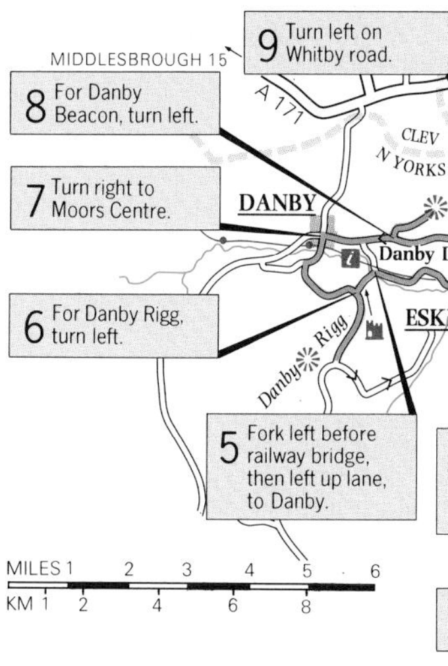

AYTON CASTLE

Opposite the Forge Valley Inn in West Ayton, a turn-off from the main road leads up to the remains of Ayton Castle. All that is left standing is the base of a fortified medieval tower, built like a Scottish peel tower both as a house and as a fortress strong enough to give protection against marauders coming by land or sea.

An unusual form of dual carriageway crosses the River Derwent in West Ayton, with the old stone bridge taking eastbound traffic, and the modern bridge the westbound.

FORGE VALLEY

The Derwent runs bubbling down this idyllic valley, with paddling places shaded by cool trees. Forge Valley takes its name from a now-vanished forge which once stood halfway along the valley. Forge Valley Woods are a small remnant of the prehistoric forest that once covered most of Britain.

HACKNESS

The Derwent valley opens out into rich cornland, where the road crosses Sea Cut – a 5 mile long channel dug between 1800 and 1810 from the Derwent to the sea north of Scarborough, to divert flood water from Forge Valley and the Vale of Pickering.

The Georgian Hackness Hall is visible through the trees to the right of the road. Hackness was the site of a monastery in Saxon times, and its much-restored medieval church has fragments of an 8th-century cross.

TROUTSDALE

The road twists up through the steep valley of Troutsdale Beck, with the conifers of Wykeham Forest rising on the left. A viewpoint marks the summit of the climb, and beyond it the moors fall away in a regular series of flat plates or 'tables', from which they get their name of 'Tabular Hills'.

THORNTON DALE

The southern edge of the moors rises steeply to the right, with the fertile lowlands of the Vale of Pickering spreading to the left. The road then leads gently down into the village of Thornton Dale, between stone-built houses with red-tiled roofs, and past the small medieval church with its pinnacled tower. At the village centre, Thornton Beck runs beside the road.

DALBY FOREST

Cars are not allowed into the tranquil Forestry Commission village of Low Dalby. It is set on the edge of Dalby Forest, rich in conifers, with a 'forest drive' of 9 miles from the tollgate at its south-western corner, to a point near Hackness on its eastern edge. A 3 mile drive through the forest brings visitors to the open space round Staindale Lake – a peaceful stretch of water with picnic tables at its edge.

An excellent visitor centre in Low Dalby has exhibits of wildlife and vegetation in the forest, including woodland sounds such as barking deer, thumping rabbits and drumming woodpeckers.

HOLE OF HORCUM

This spectacular amphitheatre, gouged in the heather-covered moorland, was created in remote geological time by spring water eroding the limestone above deeper levels of clay. According to legend, the Hole was excavated either by the Devil or by a giant named Wade who haunted the Cleveland Hills. After he had scooped out the Hole, the giant hurled the rocks more than a mile to the east, where they landed to form the outcrop known as Blakey Topping.

FYLINGDALES MOOR

From Horcum the road descends steeply, then climbs again to open, wild moorland, where the white radomes of the Fylingdales RAF early warning station burst into view. These three giant 'golf balls', 140ft in diameter, dominate the bleak landscape like abstract works of modern sculpture.

FALLING FOSS

This delightful waterfall, about 30ft high, is easier to hear than to see, as it lies among trees and shrubs that allow only occasional glimpses of its tumbling waters. From the Forestry Commission car park a track leads steeply down through oak, beech and sycamore to the waterfall.

ROBIN HOOD'S BAY

Tall, narrow houses, many of them colour-washed in pink, yellow or sky blue, crowd down the steep hill to a tiny inlet, where fishing cobles are drawn up onto the slipway with lobster pots beside them.

Though it seems unlikely that Robin Hood ever came to the port, it certainly saw plenty of lawlessness in earlier centuries, when smuggled goods passed quickly from house to house unseen by the excisemen.

South of Robin Hood's Bay a short walk along the Cleveland Way leads down to a cleft in the cliffs known as Boggle Hole. A youth hostel – a converted 19th-century mill house, with sash windows and slate roof – is tucked away by the sea. Boggle Hole can be reached by car by turning off the route beyond Fylingthorpe, on a road marked 'Beach Only'.

RAVENSCAR

The road that leads down to the Raven Hall Hotel gives a magnificent view northwards round the sweep of Robin Hood's Bay. A mile of this coast and cliff was acquired by the National Trust as the first purchase of its Enterprise Neptune campaign to safeguard the coastline, and the information centre at Ravenscar sells a 'geological trail' guide to the rock formations of the area.

A little way west of the village are the spoil heaps of an open-cast mine where alum-bearing rock was dug from the 17th century to the mid-19th century. Alum was used in all sorts of industrial processes, from dyeing wool to making Epsom salts.

Tourist information: Scarborough 372261/373333; Pickering 73791 (summer).

Water and stone in the eastern Dales

TOUR

165

—— 91 MILES ——

Winding roads meander through Pennine foothills, past ruined abbeys and a castle where a queen was imprisoned. From moorland passes there are broad views of the green Dales.

LEYBURN
Georgian shops and old inns surround Leyburn's market square, which is thronged with dalesfolk from miles around on Friday, market day. In summer a mobile information centre is parked near the ancient Market Hall. From there a five-minute walk leads to Leyburn Shawl, a long limestone ridge capped with tall pines. Its name may come from the Viking *scale* or *shiel*, meaning 'summer dwelling', and it overlooks all of Wensleydale.

A path about a mile long runs across the Shawl. According to tradition it was there, at Queen's Gap, that Mary, Queen of Scots was recaptured after escaping from Bolton Castle.

BOLTON CASTLE
Ravens swoop around the flower-hung battlements of this partly ruined castle, in which Mary, Queen of Scots was held prisoner for seven months in 1568-9. Built in the late 14th century, the castle was said to be impregnable and escape-proof – and its walls were supposed to have had ox blood mixed with the mortar to give extra strength. Despite this, Mary – who had been imprisoned by her cousin, Elizabeth I – is said to have escaped through one of the castle windows. However, she was soon caught.

The castle is open to the public every day except Monday, and there is a restaurant in the original banqueting hall. To avoid confusion, the nearby estate village is named Castle Bolton. It has a beautiful medieval church which often houses exhibitions.

AYSGARTH FALLS
Turbulent, tumbling cascades of the River Ure roar through a tree-lined gorge. There are three falls: Upper Falls, visible from the old bridge on the road, and the Middle and Lower Falls which can only be seen by taking the footpath to viewing platforms, well signposted from the car park.

Allow a good hour to see all three falls, which are at their best when the River Ure is in spate. But call first at the National Park Centre where displays show the remarkable rock formations of the falls.

Just past the centre on the left is Aysgarth Mill, a huge, former cotton mill which is now the Yorkshire Dales Carriage Museum. It houses elegant, gentlemen's carriages and coaches, a stagecoach, and farm wagons which once bounced and trundled along the Dales' roads. The museum is open at weekends and daily in the summer.

WEST BURTON
The narrow lane from the main road suddenly opens onto a broad village green and the tranquil beauty of West Burton, set at the foot of high fells. The unusual 19th-century village cross, pointed like a steeple, makes an immediate focal point. On the left, at the entrance to the village, a short path leads behind the site of the old mill to a waterfall crashing through a rocky ravine, the water churned creamy-white after rain.

The journey from West Burton to Kettlewell in Wharfedale crosses Kidstones Pass. From its summit there are breathtaking views across

the head of Bishopdale to Buckden Pike, on the left, and down into deep green Wharfedale flanked by steep-sided fells.

KETTLEWELL
Dark-grey cottages cluster around little Cam Beck, a tributary of the Wharfe as it plunges down from Great Whernside. Behind the village, pale-green pastures contrast with the grey stone of cottages and church. It is difficult to imagine that many of these cottages, with their immaculate lane-side or beckside gardens, were once lead-miners' cottages, or that the hillsides and gullies were once mined.

The village is an excellent centre for walks. For example, part of the lengthy Dales Way, which links Ilkley and Windermere, can be followed north to Starbotton or Buckden – 4 miles away. A more strenuous walk is up the steep path over Old Cote Moor to Arncliffe in Littondale, returning through Hawkswick, a route offering breathtaking views throughout.

GRASSINGTON
The narrow entrance to the main cobbled square gives this former lead-mining town an intimate, enclosed feeling. Traditional Dales cottages and 18th-century houses and shops are bright with hanging flower baskets in summer. Less obvious are the little 'folds' or courtyards that open out from the square and main street.

KISSING CHAIR *The northernmost of the weather-sculptured Brimham Rocks overlooks Nidderdale.*

ABBEY OF CHEESE *In the Middle Ages, Jervaulx Abbey was noted for the making of Wensleydale cheese.*

AYSGARTH MIDDLE FALLS *Crashing over great limestone steps, the falls are flanked by bushes and trees.*

In these were the homes of lead miners, which have now been converted into weekend cottages and holiday homes.

One cottage in the square houses the Upper Wharfedale Museum, packed with Dales bygones and relics of farming, crafts and domestic life. Most of the collection has come from local farmhouses.

A car park and picnic area on the Pateley Bridge road, next to the National Park Centre, is the starting point of a walk to Linton Falls on the River Wharfe. Go through the gate at the far end of the car park and follow the enclosed path to the riverside. Beyond the falls, proceed along the footpath to the road, and then turn left to a little Norman church which serves a number of scattered parishes in Upper Wharfedale.

Leaflets describing walks in the area, and a local footpath map, are available at the National Park Centre.

STUMP CROSS CAVERNS
The road from Grassington to Stump Cross and Greenhow climbs through a wild, bleak landscape with the occasional isolated farmhouse or the remains of an old mine – the only signs of man's hand. Stump Cross was named after an eroded medieval cross, now long vanished, on the ancient monastic road between Malham and Fountains Abbey.

The Show Cave at Stump Cross has a visitor centre with exhibitions and a video film about the caves, in which recent finds include the bones of prehistoric bears, hyenas and wolverines. A path leads through the cavern, which is richly decorated with stalactites and stalagmites. One formation, called The Sentinel, is 9ft 6in high and estimated to be at least 200,000 years old. The caverns are open daily from Easter to November, and on Sunday in the winter – weather permitting.

GOUTHWAITE RESERVOIR
Created by the flooding of a valley in 1901, this huge man-made lake, covering a hamlet and the site of an Elizabethan house, now forms a fine bird sanctuary.

At the head of the reservoir is the village of Ramsgill, where an ivy-covered inn overlooks a close-cropped village green whose huge trees give an impression of complete rural seclusion. The village stands on the site of a grange of nearby Byland Abbey.

PATELEY BRIDGE
Pretty cottages and even the more modern houses terracing the steep hillside give Pateley Bridge an almost Mediterranean flavour – especially in summer when almost every doorway and wall overflows with flowers. The little town is the 'capital' of Nidderdale, and its old workhouse is now the Upper Nidderdale Museum. This remarkable treasure house gives an insight into many aspects of 19th-century farming, and industrial and domestic life in the Dales. The museum, opposite the church, is open daily in summer and on Sunday afternoons in winter.

For a short but rewarding walk from the town centre, follow the Ripon road up the main street, bearing left then turning left up some steps marked Panorama Walk. An enclosed way soon gives extensive views across the dale, and leads through a kissing gate into the melancholy ruins of Old St Mary's Church. There are also riverside walks upstream and downstream along the Nidd.

BRIMHAM ROCKS
Worn by the wind and the rain into a variety of fantastic shapes, Brimham Rocks have been given equally fanciful nicknames. They include the Sphinx, the Blacksmith and his Anvil, the Baboon's Head, the Dancing Bear, the Druid's Cave, the Druid's Writing Desk, the Kissing Chair and the Indian's Turban.

The sandstone rocks, formed 300 million years ago, assumed their present shapes after long exposure to the elements, and their deep vertical cracks were caused by repeated attacks of biting frosts.

People began to visit Brimham Rocks in the 18th century, when a legend arose that they had been carved by the Druids – hence some of the nicknames. The rocks rise high above the surrounding heather-clad moors, and on clear days the views from them extend across the Vale of York to the North York Moors, and to the River Humber. There are several

marked paths among the rocks, and an information centre beside the rock called the Crocodile has displays on the local geology. The site, owned by the National Trust, is open daily.

FOUNTAINS ABBEY
The great tower and soaring 13th-century arches on the banks of the River Skell make Fountains Abbey the largest and finest monastic ruin in Britain. The superbly landscaped gardens of Studley Royal, laid out in 1720, are a continuation of the abbey grounds.

By the abbey gates stands the elegant Fountains Hall, built in the early 17th century with stone taken from the abbey. The hall has an exhibition and video film about the estate. Allow at least 1½ hours to explore the abbey and gardens from the Western Gate. There is also a 400 acre deer park. Owned by the National Trust, Fountains Abbey and Studley Royal are open daily.

JERVAULX ABBEY
This little abbey won a small but dramatic place in English history when its abbot, Adam Sedbergh, was involved in the so-called 'Pilgrimage of Grace' – an unsuccessful rebellion against Henry VIII. Before being hanged at Tyburn, the abbot was clapped in the Tower of London, where his name and year of imprisonment – Adam Sedber Abas Jarvall

1537 – are still carved on a wall there.

Originally founded by the short-lived Savigniac Order of monks – who moved here from Fors, in Upper Wensleydale, in 1156 – Jervaulx soon came under the jurisdiction of Byland Abbey. Jervaulx, in beautiful parkland, is open daily and is never lovelier than in late spring, when sweet-scented purple aubrieta cascades over the dark grey of the ruined walls.

EAST WITTON
It is worth turning off the main road and spending a few minutes in East Witton to enjoy its long, rectangular village green, spreading trees and handsome cottages – superbly set against the broad green of Witton Fell. There are good views across Lower Wensleydale from the churchyard of the early 19th-century church.

MIDDLEHAM
The gaunt, ruined castle of Middleham, its keep one of the largest in Britain, was for many years the home of Richard of Gloucester (1452-85), later Richard III. The weather-worn stump of a cross in the market square near the castle is thought to represent his heraldic boar. The castle is open daily.

Tourist information: (Leyburn) Wensleydale 23069 (summer); (Pateley Bridge) Harrogate 711147 (summer).

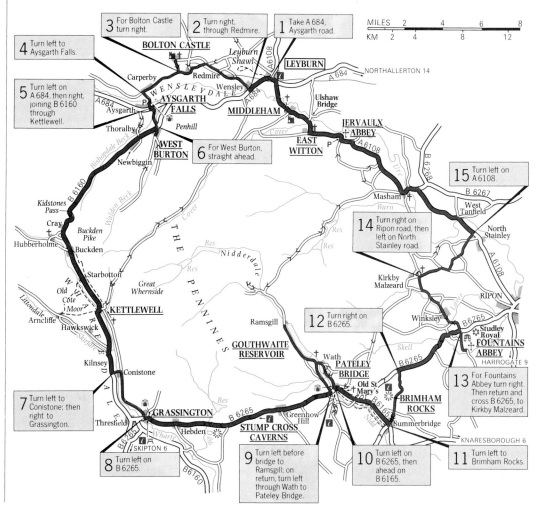

Sand and safaris on the Lancashire Plain

Golden sand dunes bordered by pine forest provide a natural windbreak for fertile farmland reclaimed from what was once a swampy moor, and beasts from Africa roam in a country park.

ORMSKIRK

Until 200 years ago the land around Ormskirk was waterlogged moorland. After being drained, it became good agricultural land, and Ormskirk developed as a market town. In the market square, now a shopping precinct, stands a clock tower erected in 1876 by the Earl of Derby, and nearby stands the church of the Stanleys, Earls of Derby. The church is unusual in having a low, square tower and a slender spire side by side.

The tower is low and square and dates from the 15th century, while its slender companion rises above it.

Inside the church the 16th-century Derby Chapel was built by the 3rd earl, and in it lies James Stanley, 7th Earl of Derby – in two coffins. A Royalist earl, he shared the fate of his king and was beheaded at Bolton for his part in the Civil War, and a short coffin holds his body while his head rests in a casket at its side.

AUGHTON

A narrow road lined by strawberry fields and potato fields leads to a pretty village dominated by the magnificent spire of St Michael's Church whose rectors are listed from 1246 onwards. Much of the church's splendid medieval architecture remains, although extensive restoration was carried out in 1914. In the bell tower are some 14th-century wooden figures depicting the Stanleys, whose leader became Lord Derby and ruler of the Isle of Man; the three legs of Man are clearly shown on the carved heraldic shields carried by the figures. In the churchyard is a sundial of 1736

which is inscribed 'I only count the sunny hours'.

Opposite the church and close to the Stanley Arms is Aughton Old Hall, not open to the public but easily visible from the road. There are the remains of a 15th-century peel tower in the front garden.

FORMBY POINT

A bumpy road slicing through an avenue of Scots pines leads from the National Trust warden's hut to a large car park beside the sand dunes. Formby Point and Ainsdale National Nature Reserve are linked by a footpath from Freshfield station and form one of the most extensive dune systems in Britain.

This is one of the last remaining strongholds of the natterjack toad, easily recognised by its running gait and prominent yellow line down its back. It breeds in the shallow salty pools, which also support a variety of plants including such rarities as dune helleborine, round-leaved winter-

green and grass of Parnassus. The drier dunes are a blaze of colourful plants. Conspicuous among them is evening primrose, extracts from which are used in medicine. There is also a red squirrel reserve.

SEFTON

A tiny hamlet clustered round a 16th-century church with a lofty spire, Sefton retains a medieval tranquillity. The church ceiling has been restored by 20th-century craftsmen; the new bosses and moulded beams match the quality of the 16th-century screens and the ornately carved pulpit of 1635. Medieval stained glass unearthed in the vestry is incorporated into the windows, and there is a beautifully preserved display of 16th-century brasses.

The box pews are among the finest in the county. They include those occupied by the dog whippers whose job was to exclude unwanted animals from the church and to control those brought by members of the congregation to protect them on their walk to and from church.

The church contains a so-called 'Treacle Bible', with some mis-translations which were corrected in the Authorised Version of 1611. For example, Jeremiah 8 v 22 reads: 'There is no more triacle (AV *balm*) in Gilead.' Another curious rendering occurs at Psalm 91 v 5: 'Thou shalt not need be afraid for any bugges (AV *terror*) by night.' The translation was the work of Miles Coverdale, later Bishop of Exeter, in 1535.

KNOWSLEY SAFARI PARK

Trumpeting elephants, grazing wildebeests and acrobatic monkeys leaping onto the boots and bonnets of slow-moving cars make a visit to Knowsley Safari Park feel like a tour of the African bush. Five miles of roads wind through parkland in the grounds of Knowsley Park, owned by the Earl of Derby. Herds of eland, buffalo, bison and zebra graze alongside the road. Lions and tigers are enclosed except for one pride of lions in the drive-through area. The safari park is open daily March to October.

BEACON COUNTRY PARK

Straddling a ridge overlooking the fertile South Lancashire Plain, the 304 acre Beacon Country Park is patch-worked by grassy meadows sheltered by belts of old oak and newly planted conifers. The visitor centre is the starting point of trails which twist and turn through trees to picnic sites overlooking a golf course.

A mile beyond the centre is the start of a walk to the summit of Ashurst's Beacon. The well-trodden path begins from a large car park just past the Beacon Inn. In Tudor times Ashurst's Beacon formed part of an Armada early warning system for Lancashire, stretching from Everton Brow to Lancaster Castle.

From the summit, Blackpool Tower and the Lakeland Hills can be seen to the north of the Mersey, the Welsh mountains to the south-west, the Peaks of Derbyshire to the south-east and the Lancashire Pennines to the north-east.

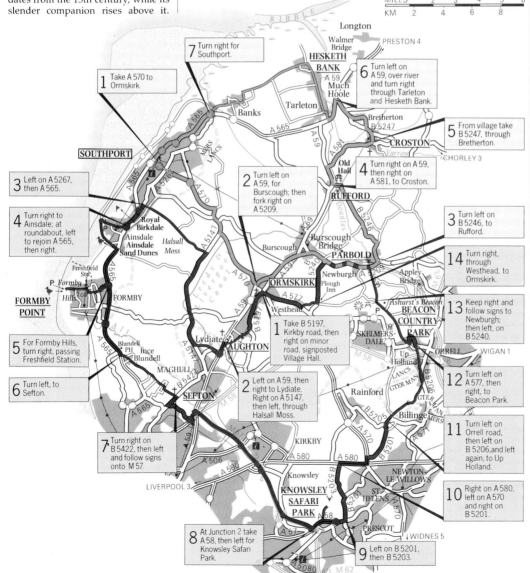

Inland from the promenades and beaches of Southport are the farmlands of the Lancashire Plain, spreading to the edge of the marshes, mud and sand flats of the Ribble estuary.

SOUTHPORT

Behind golden sands, green lawns, promenades and flowerbeds lies a town that has changed little since frock-coated gentlemen strolled along its boulevards while their wives shopped in the glass-canopied arcades. Lord Street, Southport's main thoroughfare, is a mile-long avenue of tree-shaded pavements bordered by large houses, public buildings, hotels and shops built mostly during the Victorian and Edwardian eras.

For almost their entire length the shop fronts on the west side of Lord Street are shaded by glass-and-iron canopies, and at intervals glass-roofed arcades entice the shopper into cool passageways where polished antique furniture and glittering jewellery gleams.

If an unusual number of shops seem to cater for the golfer, this is because Southport is the home of Royal Birkdale, a championship course to the south of the town.

PARBOLD

A humpback bridge spans the Leeds and Liverpool Canal in Parbold, and by it stand the stump of a tower windmill and the millhouse, both now used as business offices. Pleasure craft moor by the bridge, and at the canal edge there is a small car park from which a pleasant walk along the waterway leads to Burscough Bridge, 4 miles west.

RUFFORD

In gardens ablaze in early summer with rhododendrons and the pinks, golds and yellows of other early flowering shrubs stands Rufford Old Hall, a medieval timber-framed manor house built by the Hesketh family in the 15th century. From the large car park near the house, the first view of the black timbers and white infill of the oldest part of the hall almost overshadows the 17th-century wing built at right angles to it – but not quite, for this is a fine example of Jacobean brickwork with a hooded doorway, arched windows and gabled dormer windows. The two styles blend perfectly.

Inside the old hall there is one of the finest hammerbeam roofs in England, richly carved with angel figures, and a rare carved screen 7ft wide and intended to be movable. Rufford Old Hall is open every afternoon in summer, except Fridays.

CROSTON

Stone and brick-built cottages line one side of the village street, and on the other side the River Yarrow follows a twisting course between deep stone walls. The river is crossed by a narrow, arched stone bridge bearing the date 1682.

The 16th-century Church of St Michael stands in the centre of the village, and is approached by a narrow street of brick cottages. At the entrance to the street stands a cross mounted on a weatherworn plinth. Croston's Old English name means 'town of the Cross' and probably derives from a 7th-century wayside cross where Celtic missionaries to northern England worshipped before the church was built. The present cross, however, dates only from 1950.

Next to the church is a school founded in 1372 by John of Gaunt, virtual ruler of England during the early part of the reign of the boy king, Richard II. The school was given an endowment by the Puritan James Hyett, vicar of Croston, in 1660. Two years later Hyett was forced from the ministry for refusing to conform to the Act of Uniformity which, among other demands unacceptable to a Puritan, included the use of the revised Anglican prayer book, Hyett died in Preston in 1663 and is remembered in Croston by a stone plaque on the school wall.

HESKETH BANK

The village lies on the Ribble estuary where it is joined by the River Douglas. The road through Hesketh Bank turns sharply to the south-west, and for about 4 miles runs along the edge of salt marshes stretching into the distance and merging with the mud and sand flats of the estuary. The whole area looks wild, featureless and forbidding, but has a haunting beauty when the sun bathes it in a shimmering haze.

Tourist information: Southport 33133/ 40404.

SHIFTING SANDS *Tough marram grass binds the wind-blown sands at Formby Point, slowing their progress as the sea recedes.*

NORTHERN STYLE *Rufford Old Hall's close-set timbers and carved panelling are vivid examples of typical north country medieval building.*

TIME SPAN *Croston's 300-year-old bridge still carries local traffic.*

HEAVY TRAFFIC *Rhinos wander freely around Knowsley Safari Park.*

Historic halls near a holiday coast

TOUR

168

——— 91 MILES ———

Pretty villages and stately homes dot the attractive countryside around Preston. A few miles to the west, beaches with golden sands fringe two of the finest resorts of the Lancashire coast.

PRESTON
Street names such as Fishergate, Friargate and Stoneygate are about the only relics of Preston's medieval beginnings, and the great houses of the gentry have long since been replaced by warehouses and shops. But the fine buildings to be found in the centre of the town date from a later period of prosperity when Preston led the way in the textile industry.

Preston's heart is Market Square, perhaps the most noble site bearing such a humble name in England. It is dominated by the Harris Museum and Art Gallery, completed in 1893 from funds donated by Edmund Robert Harris, a local benefactor. Standing high above the paved square, it is of classical design with tall fluted columns supporting a massive pediment along which are sculptured reliefs much in the style of the British Museum in London. The Harris Museum contains an outstanding collection of British paintings of the 19th and 20th centuries, as well as collections of glass, ceramics and costumes.

Away from the town centre, Preston has many attractive parks.

MARTIN MERE WILDFOWL TRUST
The tone of this wildfowl conservation centre is set at the entrance buildings, built of Scandinavian pine with a turfed roof in the style of a traditional Norwegian log house. The mere itself is a 20 acre man-made lake, and also within the 360 acre site are a swan lake and pens for flamingos, black swans, geese and rare species such as the Laysan teal and Hawaiian geese.

Among the lakes and gardens some 1500 tame wildfowl are on view, and for the dedicated birdwatcher there are hides out on the marsh along two half-mile-long nature trails. In winter the marsh comes to life with up to 15,000 pink-footed geese, thousands of teal and large flocks of wigeon, ruff and pintail. Whooper swans fly here from Iceland, and Bewick's swans cross the North Sea from Russia.

An exhibition in the Southport Hall illustrates the natural history of the mere, the work of the Wildfowl Trust, and many aspects of wildlife conservation.

PARBOLD BEACON
The road from Burscough Bridge climbs past the attractive Stocks Tavern at Parbold and then winds its way to the 394ft high brow of Parbold Beacon. From a lay-by opposite the Wiggin Tree inn on the left, there are panoramic views of a wide, green valley with glimpses of the River Douglas appearing like fragments of glass among the soft folds of the hills.

STANDISH
Shops large and small line the streets of this workaday village, giving the impression of a small market town. Beyond the crossroads, where two main roads meet, the shops on one side give way to a wide square and the impressive stonework of St Wilfrid's Church.

The church dates mostly from the 16th century, except for its octagonal steeple which is not the best example of Victorian meddling. Nevertheless, the church as a whole is extremely attractive, with a two-storey porch, buttressed tower and two domed turrets where the nave and chancel meet. The pulpit is Elizabethan. The entrance to the churchyard is through a fine gateway built of the same dark red sandstone as the church but much newer, dating from 1926 when it was erected as the village's war memorial. It is in Tudor style with a small turret set at one side and a statue of St Wilfrid facing the church.

In the square stands the village cross, and below its steps the village stocks, whose well-worn holes suggest that many a miscreant must have spent unhappy hours there.

ASTLEY HALL
Few of the great houses in the north of England can compare with Astley Hall in sheer elegance and beauty, both in the house itself and in its magnificent grounds – acres of green lawns sloping down to a wooded vale and the trickling River Chor, neat flowerbeds and an ornamental lake paved with lily pads.

So lovely is the landscape that it almost distracts the eye from the house. Nothing, however, could completely subdue that splendid façade with its two huge bays rising two storeys high, the tall mullioned windows, the delicate balusters of its rooftop parapet and the arched doorway flanked by two stone lions recumbent on lofty pillars.

The oldest parts of the house date from the 16th century, but the imposing front dates from the second half of

HALL WITH A VIEW *Ranks of windows forming a wall of glass look out from Astley Hall onto a pond where swans glide among the lilies.*

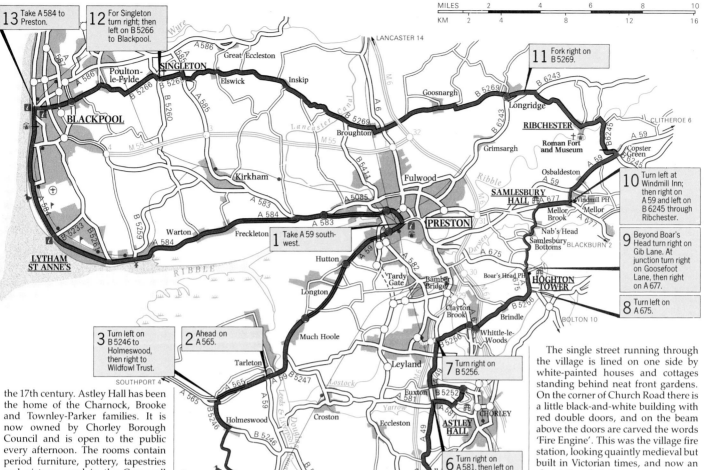

MILES 2 4 6 8 10
KM 2 4 8 12 16

13 Take A 584 to Preston.

12 For Singleton turn right; then left on B 5266 to Blackpool.

11 Fork right on B 5269.

10 Turn left at Windmill Inn; then right on A 59 and left on B 6245 through Ribchester.

9 Beyond Boar's Head turn right on Gib Lane. At junction turn right on Goosefoot Lane, then right on A 677.

8 Turn left on A 675.

7 Turn right on B 5256.

6 Turn right on A 581, then left on B 5252 (for Astley Hall turn right). At roundabout left, then right on A 49.

5 Turn left on A 49.

4 Turn right on A 59, then left on B 5241, and left again on A 5209.

3 Turn left on B 5246 to Holmeswood, then right to Wildfowl Trust.

2 Ahead on A 565.

1 Take A 59 south-west.

---

the 17th century. Astley Hall has been the home of the Charnock, Brooke and Townley-Parker families. It is now owned by Chorley Borough Council and is open to the public every afternoon. The rooms contain period furniture, pottery, tapestries and pictures, and in the Cromwell Room is a massive four-poster bed in which the Lord Protector is said to have slept.

A glass case in the Great Hall contains a pair of weathered boots, reputed to have been left behind by Cromwell because they were still wet after he arrived in heavy rain on the night of August 18, 1648.

HOGHTON TOWER

At the top of a long, rhododendron-lined drive leading up from the main road stands this historic fortified mansion, perched on a hill above the River Darwen. It is the seat of Sir Bernard de Hoghton, and has been the residence of the Hoghtons since it was built in the 16th century.

The house is built around two courtyards, the first of which is entered from the drive through a gatehouse tower which leads in turn to a terrace with fine 18th-century iron gates, and an Old English rose garden. The house contains a collection of antique dolls and dolls' houses. Its finest room is the magnificent banqueting hall where, in 1617, James I knighted a loin of beef and added sirloin to the butcher's list of prime cuts. The great carved oak table at which he sat is still in the hall.

Hoghton Tower is open to the public on Bank Holidays and Sundays throughout the summer, and also Saturdays in July and August.

SAMLESBURY HALL

This 14th-century manor house is undoubtedly one of the finest 'black and white' houses in England, its timbers cut with clover-leaf designs showing the white wall beneath, and eaves sheltering rich carvings under the leaded windows.

Inside the hall the timber roof is supported by huge oak pillars roughly carved from oaks chosen for their natural bent shape, and on a beam supporting the gallery is carved the name Thomas Southworth and the date 1532. The Southworth family owned the house from 1325 to 1679.

Samlesbury Hall's history is as chequered as its timbers. After 1679 it was sold off to pay a debt and became in turn a tenement house for weavers and labourers, an inn, a school and then a house at which Charles Dickens is said to have stayed. The house was taken over by the Samlesbury Hall Trust in 1925 and restored to its present glory. To the left of the hall is a chapel, and several rooms display antiques for sale.

Samlesbury Hall is open to the public daily except Mondays.

RIBCHESTER

Cottages of multi-coloured stone line narrow streets in this picturesque village set by a curve of the River Ribble, and encircled by the fells of Longridge and Bowland to the north, and the moors of Darwen and Bolton to the south. There are two pubs in the village, the White Bull and the Black Bull; the porch canopy of the White Bull is supported by columns said to be from Roman ruins that lie buried beneath the village.

Around AD 80 the Romans chose this site for a fort garrisoning about 500 cavalrymen. Part of the fort is visible – the ends of two granaries – outside the museum along the riverside road. The road also affords fine views across the Ribble flowing through wide meadow lands.

SINGLETON

The clue to the origins of Singleton lies in the splendid cream-painted Miller Arms at the entrance to the village, for it was the Miller family, wealthy Preston cotton-mill owners, who built the village in the 19th century. The Millers lived in Singleton Hall, out of sight from the village and not open to the public; the imposing wrought-iron gates of its south lodge stand beside the road just past the pretty little red-brick post office.

The single street running through the village is lined on one side by white-painted houses and cottages standing behind neat front gardens. On the corner of Church Road there is a little black-and-white building with red double doors, and on the beam above the doors are carved the words 'Fire Engine'. This was the village fire station, looking quaintly medieval but built in Victorian times, and now an electricity substation.

At the top of Church Road, almost hidden by trees, is St Anne's Church, built in 1860 by Thomas Miller. It occupies the site of an earlier church, whose lich gate stands by the road opposite the church.

BLACKPOOL

Blackpool Tower comes into view long before this 'Playground of the North' is reached, and its red-painted girders dominate the promenade with its endless rows of amusement centres, cafes, bingo halls, three piers and the giant Pleasure Beach. Golden sands stretch southwards all the way to Lytham St Anne's, where Blackpool's hurly-burly fades to quiet tranquillity.

LYTHAM ST ANNE'S

The town stands well back from the sea, almost as if ignoring its presence, and the wide green between the town and its sandy beaches is broken only by the outlines of a large windmill and the old lifeboat house.

This is a place for walking, with views across the Ribble estuary, or for stretching out on the grass on a warm summer's day. Lytham St Anne's offers little more for the holiday-maker, and is none the worse for it. For the sportsman there are the golf courses for which the town is famous; they include Royal Lytham St Anne's, where major international tournaments are played.

Tourist information: Preston 53731/54881; Lytham St Anne's 721222/725610; Blackpool 21623/25212.

Climbing high through two forests

TOUR
169

—— 55 MILES ——

Two forests, Bowland and Pendle,
lie close to Lancashire's heart.
Their moors and woodlands
rise above a countryside
in which historic buildings
blend with farmlands.

BLACKBURN
The cotton mills which flourished during the Industrial Revolution have mostly turned to new industries; but the past lives on in Blackburn's Lewis Textile Museum in Exchange Street. Its engrossing exhibits include full-scale working models of spinning and weaving machinery, including James Hargreaves' spinning jenny and Samuel Crompton's spinning mule, an improved version of the jenny.

Many of Blackburn's best buildings date from Victorian times, which also saw the reconstruction of the cathedral, formerly St Mary's Church.

The Blackburn Museum and Art Gallery in Library Street has a fine collection of Japanese prints, English watercolours, coins, medieval manuscripts and early printed books.

HURST GREEN
The neat little village grouped around the Shireburn Arms has changed little since the early 1800s, when enterprising local people, learning of the new road-building techniques of John Loudon McAdam, made the undulating road into Hurst Green one of the first in Britain to be 'macadamised'.

Just past a group of ornate almshouses a tree-lined road leads towards the mansion of Stonyhurst, built around 1600 for the Shireburn family. Since 1794 it has been a Roman Catholic boarding school for boys, and pupils have included the writers Sir Arthur Conan Doyle, creator of Sherlock Holmes, and J.R.R. Tolkien, author of the Hobbit books.

The splendid Tudor building is approached over a long grassy causeway between two lakes where wildfowl breed. Additions over the centuries include a magnificent chapel and an observatory in classical style. A road runs alongside the buildings, and the school is open to the public occasionally during the summer. Clearly signposted footpaths run from the village through ancient woodlands straddling the banks of the River Hodder, one of England's best salmon runs. The river features in the poems of Gerard Manley Hopkins, who taught at Stonyhurst during the mid-19th century. The scenery has not changed since Hopkins sat by the Hodder and observed:

'As kingfishers catch fire, dragonflies
   draw flame;
As tumbled over rim in roundy wells
   Stones ring . . .'

BASHALL EAVES
The tiny hamlet of Bashall Eaves rests in a cosy fold of green fields, full of sheep and gleaming gold with buttercups in summer. The Red Pump Inn gets its name from the scarlet painted pump on its forecourt.

Beyond the hamlet, along a lane passing between neat hedgerows spangled with roses and honeysuckle, lies Browsholme Hall, home of the Parker family since the 14th century. The present hall dates from 1507, and is open on Saturday afternoons in June, July and August, and at other times by appointment.

The gardens are neat and colourful and the Tudor house, refaced in red sandstone in 1604, has fine furniture, china and some stained glass removed from Whalley Abbey after its dissolution. There is also a gauge once used for measuring dogs to ensure that large animals were not kept by unauthorised owners in a royal forest area where the monarch hunted deer.

WADDINGTON
This village is named after a family which sheltered Henry VI after his defeat in the Wars of the Roses. Their descendants became engineers and bridge-builders. Sights of the village include almshouses built in 1700 and a garden commemorating Queen Elizabeth's coronation in 1953.

BOLTON-BY-BOWLAND
One long village green and a smaller one are fringed by mature trees and old stone farms and cottages. A church existed at Bolton in 1190, but the present Church of St Peter and St Paul was being constructed by Sir Ralph Pudsay when, after the Battle of Hexham on May 15, 1464, Henry VI was given refuge at the now-vanished Bolton Hall. The king took an interest in the church, and is said to have helped design the high tower, which is more typical of churches in Somerset than of those in the North.

The interior of the church is dominated by memorials to the Pudsay family, now extinct despite the virility of Sir Ralph, who married three times and fathered 25 children. A splendid limestone carving shows Sir Ralph in full armour, flanked by his three wives. Near the feet of the first wife are the Roman characters VI, denoting the number of children she bore. The number under the second wife is II, and under the third an impressive XVII. The children also appear in the carving, the boys depicted as soldiers or priests and the girls dressed in the costume of the period.

One rector of the church, Richard Dawson, was appointed in 1773 and still in office 53 years later. He appears to have been responsible for installing the church's three-decker pulpit. In the 18th century a parish clerk occupied the bottom deck and assisted the parson in the conduct of the service.

A signposted footpath follows the meanders of Tosside Beck to its junction with the Ribble, and about 2 miles farther on to the historic village of Sawley, passed earlier on the road. The village is overlooked by the ruins of Salley Abbey, a Cistercian house raised in 1147 and dissolved in 1536. Many of its stones now form part of the walls of local buildings.

GISBURN
On Thursdays Gisburn's pubs are open all day and its narrow street echoes to the sound of cattle, sheep and the patter of the auctioneer. The village has long been a market centre, and a focal point for travellers

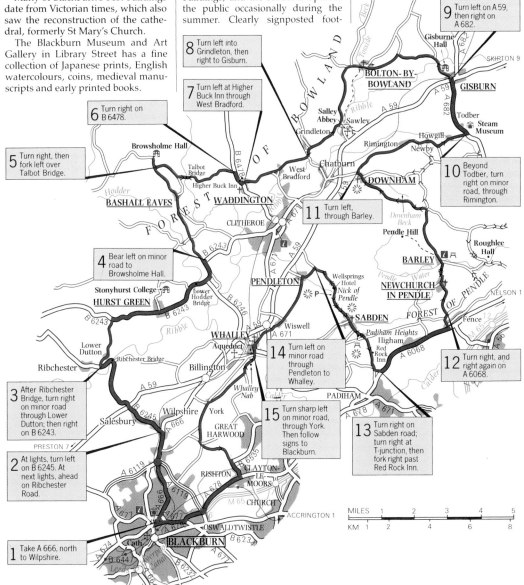

1 Take A 666, north to Wilpshire.

2 At lights, turn left on B 6245. At next lights, ahead on Ribchester Road.

3 After Ribchester Bridge, turn right on minor road through Lower Dutton; then right on B 6243.

4 Bear left on minor road to Browsholme Hall.

5 Turn right, then fork left over Talbot Bridge.

6 Turn right on B 6478.

7 Turn left at Higher Buck Inn through West Bradford.

8 Turn left into Grindleton, then right to Gisburn.

9 Turn left on A 59, then right on A 682.

10 Beyond Todber, turn right on minor road, through Rimington.

11 Turn left, through Barley.

12 Turn right, and right again on A 6068.

13 Turn right on Sabden road; turn right at T-junction, then fork right past Red Rock Inn.

14 Turn left on minor road through Pendleton to Whalley.

15 Turn sharp left on minor road, through York. Then follow signs to Blackburn.

MILES 1 2 3 4 5
KM 1 2 4 6 8

between Lancashire and Yorkshire.

Gisburne Park, formerly the family seat of Lord Ribblesdale, is now a hospital and not open to the public, but it is ringed by footpaths and its grounds are often visited by a wild herd of sika deer.

At Todber, 1 mile south, is a steam museum, and steamrollers and tractors are often heard and seen clanking and puffing along the road between Gisburn and the museum. Todber has a caravan site and a large playground for children.

DOWNHAM

Stand at the top of Downham opposite St Leonard's Church, close to the stocks under a gnarled sycamore, and look south to enjoy one of the finest views of the sinuous curve of the 1831ft Pendle Hill. The village, one of Lancashire's oldest and prettiest, has been carefully tended since the 16th century by the Assheton family, whose head is Lord Clitheroe. Even the telephone box is painted grey, blending with the cottages, which have mullioned windows and gloriously perfumed flower gardens.

Swallows, house martins and swifts nest under eaves and sweep for insects over Downham Beck, where visitors gather to feed the resident mallards.

BARLEY

The village of Barley, washed by Pendle Water, is the best starting point for the well signposted and easiest route to Pendle Hill, whose breezy, flat summit is marked by a pile of stones called the Beacon. A visitor centre beside the stream in the village caters for picnickers and walkers, and has become a focal point for visitors to Pendle. Fell races are organised throughout the year, and there are guided walks in summer.

NEWCHURCH IN PENDLE

A quaint, steep, winding village of grey stone, Newchurch dovetails into the foothills of Pendle. It was once called Goldshaw Booth, but takes its present name from the 'New Church' of St Mary which was built around 1740 onto the existing 16th-century tower. A clock was added to the tower in 1946. A much older 'eye of God' is carved on the outer wall of the tower to warn off evil spirits while the faithful were at prayer.

In the churchyard is the reputed grave of Alice Nutter, a resident of nearby Roughlee Hall, who was among the ten Lancashire witches convicted and hanged in 1612. Roughlee Hall is privately owned and not open to the public. The village shop, called 'Witches Galore', is guarded by three life-size models of wrinkled crones; an inscription on a stone over the door urges customers to part with their money by the exhortation to 'Gerrit spent'.

SABDEN

The steep descent into the once flourishing textile village of Sabden is lined in season with sparkling gorse and aromatic heather buzzing with feeding honeybees. The Church of St Nicholas, built in 1841, is surrounded

WHALLEY ABBEY *Medieval foundations pattern the lawns. A surviving wall flanks the abbot's former residence.*

WADDINGTON *St Helen's Church, largely rebuilt at the turn of the century, looks timeless in a floral setting.*

POET'S RIVER *This bridge spans the River Hodder, which inspired verses by Gerard Manley Hopkins.*

by colourful masses of azaleas and rhododendrons framing splendid views over the valley to Padiham Heights.

From the Nick of Pendle that cuts through the upland moors there are breathtaking views over the silver ribbon of the sea lapping the Fylde coast to the west and the ever-changing colours of the Lakeland hills to the north.

Hang-gliders soar over the valley, and there are artificial ski slopes at the Wellsprings Hotel.

PENDLETON

Pendleton, cut in half by a channelled brook, is both a pretty village and a working community. In the main street, between the cottages with their mullioned windows, are four working dairy farms, in which the rhythmic beat of milking machines mingles with the lowing of cows and the chattering of the nearby stream over its pebbled bed. Visiting motorists are

asked to be patient if their way is blocked by cows being taken to milking.

The church and its associated school, now used as a residential centre for youth groups, date from 1847; until then, Pendleton folk had to take one of the many green paths over the fields to church and school in Whalley.

WHALLEY

Overlooked by the heights of wooded Whalley Nab, the village is grouped around its church and abbey. An ancient corn mill once driven by the waters of the Calder is surrounded by brightly painted cottages, some selling antiques. Whalley's brief flirtation with the textile industry has left its mark in the form of red-brick Victorian town houses built in the days of prosperity.

The Cistercian abbey, open to the public, dates from the 13th century, but when Henry VIII began to

threaten the monasteries John Paslew, Whalley's last abbot, joined the revolt known as the Pilgrimage of Grace – an act which cost him his life. The abbey was dissolved. Later the abbot's residence was rebuilt for family occupation, and it is still lived in. Some walls and gateways of the abbey survive and a church conference centre is set in the grounds.

Towering over the abbey is a red-brick aqueduct more than 2000ft long, supported on 49 arches, which once carried the Blackburn to Hellifield railway over the Calder valley. The parish church of St Mary dates from around 1200 and contains chained Bibles, stained glass and amusing carved misericords – hinged choir seat shelves – one of which shows a woman beating her man with a frying pan. These medieval cartoons once decorated the abbey church.

Tourist information: Blackburn 53277; Clitheroe 25566.

Moors above the Pennine valleys

TOUR 170

35 MILES

Only a few miles from industrial Bolton there are spectacular views of moorland across a reservoir, fine country houses and gardens, and wooded nature trails with a wealth of wildlife.

JUMBLES COUNTRY PARK

From Ousel's Nest car park a gravel path descends steeply to Jumbles Reservoir and the network of tree-lined nature trails which surrounds it. One trail leads to the Water Fold picnic site and visitor centre on the opposite side of the reservoir. From the picnic site there are spectacular views across the water to Turton Moor. Tree pipits can be seen in the birches in summer, and yellow-hammers sing from the gorse-fringed hillsides.

TURTON TOWER

A drive bordered by beech and horse chestnut leads to a fine Tudor house built around an early 15th-century peel tower fortified against the Scots. This is Turton Tower, which was used as a farmhouse during the 18th century and bought and restored by industrialist James Kay in the 1830s. When the Bolton to Blackburn railway was built in the 1840s Kay insisted that the bridges close by the tower should be castellated in keeping with its style.

The tower is now a museum, with fine collections of armour, Tudor and Victorian furniture and a remarkable German chandelier made from the antlers of fallow deer. It is open from Saturday to Wednesday.

PICKUP BANK

This tiny hamlet perches on a breezy hillside dotted with sheep farms and old shepherds' cottages, many now restored. At the centre of the hamlet is the imposing Old Rosin's inn, the name of which derives from the resin used around the turn of the century to polish the inn's dance floor and musical instruments. Local people called the inn 'Old Rosin's' and this name was adopted in place of the former 'Duke of Wellington'.

Pickup Bank overlooks a fertile valley lined with trees which screen disused mills and their ponds.

TOCKHOLES

Turn off the main road at the Victoria Inn, down School Lane which descends steeply to the aptly named Ivy Cottages, draped also by sweet-smelling rambling roses. Next to the cottages is the United Reformed Chapel, founded in 1662 and a centre of nonconformity in the intolerant days of the 17th and 18th centuries.

A narrow lane beyond the chapel leads to the parish church, which has unusual lance-shaped windows. The church was rebuilt in 1832, and its outdoor pulpit is a relic of the days when large summer congregations could not be accommodated inside.

Just beyond Tockholes, a large car park and picnic site near the Royal Arms Inn is the starting point of Roddlesworth Nature Trail.

RIVINGTON

A winding but well trodden and gently sloping footpath leads to the 1190ft summit of Rivington Pike, a beacon point since at least the time of the Armada. Each Good Friday crowds of people make a pilgrimage to the summit to enjoy a picnic – an event known locally as 'Pike Fair'. The view from the top takes in a complex of reservoirs which since the mid-19th century have provided more than 11 million gallons of water a day to Merseyside.

The Rivington valley has been settled since the Bronze Age, and several historic buildings remain, even though part of the old village is now under a reservoir. Rivington Hall Barn and Great House Barn are two of Britain's few remaining Saxon 'cruck barns', their roofs supported by huge boughs or 'crucks' of oak, though their exteriors have been altered since then. Great House Barn is now a visitor centre.

The church also has Saxon origins, although it was rebuilt in 1541 and altered again in 1884, when part of the old village green was swallowed up by the new vicarage. The old village stocks are now part of the vicar's garden furniture. Rivington Hall, re-built in 1774, is now a restaurant.

SMITHILLS HALL

Surrounded by a wooded nature trail, Smithills Hall stands on an easily defended hill above Ravenden Clough. The earliest building was the work of the Knights of St John, a military religious order founded during the Crusades in the 11th century, but the present structure dates from the 14th century. There have been alterations since, but the original medieval great hall is magnificent, its four-leaf, moulded decoration still in fine condition.

The hall, now a museum, is open daily, except Thursday in summer, and Thursday and Sunday in winter. The old stables and coach house have been converted into a restaurant reached through an archway and overlooking a courtyard colourful with restored and brightly painted stagecoaches. There are a nature trail and museum in the grounds.

HALL-I'TH'-WOOD

This compact, late-15th-century half-timbered house was the home of Samuel Crompton (1753-1827), who invented the spinning mule in 1779. This produced yarn which was strong and fine enough to produce muslin, and gave Lancashire's cotton industry an unassailable advantage over its competitors. Lord Leverhulme bought the house in 1900 and restored it before giving it to Bolton as a museum. It now houses a collection of Crompton's machinery set in rooms lined with fine Tudor woodwork.

The museum and its magnificent gardens are open daily, except Thursday in summer, and Thursday and Sunday in winter.

Tourist information: Bolton 22311/384174; Blackburn 53277.

TOUR 171

45 MILES

Rivers carve deep valleys through the rocky Pennines. Weaving villages which boomed in the 18th century survive, though their populations have dwindled and the mills lie silent.

HEALEY DELL

A tree-lined valley rich in flowers forms a nature reserve beneath an aqueduct towering 105ft above the River Spodden. The 200ft long, eight-arched viaduct was built around 1880 to carry the railway from Rochdale to Bacup. It now forms part of a nature trail beginning close to the main Bacup road, and provides spectacular views over and beyond the dell. The railway closed in the 1960s, but the ruins of the old station at Broadley can still be found amid tangled vegetation. Below, the Spodden tumbles through the narrow, winding dell with waterfalls and grottoes.

BACUP

High on the breezy hills above Bacup rises the infant River Irwell which once powered the town's mighty cotton mills, all now silent. The museum of 'Bacup Nats', founded in 1878 as an artisans' naturalists' society, displays a spectacular jumble of exhibits recalling the mid-19th-century heyday of cotton and coal, clog and shawl, trap and tram. The richness of local wildlife is reflected in exhibitions of birds and butterflies, moths, mayflies and mammals.

TOWNELEY HALL

The much rebuilt 14th-century hall overlooking a lily pond was the home of the Towneley family until 1902, when Alice Mary Towneley sold it to Burnley Council. It is now Burnley's museum and has a magnificent long gallery lined with armour and furniture. Above the staircase is a 'priest hole', once a hiding place for priests.

The hall is surrounded by more than 300 acres of woods and parkland crisscrossed by nature trails starting from the adjacent visitor centre.

WORSTHORNE AND HURSTWOOD

The small green of the old village of Worsthorne is overlooked by the Victorian Church of St John and a number of inns. Wander around the 17th-century shops and cottages,

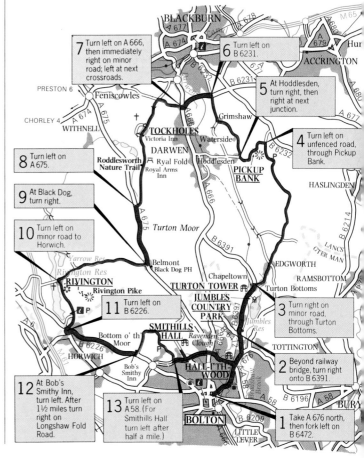

then drive the half mile to Hurst-wood, or better still stroll to it from Worsthorne's village green along a clearly marked path through the meadows. Near this village in the valley of the River Brun, according to legend, the Anglo-Saxons defeated the Danes in the 10th-century Battle of Brunenburk.

Overlooking the narrow village street is a hall built in 1579 and still a private residence, as is the ivy-clad Spensers House to its right. There, for a while, the poet Edmund Spenser lived before going to London to make his fortune writing *The Shepheardes Calender* and then to Ireland, where he wrote the *Faerie Queene*. Both poems contain more than a trace of north-country dialect. Just beyond the poet's house is a stable yard overlooked by an early 16th-century cottage. The stables, still used today, were once owned by Richard Tattersall, founder in 1766 of the London horse sales, now held at Newmarket.

HARDCASTLE CRAGS
From the well-signed car park a steep descent through a tapestry of trees leads into a valley cut by Hebden Water. The area is known as Hardcastle Crags after the large piles of angular rocks, eroded by the river, which line the valley sides. Wildlife abounds, dippers bob on stones and kingfishers breed close to the now disused Gibson's Mill and flash under the old tollbridge. The tollhouse still

bears a legible price list showing that a sheep could be taken across for a halfpenny, but a horse and trap had to pay twopence. A National Trust nature trail leads from the lodge gates to Slurring Rock, a name derived from the sound made by generations of children sliding down the rock in iron-shod clogs.

HEPTONSTALL
A village of millstone grit built on the steep slope of a hill, Heptonstall had its heyday in the 18th century as a flourishing centre of the weaving industry. Today the narrow main street is lined by cottages, an old pump set in a recess near the school, a Cloth Hall, two churches – one ancient, one modern – and a Wesleyan chapel.

The old grammar school, endowed in 1642, houses a museum. It over-looks a churchyard which is shared by the 13th-century Chapel of Thomas Becket and its modern successor dedicated to St Thomas the Apostle.

HOLLINGWORTH LAKE
Built to provide a reliable flow of water for the Rochdale Canal, the lake is now under the shadow of the bridge carrying the M62. There are boats for hire, and a ferry shuttles visitors to a wooded island with play and picnic areas and a comfortable tearoom. A visitor centre near the Fisherman's Inn provides leaflets describing the nature trails which follow the rich hedgerows and reed beds.

<u>Tourist information:</u> Hebden Bridge 843831.

STOODLEY PIKE *The hilltop peace monument was erected after the Napoleonic Wars.*

HALL-I'TH'-WOOD *Samuel Crompton's home contains machinery of the inventor.*

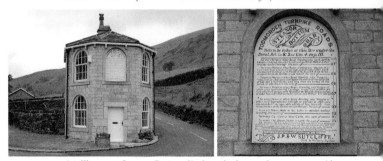

CHECKPOINT *A tollhouse at Steanor Bottom displays the fees road-users once paid.*

RIVERSIDE WALK *The sound of water accompanies the Roddlesworth Nature Trail.*

In the steps of the Vikings on the Isle of Man

Secluded beaches fringe an island of green hills and rugged glens, with wild moors at its heart. The Isle of Man is home to an independent people with Celtic and Viking ancestry.

DOUGLAS

From out at sea, Douglas – the capital of the Isle of Man – looks like a long line of white cliffs, which on closer viewing resolve themselves into the hotels that back the promenades for 2 miles between Douglas Head and Onchan Head.

Despite this, Douglas has a cosily old-fashioned air, like that of a seaside resort of the days before the Costa del Sol was dreamt of. That splendid piece of restored Victoriana, the Gaiety Theatre, certainly belongs to that era, as do the horse trams.

The excellent Manx Museum tells the story of the island during the days of the Norse occupation – and has natural history, archaeological and folklife collections besides. It is open daily except Sunday.

The Tourist Trophy motorcycle race begins and ends at Nobles Park in Douglas in the early part of June each year. The T.T. is world famous, but in fact is only one of several road races held in the island during the season.

The famous tailless cats of the Isle of Man are bred at the Manx Cattery, close by the T.T. grandstands. Douglas has long been the island's commercial centre, based on its busy harbour, now also a haven for pleasure craft. The bustling town was made the island's capital in 1869.

ONCHAN

Nowadays, Onchan is virtually a suburb of Douglas, and offers the same kind of holiday facilities. Onchan Park's diversions include an amusement centre, golf, stock-car racing, and a boating lake and sports stadium.

The residence of the Lieutenant-Governor, the sovereign's representative on the island, is on the edge of the village, and the parish register records that in 1781, William Bligh, RN, was married to Miss Betham, daughter of the island's customs officer. At that time, Bligh commanded HMS *Ranger*, engaged in suppressing smuggling in the Irish Sea, and it was not until some six years later that he took command of HMS *Bounty* – an appointment that was to confront him with the Navy's best-known mutiny.

There are some pleasant walks about the village, to the wooded Groudle Glen and Molly Quirk's Glen, and from the Promenade through Calvary Glen to Lourdes Grotto and Onchan Park.

DOUGLAS AT DUSK *As night falls, the waters of Douglas Bay reflect the lights from the hotels that line the promenades.*

GLEN MAYE *A beautiful waterfall cascades down the rugged and picturesque glen, whose deep wooded gorges open out into a secluded beach.*

CASTLE RUSHEN *Ancient walls look down on Castletown harbour.*

THREE-LEGGED SYMBOL *The Manx coat of arms is of Viking origin.*

LAXEY

The little stone harbour where cabin cruisers and dinghies lie on the shingle at low tide was once busy with fishing boats, and Laxey cattle fairs were among the most important on the island. The only vestige left of them is the Laxey Fair held in July, though it is now an occasion for carnival rather than cattle.

Throughout the 19th century, and until 1929 when Far Eastern competition put it out of business, Laxey was a lead-mining centre. The spoil heaps have long vanished but the mine pump wheel, built in 1854 and named Lady Isabella after the wife of the Lieutenant-Governor of the day, has become almost a symbol of the island itself. It is a giant of 72ft diameter that, driven by waterpower, makes two revolutions a minute and could once pump 270 gallons a minute from a depth of 1000ft.

Laxey is a station on the Manx Electric Railway, and the starting point of a mountain railway that climbs 2000ft up Snaefell.

RAMSEY

The last part of the route to Ramsey is a section of the T.T. course in reverse, which includes two dramatic hazards: the Gooseneck and the Hairpin. Below the Hairpin lies Ramsey, on a shallow bay that stretches from Maughold Head to the Point of Ayre, the northernmost tip of the island.

Though Ramsey is the second largest town on the island, it bears little resemblance to the capital. Instead of amusement arcades and casinos along the front, there is a staid

Victorian and Edwardian air. Further touches of nostalgia are the old, iron, Queen's Pier, and the Mooragh Park, 40 acres of gardens and lake claimed by diverting the estuary of the Sulby river about a century ago. Palm trees grow there among the flowers, as if to confirm Ramsey's claim that spring comes two weeks earlier to the town than to anywhere else on the island.

The Sulby, Man's greatest river, curves majestically through the town, beneath an iron swing bridge, and runs into the sea between two stone breakwaters with tall lights. The little shops and restaurants on the quays are much more akin to the older fishing port than to the Victorian resort.

CURRAGHS WILDLIFE PARK
Occupying some 26 acres of old, lush marshland in the Ballaugh Curraghs, the wildlife park has acquired a collection of birds and beasts from all over the world – llamas, monkeys, ornamental pheasants, parakeets and many others. Few, however, have an odder appearance than the native Loghtan sheep of Man with its long brown wool and, in the case of the rams, four long, curly horns sprouting from behind their ears. The park is open daily in summer.

On this section of the route several of the classic features of Man's Tourist Trophy racecourse are close at hand. They include Ballaugh Bridge (pronounced 'Bahlarf', more or less) with its humpback, and the three-fold Quarry Bends followed by the Sulby Straight, where the bikes start to make up for lost time. Laps of over 100mph are quite usual.

ST JOHN'S
Each July 5, unless it falls at a weekend, St John's presents annual confirmation that there was a good deal more to the Vikings than legend allows. This is the day of Tynwald – *Thing-Vollr*, literally, the 'assembly-field' – the yearly promulgation ceremony of the oldest continuous parliament in the world.

Tynwald, founded in AD 979, is held on a four-tiered hill and is attended by the Lieutenant-Governor, the members of the House of Keys and of the Legislative Council, and other dignitaries with such titles as Deemster, Coroner of the Sheading and Captain of the Parish – more or less judge, district council chairman and parish council chairman.

Laws which have received the Royal Assent during the past year are read out in Manx and English, newly elected coroners are presented with their wands of office, and the floor is available to any citizen of the island with a complaint or a petition.

For most of the year, however, visitors are attracted to St John's chiefly by its crafts centre in the old woollen mills. There it is possible to watch glass-blowers, potters and other craftsmen at work.

PEEL
Though hardly large enough to warrant the title of town, Peel has a cathedral and is therefore convinced it is a city. 'Sunset City', it calls itself, for

on summer evenings the dying sun builds a crimson road over the darkening water all the way from the hills of Ireland.

The cathedral is on St Patrick's Isle – now joined to Peel by a causeway – whose story summarises that of the Manx nation. Neolithic flint weapons have been found there and, very recently, the foundations of a Viking palace. St Patrick himself is said to have stayed there in AD 444, when he converted Manxmen to Christianity and banished all snakes. The roofless, 10th-century church beside the cathedral is dedicated to him, and the 50ft high Round Tower close by was built by the monks who served the church. The tower was intended as a refuge against Norse and Scottish invaders. The cathedral dates largely from the 13th century.

Sharing the islet is Peel Castle, built by the Lords of Man in the 14th century. It was besieged only once, during the Civil War, and swiftly fell to the forces of Parliament. The castle is open daily in summer.

Over all drifts a pall of fragrant smoke, a clue to the presence of the Manx kipper, which may be purchased direct from the smokeries. By the harbour is a boathouse that shelters a replica of a Viking longship.

CASTLETOWN
This little limestone town, with brightly painted front doors and gardens where palm trees battle for supremacy against a tangle of valerian and fuchsias, was for centuries the island's capital. In 1874, the House of Keys, the Manx parliament, was moved to Douglas, but Castletown still has its Parliament Square and a dignified building that used to be Parliament House, and is now the Town Hall.

Castle Rushen, commanding the square and the entire town, is built

upon and about a fortress-palace of the Old Norse kings of Man. Despite the unweathered appearance of its walls, hardly a stone was laid after the mid-14th century. It has been a prison, lunatic asylum, Parliament House and Court of Justice, which it is still. The walls of the castle look down upon the estuary of the Silver Burn and the deep canyon of the harbour.

The castle is open daily in summer, and daily except Sunday in winter.

BALLASALLA
Historians of the turf might be interested to know, as they pass Ronaldsway Airport on the way out of Castletown, that the first Derby was run not at Epsom, but a couple of hundred yards to the east of them, in 1627. It was inaugurated by the Stanley Earls of Derby, who were also Lords of Man, to encourage local horse breeding.

The course is masked by King William's College, a school founded in 1830. William IV donated his name, saying as he did so that he wished he could afford to donate cash as well.

Ballasalla village has within its boundaries the ruined Abbey of St

Mary of Rushen, beautifully set by the Silver Burn and open to the public daily in summer. It was founded by the Viking Olaf I, King of Man, in 1134, and two other Viking kings of Man are buried there: Reginald II, slain in 1250, and Magnus, who died in 1262. The abbey fell into ruin after the Dissolution, but the 14th-century Crossag, or Monk's Bridge, is still in excellent order a little upstream. There are walks up the Silverdale Glen from Ballasalla, and there is an amusement park.

As the route slants back to Douglas it goes through a leafy avenue which crosses the Santon Burn by the Fairy Bridge. It is clearly signposted, and any Manxman crossing it, however worldly he may be, will lift his hat as a mark of respect to the Little People who are said to live beneath the bridge.

Tourist information: Douglas 74323 (winter); 74328/9 (summer); Onchan 22311; Ramsey 81228; Peel 842341; Castletown 823518.

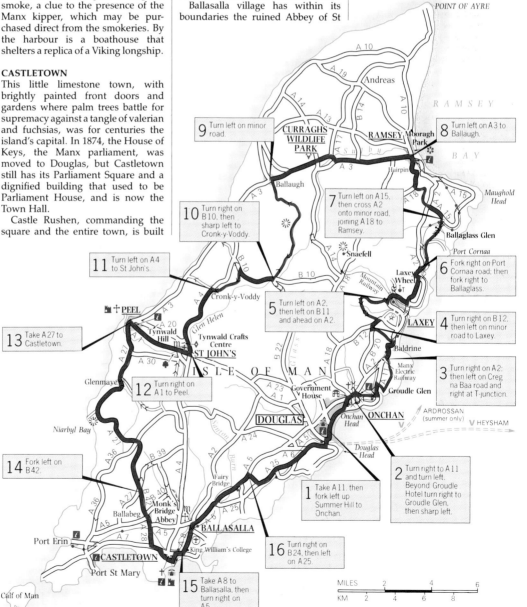

High fells in the Forest of Bowland

TOUR
173
— 66 MILES —

The wild pass of the Trough of Bowland leads to a miniature wilderness not far from the edge of industrial Lancashire. Below the breezy moors, streams link a ribbon of tiny villages.

LANCASTER

From its hilltop near the River Lune, Lancaster Castle looms over this old and dignified city. The castle was built by the Normans on the site of an old Roman fort, and its gateway, banqueting halls and towers were added in the 13th to 15th centuries. It has been used as a prison and courthouse since at least the 18th century – and is open to the public on weekdays when the courts are not sitting, and on weekends in summer.

Nearby is the imposing parish church of St Mary, built in the 14th and 15th centuries. It has a Saxon doorway and some magnificent carvings on its choir stalls. Below the hill, old alleys and streets crowd around the Market Square, where in 1651 Charles II was proclaimed king.

On the south bank of the Lune is St George's Quay, once the centre of the shipping industry which, towards the end of the 18th century, made Lancaster the fourth busiest slave-trading port in England – after London, Bristol and Liverpool. The graceful,

18th-century Custom House still stands beside the quay and now houses the maritime museum.

To the east of the city, surrounded by parkland, rises the Ashton Memorial. It was built in 1906-9 by Lord Ashton as a tribute to his late wife, and its domed elegance has led it to be dubbed 'the Taj Mahal of the North'. The view from the top is superb.

HALTON

St Wilfrid's Church, with its half-timbered porch, overlooks a peaceful grey village above the twisting River Lune. Boat House, opposite the church, is built on the site of an old ferry-stage by the river, noted for the fine quality of its salmon and trout fishing.

Surrounded by magnificent woodland and only a mile beyond Halton is the deep meander of the river known as the Crook of Lune.

HORNBY

Divided neatly by the River Wenning, a tributary of the Lune, and sheltering beneath a massive medieval-style castle, built mainly in Victorian times, Hornby is a large, attractive village. The castle is not open to the public. The old school is now a car show-

room, but the outlines of the original classrooms have been retained and the building still has some of its old character.

From the triple-arched bridge there is an attractive view down the main street, lined with substantial Georgian houses, to the gates of the 19th-century Church of St Margaret. Gaily painted shops, some with bottle-glass windows, flower-bordered cottages and a trim 18th-century hotel contrast pleasantly with the grey of the local building stone.

STOCKS RESERVOIR

Plantations of dark green spruce and majestic larch screen Stocks Reservoir, which takes its name from the village drowned during the early 1930s to create it. Sometimes, in dry summers, the level of the water falls enough to reveal cobblestones in the ruins.

When the valley was flooded, some of the stones of the village church were removed, at the villagers' insistence, and incorporated in a new church built alongside the road through the forest. Re-sited gravestones are in the new churchyard.

The reservoir is the winter haunt of large flocks of wildfowl, including

whooper swans, goosanders and Canada geese. Some geese stay and breed on a reed-fringed island which was once a high knoll overlooking the village.

SLAIDBURN

A majestic river flows under a high bridge, festooned with ferns and encrusted with grey lichen, in one of Bowland's most delightful villages. Shops selling homemade jams, a youth hostel, a grammar school dated 1717 and a splendid 17th-century church with a three-decker pulpit all lie close to the steep winding street, at the top of which is an inn named Hark to Bounty. The name is said to have come in the 19th century from the leader of a pack of hounds, whose bark could be heard above those of the other dogs and was instantly recognised by his master, who would exclaim: 'Hark to Bounty!'

Once the administrative centre of Bowland, Slaidburn is now a focal point for walkers who enjoy exploring the quiet fells.

NEWTON

This friendly village of limestone cottages crouches under the wooded slopes of Dunnow Rock. From the mid-17th century Newton was a centre for the Quakers, and their meeting house, built in 1767, still stands. Among those educated at the old Quaker school was John Bright,

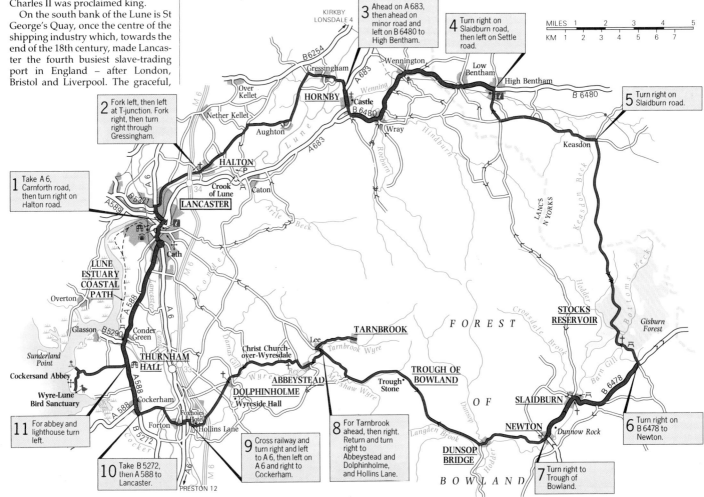

VALLEY VIEW *From the Hodder valley near Dunnow the road climbs between wooded hills and past tranquil farmsteads to the Bowland village of Slaidburn.*

the Lancashire-born politician. He was one of the leaders of a campaign in 1846 to repeal the Corn Laws which restricted grain imports. He carved his initials on the back of a bench in the House of Commons, where they can still be seen – together with the date 1826.

DUNSOP BRIDGE
Between a bridge at one end and the 18th-century Thorneyholme Hall, now a hotel, at the other, is the tranquil hamlet of Dunsop Bridge. Children paddle in the safe, clear waters of the River Dunsop – which, a short way to the east of the village, merges with the River Hodder, rushing down from the Trough of Bowland. Just beyond the junction, the Hodder feeds a trout farm, whose waters seethe with fish being fattened for the table and to stock local rivers.

TROUGH OF BOWLAND
A soaring pass climbing to more than 1000ft between Dunsop Bridge and Abbeystead, the Trough of Bowland has magnificent views over the valleys of the Hodder and the Wyre. At the summit of the pass is the Trough Stone, the old boundary stone between Lancashire and Yorkshire, now badly weathered and often smothered in bracken.

Small tributaries trickle down from moorlands spongy with moss, but with drier patches of purple moor grass and heather, the haunts of red grouse, snipe and meadow pipits. In the autumn, patches of rusty-brown bracken contrast with the dark patches of burnt heather, fired to produce succulent shoots for the grouse upon which the moorland economy depends.

TARNBROOK
Rising high on a windswept fell, the peaty waters of Tarnbrook Wyre pound through a narrow gorge and are whipped into a spray which hangs like a swirling white cloak around the alders lining the bank. The hamlet of Tarnbrook consists of scattered sheep farms, sweet-scented wood smoke curling from their chimneys, and a mountain rescue centre which is kept busy when heavy snows fall on Bowland.

In the summer visiting sandpipers nest near the water and fly low over the brook, and ring ouzels feed their young among the tufts of heather. Resident short-eared owls hunt the open moor, often sharing the area with the graceful hen harrier.

ABBEYSTEAD
A steep descent between neat beech hedges leads to Abbeystead in its sheltered valley. Built on the site of a long-vanished Cistercian abbey, the village has some farms which look like manor houses, a fine school, an ornate horse trough and a colourful tangle of cottages. Surrounded by heather moors, Abbeystead is noted for its fine grouse and its bees – many of the farms and cottages have honey for sale.

The River Wyre flows over a pebbly bed before passing through a reservoir, built in the 19th century to provide extra water for textile industries downstream at Dolphinholme and beyond. The reservoir is gradually silting up and wildfowl gather there in winter.

About a mile beyond Abbeystead is Christ Church-over-Wyresdale, known locally as the Shepherds' Church. This is because its porch faces rich green water meadows – ideal grazing land for sheep. The inscription over the church door reads: 'O ye shepherds hear the word of the Lord.'

DOLPHINHOLME
At Dolphinholme the swiftly flowing Damas Gill joins the Wyre, which at one time provided water to power a now vanished textile mill. Beside the bridge is a restored gas lamp, installed in the early 19th century.

The village is a pleasant mixture of the old and the new, with late 18th-century cottages by the bridge and more recent houses sprinkled about. The late 19th-century St Mark's Church is low-lying with a stumpy central tower. Just to the south-east of Dolphinholme is Wyreside Hall, built in the early 1800s of a dignified, dark grey stone.

THURNHAM HALL
A sweeping drive through green pastures leads to Thurnham Hall, built around a 13th-century peel tower and backed by wooded gardens and an avenue of yews. The Dalton family formerly occupied the mansion for more than 400 years and added a magnificent Elizabethan Great Hall, a fine Jacobean staircase and some beautiful panelling and plaster work. There is also a Gothic-style chapel added in the mid-1850s, and a cunningly placed priest-hole. The hall is open on most days in the summer.

Just beyond the hall a narrow road on the left winds for 3 miles through flat fields to the remains of Cockersand Abbey, founded near the coast in the 12th century.

The road ends at the Wyre-Lune Bird Sanctuary, which is open throughout the year. It is noted for the sea birds, waders and wildfowl which roost on the sea covering the surrounding mud flats.

LUNE ESTUARY COASTAL PATH
A clearly marked path begins just beyond The Stork pub in the hamlet of Conder Green. It follows a disused railway line and is banked with hawthorns and stands of yellow gorse. There is a picnic site by the coast, and not far away brightly painted boats rock at anchor.

Across the bay is the tiny port of Glasson, built in the 18th century for trade with the West Indies. Today its prosperity comes mainly from trade in animal feed, grain and fuel in northern and southern Europe. A bustling marina links the Lancaster Canal to the estuary, and a colourful assortment of boats – some with sails flapping in the breeze, some with gently purring diesel engines – often waits to pass through the locks and out into the open sea.

Tourist information: Lancaster 32878.

Halls and hamlets of the Lune valley

TOUR
174
———— 26 MILES ————

Cumbrian and Lancashire villages are set against lofty crags. The transport of an earlier age is recalled by coaching inns, a disused canal and steam railway locomotives.

STAINTON
A narrow lane running between high hedgerows follows the grassy banks of Stainton Beck away from the busy main road to this tiny rural community. There are only a few farmsteads and cottages – many of them adorned by colourful shrubs – and the atmosphere is tranquil. An old stone footbridge crosses the beck and a bench stands in the shade of a nearby sycamore.

Just beyond the village lies a disused leg of the Lancaster Canal. It resembles an overgrown lily pond, but once it was a busy waterway along which horses would draw a 'swift packet boat' to Preston, about 35 miles away, in less than seven hours.

BURTON-IN-KENDAL
Once the clatter of horses and stage coaches echoed through the village, and two coaching inns survive as reminders of that age. Narrow alleys and courtyards are hidden behind the main street, and a jumble of cottages and fine old houses, many with ivy-clad walls, is set against the wooded hillside of Dalton Crags and surrounding farmland.

Burton once had an important corn market, and tall Georgian houses around the market square are evidence of those prosperous times. Traces of leg irons can be seen in the base of the 18th-century market cross.

At the northern end of the village the simple lines of the ancient parish church are framed by a rural landscape and by the lofty, scree-covered slopes of nearby Hutton Roof Crags.

LEIGHTON HALL
From a distance, the turrets and roof castellations of Leighton Hall stand out sharply against a backcloth of rolling park and woodlands, and a horizon tinged by the purple of distant fells. The neo-Gothic façade was added to this classical mansion in about 1800.

In the public rooms are many fine examples of antique furniture including pieces by Richard Gillow, a member of the family whose home the hall has been for more than four centuries. The elegant curved stone staircase is Georgian, and delicate pillars supporting a gallery are an exceptionally fine example of early Gothic revival.

The grounds include parkland, a shrubbery walk and a long, narrow lawn originally designed for archery. An aviary contains birds of prey,

including kestrels, owls and eagles, and most afternoons in summer visitors can watch the birds in flight in a display of hawking.

WARTON
A long main street contours the lower slopes of a hillside crowned by the exposed limestone terraces of Warton Crag. Cottages and more substantial houses, all built from local stone, lead towards a parish church with important transatlantic links. George Washington (1732-99), first President of the United States, was a descendant of the local landowner who built the church tower in the 15th century. An old family crest, which includes stars

and stripes, and a Stars and Stripes banner inside the church commemorate this bond.

In the vicarage gardens across the street, carefully preserved remains of a 14th-century lay rectory can be visited. But there was a settlement here as long ago as the Bronze Age, when people made their homes among the rocky knolls high above the village.

BORWICK
A detour of less than 2 miles leads to this small, leafy hamlet dominated by its magnificent Tudor hall. The earliest building is the partly ivy-clad, 14th-century defensive peel tower

which occupies four storeys. The delightful baronial hall was built in the late 16th century after peace had been made between England and Scotland and the need for a defensive house had passed.

The 9 acres of grounds include woodlands and formal gardens. Borwick Hall is now a residential training centre, but it is open to the public for three weeks in August.

STEAMTOWN
A collection of more than 30 old steam locomotives, including famous names such as the *Flying Scotsman*, dating from 1923, makes Steamtown in Carnforth the largest operating mainline steam depot in the country. Several of the locomotives are regularly leased to British Rail for special excursions. Open every day of the year except Christmas Day, it is an attraction for

PERIOD PIECE *The imposing white neo-Gothic façade of Leighton Hall resembles a stage set in a bowl of the hills.*

VALLEY VIEW *The author John Ruskin acclaimed the view over Lune valley at Kirkby Lonsdale as 'one of the loveliest scenes in England, therefore the world'.*

WHARTON CHURCH *The 15th-century tower has links with George Washington*

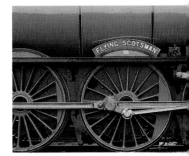

VENERABLE LOCO *The 'Flying Scotsman' is on view at Steamtown.*

all who enjoy the hiss of steam, the clanking of machinery and the smell of oily rags. Besides working locomotives and those in various stages of repair, there are model and miniature railways and a shop for collectors.

BOLTON-LE-SANDS
The whitewashed 17th and 18th-century cottages of Bolton-le-Sands lie behind a busy shopping street overlooking a delightful stretch of the Lancaster Canal. The Packet Boat Hotel, whose name recalls an earlier means of transport, now caters for the many pleasure boats moored nearby.

At the other end of the village the great Perpendicular tower of the parish church has been a landmark for seafarers over the centuries.

A lane leads over the railway to a picnic area by Morecambe Bay, with fine views of the Kent estuary.

Tourist information: Kendal 25758.

Dotted along the banks of the River Lune are clusters of old houses and colourful spreads of flowers. John Ruskin claimed the view at Kirkby Lonsdale was unsurpassed anywhere.

HALTON
An iron bridge just wide enough for a car spans the tree-lined banks of the River Lune. Norman kings chose Halton as the chief centre for their 22 Lonsdale Townships and built a castle high above the river; no trace of it remains but its site, a grassy mound marked by a flagpole, is a fine viewpoint. The village, dominated by the 15th-century tower of its church, is a delightful mix of cottages and imposing houses, all of them built in local stone.

A parking area by the southern end of the bridge is a convenient starting point for walks beside a stretch of river which is popular with anglers and oarsmen. Farther upstream the river is more turbulent, and canoeists can often be seen exercising their strength and skills in the torrents cascading over the weirs.

ARKHOLME
Beautifully preserved cottages and old stone houses with mullioned windows and colourful gardens line both sides of Arkholme's single street, leading down to the Lune. A prominent grassy dome near the water's edge was the site of a 12th-century fort.

A signposted walk through riverside meadows leads to Loyn Bridge and across the Lune to the village of Hornby and its castle.

KIRKBY LONSDALE
The town 'capital' of the Lune valley, has dignified, ivy-clad Georgian buildings and quaint cottages, narrow alleys and cobbled courtyards – with names like The Horsemarket and Salt Pie Lane. Shops and hotels mingle in a main street festooned in spring and summer with colourful flower baskets.

The parish church has a fine archway and magnificent stained glass, and from the churchyard, worn stone steps descend to the river bank, revealing a view of which John Ruskin said: 'I do not know in all my own country, still less in France or Italy, a place more naturally divine.'

Delightful riverside walks begin from the parking and picnic area by the graceful medieval spans of the Devil's Bridge.

The origin of the bridge is obscure, which has given rise to a legend that it was built by the Devil in a pact with an elderly lady. The story tells how Satan appeared one night and offered to build a bridge overnight so that the lady and her animals could cross the river, on condition that the first to cross would be his for ever. Next day Satan appeared to claim his due but the wily lady sent her dog across first and so cheated the Devil.

BARBON
A stone sign by an old bridge that carries the A683 northwards towards Sedbergh proclaims 'Main road to Barbon'. It leads to a small village clustered around its church, pub and tiny post office.

The swift-flowing Barbon Beck tumbles straight off Crag Hill, the high fell that dominates the eastern skyline. Then the beck winds through the village and under the old pack-horse bridge. Everywhere around the village, rough stone walls divide a patchwork of fields.

MIDDLETON
This scattered and far-flung parish occupies the eastern side of the Lune valley, along which Roman legionaries marched on their way to the border. Green meadows by the river-side give way in the east to the high ground of Middleton Fell, rising to nearly 2000ft and forming a natural barrier between the Lune valley and Yorkshire.

Just off the main road a massive medieval wall surrounds the remains of the 14th-century Middleton Hall. A high archway in the wall leads into the present-day farmyard.

BRIGFLATTS
Close to the banks of the River Rawthey in this tiny hamlet is the second oldest Friends' Meeting House in England. The oldest, built in 1670, is in Hertford. The plain stone building, surrounded by a small garden, was built in 1675 by the early followers of George Fox, founder of the Society of Friends – the Quakers – who came to the district to preach their gospel in the mid-17th century.

Inside the meeting house the simple oak panelling and benches create an atmosphere of enduring peace which must have comforted those who, because of persecution, had been forced to worship secretly in farm buildings or on the nearby fells. The heavily studded door is always open to visitors.

SEDBERGH
This small country town stands beneath the protective, dome-shaped peaks of Howgill Fells on raised ground above the meeting point of the Lune and Rawthey rivers. Elegant houses and gardens on the outskirts give way to a narrow main street of tall houses and busy shops and pubs. In the centre, the magnificent parish church of St Andrew dating back to Norman times is flanked by the playing fields and meadows which surround Sedbergh public school.

Steep paths lead to the top of Winder, some 1100ft directly above the town, from which the views are spectacular. To the south are the Pennines, deeply cut by the valleys of Garsdale and Dent, and farther west the broad valley of the Lune sweeps away towards the distant blue-tinged hills of the Forest of Bowland.

KILLINGTON
A narrow lane, just wide enough for a single car and sunk deep between hedgerows fragrant in spring, dips suddenly into the hidden hamlet of Killington – little more than a cluster of cottages and farms. The partly ruined Killington Hall, built in the 15th century as a fortified residence, is now a farmhouse. Its attractive front wall, half covered in thick ivy, displays heraldic symbols and handsome trefoiled windows. Opposite is a 14th-century church believed to have been once connected to the hall by a secret passage.

The road out of the village climbs steeply. Soon, hedgerows give way to open moorland scenery, varied by conifer plantations and by the bleak waters of Killington Reservoir, built during the last century to feed the Lancaster Canal.

Tourist information: Lancaster 32878; Kirkby Lonsdale 71603.

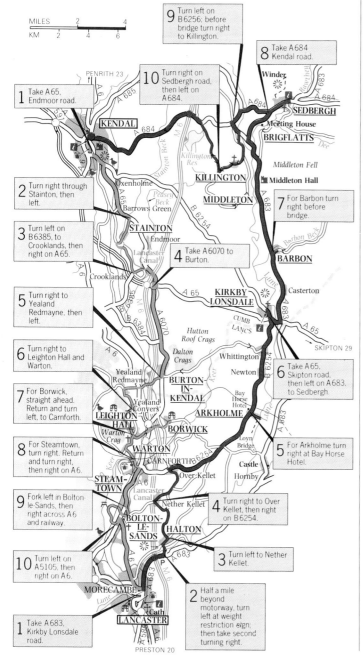

Green lanes in southern Lakeland

TOUR
176

28 MILES

Narrow roads wind through a patchwork of woodland and sheep farms, and trout streams run below the distant fells. An old hall and a castle are reminders of earlier days of conflict.

KENDAL

Pearly grey stone buildings line narrow, twisting streets in this busy market town on the banks of the River Kent. Despite a heavy influx of summer visitors it remains very much a place where the townspeople and villagers from the surrounding area do their shopping – especially on Saturdays when the street market adds its clamour to the general bustle.

Narrow lanes leading off Highgate, the main street, are said to have been built to make Kendal easier to defend during the long Anglo-Scottish wars. Troubled times are also recalled by the ruined castle perched on a steep, isolated hill above the river. It was the birthplace of Catherine Parr, Henry VIII's sixth and last wife.

Abbot Hall, an 18th-century mansion in a quiet park beside the River Kent, has been restored to its original elegance and houses an art gallery and cultural centre. There is also a museum of Lakeland life and industry in the hall's fine stable block.

WINSTER

Almost hidden among the folds of the wooded hillsides that border an upper reach of the River Winster lies this hamlet of whitewashed cottages of rough-hewn stone. A 17th-century cottage, with a magnificently studded front door and a multi-coloured rockery, houses the village post office. Its tinkling shop bell evokes memories of the days when shopping was a time for gossip as well as for buying provisions. In Winster it still is.

LYTH VALLEY

At Crosthwaite, on the north side of the Lyth Valley, a footpath from a bridge over the sparkling River Gilpin leads in both directions along the river bank.

The sheltered valley is noted for its damson orchards. The trees are magnificent in full bloom in spring, and in September the fruit can be bought from farm shops by the roadside. An impressive view of the valley, flanked by the blunt shoulder of Whitbarrow Scar, can be seen just beyond Brigsteer as the road rises before entering a strip of woodland.

LEVENS HALL

Yew and box trees sculptured to look like cones, corkscrews, circles, pyramids and other curious shapes make Levens Hall's topiary garden unique in Britain. 'Queen Catherine and her

Maids of Honour' stand in one part of the garden, and another group of clipped trees is known as 'Coach and Horses'.

The topiary was created in the late 17th century by the Frenchman Guillaume Beaumont, who had been gardener to James II. Some of the mature sculptured trees stand 20ft tall. At their feet are neat flowerbeds, surrounded by meticulously clipped box hedges.

Overlooking the garden is the old stone-built Levens Hall, mainly Elizabethan, but constructed around a 13th-century peel tower. Woodcarvings on the overmantel in the drawing room represent the four elements, the four seasons and the five senses. Some of the hall's furniture dates from the Elizabethan period.

In the grounds the hiss and clank of steam engines is heard each Sunday – weather permitting – when the hall's collection of working model steam engines is brought to life. The collection illustrates the progress of steam from 1820 to 1930, and includes traction engines, a steam wagon and a steam car. The house and gardens are open most days in summer.

SIZERGH CASTLE

Round the massive creeper-clad walls of a 14th-century peel tower, built to keep out Scottish raiders, clusters a group of buildings added over the following four centuries. Together they form three sides of a rectangular courtyard. The peel tower is easily recognisable by its turret rising above the castellated parapet.

Sizergh has been the home of the Strickland family since 1239, and its name stems from even earlier settlement in the area; it comes from the Scandinavian *Sigarith*, a personal name, and *erg*, 'a dairy farm', and dates from Viking occupation in the 9th and 10th centuries.

Several rooms have Elizabethan oak panelling from floor to ceiling, and the dining room has a richly carved overmantel bearing the date 1564. The top floor of the peel tower is now a museum, where 14th-century fireplaces and windows survive unaltered. A number of portraits of the Stuart royal family are on display, and there is also a collection of Stuart and Jacobean relics.

The Sizergh estate covers about 1500 acres and includes a rock garden of hardy ferns and dwarf conifers. A footpath leads through the grounds to Brigsteer Woods, where daffodils carpet the glades in spring. The estate is administered by the National Trust, and both the castle and the grounds are open to the public daily in summer.

Tourist information: Kendal 25758.

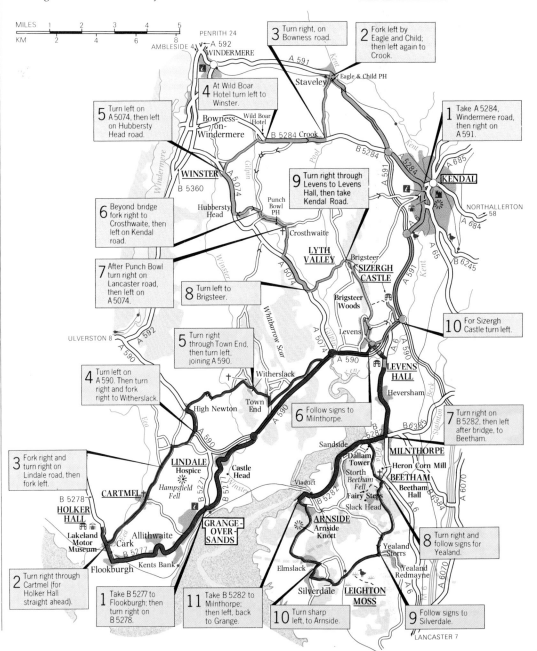

VALLEY CHURCH *A preaching cross once stood on the site of St Mary's Church at Crosthwaite, which means 'place of the cross'.*

TOUR 177

44 MILES

The golden tidal sands of Morecambe Bay fringe peat moss and salt marshes, spread below limestone peaks. Inland are narrow lanes once travelled by the monks of Cartmel Priory.

GRANGE-OVER-SANDS

Ornamental gardens and a flower-bedecked promenade give Grange-over-Sands some of the gentility of a Victorian seaside resort, to which are added the attractions of a modern holiday centre.

Behind Grange-over-Sands, the 727ft Hampsfield Fell is crowned by the Hospice, built as a shelter for travellers by Thomas Remmington, vicar of Cartmel, between 1835 and 1854. From the fell's summit there are spectacular views of the Lakeland peaks and the Pennines.

HOLKER HALL

A magnificent deer park surrounds this stately home of the Cavendish family, close to the village of Cark. Extensively rebuilt last century after a fire, Holker Hall is an impressive mixture of 17th-century, Georgian and Victorian architecture.

The Victorian wing houses the library and other rooms containing fine collections of furniture, porcelain and paintings. Formal and woodland gardens are colourful in spring and summer with rhododendrons, azaleas, magnolias and cherry trees.

A replica of Sir Malcolm Campbell's *Bluebird* is among a collection of more than 70 vintage cars and motorcycles in the Lakeland Motor Museum, converted from Holker Hall's old stables. The hall and motor museum are open most days in summer.

CARTMEL

Ivy-clad walls, old shops and pubs, and a 14th-century gatehouse owned by the National Trust, surround Cartmel's village square and market cross. A narrow street of neat, white-painted cottages with small cobbled forecourts leads across the River Eea to the cathedral-like priory church.

Dating back to the 12th century, Cartmel Priory is one of the few English monastic churches to survive the Reformation unscathed. It contains elegantly carved choir stalls and a magnificent 15th-century stained-glass east window. The church's towering belfry is a local landmark.

MILNTHORPE

The village square is the scene of a lively Friday market that has been held for more than 700 years. It is also a convenient parking place for visitors, who can then set off on foot to explore nooks and corners that recall the village's old coaching days. The most attractive part of Milnthorpe is by Dallam Tower, a stately home on the banks of the River Bela.

Just beyond Milnthorpe the route passes Dallam's deer park.

MOTORING MEMORIES *Vintage cars and a 1920's style country garage in the Lakeland Motor Museum at Holker Hall recall motoring's golden age.*

GARDENER'S WHIM *Levens Hall's topiary garden creates a fantasy world.*

BEETHAM

The cluster of cottages, ancient church and village inn beneath the wooded hillside are undisturbed by the nearby main road. In earlier days worshippers would walk several miles to the parish church, many crossing Beetham Fell by way of the 'Fairy Steps' cut into the limestone ridge above the village.

Half a mile to the south, the ruins of Beetham Hall, once a semi-fortified house, can be seen among modern farm buildings.

In the opposite direction, a signposted walk along the river behind the present mill leads to the restored water-driven Heron corn mill, which is open to the public.

The route continues towards Silverdale and Arnside through a maze of twisting lanes.

LEIGHTON MOSS

One of the rarest of English bird calls may sometimes be heard rising from a wooded valley between the villages of Silverdale and Yealand Redmayne. This is the deep resonant 'boom' of the male bittern, which breeds on the Leighton Moss bird reserve.

The reserve, administered by the Royal Society for the Protection of Birds, is open daily.

ARNSIDE

Steeply banked rows of houses built in local limestone rise up the hillside from Arnside's elegant riverside promenade. They overlook the Kent estuary and the long slender railway viaduct which crosses the water to Grange-over-Sands.

South of the village is the wooded hillside of Arnside Knott, owned by the National Trust. There are easy walks to the 520ft summit, from which can be seen a panorama of distant high fells, the Pennines and the vastness of Morecambe Bay.

LINDALE

The iron obelisk near the centre of the village is a tribute to the engineer John Wilkinson, who built the famous iron bridge over the River Severn. Before he died in 1808 'Iron-Mad' Wilkinson had an iron coffin built for himself, and in it he lies buried in an unmarked grave in Lindale's parish church.

Just outside the village, at Castle Head, is the impressive house Wilkinson built beside the River Winster. It is now an outdoor activity centre.

Tourist information: Grange-over-Sands 4331 (summer).

Up and away on two mountain passes

TOUR
178
50 MILES

Among high crags above Lakeland is Hardknott Pass, with its spectacular view of a vast Roman fort. After another stiff climb to the Wrynose Pass, Coniston offers its secluded beauty.

BROUGHTON IN FURNESS
The quiet of this town is shattered on Tuesday – market day. This is a particularly busy day at summer's end, when loud bleating and floating clouds of straw herald the arrival of sheep brought down off the fells to be auctioned.

At any time, Broughton is a place to test one's fitness. It is built on slopes and stairs. Its largest shop is the Mountain Centre, where a notice exhorts people to canoe, sail, cycle, walk and climb. Equipment for all these pursuits – including no fewer than 12 different kinds of canoe – is on sale.

The square, overhung by chestnut trees, has a set of stocks in full working order, a slate table on which fish were once displayed for sale, and a graceful obelisk commemorating the Golden Jubilee of George III in 1810. A yellow Georgian building with a small belfry houses the Jack Hadwin collection of vintage motorcycles.

The heart of the town is a 14th-century peel tower built by the Broughton family, who held the manor from Saxon times until the 1480s. An 18th-century house has been built around it – not open to the public but visible from footpaths in the grounds. The Church of St Mary Magdalene, dating partly from Norman times, has been much restored.

Only minutes from this scene is the road to Ulpha and the high passes. It is narrow; it turns and twists; yet it is exhilarating. It climbs up, under and around the high crags thrusting up through the turf and bracken and comes at last to a wide, curved prairie full of sheep noises – and with the worn mountains all about.

ULPHA
The name derives from a Scandinavian word meaning 'wolf hill'. There is not much of Ulpha – mainly a few cottages and some almshouses – but its setting among the wild fells is glorious, if lonely.

The Church of St John is handsomely set on high ground. It has wall paintings and an altar made from apple or pear wood.

BOOT
A pretty white stone oasis in the midst of the dark crags, Boot has two hotels, a miniature art gallery and some old cottages bristling with the largest and latest TV aerials – necessary with the mountains crowding all round. A lane leads down to St Catherine's Church by the chattering Esk river.

From the pub, a path leads to Whillan Beck and a water mill that has ground corn since the 1570s at least. It is still in working order, and during the summer months puts on an exhibition of milling and of the agricultural life of the district.

For a large part of its existence, however, Boot was a mining and quarrying village, producing copper, iron and granite. These called into being the narrow-gauge railway that now terminates at nearby Dalegarth. Today it is the passenger-carrying Ravenglass and Eskdale Railway, famed among train enthusiasts.

For the more energetic, there is yet another attraction – a nature trail from Dalegarth Station through a gorge to the magnificent Stanley Force.

HARDKNOTT PASS
A battery of notices at the bottom warn that the pass is a single-track road, unsuitable in winter conditions, has severe gradients (maximum 30% – 1 in 3), is unsuitable for caravans and requires extreme caution. Often an RAF Mountain Rescue truck stands by.

Though the gradients are fierce, the road is adventurous rather than terrifying. In any case, it is a challenge that should be met, for Hardknott Pass is the highlight of the tour and contains one of the great sights of England. This is Hardknott Roman Fort, the vast stone fort that the Romans called Mediobogdum and set high in the fells to command Eskdale and the road to the east.

Despite its size – it covers some 3 acres – it is remarkably easy to miss when coming from the west. The road passes it by without acknowledgment or sign, and the only clue is a small car park cut into the bank on the left about half a mile back from the summit of the pass. The fort lies just behind the car park.

Eased into a wild, sloping plateau, the outer wall – partly rebuilt – stands 10ft high and even after 1800 years the foundations of the commandant's house, and the granaries, are perfectly clear. So too are those of the bathhouse outside the wall, though the wooden barracks in which the troops lived have long vanished.

The garrison was not drawn from imperial legions, who were seldom posted to such distant stations, but from auxiliaries recruited in the provinces. The regiment at Hardknott was the 4th Cohort of Dalmatians from what is now Yugoslavia. What they thought of the Cumbrian winter winds after their sunny homeland might easily be imagined – though they could be drilled into warmth on the parade ground east of the fort. This ground was hammered out, with enormous labour, from the boulder-strewn mountainside; military priorities change little with the centuries. What gives the scene its particular attraction is how very little it can have altered since Roman days. There are the same sounds of wind and water, the same crags standing over the pass. The toy-like farms and fields

LONESOME ROAD *Down from the exhilarating Hardknott Pass, the route winds along the green valley of the Duddon.*

away down in Eskdale are tidier now, probably, than they were then. But the hard glint of the sea at the far end, and the mountain clouds touched by pillars of light, are unchanging.

WRYNOSE PASS

From the summit of Hardknott Pass, the road tips violently down to the long, lovely valley of the Duddon, then shoots up again to Wrynose Pass, the western gate to Langdale and Ambleside. It is also the eastern gate to Eskdale and Ravenglass, and therefore one of the reasons for the Roman fort on Hardknott.

It is not too stiff a climb – for those who have just accomplished Hardknott Pass, at any rate – and it reaches up to Three Shire Stone, the boundary marker of the three old counties of Cumberland, Lancashire and Westmorland. Through a gap in the wild hills the serene, civilised acres of Little Langdale can be seen. The descent to the valley is equal to Hardknott standards – a narrow ledge angling to a steep dive down the mountainside.

CONISTON

Many visitors would vote for Coniston as the most endearing of Lakeland villages. It has the mixture right. From the shore of its lake – Coniston Water – it climbs in steps up the lower slopes of its mountain, the Old Man of Coniston, whose quarries supply the silver-grey, light green and dark green slate of which the village is composed.

Gift shops and tearooms, mountaineering suppliers and bed-and-breakfast establishments are plentiful but not obtrusive. There are some toughish footpaths up and around the Old Man and, for wet afternoons, there is the Ruskin Museum, one of the finest in the area.

The museum, open daily in summer, is devoted mainly to the life and works of John Ruskin, art critic, historian and virtual dictator of the late-Victorian artistic scene. He lies beneath a delicately sculpted cross in Coniston churchyard. Close by is the grave of James Hewitson who, as a lance corporal in the Royal Lancaster Regiment, won the Victoria Cross in France in 1918.

Another local hero, Donald Campbell, is commemorated by a stone seat on the village green. He was killed while attempting to break the world waterspeed record on Coniston Water in 1967, and his body was never found.

It could be said that Coniston Water is the most satisfactory of the lakes, at least by Victorian standards of the picturesque. It neatly divides two different but complementary kinds of scenery, so that the village looks across to tiered forest rising from the lake shore. Between forest and lake is Brantwood, Ruskin's sprawling, lovely white house. Ruskin could look west to the village and the towering wilderness of the mountains behind.

Brantwood was a power house of the Victorian art world, and this is reflected in its astonishing collection of paintings, furniture and memorabilia. A special joy is a mass of drawings by J.M.W. Turner, who was Ruskin's particular favourite. The gar-

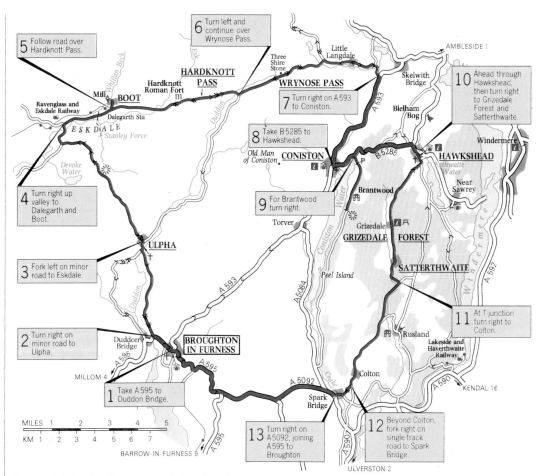

dens are delightful, with a nature trail and a waterfall, beside which is Ruskin's stone seat. The house and grounds are open daily in summer and most days in winter.

Another evocation of Coniston's yesterdays is the National Trust's flagship – in fact, the sole member of its fleet. This is Steam Yacht *Gondola*, first launched on Coniston Water in 1859. The elegant craft carries passengers on lake trips through most of the year. One of the features she passes at the southern end of the lake is Peel Island. In *Swallows and Amazons*, Arthur Ransome transported it to Windermere and called it Wild Cat Island.

HAWKSHEAD

This is a townsman's dream of a Lakeland village – cobbles, overhanging gables, twisting alleys, little squares and bowfronted shops selling such traditional Cumbrian delicacies as sausage, mint cake, gingerbread, rum and brandy butter, cheese and toffee. The village caters for the townsman's dream by excluding cars from its streets. It is pretty, without being cute.

William Wordsworth attended the Grammar School from 1778-87 and, thoughtfully for posterity, carved his name on one of the old benches. The school is open to the public most days in summer. Wordsworth lodged with a family whose cottage can still be seen on the corner of Vicarage Lane and Wordsworth Street.

Wordsworth wrote with affection of the 'snow-white church upon the hill'. That description fitted until the

building's restoration in 1875, when the whitewash was removed from the exterior walls. The church, dedicated to St Michael and All Angels, probably stands on Viking foundations but dates mostly from the 16th century.

Edwin Sandys, Archbishop of York and founder of the Grammar School, endowed much of the building. There is plenty to see in the church, including a framed 'Burial in Woollen' certificate of 1696. These certificates were introduced when, in order to foster the wool trade, Parliament decreed that all burials should be in wool only. The views from the churchyard to the surrounding mountains are superb.

Probably the oldest building in the village is the Courthouse, now a museum. It is the gatehouse of a long-vanished manor that belonged to Furness Abbey. Manorial courts, presided over by the abbot, were held on the first floor.

The museum can be visited in summer by obtaining the key from the National Trust Information Centre in the village square.

GRIZEDALE FOREST

About 8700 acres of integrated forest and farmland between Coniston Water and Windermere are run by the Forestry Commission. The introduction to the area is a glorious drive through rolling wooded hills, with meadows running up from the edge of the road to the tree line.

Car parks and picnic sites are numerous, and at the heart of the forest is the Visitor and Wildlife Centre. It stands near the site of

Grizedale Hall, which was a Second World War prisoner camp for German officers. The hall was demolished in 1956, but the outbuildings remain to provide a nucleus for the visitor centre, a forest shop, a theatre and other facilities.

Throughout the summer there is an exhibition on the natural history, archaeology and industries of the forest. Concerts, lectures and film shows are held in the theatre.

A number of waymarked trails begin at the Centre. They range from the mile-long Millwood Forest Trail to the 9½ mile Silurian Way, and provide opportunities to observe the forest's plants and animals – including red squirrels and the roe and red deer whose ancestors roamed these hills long before man came. There are observation hides in the forest, including one overlooking a tarn where wildfowl can be seen.

A nice touch by the visitor centre's exit is the notice: 'We hope previous visitors left the forest clean for your enjoyment.'

SATTERTHWAITE

The hamlet is of Viking origin, and its name means 'the clearing of the saeter (summer farm)'. It is not much more than that today, for all about it lies the vast Grizedale Forest. But it is a pretty little place, built of the same local stone as the mossy dry-stone walls, so it looks as though it grew as naturally in its place as the trees.

Tourist information: Coniston 41533 (summer); Hawkshead 525 (summer).

Lakeland scenes that inspired a poet

TOUR 179

— 44 MILES —

Craggy fells and peaceful lakes still retain the beauty that inspired the poet William Wordsworth. He lived, wrote and lies buried here, and two of his family homes are now museums.

AMBLESIDE

This is Lakeland's vortex. The streets in season are a swirl of humanity beneath the jutting boards of hotels, inns, guesthouses, teashops and restaurants, looking like banners at a medieval tournament. For visitors the accepted dress seems to be breeches, hairy stockings, massive boots, and rucksacks like Wendy houses.

Even for the less energetic, Ambleside is a pleasant place. It is a serpentine, humpbacked little town built of brown or grey-greenish stone slabs. Bridge House – a doll-sized house perched on a tiny bridge over Stock Ghyll – has been an apple store, a cobbler's and a family home; now it is a National Trust Information Centre. A little upstream is the splendid Old Mill, now a knitwear shop.

RYDAL

In all weathers, a steady stream of anoraked and booted visitors march up the hill above the village to Rydal Mount, the stone farmhouse of pleasantly jumbled periods that was the poet Wordsworth's home from 1813 until his death in 1850. His wife Mary and sister Dorothy also spent the remainder of their lives there, and the presence of the three is everywhere in the house – in the furniture, the garden they created, in the portraits and mementos. Rydal Mount is open daily, except Tuesdays in winter.

It is easy to see why Wordsworth chose Rydal, a stone and slate village with a humpbacked bridge, overlooked by the crag of Loughrigg Fell. An eyecatcher is Church Cottage, with its lattice windows, barrel-shaped chimney and garden of multicoloured heathers and fuchsias beside a little stream. St Mary's Church, where Wordsworth worshipped, has windows glowing with Pre-Raphaelite angels and cherubs. Just beyond the village, calm, reedy Rydal Water reflects the surrounding hills.

GRASMERE

If as many people read Wordsworth's works as visit his house, Dove Cottage in Grasmere, then the poet's shade must be gratified indeed. His earthly remains lie in Grasmere churchyard beside those of his beloved sister Dorothy and his wife and children.

Wordsworth also has a monument inside the church dedicated to St Oswald, a 7th-century king of Northumbria. The building probably dates from the 12th century, and its massive roof timbers resemble those of an ancient barn.

The Wordsworths lived in Dove Cottage from 1799 to 1808, and the interior remains much as it did during their occupancy. It is relatively humble; the poet had no financial security until he was appointed Distributor of Stamps in the area and moved to Rydal Mount in 1813.

Next door is a former blacksmith's shop that is now the Grasmere and Wordsworth Museum. It houses many relics of the poet and his friends, and presents a portrayal of Grasmere life as it was in their day.

Both Dove Cottage and the Wordsworth Museum are open daily from March to October.

THIRLMERE

The road along the western shore of the lake is a conifer tunnel with feathery branches of softest green reaching over to touch the high bracken. Through the black columns of the trees there are only occasional glimpses of the deep, clear lake; yet this is still the best side to see it from, looking over to the vast, smooth hummock of Helvellyn climbing up into the clouds on the far side, with the sun making gilded patterns on its flanks.

The best views are obtained from Hause Point, where railed steps lead to the top of a rock overlooking the lake, and at Armboth, where a car park has been cut through the trees almost to the water's edge. There are other parking places along the western shore, while at the northern end a forest trail leads up to Castle Rock.

CASTLERIGG STONE CIRCLE

The poet John Keats described this 3500-year-old Bronze Age monument as 'a dismal cirque of Druid stone upon a forlorn moor'. The site is today a neat, sheep-nibbled green field guarded by a National Trust sign.

None of the stones are much more than 6ft tall, and it has none of the awesomeness of Stonehenge or Avebury or the mighty stone circles of Orkney. Nevertheless, standing there on its hillock and gazing outwards to the ring of surrounding mountains, it is obvious that it was sited by someone with a magnificent sense of drama, and it remains a noble tribute to gods unknown.

THRELKELD

This is a pretty little village of two-storey stone houses and a couple of neat pubs – The Salutation and The Horse and Farrier. The place is well known for its August sheepdog trials, and even more as the headquarters of the Blencathra Fell Pack, the premier foxhound pack of the Lake District.

As with all fell packs, members of the hunt follow hounds on foot. Among the surrounding mountains is the glorious Saddleback, or Blencathra, that soars above the village to a height of over 2600ft.

AIRA FORCE

Just beyond the hamlet of Dockray, with its big, good-looking pub, there is a National Trust car park labelled Gowbarrow. A path leads from this through a steep field to the Aira Beck, a white roaring cataract running down to the dark trench of Ullswater.

Another car park farther down the road is the starting point of a path to Aira Force. There, the stream rushes under a little stone bridge and is flung, spitting spray, down a cold, green, 70ft hole lined with ferns and moss. At the bottom of the hill, below Aira Force, there is a delectable drive along the shores of Ullswater to Glenridding where there are teas, guesthouses, boats for hire and cruises on the lake. All about is walkers' and climbers' country.

KIRKSTONE PASS

The road serpentines upwards with near-sheer screes falling away down the mountainside on either hand. From the top of the pass a 3 mile minor road known locally as 'The Struggle', drops down steeply to Ambleside in one of the finest scenic rides that even Lakeland can offer the motorist. The bird's-eye view looking down on Ambleside church tower is particularly memorable.

Tourist information: Ambleside 33084 (summer); Grasmere 245 (summer).

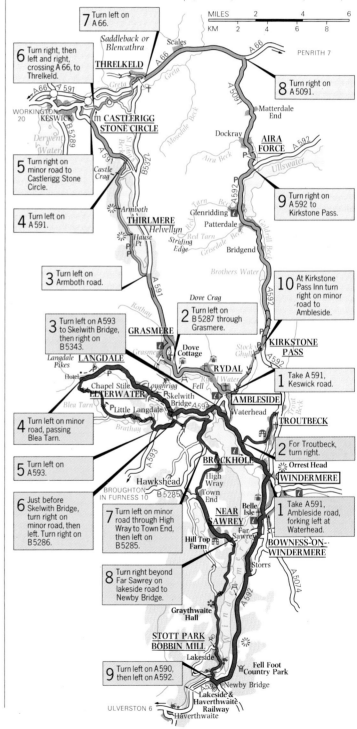

7 Turn left on A66.

6 Turn right, then left and right, crossing A66, to Threlkeld.

8 Turn right on A5091.

5 Turn right on minor road to Castlerigg Stone Circle.

4 Turn left on A591.

9 Turn right on A592 to Kirkstone Pass.

3 Turn left on Armboth road.

3 Turn left on A593 to Skelwith Bridge, then right on B5343.

2 Turn left on B5287 through Grasmere.

10 At Kirkstone Pass Inn turn right on minor road to Ambleside.

4 Turn left on minor road, passing Blea Tarn.

1 Take A591, Keswick road.

5 Turn left on A593.

6 Just before Skelwith Bridge, turn right on minor road, then left. Turn right on B5286.

7 Turn left on minor road through High Wray to Town End, then left on B5285.

2 For Troubeck, turn right.

1 Take A591, Ambleside road, forking left at Waterhead.

8 Turn right beyond Far Sawrey on lakeside road to Newby Bridge.

9 Turn left on A590, then left on A592.

292

—— 45 MILES ——

England's largest lake is fed by becks tumbling from mountains of matchless beauty. Villages whose cottages are roofed with green and blue slate are tucked away in the valleys.

WINDERMERE AND BOWNESS

The coming of the railway in the 1840s lured northern magnates to Windermere. The mansions they built overlooking the lake remain, towered, turreted and mullioned, but they are all hotels and boarding houses now. From almost opposite the station a path leads up in half a mile to Orrest Head and one of the finest views in the area.

Bowness, by the shore, is prettier, livelier and older than Windermere. It was a port that grew up around the 15th-century St Martin's Church, and is now a resort more reminiscent of the seaside than the lake shore.

The lake runs 10 miles into the dim bulk of the hills, and in the foreground is the wooded, 40 acre Belle Isle. The island, reached by ferry from Bowness, has the first perfectly round house to be built in England, dating from 1774.

About half a mile north along the lakeside road is the Steamboat Museum, open from Easter to October. Its roofed harbour houses a dozen or so old lake boats, each with an endearing history.

BROCKHOLE

A white Victorian mansion houses the Lake District National Park Visitor Centre, which is second to none of its kind in the country. Sight and sound exhibitions embrace all aspects of the area. Outside, flowery terraces look over magnificent trees to the lake.

TROUTBECK

The road up to Troutbeck is bordered by tidy estates and dry-stone walls. To the right, the headwaters of Windermere gleam pale pewter in the valley.

Troutbeck is composed almost entirely of narrow slabs of grey-brown stone. Its cottages and farms are strung along a mile-long ridge between Town End and Town Head.

Town End Farm, built in 1628 and now the property of the National Trust, contains furniture and utensils assembled by the Browne family over 300 years. Carved oak, leather bookbacks and copper pans gleam and twinkle with the polish and love of centuries, so that it seems as though the owners had only stepped out for a moment. In fact, the last Browne died in 1914. The house is open most days in summer.

ELTERWATER

The entrance to Langdale is abrupt. A quick rattle of a cattle grid under the wheels, and there in front are the ridges and heads of the Langdale Pikes, like a pride of resting lions. Just to the left of the road is Elterwater, a village built mainly of green slate slabs and gathered about a corner shop, the Britannia pub and a triangular green.

Behind the village the Great Langdale Beck leaps and cavorts in a ravine on whose banks are the remains of the juniper plantations that were the basis of Elterwater's charcoal-burning industry. The curious little first-floor galleries on some cottages are spinning galleries on which women used to spin and weave the local wool.

LANGDALE

Beyond Chapel Stile, a pretty slate-quarrying village on the Great Langdale Beck, the road twists, rises and plunges until it comes to an abrupt end at the greystone Dungeon Ghyll Hotel. The great arc of the Langdale mountains, Pike of Stickle, Harrison Stickle, Great Knott and the rest, fill the sky behind.

From the car park beside the hotel a steep path leads up to Dungeon Ghyll Force. Ribbons of water drop into an abyss, nearly 100ft deep, whose form really does suggest a dungeon. From there, the route follows a steep minor road up into fells dressed in russet, faded green and old gold, with a pale tumble of sunlit cloud over the pikes.

The road grows narrower and goes through gates and over cattle grids to stilly Blea Tarn, mirroring a topknot of firs in its water. On then to Little Langdale, with its handsome valley farms and Three Shires Inn.

NEAR SAWREY

In a green dell lies this pretty grey village where the prevailing breeze streams horizontal ribbons of grey smoke from the chimney pots. Just outside, guarded by an enormous cedar, is Hill Top Farm. In 1900 Peter Rabbit, or his royalties, bought it for Beatrix Potter, and it was later the birthplace of Tom Kitten, Jemima Puddle-Duck, Samuel Whiskers and other childhood deities.

An early publicist of the ideals of the National Trust, Miss Potter left the 17th-century Hill Top to the nation, together with her furniture, china and drawings. It is open daily in summer, except Fridays. Fans of *The Tale of Jemima Puddle-Duck* will recognise the Tower Bank Arms pub next door; this too, is the property of the National Trust.

STOTT PARK BOBBIN MILL

One of the country's more unusual museums, the Stott Park Bobbin Mill is the sole survivor of many similar factories in the area whose chief customers were the Lancashire cotton mills. From its opening in 1835, Stott Park turned out some 28,000 reels and bobbins a day until it closed in 1971.

Few alterations have been made, and the mill is still in working order. Former workers show visitors the venerable lathes, driven by wildly flapping leather belts. The mill is open daily in summer.

Tourist information: Windermere 4561; (Bowness) Windermere 2895 (summer).

MOUNTAIN GREENERY *Grassy fells crowd Ullswater's southern shores, with Place Fell's peak thrusting above Birk Fell and wooded hills tumbling to the water's edge.*

Green coast and grey hills of Cumbria

Along the Cumbrian coast the rivers flowing down from the Lakeland fells enter the sea. On their banks men have built castles, monasteries – and a nuclear power station.

WHITEHAVEN
Before trains and steamships, Whitehaven was as large a port as Liverpool. It imported tobacco from Virginia and exported coal from its own mines above the harbour to Ireland. The 18th-century War of American Independence put paid to the tobacco trade, and the mines are mostly reduced to some spectacular fragments of early 19th-century industrial archaeology.

The docks and harbours remain, however, and so massively walled that the complex looks like the flooded interior of a gigantic castle. There are still some coasters among the fishing boats along the quays, and when the tide goes out, the sands are clean and gold.

A heart of Georgian elegance shows itself in Whitehaven's wide, grid-pattern streets, in the splendid terraces and public buildings and, above all, in St James's Church. The Museum – the old Market Hall – tells the story of Whitehaven's tobacco merchants, sailors, trawlermen and miners. On Thursdays and Saturdays the James Street market offers homemade pies, Cumberland sausage, sheepskins and locally made sweets.

EGREMONT
Lying among the low hills of the Ehen valley, the little industrial town has a turn-of-the-century air that seems more in accord with the 1914 infantryman on its war memorial than with the futuristic atomic power complex on the horizon.

Egremont consists mostly of a single wide street whose two-storey, flat-fronted houses open their front doors straight onto the pavement. Windows and doors are surrounded by massive stone blocks, and probably the walls are stone too, except that they have long disappeared under cheerful coats of blue, yellow, green or cream.

The town takes its noble-sounding name from that of the castle, whose tumbled, red keep stands on a mound at the street's southern end. The legend of the Horn of Egremont, recalled in the name of a local pub and in a poem by William Wordsworth, tells of a great horn that was hung above the castle gate and could be sounded only by a true de Lucy Lord of Egremont.

Egremont has an excellent art gallery that exhibits the work of Cumbrian artists, and an annual Crab Fair which celebrates the late September season of the crab apple, and has done so since 1267. Features of the fair are an apple cart parade, a greasy pole competition and the World Gurning (ugly face) Competition.

CALDER BRIDGE
The little village sits in the midst of the oddest contrast on this coast. Less than a mile up the swift-flowing Calder river to the east is Calder Abbey, founded by the Cistercians in 1134, badly knocked about by the Scots four years later, and reoccupied by monks from Furness until the Dissolution in 1536. The ruins are serene and picturesque, but too shaky to walk among; they can be seen, however, from the road.

Then to the west, on the edge of the sea, are the domes and towers of Calder Hall nuclear power station and the nuclear fuel reprocessing plant, all part of the Sellafield complex. An exhibition, open daily, shows the development of nuclear power in Britain and the work of British Nuclear Fuels. It also sets out to allay public uneasiness about the safety of the nuclear power industry.

GOSFORTH
The western gateway to the Lake District National Park is an attractive place of sturdy stone-and-slate houses that might have been built at any time in the last 300 years. A clue is provided by the library, over whose door a plaque reads: 1628 IOHN ET MARGARAT SHEARWEN. There is an excellent crafts shop and a temptingly scented home bakery.

The chief treasures of Gosforth, however, are the church and its remarkable collection of Norse and early Christian monuments, many of which were discovered in the foundations during 19th-century renovations. Finest of all is the tall, slender cross in the churchyard whose carvings depict the triumph of good over evil.

WAST WATER
The deepest and most remote-feeling of all the English lakes is slaty-black, and the mountains rising almost sheer from its banks are bare, sending great fans of scree down from their summits to the water.

At Wasdale Head there are some sheep pastures, neatly framed by dry-stone walls of rounded boulders, and an inn famed among climbers. A footpath runs from the car park up to Sty Head Pass and Great Gable. The hamlet is said to possess the smallest parish church in England. It is certainly very small, and is roofed with massive slate tiles over beams that may have come from Viking wrecks.

The road from Wast Water to Ravenglass is idyllic, if a little narrow. It offers the lake and the savage mountains, sweet pastures governed by mossy stone walls, sudden vistas across miles of country. Then there are the white-gold sands of the Ravenglass estuary.

RAVENGLASS
The Romans established a naval base at Ravenglass to supply the militarised zone around Hadrian's Wall. Little remains of their 300 year stay but a bathhouse, one so impressive that it became known as Walls Castle. It is still one of the highest-standing Roman buildings in Britain.

The layout of Ravenglass Main Street has changed little since the 16th century, but the harbour has long been silted up. Iron ore from the mines at Boot was occasionally shipped from Ravenglass until the opening of the Ravenglass and Eskdale Railway in 1875. Though the mines and quarries up the valley are no more, the line is now one of the most popular privately owned narrow-gauge lines in Britain. Each year it carries thousands of holidaymakers through some of the loveliest country in Lakeland. The road runs east to Muncaster, though the hamlet can be

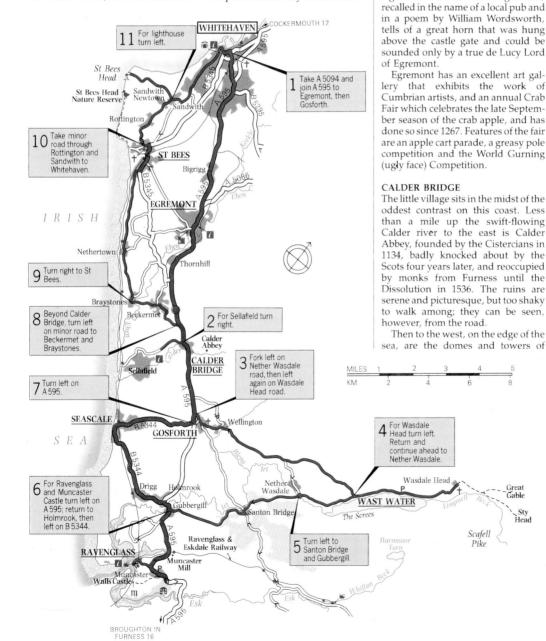

MILES | 1 | 2 | 3 | 4 | 5
KM | 2 | 4 | 6 | 8

SHELTERED VALLEY *The Lakeland fells crowd round the eastern end of Wast Water, which is fed by streams which drop from the highest summits in England.*

ANCIENT CROSS *Gosforth's cross, 14½ft high, is nearly 1000 years old.*

CALDER ABBEY *The ruins include the church and chapter house.*

FOOL'S PARADISE *Thomas Skelton, the jester who gave 'tomfoolery' to the language, is said to haunt Muncaster Castle, which Ruskin called 'the gateway to Paradise'.*

reached just as easily by footpath. The main reason for doing so is to visit Muncaster Castle, an imposing 19th-century building incorporating parts of a medieval castle, the home of the Pennington family since the 13th century.

The gardens are glorious, especially in early summer, and the house contains magnificent furniture, paintings and carvings. The castle is open most afternoons in summer.

SEASCALE
This partly Victorian seaside resort appears to have been dropped, without any visible attempt at planning, onto the windy shores of the Irish Sea. The background, at a picturesque distance, is the lovely hillscape of the Lake District National Park. The beach is dark gold, boulder-strewn sand, and bathers may or may not be encouraged by Calder Hall nuclear power station peering over the roof-tops to the north. Boating is popular on not too breezy days, and there is golf and riding on the dunes.

ST BEES
The name is a diminutive of St Bega, an Irish abbess who, according to legend, on a midsummer eve asked the Lord of Egremont for some land on which to found a nunnery, and was told that she might have as much as would be covered by snow on the following morning. Since he was a pagan and she an Irish saint, he should have known better; for sure enough on midsummer morning, some 3 square miles lay under a blanket of white. The convent thus founded was destroyed by the Danes in the 7th century, but was refounded by the Normans in 1129.

The Priory Church of St Mary and St Bega, all that is left of the Norman priory, is still in use as the parish church. Its red Norman doorway, so worn and massive, looks like a strange, natural rock formation, while within there are monuments to Norsemen, Norman priests and medieval knights.

Close by the church is St Bees School, founded in 1583 by Edmund Grindal, Archbishop of Canterbury. The original quadrangle bearing his arms is still in use, as is the bridge he gave to the village.

St Bees is a self-contained sort of place, tucked into a slanted bowl on the slope leading up to the mighty promontory of St Bees Head. Unlike the greys and greens of most of Cumbria, the older buildings in St Bees are red, the colour of the headland. The sand on the beach is gold, thickly scattered with multi-coloured pebbles worn to flat, oval discs like coins or sweets. Far out to sea is the silhouette of the Isle of Man, rising up to the peak of Snaefell.

The lighthouse on St Bees Head may be visited at the keeper's discretion; it may also be reached by road from Sandwith. On the headland too is a noted nature reserve whose cliffs are crowded with guillemots, razorbills, kittiwakes, gulls, gannets and skuas. The sandstone cliffs drop sheer to the sea, and visitors should keep to the footpath.

Tourist information: Whitehaven 5678; Egremont 820693 (summer); Ravenglass 278 (summer).

Lakes and fells at Cumbria's heart

TOUR
182
56 MILES

Five of Cumbria's loveliest lakes are linked by a tour which climbs from Borrowdale over a spectacular mountain pass, then visits a poet's birthplace and finally skirts lofty Skiddaw.

KESWICK
Its reputation as a tourist centre has not robbed Keswick of the old-world charm of a self-sufficient lakeland village. The treasure-packed Keswick Museum in Fitz Park contains a spectacular relief model of the Lake District, and at the heart of the town is the 19th-century Moot Hall, or meeting hall, now an information centre.

The Cumberland Lead Pencil Museum has a display of the pencils made at Keswick since the 16th century. Originally the graphite used as 'lead' was mined in Borrowdale, but imported material is now used.

The oldest building in Keswick is the parish Church of St Kentigern at Crosthwaite, mainly 14th to 16th century, with fragments dating from the 12th century. The poet Samuel Taylor Coleridge lived for a while at Greta Hall. Another poet, Robert Southey, lived there from 1803 to 1843.

FRIAR'S CRAG
A large car park is the usual home during the summer months of the mobile Century Theatre, which presents varied productions. From the theatre an easy stroll leads to one of Lakeland's most magnificent views. A monument to John Ruskin, who recorded his 'intense joy' at the view from the crag, looks out over Derwent Water, with a backdrop of hills including the humpbacked Cat Bells.

The viewpoint, owned by the National Trust, is often crowded in summer. However, for winter visitors the views of snow-kissed mountains turned pink by the light of the setting sun are memorable.

ASHNESS BRIDGE
A narrow road, dotted with cattle grids, leads to a tiny humpbacked bridge. A car park just beyond the bridge is the starting point of a short footpath through Ashness Wood to a cliff-edge vantage point known as the Surprise View. Breathtaking panoramas of Derwent Water and Skiddaw are framed by graceful birches and flat-topped pines. The surrounding woodlands are alive with the song of birds in the early morning.

WATENDLATH
The hamlet is reached along a narrow road bordered by stone walls. From the National Trust car park, signposted footpaths lead to Blea Tarn and Wythburn. The whitewashed houses are roofed with grey slate, their white-painted porches often filled with logs for winter fires. The scent of sawdust seems to permeate the hamlet, which echoes with the sound of water chuckling down the steep valley as it makes its way to Derwent Water.

LODORE FALLS
The waters from Watendlath Tarn drop into Borrowdale close to the Lodore Swiss Hotel. For those in a hurry the twinkling cascade – 'dashing and clashing and splashing', as Robert Southey described it in a tongue-twisting poem – can be reached through a turnstile, but for those with time to spare, a stroll through the delicate greenery of Lodore Wood is well worth while.

The upper falls can be reached along a path which follows the stream, the haunt of wagtails and dippers. Towering above is the massive bulk of Shepherds Crag, a popular practice area for climbers.

GRANGE
The hamlet on the banks of the River Derwent is usually known as Grange-in-Borrowdale, and was once a grain store for the Cistercian monks of Furness Abbey. Its tiny church is built of local slate.

Just beyond the village on the Rosthwaite road is Quay Foot Quarry car park, from which a signposted footpath leads through woods to the Bowder Stone. This 2000 ton rock was probably left perched on its narrow base by the melting of a huge glacier. Steps lead to its summit, from which there are magnificent views into Borrowdale.

ROSTHWAITE
This attractive grey-slate village is an ideal centre for the naturalist. Herons soar over the streams, and the path to Longthwaite leads across the Derwent to the National Trust's Johnny Wood, set on a knoll and rich in native oaks. The wood has a rich and varied plant life, including liverworts, mosses and ferns, and it is classified as a Site of Special Scientific Interest.

SEATHWAITE
The tiny village is reached at the end of a narrow winding road, fringed by dramatic hills and a few straggling pines and birches. Seathwaite is renowned for having one of the highest average annual rainfalls in England, 157in, but this does not diminish its popularity with fell walkers. A footpath from the village leads in less than a mile to a packhorse bridge at Stockley, from which signposted but difficult paths lead to Styhead Tarn,

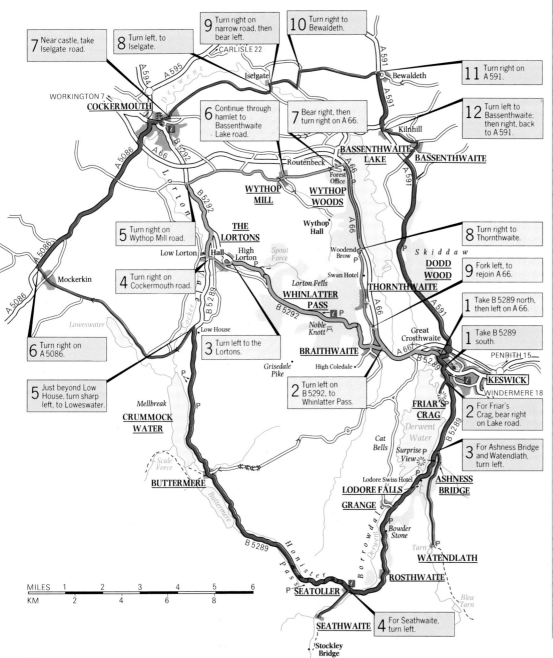

CRUMMOCK WATER *Stately roadside pines lead the eye towards the heights of Mellbreak on the lake's opposite shore.*

POET'S HOME *An open gate leads to Wordsworth's Cockermouth birthplace.*

BOATING LAKE *Yachts sail on the calm waters of Bassenthwaite Lake.*

BELOW THE BRIDGE *At Watendlath, water from the fells collected in Watendlath Tarn bubbles downstream under a humpbacked bridge festooned with ferns.*

Cockermouth's most famous son, the poet William Wordsworth. The house is owned by the National Trust and open on most days in summer. There are also remains of a castle, originally built in 1134, but now mostly 14th century, at the junction of the Cocker and Derwent rivers.

BASSENTHWAITE
The view from the village is enchanting, with the fringing hills framing but never overwhelming Bassenthwaite Lake at their feet, where, thanks to a ban on motorboats, silence reigns. The area around Bassenthwaite had Roman and Norse settlements. Thwaite is an old Scandinavian word meaning 'clearing'.

DODD WOOD
The large car park at the edge of Dodd Wood looks down over the long stretch of Bassenthwaite Lake. Near the car park are the remains of an old sawmill, and walks lead through the haunts of roe deer and red squirrels, which even casual visitors are quite likely to spot.

By the lakeside is the 17th-century Mirehouse, the home in the 19th century of James Spedding, biographer of Francis Bacon. The house contains portraits and manuscripts of Francis Bacon and some of Spedding's literary friends, including Lord Tennyson who was a frequent visitor. The house is open to the public on some days in summer, and a lakeside walk from the house is open daily.

TOUR
183

——— 25 MILES ———

From Lorton Fells, the 1043ft Whinlatter Pass looks down onto the villages of Lorton Vale. Hedged lanes lead eastwards to the wooded western shore of Bassenthwaite Lake.

BRAITHWAITE
Just beyond the Royal Oak a road to the left signposted 'Coledale' offers splendid views over the village of Braithwaite, over which looms the frowning 2593ft mass of Grisedale Pike. Well-marked walks lead 6 miles over the fells to Crummock Water and Buttermere.

WHINLATTER PASS
From Braithwaite, the road rises sharply to 1043ft at Whinlatter Pass, but the road is wide and there are several lay-bys. Noble Knott picnic site, on the left, is the starting point for many marked footpaths that often ring with bird song. At the summit of the pass a sharp right turn leads to a large car park and a well-appointed Forestry Commission visitor centre, the starting point of miles of lovely woodland walks.

The descent into Lorton Vale is dramatic. On the right, close to an old quarry, is a lay-by from which a marked footpath leads after half a mile to Spout Force, which is spectacular after rain. In the summer

Great Gable and Scafell Pike. These walks should not be attempted without a map, compass and waterproof clothing.

On the fellsides to the north-west are the spoil heaps left by mining in earlier days for plumbago, or graphite. In the 17th century it was used to make moulds for the manufacture of cannonballs and as 'lead' in the pencil industry based at Keswick.

SEATOLLER
The Lake District National Park Information Centre makes Seatoller a good stopping place before the 1176ft Honister Pass – a narrow, twisting route that is unsuitable for caravans.

The climb is spectacular, with streams and waterfalls down to the left and towering fells on the right. At the summit is a youth hostel in an old slate quarry, and behind it a car park. The descent towards Buttermere is even more dramatic, with tumbling slate scree on the left and hills rusted with bracken to the right.

BUTTERMERE
From this snug little village, walks radiate through typical Lakeland scenery. One footpath from the Fish Hotel leads left to Scale Force, 2 miles away; another route wends its way towards Crummock Water. Both walks lead through woods and mead-

ows and follow clear bubbling becks which are noisy torrents after rain.

CRUMMOCK WATER
Several lay-bys offer spectacular views across Crummock Water, which was once joined to Buttermere but is now separated from the larger lake by a three-quarter-mile strip of low-lying fields. There is a car park just beyond Rannerdale, and two at Lanthwaite from which paths yield views over the lake.

COCKERMOUTH
The pride of Cockermouth is a Georgian house at the end of its tree-lined main street. There, in 1770, was born

dippers bob on the shores of the Aiken Beck, larks sing above the fells and buzzards circle overhead.

THE LORTONS

The two hamlets of High Lorton and Low Lorton, though often visited, remain so peaceful that they seem to have been forgotten by time.

At Low Lorton is a hall, with an impressive peel tower, where the future Charles II is reputed to have stayed in 1651 when he was rallying opposition to Cromwell's rule. A chuckling beck wends its way among neat white cottages, in whose eaves swifts and martins feed their young.

Yew trees are a feature of the area, and one tree was praised by William Wordsworth in a poem as the 'pride of Lorton Vale'.

WYTHOP MILL

Reached after a pleasant drive between hedges dominated by well-trimmed holly, Wythop is an enchanting village, its blue-and-white houses huddled round an old bridge beneath which the Wythop beck chatters over a pebbled bed. From the bridge a right turn leads to Wythop Hall, while in a dip to the left is an old mill.

WYTHOP WOODS

A sharp right turn just before the road from Routenbeck reaches the main road leads to Thornthwaite Forest Office. Several footpaths traverse Wythop Woods and visitors must keep to them. Through silver birches there are views across Bassenthwaite Lake.

BASSENTHWAITE LAKE

Beyond Wythop Mill the road descends to join the main road heading south alongside Bassenthwaite Lake – the only 'lake' in the Lake District, since all the others are called meres or waters.

It is also the northernmost of the lakes and the fourth largest, measuring 4 miles long and half a mile wide. Its shallow waters are the home of the vendace, a white fish found only here and in Derwent Water.

Bassenthwaite Lake is said to be the setting described by Lord Tennyson in his *Idylls of the King*, in which Sir Bedevere hurled the mighty sword Excalibur into a lake.

THORNTHWAITE

A car park at Woodend Brow, north of the village of Thornthwaite, affords wide views of Bassenthwaite Lake, dominated by the brooding hulk of Skiddaw. From Thornthwaite village a pleasant stroll from the Swan Hotel follows a marked footpath to the lake shore. The tiny parish church can be glimpsed across green fields through an attractive belt of trees.

Tourist information: Keswick 72645; Cockermouth 822634 (summer).

A WALK AROUND THE LAKE *Surrounded by towering mountains, Buttermere stretches for 1¼ miles through the heart of Cumbria. Foaming becks feed its deep waters. A gentle walk from Buttermere village runs round the lake, passing through a cliff tunnel beside plantations of spruce.*

Mountains and meadows by the Eden

TOUR
184

——— 82 MILES ———

Roads follow the winding River Eden or cross its sparkling waters by ancient bridges. Market towns shelter in the folds of rolling moors, and castles command the river crossings.

KIRKBY STEPHEN

Perched 600ft above the fertile Eden valley, Kirkby Stephen has been an important wool town since the Middle Ages. Today its long main street is often crammed with sheep being driven from the fells to market. Nearby, brightly painted shops and old coaching inns huddle among small and attractive cobbled squares.

Just off the Market Place is the 13th-century parish church which is approached along a drive. Inside the church is a collection of stones dating from before the Norman Conquest, and part of an Anglo-Danish cemetery cross depicting Loki, the Danish form of the Devil. The bearded figure was carved in the 10th century, and is the only one of its kind in Britain.

Across the road from the church is a house with an open gallery on which the women, like so many in Cumbria and Yorkshire hill settlements, did their spinning and weaving to make the most of the daylight.

BROUGH

A turning off the main road leads past the ancient district of Church Brough, from whose square a twisting path leads to the ruins of Brough Castle. Set on a hill overlooking the Eden valley, the castle was built by the Normans on the site of the Roman fort of Verterae. In 1521 the castle was gutted by fire, and it was rebuilt in medieval style by Lady Anne Clifford in the mid-17th century. The castle, which is now in ruins, is open daily.

Church Brough's square is surrounded by neat houses and cottages, including a former Dame school and a farm that was once an inn used by packhorse drivers. A maypole stands on the site of the old market cross, and a narrow lane lined with holly and hawthorn leads to St Michael's Church. Built partly in the 11th century, its masonry includes some Roman stones from the fort. There is also a leper's squint, an opening through which lepers could watch services without mixing with the congregation.

On driving into Brough itself there are picturesque reminders of its past as a busy coaching town. Old coaching inns with cobbled courtyards and stables flank the street. The village – sometimes called Market Brough – grew up around an old ford, first bridged in 1369. It carried the road along which cattle, sheep and even geese, their feet protected with coats of tar, were driven to be sold in markets as far away as Lancashire and Yorkshire.

WARCOP

A village green is overlooked by a colourful maypole and surrounded by a tangle of cottages and sandstone houses. Warcop lies between the main road and the River Eden, which is spanned by a fine 16th-century bridge with three graceful arches. The partly Elizabethan and partly Georgian Warcop Hall stands to the north-west of the village, opposite the 12th-century Church of St Columba. The hall is not open to the public. The path to the church is lined with yew trees, whose upper branches are linked, providing shade from the sun and shelter from the rain.

APPLEBY-IN-WESTMORLAND

The former capital of the old county of Westmorland, Appleby consists of two towns: one on either side of the wide River Eden. Old Appleby is set on a high sandstone bluff, overlooking a ford, and is the site of the 10th-century village of Bongate – where Danish bondsmen used to live. New Appleby, built in the early 12th century by the Normans, is low-lying and fits neatly into a loop of the river.

The new town grew around the Norman castle, which was restored in the 1650s by its owner, Lady Anne Clifford. Lady Anne also restored the Norman Church of St Lawrence, which Scottish marauders had set on fire in 1388. Appleby Castle is now the headquarters and training centre of an industrial company, but the keep is open to the public in the summer, when rare farm animals including Vietnamese pot-bellied pigs can be seen in the grounds. The church contains the black marble tomb of Lady Anne Clifford, who died in 1676.

Lady Anne also built St Anne's Hospital, a group of almshouses which is reached through a low archway at the foot of the main street, Boroughgate. The neat houses and tiny chapel, set around a cobbled square, are still reserved for needy widows. In Boroughgate there are some handsome Georgian houses, and the 16th-century Moot Hall is now an information centre.

Each June, Appleby stages a huge horse fair, which lasts for several days. The fair was first held in 1685, by special charter of James II – and gypsies converge on the town early in

DOWN FROM THE PEAKS *The River Eamont flows from Ullswater and joins the Eden 3 miles south of Little Salkeld.*

the month. Their vividly coloured caravans – some of them very old and horse-drawn – park on Fair Hill, and the sale horses are later watered in the Eden, washed and groomed and then put briskly through their paces for their prospective new owners.

TEMPLE SOWERBY

A quiet village near an excellent stretch of fishing along the Eden, Temple Sowerby's mixture of 17th and 18th-century buildings huddles around a large sloping green. The village is named after the Knights Templars who ruled the community until their suppression in 1312. The village was then taken over by the religious military order the Knights Hospitallers, who governed the lands until the Dissolution of the Monasteries in the 1530s.

Since the Middle Ages the village has had a reputation for herbal healing, and the tradition is continued today as the National Trust Gardens at Acorn Bank – an early 18th-century manor house – has a fine collection of medicinal and culinary herbs. The red-sandstone house is now a home for the elderly and is not open to the public; but its gardens, reached by a path through a thick oak wood, are open daily in the summer.

LITTLE SALKELD AND LONG MEG

A narrow winding road just outside Little Salkeld leads to a meadow in which stands a 15ft tall column of sandstone. Long Meg, as the stone is called, together with her 66 'daughter' stones form a Neolithic circle some 300ft in diameter – one of the largest and oldest in Britain. It was possibly used for rituals associated with the changing seasons, and the setting midwinter sun is aligned with Long Meg herself. She bears some cup and ring carvings which are thought to be about 4500 years old.

In the village, red-sandstone cottages cluster near a restored, 18th-century water mill. The mill grinds flour throughout the year and is open to the public on certain afternoons in the summer. Visitors can watch the mill at work and sample freshly baked bread, scones and cakes in the tea-rooms.

There has been a hall in Little Salkeld since the Middle Ages, and the present hall stands near the small, triangular green. A large walled building, it dates mainly from the early 19th century and is now mostly divided into holiday apartments.

GREAT SALKELD

The line of the old drovers' road from Scotland to the English markets is still followed by the modern road through Great Salkeld. The 18th-century Highland Drove Inn, with its white walls and rambling roses, blends prettily with the nearby cottages.

The partly Norman Church of St Cuthbert has a sturdy defensive tower, its lower half covered with ivy, built in 1380. Villagers hid in the tower when threatened by the Scots, and were given extra protection by the iron door at the western entrance. Armour from the Civil War hangs on the church walls.

KIRKOSWALD

So that local people can hear them ringing, the bells of St Oswald's are hung in a detached stone tower on top of a grassy hill south of the village. The church itself is tucked into the foot of the hill 200yds away. There is thought to have been a bell tower on the summit since Norman times, but the present tower – complete with flagpole and weather vane – dates only from the 1890s.

The village and its church were named after King Oswald of Northumbria, who converted the area to Christianity in the 7th century. The wooden Saxon church was replaced in the 12th century by one built of stone, and despite later alterations it still has its splendid chancel arch with a Norman base. A little way to the east are the ruins of Kirkoswald Castle, most of whose 13th-century moat is intact.

Kirkoswald is a pretty village built mostly of red sandstone, and its finest building is the College, the home of the Fetherstonhaugh family since the late 16th century. The two-storeyed house, with its sloping-ended roof, was originally built about 1450 as a peel tower, and was converted into a college for priests in the 1520s. The house stands back from the road and is not clearly visible. It can be visited by special written appointment.

Two miles north-west of the village is the Nunnery Walks nature trail. Open daily, it winds through the surrounding woods and past Croglin Water, which crashes over stony rapids. The 13th-century nunnery was rebuilt in 1715 in Georgian style and is now a guesthouse.

CORBY CASTLE

Rising from the east bank of the River Eden, Corby Castle overlooks Wetheral, on the opposite bank of the river. The castle, with its bulky, 13th-century keep, was originally a defensive tower which was expanded in the 17th and early 19th centuries.

Its terraced gardens look down on the river, in which can be seen medieval, wood-and-stone salmon traps, which provided food for the castle residents. The castle and gardens are open to the public in the summer.

WETHERAL

A steep road leads from Wetheral's triangular green and ends at the edge of the River Eden. Near the site of an old ferry crossing now stands the high, five-arched viaduct carrying the Carlisle to Newcastle railway across the river.

A well-signed riverside walk to National Trust woodlands provides colourful flashes of kingfishers, and herons fish in the deeper pools. Along the riverbank are three man-made caves in which a saint called Constantine is said to have lived in the 6th century. He was probably the Cornish saint of royal birth who visited the area when it was a part of Scotland.

Nearby is the dignified Church of Holy Trinity, restored in the 1880s. A chapel to the Howard family of Corby Castle stands at the north side of the chancel and behind a wrought-iron

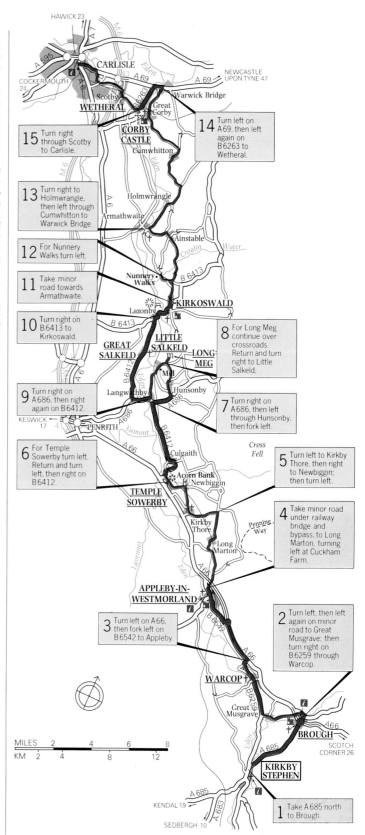

screen. The chapel was built in 1791 to house a monument showing the figure of Faith, by the sculptor Joseph Nollekens. It stands above the Howards' mausoleum, which was in use until the mid-19th century and was sealed off in the 1960s.

A short distance to the south of the church, tucked away among the trees, is the gateway and porter's lodge of Wetheral Priory – all that remains of the Benedictine priory which was founded about 1100. In the centuries after the priory was built, the surrounding countryside was ravaged by the Scots, who burnt buildings and stole animals and food. However, wrongdoers could claim sanctuary in the priory – provided they swore they would keep the peace.

Tourist information: Kirkby Stephen 71804; Brough 260; Appleby-in-Westmorland 51177.

301

Farmlands beyond the Lakeland fells

TOUR

185

—— 31 MILES ——

Amid tranquil farming country, patchworked with woods, a battlemented mansion is a reminder of clashes with the Scots. In a valley lies the grave of huntsman John Peel.

PENRITH

The squat, pyramid-topped tower on Beacon Hill, whose wooded slopes rise steeply above Penrith, is a reminder of the old town's turbulent history. Although not built until 1719, the tower marks the spot where many a warning fire was lit before peace finally came to the Anglo-Scottish border at the end of the 16th century.

In 1804, when invasion was feared during the Napoleonic Wars, Sir Walter Scott hurried home to join his regiment after, it is said, seeing the flames flickering above Penrith.

There is a footpath to the top of Beacon Hill, from which there are fine views over the Lake District.

Penrith's sandstone castle, in ruins for more than 400 years, was built at the end of the 14th century after the town had been sacked by the Scots. Its keepers included Richard Neville, Earl of Warwick – 'Warwick the Kingmaker' – and the future Richard III when he was Lord Warden of the Western Marches. The weathered walls, set in a public park, overlook the former Castlegate Foundry, established in the 19th century. The old foundry now houses the Penrith Steam Museum's traction engines, vintage farm machinery, a working blacksmith's shop and other reminders of Cumbria's past.

The partly Norman Church of St Andrew is a notable survivor of the border wars. Its tower, with walls 6ft thick, casts its shadow over stones marking the so-called 'Giant's Grave'. These are said to be the burial place of Owen Caesarius, King of Cumbria in the 10th century, but may be a collection of medieval memorials.

Near the church, a restaurant now occupies the Tudor building where Dame Birkett's School was attended by William Wordsworth, his sister Dorothy, and his future wife, Mary Hutchinson. Wordsworth twice revisited Penrith in the late 1790s and stayed at the Robin Hood Inn, where there is a plaque to him. Wordsworth also lived with his cousin John at Wordsworth House, which is now the Town Hall.

GREYSTOKE

Green hedges and broad, grassy verges line the road into this immaculate crossroads village with its tiny green and buildings of pale red stone. To the north-west rises the walled and wooded park of Greystoke Castle. The castle, which is not open to visitors, has been in the same family since Elizabeth I granted the estate to Thomas Howard, Duke of Norfolk, 400 years ago. It was largely rebuilt in the 19th century as an Elizabethan-style mansion.

Greystoke's parish church is larger than most in Lakeland. It was extended in the 14th century into a collegiate church, with a master and eight secular priests. Six chantry chapels were built, only one of which remains in use, dedicated to the Greystoke men who fell in the Second World War.

The church's magnificent medieval stained-glass east window includes the figure of St Andrew, trampling on a red, defeated devil.

HUTTON-IN-THE-FOREST

A drive through wooded parkland suddenly reveals the battlemented sandstone towers of Hutton-in-the-Forest. The mansion has been inhabited for more than 600 years and embraces building styles ranging from medieval to Victorian.

The original peel tower was built by Thomas de Hoton, or Hutton, who died in 1362. He was the hereditary keeper of the Royal Forest of Inglewood, which sprawled from Penrith to Carlisle and provided excellent cover for Scottish marauders.

East of the tower stands a wing added by Sir Richard Fletcher early in the 17th century. On the south front a three-storeyed façade of classical elegance is sandwiched between the peel and a Victorian 'Gothic' tower whose drawing room retains its original 1870s atmosphere.

One of the mansion's portraits depicts Sir Henry Vane, a radical who supported Parliament during the Civil War. Although granted a pardon after the House of Stuart's restoration, he had many influential enemies and was executed on Tower Hill in 1662.

In the grounds, stately oaks and other native hardwoods overlook lakes and a 17th-century dovecote, whose birds were an important source of eggs and fresh meat.

HESKET NEWMARKET

There are spectacular views of the slopes and summits of Blencathra, Bowscale Fell, Carrock Fell and Caldbeck Fells to the south and west before the road drops into the River Caldew's valley – the Lake District National Park's boundary – and reaches Hesket Newmarket. The village used to have a flourishing market where sheep and cattle were sold.

A small, open-sided building with a cobbled floor and slate roof was then the focal point for Hesket Newmarket and the surrounding countryside. Known as the market cross, it still stands on the long, sloping village green.

VILLAGE BELOW THE FELLS *The village of Orton lies half-hidden among trees, above which rises the early 16th-century tower of All Saints' Church.*

CALDBECK

John Peel, the huntsman and land-owner famed in song, died in 1854 at the age of 78 after falling from his horse and is buried near the porch of Caldbeck's medieval church. His headstone, carved with hunting horns and a dog, also commemorates various members of his family, including Mary Peel – the woman he married after eloping to Gretna Green – and their eldest son John, one of 13 children, who lived to 90.

Clad in a beaver hat, knee breeches and a long, grey coat, Peel was an indefatigable hunter who followed the hounds on foot and horseback. He was also a mighty drinker whose regular companions included John Woodcock Graves, the millworker who wrote *D'ye ken John Peel*. The original tune was abandoned after William Metcalfe, choirmaster at Carlisle Cathedral, composed a rousing alternative in 1868.

Caldbeck is a delightful village whose river, a tributary of the Caldew, powered woollen mills in John Peel's lifetime and produced the grey cloth for his hunting coats. The Church of St Kentigern dates from Norman times, and the arch to the nave, the entrance to the south porch and some of the windows are probably Norman. But additions were made in the 19th century, and the clerestory and north aisle windows are Victorian. St Kentigern is said to have preached at Caldbeck on his way from Scotland to Wales in AD 553.

The road from Caldbeck runs between gorse and foxgloves, climbing to nearly 950ft before sweeping down towards Dalston and Carlisle.

DALSTON

Attractive cottages, many of them with colour-washed walls, sweep round Dalston's sandstone church. Dedicated to St Michael and All Angels, it dates from the early 13th century, but was restored in 1890. A 17th-century Bishop of Carlisle is buried in the grounds, which lead to a peaceful stretch of the River Caldew.

Just over a mile to the north-east of the village is Dalston Hall, now a hotel, which is thought to have been built about 1500. However, its front dates mostly from 1899. Standing beside it is a battlemented peel tower, complete with turret.

Tourist information: Penrith 67466 (summer); Carlisle 25517.

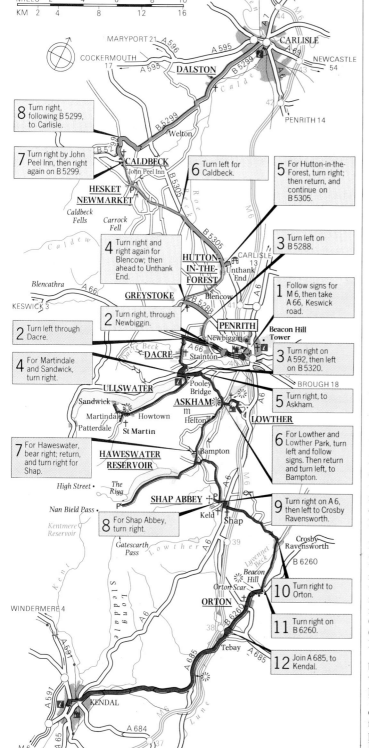

TOUR
186
—— 55 MILES ——

Winding by a wooded lake shore, the road follows a quiet river valley off which lies a remote reservoir. A final climb over limestone fells offers fine views across the Pennines.

DACRE

The steep, wooded slopes of Soulby Fell provide a green backcloth for this pretty little village in the Dacre Beck's secluded valley. According to the medieval chronicler William of Malmesbury, it was at Dacre that King Constantine of Scotland and Owen Caesarius, King of Cumbria, paid tribute to King Athelstan of England in AD 926. It is easy enough to picture a peace treaty being signed in such a peaceful place.

The medieval sandstone church probably stands on the site of an Anglo-Saxon monastery. It shelters the mutilated effigy of a knight, clad in chain mail and a surcoat, who is thought to have been a crusader. A more recent link with campaigns in far-off lands is the memorial to Charles James Salmond, a Bengal Cavalry officer killed during the Indian Mutiny of 1857.

Dacre Castle, open to visitors only by written appointment, is clearly visible from the church. Originally a peel tower, the castle dates from the 14th century and has been inhabited ever since. The last of the Dacre family fled to Scotland after taking part in an ill-fated rebellion against Elizabeth I in 1569.

ULLSWATER

A good view of Ullswater, Lakeland's longest stretch of water after Windermere, and the mountains that surround it is obtained from the narrow road which runs along the lake's eastern shore from Pooley Bridge. The road zigzags up to the remote hamlet of Martindale before reaching Sandwick, on the lakeside between Hallin Fell and Sleet Fell.

A short detour south from Martindale enters a deep valley where slopes rise steeply above the 16th-century Chapel of St Martin. Walls of uncut stone shelter the 17th-century pulpit and pews. Outside is the grave of Richard Birkett, parish priest from 1633 until his death in 1699. St Martin's was the parish church until St Peter's, on the road between Martindale and Howtown, was consecrated in 1882.

Serious walkers can explore the lake shore between Sandwick and Patterdale, or make Martindale the base for long hikes over the mountains. Visitors seeking gentler exercise should follow the path round Hallin Fell from Sandwick to Howtown, a fine high vantage point for views across Ullswater's shimmering expanse.

ASKHAM

Immaculate stone cottages with rose gardens adorn a steep, wooded bank of the River Lowther, and the upper village green looks east over the ruins of Lowther Castle to the distant Pennines. The broad green at the bottom of the village slopes down towards the parish church of St Peter, built in 1832 by Sir Robert Smirke, the architect of Lowther Castle. As well as an Elizabethan tomb chest, the church has a number of tablets to the Sandford family of Askham Hall.

The hall – not open to the public – dates in part from the 14th century and is the village's oldest building. Several cottages date from the 17th century. The area around the village has been occupied since the Stone Age, for on nearby Askham Fell there is an ancient stone circle; there are also traces of Bronze Age burial sites.

LOWTHER

A spectacular façade worthy of a Walt Disney fairy-tale was left standing when Lowther Castle was demolished in 1957. The vast mansion – all towers, turrets and battlements – was built for the Lowthers early last century by Sir Robert Smirke, designer of the British Museum, on the site of Lowther Hall, destroyed by fire in 1725. It was the home of the 5th Earl of Lonsdale, an amateur boxer who gave his name to the Lonsdale Belt – one of the sport's most coveted trophies – and was the first president of the Automobile Association.

Many generations of the Lowther family are commemorated in the village church, parts of which date from the 12th century when the Lowthers first became associated with this part of England. From a mausoleum perched on the brink of the river's wooded valley there are fine views over Askham to the Lake District's peaks.

303

Lowther Park contains the ruins of a 19th-century castle built on the site of a medieval house, woodland walks and a leisure park. There are also several groups of 'rare-breed' animals and deer. The largest is the herd of red deer, whose ancestry goes back to 1283, when Edward I granted Sir Hugh de Louther permission to create a 200 acre deer park.

A road runs through the park, and visitors may stop to picnic or walk among the animal enclosures and aviaries.

HAWESWATER RESERVOIR
Steep mountains send streams racing down to Haweswater, a reservoir created in the 1930s – by expanding a lake – to supply Manchester. There are fine views from the narrow road which wriggles along the eastern shore to a small parking area at the southern end of the lake, where the road ends. This is the starting point for long walks over the Gatescarth Path to Long Sleddale and over the Nan Bield Pass to Kentmere. Less ambitious explorers can follow a path to The Rigg, a wooded headland above what was once the village of Mardale, now submerged under the reservoir. During droughts, traces of the drowned village are sometimes revealed.

SHAP ABBEY
The ruined tower of the abbey church appears suddenly through the trees as the narrow road dips down southwards into the secluded valley of the River Lowther.

Shap Abbey's tranquil setting is a world apart from the lonely fells over which many a medieval traveller struggled in search of a night's shelter with the white canons. Founded in 1199, the abbey administered large estates until it was closed after Henry VIII renounced Roman Catholicism in 1534. Its isolation did not prevent a 15th-century abbot, Richard Redman, from becoming successively Bishop of St Asaph, Exeter and Ely.

A short walk across the fields south of the abbey leads to Keld, a hamlet whose modest little 16th-century

CROSBY RAVENSWORTH *Cottages in the village shine with flowers.*

HUNTSMAN'S GRAVE *The huntsman John Peel is buried in Caldbeck.*

METHODIST CHAPEL *The chapel in Little Blencow dates from 1877.*

LOWTHER CASTLE *Only the front of the 19th-century castle remains.*

chapel belongs to the National Trust.

In Shap village is the Church of St Michael, parts of which date from the 12th century. A stone in the churchyard is dedicated to the memory of the workmen 'who lost their lives by accidents' during work on the Shap section of the Lancaster and Carlisle Railway.

From Shap, the road runs across high limestone country before sweeping down to Crosby Ravensworth, a small, sleepy village in the valley of the River Lyvennet.

ORTON

Climbing gently but steadily through a landscape dominated by limestone outcrops known as 'scars', the road from Crosby Ravensworth reaches 1100ft where it meets the main road north of Orton. The unfenced junction with its broad, turf-clad verges is a convenient stopping place from which to enjoy the fine views along Orton Scar and south-eastwards across the Pennines to high peaks in the Yorkshire Dales National Park. A path leads to Beacon Hill, a craggy outcrop a few hundred yards east of the junction, where warning fires used to be lit when Scottish raiders were on the prowl.

Orton is a secluded village with stone houses and a spacious green. The Church of All Saints has an ancient parish chest of oak. It has three padlocks, each opened by a different key as a way of ensuring that three people were present when it was opened. There is also a fine stained-glass window by Beatrice Whistler, wife of the American artist James McNeill Whistler. The oldest of three bells, hung in a frame in the north aisle, was cast in 1530.

The Liberal Club, near the George Hotel, has a carving of William Gladstone above its doorway.

Tourist information: (Brougham) Penrith 67126; Penrith 67466 (summer); Kendal 25758.

EVENING CALM *The rays of the setting sun streak the calm waters of Ullswater, as a lone yacht sails off Howtown pier.*

LAKELAND CHURCH *St Peter's, in Martindale, dates from the 1880s.*

HOUSE PROUD *This handsome house stands in the centre of Greystoke.*

PASTORAL PEACE *Trees surround a country house near Sandwick.*

LAKE CROSSING *A passenger boat sets out across Ullswater.*

Woods and waterfalls in Upper Teesdale

TOUR

190

—— 81 MILES ——

Relics of lead mining are strewn over bleak moorlands – but within minutes the landscape changes to wooded dales with waterfalls and villages huddled under slopes.

MIDDLETON-IN-TEESDALE
Clustering on the hillside above a graceful bridge across the River Tees, Middleton has the style and dignity of a smart small town rather than a village, and is proud of its reputation as the capital of Upper Teesdale. Once little more than a hamlet, it retains some of its older cottages, agreeably assimilated into the busy mining centre which grew up from 1815 onwards.

Today the village is an ideal centre for fell walking, or for just strolling along riverside footpaths and pleasant back lanes.

BOWLEES AND HIGH FORCE
The wooded parking and picnic site of Bowlees, beside a winding stream, has a visitor centre with displays of the mining and other industries of Teesdale and Weardale, including the extraction of fluorspar for steel-making, and of the wildlife and wealth of wild flowers on the moors. A nature trail starts at the visitor centre.

At the end of a leisurely woodland walk beside small, tinkling waterfalls is the 20ft drop of Summerhill Force over the rim of Gibson's Cave, a deeply undercut limestone overhang.

About 1½ miles up the road, opposite another parking and picnic site, a ten-minute tree-lined stroll leads to the spectacular waterfall of High Force.

CAULDRON SNOUT
In this land of cliffs, fells and waterfalls, Cow Green Reservoir appears broad and tranquil at the end of a moorland road from Langdon Beck; but a nature trail from its breezy picnic site, a path suitable for wheelchairs, leads to another tumult of cataracts. Cauldron Snout is a sequence of eight cascades with a footpath following their long descent to a final steep drop, awesome to behold and to hear.

The falls are said to be haunted by the ghost of a 'Singing Lady' who threw herself into the turbulent waters after being spurned by a local miner.

ALSTON
One of England's highest market towns, at an altitude of almost 1000ft, Alston must also surely have some of England's steepest streets, several of them slippery with cobbles. It is hardly surprising that the original covered market cross was shattered by a runaway lorry in 1971 and again in 1980, to be faithfully rebuilt.

The narrow-gauge South Tynedale Railway operates hourly trips high above the delightful river valley to Gilderdale Halt, daily from late May until September, with limited services in late April and early May. The old railway station houses the town's tourist information centre.

NENTHEAD
At a height of 1450ft, Nenthead can boast of being the highest village in England. The hill on which it stands, from its lower to its upper lanes and steeply perched terraces, rises to nearly 1600ft. A vigorous walk along a path by the River Nent reveals many industrial remains, among them the arched entrance to a tunnel used for access to a mine and buildings which once housed a sawmill.

The road from Nenthead to Weardale over Killhope is the highest in England, rising to 2036ft.

KILLHOPE WHEEL
Suddenly, beyond a sheltering arm of Weardale Forest, the huge water wheel of an old lead-crushing plant rears up, a startling sight in this high, bleak region. In the 18th and 19th centuries the Pennines around Killhope were the world's most productive lead field.

By the beginning of this century the industry was in decline, and Killhope was abandoned; but restoration work began in 1982, and in 1984 a mining museum was opened on the site. Close to the car park and picnic site, a visitor centre has been laid out above the renovated stables and smithy. There are lots of buttons to push, setting in motion working models of the wagonways and wheel.

IRESHOPEBURN
Just beyond a tight turn of the road across the Ireshope Burn, which gives the village its name, Weavers Forge Cottage stands near one end of a row of attractive grey houses and cottages. In this converted 200-year-old smithy is a workshop, open daily, which sells yarns and hand-woven fabrics.

STANHOPE
The market place is almost over-powered by the main road, but it is possible to stand back and enjoy its original proportions – the church, the market cross, a couple of inns, and a sprightly mock-medieval castle erected in 1798 and enlarged in 1875.

On the right of the churchyard gate is the only surviving fragment of the 16th-century market cross. To the left is the stump of a fossilised tree from a forest of 250 million years ago.

WOLSINGHAM
Stonework in the village has an agreeable warm tinge to it, and the side streets are cosy with typical dales cottages of dressed stone and rubble walls, some with slate roofs and some protected by heavy stone slabs. Near the market place are the stately Whitfield House, built around 1700, and its beautifully restored neighbouring cottages of 1677.

From the north-west corner of Angate Square, with its little group of lime trees, a path leads to the Demesne Mill picnic area.

HAMSTERLEY FOREST
More than 1000 acres of this extensive coniferous forest between Weardale and Teesdale are open to the public. There are picnic and parking spaces by a rippling stream, waymarked walks and nature trails, and a forest drive. A visitor centre provides displays and leaflets on Hamsterley's wildlife, trees and plants. There is a toll for passing through the forest, but this can be avoided by turning south-west from Bedburn on a minor road.

Tourist information: Alston 81696.

HIGH AND MIGHTY The foaming torrent of High Force falls 70ft over sheer cliffs of volcanic rock, its thunderous roar reaching full voice after heavy rain.

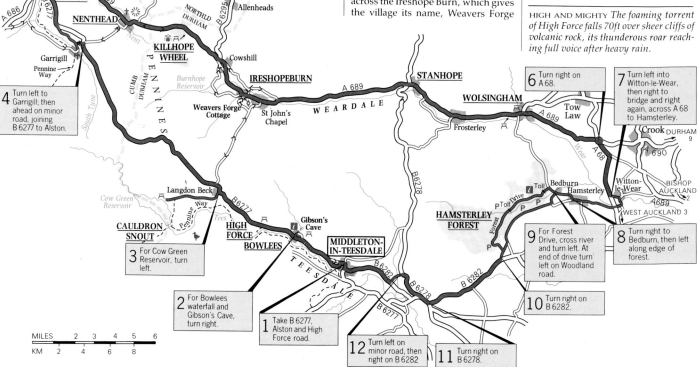

A lake at the heart of Durham's moors

The route from Durham climbs to richly hued high moors and drops into river valleys. There are nature reserves, an old priory and an open-air museum where the past lives on.

DURHAM
Norman cathedral and castle seem to rise out of the very rock of the steep, richly wooded promontory around which the River Wear makes a tight curve. One dizzying, delightful view after another is revealed from the pedestrian bridges of Framwellgate and Elvet, and from footpaths along the river banks. One path leads past a weir to an old textile mill that has been converted into a museum telling the story of the region.

High above the river stands the cathedral, and on its door is a replica of the old sanctuary knocker used by medieval fugitives from the law when seeking church protection from their pursuers. Within are the tombs of St Cuthbert and the Venerable Bede, magnificent Norman columns and stone-ribbed vaulting, a radiant 18th-century rose window, and a treasury displaying Anglo-Saxon embroidery and illuminated manuscripts.

The castle, the only one in northern England that was never captured by the Scots, also dates from Norman times. It has been inhabited for more than 900 years, and was the palace of the Bishops of Durham from 1072 to 1837. The chapel is the oldest surviving part, but it is the massive octagonal keep, high on its motte, that stands out most prominently. This keep, a copy of the original, was erected in 1840 after the castle became a student residence for Durham University. Many of the graceful houses in South Bailey and North Bailey are now the homes of university departments.

In the Market Place, the Market Tavern was the scene in November 1869 of the foundation of the Durham Miners' Association, who just under two years later held their first gala, now an annual event.

FINCHALE PRIORY
Above another of the River Wear's twists and turns, golden-tinted ruins spread themselves reflectively over an undulating, grassy bank, looking across the rippling water to a sheltering arm of wooded cliff. A neat little footbridge leads over the river to tree-shaded walks.

The site of the priory was originally occupied by a wooden chapel, built early in the 12th century by Godric, a much-travelled adventurer who, after years as a sailor and a reputed career as a pirate, withdrew from the world to become a hermit.

Much admired for his austerity and saintliness, Godric later had a stone chapel built for him. After his death in 1170 at the age of about 105 he was canonised as St Godric, and further buildings were added to make a place of retreat and relaxation for monks from Durham.

BEAMISH MUSEUM
Descending the hill to this invigorating open-air museum, the visitor sees and sometimes catches the smell of steam from an old North Eastern Railway locomotive or from a replica of George Stephenson's famous *Locomotion* of 1825. Smoke also rises from the chimneys of a reconstructed row of pitmen's cottages. Tramcars carry passengers to a rebuilt market town complete with cobbled streets, houses, shops, a public house, old-fashioned tearooms and a pretty little Victorian bandstand. The museum is open daily, except Mondays in winter.

A short walk, or a ride in a small horse-drawn carriage, leads to Beamish Hall, which houses an exhibition of items of yesteryear. The nearby Home Farm has farm animals and a display of old agricultural buildings and machinery. There is also a traditional farmhouse kitchen, where bread is often baked in a coal-fired oven.

CAUSEY ARCH
The world's oldest surviving railway bridge dominates a spacious picnic site beside the Causey Burn. It is reached after a 15 minute stroll from the car park beside a rocky gorge shadowed by tall, over-arching trees. The single stone 100ft span of Causey Arch was thrown across the Causey Burn between 1725 and 1726 as part of a wooden wagonway along which horses hauled coal from pits in the Tanfield area. The builder, a local mason named Ralph Wood, based his work on Roman techniques. Fearful of its possible collapse, he threw himself to his death from the 80ft arch before it was completed.

His fears were unfounded; though built to carry horse-drawn wagons the arch proved strong enough for the locomotives that followed, and the line continued in operation until 1962.

Another footpath from the gorge leads to Beamish Museum, and at Sunniside, near Tanfield, steam trains carry passengers along a short stretch of track on summer Sundays and Bank Holidays.

GIBSIDE CHAPEL
Set nobly at the end of a wide avenue of oak trees, the Georgian chapel, in the care of the National Trust, was designed in Palladian style in 1760 but not completed until 1812. Intended as a chapel and mausoleum for the local Bowes family, it has an interior as attractive as its exterior, with box pews and a three-tier mahogany pulpit. The building is open to the public every afternoon except Tuesday between April and September, and on Wednesday, Saturday and Sunday during October.

EBCHESTER
A few mellow old cottages provide a warm heart to what is otherwise a long, largely modern street; but below the village centre are things older still. This was the Roman station of Vindomora on the supply route of Dere Street. The parish church of St Ebba, set at one corner of the site, has Roman stone in its walls and a Roman altar set into the wall of the tower.

What was once the station yard of the now demolished Derwent Valley Railway has become a picnic site and a good place to join the Derwent Walk.

DERWENT WALK
Along the cuttings, embankments and viaducts of a disused railway, 10½ miles are now open to walkers, riders and cyclists between Swalwell and Consett. It is planned that this will eventually join up with the Waskerley Walk and another walk through the Lanchester valley.

Sometimes high on the shoulder of the Derwent valley, sometimes shaded by woodlands and lined by shrubs, the walk forms part of the Derwent Walk Country Park. There

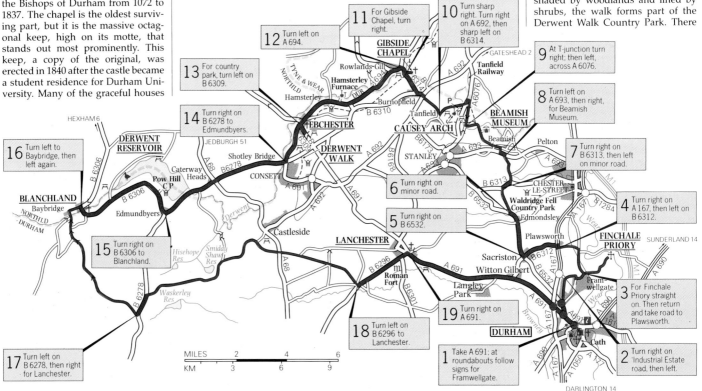

BREATHING SPACE *A sheen of clear water surrounded by a green patchwork landscape welcomes visitors to the Derwent Reservoir and Pow Hill Country Park.*

PRIVATE WORLD *The isolation of Blanchland has helped preserve its charm.*

MONKS' RETREAT *Durham monks used Finchale Priory as holiday quarters.*

CAUSEY ARCH *Britain's oldest railway bridge was used for only 50 years.*

AGE OF STEAM *Coal trucks, goods wagons and steam locomotives are among the exhibits that recall the early 1900s at Beamish Museum. There is also a coal mine re-created as it could have been in 1913 from items taken from nearby pits, now closed.*

are several picnic areas, including those at the attractive little Shotley Bridge and Rowlands Gill. Numerous other access points to both the walk and park are signposted in the nearby villages.

DERWENT RESERVOIR

The eye is caught by the first shimmering glimpse of the wide reservoir, and continues to be enchanted as the banks curve in and away, with heather and moorland plants providing a velvety contrast to the water. Pow Hill Country Park, with a small stream flowing through it, has picnic sites, walks, and a bird hide from which to observe wildlife during the winter; and there are other restful parking and picnic sites along the shore.

On the far side of the 3½ mile long reservoir, Millshield's 14 acre picnic area also offers birdwatchers several

vantage points. Permits for trout fishing can be obtained from the Utilities Building near the dam. Sailing is controlled by the Derwent Reservoir Sailing Club, and prior application for membership is essential.

BLANCHLAND

The compact village with its creamy-brown stone and slab roofs comes as a warmly tinted surprise in the green and heathery expanses of moorland and the wooded valley of the Derwent. It was developed by trustees of Lord Crewe, a 17th-century Bishop of Durham, as a housing centre for lead miners working on the fells above.

However, the village retains the contours of an earlier abbey founded in 1165 by an order of White Canons from Blanche Land in Normandy. The post office is built into what used to be the gatehouse, and the inn, the Lord

Crewe Arms, was once the abbot's lodging and guesthouse.

The abbey Church of St Mary the Virgin is the surviving north transept of the monks' church, and within it are a number of unusual tombstones. One, of the abbey forester, has carvings of his sword, an arrow, and his horn with its baldric or shoulder-strap. Another stone is ornamented with the outline of a pair of scissors, the symbol in days gone by of a woman, who in this setting must presumably have been some kind of monastic housekeeper.

LANCHESTER

This appealing, friendly place has trim little shops and arrays of houses set back from the street on raised banks. There is also a wide village green flanked on one edge by the busy main road without being really disturbed by it. The village lies half a

mile north-east of the Roman fort of Longovicium, established between AD 122 and 140. The remains of this station beside the B 6296, on private land, have been ploughed over throughout the centuries, and villagers have robbed the site of stones for use in their own homes.

Monolithic columns in the nave of the parish church of All Saints, supporting Norman arches with zigzag chevron ornamentation, are thought to have come from the Roman headquarters building. In the south porch is a Roman altar in honour of Garmangabis, a local tribal goddess happily adopted by the Romans, who frequently took regional deities into their own pantheon. Other altars and inscribed stones from the site are to be found in Durham Cathedral.

Tourist information: Durham 43720.

315

Rivers through wild Northumbria

Green pastures open up beyond the relics of Northumbria's industrial past. This was Hotspur's country, and his castle still guards the wild and lovely coastline.

SEATON DELAVAL HALL

Incongruous in the midst of wide, flat coal country is Seaton Delaval Hall, a perfect palace of dark grey stone and tall, shining windows, with flying arcades leading the eye left and right from the mightily columned central block to the detached wings. This elaborate confection is set among plain lawns running down to a sunken ha-ha wall, so that there seems no barrier between the house and the road and the house and the sea.

The hall was designed by Sir John Vanbrugh in 1718. It was his swan song, for he did not live to see it completed, and neither did his patron, Admiral George Delaval. The Delavals lived in the hall only until 1808, when the last of them died. The central block was gutted by fire in 1822 but restored in 1962.

It is now the home of Lord Hastings. The hall's treasures include fine furniture, portraits and ceramics, and in the superb stable block each stall bears the name of its original inhabitant.

Nearby is the plain little Norman Church of St Mary, containing effigies of a knight and lady of the 14th century. Also in the vicinity are some handsome, fortress-like farms, and a long, leafy avenue that reaches from the hall to the colliery village of Seaton Delaval.

SEATON SLUICE

The Delavals created the harbour in the 17th century by putting a weir across the Seaton Burn with a sluice to wash the silt away. About 100 years later they made further improvements by driving a channel 900ft long and 52ft deep through solid rock to the harbour, which for many years afterwards was busy with colliers and salt boats.

The channel has long been blocked by fallen rock and silt, but the harbour is still used by pleasure craft. Above the harbour is The Octagon, a curious building that might have been the harbourmaster's house, or a doodle of Vanbrugh's when he was building Seaton Delaval Hall. St Mary's Island, just offshore, has a graceful lighthouse and some tall old houses and cottages.

BEDLINGTON

A long sweep of square, brownish stone houses and shops curves behind steep, mown banks, with flying trees and flowerbeds. There is a very reasonable allowance of big, handsome pubs, in one of which Sir Daniel Gooch (1816-89) was born. At 21, he was locomotive superintendent of the Great Western Railway, and in later life he governed the laying of three transatlantic cables. Bedlington's other contribution to the dawn of the Steam Age was rolling the rails for the world's first public railway, the Stockton and Darlington.

The partly Norman Church of St Cuthbert has a stone inscribed Watson's Wake, in memory of a somnambulist who was climbing the building and fell to his death in 1669 when someone woke him with a shout. Durham miners still hold a June gala in the town with jazz, brass bands and a beauty contest.

Bedlington terriers are perhaps the best known local product. Whatever their cuddly image now, they were first bred for badger baiting.

BOTHAL

This estate village, of pale stone, dark slate and painted, pointed gables, was built or rebuilt all together towards the end of Victoria's reign. The partly 9th-century St Andrew's Church is almost smothered in trees chosen for their shape and leaf colour.

Just over the way is Bothal Castle which dates from the 14th century and, though small, is a fine romantic image of a castle. It does not look as though it could have put up a serious resistance for very long, though stone soldiers planted along the battlements impart a martial air. The building makes a splendid picture, but it has been turned into offices and is not open to the public.

CRESSWELL

A surprisingly large village green runs inland from a magnificent beach, protected by a reef on which the North Sea makes slow-motion thunder. Beside the green, a square, 14th-century peel tower gazes stonily out to sea from a background of dark woods. The wall about it surrounds the park of a now vanished mansion.

The route runs north along the coast behind the dunes of Druridge Bay, part of which, at Druridge Links, is protected by the National Trust.

AMBLE-BY-THE-SEA

Dunes of pale gold sand and marram grass that looks like recently coifed hair of purest sea green give the coast around Amble the status of an Area of Outstanding Natural Beauty. The sea itself is, more often than not, blackgrey carrying white breakers. About a mile offshore is Coquet Island, occupied by a lighthouse, the ruins of a Benedictine monastery and a bird sanctuary; landing is not permitted.

Queen Street has bowfronted shops selling appropriately old-fashioned things, and there are many other streets of sturdy stone Northumbrian cottages with front doors opening directly onto the pavement. For centuries, Amble had its own fleet of colliers that carried coal from mines in the vicinity to Scandinavia. The mines are closed now – though, after gales, coal from shallow offshore seams is still washed up on the beach – and the harbour is mostly concerned with pleasure craft and a few fishing boats.

WARKWORTH

At the head of the steep village street, and looking straight down it, stands Warkworth Castle, creating one of the greatest urban views in Britain. The stone houses rise uphill in steps towards the fortress.

Shakespeare's Henry IV called the castle 'a worm-eaten hold of ragged stone'; but even in its partially ruined state it is one of the realm's most imposing fortifications, with cruciform keep and graceful towers.

As the great lion on one of the towers proclaims, this is a Percy stronghold, and has been since the 1330s. Henry Percy, known as Hotspur, was born there in 1364, and there too plotted against Henry IV.

It was the Percys who fortified the 14th-century stone bridge over the River Coquet. It is one of England's few remaining fortified bridges.

ALNMOUTH

A strong curve of stone houses, grey or black and white, runs down to a wide common and a deep bay of pale gold sand. The building that most readily catches the eye is the big black-and-white Schooner Hotel, but all – houses, boutiques, guesthouses and shops – give the same impression of strength in their structure. This was done not for art's sake, but for defence against storms, one of which, on Christmas Day 1806, destroyed the church and many other buildings.

There is not much to see now of what was for centuries an important grain port; only yachts and other small craft are mirrored now in the calm waters of the Aln estuary. But many of the granaries remain, though long converted to other purposes.

Tourist information: Newcastle 610691 ext 29 or 615367.

BESIDE THE COQUET *Warkworth's Norman church overlooks the River Coquet which enfolds the village on three sides.*

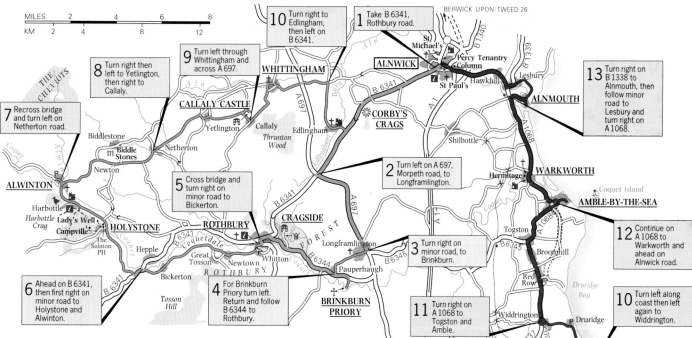

1 Take B 6341, Rothbury road.

10 Turn right to Edlingham, then left on B 6341.

9 Turn left through Whittingham and across A 697.

8 Turn right then left to Yetlington, then right to Callaly.

7 Recross bridge and turn left on Netherton road.

13 Turn right on B 1338 to Alnmouth, then follow minor road to Lesbury and turn right on A 1068.

2 Turn left on A 697, Morpeth road, to Longframlington.

5 Cross bridge and turn right on minor road to Bickerton.

6 Ahead on B 6341, then first right on minor road to Holystone and Alwinton.

4 For Brinkburn Priory turn left. Return and follow B 6344 to Rothbury.

3 Turn right on minor road, to Brinkburn.

12 Continue on A 1068 to Warkworth and ahead on Alnwick road.

11 Turn right on A 1068 to Togston and Amble.

10 Turn left along coast then left again to Widdrington.

8 Turn left on A 1068, then right on A 197 and left to rejoin A 1068 to Ellington.

9 Turn right then left on minor road to Cresswell.

7 Turn right on minor road to Hepscott then fork right and cross A 196, to Bothal.

6 Turn left on B 1331, then right on A 192.

4 Turn right on A 192.

5 Turn right on A 1068 to Plessey Woods and Bedlington.

2 Turn right on A 190 to Seaton Delaval and Seaton Sluice.

3 Take A 193 north, then turn left on minor road to New Delaval, and left on A 1061.

1 Take A 6125 north, then turn right on A 189.

TOUR 193

55 MILES

Rich upland pastures and large farmhouses announce Coquetdale's stock-breeding prosperity. However, between the snug stone villages ruined fortresses tell of a turbulent past.

ALNWICK

Quiet as a small French provincial town, handsome and well mannered as Bath, there is little to be seen now of the warrior town that held the crossing of the Aln against the Scots for centuries, and was twice razed for its pains. Of the town walls, only the Hotspur Gate remains, so old and worn that it looks as though some of the stones had melted. But the street names, Bondgate, Walkergate, Canongate, Bailiffgate and the rest, have a medieval ring to them, even if they are lined with 18th and early 19th-century shops, inns and houses and by sensible and pretty, cobbled slopes.

The Percys gained Alnwick in 1309 and, despite many ups and downs, first as Earls then as Dukes of Northumberland, hold it still. Their castle, Windsoresque in size and commanding presence, dates in part from the 11th century and reflects the battles, disasters and triumphs of the English borders ever since. The exterior is harsh and military, the interior a palace of breathtaking grandeur, with rich collections of paintings, china and furniture. The castle is open daily except on Fridays in summer.

CORBY'S CRAGS

From the brackeny, gorsey hill behind the road, there is a dizzying view down into the valley of the Edlingham Burn, crossed by a tall viaduct of the defunct Alnwick to Coldstream railway. Beside it is Edlingham hamlet, with a tough little Norman church whose tower was used as a prison by border raiders, and the broken fang of Edlingham Castle.

Edlingham is a peel tower or defensive tower house, rather than a castle, and was built by the Swinburnes in the 14th century. They stabled their horses in the basement and defied the world from the upper floors, though in a fair degree of comfort to judge by the great fireplace and the carvings.

Beyond the village, the land climbs between vast, soaring pastures dotted with sheep and cattle. The line of the Devil's Causeway, the Roman road from Hadrian's Wall to the mouth of the Tweed, crosses the route just beyond Longframlington and can be seen running to the south. Cars may be held up by flocks of sheep.

BRINKBURN PRIORY

Of near cathedral size, the 13th-century church is charmingly situated in deep woods in a crook in the River Coquet. Despoiled first by the Scots and then by Henry VIII's Commissioners at the time of the Dissolution, Brinkburn was a roofless ruin until the middle of the last century, when it was perfectly restored by Thomas Austin, a young Northumbrian architect. It is open daily.

The curious building next door may incorporate part of the monastic buildings. It is mainly Georgian, with a bit of castle added on in the 19th century.

CRAGSIDE

The route makes a winding journey through tall trees, with the River Coquet for company. Some of the trees belong to Cragside House, a wild Victorian extravaganza, part Gothic, with a lot of Tudor black-and-white timbering. The house is the creation of Sir William (later Lord) Armstrong, a Newcastle solicitor turned inventor and industrialist. He poured a fortune into the country around Rothbury, and especially into his house and park, whose exuberance reflects his personality.

Cragside's electric light – water powered – was the first to be installed in any English country house. Armstrong added hydraulic lifts and even a hydraulic spit in the kitchen. The house and park are now owned by the National Trust and open daily from April to October and at weekends in winter.

ROTHBURY

Big stone houses, some with elegant porticoes and windows, are grouped about the wide main street and sloping greens of Coquetdale's market centre. In the restored medieval

317

BAROQUE PALACE *Seaton Delaval Hall is one of Sir John Vanbrugh's creations.*

SEATON SLUICE *Ships carrying coal and salt once berthed in this peaceful harbour.*

HOLY POOL *Celtic Christian converts were baptised in Lady's Well at Holystone.*

HOME ON THE HILL *Cragside House is surrounded by more than 7 million trees.*

Church of All Saints there is a font whose pedestal is part of a Saxon cross, dating from about AD 800.

Next to the church is the doorway of the old Half Moon Inn where the Earl of Derwentwater slept in 1715 before leading his Jacobite levies to defeat at Preston.

HOLYSTONE
A pretty little jumble of stone cottages is given additional grace by a large and handsome inn called The Salmon. Behind this a footpath leads to a wood, in the midst of which is a formal pool of swimming-pool size and shape, though only a few inches deep. This is a holy well, as is apparent from the cross at its centre and the statue of a saint at its side, a representation of St Paulinus who is said to have baptised 3000 Celtic converts in the pool in one day.

Its name, Lady's Well, is an allusion to the Augustinian nuns who occupied a priory which once stood nearby. Lady's Well, however, is considerably older than both priory and saint. It was sunk by the Romans as a watering place on the link road between the Devil's Causeway and Dere Street, and still supplies water to the village.

From Campville, close by, the Forestry Commission has laid out a number of walks, including one to Dove Crag with its waterfall, said to be the home of fairies. Nearby is a

cave that legend associates with the adventurer Rob Roy.

ALWINTON

A group of low and ancient stone cottages, with thick walls and small windows, stands at the joining of the rivers Coquet and Alwin. The church, much restored in Victorian times, has a 13th-century chancel rising ten steps above the nave.

Alwinton's liveliest moment occurs when most of the tourists have departed – on the second Saturday in October, when the Border Shepherds' Show offers hound and sheepdog trials, Cumberland wrestling, fell racing and all the traditional fun of a north country fair.

Climbing 2000ft above the village are the wild and lonely Cheviots. They were not always so lonely. All about Alwinton are the hill-forts, hut circles and terraced fields of a long-vanished people.

CALLALY CASTLE

The country about is glorious – green billowing hills and high pastures. Down a shadowed drive arched over by beeches, chestnuts and pines is Callaly Castle, a classical mansion in 18th-century vein. It began as a 13th-century border peel tower, and in the 17th, 18th and 19th centuries, simply grew.

All the older parts, including the tough defensive tower, are still there,

but they are difficult to spot at first glance. There is some magnificent stucco work in the drawing room, which can be seen when the castle is open at weekends in summer.

WHITTINGHAM

A very southern-looking village at a first look, Whittingham has a tall, slim, church tower, creeper-covered walls and red pantiles. It also has a massive peel tower, built in the days when Whittingham lay in the path of the Scottish raiders; it saw plenty of action during the border wars, and later, during the Civil War. The peel tower was converted into almshouses in the 1840s, but has lost little of its original strength. The Victorian

MEANDERING RIVER *The River Aln twists and turns through farmland near Lesbury on its way to the North Sea at Alnmouth. The 25 mile long river, which rises at the edge of the Cheviot Hills, is stocked with trout and salmon.*

church tower was added to the base of a Saxon tower. The village is divided into two by the Aln river, and has a green and fine trees. A monument to the 3rd Earl of Ravensworth takes the form of a drinking fountain topped by a statue of an old man with walking stick and dog.

Tourist information: Alnwick 603120 (summer).

Roman relics above the Tyne valley

TOUR
194
—— 66 MILES ——

A road follows the straight line of Hadrian's Wall, passing the ruined forts of this outpost of Roman might. A peaceful river flows beside the birthplace of a railway pioneer.

HEXHAM
Below Hexham's great abbey, gardens shaded by copper beeches and weeping willows descend to the wooded banks of a little burn, where rustic seats are set among bluebells. It is a peaceful spot, forming an ideal frame for a view of the abbey's square tower and long north transept.

Seven centuries of devotion are represented within the abbey's walls; begun before 1200, it was not completed until this century. Among the curiosities under its lofty roofs are a wealth of carved woodwork, and a broad stone 'night stair' by which canons descended into the church from their dormitory.

The east end of the abbey forms one side of a Market Place surrounded by buildings whose contrasted styles speak vividly of Hexham's long history. There is a long market colonnade, a red-sandstone market cross, and a castle-like gate tower, or moot hall, built around 1400. Through this gate tower a passageway leads to yet another historic building – the old jail, built in 1330 in four-square Italianate style and looking like a Florentine princeling's palace; today it houses a tourist information centre.

The character of old Hexham is preserved in narrow streets lined with bowfronted houses and shops, sections of old town wall and greens lined by colour-washed stone houses. Down by·the river – here simply 'the Tyne', the North Tyne and South Tyne having merged just a mile upstream – is the Tyne Green Riverside Country Park, with picnic places and a good view of the bridge completed in 1793 after three earlier bridges had been washed away by flood.

HAYDON BRIDGE
The tree-shaded road leading down into Haydon Bridge runs beside a burn with twinkling waterfalls. The building on the left, its four battlemented towers making it look like a children's toy fort, is Langley Castle, which is privately owned and not open to the public. On the right, nearer Haydon Bridge, is a wayside cross with interlaced Celtic patterns, erected in memory of two Viscounts Langley beheaded on Tower Hill for supporting the Jacobite cause in 1715 and 1745. After climbing out of Haydon Bridge on the road heading north, there is a good view back down upon the little town of stone houses and grey slate roofs. The lonely switchback moorland road heading for the Roman wall is flanked by stony fields crisscrossed by dry-stone walls.

BROCOLITIA
The size of the car park seems excessive for the relatively insignificant remains of the Roman wall fort of Brocolitia; but the real gem of this site is hidden a few hundred yards away behind the mounds of the fort.

This is the little temple of Mithras, where Roman soldiers serving on Hadrian's Wall came to worship the Persian god of light whose cult was Christianity's main rival in the 200s. The temple, suddenly viewed in a hollow, seems surprisingly small and intimate. The altar, the columns, the broken statues and the benches upon which worshippers sat are casts of finds made on the site in 1949; the originals are in Newcastle's Museum of Antiquities.

CHESTERS
Roman walls, like Roman roads, brooked no obstacles in their straight cross-country course. At Chesters, Hadrian's builders met the River North Tyne, so they flung a bridge across it and built the fort of Cilurnum to defend it.

The site has been painstakingly excavated and is maintained with care, its buildings set off by neatly mown lawns. In the headquarters building a flight of steps leads to a grotto-like underground strongroom, where the legion's standards and pay were kept.

The highlight of Chesters, though, is the bathhouse down by the river. As many as 20 courses of bricks rise 10ft from the ground, enclosing an anteroom, boiler room, warm room, hot bath and all the other essentials of an establishment which to the Romans served not only a hygienic function but also as a social and recreational centre.

The bathhouse looks across the Tyne to the bridge abutments excavated on the opposite bank. To see these at close quarters, cross the modern bridge at Chollerford and take the marked footpath on the right. A section of the Roman wall climbing northwards is visible at Brunton Turret, reached by a marked footpath from a lay-by on the Hexham road.

HEDDON-ON-THE-WALL
A well-preserved 100yd section of Hadrian's Wall justifies a short stop in this otherwise dour main-road village. The wall, 10ft broad, is clearly visible from the Throckley road, just east of Heddon, and reached by a gate off a side road.

WYLAM
A handsome plaque depicting the early steam locomotive *Rocket*, at the top of the long hill leading down into Wylam, asserts the village's proud claim to fame as the birthplace in 1781 of George Stephenson, the railway

FARM RELICS *Donkeys and old tractors share the Hunday Farm Museum.*

HUMBLE HOME *George Stephenson, the railway pioneer, was born in this cottage.*

ARMY DEPOT *Granaries, workshops and storerooms at Corstopitum served the Roman legions from AD 208 until the 4th century.*

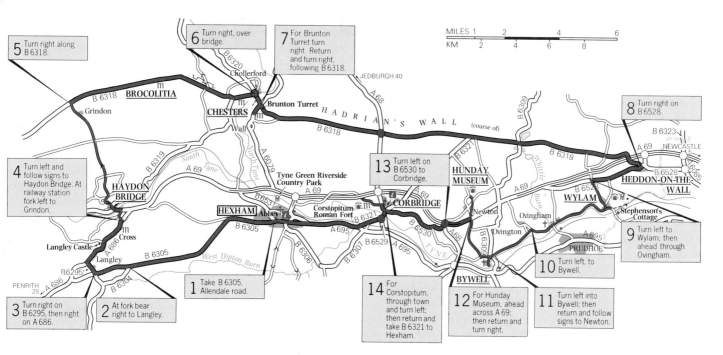

5 Turn right along B 6318.

6 Turn right, over bridge.

7 For Brunton Turret turn right. Return and turn right, following B 6318.

MILES 1   2   4   6
KM   2   4   6   8

8 Turn right on B 6528.

4 Turn left and follow signs to Haydon Bridge. At railway station fork left to Grindon.

13 Turn left on B 6530 to Corbridge.

9 Turn left to Wylam; then ahead through Ovingham.

1 Take B 6305, Allendale road.

14 For Corstopitum, through town and turn left; then return and take B 6321 to Hexham.

12 For Hunday Museum, ahead across A 69; then return and turn right.

11 Turn left into Bywell; then return and follow signs to Newton.

10 Turn left, to Bywell.

3 Turn right on B 6295, then right on A 686.

2 At fork bear right to Langley.

BROCOLITIA — CHESTERS — Brunton Turret — HADRIAN'S WALL (course of) — JEDBURGH 40 — NEWCASTLE — HEDDON-ON-THE-WALL — Stephenson's Cottage — WYLAM — HUNDAY MUSEUM — HAYDON BRIDGE — HEXHAM — Abbey — Corstopitum Roman Fort — Tyne Green Riverside Country Park — CORBRIDGE — Newton — Ovington — Ovingham — PRUDHOE — BYWELL — Langley Castle — Langley — Cross — PENRITH 28 — Grindon — Wall — West Dipton Burn — Whittle Burn

---

pioneer. The cottage in which George Stephenson's parents, with six children, occupied a single ground-floor room is reached by a half-mile footpath from a car park in the Tyne Riverside Country Park.

It is hard to imagine that this peaceful village was, in Stephenson's day, the site of a coal mine in which his father worked as an engine fireman. Coal was taken from the pit by horse-drawn wagons over wooden rails along the riverside, past the Stephensons' home, for loading onto Tyne barges farther downstream. Experiments by Wylam colliery owners with steam engines to haul the wagons are said to have inspired George Stephenson's own development of steam locomotives, such as *Rocket*, for passenger transport.

The cottage is today owned by the National Trust, and the room in which Stephenson was born is displayed by a devoted custodian on Wednesday, Saturday and Sunday afternoons in summer. A railway museum in Wylam is, awkwardly, open only on Tuesday, Thursday and Saturday mornings.

Opposite the cottage is a grassy picnic area, from which a path leads back to the car park alongside the Tyne as it runs fast over moss-covered stones. Tempting as the water looks, deep pools and strong currents make bathing dangerous.

BYWELL

A moss-covered pillar with a ball on top stands railed off in a field between two large churches less than 100yds apart. The pillar was the market cross of a thriving medieval village; and the two churches, which are all that remain of the village today, were at the edge of separate parishes.

St Peter's, with its squat tower, dates largely from around 1300 and is still in regular use; on the outside of the south wall is a scratch clock – an early form of sundial, rare in northern England, which indicated the times of services. St Andrew's, with its fine tall tower dating back to AD 950, is now disused; but it is still open to visitors, who will find inside an atmosphere of great tranquillity. Outside, set into the wall of the northern transept, are coffin lids with incised crosses dating from before 1295.

HUNDAY MUSEUM

More than 140 tractors of all sizes and all ages are the stars of the Hunday National Tractor and Farm Museum, and tractor seats set around millwheel tables furnish the museum's picnic area. Included in this intriguing display of Britain's farming history are steam-powered threshers, joiner's and blacksmith's shops, a dairy, a water wheel and tools of all types, from early veterinary instruments to thistle tongs and muck-spreading forks.

The museum shop is housed in a reconstructed circular Gin Gan, around which horses once trudged to provide power for threshing corn. One corner of the museum is devoted to living farm animals, and a narrow-gauge railway overlooks the Tyne valley.

CORBRIDGE

A visitor going no farther than the tourist information office, just off the Market Place, will have an instant glimpse of Corbridge's rich history. For the office is housed in a peel tower, built to protect the vicar of the Church of St Andrew during the border raids of the 1300s. The vaulted ground-floor room, with its heavy oak door, was probably used to stable the vicar's horses. Within the thickness of the wall a stairway mounts to his living room, which has a window overlooking the 13th-century church.

Both the peel tower and the church are built largely of stones brought from the Roman station at nearby Corstopitum; but enough remains of the station to make a visit to it an absorbing experience. Though not on the Roman wall, Corstopitum was the nerve centre for Rome's frontier system, and a military supply depot for the wall and for the legions' campaigns in Scotland.

The setting is a spectacular one. The excavated buildings of a succession of forts lie spread out against a backdrop of green hills. Below, almost hidden in its valley, the Tyne flows towards the arched road bridge at Corbridge, with the tower of St Andrew's Church prominent above it.

The Roman remains themselves are no mere tumbled heaps of stones. They are visibly the floors and walls of granaries with ventilation ducts running beneath the flagstones, and an aqueduct running into a stone water fountain, its sides worn smooth ·by soldiers sharpening their swords.

The site museum is everything a modern museum should be, the finds well displayed and set in context by reconstructions of the station in its heyday, and by an animated map that plots the movements of the legions by flashing lights.

The excavations and the museum are open daily.

Tourist information: Hexham 605225; Corbridge 2815 (summer).

HEXHAM ABBEY *Augustinian canons worshipped here from 1113.*

HAYDON BRIDGE *The bridge from which the town is named spans the South Tyne.*

An inland sea amid the border forests

TOUR

195

—— 92 MILES ——

The waters of Europe's largest man-made lake glisten at the heart of vast Kielder Forest. Narrow roads wind through lonely country into Scotland and back, to the site of a noted border battle.

BELLINGHAM

The heavy stone blocks of the walls of Bellingham's houses make the small market town look as though it has grown naturally out of the surrounding hills. St Cuthbert's Church even has a roof of stone slabs, the better to keep villagers safe in the turbulent days of the Border Reivers.

'Narrow streets and tight corners', judiciously warns a notice in the town square. One narrow street drops towards the River North Tyne, where a tranquil footpath follows the riverside for 1½ miles to join the road at Redeswood. A more spectacular walk leads up Hareshaw Burn to the waterfall of Hareshaw Linn. The path, steep in places, starts from a car park just off the main street, down the Redesmouth road. Beyond minor cataracts passed on the 1¼ mile walk the actual Linn, plunging 30ft over a series of natural terraces, is unmistakable.

KIELDER WATER

The inland sea of Kielder Water, with its 27½ mile shoreline, looks so natural a part of today's scenery that it is hard to believe that the work of damming the North Tyne to create Europe's largest reservoir began only in 1976. The Northumbrian Water Authority and the Forestry Commission have made rich amends for drowning a valley by making a superb job of landscaping the lakeshore and making it a place for many types of recreation.

A network of tracks and paths along the southern shore links a visitor centre, a field-study centre, a fishing centre, a sailing centre, viewpoints, camping sites, forest cabins and places for windsurfing, dinghy sailing, water skiing, canoeing and swimming. The northern shore, by contrast, is thickly forested, and though a regular sightseeing ferryboat zigzags across from bank to bank, only experienced hikers should venture far from the sole landing place on the north bank.

The size of the car park at Tower Knowe Visitor Centre indicates the large number of visitors expected on a fine day. A footpath leads over a footbridge to a cairn commemorating the inauguration of the Kielder Valley Water Scheme, whose creation was partly funded by European Economic Community grants.

From the heather-clad slopes behind the cairn there is a broad view out across the lake and its bright-sailed boats towards the northern slopes where conifers march to the skyline. Clouds of midges can be a nuisance at times. The visitor centre at Tower Knowe offers a film show about the reservoir, and its panoramic windows provide a view over the lake. Nearer at hand, swallows dart under the eaves of the building.

NORTH TYNE ROAD

Around the southern shores of Kielder Water runs a well-surfaced scenic drive. It was built to replace a winding road through the forested valley that is now submerged beneath 170ft deep waters. The road is lined by parking places and viewpoints, and signposted roads and tracks lead off to various recreation centres.

One of the broadest panoramas of the lake can be seen by taking the rough forest track along Bull Crag Peninsula and walking another 100yds to Otterstone Viewpoint. A forest trail following the Lewis Burn starts from a car park and picnic site signposted from the road.

KIELDER CASTLE

An old battlemented hunting lodge built in 1775 by the Duke of Northumberland now houses a Forestry Commission Visitor Centre. A permanent exhibition explains the various uses of timber and the economic necessity for the big conifer plantation through which much of this tour passes.

The castle is also the starting point of forest walks and nature trails; the 1½ mile Conifer Trail will help the visitor to identify more than a dozen different conifers – a valuable introduction to the forest.

A 12 mile Forest Drive, for which a small toll is charged, also starts from Kielder Castle. It rejoins the tour on the main road a mile south of Byrness, but the short cut involves a 12 mile drive over a loose stone surface, with a 25mph speed limit. The drive, however, gives magnificent views over forest and moorland, with occasionally a startled roe deer leaping from the roadside undergrowth. There are parking places and picnic areas beside burns and waterfalls.

KIELDER FOREST

Conifers climb the hillsides, almost to the topmost crests, where rocky heather and bracken-clad moorlands line the skyline like sand dunes above an advancing green tide. This is the Kielder Forest, Britain's largest man-made forest, covering 125,000 acres and embracing the four separate forests of Kielder, Falstone, Wark and Redesdale. So vast is the scale of

Map

HAWICK 4

4 Turn left to Bonchester Bridge; then return to junction and ahead on A 6088.

Hill Fort ▲

BONCHESTER BRIDGE — Chesters — A 6088

JEDBURGH 6

5 Bear right on A 68.

Wauchope Forest

KIELDER FOREST

CARTER BAR

Catcleugh Reservoir

A 68

CHEVIOT HILLS

SCOTLAND (BDRS) ENGLAND (NORTHLD)

Byrness

Cottonshopeburn Foot

6 For High Rochester, turn sharp left up unsignposted road.

B 6357

Kielder Burn

FOREST DRIVE

Blakehopeburnhaugh

High Rochester ▲ Bremenium

ROCHESTER

7 Straight ahead on A 696, to Otterburn.

Saughtree

Pennine Way

Rede

A 696

Toll

Kielder

KIELDER CASTLE

Percy Cross **OTTERBURN**

KIELDER FOREST

3 Turn right on B 6357.

2 From Kielder, straight ahead: narrow road, with passing places.

Tarset Burn

B 6320 DERE STREET

NEWCASTLE UPON TYNE 26

8 Turn right on B 6320; then left along A 68 (Dere Street).

KIELDER WATER

Burn

Lewis Burn

Leaplish **NORTH TYNE ROAD**

Bull Crag

Falstone

West Woodburn

North Tyne

Greenhaugh

Hareshaw Linn

CORBRIDGE 13

BELLINGHAM

9 Turn right on minor road to Bellingham.

MILES 2 4 6
KM 2 4 6 8

1 Cross river by B 6320, then sharp right to Kielder Water.

things that from the roads which snake round the hillsides the younger trees look like seedlings in a nursery garden; the more mature trees, thick-planted up the hill slopes, look blurred and out of focus.

Nearly 70 per cent of the conifers planted are Sitka spruces, but there are Norway spruces on the lower ground, pines higher up, and some lighter green larches.

Most of the area was planted between 1940 and 1970, and as spruces reach maturity in 40 or 50 years, Kielder is today in full production as a timber 'factory'. Large cleared swathes show where timber is being felled for paper, chipboard and the building industry at the rate of 100,000 tons a year.

BONCHESTER BRIDGE
After a long drive through the forest, a 3 mile diversion to Bonchester Bridge offers a small oasis of civilisation. The village, with an inn set beside its little bridge over the Rule Water, is dominated by Bonchester Hill, where there are traces of an ancient hill-fort.

CARTER BAR
A large lay-by accommodates motorists pausing to have their photographs taken beside the upright boulder which marks the border between Scotland and England. Here in medieval times the wardens of the Middle Marches met to try to resolve disputes, during four centuries of border strife which culminated in the Redeswire Fray of 1575 fought just below the pass. This was the last skirmish before the Union of the Crowns in 1603.

At 1370ft, Carter Bar offers sweeping if distant views, and on the north side a toposcope picks out hills from Rubers Law in the west to The Cheviot in the east. There are fine views all along the road southwards from Carter Bar, past Catcleugh Reservoir and beside green hills whose flanks seen at a distance look smooth enough to be bowling greens. There are marked 'scenic lay-bys' and Forestry Commission picnic areas along the road.

The picnic areas at Blakehopeburn-haugh and Cottonshopeburn Foot offer the extra attraction of having two of the longest of English place-names. Blakehopeburnhaugh is the northern end of the Forest Drive starting from Kielder Castle; from the picnic site a waymarked walk leads to the Three Kings, a group of standing stones erected nearly 2000 years ago to mark a burial site. Cottons-hopeburn Foot has picnic benches under trees by a little brook, and a forest walk.

ROCHESTER
Look out carefully for the sharp, unmarked turn off the main road, beside a war memorial, to the hamlet of High Rochester. The unusual stone-built house on the corner, once a school, has a porch built of stones from the nearby Roman fort of Bremenium. The rounded stones built into the edges of the gable were once ammunition for Roman catapults.

The narrow road climbs uphill and through a gap in a dry-stone wall into the hamlet of High Rochester, whose village green, with its scattering of houses, was once the heart of Bremenium. The fort was built in a commanding position above the Roman road of Dere Street, which the modern road follows, straight as an arrow for mile after mile, on its way to Corbridge. Catapults mounted on the fort's ramparts could be used against anyone advancing down the road. A rampart, part of a tower and the fine west gateway of the fort are still visible.

OTTERBURN
A battle in which both sides could claim some measure of victory helped to ensure that the Battle of Chevy Chase – fought in 1388 just to the north-west of modern Otterburn – became renowned in ballads from both sides of the border. The English,

WIDE WATERS *For the statistically minded, Kielder Water has a surface area of 2684 acres and holds 44 billion gallons of water. Connoisseurs of landscape can appreciate the superb blending of the reservoir with its scenic surroundings.*

with 8000 infantry and 600 spearmen under Sir Henry Percy (Harry Hotspur), killed the Earl of Douglas, leader of the 4000-strong Scottish army ravaging Northumberland; but the Scots killed 3000 of the English forces, losing only 100 of their own men, and captured Percy.

The site of the battle is marked by the so-called Percy Cross, off the main road half a mile north-west of Otterburn. Although the cross – actually a simple pillar on a stepped plinth – is only 100yds off the road it is not easy to find, being hidden in a grove of firs surrounded by a dry-stone wall. There is no parking space nearby.

Tweed is still made at Otterburn Mill, which is open to the public on weekdays. Beyond it the road crosses the River Rede by an attractive arched stone bridge. The route then turns south along Dere Street and drops towards the grey slate-roofed cottages of West Woodburn.

<u>Tourist information:</u> (Kielder Water) Bellingham 40398.

Castles on the Northumbrian border

TOUR
196

—— 65 MILES ——

Castles crown the heights near Berwick-upon-Tweed. Along Northumberland's peaceful byways, wild roses in the hedgerows frame views of the slopes of the Cheviot Hills.

BERWICK-UPON-TWEED
Swans paddle in stately procession down the Tweed, winding their way under Berwick's three bridges and below the grey stone walls that girdle the town. Behind these Elizabethan ramparts Berwick rises on a hill, its handsome buildings of pinkish-grey stone dominated by the spire of the 18th-century Town Hall. This spire makes up for the lack of one at Holy Trinity Church on Wallace Green, one of only two churches built in England during Cromwell's time.

From the elegant Georgian streets and squares east of Berwick, cobbled alleyways traverse the ramparts and lead to a wide grassy open space between the town and sea. From this vantage point it is easy to see how Berwick commanded a strategic position on the border between England and Scotland, guarded on three sides by the river and the sea.

ANCROFT
A row of long low cottages with red-tiled roofs lines the road that curves through the tiny hamlet of Ancroft. Behind them, and easily missed, St Anne's Church squats among fields where a few mounds mark the remains of cottages destroyed after the Plague in 1667.

The church tower – solid, stubby and square – was built as a fortress early in the 14th century. It is one of Northumberland's finest peel towers, meant to shelter the villagers from attack by border raiders.

CHILLINGHAM
A unique breed of cattle – small, white and woolly, with curving horns – roams wild through the hilly park that surrounds Chillingham Castle. The origin of the herd is a mystery, but it is likely that the white cattle were bred by Anglo-Saxons for religious reasons. The herd of animals is led by a single 'King' bull, which reigns for two or three years until defeated in combat by a younger bull. Visitors can see the cattle on application to the warden on any day in summer except Tuesdays. Chillingham Castle itself, with its fortifications dating from the 14th century, is closed but the little Church of St Peter can be seen, with its superb 15th-century monument to Sir Ralph Gray and his wife.

ROS CASTLE
The road climbs high onto Hepburn Moor, from where it is only a short walk along a peaty path to the summit's Iron Age fort.

Across the heather and bracken there are breathtaking views in all directions; to Berwick, 18 miles to the north, and beyond to the Scottish hills; to Alnwick in the south-east and beyond to Newcastle, 40 miles away. Bamburgh Castle, 9 miles to the north-east, seems to perch on the edge of the sea like a child's toy, with the Farne Islands dotting the water.

HARTHOPE VALLEY
The road along the valley leads to Wooler, a small town at the foot of the Cheviots, which has no fewer than seven hotels and inns to cater for the needs of Cheviot hill walkers. Most of the buildings, including St Mary's Church, are only a century old, as the town was largely destroyed by fire in 1772 and again in 1862.

A narrow lane from Middleton to Langleeford along the valley of the little Harthope Burn gives an ideal introduction to Cheviot country. From the end of the road, walkers can continue along a footpath which climbs gently along 3½ miles to the 2676ft summit of The Cheviot. The plateau at the top is one vast peat bog.

FLODDEN FIELD
A tall cross in a barley field marks the site of the bloody Battle of Flodden, fought between the Scots and the English on September 9, 1513. At least 10,000 men were slain, including James IV of Scotland, and many of them were laid to rest at the Church of St Paul in nearby Branxton.

Beside the fountain in Branxton is an unusual garden known as the 'Cement Menagerie'. It is populated with giraffes, tigers and farm animals and a motley assortment of statesmen, soldiers and countrymen – all modelled life-size in cement.

FORD AND ETAL
Louisa, Marchioness of Waterford restored Ford Castle and built generously proportioned stone houses in its grounds when she came to live there after the death of her husband in 1859. The castle is not open to the public.

Lady Waterford spent 21 years decorating the village school with religious scenes, using Ford villagers as models. The building is now a gallery of her work.

About a mile beyond Ford, the handsome three-storey stone building of Heatherslaw Mill stands on the banks of the River Till. The mill has been restored as a working museum, and visitors can buy flour that they have watched being ground by millstones driven by a huge water wheel.

About a mile farther on, a street of whitewashed houses, several of them thatched, leads up to the ruined

PEACEFUL PASTURE *Cattle graze peacefully near the gaunt ruins of the 14th-century Dunstanburgh Castle.*

ROMANTIC INSPIRATION *The ruins of Norham Castle, by the Tweed, inspired J.M.W. Turner to paint some of his most romantic works.*

SEAHOUSES *Brightly coloured fishing boats crowd the ancient harbour.*

gatehouse of Etal Castle, built with massive cubes of grey stone. The grassy bank below the castle is a favoured spot for watching salmon jump the weir on the River Till.

NORHAM

Its lofty position on a mound above the swirling River Tweed gave Norham Castle its reputation as 'the most dangerous place in England' where, in the 14th century, Sir Walter Scott's hero Sir William Marmion proved his valour single-handed against the Scots.

An attractive wide street leads down from the castle to a triangular green, where the stepped base of the village cross is worn by centuries of use as a seat. St Cuthbert's Church was begun in 1165 by Bishop de Puiset, who also built the castle five years earlier.

Tourist information: Berwick-upon-Tweed 307187 (summer), 306332 (winter); Wooler 81602 (summer).

TOUR
197

— 71 MILES —

One of Britain's least spoilt and loneliest stretches of coast has fishing villages, a nature reserve, beaches and lofty castles that are reminders of Northumberland's turbulent past.

HOLY ISLAND

At low tide Holy Island, or Lindisfarne, is a long peninsula connected to the mainland by a causeway across a vast expanse of sand flats, a nature reserve where large numbers of wildfowl and wading birds feed. The incoming tide sweeps across the sand at speed, and visitors must not try to cross the causeway if water has reached the road.

At high tide the link with the mainland is cut and the island becomes remote, peaceful and mysterious. Little wonder that King Oswald of Northumbria selected Lindisfarne as a site for a monastery, and sent St Aidan to found it in AD 634. Aidan's monastery was destroyed by the Danes in AD 793. A modern statue of the saint stands within the grounds of the later priory, built by the Benedictines in the 11th century.

Standing beside the priory, the more modest parish church of St Mary looks Victorian because of 19th-century restorations; but the round arches in the nave are 12th-century Norman.

Lindisfarne Castle peers down on the village from its vantage point in splendid isolation on a rocky crag. The castle was rebuilt in 1903, as a private house, by Edwin Lutyens around the ruin of a 16th-century fort. It is owned by the National Trust and open to visitors.

BAMBURGH

The first close view of Bamburgh Castle – as the road turns the corner beyond Budle Bay – takes the breath

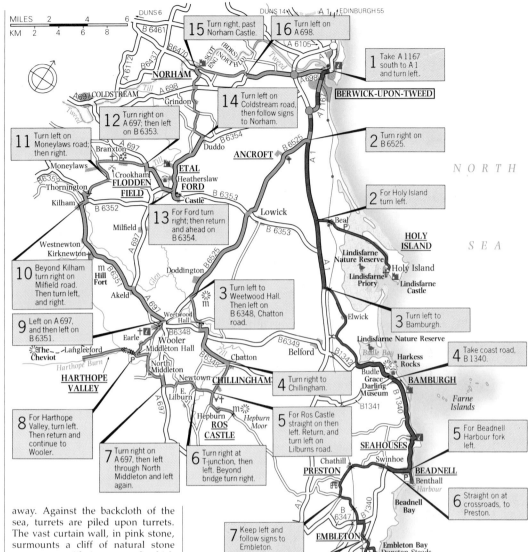

away. Against the backcloth of the sea, turrets are piled upon turrets. The vast curtain wall, in pink stone, surmounts a cliff of natural stone overgrown with ivy, around which sea birds wheel and scream.

This impressive setting dwarfs the red roofs of the little village below. Bamburgh has a fine Norman church dedicated to St Aidan who died in the village in 651.

Facing Bamburgh across what appears to be only a narrow moat of sea are the scattered rocky outcrops of the Farne Islands. It was in 1838 that the paddle steamer *Forfarshire* was wrecked on the Farnes, and Grace Darling with her father rescued nine men in a small rowing boat, or coble. Grace Darling is buried in St Aidan's churchyard, and the nearby museum named after her has a wealth of material commemorating her.

SEAHOUSES AND BEADNELL

While courting the holiday trade with fish-and-chip shops and caravan sites, the fishing villages of Seahouses and Beadnell both retain unspoilt working harbours. From Seahouses, visitors can book trips to the Farne Islands or fishing outings in one of the colourfully painted boats at the quayside.

Beside the long sandy crescent of Beadnell Bay a tiny harbour shelters a few fishing cobles. Behind the harbour are limekilns dating from 1798, now owned by the National Trust and used to store crab pots.

PRESTON

The peel tower at Preston, built for defence at the time of Scottish raids, is only half a tower, but it is impressive. One stone-vaulted room was a prison cell. It has a slit window only 3in wide.

Another room is furnished as it would have been in 1392 when the tower was built – with animal skins on the rough bed, and reeds on the floor. The tower – open daily in the summer – boasts a fine clock with a mechanism of the same type as that in the Houses of Parliament clock tower.

EMBLETON

The village is on a rise with fine views over sandy links to the sea. A peel tower has been incorporated into the vicarage beside Holy Trinity Church.

A farm at Dunstan Steads is open to

visitors on summer afternoons. From it a path leads after about a mile to Dunstanburgh Castle; because parking at Dunstan Steads is limited, it may be easier to drive to Craster and then walk back along the coast to the castle.

CRASTER

Terraces of low cottages ring the little harbour of Craster, which shelters a small fleet of fishing boats. The curiously dark stone from which the cottages are built was quarried from the whinstone on which the village stands.

From just north of Craster a footpath across fields follows the rocky shore to Dunstanburgh Castle.

Tourist information: Seahouses 720424 (summer).

Scottish Lowlands

220
DUNBAR

A 6105

A 697

COLDSTREAM
200

ROSE

Tweed

199 JEDBURGH

A 68

CHEVIOT HILLS

A 68

A 69

ENGLAND

1 FALKIRK Number of tour
and starting point

Route of tour

he turbulent River Tweed, in its final dash to the sea, today forms the eastern end of a border that once moved back and forth like an ebbing and flowing tide as Scots and English contested the 'Debatable Land'. The peaceful pastures and rolling moorland beyond the river still bear the scars and relics of that bloody past: ruined abbeys ravaged by English invaders, great defensive castles built by Scottish nobles, and fortified peel towers in which villagers took refuge when raiders descended to steal their cattle and plunder their homes.

To the south-west, more than 240 square miles of forest make up the Galloway Forest Park, a wild and rugged landscape whose scenery approaches Highland grandeur. Mountains rise to more than 2000ft, lochs glitter among the moorlands and falls cascade through winding gorges. The Mull of Galloway, a hammerhead of land projecting into the Irish Sea, is washed by the Gulf Stream; in its temperate climate subtropical trees and plants grow and gardens are glorious with colour well into the autumn. North of Galloway lie some of Scotland's favourite coastal resorts, and also places of pilgrimage for lovers of Robert Burns, the poet who lived, loved and died in this corner of Scotland. Near Lanark the Clyde crashes over spectacular waterfalls, and on the river's bank an 18th-century cotton-mill village has been restored as a living museum.

Historic sites border Southern Scotland's other great river, the Forth. Edinburgh Castle dominates the country's capital; at Falkirk, Bonnie Prince Charlie won a victory over the English; Linlithgow was the birthplace of Mary, Queen of Scots. Across the estuary in Fife are relics of an even earlier Scotland, in the stones carved by 7th-century Pictish settlers among the rolling hills between the Forth and the Tay. At Bannockburn in 1314 Robert Bruce became king of a fully independent Scotland, and at Dunfermline seven Scottish kings lie buried. History of another kind clings to St Andrews, the home of golf.

Towers by the Teviot and the Tweed

TOUR
198

———— 40 MILES ————

The high Borders country, whose peel towers recall centuries of fighting, inspired the novels of Sir Walter Scott; he loved to look out across it from a viewpoint above the Tweed.

LAUDER

The heart of Lauderdale is no metropolis. A single, long street widens out in the middle to form the Market Place. There stands the Tolbooth, which dates in part from the 14th century. Several large inns along the street – The Black Bull, The Eagle, The Golden Bannock – are reminders of Lauder's importance as a staging post in coaching days, while shops that sell such things as cattle drench and electric fence energisers reflect the area's livestock raising.

The pretty, pink-stuccoed church was built in 1673. It was constructed in the form of a Greek cross – a cross with four equal arms – so that the pulpit is sited at the centre, below the octagonal tower.

THIRLESTANE CASTLE

At the edge of Lauder, a small road to the left leads to Thirlestane Castle, a rosy confection in sandstone that belongs to all kinds of periods and is all the more interesting for it. Somewhere deep within there may be

fragments of a 14th-century fort, but most of the present shell is late Tudor or early Victorian.

Much of the interior decoration, however, is late 17th century, the work of Sir William Bruce and quite staggering in its richness; the plasterwork is particularly fine. This was done at the behest of the first and only Duke of Lauderdale, an intimate of Charles II and an astute politician who became virtual dictator of Scotland. His title died with him, though his family, the Maitlands, still live in the castle.

The sheer grandeur of the rooms apart, the chief joys are the paintings – by Gainsborough, Lawrence, Hoppner, Romney and many others. There is a Border Country Life Museum in the east wing. The formal gardens have been delightfully restored, and there are woodlands and riverside walks. The house is open most afternoons.

EARLSTON

A long stone village in the high farming country of the Borders, Earlston was the birthplace of Thomas the Rhymer, the 13th-century seer and poet. Of his many prophecies, the best known is:
'Tyde what may, whate'er betyde
Haig shall be Haig of Bemersyde'
which was regarded as being fulfilled in 1921 when the nation presented Field-Marshal Earl Haig with the estates at Bemersyde, anciently held by his family.

A fragment of Thomas's tower still stands: a thick, ancient wall at the

southern end of the village, hidden behind a café.

In the east wall of the big red parish church there is a stone on which his name is carved. But it is worn and faded with the passage of time.

SCOTT'S VIEW

The view from below the crest of Bemersyde Hill was Sir Walter Scott's favourite prospect. The lovely land is laid out in its infinite variety; the coloured woods, the curving, climbing pastures, the rich, red plough and the noble, glittering curve of the Tweed far below. In the middle distance are the triple peaks of the Eildon Hills, called the Three Sisters and rising to 1385ft.

The Eildons were a single hill, so it is said, until they were split by a demon at the command of a medieval wizard named Michael Scott. This could not be true, since the Romans knew the hills as Trimontium, and established a signal station on the highest of them. And before the Romans, the Celts had a hill-fort on the same site. King Arthur and his knights are said to lie in a vault beneath the Three Sisters, awaiting a trumpet call to action.

DRYBURGH ABBEY

Of all the great border abbeys, Dryburgh inspires the greatest affection. Its tribulations long past, it appears even in its ruined state to have achieved the serenity its founders intended.

The abbey was built in 1150 by monks from Alnwick; it was badly

mauled by English invaders in 1322 and 1385, and most savagely during the Earl of Hertford's ruthless raid of 1545. Yet a great deal of it remains – the west front with its 15th-century doorway, parts of the nave and chapter house, the refectory and other monastic buildings.

In St Mary's Aisle lies the body of Sir Walter Scott, and close by him that of Field-Marshal Earl Haig, Commander in Chief of British forces on the Western Front, 1915-18. The abbey is open daily.

SMAILHOLM TOWER

This is a different face of the Borders from the one presented by Dryburgh and the smiling valley of the Tweed. Smailholm sits on its crag like a falcon on the gauntlet, harsh and challenging and still terrible. It is probably the best surviving example of a border peel tower, a fairly simple structure with store rooms below and living quarters above; it stands five storeys high and has 7ft thick walls.

The tower was a stronghold of the Pringles, built in the 16th century when John Pringle felt it was secure enough to defy Cromwell's army, and though Parliamentarian artillery proved him wrong in the end, Smailholm's resolute defenders did not easily give in.

Sir Walter Scott's grandfather owned the neighbouring Sandyknowe Farm, and Scott played about the tower as a child. All his life it was to him an inspiration and the very embodiment of border legend. He described the tower in his epic poem *Marmion*. About sunset, when cold yellow light is reflected in the pool in front of the tower and the Eildon Hills stand black against the clouds behind, it seems that the echoes of

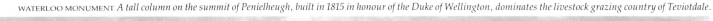

WATERLOO MONUMENT *A tall column on the summit of Penielheugh, built in 1815 in honour of the Duke of Wellington, dominates the livestock grazing country of Teviotdale.*

the reivers' hoofbeats have not quite died away.

It appears odd that this awesome and evocative building should house a museum of dolls and tapestries, but so it does, and shows them to the public in the summer.

MELLERSTAIN HOUSE
The wings of this magnificent Georgian house predate the centre, since they were probably built by William Adam in 1725; it was not until 1770 that his son Robert was commissioned by the Baillies, owners of Mellerstain, to build a central block to link the two.

The interiors are still pure Robert Adam – light and gay and colourful, with exquisite plasterwork and furniture and fine paintings. The magnificent library has a frieze of classical figures above the bookshelves.

Mellerstain's terraced gardens were laid out between 1900 and 1909. Their speciality is old roses and there are views of an ornamental lake and the distant Cheviots. One garden is laid out in Italian style. House and gardens are open most days in summer.

GORDON
In this quiet crossroads village of stone cottages, many door and window frames have been painted to add a sprightly touch of colour. The little Free Kirk of 1843 was given a tall, round turret with a clock set in it 50 years later. Clock apart, its style is strongly reminiscent of the 16th-century Greenknowe peel tower along the road.

GREENKNOWE TOWER
The red-stone Greenknowe Tower – though roofless – has a civilised air. It stands on a green knoll screened by beech trees just outside Gordon, and it has corner turrets whose design is at least partly decorative, and a magnificent fireplace. The defences are similar to those of Smailholm; a yett, or heavy iron grating over the door, and a narrow, circular staircase with a clockwise twist, so that the defender, backing up the stair, would have his sword arm clear, while his opponent's was against the wall.

The tower was built in 1581 by James Seton and his wife Jane Edmonstone, whose coats of arms are above the door. Later, it was the home of the covenanter Walter Pringle, who fought against Cromwell at Dunbar and spent most of his later years in jail, first for killing an Ironside trooper in self-defence, then, under Charles II, for nonconformity. A key to the tower is available from the key keeper in Gordon.

LEGERWOOD
The church at Legerwood stands above green hills with curves so smooth they might have been spokeshaved; and though the building has been renovated on several occasions, it still has much of its original 12th-century interior. The Norman arch of red stone is one of the finest of its kind in Scotland.

There is a large monument to John Ker of Morriston and his wife Lady Grizel Cochrane who died in 1748

aged 83 – '. . . the same who so heroically saved the life of her father the Honorable Sir John Cochrane of Ochiltree when under sentence of death at Edinburgh owing to his connection with the political troubles of 1685'. She disguised herself as a highwayman and twice waylaid the king's messenger bringing the death warrant from London, so gaining time for her father to obtain a pardon.

TOUR
199

—— 51 MILES ——

The mighty River Tweed and its tributary the Teviot run through countryside dotted with once-proud castles and peel towers. This is also rich sheep and cattle-grazing country.

JEDBURGH
Travellers coming from the south should prepare themselves for Jedburgh, for it comes upon them suddenly, around a corner, as a cliff of old rose stone. This is the abbey, founded by David I in 1138 and, despite its roofless state and numerous sackings

and pillagings down the years, is still one of the loveliest buildings in Scotland. The abbey is open daily in summer, and most days in winter.

There is not a vast amount of Jedburgh; the Earl of Hertford saw to that in a single terrible raid in 1545. But what remains is handsomely presented. Many of the old crow-stepped gabled houses in the Market Place, Canongate, High Street and Castlegate have been given a face-lift in pebbledash of various hues, a pleasant practice that seems to be catching on in many old Scottish towns.

Mary, Queen of Scots probably stayed in Jedburgh in 1566, in the house named after her. She was desperately ill; many years later, during her imprisonment in England, she cried out in despair: 'Would I had died that time in Jedburgh!' The building is a 16th-century bastel-house, a type of fortified manor house that once belonged to the Kers of Ferniehirst Castle and is now a museum open daily from spring to autumn, devoted to Mary and her sad career. One of the exhibits is said to be her death mask.

Apart from the abbey, the house is one of the oldest buildings in the town. The 12th-century castle

changed hands many times during the Border Wars, and was eventually destroyed by the Scots to keep it out of English hands. The present early 19th-century castle was built as the county jail. It is now a museum of Victorian prison life and is open daily from spring to autumn.

CESSFORD
The road to Cessford passes through one of the most important livestock-rearing areas in Scotland, and the motorist has plenty of company – indifferent sheep, inquisitive calves and suicidal pheasants.

Near the village, Cessford Castle stands like a jagged red iceberg adrift in a field. It was bombarded by the Earl of Surrey in 1523 and surrendered to him by Ker of Cessford. Ker was much criticised, since his contemporaries felt that the castle's 14ft thick walls could have withstood Surrey's cannon. They may have been right, for the old building still stands as massive as ever.

KIRK YETHOLM
Town Yetholm and Kirk Yetholm are separated from one another by the Bowmont Water. Kirk Yetholm is the older of the two; many of the Scottish knights killed at Flodden were buried in the churchyard in 1513, though the present church replaces the one of that period. Yetholm was the gypsy capital of Scotland, where gypsy queens came to be crowned. One of these, Jean Gordon, was the model for Sir Walter Scott's 'Meg Merrilees'. She died on a ducking stool in Carlisle in 1745. The last of the gypsy queens, Esther Faa Blythe, died in Yetholm in 1883. The Gypsy Palace, a tiny cottage, can still be seen.

ROXBURGH
Vanished glories are not uncommon in Scotland's story, but few have vanished quite so thoroughly as Roxburgh. It is a Cheshire Cat of a place;

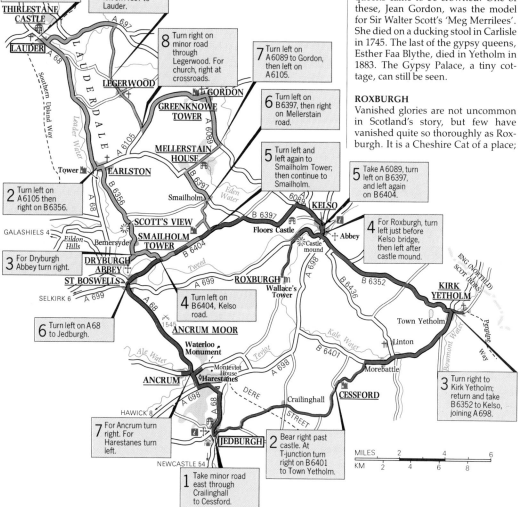

FLOORS CASTLE *The battlements and turrets of the Roxburghe family home were added in 1840 to a mansion of the 1720s.*

MELLERSTAIN HOUSE *An undulating, mile-long avenue of gigantic beeches, oaks and firs is a well-composed overture to one of the finest Scottish Georgian houses.*

KIRK YETHOLM *Gypsy queens were crowned in Scotland's old gypsy capital.*

STARK FORTRESS *Smailholm Tower still evokes memories of border battles.*

DRYBURGH ABBEY *Sir Walter Scott is buried in this 12th-century abbey beside the Tweed, which is surrounded by lawns and shielded from the world by trees.*

royal place, royal burgh, shire capital, nothing is left of them but a small, sad smile and some mouldering stones topping mighty earthworks. It was taken and retaken by Scots and English and finally demolished by the Scots after their king, James II, was killed by an exploding cannon while besieging Roxburgh in 1460.

The present village lies some 3 miles south of the original site. The medieval Wallace's Tower was the seat of Walter Ker, a 16th-century Warden of the Middle March who was as much a reiver, or cattle rustler, as he was an officer of the law.

Two great border rivers, the Teviot and the Tweed, join below the site of old Roxburgh Castle, beside the main road. Little remains of the castle, but by the meeting of the waters the road looks over to one of the finest views of Kelso. Above the silhouettes of riverside houses and mills rise the tall church spire and the soaring, breathtaking bulk of Kelso Abbey.

KELSO
Opinions as to whether Jedburgh or Kelso is the more handsome often depend on which has been visited first; judgments are affected thereby. Kelso is perhaps more austere, harder – literally so, since the setts or cobbles of its streets make the teeth rattle as the car wheels take to them. But with its tall town houses, Kelso is unquestionably elegant. The Square, big and open, with the vast Cross Keys coaching inn on one side and op-

posite, the pale stone Town House in Palladian style, suggests the plaza of a Tuscan hill city.

Like Jedburgh, Kelso has a ruined abbey of surpassing loveliness. It was brought to its present state by the Earl of Hertford who, responding to Henry VIII's order that the Scottish Borders were to be 'tourmented and occupied as much as they can be', destroyed 300 towns, villages, towers and churches during 1544 and 1545.

From the square, a street leads to the great gilded gates of Floors Castle, which was designed for the 1st Duke of Roxburghe by William Adam, and later remodelled by W.H. Playfair. The house has wonderful collections of tapestries, porcelain and paintings and is open on most days in summer.

ST BOSWELLS
Square, red-stone houses stand about an enormous and well-kept green on which were once held some of the largest livestock fairs in Scotland. The tradition is maintained by the annual gypsy fair in July.

The Tweed is at its majestic best at this point, flowing swift and strong between banks of tall trees that turn to glorious rich hues in the autumn.

ANCRUM MOOR
A couple of miles south of St Boswells, the route crosses Ancrum Moor, gradually diverging from the Roman Dere Street, whose course is marked by a line of beech trees slanting away to the left. Thereabouts, on the crest of the hill, in 1545, was fought the Battle of Ancrum Moor, or Lilliardsedge. It was very much a Borders fight, in that the English general, Sir Ralph Evers, had a number of Scottish Borderer mercenaries under his command.

Returning south, laden with loot, his force was cunningly ambushed by a smaller Scottish army under the Regent Arran and the Earl of Angus. Evers' Borderers promptly changed sides and the English were annihilated, Evers among them.

ANCRUM
Old stone and stucco houses enclose the green of a fine, wind-scoured border village. On the green stands a 16th-century cross. The village is approached by a narrow bridge over the Ale Water, in whose banks are caves which are said to have sheltered fugitives during the Border Wars.

Just south of Ancrum is the park of Monteviot House, the seat of Lord Lothian. A minor road leads into the park and to the Harestanes Woodland Centre, which comprises conifers and hardwoods. The centre is open most days in summer, and on certain days in spring and autumn.

Tourist information: Jedburgh 63435/ 63688; Kelso 23464 (summer).

SCOTT'S VIEW *Sir Walter Scott loved to stand on this hilltop near Dryburgh and look out across the country close to his heart – the Borders of ballads and legend. The triple peaks of the Eildon Hills rise 1385ft above the Tweed valley.*

A rugged coast beyond the Tweed

TOUR

200

— 70 MILES —

Trim hedgerows and neat walls throw a chequerboard pattern across the farmland north of the Tweed. On the coast are fishing villages little changed since smugglers hid there.

COLDSTREAM

Solid, grey and unpretentious, Coldstream clings to the north bank of the River Tweed. It is the first town in Scotland encountered by motorists on the main road north from Wooler, in Northumberland. A plaque on the borderline in the middle of Coldstream Bridge records that Robert Burns first set foot in England here in 1787 on his way to Newcastle. On the Scottish side of the bridge is a tiny 'Marriage House', much used by runaway lovers from England in the 18th century. The frock-coated figure who presides over the town, Nelson-like on a tall, fluted column, is Charles Marjoribanks, a well-known Victorian Member of Parliament.

Off the narrow and busy main street is Henderson Park, a formal garden overlooking the river. In the garden is an engraved stone erected by the Coldstream Guards, recording how, in 1660, the regiment crossed the Tweed behind their beloved General Monck, on the way south to crush Richard Cromwell, son of the Lord Protector, and set Charles II on the throne. Although the regiment was not raised in Coldstream it later adopted its official title in honour of the historic march south.

General Monck's headquarters, a simple building with iron gates across its large door and now two private houses, stands in the market square. Nearby, the small local history museum is open in summer.

Abbey Road leads down from the main street to where a Cistercian abbey once stood. It was dissolved in 1621 and no trace of it remains, but in 1834 human bones were dug up in the long-disused graveyard. They were thought to be from the victims of the Battle of Flodden Field (1513), when the bodies of the defeated Scots were brought to the Lady Abbess for burial.

THE HIRSEL

A white board pinned to a tree on the western edge of Coldstream marks the entrance to The Hirsel – the country home of Lord Home of The Hirsel, who, as Sir Alec Douglas-Home, was Prime Minister in 1963-4. Only the pleasant, park-like grounds are open to the public, and an attractive stable yard has been converted into a folk museum. Each stall contains a display of tools, implements and domestic equipment, under such headings as: wash house, joiner's shop, archaeology and so on. The museum, like the grounds, is open all year round. There is also a picnic site and several nature walks.

MANDERSTON

A magnificent marble staircase with a handrail made of silver is the highlight of this fine Edwardian mansion. It is open on certain days in the summer, when visitors can also view its collection of rare old biscuit tins. In the grounds is a splendid group of farm and dairy buildings.

DUNS

The great medieval scholar and religious thinker John Duns Scotus was born in this delightful old town in the 13th century. A Franciscan friar, he taught that the ultimate truth was God. In 1966, thought to be the 700th anniversary of his birth, the Franciscans put up a bust to him in the town park, and a memorial stone outside the gates of Duns Castle, 1 mile north-west of the town, which they believe to be his birthplace. A portrait of the scholar hangs in the Council Chambers.

Duns straggles up from a sturdy church on a grassy mound, behind which are narrow little streets crammed with buildings set at odd angles. From the top of Castle Street a footpath leads into Duns Nature Reserve, which has marked walks and a short, steep climb up Duns Law with fine views of the castle.

In 1639 Covenanters flew their standard from the stone on top of the Law, when their leader, General Leslie, had his headquarters in Duns Castle. The general and his troops awaited a battle with the English under Charles I which never took place because differences were solved by a negotiated settlement. The castle is not open to the public.

The Jim Clark Room, in Newtown Street, houses more than 120 trophies won by the former World Motor Racing Champion. Clark (1936-68) lived and is buried in Chirnside between Ayton and Ladykirk. The trophies, given to the town by Clark's parents after his death in a race, range from his first race win – the Border Motor Racing Club Trophy in 1957 – to the South African Grand Prix in 1968.

EDIN'S HALL

On a shoulder of Cockburn Law are the substantial remains of one of the very few Iron Age towers, or brochs, found in the south of Scotland. Edin's Hall was built within the ramparts of

ST ABB'S HEAD *The waters below the cliffs are clear and pure, and skin divers may obtain permits to explore and photograph the underwater life and scenery.*

an even earlier hill-fort, whose outlines are still clearly defined.

From the roadside pine forest a well-signed, half-hour climb starts across a suspension bridge over Whiteadder Water – which cascades down through gleaming slabs of granite. Scattered piles of stones on the nearby grassy slopes are relics of the early tribes which once inhabited the area. The imagination can picture them on this desolate hillside, huddled for protection within the tall, double-walled tower, peering fearfully out over the valley of the Whiteadder for the first warning of invaders' approach.

COLDINGHAM

In the quaint, twisting village of Coldingham are the remains of an ancient priory, restored in 1098 upon the ruins of an even earlier building. The choir of the priory is embodied in the existing parish church. An arch rises with splendid dignity from the ruined foundations, and at its feet are scattered ancient gravestones and fragments of carved masonry.

Set against a backdrop of ocean, the priory once provided sanctuary for lawbreakers. The boundary within which the fugitives had to stay was marked by crosses, the positions of which are now indicated by place names: Whitecross, Crosslaw and so on. In 1566 the priory was visited by Mary, Queen of Scots and was able to accommodate her train of about 1000 soldiers, attendants and servants.

As the traveller approaches the North Sea, the land becomes more rugged and windswept, with the bleak expanse of Coldingham Moor stretching away to the north-west.

ST ABBS AND ST ABB'S HEAD

The steep zigzag descent into the fishing village of St Abbs leads past short, irregular streets lined with neat fishermen's cottages and on into a maze of sheltered harbours. Upturned boats litter the quays among fish boxes, nets and lobster creels, backed by old stone tackle-sheds, some built into the rock. The village clings to the cliffs, overshadowed to the north by towering volcanic rocks. The sea pounds and lashes at this tough little village, often sending spray high into the air, or throwing itself in heavy waves over the harbour walls.

There is an invigorating walk out to St Abb's Head, from a car park and information centre half a mile west of the village. The walk crosses humps of smoothly cropped turf and hillocks dotted with sheep. From here there are dramatic views across the cliffs and out to sea. A gleaming white lighthouse is built into the rocks. Notices warn people to take great care when walking along the cliffs.

This desolate headland, with its wild seascape, is a National Nature Reserve harbouring more than 50,000 sea birds – including razorbills, guillemots, shags, herring gulls, fulmars and kittiwakes. It is open to the public throughout the year, and leaflets describing the reserve and its rich marine, bird and insect life are obtainable at the car park.

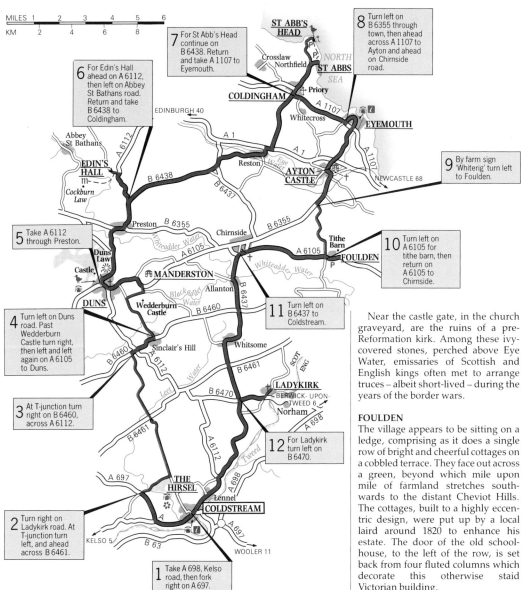

EYEMOUTH

The harbour of this thriving fishing port is crammed with all types of vessel and bustles with activity. Forklift trucks dash about, loading lorries; a derrick hoists boats from the water, and half-built ships stand in the shipyard. It was a notorious smuggling centre in the 17th and 18th centuries, and the higgledy-piggledy nature of the houses in the narrow streets leading up from the harbour was said to be designed to confuse the excisemen. It is also said that as much as half the town lies underground, a honeycomb of hiding places. Opposite the harbour, on Gunsgreen, is a splendid Georgian mansion with its own dovecote, from which secret passages are supposed to lead to the waterside.

The full story of the town and its people is told in the Eyemouth Museum. A tapestry records the name of every boat and crewman who perished in the Eyemouth Disaster on Friday, October 14, 1881. The day began bright and calm and nearly 30 boats of the fishing fleet sailed out from Eyemouth harbour. At midday, a savage hurricane suddenly struck and many of the boats were smashed to splinters. Only a few managed to return, and some of these were wrecked on the rocks outside the harbour, their crews drowning in the boiling seas within sight and hearing of the frantic, helpless women ashore. Altogether, 129 Eyemouth men lost their lives that day, almost half the adult male population, and 60 men from the surrounding district. The museum and tourist information centre, set in the Auld Kirk, are open daily from Easter to October.

AYTON CASTLE

The flamboyant, red-sandstone pile of Ayton Castle is so extravagant that local legend says it was built haphazardly, without plans or architect. In fact, it was designed in 1846 by the Scottish architect James Gillespie Graham for the Governor of the Bank of Scotland, William Mitchell-Innes. The castle is situated just beyond the village of Ayton beside the bridge over Eye Water on a site that shows off its rich colour and fantastic shape to advantage. It is open on certain days in summer; and by appointment at other times of the year.

Near the castle gate, in the church graveyard, are the ruins of a pre-Reformation kirk. Among these ivy-covered stones, perched above Eye Water, emissaries of Scottish and English kings often met to arrange truces – albeit short-lived – during the years of the border wars.

FOULDEN

The village appears to be sitting on a ledge, comprising as it does a single row of bright and cheerful cottages on a cobbled terrace. They face out across a green, beyond which mile upon mile of farmland stretches southwards to the distant Cheviot Hills. The cottages, built to a highly eccentric design, were put up by a local laird around 1820 to enhance his estate. The door of the old schoolhouse, to the left of the row, is set back from four fluted columns which decorate this otherwise staid Victorian building.

Nearby, on the edge of the churchyard, stands a well-preserved, two-storey tithe barn with outside stairs. It was used by the minister to store the grain given to him by his parishioners as stipend.

LADYKIRK

A handful of houses surround this pale pink, cross-shaped church. Its solid buttresses are topped by ornamental carvings and support the weight of a slabbed-stone roof and triple-storeyed tower.

In 1499 James IV was almost drowned crossing the Tweed here, at the head of his army, and he vowed to build a shrine, dedicated to Our Lady, in gratitude for his survival. Ladykirk, a resplendent building in a land where the House of God is often austere, was the result. And there James is said to have knelt in prayer before crossing the Tweed again on his way to his death at the Battle of Flodden in 1513. In Victorian times a bust of the monarch was placed on one wall.

Tourist information: Coldstream 2607 (summer); Eyemouth 50678 (summer).

333

Lochs and glens of Buchan country

A country town is the gateway to the John Buchan country of upper Tweeddale. A modern reservoir in a once-remote valley makes a fine recreation area in the border hills.

PEEBLES
This riverside town among wooded hills has a High Street in which the 20th century has been firmly held at bay. On the south side, the Chambers Institution with its library, museum, tourist information centre and fine war-memorial shrine was once the town house of the Dukes of Queensberry. The Tontine Hotel retains the front courtyard where stagecoaches clattered in.

Across the street, a high-set vertical sundial still shows off 'Greenwich Solar Time'. Of earlier buildings, the 13th-century Cross Kirk is preserved as an ancient monument, and St Andrews Tower is a fragment of a church established in 1195.

The River Tweed, noted for its salmon, rushes through the town, whose motto is 'Against the stream they multiply'. Pathways along both banks of the river are linked by footbridges below the High Street and at Hay Lodge Park. Other walks include a climb to viewpoints on the hill called Manor Sware, and town trails are available.

Leaving Peebles, the route passes Kailzie Gardens, open daily from April to October, and a picnic site on the edge of Cardrona Forest. Then it winds gently above the wooded banks of the Tweed.

TRAQUAIR
Written records suggest that Traquair – the home of the Maxwell Stuarts – is the oldest inhabited house in Scotland. Parts of it date back to 1107.

Traquair is a place of abiding Jacobite memories. The Bear Gates on the Cardrona road, for instance, will never be opened again until a Stuart is restored to the throne.

The house is open daily from Easter to October, and its grounds include a maze and woodland walks. Several craft workshops welcome visitors.

At the hamlet of Traquair, cattle drovers used to rest overnight before tackling the long climb of the Minchmoor track, now part of the Southern Upland Way.

ST MARY'S LOCH
The Yarrow Water flows from St Mary's Loch, which curves gently past the foot of overlapping hills rising from both its shores. A brackeny footpath climbs to the ruined St Mary's churchyard, where an open-air service in the style of the Covenanters is held on the last Sunday in July.

The loch is a noted angling and sailing centre. Tibbie Shiels Inn, at its far end, is named after a famous 19th-century licensee. The 19th-century poet James Hogg, known as the Ettrick Shepherd, lived in the district, and his statue stands below hillside woodland overlooking the inn.

GREY MARE'S TAIL
On the west side of a wild-looking glen, a spectacular waterfall spiders down from the remote, high-level bowl of hills around Loch Skeen.

The area belongs to the National Trust for Scotland, and information boards explain the geology, land use and wildlife of the area including the presence of a herd of part-wild goats.

Guided walks are arranged in July and August. One short path leads to the foot of the waterfall. Another climbs a much higher and rockier route up to the loch.

MEGGET
The landscape of this lonely, sheep-farmed valley was radically altered by the opening in 1983 of the Megget Reservoir. Picnic areas and viewpoints have been provided; there is a walk along the top of the dam, and the reservoir is stocked with trout. Nevertheless, the peace of the grass and heather hills remains unbroken.

A modern corniche-style road winds high above the reservoir, past the start of a long footpath through the northern hills to the Manor valley.

TWEEDSMUIR
The novelist John Buchan took his title of Lord Tweedsmuir from this upland valley where, since boyhood, he had enjoyed walking, angling and hearing the folklore of the border.

Tweedsmuir village is a scattered place where the Talla Water meets the Tweed. The Victorian parish church is beautifully located on a rise of ground between the rivers. To the left of the crossroads are the Standing Stones of Menzion, and straight ahead the road crosses the Tweed above a miniature but striking rock cascade.

BROUGHTON
Down in the narrow plain of the Biggar Water, the village of Broughton is set among level fields overlooked by the characteristically rounded hills.

John Buchan's father was once minister of Broughton Free Church, which has been restored as the John Buchan Centre. Open daily from April to October, it illustrates his life.

Broughton Place is a mansion designed by Sir Basil Spence in the 1930s as a modern expression of the architectural themes of the old border keeps. Part of it is open in summer as an art gallery.

DAWYCK
Generations of enthusiastic landowners have made the woodlands of Dawyck among the finest in Scotland. The Botanic Garden at the heart of the estate is now maintained by the Royal Botanic Garden of Edinburgh, and is open daily from Easter to September.

Apart from the magnificent trees in the sheltered glen of the Scrape Burn, there are azaleas, springtime daffodils and more than 120 different species of rhododendron. Footpaths winding up through the woodland lead to an elegant Dutch bridge over waterfalls.

North-east of Dawyck, the route runs through the strung-out village of Stobo. An early 19th-century castle has been converted to a health and beauty centre; but it is upstaged architecturally by the carefully restored Norman church, on a site used for worship since the 6th century.

NEIDPATH CASTLE
The riverside scenery becomes ever more dramatic, until Neidpath Castle is seen on a rise of ground dominating a curving and beautifully wooded

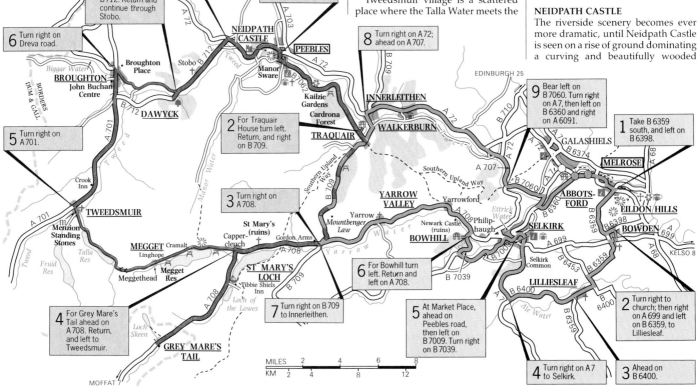

ravine. This 14th-century fortress became a family home in the 17th century. But its warlike history continued, and the walls still bear the marks of Cromwell's cannonballs.

The castle is open daily from Easter to October. Below its lawns, footpaths extend along the river banks. Opposite, in South Park Wood, roe deer browse on the hillside.

TOUR

202

—— 60 MILES ——

Three river valleys wind through a Borders landscape of rolling farmland and woods. In the beautiful Tweed valley stands the mansion house where Scott wrote his *Waverley* novels.

MELROSE
Centred on the well-kept ruins of a 12th-century Cistercian abbey, where the heart of Robert Bruce is reputedly buried, this sturdily stone-built town lies between the meadows bordering the Tweed and the foothills of the Eildons. The town lay in the path of plundering English armies during the Border Wars, and the abbey was sacked in 1322, 1485 and 1545.

Beside the ruins, the National Trust for Scotland's Priorwood Garden has two specialities: flowers grown for drying and historic strains of apple, some first established by the monks and others known since Roman times. Not far away, the Motor Museum displays cars, motorcycles, toy vehicles and vintage road signs.

The town is a fine walking centre, and paths on both banks of the Tweed, linked by a suspension footbridge of 1826, are part of the Southern Upland Way.

EILDON HILLS
The rounded summits which soar above Melrose can be explored by the exhilarating Eildon Walk. This passes steeply angled fields, extensive heather moorland, gorse thickets, conifer plantations, rough grazing and the occasional peat bog.

The main Eildon Walk, a stiff climb in its early stages, avoids the highest levels and follows a circular 4 mile route back to Melrose via the abbey. However, other paths strike out for the hilltops themselves.

Eildon Hill North was the site of a Roman signal station. The magnificent outlook is still the one the legionaries knew more than 1900 years ago, as they scanned the course of the road now called Dere Street, crossing the border hills from the Cheviot passes far away on the southern horizon.

BOWDEN
Neatly renovated houses line the main street and surround the village green at Bowden. The oldest of them was originally a 17th-century linen-weaver's cottage.

However, as a recorded settlement Bowden goes back at least 600 years before that. Its handsome parish

church, on the far side of the wooded ravine of the Bowden Burn, occupies the same site as a Norman-style church established around 1120 by the Benedictine monks of Selkirk who later founded Kelso Abbey.

LILLIESLEAF
Crossing the Ale Water, the route follows a ridge-top avenue towards the long, narrow village of Lilliesleaf. A little apart, before the entrance to the village, stands the restored parish church of 1771. Its baptismal font is far older; it may have come from the original church founded nearby in 1140. Lilliesleaf Kirk also has a fine memorial apse, with stained-glass windows lit by the morning sun.

Beyond the village, the hills and hollows around the winding Ale become more sweeping. Then the route turns north on the main Selkirk road, over high pastures, past forests of spruce and larch, before passing the rumpled hills of Selkirk Common.

SELKIRK
This is an airy hillside place, much of whose history can be read in its statues. Sir Walter Scott's, for instance, is the centrepiece of the Market Place, in front of the old courthouse where he used to sit as Sheriff. Another fine statue is of Mungo Park, the local doctor who turned to African exploration and discovered the source of the Niger in the late 18th century.

The most significant statue, however, is of Fletcher, traditionally the sole survivor of 80 Selkirk men who fought at Flodden in 1513. He returned to the town with a captured English standard, which he cast down in despair as he wordlessly brought news of the disaster. The Casting of the Colours in the Market Place is still the most emotional act of the Selkirk Common Riding, held on the second Friday in June.

Off the Market Place is the narrow Halliwell's Close with Selkirk's oldest house – the 400-year-old Halliwell's House, now restored as an information centre and museum, with an Edwardian ironmonger's shop on the ground floor and a local-history exhibition on the first.

BOWHILL
At Philiphaugh the valleys of the Ettrick and Yarrow Waters meet, and the hill triangle between them is covered by the imposing woodlands of Bowhill, the border home of the Duke of Buccleuch. The lavishly furnished Georgian mansion, with its notable collection of paintings, is open in July and early August.

In the woodlands, open from May to August, one nature trail circles a pair of lochs. Another goes by way of an elegant avenue of limes to the banks of the Yarrow, with a view to the ruined 15th-century Newark Castle.

YARROW VALLEY
Starting as a narrow gap between steeply wooded slopes, the Yarrow valley winds gently up into an open landscape of high sheep-grazed hills. Above the meadows of Yarrowford is

Broadmeadows, the oldest youth hostel in Scotland, opened in 1931. A footpath from it joins the Southern Upland Way, which follows the heathery summits forming the watershed between the valleys of the Yarrow and Tweed.

Yarrow village itself is a tiny place with a parish church built in 1640, renovated in 1826 and 1906 – and almost totally gutted by fire at Easter 1922. However, the church was soon painstakingly rebuilt.

INNERLEITHEN
This textile town beside the Tweed is described at the entrance as 'Innerleithen and St Ronan's Wells'. Ronan was adopted long ago as its patron saint, and for many years in the 18th and 19th centuries people came here to drink the healing waters from a hillside spring. In 1824, Sir Walter Scott brought these two aspects of local history together in his novel *St Ronan's Well*.

WALKERBURN
The Scottish Museum of Woollen Textiles at Walkerburn is open daily, except on Sundays, throughout the

year. It follows the history and techniques of the industry – shearing, spinning, dyeing and weaving. Displays also include traditional knitting patterns, used especially for fishermen's jerseys, with names like the Open Window of Welcome, Waves of the Sea, and Hearts in his Home.

ABBOTSFORD
In 1811, Scott bought a farm beside the Tweed, and there he wrote his *Waverley* novels, which brought him a substantial income. Much of this he used to create the Abbotsford of today. In 1822, he demolished the farmhouse and replaced it with a baronial mansion, where his descendants have lived ever since.

The house and gardens are open to the public daily from March to October. Sir Walter's study and his library of 9000 volumes are as he left them. So is the collection of historical relics – connected with figures as varied as Flora MacDonald, Napoleon, Robert Burns and Rob Roy Macgregor.

Tourist information: Peebles 20138 (summer); Melrose 2555 (summer); Selkirk 20054 (summer).

ST MARY'S LOCH *Scott praised the beauty of this loch set in Ettrick Forest.*

TWEED VALLEY *Forested slopes edge the valley near the town of Innerleithen.*

Border hills above winding Eskdale

TOUR
203
77 MILES

In Liddesdale and Eskdale, sheep graze on the hillsides and clear streams sparkle. Ruined fortresses and festivals recall the romantic, sad and violent history of the borderlands.

HAWICK

A bronze statue of an armoured youth on a charger, holding a standard above his head, is the hub of this bustling town. It marks a victory by the local callants, or youths, over a large force of English marauders in 1514. The English were encamped at nearby Hornshole while looting their way through the Borders, confident in the knowledge that the death roll from Flodden Field the previous year had reduced the fighting strength of the border towns to boys and old men. However, the callants of Hawick rode out in a brave, ragged band, routed the English force and returned with its standard.

Hawick was eventually destroyed by the English in 1570, and all that remains of the original town is incorporated into the Tower Hotel in Towerdykeside, at the far end of the High Street. There is an 8ft thick wall, once part of the Black Tower – the Borders' strongest fortress for 300 years, but destroyed by Covenanters in 1679.

Every summer Hawick celebrates the Festival of the Common Riding, in memory of the days when armed bailies and townsfolk rode round the town ensuring that no neighbouring communities had encroached on their common land. Today the week-long festival includes a celebration of the Battle of Hornshole; a cornet, an unmarried youth, is elected to carry the flag during the ceremonies.

The 19th-century Town House thrusts its baronial turrets out over the High Street. The River Teviot leads the way out of the town past extensive mill buildings, snaking over its shallow, rocky bed under the shelter of hills to the east.

DENHOLM

A huge square green offers fleeting glimpses into the wynds and closes of the village, with its neat 18th-century cottages and square-towered kirk. The elaborate monument on the green is to Dr John Leyden, born in 1775 in the tiny thatched cottage just off the north side of the square. This remarkable scholar, physician and poet, who was largely self-taught, astounded his contemporaries with his knowledge and scientific abilities. Leyden's life, part of which was spent in India, was described by Sir Walter Scott as 'bright and brief'; he was only 36 years old when he died.

Denholm is dominated by Rubers Law, to the south-east, which is most easily scaled from the southern corner of the wood on its eastern flank. From roadside car parking 3 miles south, on the way to Bonchester Bridge, an hour's climb leads over turf then up the side of a burn, with a final scramble to the rocky summit where there are remains of an Iron Age fort. Looking down across the moors, where bracken and heather break up the grassland and isolated trees cast eerie shadows, it is easy to understand why forts were built on such sites: no invader from any direction could escape detection.

The ancient fort-dwellers perhaps signalled to their neighbours in the fort on Bonchester Hill, which is reached by an easy climb from the tiny hamlet of Bonchester Bridge, and offers panoramic views.

HERMITAGE CASTLE

Even in sunshine, this angular fortress with fierce, frowning arches has an aura of cruelty. Stark and menacing on a grassy platform, it is surrounded by extensive earthworks on the banks of the swift-flowing Hermitage Water, close to the ruined Chapel of St Mary and traces of a medieval village. On all sides, bleak moorland rises to peaks from which watch could be kept for many miles.

A 14th-century tower, built round a small courtyard, can still be seen within massive additions of great square towers and walls, with corbels that once supported a continuous timber hoarding high on the exterior walls. Parts of the existing castle were reconstructed in the 19th century and at first sight it appears complete.

Hermitage has a bloody history. Nicholas de Soulis, who first built on this site in the 13th century, was believed to be a warlock who had sold his soul to the Devil in exchange for a promise that no steel could kill him. His neighbours and servants dragged him to the stone circle at Ninestone Rig, 1 mile north-east, where they wrapped him in a sheet of lead and boiled him in a cauldron.

The 11ft long grave outside the kirkyard walls is believed to contain the remains of the Cout of Keilder, a giant baron who came to slay Soulis. But the giant was thwarted in his attempt, and instead was himself drowned by the wicked lord in a deep pool of the river, still known as the Cout of Keilder Pool.

A Scottish patriot named Alexander Ramsay of Dalhousie is said to have been lowered into a pit in the prison and starved to death, after surviving for 17 days on a trickle of grain from the granary above. Mary, Queen of Scots visited Bothwell – her lover and later her third husband – at the castle. He lay wounded in a room over the bakehouse, which still has its original boiler and oven. Mary sat with Bothwell for two hours before returning to Jedburgh with a high fever, having ridden 50 miles over wild moorland.

Hermitage Castle is open all year.

NEWCASTLETON

A wide main street opens into a square, half grass, half metalled, with village pump and war memorial. Union Street, to the left just beyond the square, leads down to a peaceful picnic area on the banks of Liddel Water overlooked by a terrace of pretty cottages. Three miles south of Newcastleton, where a sign points left to Kershopefoot, a forested area across the valley was the scene of the monthly truce during the Border Wars. The warden of The Hermitage met the warden of a rival English fortress and declared a 'day of truce' between sunrise and sunset, while complaints about cattle rustling and other crimes were heard and usually resolved.

Sheep and cattle graze the pasture land, within neatly kept beech and hawthorn hedges, while in sawmill yards freshly sawn pine boles scent the air.

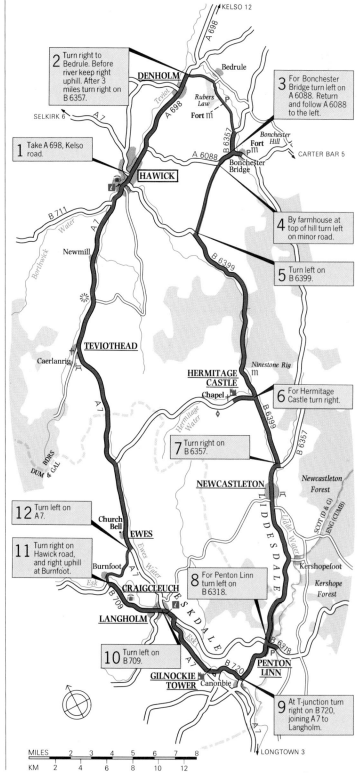

DOWN IN THE VALLEY *From the smallholding of Ryeleahead, 5 miles south of Newcastleton, there are fine views of the valley of Liddel Water and the dense woods beyond.*

BRIDGE WITH A VIEW *A row of whitewashed cottages backs onto the River Esk as it twists along its rocky course just south of Langholm, where the river is spanned by the grey-stone arches of Skipper's Bridge .*

VIOLENT PAST *The history of Hermitage Castle includes murders by starvation, drowning and boiling.*

PENTON LINN

A car park beside the bridge over Liddel Water is the starting point of a footpath beside the river. Dark, rushing water descends in a spectacular series of falls, swirling around sheer rock cliffs, drowning all other sounds as it rumbles into deep pools fringed with trees.

GILNOCKIE TOWER

High on the banks of the Esk, just north of Canonbie, stands Gilnockie Tower, once called Hollows, or Holehouse Tower. It is the recently restored fortress of a notorious 16th-century freebooter named Johnnie Armstrong.

The single tower, with crow-stepped gables and carved parapet walkway around the top, looks up the river valley towards Langholm and the hills. It is open to the public by appointment (Canonbie 245).

LANGHOLM

The River Esk, Wauchope Water and Ewes Water meet in Langholm in a flurry of converging streams. They are spanned by a variety of bridges, on one of which the engineer Thomas Telford – born locally – worked as an apprentice.

Thriving mills surround Langholm and there is a marked contrast between the narrow, twisting old part, with its Town House dominating a small market square, and the broad, more stately 18th-century houses of the 'new' town across the river, which grew as Langholm became a flourishing textile centre.

As in Hawick, a festival every summer commemorates the old Common Riding, with spirited horse races, athletics and ceremonies. Ruined Langholm Castle was the home of the Armstrongs, kinsmen of freebooter Johnnie, and the ancestors of the astronaut Neil Armstrong, first man on the moon.

CRAIGCLEUCH

If Neil Armstrong made history with a handful of moon rocks, his ancestors might have had a hand in collecting the treasures exhibited in The Scottish Explorers' Museum, at Craigcleuch House, 2 miles north of Langholm. In sheltered parkland overlooking the Esk valley, with fine views between hills known as the 'Gates of Eden' to the north, this 19th-century Scottish baronial mansion contains an extensive collection of items brought back to Britain from all over the world by early Scottish explorers.

The varied exhibits in the collection include exquisitely carved coral and ivory, African tribal sculptures, prehistoric ornaments and implements, Chinese silk paintings, wall hangings and hunting trophies.

The museum is open daily from Easter to mid-September. Pictures may be bought, and there are walks in the riverside woodlands.

EWES

In this hamlet, between steeply rising hills, a 300-year-old bell hangs in the fork of a tree in the churchyard. It was put there for safety when the old church was demolished; when the new church was built in 1867 the parishioners had become so fond of their bell in a tree that they decided to leave it there, and hang a replacement in the bell tower. The road beyond the hamlet continues up the valley of Ewes Water, and then down into Teviotdale where the River Teviot flows to join the Tweed.

The landscapes are rural, and there are several parking areas from which motorists can enjoy the views.

TEVIOTHEAD

In the churchyard at Teviot a stone set into the wall commemorates the outlaw Johnnie Armstrong and his followers. Armstrong and 36 of his men rode here from Langholm, hoping to win the favour of Scotland's teenaged king, James V, by offering their service and allegiance. The king, intent on cleaning up the lawless Borders, was apparently not to be won over. Armstrong and his men were arrested and hanged from a makeshift gallows at Caerlanrig to the south-west.

Tourist information: Hawick 72547 (summer); Selkirk 20054 (summer); Langholm 80976 (summer).

Down Annandale to the Solway Firth

An alternative to the busy main road from Scotland to England, this tour provides a leisurely leavetaking along quiet country lanes, and through agreeable lowland towns and fields.

MOFFAT

Surrounded by soft rolling hills which shelter but never overawe it, Moffat is one of the most stylish of southern Scottish towns. It is well endowed with impressive, well-groomed buildings, and its quiet back streets are smart and invariably look newly painted.

The broad main street allows room to breathe, to stand back and savour the full expanse of bright shop fronts and hotels – two of them former coaching inns on the old main highway to Glasgow.

During the 18th century, Moffat became a spa and fashionable resort. Its present town hall was once the Baths Hall, to which water was pumped from the Sulphurous Well on the outskirts of the town.

The bronze statue of a ram near the post office testifies to the lasting prosperity of the town's function as a centre of the wool trade. Visitors are welcome at Moffat Woollens mill, near the southern end of the town, and also at the viewing gallery of Moffat Pottery beside Ladyknowe camp site.

BEATTOCK

A narrow road leads to the top of Beattock Hill, beside an Iron Age hillfort, from which there are wide views over Annandale. An incline well known to railway history enthusiasts is Beattock Bank, where in the days of steam a second engine had to be coupled onto the rear of a train to help it up the slope. It used to take 20 minutes to climb the 10 miles; a modern electric unit takes seven minutes.

LOCKERBIE

This compact little market town grew up around the Johnstone Tower, or Old Tower, which was once the burgh jail. Lockerbie is noted for its sheep sales, and especially for the lamb fair held on Lamb Hill every August since 1680. The feuding Johnstone and Maxwell families fought their last battle here in 1593. Many of the defeated Maxwells had their ears cut off by a cleaver, a custom which was known along the border as 'the Lockerbie nick'.

ST MUNGO'S CHURCH

Forlorn above the bank of a stretch of the River Annan much frequented by anglers, the shell of the church is surrounded by lichen-covered gravestones. Mungo was the 6th-century 'Apostle of the Strathclyde Britons' who became Bishop of Glasgow and, after canonisation, its patron saint.

ECCLEFECHAN

Thomas Carlyle was born in Ecclefechan in 1795, and attended the village school. His house, known as The Arched House, still stands beside the village stream. The central archway, linking two whitewashed wings with glossy black doors and window surrounds, gives the building the appearance of a small coaching inn. The cobbled way through it led, in fact, to the family's own yard, stables and outhouses beyond.

The bedroom where Carlyle was born is furnished as it would have been in his time, and another room, over the arch, is a small museum containing a collection of manuscripts and other mementos of his life and work. The museum is open daily, except Sundays, between Easter and the end of October. Carlyle died in London in 1881 and is buried in the local churchyard.

ANNAN

After leaving Ecclefechan village school, Carlyle spent some time at Annan Academy before going to Edinburgh University; he later returned to teach at Annan. The Academy became the 'Hinterschlag Gymnasium' of his *Sartor Resartus*.

Built beside the River Annan north of its entry into the Solway, the town has always had busy cattle and sheep markets, a fishing industry and quays for coastal shipping.

BRUCE'S CAVE

A steeply descending footpath, from a large car park and caravan site, leads to a cave in the rock above Kirtle Water. There is evidence that the cave was occupied in Neolithic times.

In 1306, according to legend, Robert Bruce lay hidden in the cave for three months when his fortunes were at a low ebb. As he watched a spider repeatedly trying to spin a web across the cave, Bruce received fresh inspiration to continue his fight against the English for Scottish nationhood.

ANNANDALE *Cattle graze on the slopes of Beattock Hill while gentle early morning mist drifts across the soft green rolling valley of the River Annan.*

An explanation of the cave's history is available from the office of the caravan site in spring and summer.

GRETNA GREEN
Just across the border from England, the old tollhouse and smithy once competed for custom from runaway couples seeking a swift marriage under Scotland's easygoing laws, when a wedding could be legalised simply by making a declaration before witnesses. This was made illegal in 1940, but the place makes the most of its romantic past; the Blacksmith's Shop is a museum, complete with the old anvil marriage room.

Tourist information: Moffat 20620 (summer); Gretna 7834 (summer).

TOUR
205

— 46 MILES —

Around a tiny royal burgh lie villages of single-storey cottages. The boyhood home of Robert Bruce survives as a ruin, and a magnificent castle overlooks a wildlife reserve.

LOCHMABEN
The broad main street from the edge of the loch divides at its northern end around the town hall. Here stand two statues, one of Robert Bruce and the other of William Paterson, born at Torthorwald a few miles away and thought to have been educated in Lochmaben. Paterson was co-founder of the Bank of England in 1694.

Robert Bruce is thought to have been born and to have spent his childhood in Lochmaben Castle, on the south shore of Castle Loch. The castle – open to the public – is now a ruin choked by creepers, nettles and other weeds. Beside it is a parking and picnic site and all around are walks through the Castle Loch Nature Reserve, linked with the neighbouring reserve of Hightae Loch.

TORTHORWALD CASTLE
This 15th-century castle of the Kirkpatricks, and later the Carlyles, is now an unsafe ruin; but its craggy walls still retain their grandeur. It is best viewed from the road.

GLENCAPLE
Houses and cottages perch with modest chic behind little gardens above a road following the eastern shore of the Nith estuary as it broadens into the Solway Firth. Robert Burns came here frequently on his duties as an exciseman, and Walter Scott pictured Glencaple as 'Portanferry' in *Guy Mannering*.

CAERLAVEROCK CASTLE
The 13th-century moated castle of the Maxwells is a strangely proportioned triangular fortress with a huge gatehouse of glowing pink sandstone. Edward I of England captured it; Sir Eustace Maxwell, appointed its guardian by the English, declared his support for Robert Bruce whereupon the English besieged it – it held out but the Scots destroyed it, rebuilt it, destroyed it again and rebuilt it to its original plan.

In the 17th century, Robert Maxwell, the 1st Earl of Nithsdale, erected a finely carved Renaissance mansion within the castle's battlemented walls, creating the odd mixture of styles visible today. Abandoned in 1640 after being sacked by the Covenanters, the castle is now in ruins. It is open to the public daily.

CAERLAVEROCK RESERVE
Near the shore of Solway Firth, to either side of Caerlaverock Castle, are entrances to the Caerlaverock National Nature Reserve. The reserve incorporates Caerlaverock Merse, one of the largest unreclaimed salt-marsh areas in Britain. Built up by silt and sand which is intermittently flooded by the sea, the merse offers ideal conditions for many forms of small wildlife. It provides the main wintering ground for barnacle geese from Spitzbergen, and swans, ducks, plovers and curlews are here in their thousands. There are colonies of raucous natterjack toads.

There are access points from the Floorers and Castle Corner entrances. In addition, a left-hand fork down the eastern lane leads to the Wildfowl Trust's East Park Refuge, open daily from mid-September to the end of April for conducted tours.

RUTHWELL
This tiny hamlet is proud of its little museum commemorating Henry Duncan, in the cottage in which he set up the first Scottish Savings Bank. The museum contains bank archives, and room settings of the late 18th and early 19th centuries. It is open daily.

Just outside the village, dramatically displayed in the apse of Ruthwell church, is the Ruthwell Cross, 18ft high, and perhaps the finest surviving runic cross in the land. It dates from the late 7th or 8th century and bears a poem known as 'The Dream of the Rood'.

The key to the church is kept at Kirkyett Cottage, on the corner of the main road.

RAMMERSCALES
Just over 2 miles south of Lochmaben a road climbs to the Palladian frontage of this Georgian mansion. Built in 1760 for Dr James Mounsey, who became personal physician to the Tsarina Elizabeth of Russia, it commands fine views over Annandale and offers a picnic site, woodland walks and a walled garden.

The house and grounds are open on certain afternoons in summer (Lochmaben 361).

Tourist information: Dumfries 53842.

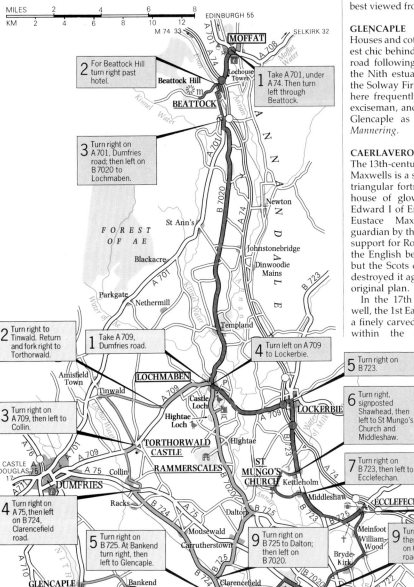

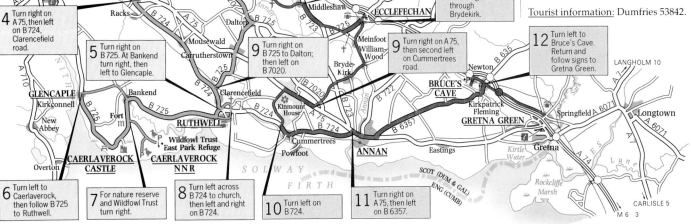

339

Land of Robert Burns and Robert Bruce

TOUR

206

——— 52 MILES ———

From the town known as the 'Queen of the South', quiet roads lead to brooding forests and trim little villages. A Renaissance castle contrasts with Robert Burns's farmhouse.

DUMFRIES

Almost every corner of this bustling market and manufacturing town shows façades, towers and steeples of sandstone as rust-red as the stone and soil of the surrounding countryside. The buildings are varied in the shopping centre, with colour-washed storeys above modern shop fronts. In contrast, Whitesands, a broad esplanade by the River Nith, breathes the air of a seaport of some consequence – as it was in the 19th century when many Scots left these quays for the New World.

Beside the far end of the graceful 15th-century bridge across the Nith stands Old Bridge House, a museum with period room displays and a dental laboratory of 1900. On the slope above stands an 18th-century windmill which now houses a camera obscura and a local history museum.

It was in Dumfries in 1306 that Robert Bruce killed the Red Comyn, his rival for leadership of the Scots, and then fled into the hills to raise forces in a struggle for independence from the English crown.

The town centre is dominated by the flamboyant tower of Midsteeple, built in 1707 as a courthouse and prison. Among plaques and relief figures on the frontage are a list of mileages from Dumfries to other towns – including that to Huntingdon, the terminus for 18th-century Scottish cattle drovers walking their beasts to England.

Robert Burns spent the last five years of his life here. He died in 1796, at the age of 37, in the house preserved in what is now Burns Street, with a few yards of the original cobbled roadway reverently maintained. His favourite chair remains in the Globe Inn, down a narrow alley off High Street. He was buried in a simple grave in St Michael's churchyard, but in 1815 was removed to a large white mausoleum with blue columns.

FOREST OF AE

Peaks and hummocks in the fields around Locharbriggs, like the ripples and billows of the sea petrified into a rich green, give way to longer, darker rollers near the forest. The largest hill is covered by a shawl of trees, with streaks of firebreaks and rides through it, often shadowed by scudding clouds chasing high above.

In the forest itself the road winds between flanks of hills thick with grass or bracken, sometimes entering avenues of trees stooped over to meet one another. A picnic site is prettily set beside a stream fringed by spruce and alder, and there are waymarked walks through the woods.

THORNHILL

Set in a fold of shallow hills, Thornhill's wide streets open up as a complete surprise – two wide boulevards lined with 100-year-old lime trees, as if the luxuriant trees all about the town had sent a small occupying force right into it. In the middle of the crossroads at the centre of the village stands a tall, slender column bearing a winged horse, emblem of the Queensberry family. It was erected in 1714, and restored after being damaged in a 1955 storm.

DRUMLANRIG CASTLE

The 'castle', family home of the Dukes of Buccleuch and Queensberry, is really a resplendent Renaissance mansion built by the 1st Duke of Queensberry in the 17th century around a 15th-century fort. Its art treasures include works by Rembrandt and Holbein, silverware, French furniture, and relics of Bonnie Prince Charlie.

The house and its grounds are open at Easter and daily from May to August, except on Fridays.

MONIAIVE

With its chunky, stony cottages painted or washed in soothing pastel shades, and one of the oldest inns in Scotland to provide a nice visual balance, Moniaive sits happily near a confluence of three burns which form the rippling, murmuring Cairn Water.

East of the village is Maxwelton House, originally a fortified home of the Earls of Glencairn, but better remembered as the birthplace of

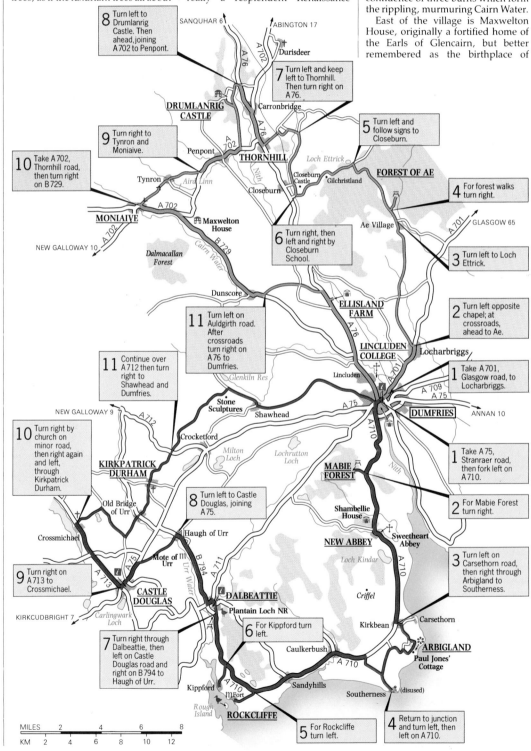

Annie Laurie, to whom William Douglas addressed his famous love lyric – only to see her marry another man. The house was refurbished in 1729 by William Adam. Annie died there in 1764 and is buried in nearby Glencairn churchyard. Rooms displaying domestic and agricultural implements are open on Wednesday and Thursday afternoons in summer, and the fourth Sunday in July and August.

ELLISLAND FARM
In 1788 Robert Burns built the farmhouse and experimented with what he hoped would be profitable new agricultural techniques. They were not a success, and he soon had to abandon farming and become an excise officer. But his struggles at Ellisland bore some fruit: it was on the riverside path that he composed *Tam o'Shanter*.

The barn, the byres and the farmhouse now form a museum of 18th-century farming life, with exhibits related to the poet, his work, and his wife and family. The museum is open daily.

LINCLUDEN COLLEGE
Tucked away behind a modern housing estate and the Lincluden Inn are the remains of a 12th-century convent for nuns, later closed down by Archibald the Grim and converted into a Collegiate Church. The choir and its carved stone sedilia have survived remarkably well.

TOUR
207

—— 67 MILES ——

Sparkling coastal resorts with long sands look out upon Solway Firth. Inland, a sandstone abbey and towns of grey stone are set amid a variety of streams, lochs and woodlands.

MABIE FOREST
A parking and picnic place on the site of an old sawmill is the base for waymarked walks of differing lengths through tangy-smelling Douglas fir, spruce, oak and beech plantations. From a number of vantage points there are sudden, breathtaking views of the granite mass of Criffel, 1868ft high, and across the Nith estuary to Caerlaverock.

NEW ABBEY
The sandstone skeleton of Sweetheart Abbey glows rosily as it rises head and shoulders above terraces of demure single-storey cottages, some with perky little dormers, about the village square. Beside a stream is an old water mill, open daily except for Thursday morning and all day Wednesday.

The abbey itself was founded in 1273 by the Lady Devorgilla, who with her husband John de Baliol had endowed Balliol College at Oxford. After his death she carried his embalmed heart around in an ivory casket, and had it buried with her in

FOREST FRINGE *Woods and fields roll towards the Lowther Hills below Gilchristland farm, on the north-west rim of the Forest of Ae.*

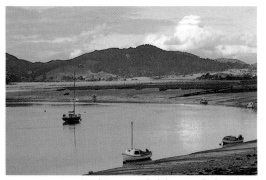
CALM KIPPFORD *Yachtsmen and fishermen find sheltered waters at the head of Rough Firth.*

LINCLUDEN COLLEGE *Green lawns fringe the red-sandstone ruins, noted for their heraldic decorations.*

what came to be known as *Dulce Cor* or Sweetheart Abbey.

North of the village, Shambellie House mounts, on most days in summer, varying displays of costume between the 18th and 20th centuries, drawn from the Royal Scottish Museum collections.

ARBIGLAND
Although the Arbigland House estate is private, the road through its quiet woodland is open to the public, and the lovingly tended gardens are open on Tuesday, Thursday and Sunday afternoons in summer.

South of the estate road stands the humble cottage where John Paul Jones was born in 1747. After imprisonment in Kirkcudbright, on suspicion of murder, he made his home in America and became one of the most daring naval heroes of the War of Independence when he commanded a force against the British.

Beyond Arbigland the road leads towards the stark pillar of Southerness lighthouse, overlooking wide sands backed by a holiday village. The route then heads west towards wooded avenues with glimpses of the firth between trees, following the lower slopes of hills sweeping right down to the shoreline.

ROCKCLIFFE
Houses are packed in between splintered elbows of granite, and ragged outcrops thrust up from the sandy shore to underpin the waterfront road of this little seaside resort. Rough Island, a National Trust for Scotland bird sanctuary, can be reached on foot at low tide from nearby Kippford.

Footpaths from Kippford curl past a pre-Roman hill-fort, the Mote of Mark, through Rockcliffe, and onto the promontory of Port o' Warren.

DALBEATTIE
The town stands square and silvery-grey in a green, rolling countryside with forest walks starting from its immediate outskirts. The greyness is that of granite hacked from great quarries on Craignar Hill which provided the basis of the Thames Embankment and of Liverpool docks, and the sinews of Dalbeattie itself. Used tastefully like this, it makes the streets look consistent and dignified.

CASTLE DOUGLAS
A straight, gently sloping main street and two subsidiary but well-designed parallel streets owe their pattern to William Douglas, a late-18th-century landlord who expanded the original village of Carlingwark into a hand-

loom weaving and carpet-making centre. Like so many small towns in the region it boasts a clock tower like a church steeple, nicely breaking the long line of the thoroughfare.

On the southern edge of the town lies broad Carlingwark Loch, lined by trees, seething with pike and perch, and studded with little islets. Two of them are Bronze Age *crannogs* – artificial islands formed by driving log piles into the bed of the lake and covering them with brushwood.

KIRKPATRICK DURHAM
In 1785 the Reverend Dr David Lamont, who had inherited great spreads of land in the neighbourhood, began to build an integrated estate village with 50 houses and a number of craft workshops. By the early 19th century the village boasted seven inns and alehouses, and although these have dwindled in number the rest of the orderly little village must be almost as Lamont knew it.

Beyond, the road climbs to wild moorland before descending to the shimmering Glenkiln Reservoir.

Tourist information: Dumfries 53862 (summer); Dalbeattie 610117 (summer); Castle Douglas 2611 (summer).

Through the Machars and the Stewartry

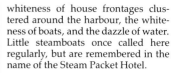

TOUR
208

—— 50 MILES ——

The low-lying peninsula of the Machars was heavily populated in prehistoric times, and has many standing stones to show for it. There are numerous memorials to martyred Covenanters.

WIGTOWN

County town before boundary changes reduced its status, Wigtown still has an air of distinction, with its sandstone courthouse and wide, main square. This broad expanse, with its narrower outlets which could be gated at night, used to shelter farm animals after dark from predators on two or four legs. It remains spacious enough to be divided now by a central garden and bowling green.

Grim memorials testify to the fate of two women who were killed in sadistic fashion because they refused to recant their adherence to the anti-episcopalian Solemn League and Covenant and accept an English-style church and prayerbook: in 1685 they were tied to stakes in the River Bladnoch and left to drown as the tide came in. A stone pillar marks the place of their martyrdom.

TORHOUSE STONE CIRCLE

In an enclosure at the roadside stands a Bronze Age stone circle erected between 1500 and 1000 BC. Three larger boulders are propped together in the centre. This must have been an ancient religious or funerary site. Today it is penned in neatly by a wall and an iron railing, but it still produces an alien, eerie effect.

PORT WILLIAM

Founded by Sir William Maxwell around 1770 as one of Scotland's earliest holiday resorts, the little port became for a time a haunt of smugglers. But today it combines holiday trade with that of sport fishing, most notably for tope – small sharks. Its road and houses hug the contour of the shoreline as if bravely welcoming the sea winds rather than wishing to huddle away from them. Misshapen boulders like abandoned beach balls are scattered over rust-coloured pebbles and shingle.

MONREITH BAY

Monreith village, like Port William a creation of Sir William Maxwell, has a long terrace of snug, low cottages set back a little way from the water. The real gem of the coast, however, lies beside a lane down to Back Bay, with its picnic site and golden sands. The ruined chapel of Kirkmaiden, tucked precariously into a cleft of the rock face, was for generations the burial place of the Maxwell family.

On the cliff top high above is a memorial to a Maxwell of the present century. The beautiful bronze otter standing alert on a crag is a moving tribute to the late Gavin Maxwell, author of *Ring of Bright Water*, who spent his childhood at House of Elrig, near Port William.

ISLE OF WHITHORN

Driving or walking onto the quayside of this luminous little port can be blinding on a sunny day, with the whiteness of house frontages clustered around the harbour, the whiteness of boats, and the dazzle of water. Little steamboats once called here regularly, but are remembered in the name of the Steam Packet Hotel.

WHITHORN

Halfway up the wide main street, with its air of quiet prosperity, an imposing archway known as the Pend, bearing the Royal Arms of Scotland, leads into Bruce Street and to Whithorn Priory ruins.

It seems that St Ninian most probably built his *Candida Casa* or 'white house' – from which the town derives its name – on this land when he returned from Rome. In the 12th century Fergus, Lord of Galloway, founded a priory under which excavations have revealed fragments of pale wall plaster which could have belonged to the older, simpler building.

GARLIESTON

The village is a smart little settlement beside an unexpectedly large harbour. Trade as a port has slackened in recent decades, but it is still a popular fishing centre.

The road around the bay offers a bright view back across the water to houses exuberantly colour-washed in pink, white and blazing yellow.

RIVER HARVEST *Nets stretched between poles on the shore of the Cree estuary just south of Creetown await the turn of the tide, and a catch of salmon.*

HOME IMPROVEMENTS *Houses as smart as new paint in Garlieston give the village a jaunty air.*

ROYAL RESTING PLACE *Mary, Queen of Scots spent her last night in Scotland at Dundrennan Abbey.*

ST CUTHBERT'S *Wooded hills rise behind the tall spire of the church which gives Kirkcudbright its name.*

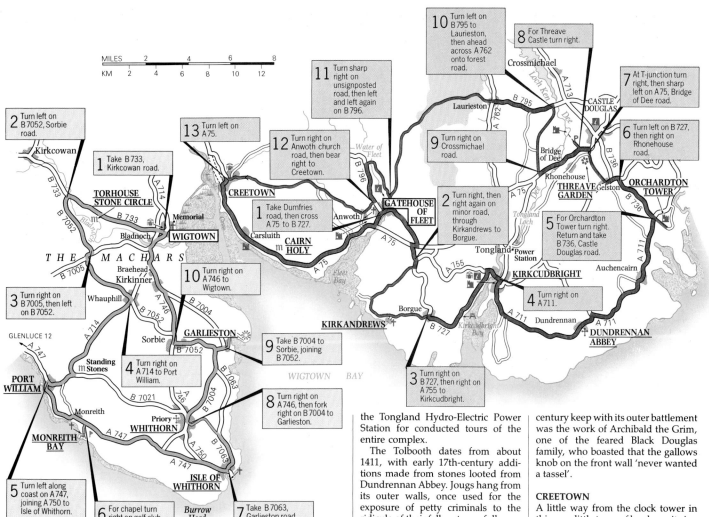

2 Turn left on B7052, Sorbie road.

1 Take B733, Kirkcowan road.

11 Turn sharp right on unsignposted road, then left and left again on B796.

10 Turn left on B795 to Laurieston, then ahead across A762 onto forest road.

8 For Threave Castle turn right.

7 At T-junction turn right, then sharp left on A75, Bridge of Dee road.

13 Turn left on A75.

12 Turn right on Anwoth church road, then bear right to Creetown.

9 Turn right on Crossmichael road.

6 Turn left on B727, then right on Rhonehouse road.

1 Take Dumfries road, then cross A75 to B727.

2 Turn right, then right again on minor road, through Kirkandrews to Borgue.

5 For Orchardton Tower turn right. Return and take B736, Castle Douglas road.

3 Turn right on B7005, then left on B7052.

10 Turn right on A746 to Wigtown.

9 Take B7004 to Sorbie, joining B7052.

3 Turn right on B727, then right on A755 to Kirkcudbright.

4 Turn right on A714 to Port William.

8 Turn right on A746, then fork right on B7004 to Garlieston.

4 Turn right on A711.

5 Turn left along coast on A747, joining A750 to Isle of Whithorn.

6 For chapel turn right on golf club road.

7 Take B7063, Garlieston road, then on minor road to Whithorn.

TOUR 209

— 78 MILES —

Farmland kept green by meandering burns is crisscrossed by lurching stone walls. Signs still call this the Stewartry, administered in medieval times by a king's 'steward'.

GATEHOUSE OF FLEET

The gatehouse which gave the place its name, now a small whitewashed wine bar behind the Murray Arms, was originally the only building at this crossing of the Water of Fleet. In the late 18th century the Murray family set about establishing cotton mills along the river bank, and encouraged the Yorkshire firm of Birtwhistle to invest in the project. All that now remain in this inviting little walking and holiday centre are derelict mill buildings beside the river.

For themselves the Murrays built the imposing 'Cally House' on the outskirts, now the Cally Palace Hotel. They also gave their name to the Murray Arms, near the clock tower; in the hotel Burns wrote 'Scots, wha hae wi' Wallace bled'.

KIRKANDREWS

The road above Fleet Bay passes some eccentric buildings, one sharing some of the properties of a church tower and a factory chimney, all part of a farm and laundry complex built by James Brown, a Manchester businessman. Even odder is Kirkandrews church, another of Mr Brown's fantasies – a tiny mock turret with Walt Disney castellations overlooking the much older graveyard. The church is reached down an unsignposted road to the right.

Among the gravestones is a Covenanting stone restored in the middle of the 18th century by Robert Paterson, a stonemason who made it his life's work to go about the countryside trimming and maintaining the memorials of those who had died for their faith: he is portrayed by Sir Walter Scott in *Old Mortality*.

KIRKCUDBRIGHT

The name means 'Church of St Cuthbert', and is pronounced 'Kircoo-bree'. The port sparkles invitingly across the estuary, dominated by a church spire, the Gothic tower of the Tolbooth, and the jagged top of MacLellan's Castle.

From the harbour there are river trips and sea-angling trips. In summer a free electric bus takes visitors to

the Tongland Hydro-Electric Power Station for conducted tours of the entire complex.

The Tolbooth dates from about 1411, with early 17th-century additions made from stones looted from Dundrennan Abbey. Jougs hang from its outer walls, once used for the exposure of petty criminals to the ridicule of their fellow townsfolk.

DUNDRENNAN ABBEY

In a hollow beside the road the gaping windows and superb arches of the ruined abbey frame green slopes and trees beyond. Farther along the road it is not difficult to identify courses of stolen abbey stones in cottages of the village.

Among relics is a relief of a murdered bishop, possibly killed by a local inhabitant who resented the arrival of Cistercian monks who came from Rievaulx to occupy the abbey in 1142.

ORCHARDTON TOWER

This round tower-house is thought to have been built by the local laird in the middle of the 15th century. It has a cellar on the ground floor, with living quarters above reached by an outer staircase, still intact.

THREAVE GARDEN

Woodland walks, plantations, and a sequence of individual gardens tended by students of the Threave School of Gardening are open to the public daily. Most plants are labelled, so that a visit is not just a visual delight but an educational experience.

Threave Wildfowl Refuge consists of a series of undisturbed feeding grounds and islands in the River Dee where grebe, ducks, geese and swans live in natural conditions. On one of the islands Threave Castle uses the river as its defensive moat. This 14th-

century keep with its outer battlement was the work of Archibald the Grim, one of the feared Black Douglas family, who boasted that the gallows knob on the front wall 'never wanted a tassel'.

CREETOWN

A little way from the clock tower in this grey little town of local granite is a museum of gems and minerals from all over the world. The museum is open daily and features a fluorescent mineral display, gem cutting and polishing.

Local granite was exported from Creetown in the 19th century, and was also used in the construction of London's Thames Embankment.

Thomas Carlyle once assured Queen Victoria that the only road in her realm which could compare with the coastal road from Creetown to Gatehouse of Fleet was the coastal road from Gatehouse of Fleet to Creetown. Even today it is difficult to quarrel with such an opinion. Little mars the gentle curve of the route as it follows the bay, passing remnants of old tower houses such as Carsluith Castle, and the four-storey, 15th-century Cardoness Castle.

CAIRN HOLY

A tortuous lane leads to the standing stones of Cairn Holy, a tomb and place of worship used by both Neolithic and Bronze Age people. Funerary fires would have been lit on the forecourt before the stones, and offerings made of shellfish and pottery. Traces of these have been found on the site, along with flint arrowheads and part of a stone axe.

Tourist information: Gatehouse of Fleet 212 (summer); Kirkcudbright 30494 (summer).

343

Forests around the lochs of Glen Trool

TOUR
210
—— 105 MILES ——

The banks of streams and the shores of lochs are clothed in dark green forests. A gently winding road leads to an airy summit between great tracts of bracken and moor grass.

NEWTON STEWART

A deceptive kink in the main street can mislead the visitor into thinking of Newton Stewart as a bright, pleasant, but none too busy little place. Then another long stretch of shops and hotels is suddenly revealed, with a sprightly clock tower, a turn across the fine bridge over the River Cree,

built by John Rennie in 1813 and, backing it all up, some welcoming riverside gardens. In one garden stands an ornate monument, 57ft high, to the 9th Earl of Galloway, who died in 1873.

Like Castle Douglas some miles to the east, the town was developed as an industrial centre by William Douglas in the late 18th century for carding and spinning wool; for a while it was known as Newton Douglas. The minor boom did not last, and the place resumed its old name and old function as a market town. Today its sheep and cattle market is no fading relic of the past, but the very pulse of the community's existence.

Exhibitions in the local museum, housed in a disused church, cover the town's changes of fortune. They include early motorcycles, farm machinery, a farmhouse kitchen and

a blacksmith's forge. Although weaving is no longer a mainstay, Glen Cree Mill still manufactures mohair. It is open to visitors from Monday to Friday, and its shop is also open on Saturdays in summer.

GLEN TROOL

The road from Newton Stewart up the valley of the Cree runs past trees and meadows with the silvery sparkle of the River Cree blinking through the foliage. To branch off into the glades and rustling plantations is to enter an even more richly wooded world, full of haunting beauty yet also full of the pain of past conflict.

At Stroan Bridge, forest trails lead from a picnic site above rushing waterfalls into the cool shadow of larch and spruce, and, near Caldons Caravan Park, to the memorial stones of several Covenanters slain because they refused to abandon their religious beliefs.

The road finishes above the waters of Loch Trool, its surface flecked with ripples so fine and slow that they

seem more like scratches and stippling on an ice rink. The Bruce Stone, a few yards beyond the car park, recalls the day in 1307 when followers of the Scottish liberator defeated an English force by rolling boulders down upon them.

Also from this spot, for the energetic there begins a 4 mile path to the summit of the 2766ft Merrick. As the path ascends there are ever-widening views over an apparently boundless panorama of glittering lochs set amid rolling moors and swathes of forest.

Returning from the glen and turning northwards, 4 miles farther on is the working hill farm of Palgowan. Visitors are welcome every afternoon except Saturday, from mid-May until the end of October, for demonstrations of sheep handling, stone dyking, horncraft, skin curing and other activities.

Beyond are more picnic places, including a restful site on the banks of the Water of Minnoch and another at Stinchar Bridge. The bridge is the point for less restful three and four-hour walks.

STRAITON

The descent from the lonely fells levels out beside fields and coppices as trim and domesticated as landscaped parkland, to reach an equally trim little stone village. There, a long, low-slung inn hides among equally low-slung cottages, noted for their spring and summer flower displays.

The church tower and bell were added in 1901. A loftier monument on the hillside above is a column in memory of Colonel James Hunter-Blair, killed during the Crimean War.

From the centre of the village the road to Dalmellington leads back into open country where wandering sheep, not content with the hillsides, claim priority on the road as well.

DALMELLINGTON

A tall cone of slag incongruously dominates the broad marshy vale, and rows of miners' cottages make white lines along the far slope. Dalmellington's coal and iron industries have all but disappeared, but their heritage is being preserved.

A former iron works is to become an open-air museum, where steam 'pugs' will run in summer for railway enthusiasts. Old weavers' cottages at Cathcartson now accommodate a small museum.

LOCH DOON

The drive along the western shore of the loch offers fold upon fold of mountains, some appearing to overlap and then sidle away from each other in a changing light which never falls the same on any two peaks or slopes.

Great blocks of stone from the loch shore were taken – some trimmed, some roughly mortared together – to build Loch Doon Castle, originally set on an islet and fought over by Scots and English until it was finally sacked by James V. When a hydroelectric scheme in the 1930s threatened to submerge the castle, the ruin was removed stone by stone and re-erected on its present site on the bank.

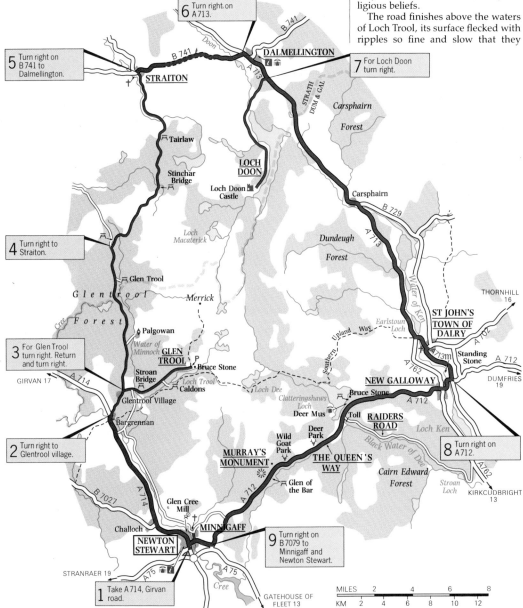

BANKS OF BONNIE DOON *Tranquil Loch Doon narrows northwards to form the River Doon, which Robert Burns called 'bonnie'.*

LEGENDARY LOCH *Legends galore have arisen about Loch Trool as a haunt of thieves, cattle robbers and murderers.*

GRANITE LINK *Built of granite in 1813, the graceful Cree Bridge links Newton Stewart with the village of Minnigaff.*

best-known novel, *The Raiders*, was published in 1894. Set in the aftermath of the Stuart rising of 1715, it tells how the Galloway hill country was the haunt of armed gypsy cattle thieves. One of the most exciting sections of the book recounts a raid in which the robbers steal the cattle from the Maxwell estates on the Solway and drive them along the Black Water of Dee and up into the hills surrounding Loch Dee.

The 10 mile forest toll road, open from June to September, closely follows the route taken by the raiders. Much of the drive goes through woodland no more than 25 years old. However, near Loch Stroan and by Loch Ken are older groups of Douglas fir and Sitka spruce. Planted about 50 years ago, the trees are now nearing their maturity.

The road runs beside the river, in which at one point stands a bronze statue of an otter, its head burnished by the stroking of countless young hands. There is a speed limit of 20mph along the drive and motorists should be careful when driving off the road to park, as there are no hard shoulders and cars can easily become bogged down.

MURRAY'S MONUMENT
A small parking place marks the start of a stroll beside a convergence of burns and little waterfalls. In a hollow ahead lies what at first looks like a heap of stones to match the bare granite thrusting from the hillside, but which proves to be the shell of the cottage where Alexander Murray was born in 1775.

From the ruins of his birthplace can be seen an obelisk crowning a nearby peak, erected in 1834 in memory of Murray, the shepherd boy who rose to become Professor of Oriental Languages in Edinburgh University. A footpath up to the monument offers breathtaking views down the valley.

MINNIGAFF
Today a suburb of Newton Stewart, Old Minnigaff actually stood by the River Cree long before its larger neighbour. Its pre-Reformation church, now mere ruins strangled by ivy, was used until the building of the present one in 1836. The interior of the newer kirk is polished, dignified, and most inviting, best viewed from its spacious galleries. The font was a gift from the private chapel at Galloway House, Garlieston, by the Earl of Galloway, whose private pew at Minnigaff was reached through a doorway halfway down the south aisle.

The yew tree in the churchyard is said to be more than 800 years old. It keeps company with gravestones telling long family histories, and one with a coat of arms recalling bygone loyalties: the emblem of a raven transfixed by an arrow, surmounting two transfixed by a single arrow, was bestowed on their family after the McKie brothers, Murdoch and his half-brother McClurg, had shown their prowess with one shot each.

Tourist information: Newton Stewart 2431 (summer); Dalmellington 550145 (summer).

ST JOHN'S TOWN OF DALRY
Sprawling down a hillside towards the Water of Ken, Dalry is a cheerful meeting place for fishermen on the river and the loch. At its eastern end stands a chair-shaped stone on which, legend has it, John the Baptist sat during travels through Britain. He was patron saint of the Knights Hospitaller who once owned the land and gave it its full name.

A ferry once took pilgrims over the Water of Ken on their way to St Ninian's shrine at Whithorn. Today the river can be crossed by stepping stones, reached down a shaded footpath beside the town hall, with its spire and clock, and the Clachan Inn.

It was a story of witches dancing in Dalry churchyard that inspired Burns to write 'Tam o'Shanter', though he changed the setting to his birthplace, Alloway.

NEW GALLOWAY
The town contains taller buildings than are usually found in this region. And the high clock tower of the town hall, and dignified houses with fine gardens on the outskirts, retain some of the swagger which the place must have known when it was created Scotland's smallest royal burgh by Charles I. Below the town hall's coat of arms hang the Scottish form of pillory – jougs, one of the hinged iron collars in which malefactors were confined.

Cairn Edward Forest, to the southwest, is named in honour of Edward, brother of Robert Bruce, who held enemies at bay in Galloway while Robert set off to rally support elsewhere.

THE QUEEN'S WAY
In 1977 Princess Anne formally gave this title to the superb scenic road between New Galloway and Newton Stewart, marking the Silver Jubilee of her mother, Elizabeth II. It has been generously supplied with parking and picnic places, and forest trails up hillsides which sometimes close in on a curve of the road only to fold back and offer more ravishing views ahead.

Near the shore of Clatteringshaws Loch Reservoir a second Bruce Stone, sometimes called the King's Stone, bears the claim that King Robert leant upon it while directing another 1307 skirmish. In a more formal setting than the dramatic one above Loch Trool, it stands on a level green sheltered by a crescent of trees which stand like deferential courtiers.

A converted farmhouse nearby houses Galloway Deer Museum, dealing not only with the life of deer in the neighbourhood but with other aspects of wildlife and geology, and displaying a reconstructed Bronze Age dwelling discovered during work on the dam.

Farther west are a deer park, with observation hides, and a wild goat park where the animals are enclosed for easier viewing.

RAIDERS ROAD
Opposite Clatteringshaws dam is the entrance to the Raiders Road, so called in tribute to the Scottish minister and author S.R. Crockett, whose

The gentle side of rugged Galloway

TOUR
211

— 85 MILES —

Despite the awesome cliffs of its Mull, Galloway wears a mostly gentle face. The Gulf Stream warms its tides and mellows its landscape, in which white farmhouses dot the fields.

STRANRAER
Set in the shelter of Loch Ryan, Stranraer has for more than a century served as the Scottish anchorage for traffic to and from Larne in Northern Ireland. But with its narrow back streets, its pleasant corners and its gardens it is more like a friendly seaside resort than a commercial harbour.

A paddling pool and marine lake has been created in a corner of Loch Ryan, with a sandy beach. Behind it is Agnew Park which contains a granite memorial to 128 people who died when the Irish ferry *Princess Victoria* sank in a gale in 1953.

Near the centre of the town is the 16th-century castle of St John, built by Adair of Kilhit. It once served as a prison for captured Covenanters, and was later used as the town jail. A large hotel called the North West Castle, built in the shape of a ship, was originally the home of Sir John Ross, the 19th-century polar explorer who sought the North West Passage round the north coast of America. One of his Arctic explorations established the true position of the North Magnetic Pole.

LOCHNAW CASTLE
The road to the castle, begun in the 15th century and enlarged in the 17th and 18th centuries, goes through the picturesque Glen of Aldouran and runs above a restful loch whose banks glow with rhododendrons in late spring. The fortified house which rises solid and proud against the skyline was once the home of the Agnews, who were Sheriffs of Galloway. It is still privately owned, as a guesthouse, and open only by appointment; but there is a craft shop in the courtyard, where fishing permits are obtainable.

PORTPATRICK
The road swings down from sheep and cattle pastures to an abrupt confrontation with tumultuous seas pounding into a tight little harbour. Attempts last century to make Portpatrick a profitable terminus for Irish ferries were doomed to failure because stone and concrete reinforcements to the raw granite teeth of the cove were repeatedly shredded by seething breakers. A massive pile of broken granite and concrete slabs at the harbour entrance is all that remains of efforts to develop the port.

Traffic was finally transferred to

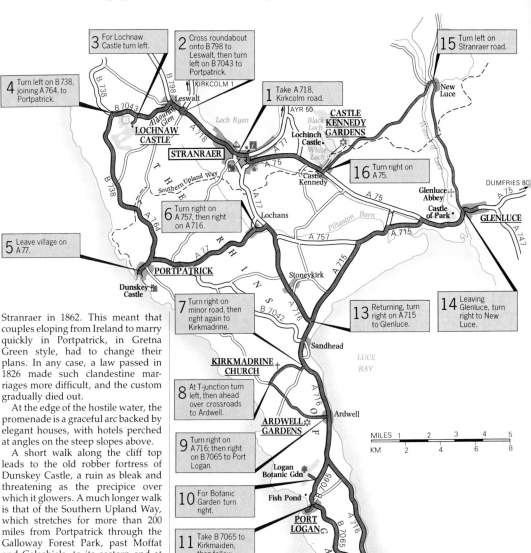

Stranraer in 1862. This meant that couples eloping from Ireland to marry quickly in Portpatrick, in Gretna Green style, had to change their plans. In any case, a law passed in 1826 made such clandestine marriages more difficult, and the custom gradually died out.

At the edge of the hostile water, the promenade is a graceful arc backed by elegant houses, with hotels perched at angles on the steep slopes above.

A short walk along the cliff top leads to the old robber fortress of Dunskey Castle, a ruin as bleak and threatening as the precipice over which it glowers. A much longer walk is that of the Southern Upland Way, which stretches for more than 200 miles from Portpatrick through the Galloway Forest Park, past Moffat and Galashiels, to its eastern end at Cockburnspath on the North Sea coast.

KIRKMADRINE CHURCH
On a low hillside between almost treeless undulations, a long avenue of trees climbs to a tiny, isolated church. Behind a plate-glass wall in the porch are ancient inscribed stones and other fragments unearthed from the graveyard.

Two of the stones praise the virtues of 5th-century Celtic priests or bishops and bear the chi-rho monogram, one of the first Christian symbols adopted by the Romans and Romano-Britons; these stones served for many generations as churchyard gateposts. Together with a third stone bearing only a few identifiable letters, they are three of the oldest Christian stones known in Britain.

ARDWELL GARDENS
Around the restored 18th-century Ardwell House, with its crow-stepped gables, are extensive grounds open to the public in summer. The garden layouts are imaginative but happily informal. They include a front garden, a walled garden, a hawthorn avenue, a wooded walk around the

moat, and a green where donkeys graze.

At appropriate times of the year there are lavish spreads of daffodils, azaleas, roses, or rock plants. Even as late as October the shrubs and flowerbeds can be a riot of colour.

PORT LOGAN
Houses are sunk below the level of the road in this small fishing village. It is said that this peculiarity dates from the time when a feudal laird, who wanted to drive the residents away, raised the road to overshadow their homes. They refused to budge, and in retaliation added extra storeys to their cottages to look over the road's edge.

A mile north across the little sandy bay – and reached by a footpath from the coastal road – is Port Logan Fish Pond, a basin hollowed from the rock

in 1800 as a fresh-fish larder for the owners of the Logan estate. Still stocked with fish, mainly cod, it can be visited daily by the public in summer, except Tuesdays and Saturdays. Some fish are so tame that they can be summoned to the pondside by the ringing of a bell, and can then be fed by hand.

Port Logan, like the rest of the Galloway coast, is warmed by the Gulf Stream. In this temperate climate, exotic shrubs, ferns and flowers flourish around the lagoon of Logan Botanic Garden, a horticultural treasure house open daily in summer.

Near the entrance to the garden stand soaring cabbage palms from

New Zealand. The scarlet Chilean fire bush glows brilliantly in early summer. In another part of the garden dwarf rhododendrons bloom on terraces of local peat.

The garden was created in the late 19th century by the McDouall family, who owned the land from the 12th to the 20th century, in what were once the grounds of their medieval castle. The castle ruins still stand, overlooking the gardens from the west. In 1969 management of the gardens passed to the Royal Botanical Gardens at Edinburgh.

MULL OF GALLOWAY
A great thrust of towering cliff marks the southernmost tip of Scotland. Sea birds wheel overhead, and on a clear day it is possible from here to see Ireland, England and the Isle of Man. A climb to the top of the rugged headland ends at a soaring lighthouse built in 1830 above the race where nine tides are said to meet.

In East Tarbet bay the sheltered water can be calm and smooth while, a few hundred yards away, West Tarbet bay will be white-flecked and stormy. Seas pinch in from both sides as if to snap off the fragile ankle of the long leg of Galloway – but then the foot broadens and juts bluntly into the sea as if to kick out any invader.

According to legend, the secret of the Pictish brew Heather Ale was lost over the cliffs of the Mull. As the Scots wiped out the Picts, the only survivors of the race – an old man and his son – were ordered to reveal the recipe of the brew described as 'sweeter far than honey, stronger far than wine'. Rather than betray the secret, the old man let the Scots throw his son from the cliff and then flung himself after him.

A little more than half a mile north of the eastern bay are fragments of a chapel from which it is said that St Medan, an Irish princess much influenced by St Ninian, fled from an over-eager lover to seek sanctuary by floating on a rock across Luce Bay to the Wigtownshire peninsula – St Ninian's own religious stronghold.

DRUMMORE
Whitewashed houses climb the slopes above a compact little harbour used by fishermen and sailing clubs. This is Scotland's southernmost village, farther south, in fact, than Durham in England. Its sheltered setting facing out across Luce Bay has made it a favoured holiday resort.

The parish church dates from 1639. In the churchyard is a gravestone in the form of a lighthouse.

North of the village the road runs close to the beach and the wide bay for several miles, sometimes on a level with the water and sometimes seeming almost to dip below it.

GLENLUCE
A brisk and welcoming little village, Glenluce offers some unexpected pleasures behind its busy main street. The abandoned railway line has become a wide footpath, with parking space on the site of the old station and a bonus in the form of a walk right across the towering viaduct. The glen

which gives the place its name can be missed by the casual visitor; it is reached by a little side turning off the main street, over a bridge crossing the burn, and between two leaning gateposts.

Beside the main road entering the village is Castle of Park, a noble castellated mansion which was built by Thomas Hay of Park in 1590. It was extensively repaired in the 1970s, and is not open to the public.

A short distance up the New Luce road, beside the meadows of the Water of Luce, the sky gleams through the blank eye sockets of ruined Glenluce Abbey. Founded by a 12th-century Earl of Galloway to house Cistercian monks, it is one of the most attractively placed monastic ruins in the region, with substantial remains of its remarkable vaulted chapter house. The abbey ruins are open daily in summer and at weekends in winter.

At the Reformation the lands were acquired by Gilbert Kennedy, Earl of Cassilis, who persuaded a monk to forge the abbot's signature on a lease, hired an assassin to kill the monk, and then hastily prosecuted and executed the murderer.

CASTLE KENNEDY GARDENS
The entrance drive gives little hint of the wealth of colour and landscaped beauty waiting beyond. Sweeping terraces look out regally over the Black Loch and the White Loch. A large lily pond is embedded within surrounds of trees, shrubs, azaleas and rhododendrons. Avenues leading away from it are skilfully devised to lead the eye towards outstanding views.

There are, in fact, two castles in the gardens. Castle Kennedy was once the seat of the powerful Kennedy family of Galloway and Ayrshire. In 1716 fire raged through the building, leaving only the high walls which now tower above the flowerbeds. Most of the surrounding garden design was the work of the 2nd Earl of Stair, in the early 18th century. As a field-marshal he drew free labour from his troops in laying out gardens inspired by Versailles. Some of his military campaigns are commemorated in the grounds by the names of Mount Marlborough and Dettingen Avenue.

By 1840 the place was overgrown, but the 8th Earl found the original plans and restored many of the main features.

The monkey-puzzle avenue frames a distant picture of the second castle – Lochinch – built in 'Scots baronial' style in 1864; it is now the home of the present Earl and Countess of Stair. The castle is set in its own gardens, formally laid out in Victorian style, including a sunken garden which contains rhododendrons and several large eucalyptus trees. The castle's appearance is impressive when it is viewed at close quarters from the path to the sunken garden.

Castle Kennedy Gardens are open daily in summer.

Tourist information: Stranraer 2595 (summer).

MULL OF GALLOWAY *Towering cliffs hold back the sea at Scotland's southernmost tip.*

GLENLUCE ABBEY *The 15th-century chapter house survives almost intact.*

LOGAN GARDENS *Exotic ferns grow in the mild climate of this part of Galloway.*

PORTPATRICK PARADE *Bright, colour-washed houses look across the sea to Ireland.*

Through Ayr in the footsteps of Burns

TOUR
212
—— 62 MILES ——

In the Ayrshire countryside Robert Burns farmed – and met the mouse to which he addressed a poem. There is a hillside memorial to another Scottish hero, Sir William Wallace.

AYR

With the coast on one side and farmland on the other, the town of Ayr is split in two by the river of the same name. It has three major parks, three 18-hole golf courses, many fine gardens and, every August, the biggest flower show in Scotland.

Ayr racecourse is the main centre of Flat and National Hunt racing in Scotland. Its prestige events include the Scottish Grand National.

The 17th-century Auld Kirk, where Robert Burns was baptised, stands off the High Street. Not far from it is the Tam o'Shanter Museum, which has a collection of Burns mementos and is open on weekdays all year and on Sundays also in summer. A painting over the door of the thatched building shows Tam o'Shanter, the hero of Burns's poem of that name.

From Burns Statue Square, the heart of the town, the route heads along Holmston Road, where there are several entrances to the peaceful River Ayr Walk. Soon it turns onto a quiet little ridge-top road on the peninsula formed by the River Ayr and its tributary, the Water of Coyle.

STAIR

The River Ayr sweeps round a tree-banked curve to enclose a tiny settlement beside a crescent of grazing land. Stair today is composed of little more than Stair House, an inn and a pleasant mid-Victorian parish church. But it used to send its products all over Europe and North America. The resoundingly titled Water of Ayr and Tam o'Shanter Hone Works were established in 1789 to take advantage of a deposit of whetstone – used for sharpening knives, scythes and sickles.

TARBOLTON

This former weaving and mining village was the centre of Robert Burns's social life when he worked on his father's farm nearby. He joined a dancing class in Tarbolton 'to give my manners a brush' and helped to found a debating society called the Bachelors' Club. The club's premises have been restored as a museum, which is open daily from April to October.

Burns began writing poems about people he knew in the village. One of his first satires, *Death and Doctor Hornbook*, poked fun at John Wilson, the local schoolmaster and an amateur apothecary.

TROON

The approach to this comfortable resort town shows off the five separate 18-hole golf courses surrounding it. Royal Troon has played host on several occasions to the British Open. Another course, the Fullarton, takes its name from the dismantled mansion of the Dukes of Portland, whose grounds are now laid out with picnic areas and woodland walks.

An uninterrupted South Beach looks across the Firth of Clyde to Arran. Troon also has a marina at the old inner harbour – and one of Scotland's rare real tennis courts.

DUNDONALD

Over the hills inland from Troon, the village of Dundonald is dominated by the ruin of its 14th-century castle, which was a favourite residence of the earliest Stuart kings.

The route follows a winding road to Symington, with its whitewashed cottages and restored Norman church. A few miles beyond, through narrow climbing lanes, is Barnweil Tower, on a hilltop among trees. This Victorian baronial monument to Sir William Wallace is the finest all-round viewpoint in the area.

The route later passes two farms once worked by Robert Burns. His father was tenant of Lochlea, and after his death Burns and his brother Gilbert rented Mossgiel. Neither farm is open to the public, but a roadside field at Mossgiel, on the outskirts of Mauchline, was the scene of the harvest-time encounter that inspired the poem *To a Mouse*.

MAUCHLINE

When Burns was farming at Mossgiel, Mauchline was where he went to relax, and the place has never forgotten him. The route enters the town at the National Burns Memorial.

In 1788, Burns and his wife Jean Armour set up house in Castle Street. The two-storey building where he rented an upstairs room is now a Burns museum, open daily from Easter to October. It also has an extensive local history collection. One display features the game of curling. Granite curling stones made in Mauchline are used wherever the game is played.

Poosie Nansie's tavern in Loudoun Street was the scene of the uproarious happenings which Burns worked into *The Jolly Beggars*.

Many of the poet's Mauchline contemporaries lie in the parish churchyard. Several of them were the butt of his most biting satires – expressions of the distaste felt by the liberal wing of the 18th-century church for the Calvinist establishment. William Fisher, for instance, figured in the withering *Holy Willie's Prayer*. Fisher was a kirk elder who fell into a ditch while drunk and drowned.

From Mauchline the route is pleasantly flanked by trim hedges and belts of trees. The road dips down again into the valley of the River Ayr.

SORN

The village laid out around 1770 on the banks of the Ayr was originally called Dalgain, but the presence of Sorn Castle soon led it to change its name. The castle has a 15th-century tower and lavish Victorian additions.

As long ago as 1798, Sorn was recorded as a place of keen gardeners.

MODEL VILLAGE *Tucked away in a corner of the Carrick hills is the village of Barr – a model of neatness with its rows of whitewashed cottages beside lines of trees.*

FALLING WATER *A frothy stream tumbles down tiny waterfalls in Bargany gardens.*

ROUND AND ROUND *Culzean Castle has a magnificent oval staircase.*

GREY WALLS *Castle ruins top the rocky hill above Dundonald.*

WHITE WALLS *Cottages climb the hilly main street at Ochiltree.*

And now the village is a frequent winner in the Britain in Bloom competition. The parish church, with traditional outside stairways, was built in the 1650s.

AUCHINLECK
Two very different 18th-century personalities are commemorated in a museum in the old parish church here. One is James Boswell, son of the Laird of Auchinleck and biographer of Samuel Johnson. The other is William Murdoch, son of a tenant farmer and miller on the Boswell estates. He was a brilliant mechanic and engineer, worked with James Watt and invented gas lighting in 1792.

Boswell and many members of his family are buried in the mausoleum added in 1754. The route leaves Auchinleck by a tree-lined avenue planted by James Boswell's father.

OCHILTREE
West of the Barony Colliery – one of the two remaining pits in the Ayrshire coalfield – the road crosses the Lugar Water and rises again into Ochiltree, where most of the houses are 'stepped' up a sharply climbing street.

Ochiltree was the childhood home of the turn-of-the-century novelist George Douglas Brown. His most famous book, *The House with the Green Shutters*, is a bitter indictment of narrow-minded village life in a town called 'Barbie'. Brown once claimed, however, that not one of the characters was drawn from Ochiltree.

The village seems to have accepted his assurance. His birthplace, now a Royal British Legion Club, has had the appropriate green shutters fixed.

Tourist information: Ayr 284196; Troon 315131 (summer).

TOUR
213
--- 65 MILES ---
From the birthplace of Robert Burns, lonely roads in the Carrick hills lead to a treasure house of Pre-Raphaelite art. A clifftop castle stands in the heart of Scotland's first country park.

ROZELLE
In its 96 acres this park contains woodlands, lawns, playing fields, a sculpture garden, nature trails and wildfowl ponds. It is centred on the elegant Georgian mansion of Rozelle House, built in the 1750s for Robert Hamilton who named it after a property in the West Indies.

Rozelle House is used for local history exhibitions. The stable block, built round a courtyard, has been restored as an art gallery.

ALLOWAY
Biographical fact and poetic fiction come mesmerisingly close together in Alloway, the very heart of Robert Burns country.

The thatched cottage where Burns was born in 1759 is now linked with a museum. A few minutes' stroll away

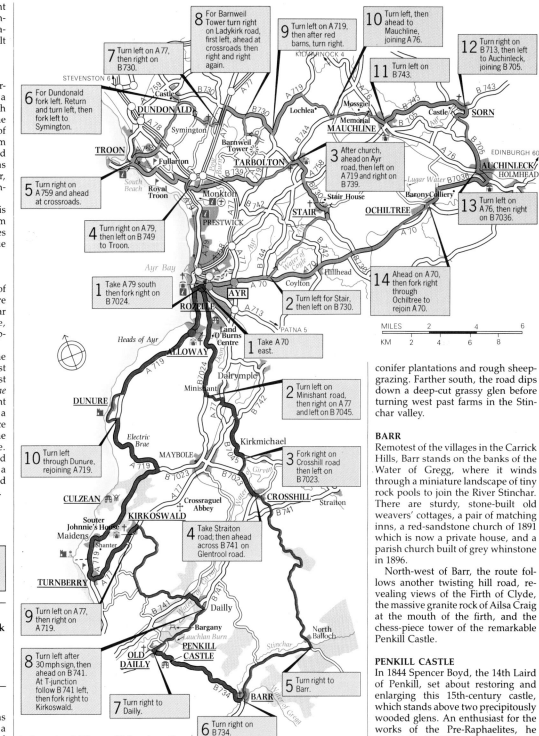

is the ruined Alloway Kirk, where the witches and warlocks were disturbed at their midnight revels in the rollicking ballad of *Tam o' Shanter*. The poet's father is buried in the churchyard. The Auld Brig o'Doon, a simple, single-arched bridge, is where Tam's mare lost her tail in the hectic chase that followed.

Overlooking the bridge is the Burns Monument, built in 1823. The Land o'Burns Centre opposite the old church houses a permanent exhibition, and an audio-visual account of the poet's life and times is given in its theatre. The centre has extensive landscaped gardens in which there are picnic areas.

Beyond Alloway the route runs

above well-wooded estates and rich, rolling farmland towards the hill country of Carrick, which forms the backdrop to the river-valley village of Crosshill.

CROSSHILL
Set in a hollow beside the Water of Girvan, Crosshill grew up in the early 19th century when Irish immigrants arrived to make it a prosperous centre of handloom weaving. The long main street with its single-storey cottages remains very much as they must have known it.

Leaving Crosshill, the route climbs into a high, deserted moorland of

conifer plantations and rough sheep-grazing. Farther south, the road dips down a deep-cut grassy glen before turning west past farms in the Stinchar valley.

BARR
Remotest of the villages in the Carrick Hills, Barr stands on the banks of the Water of Gregg, where it winds through a miniature landscape of tiny rock pools to join the River Stinchar. There are sturdy, stone-built old weavers' cottages, a pair of matching inns, a red-sandstone church of 1891 which is now a private house, and a parish church built of grey whinstone in 1896.

North-west of Barr, the route follows another twisting hill road, revealing views of the Firth of Clyde, the massive granite rock of Ailsa Craig at the mouth of the firth, and the chess-piece tower of the remarkable Penkill Castle.

PENKILL CASTLE
In 1844 Spencer Boyd, the 14th Laird of Penkill, set about restoring and enlarging this 15th-century castle, which stands above two precipitously wooded glens. An enthusiast for the works of the Pre-Raphaelites, he turned the Penkill stable block into a studio for artists such as Holman Hunt, Dante Gabriel Rossetti, Edward Burne-Jones and William Bell Scott, who all contributed to the restoration.

Penkill's furniture, portraits, tapestries and architectural details – as well as a splendid curving mural which follows the staircase in the main tower – are on show between April and September. Guided tours are available to parties by arrangement (Old Daily 226).

OLD DAILY
Spencer Boyd and his sister Alice, who shared his liking for Pre-Raphaelite art, lie beneath suitably

ornamental tombstones in the ruined churchyard of this hamlet in the Girvan valley.

East of Old Dailly are the richly wooded grounds of Bargany estate, open daily from February to October.

KIRKOSWALD
At the age of 17, Robert Burns came to Kirkoswald to study surveying with the village schoolmaster. There were many distractions. A girl who lived next door to the school, he recorded, took his mind completely off trigonometry. And at the village inn he fell in with a hard-drinking crew, including Douglas Graham from the nearby farm of Shanter and the souter, or shoemaker, John Davidson.

Fifteen years later he recalled those rowdy nights in *Tam o' Shanter*. Set in a tavern in Ayr, Tam was based on Douglas Graham, and John Davidson was the model for the thirsty Souter Johnnie. The shoemaker's cottage is now a museum, open daily except on Fridays, from April to September. Davidson and Graham are buried in the village churchyard, but their roistering alter egos remain as larger-than-life statues in the cottage garden.

TURNBERRY
Reaching the coast, the route turns north at this golfing resort, with its spectacular outlook to Ailsa Craig and the peaks of Arran.

Turnberry also has a fine sandy beach, with a lighthouse within the tumbled ruins of a castle on a rocky point at the northern end. A walk to the lighthouse reveals that the golf courses are crossed by unexpected airfield runways. Above one of the greens is a monument to airmen who trained there in both world wars.

CULZEAN
Once the most magnificent private estate in Ayrshire, Culzean – pronounced 'Cull-ayn' – is now a 531 acre country park based on Robert Adam's cliff-top castle.

Notable features of the castle – built in the 18th century for the 10th Earl of Cassillis – include an oval staircase and the inspired Round Drawing Room overlooking the firth. There are guided tours of the castle daily from April to October.

North of Culzean, the route makes for the Electric Brae where, by an optical illusion, motorists sometimes feel they are going downhill, when in fact they are going uphill.

DUNURE
The sturdy little 19th-century harbour at Dunure is now used mostly by pleasure sailors. But the original fishermen's cottages remain, overlooked by ruined Dunure Castle.

Tourist information: Ayr 284196.

HILL AND DALE *Thick forest forms a protecting cordon round cattle and sheep grazing peacefully on the outskirts of North Balloch. Beyond tower high fells on the edge of the Galloway Forest Park.*

A countryside park near the Clyde coast

A route steeped in history starts near the site of the battle that forced the Vikings to relinquish the Hebrides, and passes through a regional park where wildlife abounds.

LARGS

Here, in 1263, Alexander III's army fought off the Vikings in the battle which ended foreign control of the Western Isles. Now Norwegians invade the town peacefully every September to take part in the Viking Festival.

A car ferry leaves Largs for the attractive island of Great Cumbrae in the Firth of Clyde, and it is also a port of call on the summer sailings of the *Waverley*, the world's last seagoing paddle-steamer.

Largs is a busy watersports centre, and land recreations include golf on two fine courses. At Douglas Park a hill walk, with a flight of 138 steps up the final escarpment, leads to a superb viewpoint over the islands in the Firth of Clyde.

In the heart of the town is the Kirkgate, where the 17th-century burial aisle of the Montgomerys of Skelmorlie Castle is maintained as an ancient monument, open daily in summer. Nearby is a museum run by the local history society, open on weekday afternoons in summer. North of Largs the route follows the rocky red-sandstone coast, with windswept trees to landward.

INVERKIP

The lagoon formed by the Kip Water just before it flows into the firth is the site of an extensive marina. But Inverkip itself is slightly away from the sea, its main street now freed of main-road traffic.

In the upper fringe of the village, the route passes the fragmentary remains of the original pre-Reformation church. Buried in the churchyard is Dr James 'Paraffin' Young, who started the world's first commercial oil works at Bathgate, Lothian, in 1851.

CLYDE MUIRSHIEL PARK

After winding between trees and hedges from Inverkip, the route comes onto high open moorland on the fringes of the 30,000 acre Clyde Muirshiel Regional Park. The visitor centre at Cornalees Bridge, open all the year round, is a source of information not only about the moorland wildlife, but also about a fascinating industrial monument – Loch Thom Reservoir and the Greenock Cut.

Robert Thom's complex system of reservoirs and 'cuts' or channels to supply water to Greenock's mills and factories opened in 1827. It continued in its original form until 1971, when tunnels took the place of the old open channels. The main Greenock Cut, contouring Dunrod Hill, and its associated sluice gates were then designated an ancient monument.

Farther on, at Kilbarchan, the Weaver's Cottage of 1723 has been restored by the National Trust for Scotland as a museum of handloom weaving and village domestic life in the past. The cottage is open from late April to October, and on some days a weaver produces cloth on a re-installed 200-year-old loom. From the front door of the cottage there is a view along Shuttle Street to the Steeple, dating from 1755.

A road following a narrow, dead-end glen of the River Calder leads towards high-level grouse moors and another section of the Clyde Muirshiel Park. This is Muirshiel Country Park, a former private estate which has a visitor centre. Way-marked nature trails explore broad-leaved woodland, conifer plantations, rhododendron scrub, a waterfall and the moorland viewpoint summit of Windy Hill.

LOCHWINNOCH

Centred on a High Street with colour-washed, two-storey houses of the early 19th century, Lochwinnoch is a village which has seen many industries, and still has a substantial trade in the making of casks and barrels.

St Winnoch Road leads to Castle Semple Loch, which has facilities for sailing, canoeing and coarse fishing. The loch has its own information centre.

Off the main road south-east of Lochwinnoch, a nature centre and reserve run by the Royal Society for the Protection of Birds is open from Thursday to Sunday. There is a first-floor observation tower. More than 150 species of birds have been recorded on the reserve, which includes open water and areas of reedy marshland.

KELBURN COUNTRY CENTRE

This beautifully wooded property, based on the glen of the Kel Burn, has been the home of the Boyle family – originally the de Boyvilles – since around 1140. They were created Earls of Glasgow in 1703.

In Victorian times, the 6th Earl endowed churches all over Scotland – to the extent that he put himself almost a million pounds in debt. In 1888 all his extensive estates were auctioned off. Only Kelburn remained in the family's hands.

The grounds are open daily from April to September, and at weekends in winter. They include a network of woodland walks. There are bridges across the Kel Burn, and several waterfalls.

The South Offices, or home farm buildings, have been restored as a visitor centre. And from the walled garden there is a clear view of the site of the Battle of Largs, in which the Vikings were driven off more than 700 years ago. This event is commemorated by a monument – a round tower known locally as 'The Pencil'.

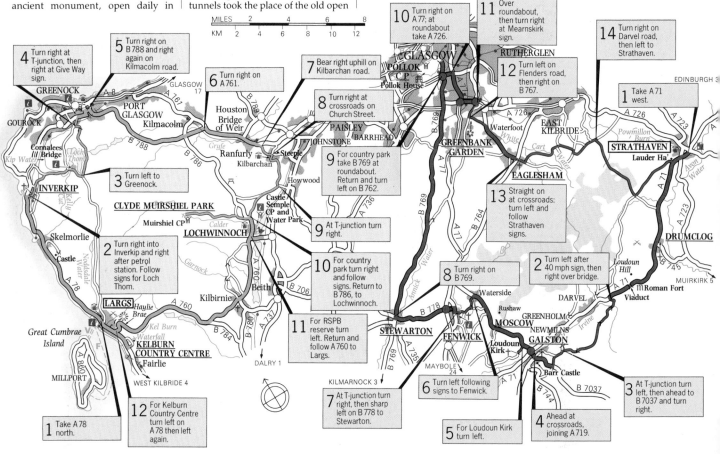

From the town where Sir Harry Lauder spent his last years, the tour follows the trail of the 17th-century Covenanters and passes through Moscow to a park full of treasures.

STRATHAVEN

This pleasant country town (pronounced 'Stray-ven') once echoed to the clack of hundreds of handlooms. They were installed in the ground-floor rooms of cottages which still line the older streets.

A convenient way to explore the town is to follow the Powmillon Burn as it flows through three public parks – one of them, the John Hastie, having a local history museum. The burn then disappears briefly before it swings through a gorge dominated by the hilltop ruin of the 16th-century Strathaven Castle; the castle was last garrisoned by troops hunting the Covenanters, fighters for Protestant freedom. Below the castle the burn plunges past the Old Town Mill, now an arts centre.

Leaving Strathaven, the route passes Lauder Ha', where the entertainer Sir Harry Lauder lived from 1934 until his death in 1950. It is visible from the main road, but not open to the public.

DRUMCLOG

The Covenanters' most famous victory was achieved in a battle fought on June 1, 1679, in the hills 1 mile north-west of this tiny crossroads settlement. A service in their honour is held on the first Sunday in June in the Drumclog Memorial Kirk.

Behind the church is the grassed-over embankment of the Strathaven to Darvel railway line. The main road follows the railway, passing a surviving viaduct below the craggy top of Loudoun Hill. Historically, this was an important 'gap' route. The Romans established a fort to guard it, and English forces were twice beaten here – by Wallace in 1297 and Bruce in 1307.

GALSTON

Much of Galston is built of locally quarried red sandstone, like Barr Castle on a side street to the south. This well-preserved 80ft tower is still used by the local masonic lodge.

The most exotic building in the town is the Roman Catholic Church of St Sophia. In two-coloured brick, it was erected in 1886 on the pattern of the similarly named church in Istanbul.

MOSCOW

Climbing out of the Irvine valley, the main road passes through the crossroads hamlet of Moscow. Before 1812 the name was pronounced 'Moss-haw', but the present spelling was adopted in celebration of Napoleon's retreat. It is purely a coincidence that a local farm is called Rushaw; but it must have been a joker who named a tributary of the Irvine which runs behind the older cottages – it is the Volga Burn.

FENWICK

Bypassed by the Glasgow to Kilmarnock road, this village is set among spreading acres of dairy farms. High Fenwick was originally a colony of shoemakers. At Low Fenwick, hand-loom weavers worked in cottages which have been neatly restored.

These were the men who founded the Co-operative Movement – or so it is claimed locally, despite the conflicting claims of Rochdale. The Fenwick Weavers' Society of 1769 not only acted as a trade guild, but also made bulk purchases of food for sale at a fair price to its members.

STEWARTON

Woollen bonnets are still made in Stewarton, which has been known for centuries as the 'Bonnet Town'. In the third week of June, a festival is run by the revived Bonnet Guild.

The original guild regulated the trade; its modern successor is a charitable organisation whose members wear the traditional Stewarton bonnet – a navy blue tam-o'-shanter with red and navy blue diced trim.

POLLOK COUNTRY PARK

Nature trails, gardens, woodlands and riverside walks are all part of this 361 acre parkland. But its centrepiece is the magnificent Burrell Collection. This was opened in 1983 to show the collection of paintings, sculptures, tapestries, stained glass, bronzes, ceramics, furniture and furnishings – 8000 items in all – given to his native city by the millionaire shipowner Sir William Burrell.

When the Maxwell Macdonald family handed the park over to the city in 1966, their gift included the elegant Georgian mansion of Pollok House which, like the Burrell Collection, is open daily. Its contents include one of the finest collections of Spanish art in Britain – with paintings by Goya, Murillo and El Greco.

GREENBANK GARDEN

The 16 acres of Greenbank, owned by the National Trust for Scotland, include a walled garden, a picnic area, a short woodland walk and a special garden for the disabled. The estate is open daily.

Beyond Greenbank the route rejoins the valley of the White Cart Water, last seen in Pollok Park.

EAGLESHAM

When the 10th Earl of Eglinton decided to build a model village here in 1769, he settled on an unusual A-shaped plan which survives as a conservation area to the present day. Montgomery Street and Polnoon Street, once the homes of weavers, start at a low level and climb to meet each other – with an ever-narrowing public park known as the Orry squeezed between.

Tourist information: Kilmarnock 39090; Largs 673765; Greenock 24400.

DOWN IN THE GLEN *The River Calder winds between grassy moorlands in the Calder Glen – part of the Muirshiel Country Park.*

FAIR HAVEN *The marina at Inverkip is one of the largest in Scotland, and has the advantage that boats can enter or leave at any state of the tide.*

FENWICK CHURCH *Several Covenanters lie buried beside the 17th-century church.*

Up the Clyde to the Lowther Hills

TOUR

216

—— 84 MILES ——

Deep river gorges slice through moorlands south of the Clyde valley. Roads made of the local pink stone pass ruined strongholds and a stream where gold was once panned.

LANARK

The agricultural market centre of lower Strathclyde stands 700ft high on a plateau above the steep banks of the River Clyde. Its main street – divided down the centre by a long flowerbed studded with chain-linked pillars – slopes down to the 18th-century parish church, standing like a bulwark at the bottom.

In a canopied niche in the face of the tall, colour-washed church tower is a statue of William Wallace. Wallace lived in Lanark and it was from here, in 1297, that he first took up arms against the English in his fight for Scotland's independence. This huge, genial Father Christmas-like figure, who seems embarrassed by his bare, fat knees, was presented to the town in 1817 by its sculptor, Robert Forrest.

The route leaves Lanark from the opposite end of the main street. On a hairpin bend, as the road turns down into New Lanark, there is a preview of the distant Falls of Clyde, with a mist of spray rising among trees above a glint of foaming water.

NEW LANARK

Built in the 18th century as a model cotton-mill village, the austere buildings of New Lanark are being preserved as a living museum, and as a memorial to a remarkable experiment in social reform.

The mill was built in 1788 by a Glasgow merchant, David Dale, in partnership with Richard Arkwright, inventor of a spinning frame, and was powered by 11 water wheels driven by the Clyde. In 1800 Dale's son-in-law Robert Owen took over the management of the mill, and he was determined to give the workers better conditions than existed elsewhere.

Owen began by building tenement blocks for his 1800 workers. The terraces, built of sandstone with slate roofs, are still sound. Owen also set about reforming working conditions. He banned work by children under ten, and reduced working hours from 13 a day to 10½. Children and adults were educated in his Institute for the Formation of Character, and workers earned tokens that could be exchanged for low-priced goods at the village shop, the forerunner of the Co-operative Movement.

FALLS OF CLYDE

At the far end of New Lanark, steps descend to a path leading to the Falls of Clyde Nature Reserve. The walk is a 2 mile wonder, and follows the bank of the Clyde upstream past the Bonnington hydroelectric power station to the waterfall of Corra Linn. Here the Clyde thunders over slabs of black sandstone, falling more than 80ft in three steps to a dark pool set in an amphitheatre of rock, hung with ever-damp vegetation and precariously rooted trees.

At the top of the fall on the other side of the river, the ruin of Corra Castle, or Wallace's Tower, clings perilously to its rock pinnacle. Built in the 15th century, it is now too dangerous to enter.

Above Corra Linn the Clyde roars through a magnificent vertical-sided gorge fringed with oak and pine. At the top of the defile, nearly a mile from the lower waterfall, is Bonnington Linn, the second of the famous 'Falls of Clyde', so beloved of poets and romantic painters.

This stretch of the river is now harnessed for hydroelectric power, and in summer is often robbed of its full splendour. However, in winter, or when the power station is switched off, the river pours over the falls in a mass of spray, which rises like smoke above the trees. There is a visitor centre for the reserve in the Dyeworks beside the river in New Lanark.

A different view of the falls can be had from the other side of the Clyde. This can be reached from the car park at Corehouse farther on in the tour.

CARTLAND CRAGS

As the busy main road sweeps west from Lanark, it is easy to miss the long chasm below Cartland Crags at Cartland Bridge. Immediately after the bridge, the left turn to Nemphlar provides safe parking off the road.

From the centre of the 129ft high bridge, built by Thomas Telford in 1822, there is a view up the gorge between precipitous, tree-hung cliffs. From a small quarry on the right, just beyond the bridge, an unfenced path leads perilously up along the top of the crags, with the innocent-sounding Mouse Water gushing through the chasm far below. William Wallace is thought to have taken refuge in a cave above the bridge.

Roads of pink stone wind up and down over moorland, between beech hedges and bracken-clad slopes, with wide views across smooth, round-topped hills. In autumn sunshine the hedgerows blaze with copper, bronze and gold, laced with crimson and russet berries of the wild briar and hawthorn.

A steep, zigzag road climbs to an unfenced, green plateau where shaggy cattle roam among old thorn trees.

CRAIGNETHAN CASTLE

The impressive ruins of the 16th-century castle, built by Sir James Hamilton of Finnart, stand on a spur beside the deeply eroded bed of the River Nethan. Excavations in 1962 unearthed a rare 'carponier'. Buried for nearly 400 years, this dank, stone-roofed vault, which was built to protect and conceal hand gunners defending the castle, still contained bones of cattle, sheep, rabbits and chickens from the meals of the 16th-century gunners. Through turbulent

FARMING VALLEY *The Crawick valley and its remote farms shelter below the rising moorlands of the Lowther Hills.*

MODEL HOMES *The houses at New Lanark provided one room for each family, a high standard for workers' homes in the 18th century, and are now modernised.*

WANLOCKHEAD *A beam pump is part of the village's lead-mining museum.*

years of religious conflict and family feuds, the fortunes of the castle rose and fell with those of the owners. It was given to the State in 1949 by the 14th Earl of Home, who as Alec Douglas-Home was Prime Minister, 1963-4, and later became Lord Home of the Hirsel; the castle is open daily.

The castle is said to have been the inspiration for Sir Walter Scott's Tillietudlem Castle, in his novel *Old Mortality* (although the author himself denied this). A nearby halt on the long-disused branch railway was called Tillietudlem in its honour.

As the road flattens out along the Nethan river, there is a fine view up to the castle perched on its crag.

An easy climb from a small lay-by to the top of Blackhill, crowned by an Iron Age hill-fort, is rewarded by sweeping views across the Clyde valley and away to distant hills in the south, and to the spires of Lanark to the east.

SANQUHAR

A granite monument in Sanquhar commemorates the two declarations made by Covenanters in 1680 and 1685. The first, made by Richard Cameron, renounced allegiance to Charles II and was affixed to the mercat cross which the monument now replaces; the second was made by James Renwick against James VII of Scotland (James II of England).

At the top of the High Street stands a Tolbooth of 1735, with a clock tower. Inside is a small local history museum. Nearby is Britain's oldest post office; it dates from 1763, 21 years before the coming of the mail coach service.

The Admirable Crichton, whose name James Barrie used for his popular play, was born at Eliock House, a tower-house 2 miles south-east of Sanquhar. In the 16th century, James Crichton astounded Europe with his intellectual genius – he could speak 12 languages while still in his teens – but was killed in a brawl in Italy at the age of 22.

WANLOCKHEAD

The climb beside Mennock Water, along a narrow valley between steeply rising hills, is so gentle that it is hard to believe that Wanlockhead, at the top, is 1380ft above sea level. The village comprises a wedge-shaped cluster of houses built on mounds of turf. To the left, past the Museum of Scottish Lead Mining, stands a 'beam pump', a relic of the days of lead mining, and farther on, across the burn, is a disused mine which is part of the museum complex. Visitors can walk into the mine, Loch Nell, which was worked from the early 1700s to 1860. There is also a water tunnel that took 11 years to cut through the rock, and a Lead Miners' Library founded in 1756. In the museum are relics from 250 years of lead-mining, and a reconstruction of a miner's kitchen in the 1800s. The museum is open daily in summer.

Gold was once panned from the neighbouring streams; one nugget found in the area and weighing some 4oz is now in the British Museum. The lonely, heather-covered moors were

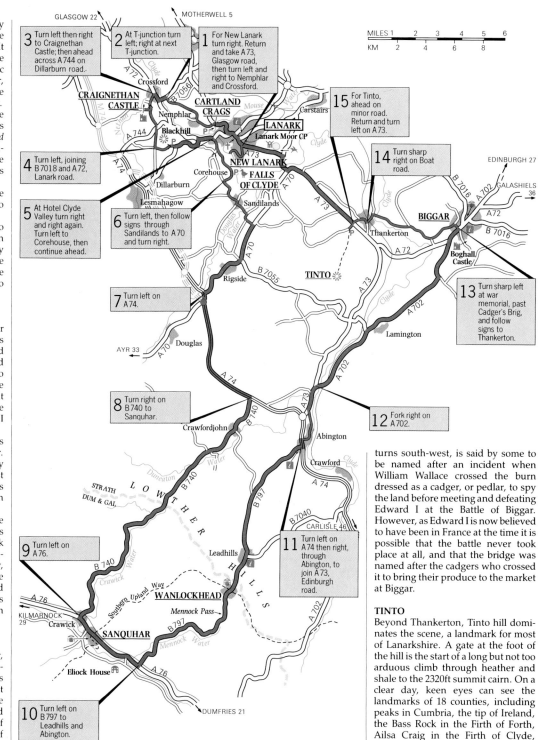

much used in the times of the Covenanters for the holding of religious meetings. The Southern Upland Way long-distance path passes through this isolated village.

In the small, windswept cemetery above Leadhills, only a few feet lower than Wanlockhead, lie the remains of John Taylor who is said to have died at the age of 137, having worked for more than 100 years in the lead mills. The village was the birthplace of the 17th-century poet Allan Ramsay.

BIGGAR

The town is spread out along its broad main street, one of the widest in Scotland, and a street of 19th-century shops is re-created in the Gladstone

Court Museum, open daily from Easter to October.

Even earlier times are recalled in the nearby Greenhill Covenanters' House, a rebuilt farmhouse in which models and reconstructions tell the story of the troubled decades of the 17th century preceding the union of Scotland and England in 1707. Greenhill is open every afternoon from Easter to October.

Mary Fleming, one of the four Marys who were ladies-in-waiting to Mary, Queen of Scots, lived at Boghall Castle, of which only a tower remains. Biggar remembers Mary each June with the Crowning of the Fleming Queen.

Cadger's Brig, where the route

turns south-west, is said by some to be named after an incident when William Wallace crossed the burn dressed as a cadger, or pedlar, to spy the land before meeting and defeating Edward I at the Battle of Biggar. However, as Edward I is now believed to have been in France at the time it is possible that the battle never took place at all, and that the bridge was named after the cadgers who crossed it to bring their produce to the market at Biggar.

TINTO

Beyond Thankerton, Tinto hill dominates the scene, a landmark for most of Lanarkshire. A gate at the foot of the hill is the start of a long but not too arduous climb through heather and shale to the 2320ft summit cairn. On a clear day, keen eyes can see the landmarks of 18 counties, including peaks in Cumbria, the tip of Ireland, the Bass Rock in the Firth of Forth, Ailsa Craig in the Firth of Clyde, Arran and Jura.

Tinto is wrapped in legend: Wallace camped on the hill with his army, and the depression in the boulder at the top is called Wallace's Thumbmark. The name Tinto is derived from the Gaelic *teinteach* – 'place of fire' – suggesting that it may have been a site of the ancient pagan fire-rites of Beltane.

Returning to Lanark over Hyndford Bridge, the route passes Lanark Moor Country Park, on the right beyond the racecourse. From the car park there are pleasant walks down to a small pine-fringed loch.

Tourist information: Lanark 2544; Biggar 21066 (summer); Crawford 436.

Into the Pentland and Moorfoot Hills

TOUR
217

— 66 MILES —

Only a few miles from Edinburgh Castle and the busy streets of Scotland's capital are hills where Covenanters fought and valleys where rivers flow shallow and fast over rocky beds.

CRAIGMILLAR CASTLE

The massive ruins of Craigmillar, to be found down Craigmillar Castle Road, stand proudly above a straggle of modern building developments which have so far failed to encroach upon the aloof and regal splendour of the castle.

Its well-preserved walls, dating from the 14th century, have witnessed some dark moments of Scottish history. In 1479, James III im-

prisoned his brother John, Earl of Mar, in the keep for suspected conspiracy and sorcery; later, Mar died from 'overzealous bloodletting . . .'

Craigmillar was the favourite country retreat of Mary, Queen of Scots, and it was here in 1566, at the Craigmillar Conference, that she was urged by her lords – including Bothwell, who later married her – to divorce Lord Darnley. It is not known whether she was party to the subsequent plot to murder Darnley.

The great banqueting hall on the first floor is served by four stairways, and it is easy to imagine hanging tapestries, rushes on the flagged floor, blazing logs in the vast hearth and minstrels in the gallery below the barrel-vaulted ceiling. In the 15th century the central tower was enclosed by a curtain wall which still survives. A gun port in one of the towers is an early example in Scotland of provision for artillery in the defence of a castle.

The view from the roof takes in Arthur's Seat, the Firth of Forth with the hills of Fife beyond, and the soft contours of the Pentland Hills on the south-western horizon. The castle is open daily.

Beyond the suburbs of Edinburgh, the northern foothills of the Pentlands rise ahead. The dry ski slope at Hillend – the largest of its kind in Europe – stands out plainly just above the road. From the main road there are views across the valley on the left to the distant Moorfoot Hills, and up the nearer flank of the Pentlands to the right.

CASTLELAW

Between high beech hedges the road climbs to a farm and a parking area. A short walk over turf between gorse scrub leads to the grass-covered ramparts of an Iron Age fort, on the far side of which a wrought-iron gate leads down into a well-preserved souterrain, or earth house. It consists of a long passage with a round chamber, lit by windows in the roof so that the interior can be seen.

Standing among the remains of this prehistoric fort in the early morning,

with the sun rising over the Moorfoots to the south-east and bathing the Pentlands in a pinkish light, is a breathtaking experience that well rewards a dawn reveille.

A footpath from the parking area leads to several good signposted walks in the hills.

GLENCORSE RESERVOIR

Cars must be left in the park beyond Flotterstone Inn, which has gardens beside the Glencorse Burn. A pleasant mile-long walk beside the burn leads to the Glencorse Reservoir, pine-fringed and tranquil, reflecting the surrounding hills. Its receding waterline often indicates a shortage of rain. The reservoir was opened in 1822, and was the first in the Pentlands to supply water for Edinburgh.

Beneath the surface of the reservoir lie the ruins of the Church of St Katherine in the Hopes, built by William Sinclair in gratitude for land he was given by Robert Bruce in the 14th century and on which he built Roslin Castle.

Tracks lead to more hill walks where, among the folds of the grassy slopes, shepherds may often be seen with their dogs, herding sheep. The sound of falling water suddenly reveals burns cascading down the hillside.

At Carlops, 6 miles farther on, the name of the Allan Ramsay Hotel is a reminder of the Scots poet whose pastoral comedy *The Gentle Shepherd*, written in 1725, was based on this area, which he often visited.

WEST LINTON

A carved statue of a woman, hands folded, stands in relief on one wall of the local clock tower. She is the wife of James Gifford, a 17th-century stonemason who immortalised his wife and four children in a group.

When Mrs Gifford unexpectedly had a fifth child, the only free place remaining on the memorial was on top of the mother's head, and here the latecomer was placed. Time and weather erased the first four children and the fifth has been removed to nearby Spitalhaugh House.

DUNSYRE

On the wall of the kirk above the tiny village of Dunsyre, an ancient 'jougs' – an iron collar that was a Scottish form of pillory – is preserved in a glass case. In the churchyard several tombstones have primitive carvings, including a skeleton and hour-glass symbols. Inside the simple kirk is an engraved 'Covenanters' Stone' – a relic from the days when Covenanters hid in the glens above.

From Carnwath, the road runs straight as an arrow through pine woods, desolate uplands and heather-clad peat bogs.

MALLENY HOUSE GARDENS

Beside the Water of Leith, in Balerno, lies this 18th-century house. It is not open to the public, but it forms a charming focal point for the formal gardens, which are open in summer. These contain clipped yews, rhododendrons, a particularly good collection of rare shrub roses and a variety of other plants.

Map directions

1 Take A7, then turn left on A68, Jedburgh road.

2 Turn right on A720.

2 For Roslin Chapel turn right on B7003, then right again on B7006.

3 Turn left on A702.

7 Turn left on Riccarton Mains Road, then right on A71.

6 For Malleny House turn right.

13 Turn right beyond bridge to Carrington, then right and right again.

14 Turn left on A7.

12 Turn left through Gorebridge to Temple.

11 For Crichton Castle fork right.

10 Turn left on A7, then right through Borthwick and right at crossroads.

1 Take A6094 south.

3 Turn left on B6372, Gorebridge road.

4 Turn right on minor road, past reservoir.

5 For reservoir turn left.

9 Straight ahead on B7007.

6 Turn left on A703.

7 Turn left on A72.

8 Turn left on B709.

4 Turn right and follow signs to Dunsyre and Newbigging.

5 Turn right on A721 to Carnwath, then right on A70.

A trip through the windswept Moorfoot Hills offers some fine walking country and a wealth of history and legend. A palace and two castles have links with Mary, Queen of Scots.

DALKEITH

In spite of being at the confluence of busy main roads, Dalkeith retains its stateliness. Its wide, cobbled High Street is flanked by many fine old buildings, and at the eastern end is the imposing entrance to the palace and park.

Dalkeith Palace is not open to the public, but its fine façade can be seen from the park, which is open in summer. It provides a gracious background to nature trails through the park and to the well-designed play area for children.

The present palace, built around the old castle, is a large reddish structure with a recessed centre and two projecting wings. It was designed in the 18th century by James Smith.

In the 16th century the palace was known as the Lion's Den because James Douglas, Earl of Morton, the sinister Regent of Scotland, lived there. He figured prominently in the murder of David Rizzio, secretary and reputed lover of Mary, Queen of Scots, and was implicated in the plot which led to the murder of Mary's husband, Lord Darnley – a plot in which Mary herself may have been involved. While he was lying sick at the palace in 1572, Morton held a council with the aim of bringing Mary to trial. He was executed in 1581 – nearly six years before Mary herself was beheaded – for his part in the killing of Darnley.

ROSLIN

Towering above the treetops of Roslin Glen and reached by a narrow bridge, Roslin Castle retains its medieval character.

William Sinclair, Earl of Orkney, lived here sumptuously in the 15th century. He decided to build a church, in which a group of clergy were bound, by deed, to sing masses and pray for the souls of the founder and his family.

The church, an enormous cruciform design, was never finished: the only parts completed were the existing lady chapel, a chancel and part of a transept, with a burial vault below.

Eyes are drawn to the Prentice Pillar on the south side of the lady chapel. Its carving is extraordinarily delicate.

The chapel is open in summer and for episcopalian worship on Sundays. Access can be arranged at other times by the curator at College Hill House next door.

GLADHOUSE RESERVOIR

On the way from Roslin to Gladhouse, grassy uplands where the shape of the trees shows the force of the prevailing winds give way to

THE PENTLANDS *With gentle majesty, the hills rise above a rural landscape near the village of Leadburn, south-west of Edinburgh.*

CURRIE CHURCH *This 18th-century building, on the Water of Leith near Balerno, beckons through the trees. Currie is a centre for walks in the Pentland Hills.*

HIGH FORT *Borthwick Castle has had few attackers in its 500 years.*

TEMPLE RUIN *The site is named after the crusading Knights Templar.*

marsh and pine plantations and wide expanses of desolate peat bog and heather. The reservoir is a peaceful, pine-fringed loch – popular with birdwatchers, nature lovers and fishermen. It is an excellent picnic site but dogs are barred.

EDDLESTON

This charming hamlet of old white cottages has a castle, dating from the 15th century, which is now privately owned. It looks down over the valley of Eddleston Water towards the Moorfoot Hills.

GLENTRESS FOREST

Several well-signposted walks lead from the car park. They include a 2½ mile trail up to Cardie Hill Fort, and another to the ancient Shieldgreen Tower – little more than a pile of stones.

On the right of the car park are three tall wooden figures, graceful in their simplicity. They are the Tent Peg Men, carved from fir out of Glentress Forest by a local man for the 50th anniversary of the Forestry Commission in 1969. The trio – foresters in deep conversation – was shown at the original anniversary exhibition near Edinburgh.

BORTHWICK

Now a private hotel, Borthwick Castle is 500 years old and the largest peel tower in Scotland, 100ft tall with walls 12-14ft thick. The castle owes its state of preservation to an almost undisturbed history. Though built as a fortress, it stood aloof from war and feud, except during the Civil War when it suffered slight damage from Cromwell's cannons.

Mary, Queen of Scots and the Earl of Bothwell stayed briefly at Borthwick after their marriage in 1567.

CRICHTON CASTLE

Within sight of Borthwick the ruins of Crichton Castle stand on a grassy plateau, magnificent above a deep valley. It is of 14th-century origin. Mary, Queen of Scots paid several visits to Crichton – once when she was fleeing from Borthwick, disguised and alone. The castle is open daily in the summer and at weekends throughout the year.

TEMPLE

In a walled churchyard on a hillside beside a burn stands the roofless ruin of a 14th-century church. It was built on the site of a 12th-century church of the Knights Templar, who had their Scottish headquarters here until their suppression by the Pope in 1312.

Tourist information:
Edinburgh 226 6591.

Castles and coves of the Lothian coast

TOUR
219

——— 52 MILES ———

Roads through the fertile farmlands of Lothian lead to a coast of dramatic seascapes. Mines and motor cars have museums – and castles of the turbulent past are never far away.

NORTH BERWICK
Narrow streets lead down to a tiny, sheltered harbour, packed with boats and bordered by warehouses now converted into flats. Lobster creels and fishing nets lie on the quay alongside pleasure boats and sailboards. The ruin of the 12th-century Auld Kirk stands on a spit by the harbour.

The stark cone of North Berwick Law, 613ft high, dominates the scene. This was once part of a chain of warning beacons: it is crowned by a watchtower built in the Napoleonic Wars and has another lookout post dating from the Second World War. The climb up the Law is fairly tough, but an indicator at the summit points out the rewardingly large range of sights to be seen.

North Berwick is surrounded by golf courses and fringed to seaward by volcanic rocks including the Bass Rock, Fidra and Craigleith.

DIRLETON
This is a peaceful backwater with pantiled cottages, a 17th-century church, a session house, an old school and inns, all grouped round two wide, tree-fringed greens in the style of a medieval feudal township. Dominating everything is the 13th-century castle, standing on a crag within a high wall and surrounded by lawns and gardens. Other features are a 17th-century bowling green and a 16th-century dovecote with more than 1000 nests. The castle is open throughout the year.

GULLANE
Famous for its golf links, Gullane fights a continual battle against encroaching sand. But the links of the area – including the championship course at Muirfield, to the north-east – have turf unrivalled anywhere.

Aberlady Bay is steadily silting up, but it is a fascinating nature reserve with more than 200 recorded bird species. Brooding over the bay is Luffness Castle, a 16th-century building with a 13th-century keep. It can be visited by appointment in summer.

COCKENZIE
At Cockenzie a right turn into Seton Place leads down to quays where fish curers have their wooden cabins.

Prestonpans, 1 mile west, gets its name from the time, more than 700 years ago, when monks heated sea water in metal pans to extract salt, using local coal. A cluster of old buildings stands back above the coast road. Elegant 17th-century Hamilton House, owned by the National Trust for Scotland, is open by appointment.

On the town's outskirts, beside the Firth of Forth, is the Prestongrange Mining Museum. Standing on the site of a former colliery, it is part of the Scottish Mining Museum and the start of a 13 mile heritage trail covering more than 700 years of mining history. It is open daily in summer, closed on Saturdays in winter, and has an introductory audiovisual show and exhibition.

South of Prestonpans a cairn commemorates Bonnie Prince Charlie's victory in a ten-minute battle in 1745.

SETON MAINS
Approached through woodland backed by the Firth of Forth, the collegiate church of the 15th and 16th centuries has a spire which was well restored in the 19th. Here clerics prayed for the souls of the Seton family, whose castellated Robert Adam mansion can be seen through the trees. The church is open daily.

MYRETON MOTOR MUSEUM
The museum, which is surrounded by farmland, houses the largest display of motor vehicles in Scotland. In addition to vintage cars and motorcycles, there are fine collections of Second World War military vehicles, old road signs, advertisements and petrol pumps. The museum is open daily.

Not far south is The Chesters, an early Pictish fort with clearly defined ramparts. It is reached by an easy climb through an orchard and gives good views to the north.

About a mile farther south, a steep path reaches the Hopetoun Monument, a tall pillar erected in memory of the 4th Earl of Hopetoun, a distinguished soldier in the Napoleonic Wars.

HADDINGTON
A cameo view down a narrow wynd; the glint of clear water beneath a 16th-century bridge . . . history breathes over Haddington as if the past has cast a spell. Among the fine buildings is the 18th-century Town House, with a spire added in 1831 by Gillespie Graham. Carlyle's House – named after the writer Thomas Carlyle – in Lodge Street has a rich Corinthian façade. Jane Welsh, who was to become his wife, lived in the house behind – and her restored rooms are open on Wednesday, Thursday, Friday and Saturday afternoons in summer.

ATHELSTANEFORD
In the churchyard of this tiny village the St Andrew's Cross flies proudly above a brass mural depicting a 10th-century battle. Here the Scottish Picts defeated the Northumbrians under the Saxon King Athelstan. A white saltire – St Andrew's Cross – is said to have appeared mysteriously in the sky – thus providing the inspiration for the Scottish flag.

Just beyond Athelstaneford is the Museum of Flight at East Fortune airfield. Relics of early flying days are displayed in and around the hangars. It is open daily in July and August.

PRESTON MILL
The mill, restored by the National Trust for Scotland, is partly 17th century, but its several-sided kiln is believed to date from 200 years earlier. The water wheel and machinery are in working order. The mill and the

LENNOXLOVE *A cannon guards this entrance to a house of art and history.*

TANTALLON CASTLE *An air of menace clings to the ruined fortress above the sea. When the Douglases held sway here, three ditches to landward repelled invaders.*

PRESTON MILL *A millstream works its magic. The mill machinery works, too.*

CALM STONES *In a valley of the Lammermuir Hills trees fringe the village of Garvald whose name, meaning 'rough water', belies its atmosphere of peace.*

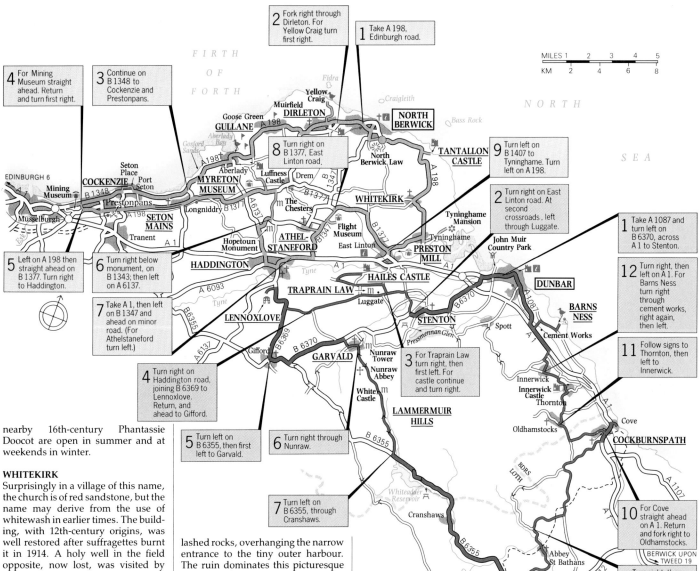

2 Fork right through Dirleton. For Yellow Craig turn first right.

1 Take A 198, Edinburgh road.

4 For Mining Museum straight ahead. Return and turn first right.

3 Continue on B 1348 to Cockenzie and Prestonpans.

9 Turn left on B 1407 to Tyninghame. Turn left on A 198.

8 Turn right on B 1377, East Linton road.

2 Turn right on East Linton road. At second crossroads, left through Luggate.

1 Take A 1087 and turn left on B 6370, across A 1 to Stenton.

5 Left on A 198 then straight ahead on B 1377. Turn right to Haddington.

6 Turn right below monument, on B 1343; then left on A 6137.

12 Turn right, then left on A 1. For Barns Ness turn right through cement works, right again, then left.

7 Take A 1, then left on B 1347 and ahead on minor road. (For Athelstaneford turn left.)

11 Follow signs to Thornton, then left to Innerwick.

4 Turn right on Haddington road, joining B 6369 to Lennoxlove. Return, and ahead to Gifford.

5 Turn left on B 6355, then first left to Garvald.

6 Turn right through Nunraw.

3 For Traprain Law turn right, then first left. For castle continue and turn right.

10 For Cove straight ahead on A 1. Return and fork right to Oldhamstocks.

7 Turn left on B 6355, through Cranshaws.

9 Turn right, then left, to Cockburnspath.

8 Turn left to Abbey St Bathans.

Map labels: FIRTH OF FORTH, NORTH SEA, Fidra, Yellow Craig, Craigleith, Bass Rock, Muirfield, DIRLETON, Goose Green, NORTH BERWICK, GULLANE, North Berwick Law, TANTALLON CASTLE, Aberlady Bay, Gosford Sands, Aberlady, Luffness Castle, Drem, WHITEKIRK, EDINBURGH 6, Seton Place, Port Seton, COCKENZIE, MYRETON MUSEUM, The Chesters, Tyninghame Mansion, Mining Museum, Prestonpans, Longniddry, Flight Museum, Tyninghame, John Muir Country Park, DUNBAR, BARNS NESS, Musselburgh, SETON MAINS, Tranent, Hopetoun Monument, ATHEL-STANEFORD, East Linton, PRESTON MILL, Cement Works, HADDINGTON, HAILES CASTLE, Luggate, STENTON, Spott, Innerwick, Innerwick Castle, Thornton, TRAPRAIN LAW, LENNOXLOVE, Gifford, GARVALD, Nunraw Tower, Nunraw Abbey, White Castle, LAMMERMUIR HILLS, Oldhamstocks, Cove, COCKBURNSPATH, BERWICK UPON TWEED 19, Whiteadder Reservoir, BDRS LOTH, Cranshaws, Abbey St Bathans, Southern Upland Way, Whiteadder Water

MILES 1 2 3 4 5 / KM 2 4 6 8

nearby 16th-century Phantassie Doocot are open in summer and at weekends in winter.

WHITEKIRK

Surprisingly in a village of this name, the church is of red sandstone, but the name may derive from the use of whitewash in earlier times. The building, with 12th-century origins, was well restored after suffragettes burnt it in 1914. A holy well in the field opposite, now lost, was visited by pilgrims in the 15th century.

TANTALLON CASTLE

The proud ruin of the 14th-century Tantallon Castle stands on the edge of a sheer cliff, overhanging the booming sea between two bays, with Bass Rock beyond. The castle – open daily – was a stronghold of the powerful Douglas family until it was wrecked by General Monck in the 17th century.

Tourist information: North Berwick 2197.

TOUR
220
— 67 MILES —
From the burgh of Dunbar the tour leads through the Lammermuir Hills and explores some hidden villages. The hump of Traprain Law gives the region its centrepiece.

DUNBAR

Only one red, fang-like tower and a few scattered stones remain of Dunbar's castle, once an extensive fortress sprawled across menacing, sea-lashed rocks, overhanging the narrow entrance to the tiny outer harbour. The ruin dominates this picturesque corner with its cobbled quays, restored warehouses, coastguard station, fishing boats and pleasure craft.

Lauderdale House, to which Robert Adam added the two wings and semicircular portico, was once military headquarters. It forms the seaward end of the wide, rectangular High Street. The barrack square provides a view of the castle, which dates from the 11th century. Mary, Queen of Scots took refuge here and it was destroyed after her defeat.

On the western outskirts the John Muir Country Park, named after a Dunbar-born conservationist, has 1667 acres of wild and beautiful coastland around the mouth of the Tyne, with cliff walks, sports and a variety of birdlife.

STENTON

On entering the village, the 16th-century Rood Well, to the right – known locally as the Cardinal's Hat – can easily be missed. It is in a hollow carpeted with St John's wort.

In the shadow of the tall pinnacles of Stenton church lie the ruins of the old kirk with its crow-stepped tower and dovecote.

A restored tron – a weighing machine used at a wool fair – stands on a tiny green, which is surrounded by red-sandstone cottages with pan-tiled roofs.

A left fork by the school leads after 1 mile to Pressmennan Glen, a long, wooded hanging valley, where Bennet's Burn was dammed in 1819 to form an artificial loch – a deep, dark snake of water, haunt of wildfowl and trout. A 2 mile forest trail, peaceful and beautiful, has six stops and viewpoints.

TRAPRAIN LAW

The 734ft high, whaleback hump of Traprain Law was the capital of the Votadini, one of the tribes occupying Lowland Scotland in Roman times. An extensive town grew up on the summit of the hill, which was a focus for the farmers living on the rich, fertile lands below. Parts of the defensive ramparts can still be traced.

In 1919 a hoard of Roman and Christian treasure was found. It was probably either a subsidy paid by the Romans to the local king or loot from the Empire. It is now in the National Museum of Antiquities in Edinburgh and includes silver-gilt bowls, goblets, cups and clasps.

Traprain Law was part of a volcanic seam running far out into the Forth, and it acts as a conductor of sound. An ear to the ground on the summit will pick up the throb of a boat engine, however small, out on the water.

HAILES CASTLE

On a rock above the River Tyne, where it surges through a narrow defile, stands the 13th-century Hailes Castle, once a feudal stronghold. Enlarged in the 14th century by the Hepburns – later Earls of Bothwell – and demolished by Cromwell, it was strategically sited on the main highway and able to extract tolls from passing travellers. Mary, Queen of

359

Scots and her third husband, James Hepburn, 4th Earl of Bothwell, sheltered here on their way to Dunbar. The castle is open daily.

LENNOXLOVE

The home of the Duke of Hamilton and Brandon is in pleasant woodland overlooking the Lammermuirs. The keep has parapet gargoyles and a watchtower penthouse. The keep and the 17th and 18th-century house contain paintings by Raeburn, Van Dyck, Janssens, Lely, Augustus John and de Laszlo, as well as fine porcelain and furniture.

There is also the death mask of Mary, Queen of Scots and her silver casket in which were found letters – possibly forged – incriminating her in the murder of her second husband, Lord Darnley. The house is open on Wednesday, Saturday and Sunday afternoons from April to September.

GARVALD

The name is derived from the Gaelic *garbh-allt*, 'rough water'. Garvald is a tiny village in a deep valley beside the rushing Papana Water.

Jougs, a metal neck collar used to punish miscreants, can be seen in a grille on the church wall, and there is a sundial dated 1633. Set back from the road in trees above the village is Nunraw, a 16th-century tower house built into a 19th-century mansion. Founded as a nunnery in the 12th century, it was abandoned at the Reformation, and bought by Irish Cistercians in 1946.

LAMMERMUIR HILLS

The road climbs through beech woods, past the Iron Age hill-fort of White Castle on the left, into the smoothly rounded summits and deep valleys of the ever-changing Lammermuirs. In summer, sheep graze among heather and gorse; skylarks sing and wild thyme scents the air.

Whiteadder Reservoir lies dark and mysterious in a bowl of wooded hills. Below the dam is a sheltered picnic site. In the narrow, wooded valleys, pheasants fly up in explosions of russet and green.

COCKBURNSPATH

Between the eastern edge of the Lammermuirs and the North Sea, Cockburnspath hides from the busy highway. In the village square is a church with a 30ft high round tower in the middle of the west gable.

BARNS NESS

The road runs straight out between stone walls to the lighthouse on its rocky promontory beyond a camp site. Here there are a wildlife preserve, a geology trail with an old limekiln, and good bathing.

Tourist information: Dunbar 63353.

FISHERS' HAVEN *The quiet little harbour at Cove, under the cliffs near Cockburnspath, could well be haunted by ghosts from its busier past. Once the quays were used by smugglers, and today's lobster traps by the harbour wall recall richer harvests in the days gone by.*

Hills and towns of the Forth lowlands

TOUR 221

— 51 MILES —

The River Carron surges through a valley of farmland to the north-west of Falkirk. Beyond are a proud castle, a handsome house and the remains of the fortified Antonine Wall.

FALKIRK

Once a cattle-drovers' meeting place, Falkirk was later a thriving iron-working town. The small museum in Orchard Street traces the history and development of the area. A 20 ton cast-iron gate, made for the Edinburgh International Exhibition of 1886, stands in Gowan Avenue.

The two battles of Falkirk are also the subjects of displays in the museum. The first battle took place in 1298, when the Scottish nationalist William Wallace was beaten by the forces of Edward I. The second occurred in 1746, when Bonnie Prince Charlie defeated the English under General Hawley. Prince Charlie is said to have spent the night after the battle in a cupboard-bed in the room above the door of what is now John Menzies' shop at 121 High Street.

On the night before the battle General Hawley stayed in Callendar House, which stands in Callendar Park among pleasant woodland walks beside a boating lake. The house – which is not open to the public – forms a splendid centrepiece to the surrounding parkland and pitch and putt course.

CARRON VALLEY

A bridge across the River Carron, rushing in white tumult over its stony bed, leads to a charming picnic area among spruces. Here a wooden footbridge crosses to a grassy island within two arms of the river. Nearby, the Carron Valley Reservoir unfolds against a backdrop of thickly wooded hills. A forestry track leads away from the reservoir and forks right to the scanty ruins of Sir John de Graham's castle set on a plateau.

Just past Loch Walton a small bracken-clad knoll on the left is immediately followed by a lay-by from which a path leads over the hill to the Loup of Fintry. There Endrick Water cascades in long creaming falls to the valley below.

CULCREUCH CASTLE

The Galbraith clan built this imposing castle – which stands by a loch in wooded parkland above Fintry – in 1296. In 1630 the clan chief, Robert, fled to Ireland after murdering a guest. It has had various owners since then, and – together with its massive keep – is remarkably well preserved. There is a walled garden and a pinetum planted in 1842. The castle is open most days in summer, and travellers can spend the night in the castle.

Once past the castle, the road winds up through the lonely moorland of Campsie Fells, where sheep graze and brooding hills stand out against the sky. From the car park above Clachan of Campsie, an easy climb leads to a summit with extensive views over Campsie Glen. Lennox Castle, a 19th-century house which is now a nurses' home, stands in the valley.

COLZIUM HOUSE

Clearly signed beyond Kilsyth – and set among rhododendrons, poplars and landscaped gardens – Colzium House has a local history museum, open on Wednesday afternoons. Other rooms in the house, which include the banqueting hall and two rooms displaying paintings by local artists, can be seen on request to the caretaker. The walled gardens, in which grow heathers and conifers, are a favourite retreat in summer.

Nearby, the site of the battle in 1645, at which the Marquis of Montrose defeated the Covenanters, lies submerged beneath the waters of Banton Loch, a reservoir built in the 18th century. In drought years, various weapons from the battle have been found in the mud, including broadswords and cannonballs.

Not far away, at Dullatur, excavations have revealed a soldier on horseback, perfectly preserved in the peat bog in which he had become trapped when fleeing after the battle.

Passing on through open country, the route runs alongside the Forth and Clyde Canal, then crosses it at Banknock. From the narrow road across the canal can be seen traces of the Antonine Wall.

ROUGH CASTLE

One of the best-preserved sections of the Antonine Wall includes the fort called Rough Castle. The wall was built about AD 140 by the Roman army on the orders of Emperor Antonius Pius, and stretched 37 miles from Forth to Clyde to form the north-western frontier of the Roman Empire for 20 years. It consisted of a turf rampart on a stone base, fronted by a ditch more than 40ft wide and 12ft deep, and there were forts at intervals of about 2 miles.

The wall was built less than ten years after Hadrian's Wall, 20 miles to the south, which was abandoned for some 15 years in favour of this new frontier. There were at least 16 forts, and most were built behind the wall, with stone granaries, bathhouse and headquarters. Each had its own ramparts; at Rough Castle these were 20ft thick, with narrow double ditches. Rough Castle was one of the smaller wall forts. Its ramparts and ditches survive, though no stone buildings are visible.

TOUR 222

— 37 MILES —

Quiet country roads dip and rise through rural uplands, past rounded hills and remote farms. This tranquil oasis seems far away from the bustle of the communities by the Forth.

LINLITHGOW

The old vies with the new in this small, historic town. But the modern buildings on the west side do not detract from the charm of the Square, with its central Well Cross, elaborately carved by a one-handed stonemason in 1807. It stands in front of the imposing 17th-century Town House, with a double flight of balustraded steps. Beside it is the white, roughcast Cross House.

From the Cross, Kirkgate leads up through an arched gateway to St Michael's Church and the ruins of Linlithgow Palace. Set on the gentle slopes of a grass mound overlooking Linlithgow Loch, the mellow ochre walls of the palace rise to five storeys – forming a roofless square. One of Scotland's four royal palaces, it was built in the 15th century for James I of Scotland and was the birthplace of James V in 1512. It is open daily.

After the 13th century, many of Scotland's kings and queens worshipped in the nearby Gothic Church of St Michael. The church was restored in the 19th century, and in 1964 its tower was topped by an aluminium 'Crown of Thorns'.

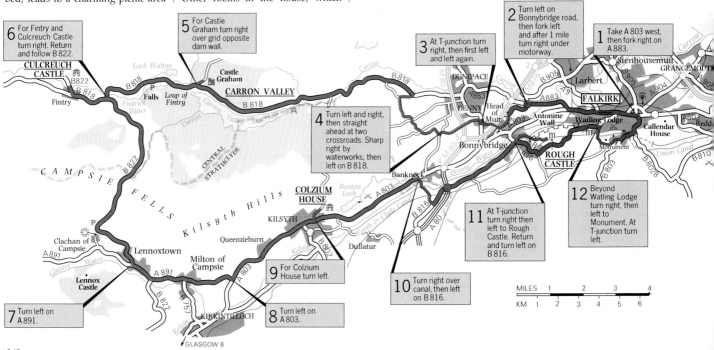

6 For Fintry and Culcreuch Castle turn right. Return and follow B 822.

5 For Castle Graham turn right over grid opposite dam wall.

2 Turn left on Bonnybridge road, then fork left and after 1 mile turn right under motorway.

3 At T-junction turn right, then first left and left again.

1 Take A 803 west, then fork right on A 883.

4 Turn left and right, then straight ahead at two crossroads. Sharp right by waterworks, then left on B 818.

9 For Colzium House turn left.

11 At T-junction turn right then left to Rough Castle. Return and turn left on B 816.

12 Beyond Watling Lodge turn right, then left to Monument. At T-junction turn left.

10 Turn right over canal, then left on B 816.

7 Turn left on A 891.

8 Turn left on A 803.

MILES 1 2 3 4
KM 1 2 3 4 5 6

COCKLEROY

From the car park, a path leads through a dense pinewood to a stile from which a short walk over turf and vivid green patches of moss climbs to the top of Cockleroy.

On a nearby cairn, a plaque points to 36 landmarks which can be seen on a clear day – including Goat Fell, 66 miles away, on the island of Arran.

TORPHICHEN PRECEPTORY

The Scottish Order of the Knights of St John of Jerusalem was founded in Torphichen in 1153. All that remains of the preceptory are the 13th-century tower and vaulted transepts – although the nave, rebuilt in the 18th century, is now the parish church.

The preceptory is set amid lawns backed by bracken-clad hills, and is open most days in summer.

CAIRNPAPPLE HILL

A short, easy climb from the road leads up the hill to a windswept, prehistoric burial ground – with extensive views in all directions. On this bleak summit there was once a circle of large stones within a ditch, forming a Stone Age temple. Later a cairn, or burial tomb, was built. This has been restored, and visitors can enter to see the burial cists, or chambers. It is open daily, except Fridays in summer and Monday afternoons in winter.

BEECRAIGS COUNTRY PARK

Within its 700 acres, Beecraigs offers all kinds of activities – including woodland walks, sailing and canoeing on the loch, fly fishing, archery, orienteering, rock-climbing and visits to a red deer farm and a trout farm.

HOPETOUN HOUSE

The simple, classical beauty of this mansion is best appreciated from the end of the avenue leading to it. The heart of the house was begun in 1699. An extra storey and two wings – with

BELOW THE FINTRY HILLS *Modern Fintry sprawls across the valley floor, watched over by the grandmotherly Culcreuch Castle.*

HOPETOUN HOUSE *Sir William Bruce, who rebuilt Edinburgh's Holyrood Palace, built the original house, which was later enhanced by the elegant architecture of the Adam family. The rooms are superbly furnished, and hung with oil paintings.*

domed, octagonal towers – were designed by William Adam in the 18th century and completed by his sons.

The home of the Marquis of Linlithgow, the house is sumptuously furnished, with walls lined with silk damask, and hung with paintings by Rembrandt, Van Dyck, Titian, Reubens and Canaletto among others. The formal gardens give unbroken views across the Forth. The house is open at Easter and in the summer, and the garden centre is open daily.

THE BINNS

The father of General Tam Dalyell (pronounced 'Di-el'), who raised the Royal Scots Greys here in 1681, built this manor house in 1612-30. The grounds, crowned by a viewing tower, have woodland walks and picnic areas.

The house has handsome plaster ceilings and antique furniture, and contains several of General Tam's possessions, including his sword and Bible. Known by his troops as 'Bluidy Tam', he ruthlessly suppressed the Covenanters – who sought civil and religious freedom – and was said to be on speaking terms with his ally, the Devil. The house is open most days in summer, and the grounds daily.

BLACKNESS CASTLE

Lapped by water on three sides, Blackness Castle thrusts out into the Firth of Forth, the northern limit of its walls pointed like the prow of a massive battleship. The castle's first historical mention was in 1449, when it served as a state prison. Cromwell's troops captured the castle in 1650 during their conquest of Scotland. Covenanters were imprisoned there in the first half of the 17th century. After 1707, when England and Scotland finally became united, it was kept in repair with a small garrison. It is open daily.

BO'NESS

The Scottish Railway Preservation Society runs the Bo'ness and Kinneil Railway from Bo'ness, beside the Firth of Forth. Steam trains run every weekend in summer from the neat station, built from old station buildings salvaged from around the country.

Just to the east, at Bridgeness, is the eastern end of the Antonine Wall. As each section was completed, commemorative 'distance slabs' were put up, and a replica of one such slab is now set in a wall by the tower at Bridgeness.

KINNEIL HOUSE

A steep, twisting drive above the Firth of Forth leads to Kinneil House, built in the mid-16th century by the 2nd Earl of Arran on the line of the Antonine Wall. Added to over the years, it fell into disrepair and in 1936 it was due to be demolished. As workmen attacked the decaying walls, 16th and 17th-century wall paintings were uncovered in two of the first-floor rooms. These chance discoveries saved the building, and its wall and ceiling paintings can be seen.

In the Arbour Room are paintings of two periods, the 16th and 17th centuries. The earlier paintings are a riot of foliage intermingled with birds, animals and heraldic beasts. Set high on the walls are roundels depicting Samson and Delilah, the Temptation of Anthony, the Sacrifice of Isaac, and David and Bathsheba. The paintings in the Parable Room include a panel of six cartoons showing the Parable of the Good Samaritan. The house is open most days throughout the year.

In a small building at the back of the house, James Watt built his first full-scale steam engine, in 1769.

Nearby Kinneil Museum covers the history of the estate; it is open daily in summer except on Sundays. Also in the grounds is an excavated Roman fortlet of the Antonine Wall.

Tourist information:
Linlithgow 844600.

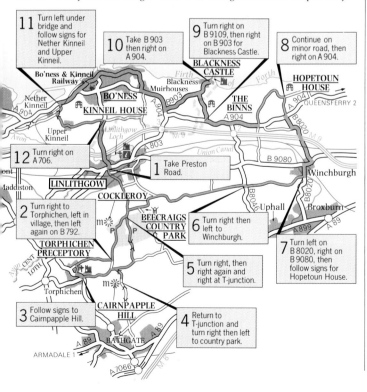

11 Turn left under bridge and follow signs for Nether Kinneil and Upper Kinneil.

10 Take B 903 then right on A 904.

9 Turn right on B 9109, then right on B 903 for Blackness Castle.

8 Continue on minor road, then right on A 904.

BLACKNESS CASTLE
Bo'ness & Kinneil Railway
Blackness Muirhouses
Nether Kinneil
BO'NESS
KINNEIL HOUSE
Upper Kinneil
Firth of Forth
THE BINNS
A 904
HOPETOUN HOUSE
QUEENSFERRY 2

12 Turn right on A 706.

1 Take Preston Road.

Linlithgow Loch
Union Canal
B 9080
Winchburgh

LINLITHGOW
COCKLEROY

2 Turn right to Torphichen, left in village, then left again on B 792.

6 Turn right then left to Winchburgh.

BEECRAIGS COUNTRY PARK
Uphall
Broxburn

TORPHICHEN PRECEPTORY
Torphichen

5 Turn right, then right again and right at T-junction.

7 Turn left on B 8020, right on B 9080, then follow signs for Hopetoun House.

3 Follow signs to Cairnpapple Hill.

CAIRNPAPPLE HILL
BATHGATE

4 Return to T-junction and turn right then left to country park.

ARMADALE 1

Valleys below the rugged Ochil Hills

TOUR
223
— 63 MILES —

The distant Ochils drop down to the flat Forth valley, with the fortified town of Stirling on its crag. Beyond nearby Bannockburn lies a port where the 16th century lives on.

DUNFERMLINE

Standing above the town like sentinels, Dunfermline's abbey and palace recall the days when this was the capital of Scotland. Pittencrieff Park slopes away to the south and west, and the town is spread out below – an endearing mixture of ancient ruins, Scottish baronial and modern architecture. In the 18th and 19th centuries the town was a prosperous textile centre, noted for its fine linen.

From a terraced car park, steps lead up to the abbey and ruined palace. The original abbey was founded for Benedictine monks by Margaret, saint and queen, the wife of Malcolm Canmore – Malcolm III – in the 11th century. Frequently sacked and burnt over the centuries, the present building is a jigsaw of different styles and periods. The nave dates from the 12th century.

In the 19th century, during the building of the present church on the site of the old abbey choir, a stone coffin was found. It contained the skeleton of the early 14th-century Scottish monarch, Robert Bruce. The breastbone had been severed for the removal of his heart, which now lies in Melrose Abbey. After the discovery the royal remains were re-interred and are under a brass plate in the church. The square, central tower has a parapet with the words 'King Robert the Bruce' in stone lettering extending around four sides. Dunfermline is a traditional burial place for Scottish kings, and Malcolm III and Queen Margaret lie in a shrine to the east of the abbey.

The palace – built by Malcolm III and rebuilt in 1500 by James IV – fell into disrepair in the 17th century. Its ruins are opposite the abbey church. The abbey is open daily.

Opposite the abbey, a gate leads into Pittencrieff Park, which was given to the town by its most renowned son – the millionaire philanthropist Andrew Carnegie (1835-1919). As a boy, Carnegie, the son of a poor weaver, was not allowed into the privately owned park. He later emigrated to America, made his fortune in steel, and bought the park on a return visit to Dunfermline. He gave it to the town so that 'no wee child should ever feel locked oot of it, as I was'. The public can stroll among beautiful shrubs, flowers and fine trees, along the steep sides of a wooded glen, with a burn tumbling below.

Just above the burn are the remains of Malcolm Canmore's Tower. He and his wife lived there before their palace was built. Not far away is Pittencrieff House, built in 1610; it has a typical projecting staircase turret and, on the upper floor, a barrel ceiling of richly carved plaster. The house is open in summer as a costume museum, with exhibits from about 1800 and local history displays.

A short walk from the abbey is Andrew Carnegie's birthplace, at the junction of Moodie Street and Priory Lane. The old weaver's cottage is furnished as it might have been in Carnegie's youth, and the adjoining Memorial Hall has displays on the millionaire's life and charitable works. The exhibits include a re-creation of Carnegie's study, with a model of him seated at his desk, and a 'Dunfermline Heritage' room. The cottage and hall are open daily.

RUMBLING BRIDGE

It would be easy to cross the River Devon at Rumbling Bridge without realising what lies below, so narrow and steep is the tree-clad gorge. Immediately beyond the bridge, a gate on the right leads to a path that skirts this breathtaking chasm, more than 120ft deep, yet remarkably narrow in places.

A riverside walk winds upriver from the bridge, securely fenced to allow safe views of the spectacular gorge. Green ferns, climbing plants and trees grow out of the limestone rock face, and the river cascades in rumbling torrents far below.

Picnic areas have been laid out along the walk, up to Devil's Mill where the thumping noise of the water on the boulders is reminiscent of a mill. At Cauldron Linn, downstream from the bridge, the waterfall has a double cascade, particularly impressive after rain. The present bridge, built in 1816, spans the old one, built in 1713 – and this leapfrog effect is clearly seen from the path. The lower bridge, very narrow and without a parapet, was once the main highway. Beyond Rumbling Bridge the road twists through purple moorland, between banks topped by beeches and neat hedges, skirting the Ochils. After crossing the main road, a single-track lane climbs into the Ochil foothills.

CASTLE CAMPBELL

This ruined fortress soars in lofty isolation on a narrow spur above the rocky, tree-lined ravines of the Burn of Care and the Burn of Sorrow, backed by a dramatic crescent of bracken-covered hills. The approach road drops steeply down from the car park past a footbridge over a rushing burn and then on up into the Ochil Hills, up Dollar Glen, with its numerous paths, to the castle.

The fortress, once known as Castle Gloom, has a 14th-century square tower joined to a 16th-century wing. The tower is the most complete part of the castle buildings, with massive walls and an overhanging parapet.

The site was a stronghold of the Stewarts of Innermeath and Lorne, but was later acquired, through marriage, by the Campbells of Argyll, who in 1489 changed its name by Act of Parliament. In the 1650s it was garrisoned by the English, who, under General George Monck, eventually set fire to it. The castle gradually fell into disrepair, and by the late 19th century was in a tumbledown condition.

The castle is in the care of the Ancient Monuments branch of the Scottish Development Department. It is open to the public on most days throughout the year.

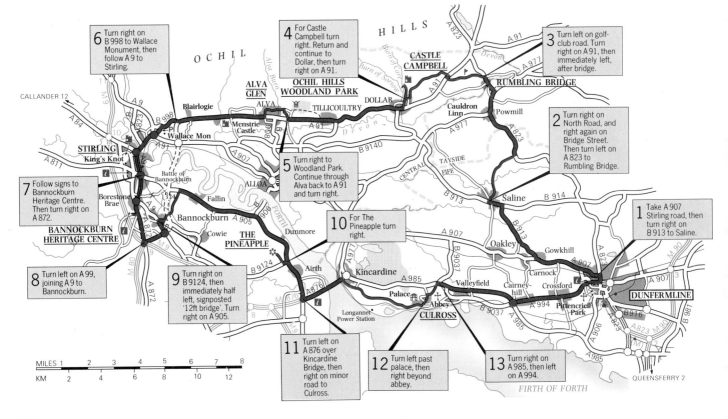

OCHIL HILLS WOODLAND PARK

The Ochils brood over a wide, wooded valley running west from Dollar through the old mill town of Tillicoultry. A clearly marked track leads past a farmstead to the Ochil Hills Woodland Park, which has a car park and a children's play area. A footpath winds back through the woods to Tillicoultry, giving extensive views across the valley.

ALVA GLEN

A plaque beside the Johnson Arms on the corner of Brook Street indicates zigzag walks up to MacArthur Braes and into Alva Glen, a dramatic gorge cut into the Ochils. There are silver mines, waterfalls and spectacular views across the lowlands below the Forth estuary.

About 2½ miles west is the 16th-century Menstrie Castle, which rises from the middle of a modern housing estate. The castle was the birthplace of Sir William Alexander (1567-1640), statesman and poet, who under James VI of Scotland (James I of England) was in charge of the colonisation of Nova Scotia in 1621. There are two commemorative rooms open to the public on Wednesday, Saturday and Sunday afternoons in summer. Blairlogie, 1½ miles farther west, is reached by turning off the main road through a concealed entrance, marked The Square. The tiny village is an enchanting muddle of old houses built along narrow winding streets on a ledge below the Ochils.

STIRLING

Halfway up the 360ft Abbey Craig, a footpath from the car park climbs to the Wallace Monument, 220ft high and visible for miles around. Overlooking the site of the Battle of Stirling Bridge – where the Scottish nationalist Sir William Wallace's troops defeated Edward I's army in 1297 – this towering memorial contains his 5ft 4in long sword.

There are audio-visual shows telling the battle's history and a Hall of Heroes, with busts of some of Scotland's most celebrated sons. A staircase of 246 steps twists up to a parapet with dizzying views across the Carse of Forth to Stirling Castle on its rocky perch.

Rising abruptly from the flat plains, the fortress-crowned rock – with the town of grey stone clinging to its steep slopes – is an impressive sight. Stirling was sited at the highest navigable point of the River Forth, guarding the main north-south and east-west routes across Scotland. From the town centre, signs point the way uphill to the castle past an unfinished, 16th-century mansion house called Mar's Wark – intended as the home of the regent, the Earl of Mar – and the Church of the Holy Rude. The castle is open throughout the year, and admission tickets – which include a ten-minute introductory film – can be bought at the visitor centre off the castle esplanade.

The castle was first mentioned historically in the 12th century, when it was the home of the Scottish monarch Alexander I. In 1174 Henry II of England took it as part payment for the release of William the Lion, King of Scotland, who was captured at the Battle of Alnwick. At that time the castle was made mostly of timber; it was rebuilt in stone in the 13th century. From then on, there were frequent alterations, additions and restorations.

From the castle there is a view of a curious, geometrically stepped grass mound, officially known as the King's Knot. It lies at the centre of a 'knot garden' – so called because of its intricate design – which was once part of the King's Park. It is easy to see why locals have dubbed the Knot the Cup and Saucer.

BANNOCKBURN CENTRE

A heritage centre at Borestone Brae, scene of some of the fighting in the Battle of Bannockburn in June 1314, tells the story of Robert Bruce's victory over the forces of Edward II, which established Robert as king of the independent Scots. There is a shop, as well as a tearoom and a car park leading to the Bruce Memorial Statue. The centre is open daily from March to October.

The present village of Bannockburn, to the south-east of the battle site, grew up in the 19th century when the Industrial Revolution brought mills to the area. Behind the village there are fine views of Stirling flanked by the Wallace Monument at Abbey Craig.

THE PINEAPPLE

A National Trust for Scotland sign points the way to The Pineapple, a 45ft retreat, built in 1761 and standing in a 16 acre walled garden. Young trees and grass are all that is left of the garden, but perched on the back wall is a vast carved stone pineapple. There are records of pineapples being grown in Scotland in 1732, and there may have been greenhouses for their cultivation here. The garden is open all year. Farther on, the Longannet Power Station overlooks the twisting road along the northern shore of the Firth of Forth.

CULROSS

Driving into this once bustling port is like travelling backwards in time. For Culross – which stands on the shores of the Firth of Forth – has been preserved by the National Trust for Scotland as a perfect example of a small Scottish burgh of the 16th and 17th centuries. Its steep, narrow, cobbled streets and wynds should be explored on foot. They go past restored cottages, Bishop Leighton's house, known as The Study, the old mercat (market) cross in the tiny square, and on up to the Cistercian abbey which stands above the town. The abbey was founded in 1217 by Malcolm, Earl of Fife, and dedicated to St Mary and St Serf. A religious building is thought to have stood on the lofty site since about the 6th century AD, when St Serf rescued the infant St Mungo, the patron saint of Glasgow, whose mother was washed up on the shore on the eve of his birth.

Level with the firth is Culross Palace, built between 1597 and 1611 by a prosperous salt and coal merchant, Sir George Bruce. As Bruce's wealth expanded, so did his house.

The palace has a steeply sloping walled garden and boasts some fine paintings on walls and ceilings. It is open daily throughout the year.

Tourist information: Dunfermline 720999 (summer); Stirling 75019; Bannockburn 812664 (summer); Kincardine Bridge 422 (summer); Forth Bridge 417759 (summer).

CASTLE CAMPBELL *A natural amphitheatre backs the 600-year-old ruined fortress, once called Castle Gloom.*

SUNLIT SLOPES *Light and shadow work their magic on the Ochil Hills, rising in splendour behind woodland.*

CULROSS *Cottages in pink and white welcome the visitor to this charming old royal burgh, which was once a thriving port.*

Through Royal and Ancient Fife

TOUR
224

—— 81 MILES ——

Behind St Andrews, hills stretch between the Firths of Forth and Tay. The Picts created a kingdom here; the Stuarts built a royal palace; and the ruins of a once powerful abbey remain.

ST ANDREWS
Much of the pale grey and golden stone used to build the old houses in St Andrews was taken from what was once the largest cathedral in Scotland, now a majestic ruin on the eastern edge of the town. Beside it stands the 12th-century St Rule's Tower, named after the saint who, according to legend, was shipwrecked here in the 8th century, carrying the bones of the apostle St Andrew. Crosses in the cobbled streets mark the sites where martyrs were burnt at the stake.

On the western side of the town stands the Royal and Ancient Golf Club, the senior golf club in the world, with responsibility for determining the rules of the game. Beside the golf links, the West Sands stretch for more than 2 miles.

CRAIGTOUN COUNTRY PARK
Two miles from St Andrews the route passes the imposing entrance to Craigtoun Country Park. Its 50 acres of lawns, pastures and woodland, laid out around Mount Melville House, now a hospital, are open to the public.

Traces of the grandeur of Edwardian living are still discernible in the Italian garden and the castellated 'Dutch village' which raises its miniature white walls from the middle of an ornamental lake. The 'village', reached by a bridge, was built in 1918 as a place for afternoon teas and picnics; it is still in use.

LOWER LARGO
Just beyond Largoward the road starts its descent to the Forth, skirting the dramatic hump of Largo Law and giving fine views over the firth to the Lothian coast. It finally reaches the sea at Lundin Links. From here a short detour leads to Lower Largo with its whitewashed stone cottages, narrow streets and tiny, red-sandstone harbour. Alexander Selkirk, the original Robinson Crusoe, was born in Lower Largo in 1676; his goat-skin clad statue stands in the centre of the village.

LETHAM GLEN PARK
Immediately to the right of the roundabout on the outskirts of Leven is Letham Glen Park. Lawns and flowerbeds are laid out beside a burn, and a path leads to a nature centre which houses pets and domestic animals. Information about the wildlife in the park is also provided.

Craft exhibitions are held in the nature centre during July and August. Beyond it, a mile-long circular trail runs past the scant remains of Scotland's only ochre mine, which operated during the middle years of the last century. The trail continues into the woods of Sillerhole Glen with its oaks, elms, beeches and silver birches.

MARKINCH
The main street of Markinch appears suddenly as the route swings over the railway bridge at its southern end. At the northern end of the main street stands a small hill, with a church on its summit overlooking the whole burgh. Markinch parish church proudly proclaims that the Word of God has been preached from this hillock for 14 centuries. The present church dates from 1788, though its square tower is late Norman and is one of only five such towers in Scotland.

FALKLAND
The ancient burgh of Falkland clings to the lower slopes of the Lomond Hills. It looks out across the fertile Howe of Fife, once a royal forest, the haunt of deer and boar.

Falkland's magnificent Royal Palace was built in the 15th and 16th centuries as the hunting lodge of the Stuarts. It is a jewel of early Renaissance architecture. The buildings are compact and ornate, with thick walls and heavily barred windows as a precaution against attack. Much of the palace has been restored.

Gardens and orchards are laid out behind the palace to the 17th-century royal plans. In the midst of them is the Royal Tennis Court, the oldest tennis court in Britain, built in 1539. The palace and gardens are maintained by the National Trust for Scotland. They are open daily from April to September.

Beyond the railings in front of the palace is the High Street, lined with quaint old stone houses. And beyond the market square the High Street becomes a narrow, winding lane as it follows the Maspie Burn and climbs the wooded shoulder of East Lomond Law. On the summit, at Craigmead, is an extensive car park and picnic area. Walks are marked to the heights of each of the nearby Lomond Hills, and the view in all directions is stupendous.

LOCH LEVEN
Along the southern shore of Loch Leven there are fine views of the loch, the hills that surround it and St Serf's Island, on which stand the remains of a 12th-century priory. The loch is a nature reserve, and many species of waterfowl breed on it. Autumn evenings see the arrival of hundreds of migrating geese; and in winter small flocks of waders huddle together on the shore. The Royal Society for the Protection of Birds has an observation hut at Vane Farm, on the southern shore.

HILLTOP HARMONY *Hill of Tarvit Mansion House and its gardens blend perfectly into the panorama of the Howe of Fife valley.*

MUSEUM PIECE *The Fife Folk Museum at Ceres is housed in two cottages and a 17th-century Tolbooth weigh house, itself a relic of a past way of life.*

FALKLAND PALACE *Once a Stuart residence, the palace is owned by the Queen.*

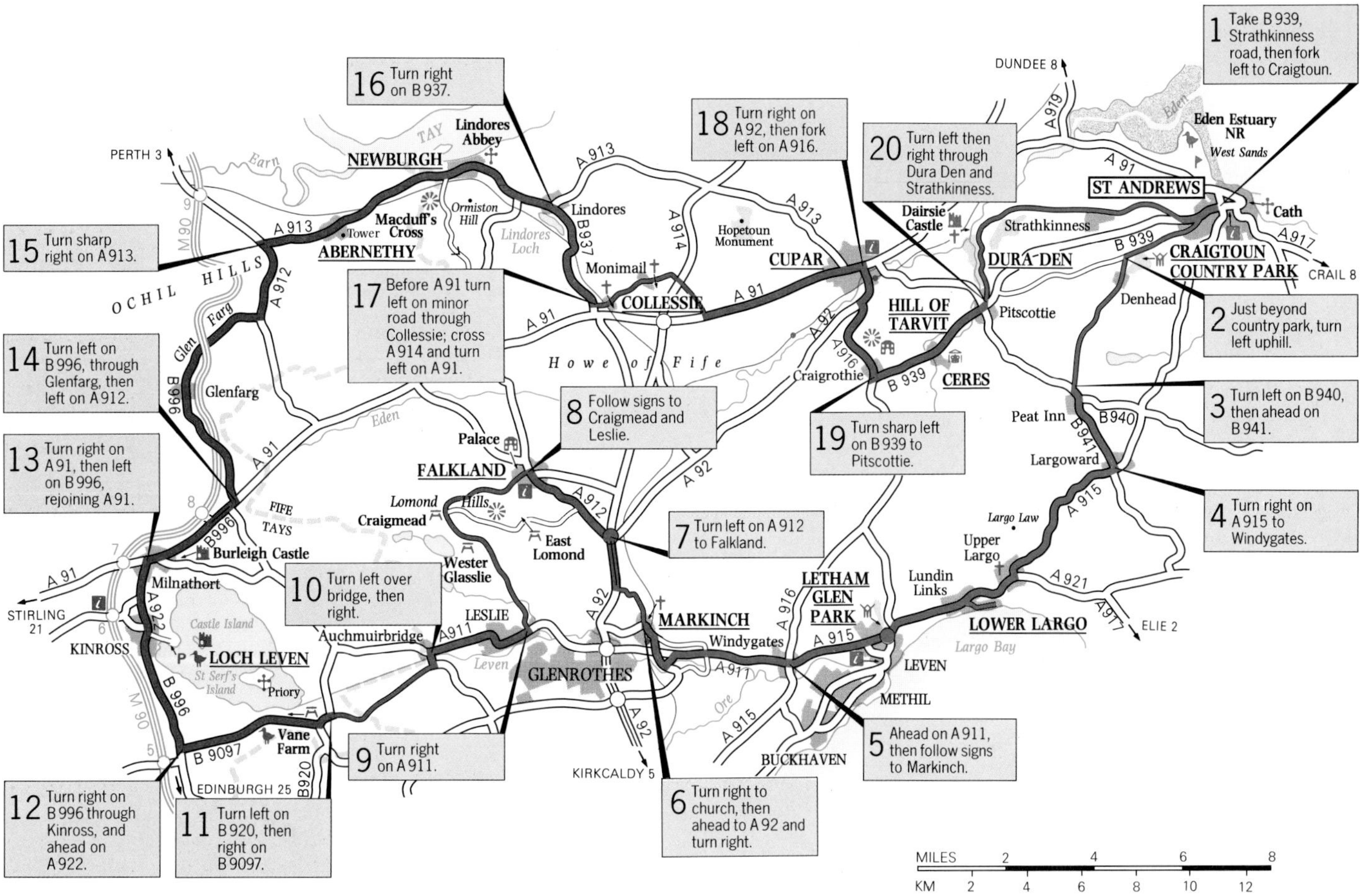
1 Take B939, Strathkinness road, then fork left to Craigtoun.
2 Just beyond country park, turn left uphill.
3 Turn left on B940, then ahead on B941.
4 Turn right on A915 to Windygates.
5 Ahead on A911, then follow signs to Markinch.
6 Turn right to church, then ahead to A92 and turn right.
7 Turn left on A912 to Falkland.
8 Follow signs to Craigmead and Leslie.
9 Turn right on A911.
10 Turn left over bridge, then right.
11 Turn left on B920, then right on B9097.
12 Turn right on B996 through Kinross, and ahead on A922.
13 Turn right on A91, then left on B996, rejoining A91.
14 Turn left on B996, through Glenfarg, then left on A912.
15 Turn sharp right on A913.
16 Turn right on B937.
17 Before A91 turn left on minor road through Collessie; cross A914 and turn left on A91.
18 Turn right on A92, then fork left on A916.
19 Turn sharp left on B939 to Pitscottie.
20 Turn left then right through Dura Den and Strathkinness.
DUNDEE 8
PERTH 3
STIRLING 21
EDINBURGH 25
KIRKCALDY 5
ELIE 2
CRAIL 8
ST ANDREWS
Eden Estuary NR
West Sands
Cath
CRAIGTOUN COUNTRY PARK
Denhead
Strathkinness
DURA DEN
Dairsie Castle
Pitscottie
HILL OF TARVIT
CUPAR
Hopetoun Monument
Craigrothie
CERES
Peat Inn
Largoward
Largo Law
Upper Largo
Lundin Links
LOWER LARGO
Largo Bay
LEVEN
METHIL
BUCKHAVEN
LETHAM GLEN PARK
Windygates
MARKINCH
GLENROTHES
LESLIE
Leven
Ore
Auchmuirbridge
Wester Glasslie
East Lomond
Lomond Hills
Craigmead
FALKLAND
Palace
Howe of Fife
COLLESSIE
Monimail
Lindores
Lindores Loch
Ormiston Hill
Lindores Abbey
NEWBURGH
TAY
Earn
Macduff's Cross
Tower
ABERNETHY
OCHIL HILLS
Glen Farg
Glenfarg
Eden
FIFE TAYS
Burleigh Castle
Milnathort
KINROSS
Castle Island
LOCH LEVEN
St Serf's Island
Priory
Vane Farm
M90
A91
A92
A911
A912
A913
A914
A915
A916
A917
A919
A921
A922
B920
B937
B939
B940
B941
B996
B9097
MILES 2 4 6 8
KM 2 4 6 8 10 12

Half a mile offshore, on Castle Island, stands the small, grey keep of a 15th-century fortress which held Mary, Queen of Scots prisoner for a year in 1567-8. Between April and September a ferry makes regular trips to the island.

ABERNETHY

The route into this ancient village skirts the Ochil Hills with the fertile Strathearn to the left. Abernethy is dominated by a slender round tower, built in the 11th century in the Irish Celtic style and one of only two such towers in Scotland. Set into its base is a superbly carved 7th-century stone slab decorated with mysterious Pictish symbols. Hanging from the base of the tower are the village jougs, an iron collar which used to be locked round the neck of a miscreant as a public humiliation before he was taken to the church for a formal reprimand.

Abernethy was a royal capital in Pictish times, and the centre of the Celtic church in Scotland for centuries. It was here, in the graveyard at the foot of the tower, that William the Conqueror received the homage of Malcolm Canmore, King of Scots, in 1072.

The key to the tower is kept at the post office, and the view from the top, 72ft above the little village square, is splendid. Strathearn, the mighty river Tay and the Carse of Gowrie stretch to the north; the medieval character of the old town can be seen in the orchards and vegetable strips that stretch behind the pantiled houses of the main street.

NEWBURGH

The prosperous 18th-century houses on either side of the broad main street were built by successful merchants and traders in the days when Newburgh was a thriving port. From the harbour, the town rises up craggy Ormiston Hill, near the summit of which stands the sandstone stump of MacDuff's Cross, an ancient monument. There are views down the Tay and across to the Grampians.

The red-sandstone ruins of Lindores Abbey, on the eastern outskirts of Newburgh, are all that remain of an ecclesiastical centre founded by the Benedictines in the 12th century. The image of a bear – the symbol of the abbey – has been cut in the turf on the hill opposite.

COLLESSIE

East of Newburgh the Ochil Hills become a cluster of small hillocks, each with views of different straths – broad valleys. Collessie village is built on top of one of the smallest and southernmost hillocks; its neat pantiled cottages cluster about the church, turning their backs on the fine view of the Howe of Fife beyond.

One and a half miles farther on, Monimail is hardly a village at all – more a hamlet which has grown up in the shadow of Melville House, the massive 18th-century seat of the Earls of Melville, now a school.

The small country road, overhung by mature oak and beech trees, passes a charming 18th-century church set in a neat clearing. Built in the Dutch style, with a central pulpit and box pews, the interior of the church has an austere elegance, complemented by Robert Adam's simple ceiling decoration, reminiscent of early Wedgwood china. It was built by the Melvilles, and a family gallery runs around three sides of the church.

CUPAR

The landscape on the left of the road into Cupar is dominated by the Hopetoun Monument, more than 100ft high. It was erected in 1826 in memory of the 4th Earl of Hopetoun who commanded the British Army during the last stage of the Peninsular War.

Cupar has all the cheerful bustle of a market town. Elegant 18th-century houses built of honey-coloured stone stand on either side of the broad main street, at one end of which is a mercat cross surmounted by a staff and unicorn and dated 1683.

HILL OF TARVIT

Fine views of the Howe of Fife open up as the road leaves Cupar and climbs Hill of Tarvit. The panorama from the monument on the summit of the hill is spectacular. This is reached either from the road or from the gardens of Hill of Tarvit Mansion House, built originally in the 17th century but rebuilt in 1906 by Sir Robert Lorimer. It is now in the care of the National Trust for Scotland and open each afternoon in summer, except Fridays.

The house, still occupied, provides an appropriately domestic setting for an excellent collection of 18th-century French and English furniture, tapestries, porcelain and paintings.

CERES

Ceres is the quintessential Fife village. As the road from Craigrothie approaches the village green, the sudden impression of pastoral peace is remarkable. The green itself is wide enough to accommodate an annual Highland Games, held to commemorate the Ceres men who fought at Bannockburn in 1314. Along one side of it bubbles the Ceres Burn, and on the other side is a row of low cottages built of mellow stone, with deep orange, pantiled roofs.

A 17th-century humpbacked bridge crosses the burn, and to the right an even older structure, the Bishop's Bridge, leads to the Fife Folk Museum. The museum displays the life of an agricultural community of a century or more ago.

DURA DEN

At Pitscottie crossroads, the Ceres Burn turns north into Dura Den, a wooded gorge where many fish fossils have been found. The ruins of a number of linen and jute mills stand on the bank of the stream, and close to where it joins the River Eden is a fine old bridge. Just above the bridge stand an ancient church and the ruined Dairsie Castle.

David II, the son of Robert Bruce, lived for a time in Dairsie Castle, although the present ruin dates mainly from the late 16th century. The church, built in 1621, has some fine carved gargoyles.

Tourist information: St Andrews 72021; Leven 29464; Kinross 63680 (summer); Cupar 53722 (summer).

Scottish Highlands

The drama of the Highlands starts not far north of Scotland's densely populated central belt. At their western end they rise in the lovely Trossachs, where passes swoop over birch-clad hills and down to crystal-clear lochs. Farther east the waters from long lochs and high peaks among the Grampians drop by rivers such as the Esk and the Tay to the lowlands of Strathmore, dotted with relics of Scottish history since the time of the Picts.

On the north-eastern shoulder of Scotland the main settlements cling to the coast, at the mouths of rivers lined by royal castles and patient anglers. Inland the traveller is soon heading up lonely wooded straths towards moorlands where cloud shadows chase each other across the heather. Noted salmon rivers such as the Spey, the Don and the Dee tumble over stony beds, and beyond their tree-lined banks is revealed the breathtaking scenery of the Cairngorm Mountains, among whose granite domes eagles and ptarmigans nest and patches of snow linger even in high summer. From Inverness the Great Glen slices south-westward across the country to a very different coastline. Here high peaks march beside long sea lochs, then crumble off into a fringe of spiky islands where sea birds wheel, wild flowers bloom and the saga of Bonnie Prince Charlie's ill-fated Uprising of 1745 seems a memory of only the day before yesterday.

Farther north uprears the wildest countryside in Britain. Few roads cut across the gaunt uplands of Caithness and Sutherland, and those that do are narrow ones, demanding caution. But for the adventurous motorist there is ample reward in the scenic grandeur of landscape formed from some of the world's oldest rocks, the utter peace and the sense of the supremacy of nature over man. Signs of the notorious 19th-century Highland Clearances remain in ruined crofts and in the fishing villages built to house the refugees along a rugged coastline that stretches to the northernmost tip of mainland Britain.

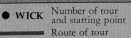

250 ● WICK — Number of tour and starting point

Route of tour

Rob Roy country beyond the Trossachs

Little more than a mile from a holiday resort's main street lies a world in which forests and soaring mountains are reflected in the clear waters of some of Scotland's most beautiful lochs.

CALLANDER

Set above the meadows of the meandering River Teith, and backed by steeply rising wooded hills, Callander is largely a Georgian and Victorian creation. The town centres around the gracious, late 18th-century Ancaster Square, where the houses still have many of their original features. These include guarded windows where stagecoach mail was delivered and, above the front doors, 'marriage lintels', on which the initials of the occupants and the date of their wedding were carved.

There are some splendid scenic walks around the town, including the Wood Walks which lead to steeper footpaths up the 1000ft Callander Crags. At nearby Bracklinn Falls the Keltie Water tumbles down a ravine.

PASS OF LENY

Beyond Callander the road suddenly enters a deep cleft in a wooded ridge. This is the entrance to the Pass of Leny, where the Lowlands abruptly cannon into the Highlands: it lies across the line of the Highland Boundary Fault, a deep fissure in the Earth's crust, which divides the Highlands from the Lowlands. Pathways follow an old charcoal-burners' track to a summit viewpoint.

STRATHYRE

Strathyre village, beyond the head of Loch Lubnaig, has a Forestry Commission visitor centre which is open daily in summer. A marked walk east of the road passes many specimen trees including Douglas fir, oak and willow.

By the roadside stands a memorial fountain to the Gaelic poet Dugald Buchanan, born in 1716 in old Strathyre, across the River Balvaig.

BALQUHIDDER

Directly west from the King's House Hotel, built in 1747 for Highland cattle drovers, is the valley of Balquhidder – the country of the outlaw Rob Roy Macgregor, whose exploits were romanticised by Sir Walter Scott. In the 18th century Rob Roy stole cattle from Lowland farmers, from whom he also levied 'protection money'.

Bright cottages and farmhouses line the first part of the Balquhidder road, where the hillsides rise steadily from the valley floor. Away to the west is the forbidding range of mountain peaks around Inverlochlarig, once Rob Roy's home.

Rob Roy died peacefully in 1734 at the age of 63 and was buried in the churchyard at Balquhidder. In 1975 a special service was held in the church, and a memorial plaque was placed over his grave and those of his wife Mary and two of their sons.

LOCHEARNHEAD

This water-sports centre on the shore of Loch Earn offers water-skiing, windsurfing, canoeing, dinghy sailing, angling and parascending – an exhilarating cross between water-skiing and parachuting.

Lochearnhead is also the starting point of a fine circular walk in the wooded Glen Ogle.

CRIANLARICH

The trim and pleasant village of Crianlarich is ringed by some of Scotland's mightiest mountains: Ben More, Stobinian, Cruach Ardrain and Ben Lui, all more than 3000ft high. To the south-west, the route winds down through the narrow Glen Falloch. All-weather footpaths lead to the Falls of Falloch, where the river cascades over a series of angled ledges to a dark rock pool below.

Near the foot of the glen is the Drovers' Inn of Inverarnan, built in 1705. A quarter of a mile above the inn, a footbridge over the River Falloch allows walkers on the West Highland Way to break off from the hard slog between the east side of Loch Lomond and Crianlarich.

TARBET

South of Ardlui, the Loch Lomond-side road winds past a succession of wooded shingle bays on the loch's western shore. There is a car park and picnic site at Inveruglas, with a spectacular hilltop viewpoint. The Loch Lomond pleasure cruiser calls at Tarbet pier. Other boats run their own summer cruises, and the linking timetables allow visitors to fit in walks along the roadless eastern shore.

LUSS

Restored cottages of reddish stone, with rose gardens, line the road to the pier in the village. The parish church was built in 1875 in memory of a Colquhoun laird who was drowned in a storm while sailing back from the deer-park island of Inchlonaig.

BALLOCH

On the way to Balloch, at Duck Bay, Auchendennan, a lochside parking and picnic area, has unsurpassed low-level views across to Ben Lomond. Offshore is Inchmurrin, the largest of the 30 or more islands on Loch Lomond.

Beyond Auchendennan, the Cameron estate contains a large pleasure park and children's playground open daily in summer.

Balloch lies at the southern end of Loch Lomond, with boatyards, moorings and a pier by the River Leven. The 200 acres of Balloch Castle Country Park beside the loch contain numerous conifers, azaleas and other shrubs. There is a walled garden and a Fairy Glen. The visitor centre, with information about the nature trails and guided walks in the summer, is situated in the old castle. The park is open to the public daily throughout the year.

Map labels:

TYNDRUM 2
Ben Lui
4 Turn left on A82.
ABERFELDY 20
Killin
Glen Dochart
Loch Tay
CRIANLARICH
A82
A85
Glen Falloch
Ben More
Falls of Falloch
Cruach Ardrain
3 Straight ahead, on A85.
LOCHEARNHEAD
Ardlui
CRIEFF 14
Loch Earn
Glen Ogle
BALQUHIDDER
Loch Voil
King's House Hotel
2 For Balquhidder turn left.
Inveruglas
Inversnaid Hotel
Ben Shian
STRATHYRE
5 Keep left on A82.
INVERARAY 18
Loch Arklet
Loch Lubnaig
PASS OF LENY
3 For Loch Katrine, straight ahead; then return and turn right.
Arrochar
TARBET
LOCH KATRINE
Ben Lomond
The Trossachs
BRIG O'TURK
Ben Ledi
2 Turn left on A821.
Falls of Leny
1 Take A84 west.
CALLANDER
Bracklinn Falls
THE DUKE'S ROAD
Loch Achray
Invertrossachs
Achray Forest
Samson's Stone
LOCH VENACHAR
Rowardennan Hotel
Loch Ard
Inverbeg
4 Fork left on A81.
ABERFOYLE
Loch Ard Forest
Priory
LAKE OF MENTEITH
Lake Hotel
DOUNE 1
Thornhill
Flanders Moss
LUSS
Inchlonaig
5 For lake, turn right on B8034.
STIRLING 6
Inchcailloch
DRYMEN
Inchmurrin
GARTOCHARN
Buchlyvie
KIPPEN
HELENSBURGH
Balloch Castle
Cameron
BALLOCH
6 Turn left on A811. At next roundabout turn left, then right on Balloch road.
8 Turn left through Drymen and rejoin A811.
9 Turn left on A81 then immediately right on A811.
10 Turn right on B8037 to Kippen; then left on B822 and straight across A811.
11 Turn left, still on B822, through Thornhill, joining A81 to Callander.
Alexandria
7 Turn left to country park. From park straight ahead, then left on A811.
GLASGOW 15

MILES 2 3 4 5 6 7 8
KM 2 4 6 8 10 12

GARTOCHARN

A side road in this charming village leads to the footpath up Duncryne Hill, from whose summit there is a superb all-round view. The wooded islands – Inchmurrin, Creinch, Torrinch and Inchcailloch – which march across Loch Lomond from Auchendennan mark the line of the Highland Boundary Fault.

DRYMEN

Although there is a pub here called The Three Dry Men, the village name comes from the Gaelic word *druim*, meaning 'a ridge'. The centre of the village is clustered around a small, 19th-century green. From the rose garden opposite the Buchanan Arms Hotel, a pathway leads to a hilltop viewpoint.

KIPPEN

Kippen is the largest village on the rising ground above the flat landscape of Flanders Moss – beyond which the Perthshire Highlands line the northern horizon. There are many carefully restored 18th and 19th-century houses in the main streets and down unobtrusive lanes.

The handsome parish church was built of red sandstone in 1827 and is set among well-tended lawns and gardens. Since 1924 it has undergone a long series of renovations, which were originally inspired by the Scottish painter Sir David Young Cameron, who worshipped at the church for almost 50 years until his death in 1945.

Tourist information: Callander 30342 (summer); (Balloch) Alexandria 53533 (summer).

TOUR
226
— 32 MILES —

The mountain passes, forests and lochsides of the Trossachs comprise a Highland world in miniature. The road climbs to heather-topped hills, then drops through birchwoods.

LOCH VENACHAR

On the far side of the River Leny, a picnic place behind a bank of broom leads to the public footpath along the old track-bed of the Callander to Oban railway. High up on Bochastle Hill, Samson's Putting Stone is the fanciful name for a boulder poised there in the wake of a retreating glacier about a million years ago.

Loch Venachar is popular with yachtsmen and small-boat sailors. On the south shore is Invertrossachs, a mansion house originally called Drunkie, but tactfully re-named before a visit by Queen Victoria.

BRIG O'TURK

This attractive and intriguingly named hamlet is not quite as exotic as it sounds – *tuirc* is Gaelic for a 'wild boar'. Beside the post office, in a building called the Post House, is a fascinating audio-visual display of

EVERGREEN HILLS *Mountain slopes clad with spruce, larch and pine shelter the waters of Loch Lubnaig, the 'curved loch'.*

RED BRIDGE *The graceful arches of Callander's sandstone bridge, built in 1908, span the River Teith. From the bridge there is a magnificent view of Ben Ledi.*

PORT OF MENTEITH *Small boats and a ferry use the lakeside harbour.*

FLOWERY WAY *Cottages at Luss line the street leading down to Loch Lomond.*

local wildlife. Beyond Brig o'Turk set among steep, wooded hills, is the watersports centre of Loch Achray.

LOCH KATRINE

The pass between Loch Achray and Loch Katrine is the authentic Trossachs – Gaelic for the 'bristly country' of abrupt little hills and valleys, heathery crags and tangled birchwoods.

Trossachs Pier has a car park below bare rock faces and towering cliffs. A visitor centre illustrates the work of the Lower Clyde Water Board, which supplies 100 million gallons of Loch Katrine water every day to the city of Glasgow and several Lowland towns. The turn-of-the-century steamer *Sir Walter Scott*, with its elegant red-and-white striped awnings, is based at the pier for summer cruises.

THE DUKE'S ROAD

Named after the Duke of Montrose, who built it as a carriageway in 1820, this magnificent route over the pass from Loch Katrine to Aberfoyle runs through the Queen Elizabeth Forest Park. There are many attractive walks, a superb hilltop viewpoint, a 7 mile forest road drive, and a course laid out for wayfaring – a less arduous and non-competitive form of orienteering. The Forestry Commission's visitor centre is in a lodge overlooking Aberfoyle.

ABERFOYLE

As well as enjoying this bright and bustling tourist resort, the visitor can explore the old slate quarries and the site of the Aberfoyle Quarries village in the hills above Aberfoyle. The village was abandoned in the 1930s.

Achray Forest covers the steep slopes to the north, while farther south and west there are forest walks in the gentler terrain of Loch Ard Forest.

LAKE OF MENTEITH

The only natural 'lake' in Scotland, this attractive stretch of water with its woodland fringe was called a loch until a Victorian map-maker mistakenly Anglicised it. At the north-east corner is the Lake Hotel with its tiny harbour, and a pier for the Inchmahome ferry.

Inchmahome is the largest of the three lake islands, with the beautifully preserved ruin of a 13th-century Augustinian priory set among lawns and woodland.

Tourist information: Callander 30342 (summer); Aberfoyle 352 (summer).

Lochs below the peaks of North Argyll

TOUR
227
——— 103 MILES ———

Along Argyll's jagged coastline great sea lochs thrust inland among wild Highland peaks. In a mountain cavern is the world's second largest hydroelectric power station.

OBAN

Rising in tiers above curving seafront streets, Oban is a bustling holiday resort and trading centre. It is built around Oban Bay, which is protected from the open waters of the Firth of Lorn by the flat-topped hills of the long green island of Kerrera. North from Oban, a road runs below the hilltop ruin of Dunollie Castle, seat of the MacDougall Lords of Lorn, who, in the 13th century, ruled over much of Scotland. Beyond lie the sandy beaches of Ganavan.

Two miles farther on, a side road leads to the ruin of the 13th-century Dunstaffnage Castle which overlooks a sheltered anchorage at the entrance to Loch Etive.

CONNEL

This Victorian village grew up after 1880 around a station on the newly opened Oban railway. A cantilever bridge across the narrows of Loch Etive straddles the Falls of Lora, where the reduced width of the sea loch and the presence of an under-water reef create rare saltwater falls at the ebb and flow of the tide.

The village church, St Oran, is based on the design of Iona Abbey. One of its stained-glass windows depicts the span of the bridge which can be seen, full size, outside.

Beyond Connel, the main road winds round a series of beautiful curving bays, then skirts the plantations of Fearnoch Forest. A road on the left leads to the garden of Achnacloich, open from early April to mid-June when its rhododendrons, azaleas and primulas are at their best.

GLEN NANT

Woods of oak, birch and hazel clothe both sides of this narrow glen – an unusual sight today in the West Highlands, where much of the natural tree cover has long since gone. Charcoal-burners once worked in the woods, making fuel for the iron furnace at Bonawe, near Taynuilt. The sites of several charcoal hearths can be seen on a forest trail starting from a signposted car park about 1¼ miles down a gravel road to the right, off the main road.

Beyond Glen Nant the route reaches more open country – rough moorland grazing – with splendid views north-eastwards to the peaks and ridges of Ben Cruachan.

KILCHRENAN

This remote village is the heart of a parish which takes in the hill country on both sides of Loch Awe. Built into one wall of the parish church is the tombstone of Sir Colin Campbell of Lochawe, the 13th-century founder of the family now headed by the Duke of Argyll.

A road to the left leads to the Victorian mansion of Ardanaiseig, now a hotel where woodland gardens with a collection of specimen trees and flowering shrubs are open from April to October.

Near Kilchrenan is the separate settlement of Taychreggan, once the north port of a busy ferry route across Loch Awe, the longest inland loch in Scotland, its three arms giving it a total length of 25½ miles. There is excellent fishing on Loch Awe, and boats can be hired. Catches include salmon and brown trout.

INVERLIEVER FOREST

A narrow and adventurous switch-back road through Inverliever Forest follows the west side of Loch Awe from Kilchrenan to Ford. Inverliever is the oldest state forest in Scotland, established in 1908.

Off the single-track road, north and south of the forestry village of Dalavich, are a number of waymarked forest walks. They take in hilltop viewpoints, waterfalls on the River Avich and River Inan, and the ruins of New York, a settlement established in the 18th century by the York Building Company of London. Red deer, roe deer and badgers live in the forest, while buzzards, sparrowhawks and, occasionally, golden eagles may be seen quartering the sky.

EREDINE FOREST

Along the narrow lochside road through the fringes of Eredine Forest there are informal picnic places at shingle bays. Occasional views through the screen of trees reveal islands like Innis Chonnell, with its ruined but still forbidding castle, the original stronghold of the Campbells of Lochawe.

There are no longer any ferries or cruises on Loch Awe, but boats may be hired at Portsonachan, the south port of the old ferry route from Tay-chreggan. Its Victorian fishing hotel is on the site of a ferry inn whose records go back to the 15th century.

From Portsonachan the route bends round the north-east corner of Loch Awe, providing a succession of striking views to secluded bays, wooded peninsulas and islands, and a splendid mountain skyline.

LAKESIDE FORTRESS *Kilchurn Castle, on Loch Awe, was used to house English troops during the 1745 uprising.*

NEW ROLE *Connel's former railway bridge now carries only road traffic.*

BARDIC CROWN *Duncan Ban MacIntyre's memorial stands above Dalmally.*

HIGH IDEAL *The banker, art critic and philanthropist John McCaig built the Colosseum-like tower above Oban in 1897, to provide work for the unemployed.*

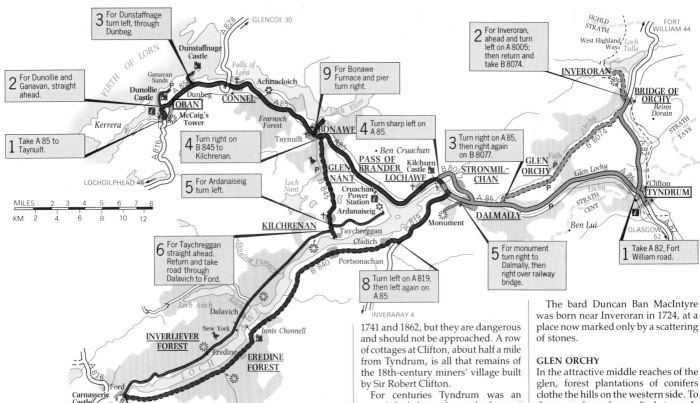

Box 3: For Dunstaffnage turn left, through Dunbeg.

Box 2: For Dunollie and Ganavan, straight ahead.

Box 1: Take A 85 to Taynuilt.

Box 4: Turn right on B 845 to Kilchrenan.

Box 5: For Ardanaiseig turn left.

Box 6: For Taychreggan straight ahead. Return and take road through Dalavich to Ford.

Box 7: Turn left on B 840.

Box 8: Turn left on A 819, then left again on A 85.

Box 9: For Bonawe Furnace and pier turn right.

Box 4: Turn sharp left on A 85.

Box 3: Turn right on A 85, then right again on B 8077.

Box 5: For monument turn right to Dalmally, then right over railway bridge.

Box 2: For Inveroran, ahead and turn left on A 8005; then return and take B 8074.

Box 1: Take A 82, Fort William road.

LOCHAWE

Like Connel, this holiday and angling resort developed in Victorian times round a station on the Oban railway. Its most important building is St Conan's Kirk, which was designed and built by Walter Campbell, owner of the island of Innis Chonain on Loch Awe.

Begun in 1881, the kirk is a deliberate mixture of elements of many centuries of church design, from an entirely ornamental cloister garth to a stately semicircular apse and a memorial chapel to Robert Bruce, who defeated the MacDougalls in a battle within sight of here in 1308.

PASS OF BRANDER

Beyond Lochawe village, the main road has so little space between the wooded cliffs to the right and the water's edge to the left that it has had to be built up on stilts as it heads for the narrow Pass of Brander. There the fields and woodlands on the far shore of Loch Awe give way to rocky crags and precipitous scree runs.

At the entrance to the pass is the North of Scotland Hydro-Electric Board's visitor centre for the Cruachan power station. Minibus tours along nearly a mile of road tunnel take visitors to see the machine hall, where the turbine generators hum in a vast cavern excavated from the heart of the mountain.

BONAWE

On rising ground above Loch Etive stand the meticulously restored ironworks of Bonawe Furnace. Established in 1753, the works smelted iron ore which was shipped in from Ulverston, using blast furnaces fuelled by charcoal produced in the local woodlands.

Inside the furnace, which is open daily from April to September, exhibitions explain the techniques of iron smelting and the history of Bonawe until production stopped in 1876.

Bonawe Pier is the base for summer cruises on Loch Etive, through magnificent scenery, in the lonely and roadless mountain country between Ben Cruachan and Glencoe.

Tourist information: Oban 63122/63551; Lochgilphead 2344 (summer).

TOUR
228
45 MILES
Cattle drovers passed this way on their journeys between the Highlands and Lowlands. Their route is now a long-distance path, through mountains that inspired a poet.

TYNDRUM

Majestic peaks, snow capped in winter, surround this village at the junction of Strath Fillan and the steep-sided Glen Lochy. Across Glen Lochy stands the 3708ft Ben Lui, with its spectacular northern corrie.

The best view in the village is the panorama of mountains and forests visible from Tyndrum Upper railway station. Near the base of Ben Lui can be seen the scar of abandoned lead mines which were worked between 1741 and 1862, but they are dangerous and should not be approached. A row of cottages at Clifton, about half a mile from Tyndrum, is all that remains of the 18th-century miners' village built by Sir Robert Clifton.

For centuries Tyndrum was an overnight halt on the cattle-drovers' route from Glencoe to the Lowlands. This became a military road in 1752, and was adopted in 1980 as part of the West Highland Way, a 95 mile long-distance path from Milngavie, north of Glasgow, to Fort William.

Just south of Tyndrum is Dail Righ, a narrow defile where, in 1306, Robert Bruce was ambushed by MacDougall of Lorne and barely escaped with his life.

Leaving Tyndrum on a sweeping climb, the 3530ft conical peak of Beinn Dorain soon comes into sight. This peak inspired the poetry of Duncan Ban MacIntyre, one of the most highly regarded Gaelic bards in the mid-18th century, when his poems were recited at firesides all over the Highlands.

BRIDGE OF ORCHY

This crossroads village is no more than a hotel, a railway station, a tiny church and a handful of houses. It is the only sizable settlement for miles in any direction, and its inhabitants have to be prepared to offer shelter to travellers delayed by winter snows.

The route turns left off the main Fort William road, across the bridge over the rocky course of the River Orchy, then runs above the shore of Loch Tulla, through the trees of a carefully preserved pine wood.

INVERORAN

As their cattle grazed at an overnight 'stance' at Inveroran, the old-time drovers would carouse at a lochside inn dismissed by the poet Robert Southey in 1819 as 'a wretched hovel'. Even as he wrote, it was being replaced by a coaching inn which is now a base for climbers, walkers, skiers and anglers. The view from the village is to the spectacular peaks and ridges, corries and cascading burns of the Black Mount deer forest.

The bard Duncan Ban MacIntyre was born near Inveroran in 1724, at a place now marked only by a scattering of stones.

GLEN ORCHY

In the attractive middle reaches of the glen, forest plantations of conifers clothe the hills on the western side. To the east, sheep farms climb towards craggy summits. But the great attraction is the River Orchy itself. There are parking places beside gentle stretches where fly fishermen concentrate on the rise of trout or salmon, and at a series of falls and rapids where the thundering river has carved channels through rugged outcropped rock.

STRONMILCHAN

A turning off the main road on the outskirts of Dalmally leads through the farming hamlet of Stronmilchan and provides a dramatic close-up view of the huge eastern corries of Ben Cruachan, rising to 3695ft.

Back on the main road, a half-mile footpath leads to the ruin of Kilchurn Castle, a Campbell stronghold strikingly placed on a low peninsula reaching out into Loch Awe. After centuries of neglect, its ancient walls are being preserved, but the roof timbers have long since gone into the building of the parish church.

DALMALLY

A centre for angling and hill-walking, Dalmally is another village which expanded after the arrival of the West Highland Railway. Many of its houses are built of Ben Cruachan granite, quarried by a workforce drafted from a Glasgow jail.

The pillared memorial to Duncan Ban MacIntyre on the summit of Monument Hill is an impressive viewpoint. A public road from Dalmally station finishes at a pass below the monument, from which there is a 200yd walk up to the top. Westwards, Loch Awe and its wooded islands are towered over by the majestic Cruachan range.

Tourist information: Tyndrum 246 (summer); Oban 63122/63551.

Mountains above the lochs of Mull

TOUR
229

— 105 MILES —

Sea lochs and cliffs fringe a beautiful island of forests and mountains. A Spanish galleon lies near its coast, and an ancient castle of the Macleans has been restored.

CRAIGNURE

Facing the deserted mainland hills of south-east Morvern across the Sound of Mull, Craignure sits at the foot of wooded cliffs which line a sheltered bay. As the port for the car ferry from Oban, the village is much busier than its size suggests. But not all the shipping calls in; other steamers pass by on their way through the Sound of Mull to and from Coll and Tiree, Barra and South Uist.

Just outside Craignure stands a signpost to Java Point, which recalls a former landowner who made his fortune in the East Indies. The route continues through forest and farmland, below brackeny hill slopes and above sweeping bays, with extensive views along the Sound of Mull. Beyond Scallastle Bay, a side road leads through conifer plantations to a picnic site and jetty at Fishnish.

GLEN FORSA

The route passes through deer-fenced farmland and scattered forest at the foot of Glen Forsa. To the south, up the valley of the well-known angling water of the Forsa river, stands one of Mull's most striking and well-proportioned mountains. The conical peak of Beinn Talaidh, 2496ft, is framed by the steeply angled slopes of neighbouring hills, in the heart of what was once an area of vast volcanic convulsions.

Between a Scandinavian-style hotel and the sea runs a grass airstrip, the only one on Mull. It is used by private planes, charter flights and the Air Ambulance service.

SALEN

This 'model' village was built early in the 19th century by a man who operated on a far grander scale on the other side of the world. Major General Lachlan Macquarie, born on Ulva, a smaller island off the west coast of Mull, became Governor of New South Wales, and is regarded as the 'Father of Australia'.

Salen is the pivot of the island's road system. A few white cottages and a hotel stand beside the main road, and several stone villas line a side road leading to a once-busy pier whose traffic has moved away. The village contains a number of fine craft workshops. Local fishing boats are beached beside Salen Bay, which curves into the narrow tidal estuary of the Aros River.

AROS COTT

The hamlet is attractively placed at the mouth of the Aros River beside an old stone bridge. On the hillside above, reached by the tree-lined lane to Aros Mains, stands the ruin of the 14th-century Aros Castle, one of a series of fortresses along the Sound of Mull. Each castle was in clear sight of two others, so that urgent messages could be passed by signal fires.

In 1608, James VI decided to bring the troublesome island chiefs finally to heel. He sent a fleet to Aros, and his viceroy, Lord Ochiltree, won the day without a shot being fired. The chiefs were invited to a conference, then entertained to dinner on the flagship. Finally, Ochiltree rose to announce that they could now consider themselves the king's prisoners, upped anchor and sailed away with them still on board.

AROS PARK

This wooded estate on a hillside running down to the sea was once the home of a family who devoted a great deal of effort to 'amenity' planting. It has been owned since 1954 by the Forestry Commission and is open to the public all year round.

From a grassy picnic place on the site of the former mansion house, a network of woodland walks leads round a peaceful loch overlooked by birch-banked crags, and past high,

thundering waterfalls. The Shore Path follows a ledge part-way up a rocky cliff; from here there is a fine landward view of Tobermory, where freshly colour-washed buildings – red, yellow, blue, beige and olive-green – front the bay.

TOBERMORY

The 'capital' of Mull was built on land bought in 1788 by the British Fisheries Society. It is laid out on a curving hillside round a splendid natural harbour.

Tobermory is a well-equipped holiday centre, especially popular with yachtsmen. In summer, a museum of local history is open in the old Baptist church. The malt-whisky distillery offers guided tours, and other Tobermory products range from pottery to exotically flavoured chocolate.

A wooded footpath follows the north side of the bay, below the hillside golf course, to Rubha na Gall lighthouse. Eastwards across the Sound of Mull is the entrance to Loch Sunart. On the silty bottom of the bay lie the remains of a galleon of the Spanish Armada, which was blown up while sheltering here in 1588. Legend says the vessel was the Armada's treasure ship, but latest research suggests it was in fact a warship and troop-carrier, with no gold on board.

West of Tobermory the route climbs back into the hills, past conifer plantations and the trout waters of the Mishnish lochs and Loch an Torr. Beyond Loch an Torr, the road hairpins up through woodlands to a cairn from which there is a distant view of Loch Frisa, the largest freshwater loch in Mull, nestling in a narrow valley banked by forest. Beinn Talaidh stands clear on the south-east horizon.

DERVAIG

The road winds downhill again to the village of Dervaig, most of which lines a short side road leading to a pleasant walk above Loch a' Chumhainn, a narrow and rocky inlet of the sea.

A fine stone bridge spans the Bellart river which flows through saltings to Loch a' Chumhainn. Overlooking the bridge stands Kilmore parish church, which has an unusual Irish-style pencil tower dating from the church's rebuilding in 1905.

Dervaig has what is probably the smallest professional theatre in Britain. Mull Little Theatre, housed in a converted barn, produces plays with a cast of two to four, in front of an audience limited to 40.

The route continues through a moorland glen, into forest plantations and then down the valley of the Aros River to return to Salen, where it turns off to circle the spectacular mountains of southern Mull.

GRULINE

As the road approaches the head of Loch na Keal, a sign erected by the National Trust of Australia points past Gruline Home Farm, to the mausoleum, in a walled grass enclosure, of Major General Lachlan Macquarie. Gruline estate was Macquarie's home on Mull in his later life.

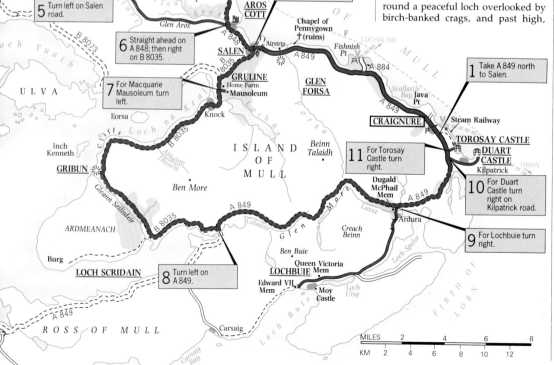

PEACEFUL WATERS *The stony bay of Loch Beg is tucked away at the head of Loch Scridain on Mull's remote west coast. In the distance is the 2354ft summit of Ben Buie.*

Beyond Gruline, an attractive lochside road wanders above the rocky shore. At the mouth of Loch na Keal lies Ulva, an island of flat grassy terraces and low guardian cliffs. This was General Macquarie's birthplace.

The view inland changes from rounded foothills to the sculptured summit peak of Ben More. At 3169ft it is the highest mountain on any of the Scottish islands apart from Skye. Hill walkers often approach Ben More by the Dhiseig Burn which tumbles down the north-western corrie.

GRIBUN
At the mouth of Loch na Keal the coast road bends to the south at the towering, 1000ft basalt cliffs of Gribun. Some rise directly from the roadside, and others are at the top of almost impossibly steep-looking grass slopes. Rock falls are common, and this is not a place in which to linger.

From the brow of the hill beyond a tiny crofting hamlet there is a magnificent seaward view, to the distant outline of the Treshnish Isles and the nearer island of Staffa. A look through binoculars reveals, at the southern end of Staffa, the great basalt columns around Fingal's Cave, home of the legendary Celtic hero Finn mac Cool.

LOCH SCRIDAIN
Over a pass from Gribun, the route runs down through forest to Loch Scridain, a long sea loch separating the hilly peninsulas of Ardmeanach and the Ross of Mull. Nearing the

tangle of salt marsh at the head of Loch Scridain there are striking views north to Ben More. Then the route heads up the long, wild, glaciated valley of Glen More, littered with boulders left behind by the retreating ice sheets.

Over the watershed, the road comes down through forest to the junction at Ardura. A memorial tower here commemorates Dugald McPhail, composer of the island's Gaelic anthem, *An t'Eilean Muileach* – 'The Island of Mull'. The memorial was built of stones from the long-since ruined house in Glen More where McPhail was born.

LOCHBUIE
From the road junction at Ardura, through woods of birch and hazel, a detour from the main route makes for the stony bays of Loch Spelve. Above the head of the loch rise the impressively rugged ravines of 2289ft high Creach Beinn. Less than half a mile of flattish land separates the saltwater Loch Spelve from the attractive freshwater Loch Uisg, which is dominated to the north by substantial wooded crags.

To the right of the lochside road to Lochbuie stands a stone pyramid erected by 'Lochbuie and his Highlanders' on the occasion of Queen Victoria's Diamond Jubilee. He was the chief of the Maclaines of Lochbuie, who took their hereditary title from the sea loch and village at the end of the road. By the shore of the loch stands another monument,

of triangular design, commemorating Edward VII.

At Lochbuie a scattering of houses set back from a gorse-lined road look south-west to the open sea. A half-mile walk along the loch shore leads to the 15th-century Moy Castle, once the Maclaine stronghold. Entry to the castle is now prohibited because of the danger of falling stonework.

On the north side of the loch, a 5½ mile path along farm tracks and footpaths leads to the massive cliffs at Carsaig Bay.

DUART CASTLE
Although the landward approach to Duart is gentle, most visitors will already have seen the castle from the Oban ferry as a forbidding cliff-top fortress, guarding the entrance to the Sound. It was built by the Macleans when they ousted the MacDonalds from their supremacy as Lords of the Isles.

The Macleans of Duart and Morvern are first mentioned in a document of 1390. But this once-powerful Jacobite clan fell foul of the ambitious Campbells, and on the orders of the king surrendered Duart Castle and their fort on one of the Treshnish Islands in 1692. Duart lay in ruins until 1912, when the 26th chief, Sir Fitzroy Maclean, then 76 years old, completed an impressive restoration.

Macleans from all over the world visit the castle, which is open to the public daily from May to September. As well as rooms devoted to family and clan history, there is an exhibition

on Scouting. Lord Maclean, the 27th chief of the clan, served for many years as Chief Scout of the Commonwealth.

TOROSAY CASTLE
Across the bay from Duart stands a castle of an entirely different character. Torosay has no history of feuds and battles. It was built in 1856, in the Scottish baronial style favoured by the architect David Bryce, and has remained in the hands of one family ever since.

The castle contains good furniture and pictures, and photographic displays of life at the turn of the century. The castle is open to the public daily from April to October, the gardens all the year round.

Torosay is set in splendid gardens – the finest on Mull – built on three levels of terraced lawns, with an Italian-style statue walk. They are open all year round. A pleasant 1 mile stroll through rhododendrons, birches and spruce plantations leads back to Craignure.

From April to September, steamhauled trains run scheduled services on a narrow-gauge line between Torosay Castle and Craignure – Scotland's only island railway. The journey takes 20 minutes, seven of which are spent at the watering point of Tarmstedt Loop, so that passengers can take photographs against the background of the Sound of Mull.

Tourist information: Tobermory 2182 (summer).

From Loch Tummel to the silvery Tay

TOUR
230
—— 91 MILES ——

The mountains of Schiehallion and Ben Lawers dominate most of the country around Aberfeldy. Their peaks rise above forests and braes, and are reflected in the waters of three lochs.

ABERFELDY
The waters of the Urlar Burn surge over the Falls of Moness and down into Aberfeldy. On the outskirts of the town the burn joins the River Tay near the 400ft long military bridge built in 1733 by General George Wade, the English overlord of the Highlands. Wade built 35 bridges, and Aberfeldy Bridge is the only one still used as a public highway. At one time it was the only bridge over the Tay, making the town an important meeting point of routes. Prince Charles Edward Stuart crossed the bridge on his retreat north in 1746.

The river banks are overlooked by a monument built in 1887 to mark the incorporation of the Black Watch Regiment into the British Army in 1740. The regiment was named for its dark tartan and its first task – watching the braes which were full of Jacobite rebels.

KENMORE
Five years after bridging the River Tay here in 1774, the 3rd Earl of Breadalbane built a model village to give free housing to his estate workers. The village also provided safety

when brigands were preying on the district. In 1787 Robert Burns was so impressed with the view from the bridge that he wrote a verse about it on the wall above a fireplace. A framed copy of the poem can be seen in the Kenmore Hotel.

The salmon fishing on Loch Tay is amongst the best in Scotland; boats can be hired from Kenmore, which also has a sandy bathing beach. From the lochside picnic site at Rustic Lodge, off the main road just west of the town, signposted nature trails lead up into the conifer forests. There are spectacular views over Loch Tay towards the towering hulk of 3984ft Ben Lawers.

GLENGOULANDIE DEER PARK
Highland cattle, rare breeds of sheep and a magnificent herd of red deer, graze close to the military road built by General Wade after the 1715 Jacobite uprising. A rutted, winding road circles the park and passes close to the animals; there is a picnic site and car park at the halfway point. Close to the car park a waterfall tumbles through a narrow gorge lined with mature birches. Glengoulandie is open daily from Easter to September.

BRAES OF FOSS
The 3547ft pyramid of Schiehallion towers above the Braes of Foss, and a long walk to its summit begins at the Forestry Commission's car park. The early stages are easily managed, and the views from the lower slopes over Loch Rannoch are majestic.

In the car park, a plaque records how in 1774 the Reverend Nevil Maskelyne set up observatories on

opposite sides of the mountain and noted how plumb lines were attracted towards Schiehallion. He called this 'the attraction of mountains'.

RANNOCH WOODLANDS
A sparkling loch and delicate birch trees whose leaves stir in the gentlest of breezes give charm to Rannoch Woodlands. The woods include the 'black wood', a remnant of the ancient Caledonian forest where Scots pines add their own beauty.

At Carie is a car park deep in the forest from which radiates a series of forest walks which take from 30 minutes to three hours to walk. The longest trail strikes deep into the forest towards Glen Lyon, with breathtaking views over Loch Rannoch. At the western end of Loch Rannoch the Bridge of Gaur marks the start of the historic 'Road to the Isles'.

KINLOCH RANNOCH
Compact stone cottages draped with virginia creeper and roses stand beside a loch splashed with the colourful sails of boats from a nearby adventure centre. Through the trees several lochside car parks offer startlingly different views of Schiehallion.

Kinloch Rannoch's church is sheltered by a massive old oak, and behind it a waterfall plunges from the glowering hulk of Beinn a' Chuallaich into the River Tummel.

TUMMEL FOREST
Exciting views over quiet waters towards some of Scotland's grandest mountains are a feature of the drive along the road hugging the north bank of Loch Tummel. The best vantage point is Queen's View,

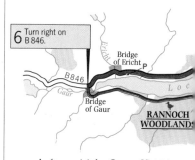

6 Turn right on B 846.

Bridge of Ericht

B 846

Bridge of Gaur

RANNOCH WOODLANDS

named after a visit by Queen Victoria in 1866, where a view indicator identifies the mountains in sight.

In a tree-lined dip below the viewpoint, a visitor centre has a display of the history of forestry. From a car park a quarter of a mile west, four trails lead into the forest. Clearly signposted is an 8th-century ring fort from where panoramic views over Loch Tummel may be enjoyed. Another sign leads to a 17th-century clachan or farm settlement, now restored and with picnic tables overlooking the loch.

A car park at Garry Bridge, 3 miles east, is the start of the Linn of Tummel woodland walk which crosses and then follows the east bank of the River Garry for 2 miles towards Killiecrankie. The patient observer may see a family of roe deer or even a capercaillie or wood grouse, the male distinguished by his red wattles and fanlike tail.

KILLIECRANKIE
Gnarled birches and rowans, damp fern-clad crevices and thundering waterfalls feeding the roaring River Garry are reached along a steep winding path from the National Trust for Scotland Visitor Centre.

The Battle of Killiecrankie in 1689 provided a rare victory for the Jacobites over William III's troops; and one terrified English soldier leapt for his life 18½ft across the ravine – a feat immortalised as The Soldier's Leap. The visitor centre is signposted from the main road.

WEEM
The town's only hotel, the Weem Hotel, bears as its sign a portrait of General Wade, who lodged there in 1733 while Aberfeldy Bridge was being built.

The kirk behind the hotel is thought to have been founded by St Cuthbert in AD 650. The present building, dedicated to the saint, is late 15th century and was used as the parish church until 1836, when it was given to the Menzies family as a mausoleum. Tastefully restored, it contains a stone cenotaph of 1616, in memory of the ladies of the clan, and, recording the lineage of the clan, a fine collection of funeral coats of arms.

Even older relics are a number of tombstones and two sanctuary crosses, originally belonging to an 8th-century monastery at Dull, about 4 miles west of Weem.

SALMON WATERS A lone angler near Aberfeldy enjoys one of the many delights provided by the Tay in its 120 mile course.

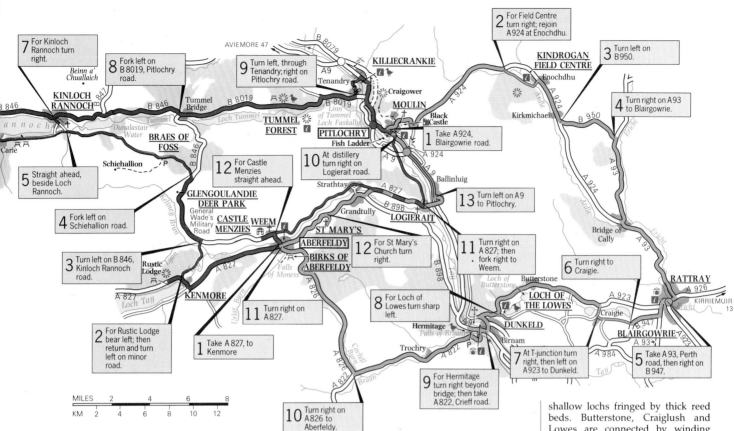

CASTLE MENZIES

Set in a field of golden barley, with a wooded cliff behind it, Castle Menzies lives again after centuries of neglect. The original castle was built in 1485 to defend the road to Rannoch. It was destroyed in 1502 and the present building is a fine example of a Z-plan tower house dating from the mid-16th century. In 1957 it was bought by the Menzies Clan Society who lovingly restored it. The castle is open daily in summer.

Tourist information: Aberfeldy 20276 (summer).

TOUR 231

78 MILES

Quiet roads meander through strawberry and raspberry fields, towards a different landscape where moors and mountains tower high above swirling rivers and peaceful lochs.

PITLOCHRY

Towering mountains surround Pitlochry, and trout and salmon streams pour down mossy slopes and through steep wooded gorges into Loch Faskally. This is an artificial loch, made by damming the River Tummel as part of a hydroelectric scheme.

The generating station is open to the public, and it has a 1000ft long fish pass used by salmon on their way to spawn. A viewing chamber allows visitors to watch the fish struggling upriver against the current.

Pitlochry was built mainly in the 1890s as a health resort, for the Moulin Burn, which twists through the town, was said to have healing properties. Today, however, visitors mostly flock to Pitlochry for the superb riverside, forest and mountain walks. Highland Games are held in the second week of September, and the Festival Theatre, situated on a wooded hillside above the Tummel, presents plays from May to October.

MOULIN

A peaceful village of cottages grouped around a 17th-century church, Moulin stands on a knoll overlooking Pitlochry. The walls of the timbered Moulin Inn, once on a main road, still bear rings to which the horses of Bonnie Prince Charlie's army were tethered on their way to Culloden. Set in the church grounds is a bell dated 1749 and there are two gravestones of medieval warriors, their profession symbolised by engraved swords.

A 3 mile, well-marked walk starts from the Moulin Inn and follows a winding path through woodlands to the 1300ft Craigower Fell. From the summit there are spectacular views of the green water meadows alongside the Tummel, which in late summer contrast with the fields of golden barley grown for the local whisky distilleries.

A path leads from the church to the ruined Black Castle, built about 1320 by a nephew of Robert Bruce. Originally the castle stood on an island in the middle of a shallow loch, and was connected to the bank by a stone causeway. The damp land surrounding the ruins has a colourful tangle of marsh plants in spring and early summer including the red of ragged robin, and the mauve cuckoo flower.

KINDROGAN FIELD CENTRE

Motorists who drive slowly along the rough road to Kindrogan may be rewarded by the sight of roe deer trotting from the fields where they feed into the shelter of the Forestry Commission plantation.

A nature-trail leaflet available at the field centre directs visitors along the banks of the peat-stained River Ardle and through a leafy glade where a plaque marks the spot where Queen Victoria took tea during her tour of the Highlands.

From the field centre there is a gentle, 4 mile long climb to Kindrogan Hill, at whose summit a view indicator identifies all the Perthshire mountains.

BLAIRGOWRIE AND RATTRAY

The fast-flowing River Ericht flows swiftly between the two towns, which were joined together in 1928. The burgh's prosperity comes mainly from farming and tourism, which flourishes in winter as well as summer, as it is the nearest town to the ski centre at Glen Shee, some 24 miles to the north. The district produces vast quantities of raspberries – about three-quarters of those grown in the Western Hemisphere.

The waters of the Ericht once powered jute and flax mills on its banks, and one of them has recently been restored as a craft centre.

LOCH OF THE LOWES

A narrow seesaw road, twisting and turning between fields of strawberries and raspberries, passes close to three shallow lochs fringed by thick reed beds. Butterstone, Craiglush and Lowes are connected by winding streams, whose banks are scented with water mint and meadowsweet. Loch of the Lowes is home to a pair of breeding ospreys which, from May to September, can be seen diving down to the water for fish, then raising a glistening trout aloft in their rough-scaled talons.

Lowes is a nature reserve administered by the Scottish Wildlife Trust. It has a car park, a two-storey hide open daily, and a visitor centre open on most days during the osprey season until 8.30pm. The loch itself is surrounded by magnificent woodlands, which are reflected in the tranquil waters.

DUNKELD

One of the engineer Thomas Telford's most spectacular bridges, built early in the 19th century, spans the sparkling waters of the Tay at Dunkeld. From it, Dunkeld Cathedral can be seen on a grassy tree-lined bank, close to where the Braan joins the larger river. A place of Christian worship has stood on the site since AD 570, and some of the present building, built between 1312 and 1501, has red-sandstone blocks from a cathedral erected there in AD 848.

Many of the small houses on Cathedral Street have been restored by the National Trust for Scotland, whose local headquarters, called the ell shop, occupies one corner. An ell was a cloth measure of about a metre – and a metal ell is embedded in the wall of the shop.

Nearby, the Hermitage woodlands contain an 18th-century folly built in the style of an Oriental pavilion. This overlooks the spectacular Falls of Braan, which crash through a narrow gorge filling it with spray.

BIRKS OF ABERFELDY

Purple heather moors lie on both sides of the road which sweeps down 1200ft into a valley lined with birch trees, or birks, sheltering the town of Aberfeldy. Parts of the modern road lie on top of one of General Wade's military roads built in 1725-33 to speed the movement of troops kept busy by rebellious Highlanders. In places the two are separate, and the military road can be seen as a pale grey narrow ribbon.

A footpath leads from a car park among trees just off the road through stands of delicate birches and stately Scots pines. Graceful buzzards soar and hover over jagged rocks and spectacular waterfalls, and wildcats are occasionally seen scurrying across the open glades.

ST MARY'S CHURCH

One of the most beautifully decorated churches in Scotland is reached along a rough but clearly signposted road which twists through the Nether-Pitcairn farm buildings to a car park. The church was endowed in 1533 by Alexander Stuart of Grandtully, but it was in 1636 that his descendant Sir William Stuart added its remarkable, coloured, wooden ceiling. This is divided into 29 panels illustrating texts from the Bible, as well as having the coats of arms of the Stuarts and other local landowners and the royal arms of Scotland, England and France. The panels are separated by paintings of fruit, vases of flowers and farmyard birds.

The white-painted church was used until 1892, when it was replaced by a building nearer to Aberfeldy – after which the interior of the old barn-like church was divided by a cross wall. The eastern end, with the painted ceiling, was left alone whilst the western section was used as a byre and farm store. In 1954 the entire building was given to the state and it has been preserved.

LOGIERAIT

The waters of the Tummel join those of the Tay at Logierait in a narrow gorge which for centuries was strategically important to military commanders as troops moving northwards could move upriver from this point. And in the late 14th century the village was one of the hunting seats of Robert II of Scotland.

In the churchyard are three mort-safes, used in the early 19th century to protect corpses from the attentions of body snatchers. The coffins were placed inside metal frames, which were then padlocked and buried. After the bodies had decayed, making them useless for medical research, the graves were reopened and the mort-safes removed for future use.

Tourist information: Pitlochry 2215; Blairgowrie 2960 (summer); Dunkeld 688 (summer).

FIT FOR A QUEEN *The view of Loch Tummel from the northern banks of the loch was one of the spectacles praised by Queen Victoria during her tour of the Highlands in 1866.*

Relics of the Picts in north Tayside

TOUR
232
——— 70 MILES ———

Woods notable for their glorious autumn colour fringe the route from Dundee towards a haunted castle and a fort that recalls a queen's illicit love. A waterfall adorns the Grampian foothills.

BROUGHTY FERRY

Although its fishing fleet is gone, some of Broughty Ferry's fishermen's cottages remain, and there is a feeling of the old lifestyle in the narrow wynds and closes leading off Fisher Street on the seafront.

The tower and battlements of Broughty Castle stand on a rocky spur, towering over a tiny harbour that dries out at low tide. Built in the 15th century on the site of a Pictish fort, the castle's purpose was to levy a toll from ships entering the Tay. The Gray family, who owned it, also controlled the lucrative ferry that linked Broughty with Fife.

After the 4th Lord Gray sided with the English in a plot to capture the infant Mary, Queen of Scots, as a bride for Edward VI, the English occupied the castle for three years until it was recaptured in 1550.

Extensively restored in 1860, Broughty Castle now contains a museum, open most days in summer, with one gallery devoted to the whaling industry that once thrived along this coast. A mile north-west of Broughty Ferry stands the 16th-century Claypotts Castle, its four-storey angle towers with crow-stepped gables rising incongruously within a modern housing estate. The castle is open daily in summer.

ARDESTIE

A clear sign marks the start of a path leading to one of two well-preserved souterrains in the area. These underground earth houses, which were once roofed with stone, have chambers and passages, and were the byres, silos and living quarters of the Picts in the 1st and 2nd centuries. A similar souterrain at Carlungie, 1 mile north, is signposted from the minor road leading to the right.

Just before Monikie, opposite the sign for Pitairlie, there is a superb view over farmland to the sea. Due south, where the Tay meets the North Sea, constantly shifting sandbanks have claimed many ships.

MONIKIE

A country park which surrounds a reservoir offers waterside walks and also boating. There are several pleasant picnic sites, and a car park near the gate.

Beyond Monikie the road runs back towards the coast, giving wide views over the sea. Afterwards it turns inland again to climb gently over a ridge on which the trees are kept strikingly wedge-shaped by the strong prevailing wind.

GLAMIS

In a wooded dell just off the main road, Glamis is a cluster of houses between two entrances to Glamis Castle. A thatched cottage beside the Strathmore Arms is an unusual sight among the slated and pantiled roofs of this part of Scotland.

In Kirkwynd is the Angus Folk Museum, housed in a row of converted 19th-century cottages with stone-slabbed roofs and colourful front gardens bordered by paved terraces. It is open daily in summer.

In the manse garden beyond the museum stands the 9ft high Glamis Stone, which bears intricate Pictish carvings. Legend has it that Malcolm II was slain here in 1034, and it is known also as King Malcolm's Stone.

Glamis Castle is approached down a wide, tree-lined avenue. Backed by distant hills, the pink-grey castle gives an impression of grandeur rather than beauty, with its turrets, wings, gables, parapets and heraldic embellishments. The central six-storey tower is 15th century, and remains of an earlier fortress are incorporated in the lower parts of the castle.

Glamis is said to be the most haunted castle in Scotland. Among its company of ghosts is 'Earl Beardie' Crawford. Nobody dares to enter the sealed room, where the huge red-bearded earl is said to have played cards with the Devil on the Sabbath. The castle has Dutch and Italian gardens, and extensive parkland planted with fine trees. It is open most days in summer.

REEKIE LINN

Legendary 'kelpies' or water sprites are said to live in Reekie Linn, a dramatic waterfall reached by a footpath starting near a lay-by just across the Bridge of Craigisla. The River Isla, constricted by narrow rock walls, plunges into a deep gorge in a single, foaming cascade, making a whirlpool in the dark water below and sending up spray like clouds of steam.

BARRY HILL

Park on the narrow verge at the foot of Barry Hill, from where a short, steep climb through gorse and bracken leads to the summit. In a slight depression stands the ruin of a large Pictish fort, its oblong shape punctuated with round turrets and its grass-covered ramparts still clearly defined. Legend has it that King Arthur's wife, Guinevere, was imprisoned here for her romance with a Pictish prince. The view rewards the climb.

Beyond Alyth, in Meigle, poor unfaithful Guinevere is said to be buried. In a small museum, open daily except Sundays, there is a remarkable collection of early Christian and Pictish stones of the 7th to 10th centuries. Their elaborate carvings show sophisticated clothing and weapons.

Tourist information: Dundee 27723.

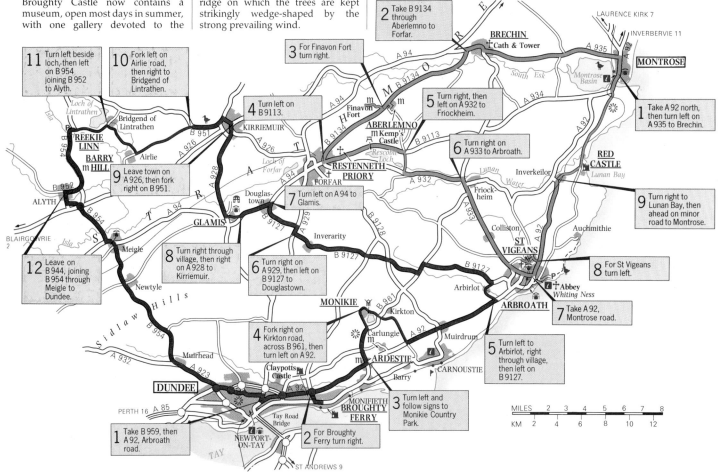

1. Take A 92 north, then turn left on to A 935 to Brechin.
2. Take B 9134 through Aberlemno to Forfar.
3. For Finavon Fort turn right.
4. Turn left on B 9113.
5. Turn right, then left on A 932 to Friockheim.
6. Turn right on A 933 to Arbroath.
7. Take A 92, Montrose road.
8. For St Vigeans turn left.
9. Turn right to Lunan Bay, then ahead on minor road to Montrose.
5. Turn left to Arbirlot, right through village, then left on B 9127.
4. Fork right on Kirkton road, across B 961, then turn left on A 92.
3. Turn left and follow signs to Monikie Country Park.
2. For Broughty Ferry turn right.
1. Take B 959, then A 92, Arbroath road.
6. Turn right on A 929, then left on B 9127 to Douglastown.
7. Turn left on A 94 to Glamis.
8. Turn right through village, then right on A 928 to Kirriemuir.
9. Leave town on A 926, then fork right on B 951.
10. Fork left on Airlie road, then right to Bridgend of Lintrathen.
11. Turn left beside loch, then left on B 954 joining B 952 to Alyth.
12. Leave on B 944, joining B 954 through Meigle to Dundee.

MILES
KM

—— 52 MILES ——

Ancient Scottish history has left its traces across the Strathmore countryside, and almost every village has Pictish relics. At Arbroath the Scots declared their independence in 1320.

MONTROSE
With sea to the east, the River South Esk to the south and a wide tidal basin to the west, Montrose is almost an island, with an airy, spacious feeling. The High Street, as wide as a market square, is lined with houses built gable-end-on. Closes lead to 19th-century courtyards.

Some 10,000 pink-footed geese, a tenth of the world's population, migrate annually in November to the tidal basin from their Arctic breeding grounds. This haunt of many species of wildfowl, which drains at low tide to reveal mussel beds on its mud flats, offers a peaceful contrast to the bustling town with its docks and shipping, its sturdy buildings and oil-related prosperity.

BRECHIN
The red-sandstone cathedral and attached round tower are the focal points in this attractive town. The tapering round tower, dating from the 11th century, was restored in 1960.

The cathedral, now a parish church, dates from the 13th century. It was restored in 1900 but still has a spire dating from 1360. Inside are Pictish relics as well as a 16th-century font and 17th-century pewter and silver.

ABERLEMNO
In this tiny hamlet stand four intricately carved Pictish stones dating from the 7th century. Three are on the left of the road, with parking in front of the village hall on the right.

The finest stone of all is farther on, in a churchyard down a small turning to the left. The 7ft high stone bears a remarkably clear carving of a Celtic cross flanked by intertwined creatures on one side, and a battle scene on the other.

Beyond Aberlemno a turning on the right leads to Finavon Hill, crowned by a fine Iron Age fort. Its ramparts are easily seen, though covered by turf, and there is a central well or spring. Excavations have revealed evidence of metal-working, pot-making and weaving on this lofty summit, from which there are views up Strathmore to the Mearns, and west to Blairgowrie.

RESTENNETH PRIORY
Surrounded by gently sloping meadows and scattered clumps of trees, the ruin of Restenneth Priory rises from marshy ground. The priory originally stood on a peninsula jutting out into a shallow loch, but the loch was drained in the late 18th century. Incorporated in the remains of the Augustinian priory church is an early

SILVER AND GOLD *Lunan Water traces a silvery path between golden beaches as it threads its way to meet the sea in Lunan Bay.*

ECHOES OF FRANCE *The chateau-like turrets and parapets of Glamis Castle were added in the 17th century, and the style became known as Scottish Baronial.*

TRADE ENTRY *Lay visitors entered Arbroath Abbey by the north-west gate.*

FOLK MUSEUM *Cottages in Glamis house a display of local history.*

porch, possibly dating from the 11th century; it was later heightened to form a tower and was capped by a spire in the 15th century.

Rescobie Loch, just beyond Restenneth, offers a pleasant picnic site. The little fishing loch is fringed by rushes and backed by trees.

ARBROATH
The well-preserved ruin of a red-sandstone abbey rises from the heart of this thriving seaside town. The abbey was founded in the 12th century, but most of what remains dates from the 13th century. The south transept has a round rose window where, according to tradition, a light was burned at night in ancient times as a guide to ships.

It was in Arbroath Abbey that the most important document in Scottish history, the Declaration of Arbroath, was signed in 1320. Nobles who signed it acknowledged Robert Bruce as king in their fight against the English.

In the backyards of Arbroath's 'fisher-town', between the harbour and the abbey, haddock is smoked over wood-chip fires to provide the Arbroath 'Smokies' which can be bought from many of the cottages.

From Whiting Ness, north of the wide promenade, a path winds for 3 miles along the cliff top to the picturesque fishing village of Auchmithie. Waves lick at the rocks below, honeycombed with caves.

On a clear day the Bell Rock lighthouse is visible 12 miles to the east, marking the Inchcape Rock.

ST VIGEANS
Less than 2 miles north of Arbroath, a left turn leads to St Vigeans, an unexpected gem of a village in a dip below modern housing developments. Park near the railway bridge and cross the Brothock Burn on foot.

The small redstone church is perched on top of a steep, natural mound, 40ft high, neatly kept and dotted with gravestones. Extensive 19th-century renovations tend to disguise the 12th-century origins of the church, although some of the original stones were used in the renovation. Below the church pretty, redstone cottages with stone-slabbed roofs form a semicircle. One cottage is now a museum containing a collection of Pictish stones, including the Drosten Stone, which bears an early Christian inscription.

RED CASTLE
Park on the verge at the far side of the wood beyond Redcastle. From a gate, a short path climbs steeply through trees to a 15th-century ruin jutting out on a cliff, high above the sea, dominating Lunan Bay and Lunan Water.

Red Castle stands on the site of an old fort built to protect the coast from Danish pirates. Cows now graze where bloody battles once raged.

The route winds northwards along the coast, and from the final crest there is a wide view of Montrose.

Tourist information: Montrose 72000; Brechin 3050 (summer); Arbroath 72609/76680.

From Royal Deeside to the coast

TOUR

234

— 108 MILES —

For more than a century Balmoral has been a favourite home of the royal family. Other historic castles line the Dee valley on its long course through breathtaking Highland scenery.

BANCHORY

Rising in a series of terraced streets above the River Dee, this ancient little town provides a good base from which to explore the surrounding area. There are several easy forest walks, and across the river a well-marked path leads to the top of the 1000ft Scolty Hill, which is topped by a monument to General Burnett, an officer in the Napoleonic Wars whose home was Crathes Castle.

At the east end of the town, the Ingasetter lavender distillery welcomes visitors on weekdays. A 5 acre field of lavender behind the factory is in full and fragrant bloom only briefly before harvesting in July or August.

CRATHES CASTLE

Round and square towers sprout from the upper storeys of this 16th-century castle whose little pepper-pot roofs and crenellations give it the look of a French chateau. Finely built yet immensely solid, its high walls slope inwards towards the top to increase stability.

Inside the castle there are wooden floors, panels and ceilings with symbolic figures painted between the joists. One bedroom, the Room of the Nine Nobles, has nine great heroes from the past intricately painted on its ceiling. The Long Gallery at the top of the castle, where the laird used to hold court, has a superb oak-panelled ceiling.

The castle's 4 acre garden, bordered by carefully shaped 18th-century yew hedges, is divided into eight smaller gardens which provide a succession of dazzling colours from spring to autumn. The castle is open daily in summer.

DRUM CASTLE

Comprising a massive 13th-century tower, 70ft high with walls 12ft thick, linked to a gracious Jacobean wing, Drum Castle is set in 400 acres of the oldest surviving part of the ancient Caledonian Forest. It was owned by a single family, the Irvines, for 653 years until it was bequeathed to the National Trust for Scotland in 1976. It is open to the public daily in summer.

The tower has changed little, apart from the addition of a large Victorian window when the hall was turned into a library. The Jacobean wing was added in the early 17th century by the 9th laird, Alexander Irvine.

A well-marked woodland walk through the castle grounds starts from the car park and picnic area.

BRIDGE OF FEUGH

The bridge is a narrow, 18th-century span with niches for pedestrians, and a car park nearby. Its river, the Water of Feugh, flows through a valley of tall limes, sycamores and beeches.

Just upstream from the bridge the river turns into a torrent, a near-waterfall that pours over and around crags, pools and basins of rock.

KNOCK CASTLE

From the road, a steep, stony track leads to the late-16th-century Knock Castle, a bare ruin of a keep set neatly in well-trimmed grass. The place has a gruesome story attached to it, concerning the Gordon family, owners of Knock in the 16th century.

One day, seven Gordons were out cutting peat on the land of their neighbours, the Forbes. Forbes men overwhelmed the trespassers, killed them, and cut off their heads, which they stuck onto peat-cutting spades. A horrified servant rushed back to Knock and blurted out the news to the father, who was so shocked that he fell down the stairs and was killed.

BALMORAL CASTLE

At Balmoral, wrote Queen Victoria, 'all seemed to breathe freedom and peace and to make one forget the world and its sad turmoils'. In 1852 Prince Albert bought Balmoral and two neighbouring estates, and there the couple lived, in the words of one visitor, 'like very small gentlefolks'.

The old castle, however, was too small to accommodate their growing family and their guests, so they decided to rebuild. The new house, its building in Scottish baronial style closely supervised by Albert, was completed in 1859.

The Scottish influence is obvious in the light grey local granite, the central keep-like tower and the conical roofs of the turrets. The two main blocks have two or three storeys, giving the impression of a large, rambling family house. The house and grounds are open to the public in May, June and July.

Just beyond the car park, over the Dee, is the small parish church of Crathie, in which the royal family have worshipped since 1848. The church of local blue-grey granite stands on a hillside. Rebuilt in 1895, its inspiration is medieval, with a barrel-vaulted wooden ceiling and Gothic arches.

BRAEMAR

Two huge Victorian hotels dominate a village which has three claims to fame – its setting, its games and its castle. It

DEFIANT FORTRESS *In 1652 Dunnottar Castle guarded the Scottish Crown Jewels from Cromwell's besiegers for eight months.*

DOUBLE CROSSING *Near Cambus o' May, between Ballater and Dinnet, a double footbridge spans the Dee and crosses a disused railway track, now a scenic walk.*

CRATHES CASTLE *Cheerful gardens belie tales of a ghost within.*

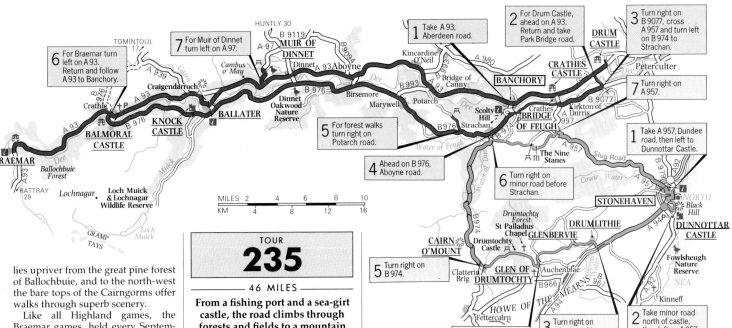

Map labels (reading across the map):

HUNTLY 30

TOMINTOUL 17

1 Take A 93, Aberdeen road.

2 For Drum Castle, ahead on A 93. Return and take Park Bridge road.

3 Turn right on B 9077, cross A 957 and turn left on B 974 to Strachan.

DRUM CASTLE

Peterculter

6 For Braemar turn left on A 93. Return and follow A 93 to Banchory.

7 For Muir of Dinnet turn left on A 97.

B 9119

MUIR OF DINNET

A 97

Dinnet

A 93 Aboyne

Kincardine O'Neil

A 980

CRATHES CASTLE

Bridge of Canny

BANCHORY

7 Turn right on A 957.

Cambus o' May

Cairn

Craigendarroch

BALLATER

Dinnet Oakwood Nature Reserve

B 976

Birsemore

Marywell

B 993

Dee

Potarch

Crathes

B 9077

Kirkton of A Durris

A 957

Crathie

A 93

KNOCK CASTLE

B 976

5 For forest walks turn right on Potarch road.

4 Ahead on B 976, Aboyne road.

B 976

Scolty Hill

Strachan

BRIDGE OF FEUGH

The Nine Stanes

1 Take A 957, Dundee road, then left to Dunnottar Castle.

BALMORAL CASTLE

Ballochbuie Forest

BRAEMAR

A 93

RATTRAY 29

Lochnagar

Loch Muick & Lochnagar Wildlife Reserve

Loch Muick

GRAMP TAYS

Water of Feugh

B 974

6 Turn right on minor road before Strachan.

Cowie Water

STONEHAVEN

NORTH

Black Hill

A 94

Slug Road

DUNNOTTAR CASTLE

Fowlsheugh Nature Reserve

SEA

Kinneff

MILES 2 4 6 8 10
KM 4 8 12 16

Drumtochty Forest

St Palladius Chapel

Drumtochty Castle

GLENBERVIE

DRUMLITHIE

5 Turn right on B 974.

CAIRN O'MOUNT

Clatterin Brig

GLEN OF DRUMTOCHTY

Auchenblae

B 966

HOWE OF THE MEARNS

Fettercairn

A 94

Bervie Water

B 967

2 Take minor road north of castle, then left on A 957, joining A 94.

3 Turn right on minor road to Auchenblae.

4 Turn right to church, and then take 'Cemetery' road.

TOUR

235

—— 46 MILES ——

From a fishing port and a sea-girt castle, the road climbs through forests and fields to a mountain pass once crossed by Macbeth. In the valleys, burns chatter over rocky beds.

---

lies upriver from the great pine forest of Ballochbuie, and to the north-west the bare tops of the Cairngorms offer walks through superb scenery.

Like all Highland games, the Braemar games, held every September, have their origins in the 11th century when, it is claimed, Malcolm III held contests to select the strongest fighters for his struggle against the Normans. The present games, which were reinstituted in 1832, owe more to entertainment than war, with their arrays of pipers, dancers, caber-tossers and shot-putters.

Braemar is in a key position to control the upper Dee valley, which until 1745 was a hotbed of warring factions. The authority of the local earls needed constant reassertion, and in 1628 John Erskine, Earl of Mar, built 'a great body of a house' just outside the village. The house – Braemar Castle – still stands, austere and fortress-like, on a rough knoll surrounded by unkempt grass. The castle is open daily from May to October.

BALLATER
A wooded hillside above the River Dee, in the shadow of the 3786ft Lochnagar, is the setting for this holiday resort renowned for its dry, clear atmosphere. It was founded in the 18th century when a local laird decided to exploit the healing benefits of a nearby spa – now the Pannanich Wells Hotel.

Behind Ballater, a well-trodden path leads to the 700ft summit of Craigendarroch – 'The Hill of Oaks' – from where there are dramatic views down the Dee valley to Aboyne, and across to the forbidding north face of Lochnagar.

MUIR OF DINNET
Leaving the Highlands behind, the land flattens into a lowland expanse of heather, woodland, loch and bog. The Muir of Dinnet, the terminal moraine of an Ice Age glacier that ground its way out of the Cairngorms, contains a wealth of land forms and plant life and is now a 3500 acre nature reserve.

Tourist information: Banchory 2066; Ballater 55306 (summer); Braemar 600 (summer).

STONEHAVEN
The Old Town of Stonehaven, the fishing port, has been there for centuries, but its New Town is mostly Georgian, the creation of a colourful 18th-century figure, Robert Barclay of Ury. They are given unity, however, by the attractive pinky-beige sandstone used as building stone, which makes harbour walls, houses and handsome Victorian courthouse seem all of a piece.

In a sense, there is a third town too, the resort that is taking the place of the slowly declining fishing industry. All the same, there are a few fishing boats among the pleasure craft in the harbour, and piles of lobster pots and fish boxes along the quay.

The Old Tolbooth by the harbour is something of an Episcopalian shrine. Three ministers were imprisoned there for six months in 1748 as part of the reprisals for the town's part in the Jacobite rising of 1745. However, they continued to baptise children through the barred window of their cell. The building now houses the town museum.

At the top of the High Street, beside the Mercat Cross, stands the 18th-century Town Steeple. At the south end of Market Square a bronze plaque marks the birthplace in 1822 of Robert Thomson, inventor of the pneumatic tyre.

DUNNOTTAR CASTLE
Crouched on a dark crag around which the sea restlessly sighs and heaves, Dunnottar Castle appears sinister, an impression not belied by its story. Despite its apparent impregnability, at least two of its garrisons, English and Scots, have been forced to surrender, and in 1685, 167 Covenanter prisoners were herded into a cellar known as Whigs' Vault. Many of them died of ill treatment and they now lie in Dunnottar Kirkyard.

The most dramatic incident in Dunnottar Castle's history was the siege of 1652, when a Royalist garrison held out for eight months against the forces of Parliament. The Parliamentarians' chief interest was that the Honours of Scotland – the Scottish Crown Jewels – had been sent to Dunnottar for safe keeping, and when they mounted artillery on Black Hill, the garrison knew the end could not be far off.

The Honours were smuggled out in a basket of flax, so it is said, probably by the wife of the minister of nearby Kinneff, and when the Royalists surrendered, the regalia were already safely hidden beneath the floor of Kinneff church. There they remained until the Restoration of Charles II, nine years later, when they were taken in triumph to Edinburgh Castle, where they can still be seen.

Dunnottar Castle is open daily but is closed on Saturdays in winter.

DRUMLITHIE
The road wanders through the rolling farmlands of the Howe of the Mearns to Drumlithie, surrounded in early summer by barley fields and acre upon acre of glowing oil-seed rape. The village has a nucleus of stone cottages where weavers once lived and worked. Their lives were regulated by the ringing of a bell from the slender red-stone belfry, built in 1777, which called them to work. The bell rings still, but only for village weddings, and to bring in the New Year.

GLENBERVIE
This uphill-and-down-dale parish is set in a bowl of wooded hills. The churchyard is perched on a grassy knoll, one side of which drops down a steep bank a-sparkle with wild flowers, to the chattering burn at its foot. The plot is a place of minor pilgrimage, since among a collection of ornate tombs are those of Robert Burns's great-grandfather and great-grand-uncle. They spelt their name 'Burnes', and died long before the poet was born in Ayr. Nevertheless, the local Burns Society paid for the shelter erected to protect the tombstones in 1968.

GLEN OF DRUMTOCHTY
Beyond the Bervie Water, the route runs through Auchenblae, a quiet village attractively set in a chequer-board vale of green fields and red plough land. Beyond is the Glen of Drumtochty, Forestry Commission country mostly, but look out on the right for the astonishing Chapel of St Palladius, a blend of Walt Disney castle and Russian basilica. It stands just beyond the lodge entrance to the privately owned Drumtochty Castle, a few of whose Scottish baronial turrets stick above the trees.

Along the road, the Mearns Forest car park and picnic area is the start of a short forest walk which climbs a rustic stair and runs west into the trees. The road continues through a steep, pretty gorge to the Slack Burn and Clatterin' Brig.

CAIRN O' MOUNT
This is the classic pass through the eastern Grampians, linking Fettercairn with Banchory. Macbeth fled this way, and Edward I, Montrose and John Graham of Claverhouse (Bonnie Dundee) all brought their armies over it at various times in Scotland's battered history. Now its chief appeal is its view, which is gained by ascending 1070ft in 2 miles, though the gradients are never more than 1 in 5.

At the summit, the car park at Cairn o' Mount has compelling views over dark, heathery hills and pine forests, and range upon range of black mountains stretching far to the north and west.

Tourist information: Stonehaven 62806 (summer).

Rugged castles and cliffs of Buchan

TOUR
236
——— 66 MILES ———

Sweeping hills and distant horizons mark the way to the peak of Bennachie. To the south, three great estates offset the bleak grandeur of this north-eastern shoulder of Scotland.

PETERHEAD

Peterhead is the largest fish-landing port in Europe, and down at the harbour more than 400 fishing vessels crowd the five pools. Lines of single and two-storey granite cottages in the Buchanhaven area also testify to the strength of the town's fishing traditions. Fish sales are still held beside the innermost harbour from 8.30am daily.

Except for three decades in the late 19th century, when steam drifters briefly made many fishermen redundant, Peterhead has been an important fishing town almost since its foundation in 1593. As a whaling centre it was unrivalled in Scotland, and its history in this role is recalled in the Arbuthnot Museum.

The town's newest and largest basin, Peterhead Bay, is a major base for the North Sea oil industry. To the south, on Sandford Bay, are the stark, impressive lines of Boddam power station.

INVERUGIE

The Ugie is a good river for catching trout, sea trout and salmon, and the bridge at Inverugie is one of several offering ready access to the fast-flowing, rushy waters. The bridge is narrow, but there is a car park beside it. Licences to fish in the sheltered, leafy dell can be obtained at Peterhead and Fraserburgh. Beside the river are the ruins of Inverugie Castle.

LONGSIDE

Set about with trees and well-kept gardens, this attractive village has two contrasting churches – and the ruins of a third. On the left of the road into the village is a small but stately Episcopalian church that is a gem of 19th-century architecture, built of blue-grey stone and with windows by the pre-Raphaelite artist Edward Burne-Jones.

The parish church, in the middle of the village, is a spacious 18th-century hall, with a large gallery, and it stands next to its ruined 17th-century predecessor, open to the sky.

ADEN COUNTRY PARK

Aden – centred on a semicircular 'steading' of farmhands' houses, a coach house and the great house itself – was once the estate of the 18th-century laird Alexander Russell. Early this century the estate declined with the Russell family's fortunes. Now restored, it recalls former glories.

TOLQUHON CASTLE *The ruins of this ancient monument lie in a leafy valley about 2 miles south of the village of Tarves.*

PITMEDDEN GREAT GARDEN *Built as a summerhouse, this stone pavilion has a fireplace for use when the weather is chilly.*

BOOKS AND BUSTS *Sculptured heads guard part of the extensive library in a corridor at Haddo House.*

Although the great house at Aden – pronounced 'Adden' – is a ruin, the farm buildings, 230 acres of field and forest and the walled nursery garden are open to the public free of charge.

An exhibition centre illustrates local farming life in the past. Walks through the woodlands, by the lake and along the South Ugie Water offer glimpses of deer, rabbits and, sometimes, a fox.

OLD DEER ABBEY

Behind a massive stone wall lie the ruins of Old Deer Abbey, founded in 1219. Although only the lowest stoneworks survive, they clearly show the ground plan of a great Cistercian monastery – the last expression of a monastic tradition stretching back to the 6th century. The abbey was once a powerful influence locally, for in the Middle Ages the large district of Deer came under its direct administration. However, all that changed with the Reformation, and the district was divided into Old and New Deer.

WHITE COW WOOD

From a car park, two marked walks – one of a mile, the other of 3 miles – lead through Forestry Commission woods, with numerous smaller paths winding off into the dense conifers. The short walk passes a badger sett which has been there for several years.

Beyond the wood, on the road down to Strichen, there is a fine view of Mormond Hill, with a white horse etched into the slope beneath a topknot of radar dishes.

NEW DEER

The village's carefully planned but uninspired High Street leads to the Hill of Culsh, and an austere monument to a local landlord, William Fordyce. From here, there is a windswept, all-round view across to Mormond Hill over the bare, green, rolling hills of Buchan towards the Bennachie range of hills.

The straight and high-flying road southwards to Methlick has the best and longest view of the tour. The Bennachie hills can be seen rising in the distance like an island beyond a sea of lesser hills.

HADDO HOUSE

Built in the early 18th century, this house is very different from the formidable castles of Scottish tradition. It has two wings which reach forward as if to embrace the grounds – an enchanting sight with their gardens, squared terraces, lakes, woodland walks and flowing lawns.

The house was built by William Gordon, 2nd Earl of Aberdeen, and its name figures in another of the family's titles – Lord Haddo. The earls were by turns, and sometimes simultaneously, colourful, brilliant and eccentric. The 3rd, known as the 'wicked earl', had a wife and at least three permanent mistresses. The 4th was a scholar, designer of Haddo's gardens and the prime minister who in 1854 led Britain into the Crimean War. The 5th was a religious man who gave away much of his wealth, while the 6th ran away to become a merchant seaman in America under the name of George Osborne and was lost at sea.

The family's fortunes declined over the last century. In 1872, the 7th earl had 75,000 acres. In 1934 the estate had shrunk to 15,000 acres. When the National Trust for Scotland took it over in 1979, it assumed responsibility for just 180 acres. Queen Victoria slept at Haddo one night in 1857, and her little bedroom, dominated by a four-poster with simple hangings, is preserved almost unchanged.

The house is open each afternoon in the summer, and the gardens are open throughout the year.

TOLQUHON

The pinkish-grey stones of this ruin lie at the end of a wooded lane. In the late 16th century, the original grim tower of Tolquhon (pronounced 'Tullchon' locally, with a guttural *ch*) was extended by William Forbes, the 7th laird, into a cross between a large house and a castle.

Even as a ruin, the castle has a domestic intimacy about it, despite reminders of grimmer times – apertures for guns on either side of the main gatehouse and a pit, or narrow prison cell, into which visitors can climb. William Forbes is buried in an ornate tomb in Tarves.

In 1718 Tolquhon was sold to the Earl of Aberdeen (father of the earl who built Haddo). The castle decayed from the middle of the last century, but is now well tended.

PITMEDDEN

The ornate heraldic designs formed with 40,000 plants and 3 miles of tiny boxwood hedges make the Great Garden of Pitmedden a horticultural jewel. Pitmedden was bought by the Seton family in 1603. A century later Sir Alexander Seton, Lord Pitmedden, who opposed James II's efforts to restore Catholicism and fell into disfavour at court, retired here to devote himself to his gardens.

He found his inspiration in the classical formality of French gardens, but applied the principles to create floral displays of wonderful intricacy. In the mid-19th century the estate decayed, but in 1952 the National Trust for Scotland acquired Pitmedden and set about restoring the beds, using contemporary designs for gardens Sir Alexander would surely have known.

In the 3 acres of sunken, walled garden, the plants and hedges form a variety of designs – the Seton coat of arms, mottoes, St Andrew's crosses and Scottish thistles – all of which can be seen from the surrounding walls. The garden is open all year.

CRUDEN BAY

At Cruden Bay, the road reaches Buchan's rugged coast. The ruggedness is briefly modified by sand dunes and by a pretty harbour, Port Erroll.

But the cliffs soon assert themselves. To the north, they are capped by the stark ruins of Slains Castle, often known as Count Dracula's Castle because they supposedly inspired Bram Stoker, author of *Dracula*, who used to visit Cruden Bay. The castle was built by the Earl of Erroll in the early 17th century and extended by his descendants. It was the scene of numerous high-society gatherings in Victorian and Edwardian days before it was abandoned and partially demolished in 1925.

A footpath runs to the ruins from Cruden Bay up a wooded gorge. Cars can reach the castle along a stone track, though visitors should beware of the sheer and unfenced drops.

BULLERS OF BUCHAN

The sea has carved in the cliffs a cauldron and a cave, through which the waters surge. These bullers – the old Scottish word for 'boilers' – lie beneath a cliff-top path that leads 100yds from a cluster of cottages along a razor-edged route round the 150ft deep cauldron. Gulls, kittiwakes and guillemots scream and wheel in the maze of cliffs and stacks that make up this convoluted chunk of coast.

Tourist information: Ellon 20730 (summer); Banff and Buchan Tourist Board, Banff 2419.

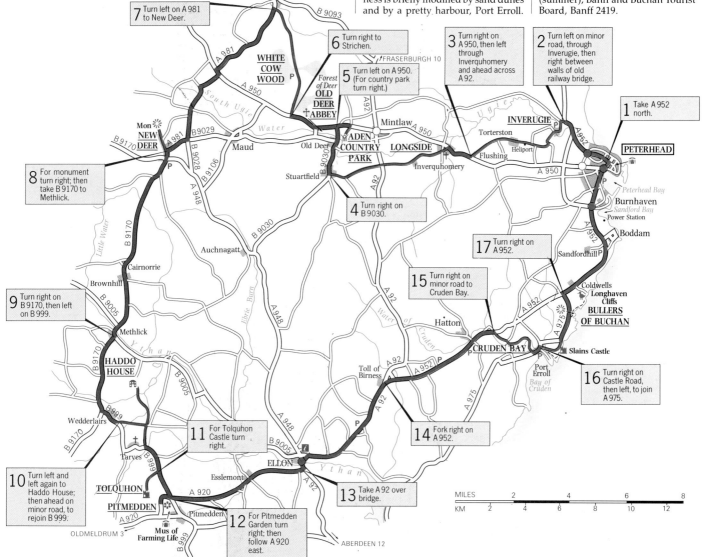

From Culloden to the shores of Moray

TOUR
237
—— 84 MILES ——

Major events in Scottish history and legend have occurred close to the Moray Firth west of Nairn. Inland are fertile valleys, wooded hills and pine forests along the River Spey.

NAIRN
The opening of the Inverness and Nairn Railway in 1855 transformed Nairn from a prosperous county town into a fashionable Victorian watering place. Nairn is still one of Scotland's most elegant resorts, with two sandy beaches. In the summer, holiday-makers sit for hours on the seafront, entranced by the waters of the Moray Firth and the low blue hills of Cromarty. In old Fishertown, narrow alleys crowded with former fisher-men's cottages lead to the harbour.

FORT GEORGE
With its bastioned ramparts occupying the tip of a pointed peninsula, where the Moray Firth is only a mile wide, Fort George is one of Europe's outstanding artillery fortifications. The defences enclose 16 acres of land including a parade ground, barrack

ranges, ordnance stores and a chapel. Fort George was built soon after the Jacobite rising of 1745 to forestall any further threats to Hanoverian law and order. The regimental museum of the Queen's Own Highlanders and some parts of the fort are open daily.

CULLODEN
A fierce gale was blowing on April 16, 1746, when the armies of Prince Charles Edward Stuart and the Duke of Cumberland confronted each other across Culloden Moor. Within an hour, the prince's army of 5000 Highlanders had been routed by the cannon, grapeshot and, finally, bayonets of the government troops. All that was left was a barren field of slaughter where more than 1000 men lay dead.

The audio-visual display at the visitor centre, which is run by the National Trust for Scotland, brings the Battle of Culloden vividly to life.

The display provides a useful starting point for retracing the scenes of the battle. From the visitor centre, paths lead past the graves of the dead clans and stones marking the positions in which the two opposing commanders stood at the start of the battle.

CLAVA CAIRNS
The Nairn valley is rich in prehistoric remains. One of the best examples is hidden among the trees 1 mile east of Culloden. The Clava Cairns are surrounded by circles of standing stones, and date from the late Stone Age (1800-1500 BC). They originally contained domed burial chambers with passage entrances.

LOCH MOY
Set in a wooded glen beside the road, the waters of Loch Moy lap round an island on which stand the ruins of the 14th-century Castle of Moy and an obelisk to a 19th-century Mackintosh chief. The loch may be reached by a path which leads off the road running to the parish church. It is surprisingly peaceful here, despite the nearness of a busy road.

CARRBRIDGE
A narrow defile carries the main road past the Slochd summit, and as the road descends, leaving the wind-swept hills behind, it bypasses Carrbridge.

The village takes its name from the narrow 18th-century bridge which spans the River Dulnain just to the west of the present bridge. From the Landmark Visitor Centre, imaginative forest walks have been laid out in the pinewoods beside the road. These include a 'treetop trail', a contemporary sculpture trail with work by Antony Caro and Eduardo Paolozzi

among others, and a nature trail which draws attention to the local wildlife and plants.

An exhibition in the visitor centre traces the progress of everyday life in the Highlands from prehistoric times until today.

CAWDOR
William Shakespeare immortalised Cawdor in *Macbeth* – as the scene of Duncan's murder. But the castle and its history are colourful enough without the aid of myth. A turreted 14th-century tower, protected on one side by a gully and on the other by a dry moat, rises majestically from the woods of the Nairn valley.

Since the 17th century the small defensive fort has been transformed into a large family mansion, and the impression of a black and bloody past has been tamed by centuries of civilisation. Inside, the walls are luxuriously hung with Flemish tapestries and family portraits; and outside the walled flower garden is an extravagant blaze of colour.

Unlike many Highland villages which are simply strung out along either side of a main street, the layout of Cawdor village is more haphazard and more interesting. Its compact stone cottages straggle along the banks of a stream before leading through a leafy lane past an imposing 17th-century parish church – built by the 12th thane, allegedly to fulfil a vow made when he was in danger of shipwreck.

Tourist information: Inverness 234353; Nairn 52753 (summer); Carrbridge 630 (summer).

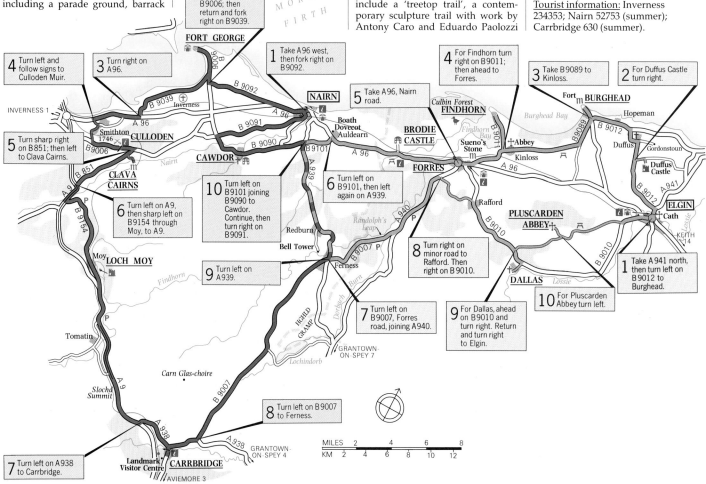

— 73 MILES —

Acre upon acre of barley fields cover the region known as the 'Granary of the North'. A village south-west of Elgin has connections with an American city of the same name.

ELGIN
The stone walls of Elgin glow with a mellow dignity befitting its status as a city, and an ancient royal burgh. Over 1000 years ago a settlement started to grow up along a low ridge between the loops of the River Lossie. And today, although many of the houses date from the 18th and 19th centuries, the city keeps its medieval street plan.

From a mound in the west, on which stands a fragment of Elgin's original royal castle, the High Street runs to the ruined 12th-century cathedral in the east.

BURGHEAD
Some of the grain produced by the barley fields of Moray was once shipped from Burghead, where stone granaries still line the harbour. Burghead is a former fishing port which juts out along a promontory to the Moray Firth. From the coastguard station above the harbour a 5 mile sweep of sandy beach stretches west to Findhorn.

FINDHORN
The golden sands, fringed by trees, which face the village of Findhorn from across the narrow mouth of its bay are a last line of resistance against the forces of nature. The village is now on its third site for, over the centuries, the shifting sands to the west of Findhorn have drifted eastwards, gradually swallowing acre after acre of fertile farmland.

The present village was a busy port in the 18th century; and the cluster of houses around the Crown and Anchor inn at the heart of the village includes traces of an old warehouse and granary.

FORRES
A 23ft high monolith known as Sueno's Stone – the name may be a variation of Sweyn – carved by the Picts in the 9th or 10th century stands sentinel over the eastern approach to Forres. On the hill above, a 70ft battlemented tower built to commemorate Admiral Nelson watches over the town.

Although most of its buildings are 19th century, the layout of this ancient royal burgh dates from the Middle Ages. Its main street widens to accommodate the market place, and narrow alleys – or wynds – lead enticingly off towards some of the remaining 18th-century houses.

BRODIE CASTLE
There have been Brodies at Brodie for more than 800 years, but it was the 12th laird who began the present buildings in 1567. His castle took the

RIOT OF COLOUR *Bright blooms soften the grey lines of Cawdor Castle, home of the Thanes of Cawdor for 600 years.*

JOURNEY'S END *A boulder marks the grave of the Stewarts who died in Bonnie Prince Charlie's front line at Culloden.*

GUN POINT *A Victorian 64-pounder, the sole survivor of its type, commands the Moray Firth at Fort George.*

WHITE WALLS *Gables and pinnacles rise above the lime-plastered façade of 400-year-old Brodie Castle.*

form of a tower-house with the corbelled battlements so typical of 16th-century Scottish fortified houses.

Inside, however, there is none of the chill or menace that pervades many such houses. The ceilings are decorated with elaborate plasterwork and the walls are hung with elegant family portraits. The castle is open daily in summer.

From Brodie the route goes to Auldearn, where a signposted road leads to a 17th-century dovecote.

The route crosses the River Findhorn then follows its bank to Randolph's Leap, where the river rushes through a narrow gorge. A footpath from a lay-by leads down to the river.

DALLAS
The line of stone cottages which straggles along the main street of this upland village could hardly bear less resemblance to the Texan city of skyscrapers and oil tycoons with which it is connected. One of the descendants of the Dallas family who used to own the local estate was George Mifflin Dallas, a 19th-century Vice-President of the United States; and it was after him that Dallas, Texas, was named.

PLUSCARDEN ABBEY
Halfway along a peaceful wooded valley, a massive central tower flanked by two transepts rises above the trees. The setting may have

reminded the French monks who moved here in the 13th century of their parent house, the Priory of Val des Choux in Burgundy.

After the Reformation the Priory of Pluscarden fell into disrepair. The roofs collapsed and ivy crept over the walls. It was not until 1948, when the property was taken over by the Benedictines, that an active community of monks began to restore the buildings to their former glory and to imbue them once again with an atmosphere of quiet devotion. The priory was elevated to abbey status in 1974. It is open daily.

Tourist information: Elgin 3388/2666; Forres 72938 (summer).

Castles and gardens in the Grampians

TOUR

239

—— 93 MILES ——

Salmon rivers and peaty streams flow beside roads that climb high into the Grampians. Gaunt ruins of castles stand sentinel over the glens, and there are two colourful gardens.

TOMINTOUL

Perched high on a heather moor, Tomintoul's pale limestone houses reflect every beam of sunlight and illuminate the central square. A centre for winter sports and summer shooting and fishing, the village was founded astride a military road by the 4th Duke of Gordon in 1776. It lies at 1160ft and like Dalwhinnie is one of the highest villages in the Highlands. One of Tomintoul's largest buildings houses a visitor centre and a museum of local history.

MORTLACH CHURCH

This is one of Scotland's oldest churches. St Moluag, from Ireland, set up a religious cell at Mortlach in the 6th century, and parts of the present church may date from the 11th century. It was restored in 1931, but the original squint – an opening through which segregated lepers watched the service in medieval times – has been retained.

In the vestibule is a pre-Christian stone with an engraving of an animal looking surprisingly like an elephant. Another Pictish stone stands in the churchyard and recalls Malcolm II's victory over the Danes in 1010.

DUFFTOWN

The tumbling waters of the River Fiddich and Dullan Water meet at Dufftown. Its grey-stone buildings converge on a spacious square, overlooked by a clock tower housing a museum and information centre. Although some of the rambling cottages and twisting alleys of Dufftown give the impression of an older settlement, it was only in 1817 that James Duff, the 4th Earl of Fife, planned the town he called Balvenie but which now bears his name.

GLENFIDDICH DISTILLERY

The brown peaty waters of a stream run down granite hills towards the River Fiddich and are diverted into Glenfiddich distillery to help to give the malt whisky produced there its distinctive flavour. The warehouse walls bear a lichen nourished by the sweet fumes that evaporate from the barrels of maturing whisky.

Visitors can chew the surprisingly sweet ears of malted barley, smell the steaming vats of extracted sugar and see the copper stills which distill the spirit. The process here has changed little since the Grant family first produced malt whisky at Glenfiddich on Christmas Day 1887.

Visitors can tour the distillery daily in summer, and on weekdays in winter; the visit includes a film showing the process of whisky making from 'barley to bottle'.

BALVENIE CASTLE

This dominating ruin stands on a grassy mound, its gateway protected by circular towers and a dry moat. Balvenie was one of the earliest of Scotland's stone castles. From the 13th century it secured the passes to Huntly, Keith and Cullen, and was the key to the green roads to Rothes and Elgin.

In the Civil War of the 1640s Royalists and Government forces

TOMINTOUL VALLEY *Cattle graze on the green rolling hills beside Conglass Water, just outside the village of Tomintoul, as the evening shadows lengthen.*

FRAGRANT GARDENS *The mingling scents of catmint, honeysuckle, heather and roses pervade the gardens of Leith Hall.*

CORGARFF CASTLE *Government troops garrisoned in this Highland castle in 1748 added the star-shaped defensive wall.*

ROAD STONE *A plaque commemorates the builders of the military road.*

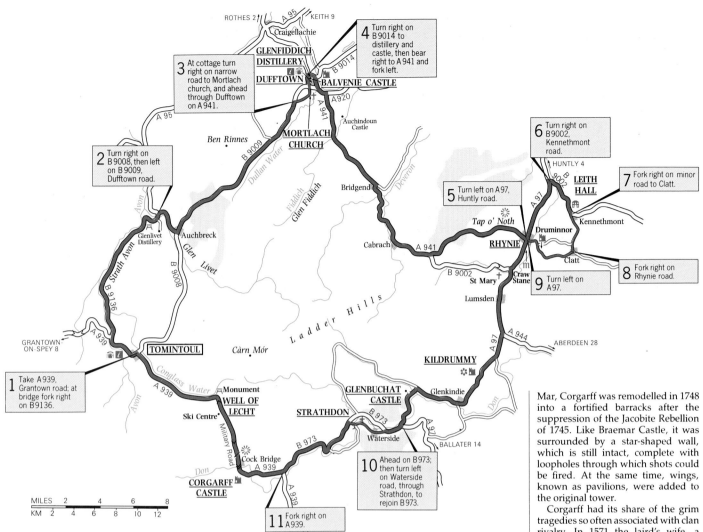

ROTHES 2 A 95 **KEITH 9**

Craigellachie

B 9014

3 At cottage turn right on narrow road to Mortlach church, and ahead through Dufftown on A 941.

GLENFIDDICH DISTILLERY
DUFFTOWN 𝄞 **BALVENIE CASTLE**

4 Turn right on B 9014 to distillery and castle, then bear right to A 941 and fork left.

A 95

A 941

A 920

Auchindoun Castle

Ben Rinnes

6 Turn right on B 9002, Kennethmont road.

B 9009

MORTLACH CHURCH

HUNTLY 4

B 9002

LEITH HALL

2 Turn right on B 9008, then left on B 9009, Dufftown road.

Dullan Water

Fiddich

Glen Fiddich

Deveron

Bridgend

5 Turn left on A 97, Huntly road.

7 Fork right on minor road to Clatt.

A 97

Kennethmont

Tap o' Noth

Druminnor

Glenlivet Distillery

Auchbreck

Cabrach

A 941

RHYNIE

Strath Avon

Glen Livet

B 9008

B 9136

B 9002

St Mary

Craw Stane

Clatt

8 Fork right on Rhynie road.

9 Turn left on A 97.

Lumsden

GRANTOWN-ON-SPEY 8

A 939

Ladder Hills

Càrn Mór

TOMINTOUL

Conglass Water

A 97

A 944

ABERDEEN 28

1 Take A 939, Grantown road; at bridge fork right on B9136.

A 939

Monument

WELL OF LECHT

KILDRUMMY

Ski Centre

Military Road

GLENBUCHAT CASTLE

Glenkindie

Mar, Corgarff was remodelled in 1748

Avon

Cock Bridge

STRATHDON

Don

B 973

10 Ahead on B973; then turn left on Waterside road, through Strathdon, to rejoin B973.

Don

A 939

Waterside

A 97

BALLATER 14

CORGARFF CASTLE

A 939

11 Fork right on A 939.

MILES 2   4   6   8
KM   2 4 6 8 10 12

confronted each other under its walls.

In 1689, the victorious Jacobites returned to Balvenie after the Battle of Killiecrankie.

After the Jacobite rising of 1745 the castle fell into disrepair. But, seen from the green lawns, the gaunt walls and single stone archway defended by double iron gates still convey massive strength. Balvenie is open on most days.

Two miles beyond Balvenie, the grim and neglected ruins of the 15th-century Auchindoun Castle stand on a commanding bluff overlooking the River Fiddich. The castle was burnt down in a clan feud of 1592, and the ruins are now too dangerous to enter but can be viewed from the outside.

LEITH HALL
Herbaceous borders line the sweeping gravel drive leading to this white-painted 17th-century mansion, set in one of Scotland's most attractive gardens. Leith Hall was the home of the Leith-Hay family, but has been in the care of the National Trust for Scotland since 1945. The design of the house is typically Scottish baronial, with 'witch's hat' turrets projecting from the corners, crow-stepped gables and dormer windows. The style was adhered to in 1900 when two conical-roofed towers were added. Inside are gems of Jacobite history, including a writing case given by the Young Pretender to Andrew

Hay on the eve of the Battle of Culloden in 1746.

Two nature trails, each about 2 miles long, lead from the car park through woodlands past a fine 18th-century ice house. The castle is open daily in summer, and the gardens are open all the year.

RHYNIE
A grey village set around a green square, Rhynie stands amid dramatic scenery. Nearby is Druminnor, a 15th-century castle now surrounded by fields of waving barley and backed by birches and Scots pine. Druminnor is an early example of the 'palace style' of castle, having formidable defences yet great beauty. It is not open to visitors.

Just outside Rhynie, in the fold of a hill, is a single standing stone carved with much-eroded Pictish symbols. It is called the Craw Stane (crow stone), and is reached from the only lay-by on this stretch – opposite a farm gate.

KILDRUMMY
Sheltered by an ancient quarry and a canopy of mighty beeches, Kildrummy Garden is overlooked by the ruins of a 13th-century castle. The walls of its hall, kitchen and chapel survive almost intact.

The castle is open daily and the garden is open daily in summer. They are run independently and have separate car parks.

GLENBUCHAT CASTLE
Twisting paths climb steeply from the car park to the ruins of Glenbuchat Castle. These paths, dovetailing into the contours of towering hills, were once trodden by smugglers carrying whisky from illicit stills.

Glenbuchat's original Z-plan design can still be seen, as can the unusual feature of two stair turrets supported by French style 'tromps' – flying arches. When the castle is seen in fading light against the setting sun it is easy to understand why John Gordon, who built it in 1590, loved it so and recorded the fact with inscriptions carved on the wall. The castle is not open to the public, but may be viewed from the outside.

STRATHDON
Pipe-skirling, prize salmon, canoes on the river and Highland Games in mid-August make Donside one of the joys of Scotland. The Strathdon village, dominated by its church spire, is the starting point for riverside walks fringed by delicate birches and gnarled oaks. The more adventurous will enjoy climbing on the heathery slopes.

CORGARFF CASTLE
This hauntingly attractive slate-roofed tower, with white-painted walls, stands alone on a mound surrounded by rolling hills. Built in 1537 as a hunting lodge by the Earl of

Mar, Corgarff was remodelled in 1748 into a fortified barracks after the suppression of the Jacobite Rebellion of 1745. Like Braemar Castle, it was surrounded by a star-shaped wall, which is still intact, complete with loopholes through which shots could be fired. At the same time, wings, known as pavilions, were added to the original tower.

Corgarff had its share of the grim tragedies so often associated with clan rivalry. In 1571 the laird's wife, a Campbell, was burned to death in the castle by the Gordons, along with her family and servants.

The interior has been restored to show the stark, draughty reality of an 18th-century barracks complete with huge wooden bunks, recesses for muskets and enormous stone fireplaces. The castle is open daily in summer.

WELL OF LECHT
With sweeping expanses of heather-clad slopes on all sides, the road beyond Cock Bridge climbs steeply to 2090ft, following the old military road from Corgarff to Tomintoul. There are panoramic views from the ski-lift area. The lifts themselves operate only in winter, when ski lessons are available, but the café and other facilities are also open from June to September.

A carved stone commemorating the labours of General George Wade and his team of soldier-builders stands in the car park and picnic spot at the Well of Lecht – to the right of the road just below the ski lifts. From here the pale winding ribbon of the military road can be seen, using every contour of the hills to assist drainage and avoid ambush.

Tourist information: Elgin 2666; Tomintoul 285 (summer); Dufftown 20501 (summer); Alford 2052 (summer).

Lochs and falls along the Great Glen

The 60 mile long Great Glen splits the Highlands in two. Its lochs are linked by a series of cuttings to form the Caledonian Canal, a waterway from coast to coast.

INVERNESS

There is no better springboard for a tour of northern Scotland than Inverness, 'capital of the Highlands'. The town stands at the eastern end of the Great Glen, and is a terminus of the Caledonian Canal.

The city centre is dominated by a pink sandstone castle on a steep grassy bank overlooking the River Ness. It was built in the 19th century to replace two earlier fortresses, the last of which was blown up by Jacobites in the 1745 rebellion. Inverness Museum in Castle Wynd has many Jacobite relics. Across the river stands St Andrew's Cathedral, built in the 1860s. Its font is a copy of one in Copenhagen Cathedral, Denmark.

BEAULY

The French monks who built the priory here in 1230 named the site *beau lieu*, meaning 'beautiful place'. And it still is, despite the main road which trundles through the town. At one end of the central square stand the ruins of the priory – one of only three houses outside France belonging to the Valliscaulian order.

The square is dominated by a monument built in 1905 to commemorate the raising by Lord Lovat of Scouts for service in the Boer War.

Until earlier this century, when the river estuary silted up, Beauly was a port with a harbourmaster. The jetties have now vanished; but the narrow towpath at the bottom of Ferry Lane makes a pleasant walk along the river bank.

The road to the west follows the course of the River Beauly. There are plenty of lay-bys from which to admire breathtaking views along gorges carved out of the solid rock.

CULLIGRAN FALLS

The falls themselves may be no more dramatic than many other Highland waterfalls; but the journey to reach them leads through some of the most spectacular and secluded scenery in Britain.

Just before Struy Bridge a road to the right leads to Glen Strathfarrar. The adventure has begun. But first the motorist must get a vehicle pass from the cottage beside the gate where the public road ends. The falls are reached after driving for 2 miles, amid peaceful woodlands.

CORRIMONY

At the head of Glen Urquhart, a side road crosses the River Enrick and leads westwards to a separate valley which is steeped in thousands of years of history. It was among these gentle farmlands that Mony, a Norse prince who invaded Scotland, is said to have been killed and buried. Corrimony is also the site of a chambered cairn about 4000 years old.

DRUMNADROCHIT

At the foot of fertile Glen Urquhart, Drumnadrochit is a popular stopping-off place for visitors to Loch Ness. An exhibition centre chronicles the various accounts of the legendary Loch Ness monster – from a sighting in the 6th century attributed to St Columba to more recent film coverage of disturbances in the deep waters of the loch, and the results of sonar patrols. It also reveals the remarkable ingenuity displayed by searchers in their quest for the monster.

A side road south of the village goes 2 miles up Glen Coiltie to the Divach Falls, where a cataract cascades 100ft down the rocks of a steep wooded valley. Perched romantically on a ledge above the falls is Dhivach Lodge where J.M. Barrie (1860-1937), the author of *Peter Pan*, once stayed.

LOCH NESS

The road from Urquhart Castle to Invermoriston runs alongside the wooded slopes of Loch Ness, with plenty of lay-bys at good viewpoints. Mountains tower menacingly on either side of the loch's sometimes choppy waters which, at a depth of up to 754ft, are deeper than much of the North Sea. The loch was created some 400 million years ago by a huge rift which split Scotland along the Great Glen. Later, glaciers moulded the scenery until the last retreat of the ice, only 10,000 years ago.

INVERMORISTON

At Invermoriston, the forests rise sharply behind the low-lying pastures at the mouth of the River Moriston. The village is small and sparsely populated – like the rest of the Glen which was a victim of the Highland Clearances of the 19th century, when the inhabitants were evicted to make way for sheep. But there is an inn, now called the Glenmoriston Arms Hotel, in which Dr Johnson and Boswell were said to have planned their epic tour of the Hebrides. Just before the bridge, a path branches off along the bank of the River Moriston towards Loch Ness.

WHITEBRIDGE

The route from Fort Augustus rises through rougher country, over moors where hidden lochs and lochans, or small lochs, gleam amidst the heather. In stretches the road runs arrow straight, for it follows the course of General Wade's military road constructed after the Jacobite rebellions to connect strategically sited forts in the Highlands and to move troops quickly in the event of another uprising.

At Whitebridge a fine humpbacked bridge, built by Wade in 1732, arches over the River Fechlin; but it is no longer used. There is also a hotel which was once a military rest house.

One mile beyond Whitebridge the route leaves the military road to follow a narrow winding road which clings to the bank of the wooded valley of the River Foyers. It passes a picnic area beside the river, and provides a marked contrast both to General Wade's road and to the lonely moorland road along Strathnairn.

ABERCHALDER GARDENS

A sheltered glen scooped out of the purple hills provides a perfect setting for Aberchalder Alpine Gardens. The scent of pine hangs heavily on the small ornamental rock gardens; and the peace is disturbed only by the buzzing of bees and the gurgle of the river as it trickles over the boulders at the bottom of the garden.

Tourist information: Inverness 234353.

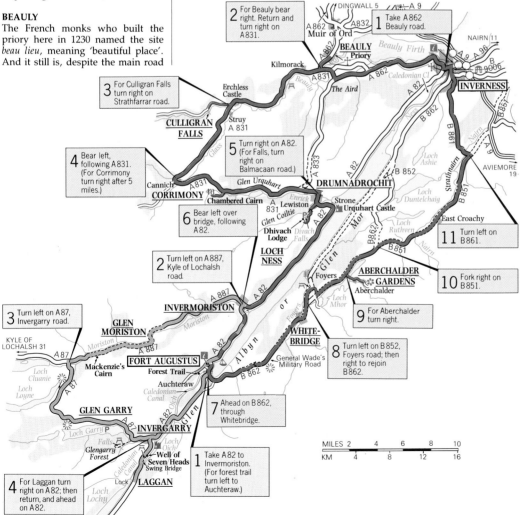

TOUR
241
— 52 MILES —

Sweet-scented pine forests in which deer roam give way to bleak and windswept moors. A ruined castle recalls the Jacobite Wars, and Loch Ness preserves an air of mystery.

FORT AUGUSTUS

The best approach to Fort Augustus is along the side road which rises along the east bank of the River Tarff. Down below, the grey clock tower and belfry of St Benedict's Abbey rise above the trees which line the deep, blue waters of Loch Ness.

The abbey, which houses a school, was built in the 19th century and stands on the site of one of a chain of forts built across the Highlands by General Wade after the Jacobite rising of 1715. It was named after Prince William Augustus, Duke of Cumberland, the victor of Culloden in 1746. More information on the Great Glen since prehistoric times is provided by the Great Glen Exhibition.

At the heart of the village a flight of six locks designed in the early 19th century by the engineer Thomas Telford connects Loch Ness with the Caledonian Canal. The grass banks on either side are a good place to observe the varying degrees of skill with which the pleasure boats negotiate the locks. Fort Augustus is now a pleasant, pine-scented Highland resort – a centre for boating, hill walking and fishing.

Only 2 miles from the town centre is the Inchnacardoch Forest Trail, reached by turning left on a road signposted 'Auchterawe'. The trail displays fine examples of trees such as juniper, oak, birch, beech and ash among which deer can sometimes be seen roaming.

GLEN MORISTON

At Invermoriston the route leaves the Great Glen and passes through the heavily wooded lower reaches of Glen Moriston. Although this is one of the major routes to the West Coast, the trees on either side give the feeling of seclusion; and the road narrows to a single track as it crosses the bridges over the river. Dr Johnson and Boswell travelled this route in 1773 on their epic tour of the Highlands and Islands.

At one point, the route passes a small cairn on the left of the road. An inscription relates how, on this spot, a Jacobite officer named Roderick Mackenzie was mortally wounded in 1746. Mackenzie was 'of the same size and of similar resemblance' to Prince Charles Edward Stuart, and the government troops who captured him, encouraged by the £30,000 ransom on the prince, believed that they had caught him at last. Gallantly Mackenzie did not disillusion them – for the sake of his prince who was hiding in a nearby cave. According to tradition, Mackenzie told the redcoats, 'Gentlemen, you have murdered your prince!'

SAILING SAFE *Sailing boats find a tranquil haven in the waters of Fort Augustus, at the south-west corner of Loch Ness.*

URQUHART CASTLE *In 1692 the castle was blown up to prevent it falling to the Jacobites. Its ruins jut out from the west bank of Loch Ness, by Urquhart Bay.*

ROOFLESS REMAINS *All that is left of Beauly Priory is the shell of its church.*

BEAULY VALLEY *The River Beauly twists through the valley's tree-clad banks.*

GLEN GARRY

The road which climbs up the windswept moorland between Loch Loyne and Loch Garry is a stark contrast to the sheltered woods of Glen Moriston; but the traveller is rewarded by magnificent views on either side. Soon, however, the road descends to the wooded slopes of Loch Garry.

Just beyond the end of the loch, a track to the right leads over a bridge to a car park and picnic area in Glengarry Forest. From there, a marked walk of just under 2 miles leads to the pretty Falls of Garry.

INVERGARRY

The chiefs of the Clan Macdonnell made their home at Invergarry Castle. However, because of their support for the Jacobite cause, the castle was burnt and rebuilt several times. It was finally set fire to in 1746 and all that remains now are ruins perched on the steep slopes of Loch Oich.

It was the Macdonnells, too, who in 1812 had a monument built half a mile south of the village. The monument, known as the Well of Seven Heads, is carved with the heads of seven murderers as 'a memorial of ample and summary vengeance'. Inscriptions tell a gruesome tale in four languages – Gaelic, Latin, French and English. In the 1660s the young Chief of Keppoch and his brother, both kinsmen of the Macdonnell chief, were murdered by seven of their jealous relatives. And so, on the orders of Lord Macdonnell, 'in the swift course of feudal justice', the heads of the murderers were presented to him once they had been washed in the waters of the spring.

According to tradition, the heads were laid at the Chief's feet by the family bard, Ian Lorn.

LAGGAN

Streams course down the hillsides above Laggan towards the Caledonian Canal. This was built between 1804 and 1822 to link the Atlantic Ocean at Corpach with the North Sea at Inverness, so bypassing the dangerous Pentland Firth. The extraordinary piece of engineering – 22 miles of man-made cuttings and 38 miles of lochs – was designed and built by Thomas Telford and took 44 years to complete. The stretch at Laggan has a swing bridge in the east and a set of locks in the west.

Tourist information: Fort Augustus 6367 (summer).

Granite domes beside the Spey valley

Sweeping ranges of heather-clad mountains, often capped with snow, rise above the valley of the River Spey. Narrow roads, with few petrol stations, twist and turn through fine scenery.

NEWTONMORE

Overlooked by the splendour of the Monadhliath Mountains to the north, Newtonmore, with its gaily painted, stone-built hotels and guesthouses, stands at the gateway to the Spey valley. A long winding path leads from the village for more than 4 miles among the stately rowans and wind-bent birches of Glen Banchor, to Loch Dubh, below the 3087ft summit of Carn Ban. From those high slopes there is a view across the Spey valley to the Cairngorms, which are never without patches of snow in their high hollows. Nearer at hand, in summer, lines of ponies can be seen trekking from the local hotel.

The surrounding glens were once populated by the Macphersons, whose clan museum is in Newtonmore. Black musical pipes made in the 15th century, battle banners, and an assortment of fearsome weaponry are among the reminders of this once powerful clan.

KINGUSSIE

Rolling hills with granite outcrops, sparkling streams and the smell of resin from the surrounding forests give Kingussie an invigorating air. A folk museum showing Highland and Island life, originally founded on Iona in 1934-5 and the oldest in Britain, has indoor and open-air exhibits. A small Hebridean black-house – with a turf roof providing nest sites for starlings and house sparrows – and a shooting lodge stand in a green field planted with roses.

A small 'clack mill' – named after the noise it makes when grinding corn – is powered by the tiniest of streams. It is next to a set of overlapping, mushroom-shaped stackle, or stad-dle, stones. These were linked by planks of wood on which cereal crops were stacked to dry, helped by the air circulating between the stones – which also kept out hungry rodents. Inside the museum are old farm implements, a peat-cutting display and vintage vehicles, including a steam-powered fire engine. There is also a display of local crafts. The museum is open daily in summer and on weekdays in winter.

Kingussie is also a popular centre for winter sports in the Cairngorms.

RUTHVEN BARRACKS

On a prominent grassy mound beside the road stand the stark ruins of Ruthven Barracks, built to house troops brought in to control the Highlanders after the 1715 rebellion. The barracks survived for less than 30 years. They were captured by Bonnie Prince Charlie's forces during the 1745 uprising. After their defeat at Culloden in 1746 many of the prince's men gathered at Ruthven to await fresh orders which never came. Before dispersing they set fire to the barracks and only the walls remain. The ruins are open daily.

ROCK WOOD PONDS

A drive fragrant with the smell of fresh-cut timber and noisy with flocks of chaffinches leads to a car park close to a tranquil loch. From the car park the Rock Wood Ponds Trail follows a 2 mile circular route along deer paths and through open rides with spectacular views of tiny lochs reflecting the trees in their peaty waters. Here is a quiet spot to stop, stare and listen to the high-pitched calls of goldcrests and crossbills as they feed in the upper branches of the conifers.

INSH CHURCH

Perched high on a rocky knoll overlooking the reedy shallows at the northern tip of Loch Insh is a tiny white-painted church. It was built in the 18th century, but the site has been in continual use since the 7th century. Inside is an 8th-century bronze hand bell, used to call worshippers in the days before bells were hung in steeples.

In the loch lurks an Arctic species of char, once migratory until cut off from the sea during the ice ages. The fish stay in the cool depths and spawn along the upper reaches of the loch's feeder streams.

HIGHLAND WILDLIFE PARK

Wolves prowl the woodlands, wild boar and bison crash through the undergrowth and pine martens chase squirrels through the branches of the trees, taking visitors back in time to the wildwoods of ancient Britain. This is the Highland Wildlife Park near Kincraig. It is open daily from spring to autumn.

No pets are allowed to remain in the cars entering the park, but kennels are provided at the entrance. Beavers, wildcats, otters and badgers can all be seen, and from the reception building there is sometimes an osprey to watch as it fishes in the nearby lake.

AVIEMORE

Souvenir shops, hamburger bars, amusement arcades, a busy railway station and throngs of tourists give Aviemore today the atmosphere of a bustling seaside resort. But before 1960 Aviemore was a sleepy little village straddling the Spey valley; its name derives from *Agaidh Mohr*, 'the big gap'. Copper retorts, hundreds of

LOCH INSH *Above Kincraig Bridge this widening of the Spey is at its most tranquil. It is also a sailing and canoeing centre.*

brands of whisky both malt and blended, and old illicit stills taken from Highland hide-outs are features of the Whisky Centre and Museum at Inverdruie, just south of the town. A whisky trail map shows the position of each distillery open to the public.

In winter, Aviemore is full of skiers in search of Cairngorm snow. In summer the town is a good gathering point for visitors before they disperse into the tranquillity of the unspoilt Spey valley.

Loch an Eilein, 2 miles south of Aviemore, is surrounded by pine forests. In the 15th century, the ruined castle on an island in the loch was a stronghold of Sir Alexander Stuart, son of Robert II.

The loch is part of the vast Cairngorms National Nature Reserve, which covers about 100 square miles. There is a visitor centre on the north side of the loch, open from May to September. A nature trail, just over 3 miles long, starts at the centre and goes around the loch, passing some of the finest remnants of the ancient Caledonian Forest.

GLENMORE FOREST PARK

The waters of Loch Morlich reflect the savage but haunting scenery of the Cairngorms. Patches of snow remain to reflect the sunlight of high summer. Reindeer, introduced from Lapland in the 1950s, lie cooling themselves in the drifts of snow, resident ptarmigans feed off the new green shoots of heather, and visiting dotterel quietly incubate their eggs.

Waymarked walks lead from car parks through belts of planted conifers screening caravan sites and outdoor centres. Native Scots pines give shelter from winter snow and summer heat, their fissured red trunks reflecting a warm friendly light onto the forest floor. Gaps through the trees reveal kaleidoscopic variations in the colour of mountain, moor and loch. South of the forest lies the mighty Cairn Gorm, 4084ft high, where chair lifts from the car parks carry visitors to a different world of granite peaks. The main chair lift, which goes almost to the summit of Cairn Gorm, operates all year round, weather permitting.

BOAT OF GARTEN

The smooth deep waters of the Spey sweep gently around the village, providing an obvious site for the ferry which gave the Boat of Garten its name. The ferry was replaced in 1898 by a wooden trestle bridge which carried traffic until the early 1970s, when the elegant concrete and steel span was constructed.

In the centre of the village is the terminus of the Strathspey Railway, whose steam-hauled trains take about 20 minutes to reach Aviemore along a scenic route. The service operates on Saturdays and Sundays from mid-May to mid-October, daily except Friday in July and August, and on Sundays from mid-April to mid-May. Signs, signals, points, photographs and rolling stock are scattered in and around the old waiting room, which is now used as a museum.

Boat of Garten describes itself as the

'Osprey village', but the RSPB reserve at Loch Garten is 2 miles farther east, up a signposted road off the main road. The hide overlooks the pine-fringed loch, and the ospreys are present around their nesting tree from June to September. Red squirrels, roe deer, capercaillie and crossbills are resident, while in winter the loch echoes to the calls of visiting wildfowl, often including whooper swans. Visitors must keep to the marked path to the hide, which is open daily from the end of April to the end of August. Elsewhere access is confined to the pinewood paths.

MARYPARK

Old stone cottages with neat and colourful gardens mingle with a few modern bungalows in this pretty hamlet. Marypark often vibrates to the sound of bagpipes coming from the workshop of George Kilgour, Highland bagpipe maker. The bags are made from hide and sheepskin and the pipes on which the melodies are played are hand turned and mounted with nickel. Blocks of ivory and sterling silver lie about waiting to be used in the finishing touches.

The nearby Glenfarclas Distillery is open daily from Monday to Friday and at weekends too in the summer. A guided tour follows whisky production from the delivery of barley and peaty water to the time the spirit is stacked in barrels and left for at least seven years to mature.

KNOCKANDO

An avenue of sycamores dripping with nectar and buzzing with bees in summer leads from a roadside lay-by to the 18th-century Knockando church. In the grounds are Pictish stones and inside is an impressive gallery. Memorials to the Grants and other whisky families line the walls.

Opposite the lay-by a sign indicates a gentle walk down to a riverside woollen mill. No museum this, but a hard-working mill operated by one man, its most modern piece of machinery being a loom built in Rochdale in 1919. The mill is now powered by electricity, but the old water-driven wheel can still be seen, surrounded by nettles and with an old blackbird's nest set between two of the wooden gear cogs.

Just under half a mile beyond the mill, along a well-signposted narrow road, is Tamdhu Distillery, open on summer weekdays and marked on the whisky trail map.

Archiestown, 4 miles east of Knockando, is set around a square and has another old working mill producing tough tartans used, as the owner says, by 'fishermen and those who kill the birds upon the hills'.

CRAIGELLACHIE

Overhung by precipitous rocks and precariously balanced Scots pines stands Thomas Telford's single-span bridge, its supports washed by the swirling waters of the Spey. Cast in iron in 1815, and closed to traffic since the opening of the new bridge in 1972, Telford's castellated masterpiece has now been restored. The pale shingle of the riverbed reflects every ray of

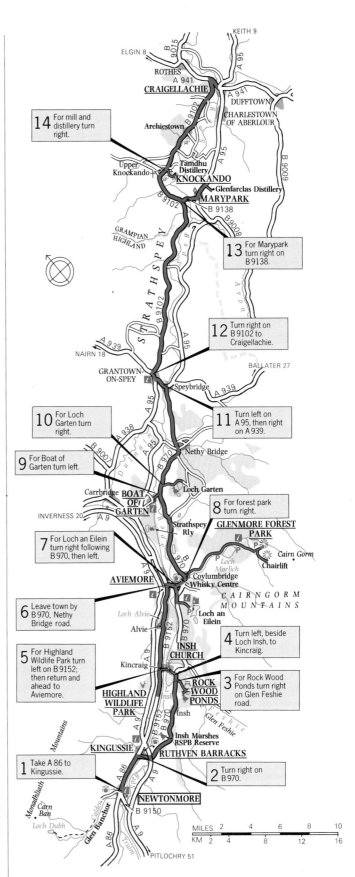

sunshine, highlighting the fringing vegetation of hemp-agrimony, ragwort, rosebay and monkey flower. Sandpipers and swifts are seen.

From Craigellachie, a town famous for the distilling and blending of whisky and the associated barrel making, waymarked paths run alongside the often turbulent waters of the

Spey. There are spectacular views of ravens, occasionally buzzards, and on rare occasions eagles soaring on the thermals of warm air.

Tourist information: Newtonmore 274 (summer); Kingussie 297 (summer); Aviemore 810363; Elgin 3388; Boat of Garten 307.

Loch shores on the Road to the Isles

TOUR
243

— 112 MILES —

A coastal village is the base for an adventurous drive through the spectacular Highland scenery of Moidart, where the 1745 Jacobite rising had its beginning and its end.

ARISAIG

Built round the head of a shallow sea loch, where wild flowers brighten a succession of grass-backed rocky bays, the village of Arisaig looks out over jumbled reefs and skerries towards the Cuillin peaks of Skye, the spiky summits of the lesser Cuillin on the Nature Conservancy island of Rhum, and the crouching, sphinx-like outline of Eigg. All the islands are reached by summer cruises from Arisaig harbour.

The surrounding country has always been Roman Catholic, and was therefore sympathetic to the cause of Bonnie Prince Charlie. This, together with its remoteness, was why the prince chose the village as his base of operations in 1745. The church in

Arisaig is still Roman Catholic, and its spire a famous local landmark. The church clock is a memorial to Alasdair MacMhaighstir Alasdair, a much revered Gaelic poet who fought alongside the prince at Culloden.

The village has a station on the West Highland Railway, opened in 1901 to link Fort William with the newly created port of Mallaig. During the summer, several of the trains are steam-hauled.

Arisaig's white sandy bays and rocky islets are pleasant to explore. Sometimes seals and human bathers eye each other with the same polite curiosity. But the most impressive sight is when the towering golden-red cloudbanks of a West Highland sunset form a backdrop for the dark silhouettes of Eigg and Rhum.

LOCH NAN UAMH

East of Arisaig, the narrow main road twists and turns through shaded woodland glens before curving along the bouldery shore of Loch nan Uamh. High above a fringe of oaks, the terraced crags of Druim Fiaclach brood over a place of Jacobite regrets. It was on the shores of this loch that Prince Charles Edward Stuart landed in July 1745 with the dream of gaining the throne of England.

A memorial cairn by the shore marks the spot where Bonnie Prince Charlie left for France, on a

September day in 1746 when the Jacobite cause, in military terms, was abandoned forever.

Under a railway viaduct, the road leaves Loch nan Uamh and climbs over a pass. On a hilltop, an isolated white church is outlined against the bulk of Rois-Bheinn, dominating the far shore of Loch Ailort.

LOCH AILORT

The tidemark shows that this splendid loch, between Rois-Bheinn and the rocky Ardnish peninsula, is not landlocked, as first impressions suggest. It curves westwards to the hidden sea.

Lochailort village is a quiet place, centred on a hotel and a hillside railway station. But at the turn of the century it was the site of a bustling construction camp where 2000 railway navvies lived. Now, it is the headquarters of an extensive fish-farming operation. Beyond the mouth of Loch Ailort there are parking and picnic places among jagged rock outcrops, with fine views across the Sound of Arisaig.

GLENUIG

Until the 1960s, this settlement of houses facing the sea on a tiny bay and climbing the steep glen behind had no road access from any direction. Now Glenuig is the starting point for summer cruises to the isle of Eigg.

A narrow side road turns off towards the sandy beach of Samalaman

Bay. At the end of the road there are two exhilarating walks. A rough half-mile track crosses a pass to the restored cottages of the tiny coastal settlement of Smirisary. Another heads through a mile of wild country to Loch na Bairness, dotted with wooded islets.

Back on the main road, the route climbs through the outcropped rocks and heather of Glen Uig to a summit viewpoint over the mainland hills, the substantial islands and the maze of tidal inlets at Loch Moidart which at low tide consists mostly of sandflats.

LOCH MOIDART

The area known as Moidart, between Loch Ailort and Loch Shiel, is the very heart of Jacobite country. The road slants down a hillside of birch woods and heather, then runs along the lochside to the hamlet of Kinlochmoidart, passing a living Jacobite memorial. In a meadow stand seven beech trees, known as the Seven Men of Moidart, commemorating the group of men who accompanied Bonnie Prince Charlie from France in 1745.

During the rising the MacDonalds of Kinlochmoidart were among the prince's most faithful followers, and Kinlochmoidart was his secret planning base.

Beyond the head of the loch there is a climb through conifer plantations to a bare summit. Three stone cairns mark the place where funeral parties, carrying coffins across country for burial on nearby St Finnan's Island in Loch Shiel, traditionally paused for a rest. Then the route winds down into the great glacial valley of Loch Shiel.

ACHARACLE

The mile-long village of Acharacle looks over peat mosses at the foot of Loch Shiel to the range of mountains which holds the middle and upper reaches of the loch in a giant grasp.

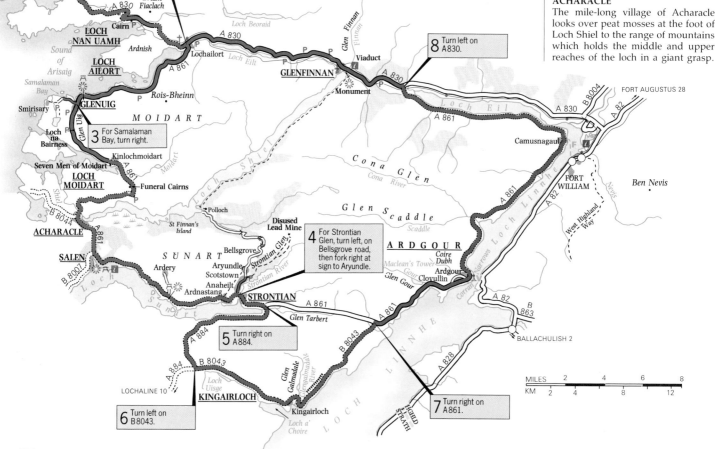

CORRAN *A car ferry runs between the west and east banks of Loch Linnhe.*

DOWN THE LOCH *From the Jacobite monument at the head of Loch Shiel the shimmering stretch of fresh water, nowhere wider than 1 mile across, is broken only by a wooded island below the bare slopes of Meall nan Creag Laec.*

STRONTIAN *The village post office also serves as a supply shop for visitors.*

Acharacle is a fine base for loch and river fishing, sailing, canoeing, hill-walking and pony trekking. Dinghies can be hired from the pier.

Five miles from Acharacle, along the southern shore of Loch Shiel, the mountains enclose one of the very few islands in this narrow deep-water loch. Eilean Fhianain has St Finnan's Island – a centuries-old burial ground with a ruined chapel dedicated to St Finnan, a contemporary of St Columba.

SALEN

Over a wooded pass from Acharacle is Salen, a smaller village set round the rocky shores of a narrow inlet of Loch Sunart. The best view of it is from a waymarked mile-long trail which starts at a Forestry Commission car park and leads through attractive oak woods to a picnic site and tourist information point overlooking the loch where it opens out to the sea.

About 5 miles farther on, the forest car park at Ardery is the start of a short walk over a wooded promontory to a quiet bay with peaceful loch and island views.

Loch Sunart is noted for its wildlife. Along the shoreline, plants such as sea plantain, thrift and scurvy grass survive the salt spray and high spring tides. Otters and common seals are often seen, and there is good fishing for sea trout, skate, mackerel and salmon. Many sea birds live on or visit the loch, including several species of gull, terns, eider ducks and black guillemot.

STRONTIAN

This substantial village extends along both sides of a bay and up the valley of the Strontian River. The estate was bought by the Crown in 1920, to guarantee land to crofters back from the First World War. There are salmon and sea-trout fishing, craft work-

shops, and a selection of walks with extensive mountain views, such as the track from Ardnastang, 1 mile west of Strontian, above the croftlands of Anaheilt.

A leaflet available in the village describes the 7 mile Aryundle Nature Trail starting from a car park in Strontian Glen. It passes through plantations of lodgepole pine and a fine oak wood preserved by the Nature Conservancy; then it crosses a high moorland to the site of one of the lead mines which operated in the district for a century and a half from 1722. One of the minerals extracted from the mines was strontianite, from which strontium 90 was isolated – the same isotope that occurs as a by-product of nuclear fission.

Beyond Strontian, the route rounds the head of Loch Sunart before turning south to tackle the lonely hill and forest country of Kingairloch.

KINGAIRLOCH

Narrow and twisting, the only road through Kingairloch runs at first over a wild heathery moorland, then down alongside the deep gorge of the river which drains Loch Uisge, through forest plantations to the sea.

At the edge of Loch a' Choire is the beautifully located hamlet of Kingairloch. Backed by steeply rising wooded hills, the single line of houses faces a beach of pink, white and grey pebbles, separated by the windings of the Glengalmadale river from a series of shingle lagoons.

Glen Galmadale itself is unexpectedly dramatic, with a ring of 2000ft ridges. After it, the road runs between the shore of Loch Linnhe and a line of reddish cliffs, with massive boulders tumbled down from them – an open-air geology classroom on the Great Glen Fault, which runs from south-west to north-east, cutting the Highlands in two.

ARDGOUR

The mountains of Ardgour crowd the road against the Loch Linnhe shore. There are only occasional stretches of level ground, as at the crofting fields of the bypassed village of Clovullin. On the wild mountainside above, a high-level waterfall called Maclean's Tower can be seen foaming down from Coire Dubh, the 'Black Corrie'.

Ardgour village starts with a road-side lighthouse, marking the entrance to the tide-race of the Corran Narrows, where a car ferry crosses Loch Linnhe. The cages of a salmon farm are moored in a bay where eider ducks cruise.

Running mostly through birch woods, the route continues to Camusnagaul – where a passenger ferry runs to Fort William – and the towering mass of Ben Nevis is seen directly across Loch Linnhe.

GLENFINNAN

In one of the most stunning inland views of Scotland, peak after mountain peak appears to march away down Loch Shiel. Against this background an elegant lochside tower – open daily in the summer – commemorates August 19, 1745, when Bonnie Prince Charlie arrived by boat to raise the Jacobite standard in front of more than 1000 Highland fighting men.

Had the spot been deliberately chosen to enhance the grandeur of the moment, the prince could not have done better. From a wide green meadow, the mountains reach up to the ragged base of the clouds, framing the waters of Loch Shiel. But the choice was strategically made. Glenfinnan lay in the country of Mac-Donald of Clanranald, who had already committed his clan, and its position at the head of three glens made it accessible to other clans.

Most important of these were the Camerons, whose chieftain, Cameron of Lochiel, was a man of great

influence. If he refused to rise, other clans would follow suit, and a few days earlier, seeing no sign of the French support promised by the prince, he had demurred. Charles replied that he had intended to raise the clans come what may, and Lochiel could 'stay at home and learn from the News Sheet the fate of his Prince'.

However, at about 2pm, a skirl of pipes was heard in the hills and 700 Camerons, with Lochiel at their head, came swinging over the ridge and down a zigzag path not far from where the viaduct of the West Highland Railway now stands. Warriors from other clans arrived and in the late afternoon the silken banner of white and crimson was unfurled, the prince's father was proclaimed James III of Great Britain – and the prince himself Regent of the Kingdom.

The west side of Loch Shiel is trackless. But an invigorating 15 mile walk on a forest road, starting about 2 miles east of Glenfinnan, leads down the other shore to Pollock, a hamlet linked by road with Strontian.

Across the road from the monument is an information centre. Behind it, the railway crosses Glen Finnan on its spectacular curving viaduct, one of the pioneering designs of Sir Robert McAlpine, 'Concrete Bob'.

Glenfinnan pier is used by anglers and the Loch Shiel cruise boats. Uphill, beside the main road, is the Victorian Gothic Church of St Mary and St Finnan. In a wooden frame nearby hangs a bell – intended for a tower which was never built.

The rest of Glenfinnan village is beside the station. Beyond, the route runs past craggy, birch-scattered hills above narrow Loch Eilt before dipping down again to Lochailort.

Tourist information: Fort William 3781; Mallaig 2170 (summer); Salen 622 (summer).

Crofts and castles on the coast of Skye

TOUR

244

——— 125 MILES ———

Coastal roads on a wild and beautiful island lead to quiet fishing and crofting villages. On the way are ruined castles, waterfalls, craggy summits and weird rock formations.

KYLEAKIN

This seafront village of white houses, hotels, shops and numerous churches is the main ferry port in Skye. Its name comes from the Norse King Hakon, whose fleet assembled here in 1263 before sailing south to defeat in the Battle of Largs – which freed the Hebrides from Viking control. Kyle Akin means Hakon's Strait, where fast tides rush through between Skye and the mainland.

On a bluff overlooking the strait stand the ruins of Castle Moil. There was a fortress here in Viking times,

controlling the strait. Parts of the present ruins date from the 13th century, when the castle was a stronghold for the MacKinnons.

Westwards, the road runs between forest and coast, with views to the islands in the Inner Sound. The motorist passes by Skye's only airstrip and onto the crofting fields of Upper and Lower Breakish.

BROADFORD

The largest village in the south of Skye attracts walkers, cyclists, anglers, birdwatchers and fossil-hunters. Broadford is built round three sides of a rocky bay. On the west side, a tree-lined road leads to a harbour now used mainly by yachts and dinghies, although Broadford is still the registration port for Skye-based fishing boats. On the east side, the houses at Waterloo recall that this part of the village was first settled by veterans of the Napoleonic Wars.

Beyond the mouth of Broadford Bay is the low-lying island of Pabay, whose souvenir postage stamps, issued locally, are on sale in the village.

Beyond Pabay can be seen the Crowlin Islands, backed by the mainland mountains of Applecross.

The white hotel at the bridge over the Broadford River stands on the site of an old inn where, in 1746, one of the MacKinnons welcomed the fugitive Bonnie Prince Charlie after his defeat at the Battle of Culloden. The prince asked for a liqueur, made to his own recipe of whisky, honey and other secret ingredients, which later became known as Drambuie – from *dram buidheach*, Gaelic for 'the drink that satisfies'. The secret recipe has remained with the MacKinnon family ever since.

Inland, there is a fine view over the Broadford River to the peak of Beinn na Caillich, rising from moorland and a forerunner of the magnificent mountains to come. Beyond Broadford, the main road runs between conifer plantations to Corry picnic area, from which a short walk leads to a quiet bay facing the wooded and hilly island of Scalpay.

STROLLAMUS

Protected from the northerly winds by the bulk of Scalpay island, Strollamus is the first of a series of crofting villages on the coast road beyond Broadford. A centre for sea angling and pony trekking, it merges with Dunan, where a local craftsman makes small ornaments, ashtrays and paperweights from Skye marble.

The road runs along the shore of Loch Ainort and through the hamlet of Luib, where an old thatched cottage has been turned into a museum of crofting, open daily in summer.

Beyond Luib, a pass sweeps up to a ridge of wedge-shaped peaks, the Red Hills. They rise from heather and rough moorland – where mountain torrents dash down steeply angled gullies – up to the craggy 2542ft summit of Glamaig.

Down below, on the shore of Loch Sligachan, is the crofting town of Sconser. It has a golf course whose fairways are grazed by sheep. Nearby is the car-ferry slip for the beautiful offshore Island of Raasay.

SLIGACHAN

Standing beyond the head of the loch, Sligachan Hotel has been a renowned climbing centre since Victorian times, when enthusiasts pioneered mountaineering in Skye. The southern skyline is ringed by the soaring peaks, saw-toothed ridges and pinnacles of

the Cuillin Hills, several of whose summits rise to more than 3000ft. These are the finest climbing mountains in Scotland, their coarse rock providing solid handholds and footholds.

Many parts of the Cuillin ridge are accessible only to rock climbers. Even the so-called 'tourist route' from Sligachan to the 3166ft summit of Sgurr nan Gillean, 3 miles away, calls for agility and strength. However, a less arduous, low-level route which offers magnificent views of the rock faces starts from the old bridge of Sligachan. A rough track leads up the glaciated valley of Glen Sligachan to the foot of the crags of Blà Bheinn.

LOCH HARPORT

Beyond Sligachan, the road crosses the moorlands of Glen Drynoch to the head of Loch Harport, where white houses line the steep hillside above the south-western shore.

At Carbost, the side road descends to sea level and then hairpins sharply uphill again. At the north-west end of the village are the pagoda-roofed, malt-drying kilns of Talisker Distillery – the only place in Skye where malt whisky is made.

LOCH BRACADALE

From the head of Loch Harport, the route climbs over a shoulder of hills and then descends to the coast at Loch Bracadale. This splendid sea loch, studded with islands and with numerous hilly peninsulas providing sheltered anchorages, is where Hakon's fleet regrouped after its defeat at the Battle of Largs.

One of the narrower inlets is Loch Beag, which is crossed by a modern causeway. The motorist then goes inland, across lonely moorlands and through forest plantations, and crosses a bridge over the Snizort, the longest river in Skye and the haunt of trout and salmon anglers. Beyond the Snizort, the road runs through crofting country and joins the main road around the dramatic landscape of the Trotternish peninsula.

UIG

A roadside viewpoint reveals the well-wooded setting of this attractive inshore fishing port. Its white houses are set in green fields which sweep up from a bay flanked by high cliffs. A round stone tower downhill from the viewpoint is a 19th-century folly.

Uig is the car-ferry terminal for Harris and North Uist. Beyond the village, the main road twists uphill, past a short cut to Staffin on the east coast, and goes on through crofting towns in the district once known as 'the granary of Skye'.

KILMUIR

At the turnoff for Heribusta, four thatched cottages have been converted into the Skye Cottage Museum. Exhibits portraying crofters' life in the 19th century include a handloom and a collection of contemporary letters and documents. The museum is open daily in summer except Sundays.

The old churchyard of Kilmuir is the burial place of the Scottish heroine

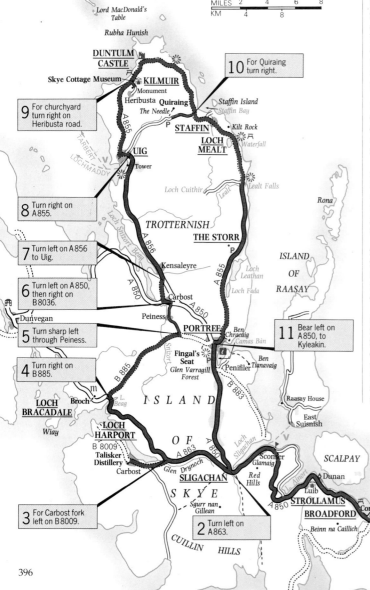

MILES 2 4 6 8
KM 4 8

10 For Quiraing turn right.

9 For churchyard turn right on Heribusta road.

8 Turn right on A855.

7 Turn left on A856 to Uig.

6 Turn left on A850, then right on B8036.

5 Turn sharp left through Peiness.

4 Turn right on B885.

3 For Carbost fork left on B8009.

2 Turn left on A863.

1 Take A850, Broadford road.

11 Bear left on A850, to Kyleakin.

Flora MacDonald, who in 1746 helped Bonnie Prince Charlie to escape to Skye as English troops closed in on his hide-out on Benbecula in the Outer Hebrides. Her grave is marked by a tall Celtic cross.

DUNTULM CASTLE

The crumbling walls of Duntulm Castle stand on top of a cliff which drops sheer on three sides to the rocks below. The castle – a short walk from the roadside over a grassy headland – was built on the site of a Celtic fortress.

Out to sea lies a line of curiously shaped rocks and islands, suggesting the humps of fabulous sea monsters. The flat-topped island is known as Lord MacDonald's Table.

STAFFIN

Crofting and fishing settlements spread across rising ground above Staffin Bay. Inland, the road to Uig rises through a fantastic landscape – the rock pinnacles of the Quiraing. From a car park above the top hairpin, a path wanders along the foot of cliffs and screes, a garden of arctic-alpine flowers, towards some weathered basalt pillars. The most prominent of these is the elegant 120ft column, The Needle.

Staffin Bay is reached by the narrow road to Staffin Slip. It crosses the rocky bed of the Stenscholl river and goes below cliffs from which boulders have tumbled down towards the sea. Staffin Island, just offshore, has tall wooden frames on which fishermen hang their nets to dry.

LOCH MEALT

There is just enough space between Loch Mealt and the sea cliffs immediately east of it for the main road and a cliff-top car park. North of the car park the view looks back up the coast to Kilt Rock, so named because its markings resemble the pleats and patterns of a kilt.

The river which drains Loch Mealt is one of the shortest in Scotland, flowing for only 50yds before it plunges down a feathery waterfall nearly 200ft to the sea below. There are more falls, 2½ miles south, in the wooded gorge of the Lealt River. Opposite the falls a side road, which changes from tarmac to loose gravel, leads to Loch Cuithir – one of the few sites in Skye on which industry has left a mark.

The loch contains large quantities of diatomite, a powdery deposit used in industrial filtering processes. Since the 1880s, attempts have been made to mine the deposits – but without success.

THE STORR

All the way from Staffin, the route follows the meandering escarpment which forms the backbone of the Trotternish peninsula. At its southern end are the spectacular cliff faces and buttresses of The Storr. Standing out from the main face is the Old Man of Storr, the tallest of a series of detached and weathered pinnacles. This huge monolith of basalt is 160ft tall and 40ft in diameter, and dramatically overhangs its base all the way round.

BAY OF REFUGE *In 1746 Bonnie Prince Charlie landed at Uig Bay when he fled to Skye disguised as Flora MacDonald's maid.*

KING'S PORT *The name Portree comes from the Gaelic for 'king's port'. It refers to the time in 1540 when James V sailed there to win over the Skye chieftains.*

DUNTULM CASTLE *Until the 1720s the castle was the MacDonald chiefs' home.*

SKYE COTTAGE MUSEUM *Among the exhibits is a reconstructed smithy.*

Nearby pinnacles are the Old Man's 'wife', 'castle' and 'dog'. Around The Storr are beautifully marked crystalline rocks, including basalt, and the area – like the Quiraing – is a wonderland of alpine flowers.

South-east of the cliffs, a roadside car park below a conifer plantation leads into a short forest walk. This links up with a more exposed footpath towards the Old Man. Beyond the car park, the route passes The Storr lochs – Leathan and Fada – stocked with trout.

PORTREE

The port and chief town of Skye rises from a fishing harbour protected by the Island of Raasay from the open waters of the Inner Sound. White and colour-washed houses, shops and hotels face the bay, and others are banked behind them.

The Royal Hotel incorporates the old inn where, in 1746, Bonnie Prince Charlie said farewell to Flora Mac-Donald before setting sail for Raasay and eventual exile in France. Flora was captured by Government troops soon after and served time aboard the infamous prison ship, the *Furnace*.

Directly above the harbour is the hilly, wooded peninsula called The Lump, where the Portree Highland Games are held in August. The island's oldest building, Meall House, is on The Lump. Built in the early 18th century, it was once the jail and is now the tourist information centre.

A turning off the Staffin road, towards the Coolin Hills Hotel, leads to a shoreline path beside the bay. There is a choice of continuing around a point or climbing above the cliffs of Ben Chracaig. West of Portree, off the Struan road beside the old golf course, a track leads to Fingal's Seat, a hilltop viewpoint.

To the right of the main road south of Portree are two waymarked walks in the hillside spruce and larch plantations of Glen Varragill. The next side road on the left leads to the hamlet of Penifiler and the start of a footpath to the wide sandy beach of Camas Bàn. From there an exhilarating walk goes high above the cliffs of Ben Tianavaig.

Tourist information: Broadford 361/463 (summer); Portree 2137.

High peaks around Loch Torridon

Narrow roads twist along loch shores, through lonely glens and over high mountain passes. Spectacular peaks rise above forested slopes, and a Jacobite castle stands on an island.

LOCHCARRON

Facing the sunrise over the mountains of the Attadale deer forest, this village of whitewashed houses and colourful gardens spreads for 4 miles along the west shore of Loch Carron. There are crofters' fields by the lochside and on the hillside behind.

The Allt nan Carnan Burn tumbles down a half-hidden gorge into the heart of the village. Its banks form a nature reserve, thickly wooded with birch and hazel, oak, ash, elm and Scots pine.

South of the village, a weather vane in the shape of a woman at a spinning wheel marks the tartan mill run by Lochcarron Weavers, which is open to visitors daily except weekends.

Leaving Lochcarron, the single-track main road climbs to bare moorland before plunging down a narrow and steep-sided glen where rocky crags, scree-runs and birch scrub are split by zigzag waterfalls.

LOCH KISHORN

Across the loch tower the mountains of the Applecross peninsula, dwarfing the North Sea oil platform yard at their foot.

From Tornapress Farm a road rises to the 2053ft Pass of the Cattle, also called Applecross Scenic Route and one of the most exciting roads in Scotland. The final hairpin bends twist through an Alpine landscape ringed by cliffs and rock buttresses. From a car park beyond the summit, the outlook is over dozens of silvery lochans in the Applecross hills to the mountain peaks of Skye.

Rassal Ashwood, a mile beyond Tornapress on the main road, is part of a National Nature Reserve. Ash trees grow from niches in a fertile limestone outcrop, and the ground is carpeted with primroses in spring.

SHIELDAIG

Six miles beyond Rassal Ashwood, a wood of stately Scots pines climbs from Loch Dughaill up the lower slopes of Ben Shieldaig. Then it gives way to birches, as a series of rock terraces takes the eye to the summit.

Shieldaig is a holiday village of slate-roofed white houses facing the sea loch of the same name. Lobster pots are piled up at the little jetty, and

fishing boats anchor off the sheltered western shore.

Craggy Shieldaig Island, covered in Scots pines, is owned by the National Trust for Scotland. Since the island cuts off the outlook to the open sea, the best viewpoint is a grassy car park on the hillside above the village.

UPPER LOCH TORRIDON

Turning east from Shieldaig, the route runs high above the superb curving bays of Upper Loch Torridon. Across the loch are the peaks and corries of Ben Alligin, with the houses of Alligin and Wester Alligin dotted over croft land rising from the water's edge.

After a river bridge 3 miles beyond Shieldaig, a gate in the high deer fence marks the start of a short riverside footpath to the cascades of the Falls of Balgy. A high-level viewpoint 1½ miles farther on looks directly across the loch into the ravine of the Coire Mhic Nobuil, which separates 3232ft high Ben Alligin from the massive 3456ft ridge of Liathach.

Beyond the woodlands and rhododendrons surrounding a Victorian hotel, the road dips down to sea level again at the crofting township of Annat.

TORRIDON

Beside the turnoff to Alligin is the National Trust for Scotland's summer visitor centre. The trust owns 16,000 acres around Torridon, including Ben Alligin and Liathach.

From the centre there is a neck-craning view of the rock ledges and terraces of Liathach, rising precipitously to the pinnacled summit. A short walk away at Torridon Mains, the trust's deer museum features displays on the life cycle of the red deer. The deer spend the summer in

the remoter mountain corries, but may sometimes be glimpsed at the roadside early and late in the day as they come to the river to drink.

GLEN TORRIDON

This glaciated valley is overlooked by wild slopes of rock and heather, deep-cut gullies and spidery mountain burns. From a car park in the heart of the valley there is an 8 mile footpath all the way round the back of Liathach to meet up with the Alligin road.

On the south side of Glen Torridon, tree-ringed Loch Clair marks the start of the classic 9 mile walk past Loch Coulin, over the Coulin Pass to Glen Carron.

BEINN EIGHE

Liathach's north-eastern neighbour is the splendid range of Beinn Eighe, whose southern peaks have white quartzite screes giving the appearance of a permanent dusting of snow. Beinn Eighe was the first National Nature Reserve in Britain, established in 1951. More than 10,000 acres of mountain and moorland habitats, unusual rock formations and native pine forest overlook Loch Maree and have been designated a Biosphere Reserve by UNESCO under its Man and Biosphere Programme, making it one of the premier conservation areas in the world.

The main access to the reserve is north-west of the village of Kinlochewe, a climbing, walking and fishing centre. Two miles beyond the cottage visitor centre at Aultroy is a car park and picnic place in a birch wood beside Loch Maree.

From the car park the 1 mile Glas Leitire Trail climbs through a protected remnant of the ancient Caledonian pine forest to a height of about

350ft. Here a turf-roofed Conservation Cabin looks across the loch to the 3215ft peak of Slioch, whose name means 'the spear'.

East of Kinlochewe, the route heads up lonely Glen Docherty, with a viewpoint at a car park looking back down towards Loch Maree. Then, among more rounded hills, it runs alongside Loch a' Chroisg where there are informal picnic places on the loch shore.

ACHNASHEEN

Founded after the railway arrived in 1870, Achnasheen is still the passing place for trains on the single-track Kyle of Lochalsh line; it is also an isolated main-road junction with hotels and a scattering of houses.

South of Achnasheen the route crosses a moorland watershed and heads down Glen Carron. Gradually the River Carron sinks into a deeper-cut ravine, with forests on both sides. Achnashellach, where conifer plantations and rhododendrons surround a Victorian shooting lodge, is the southern end of the track across the Coulin Pass to Loch Clair.

STRATHCARRON

From the level-crossing at Strathcarron Station, the road leads along the east shore of Loch Carron. It runs parallel with the railway at the foot of unstable cliffs, where chain-link netting and an avalanche shelter guard against rock falls.

Soon the road tackles steep gradients, up and downhill, on the way to South Strome Forest. A viewpoint overlooks Loch Carron and the village of Stromeferry, named after the ferry which used to link it to Stromemore across the loch. The ferry was replaced in 1970 by a road around the lochside.

From Stromeferry, a 1½ mile forest walk leads through larch, spruce and cypress to viewpoints above the loch.

Beyond the Stromeferry turning,

SUMMIT MEETING *Across Upper Loch Torridon the red-sandstone peaks frame the 3456ft crest of Liathach.*

the route goes through the forestry village of Achmore in lovely Strath Ascaig. It then continues on a narrow road cut into the cliffside high above Loch Carron.

PLOCKTON
Holiday village, sailing centre and artists' delight, Plockton is beautifully situated round a series of sheltered rocky bays. A farm track high above the main street makes a pleasant walk. So does a splendid footpath round the inner bay, then uphill into the Duncraig Castle woods.

From Plockton Station, a side road leads past an airstrip to Nead-an-Eoin – 'the Bird's Nest' – a house whose woodland garden, looking out to sea, is open daily except Sunday from May to September.

Leaving Plockton, the road passes the crofting village of Duirinish, built in lines along both banks of a burn; the gardens of Duirinish Lodge are open to the public.

KYLE OF LOCHALSH
Before 1897, Kyle was no more than a barren and rocky promontory with four or five houses and an inn, looking across a narrow strait to Skye. In that year, the railway was extended beyond its original terminus at Stromeferry to Kyle, which grew to its present status as a railhead. It is now the main car-ferry terminal for Skye, a shopping centre, inshore fishing station and supply depot for the Royal Navy.

From a hilltop viewpoint, reached by Plock Road and then a short footpath through gorse, birch and rowan, there are views to Applecross, Skye and a scattering of smaller islands, reefs and skerries.

BALMACARA
East of Kyle, the main road runs above the shore of Loch Alsh towards the three-part village of Balmacara. A side road leads to Lochalsh Woodland Garden, owned by the National Trust for Scotland and open daily. It is crisscrossed by sheltered footpaths, and the old coach house is a visitor centre, open in summer.

At Reraig, a lochside picnic place looks directly down the narrow Sound of Sleat.

EILEAN DONAN
Beyond Balmacara, the route curves round towards the former fishing village of Dornie at the junction of Loch Alsh, Loch Duich and the narrower Loch Long.

On the outskirts of Dornie, set against a background of forested hills sweeping up from the shoreline of Loch Duich, stands Eilean Donan Castle, on a rocky island linked to the mainland by a fine stone causeway and three-arched bridge.

Established as a royal stronghold in the 13th century, Eilean Donan later passed into the ownership of the Mackenzies of Kintail. In 1719, during the Jacobite rising, it was held by a Spanish garrison for the Old Pretender, son of the deposed James II, and was pounded into ruins by the English warship *Worcester* . The castle remained a ruin until 1932, when restoration began.

Notable features of the rebuilt castle include the Billeting Room, with its spectacular curved stone ceiling, and the Banqueting Hall, where Jacobite relics are on display. Eilean Donan is open daily from Easter to September.

There is also a memorial to the Clan Macrae, who held the castle as hereditary Constables for the Mackenzies.

Tourist information: Kyle of Lochalsh 4276 (summer).

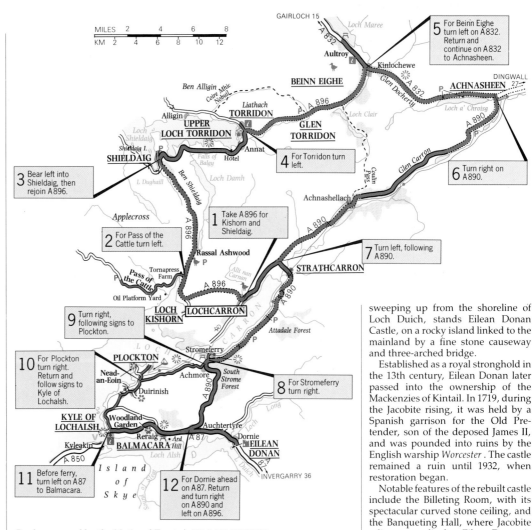

MILES 2 4 6 8
KM 2 4 6 8 10 12

5 For Beinn Eighe turn left on A 832. Return and continue on A 832 to Achnasheen.

GAIRLOCH 15

Loch Maree

Aultroy

Kinlochewe

BEINN EIGHE

DINGWALL 27

ACHNASHEEN

Ben Alligin

Coire Mhic Nobuil

Liathach

TORRIDON

GLEN TORRIDON

Loch Clair

Loch a' Chroisg

Alligin

UPPER LOCH TORRIDON

Annat

Hotel

4 For Torridon turn left.

3 Bear left into Shieldaig, then rejoin A896.

Loch Shieldaig

Shieldaig I.

SHIELDAIG

Falls of Balgy

Loch Damh

Achnashellach

6 Turn right on A890.

Glen Carron

Coulin Pass

L Dughaill

Ben Shieldaig

Applecross

1 Take A896 for Kishorn and Shieldaig.

2 For Pass of the Cattle turn left.

Rassal Ashwood

STRATHCARRON

7 Turn left, following A890.

Tornapress Farm

Pass of the Cattle

Oil Platform Yard

Allt nan Carnan

LOCH KISHORN

LOCHCARRON

9 Turn right, following signs to Plockton.

Stromeferry

Attadale Forest

10 For Plockton turn right. Return and follow signs to Kyle of Lochalsh.

PLOCKTON

Nead-an-Eoin

Duirinish

Achmore

South Strome Forest

8 For Stromeferry turn right.

KYLE OF LOCHALSH

Woodland Garden

Reraig

Kyleakin

BALMACARA

Ard Hill

Auchtertyre

Dornie

EILEAN DONAN

A 850

Loch Alsh

Island of Skye

11 Before ferry, turn left on A87 to Balmacara.

12 For Dornie ahead on A87. Return and turn right on A890 and left on A896.

INVERGARRY 36

ENFOLDED BAY *Plockton's serene little harbour shelters beneath a ring of mountains.*

LIVE EXHIBIT *Young deer can sometimes be seen near Torridon deer museum.*

LOCHMAREE 9½
KINLOCHEWE
ACHNASHEEN 10
SAFETY FIRST

WORDS OF WARNING *An early motoring sign still welcomes cautious drivers.*

Wild moorland above Dornoch Firth

TOUR
246
——— 91 MILES ———

From a town by the sea the route climbs to wild moors, then drops to low-lying farmland and sheltered seaside places. Pictish remains and old crafts maintain links with the past.

TAIN

It is no accident that the ancient royal burgh of Tain appears to have grown naturally out of its landscape. For the honey-coloured sandstone from which most of its houses are built was quarried only 2 miles away. From the High Street, dominated by the turreted 18th-century Tolbooth, leafy side streets and well-tended gardens tumble eastwards down a slope towards the Dornoch Firth.

In one of these streets, Castlebrae, stands the museum – a labour of local pride and love. It contains craftsmen's tools, reproductions of royal charters, fragments of tartan and corners crammed with local memorabilia. The street continues down the slope to the graveyard of the ruined St Duthac's Chapel, destroyed by fire in 1427.

St Duthac was born in Tain about AD 1000 and died in Ireland in 1065. His remains were brought to Tain and buried in a chapel built on the reputed site of his birthplace, now an ivy-covered ruin north of the town. They were later transferred to a more fitting shrine; this became a place of pilgrimage – James IV was a frequent visitor – and it was here that the wife, daughter and sisters of Robert Bruce took refuge from the armies of Edward I in 1306. They were betrayed by the Earl of Ross and imprisoned until their release after Bruce's victory over the English at Bannockburn in 1314.

Near the ruined chapel is the Collegiate Church of St Duthac, built in 1371 by the Bishop of Ross.

At Blarliath, on the north-west outskirts of the town, visitors can watch traditional Highland cheeses such as crowdie and caboc being made. Blarliath is reached down Shore Road.

A short diversion from the main road 2 miles outside Tain runs along a sand-spit peninsula, barely 200yds wide in places, which thrusts out into the Dornoch Firth towards Meikle Ferry. From a car park 1 mile farther along the main road, Forestry Commission walks lead up the wooded slope at Redburn, rising above the golden Edderton Sands.

EDDERTON

A side road leads northwards through the village and into the Ardmore peninsula. It passes a 10ft high Pictish stone, inscribed with a fish symbol and standing in the middle of a field. Farther on is the Balblair Distillery, founded in 1749 but moved to its present site below Struie Hills in the 19th century to take advantage of the railway line and, it is said, of the quality of the local peat. Today it is possible – preferably by prior arrangement (Edderton 273) – to tour the distillery and see how malt whisky is made, from the grinding mills and fermenters to the casks in which the whisky matures.

Beyond Edderton the tree-lined main road twists and turns as it skirts the placid waters of Dornoch Firth.

STRATH RORY

The road southwards towards Strath Rory winds up the slope of Struie Hills onto broad expanses of purple moorland. From a viewpoint beside the road there are fine views back over the coastal farmlands, green or golden with the changing seasons.

From the car park at Strathrory Bridge it is possible to walk back over a cattle grid to pick up a forestry track following the northern bank of the Strathrory River. Cnoc an Duin, the hill which rises in front, guarded by the ruins of a Pictish hill-fort, may be reached by a 2 mile walk. Little remains of the fortified walled enclosure, but there are fine views from the top of the hill.

Four miles farther on, the road crosses the River Averon, beyond which, among the Highland scenery on the right of the road, stands a replica of the gates of an Indian town.

In 1782 General Sir Hector Munro had the gates constructed on Cnoc Fryish to commemorate his capture of Negapatam (now Nagapattinam) in Southern India the year before, when he commanded the Black Watch. The main purpose of this apparent act of self-glory was to provide work during a time of high unemployment.

The monument may be reached by a footpath which leads from a car park on the Boath Road.

BLACK ROCK GORGE

Precipitous paths are perched 200ft above a narrow ravine carved by the waters of the River Glass, which snake through mossy clefts in the rock little more than 10ft wide. The lower reaches of Glen Glass are approached down a track starting on the left of the road from Evanton. A wooden bridge spans the gorge, where the river tumbles and foams some 70ft below on its tumultuous way to join the Cromarty Firth.

FOULIS CASTLE

Members of the Clan Munro come from all over the world to visit the seat of their chieftain, which has been at Foulis since the 11th century. The present house, however, is built in Dutch style and dates from the 1750s when it replaced a former castle which was burnt down by the Mackenzies at the time of the Jacobite uprising of 1745. During the uprising the Munros took the side of the government against the Jacobites while their neighbours and old enemies, the Mackenzies, supported the Young Pretender. Foulis Castle may be visited by arrangement with the

HILLS ACROSS THE FIRTH *Fields and trees drop to the tide-streaked waters of Dornoch Firth, while on the northern skyline distant peaks scrape the clouds.*

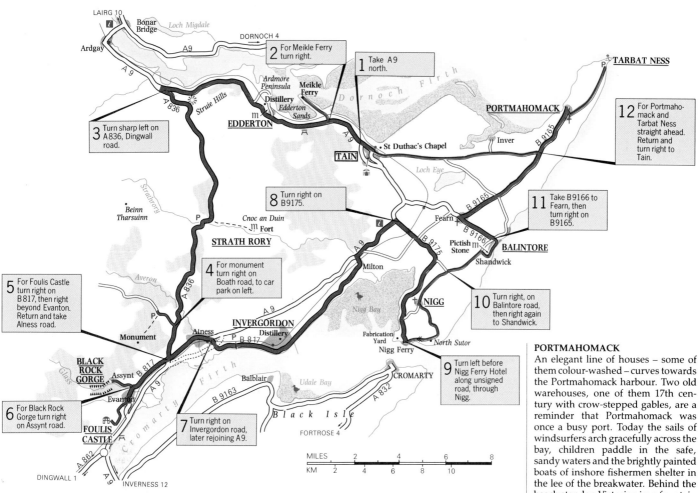

LAIRG 10

Bonar Bridge

Loch Migdale

Ardgay

DORNOCH 4

A9

Ardmore Peninsula

Meikle Ferry

Distillery

Edderton Sands

EDDERTON

Dornoch Firth

2 For Meikle Ferry turn right.

1 Take A9 north.

TARBAT NESS

PORTMAHOMACK

Inver

12 For Portmahomack and Tarbat Ness straight ahead. Return and turn right to Tain.

3 Turn sharp left on A836, Dingwall road.

Struie Hills

A836

St Duthac's Chapel

TAIN

B 9165

Beinn Tharsuinn

Strathrory

P

Cnoc an Duin

Fort

Loch Eye

8 Turn right on B9175.

Fearn

11 Take B9166 to Fearn, then turn right on B9165.

STRATH RORY

A 836

B 9166

B 9175

Pictish Stone

BALINTORE

Shandwick

4 For monument turn right on Boath road, to car park on left.

Milton

5 For Foulis Castle turn right on B817, then right beyond Evanton. Return and take Alness road.

Averon

P

A9

Nigg Bay

NIGG

10 Turn right, on Balintore road, then right again to Shandwick.

Monument

INVERGORDON

Alness

Distillery

B 817

Fabrication Yard

Nigg Ferry

North Sutor

BLACK ROCK GORGE

Assynt

B 817

A9

Glass

Balblair

Udale Bay

CROMARTY

9 Turn left before Nigg Ferry Hotel along unsigned road, through Nigg.

6 For Black Rock Gorge turn right on Assynt road.

Evanton

Cromarty Firth

FOULIS CASTLE

A 862

A9

B 9163

A 832

Black Isle

FORTROSE 4

7 Turn right on Invergordon road, later rejoining A9.

DINGWALL 1

INVERNESS 12

MILES 2 4 6 8

KM 2 4 6 8 10

---

owner, the 30th chieftain (Evanton 830212). The Munro room houses a collection of clan memorabilia.

INVERGORDON

The northern shore of the Cromarty Firth offers a stark contrast to the rural scenery of the rest of the tour. For around Invergordon the landscape is primarily industrial. The normally salty air of the firth is heady with the whiff of whisky production from the Invergordon Distillery. North Sea oil has left its impact on the landscape in the form of equipment-repairing and servicing installations. Finally, there is a naval fuel depot. The town dates mainly from the 18th century, when it was laid out by Sir William Gordon of Embo, who changed its name from Inverbeakie.

During the First World War, Invergordon became a large naval base because of the deep-water anchorage provided by the firth. In 1931 it was the scene of a mutiny. A cut in sailors' pay – in some cases more than 10 per cent – caused men of the Home Fleet on ships at Invergordon to refuse duty. During the Second World War the naval base was also used by seaplanes, and it continued in operation until 1956.

NIGG

Skeletal cranes haunt the landscape around Nigg Ferry, once the starting point for the ferry to Cromarty, and oil-production platforms towed in from the North Sea for repair at Invergordon rise above the low-lying

pastures and cornfields of the shore.

It is a meeting of two worlds – the industrial and the agricultural. The south-east corner of Nigg Bay now houses a vast fabrication yard, where platforms are built. But it is easy to escape by driving east up the steep road which climbs to the high head-land of the North Sutor whose red-sandstone cliffs shelter the bay. In places the road degenerates into little more than a dirt track, but the reward is a view from the top, with the old port town of Cromarty shimmering across the firth's narrow mouth.

A grassy mound on the headland is the site of a fort probably built by William the Lion in 1179. Within the bay the Sands of Nigg form a nature reserve, the habitat of a wide range of ducks, geese and wading birds.

As the road passes through a large farm, it takes a turn left to the village of Nigg. Here, a long, low, parish church contains a carved Pictish stone dating from the 9th or 10th century. In the churchyard is a small, round, flat stone known as the Cholera Stone. Legend has it that during the great cholera epidemic of 1832 Jasper Vass, a church elder, saw the plague float-ing in the form of a small cloud. Bravely he is said to have caught the cloud in a linen bag and buried it under the stone – which has never been moved in case the cholera escapes.

BALINTORE

The road to Balintore passes a sad memorial called the Clach a Charridh, or Stone of Sorrow. It is a Pictish stone

which marks the spot where unbap-tised infants who died in the parish were buried.

The Stone of Sorrow stands 10ft high, and for centuries served also as a seamark for shipping. On its reverse side is a remarkably well-preserved panel of carved animals, including stags and wolves.

A straggle of single-storey cottages lines Shandwick Bay, linking the villages of Shandwick, Balintore and Hilton of Cadboll leading to Balintore harbour. This was once a port, export-ing grain and potatoes and importing coal; but it is now used mainly for fishing.

Lobster pots are piled high in places along the harbour wall, and salmon nets are strung out to sea to catch the fish or are slung from poles on the grass by the shore to dry. The massive harbour wall protects the village from the fury of winter gales, and also provides a useful haven for small pleasure craft.

From Balintore the route leads about 2 miles inland through low-lying farmland to Fearn, where the remains of an abbey are now incor-porated into the parish church. The abbey was originally founded in 1221 at Mid Fearn, north of Edderton. But, possibly because the Augustinian monks realised the present site was better for farming, the abbey was transferred to Fearn in 1238.

In 1742 the church was struck by lightning during a service and the stone roof fell in, killing 38 members of the congregation.

PORTMAHOMACK

An elegant line of houses – some of them colour-washed – curves towards the Portmahomack harbour. Two old warehouses, one of them 17th cen-tury with crow-stepped gables, are a reminder that Portmahomack was once a busy port. Today the sails of windsurfers arch gracefully across the bay, children paddle in the safe, sandy waters and the brightly painted boats of inshore fishermen shelter in the lee of the breakwater. Behind the beach stands a Victorian iron fountain of 1887, erected to mark the introduc-tion of 'Gravitational Water' to the village. With its sheltered position, Portmahomack is now popular with holidaymakers.

On higher ground, behind the village, stands the disused parish church, its domed belfry adding a slightly incongruous Mediterranean feel to the village. The belfry dates from the early 18th century, but its purpose remains a mystery. Aper-tures in the dome suggest that these were intended for the dispersal of smoke from a brazier if the belfry had been used as a seamark. But there is no evidence that it was ever used for this purpose.

The 18th-century church stands above a medieval crypt, but its history probably stretches even farther back because in 1899 a Viking silver hoard was discovered by accident only a few yards from the east gate.

TARBAT NESS

A striking red-and-white striped lighthouse dominates the flat ground between Portmahomack and Tarbat Ness. It was built in 1833 and is one of several in Scotland designed by the Stevensons, ancestors of the novelist Robert Louis Stevenson. The light-house is open to the public. Beyond it ledges of rock shelve gently down to the sea, making it possible to sit and fish for cod or simply to explore the rock pools.

Tourist information: Strathpeffer 415; (Ross and Cromarty) Kessock 505.

Peaks and valleys in wild Sutherland

TOUR
247

— 130 MILES —

Settlements are rare on this dramatic route through the wilderness of Sutherland. It leads inland from the coast to imposing mountain peaks and the chilly waters of Loch Drumbeg.

LOCHINVER

Hills of rock, birch scrub and heather enclose the bay of Loch Inver on three sides like an amphitheatre. The road leads past a line of houses and squeezes round the Culag Burn to the quayside, with its huddles of fishing vessels.

Lochinver was founded as a fishing village in 1812, soon after clearances for sheep inland forced crofters to resettle on the coast. One of the first buildings to go up was the Culag Hotel, built originally as a hunting lodge for the Dukes of Sutherland. It burned down in the late 19th century, but in response to the growing demand for accommodation for shooting and fishing parties it was rebuilt in ornamental Victorian style. It burned down again in the 1930s and was again ornately rebuilt.

Visitors can take boat trips from the pier to seal colonies and islands thronged with birds, watch the unloading of the fish catches, and see craftsmen at work in a pottery at nearby Baddidarroch. Lochinver's Assynt Angling Club controls 34 lochs, and

there is a school of casting. Salmon and trout fishing is available on various rivers, burns and lochs in the area.

To the east of the village the awesome Suilven rises a craggy 2399ft to its twin peaks. Its rocks are among the oldest in Britain, thrust up when the Earth was new more than 2600 million years ago.

ARDVRECK CASTLE

A fine new road leading east from Lochinver bowls along past Loch Assynt on the right and the steep sides of 2651ft Quinag on the left. These mark a change from the small-scale landscape of the coastal area to the more massive scenery inland.

In this dramatic setting the ruin of Ardvreck Castle rears up on a grassy point above a small pebble cove. Opposite the steep flanks of Beinn Gharbh with its twin waterfalls, Ardvreck captures the essence of the Highlands' stark and romantic beauty. The castle, built in the 1590s, was a Macleod stronghold and here, in 1650, the Marquis of Montrose sought refuge after his disastrous defeat at Carbisdale while attempting to win Scotland for the exiled Charles II. The price put on his head proved too great a temptation to Neil Macleod, who betrayed his guest to the Roundheads. Montrose was taken to Edinburgh and hanged.

INCHNADAMPH

The hotel at Inchnadamph, at the head of Loch Assynt and near the 3273ft Ben More Assynt, is a centre for birdwatchers, geologists, botanists and anglers. The area stands on a

geological border created when old rock, of which Ben More is made, thrust up over much younger rock.

A 3200 acre National Nature Reserve protects some rare limestone vegetation as well as such creatures as wildcat, mountain hare and red deer, but the reserve has no facilities for visitors and is hard to penetrate. In the limestone, there are potholes – best left to experienced potholers – and caves that bore traces of pre-historic human habitation when they were excavated in the 1920s, but which are now empty.

Hill walkers flock to the slopes and crags of nearby peaks: Ben More Assynt, Quinag, Suilven and Canisp. The Inchnadamph hotel has several boats on Loch Assynt, which contains salmon and brown trout.

KNOCKAN

Approaching Knockan, the road winds beneath a black cliff towering to the left. On the right, small lochs and peat bogs stretch away towards the sandstone peaks of Cul Beag and Cul Mor. These form part of Inverpolly National Nature Reserve, 27,000 acres of mountain, cliff and scree which form the second largest reserve in Britain after the Cairngorms. Here, on the barren uplands, birds such as the ptarmigan breed, and red deer roam the slopes.

An information centre offers a comprehensive guide to the area's prehistory, and a mile-long, well-signposted trail, cut into the scree beneath Knockan Cliff, displays some of the rocks and plants of north-west Scotland.

The cliff is known to geologists the world over for its peculiar formation. Normally, younger rocks lie above older ones. At Knockan, however, the cliffs are older than the rocks beneath. In the 19th century, this was the subject of considerable scientific debate. Then, around 1868, geologists realised that massive earth movements could thrust enormous tongues of very ancient rock up and over younger rocks.

The path which runs below the cliff is also a nature trail. It has pointers to lichens, mosses and plants which explain the origins and disappearance of the great forests that once covered Scotland – and also the build up of peat from moss and heather.

OYKEL BRIDGE

The River Oykel flows down the slopes of Ben More Assynt and through the broad, ice-gouged valley of Glen Oykel to Oykel Bridge. A lonely hotel stands by the roadside, where two bridges span turbulent rapids, and a little way to the west are picturesque falls. South-east of the bridges the Oykel is joined by the Einig.

CASSLEY WATERFALL

A narrow stone bridge and a wooded lane lead up to a mile-long series of falls and rapids, formed by the River Cassley as it tumbles down between wooded banks and over flat rocks and boulders capped with trees. There are good walks over soft grass and pine needles, and in season anglers fish for salmon and sea trout.

LAIRG

This popular resort and fishing village on the south-eastern shores of Loch Shin is a magnet for anglers seeking salmon and trout. New houses give

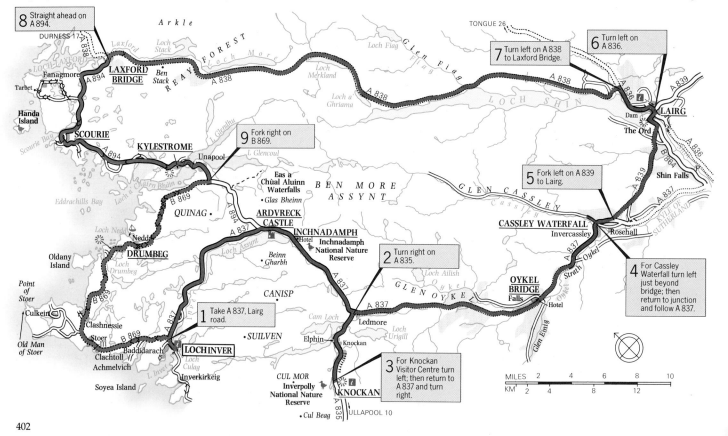

LONELY LOCH *Snow-dappled mountains and furrowed, gunmetal-blue waters make an awesome setting for a lonely crofter's house on the shore of Loch Stack.*

ROCKY RIVER *The Oykel threads its way through an avenue of tilted rocks at Oykel Bridge.*

SCOTS POTS *The coiled lines of lobster pots at Scourie add their splash of colour to Scourie's small bay.*

SEA HAVEN *Sailing boats find sheltered anchorage on the glass-calm waters of Loch Nedd.*

Lairg a trim and modern appearance which contrasts sharply with the surrounding untamed and ruggedly beautiful countryside. The River Shin flows alongside the village, away from the hydroelectric dam across the southern end of Loch Shin, and onto some impressive, wood-surrounded waterfalls 3 miles to the south.

On the west bank of the river, just across from the village, a half-mile track leads to the top of a hill called The Ord, from which there are clear views up Loch Shin.

LAXFORD BRIDGE
The road to Laxford Bridge, past Loch More and Loch Stack, leads first through towering sandstone mountains, like the bare grey whaleback of Arkle and the boulder-strewn Ben Stack, and then onto a totally different landscape of tightly packed rocky hillocks. These knolls and folds are of Precambrian rock, formed between

2800 and 1400 million years ago. The rock seems to close in on the single-track road, with its tight bends and blind crests. However, today's road is a great improvement on the earlier 9ft lane – sections of which can be seen on either side. Loch Laxford spreads fanwise towards the open sea, and is dotted with rocky islets and pierced by tiny bays and creeks. Beyond Laxford Bridge, the road widens again and the feeling of being enclosed vanishes. Here the road passes through a wild and remote area of peat bogs and lochans, some scattered among rocky hillocks and others side-stepped as the road winds towards the coast.

SCOURIE
Set in a tiny sheltered bay, Scourie has a beautiful sandy beach with rock pools at low tide.

The sparsely populated hamlet is a popular base for geologists, wild-

flower enthusiasts – the mild climate encourages the growth of varieties of dwarf orchids – and birdwatchers, who can take boats from Tarbet, to the north, to the Handa Island Nature Reserve. A large variety of sea birds inhabit the island, including razorbills, guillemots, puffins, kittiwakes, fulmars and the great skua.

Until 1846 the island, now uninhabited, was populated by 12 families who appointed their own queen, the oldest widow in the community, and elected their own parliament. There is good sea trout and salmon fishing on the many local lochs.

KYLESTROME
A viewpoint, with a telescope, above the great cleft of Loch a' Chàirn Bhàin gives a panoramic view of the many-peaked mass of Quinag and Glas Bheinn's steeply scalloped sides. A new bridge sweeps grandly over the inlet and past the old ferry point –

which has become a secluded backwater at the meeting of Lochs Glendhu and Glencoul.

A boat trip up Loch Glencoul offers views of Britain's highest waterfall, Eas a Chùal Aluinn – a 650ft drop. There is no access to the falls by road, and the steep, 3 mile walk from the road by Loch Ganvinch takes a full day for the round trip.

DRUMBEG
The little single-track road round the coast to Lochinver leaps and twists over the flanks of Quinag, playing hide-and-seek with glorious views of the various islands and lochs – including Loch Drumbeg. The hamlet of Drumbeg has a hotel, which is popular with trout fishermen, a car park where an indicator pinpoints outlying islands, and a craft shop.

Tourist information: Lochinver 330 (summer); Lairg 2160 (summer).

Lonely crofts and a valley of gold

TOUR
248
— 79 MILES —

From a coast of craggy headlands and sandy beaches, fertile valleys gouged out by the meltwaters of a great ice sheet 10,000 years ago pierce inland towards a wild sweep of moors.

BETTYHILL
The settlement scattered over a hill overlooking Torrisdale Bay is named after Elizabeth, Countess of Sutherland, who granted land there to inland crofters evicted in the Clearances.

Half a mile east of Bettyhill is Farr church, a large white 18th-century building which now houses Strath-naver Museum. Much of the museum is devoted to Clearance history. From the massive pulpit the minister read eviction notices on behalf of the landlord.

In the churchyard stands the 9th-century Farr Stone, an early Christian gravestone intricately carved with a Celtic cross and panels decorated with key patterns, spirals, interlacing and an animal motif. These carvings are most clearly visible when a mid-day sun throws them into relief; there is a photograph of the cross in the museum. The stone probably commemorated a local Pictish religious or political leader. Other rough stones may mark graves of the same period.

ARMADALE
The village of Armadale is a small crofting community, the walls of its cottages piled high with peat for burning in winter. There is a fine view of Armadale Bay, with its sandy beach and long sweep of shallow water.

The main road beyond Armadale leads over two burns, the Allt Beag and the Armadale. Both have twin stone bridges, old and new. Both burns show, in different ways, evidence of their Ice Age origins. The Allt Beag has a flat floor chaotically rock-strewn with debris dropped by the retreating ice; the Armadale is steeply V-shaped, carved by a torrent many times larger than the stream that follows it today.

STRATHY POINT
A single-track road flanked by rolling waves of grass leads up to a stocky lighthouse, opening up dramatic and contrasting views along the coast in both directions.

To the west is a natural arch carved by pounding seas, which flanks a geo, or collapsed cave; to the east rises the golfball-like atomic reactor of Dounreay, 10 miles away, and 12 miles farther looms Dunnet Head – the most northerly point of mainland Britain.

MELVICH
Melvich looks down on grassy dunes and an apron of brilliant sand, accessible by a footpath signposted from the village. The sands reach a mile inland along the estuary of the River Halladale, which has good fishing.

FORSINARD
A hotel and a railway station make this tiny community a good base for exploring Strath Halladale. The Halladale has good salmon fishing, and the hotel has access to six trout lochs. The lochs and peaks are homes for buzzards, ospreys, eagles, greenshanks, lapwings and pine martens.

INVERNAVER
The Naver runs along a wooded and fertile valley, which supported hundreds of crofters before the Clearances, to an estuary that spreads out into great tidal flats edged by hills and dunes. The dunes, which were built by the high winds that sweep in from Torrisdale Bay, suggest the Sahara Desert rather than northern Scotland.

A half-mile walk across coarse grass and sand leads to a plateau, the site of Baile Marghait which was a Neolithic community. There are graves, hut circles and, to the west, a broch – a defensive round tower – on top of a 200ft rocky slope.

The hills mark the edge of Invernaver Nature Reserve. The area is rich in lime and supports an array of unusual flowers, in particular the small, white mountain avens, saxifrages and dwarf willow and juniper.

Tourist information: Bettyhill 342 (summer); Wick 2596.

TOUR
249
— 95 MILES —

Few roads penetrate the wilderness heart of Sutherland, but some that do are followed on this tour, past foaming rivers and wind-textured lochs, and back to a castle by the sea.

HELMSDALE
The Duke of Sutherland replanned Helmsdale in the early 19th century, to house crofters evicted by him from the Helmsdale valley, the Strath of Kildonan. Some 10,000 people throughout Sutherland were evicted from their homes by the duke, so that sheep could be reared on the coarse peaty grass. The original road bridge, built by Thomas Telford in 1811-12, still stands upstream from the new bridge carrying the main coast road. Helmsdale's streets are laid out in a neat gridiron pattern and named after the duke's estates in Scotland and England.

The River Helmsdale, some 30yds wide and noted for its salmon, flows

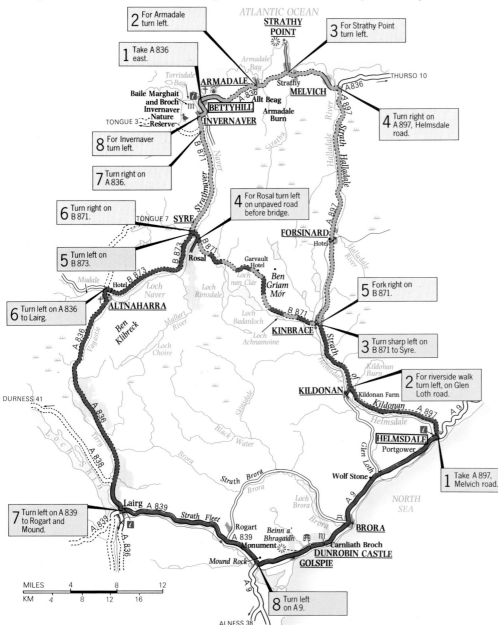

out through a well-enclosed harbour, flanked by a rocky shoreline. A small road leads along an undercliff to the shore, where visitors can sometimes find fossilised coral.

KILDONAN

A single-track road, with passing places, leads up the broad valley of the Strath of Kildonan until the hills crowd in at a little stone bridge over Kildonan Burn. The tents pitched at a site beside the burn are mostly those of gold-panners; Kildonan and the surrounding area was the focus of a minor gold rush in 1869-70, and gold is found there still.

In the early 19th century, a half-ounce nugget was picked up in the valley and given to the Duke of Sutherland, who had a ring made from it. In 1868, a local man, Robert Gilchrist, returned from the Australian goldfields and began panning on the tributaries of the Helmsdale. Others followed. Soon 500 gold-hungry prospectors were at work. The spot was optimistically named Baile an Or, 'The Town of the Gold'.

Perhaps, though, the gold-panners are drawn as much by the wild beauty of the steep hills, the tumbling burns and the rushing Helmsdale itself, which, beyond Kildonan Farm, foams past crags made accessible by a wire-and-wood hanging bridge.

A little to the north a side road leads to a railway station – a surprising sight in such a remote spot. A path from the road leads northwards to a little promontory offering fine views of foaming rapids, and of leaping salmon when they are running.

KINBRACE

Towards Kinbrace – a dozen houses and a railway station – the road emerges onto high, treeless peat moors dominated by the peak of Ben Griam Mór, poised like a breaking wave. At Kinbrace, the route makes a hairpin left turn and follows the Helmsdale to its source in Loch Achnamoine.

Beyond lies Loch Badanloch, one of three interconnecting lochs noted for their trout. The only building in sight is the Garvault Hotel, standing in isolation beneath Ben Griam Mór.

SYRE

The road drops down to the woods and fields of Strathnaver, past an unpaved road and over a bridge. Set back from the road junction is a white, gabled house, roofed with red corrugated iron, which belonged to Patrick Sellar, the man employed by the Duke of Sutherland to evict the crofters at the time of the Clearances.

Opposite, along the unpaved road, are the remains of the village of Rosal, one of the Strathnaver villages Sellar cleared in 1814.

The site lies 1 mile along the road and half a mile along a track through firs. The low stone walls are scattered over an open hillside.

ALTNAHARRA

The road to Altnaharra follows every little bay and inlet along the shore of Loch Naver, then crosses the River Mudale into the village – a church, a dozen houses and a hotel popular with anglers. The Altnaharra Hotel was built of timbers taken from a church in Achness, a village which used to stand at the eastern end of Loch Naver, which was destroyed in the Clearances.

Ben Klibreck, more than 3000ft high, towers above the village and the road heading south to Lairg.

GOLSPIE

Past the towering crag of Mound Rock the road runs along a tree-lined rise, with fields falling away to the sea, to this busy holiday village of single-storey stone cottages.

The village is overlooked by a formidable monument to the 1st Duke of Sutherland. His statue, perched on an octagonal tower, stands on the peak of Beinn a' Bhragaidh. From the end of Fountain Road, a steep but well-trodden track (signposted 'Ben Bhraggie Footpath') leads for three-quarters of a mile through trees and then up over peaty soil and treeless heath. The view from the top is dramatic, across the open expanse of the Dornoch Firth and round to ridge upon ridge of inland mountains.

At the northern end of the village the Orcadian Stone Company, which takes its name from the lake that covered central Scotland 400 million years ago, sells geological specimens. Some 2000 examples of stone and mineral are exhibited, and there are displays explaining the geology of the Highlands.

DUNROBIN CASTLE

The Earls and Dukes of Sutherland have lived in Dunrobin Castle since the 14th century, but the white-stone chateau that almost entirely encases the castle's late 13th-century heart looks as though it has been transported stone by stone from France.

In 1840 the 2nd Duke, who had spent his childhood in France and was impressed by its architecture, commissioned Sir Charles Barry, architect of the Houses of Parliament, to turn Dunrobin from a dour Scottish castle into a glowing chateau, standing in gardens set out in the formal French style of Versailles. Inside the castle, which is open daily in summer, high-ceilinged rooms lead directly into each other. Among the many paintings is a fine portrait of the 18th Earl of Romsey. One room contains the castle's early 20th-century steam-driven fire engine.

BRORA

Straddling the mouth of the river from which it takes its name, Brora is both an industrial town with a wool mill and a distillery, and a holiday resort. Over the bridge a road signposted 'Fascally' leads to a picnic spot beside the river.

Beside the road 5 miles north of Brora stands the Wolf Stone, said to be the site of the shooting of Scotland's last wolf about 1700. It must have been a remarkable animal, since at least two other places make the same claim.

Tourist information: Helmsdale 640 (summer); Wick 2596.

TORRISDALE BAY *Farmsteads look down on sand dunes which form part of the Invernaver Nature Reserve.*

PICTISH FORT *Carnliath Broch lies beside the road between Dunrobin and Brora.*

BONANZA BURN *Prospectors still visit Kildonan in search of gold.*

FRENCH CONNECTION *French and Scottish styles meet at Dunrobin Castle.*

Wave-torn capes at John o'Groats

TOUR

250

—— 119 MILES ——

At Britain's north-east corner, highland gives way to peat moors edged by towering cliffs. The countryside is dotted with relics of the Stone Age, the Bronze Age and the Picts.

WICK
A bustling, sturdy little fishing port is set securely back in its bay at the mouth of Wick River. Wick comes from the Norse word *vik*, meaning 'creek' – from which the Vikings themselves take their name.

Wick became a royal burgh in 1589. In the 19th century it was the world's largest herring-fishing port. More than 1100 boats once worked from its three harbours, laid out by the engineer Thomas Telford. That way of life declined with the coming of huge factory ships in the 1960s and 1970s; but it is recalled by the Heritage Museum near the harbour.

At the Caithness Glass factory, south of the town, visitors can watch craftsmen heating glass in roaring ovens and blowing it into paperweights, glasses and ornaments. The factory was set up in 1960 to employ young people who might otherwise have been out of work as herring fishing declined. It still takes apprentices.

Old Wick Castle, signposted from the main road south of the town, is a gaunt shell of a tower dating from the 12th century. It is set on a promontory, behind a defensive ditch. The castle is one of the oldest in Scotland and still stands three storeys high.

GIRNIGOE
A romantic ruin, as craggy as the weathered rocks it stands on, crowns a miniature peninsula above a little sheltered cove. Its position and its protective ditch recall Old Wick Castle, but it is more extensive.

The castle has two wings reaching out from a powerful keep. The east wing is 15th century, while the 17th-century westward extension is known as the Castle Sinclair – misleadingly, for the Sinclairs, who as earls ruled Caithness from here for 200 years, treated the sections as one castle.

It is said that one of the earls fell out with his son and imprisoned him in the dungeon, where he died six years later after he had been driven mad by being fed salt meat and denied drinking water.

The castle was besieged in 1690 during a feud between members of the family over succession to the earldom; it was eventually abandoned and never reoccupied. The outside walls still stand, falling sheer to the sea, but nothing remains of the upper storeys inside.

There is no path to the ruin. Visitors must park short of the lighthouse and walk across the grass for 600yds.

LYTH
This tiny community of moorland houses has become a showcase for local artists and craftsmen. The old school house has been converted into a well-lit and roomy Arts Centre, with displays of paintings, ceramics, sculpture, photographs and textiles.

Nearby, there is a ceramic workshop in a once-derelict smithy. The workshop runs a small summer school which draws students from Europe and North America.

AUCKENGILL
The former school house has been turned into a museum, named after a local 19th-century antiquarian, John Nicolson, who lived opposite in a house which still stands, and spent much of his life researching the archaeology of the region. The museum provides information about the area's early history – particularly the Pictish round towers known as brochs, which are found on some 100 sites in Caithness.

DUNCANSBY HEAD
On the way to the most dramatic stretch of the Caithness coast, visitors may call at the two perfumed and waxy rooms of a local craft shop, Caithness Candles. A wide range of handmade candles is on sale.

A mile and a half beyond lies a car park, the start of a windswept half-mile stroll over grass to well-fenced cliffs. There are views down to five sandstone rock stacks rising from the sea. The largest is the Muckle Stack, 300ft high. On the head itself stands a lighthouse which is open in the afternoons at the keeper's discretion. It is a reminder of the treacherous 12 knot tides in the Pentland Firth, the 6 mile wide strait between the mainland and the Orkneys. More than 400 ships have been wrecked there in the last 150 years.

JOHN O'GROATS
The first view of John o'Groats is glorious. When seen from the car as the main road breasts the crest of rolling peat moors, the village forms a small part of a superb panorama of coast and island, with Stroma lying in the Pentland Firth like a stepping stone to the Orkneys, edged in the west by the 1200ft cliffs of Hoy.

John o'Groats itself is a scattered collection of houses, hotels, cafés and souvenir shops. The last hotel, John o'Groats House, has an eight-sided tower as a memorial to the village's Dutch founder, Jan de Groot.

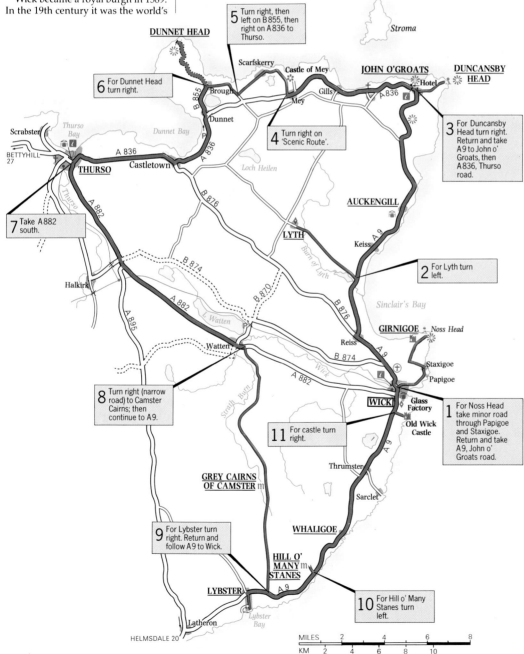

5 Turn right, then left on B855, then right on A836 to Thurso.

Stroma

DUNNET HEAD

Scarfskerry

Castle of Mey

JOHN O'GROATS   DUNCANSBY HEAD

Hotel

6 For Dunnet Head turn right.

Brough   Gills   A 836

Mey

Dunnet

3 For Duncansby Head turn right. Return and take A9 to John o' Groats, then A836, Thurso road.

Scrabster

Thurso Bay

Dunnet Bay

4 Turn right on 'Scenic Route'.

BETTYHILL 27

A 836

THURSO   Castletown

Loch Heilen

AUCKENGILL

7 Take A882 south.

B 876

LYTH

Keiss

2 For Lyth turn left.

Halkirk

B 874

Burn of Lyth

A 882

B 870

Sinclair's Bay

L. Watten

GIRNIGOE   *Noss Head*

Watten

Reiss

B 874

A 9

Staxigoe

Papigoe

8 Turn right (narrow road) to Camster Cairns; then continue to A9.

Strath Byrn

Wick

A 882

WICK   Glass Factory

Old Wick Castle

1 For Noss Head take minor road through Papigoe and Staxigoe. Return and take A9, John o' Groats road.

11 For castle turn right.

GREY CAIRNS OF CAMSTER

Thrumster

Sarclet

9 For Lybster turn right. Return and follow A9 to Wick.

WHALIGOE

HILL O' MANY STANES

LYBSTER

A 9

10 For Hill o' Many Stanes turn left.

Latheron

Lybster Bay

HELMSDALE 20

MILES   2   4   6   8
KM   2   4   6   8   10

De Groot arrived with his two brothers in 1496 bearing instructions from the Scottish king, James IV, to establish a ferry linking the mainland more securely to Orkney, newly acquired from the King of Denmark and Norway. The de Groots prospered, and every year celebrated their success with a dinner.

After 50 years, when there were eight of them, they quarrelled over who should sit at the head of the table. Jan solved the problem by adding to his house an octagonal room with an octagonal table, so that all could be said to sit at the head. The house has gone, but the hotel's octagonal tower serves as a reminder.

John o'Groats is not the mainland's northernmost spot – Dunnet Head lies farther north. Neither is it the most distant point from Land's End – Duncansby Head is more than a mile farther. But it is the farthest *inhabited* spot from Land's End – 876 miles away by road.

DUNNET HEAD
From the coastal road, Britain's most northerly point looms as a mass of bare, rolling peat, edged by a 300ft cliff. There is a car park and an octagonal viewing platform which provides a 360 degree view from Cape Wrath in the west to Duncansby in the east, from mist-veiled Orkney in the north to the moors inland.

Below the viewpoint is Dunnet Head's lighthouse. Though 300ft above the sea, stone thrown up by winter storms in the Pentland Firth sometimes batter its walls.

THURSO
The road into Thurso leads over an elegant stone bridge to an equally elegant 18th-century square named after Sir John Sinclair. As well as being a writer, agriculturalist and politician, Sir John, whose statue stands in the square, was also an accomplished town planner. He laid out the gridwork of streets and neat brownstone houses that still forms the centre of the town.

The ruins of Old St Peter's Kirk stand between the Thurso river and the bay. Founded in 1220, it was superseded in 1832 by an imposing new building in Gothic style.

Thurso has continued to prosper since Sir John's time. In the 19th century the railway came, and since then has linked the town to the south. Local flagstone from Scrabster underpinned Thurso's wealth. In the 1950s the building of Dounreay nuclear power plant drew in more people, until now, with 10,000 inhabitants, Thurso has more than a third of the entire population of the Caithness district.

The town has a museum next to the Town Hall. It includes displays on local geology and history, and a reconstruction of a croft kitchen.

GREY CAIRNS OF CAMSTER
A single-track road, which must be one of the most desolate in Britain, leads south over a deserted and treeless peat moor. In good weather, motorists will see low hills and one or two distant houses. In rain or mist, all clues to context, human or natural, vanish. In such a setting visitors can easily imagine that they are driving out of time, the more so when they see, to their right, two low piles of stone – the Grey Cairns of Camster.

These tombs, put up by Stone Age people between 4000 and 1500 BC, are well restored, with boardwalks over the spongy peat, skylights in the enclosed burial chambers and iron wicket gates guarding the low entrance tunnels. One tunnel, 50ft long, is only 2ft 6in high.

There are two cairns. One is 55ft in diameter and 12ft high and contains a single tomb; the other is 200ft long and made up of perhaps 3000 tons of stone, and contains two tombs. The people would have used the cairns over the course of many generations to bury their chiefs, adding to the pile of stones at each burial. It is not hard to imagine a burial procession winding towards the cairns from the wooded defile farther along the road – a site that could well have been the home of a prosperous Stone Age farming community.

LYBSTER
Lybster – pronounced 'Lie-bster' – seems to be two places in one. An impressively broad thoroughfare leads seawards, but then the road dips to the right down to a picture-book harbour.

The basin was a rarity when it was built in the 19th century, for it was scooped out inland, rather than being built up into the sea, to create a secure haven for several hundred fishing vessels. A lighthouse stands at the harbour entrance, overlooked by a ruined mill, which is reached by a pretty bridge over a craggy glen. Lybster retains all its charm, though its few crab and lobster boats are but a distant echo of the bustle that characterised the place until after the Second World War.

HILL O' MANY STANES
On a hillock behind three houses, some 200 stones, each only a foot or two high, are set out roughly in a fan shape that converges towards a low rise. There are about 20 similar sites elsewhere in Caithness and Sutherland, but none elsewhere.

All date from the Bronze Age, between 2000 and 600 BC, but their function is unclear. Possibly their purpose was astronomical, but the site suggests that positions were set for a regular ritual.

WHALIGOE
A staircase of 365 stone steps winds steeply down to where the old harbour cliffs enclose a grassed-over quay, with only a few ruined walls to recall the days of the great herring fleets.

The steps are slippery when wet, and visitors descending them should take great care. They are reached by turning off the main road at the phone box. Park by the line of cottages and carry on downhill on foot, round the old mill house.

Tourist information: Wick 2596; John o'Groats 373 (summer); Thurso 62371 (summer).

CLIFF-TOP SENTINEL *An escape route runs right through Castle Girnigoe. A vaulted passage, large enough to take a man on horseback, leads to a trap door to the sea.*

WHERE TO FIND OUT MORE ABOUT BRITAIN

TOURIST INFORMATION

At the end of each tour in this book appears the telephone number of the appropriate Tourist Information Centres for the areas through which the tour passes. Where two tours start from the same town, the information centres are listed at the end of the second tour.

A phone call to these centres will bring you leaflets and maps of the area, accommodation lists and programmes of forthcoming events. Although general information about opening times of places of interest is given in the text, it is wise to check these details with the local Tourist Information Centre before setting out.

For further help in planning your tours, contact the appropriate national or regional tourist board listed below:

English Tourist Board,
   Thames Tower, Black's Road,
   Hammersmith, London W6 9EL.
   Tel. (01) 846 9000.

Scottish Tourist Board,
   23 Ravelston Terrace,
   Edinburgh EH4 3EU.
   Tel. (031) 332 2433.

Wales Tourist Board,
   Brunel House, 2 Fitzalan Road,
   Cardiff CF2 1UY.
   Tel. Cardiff 499909.

Cumbria Tourist Board,
   Ashleigh, Holly Road, Windermere,
   Cumbria LA23 2AQ.
   Tel. Windermere 4444.

East Anglia Tourist Board,
   Toppesfield Hall, Hadleigh,
   Suffolk IP7 5DN.
   Tel. Hadleigh 822922.

East Midlands Tourist Board,
   Exchequergate, Lincoln,
   Lincolnshire LN2 1PZ.
   Tel. Lincoln 31521.

Heart of England Tourist Board,
   Trinity Street, Worcester, Hereford
   and Worcester WR1 2PW.
   Tel. Worcester 29511.

Isle of Man Tourist Board,
   13 Victoria Street, Douglas,
   Isle of Man.
   Tel. Douglas 74328/9 (summer),
   74323 (winter).

Isle of Wight Tourist Board,
   21 High Street, Newport,
   Isle of Wight PO30 1JS.
   Tel. Newport 524343.

Northumbria Tourist Board,
   9 Osborne Terrace, Jesmond,
   Newcastle upon Tyne NE2 1NT.
   Tel. Newcastle upon Tyne 817744.

North-West Tourist Board,
   The Last Drop Village, Bromley Cross,
   Bolton, Lancashire BL7 9PZ.
   Tel. Bolton 591511.

South-East England Tourist Board,
   1 Warwick Park, Tunbridge Wells,
   Kent TN2 5TA.
   Tel. Tunbridge Wells 40766.

Southern Tourist Board,
   Town Hall Centre, Leigh Road,
   Eastleigh, Hampshire SO5 4DE.
   Tel. Eastleigh 616027.

Thames and Chilterns Tourist Board,
   8 The Market Place, Abingdon,
   Oxfordshire OX14 3UD.
   Tel. Abingdon 22711.

West Country Tourist Board,
   Trinity Court, 37 Southernhay East,
   Exeter, Devon EX1 1QS.
   Tel. Exeter 76351.

Yorkshire and Humberside Tourist
   Board,
   312 Tadcaster Road, York,
   North Yorkshire YO2 2HF.
   Tel. York 707961.

MOTORING INFORMATION

Information and advice on all aspects of motoring is available to Automobile Association members from AA Centres throughout England, Wales, Scotland and Northern Ireland. The AA's services are directed through the regional head-quarters listed below. New members can enrol through any AA Centre, or by writing to AA Freepost BZ47, Basingstoke, Hants RG21 2BR.

West and Wales Region,
   Fanum House, Park Row,
   Bristol BS1 5LY.
   Tel. Bristol 297272.

South-East Region,
   Fanum House, 52 London Road,
   Twickenham TW1 3RN.
   Tel. (01) 891 1441.

Midlands Region,
   Fanum House, Dogkennel Lane,
   Halesowen, West Midlands B63 3BT.
   Tel. (021) 550 4721.

North Region,
   Fanum House, Station Road,
   Cheadle Hulme, Cheadle,
   Cheshire SK8 7BS.
   Tel. (061) 485 6188.

Scotland and N. Ireland Region,
   Fanum House, Erskine Harbour,
   Erskine, Renfrewshire PA8 6AT.
   Tel. (041) 812 0144.

WILDLIFE AND NATURE CONSERVANCY

Several organisations will supply information on wildlife, natural history and nature conservancy. They include:

British Trust for Ornithology,
   Beech Grove, Tring,
   Hertfordshire HP23 5NR.
   Tel. Tring 3461.

Council for the Protection of Rural
   England,
   4 Hobart Place,
   London SW1W 0HY.
   Tel. (01) 235 9481.

Council for the Protection of Rural
   Wales,
   31 High Street, Welshpool,
   Powys SY21 7SD.
   Tel. Welshpool 2525.

Forestry Commission,
   231 Corstorphine Road,
   Edinburgh EH12 7AT.
   Tel. (031) 334 0303.

Nature Conservancy Council,
   Norminster House,
   Peterborough PE1 1UA.
   Tel. Peterborough 40345.

Royal Society for Nature Conservation,
   The Green, Nettleham,
   Lincoln LN2 2NR.
   Tel. Lincoln 752326.

Royal Society for the Protection of Birds,
   The Lodge, Sandy,
   Bedfordshire SG19 2DL.
   Tel. Sandy 80551.

Scottish Ornithologists' Club,
   21 Regent Terrace,
   Edinburgh EH7 5BT.
   Tel. (031) 556 6042.

Scottish Wildlife Trust,
   25 Johnston Terrace,
   Edinburgh EH1 2NH.
   Tel. (031) 226 4602.

NATIONAL PARKS

A number of tours explore parts of Britain's ten National Parks. Information offices can supply leaflets on the wildlife, scenery, recreational facilities and other features of the parks:

Brecon Beacons National Park,
   7 Glamorgan Street, Brecon,
   Powys LD3 7DP.
   Tel. Brecon 4437.

Dartmoor National Park,
   Parke, Haytor Road, Bovey Tracey,
   Devon TQ13 9JQ.
   Tel. Bovey Tracey 832093.

Exmoor National Park,
   Exmoor House, Dulverton,
   Somerset TA22 9EN.
   Tel. Dulverton 23665.

Lake District National Park,
   Brockhole, Near Windermere,
   Cumbria LA23 1LJ.
   Tel. Windermere 2231.

Northumberland National Park,
   Eastburn, South Park, Hexham,
   Northumberland NE46 1BS.
   Tel. Hexham 605555.

North York Moors National Park,
   The Old Vicarage, Bondgate,
   Helmsley, North Yorkshire YO6 5BP.
   Tel. Helmsley 70657.

Peak District National Park,
   Aldern House, Baslow Road,
   Bakewell, Derbyshire DE4 1AE.
   Tel. Bakewell 4321.

Pembrokeshire Coast National Park,
   County Offices, Haverfordwest,
   Dyfed SA61 1QZ.
   Tel. Haverfordwest 4591.

Snowdonia National Park,
   Penrhyndeudraeth,
   Gwynedd LL48 6LS.
   Tel. Penrhyndeudraeth 770274.

Yorkshire Dales National Park,
   Yorebridge House, Bainbridge,
   Leyburn, North Yorkshire DL8 3BP.
   Tel. Wensleydale 50456.

HISTORIC PLACES

Information on ancient monuments, historic houses, castles, stately homes and gardens can be obtained from:

English Heritage,
   Historic Buildings and Monuments
   Commission for England,
   PO Box 43, Ruislip,
   Middlesex HA4 0XW.

Historic Buildings and Monuments,
   Scottish Development Department,
   3-11 Melville Street,
   Edinburgh EH3 7QD.
   Tel. (031) 226 2570.

The National Gardens Scheme,
   57 Lower Belgrave Street,
   London SW1W 0LR.
   Tel. (01) 730 0359.

The National Trust,
   36 Queen Anne's Gate,
   London SW1H 9AS.
   Tel. (01) 222 9251.

The National Trust for Scotland,
   5 Charlotte Square,
   Edinburgh EH2 4DU.
   Tel. (031) 226 5922.

Welsh Office, Ancient Monuments
   Branch,
   Cadw, Brunel House, Fitzalan Road,
   Cardiff CF2 1UY.
   Tel. Cardiff 465511.

COUNTRY PARKS, NATURE TRAILS AND WALKS

Recommended stopping places on the tours include many of Britain's 200 country parks, recognised by the Countryside Commission and run by county councils. Tours also offer opportunities for walkers to sample sections of the long-distance paths, and many shorter routes and nature trails. Particulars of walking in Britain may be obtained from:

Countryside Commission,
   John Dower House,
   Crescent Place, Cheltenham,
   Gloucestershire GL50 3RA.
   Tel. Cheltenham 521381.

Countryside Commission for Scotland,
   Battleby, Redgorton,
   Perth PH1 3EW.
   Tel. Perth 27291.

The Ramblers' Association,
   1/5 Wandsworth Road,
   London SW8 2LJ.
   Tel. (01) 582 6878.

INDEX

NORTHERN BRITAIN

The starting points of the 250 tours are indicated on this map and on the map of Southern Britain on the end-papers at the front of the book. The tours are grouped into eight regions, as shown on the left of this page; further guidance on how to reach the start of each tour is given on the larger-scale regional maps on the pages indicated.

194 Hexham	Number of tour and starting point
	Boundary of region
	Motorway
	Main road

MILES 20 40 60
KM 20 40 60 80

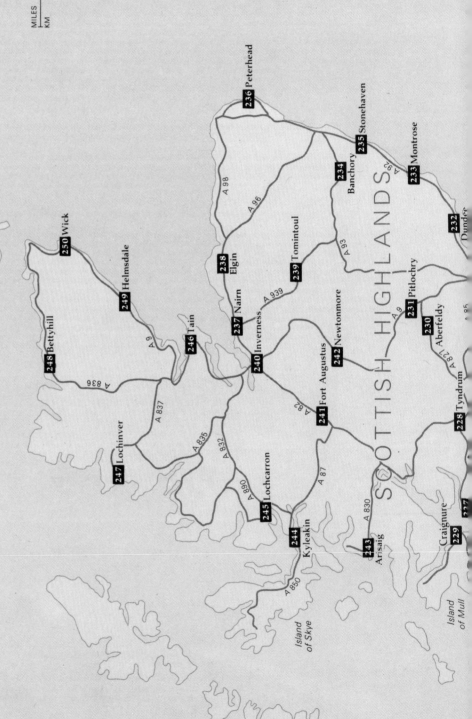

WHERE TO FIND THE TOURS

WEST COUNTRY
Tours 1–32
Map on pages 8–9

EASTERN ENGLAND
Tours 136–151
Map on pages 222–223

THE SOUTH-EAST
Tours 33–72
Map on pages 62–63

NORTH COUNTRY
Tours 152–197
Map on pages 248–249

WALES
Tours 73–102
Map on pages 124–125

SCOTTISH LOWLANDS
Tours 198–224
Map on pages 326–327

CENTRAL SHIRES
Tours 103–135
Map on pages 170–171

SCOTTISH HIGHLANDS
Tours 225–250
Map on pages 368–369

SCOTTISH HIGHLANDS
SCOTTISH LOWLANDS
NORTH COUNTRY
CENTRAL EASTERN SHIRES ENGLAND
WALES
THE SOUTH-EAST
WEST COUNTRY

SCOTTISH HIGHLANDS

236 Peterhead
235 Stonehaven
234 Banchory
233 Montrose
232 Dundee
250 Wick
249 Helmsdale
248 Bettyhill
247 Lochinver
246 Tain
245 Lochcarron
244 Kyleakin
243 Arisaig
242 Newtonmore
241 Fort Augustus
240 Inverness
239 Tomintoul
238 Elgin
237 Nairn
231 Pitlochry
230 Aberfeldy
229 Craignure
228 Tyndrum
227

Island of Skye
Island of Mull

A 98 A 96 A 93 A 939 A 9 A 82 A 87 A 832 A 835 A 837 A 836 A 890 A 830 A 850 A 92 A 95 A 827